Brain Development and Cognition

B

BRAIN DEVELOPMENT AND COGNITION

A Reader

Edited by
Mark H. Johnson

BLACKWELL
Oxford UK & Cambridge USA

First published 1993
Reprinted 1994

Blackwell Publishers
108 Cowley Road, Oxford, OX4 1JF, UK

238 Main Street
Cambridge, Massachusetts 02142, USA

British Library Cataloguing in Publication Data
A CIP catalogue record for this book is available from the British Library.

Library of Congress Cataloging in Publication Data

Brain development and cognition: a reader/edited by Mark H. Johnson.
  p. cm.
  Consists of a collection of classic articles and commissioned chapters.
  Includes bibliographical references and index.
  ISBN 0–631–18222–5 (alk. paper). — ISBN 0–631–18223–3 (pbk.: alk. index)
  1. Cognitive neuroscience. 2. Cognition in children.
I. Johnson, Mark H. (Mark Henry), 1960– .
  [DNLM: 1. Brain—growth & development—collected works. 2. Brain—growth & development—essays. 3. Cognition—physiology—collected works.
4. Cognition—physiology—essays. 5. Neuronal Plasticity—collected works.
6. Neuronal Plasticity—essays. WL 300 B81238]
QP360.5.B73 1992   612.8'2–dc20   92–17620   CIP
DNLM/DLC
for Library of Congress

Typeset in 9½ on 11pt Ehrhardt
by Pure Tech Corporation, Pondicherry, India
Printed in Great Britain by T. J. Press Ltd, Padstow, Cornwall

This book is printed on acid-free paper

Contents

Contributors

JOCELYNE BACHEVALIER: University of Texas Health Science Center, Houston, Texas
ELIZABETH A. BATES: University of California, San Diego, California
URSULA BELLUGI: Salk Institute for Biological Studies, La Jolla, California
JAMES E. BLACK: University of Illinois, Urbana-Champaign, Illinois
M. P. BRYDEN: University of Waterloo, Waterloo, Canada
JEAN-PIERRE CHANGEUX: Institut Pasteur, Paris, France
HARRY T. CHUGANI: University of California, Los Angeles School of Medicine, Los Angeles, California
STANISLAS DEHAENE: INSERM and CNRS, Paris, France
ADELE DIAMOND: University of Pennsylvania, Philadelphia, Pennsylvania
JEFFREY L. ELMAN: University of California, San Diego, California
WILLIAM T. GREENOUGH: University of Illinois, Urbana-Champaign, Illinois
RICHARD HELD: Massachusetts Institute of Technology, Cambridge, Massachusetts
GABRIEL HORN: University of Cambridge, Cambridge, UK
PETER R. HUTTENLOCHER: University of Chicago, Chicago, Illinois
JERI S. JANOWSKY: Oregon Health Sciences University, Portland, Oregon
JACQUELINE S. JOHNSON: University of Virginia, Charlottesville, Virginia
MARK H. JOHNSON: Carnegie Mellon University, Pittsburgh, Pennsylvania
ANNETTE KARMILOFF-SMITH: MRC Cognitive Development Unit, London, UK
JOSEPH B. KELLER: Stanford University, Stanford, California
PATRICIA A. KENNY: Hunter College of the City University of New York, New York
EDWARD S. KLIMA: University of California, San Diego and Salk Institute for Biological Studies, La Jolla, California
BRYAN KOLB: University of Lethbridge, Lethbridge, Canada
ERIC H. LENNEBERG: Harvard Medical School, Cambridge, Massachusetts
KONRAD LORENZ*: Max Plank Institute Für Verhaltensphysiologie, Seewiesen, Germany
I. C. MCMANUS: University College, London, UK
PETER MARLER: University of California, Davis, California
JOHN C. MAZZIOTTA: University of California, Los Angeles School of Medicine, Los Angeles, California
KENNETH D. MILLER: California Institute of Technology, Pasadena, California
MORTIMER MISHKIN: National Institute of Mental Health, Bethesda, Maryland

HELEN J. NEVILLE: Salk Institute for Biological Studies, La Jolla, California
ELISSA L. NEWPORT: University of Rochester, Rochester, New York
R. S. NOWAKOWSKI: Robert Wood Johnson Medical School, Piscataway, New Jersey
DENNIS D. M. O'LEARY: Salk Institute for Biological Studies, La Jolla, California
SUSAN OYAMA: City University of New York, New York
MICHAEL E. PHELPS: University of California, Los Angeles School of Medicine, Los Angeles, California
JEAN PIAGET*: University of Geneva, Geneva, Switzerland
HOWARD POIZNER: Rutgers University, Newark, New Jersey
P. RAKIC: Yale University School of Medicine, New Haven, Connecticut
JOAN STILES: University of California, San Diego, California
MICHAEL P. STRYKER: University of California, San Francisco, California
DONNA THAL: San Diego State University, San Diego, California
ESTHER THELEN: Indiana University, Bloomington, Indiana
GERALD TURKEWITZ: Hunter College of the City University of New York and Albert Einstein College of Medicine, New York
CHRISTOPHER S. WALLACE: University of Illinois, Urbana-Champaign, Illinois

* Deceased

Preface

Several times in my scientific career I have felt pressure to classify myself as being either a "cognitive neuroscientist" or a "developmentalist". However, the more I considered which of these two I really was, the more I realized that the two enterprises are inextricably entwined. Indeed, I have come to the belief that significant progress in either field is crucially dependent upon its interaction with the other. This book represents a initial attempt to convince others that this might be the case.

The book was prepared with two types of reader in mind. The first type is students on courses in cognitive neuroscience and cognitive development. I hope this book will fill the gap that those of us who run such courses know to exist. The second type of reader I have in mind is the established researcher/teacher in cognitive science, neuroscience, or neuropsychology who feels that he or she ought know something about the relation between the developing brain and mind. I hope these people find this a useful and stimulating reference volume.

I have no doubt that the particular choice of readings and new authors reflects my own particular biases, and that any other editor's selection would have been different. However, I have gone to some lengths to find out from others in the field what readings they would have chosen for a course on this topic. These consultations, and space limitations, have resulted in my making the difficult decision to drop some of my own personal favorites. Some of these have found their way into the further reading sections at the end of each of the part introductions. When the reactions to my current selection of readings began to vary from them being overall "too cognitive" to being overall "too neural", I realized that I must have got the balance about right! The best I can hope for is that readers familiar with the area will find that the selection includes at least the majority of those that they would have included.

The book would not have seen the light of day without at least two other people: first, Stephan Chambers of Basil Blackwell, with whom the idea for the book was originally born, and who nurtured it carefully from conception to publication; second, Leslie Tucker, whose cheerful application to the many chores associated with a book such as this never ceased to amaze me. Leslie also assisted indirectly by running my lab so efficiently that I have time to spend on projects such as this one. While Leslie labored in Pittsburgh, Judith Harvey and Pam

Shahen did likewise in Blackwell's office in Oxford. Together they formed a formidable team.

Rarely can a prospective book have been given such a thorough testing bed as that provided by the students and postdocs who attended my fall 1991 "Brain Development and Cognition" course at Carnegie Mellon (Dan Appelquist, Maxwell Drain, Matt Isaak, Randy O'Reilly, Cathy Reed, Hermi Tabachnek, Shaun Vecera, Marcie Wallace and Gene Zilberstein). It was a joy to have such incisive and interested fellow travellers on my voyage of discovery.

Other people who provided advice on particular topics or readings were Jeri Janowsky, Annette Karmiloff-Smith, Yuko Munakata, and Joan Stiles. Thanks are also due to Bob Seigler and Annette Karmiloff-Smith who commented on the comprehensibility of my introductions to each of the sections. Needless to say, none of the above is in any way responsible for the views expressed in the final version.

Thanks are also due to the various publishers and authors who contributed to the book in ways big and small.

To my parents and sisters I owe thanks for putting up with my long absences, and neglect of family events, over the years.

Thanks are insufficient for Anoushka, who has brought so much that is good into my life.

Part I

Perspectives on Development

Introduction

Few subjects in science can have provoked such acrimonious and impassioned debate as development. These debates have often been centered on particular dichotomies, with each side characterizing the other's viewpoint as at an extreme end of the dichotomy, even though both may have been closer to the middle ground than their opponents would care to admit. Throughout the book, these dichotomies, such as nature versus nurture, and selection versus learning, will keep recurring in a variety of different contexts. We will discover that the same debates often rage simultaneously in the domains of neural, behavioral, and cognitive development. In this first section we begin by bringing some of these major issues out in the open in a number of writings by authors who have explicitly championed particular viewpoints on development.

The first two readings in this section put the case for and against the use of the nature versus nurture dichotomy (Lorenz for, and Oyama against). Although most researchers now agree that the study of development should be about unravelling the *interaction* between genetic specification and environmental influence, debates still rage about whether the role of experience is in structuring or organizing the mind/brain (Piaget), or whether its role is more that of a releaser of propensities already latent within the organism (Lenneberg).

Lorenz defends the utility of the innate – learned dichotomy as a powerful tool for discovering important facts about development. The section reprinted is from a book written fairly late in his career and designed to answer the criticism of his earlier work, in which he argued for "innate" and "learned" components of behavior as being opposed and mutually exclusive. When it became clear from a number of experimental examples that the distinction between these two is often blurry, several critics (Lehrmann (1953) perhaps foremost among them) argued that the search for purely "innate" behaviors was not only futile, but also misleading. Lorenz responds in the reprinted article by conceding that his earlier claims about the innate and learned being mutually exclusive were incorrect. "Learning" has to involve an innate component in two senses. First, a species has to be adapted to learn – it needs to have brain circuits that have been selected to be appropriately plastic at certain points in development. The second sense in which innate information is important is that it often acts as a teacher, "the innate schoolmarm," for learning. This latter point re-emerges in part VI of this volume (Constraints on Plasticity).

Lorenz refuses to yield with regard to the usefulness of the concept of the "innate" for two reasons. First, he argues that certain components of behavior are present without experience of the environment. In some cases, these systems have to be impervious to learning for them to be simultaneously efficient, fast acting, and relatively complex. Second, he argues that investigating the extent to which components of behavior are innate is the best, and may be the only, strategy for unpacking developmental processes scientifically.

The next reading, due to Susan Oyama, presents a recent and very comprehensive attack on the nature/nurture dichotomy. Oyama attempts to show how even the implicit use of this dichotomy can mislead investigations of development. She argues that the nature/nurture dichotomy is partly the result of the scientific need to think in dichotomies, and partly the result of addressing the wrong question. She also maintains that the current scientific approaches to development are more deeply influenced by cultural traditions than we think. That is, both religion and science have looked for a source of prespecified instructions (information) outside the developmental process itself. While religion has attributed the emergence of structure or form to an outside creator, scientists have proposed that the source of prespecified instructions is to be found in the gene.

The first scientists interested in ontogeny hypothesized that a completely formed being existed within the "germ," either the egg or the sperm. In both varieties of the theory, the other partner's contribution was said merely to diffuse into the preformed being. Gradually, as scientific knowledge grew, the prespecifications for form became enclosed within the genetic material. In recent years, ever more elaborate metaphors have been devised as it becomes clear that the majority of genes cannot do the job of regulating development in isolation. The orchestration of development is now hypothesized to be controlled by "switching" genes, but these in turn are regulated by other "switching" genes, leading us, Oyama states, into an infinite regress. While there has been much debate between those concerned with whether the genes act as a blueprint, hypothesis generator, program, code, plan, or set of rules for development, no one has yet proposed that these views might *all* be wrong, she maintains.

Oyama believes that in understanding development we should be concerned more with change than with the steady state, with the process not the phenotypic state at any point in time.

> Nativism and empiricism require each other as do warp and weft. What they share is the belief that information can pre-exist the processes that give rise to it. Yet information "in the genes" or "in the environment" is not biologically relevant until it participates in phenotypic processes. Once this happens, it becomes meaningful in the organism only as it is constituted by its developmental system. The result is not *more* information but *significant* information. (Oyama, her chapter 2, p. 13)

The difference between Oyama and Lorenz is brought out clearly in one metaphor employed by the latter. Lorenz states that it is not the bricks and mortar which regulate the building of a cathedral, but a pre-existing plan that has been devised by an architect. For Oyama, it is precisely the notion of a pre-exisiting plan that is misguided. When considering living forms, she argues that the "plan" is contained in each and every brick and piece of mortar.

What are the implications of these arguments for the study of cognitive development? Oyama urges us not to focus on constancy during development, since this inevitably leads us to look for an injection of pre-existing information from either the genes or the environment to account for changes. With few exceptions, this focus on constancy is a characteristic of models of cognitive development. This is partly because it is simply easier to describe particular stages in development than to account for the dynamic processes of change, and partly because of influential logical arguments such as those put forward by Jerry Fodor. Fodor argues, for example, that it is impossible to learn a language of thought whose predicates express extensions unexpressable in the previously available language. In Oyama's view, Fodor's arguments are based on a very static and stage-like conception of development. The emergence of a new language of thought should not be attributable to either learning or maturation (the latter of which Fodor settles for), but rather should be seen as a product of the preceding developmental system. Despite the obsession of some of his followers with particular static *stages* of development, perhaps only in Jean Piaget's original writing is there the beginning of an attempt to address increases in significant information as part of the developmental process itself.

In the reprinted section from his volume *Biology and Knowledge*, Piaget discusses the notion of stages of development. While arguing for their usefulness if they are carefully defined, he also stresses that a stage is not a static phenomenon, but rather the temporarily balanced "dynamic equilibrium" of a variety of continually competing factors. Transition from one of these stages to the next is provoked by a disturbance of this equilibrium, a disequilibrium. Piaget argues for a particular kind of relation between one stage and the next, in which the previous stage is always crucial for the present one, without the present stage being in any sense contained within the previous one.

It is worth noting here that Piaget's conception of stages and the transitions between them is very different from the static "stages of development" notion criticized by Oyama. For Piaget, both the transitions and the stages are the products of dynamic interaction between a variety of factors, some related to the genes and others related to the environment. The transition phases occur when these competing factors become uneven, provoking disequilibrium. This conception is markedly different from the idea that either the genes or the environment push the organism from one stable static state to another. Indeed, Piaget sees the agenda for developmental psychology as

> to explain in detail how, in the field of knowledge as in that of organic epigenesis, this collaboration between the genome and the environment actually works – especially those details which concern autoregulations or progressive equilibrations which admit of the exclusion of both preformism and the notion of a reaction caused entirely by environment. (p. 33).

Thus, Piaget distances himself from both nativists on the one hand, and empiricists on the other, suggesting that heredity opens up possibilities that have to be actualized by collaboration with the environment (see also Bates and Elman, part VIII).

Piaget presents us with a paradox: while there is no sense in which we can consider formal logical thinking to be specified in the genome, it is virtually always attained by a certain age in normal children, and always preceded by a certain sequence of earlier stages. He attempts to resolve this paradox by invoking a concept originally devised by the geneticist C. H. Waddington, that of necessary epigenetic routes or "chreods" (see Waddington, 1975, for further reading). Waddington proposed that development could be visualized in terms of an "epigenetic landscape" (see figure 1) in which processes tended to take only certain channels. Self-regulatory processes, such as "homeorhesis," ensure that the organism returns to its channel following small perturbations to the system (while very large peturbations can result in a quite different channel being taken). Thus, for the normal child, the same endpoint will be reached regardless of any small deviations that take place earlier. Piaget also sees chreods as being important on the temporal dimension; processes of organization in particular domains have their own "time tally," rhythm, or schedule. Thus while some degree of acceleration can occur during some stages, the amount is limited.

In the extract from *Biological Foundations of Language*, Eric Lenneberg, while appreciating that both the genome and the environment are important in development, places a good deal less importance on the structuring role of the environment than does Piaget. Lenneberg argues that since the same environment is commonly shared by widely differing species, that environment cannot be crucial in shaping some of the species-specific characteristics of behavior. (We shall see later, in part VI, that during development many species appear to increasingly select aspects of their environment to interact with. So while two or more species may live in the same general environment, such as a pond, they may have very different effective environments.) For Lenneberg, the environment's role in development is similar in some respects to that proposed by Lorenz – it is a *releaser* rather than an *organizer*.

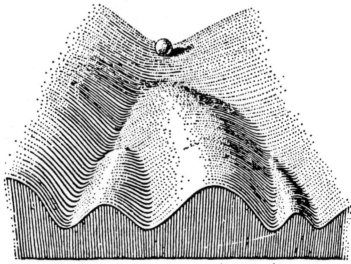

Figure 1 The epigenetic landscape. Reproduced from: C. H. Waddington *The Evolution of a Evolutionist* (Edinburgh University Press, 1975) by kind permission.

In common with Piaget, Lenneberg believes that it is fruitful to think of transitions between points in development in terms of disequilibrium (factors being out of balance). The disequilibrium leads to rearrangements of the system until a period of relative stability is reached. The difference between these two authors is that, at least for language acquisition, Lenneberg believes that the disequilibrium is specifically brought about by neural development, resulting in a state he refers to as "language-readiness." This state waits until it "resonates" to language input. If no language input is received by a certain age, the language readiness state declines. Thus, for Lenneberg, disequilibrium is brought about by the maturation of the nervous system resulting in a temporally limited period of maturational readiness.

In Lenneberg's writing, a distinction is made between the *latent structure* and the *realized structure* of language. The former corresponds to Chomsky's universal grammar, and the latter to particular grammars. In part III we shall see that this distinction is quite general, and may be relevant to aspects of neural development as well as to aspects of cognitive development.

FURTHER READING

D'Arcy Thompson (1917 – abridged edition 1961) *On Growth and Form*. Cambridge: Cambridge University Press. (A classic introduction to fundamental issues surrounding development.)

Boden, M. (1979) *Piaget*. Fontana: London. (A good psychological – philosophical introduction to Piaget's thinking.)

Braintenberg, V. (1984) *Vehicles: Experiments in Synthetic Psychology*. Cambridge, MA: MIT Press. (A wonderful collection of invented organisms that evolve ever more complex behaviors.)

Donaldson, M. (1978) *Children's Minds*. Fontana: London. (A basic psychological – experimental introduction to Piaget, with an excellent appendix outlining aspects of his theory.)

Johnson, M. H. and Morton, J. (1991) *Biology and Cognitive Development: the Case of Face Recognition*. Oxford: Blackwell. (Chapter 1 is relevant to the issues addressed in this part.)

Lehrmann, D. S. (1953) A critique of Konrad Lorenz's theory of instinctive behavior. *Quarterly Review of Biology*, 28, 337–63. (A prominent critique of Lorenz's early writing.)

Piatelli-Palmarini, M. (ed.), (1980) *Language and Learning. The Debate between Jean Piaget and Noam Chomsky*. London: Routledge & Kegan Paul. (A collection of position papers centered on the debates between Piaget and Chomsky at the Abbey de Royaumont conference.)

Tinbergen, N. (1951) *The Study of Instinct*. Oxford: Clarendon Press. (The classic introduction to the ethological analysis of ontogeny.)

Waddington, C. H. (1975). *The Evolution of an Evolutionist*. Edinburgh: Edinburgh University Press. (A series of essays about evolution and ontogeny. Waddington's ideas on this topic greatly influenced Piaget and other constructivists.)

1

Critique of the Modern Ethologists' Attitude

KONRAD LORENZ

What I propose to discuss here is mainly the assumptions already mentioned in the introduction: that "what we formerly called innate" and what we formerly called "learned" represent only the extreme ends of a continuum of insensibly graduated mixtures between the two, and that all behaviour, down to its smallest elements, owes its adaptedness to both processes. I think I can show that this assumption is not only bad strategy of research but completely unfounded and in all probability false.

In discussing the first behavioristic argument,[a] I have attempted to demonstrate the fallacy of treating the "innate" and the "learned" as opposed, mutually exclusive concepts. I tried to show that, while all learning is performed by mechanisms which do contain phylogenetically acquired information, no reasons exist for assuming that individually acquired information "enters into" every kind of phylogenetically adapted behaviour. For millions of years our planet has been inhabited by creatures possessing quite elaborate behaviour patterns which owed none of their adaptedness to any of the higher and typical forms of learning. We are certain that habituation and its counterpart, sensitization, are the only forms of adaptive modification of behaviour ever found in protozoa and in organisms with a diffuse nervous system. When, eons later, at a comparatively high level of neural organization, modifiability of behavior began to increase, a tremendous selection pressure must have been brought to bear on the development of mechanisms adaptively modifying individual behavior. The intensity of this pressure can be inferred from the omnipresence of its effect in all phyla of

[a] The "first behavioristic argument" refers to the argument that the dissociation of behaviors into "innate" and "learned" components is not analytically valid since hitherto the only definition of "innate" is that which is not learned. (Editor's note.)

"Critique of the Modern Ethologists' Attitude" is an excerpt from: Konrad Lorenz, *Evolution and the Modification of Behavior* (University of Chicago Press, 1965, chapter 5, pp. 29–48) and is reprinted by kind permission.

organisms which, independently of each other, have evolved a centralized nervous system.

Everything that has been said in criticism of the first behavioristic argument is a reason for not assuming an unlimited, diffuse mutual permeability and mixability of phylogenetic adaptation and learning. Only confirmed "preformationists" can doubt the fact that any specialized adaptive modifiability of behaviour, such as we find in vertebrates, arthropods, and cephalopods, can never be a product of chance, but has to be regarded as the function of a nervous apparatus which is highly organized and which owes its origin, as all organization does, to the process of "pure induction" conducted by the evolution of every species. To assume diffuse permeability of phylogenetic adaptation and learning implies the assumption of an infinite number of such organizations, which is strictly contradicted by the hackneyed fact that there are, for each animal species, only limited numbers of highly specific stimulus situations that will act as reinforcements.

The notion that learning or any other change of behavior achieving survival value could possibly be the function of a non-specifically organized and programmed aggregation of neural elements, is absolutely untenable.

It is a matter of surprise and concern to me that this fallacy has been voiced in *Behaviour*[b] with great self-confidence and without arousing the least contradiction on the part of English-speaking ethologists. Ethology loses its character of a biological science if the fact is forgotten that adaptedness exists and needs an explanation. There is no hope of gaining greater "exactitude" by shedding biological knowledge and clinging to allegedly operational concepts. All conceptualizations employed in the scientific study of nature are fundamentally operational, and if the operations underlying the concepts used in phylogenetics are complicated and presuppose considerable knowledge, this furnishes no excuse for neglecting important and well-known facts. It is a great error to believe that "exactitude" can be gained by restricting research to one experimentally – and mentally – simple operation. The damage done by this type of procedure is best illustrated by Jensen's paper "Operationism and the Question 'Is This Behavior Learned or Innate?' " (1961).

Jensen argues in the following manner:

> The possibility of differences in behavior being neither innate (selected) nor learned (trained) but something else (produced by other operations) allows the separate classification of various types of operations or antecedent differences to which behavioral differences can be attributed. [A list of such operations, including food schedule, hormones, and even nervous system lesions, etc. follows.]
>
> Since behavioral differences may be attributed to effects and interactions of many factors, the original question can be rephrased in an unrestricted way. Instead of: "Is this behavior innate or learned?" we can ask: "What causes this difference in behavior?" So asked, the question becomes a matter for research instead of argument.

There is not and there cannot be any argument about the fact that the Kuenzers' (1962) young *Apistogramma* responded selectively to the configurational

b *Behaviour* is an international journal which publishes ethological studies of animal behaviour. (Editor's note.)

key stimulus of a yellow and black pattern by the specific activities of following the parent and that a mother *Apistogramma* is indeed striped black and yellow. Nor is it a matter of argument that a stickleback responds to the key stimulus "red below" by performing the motor patterns of rival fighting and that a male stickleback is indeed red on the ventral side. Only if we should forget these central facts of adaptedness, and only then, should we have to resort to the desperate strategy of research which Jensen recommends to us, unless we should prefer to give up as hopeless any further attempt to analyze behavior.

Non-adaptive differences in structure and behavior are of but secondary interest to the biologist, while they are the primary concern of the pathologist. A living organism is a very complicated and very finely balanced system, and there is precious little about it that cannot, at least on principle, be understood on the basis of phylogenetic adaptation and adaptive modification. Neither in an animal's body nor in its behavior are there many characters that may be changed by "other operations" without leading to destruction.

As students of behavior, we are not interested in ascertaining at random the innumerable factors that might lead to minute, just bearable differences of behavior bordering on the pathological. What we want to elucidate are the amazing facts of adaptedness. Life itself is a steady state of enormous general improbability and that which does need an explanation is the fact that organisms and species miraculously manage to stay alive. The answer to this question in respect to bodily structure as well as to behavior always hinges on the provenience of the information contained in and indispensable for the molding of the organism in such a way that it fits its environment and is able to cope with it. In the special case of our baby *Apistogramma* and of our male stickleback we want to know how the former can possess information on the external characteristics of its mother and how the latter can "know" what its rival looks like.

Instead of being faced, as Jensen's proposal would make it seem, with a Herculean task promising only uninteresting results, we have before us a program of practically feasible experiments which simply cannot fail to give interesting results one way or the other. All we have to do is to rear an animal, as perfectly as we can, under circumstances that withhold the particular information which we want to investigate. We need not bother about the innumerable factors which may cause "differences" in behavior as long as we are quite sure that they cannot possibly relay to the organism that particular information which we want to investigate. If our baby *Apistogramma*s, who have never seen an adult female of their species, selectively respond to a certain black and yellow pattern by following it and staying with it (as they would with their real mother) or if our stickleback responds to an object which is red below with the highly specific motor patterns used in fighting a rival, we are justified in asserting that the information which these fishes possess concerning these two objects is fully innate. In other words, the fish's genome must contain the blueprint of a perceptive apparatus which responds selectively to certain combinations and/or configurations of stimuli, and which relays the message "mother present" or "rival male present" to effector organizations equally adapted to dealing with this fact. That much we know, and this is, in my opinion, intensely interesting knowledge. Furthermore, it is knowledge which raises new questions.

First among these are the problems of ontogeny. It is a hackneyed fact that it is never more than just such a blueprint which is inherited and that between this inheritance and its final realization in bodily structures and functions lies the whole process of individual development of which experimental embryology (*Entwicklungsmechanik*) tries to gain causal understanding. This indeed is the truth contained in the statement that organs or behavior patterns must not be called innate. The experimental embryologists, while trying to gain insight into the physiological causality of development, have always acted on the knowledge that any structure which is elaborately adapted to functions and environmental givens to be faced only much later in individual life must be blueprinted in the genome. They also know that adaptive epigenetical regulation can only be expected on the basis of such information that one part of the embryo can receive from another. The ectoderm must have all the information about how to build a neural tube. What the ectoderm can "learn" from the organizer emanating from the chorda is only where to do so. If investigators never put this into words, it was because all this was a matter of course to all of them, but they certainly would not have gained the results they did had they allowed their approach to be narrowed by the attitude exemplified in Jensen's paper.

Any investigator of the ontogeny of animal behavior is well advised to begin with the time-honored procedure of first searching for whatever may be blueprinted by heredity. This is good strategy and not only for the simple reason that anatomy regularly begins with the investigation of the skeleton; in any system whose function consists of the interaction of many parts, the least changeable are the best point of departure, because their properties appear most often as causes and least often as effects in the interaction that is to be studied. An even better reason is that phylogenetically adapted structure represents, in the ontogeny of behavior, the indispensable prerequisite for guiding modification in the generally improbable direction of adaptedness. We cannot ever hope to understand any process of learning before we have grasped the hereditary teaching mechanism which contains this primary programming.

The emphasis which I am putting on the fact that we know about some indubitably inherited blueprints of motor patterns as well as of receptor organizations must not mislead anyone into thinking that I deem it unnecessary to investigate the ontogeny of behavior. The very opposite is true, particularly as far as receptor patterns (in other words, releasing mechanisms) are concerned. Among these, there is hardly one which, though indubitably based on innate information, is not rendered more selective by additional learning. A flashlike conditioning can take place at the very first function of a releasing mechanism and has to be taken into consideration in order to avoid the danger of mistaking what had actually been learned in the first experiment for innate information in later ones. In order to assess correctly the amount of innate information contained in a releasing mechanism, it is literally necessary to pull it to bits – no pun intended. The method of doing so will be discussed in the chapter on the deprivation experiment[c].

At present, one example is sufficient to illustrate the point. The behavior by which an inexperienced turkey hen responds to her first brood of chicks is dependent on a single phylogenetically adapted receptor mechanism. As Schleidt

[c] On page 89 of the book. (Editor's note.)

and Schleidt (1960) have conclusively shown, she treats every moving object within the nest as an enemy, unless it utters the specific note of the chick. A deaf hen invariably kills all of her own progeny immediately after hatching. A hen with normal hearing accepts and mothers any stuffed animal, if it is fitted with a small loudspeaker uttering the correct call notes. Under natural circumstances with a young turkey hen hatching her own young, the one phylogenetically adapted auditory reaction effects so rapid a conditioning of maternal responses to other stimuli emanating from the baby birds that after a few hours the unconditioned stimulus can be dispensed with and the mother is ready to brood the young even when they are silent. Nevertheless, the babies' call notes continue to enhance maternal activities.

The Schleidts did not succeed in finding an artificial substitute for the reinforcement of maternal behavior effected by the turkey chick's call note. Although it was possible with the utmost patience to sufficiently habituate some deaf hens to the presence of little chicks so that these were no longer killed on sight, it proved to be quite impossible to condition any deaf mother's maternal activities so as to respond to the babies. All that could be achieved was that the deaf birds behaved as if there were no chicks present, in spite of the fact that they were in exactly the right phase of their reproductive cycle and so tame that all kinds of manipulation were possible in the attempt to establish a contact between them and their progeny.

My point in telling about these highly interesting results is that they could never have been obtained by using the conceptualizations and methods proposed by Jensen. The operation of withholding specific information underlying adaptedness is only one among literally millions of possible changes "causing differences in behavior," and the chances of finding the effective conditioning mechanism which the Schleidts found by these methods is correspondingly small.

No biologist in his right senses will forget that the blueprint contained in the genome requires innumerable environmental factors in order to be realized in the phenogeny of structures and functions. During his individual growth, the male stickleback may need water of sufficient oxygen content, copepods for food, light, detailed pictures on his retina, and millions of other conditions in order to enable him, as an adult, to respond selectively to the red belly of a rival. Whatever wonders phenogeny may perform, however, it cannot extract from these factors information which simply is not contained in them, namely, the information that a rival is red underneath.

We must be quite clear about what we call a "behavior element." If the Kuenzers' baby *Apistogrammas* responded selectively to a certain color configuration which roughly but sufficiently corresponds to the coloration of the mother they have to follow, we certainly must assume a nervous mechanism which, among innumerable other possible visual stimulus situations, selects this particular one and connects it with effector patterns phylogenetically adapted to keep the little family together. This mechanism is, of course, dependent on a structure built during ontogeny on the basis of a genetical blueprint. The whole function of specifically responding to the maternal color patterns involves functions other than that of this particular mechanism. Many of the processes which take place on the way from sensory stimulation to the response are less specific than the latter. Not only the processes of visual stimulation in the retina, but much more highly integrated functions, like those of perception (including depth perception, color constancy, and so on), are used in very many other responses and/or activities of the animal. Among these functions there may be some that require ontogenetically acquired information for their full development. Even the function of retinal elements requires "practice"; it is well known that retinal elements are subject to atrophy if not sufficiently used. The faculty of point discrimination, probably performed by the ganglion retinae, is lost to a large extent if not practiced, even if diffused light and unfocused images do impinge on the retina. If a person's vision is impaired for a long period by purely optical deficiencies of the eye, point discrimination remains seriously damaged even after correction of the optical apparatus, a state of affairs termed *amblyopsia ex anopsia* by oculists.

It is a matter of taste whether or not one chooses to call it learning when an activity is necessary to prevent atrophy and disintegration of a physiological mechanism, but it can be regarded as adaptive modification and it may well involve ontogenic acquisition of information. Much the same is true of the effector side of the reaction. Orientation mechanisms, motor patterns, etc. functioning in a stickleback fighting a rival or in an *Apistogramma* baby following its mother may also be elements of behavior that occur in other contexts as well. Among them, too, there may be some that need an inflow of individually acquired information for their full functional development.

These modifications adapting the less specific elements of a more specific response are indispensable requisites for the proper functioning of the latter. They must, therefore, never be forgotten or overlooked in our attempts to analyze this function. On principle, however, they are no obstacle to the solution of our fundamental question concerning the provenience of the information underlying each point of adaptedness in behavior. Nor do they represent a very serious source of error quantitatively. What may be overlooked is the effect of a little sensory adaptation making an afferent process a little more selective, or that of a little practice smoothing out a motor coordination. But there is little danger, with circumspect experimentation and with an experimenter knowing its pitfalls, that any process of true learning, particularly classical conditioning, might pass unnoticed.

It must not be thought that the learned prerequisites for the proper functioning of innate information are only made up of the primitive types of adaptive modification of behavior. True conditioning does figure among them. A good example of this is furnished by the copulatory response of some geese. Greylags (*Anser anser*), greater snow geese (*Anser hyperboreus atlanticus*), and probably many others possess perfectly good phylogenetic information about how a fellow member of the species behaves when inviting copulation, but they have to learn what a fellow member of the species looks like. The genetic information may be verbalized as follows: copulate with a conspecific who is lying low in the water and is stretched out along its surface. Hand-reared greylags, usually born in the first days of May, usually do not meet their human foster parents swimming in the water earlier than June (in our climate). They then regularly attempt to tread them. As a human swimmer is much longer than any goose and also is lying much lower in the water, he represents a supernormal object for the copulatory response of all those geese which regard him as a conspecific. Even in very young fledgling geese and also in females, which normally never show any copulatory movements, attempts to tread can reliably be released by this supernormal stimulation. These phenomena definitely are not a consequence of imprinting. The geese behaving thus remain otherwise quite normal in respect to their sexual objects and do not persist in trying to copulate with humans. Nor do they ever attempt copulation with any other randomly chosen object that happens to be elongated and lying low in the water. These configurational properties are effective as key stimuli only if they pertain to an object which the goslings have learned to know as a fellow member of their species, and this learning is achieved by all the many conditioning processes which attach the gosling to its parents and its siblings.

Much ontogenetically acquired adaptive modification of behavior may be involved in a functional whole, such as fighting a rival in the stickleback, following the mother in *Apistogramma*, or copulating with a conspecific in geese; however, it does not affect either the correctness or the justification of our statement that certain parts of the information which underlie the adaptedness of the whole and which can be ascertained by the deprivation experiment are indeed innate.

It is obviously this information alone to which we have a right to apply the term innate. We cannot, however, think of any way for this information to express itself in adapted behavior other than by the function of a neural structure. It is the distinctive property of this structure to select, from among innumerable other possible stimulus situations, the one which specifically elicits the response. This property definitely is a character of the species. The neural mechanism is an organ and not a character. A character in *The Oxford English Dictionary* is a "distinctive mark."

When some geneticists and, following them, many modern ethologists contend that characters must never be called innate, I have a suspicion that they are confounding the concepts of a character and of an organ. The latter, of course, really must not be called innate nor, indeed, must a behavior pattern. The formulation that it is not characters but differences between characters which may be described as innate is, in my opinion, an unsuccessful attempt to arrive at an operational definition. If we rear two or more organisms under identical conditions, any differences shown by them may be regarded as caused by differences in the genome. Theoretically this is all right, but I doubt whether the definition can be put into operation. If we rear a number of larval fish in the same tank under "identical conditions," for instance with very few larval crustacea present, the few fish which happen to catch these few nauplii will grow much faster than those that don't. How can we prevent, on principle, analogous sources of error? It seems to me that the opposite formulation is at least as workable: calling innate the similarities of characters developing under dissimilar rearing conditions. If we observe that all mallard drakes – and many other male dabbling ducks – whether reared in the wild or in captivity, by their own mothers or by a human keeper, under good or under highly unnatural conditions, perform the grunt-whistle in very nearly the same way, the breadth of variability being almost negligible in the confines of one species, our assertion that this similarity is innate, that is, based on genetical information, has at the very least the same likelihood of being correct as the opposite one, that dissimilarities in identically reared organisms are innate. It is, indeed, the similarity of individuals that tells the taxonomist what a species really is, and he was never mistaken in applying this indubitably genetical concept even in Linné's time.

Our question, "Whence does the organism derive the information underlying all adaptedness of behavior?" leads directly to more special and to more general questions. What rules ontogeny, in bodily as well as in behavioral development, is obviously the hereditary blueprint contained in the genome and not the environmental circumstances indispensable to its realization. It is not the bricks and the mortar which rule the building of a cathedral but a plan which has been conceived by an architect and which, of course, also depends on the solid causality of bricks and mortar for its realization. This plan must allow for a certain amount of adaptation that may become necessary during building; the soil may be looser on one side, necessitating compensatory strengthening of the fundaments. The phylogenetically adapted blueprint of the whole may rely on subordinate parts adaptively modifying each other. The prospective chorda exerts a very specific adaptively modifying effect on the neighboring ectoderm, causing it to form a neural tube in exactly the right place. The adaptive modification effected by one part on the other may even take the form of true learning. The gosling "knows innately" that it should copulate with a fellow member of the species stretching out low in the water, but it has to learn what a fellow member of the species is. Any such adaptive regulations, however, presuppose at the very least as much information contained in the genetical blueprint as any elements of little or no modifiability do. In other words, the apparatus which makes adaptive modifiability possible is genetically blueprinted itself, and it is in a very complicated form, particularly if it allows so much scope to regulations as we find in embryogeny.

Because all the causal chains of development begin with the hereditary information contained in the genome (and the plasma) of the egg, our first question concerning the ontogeny of an organism and its behavior is: "What is blueprinted in its genome?" The second is: "What are the causal chains which begin at the blueprints given in the genome and which end up, by devious and often highly regulative routes, by producing adapted structure ready to function?" We are fully aware that the processes of growth can be separated from those of behavior only by an injunctive definition permitting intermediates. We think, however, that the processes of individual learning is sufficiently distinct from other processes of adaptive modification, and particularly from those regulating structural growth, that we are justified in leaving, at least for the time being, to the care of the experimental embryologists all those questions which are concerned with the chains of physiological causation leading from the genome to the development of such neurosensory structures. These structures, like the releasing mechanism of the stickleback's rival fighting or like that of the turkey hen's response to the chick's call, demonstrably owe their specific adaptedness to information acquired in phylogeny and stored in genes.

Not being experimental embryologists but students of behavior, we begin our query, not at the beginning of the growth, but at the beginning of the function of such innate mechanisms. The modern English-speaking ethologists are generally agreed that the concept of the "innate" is valuable and valid only if defined as "not caused by modification." This cautious definition, although of course quite true as far as it goes, states only the less important side of the problem.

The important one is that the phylogenetically adapted structures and their functions are what affect all adaptive modification. In regard to behavior, the innate is not only what is not learned, but what must be in existence before all individual learning in order to make learning possible. Thus, consciously paraphrasing Kant's definition of the *a priori*, we might define our concept of the innate.

This definition is truly operational, as can be seen in the Schleidts' and many other people's investigations. On the other hand, I defy anybody to put into practical operation the allegedly operational definition proposed by Jensen. Whoever tries it, will, with an overwhelming probability, die of old age before reaching publishable results. Hence the acceptance of this definition must discourage any investigation of the ontogeny of behavior.

Obviously it is the best strategy of research if, in our attempt to analyze the ontogeny of behavior, we first concentrate on the question: "What are the teaching mechanisms?" and second on the question: "What do they teach the animal?" In asking these questions, we may seem to neglect, at least for the time being, those "behavioral differences" which are "neither innate (selected) nor learned (trained) but something else (produced by other operations)." When we rear, in our experiments, an organism under circumstances which are calculated to withhold from it some specific information, we do our very best to avoid that kind of difference in behavior. In other words, we try to produce an individual whose genetical blueprints have been realized unscathed in the course of healthy phenogeny. Should we fail in this, we would incur the danger of mistaking some defects in our subject's behavior for the consequences of information withheld, while they really are the pathological results of stunted growth. This danger is very great if the investigator is not aware of it, if he does not know the system of actions of his subjects inside out, and if he does not possess what is called the "clinical eye." Otherwise, the danger is almost negligible.

Of course, the behavior of an otherwise perfectly healthy mandarin drake (*Aix galericulata L.*) whose sexual responses are fixated by the process of imprinting on mallard ducks (*Anas platyrhynchos L.*) is also indubitably pathological, particularly from the viewpoint of survival, as the bird is rendered permanently unable to reproduce. But not only do we know what behavioral system we have damaged in this mandarin by the intentional misinformation furnished to it at a critical stage of its ontogeny, but even if we did not know the previous history of the individual, we could still, with great certainty, deduce it from the symptoms.

In the present chapter, criticizing the assumption of a general and diffuse modifiability of phylogenetically adapted behavior mechanisms, I need only say that the enormous symptomatic difference between behavior defects caused by withholding information and defects "produced by other operations" is in itself extremely strong and convincing evidence against that assumption.

Finally, I want to discuss a speculative but, to me, rather convincing argument against assuming a diffuse modifiability of phylogenetically adapted behavior through learning. I have already said that with the increasing complication of an adapted system, the probability decreases that random change in any of its parts may produce anything but disadaptation. The power of the argument illustrated by the sports car is multiplied greatly when we consider really complicated neural systems, for instance, those performing real computations. Phylogenetic adaptation has created mechanisms of such subtle complication here that even a really brilliant physiological cyberneticist is barely able to gain a tolerably complete insight into their workings. After carefully reading and rereading Mittelstaedt's paper (1957) on the complex feedback mechanism enabling a mantid to aim a precise stroke at its prey, my own understanding of that mechanism is insufficient to permit sensible suggestions for its improvement. So I find it difficult to believe that the insect should be superior to myself in that respect, unless, of course, it possesses special built-in calibrating or adjusting mechanisms. I argue that this type of complicated neural mechanism must be highly refractory to random change by individual modification. The complexity and precision with which the processes of evolution have endowed these mechanisms would be destroyed immediately if individual modification by learning were allowed to tamper with them.

Even in man, computing mechanisms of this kind, particularly those of perception, are built in such a way as not to let learning "enter into" them. Although these mechanisms very often perform functions so closely analogous to rational operations that Brunswik (1957) termed them "ratio-morphous" processes, they stubbornly refuse to have anything to do with rational processes, least of all to let themselves be influenced by learning. As von Holst (1955, 1957) has shown, all so-called optical illusions, with very few exceptions, can be regarded as the results of ratio-morph operations which are caused to miscarry by the introduction of one erroneous "premise." From these, a perfectly logical computation draws a false conclusion. These mechanisms are not only inaccessible to self-observation but also refractory to learning.

If we consider learning as a specific function achieving a definite survival value, it appears as an entirely unfounded assumption that learning must necessarily "enter into" all other neurophysiological processes determining behavior. It is, however, by no means this theoretical consideration alone which causes us to reject that assumption; all experimental and observational evidence points that way. Not once has diffuse modifiability been demonstrated by experimentally changing arbitrarily chosen elements of phylogenetically adapted behavior mechanisms. On the other hand, innumerable observations and experiments tend to show that modifiability occurs, if at all, only in those preformed places where built-in learning mechanisms are phylogenetically programmed to perform just that function. How specifically these mechanisms are differentiated for one particular function is borne out by the fact that they are very often quite unable to modify any but one strictly determined system of behavior mechanisms. Honey bees can learn to use irregular forms, like those of trees or rocks, as landmarks by which to steer a course to and from the hive; but, they cannot, even by the most subtle conditioning technique, be taught to use these same forms as positive or negative signals indicating the presence or absence of food in a tray, as von Frisch (1914) has shown. As signals for food, bees can distinguish different forms only if they are geometrically regular, preferably radially symmetrical (Hertz, 1937).

In other words, the old and allegedly naïve theory of an "intercalation" of phylogenetically adapted and of individually modifiable behavior mechanisms, far from having been refuted by new facts, has proved to agree with them in a quite surprising manner. Scientists working on entirely different problems, such as the selectivity of innate releasing mechanisms, bird navigation, feedback mechanisms of aiming, circadian rhythms, etc. have one and all found that if modifiability existed at all, it was restricted to one particular link in the chain of neural processes determining behavior.

REFERENCES

Brunswik, E. (1957) Scope and Aspects of the Cognitive Problem. In J. S. Bruner et al., *Contemporary Approaches to Cognition*. Cambridge, MA: Harvard University Press.

Frisch, K., von. (1914) Der Farbensinn und Formensinn der Biene. *Zool. Jahrb.*, 35, 1–188.

Hertz, M. (1937) Beitrag zum Farbensinn und Formensinn der Biene. *Z. vgl. Physiol.*, 24, 413–21.

von Holst, E. (1955) Regelvorgänge in der optischen Wahrnehmung. *Rept, 5th Conf. Soc. Biol. Rythmn*, Stockholm.

von Holst, E. (1957). Aktive Leistung der menschlichen Gesichtswahrnehmung. *Studium Generale*, 4, 231–43.

Jensen, D. D. (1961) Operationism and the Question "Is This Behavior Learned or Innate?" *Behaviour*, 17, 1–8.

Kuenzer, E. and Kuenzer, P. (1962) Untersuchungen zur Brutpflege der Zwergcichliden *Apistogramma reitzigi* und *A. borrellii*. *Z. Tierpsychol.*, 19, 56–83.

Mittelstaedt, H. (1957) Prey capture in Mantids. *Recent Advances in Invertebrate Physiology*. University of Oregon Publ., 51–57.

Schleidt, W. and Schleidt, M. (1960) Störung der Mutter-Kind-Beziehung bei Truthühnern durch Gehöverlust. *Behaviour*, 16, 3–4.

2

The Problem of Change

SUSAN OYAMA

In thinking about forms, we tend to focus on constancy rather than change – constancy of a character through time, in spite of turnover in constituent materials and shifting conditions, similarities among related individuals or members of a species, continuity across generations or among related species. In fact, though, change and variability are as basic to biological processes as uniformity. Change and variability are not the same thing, though they are associated in important ways, and they both pose difficult problems for the conception of the directive gene. We will consider change in an entity first.

Embryogeny, as orderly, recurrent sequences of change, is the perfect synthesis of constancy and change. From day to day, sometimes from minute to minute, the entire system, increasingly intricate, changes – forms shift and disappear, lift and fold, divide and spread – yet each phase is largely predictable, at least in its outlines, as its end.[1]

Students of development in the seventeenth, eighteenth and nineteenth centuries discovered more astonishing complexity of change than had been previously imagined, and it was then that the preformationist and epigenetic views became engaged in an increasingly subtle dialectic, coalescing by the late nineteenth century in what Oppenheim (1982, p. 37) describes as an essentially modern position: "transmission of a *predetermined* (or rather, a preorganized) germ plasm in the nucleus that in the course of ontogeny is expressed via cytoplasmic *epigenesis*." It will be recalled that Oppenheim uses "epigenesis" for progressive ontogenetic change. It is also important to bear in mind that the course of development was agreed by preformationists and epigeneticists alike to be predetermined in some sense; the question was how this was to be understood. Gould says:

> The solution to great arguments is usually close to the golden mean, and this debate
> is no exception. Modern genetics is about as midway as it could be between the

"The Problem of Change" is an excerpt from: Susan Oyama, *The Ontogeny of Information* (Cambridge University Press, 1985, chapter 3, pp. 24–35) and is reprinted by kind permission.

extreme formulations of the eighteenth century. The preformationists were right in asserting that some preexistence is the only refuge from mysticism. But they were mistaken in postulating performed structure, for we have discovered coded instructions. (It is scarcely surprising that a world knowing nothing of the player piano – not to mention the computer program – should have neglected the storage of coded instructions.) The epigeneticists, on the other hand, were correct in insisting that the visual appearance of development is no mere illusion. (Gould, 1977, p. 18)

I, on the other hand, tend to be skeptical of golden mean solutions, because when two great traditions battle for long periods, there is generally, along with their disagreements, some basic misapprehension that they share, and from which, therefore, they do not attempt to dissuade each other. Preformationism did offer a refuge from mysticism in the sense of vitalistic forces acting directly on development each time it occurred, but only at the price of postulating a one-time-only simultaneous creation of all things (and no need, therefore, for real development). Though contemporary thought rejects nested bodies, it does not often balk at preformed targets and instructions. The pre-existence that the preformationists, the epigeneticists and current orthodoxy all agree upon is form, whether miniaturized and encapsulated, re-created by a vitalistic force or inscribed on a molecule. The corollary is that the pre-existing form must be the "same" as the final one; for the preformationists both were concretely material, for the epigeneticists form was first disembodied, then embodied, and for the modern thinker it is initially material but cryptic, then manifested in the phenotype. In fact, preformationism was not as naive as is often claimed; the important versions during biology's early years acknowledged differences in the relative position and shape of encapsulated organs, agreeing that if the embryo were enlarged it would not look like a finished organism (Gould, 1977, p. 20; Oppenheim, 1982). This brings them closer both to their traditional opponents and to modern views.[2]

Though Gould states that the preformationists were in error in postulating preformed structure, there is really nothing problematic about this idea. What is misguided, not only about the preformationist belief, but the modern version as well, is the assumption of correspondence between initial and final structure. The chromosomes are indeed highly structured, as are the cell organelles, the chemical substrates and the extracellular environment.

Emphasis on the structure in the genome without full acknowledgment of structure in the surround is common. Gould (1977, pp. 21–2) claims that the preformationist critique of epigenesis is still valid: if the egg is "truly unorganized, how could it yield such consistent complexity without a directing entelechy. It does so, and can only do so, because the information – not merely the raw material – needed to build this complexity already resides in the egg." Preformationists and epigeneticists agreed that a formless egg required form from without. Preformationists placed accomplished form inside the egg, while epigeneticists rejected this solution and instead posited an additional force. Gould appears to accept the vision of the formless egg and to place the entelechy-as-program inside. (See also Mayr, 1982, pp. 105–6.)

The situation is thus quite peculiar. What scientists say in some contexts is contradicted by what they say, know and do in others. It is therefore difficult to grasp what is happening without following arguments or trains of thought quite closely, and this is one of my tasks in this book. In fact, no biologist seriously limits structure to the chromosomes; they sometimes sound as if they do because *they assign formative relevance only to the DNA, where the encoded representation of the phenotype (or of the instructions for building it) is thought to reside.* This is the error, along with the associated idea that unless such a representation exists, development cannot be structured, and it is a pervasive and fundamental error indeed.[3]

If matter and form are distinct, as one part of our classical tradition tells us, and matter is inert (recall Toulmin's (1967) argument about seventeenth-century thought), then both the emergence of form and change in that form must be explained. We tend to see the "biological" as that which has the power to effect change without being changed. Maturation, conceived causally rather than descriptively, is seen as a force bringing basic characters into being, without requiring, indeed, without permitting, more than minimal environmental influence (Oyama, 1982). Maturation in turn is seen as driven and guided by the genes, which "initiate and direct" development (Gesell, 1945, p. 19), which are potentially immortal (Williams, 1974, p. 24), and which, of course, are not generally altered by their cellular interactions. To continue the causal progression, the genes are formed by random variation and natural selection. Gatlin has noted that "the words 'natural selection' play a role in the vocabulary of the evolutionary biologist similar to the word 'God' in ordinary language" (1972, p. 164), and Montalenti observes that natural selection is the biological *primum movens* (1974, p. 13). Just as traditional thought placed biological forms in the mind of God, so modern thought finds many ways of endowing the genes with ultimate formative power, a power bestowed by Nature over countless millennia.

"But wait," the exasperated reader cries, "everyone nowadays knows that development is a matter of interaction. You're beating a dead horse."

I reply, "I would like nothing better than to stop beating him,[4] but every time I think I am free of him he kicks me and does rude things to the intellectual and political environment. He seems to be a phantom horse with a thousand incarnations, and he gets more and more subtle each time around. Just look at the horselets, infrahorses and metahorses described in this book. What we need here, to switch metaphors in midstream, is the stake-in-the-heart move, and the heart is the notion that some influences are more equal than others, that form, or its modern agent, information, exists before the interactions in which it appears and must be transmitted to the organism either through the genes or by the environment. This supports and requires just the conceptions of dual developmental processes that make up the nature – nurture complex. Compromises don't help because they don't alter this basic assumption."

Jacques Monod, who, with Jacob, presided over some of the most exciting developments in molecular biology, describes in minute detail various macromolecular processes and their organizing functions. When he engages in straightforward description, the complexity and interdependence of causes are clear. When he interprets these processes in more general terms, however, an interesting thing occurs. He says, for example, that the genome "entirely defines" protein function, and asks if this is contradicted by the statement that the protein's three-dimensional structure has a "data content" that is "*richer* than the direct contribution made to the structure by the genome." His answer is

that, because the three-dimensional, globular structure appears only under "strictly defined initial conditions," only one of all possible structures is realized.
"Initial conditions hence enter among the items of information finally enclosed
within the globular structure. Without specifying it, they contribute to the
realization of a unique shape by eliminating all alternative structures, in this way
proposing – or rather, imposing – an unequivocal interpretation of a potentially
equivocal message" (Monod, 1971, p. 94, emphasis in original). But if initial
conditions select one folded structure among an array of possible ones, thus
contributing to the unique shape, they *do* specify it, in cooperation with the
linear structure. The particular globular shape results only when particular chains
fold under particular conditions. Monod is forced, in his terms, to admit that
the structure therefore "contains" more information than it would if such
conditions were not critical. But his commitment to the power of the gene
entirely to define leads him to withhold "specifying" power from the cellular
environment. This is not due to idiosyncratic use of "specify"; elsewhere he
makes much of the *specificity* of enzyme action – that is, the selective interaction
with only one or two molecule types from many.

Earlier in the same book (p. 84), he asserts that he uses "epigenesis" for all
structural and functional development, not in the old sense of the epigeneticists,
who, in contrast to the preformationists, "believed in an *actual* enrichment of
the initial genetic information." Since the eighteenth and nineteenth centuries
lacked the contemporary notion of genetic information, one can only speculate
on the precise meaning of this assertion, but in the light of Monod's general
position it seems reasonable that he was distancing himself from any view that
attributes real formative power to anything other than the gene. Again, in
discussing the preformation – epigenesis dispute, he says:

> No preformed and complete structure preexisted anywhere; but the architectural
> plan for it was present in its very constituents. It can therefore come into being
> spontaneously and autonomously, without outside help and without the injection of
> additional information. The necessary information was present, but unexpressed, in
> the constituents. The epigenetic building of a structure is not a *creation*; it is a
> *revelation*. (Monod, 1971, p. 7; emphasis in original)

And, after another vivid description of development, he concludes, "The
determining cause of the entire phenomenon, its source, is finally the genetic
information represented by the sum of the polypeptide sequences, interpreted –
or, to be more exact, screened – by the initial conditions" (p. 95). If, by initial
conditions, he means only the intracellular environment when the molecular chain
folds through the third dimension, he is excluding from this story all other
nongenetic conditions, including substrates, intracellular machinery, factors influencing occurrence and rate of enzymatic action, as well as interactions at the
tissue, organ and organism levels that can, at best, be only partially explained
by stereospecific interactions among molecules. Even if he includes these sources
of specificity (and therefore of "information"), they evidently do not qualify as
"determining causes" or "sources" of the phenomenon itself.

I dwell on Monod at length because he is a skilled and expressive writer,
because it is difficult to question his credentials in molecular biology, because

he has chosen to address issues beyond that field, such as ontogeny, evolution and values, and because, given his standing as a scientist, he has unusual authority when he does so. He is thus in a powerful position to influence the thinking of his colleagues and of the general public, particularly because this conceptual ground is so well prepared.

In reviewing *Chance and Necessity*, Toulmin (1982a) places Monod's thinking (and his rhetorical style) in the context of a French intellectual tradition that has been slow to relinquish progressivist ideas of evolution. Monod's emphasis on the role of the random in evolution and on the one-way flow of information from gene to protein is perhaps best understood in this light. Ravin (1977) points out that this latter notion of unidirectional transfer of information, Crick's "central dogma," is a denial of the inheritance of acquired characters. It is, however, unnecessary to deny nongenetic contributions to biological form in order to deny Lamarckian inheritance. As Toulmin points out in the above review, even randomness of variation is not essential to an anti-Lamarckian argument, though "decoupling" of variation from selection is.

One might argue that Monod is concerned, not so much with the particulars of Lamarckian evolution (some of which Darwin did not himself reject), as with Lamarckianism as emblematic of an unscientific vitalism. Not being above using "vitalistic" and "preformationistic" as terms of abuse myself, I would point out two things. First, both are descriptive of particular kinds of attitudes and explanations, as well as of broad philosophical–theoretical positions, and they can coexist within theories and within persons. Second, any approach to biological processes that begins with inert raw materials requires a mindlike force to fashion this matter into a functioning animal-machine. This approach is at odds with what we know about physics and chemistry, including Monod's own findings about the interactions of complex molecules. The implications of this kind of view of development as revelation will be elaborated in later chapters. At this point, however, lest it seem that I am singling out a scholar whose primary field is not development, and in fact one who has every reason to be particularly impressed with genetic functioning, let me point out that the views described are not at all peculiar to Monod, or to molecular biologists. They exemplify much thinking in biology and psychology. Indeed, if this were not so I would not be writing this book.

Decades ago, a sensitive and sophisticated observer of human development, who understood ontogenetic processes very well indeed, made similar statements about the causal primacy of the gene. In his much-quoted pronouncement, Arnold Gesell (1954) declared that environmental factors "support, inflect, and specify, but they do not engender the basic forms and sequences of ontogeny" (p. 354; see discussion in Oyama, 1982). Oppenheim (1982) has argued that Gesell sometimes belied his understanding of development in his efforts to counteract excessive environmentalism. This seems correct and important to me, and it is often the case that we must temper our reading of documents with such historical perspective. As was the case with Monod's polemic for scientific Darwinism and against mystical Lamarckianism, however, it is important to distinguish justifiable implications from false ones. One of the problems with these grand oppositions is that, while they may fuel investigation and theoretical advance, by placing those activities in an erroneous context they make correct inference improbable.

Opponents tend to pay more attention to refuting each other's claims than to examining the logical bases for those claims. By combatting environmentalism with special formative, engendering genetic causes, Gesell only legitimized the underlying assumption that genetic and environmental causes could and should be distinguished in this way. He thus helped perpetuate the environmentalist–nativist opposition, when, as Oppenheim and I point out, his approach potentially transcended it.

It is the structure of the argument, finally, that intrigues and troubles. Almost three hundred years ago, preformationists wondered whether the germ, the complete but inert form, was in the sperm or the egg. Because fertilization was necessary to activate development, there were, as for Gesell and Monod, two necessary sets of interactants, neither sufficient to produce the organism. Both influences were granted power to affect the outcome (the parent who did not contribute the germ could still impart some qualities to the offspring). The basic form, however, was contributed by only the egg or only the sperm, depending on which camp one was in (Jacob, 1973, pp. 57–9).[5]

The assumption seems to be that change of the sort we see in developmental processes must have a single, fundamental source; since such change is ordered and directional, the problem becomes essentially that of the origin of form. Having defined an induced pattern as one that is "imposed . . . by the immediate environment," Bonner (1974) comments that the pattern resulting from embryological induction lies not in the inductor but "largely in the stimulated tissues" (pp. 221, 249). Much of the history of embryology has been the chronicle of attempts to locate patterns in tissues or in chemicals (see Waddington, 1962, pp. 190–195, on patterns and prepatterns), as that of the study of behavioral development has frequently been an exercise in pronouncing patterns to be inborn or learned. The problem, of course, is that patterns as such don't exist anywhere before they are realized – constructed by reciprocal selection (or coaction, McClearn and DeFries, 1973, p. 311; Oyama, 1981) in ontogeny.

Yund and Germeraad (1980) follow standard procedure in declaring that development results from a "highly coordinated program of gene activity. The genome itself is the program. It must contain all the information for its own regulation." They admit, though, that little is known about the "branching" of the developmental program governing gene expression in multicellular organisms (p. 317). They go on to describe cellular determination as "commitment" to a "particular branch of the developmental program" and outline the methods of investigating the time of determination by looking at subsequent differentiation of cells *in vitro* or after transplantation. Interestingly enough, they remark that the more sophisticated the manipulation, the fewer are the cases of completely stable, irreversible commitment. (See also Alberts et al. (1983, p. 835), who state that the crucial characteristic of determination is not irreversibility, but heritability, defined as "self-perpetuating change of internal character that distinguishes it [the cell] and its progeny from other cells in the embryo and that commits these progeny to a specialized course of development." Note that "heritability" here refers not to genetic changes but to enduring alterations in cellular processes that distinguish the cell and its progeny from other cells. See also Margulis, 1981, pp. 164, 177, and 224.) So dependent is commitment on the method of investigation and the particular question asked that its strict definition as stable cell fate has been abandoned. In its place is a conception in which a "separate decision, regardless of its stability, occurs at each branch in the program." One can say only that a cell is on a particular path at a particular time, and investigate the mechanisms and relative stability of the decision. Its developmental potential, say the authors, narrows with each decision (Yund and Germeraad, 1980, pp. 317–19). Surely this is not consistent with the idea that the cell's genetic program contains "information for its own regulation," but rather with an indeterminate process in time, whose regulation depends on conditions. "Decisions" are not written in the nucleus but are made on the basis of developmental contingency. It is no wonder that determination becomes largely a matter of methodology, in fact, since "decision" is merely an anthropomorphic locution for a consequence. Individuals may decide to become this or that, and resolutely commit themselves to a course of action. Cells change states or not, depending on their competence, which may change, and their surroundings, which may also change. Their "commitment" must therefore be assessed with respect to those considerations.

Under some circumstances, a peculiar phenomenon known as transdetermination may be observed. Transplanted imaginal disc tissue from the larva of the fly *Drosophila*, for example, usually behaves in a very "programmed" manner, apparently being determined or committed very early in development to give rise to certain adult structures. It will sometimes, however, differentiate into structures characteristic of *other* discs. This new determined state can be propagated by serial cloning. Furthermore, transdetermination may occur repeatedly, with successive transplantations. The authors note that the ability to transdetermine depends on the developmental state of the cells, especially age, and on original position in the imaginal disc (Yund and Germeraad, 1980, pp. 333–5). Once again we observe that investigators' descriptions of actual phenomena give the lie to their general pronouncements on the nature of development. It is not even the case that each developmental decision narrows the cell's potential, any more than an individual's does; in transdetermination, potential seems to shift and increase in scope (Alberts et al., 1983, pp. 833–40).

Conceptually the problem of determination is parallel to that of the sensitive period as fixer of developmental fate. The behavioral notion of the sensitive period is in fact derived from the embryological one of critical period and tissue determination (Oyama, 1979). Detailed investigation in both cases reveals a phenomenon that is not absolute and definitive, but complex and relative, one that is much more consistent with the model of development being elaborated here than with any fixed program.

A corrective for a person who tends to think too much in terms of potters molding clay or of computers printing out messages might be the idea of campers raising and stabilizing a tent pole by pulling in opposite directions. Stability is dynamic, clearly depends on both participants, and may be maintained to the extent that variation from one or both directions can be compensated for. Attributing the general outcome to one camper and trivial details to the other would falsify the process. I hasten to add that I don't consider this an adequate metaphor for ontogeny, but rather an illustration of a fairly simple point about causation: that it is multiple, interdependent and complex. Even the potter, in fact, does not command absolutely. An artisan respects the qualities and limits of the material as much as he or she does his or her own; much of artistry, in fact, lies in just this respect for, and sensitivity to, the medium and the developing form. Finally, a program, to be useful, must be responsive to its data; outcomes are jointly determined.

It would seem that polemics do not justify arguments of the Monod–Gesell type, which, being characterized by their structure, pre-date these two scientists and can be found on the environmentalist side as well. They do not adequately represent the analytic reality that the author is attempting to convey. In fact, by misattributing the orderliness of these processes, they diminish the impact of the argument.

Change, then, is best thought of not as the result of a dose of form and animation from some causal agent, but rather as a system alteration jointly determined by contemporary influences and by the state of the system, which state represents the synthesis of earlier interactions. The functions of the gene or of any other influence can be understood only in relation to the system in which they are involved. The biological relevance of any influence, and therefore the very information it conveys, is jointly determined, frequently in a statistically interactive, not an additive, manner, by that influence and the system state it influences.

In mice, many cell types contain the same androgen receptor protein, but different types of cells respond to androgen stimulation by activating different genes (Paigen, 1980). Again, the *Drosophila engrailed* mutation influences sex combs, bristles or vein patterns, depending on the appendage. The authors who cite this research observe that organs seem not to have their own "subplans" but to use general mechanisms in specific ways (Leighton and Loomis, 1980, p. xvi). The impact of sensory stimuli is a joint function of the stimuli and the sensing organism; the "effective stimulus" is defined by the organism that is affected by it. That one creature's sensory meat is another's poison, or that the same stimulus may have different effects on the same organism at different times, does not render stimulation causally irrelevant or merely permissive (as opposed to formative). The concepts of motivation, personality and maturation have been developed in part to address such contingency of stimulus effects. Similarly the gene controls by being controlled or selected, sometimes by other parts of the genome, and even regulatory genes regulate by being regulated (Kolata, 1984). One of the prime questions of developmental biology, in fact, is that of differential gene activation.

Causation is endlessly interlocked, and the biological "meaning" of changes depends on the level of analysis and the state of the whole. This perspective may make it more difficult to say with confidence what constitutes a "whole" or a "system" in any given case, but since the material of life is neither structureless nor inert, there is no need for animistic forces; form and control are defined in life processes, not the other way around. (See also Waddington, 1972, p. 111.)

In describing the nested feedback loops (which, by definition, involve reciprocal control) through which the environment influences developmental processes, Bonner declares the search for ultimate control factors to be futile, unless one conceives of ultimate control as that which

> comes from the power gained by repeated, successive life cycles. Only in this way can one achieve a vast array of complex, interacting events. Successive life cycles

allow the accumulated information of millions of years to be used at a moment's notice. As far as control mechanisms go, there is no end: they go back to the beginning of life and are part of what we have called evolutionary development. The products of that control information are realized in each life cycle. (Bonner, 1974, pp. 156–7)

When Bonner asserts that life cycles may use "information" developed in previous cycles, he is referring primarily to cell products and structures already in place when a new sequence of ontogenetic differentiation begins. His discussion of nongenetic inheritance, in which "direct inheritance from one generation to the next is not restricted to the DNA of the genome, but many other substances and structures are built up from previous cell cycles" (p. 180), could readily be extended to include extracellular, even extraorganismic influences. The notion of life cycles as nested feedback loops (or at least, nested sets of relationships) is a crucial one that deserves wider generalization to include not only pheromonal cycles in social insects, which Bonner considers to be the largest ontogenetic loop, but other essential ecological relationships as well, *even when they involve the inanimate world or other organisms.*

What we are moving toward is a conception of a developmental system, not as the reading off of a pre-existing code, but as a complex of interacting influences, some inside the organism's skin, some external to it, and including its ecological niche in all its spatial and temporal aspects, *many of which are typically passed on in reproduction* either because they are in some way tied to the organism's (or its conspecifics') activities or characteristics or because they are stable features of the general environment. It is in this ontogenetic crucible that form appears and is transformed, not because it is immanent in some interactants and nourished by others, or because some interactants select from a range of forms present in others, but because any form is created by the precise activity of the system. Since even species-typical "programmed" form is not one but a near-infinite series in transition throughout the life cycle, each whole and functional in its own way, to refer to the type or the typical is also to refer to this series and the constant change that generates it.

If the genome, highly structured and integrated as it is, cannot by itself explain the products of ontogenetic change (the cognitive, planning function), can it at least be seen as the driving force (the causal, volitional, energetic function) of such change? Much is written about the genes initiating, engendering and originating, and the idea of diminutive chemical engines powering biological processes is appealing. In fact, of course, a gene initiates a sequence of events only if one chooses to begin analysis at that point; it occupies no privileged energetic position outside the flux of physical interactions that constitutes the natural (and the artificial) world. A seed may remain dormant for years, and though plants frequently show this kind of developmental passivity,[6] it is observed among animals as well (Clutter, 1978). Genes affect biological processes because they are reactive, and this reactivity is a prime characteristic of our world, at all levels of analysis, from the subatomic through the social to the astronomical. To describe biological processes as the product of exchanges of energy, matter and information, while consistent with the temper of the times, is misleading in seeming to postulate a third, quasi-physical force at work in the world. Both the initiation and the course of biological change are a function of developmental systems, and there is no evidence that our notions of matter and energy exchanges, themselves admittedly evolving, are inadequate to describe them. Adding information to matter and energy is something like speaking of nations exchanging dollars, yen and profits. The third term belongs on a different level. Not another form of currency, it describes a certain disposition and use of currencies. Just as time or information can, under certain circumstances, "be" money, matter and energy can sometimes "be" information.

It may be objected that this view of development as the result of changing and widely ramified systems is too complex and multiple, that its boundaries are too indistinct, potentially extending to anything and everything in the universe. In fact, when we attempt to provide artificial conditions for proper development of captive animals, we are often forcefully reminded of the breadth and variety of linkages between biological processes and extraorganismic factors. When feeding or reproductive "instincts" fail in captivity, we are prompted to search for missing factors in the vital system, often without success. What is programmed, committed or determined, switched or triggered, depends on external considerations that are as causally basic to the design of the phenomenon as internal factors, whether or not they are included in the design of the researcher, and however they are designated after the fact.

In living beings, no agent is needed to initiate sequences of change or to guide them to their proper goals. Matter, including living matter, is inherently reactive, and change, far from being an intrusion into some static natural order, is inevitable.

NOTES

1 Because ontogeny continues at least to the adult period, and, some would argue, through senescence to death (Bonner, 1974, pp. 167–8, for instance), what is considered the "end" is somewhat arbitrary. Though the adult is traditionally seen to be the end of development, both in the sense of goal and in the sense of terminus, with everything else either an incomplete transition to, or a degeneration from, this basic form, a strong argument can be made that ontogenesis is continuous with the life cycle. Every stage is thus equally the "end" of development. Unlike a machine, which is generally useless until it is completely assembled, an organism "works" at all points in its development. For a view of development that places ends in genomes, this implies that not only the standard adult form but also every stage of the life cycle must be "in" the genes. When norms of reaction or sets of potentials are thought of as being encoded, the genomic freight rapidly becomes prodigious.

2 Gasking (n. d.) distinguishes between preformationism as a *prediction* of what would be seen in the germ, especially if parts were hardened and made visible, and as an *explanation* of development. It was the latter that was generally primary, and it was quite consistent with gradual appearance during embryogeny (pp. 48–50).

3 These points become especially interesting and important in Gould's case, for unlike many of the other writers cited in these pages, he has been persistent in his opposition to various kinds of genetic determinism and alert to their consequences (Gould, 1981, and numerous columns in the magazine *Natural History*, for instance). Over the last several years his writings on these issues has become steadily more interactionist. Program metaphors seem to have dropped out, and in their place is an opposition

between biological determinism as a "theory of limits" and, on the other hand, "biological potentiality" "viewed as a range of capacity" (Gould, 1984, p. 7). For reasons that will become clear later, this formulation unfortunately does not quite solve the problem. It neither distinguishes his position from those of the workers he criticizes (many of whom use an interactionist vocabulary of sorts and readily speak of potential rather than fate) nor, much the same thing, fully detaches him from the notion of fixed limits (often expressed, in fact, as biologically encoded potential). What are limits, in fact, but the boundaries of the range of capacity? Gould's eloquence and moral commitment are considerable; we will all benefit from his continued thinking about these matters.

4　In *The Ghost in the Machine*, Arthur Koestler gives a hierarchical systems account of ontogeny, phylogeny and creativity, covering some of the problems treated here but in the service of a quite different aim. Having been accused of criticizing behaviorism once too often, he advocates the formation of the SPCDH, the Society for Prevention of Cruelty to Dead Horses (Koestler, 1967, p. 349). For an interesting treatment of Koestler's work, see the three reviews by Stephen Toulmin collected in Toulmin (1982b).

5　It is perhaps significant that the arguments the preformationists had used against each other in the ovist – animalculist controversy were deployed in the mid eighteenth century by Maupertuis against the preformationists themselves (Gasking, n. d., pp. 70–8).

6　"Active" and "passive," as should be clear from this discussion, do not generally characterize entities, but only signal focus on sources of perturbation and effects of perturbation, respectively.

REFERENCES

Alberts, B., Bray, D., Lewis, J., Raff, M., Roberts, K. and Watson, J. D. (1983) *Molecular Biology of the Cell*. New York: Garland.

Bonner, J. T. (1974) *On Development*. Cambridge, MA: Harvard University Press.

Clutter, M. E. (1978) *Dormancy and Developmental Arrest*. New York: Academic Press.

Gasking, E. (n. d.) *Investigations into Generation: 1651–1828*. Baltimore, MD: Johns Hopkins University Press.

Gatlin, L. L. (1972) *Information Theory and the Living System*. New York: Columbia University Press.

Gesell, A. (1945) *The embryology of behavior*. Westport, CT: Greenwood Press.

Gesell, A. (1954). The ontogenesis of infant behavior. In L. Carmichael (ed.), *Manual of Child Psychology*, 2nd edn. New York: Wiley, 335–73.

Gould, S. J. (1977) *Ontogeny and Phylogeny*. Cambridge, MA: Harvard University Press (Belknap Press).

Gould, S. J. (1981) *The Mismeasure of Man*. New York: Norton.

Gould, S. J. (1984) Similarities between the sexes. *New York Times Book Review*, August 12, 7.

Jacob, F. (1973) *The Logic of Life: a History of Heredity* (B. E. Spillman, trans.). New York: Pantheon Books (original work published 1970).

Koestler, A. (1967) *The Ghost in the Machine*. New York: Macmillan.

Kolata, G. (1984). New clues to gene regulation. *Science*, 224, 588–9.

Leighton, T. and Loomis, W. F. (1980) Introduction. In T. Leighton and W. F. Loomis (eds), *The Molecular Genetics of Development*. New York: Academic Press, xiii – xxiii.

Margulis, L. (1981) *Symbiosis in Cell Evolution: Life and Its Environment on the Early Earth*. San Francisco: Freeman.

Mayr, E. (1982) *The Growth of Biological Thought*. Cambridge, MA: Harvard University Press (Belknap Press).

McClearn, G. E. and DeFries, J. C. (1973) *Introduction to Behavioral Genetics*. San Francisco: Freeman.

Monod, J. (1971) *Chance and Necessity* (A. Wainhouse, trans.). New York: Knopf.

Montalenti, G. (1974) From Aristotle to Democritus via Darwin. In F. J. Ayala and T. Dobzhansky (eds), *Studies in the Philosophy of Biology*. Berkeley, CA: University of California Press, 3–19.

Oppenheim, R. W. (1982) Preformation and epigenesis in the origins of the nervous system and behavior: issues, concepts, and their history. In P. P. G. Bateson and P. H. Klopfer (eds), *Perspectives in Ethology*, vol. 5. New York: Plenum, 1–100.

Oyama, S. (1979) The concept of the sensitive period in developmental studies. *Merrill-Palmer Quarterly*, 25, 83–103.

Oyama, S. (1981) What does the phenocopy copy? *Psychological Reports*, 48, 571–81.

Oyama, S. (1982). A reformulation of the concept of maturation. In P. P. G. Bateson and P. H. Klopfer (eds), *Perspectives in Ethology*, vol. 5. New York: Plenum, 101–31.

Paigen, K. (1980) Temporal genes and other developmental regulators in mammals. In T. Leighton and W. F. Loomis (eds), *The Molecular Genetics of Development*. New York: Academic Press, 419–70.

Ravin, A. W. (1977) The gene as catalyst; the gene as organism. In W. Coleman and C. Limoges (eds), *Studies in History of Biology*. Baltimore, MD: Johns Hopkins University Press, 1–45.

Toulmin, S. (1967) Neuroscience and human understanding. In G. C. Quarton, T. Melnechuk and F. O. Schmitt (eds), *The Neurosciences: a Study Program*. New York: Rockefeller University Press, 822–32.

Toulmin, S. (1982a), Jacques Monod. In S. Toulmin (ed.), *The Return to Cosmology*. Berkeley, CA: University of California Press, 140–55.

Toulmin, S. (ed.) (1982b) *The Return to Cosmology*. Berkeley, CA: University of California Press.

Waddington, C. H. (1962) *New Patterns in Genetics and Development*. New York: Columbia University Press.

Waddington, C. H. (1972). Form and information. In C. H. Waddington (ed.), *Towards a Theoretical Biology*, vol. 4. Edinburgh: Edinburgh University Press, 109–45.

Williams, G. C. (1974) *Adaptation and Natural Selection*. Princeton, NJ: Princeton University Press.

Yund, M. A. and Germeraad, S. (1980) Drosophila development. In T. Leighton and W. F. Loomis (eds), *The Molecular Genetics of Development*. New York: Academic Press, 237–360.

3

The Epigenetic System and the Development of Cognitive Functions

JEAN PIAGET

1 Preformation and Epigenesis

The problem that has always arisen before one could tackle ontogenesis has been preformation or epigenesis. With the usual veering of fashion in the history of ideas, the tendency of many writers today is to return to the more or less strict preformation standpoint. Their grounds for this are that the chain or helical structure of the DNA or deoxyribonucleic acid molecule is susceptible of a combinatorial arrangement of its elements where "combinatorial" covers, by definition, the set of all possibilities. But if it is difficult, from the phylogenetic point of view, to conceive of man as preformed in bacterium or virus, it is every bit as hard to make out how, from the ontogenetic point of view, the main stages of "determination" or induction, and, most important, of the final functional "reintegration" of differentiated organs, could already be present in the initial stages of segmentation. Furthermore, Waddington has stated categorically that the idea of an entirely predetermined system in the DNA, however fashionable it may be at the moment, is just unacceptable in embryology[a]. At the symposium on this subject at Geneva in 1964, in the course of discussion about the regulations of development, he made a very profound comparison between epigenetic construction and a progression of geometric theorems in which each is rendered indispensable by the sum of those preceding it, though none is directly derived from the axioms underlying the original one.

---

[a] See Waddington (1975) – cited under Further reading. (Editor's note.)

"The Epigenetic System and the Development of Cognitive Functions" is an excerpt from: Jean Piaget, *Biology and Knowledge* (Edinburgh University Press and University of Chicago Press, 1971, section 2, pp. 14–23) and is reprinted by kind permission.

The comparison of epigenesis with a progressive mathematical construction comes home to us all the more forcibly because the growth of elementary logico-mathematical operations during the ontogenesis of intelligence in a child raises the same problem of preformation or epigenetic construction as that which forms the basis of discussion about causal embryology.

We shall, indeed, find ourselves compelled to trace the origin of logico-mathematical operations back to an abstraction made from the general coordination of actions. On the one hand, such operations cannot possibly be based on the objects themselves, since abstraction from objects can give rise only to non-necessitous statements (in the sense of deductive necessity) or, to put it more precisely, to judgements which are merely probable, whereas it is characteristic of logico-mathematical operations that they have an internal necessity attributable to their complete reversibility (and therefore not physical): for example, if $i = \sqrt{-1}$, then $i \times i = -1$. On the other hand, reunion, order, and interchangeable schemata are to be found in the general coordination of action, and these constitute the practical equivalent and even the motor equivalent of future interiorized operations.

If these elementary logico-mathematical operations are based on the coordination of actions, by means of reflective abstraction[b] drawn from sensorimotor schemata, do we have to conclude that the whole of mathematics is laid down in advance to our nervous system? Not only is this unthinkable, but the facts prove that logic itself, even in its most "natural" forms, is by no means innate in human beings in the sense that it exists at any age. Even the transitivity of equals or of cumulative differences ($A = C$ if $A = B$ and $B = C$, or $A < C$ if $A < B$ and $B < C$) is by no means obvious to a child of four to six years when he has to make a comparison between lengths and weights on first perceiving A and B simultaneously, next B and C, but not A and C (A subsequently being hidden and so presenting the problem).

The task of finding out about this transitivity raises all the main problems of epigenesis. Is this transitivity inherent in the genotype of the human species? If so, why does it not automatically come into play at about seven or eight years (and about nine or ten for weights)? Because, it will be said, new conditions are indispensable if the inherent virtual is later to become actual: for example, the intervention of regulatory genes or the collaboration of a number of genes not so far synergic (by reference to genetic or genic coadaptation, to use the currently accepted term). However, as these differentiated regulations are not made at any definite age in the particular case but may be accelerated or retarded according to conditions of exercise or acquired experience, they certainly exercise factors which are indirectly connected with environment.

Can it then be said that transitivity is utterly unconnected with the actions of the genome and solely dependent on phenotypic actions of the organism in relation to environment? In that case, how can it become "necessary" and generalizable? Because those actions which exert an influence on environment

---

[b] Piaget defines "reflective abstraction" as the process of "reconstruction with new combinations, which allows for any operational structure at any previous stage or level to be integrated into a richer structure at a higher level" (section 20, part 4, p. 320 of *Biology and Knowledge*). (Editor's note.)

are influenced in their turn by the more generalized forms of internal coordinations of action? If that were so, would then generalized coordinations depend, in their turn, on the most common and deep-seated coordinations of the nervous system, which brings us back to the genome?

The evidence thus proves that the problem of preformation or epigenesis has nothing about it that appertains specially to organic embryogenesis, and it crops up in its most acute form every time we discuss the ontogenesis of cognitive functions. It may be objected that the problem is settled in advance, since the various aspects of intellectual behavior are phenotypic reactions and a phenotype is the result of interaction between the genotype and the environment. That is indisputable, but one still needs to explain in detail how, in the field of knowledge as in that of organic epigenesis, this collaboration between the genome and the environment actually works – especially those details which concern autoregulations or progressive equilibrations which admit of the exclusion of both preformism and the notion of a reaction caused entirely by environment.

2 The Sequential Character of Stages

In this attempt at elucidation, the first step forward should be an examination of the sequential character of development. We call sequential a series of stages, each one of which is a necessary part of the whole and a necessary result of all the stages that precede it (except for the first one), as well as naturally leading on to the next stage (except for the last one). This seems to be the case with the embryogenesis of Metazoa, since the main stages constantly repeat themselves in the same order. However, no experiments have yet been done to control the impossibility of doing away with one stage, though these will doubtless be performed some day if someone succeeds in isolating processes which entail considerable speeding up or slowing down of the succession of stages. A further argument in favor of the sequential character and generality of the stages is the fact that, in mosaic-type embryos, namely at the initial level studied, those which have shown incomplete regeneration when separated from a blastomere reach a stage of partial control if the seed is split at the virgin egg stage (Ascidies de Dalcq).

Now this same problem about the sequential character of stages appears again in psychology in connection with the development of the cognitive functions. It is important to note that in this sphere the stages became increasingly clear and sequential in relation to controls that are better differentiated and of wider application.

Psychologists have relied too much on the notion of stage. Some speak as though it were nothing but a series of actions, not always, though "generally," in a constant order, and supposedly sharing a dominant characteristic, nothing more – which opens the door to arbitrary thinking. This is what Freud means by stages, for example, as far as the affective is concerned.

When it comes to intelligence, however, we use the term stage where the following conditions are fulfilled: first, where the series of actions is constant, independently of such speeding up or slowing down as may modify the middle range of chronological age[1] in terms of acquired experience and social environment (like individual aptitude); second, where each stage is determined not merely by a dominant property but by a whole structure which characterizes all further actions that belong to this stage; third, where these structures offer a process of integration such that each one is prepared by the preceding one and integrated into the one that follows. For example, without going into great detail about particular stages, three main periods can be seen in the case of operative intelligence:

A. A sensorimotor period (from birth up to one and one-half to two years) during which sensorimotor schemata ranging up to acts of practical intelligence by means of immediate comprehension (using a stick or a piece of string, etc.) are established as well as practical substructures of future notions (permanent object schema, spatial deplacement "group," sensorimotor causality, etc.).

B. A period that begins when the semiotic function (language, game symbols, picture making) manifests itself and goes through the preparatory phase of preoperative representation (nonconservation, etc.). This ends not later than the eighth or ninth year with the setting up of operations which are called "concrete" because they still have a bearing on objects (classifying things, putting them in series, noting connections, understanding numbers).

C. A period beginning at about the age of eleven or twelve which is characterized by propositional operations (implications, etc.) with their combinatorial quality and their possible transformations made by relation to a quaternary group – a combination of two elementary reversibility forms (inversion or negation and reciprocity).

A stage system of this kind (stages which can actually be even further differentiated into substages) makes up a sequential process: it is not possible to arrive at "concrete" operations without undergoing some sensorimotor preparation (which explains why, for example, blind people, having badly coordinated action schemata, may be retarded). It is also impossible to progress to propositional operations without support from previous concrete operations, etc. Thus, one is confronted with an epigenetic system whose stages may be characterized by fairly precise structures: coordination of sensorimotor schemata reaching certain invariables and an approximate reversibility (though in successive actions); "groupings" of concrete operations, that is, those elementary structures which are common to classifications and serializations, etc.; and combinatorial with a quaternary group at the third degree.[2]

By contrast, in the field of primary perceptions (or field effects) no comparable system of stages is to be found, and, as to behavior of medium complexity (perceptive activity in exploration, etc., and mental images), an intermediary situation is found halfway between an absence of stages and stages limited by their progressive integrations. Thus, everything seems to happen as though the more complex – in their organization and autoregulation systems – cognitive systems are, the more their formation is dependent on a sequential process comparable to a biological epigenesis.

3 Chreods

If a detailed study is to be made, that is, if the evolution of broad concepts or of particular operative structures is to be studied separately, then each one may give rise to its own respective stages in the midst of which is to be found the same sequential process. But the interesting thing about this point is that it presents us with differentiated channels, each one of which is nevertheless relatively even and follows its own course while still giving proof of varied interactions with the rest.

Waddington has suggested the name "chreods" (necessary routes) to describe developments particular to an organ or a part of an embryo, and he applies the term epigenetic system (or, epigenetic "scene") to the sum of the chreods, taken as being – to a greater or a lesser degree – channeled[c]. But the main interest of this idea is not just in the names he gives things (or in the symbolic patterns thereby presented to us, of channels, some wide, some narrow, that the processes must follow). It is, rather, in a new concept of equilibrium as something which is, as it were, kinematic and which, in determining such processes, is nevertheless quite distinct from homeostasis: there is a kind of "homeorhesis" when the formatory process, deviating from its course under outside influence, is brought back on course by the interplay of coercive compensations. In Waddington's opinion, such a mechanism is dependent upon a network of interactions rather than upon the action of individual genes; each group of genes is not even homeorhetic, and its return to a moral course or chreod presupposes, in this way, a complex interplay of regulations. It is true that some influence systematically exerted by the environment may eventually lead to lasting deviations in the chreod and to the consolidation of a new homeorhesis, but this is not the moment to raise such a problem. On the contrary, we would do better to emphasize the fact that the chreod and its homeorhesis do have a space–time aspect, not merely a space one. Differentiation in chreods is regulated in both time and space. The various channelings as well as the autocorrections which assure their homeorhetical equilibrium are under the control of a "time tally," which might well be described as a speed control for the processes of assimilation and organization. It is, then, only at the completion of development or at the completion of each structural achievement that homeorhesis gives place to homeostasis or functional equilibrium. In the latter case, the question naturally arises of determining the relationship between the two.

It is impossible to take note of such a picture without immediately thinking of the far-reaching analogies it has with the development of schemata or ideas in the intelligence, and with that of operational structures.

To put the matter in a familiar way, let us begin by noting that these analogies are very far from being universally accepted; very rarely have I been able, in America, to expound any aspect of my stage theory without being asked, "How can you speed up this development?" And that excellent psychologist, J. Bruner, has gone so far as to state that you can teach anything to any child at any age if only you set about it the right way. My answer to this is in the form of two questions: first, would it ever be possible to make the theory of relativity or even the simple handling of propositional or hypothetico-deductive operations comprehensible to a four-year-old? And, second, why does a human baby not discover the continued presence of something that he sees you hide beneath a screen until he reaches the age of nine months and upward, whereas kittens (in a study made

[c] See Editors note a.

by H. Gruber when he discovered the same preliminary stages in them as in us) do so at three months, even though they make no further progress in coordinating successive positions?

The truth, it seems to me, is that every notional or operational construction implies some optimum length of time, the expression of the most favorable transformation or assimilation speeds. This is because such a construction contains a certain number of necessary stages whose itinerary is the equivalent of a "chreod." In the sphere of the mind, where social influences are added to factors of physical experience (material environment), deviations easily occur, and short circuits too. Thus, the natural way for the mind to attain the concept of whole numbers consists of syntheses of inclusion of classes and the sequence of transitive asymmetrical relationships, in spite of the fact that the latter two systems develop along partly independent lines. Now the natural structure of the number concept can be modified in various ways. First of all, as is done by many parents, it can be taught the child verbally – ten to twenty, etc. But this only modifies the child's comprehension very slightly; we are constantly coming across subjects of four to five years old who will deny the equality of two piles of objects, even though they have counted what is in each pile as being perhaps seven or ten, because the way the objects were arranged in space or subdivided into small groups was changed each time. In such cases, outside influences, such as counting out loud, only produce a slight deviation leading back to the "chreod" at the four- to five-year-old level, for lack of any means of assimilation at higher levels. In other cases, a genuine acceleration can be set up, but only at one point (for example, in experiments where transfers are made one at a time in succession, thus facilitating, by repetition of the same actions, the synthesis of inclusions and the serial order).[3] This local synthesis is not necessarily followed by comprehension, nor will it guarantee retention of the number in transfer experiments between groups of objects arranged differently on different planes.

Briefly, intellectual growth contains its own rhythm and its "chreods" just as physical growth does. This is not, of course, to say that the best teaching methods, by which we mean the most "active" ones, cannot, to a certain extent, speed up the critical ages dealt with so far, but this speeding up cannot be indefinitely continued.

4 Maturation and Environment

The epigenesis of the cognitive functions, like any other, does, in fact, presuppose an increasingly close collaboration between the factors of environment and the genome, the former increasing in importance the larger the subject grows.

The factors relative to the genome are certainly not to be left out of account, in spite of what some scholars, empirically oriented, have said about all knowledge being drawn from outside experience. At this stage of our knowledge, these factors certainly cannot be tested in detail, but the best indication that they do intervene is the fact that the maturation of the nervous system is continuous right up to the age of fifteen or sixteen years. This, of course, in no way implies that ready-made knowledge is written into the nervous system from the outset in the way that "innate ideas" are, and, even if this idea proves acceptable in the case of certain instincts, there does not seem to be any similar phenomenon where human knowledge is concerned. On the contrary, heredity and maturation open up new possibilities in the human child, possibilities quite unknown to lower types of animal but which still have to be actualized by collaboration with the environment. These possibilities, for all they are opened up in stages, are nonetheless essentially functional (having no preformed structures) in that they represent a progressive power of coordination; but this very power is what makes possible the general coordinations of action on which logico-mathematical operations are based, which is why the continuous maturation of the nervous system that goes on until fifteen or sixteen years is a factor by no means to be ignored.

Such maturation does not, moreover, depend solely on the genome. But it does depend on that among other things (with the intervention of exercise factors, etc.), and, in general terms, it is admitted today that every phenotypic growth (including, therefore, cognitive functions in general) is the product of close interreactions between the genome and the environment.

The analysis of this collaboration remains, it is true, very complex and has scarcely been touched on so far. At this point we might begin by referring to an idea for which we are indebted, once more, to Waddington. This time it dates back to the work he did in 1932 on the phenomena of induction in the embryos of hens and ducks, to the idea of "competence," or the physiological state of a tissue, which permits it to react in a specific way to given stimuli. Competence is naturally subject to time conditions such as we talked about earlier, and a tissue may be competent at one particular phase without having been so previously or even remaining so afterward.

Surely no one can fail to see the analogy between this notion in relation to the embryonic mechanism and the facts brought out by experiments in the field of learning in logico-mathematical operations. The work of such people as Inhelder, Sinclair, and Bovet opened this up. When mechanisms favorable to the acquisition of knowledge are thus presented (for example, retaining the idea that there is the same amount of liquid when changing it from one vessel to another of a different shape), the results are utterly different according to the stage of the child's development, and the particular presentation which causes one subject to learn more quickly about a constant quantity will leave another utterly unmoved. The explanation of this again lies in the fact that sensitivity to stimuli (not only perceptual stimuli but in some cases those which set up a reasoning process) is a function of such assimilation schemata as are available to the subject. In this case, then, "competence" is a particular instance of what we call cognitive "assimilation," but assimilation schemata are built up by the interplay among the subject's powers of coordination and by the data of experience and environment.

To put it briefly, the epigenetic process which is the basis of intellectual operations is rather closely comparable to embryological epigenesis and the organic formation of phenotypes. Of course, the part played by environment is much larger, since the essential function of knowledge is to make contact with environment. To the effects of physical environment we must add those of social environment (for the individual genome is always the reflection of multiple crossbreedings and of a fairly broad range of "population"). But the essential question does not concern the quantitative sum of the respective influences exerted by endogenitive and external factors; rather, it has to do with qualitative analogies, and from that point of view it seems obvious that internal coordinations of the necessary and constant type, which make possible the integration of exterior cognitive aliment, give rise to the same biological problem of collaboration between the genome and the environment as do all the other forms of organization which occur in the course of development.

NOTES

1 In psychology the distinction is always made between chronological and mental age.
2 This sequential character of the stages of intelligence certainly seems to prove the necessity of an endogenic factor in nervous maturation, but by no means excludes either the intervention of the environment (experience) or, more particularly, the interaction of environment and maturation at the center of a process of equilibration or progressive autoregulation.
3 In this case, it was the putting of beads, simultaneously, one in each hand, into transparent bottles. See Inhelder and Piaget, *La formation des raisonnements récurrentiels*, Etudes d'épistémologie génétique, 17 (Presses Universitaires de France, 1963), chapter 2.

4

Toward a Biological Theory of Language Development

ERIC H. LENNEBERG

1 Five General Premises

The language theory to be proposed here is based upon the following five empirically verifiable, general biological premises.

(i) *Cognitive function is species-specific.* Taxonomies suggest themselves for virtually all aspects of life. Formally, these taxonomies are always type-token hierarchies, and on every level of the hierarchy we may discern differences among tokens and, at the same time, there are commonalities that assign the tokens logically to a type. The commonalities are not necessarily more and more abstract theoretical concepts but are suggested by physiological and structural invariances. An anatomical example of such an invariance is cell-constituency – it is common to all organisms. In the realm of sensory perception there are physiological properties that result in commonalities for entire classes of animals, so that every species has very similar pure stimulus thresholds. When we compare behavior across species, we also find certain invariances, for instance, the general effects of reward and punishment. But in each of these examples there are also species differences. Cells combine into a species-specific form; sensations combine to produce species-specific pattern-recognition; and behavioral parameters enter into the elaboration of species-specific action patterns.

Let us focus on the species-specificities of behavior. There are certain cerebral functions that mediate between sensory input and motor output which we shall call generically *cognitive function.* The neurophysiology of cognitive function is largely unknown but its behavioral correlates are the propensity for categorizing in specific ways (extraction of similarity), the capacity for problem solving, the

"Toward a Biological Theory of Language Development" is an excerpt from: Eric H. Lenneberg, *Biological Foundations of Language* (John Wiley & Sons Inc., 1967, chapter 9, pp. 371–80) and is reprinted by kind permission.

formation of learning sets, the tendency to generalize in certain directions, or the facility for memorizing some but not other conditions. The interaction or integrated patterns of all of these different potentialities produces the cognitive specificities that have induced von Uexkuell, the forerunner of modern ethology, to propose that every species has its own world-view. The phenomenological implications of his formulation may sound old fashioned today, but students of animal behavior cannot ignore the fact that the differences in cognitive processes (a) are empirically demonstrable and (b) are the correlates of species-specific behavior.

(ii) *Specific properties of cognitive function are replicated in every member of the species.* Although there are individual differences among all creatures, the members of one species resemble each other very closely. In every individual a highly invariable *type* of both form and function is replicated. Individual differences of most characteristics tend to have a normal (Gaussian) frequency distribution and the differences within species are smaller than between species. (We are disregarding special taxonomic problems in species identification.)

The application of these notions to (i) makes it clear that also the cognitive processes and potentialities that are characteristics of a species are replicated in every individual. Notice that we must distinguish between what an individual actually does and what he is capable of doing. The intraspecific similarity holds for the latter, not the former, and the similarity in capacity becomes striking only if we concentrate on the general type and manner of activity and disregard such variables as how fast or how accurately a given performance is carried out.

(iii) *Cognitive processes and capacities are differentiated spontaneously with maturation.* This statement must not be confused with the question of how much the environment contributes to development. It is obvious that all development requires an appropriate substrate and availability of certain forms of energy. However, in most cases environments are not specific to just one form of life and development. A forest pond may be an appropriate environment for hundreds of different forms of life. It may support the fertilized egg of a frog or a minnow, and each of the eggs will respond to just those types and forms of energy that are appropriate to it. The frog's egg will develop into a frog and the minnow's egg into a minnow. The pond just makes the building stones available, but the organismic architecture unfolds through conditions that are created within the maturing individual.

Cognition is regarded as the behavioral manifestation of physiological processes. Form and function are not arbitrarily superimposed upon the embryo from the outside but gradually develop through a process of differentiation. The basic plan is based on information contained in the developing tissues. Some functions need an extra organismic stimulus for the initiation of operation – something that triggers the cocked mechanisms; the onset of air-breathing in mammals is an example. These extra-organismic stimuli do not shape the ensuing function. A species' peculiar mode of processing visual input, as evidenced in pattern recognition, may develop only in individuals who have had a minimum of exposure to properly illuminated objects in the environment during their formative years. But the environment clearly does not shape the mode of input processing, because the environment might have been the background to the visual development of a vast number of other types of pattern-recognition.

(iv) *At birth, man is relatively immature; certain aspects of his behavior and cognitive function emerge only during infancy.* Man's postnatal state of maturity (brain and behavior) is less advanced than that of other primates. This is a statement of fact and not a return to the fetalization and neotony theories of old.

(v) *Certain social phenomena among animals come about by spontaneous adaptation of the behavior of the growing individual to the behavior of other indiviuals around him. Adequate environment* does not merely include nutritive and physical conditions; many animals require specific social conditions for proper development. The survival of the species frequently depends on the development of mechanisms for social cohesion or social cooperation. The development of typical social behavior in a growing individual requires, for many species, exposure to specific stimuli such as the presence of certain action patterns in the mother, a sexual partner, a group leader, etc. Sometimes mere exposure to social behavior of other individuals is a sufficient stimulus. For some species the correct stimulation must occur during a narrow formative period in infancy; failing this, further development may become seriously and irreversibly distorted. In all types of developing social behavior, the growing individual begins to engage in behavior as if by resonance; he is maturationally ready but will not begin to perform unless properly stimulated. If exposed to the stimuli, he becomes socially "excited" as a resonator may become excited when exposed to a given range of sound frequencies. Some social behavior consists of intricate patterns, the development of which is the result of subtle adjustments to and interactions with similar behavior patterns (for example, the songs of certain bird species). An improverished social input may entail permanently impoverished behavior patterns.

Even though the development of social behavior may require an environmental trigger for proper development and function, the triggering stimulus must not be mistaken for the cause that *shapes* the behavior. Prerequisite social triggering mechanisms do not shape the social behavior in the way Emily Post may shape the manners of a debutante.

2 A Concise Statement of the Theory

(1) Language is the manifestation of species-specific cognitive propensities. It is the consequence of the biological peculiarities that make a human type of cognition possible.[1] The dependence of language upon human cognition is merely one instance of the general phenomenon characterized by premise (i) above. There is evidence that cognitive function is a more basic and primary process than language, and that the dependence-relationship of language upon cognition is incomparably stronger than vice versa.

(2) The cognitive function underlying language consists of an adaptation of a ubiquitous process (among vertebrates) of categorization and extraction of similarities. The perception and production of language may be reduced on all levels to categorization processes, including the subsuming of narrow categories under more comprehensive ones and the subdivision of comprehensive categories into more specific ones. The extraction of similarities does not only operate upon physical stimuli but also upon categories of underlying structural schemata. Words label categorization processes.

(3) Certain specializations in peripheral anatomy and physiology account for some of the universal features of natural languages, but the description of these human peculiarities does not constitute an explanation for the phylogenetic development of language. During the evolutionary history of the species form, function and behavior have interacted adaptively, but none of these aspects may be regarded as the "cause" of the other. Today, mastery of language by an individual may be accomplished despite severe peripheral anomalies, indicating that cerebral function is now the determining factor for language behavior as we know it in contemporary man. This, however, does not necessarily reflect the evolutionary sequence of developmental events.

(4) The biological properties of the human form of cognition set strict limits to the range of possibilities for variations in natural languages. The forms and modes of categorization, the capacity for extracting similarities from physical stimulus configuration or from classes of deeper structural schemata, and the operating characteristics of the data-processing machinery of the brain (for example, time-limitations on the rate of input, resolution-power for the analysis of interwined patterns such as nested dependencies, limits of storage capacities for data that must be processed simultaneously, etc.) are powerful factors that determine a peculiar type of form for language. Within the limits set, however, there are infinitely many variations possible. Thus the outer form of languages may vary with relatively great freedom, whereas the underlying type remains constant.

(5) The implication of (1) and (2) is that the existence of our cognitive processes entails a potential for language. It is a capacity for a communication system that must necessarily be of one specific type. This basic capacity develops ontogenetically in the course of physical maturation; however, certain environmental conditions also must be present to make it possible for language to unfold. Maturation brings cognitive processes to a state that we may call *language-readiness*. The organism now requires certain raw materials from which it can shape building blocks for its own language development. The situation is somewhat analogous to the relationship between nourishment and growth. The food that the growing individual takes in as architectural raw material must be chemically broken down and reconstituted before it may enter the synthesis that produces tissues and organs. The information on how the organs are to be structured does not come in the food but is latent in the individual's own cellular components. The raw material for the individual's language synthesis is the language spoken by the adults surrounding the child. The presence of the raw material seems to function like a releaser for the developmental language synthesizing process. The course of language-unfolding is quite strictly prescribed through the unique maturational path traversed by cognition, and thus we may say that language-readiness is a state of *latent language structure*. The unfolding of language is a process of *actualization* in which latent structure is transformed into *realized structure*. The actualization of latent structure to realized structure is to give the underlying cognitively determined type a concrete form.[2]

(6) The actualization process is not the same as "beginning to say things." In fact, it may be independent from certain restraints that are attending upon the capacity for making given responses. Actualization may take place even if responses are peripherally blocked; in this case actualization is demonstrable only

through signs of understanding language. In cases where the proper raw material for language synthesis cannot be made available to the growing child (as in the deaf), the latent structure fails to become actualized either temporarily or permanently.

(7) The maturation of cognitive processes comes about through progressive differentiation. Physiological (and, therefore, cognitive) functions assume characteristics and specificities much the way cells and tissues do during ontogeny. Organs do not suddenly begin to function out of a state of silence, but every function in the mature individual is a derivative of embryologically earlier types of function. Although the primitive functions may often be different from the mature ones, we cannot say just when a later or derived process had its beginning. If language is an aspect of a fundamental, biologically determined process, it is not scientifically profitable to look for a *cause* of language development in the growing child just as we do not look for a *cause* for the development of his ears. It might be more fruitful to think of maturation, including growth and the development of behavior such as language, as the traversing of highly unstable states; the disequilibrium, of one leads to rearrangements that bring about new disequilibria, producing further rearrangements, and so on until relative stability, known as *maturity*, is reached. Language-readiness is an example of such a state of disequilibrium during which the mind creates a place into which the building blocks of language may fit.

(8) The disequilibrium state called language-readiness is of limited duration. It begins around two and declines with cerebral maturation in the early teens. At this time, apparently a steady state is reached, and the cognitive processes are firmly structured, the capacity for primary language synthesis is lost, and cerebral reorganization of functions is no longer possible.

(9) The language potential and the *latent structure* may be assumed to be replicated in every healthy human being because they are a consequence of human-specific cognitive processes and a human-specific course of maturation. In other words, universal grammar is of a unique type, common to all men, and it is entirely the by-product of peculiar modes of cognition based upon the biological constitution of the individual. This notion of replication, which is a cornerstone of the present theory, also leads us to assume that the actualization process from latent to realized structure is universal because of replicated sequences of similar states of disequilibrium, and there is evidence for this assumption in the regularity of language-acquisition strategies discussed in earlier chapters.

(10) Because latent structure is replicated in every child and because all languages must have an inner form of identical type (though an infinity of variations is possible), every child may learn any language with equal ease. The realized structure or outer form of the language that surrounds the growing child serves as a mold upon which the form of the child's own realized structure is modeled. This maneuver is possible only because all languages are so constructed as to conform to the stringent requirements imposed upon them by cerebral language-data processing mechanisms. Insistence upon universal, underlying identity of type in all languages may be difficult to understand in the face of differences in rules of syntax and semantic divergences. This puzzle is solved by considering the remarkable freedom allowed individual speakers to make creative

and novel use of word-meanings, to reclassify words into various syntactic categories, and to take creative freedoms with rules of syntax. All aspects of outer form or realized structure are in a state of fluidity (of relatively high viscosity) indicating that it is our "mode of calculating with categories" that is universal, but the categories themselves are not fixed, nor the particular choice of the many possible operations.

(11) The raw material from which the individual synthesizes building blocks for his own language development cannot be the cause of the developing structure as evidenced by the autochthonous beginnings in the infant's language acquisition. Primitive stages of language are simply too different from adult language to be regarded as a direct mirroring of the input. Nor is there any evidence that the adults surrounding the child are the causative or shaping agents that determine language onset or his course of development. Purposiveness cannot, logically, be the mainspring for language development.

(12) Social settings may be required as a trigger that sets off a reaction. Perhaps a better metaphor still is the concept of resonance. In a given state of maturation, exposure to adult language behavior has an excitatory effect upon the actualization process much the way a certain frequency may have an excitatory effect upon a specific resonator; the object begins to vibrate in the presence of the sound. In the case of language onset, the energy required for the resonance is, in a sense, supplied by the individual himself; if the trigger-analogy, is preferred, we might say that he unwinds himself. The resonance analogy, on the other hand, illustrates more vividly how slight variations in the frequencies that impinge on the resonator may affect the quality or nature of the resonance; it is comparable to the child's hearing of French resulting in his speaking of French, each natural language being a selected frequency band from the limited possible frequency range that is capable of eliciting resonance. Once the critical period during which resonance may occur is outgrown, one language is firmly established, and exposure to new and different natural languages is no longer resonated to.

Thus the propagation and maintenance of language behaviour in the species are not comparable to cultural tradition which is handed down from generation to generation. The individual does not serve as a passive vehicle or channel through which information is transmitted; instead, he is an autonomous unit constituted in very much the same way as other units around him, ready to behave in the same fashion as they do. His behavior is activated by social contact, and there is some superficial adaptation to the structure of their behavior, but it may be well to remember that he can only function if he can synthesize (recreate might be another word) the entire language mechanism out of the raw material available to him. The raw material is of no use unless it can be broken down as food proteins are broken down into amino acids and built up again into the pattern of his in-dwelling latent structure. Thus, the individual is seen as functioning by virtue of his own power supply, so to speak; he constructs language by himself (provided he has the raw material to do it with), and the natural history of his development provides for mechanisms by which he will harmonize his function with that of other equally autonomously functioning individuals around him; the outer form of his language will have the outer form of the language of his native community.

(13) Even though biological constitution of the individual is an essential replica of its progenitors, there are, naturally, individual variations. In fact, there are two distinct levels that are relevant to language: in the formation of the latent structure and in the actualization process from latent to realized structure. The former may be due to variations in the operation of cognitive processes or due to variations in the maturational course; the latter is primarily due to variations in peripheral function and structures such as the vocal tract or the ears. Variations on these two levels explain the main facts about language constancies, language change, and language universals.

3 Explanatory Power of the Theory

These are the essentials of the theory. Most of its tenets are merely special instances of the general premises (i) through (v) cited at the beginning of the chapter and may, therefore, be considered as fairly common biological phenomena. A few of the tenets, however, may seem novel introductions into the armamentarium of explanations for behavior. But within the wider horizon of biological theory they should not at all look like theoretical innovations or logically illegitimate freedoms. The natural history of species-specific behavior is proposed here to partake of most of the characteristics and peculiarities encountered in the history of differentiated anatomical structures or physiological functions. Sections (5) and (12) particularly make no stronger assumptions than those made by the theory of morphogenesis or general physical development. It is true that the most crucial questions surrounding embryology have yet to be answered, and the same is true of the molecular mechanisms that would underlie the phenomena proposed here. Just as the present state of embryological theory, my theory of language development is essentially an interpretive commentary on observable facts.

The observable facts are the absence of any need for teaching of language as well as the relative ineffectiveness of programmed training upon the rate of language acquisition; the resonance phenomenon is most beautifully seen in the language development of twins who influence each other in the actualization process, sometimes resulting in peculiar deviations in their realized structure or outer form when compared to the model form of the language surrounding them. The regularity of language-onset as a milestone that fits into an ordered and fairly constant sequence of other maturational milestones is another observable fact and so is the apparent similarity in language acquisition strategies, the universal similarity of primitive stages, and the difference in outer form between primitive stages and adult language. Other observable facts are the differences between children and adults in their recovery from acquired aphasia. Furthermore, nothing short of statement (5) can account for the perfect ease with which blind children learn meanings and even blind-and-deaf children may acquire the fundamentals of language, although they may have to recode input and output.

Sometimes it is said that the general claim of species-specificity of behavior or the postulation of innate factors that determine such behavior is a return to the preformist position of eighteenth-century developmental theory. Nothing could be farther from the truth. Modern ethology is as epigenetic as embryology itself is today. The preformist believed that the ovum contained a miniature specimen of the adult individual, whereas the epigenetic doctrine teaches that the adult form is the result of gradual formation of structure through a continuing process of reconstitution of molecules, and that every individual is, therefore, created anew, so to speak. It is obvious, however, that the laws of formation must be duplicated in every growing individual and that these laws follow from information or guidelines that are encoded in the genic material of the first cell. Environmental conditions, such as gravity, temperature, availability of oxygen, space to expand in, etc., are, in many cases, necessary factors for proper development, but they are never sufficient to determine the formation of the structural plan peculiar to a given species of complex animals. Clearly, our proposal of how language develops in the individual is in no way counter to an epigenetic view.

NOTES

1 It is true that this statement introduces some profound problems in the theory of evolution, but our preoccupation with language should not oblige us to solve, at the same time, the general problems that affect all evolutionary phenomena. The emergence of celestial navigation in birds or the diving abilities of whales are no less mysterious than the emergence of a language-enabling cognition.
2 This formulation might be regarded as the biological counterpart to what grammarians have for centuries called *universal* and *particular* grammar. Latent structure is responsible for the general type of all features of universal grammar; realized structure is responsible both for the peculiarities of any given statement as well as those aspects that are unique to the grammar of a given natural language.

Part II

Brain Maturation

Introduction

One of the earliest roots of development psychology in the United States was the study of how brain maturation gives rise to motor development (see Carey 1980 – further reading, part III; Thelen, part VII). During the behaviorist era, this approach fell out of favor, and the infant was viewed as more of a *tabula rasa*, albeit one containing some powerful learning algorithms. As mentioned earlier, part of the purpose of this book is to redress the balance, and to enquire more closely into the relation between the developing brain and cognitive change. To do this, however, we need to review what is known about the pre-and post-natal development of the brain. In this and the following part, we focus on intrinsic determinants of developmental change. In contrast to this, parts IV and V focus on the influence of external experience on neural and cognitive development.

Developmental neurobiology is a large and rapidly growing field of enquiry, at least as large as cognitive development. The articles that are contained in this part only present a tiny proportion of what is known. However, they serve to illustrate that brain development is not a uniform process. There are variations not only in the timing of development between brain regions, but also between aspects of neuronal development within a brain region. Some of the conclusions for this part may be summarized as follows:

1 Different regions of the brain develop at different times and rates (Chugani et al., Huttenlocher).
2 Different progressive and regressive events in neurogenesis often occur at different times within any given region (Nowakowski, Rakic, Huttenlocher).
3 Many (but not all) markers of neurogenesis show an "inside-out" pattern of growth within the cerebral cortex, but the opposite pattern in other regions of the brain (Rakic, Huttentlocher).
4 Major regressive events occur during postnatal brain development (Chugani et al., Huttenlocher).

In the first reading of this part, Nowakowski reviews studies of the development of the brain from its earliest embryonic stages to around the time of birth. He distinguishes among "the *when*, the *where*, and the *what*" questions. The "when" question can be further divided into issues surrounding the *absolute* time frame, and issues surrounding the *relative* timing of events. With regard to the latter he points out that development is a sequential cascade of events where particular events can affect those that follow it, but not those that precede it. One example of this concerns the relative numbers of certain types of cells generated for the cerebellar cortex, a part of the brain involved in coordinating motor behavior. Cell types that are generated slightly earlier in development (Purkinje cells) appear to have a role in regulating the number of cells of a different type generated slightly later in development (granule cells), but not vice versa. Thus, data on the relative timing of developmental events can be crucial in unravelling causal relations in development.

The importance of "where" questions is illustrated by Nowakowski's discussion of the importance of the three dimensions of the neural tube (length, circumference, and radial dimensions), the first manifestation of what will subsequently become the brain in the vertebrate embryo (see figure 3 in Nowakowski's chapter). The major divisions of the nervous system are produced along the longitudinal dimension of the neural tube, with one end becoming the spinal cord and the other forebrain. Differentiation along the radial dimension of the neural tube gives rise to many of the laminar structures found within vertebrate brains.

The cerebral cortex, like some other brain regions, is highly structured in both the vertical and horizontal planes. In the vertical plane, functionally organized "columns" form, while in the horizontal plane layers with particular cell types and connectivity patterns form. Nowakowski spends a considerable portions of the chapter discussing evidence relating to the "what" question. That is, how do cells differentiate into types and gain their specific connectivity patterns? In some brain regions, cells reach their final destination by being passively pushed away from the proliferative zone by more recently generated cells. This results in an "outside to inside" pattern developing, with the most developed cells being furthest away from the site of origination. In more distinctly layered structures, such as the cerebral cortex, the opposite pattern is found: the most recently generated cells migrate past their older relatives, resulting in the cells closest to the proliferative zone (the deeper layers – 5 and 6 – of the mammalian cortex) being the first to develop. Some computational consequences of this characteristic "inside to outside" pattern of growth are investigated in part III (Johnson). The cells migrate by a mechanism that may help to create the vertical structure of the cortex: they become attached to a radial glial fibre that acts like a climbing rope to guide them to their appropriate location. This mechanism is discussed in more detail by its main proponent, Pasko Rakic, in the next reading.

Rakic's "radial unit model" of neocortical parcellation gives an account of how both the vertical (columnar) and the horizontal (layer) structure of the mammalian cerebral cortex arise. The vertical columnar organization of the cerebral cortex is determined by the fact that each proliferative unit gives rise to about 100 neurons that all migrate up the same radial glial fibre, with the latest born travelling furthest, and past their older relatives (resulting in the inside-out pattern of growth mentioned earlier). Rakic speculates that regulatory genes, known as homeobox genes, may be involved in parcellating the proliferative zone into a basic protomap of cortical cytoarchitectonic areas. The scaffolding provided by the radial glial fibres simply enable the translation of this 2D map from one location to another. While the general boundaries between cortical areas may be partly regulated by genetic control, Rakic also discusses evidence that thalamic inputs adjust the relative sizes of these areas in a use-dependent way (see also the reading by O'Leary in part IV). That is, competitive interactions between thalamic inputs to the cortex may determine the number of proliferative units that are devoted to that input (see also reading by Johnson, part VIII). While there is, as yet, no strong evidence that this fetal vertical organization maps directly onto the functional cortical columns found in the adult, it is possible that they correspond in some respect.

With regard to the horizontal lamination of the cerebral cortex, Rakic explores the possibility that cells only differentiate once they have reached their appropriate vertical location. By this account, certain genes would be expressed according to the local biochemical environment at certain vertical distances from the proliferative zone. But, since we know that in the adult cortex different cell types appear within the same layer, this cannot be the whole explanation. Furthermore, Rakic cites some recent evidence that cells begin to differentiate before they reach their final vertical location. For example, in the genetic mutation "reeler" mice, cells that acquire inappropriate laminar positions within the cortex still differentiate into neuronal types according to their time of origin rather than the types that would normally be expected at their new location. This implies that the information required for differentiation is present at cell birth in the proliferative zone, rather than it being dependent upon vertical spatial location.

Rakic also discusses the role of genetic regulation in species differences. He points out that a single round of additional symmetric cell division at the proliferative unit formation stage would double the number of ontogenetic columns, and hence the area of cortex. In contrast, an additional single round of division at a later stage, from the proliferative zone, would only increase the six layers of a column by one cell (about 1 percent). With this in mind he points out that there is very little variation between mammalian species in the layering of the cortex, while the total surface area of the cortex varies by a factor of 100 or more between different species.

Chugani and colleagues report the results of a position emission tomography (PET) study of the functional development of the human brain. Owing to the potential hazards of the procedure, the study is based on data from children who had to undergo PET scanning for clinical reasons. This study yielded two main conclusions. The first is that particular regions of the brain develop at different times and rates. Thus, while the sensorimotor cortex and some subcortical regions showed high levels of activation from birth, frontal regions did not show a maturational rise in glucose metabolism until six to eight months of age. The second, and perhaps more surprising, observation is that the absolute rates of glucose metabolism rise postnatally until they *exceed* adult levels, before returning to adult levels by about nine years of age. For most cerebral cortical regions the levels reached are about double those found in the adult. Of several reasons that the authors give for this developmental pattern of glucose uptake, possibly the most attractive is that it corresponds to the overproduction of synapses known to occur in many primate brain regions. The topic of exuberant connectivity is taken up at the neuroanatomical level in the next reading.

Huttenlocher focuses on quantitative neuroanatomical evidence from two comparatively well studied regions of the human brain – the primary visual cortex and a part of the prefrontal cortex. In both regions, the density of synapses (contact points between neurones) shows a characteristic increase during childhood to levels about twice that found in the adult. This is then followed by a period of synaptic loss. Huttenlocher suggests that this initial over-production of synapses may have an important role in the apparent plasticity of the young brain. This issue will be discussed in more detail in part V (Changeux and Dehaene; Editor's introduction).

The inside-out pattern of cortical growth described earlier for neurons is also apparent in terms of the growth of dendrites and dendritic trees. For example, while the mean total length of dendrites for pyramidal cells of layer III of the human primary visual cortex is only 30 percent of the maximum at birth, in layer V (a deeper layer) it is already 60 percent of the maximum. Interestingly, this inside-out pattern of growth is not evident in the later occurring rise and fall in synaptic density. For this measure, there are no clear differences between cerebral cortical layers.

Consistent with the PET findings of Chugani and colleagues, Huttenlocher reports clear evidence of a difference in the timing of postnatal neuroanatomical events between the primary visual cortex and the frontal cortex, with the latter reaching the same developmental landmarks considerably later in postnatal life than the former.

FURTHER READING

General introductions to neurobiology

Crick, F. and Asanuma, C. (1986) Certain aspects of the anatomy and physiology of the cerebral cortex. In J. L. McClelland and D.E. Rumelhart (Éds), *Parallel Distributed Processing*. Cambridge, MA: MIT Press.

Shephard, G. M. (1983) *Neurobiology*. Oxford: Oxford University Press.

Sejnowski, T. and Churchland, P. S. (1990) Brain and cognition. In M.I. Posner (ed.), *Foundations of Cognitive Science*. Cambridge, MA: MIT Press.

Introductions to neural development

Brown, M. C., Hopkins, W. G. and Keynes, R. J. (1991) *Essentials of Neural Development*. Cambridge: Cambridge University Press. (A useful short introduction to neural development.)

Purves, D. (1988) *Body and Brain: a Trophic Theory of Neural Connections*. Cambridge, MA: Harvard University Press. (Explores the evidence and implications of trophic theories of neural development.)

Purves, D. and Lichtman, J. W. (1985) *Principles of Neural Development*. Sunderland, MA: Sinauer Associates. (An excellent comprehensive introduction to developmental neurobiology.)

Others

Conel, J. L. (1939–1967) *The Postnatal Development of the Human Cerebral Cortex, Volumes I–VIII*. Cambridge, MA: Harvard University Press. (The original volumes describing in detail the postnatal growth of the human cortex. It remains an excellent reference source despite being written before more recent quantitative techniques in neuroanatomy.)

Ebbesson, S. O. E. (1984) Evolution and ontogeny of neural circuits. *Brain and Behavioral Sciences*, 7, 321–66. (A full *BBS* treatment concerned with the factors that cause synaptic and cell loss during brain development and evolution.)

Marin-Padilla, M. (1990) The pyramidal cell and its local-circuit interneurones: a hypothetical unit of the mammalian cerebral cortex. *Journal of Cognitive Neuroscience*, 2, 180–94. (Presents an alternative hypothesis about the development of the cortex based around pyramidal cells.)

Rabinowicz, T. (1986) The differential maturation of the cerebral cortex. In F. Falkner and J. M. Tanner (eds), *Human Growth, Volume 2: Postnatal Growth and Neurobiology*, 2nd edn. New York: Plenum Press. (A review of further studies of the postnatal maturation of the human cortex.)

Rakic, P. et al. (1986) Concurrent overproduction of synapses in diverse regions of the primate cerebral cortex. *Science*, 232, 232–5. (Evidence that the over-exuberance of synapses reduces in several parts of the cortex at around the same age in some non-human primates.)

5

Basic Concepts of CNS Development

R. S. NOWAKOWSKI

The human central nervous system (CNS) is, without a doubt, the single most complicated organ in the body, and the processes involved in its development are commensurately complex. These processes are often treated in a cursory fashion in the early chapters of developmental psychology textbooks, and it is sometimes assumed that the "hardware" being shaped by these developmental processes places few constraints on behavioral development. To a certain extent this is true; however, the nature versus nurture controversy that pervades modern biology and psychology also extends into the analysis of the development of the CNS. The current focus of the controversy in this field is directed at understanding the contributions of processes *intrinsic* to the CNS relative to the contributions of influences from *extrinsic* sources, such as behavioral experience, trauma, nutrition, hormonal states, etc. In other words, in contemporary neurobiology, the issue is not whether nature or nurture is the major contributor but which contributes what to the development of specific structures and areas. For the developing CNS, this analysis continues on a variety of levels, ranging from the level of the organism (influences intrinsic to the organism *vs* influences from the environment), through the level of the organ (influences intrinsic to the brain *vs* influences from elsewhere in the body), and the level of a given structure (influences intrinsic to one brain structure *vs* influences from other parts of the brain), to the level of interactions between cells (influences intrinsic to a single cell *vs* influences on that cell from other cells).

For each level of analysis the technology and avenues of experimentation vary, but the questions asked and the concepts being utilized are essentially identical. Furthermore, each level of analysis leads to questions at both the next higher and the next lower level. For example, recent research has shown that there is considerable *biological* variation in the early processes of neurogenesis (e.g.

"Basic Concepts of CNS Development" first appeared in *Child Development* 58 (1987), pp. 568–95, and is reprinted by kind permission.

O'Rahilly et al., 1984; Zimmerman et al., 1983), and, furthermore, that this variation may underlie a number of developmental psychopathologies, including dyslexia (Galaburda et al., 1983; Kemper, 1984; Sherman et al., 1985) and schizophrenia (Kovelman and Scheibel, 1983). However, the link between the biological processes occurring during CNS development and behavioral pathologies or behavioral capacities exhibited by adults or during behavioral development is obviously not easy to establish. Specifically, in order to arrive at an understanding of how a modification in a developmental process exerts its influence on a particular behavior, it is necessary to understand where the developmental process is being modified (e.g. which kinds of cells and in which part of the brain), how the structure (e.g. the "wiring," etc.) of the mature brain will be changed, and also how the structural changes that are produced will change the ability of the brain to process the information it confronts during a complex behavioral task (for a review, see Nowakowski, 1985). Therefore, in this article, the relationship between the basic organization of the embryonic CNS and the adult CNS will be reviewed in order to provide a useful and, by necessity, simplified set of principles for understanding the complex anatomy of the adult brain. Also, the special embryological mechanisms that are involved in generating the diversity that characterizes the adult CNS will be reviewed in order to provide a set of concepts to aid in understanding the variety of complex processes occurring during CNS development. Finally, during this discussion examples describing how modifications of the normal development of the CNS by traumatic injury, by environmental and experiential influences, and by genetic variation may affect and modify the development of the CNS and thereby influence the resultant structure and function of the adult CNS will be included.

Modifications of Developmental Processes

Although it may not be intuitively obvious, the only way that diversity in the structure of the brain can be generated during development is to modify one of the basic developmental processes of cell proliferation, cell migration, or cell differentiation. This can be brought about by any of a variety of interventions, such as traumatic injury, behavioral experience, genetic variations, etc. It cannot be emphasized too strongly that *the kind of modifications resulting from any particular intervention are directly related to: (1) what is happening in the developing CNS at the time that the intervention occurs, and (2) which cell types and developmental processes are affected by the intervention.* In the following paragraphs, specific examples of how a variety of interventions can affect CNS development are given. Note, however, that the effects of early behavioral experience will not be discussed here. The interested reader is referred to the review by Greenough et al. (see part IV).

The Problem and Its Magnitude

Perhaps the most perplexing aspect of the organization of the CNS is the fact that each division and subdivision of the brain has its own characteristic structure

and function. The problem faced by the neuroembryologist is to try to understand: (1) how this tremendous diversity in form is generated, and (2) how each
portion of the CNS is integrated into the whole to produce a functional entity.
Clearly, these are not trivial issues, especially since modern biology requires that
they be addressed not only in terms of relatively gross changes in the architecture
of the developing CNS but also in terms of the "behavior" of its cellular
constituents and of changes in gene expression within the cells.

The magnitude of this problem is at least partially reflected in the fact that
there are between 10 and 20 billion (i.e. approximately 10^{10}) neurons in the
cerebral cortex of an adult human (note that this is *not* the whole brain) and
that there are 5–10 times as many glial cells (Blinkov and Glezer, 1968). Although
the glial cells certainly contribute in important ways (Kuffler et al., 1984), it is
the diversity in shape, form, and interconnections of the neurons that is ultimately responsible for the ability of the CNS to process all of the various sorts
of information that it confronts every minute of every day. For this reason, the
"life history" of the neurons of the CNS is of primary importance in understanding CNS development because the neurons are the components that are
"assembled" into a functional network, and it is the network that controls
function. In particular, it is important to define the common features, influences,
and capabilities of the differentiating neurons of the CNS. As is true in any
developmental analysis, the elucidation of such similarities provides a set of
"concepts" or "rules" that make understanding a complex system easier.

Another reflection of the complexity of these issues stems from recent evidence
suggesting that approximately 30 percent of the entire genome is expressed only
in the brain (Sutcliffe et al., 1984). (Presumably even more of the genome may
be involved if allowances are made for genes that are expressed only transiently
during development.) Other evidence for such a high proportion of the genome
is provided by the recent compilations of mutations in mouse (Green, 1981) and
man (McKusick, 1983), both of which catalog a large number of genetic loci that
are primarily involved in nervous system structure and/or function and an even
larger number that seem to affect the nervous system secondarily. A rigorous
analysis of the changes in gene expression during the development of the CNS
is only now becoming possible, and, in the next few years, dramatic changes in
our understanding of this important issue are likely to occur.

The Basic Questions

A useful organizational scheme for conceptualizing the complicated events and
processes that contribute to generating the diversity and complexity of the mature
CNS is to ask the question, "*what* is happening *where, when?*" Answering each
of these questions is, of course, not a simple task, because there are many issues
and simultaneously occurring processes that must be considered and dealt with.
However, the three words *when, where,* and *what* do provide a simple framework
for the discussion of the key issues involved in the analysis of CNS development,
and answering the question posed by each of them results in a reasonably
complete description of the phenomena underlying CNS development. Furthermore, this knowledge is the essential background needed to ask *how* processes

during CNS development are controlled (i.e. Which cells and cellular interactions affect the fate of other cells? Which genes are expressed in which cell type and when are they expressed? Does the maturation of one region of the CNS affect the maturation of other regions of the CNS? etc.). In the following paragraphs, I shall use these four simple questions (*when? where? what?* and *how?*) to describe the major issues confronted by contemporary neuroembryologists. When possible, relevant work in human development will be cited.

"When?": A Question of Time and Timing

"When?" is answered by consideration of the time that an event occurs. For example: when do neurons first appear? When do axons grow into a certain region? When does a particular behavioral competency first appear? Also, these questions are clearly related to the general issue of critical periods during development. Each of these questions can be answered in two ways. First, there is the issue of an absolute time frame. For most experimental animals, this is usually measured simply as days (or some other convenient unit) after conception and days after birth. In table 5.1 the gestation periods of some common laboratory animals are listed. Sometimes, for greater precision, staging systems are used in order to reduce problems resulting from differences in diet or environment, different rates of development in various strains, or simply because some species develop rapidly. Staging systems are based on readily observable features of the embryo (e.g. eye opening, fusion or separation of fingers and toes, etc.). For the staging of human embryos and fetuses, the same principles apply except that gestation is generally measured from the time of occurrence of the last menstrual period rather than from the day of conception. With this method human gestation is considered to be 40 weeks long, even though the conceptus is only present

Table 5.1 Development period of various species

Species	Length of relevant developmental period	Staging system
Xenopus	–[a]	Niewkoop and Faber (1956)
Frog (*Rana pipiens*)	–[a]	Shumway (1940)
Chick	21 days[b]	Hamburger & Hamilton (1951)
Mouse	19 days	Theiler (1972)
Mouse	21–22 days	
Chinese hamster	13 days	–
Rhesus monkey	165 ± 5 days[c]	–
Human	40 weeks after last menstrual period; 38 weeks after conception	Streeter (e.g. Oliver and Pineau 1961; O'Rahilly et al. 1984)

[a] Absolute times are rarely used for these species because the rate of development is too dependent upon ambient temperature.
[b] The early development of the chick embryo is so rapid that the staging system of Hamburger and Hamilton is invariably used.
[c] From Macdonald (1971).

for 38 weeks. The staging system for human embryos and fetuses (e.g. Olivier and Pineau, 1961) relies upon easily measurable features such as greatest length (GL) or crown-to-rump length (CRL). The gestation period of humans is generally divided into trimesters, each lasting about 13 weeks.

It is of great significance that the development of CNS is not confined to the gestational period. For example, during the intrauterine period the brain grows from almost nothing to about 350 grams (Blinkov and Glezer, 1968). During this period, most of the neurons of the CNS are produced (see below). However, after birth the brain continues to grow, reaching a size of about 1350 grams at 20 years of age (Blinkov and Glezer, 1968). Most of the postnatal growth occurs within the first three or four years after birth (Blinkov and Glezer, 1968), but changes in myelination (Yakovlev and LeCours, 1967) and in other measures (e.g. cortical surface areas, numbers of glial cells, etc.) continue to be apparent even 70–80 years after birth (Blinkov and Glezer, 1968). In this review, the early prenatal periods of CNS development are being emphasized. It should be emphasized that the time of birth is not correlated with most measures of the maturity of the CNS. This means, for example, that events occurring prenatally in some species may occur postnatally in another species. One example of this variation is the maturation of the cerebral cortex. In rats and mice most of the cells destined to comprise the cerebral cortex are generated during the second half of gestation, ending only a few days before birth (Angevine and Sidman, 1961; Berry and Rogers, 1965; Miller, 1985). In contrast, in monkeys and humans these same events are completed about the time of the end of the second trimester, well before birth (Kostovic and Rakic, 1980; Rakic, 1972, 1975a, 1975b; Rakic et al., 1974). For this reason, it is critical to consider the species being examined before a general conclusion is made.

Second, there is the issue of the *relative* timing of events, that is, the sequence of occurrence. This is an important issue, because knowledge of the order of occurrence of developmental events can provide information about the presence or absence of a causal relationship between the two events. In many cases such knowledge provides a clear-cut answer to important questions. For example, one important question is, How is neuron number regulated in the developing CNS? This question has been addressed in studies of the development of the cerebellar cortex. This region of the CNS is involved in controlling coordinated motor behaviors (e.g. Eccles et al., 1967) and has a regular, almost rectilinear, organization that makes it an ideal structure for the analysis of intercellular interactions during development. Furthermore, the cerebellar cortex contains only five types of neurons that are found in discrete laminae (Palay and Chan-Palay, 1974). In figure 5.1, the relationship of two of these neuron types, the Purkinje cells and the granule cells, is illustrated (see the legend for an explanation). In humans, there are approximately 1000 granule cells for each Purkinje cell (Blinkov and Glezer, 1968). Thus, it is relevant to ask, how is this ratio determined? Is the number of granule cells affected by the number of Purkinje cells? Or vice versa?

A partial answer to these questions is obtained from the knowledge that the generation of the Purkinje cells *precedes* the generation of the granule cells. The best evidence for this fact comes from experiments in animals in which tracing techniques were used to determine the birthdays of the various cell types (Sidman, 1970). As it turns out, in mice, the Purkinje cells are generated between embryonic day 11 (E11) and E13, whereas the granule cells are generated between E15 and postnatal day 21 (P21) (Miale and Sidman, 1961). (Comparison of monkey and human specimens indicates that during the development of the human cerebellar cortex there is a similar sequence of events; Zecevic and Rakic, 1976.) This information clearly indicates (1) that the possibility that the number of Purkinje cells generated is dictated by the number of granule cells is *not* viable, and (2) that the converse, namely that the number of granule cells generated is influenced by the number of Purkinje cells, is, on the other hand, possible. Corroborating evidence has been obtained using a variety of experimental methods and by examining the anatomy of the cerebellum in a variety of pathological conditions, such as disruption of cell proliferation using toxic substances (Sotelo and Rio, 1980), X-rays (Altman et al., 1969) and the examination of cerebellar development in a variety of mutant mice (Caviness and Rakic, 1978; Herrup and Mullen, 1979). Human developmental conditions in which the balance between granule cell production and Purkinje cell number is disrupted include medulloblastoma and both the viral and genetic forms of granuloprivic cerebellum (Johnson, 1982; McKusick, 1983).

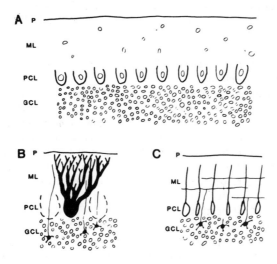

Figure 5.1 Schematic diagram of the organization of the cerebellar cortex. A, The cerebellar cortex has a three-layered organization. Three types of neurons are included in this diagram: (1) the Purkinje cells are large cells which form a single layer of cells (PCL) sandwiched between the molecular layer (ML) and the granule cell layer (GCL), (2) the granule cells are small cells found in a thick layer beneath the Purkinje cells, and (3) the molecular layer interneurons are medium-sized cells found scattered in the molecular layer. B, When the Golgi or other special methods are used, the dendritic trees and axonal aborizations of the various neuronal cell types can be seen. This diagram illustrates the large dendritic tree of one of the Purkinje cells and the short dendrites and part of the axon of the granule cells. C, In the plane perpendicular to that shown in C the dendrites of the Purkinje cells are narrow and confined to only a limited portion of the molecular layer. Also, in this plane the T-shaped axon of the granule cells is clearly seen.

The above examples of the analysis of the development of the cerebellum serve to emphasize two important points. First, they demonstrate that the knowledge of *when* particular developmental events occur relative to other events is crucial for the posing of germane questions. This is simply because if event A occurs before event B, then it is possible for A to influence B but not for B to influence A. It does not, however, necessarily follow that just because A preceded B that A influences B. It is most certainly possible that B proceeds independent of A or that both A and B are influenced by some common event occurring prior to (or concurrent with) both of them. Second, these examples illustrate the general principle that development occurs as a cascade of events, and that any one event *may* influence those that follow it but *not* those that precede it. A corollary to the cascade concept is that the earlier during development that a particular event occurs the greater is its *potential* influence on subsequently occurring events. This also means that the disruption of an early event is likely to have a greater effect on the adult structure than the disruption of a later occurring event. At this point it is perhaps useful to emphasize that a large number of "events" influence the development of any given region of the nervous system, and even of any given cell type, and that it is the summation of these events that produces the mature functioning whole. For example, if A is the production of Purkinje cells and B is the subsequently occurring Purkinje cell death, both events A and B influence the total *number* of Purkinje cells in the adult animal. Additional events (e.g. C, D, etc.) could also affect cell number, but *only events occurring prior to or during* the time that event A occurs could affect Purkinje cell number by affecting cell proliferation.

A potentially important use for the knowledge of *when* something occurs is to corroborate and/or eliminate possible biological bases for behavioral critical periods. For example, Greer et al. (1982) have shown that an enriched behavioral experience during the developmental period can increase cell number in the adult cortex. It is known that the cells comprising the adult cortex are generated before this critical period. This knowledge definitely eliminates an influence on cell proliferation as being responsible for Diamond's observations. The likely mechanism is, therefore, a reduction in cell death (i.e. hypothanasia) (Hollyday and Hamburger, 1976). Cell death is a normal aspect of CNS development (Oppenheim, 1981), including the cerebral cortex (Finlay and Slattery, 1983). Knowledge of the time that something occurs is also important when assessing the possible trauma produced by events like the development of a tumor (e.g. Gilles, 1985), malnutrition (e.g. Morgane et al., 1978), or exposure to alcohol (e.g. Miller, 1986, 1987; Rosett et al. 1983) or radiation (Otake and Schull, 1984). For the last example mentioned, a particularly striking relationship has been shown between mental retardation in children who were exposed *in utero* to the high radiation levels associated with the atomic bombs dropped on Hiroshima and Nagasaki and the gestational age of the children at the time of the exposure. Otake and Schull (1984) showed that during a critical period lasting from the eighth to the fifteenth week of gestation the risk of developing mental retardation later in life was directly proportional to the dose of radiation received. However, for embryos exposed before the eighth week there was no risk, and for embryos exposed after the fifteenth week the risk of developing mental retardation was less than one-fifth that of the risk associated with the critical period. The time of occurrence of this critical period allowed Otake and Schull (1984) to hypothesize that the proliferation and migration of neurons destined for the cerebral cortex were severely compromised by the radiation (see below for a description of these processes).

"Where?": The Three Dimensions of the Neural Tube

The structural and functional diversity of the various subdivisions of the adult CNS requires that during development each subdivision be recognized and

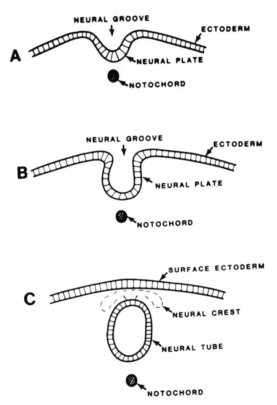

Figure 5.2 Neurulation. The process of neurulation begins at the end of the third week after conception. During the next few days, the outer surface of the embryo (or ectoderm) folds in upon itself to form the neural tube. A, At the beginning of neurulation a shallow groove appears to mark the position of the neural plate (A). B, Subsequently, the groove deepens and (as seen in C) the lateral edges of the neural plate fuse to become the neural tube. A small group of cells just lateral to the edge of the neural plate and some cells from the dorsal-most portion of the neural tube (arrows in C) become the neural crest. The neural tube is the forerunner of the central nervous system (i.e. the brain and spinal cord), whereas the neural crest cells produce most of the peripheral nervous system (LeDourain, 1982). Together the neural tube and the neural crest are often referred to as the neuroectoderm.

located for subsequent analysis. Consequently, *where* in the CNS a particular event occurs is defined by a coordinate system that delineates three dimensions. This coordinate system based on developmental principles is useful because: (1) developmental subdivisions precede and presage functional subdivisions, and (2) it becomes somewhat easier to understand the organization of the adult CNS once the organization of the simpler developing CNS is understood. The definition of the three dimensions of the CNS stems from its first appearance in the embryo at the beginning of a process known as neurulation (for explanation see figure 5.2). The end result of the process of neurulation is the neural tube. Just like any other tube, the wall of the neural tube can be considered to have three dimensions: length or a longitudinal dimension, a circumferential or tangential dimension, and a radial or laminar dimension (across its thickness) (see figure 5.3). During subsequent development, the lumen of the neural tube becomes the ventricles of the brain and the central canal of the spinal cord, whereas the wall of the neural tube grows at different rates along each of these three dimensions. As it turns out, differentiation of the neural tube along these three dimensions is a useful way to conceptualize the primitive organization of the mamalian CNS. Along the length of the neural tube, the major divisions of the nervous system are produced; around its circumference, functionally distinct

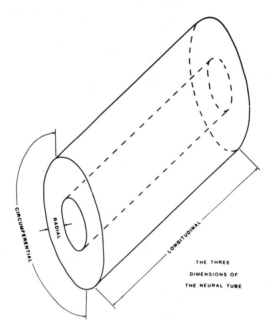

Figure 5.3 Stylized representation of the neural tube. During their development, the brain and spinal cord are derived from the neural tube. Just like any other tube, the neural tube can be considered to have three dimensions: length or a longitudinal dimension, a circumferential or tangential dimension, and a radial dimension. Differentiation of the neural tube along these three dimensions is a useful way to conceptualize the primitive organization of the mammalian CNS. See the text for further details.

subdivisions within the division arise; and along the radial dimension, the wall of the neural tube develops laminae or layers that are distinct for each subdivision.

Differentiation Along the Longitudinal Dimension

Already at the time of neurulation the head and tail ends of the embryo have been determined, and, in fact, neurulation proceeds at a different rate in the different parts of the neural tube. Eventually, about 50 percent of the tail or caudal end of the neural tube becomes the spinal cord, which becomes organized segmentally, that is, it becomes organized in repeated units called segments, each of which is associated with the sensory and motor innervation of a small part of the body. The head or cephalic portion of the neural tube acquires, for the most part, a suprasegmental organization, which means: (1) that its organization does not repeat, and (2) that a substantial portion of its innervation and output is not devoted to or derived from a single body segment but rather to the segmental parts of the nervous system. It is this suprasegmentally organized part of the neural tube that becomes the brain.

In humans, it is the cephalic portions of the neural tube (i.e. the head portions; see table 5.2) that grow tremendously, and this disproportionate emphasis of the suprasegmental portions of the neural tube is referred to as "encephalization." Even before the closure of the neural tube is complete, the cephalic end of the neural tube differentiates into three primary vesicles (i.e. "bulges") that form from its wall (see figure 5.4). From rostral to caudal (i.e. from front to back, literally "beak to tail") these vesicles are: (1) the prosencephalon or forebrain, (2) the mesencephalon or midbrain, and (3) the rhombencephalon or hindbrain. Subsequently, the prosencephalon becomes subdivided into the telencephalon and

Table 5.2 The "Encephalons"

Prosencephalon ("forebrain")	*proso*, forward + *enkephalos*
Telencephalon ("endbrain")	*telos*, end + *enkephalos*
Diencephalon ("throughbrain")	*dia*, through or across + *enkephalos* (many ascending and descending pathways cross or pass through the diencephalon on their way to or from the telencephalon)
Mesencephalon ("midbrain")	*mesos*, middle + *enkephalos*
Rhombencephalon ("rhombic-brain")	*rhombos*, rhombic + *enkephalos* (at this level of the brain, the ventricle is shaped like a rhombus)
Metencephalon ("afterbrain")	*meta*, after or post + *enkephalos*
Myelencephalon ("medulla")	*myelos*, marrow + *enkephalos* (the spinal cord is the "marrow" of the vertebral column and the medulla is the spinal-most portion of the brain)

Note: At first, the names of the subdivisions of the embryonic brain seem formidable, but an examination of their root meanings facilitates becoming comfortable with their usage. In all cases, the second part of the name is derived from the Greek word *enkephalos* (*en*, in + *kephalos*, head). Each prefix has a similarly descriptive root that is derived either from its relative position in the neural tube or some other salient feature; see figure 5.4.

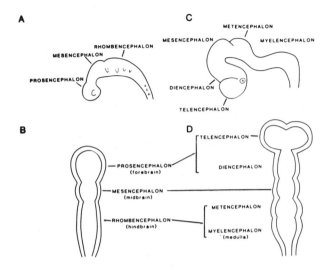

Figure 5.4 Longitudinal differential of the neural tube. A, A drawing of a lateral view of the brain of a 4-week-old human embryo. This is only shortly after neurulation, and already the three primary brain vesicles (the prosencephalon, mesencephalon, and rhombencephalon) are present. B, A stretched out and cut-away dorsal view of the 4-week-old brain as seen in A. C, A drawing of a lateral view of the brain of a 5-week-old human embryo. At this age, the prosencephalon has become divided into the telencephalon and diencephalon, and the rhombencephalon has become divided into the metencephalon and myelencephalon. D, A stretched out and cut-away dorsal view of the 5-week-old brain as seen in C.

the diencephalon, and the rhombencephalon becomes subdivided into the metencephalon and myelencephalon, and thereby *five* secondary vesicles are formed. In the human embryo, these five secondary vesicles are already recognizable at the fifth week of gestation (Hochstetter, 1919). Thus, at a very early stage in development the major structural subdivisions of the brain in the adult are defined by these vesicles. In fact, their names are used to refer to parts of the adult brain. Examples of major adult structures derived from each of these secondary vesicles are: (1) the cortex is derived from the telencephalon, (2) the thalamus and hypothalamus are derived from the diencephalon, (3) the midbrain is derived from the mesencephalon, (4) the pons and cerebellum are derived from the metencephalon, and (5) the medulla is derived from the myelencephalon.

Once these basic longitudinal subdivisions have appeared, each of them is subsequently modified by further differentiation in the other two dimensions of the neural tube. However, developmental *errors* in neural tube closure and in the subsequent longitudinal parcellation of the nervous system lead to profound disturbances of the nervous system. (This is presumably because neural tube closure and the subsequent parcellation of the longitudinal subdivisions into the various "encephalons" is one of the early events of CNS development.) The two most common places for the failure of the neural tube to close are its two ends, that is, in the spinal cord and prosencephalon (Friede, 1975). When the neural tube fails to close at the caudal end, a severe form of spina bifida known as *rachischisis* occurs. In rachischisis, the spinal cord, the vertebrae, and the overlying skin are malformed such that the central canal of the spinal cord (i.e. the lumen of the neural tube) is open (Friede, 1975). As a result this malformation is detectable by ultra sonography and/or by measurement of serum alpha-fetoprotein (Bell and Gosden, 1978). Rachischisis is the result of a very early failure of neural tube closure; later closures result in less deleterious forms of spina bifida (Friede, 1975). Similar malformations occurring at the rostral end of the neural tube result in anencephaly, which is a malformation in which the derivatives of the prosencephalon do not form (Friede, 1975). A variety of neural tube defects in man are similar to a class of mutations in the mouse in a part of the chromosome known as the T-locus (Bennett, 1975; Fellous et al., 1982) and to other known mouse mutations (Kalter, 1985). In addition, certain viral infections can also produce neural tube closure defects (Johnson, 1982), but, in many cases, the precise etiology is unknown (Bell and Gosden, 1978; Friede, 1975).

Differentiation in the Circumferential or Tangential Dimension

Specializations also develop *circumferentially* around the neural tube (i.e. *tangential* to its surface) (figure 5.3). These specializations are most easily described for the future spinal cord, which can be divided into four circumferentially defined zones or "plates": the floor plate, paired lateral plates, and the roof plate (figure 5.5). Each lateral plate is usually divided into a basal plate and an alar plate. The adult spinal cord receives a substantial contribution only from the alar and basal plates, which become the dorsal and ventral horns of the spinal cord, respectively. In the lower brainstem,[1] the same four circumferential subdivisions exist, and, despite the fact that the roof and floor plates distort the shape of the neural tube, the relation of sensory and motor to alar and basal plate is retained (figure 5.5B). The significance of this circumferential differentiation is that: (1) it *precedes the functional* organization of the spinal cord into sensory and motor subdivisions, and (2) it presumably reflects developmental processes that extend beyond the borders of any single longitudinal subdivision.

An important common feature of differentiation in both the longitudinal and circumferential dimensions is that the developmental processes underlying both produce subdivisions of the neural tube that are discernible very early during the development of the CNS. To a significant degree, the early appearance of these subdivisions precedes the functional differentiation of the CNS. One inference that can be drawn from this observation is that the wall of the neural tube, even at very early stages, is mosaic, that is, each portion has different potential and developmental capabilities (Rakic and Goldman-Rakic, 1982). The existence and nature of these differences continues to be the subject of a wide variety of experiments.

Differentiation in the Radial or Laminar Dimension.

From the description outlined above, it should be clear that the different areas of the CNS are discernible very early during development, and that differentiation of the neural tube along its length and circumference defines its basic

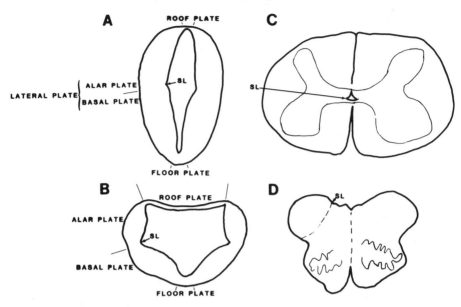

Figure 5.5 Circumferential differentiation of the neural tube. A and C, The circumferential zones or "plates" are best seen in the developing spinal cord, where there are four of them: a floor plate, two paired lateral plates, and a roof plate. Each lateral plate is usually divided at the sulcus limitans into a basal plate and an alar plate, which become the motor and sensory portions of the spinal gray, respectively. The names of these plates are derived from their position around the tube (alar is derived from the Latin word *ala*, wing). B and D, In the medulla, the roof plate becomes wide and attenuated and displaces the alar and basal plates laterally. Nevertheless, the sulcus limitans continues to mark the border between the basal and alar plates, and, in the adult, the morphological relation between the sensory and motor derivatives of these two plates is similar to that found in the spinal cord, except that they are displaced laterally by the extension of the roof plate.

organizational plan. There is, however, tremendous further refinement in the structure of the CNS before it can be considered to be mature. For the most part, this additional differentiation arises from its internal organization and consists of a series of changes in the radial dimension to produce a variety of laminar schemes in various parts of the neural tube. What is happening to produce this variety of lamination patterns in the various parts of the CNS is discussed in the following section.

"What?": Cellular Actions and Interactions during Development

The question "what is happening in a particular part of the developing CNS at a particular time?" can best be answered in terms of cellular processes, and, at the simplest level of analysis, there are three of these to consider: cell proliferation, cell migration, and cell differentiation. Needless to say, each of these processes describes a complicated set of events, but it is possible to describe a considerable portion of the development of the CNS by using them. Perhaps the most useful way to deal with these concepts is to realize that the "life history" of a single neuron or a glial cell can be traced by considering each of these processes as a developmental "step" through which each cell must pass. Thus, as discussed earlier, these steps represent a cascade of developmental events of which the earliest occurring ones may influence the subsequently occurring ones, but the later occurring ones cannot influence the earlier occuring ones. Also, as will become clear in the descriptions that follow, cell proliferation, cell migration, and cell differentiation can occur simultaneously in every division and subdivision of the developing CNS. For this reason, in order to complete the description of CNS development in cellular terms, it is necessary to add the additional concept of intercellular interactions as a way for one cell to influence the fate of another cell. Intercellular interactions can occur between cells in the same state of maturation (e.g. one differentiating cell can influence another) or between cells of different levels of maturation (e.g. a migrating cell can interact with a differentiated cell). In the following paragraphs, the processes and events associated with cell proliferation, cell migration, and cell differentiation are described. Emphasis will be placed on these processes as they apply to neurons, and, in general, the opportunities for intercellular interactions will only be pointed out when especially good examples are known.

Cell Proliferation and Lineage Relationships

There is no proliferation of neurons in the adult primate[2] CNS (Nowakowski and Rakic, 1981; Rakic, 1982, 1985) and, therefore, the neurons of the adult CNS are produced during the developmental period. Shortly after the closure of the neural tube, its wall becomes specialized such that the proliferating cells are found surrounding the lumen of the tube (see figure 5.6). With only a few exceptions, most of the cells of the CNS are produced by one of two proliferative zones adjacent to the future ventricular system. The first of these two zones to appear is the "ventricular zone" (Boulder Committee, 1970), which is a pseudostratified columnar epithelium (for explanation see figure 5.6). In some parts of the developing CNS, the ventricular zone is the only proliferative zone to appear, and thus it is reasonable to assume that it produces all of the cell types (figure 5.6*A–E*). In other parts of the developing CNS, however, a second proliferative zone appears (figure 5.6*F, G*). This second zone, known as the subventricular zone differs in several ways from the ventricular zone (for explanation see figure 5.6). It is attractive to speculate that the subventricular zone is a phylogenetically recently acquired specialization. For example, the hippocampus is classified as an archicortical (i.e. "old" cortex) structure, and the neurons of its major subdivisions (areas CA1, CA2, and CA3) are all derived from the ventricular zone (Nowakowski and Rakic, 1981). In contrast, in the neocortex (i.e. "new" cortex), the subventricular zone is substantial and is believed to contribute large numbers of neurons to the developing cortex (Nowakowski and Rakic, 1981). A similar contrast occurs in the developing diencephalon (Rakic, 1977). These differences in the distribution of proliferative zones along the ventricular surface reflect the existence of mosaicism as discussed above. The fact that these differences in cell proliferation arise just as the first

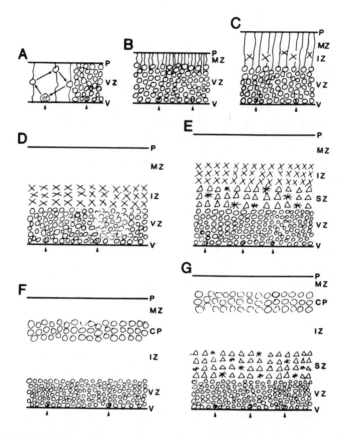

Figure 5.6 Radial differentiation of the neural tube. A, B, and C are schematic diagrams of the early stages of the radial differentiation of the neural tube through which every part of the CNS passes. D, E, F, and G are schematic diagrams of various options for the later stages of the radial differentiation of the neural tube. Each of these options is characteristic of a different part of the neural tube. A, At the time of closure of the neural tube its wall consists of a population of proliferating cells organized into a pseudostratified columnar epithelium, known as the ventricular zone (VZ). In this proliferative zone, the nuclei of the cells are stratified, but each cell has processes that contact the ventricular (V) and pial (P) surfaces of the neural tube. As diagrammed on the right-hand side of the drawing, mitosis occurs at the pial surface (arrowheads), and during the cell cycle the nucleus of each cell moves to a different level. DNA synthesis, for example, occurs in the outer half of the ventricular zone. This to-and-fro movement of the cell nuclei is known as interkinetic nuclear migration and means that all cells, even though they are apparently at different levels, are part of the proliferative population. B, The next zone to appear during the radial differentiation of the neural tube is the marginal zone (MZ), which is an almost cell-free zone between the ventricular zone and the pial surface. C, The intermediate zone (IZ), which contains the first postmitotic cells in the nervous system, is the next to form. This zone is located between the ventricular zone and the marginal zone. D, In some parts of the neural tube, such as the spinal cord, the postmitotic cells derived from the ventricular zone aggregate and mature in a densely populated intermediate zone. E, In some areas, such as the dorsal thalamus, a second proliferative zone, the

neurons are being produced (Nowakowski and Rakic, 1981) indicates that one level of functional differentiation, the development of the major subdivisions of the CNS, is well under way even at a very early stage (in humans this would be occurring during the second month of gestation).

The proliferating cells of the ventricular and subventricular zones differ from each other in their mode of proliferation, and, moreover, the proliferating cells within each zone differ from each other. The best evidence for this is the studies of Levitt et al. (1981, 1983), who identified two distinct classes of cells, some containing a marker for glial cells and some not. This observation demonstrates that separate neuronal and glial lines coexist within the proliferative populations. The appropriate designations of cells belonging to these separate populations are neuroblasts for those cells that are still proliferating whose descendants will become neurons, and glioblasts for those cells that are still proliferating whose descendants will become glia. (Cells that are no longer proliferating and have begun to migrate and/or differentiate into neurons are properly designated *young neurons*; see Boulder Committee, 1970.) There is also evidence that the neuroblasts within the proliferative populations are destined to produce a definite and limited number of neurons. For example, in the developing cerebellar cortex, it seems that early in development a few proliferating cells (i.e. less than a dozen) are destined to produce the Purkinje cells of the cerebellar cortex, and each precursor cell produces a clone[3] of about 10 000 cells (Oster-Granite and Gearhart, 1981; Wetts and Herrup, 1982c). Glial cells are also clonally produced (Miller et al., 1985; Temple and Raff, 1986). This clonal organization of proliferative populations and early restriction in clone size suggests (1) that within the population of neuroblasts there are subpopulations (or lineages) destined to produce specific types of neurons, and (2) that, for at least some cells in the proliferative populations, the "signal" to stop proliferating and leave the proliferative zone is self-contained. It is not known, however, if this latter suggestion is true for all of the cells in the proliferating populations, and it has been suggested that the time of origin and relative position ultimately achieved are crucial for the determination of cell class in the cerebral cortex (Caviness and Rakic, 1978; McConnell, 1985).

Is it possible for there to be a developmental defect that affects only cells of one lineage and not those of another lineage that is proliferating *at the same time*? In short, yes it is, and there are some good examples of this. First, there is the

subventricular zone (SVZ), is formed between the ventricular zone and the intermediate zone. In the subventricular zone, interkinetic nuclear migration does not occur; instead, mitotic figures (asterisks) are found scattered throughout the thickness of the zone. (DNA synthesis also occurs throughout the thickness of the subventricular zone.) The postmitotic cells derived from both the ventricular and subventricular zones aggregate and mature in a densely populated intermediate zone. (Note, however, that any cells derived from the ventricular zone must cross the subventricular zone.) F, In the hippocampus, the postmitotic cells derived from the ventricular zone migrate across a sparsely populated intermediate zone to form a cortical plate. G, In the cerebral cortex, postmitotic cells derived from both the ventricular and subventricular zones migrate across a sparsely populated intermediate zone to form a cortical plate. Abbreviations: V, ventricular surface; VZ, ventricular zone; SZ, subventricular zone; IZ, intermediate zone; CP, cortical plate; MZ, marginal zone; P, pial surface.

weaver mutant mouse, in which a single autosomal recessive gene produces a defect in the granule cells of the cerebellum. In this mutant mouse, the granule cells of the cerebellar cortex are affected such that they do not migrate properly, but another population of cells (the stellate and basket cells of the molecular layer) that is produced in the same proliferative zone at the same time is not affected (Goldowitz and Mullen, 1982; Hatten et al., 1986; Rakic and Sidman, 1973). As a result, these mice are ataxic.

Other neurological mutations in the mouse also affect specific populations of cells that are presumably derived from a single lineage. Examples include staggerer (gene symbol: *sg*), another mutation that produces ataxia because of a deficit of granule cells in the cerebellum, but in *sg* the granule cells die *after* migrating, secondary to a defect in the Purkinje cells (Herrup, 1983; Landis and Sidman, 1978; Sonmez and Herrup, 1984). Lurcher (gene symbol: *Lc*) mice are also mildly ataxic because of Purkinje cell death resulting from an action of the *Lc* gene *intrinsic* to the Purkinje cells (Wetts and Herrup, 1982a, b). Mice with retinal degeneration (gene symbol: *rd*) are almost totally blind because of a rapid postnatal loss of the rod photoreceptors; in contrast, the cone photoreceptors degenerate slowly and may even persist for the life of the animal (Carter-Dawson et al., 1978; LaVail and Sidman, 1974; Wegmann et al., 1971). In all of these examples, the disappearance of the cell population occurs only after it has been produced. There are, however, examples of viral infections that specifically affect the production of the granule cells of the cerebellar cortex without affecting the production of other cell types from the same proliferative zone (Herndon et al., 1971; Johnson, 1982). Also, there is one mutant mouse, the dreher mouse (gene symbol: *dr*), in which it has recently been found that the granule cells of the dentate gyrus (a part of the hippocampal formation) are frequently missing, and, furthermore, when they are missing it appears that they are never formed (Nowakowski and Wahlsten, 1985a). It is possible that the dreher mutation somehow affects lineage relationships in the developing dentate gyrus.

Cell Migration Influences Ultimate Cell Position

As illustrated in figure 5.6, the zones where cell proliferation occurs are, in general, physically separate from the ultimate destination of the cells they produce. This means that the postmitotic young neurons must move from the site of their proliferation to their final position. There are two essentially different ways that cells make this movement. In some parts of the developing nervous system the postmitotic neurons leave the proliferative population (presumably under the influence of some unknown signal or signals) and move only a very short distance from the border of proliferative zone. Subsequently, these cells are displaced outward away from the proliferative zone by newly produced cells (see figure 5.7). This type of cell movement does not seem to require active locomotory activity by the moving cell and is generally considered to be a *passive cell displacement*. In other parts of the developing nervous system the moving cells play a much more active role in reaching their final position. In these cases, the neurons leaving the proliferative zone move a much greater distance, and, in addition, in many instances the earliest neurons to be generated are bypassed by the progressively later-generated neurons (see figure 5.8). This type of cell

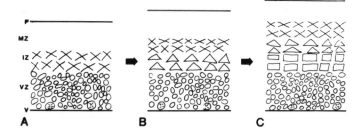

Figure 5.7 Cell movement by passive displacement. Some cells leave the proliferative zones and move only a short distance from the outer edge of the zone. Subsequently, these cells are displaced outward away from the proliferative zone by newly produced cells. This sequence of events is illustrated in diagrams A–C. In A, the first neurons to leave the ventricular zone are shown as X's. In B, the next neurons to form (shown as triangles) move away from the ventricular zone displacing the earlier generated ones outward. Finally, in C, the last neurons to form (shown as rectangles) move away from the ventricular zone and displace both populations of earlier-generated neurons. This sequence of events results in a specific distribution of neurons generally known as an outside-to-inside spatiotemporal gradient. Abbreviations: V, ventricular surface; VZ, ventricular zone; IZ, intermediate zone; CP, cortical plate; MZ, marginal zone; P, pial surface.

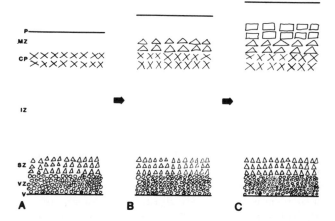

Figure 5.8 Cell movement by active migration. In many parts of the developing nervous system, cells leaving the proliferative population move a considerable distance from the proliferative zone. For example, in the cerebral cortex, the later-generated cells bypass the earlier-generated cells and take up a position even more distant from the proliferative zone. In A, the first neurons to leave the proliferative zones are shown as X's. These cells form a cortical plate between the intermediate and the marginal zones. In B, the next neurons to form (shown as triangles) leave the proliferative zones, migrate across the intermediate zone and *past* the previously generated cells to the top of the cortical plate. In C, the final neurons to reach the cortical plate are shown as rectangles. These cells have also migrated across the intermediate zone and *past* the previously generated cells to the top of the cortical plate. This sequence of events results in a specific distribution of neurons generally known as an inside-to-outside spatiotemporal gradient. Abbreviations: V, ventricular surface; VZ, ventricular zone; SZ, subventricular zone; IZ, intermediate zone; CP, cortical plate; MZ, marginal zone; P, pial surface.

movement clearly requires the active participation of the moving cell itself in its own displacement. This active process of cell movement is generally referred to as *neuronal migration* (Sidman and Rakic, 1973).

In the parts of the developing CNS in which passive cell displacement is the only type of cell movement that occurs after the young neurons leave the proliferative population, the neurons that are generated earliest are located furthest away from the proliferative zone and subsequently generated neurons are found at levels progressively closer to the position of the proliferative zone (figure 5.7). This correlation of the distribution of neurons with their time of origin is referred to as an "outside-to-inside" spatiotemporal gradient. In this case, outside and inside are defined with respect to the position of the cells with respect to the proliferative zone. (This usually, but not always, corresponds with the outside and inside of the neural tube.) It should be noted, however, that the presence of an outside-to-inside spatiotemporal gradient does not necessarily imply that the neurons of that region moved only by passive displacement. As will be pointed out below, the key factor in determining whether or not a neuron migrates (i.e. actively contributes to its own displacement) seems to be the distance it must move from the proliferative zone. Areas of the nervous system in which the outside-to-inside spatiotemporal pattern is present include the thalamus (Altman and Bayer, 1979; Angevine, 1970; Rakic, 1977), hypothalamus (Ifft, 1972), spinal cord (Nornes and Das, 1974), many regions of the brainstem (Altman and Bayer, 1981; Taber-Pierce, 1972), the retina (Sidman, 1961; Walsh et al., 1983), and the dentate gyrus of the hippocampal formation (Angevine, 1965; Bayer, 1982; Bayer et al., 1983; Nowakowski and Rakic, 1981; Wyss and Sripanidkulchai, 1985).

In many parts of the developing CNS, however, the migrating young neuron actively contributes to its displacement away from the proliferative zones. In these cases, the migrating young neuron may bypass the previously generated cells (see figure 5.8). When this happens, the result is an "inside-to-outside" spatiotemporal gradient. This pattern is found in most portions of the cerebral cortex (Angevine, 1965; Angevine and Sidman, 1961; Caviness, 1982; Caviness and Sidman, 1973; Hinds, 1968; Miller, 1985, 1987; Rakic, 1975b; Rakic and Nowakowski, 1981; Wyss and Sripanidkulchai, 1985) and in several subcortical areas (Cooper and Rakic, 1981; Hickey and Hitchcock, 1984). What all of these areas have in common is that they are all *well-laminated* structures (which means that they are divided up into tangentially oriented layers that run *parallel* with the surface of the proliferative zone). In other words, this inside-to-outside pattern of distribution of neurons is best correlated with the eventual organization of the region of the CNS to which the migrating neurons will eventually belong.

How do migrating neurons "know" where their eventual destination is? A partial answer was provided by Rakic (1971, 1972), who discovered that migrating neurons in the developing cerebral and cerebellar cortex use radial glial fibers as guides during their migration (see figure 5.9). This finding has since been confirmed for other parts of the cerebral cortex, and it is now widely accepted that during the development of the cerebral cortex young neurons are intimately apposed to radially aligned glial fibers that provide guidance (Nowakowski and Rakic, 1979; Rakic, 1971, 1978, 1982; Rakic et al., 1974) and may provide the scaffolding for the columnar organization of the adult cortex (Eckenhoff and

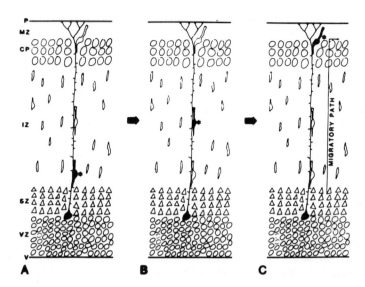

Figure 5.9 Interaction between migrating neurons and radial glial cells. As a young neuron moves from its site of origin in the proliferative zone to its final position in the cortical plate it is guided by a radially aligned glial cell. In this figure, the movement of a young neuron is depicted by a single black cell (marked by an asterisk) in each of the three drawings. This migratory process can be divided into three phases. Initially (A), a young neuron leaves the proliferative population, becomes apposed to a radial glial fiber, and acquires a polarity directed toward the pial surface (P). Next (B), it must traverse the intermediate zone (IZ); while doing this it maintains it apposition to the radial glial fiber and its polarity. Finally (C), as it reaches the top of the cortical plate, it stops its forward progress, loses its apposition to the radial glial fiber, and reorganizes its polarity in order to become a mature neuron. Disruption of any of these three steps could lead to neuronal heterotopias. Abbreviations: V, ventricular surface; VZ, ventricular zone; SZ, subventricular zone; IZ, intermediate zone; CP, cortical plate; MZ, marginal zone; P, pial surface.

Rakic, 1984; Mountcastle, 1978; Rakic, 1978, 1982; Smart and McSherry, 1982). This interaction of migrating young neurons with radial glial fibers is one of the best-documented examples of cell–cell interactions in the developing CNS. The process of neuronal migration is a complicated process consisting of at least three phases (for review, see Nowakowski, 1986a). First, a young neuron starts its migration. During this phase, a cell in the proliferating population makes the transition from neuroblast to young neuron, becomes apposed to a radial glial fiber, and establishes an axis of polarity away from the ventricular surface. In the second or locomotory phase, a young neuron propels itself along the surface of the radial glial cell, while maintaining its apposition to the radial fiber and its axis of polarity. Finally, in the third phase of its migration, a young neuron "recognizes" that it has reached its final destination and stops its migration. During this phase, the specific attachment of the migrating neuron to the radial glial fiber is lost and the young neuron can continue to differentiate. Also, as a result of this detachment the surface of the radial glial fiber is made available for the guidance of subsequently generated neurons that migrate past those that were previously generated (Pinto-Lord et al., 1982).

If neuronal migration is disrupted, an *abnormality in cell position results*. When this happens, the neurons are said to be heterotopic (Rakic, 1975a). A variety of defects in neuronal migration have been detected and described. In humans, the best-studied examples of defects in neuronal migration are in the cerebral cortex, where defects in neuronal migration have been associated with a variety of syndromes and diseases, ranging from behavioral disorders to extremely severe mental retardation and failure to thrive. Behavioral disorders that have been associated with a disruption of neuronal migration include some forms of schizophrenia and of dyslexia. Specifically, Kovelman and Scheibel (1983) have found clear evidence for the presence of heterotopic neurons in one subdivision of the hippocampus (area CA1) in the brains of patients with schizophrenia, and Galaburda et al., (1983) have found islands of heterotopically positioned neurons in the neocortex of severe dyslexic.[a] More severe disorders associated with disruption in neuronal migration include ethanol exposure, hydrocephalus, mental retardation, seizures, lissencephaly, methylmercury poisoning, craniofacial anomalies, etc. (Choi and Kudo, 1981; Evrard et al., 1978; Mikhael and Mattar, 1978; Miller, 1986, 1987; Richman et al., 1975; Zimmerman et al., 1983).

What is the developmental fate of neurons that fail to migrate to their proper position? Do these abnormally positioned neurons make connections with the rest of the brain? If so, do they make connections with their normal targets or some other targets, and how does this affect the function of the area of the brain in which these cells were supposed to have ended up? The answers to these questions are by no means completely known, but some insight into these issues is coming from studies of mutant mice that have defects in neuronal migration (see table 5.3). Four of these mutant mice have neurons that are not in their normal position, and in the fifth mutant, the weaver mouse (Rakic and Sidman, 1973), the neurons that fail to reach their final position die. This ability and inability to survive illustrates dramatically that the fate of all neurons that fail to reach their final position is *not* the same. What is the ability of the abnormally positioned neurons that do survive to make interconnections with other neurons in the brain? Considered abstractly, there are four possibilities for rearrangements of the synaptic connections of abnormally positioned cells. Two of these possibilities are for the input to the abnormally positioned cells. (1) The axons of normally positioned cells will follow a normal trajectory and therefore fail to find their normal target (because it is not where it belongs). (2) The axons of normally positioned cells will follow an abnormal trajectory in order to reach their normal target. The remaining two possibilities are for the output from the abnormally positioned cells. (3) The axons of the abnormally positioned neurons successfully find their normal targets. (4) The axons of the abnormally positioned neurons fail to find their normal targets.

What is the significance of these possibilities for the development of normal functions in the CNS? In order for normal connections to be made and presumably for normal functions to be established, both the inputs to a population of abnormally positioned cells and the outputs from the abnormally posi-

---

[a]   This initial finding still needs to be established beyond dispute. (Editor's note.)

Table 5.3 Mouse mutation affecting cerebral cortical development

	Mutant	Developmental deficit
1	Dreher	Proliferation and migration of neurons
2	Reeler	Migration of all neurons
3	NZB/BINJ	Migration of granule and pyramidal cells
4	*Hld*	Migration of pyramidal cells

tioned cells must *both* succeed in finding their normal targets. In the case of the input to the abnormally positioned cells, it will only be the axons that deviate from their normal trajectory and seek out their now abnormally positioned targets (possibility 2) that can succeed in making normal connections and, therefore, will be able to function normally. The axons that do not deviate from their normal trajectory (possibility 1) will not be able to carry out their normal functions with their normal synaptic partners. In the case of the axons comprising the output from the abnormally positioned neurons themselves, they must also seek out and find their normal targets (possibility 3). In other words, the establishment of normal synaptic connections is dependent on two presumably independent events.

How do these theoretical possibilities fit with reality? Do axons find their normal targets or not? So far, of the mouse mutations listed in table 5.3, these possibilities have been addressed to some extent for the reeler (gene symbol: *rl*) mutation, the hippocampal lamination defect (gene symbol: *Hld*) mutation, and the dreher (gene symbol: *dr*) mutation. Interestingly, the available results indicate that the the way abnormally positioned neurons make and receive connections with other neurons in the brain varies.

The reeler mutation produces a widespread change in relative cell position in many parts of the CNS (for review, see Caviness and see Rakic, 1978). For the most part, axons in the reeler mouse find their way to their appropriate target. In doing so, these axons may change their normal trajectory considerably in order to reach the appropriate portion of their normal target's dendritic tree (e.g. Stanfield et al., 1979). Thus, in reeler, the abnormally positioned neurons find their normal targets (i.e. possibility 3, as listed above), *even though the normal target may also be abnormally positioned*. The functional capacities of these connections has been tested in the visual cortex, and it appears that these connections are capable of processing information normally (Dräger, 1976, 1977; Lemmon and Pearlman, 1981; Pearlman, 1985; Simmons et al., 1982; Simmons and Pearlman, 1982, 1983). This change in trajectory does not occur everywhere in the brain of the reeler mouse (Devor et al., 1975). For example, the axons of the lateral olfactory tract remain a tightly collimated bundle following their normal trajectory, and, as a result, they do not contact the appropriate part of the dendrites of their target cell (i.e. possibility 1, as listed above).

Hld is an autosomal dominant mutation that produces a malformation confined to a small portion of the hippocampus (Nowakowski, 1984, 1985, 1986a; Nowakowski and Davis, 1985). Only the late-generated pyramidal cells are in the wrong position, and adjacent areas of the hippocampal formation seem to be unaffected by the mutation (Nowakowski, 1984, 1985, 1986a; Nowakowski and Davis, 1985). This situation provides an ideal setting for determining which of the above four

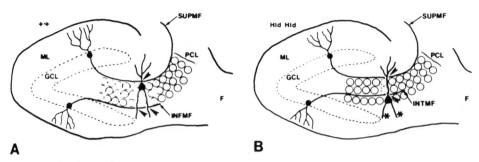

Figure 5.10 A schematic drawing of the differences in the inputs of the mossy fibers onto late-generated pyramidal cells in the area CA3c of normal (A) mouse and *Hld/Hld* (B) mouse. In each diagram, the neuron with the blacked-in dendrites represents a late-generated pyramidal cell. The arrowheads indicate the points of contact between the mossy fibers and the dendrites of the pyramidal cells. Note that in the *Hld/Hld* mutant (B), the axons of the granule cells of the dentate gyrus do not change their trajectory in order to innervate the basal dendrites of the abnormally positioned cells (in the area indicated by the asterisks). As a result the information being transmitted by the dentate gyrus to the hippocampus may not be interpreted in the normal way (for further details, see Nowakowski & Davis, 1985). Abbreviations: F, fimbria; GCL, granule cell layer of the dentate gyrus; INFMF, *infra*pyramidal mossy fiber layer; INTMF, *infra*pyramidal mossy fiber layer; ML, molecular layer of the dentate gyrus; PCL, pyramidal cell layer; SO, stratum oriens; SR, stratum radiatum; SUPMF, *supra*pyramidal mossy fiber layer; SR, stratum radiatum. Drawing modified from Nowakowski and Davis (1985).

possibilities are implemented, for determining how the wiring of the hippocampus is modified by the presence of abnormally positioned cells, and what effect the modified circuitry has on the behavior of the animal. The normal anatomy of a small portion of the hippocampal area of a mouse is illustrated in figure 5.10A. The granule cells of the dentate gyrus project to the pyramidal cells of the adjacent hippocampus, forming two bundles of "mossy fibers," one just above the cell bodies of the pyramidal cells and the other just below the cell bodies of the pyramidal cells. Thus, the points of contact of the mossy fibers with the dendrites of the pyramidal cells are confined to two narrow regions. In the *Hld* mutant mouse (figure 5.10B) the mossy fibers also form two narrow zones of contact with the dendrites of the pyramidal cells, but the late-generated pyramidal cells are now in the wrong place! Normally, the late-generated cells migrate past the previously generated cells to the top of the cortical plate (figure 5.11), but in the *Hld* mouse the late-generated cells stop before reaching their final position (Nowakowski, 1985, 1986a) and end up below the lower of the two mossy fiber bundles. As a result, in the *Hld* mouse (figure 5.10B) the mossy fibers from the denated gyrus contact the apical dendrites of the late-generated cells in *two* places, whereas in the normal mouse (figure 5.10A) the mossy fibers contact both the apical dendrites (in one place) and the basal dendrites of the pyramidal cells. Note that the bundle of mossy fibers axons does not change its trajectory to make contact with the basal dendrites of the late-generated cells which are, in fact, its normal target (Nowakowski and Davis, 1985). Thus, this aspect of the rewiring of the hippocampus as a result of a disruption of a particular population of cells is consistent with possibility 1 as listed above. It is not yet known how the abnormally positioned pyramidal cells themselves make connections with their normal counterparts.

Presumably, the anatomical rearrangements produced by the *Hld* genotype affect the behavior of the animal, but it is not yet clear how. Experiments have been done to test the affect of this gene on two behaviors commonly believed to involve hippocampal function – active avoidance and exploratory activity – but neither of these behaviors could be shown to be affected in *Hld/Hld* mice (Peeler and Nowakowski, in press). Thus, despite the fact that a clear relationship has been shown between the anatomical organization of mossy fibers and similar behaviors (Schwegler and Lipp, 1981, 1983; Schwegler et al., 1981), the particular rearrangements produced by the *Hld/Hld* genotype do not seem to affect these behaviors in the same way. Further work is in progress to analyze these differences and also to test the affect of the *Hld/Hld* genotype on other behaviors believed to involve hippocampal function.

The dreher mouse is the third mutant mouse in which these possibilities have been examined. The mutation is particularly interesting because it has differential penetrance, which means that there is variation from animal to animal in the extent of the malformations produced (Nowakowski and Wahlsten, 1985a, b;

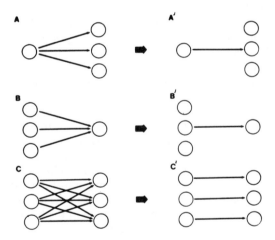

Figure 5.11 There are two types of exuberant projections that occur during the development of the CNS. In A, the transient *divergence* of a single source of axons is illustrated. In this case, the circle represents a single source of axons (a cell or population of cells) that projects to an area broader than its eventual adult distribution. Subsequently, some portion of the projection is withdrawn (through a variety of mechanisms) to produce the adult pattern (A'). In B, the transient *convergence* of projections from more than one source (i.e. from more than one cell or population of cells), all terminating on a single target is illustrated. In this case, the projections from some of the sources are lost in order to establish the adult pattern (B'). In C, the simultaneous presence of both transient divergence and convergence is illustrated. In this case, both types of exuberant projections have to be lost in order to establish the adult pattern of connections (C').

Wahlsten et al., 1983). In fact, there is also variation between the two sides of
the brain of the same mouse (Nowakowski and Wahlsten, 1985b). In the
hippocampal formation of *dr/dr* mice, both proliferation and migration of both
the granule cells of the dentate gyrus and the pyramidal cells of the hippocampus
are affected (Nowakowski and Wahlsten, 1985a, b). In the dentate gyrus, large
portions of the granule cell layer are often missing, and there are often small
clusters of granule cells abnormally positioned in the molecular layer (i.e. *beyond*
their normal position in the granule cell layer). Also, there are often pyramidal
neurons and sometimes even granule cells abnormally positioned in the stratum
oriens, apparently occupying an area through which they normally migrate. These
abnormally positioned cells seem to be distributed along their normal migration
routes. Interestingly, special histochemically stained preparations indicate that
the abnormally positioned granule cells send a small bundle of mossy fibers to
terminate on the abnormally positioned pyramidal cells (Nowakowski and
Wahlsten, 1985a, b). Curiously, they do not seem to send any input to the basal
dendrites of normally positioned CA3c pyramidal neurons, even though this
otherwise normal target is closer. This is most consistent with possibility 4, as
listed above, because these abnormally positioned granule cells do not find their
normally situated target but instead end up terminating on another abnormally
positioned population.

Finally, it has recently been discovered that in the NZB/BINJ inbred strain
there are anatomical abnormalities indicating the existence of a fourth mutation
that affects the development of the hippocampal formation (Nowakowski, 1986b).
The NZB/BINJ mice have two abnormalities in cell position in the hippocampal
formation. In the dentate gyrus there are clusters of abnormally positioned
granule cells in the molecular layer, and in area CA3 there are small clusters of
pyramidal cells abnormally positioned in the stratum lucidum and stratum
radiatum. In both cases it appears that the abnormally positioned neurons have
migrated *beyond* their normal positions. Both the abnormalities in cell position
in the dentate gyrus and in the hippocampus occur most frequently in the ventral
half of the hippocampal formation. The existence of this abnormality in the
NZB/BINJ inbred strain is interesting for two reasons. First, the abnormally
positioned cells in NZB/BINJ have *migrated too far*. This is in marked contrast
to the cell-position defects found in the hippocampal formation of the *Hld*,
dreher, and reeler mice in which the abnormally positioned cells have *not migrated
far enough*. Second, this abnormality in cell position in the hippocampal formation
is similar to that recently described by Sherman et al. (1985) for the neocortex
of NZB/BINJ mice. Sherman et al. (1985) have described islands of abnormal
neurons in layer I of the neocortex in about 30 percent of NZB/BINJ mice.
Furthermore, they have noted that this abnormality is similar to those they have
described in the brains of human dyslexics, and suggested that both the murine
and the human abnormalities may be related to autoimmune disorders (Sherman
et al., 1985). Experiments in this laboratory are presently in progress to determine: (1) if the neuronal migration abnormality in the hippocampal formation is
produced by one or more than one gene, (2) if the neuronal migration abnormalities in the hippocampal formation and in the neocortex are produced by the
same gene (or genes), and (3) if either or both of the neuronal migration
abnormalities are produced by any of the genes carried by NZB/BINJ mice that

are responsible for the autoimmune deficiencies characteristic of this inbred strain (Datta et al., 1982; Raveche et al., 1981).

The effect of each of these mutations on developmental processes and, hence, on the organization of the adult hippocampal formation is different (table 5.3). The dreher mutation seems to affect both cell proliferation and migration but not of all cell populations (Nowakowski and Wahlsten, 1985a, b). The reeler mutation affects the migration of all neurons but has minimal affects on cell number (Stanfield and Cowan, 1979a, b; Stanfield et al., 1979). In NZB/BINJ mice, it seems that migration of both pyramidal and granule cells are affected. Finally, the *Hld* mutation seems to affect the migration of only the late-generated pyramidal cells that are destined for area CA3c. Thus, the effects of these four mutations on the development of the hippocampal formation ranges from dramatic effects on both cell proliferation and migration to a very restricted effect on neuronal migration. This indicates (1) that the mutant genes are probably expressed in different cell types, (2) that the mutant genes are probably expressed at different times during development, and (3) that a basic developmental process such as neuronal migration is influenced and perhaps controlled by a variety of cell–cell interactions that are functionally related to several different genes. Also, in the different mutants that have been examined so far, different rewiring patterns are present. This indicates that the ways that heterotopically positioned neurons become interconnected with other neurons in the developing CNS are dependent on the reasons that they have come to reside in the wrong position in the first place. At present, it is not known how these various rewiring patterns affect function (defined either physiologically or behaviorally), and experiments pursuing these goals are currently in progress in this laboratory.

These four genetically produced defects in cell position provide a significant new way to explore cerebral cortical development in general and neuronal migration in particular. Recently, evidence for the possible existence of other mutations affecting neuron number (possibly through affects on cell proliferation) during cerebral cortical development has been presented (Wimer and Wimer, 1985). Thus, the foundation is being laid for future experiments that will lead to a new understanding of how genes influence a variety of events during both normal and abnormal CNS development.

Cell Differentiation Is the Final Complication

Once a neuron or glial cell has left the proliferative population and reached its final position, it enters the final phase in its life history, that is, its differentiation. The differentiation of neurons and glia is an extraordinarily complicated process that is responsible for the generation of a large proportion of the diversity of the adult CNS. During its differentiation, each neuron grows out of its axon and its dendrites. In many cases the axon grows a long distance over a complicated terrain before reaching its final target. The dendrites grow out and form their characteristic pattern of arborization for the particular cell class. Each differentiating neuron also must acquire the specific enzymes it requires in order to produce the neurotransmitter(s) it will use. Also, each postsynaptic site must acquire the receptors it needs to receive input from its presynaptic partner. In addition, the axons of some neurons will become myelinated, whereas others will not. Simultaneous with the acquisition of mature properties by the neurons, the glia cells are also differentiating into oligodendrocytes that make myelin and astrocytes that perform other functions (Temple and Raff, 1986; ffrench-Constant and Raff, 1986). For example, in humans the myelination of most pathways in the CNS continues long after birth (for review, see Richardson, 1982), and, in fact, the classical work by Flechsig (1920) on myelination in the developing human cerebral cortex provided the basis of the traditional classification of cortical areas into primary, secondary, and association areas. Many aspects of cell differentiation in the CNS are beyond the scope of this review, and, for this reason, the discussion below will be confined to limited aspects of axon–target interactions. For other topics the reader is referred to recent reviews (Easter et al., 1985; Jacobson, 1978; Jonakait and Black, 1986; Purves and Lichtman, 1985; Wiesel, 1982).

The growth of axons in the CNS involves the extension of a process from the cell body to a target or postsynaptic cell. Each growing axon must find its way through a complicated terrain to its target area, and once there it must select the appropriate target cell and even the appropriate part of the dendritic tree in order to make its synapses. This is clearly a complicated process, and it is likely that the growing axon makes use of a variety of mechanisms to find its way to its final target. Recently, however, it has become clear that in many parts of the developing CNS the growing axons do not grow directly to their final targets, but instead grow "exuberantly" such that they transiently innervate areas and cells that they do not normally contact in the adult. Two types of transient connections are made (see figure 5.11), divergent and convergent. Divergence means that one neuron (or population of neurons) innervates more cells (or a greater area) than it normally does in the adult (figure 5.11A). During develop-ment, the extra collaterals of the divergently projecting population are eliminated such that the projection area is reduced to its adult size (figure 5.11A′). Convergence, which is the converse of divergence, means that several neurons (or populations of neurons) innervate one target neuron (or area) (figure 5.11B), whereas in the adult only one of these neurons (or populations) innervates that target (figure 5.11B′). These two types of transient projections are not mutually exclusive, and it is possible that both could be found within a single population of cells (figure 5.11C), in which case both the divergent and convergent projec-tions would have to be eliminated in order to establish the adult pattern of connections (figure 5.11C′).

How are transient connections eliminated? There seem to be two distinctly different regressive phenomena responsible, neuronal death and the reorganiza-tion of axonal and dendritic trees (Cowan et al., 1984; Innocenti et al., 1986; Segraves and Innocenti, 1985). The *elimination* of the divergent connections occurs via two mechanisms: (1) in the case of a single neuron projecting to a wider target than in the adult, the transient connections can be removed by a retraction of the collaterals of the neuron's axon or by a shrinking of the terminal arborization of the axon, and (2) in the case of a population of neurons projecting to a wider target than in the adult, the transient connections can be removed through selective cell death, such that the neurons projecting beyond their normal adult territory die. Both of these mechanisms of elimination are known to occur. For example, during the development of the cerebral cortex, pyramidal neurons in the visual cortex send collaterals to targets, such as the spinal cord, which they do not ordinarily innervate in the adult animal. As the animal matures, some of the collaterals of these cells are lost, whereas other collaterals persist (O'Leary and Stanfield, 1985; Stanfield and O'Leary, 1985a, b). In many parts of the CNS there is extensive neuron death during the normal course of development. It has been hypothesized (Cowan et al., 1984; Oppenheim, 1981) that some of this neuron death contributes to the elimination of divergently projecting collaterals. The elimination of the *convergent* projections also may involve cell death (Cowan et al., 1984; Oppenheim, 1981) and in addition seems to involve a retraction of the terminal synaptic field (Cowan et al., 1984; Oppenheim, 1981; Wiesel, 1982). Thus, it is of great interest (and some irony) that an important set of processes during the development of the nervous system, which is generally thought of as being a series of *progressive* events, are *regressive* events involving the retraction of axons and the death of cells.

How is it decided which connections persist and which are eliminated? There are three views (for review, see Marler and Terrace, 1984): (1) the preformist view, in which it is considered that experience does not have any direct effect on the highly ordered anatomy of the brain; (2) the empiricist view, in which it is considered that the initial state is a *tabula rasa* (i.e. a blank slate) and that the environment (including experience) is of primary importance in determining the wiring patterns of the maturing nervous system; and (3) the selectionist view, which is essentially an intermediate perspective in which it is considered that the neuronal networks that are initially established are modified by subsequent environmental and experiential influences and are subsequently selectively stabilized by as yet unidentified mechanism(s) (Changeux and Danchin, 1976; Cowan et al., 1984; Innocenti et al., 1986; Segraves and Innocenti, 1985; see also Greenough et al., 1987, See part IV). Suggestions that competition for limited synaptic space or for a "growth factor" usage, or electrical activity, are possible mechanisms for the selective stabilization of synapses during development have been made (e.g. Fawcett et al., 1984; Henderson et al., 1986; Purves and Lichtman, 1985; Schmidt, 1985a, b; Schmidt and Tieman, 1985; Toulouse et al., 1986), and it seems likely that all of these mechanisms will be found to contribute to the elimination of transient exuberant connections (e.g. Easter et al., 1985).

The elimination of transient connections not only involves the actual loss of axons and axon collaterals (Crespo et al., 1985; Rakic and Riley, 1983) but also an actual decrease in synaptic numbers and densities (Oppenheim, 1981; Rakic et al., 1986). It has been suggested (Rakic et al., 1986) that the emergence of full functional and behavioral competence involves not only the elimination of excess synapses but also the acquisition of synaptic efficiency at the molecular level and the reorganization of synapses without a concomitant increase in their numbers. Finally, it is interesting to note that some of these processes involved in the differentiation of the nervous system are known to be influenced by steroidal hormones (Arnold and Breedlove, 1985; Arnold and Gorski, 1984; Nordeen et al., 1985) and may continue on into adulthood (Nottebohm, 1985; Purves and Hadley, 1985; Toulouse et al., 1986), when they are obvious candidates for participants in the learning process (for a review, see Marler and Terrace, 1984).

The existence of regressive processes such as cell death, the retraction of axonal processes, and the elimination of synapses during CNS development is of potentially tremendous importance for a variety of reasons. For example, in a variety of human disorders, such as some forms of dyslexia (Galaburda et al., 1983; Kemper, 1984), some forms of schizophrenia (Kovelman and Scheibel, 1983), fetal alcohol syndrome (Miller, 1986, 1987), methylmercury poisoning (Choi et al., 1978), and others (e.g. Choi and Kudo, 1981; Otake and Schull, 1984; Zimmerman et al., 1983), neuronal migration is disrupted in some way. It seems reasonable to presume that the abnormally positioned neurons do not make normal connections, and, as a result, normal functional competence is not achieved. Exactly how severe the functional consequences of abnormal position are is not clear at this time, but it is possible to predict that populations of neurons that are normally innervated by exuberantly projecting axons (i.e. divergent projections) are more likely to be able to become normally innervated and thereby achieve normal function. This prediction also applies to the output from the abnormally positioned neurons. Testing this hypothesis in humans is obviously not possible, but the availability of ways to produce abnormally positioned neurons in animals by genetic means (e.g. Caviness and Rakic, 1978; Nowakowski, 1985, 1986a, b; Nowakowski and Wahlsten, 1985a, b; Pearlman, 1985) and by other experimental avenues (e.g. Miller, 1986, 1987) will provide a useful test of this hypothesis. These experimental systems will also allow a rigorous assessement of the functional and behavioral consequences of these sorts of malformations.

Questions for the Future

"How" are cell proliferation, cell migration, and cell differentiation controlled? As discussed in the introduction to this article, the simple answers are that they are each controlled by processes intrinsic to the cell or by processes extrinsic to the cell, that is, by cell–cell interactions, by interactions of cells with hormones, etc. This is simple to state, but reliable confirmation and the sorting out of which events are controlled at which level is not. Answers will come from experiments utilizing a variety of experimental and clinical approaches and techniques. Clearly, one important new approach is the availability of the recombinant DNA technology (e.g. Sutcliffeet et al., 1984), which will allow questions concerning developmental changes in gene expression to be posed and answered, that is, what genes are expressed when and where (i.e. in which cells and in which part of these cells?). This approach will certainly provide new and important insights into the wonders and complexities of CNS development. The power of this approach is illustrated by the recent cloning of the gene for the brain amyloid protein which accumulates in patients with Alzhemier's disease and Down syndrome (Goldgaber et al., 1987). Simultaneously, Tanzi et al. (1987) have provided evidence that the chromosomal location of this gene indicates that it may be defective in the inherited, autosomal dominant form of Alzheimer's disease. In particular, when it is utilized in an interdisciplinary fashion in combination with the traditional anatomical (Rakic, 1978, 1982, 1985), physiological (Schmidt, 1985a, b; Schmidt and Tieman, 1985; Wiesel, 1982), genetic

(Nowakowski, 1985, 1986a; Wimer and Wimer, 1982a, b, 1985), and behavioral (Greenough et al., 1987; Goldman-Rakic, 1987) methods and with new technologies, such as PET and MRI (Chugani and Phelps, 1986; Zimmerman et al., 1983) and Brain Electrical Activity Mapping (Duffy et al., 1984), it is virtually certain that in the next decades we will bear witness to a tremendous and marvelous expansion in our knowledge of CNS development. Our ability to provide meaningful treatments when CNS development goes áwry will also increase as this new knowledge is applied to specific clinical conditions. This progress will not, however, come easily and will require the establishment of communication between scientists of many disciplines.

ACKNOWLEDGEMENTS

This work was supported by grants from the NIH (NS23647) and from the GRS program of the Robert Wood Johnson Medical School.

NOTES

1 In the prosencephalic derivatives, it is difficult to define the extension of the alar, basal, roof, and floor plates (His, 1904; Johnston, 1902; Kingsbury, 1922; Schulte and Tilney, 1915). However, differentiation in the tangential dimension is still obvious. For example, in the diencephalon. His (1904) defined three sulci that divide the wall of the diencephalon into four zones that become the epithalamus, dorsal thalamus, ventral thalamus and the hypothalamus, respectively (Kuhlenbeck, 1973; Miura, 1933; Sidman and Rakic, 1982). Similarly, in the telencephalon, the archicortex is derived from the medial wall of the lateral hemisphere, the neocortex from the dorsolateral wall, and the paleocortex from the lateral wall of the hemisphere (Kuhlenbeck, 1977; Poljakov, 1949; Sidman and Rakic, 1982).

2 There have, however, been reports of neuron production in the adult canary (Goldman and Nottebohm, 1983; Nottebohm, 1985) and also in the adult rat (Bayer, 1982; Bayer et al., 1982; Kaplan, 1977; Kaplan and Hinds, 1977).

3 A *clone* is a group of cells derived from a single precursor cell. Thus it is a relative term dependent on which proliferating cell is specified to be the progenitor. Often, the term *lineage* or *lineage relations* is used to avoid some of the connotative difficulties associated with the word "clone."

REFERENCES

Altman, J., Anderson, W. J., & Wright, K. A. (1969). Early-effects of X-irradiation of the cerebellum in infant rats: Decimation and reconstitution of the external grapular layer. *Experimental Neurology*, 24, 196–216.

Altman, J., & Bayer, S. A. (1979). Development of the diencephalon in the rat: V. Thymidine-radiographic observations on internuclear and intranuclear gradients in the thalamus. *Journal of Comparative Neurology*, 188, 473–500.

Altman, J., & Bayer, S. A. (1981). Development of the brain stem in the rat: V. Thymidine-radiographic study of the time of origin of neurons in the midbrain tegmentum. *Journal of Comparative Neurology*, 198, 677–716.

Angevine, J. B., Jr. (1965). Time of neuron origin in the hippocampal region: An autoradiographic study in the mouse. *Experimental Neurology Supplement*, 2, 1–71.

Angevine, J. B., Jr. (1970). Time of neuron origin in the diencephalon of the mouse: An autoradiographic study. *Journal of Comparative Neurology*, 139, 129–188.

Angevine, J. B., Jr., & Sidman, R. L. (1961). Autoradiographic study of cell migration during histogenesis of cerebral cortex in the mouse. *Nature*, 192, 766–768.

Arnold, A. P., & Breedlove, S. M. (1985). Organizational and activational effects of sex steroids on brain and behavior: A reanalysis. *Hormones and Behavior*, 19, 469–498.

Arnold, A. P., & Gorski, R. A. (1984). Gonadal steriod induction of structural sex differences in the central nervous system. *Annual Review of Neuroscience*, 7, 413–442.

Bayer, S. A. (1982). Changes in the total number of dentate granule cells in juvenile and adult rats: A correlated volumetric and 3H-thymidine autoradiographic study. *Experimental Brain Research*, 46, 315–323.

Bayer, S. A., Yackel, J. W., & Puri, P. S. (1982). Neurons in the rat dentate gyrus granular layer substantially increase during juvenile and adult life. *Science*, 216, 890–892.

Bell, J. E., & Gosden, C. M. (1978). Central nervous system abnormalities – contrasting patterns in early and late pregnancy. *Clinical Genetics*, 13, 387–396.

Bennett, D. (1975). The T-locus of the mouse. *Cell*, 6, 441–454.

Berry, M., & Rogers, A. W. (1965). The migration of neuroblasts in the developing cerebral cortex. *Journal of Anatomy*, 99, 691–709.

Blinkov, S. M., & Glezer, I. I. (1968). *The human brain in figures and tables: A quantitative handbook*. New York: Plenum.

Boulder Committee. (1970). Embryonic vertebrate central nervous system: Revised terminology. *Anatomical Record*, 166, 257–261.

Carter-Dawson, L. D., LaVail, M. M., & Sidman, R. L. (1978). Differential effect of the rd mutation on rods and cones in the mouse retina. *Investigative Ophthalmology and Visual Science*, 17, 489–498.

Caviness, V. S., Jr. (1982). Neocortical histogenesis in normal and reeler mice: A developmental study based upon [^{3}H] thymidine autoradiography. *Developmental Brain Research*, 4, 293–302.

Caviness, V. S., Jr., & Rakic, P. (1978). Mechanisms of cortical development: A view from mutations in mice. *Annual Review of Neuroscience*, 1, 297–326.

Caviness, V. S., Jr., & Sidman, R. L. (1973). Time of origin of corresponding cell classes in the cerebral cortex of normal and reeler mutant mice: An autoradiographic analysis. *Journal of Comparative Neurology*, 148, 141–151.

Changeux, J. P., & Danchin, A. (1976). Selective stabilization of developing synapses as a mechanism for the specification of neuronal networks. *Nature*, 264, 705–712.

Choi, B. H., & Kudo, M. (1981). Abnormal migration and gliomatosis in epidermal nevus syndrome. *Acta Neuropathologica*, 53, 319–325.

Choi, B. H., Lapham, L. W., Amin-Zaki, L., & Saleem, T. (1978). Abnormal neuronal migration, deranged cerebral cortical organization, and diffuse white matter astrocytosis of human fetal brain: A major effect of methylmercury poisoning in utero. *Journal of Neuropathology and Experimental Neurology*, 37, 719–733.

Chugani, H. T., & Phelps, M. E. (1986). Maturational changes in cerebral function in infants determined by [18]FDG positron emission tomography. *Science*, 231, 840–843.

Cooper, M. L., & Rakic, P. (1981). Neurogenetic gradients in the superior and inferior colliculi of the rhesus monkey. *Journal of Comparative Neurology*, 202, 309–334.

Cowan, W. M., Fawcett, J. W., O'Leary, D. D., & Stanfield, B. B. (1984). Regressive events in neurogenesis. *Science*, 225, 1258–1265.

Crespo, D., O'Leary, D. D., & Cowan, W. M. (1985). Changes in the numbers of optic nerve fibers during late prenatal and postnatal development in the albino rat. *Brain Research*, 351, 129–134.

Datta, S. K., Owen, F. L., Womack, J. E., & Riblet, R. J. (1982). Analysis of recombinant in bread lines derived from "autoimmune" (NZB) and "high leukemia" (C58) strains:

Independent multigenic systems control B cell hyperactivity, retrovirus expression, and autoimmunity. *Journal of Immunology*, 129, 1539–1544.

Devor, M., Caviness, V. S., Jr., & Derer, P. (1975). A normally laminated afferent projection to an abnormally laminated cortex: Some olfactory connections in the reeler mouse. *Journal of Comparative Neurology*, 164, 471–482.

Dräger, U. C. (1976). Reeler mutant mice: Physiology in primary visual cortex. *Experimental Brain Research Supplement*, 1, 274–276.

Dräger, U. C. (1977). In G. S. Stent (ed.), *Function and formation of neural systems* (pp. 111–138). Berlin: Dahlem Konferenzen.

Duffy, F. H., McAnulty, G. B., & Schachter, S. C. (1984). Brain electrical activity mapping. In N. Geschwind & A. M. Galaburda (eds.), *Cerebral dominance: The biological foundations* (pp. 53–74). Cambridge, MA: Harvard University Press.

Easter, S. S., Jr., Purves, D., Rakic, P., & Spitzer, N. C. (1985). The changing view of neural specificity. *Science*, 230, 507–511.

Eccles, J., Ito, M., & Szentagothai, J. (1967). *The cerebellum as a neuronal machine*. New York: Springer-Verlag.

Eckenhoff, M. F., & Rakic, P. (1984). Radial organization of the hippocampal dentate gyrus: A Golgi, ultrastructural, and immunocytochemical analysis in the developing rhesus monkey. *Journal of Comparative Neurology*, 223, 1–21.

Evrard, P., Caviness, V. S., Jr., Prats-Vinas, J., & Lyon, G. (1978). The mechanism of arrest of neuronal migration in the Zellweger malformation: An hypothesis based upon cytoarchitectonic analysis. *Acta Neuropathologica*, 41, 109–117.

Fawcett, J. W., O'Leary, D. D., & Cowan, W. M. (1984). Activity and the control of ganglion cell death in the rat retina. *Proceedings of the National Academy of Sciences USA*, 81, 5589–5593.

Fellous, M., Boue, J., Malbrunot, C., Wollman, E., Sasportes, M., VanCong, N., Marcelli, A., Rebourcet, R., Hubert, C., Demenais, F., Elston, R. C., Namboodiri, K. K., & Kaplan, E. B. (1982). A five-generation family with sacral agenesis and spina bifida: Possible similarities with the mouse T-locus. *American Journal of Medical Genetics*, 12, 465–487.

ffrench-Constant, C., & Raff, M. C. (1986). Proliferating bipotential glial progenitor cells in adult rat optic nerve. *Nature*, 319, 499–502.

Finlay, B. L., & Slattery, M. (1983). Local differences in the amount of early cell death in neocortex predict local specialization. *Science*, 219, 1349–1351.

Flechsig, P. (1920). *Anatomie des menschlichen Gehirns und Ruckenmarks auf myelogenetischer Grundlage*. Leipzig: Georg Theime.

Friede, R. L. (1975). *Developmental neuropathology*. New York: Springer-Verlag.

Galaburda, A. M., Sherman, G. F., & Geschwind, N. (1983). Developmental dyslexia: Third consecutive case with cortical anomalies. *Society of Neuroscience Abstracts*, 9, 940.

Gilles, F. H. (1985). Classifications of childhood brain tumors. *Cancer*, 56, 1850–1857.

Goldgaber, D., Lerman, M. I., McBride, O. W., Saffiotti, U., & Gajdusek, D. C. (1987). Characterization and chromosomal location of a cDNA encoding brain amyloid of Alzheimer's disease. *Science*, 235, 877–880.

Goldman, S. A., & Nottebohm, F. (1983). Neuronal production, migration, and differentiation in a vocal control nucleus of the adult female canary brain. *Proceedings of the National Academy of Sciences USA*, 80, 2390–2394.

Goldman-Rakic, P. S. (1987). Development of cortical circuitry and cognitive function. *Child Development*, 58, 601–622.

Goldowitz, D., & Mullen, R. J. (1982). Granule cell as a site of gene action in the weaver mouse cerebellum: Evidence from heterozygous mutant chimeras. *Journal of Neuroscience*, 2, 1474–1485.

Green, M. C. (1981). *Genetic varaints and strains of the laboratory mouse*. Stuttgart: Gustav Fisher.

Greenough, W. T., Black, J. E., & Wallace, C. S. (1987). Experience and brain development. *Child Development*, 58, 539–559.

Greer, E. R., Diamond, M. C., & Tang, J. M. (1982). Environmental enrichment in Brattleboro rats: Brain morphology. *Annals of the New York Academy of Sciences*, 394, 749–752.

Hamburger, V., & Hamilton, H. (1951). A series of normal stages in the development of the chick embryo. *Journal of Morphology*, 88, 49–92.

Hatten, M. E., Liem, R. K. H., & Mason, C. A. (1986). Weaver mouse cerebellar granule neurons fail to migrate on wild-type astroglial cells in vitro. *Journal of Neuroscience*, 6, 2676–2683.

Henderson, C. E., Benoit, P., Huchet, M., Guenet, J. L., & Changeux, J. P. (1986). Increase of neurite-promoting activity for spinal neurons in muscles of "paralyse" mice and tenotomised rats. *Brain Research*, 390, 65–70.

Herndon, R. M., Margolis, G., & Kilham, L. (1971). The synaptic organization of the malformed cerebellum induced by perinatal infection with feline panleukopenia virus (PLV): I. Elements forming the cerebellar glomeruli. *Journal of Neuropathology and Experimental Neurology*, 30, 196–205.

Herrup, K. (1983). Role of staggerer gene in determining cell number in cerebellar cortex: I. Granule cell death is an indirect consequence of staggerer gene action. *Brain Research*, 313, 267–274.

Herrup, K., & Mullen, R. J. (1979). Staggerer chimeras: Intrinsic nature of Purkinje cell defects and implications for normal cerebellar development. *Brain Research*, 178, 443–457.

Hickey, T. L., & Hitchcock, P. F. (1984). Neurogenesis in the cat lateral geniculate nucleus: A ³H-thymidine study. *Journal of Comparative Neurology*, 228, 186–199.

Hinds, J. W. (1968). Autoradiographic study of histogenesis in the mouse olfactory bulb: I. Time of origin of neurons and neuroglia. *Journal of Comparative Neurology*, 134, 287–304.

His, W. (1904). *Die Entwicklung des menschlichen Gehirns wahrend der ersten Monate.* Leipzig: Herzel.

Hochstetter, F. (1919). *Beitrage zur Entwicklungsgeschichte des menschlichen Gehirns.* Leipzig: Deuticke.

Hollyday, M., & Hamburger, V. (1976). Reduction of the naturally occurring motor neuron loss by enlargement of the periphery. *Journal of Comparative Neurology*, 170, 311–320.

lift, J. D. (1972). An autoradiographic study of the time of final division of neurons in the rat hypothalamic nuclei. *Journal of Comparative Neurology*, 144, 193–204.

Innocenti, G. M., Clarke, S., & Kraftsik, R. (1986). Interchange of callosal and association projections in the developing visual cortex. *Journal of Neuroscience*, 6, 1384–1409.

Jacobson, M. (1978). *Developmental neurobiology*, 2d. ed. New York: Plenum.

Johnson, R. T. (1982). *Viral infections of the nervous system.* New York: Raven.

Johnston, J. B. (1902). An attempt to define the primitive functional divisions of the central nervous system. *Journal of Comparative Neurology*, 12, 87–106.

Jonakait, G. M., & Black, I. B. (1986). Neurotransmitter phenotypic plasticity in the mammalian embryo. *Current Topics in Developmental Biology*, 20, 165–175.

Kalter, H. (1985). Experimental teratological studies with the mouse CNS mutations cranioschisis and delayed splotch. *Journal of Craniofacial Genetics and Developmental Biology*, 1(Suppl.), 339–342.

Kaplan, M. S. (1977). Neurogenesis in the 3-monthold rat visual cortex. *Journal of Comparative Neurology*, 195, 323–338.

Kaplan, M. S., & Hinds, J. W. (1977). Neurogenesis in the adult rat: Electron microscopic analysis of light radioautographs. *Science*, 197, 1092–1094.

Kemper, T. L. (1984). Asymmetrical lesions in dyslexia. In N. Geschwind & A. M.

Galaburda (Eds.), *Cerebral dominance: The biological foundations* (pp. 75–89). Cambridge, MA: Harvard University Press.

Kingsbury, B. F. (1922). The fundamental plan of the vertebrate brain. *Journal of Comparative Neurology*, 34, 461–491.

Kostovic, I., & Rakic, P. (1980). Cytology and time of origin of interstitial neurons in the white matter in infant and adult human and monkey telencephalon. *Journal of Neurocytology*, 9, 219–242.

Kovelman, J. A., & Scheibel, A. B. (1983). A neuroanatomical correlate of schizophrenia. *Society of Neuroscience Abstracts*, 9, 850.

Kuffler, S. W., Nicholls, J. G., & Martin, A. R. (1984). *From neuron to brain: A cellular approach to the function of the nervous system*, 2d ed. Sunderland, MA: Sinauer.

Kuhlenbeck, H. (1973). *The central nervous system of vertebrates: Vol. 3, Pt. 2. Overall morphologic pattern*. Basel: Karger.

Kuhlenbeck, H. (1977). *The central nervous system of vertebrates: Vol. 5, Pt. 1. Derivatives of the prosencephalon: Diencephalon and telencephalon*. Basel: Karger.

Landis, D. D. M., & Sidman, R. L. (1978). Electron microscopic analysis of postnatal histogenesis in the cerebellar cortex of staggerer mutant mice. *Journal of Comparative Neurology*, 179, 831–863.

LaVail, M. M., & Sidman, R. L. (1974). C57BL/6J mice with inherited retinal degeneration. *Archives of Ophthalmology*, 91, 394–400.

LeDouarin, N. (1982). *The neural crest*. Cambridge: Cambridge University Press.

Lemmon, V., & Pearlman, A. L. (1981). Does laminar position determine the receptive field properties of cortical neurons? A study of corticotectal cells in area 17 of the normal mouse and the reeler mutant. *Journal of Neurosciences*, 1, 83–93.

Levitt, P., Cooper, M. L., & Rakic, P. (1981). Coexistence of neuronal and glial precursor cells in the cerebral ventricular zone of the fetal monkey: An ultrastructural immunoperoxidase analysis. *Journal of Neurosciences*, 1, 27–39.

Levitt, P., Cooper, M. L., & Rakic, P. (1983). Early divergence and changing proportions of neuronal and glial precursor cells in the primate cerebral ventricular zone. *Developmental Biology*, 96, 472–484.

Macdonald, G. I. (1971). Reproductive patterns of three species of macaques. *Fertility and Sterility*, 22, 373–377.

Marler, P., & Terrace, H. (1984). *The biology of learning*. Berlin: Springer-Verlag.

McConnell, S. K. (1985). Migration and differentiation of cerebral cortical neurons after transplantation into the brains of ferrets. *Science*, 229, 1268–1271.

McKusick, V. A. (1983). *Mendelian inheritance in man*, 6th ed. Baltimore: Johns Hopkins University Press.

Miale, I., & Sidman, R. L. (1961). An autoradiographic analysis of histogenesis in the mouse cerebellum. *Experimental Neurology*, 4, 277–296.

Mikhael, M. A., & Mattar, A. G. (1978). Malformation of the cerebral cortex with heterotopia of the gray matter. *Journal of Computer Assisted Tomography*, 2, 291–296.

Miller, M. W. (1985). Cogeneration of retrogradely labeled corticocortical projection and GABA-immunoreactive local circuit neurons in cerebral cortex. *Developmental Brain Research*, 23, 187–192.

Miller, M. W. (1986). Effects of alcohol on the generation and migration of cerebral cortical neurons. *Science*, 233, 1308–1311.

Miller, M. W. (1987). The effect of prenatal exposure to alcohol on the distribution and the time of origin of corticospinal neurons in the rat. *Journal of Comparative Neurology*, 257.

Miller, R. H., David, S., Patel, R., Abney, E. R., & Raff, M. C. (1985). A quantitative immunohistochemical study of macroglial cell development in rat optic nerve: In vivo evidence for two distinct astrocyte lineages. *Developmental Biology*, 111, 35–41.

Miura, R. (1933). Über die differenzierung der Grundbestandteile im Zwischenhirn des Kaninchens. *Anatomischer Anzeiger*, 77, 1–65.

Morgane, P. J., Miller, M., Kemper, T., Stern, W., Forbes, W., Hall, R., Bronzino, J., Kissane, J., Hawrylewicz, E., & Resnick, O. (1978). The effects of protein malnutrition on the developing central nervous system in the rat. *Neuroscience and Biobehavioral Reviews*, 2, 137–230.

Mountcastle, V. B. (1978). An organizing principle for cerebral function: The unit module and distributed system. In G. Edelman & V. B. Mountcastle (Eds.), *The mindful brain* (pp. 7–50). Cambridge, MA: MIT Press.

Nieuwkoop, P. D., & Faber, J. (1956). *Normal table of Xenopus laevis (Daudin)*. Amsterdam: North Holland.

Nordeen, E. J., Nordeen, K. W., Sengelaub, D. R., & Arnold, A. P. (1985). Androgens prevent normally occurring cell death in a sexually dimorphic spinal nucleus. *Science*, 229, 671–673.

Nornes, H. O., & Das, G. D. (1974). Temporal patterns of neurons in spinal cord of rat: I. An autoradiographic study – time and sites of origin and migration and settling pattern of neuroblasts. *Brain Research*, 73, 121–138.

Nottebohm, F. (1985). Neuronal replacement in adulthood. *Annals of the New York Academy of Sciences*, 457, 143–161.

Nowakowski, R. S. (1984). The mode of inheritance of a defect in lamination in the hippocampus of the BALB/c mouse. *Journal of Neurogenetics*, 1, 249–258.

Nowakowski, R. S. (1985). How do genes influence behavior? Some examples from mutant mice. In S. D. Smith (Ed.), *Genetics and learning disabilities* (pp. 125–151). San Diego: College Hill Press.

Nowakowski, R. S. (1986a). Neuronal migration in the hippocampal lamination defect (*Hld*) mutant mouse. In H. J. Marthy (Ed.), *Cellular and molecular control of direct cell interactions* (pp. 133–154). New York: Plenum.

Nowakowski, R. S. (1986b). Abnormalities in neuronal migration in the hippocampal formation of the NZB/BINJ mouse. *Society of Neurosciences Abstracts*, 12, 317.

Nowakowski, R. S., & Davis, T. L. (1985). Dendritic arbors and dendritic excrescences of abnormally positioned neurons in area CA3c of mice carrying the mutation "Hippocampal lamination defect." *Journal of Comparative Neurology*, 239, 267–275.

Nowakowski, R. S., & Rakic, P. (1979). The mode of migration of neurons to the hippocampus: A Golgi and electron microscopic analysis in foetal rhesus monkey. *Journal of Neurocytology*, 8, 697–718.

Nowakowski, R. S., & Rakic, P. (1981). The site of origin and route and rate of migration of neurons to the hippocampal region of the rhesus monkey. *Journal of Comparative Neurology*, 196, 129–154.

Nowakowski, R. S., & Wahlsten, D. (1985a). Anatomy and development of the hippocampus and dentate gyrus in shaker-short tail (sst) mutant mouse. *Anatomical Record*, 211, 140A.

Nowakowski, R. S., & Wahlsten, D. (1985b). Asymmetric development of the hippocampal region in shaker-short tail (*sst*) mutant mouse. *Society of Neuroscience Abstracts*, 11, 989.

O'Leary, D. D., & Stanfield, B. B. (1985). Occipital cortical neurons with transient pyramidal tract axons extend and maintain collaterals to subcortical but not intracortical targets. *Brain Research*, 336, 326–333.

Olivier, G., & Pineau, H. (1961). Horizons de Streeter et age embryonaire. *Bulletin of the Association of Anatomy (Nancy)*, 47e, 573–576.

Oppenheim, R. W. (1981). Neuronal cell death and some related regressive phenomena during neurogenesis: A selective historical review and progress report. In W. M. Cowan (ed.), *Studies in developmental neurobiology* (pp. 74–133). New York: Oxford University Press.

O'Rahilly, R., Müller, F., Hutchins, G. M., & Moore, G. W. (1984). Computer ranking of the sequence of appearance of 100 features of the brain and related structures in staged human embryos during the first 5 weeks of development. *American Journal of Anatomy*, 171, 243–257.

Oster-Granite, M. L., & Gearhart, J. (1981). Cell lineage analysis of cerebellar Purkinje cells in mouse chimeras. *Developmental Biology*, 85, 199–208.

Otake, M., & Schull, W. J. (1984). In utero exposure to A-bomb radiation and mental retardation: A reassessment. *British Journal of Radiology*, 57, 409–414.

Palay, S. L., & Chan-Palay, V. (1974). *Cerebellar cortex*. New York: Springer-Verlag.

Pearlman, A. L. (1985). The visual cortex of the normal mouse and the reeler mutant. In E. G. Jones & A. A. Peters (eds), *The cerebral cortex: Vol. 3. Visual cortex* (pp. 1–18). New York: Plenum.

Peeler, D. F., & Nowakowski, R. S. (in press). Genetic factors and the measurement of exploratory activity. *Behavioral Biology*.

Pinto-Lord, M. C., Evrard, P., & Caviness, V. S., Jr. (1982). Obstructed neuronal migration along radial glial fibers in the neocortex of the reeler mouse: A Golgi-Em analysis. *Developmental Brain Research*, 4, 379–393.

Poljakov, G. I. (1949). Strukturnaja organizatsija kory boljshogo mozga cheloveka po dannym razvitija ee v ontogeneze. In S. A. Sarkisov, I. N. Filimonov, & N. S. Prjeobrazhjenskaja (Eds.), *Tsitoarkhitjektonika Kory Boljshogo Mozga Cheloveka* (pp. 33–92). Moscow: Medgiz.

Purves, D., & Hadley, R. D. (1985). Changes in the dendritic branching of adult mammalian neurons revealed by repeated imaging in situ. *Nature*, 315, 404–406.

Purves, D., & Lichtman, J. W. (1985). *Principles of neural development*. Sunderland, MA: Sinauer.

Rakic, P. (1971). Neuron-glia relationship during granule cell migration in developing cerebellar cortex: A Golgi and electron microscopic study in macacus rhesus. *Journal of Comparative Neurology*, 141, 283–312.

Rakic, P. (1972). Mode of cell migration to the superficial layers of fetal monkey neocortex. *Journal of Comparative Neurology*, 145, 61–83.

Rakic, P. (1973). Kinetics of proliferation and latency between final division and onset of differentiation of the cerebellar stellate and basket neurons. *Journal of Comparative Neurology*, 147, 523–546.

Rakic, P. (1975a). Cell migration and neuronal ectopias in the brain. *Birth Defects: Original Article Series*, 11(7), 95–129.

Rakic, P. (1975b). Timing of major ontogenetic events in the visual cortex of the rhesus monkey. *In Brain mechanisms in mental retardation* (pp. 3–40). New York: Academic Press.

Rakic, P. (1977). Genesis of the dorsal lateral geniculate nucleus in the rhesus monkey: Site and time of origin, kinetics of proliferation, routes of migration and pattern of distribution of neurons. *Journal of Comparative Neurology*, 176, 23–52.

Rakic, P. (1978). Neuronal migration and contact guidance in the primate telencephalon. *Postgraduate Medical Journal*, 54, 25–40.

Rakic, P. (1982). Early developmental events: Cell lineages, acquisition of neuronal positions, and areal and laminar development. *Neuroscience Research Program Bulletin*, 20, 439–451.

Rakic, P. (1985). DNA synthesis and cell division in the adult primate brain. *Annals of the New York Academy of Sciences*, 457, 193–211.

Rakic, P., Bourgeois, J.-P., Eckenhoff, M. F., Zecevic, N., & Goldman-Rakic, P. S. (1986). Concurrent overproduction of synapses in diverse regions of the primate cerebral cortex. *Science*, 232, 232–235.

Rakic, P., & Goldman-Rakic, P. S. (1982). The development and modifiability of the cerebral cortex: Overview. *Neuroscience Research Program Bulletin*, 20, 433–438.

Rakic, P., & Nowakowski, R. S. (1981). The time of origin of neurons in the hippocampal region of the rhesus monkey. *Journal of Comparative Neurology*, 196, 99–128.

Rakic, P., & Riley, K. P. (1983). Regulation of axon number in primate optic nerve by prenatal binocular competition *Nature*, 305, 135–137.

Rakic, P., & Sidman, R. L. (1973). Sequence of developmental abnormalities leading to granule cell deficit in cerebellar cortex of weaver mutant mice. *Journal of Comparative Neurology*, 152, 103–132.

Rakic, P., Stensaas, L. J., Sayre, E. P., & Sidman, R. L. (1974). Computer-aided three-dimensional reconstruction and quantitative analysis of cells from serial electron microscopic montages of foetal monkey brain. *Nature*, 250, 31–34.

Raveche, E. S., Novotny, E. A., Hansen, C. T., Tjio, J. H., & Steinberg, A. D. (1981). Genetic studies in NZB mice: V. Recombinant inbred lines demonstrate that separate genes control autoimmune phenotype. *Journal of Experimental Medicine*, 153, 1187–1197.

Richardson, E. P., Jr. (1982). Myelination in the human central nervous system. In W. Haymaker & R. D. Adams (Eds.), *Histology and histopathology of the nervous system* (Vol. 1, pp. 146–173). Springfield, IL: Thomas.

Richman, D. P., Stewart, R. M., Hutchinson, J. W., & Caviness, V. S., Jr. (1975). Mechanical model of brain convolutional development. *Science*, 189, 18–21.

Rosett, H. L., Weiner, L., Lee, A., Zuckerman, B., Dooling, E., & Oppenheimer, E. (1983). Patterns of alcohol consumption and fetal development. *Obstetrics and Gynecology*, 61, 539–546.

Schmidt, J. T. (1985a). Selective stabilization of retinotectal synapses by an activity-dependent mechanism. *Federation Proceedings*, 44, 2767–2772.

Schmidt, J. T. (1985b). Activity-dependent synaptic stabilization in development and learning: How similar the mechanisms? *Cellular and Molecular Neurobiology*, 5, 1–3.

Schmidt, J. T., & Tieman, S. B. (1985). Eye-specific segregation of optic afferents in mammals, fish, and frogs: The role of activity. *Cellular and Molecular Neurobiology*, 5, 5–34.

Schulte, H. von W., & Tilney, F. (1915). Development of the neuraxis in the domestic cat to the stage of twenty-one somites. *Annals of the New York Academy of Sciences*, 24, 319–346.

Schwegler, H., & Lipp, H. P. (1981). Is there a correlation between hippocampal mossy fiber distribution and two-way avoidance performance in mice and rats? *Neuroscience Letter*, 23, 25–30.

Schwegler, H., & Lipp, H. P. (1983). Hereditary covariations of neuronal circuitry and behaviour: Correlations between the proportions of hippocampal synaptic fields in the regio inferior and two-way avoidance in mice and rats. *Behavioral Brain Research*, 7, 1–38.

Schwegler, H., Lipp, H. P., Van der Loos, H., & Buselmaier, W. (1981). Individual hippocampal mossy fiber distribution in mice correlates with two-way avoidance performance. *Science*, 214, 817–819.

Segraves, M. A., & Innocenti, G. M. (1985). Comparison of the distributions of ipsilaterally and contralaterally projecting corticocortical neurons in cat visual cortex using two fluorescent tracers. *Journal of Neuroscience*, 5, 2107–2118.

Sherman, G. F., Galaburda, A. M., & Geschwind, N. (1985). Cortical anomalies in brains of New Zealand mice: A neuropathologic model of dyslexia. *Proceedings of the National Academy of Sciences USA*, 82, 8072–8074.

Shumway, W. (1940). Stages in the normal development of *Rana pipiens*: I. External form. *Anatomical Record*, 78, 139–148.

Sidman, R. L. (1961). Histogenesis of mouse retina studied with thymidine-H^3. In G. Smelser (Ed.), *Structure of the eye* (pp. 487–506). New York: Academic Press.

Sidman, R. L. (1970). Autoradiographic methods and principles of study of the nervous system with thymidine-H^3. In W. J. H. Nauta & S. O. E. Ebbesson (Eds.), *Contemporary research methods in neuroanatomy* (pp. 252–274). New York: Springer-Verlag.

Sidman, R. L., & Rakic, P. (1973). Neuronal migration with special reference to developing human brain: A review. *Brain Research*, 62, 1–35.

Sidman, R. L., & Rakic, P. (1982). Development of the human central nervous system. In W. Haymaker & R. D. Adams (eds), *Histology and histopathology of the nervous system* (pp. 3–145). Springfield, IL: Thomas.

Simmons, P. A., Lemmon, V., & Pearlman, A. L. (1982). Afferent and efferent connections of the striate and extrastriate visual cortex of the normal and reeler mouse. *Journal of Comparative Neurology*, 211, 295–308.

Simmons, P. A., & Pearlman, A. L. (1982). Retinotopic organization of the striate cortex (area 17) in the reeler mutant mouse. *Brain Research*, 256, 124–126.

Simmons, P. A., & Pearlman, A. L. (1983). Receptive-field properties of transcallosal visual cortical neurons in the normal and reeler mouse. *Journal of Neurophysiology*, 50, 838–848.

Smart, I. H. M., & McSherry, G. M. (1982). Growth patterns in the lateral wall of the mouse telencephalon: II. Histological changes during and subsequent to the period of isocortical neuron production. *Journal of Anatomy*, 134, 415–442.

Sonmez, E., & Herrup, K. (1984). Role of staggerer gene in determining cell number in cerebellar cortex: II. Granule cell death and persistence of the external granule cell layer in young mouse chimeras. *Brain Research*, 314, 271–283.

Sotelo, C., & Rio, J. P. (1980). Cerebellar malformation obtained in rats by early postnatal treatment with 6-aminonicotinamide: Role of neuron-glia interactions in cerebellar development. *Neuroscience*, 5, 1737–1759.

Stanfield, B. B., Caviness, V. S., Jr., & Cowan, W. M. (1979). The organization of certain afferents to the hippocampus and dentate gyrus in normal and reeler mice. *Journal of Comparative Neurology*, 185, 461–484.

Stanfield, B. B., & Cowan, W. M. (1979a). The morphology of the hippocampus and dentate gyrus in normal and reeler mice. *Journal of Comparative Neurology*, 185, 393–422.

Stanfield, B. B., & Cowan, W. M. (1979b). The development of the hippocampus and dentate gyrus in normal and reeler mice. *Journal of Comparative Neurology*, 185, 423–460.

Stanfield, B. B., & O'Leary, D. D. (1985a). The transient corticospinal projection from the occipital cortex during the postnatal development of the rat. *Journal of Comparative Neurology*, 238, 236–248.

Stanfield, B. B., & O'Leary, D. D. (1985b). Fetal occipital cortical neurons transplanted to the rostral cortex can extend and maintain a pyramidal tract axon. *Nature*, 313, 135–137.

Sutcliffe, J. G., Milner, R. J., Gottesfeld, J. M., & Reynolds, W. (1984). Control of neuronal gene expression. *Science*, 225, 1308–1315.

Taber-Pierce, E. (1972). Time of origin of neurons in the brain stem of the mouse. *Progress in Brain Research*, 40, 53–66.

Tanzi, R. E., Gusella, J. F., Watkins, P. C., Bruns, G. A. P., George-Hyslop, P. S., Van Keuren, M. L., Patterson, D., Pagan, S., Kurnit, D. M., & Neve, R. L. (1987). Amyloid β protein gene: cDNA, mRNA distribution, and genetic linkage near the Alzheimer locus. *Science*, 235, 880–884.

Temple, S., & Raff, M. C. (1986). Clon.l analysis of oligodendrocyte development in culture: Evidence for a developmental clock that counts cell divisions. *Cell*, 44, 773–779.

Theiler, K. (1972). *The house mouse*. Berlin: Springer-Verlag.

Toulouse, G., Dehaene, S., & Changeux, J. P. (1986). Spin glass model of learning by selection. *Proceedings of the National Academy of Sciences USA*, 83, 1695–1698.

Wahlsten, D., Lyons, J. P., & Zagaja, W. (1983). Shaker short-tail, a spontaneous neurological mutant in the mouse. *Journal of Heredity*, 74, 421–425.

Walsh, C., Polley, E. H., Hickey, T. L., & Guillery, R. W. (1983). Generation of cat retinal ganglion cells in relation to central pathways. *Nature*, 302, 611–614.

Wegmann, T. G., LaVail, M. M., & Sidman, R. L. (1971). Patchy retinal degeneration in tetraparental mice. *Nature*, 230, 333–334.

Wetts, R., & Herrup, K. (1982a). Interaction of granule, Purkinje and inferior olivary neurons in Lurcher chimaeric mice. *Journal of Embryology and Experimental Morphology*, 68, 87–98.

Wetts, R., & Herrup, K. (1982b). Interaction of granule, Purkinje and inferior olivary neurons in Lurcher chimaeric mice: II. Granule cell death. *Brain Research*, 250, 358–362.

Wetts, R., & Herrup, K. (1982c). Cerebellar Purkinje cells are descended from a small number of progenitors committed during early development: Quantitative analysis of Lurcher chimaeric mice. *Journal of Neuroscience*, 2, 1494–1498.

Wiesel, T. N. (1982). Postnatal development of the visual cortex and the influence of environment. *Nature*, 299, 583–591.

Wimer, R. E., & Wimer, C. C. (1982a). A biometrical-genetic analysis of granule cell number in the area dentata of house mice. *Developmental Brain Research*, 2, 129–140.

Wimer, R. E., & Wimer, C. C. (1982b). A geneticist's map of the mouse brain. In I. Lieblich (Ed.), *Genetics of the brain* (pp. 395–420). Amsterdam: Elsevier.

Wimer, R. E., & Wimer, C. C. (1985). Animal behavior genetics: A search for the biological foundations of behavior. *Annual Review of Psychology*, 36, 171–218.

Wyss, J. M., & Sripanidkulchai, B. (1985). The development of Ammon's horn and the fascia dentata in the cat: A [^{3}H]thymidine analysis. *Developmental Brain Research*, 18, 185–198.

Yakovlev, P. I., & Lecours, A. R. (1967). The myelogenetic cycles of regional maturation of the brain. In A. Minkowski (Ed.), *Regional development of brain in early life* (pp. 3–70). Oxford: Blackwell Science Publications.

Zecevic, N., & Rakic, P. (1976). Differentiation of Purkinje cells and their relationship to other components of developing cerebellar cortex in man. *Journal of Comparative Neurology*, 167, 27–48.

Zimmerman, R. A., Bilaniuk, L. T., & Grossman, R. I. (1983). Computed tomography in migratory disorders of human brain development. *Neuroradiology*, 25, 257–263.

6

Intrinsic and Extrinsic Determinants of Neocortical Parcellation: a Radial Unit Model

P. RAKIC

Introduction

In this chapter, I will review some developmental principles and several lines of evidence in support of the radial unit model of neocortical ontogeny and phylogeny. This model, which involves the kinetics of cell proliferation, neuronal migration, competitive interactions, and selective cell elimination, has implications for understanding the genetic and epigenetic regulation of neocortical parcellation during development, and provides a new view on the pathogenesis of certain cortical malformations in man.

I will draw background information mostly from the analysis of cortical development in rhesus monkeys, which has become accessible to experimental analysis with modern methods including axonal tracing, electron microscopy, immunocytochemistry, *in situ* hybridization, receptor binding, and ^{3}H-thymidine autoradiography. Advances made in techniques of neurosurgery on the fetal cerebrum *in utero* make experimental manipulations that were traditionally limited to avain and amphibian embryos possible in large mammals (Rakic and Goldman-Rakic, 1985). The size of the monkey's cerebrum during the second half of gestation and the presence of visible morphological landmarks at its surface allow precise localization for excision of specific cortical areas, while protracted development provides high temporal resolution of cellular events. Finally, the similarity between man and monkey of the convoluted cerebral surface and of distinct boundaries between major cytoarchitectonic fields enables comparison between

"Intrinsic and Extrinsic Determinants of Neocortical Parcellation: a Radial Unit Model" first appeared in *Neurobiology of Neocortex*, edited by P. Rakic and W. Singer (John Wiley & Sons, 1988, pp. 5–27), © S. Bernhard, Dahlem Konferenzen, 1988, and is reprinted by kind permission.

findings obtained from animal research and findings from normal and pathological human autopsy specimens.

I will concentrate on the formation of cytoarchitectonic areas during ontogenetic and phylogenetic development. A comparison of cytoarchitectonic maps in various species reveals four important points relevant to the proposed developmental model. First, the neocortex expands enormously during phylogeny (e.g. the surface of rat's neocortex is less than 1 percent of a monkey's and 0.1 percent of a human's). Second, all cytoarchitectonic areas do not expand equally (e.g. striate cortex occupies only 3 percent of the cerebral surface in humans but more than 15 percent of the cerebral surface in monkeys). Third, new cytoarchitectonic areas become introduced during evolution (e.g. monkeys do not have Broca's area). Fourth, there are large interspecies variations in the sizes of cortical areas, as well as differences between the hemispheres of the same individual (e.g. the auditory cortex may be three times larger on the left side in right-handed humans).

How are differences in cortical parcellation between species and individuals generated? Is the number of neurons in each cytoarchitectonic area genetically determined? Do environmental factors and functional activity play any role? If so, when does the capacity for structural change stop? To answer some of these questions, we first must know when and where cortical neurons are generated and how they assume their positions within the cortex. Then we have to determine whether their fate can be experimentally manipulated.

Origin of Cortical Neurons

Classical histological studies suggested that the majority of cortical neurons in man are generated outside of the cortex itself, probably well before birth (Sidman and Rakic, 1973). However, only the introduction of the DNA labeling method using ^{3}H-thymidine provided sufficiently precise data on the onset and end of corticogenesis. For example, analysis of a series of adult rhesus monkeys that were exposed to ^{3}H-thymidine during various pre-and postnatal stages revealed that all cortical neurons in this species are generated during the middle of gestation (Rakic, 1974; Rakic and Goldman-Rakic, 1982). The first cortical neurons arise around the 40th embryonic day (E40); the last at a more variable time. Thus, corticogenesis in the cingulate cortex stops at E70; in the striate cortex at E100. No neocortical neurons are produced during the last two prenatal months nor at any time after birth, which in rhesus monkeys occurs around E165 (Rakic, 1985). This contrasts with reports of neurogenesis in the cortex of mature rodents (Kaplan, 1981). Comparative cytological analysis indicates that in humans, with a normal gestation of about E265, the first cortical neurons are also generated around E40, and their production is complete by E125 (Rakic, 1978). Thus, unlike rodents, where the last neocortical neurons are produced close to or shortly after birth (Angevine and Sidman, 1961; Berry and Rogers, 1965; Smart and Smart, 1982), primates including man acquire their full complement of neurons by midgestation.

The high proportion of mitotic figures at the ventricular surface suggested to the early neuroanatomists that most cortical neurons might be produced there

(His, 1904; Ramon y Cajal, 1911). Again, the direct evidence for this conclusion came from ^{3}H-thymidine autoradiographic analysis. A series of monkey embryos sacrificed within two hours after injection of isotope showed that all neurons of the neocortex are produced in the proliferative zone near the cerebral ventricle (Rakic, 1978; Rakic and Goldman-Rakic, 1982). Therefore, cortical neurons must migrate to the cortex after their last mitotic division. Golgi, electron microscopic, autoradiographic, and immunocytochemical analyses have revealed that both neuronal and glial cells coexist in the proliferative zone from the onset of corticogenesis (Levitt et al., 1983; Rakic, 1972b; Schmechel and Rakic, 1979). The point relevant to the proposed radial unit model of cortical development is that interaction between glial fibers and postmitotic neurons has to be taken into account when considering mechanisms of neuronal migration and cortical parcellation (Rakic, 1972b).

Neurons Migrate Along Radial Glial Grids

Although the most massive migration of neurons in primates occurs during the rapid and differential growth of the cerebral wall that causes buckling of its surface, postmitotic neurons nevertheless find their way through the intricate cellular lattice of the intermediate and subplate zones. Electron microscopic studies revealed that the pathways of migrating cells are established by a guidance mechanism that depends on interaction with the shafts of radial glial cells that stretch across the developing telencephalic wall (Rakic, 1972b). Therefore, the migrational pattern of these neurons is imposed by the shape and nature of non-neuronal scaffolding, which is provided by the fascicles of radial glial fibers. This scaffolding is particularly prominent during a period of about two months when most radial glial cells do not divide (Schmechel and Rakic, 1979). Possible cellular and molecular mechanisms underlying the translocation of migrating cells and their guidance to the cortex have been reviewed elsewhere, and several candidate molecules have been tested *in vitro* (Edelman 1983; Hatten and Mason 1986; Lindner et al., 1983). Here, I will focus only on the significance of the glial scaffolding for columnar compartmentalization of the neocortex as it relates to the radial unit hypothesis.

Migrating neurons in the large primate cerebrum have to pass through a long and often tortuous pathway across the intermediate zone and, at later stages, across the subplate zone before arriving at their proper destination (figure 6.1). The intermediate zone increases in thickness by the addition of axonal fascicles of various origins. After most of these axons acquire their myelin sheath, this zone is transformed into the subcortical white matter. The transient subplate zone, which is situated below the developing cortical plate, consists of early generated interstitial neurons dispersed among incoming thalamic afferents (Kostovic and Rakic, 1980; Rakic, 1977; Rakic and Goldman-Rakic, 1982; Shatz and Luskin, 1986) and, at later stages, among corticocortical afferents as well (Goldman-Rakic, 1981; Rakic and Goldman-Rakic, 1982). It has been suggested that the subplate zone might be a waiting compartment where afferent fibers make temporary contacts with interstitial cells and migrating neurons before their entry into the cortex (Rakic, 1977). We do not yet understand the nature of these contacts or

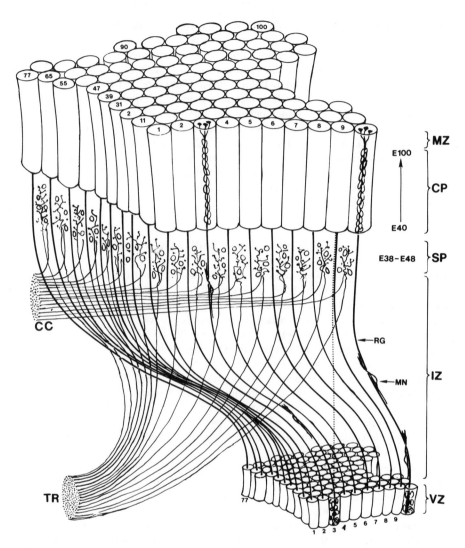

Figure 6.1 The relationship between a small patch of the proliferative, ventricular zone (VZ) and its corresponding area within the cortical plate (CP) in the developing cerebrum. Although the cerebral surface in primates expands during prenatal development, resulting in a shift between the VZ and CP, ontogenetic columns (outlined by cylinders) remain attached to the corresponding proliferative units by the grid of radial glial fibers. All cortical neurons produced between E40 and E100 by a given proliferative unit migrate in succession along the same radial glial guides (RG) and form a single ontogenetic column. Each migrating neuron (MN) traverses the intermediate (IZ) and subplate (SP) zones that contain "waiting" terminals of thalamic radiation (TR) and corticocortical afferents (CC). After entering the cortical plate, each MN bypasses deeper-lying earlier generated neurons and assumes the most superficial position at the interphase between the CP and marginal zone (MZ). As a result, the set of proliferative units 1–100 produce a set of ontogenetic columns 1–100 in the same relative position to each other. Glial scaffolding prevents a

their significance, although the presence of synapses, neurotransmitters, and neuromodulators, indicates neuronal interaction (Chun et al., 1987; Kostovic and Rakic, 1980).

The proliferative zone can be regarded as a mosaic of proliferative units, each of which provides about one hundred generations of neurons that follow the same radial glial pathway (figure 6.1). The cohorts of genealogically related cells finally end up in the cortical plate stacked one above the other in the form of ontogenetic columns (Rakic, 1974, 1978; Rakic and Goldman-Rakic, 1982). Confinement of several generations of postmitotic cells to a common glial guide may serve to divide the cerebral wall into radial units that extend from the proliferative units across the migratory intermediate zone to the ontogenetic columns in the cortex (figure 6.1). The number of proliferative units, therefore, determines the number of ontogenetic columns (Rakic, 1978). A set of regulatory genes analogous to the homeotic genes, which govern segmental differentiation in drosophila (Lewis, 1978; Morata and Lawrence, 1977; Scott, 1984), may parcellate proliferative units within the ventricular zone into a proto-map of basic cytoarchitectonic areas. The radial glial scaffolding simply enables translation of such a map from the ventricular zone to the expanding cortical plate. The use of the term "proto-map" in this context implies that a given site (proliferative unit) of the ventricular zone generates neurons that form area-specific ontogenetic columns. After the number of proliferative units is established, homeotic genes may turn on another set of genes that determine individual phenotypes of cells produced in each proliferative unit. Therefore, this hypothesis is based on the assumption that (a) within the ventricular zone some proliferative cells have been committed to differentiate into a particular cortical area; and (b) cells produced within an ontogenetic column are genealogically related (Rakic, 1972b, 1978, 1988; Rakic and Goldman-Rakic, 1982). Thus, the complex three-dimensional organization of the adult cortex can be explained by genetic specification as well as spatial and temporal gradients originating from the two-dimensional map of the proliferative zone (figure 6.1).

Laminar Position and Phenotype of Neurons Are Time-Specific

As suspected from the examination of Golgi impregnated tissue (Köelliker, 1896; Ramon y Cajal, 1911; Vignal, 1888) and proven by ^{3}H-thymidine autoradiography in a variety of species (Angevine and Sidman, 1961; Berry and Rogers, 1965; Luskin and Shatz, 1985; Rakic, 1974; Smart and Smart, 1982), neurons destined for deeper cortical layers are generated earliest and are bypassed by those of the more superficial layers. The relationship between the time of neuronal origin and their laminar position, referred to as an "inside-out" gradient of neurogenesis,

mismatch between proliferative unit 3 and ontogenetic column 9 (dashed line). According to the radial unit model, the tangential coordinates of cortical neurons are determined by the position of their ancestors at the ventricle, while their radial positions are determined by the time of genesis and rate of neuronal migration. Thus, the basic topography and/or modality is specified by the spatial distribution of proliferative units, while the neuronal phenotypes within units are specified by time. Modified from Rakic (1978, 1982).

is particularly sharp in primates where each injection of ^{3}H-thymidine labels a highly selective sample of cortical neurons (Rakic, 1974). This gradient is present throughout the entire cortex, although simultaneously generated neurons destined for various areas display small differences in their laminar position (Rakic, 1974, 1978; Rakic and Goldman-Rakic, 1982; Sidman and Rakic, 1973; Smart and Smart, 1982). The inside-out gradient is characteristic of the mammalian telencephalon, since in reptiles telencephalic neurons settle in an opposite (outside-in) gradient (Goffinet et al., 1986).

On a given day, one area may receive pyramidal cells of layer V, while on the next day it may receive stellate neurons of layer IV. On the other hand, both types of neurons within one layer can be generated simultaneously. It remains possible that different phenotypes of the same ontogenetic column may originate from two or more clones situated in the single proliferative unit (Rakic, 1978; Rakic and Goldman-Rakic, 1982). At present, we are not able to follow the lineage of cortical neurons as has been done for neurons in some simple invertebrates, but we can determine when they become committed to their phenotypes.

Several lines of evidence suggest that a neuron's fate may be determined before the cell assumes its final position. First, in reeler mutant mice, cells that acquire inappropriate laminar positions within the cortex nevertheless differentiate into neuronal types corresponding to the time of their origin rather than the types expected in their new location (Caviness and Rakic, 1978). Second, neurons that remain close to their origin near the ventricular surface due to X-irradiation, which prevents their migration, assume their appropriate phenotype and also establish appropriate efferent connections (Jensen and Killackey, 1984). Third, ventricular cells transplanted into a host's proliferative zone migrate to the positions and assume morphological characteristics similar to those of normal cortical neurons with the same birthdates (McConnell, 1985, 1987). Finally, a subset of callosal neurons destined for layer III in the monkey fetus sends its axons to the opposite hemisphere before entering the cortical plate (Schwartz and Goldman-Rakic, 1986). These findings collectively suggest that the basic properties of neurons such as their morphology and/or prospective synaptic contacts may be specified early, i.e. determined before cells reach their final positions. A similar conclusion has been draw for the neuronal classes of the cerebellar cortex (granule cells, interneurons of the molecular layer, and Purkinje cells), which originate from different precursors (Rakic, 1972a). More recently, it has been suggested that all Purkinje cells arise from a few clones established early in the proliferative zones (Herrup, 1986). It should be emphasized, however, that determination of the basic types of neurons (e.g. pyramidal versus stellate) does not address the larger issue of their areal specificity (e.g. area 17 versus area 18), or modal specificity (e.g. visual versus auditory). Knowing how and when neurons differentiate into certain types does not tell us how they find their areal and laminar positions, what controls their number, or how they become an integral part of the cortex as a whole.

Fetal Cortex Consists of Ontogenetic Columns

According to the radial unit hypothesis, proliferative units should have corresponding ontogenetic columns in the cortex (Rakic, 1978). In monkey embryos at midgestation, each ontogenetic column may contain between 80 and 120 neurons stacked on top of one another, separated by intercolumnar spaces. In some areas like the cingulate cortex, where neurogenesis lasts about one month, ontogenetic columns have fewer neurons, whereas the visual cortex, which is produced over almost two months, has columns with a higher number of neurons (Rakic, submitted). However, final numbers of neurons within the columns may be subsequently modified by differential cell death (Finlay and Slattery, 1983).

The total number of proliferative units and the number of units subserving specific cytoarchitectonic areas very between species and among individuals of the same species. We estimate that in the fetal monkey, the number of proliferative units in the cerebral ventricular zone and the number of ontogenetic columns in the cortical plate may be in the vicinity of 15 to 20 million. In humans, the number is probably ten times higher, while in the rat, probably ten times smaller. The number of ontogenetic columns comprising various areas has not been precisely determined in any species, but it is likely that the average striate cortex in a rhesus monkey contains between 2.5 and 3 million (Rakic, unpublished). These numbers are rough approximations complicated by large individual variations. Subsequent neuronal growth, elaboration of dendrites, ingrowth of afferents, formation of synapses, and proliferation of glial cells distort the initially simple radial organization. Although in most areas the fetal type of radial organization disappears by the time the cortical plate acquires its horizontal lamination, its vestiges can still be discerned in some areas, even in an adult.

Columnar deployment of neurons in the adult neocortex was recognized over fifty years ago (Lorente de No, 1938), but most subsequent research focused on its laminar organization. It was Mountcastle (1957) who established the functional significance of radial organization in the cerebral cortex by discovering that all neurons within a single column respond to the same stimulus. His work revealed that the cortex can be conceived of as a mosaic of interrelated cellular columns concerned with one specific modality (touch, pressure, joint movement, etc.) and with a single point (receptive field) at the periphery (Mountcastle, 1957, 1979). Projections from a given thalamic nucleus or from its parts may terminate in the form of stripes that innervate arrays of ontogenetic columns arranged as "colonnades", or parallel rows of columns (Eccles, 1984; Mountcastle, 1979; Szentagothai, 1978). Similar functional or anatomical columns have been observed in other sensory areas (Hubel and Wiesel, 1977; Jones et al., 1975; Jones, 1981) as well as in association cortex (Goldman and Nauta, 1977; Goldman-Rakic and Schwartz, 1982). However, the present article is not concerned with the columnar terminal fields of thalamic or corticocortical connections. Rather, it is focused on the cohorts of genealogically related neurons that may provide the developmental basis for the columnar organization of neurons and their function in the adult cortex (Rakic, 1978).

Cortex Expands Mainly by Addition of Radial Units

There is little doubt that the neocortical mantle enlarges during evolution by unequal growth of existing cytoarchitectonic areas and by the addition of new ones (e.g. Brodmann, 1909; Ebbesson, 1980; Kaas, 1987; Sanides, 1972). This is accomplished by the addition of ontogenetic columns, which in turn are produced by the proliferative units in the ventricular zone. The hypothesis consistent with our findings is that cells of the proliferative units arise mainly by symmetrical cell divisions, while later they produce cortical cells mainly by asymmetrical divisions. The number of units in each individual, therefore, must be determined early, before the onset of neurogenesis. A single additional round of symmetrical cell divisions at the stage of unit formation would double their number as well as the number of ontogenetic columns that they subsequently produce. Conversely, the number of neurons within the ontogenetic columns depends on the rate of cell production by asymmetrical division in the proliferative units. An additional cell division would increase the number of neurons within a given ontogenetic column by only one. Indeed, the number of cells in ontogenetic columns, reflected in the thickness of the cortex, changes relatively little during evolution (Rockel et al., 1980). It may not be coincidental that the size of the columnated afferent terminal fields in the cortex is relatively constant, even in species with large differences in the cerebral surface (Bugbee and Goldman-Rakic, 1983). Although an increase in the number of ontogenetic columns explains the expansion of the cortical surface as a whole, it does not address the issue of a differential increase in the surface of various Cytoarchitectonic areas.

Two basic cellular mechanisms, or their combination, could account for differential expansion of cytoarchitectonic fields. According to one hypothesis, the areal specificity of cortical neurons is rigidly determined within the ventricular zone (i.e. the number of proliferative units devoted to each area is fixed). The differential increase in the number of units producing area-specific columns can be regulated at early embryonic stages by homeosis, meaning the "assumption of one member of a metric series of the form to another member of the series" (Bateson, 1894). More recently, genes that regulate such developmental changes, the so-called homeotic genes, have been demonstrated in a variety of species (Gehring, 1985; Lewis, 1978; Scott, 1984). It is likely that such master genes, at later stages, control production of neuronal phenotypes within the proliferative units, thereby generating variations on the common neural pattern in ontogenetic columns subserving individual cytoarchitectonic areas. Therefore, regulatory genes may preserve an evolutionary component and provide instruction both for duplication and for changes in the mosaic of proliferative units at the ventricular surface.

An alternative possibility is that the areal positions and modal specificity of neurons are not determined in the proliferative units, and that their phenotype and function are decided later by the type of input they receive from the periphery via the thalamus (Creutzfeldt, 1977; Mountcastle, 1957). Although this hypothesis provides a logical and attractive explanation for the diversification of cytoarchitectonic areas, it is difficult to reconcile it with a variety of evidence indicating that the information from the receptors of the periphery cannot be the sole determinant of cortical areas. For example, the basic pattern of geniculocortical connections is present not only before the formation of contacts with the retinal receptors (Nishimura and Rakic, 1986), but they develop appropriate topography and are maintained in the absence of both eyes (Olivaria and van Sluyters, 1984; Rakic, 1988; Rakic and Williams, 1986). Results of these and other studies, some of which are reviewed in preceding sections, indicate that certain areal markers must be present in the cortical plate independently of input from the periphery.

There is a third possibility which combines features from both above-mentioned hypotheses and is compatible with most of the available information. According to the radial unit model, proliferation units produce area-specific ontogenetic columns, but their final number devoted to a given area can be adjusted downward by a complex input/output relationship. This model would be in general accord with the theories of selective stabilization (Changeux and Danchin, 1976), neuronal group selection (Edelman and Finkel, 1984), and competitive elimination (Rakic, 1986), which were proposed to explain the fine tuning of synaptic connections within a given system. We are now at a point where the various hypothesis proposed for cortical parcellation can be experimentally tested.

Experimental Manipulation of Cytoarchitectonic Areas

To distinguish between mechanisms of cortical parcellation discussed in the preceding section, a number of axons in a specific thalamocortical or corticocortical system should be altered at early embryonic stages and the effect on cortical areas examined. We have recently found that binocular enucleation performed on monkey embryos in the first half of gestation provides a useful test of the role thalamic afferents may play in the regulation of cytoarchitectonic fields. When enucleation is performed around E60, after all neurons of the lateral geniculate nucleus have been generated, but prior to ingrowth of their axons into the developing cortical plate (Rakic, 1977), this thalamic nucleus comes to contain less than one-half of the neurons present in the age-matched controls (Rakic, submitted; Rakic and Williams 1986; Rakic, unpublished). The occipital lobe in enucleated animals displays dramatic changes in the pattern of convolutions but has topographically well-defined residual connections with the diminished lateral geniculate nucleus. Since geniculocortical axons project to the striate cortex in a predictable manner (figure 6.2A), the presence of fewer fibers during corticogenesis could affect the size of the primary visual cortex in at least three ways: (a) the number and height of the ontogenetic columns may remain the same as in controls, resulting in dilution of geniculocortical afferents (figure 6.2B); (b) the number of columns devoted to area 17 could remain the same, but their height may be diminished by the process of second order transneuronal degeneration (figure 6.2C); (c) the number of ontogenetic columns can be reduced, while their height (i.e. the number of cells in each column) remains the same (figure 6.2D).

The results support the model illustrated in figure 6.2D. The striate cortex in enucleates was well-defined by a sharp border with the adjacent area, indicating that a morphological distinction between them develops in the absence of any information from the retina. Most unexpectedly, the thickness of the striate cortex and its characteristic complement of layers and sublayers was within the normal range (Rakic, 1988; Rakic and Williams, 1986). However, most importantly, the area of the striate cortex in enucleates was less than half the size it was in the age-matched controls. Thus, despite the absence of retinal input to

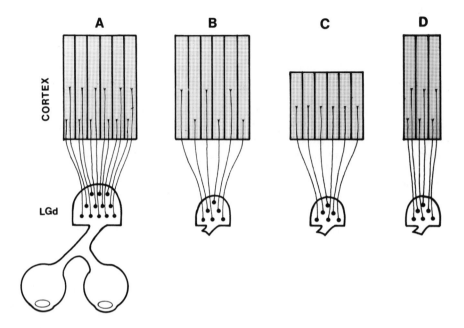

Figure 6.2 Schematic of the possible consequences of diminished afferent input to the visual cortex from the dorsal lateral geniculate nucleus (LGd) in animals binocularly enucleated at early embryonic stages. The normal numerical relationship between geniculocortical projections and ontogenetic columns in the cortex schematically illustrated in A can be altered in three basic ways (B, C, D), discussed in the text.

the lateral geniculate nucleus and the severely reduced number of geniculocortical afferents, the striate cortex had the normal number of neurons per layer and per ontogenetic column, while the total number of neurons in the area and its surface was diminished in proportion to the loss of geniculate neurons (Rakic, 1988; Rakic and Williams, 1986; Rakic, unpublished). The method of this reduction is not understood, and our working hypotheses are illustrated in figure 6.3: the striate cortex (area 17) can simply lose a number of ontogenetic columns, diminishing the total size of the cortex (figure 6.3B). Alternatively, the prestriate cortex (area 18), which normally receives input from the adjacent thalamic nucleus (pulvinar) and from the other parietal and temporal cortices, could take over some of the territory from area 17 (figure 6.3C). Finally, a number of columns that were specified for area 17 (X in figure 6.3D) could, in the absence of normal afferents, receive input from the pulvinar and other cortical areas, thus becoming a new cytoarchitectonic area that is genetically striate (area 17) and connectionally prestriate (area 18). Our preliminary data favor the last hypothesis (figure 6.3D), but additional experiments need to be done.

So far, results obtained from our experiments are in harmony with the observation that the human left cerebral hemisphere with a larger auditory cortex also has a larger medial geniculate nucleus (Eidelberg and Galaburda, 1982). Finally, it may be relevant to mention that the laminar distribution of major

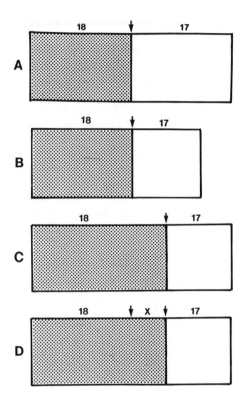

Figure 6.3 Schematic of the relationship between the striate (area 17) and prestriate (area 18) cortex in a normal animal (A) and the possible mechanisms responsible for the reduction of area 17 in binocular enucleates (B–D): the striate cortex can be diminished by differential cell death due to diminished input (B); encroachment of area 18 into its territory (C); or by formation of a new area (X), which is genetically striate but receives input characteristic for area 18 (D). Further explanation in the text.

neurotransmitter receptors within the striate area in early enucleated monkeys retains the appropriate pattern (Rakic et al., 1987), and that synaptic density within each layer, as revealed by quantitative electron microscopy, develops within the normal range (Bourgeois and Rakic, 1987). Thus, our data demonstrate that the number of specific thalamic afferents affects the final number of ontogenetic columns in the corresponding cortical area, but does not alter the number of neurons within each ontogenetic column or their phenotype.

Thalamic regulation may be only part of a more complex interactive process that occurs during development and parcellation of the neocortex. Prenatal resection of the fetal cortex, which eliminates or decreases specific corticocortical input to the subplate at early stages, has a profound effect on the gyral pattern and anatomy of the other, unoperated areas on both sides (Goldman-Rakic, 1980; Goldman-Rakic and Rakic, 1984; Rakic, 1988). On the basis of experiments in other systems, one can predict that multiple inputs to a given cytoarchitectonic area could have an effect on its final size. For example, we have found that initially overproduced retinogeniculate axons compete for their territory and for their survival (Rakic, 1981; Rakic and Riley, 1983). This can be demonstrated by early monocular enucleation, as graphically presented in figure 6.4A–C. In this series of experiments we found that by midgestation, about 3 million axons originating from each eye terminate in an overlapping manner in the lateral geniculate nucleus, but that their number diminished during the period of segregation to about 1.2 million. However, if one eye is removed at the stage of retinogeniculate overlap, the remaining eye retains a larger number of ganglion cells and their axons than it otherwise would, but this number is still smaller than the sum of two normal eyes (Rakic and Riley, 1983).

Our preliminary data indicate that the same general principle of competitive elimination may apply for cortical areas that share some common synaptic targets during development (figure 6.4D, E). For example, unilateral resection of the occipital cortex at midgestational periods results in an enlarged inferior parietal lobule on the side of the lesion (Goldman-Rakic and Rakic, 1984; Rakic,

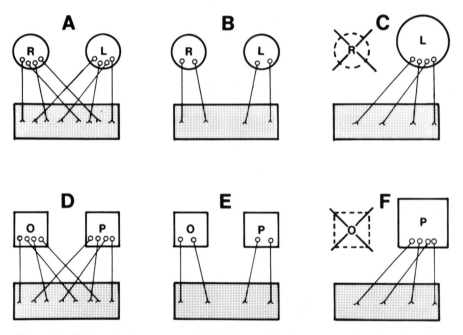

Figure 6.4 Diagrammatic representation of the model of competitive interaction between structures with supernumerary projections that share common synaptic targets (shaded boxes). A, Projections from the right (R) and left (L) eye to the brain are initially overproduced and intermixed. B, These projections become segregated by competitive elimination during normal development. C, Removal of the competition from one eye at the critical period results in retention of a larger number of neurons and axons in the remaining eye. Views D–F are diagrammatic representations of the similar type of competitive interaction that may occur between neurons of the occipital (O) and parietal cortex (P) which share a common synaptic target during embryogenesis. Further explanation in the text.

unpublished). One hypothesis to explain this dramatic result is that supernumerary cells in the parietal lobe may survive in the absence of competition with projections from the occipital lobe in the subcortical structures, or in the other cortical areas with which they share common synaptic targets (Figure 6.4D, E). Another hypothesis is that input from the remaining areas spreads to the territories normally occupied by the removed region. In cortical ablation experiments and in thalamic reduction experiments (described above), ontogenetic columns genetically specified for one area receive afferents characteristic of another area. As a result, we may have experimentally created a new cytoarchitectonic area that could contain different synaptoarchitecture. This is an important goal of future research as it may hold a key to understanding how new cytoarchitectonic areas may be introduced during evolution.

Reorganization of Cortical Representation Within Areas

Development and modifiability of the cortical representation is related, but is a somewhat different issue since it involves the intra-areal changes in maps (within a single area), rather than inter-areal changes (between different areas). Nevertheless, the results of intercortical manipulation in nonhuman primates are in general agreement with the "intracortical principles of magnification", according to which more densely innervated parts of the periphery have a larger representation in the somatosensory (Woolsey et al., 1942), visual (Daniel and Whitteridge, 1961), and auditory (Suga and Jen, 1976) areas. For example, in the trigeminal system in rodents, the number of sensory axons innervating a given vibrissal follicle and the size of the corresponding barrel in the cortex are closely correlated (Lee and Woolsey, 1975; van der Loos, 1979). Manipulation of the size of trigeminal innervation by a neonatal lesion in neighboring follicles or by selective inbreeding of mice with an "extra" whisker indicate that the "size of the somatory map and of its parts, while relating to the number of nerve fibers innervating the corresponding sensory periphery, is not an invariable function of it" (Welker and van der Loos, 1986). Recently, it has been shown that the forepaw and hindpaw representations in the somatosensory map also can be changed by damage to the periphery in newborn rodents (Dawson and, Killackey 1987; Seo and Ito, 1987). Likewise, peripheral nerve injury in developing rats changes the representational pattern in the motor cortex (Danoghue and Sanes, 1987).

Physiologically defined shifts in the borders of somatosensory representations have also been demonstrated in adult monkeys and cats. For example, peripheral nerve transection or digit amputation in adult primates (Merzenich et al., 1983) alters the borders between areas representing these digits. Likewise, in adult cats elimination of thalamic input to the motor cortex results in the reorganization of corticocortical projections (Asanuma et al., 1985). Although no anatomical substrate has thus far been demonstrated for these changes, they indicate considerable competitive interaction among various cortical connections in the adult cortex. Data from such a heterogenous set of experimental results obtained by different methods in various species are not easily comparable and are still far from being conclusive. Nevertheless, they support the notion that, although areal specificity and representation of the periphery may be already indicated at the time of cell production within the proliferative zone, the final number of ontogenetic columns devoted to a given receptive field or area may be to some extent regulated by competive interaction among participating neurons.

Radial Unit Model Can Explain the Pattern of Some Human Cortical Malformations

Another source of evidence supporting the radial unit hypothesis comes from the pattern of major cortical malformations in humans. Among abnormalities of the cortical mantle caused by defective proliferation and/or migration of cortical neurons, lissencephaly and polymicrogyria are the most prominent (reviewed in Volpe, 1981). There are several variations of these two basic types of malformations but in general, lissencephalic brains have a smooth cerebral surface, diminished total area, and approximately normal cortical thickness, whereas polymicrogyria is characterized by a highly convoluted cerebrum with nearly normal surface area, and thin cortex (Richman et al., 1974; Volpe, 1981). Since the etiology of these two malformations is a mystery, their classification in the past has been based on the appearance of the cortex at the time of death.

These types of cortical malformation can now be classified into two major categories on the basis of developmental mechanisms outlined by the radial unit hypothesis. The first category consists of malformations in which the number of ontogenetic columns in the cortex is diminished, while the number of neurons within each ontogenetic column remains relatively normal. The second category consists of malformations in which the number of ontogenetic columns in the cortex remains normal, while the number of neurons within each column is diminished. Although most malformations predominantly display features of one or the other of these two categories, some are a mixture of both types.

It can be expected that the first category is the result of an early defect that occurs at the time when proliferative units are being formed within the cerebral ventricular zone. The defect in this case should precede the onset of neurogenesis and therefore probably occurs in humans within the first seven weeks of gestation. Once the number of proliferative units in the ventricular zone has been established, each unit produces the usual number of neurons that form ontogenetic columns of normal height. As a result, the cortex has normal thickness but a smaller surface.

The defect in the second category of malformations begins after the normal number of proliferative units have been established. This defect should, therefore, occur after the seventh week of gestation, and should not greatly affect the number of ontogenetic columns. However, it can be expected that it affects the number of neurons produced within each proliferative unit. As a result, onto-genetic columns should have fewer neurons and consequently a thinner cortex. It should be emphasized that a smaller number of cells in the ontogenetic columns could be the result of low production in the proliferative unit, subsequent cell death, or a failure of their migration. In the latter case, some cortical neurons may survive in ectopic positions within the white matter, as frequently occurs in polymicrogyric brains (Volpe, 1981). Although the proposed classification of cortical malformations does not address the issue of their primary etiology, it suggests possible developmental mechanisms and delineates the timing and sequence of cellular events. The pattern of cortical malformations, on the other hand, supports the radial unit hypothesis by exposing the possible consequences of defects occurring during the stages when proliferative units or columns are forming.

Unsolved Questions and Future Prospects

The *radial unit model* can explain how the immense cellular mass of the neocortex disperses so that postmitotic cells generated near the cerebral ventricle find their final laminar and regional positions in appropriate cytoarchitectonic areas with species-specific and individual-specific differences in their size. This model assumes that cortical areas are the end-product of genetic information that can be modified by epigenetic variables. Advances in genetic and experimental manipulation of cortical development provide an opportunity to examine the validity of the radial unit model of cortical parcellation, and to determine the role of intrinsic and extrinsic factors in regulating the size of cytoarchitectonic areas. Furthermore, the fact that the radial unit model is consistent with the observed pattern of cortical abnormalities in major cortical malformations allows its validation at the genetic level.

Although the proposed model and its experimental testing have settled some issues, it has also led to a new set of questions. For example, we have learned that the number of radial columns devoted to the striate area can be altered by manipulation of the input it receives, but we do not understand the mechanisms involved in this regulatory process (figure 6.3). We do not even have some rather basic facts. For example, is the area of the striate cortex in early enucleates diminished by differential neuronal elimination, or by a shifting of the adjacent peristriate area into the territory normally occupied by the striate columns? If the latter possibility is the case, should this region be considered an enlarged area 18, or a new type of cortex which has input appropriate for area 18, but ontogenetic columns appropriate for area 17? What is the pattern of connectivity and what is the function of this artificially formed cortical area? What is the best research strategy to mark the embryonic site of the prospective areal borders before afferents invade the cortical plate and cytoarchitectonic characteristics emerge? Modern methods and research strategies using a combination of prenatal neurosurgery, transgenetic animals, cDNA and mRNA probes, or retrovirus-mediated gene transfer to label and to follow the progeny of neuronal clones from the site of their origin in the proliferative units to their final positions in the ontogenetic columns promise to provide further testing of the radial unit model of cortical development.

ACKNOWLEDGEMENTS

This work from the author's laboratory was supported by grants NS14841, EY02593, and Program Project NS22807.

REFERENCES

Allman, J. 1986. Maps in context: some analogies between visual cortical and genetic maps. In *Matters of Intelligence*, ed. L. Vaina, pp. 347–370. Holland: Reidel.

Angevine, J. B. Jr., and Sidman, R. L. 1961. Autoradiographic study of cell migration during histogenesis of cerebral cortex in the mouse. *Nature* 192: 766–768.

Asanuma, H.; Kosar, E.; Tsukuhora, N.; and Robinson, H. 1985. Modification of the projection from the sensory cortex to the motor cortex following the elimination of thalamic projections to the motor cortex in cat. *Brain Res.* 345: 79–86.

Bateson, W. 1894. *Materials for the Study of Variation Treated with Especial Regard to Discontinuity in the Origin of the Species.* London: Macmillan.

Berry, M., and Rogers, A. W. 1965. The migration of neuroblasts in the developing cortex. *J. Anat.* 99: 691–709.

Bourgeois, J.-P., and Rakic, P. 1987. Distribution, density and ultrastructure of synapses in the visual cortex in monkeys devoid of retinal input from early embryonic stages. *Soc. Neurosci. Abst.* 13: 1044.

Brodmann, K. 1909. *Lokalisationslehre der Grosshirnrinde in ihren Principien dargestellt auf Grund des Zellenbaue.* Leipzig: Barth.

Bugbee, N. M., and Goldman-Rakic, P. S. 1983. Columnar organization of corticocortical projections in squirrel and rhesus monkeys: similarity of column width in species differing in cortical volume. *J. Comp. Neurol.* 220: 355–364.

Caviness, V. S. Jr., and Rakic, P. 1978. Mechanisms of cortical development: a view from mutations in mice. *Ann. Rev. Neurosci.* 1: 297–326.

Changeux, J.-P., and Danchin, A. 1976. Selective stabilization of developing synapses as a mechanism for the specialization of neural network. *Nature* 264: 705–712.

Chun, J. J.; Nakamura, M. J.; and Shatz, C. J. 1987. Transient cells of the developing mammalian telencephalon are peptide-immunoreactive neurons. *Nature* 325: 617–620.

Creutzfeldt, O. D. 1977. Generality of the functional structure of the neocortex. *Naturwissenschaften* 64: 507–517.

Daniel, P. M., and Whitteridge, D. 1961. The representation of the visual field on the cerebral cortex in monkeys. *J. Physiol.* 159: 203–221.

Danoghue, J. P., and Sanes, J. N. 1987. Peripheral nerve injury in developing rats reorganizes representation pattern in motor cortex. *Proc. Natl Acad. Sci. USA* 84: 1123–1126.

Dawson, D. R., and Killackey, J. P. 1987. The organization and mutability of the forepaw and hindpaw representations in the somatosensory cortex of the neonatal rat. *J. Comp Neurol.* 256: 246–256.

Ebbesson, S. O. E. 1980. The parcellation theory and its relation to interspecific variability in brain organization, evolutionary and ontogenetic development, and neuronal plasticity. *Cell Tissue Res.* 213: 179–212.

Eccles, J. C. 1984. The cerebral neocortex. A theory of its operation. In *Cerebral Cortex*, vol. 2, eds E. G. Jones and A. Peters, pp. 1–36. New York: Plenum.

Edelman, G. M. 1983. Cell adhesion molecules. *Science* 219: 450–457.

Edelman, G. M., and Finkel, L. H. 1984. Neuronal group selection in the cerebral cortex. In *Dynamic Aspects of Neocortical Function*, eds G. M. Edelman, E. W. Gall, and W. M. Cowan, pp. 653–694. New York: Wiley & Sons.

Eidelberg, D., and Galaburda, A. M. 1982. Symmetry and asymmetry in the human posterior thalamus. *Arch. Neurol.* 39: 325–332.

Finlay, B. L., and Slattery, M. 1983. Local differences in the amount of early cell death in neocortex predict adult local specialization. *Science* 219: 1349–1351.

Gehring, W. J. 1985. The homeobox: a key to the understanding of development. *Cell* 40: 3–5.

Goffinet, A. M.; Doumierie, C.; Langerwerf, B.; and Pieau, C. 1986. Neurogenesis in reptilian cortical structures: ³H-thymidine autoradiographic analysis. *J. Comp. Neurol.* 243: 106–116.

Goldman, P. S., and Nauta, W. J. H. 1977. Columnar organization of association and motor cortex: autoradiographic evidence for cortico-cortical and commissural columns in the frontal lobe of the newborn rhesus monkey. *Brain Res.* 122: 369–385.

Goldman-Rakic, P. S. 1980. Morphological consequences of prenatal injury to the primate brain. *Prog. Brain Res.* 53: 3–19.

Goldman-Rakic, P. S. 1981. Development and plasticity of primate frontal association cortex. In *The Organization of the Cerebral Cortex*, eds F. O. Schmitt, F. G. Worden, S. G. Dennis, and G. Adelman, pp. 69–97. Cambridge, MA: MIT Press.

Goldman-Rakic, P. S., and Rakic, P. 1984. Experimental modification of gyral patterns. In *Cerebral Dominance: The Biological Foundation*, eds N. Geschwind and A. M. Galaburda, pp. 179–192. Cambridge, MA: Harvard Univ. Press.

Goldman-Rakic, P. S., and Schwartz, M. L. 1982. Interdigitation of contralateral and ipsilateral columnar projections to frontal association cortex in primates. *Science* 216: 755–757.

Hatten, M. E., and Mason, C. A. 1986. Neuron-astroglia interactions in vitro and in vivo. *Trends Neurosci.* 9: 168–174.

Herrup, K. 1986. Cell lineage relationship in the development of the mammalian central nervous system: role of cell lineage in control of cerebellar Purkinje cell number. *Dev. Biol.* 115: 148–154.

His, W. 1904. *Die Entwicklung des menschlichen Gehirns während der ersten Monate.* Leipzig: Hirzel.

Hubel, D. H., and Wiesel, T. N. 1977. Ferrier lecture. Functional architecture of macaque monkey visual cortex. *Proc. R. Soc. Lond. B.* 198: 1–59.

Jensen, K. F., and Killackey, H. P. 1984. Subcortical projections from ectopic neocortical neurons. *Proc. Natl Acad. Sci. USA* 81: 964–968.

Jones, E. G. 1981. Anatomy of cerebral cortex: columnar input-output organization. In *The Organization of the Cerebral Cortex*, eds F. O. Schmitt, F. G. Warden, G. Adelman, and S. G. Dennis, pp. 199–235. Cambridge, MA: MIT Press.

Jones, E. G.; Burton, H.; and Porter, R. 1975. Commissural and cortico-cortical "columns" in the somatic sensory cortex of primates. *Science* 190: 572–274.

Kaas, J. H. 1987. The organization and evolution of neocortex. In *Higher Brain Functions*, ed. S. P. Wise.

Kaplan, M. S. 1981. Neurogenesis in the 3-month-old rat visual cortex. *J. Comp. Neurol.* 195: 323–338.

Koelliker, A. 1896. *Handbuch der Gewebelehre des Menschen. Vol. 2, Nervensystem des Menschen und der Thiere.* Leipzig: W. Engelmann.

Kostovic, I., and Rakic, P. 1980. Cytology and time of origin of interstitial neurons in the white matter in infant and adult human and monkey telencephalon. *J. Neurocytol.* 9: 219–242.

Lee, K. J., and Woolsey, T. A. 1975. A proportional relationship between peripheral innervation density and cortical neuron number in the somatosensory system of the mouse. *Brain Res.* 99: 349–353.

Levitt, P.; Cooper, M. L.; and Rakic, P. 1983. Early divergence and changing proportions of neuronal and glial precursor cells in the primate cerebral ventricular zone. *Dev. Biol.* 96: 472–484.

Lewis, E. B. 1978. A gene complex controlling segmentation in *Drosophila. Nature* 276: 565–570.

Lindner, J.; Rathjen, F. G.; and Schachner, M. 1983. LI mono-and polyclonal antibodies modify cell migration in early postnatal mouse cerebellum. *Nature* 305: 427–430.

Lorente de No, R. 1938. Architectonic structure of the cerebral cortex. In *Physiology of the Nervous System*, ed. J. F. Fulton, pp. 291–339. London: Oxford Univ Press.

Luskin, M. B., and Shatz, C. J. 1985. Neurogenesis of the cat's primary visual cortex. *J. Comp. Neurol.* 242: 611–631.

McConnell, S. K. 1985. Migration and differentiation of cerebral cortical neurons after transplantation into brain of ferrets. *Science* 229: 1268–1271.

McConnell, S. K. 1987. Fates of transplanted visual cortical neurons. Thesis. Cambridge, MA: Harvard Univ.

Merzenich, M. M.; Kaas, J. H.; Wall, J.; Nelson, R. J.; Sur, M.; and Fellman, D. J. 1983. Topographic reorganization of somatosensory cortical areas 3b and 1 in adult monkeys following restricted deafferentiation. *Neurosci.* 8: 33–55.

Morata, G., and Lawrence, A. 1977. Homeotic genes, compartments and cell determination in *Drosophila*. *Nature* 265: 211–216.

Mountcastle, V. B. 1957. Modality and topographic properties of single neurons of cat's somatic sensory cortex. *J. Neurophysiol.* 20: 408–434.

Mountcastle, V. B. 1979. An organizing principle for cerebral function: the unit module and the distributed system. In *The Neurosciences: Fourth Study Program*, eds F.O. Schmitt and F. G. Worden, pp. 21–42. Cambridge, MA: MIT Press.

Nishimura, Y., and Rakic, P. 1986. Development of the rhesus monkey retina. II. Three dimensional analysis of microcircuitry in the inner plexiform layer. *J. Comp. Neurol.* 241: 420–434.

Olivaria, J., and van Sluyters, R. C. 1984. Callosal connections of the posterior neocortex in normal-eyed, congenitally anophthalmic, and neonatally enucleated mice. *J. Comp. Neurol.* 230: 249–268.

Rakic, P. 1972a. Extrinsic cytological determinants of basket and stellate cell dendritic pattern in the cerebellar molecular layer. *J. Comp. Neurol.* 146: 335–354.

Rakic, P. 1972b. Mode of cell migration to the superficial layers of fetal monkey neocortex. *J. Comp. Neurol.* 145: 61–84.

Rakic, P. 1974. Neurons in rhesus monkey visual cortex: systematic relation between time of origin and eventual disposition. *Science* 183: 425–427.

Rakic, P. 1977. Prenatal development of the visual system in the rhesus monkey. *Phil. Trans. R. Soc. Lond.* B 278: 245–260.

Rakic, P. 1978. Neuronal migration and contact guidance in primate telencephalon. *Postgrad. Med. J.* 54: 25–40.

Rakic, P. 1981. Development of visual centers in primate brain depends on binocular competition before birth. *Science* 214: 928–931.

Rakic, P. 1985. Limits of neurogenesis in primates. *Science* 227: 154–156.

Rakic, P. 1986. Mechanisms of ocular dominance segregation in the lateral geniculate nucleus: competitive elimination hypothesis. *Trends Neurosci.* 9: 11–15.

Rakic, P. 1988. Specification of neocortical areas: radial unit hypothesis. *Science*, in press.

Rakic, P., and Goldman-Rakic, P. S. 1982. Development and modifiability of the cerebral cortex. *Neurosci. Res. Prog. Bull.* (Edited volume for MIT Press, Cambridge, MA) 20: 429–611.

Rakic, P., and Goldman-Rakic, P. S. 1985. Use of fetal neurosurgery for experimental studies of structural and functional brain development in nonhuman primates. In *Prenatal Neurology and Neurosurgery*, eds R. A. Thompson and J. R. Green, pp, 1–15. New York: Spectrum Press.

Rakic, P.; Kritzer, M.; and Gallager, D. 1987. Distribution of major neurotransmitter receptors in visual cortex of monkeys deprived of retinal input from early embryonic stages. *Soc. Neurosci. Abst.* 13: 358.

Rakic, P., and Riley, K. P. 1983. Regulation of axon number in primate optic nerve by binocular competition. *Nature* 305: 135–137.

Rakic, P., and Williams, R. W. 1986. Thalamic regulation of cortical parcellation: an experimental perturbation of the striate cortex in rhesus monkeys. *Soc. Neurosci. Abst.* 12: 1499.

Ramon y Cajal, S. 1911. *Histologie du Systeme Nerveus de l'Home et des Vertebres. Reprinted by Consejo Superior de Investigaciones Cientificas.* Paris: Maloine.

Richman, D. P.; Stewart, R. M.; and Caviness, V. S. Jr. 1974. Cerebral microgyria in a 27 week fetus: an architectonic and topographic analysis. *J. Neuropath. Exp. Neur.* 33: 374–384.

Rockel, A. J.; Hiorns, R. W.; and Powell, T. P. S. 1980. The basic uniformity in structure of the neocortex. *Brain* 103: 221–244.

Rose, J. E., and Woolsey, C. N. 1949. The relations of thalamic connections, cellular structure and evocable electrical activity in the auditory region of the cat. *J. Comp. Neurol.* 91: 441–466.

Sanides, F. 1972. Representation in the cerebral cortex and its areal lamination patterns. In *Structure and Function of Nervous Tissue, vol. 5,* ed. G.H. Bourne, pp. 329–453. New York: Raven.

Schmechel, D. E., and Rakic, P. 1979. Arrested proliferation of radial glial cells during midgestation in rhesus monkey. *Nature* 277: 303–305.

Schwartz, M. L., and Goldman-Rakic, P. S. 1986. Some callosal neurons of the fetal monkey frontal cortex have axons in the contralateral hemisphere prior to the completion of migration. *Soc. Neurosci. Abst.* 12: 1211.

Scott, M. P. 1984. Homeotic gene transcripts in the neural tissue of insects. *Trends Neurosci.* 7: 221–223.

Seo, M. L., and Ito, M. 1987. Reorganization of rat vibrissa barrelfield as studied by cortical lesioning on different postnatal days. *Exp. Brain. Res.* 65: 251–260.

Shatz, C. J., and Luskin, M. B. 1986. The relationship between the geniculocortical afferents and their cortical target cells during development of the cat's primary visual cortex. *J. Neurosci.* 6: 3655–3668.

Sidman, R. L., and Rakic, P. 1973. Neuronal migration, with special reference to developing human brain: a review. *Brain Res.* 62: 1–35.

Smart, I. H. M., and McSherry, G. M. 1982. Growth patterns in the lateral wall of the mouse telencephalon. II. Histological changes during and subsequent to the period of isocortical neuron production. *J. Anat.* 134: 415–442.

Smart, I. H., and Smart, M. 1982. Growth patterns in the lateral wall of the mouse telencephalon: I. Autoradiographic studies of the histogenesis of the isocortex and adjacent areas. *J. Anat.* 134: 273–298.

Suga, N., and Jen, P. H.-S. 1976. Disproportionate tonotopic representation for processing species-specific CF-FM sonar signals in the mustached auditory cortex. *Science* 194: 542–544.

Szentagothai, J. 1978. The neuronal network of the cerebral cortex: a functional interpretation. *Proc. R. Soc. Lond. B* 201: 219–248.

van der Loos, H. 1979. The development of topographical equivalences in the brain. In *Neural Growth and Differentiation,* eds. E. Meisami and M. A. B. Braizer, pp. 331–336. New York: Raven Press.

Vignal, W. 1888. Recherches sur le development des elements des couches corticales du cerveau et du cervelet chez l'homme et les mammiferes. *Arch. Physiol. Norm. Path. (Paris) Ser. IV* 2: 228–254.

Volpe, J. J. 1981. *Neurology of the Newborn.* Philadelphia: Saunders.

Welker, E., and van der Loos, H. 1986. Quantitative correlation between barrelfield size and the sensory innervation of the whisker pad: a comparative study in six strains of mice bred for different patterns of mystacial vibrissae. *J. Neurosci.* 6: 3355–3373.

Woolsey, C. N.; Marshall, W. H.; and Bard, P. 1942. Representation of cutaneous tactile sensibility in the cerebral cortex of the monkey as indicated by evoked potentials. *Bull. Johns Hopk. Hosp.* 70: 399–441.

7

Morphometric Study of Human Cerebral Cortex Development

PETER R. HUTTENLOCHER

Introduction

Recent morphometric studies of human cerebral cortex during development provide interesting insights into the anatomical substrate of emerging cortical functions in the infant and child. They give evidence for a dynamic, changing system, at least into the late childhood years, an age at which cortical structure had been thought to be relatively stable. The quantitative approach has been especially productive in the area of synaptogenesis. However, quantitative data on cortical volume, neuronal number,
and dendritic growth also have yielded important findings.

As yet, there has been little attempt to correlate developmental changes in these different components of the neuropil.[a] Extensive data are now available for specific cortical areas, especially for primary visual cortex. These make it possible to obtain a fairly comprehensive picture of the changes that occur in cortical neurons during pre-and postnatal development. The present report is concerned with an analysis of extant data, emphasizing those in visual cortex, comparing them to findings in frontal cortex and stressing relationships between dendritic and synaptic growth.

Volume of Visual Cortex (Area 17)

Most quantitative morphologic data are obtained in terms of densities, i.e. number of structure per unit volume. For these to be meaningful, they have to

---

[a] Neuropil refers to the mass of interwoven dendrites and axons within which the nerve cell-bodies of the brain are embedded. (Editor's note.)

Reprinted with permission from Huttenlocher 'Morphometric Study of Human Cerebral Cortex Development' from *Neuropsychologia* (1990, Pergamon Plc) pp. 517–27.

be correlated with the total volume of the tissue. This is especially important during early development, when volume expansion of brain is an important factor. Measurements of volume of most cortical regions are difficult if not impossible, due to the fact that structural changes from one area to the other tend to be subtle, and transitions gradual. The primary visual cortex (area 17) forms a notable exception. It is clearly demarcated by its characteristic anatomy, with a very large granular layer, transsected by a prominent bundle of fibers, the stria of Gennari. Measurements of volume of area 17 during development have been made by Huttenlocher *et al.* [22, 23] and by Sauer *et al.* [37]. The two studies show similar findings, i.e. rapid expansion of cortical volume during fetal life and during the first four postnatal months. During late childhood there is a small but statistically significant contraction in cortical volume. The values used for the present calculations of total number of neurons (table 7.1) and synapses (figure 7.1) are those published by Huttenlocher *et al.* [22, 23]. Some of the other quantitative data analyzed in this report, including synapse counts and counts of neuronal number, were carried out on the same brains. Tissue shrinkage or swelling during the agonal period and during fixation and embedding therefore is apt to be approximately the same for the volume and synaptic and neuronal density data, making it possible to examine relationships between them.

The very early growth of visual cortex, with maximum volume reached at about age four months, is somewhat surprising when one considers the size of the brain as a whole, which at four months is only about half that of the adult. It is likely that cortical association areas, especially frontal cortex, grow more

Table 7.1 Volume, neuronal density, and total number of neurons in striate cortex (area 17) at various ages

Age	Volume (mm^3)	Neurons/mm^3 ($\times 10^4$)	Total neurons ($\times 10^7$)
28 wk GA	230	61.9	14.2
Newborn	920	9.6	8.8
6 days	1270	9.4	11.9
2 wk	1330	10.9[a]	14.5
2 mon.	2720	5.2	14.1
4 mon.	3800	3.5	13.5
19 mon.	4170	3.0	12.5
$3\frac{9}{12}$ yr	4430	3.1	13.7
5 yr	4310	2.5[a]	10.8
11 yr	3620	2.5	9.1
13 yr	3620	2.9[a]	10.5
26 yr	3790	3.6	14.6
71 yr	3850	4.2	16.2

The cortical volume and neuronal density data are not corrected for tissue shrinkage, since the neuronal density values published by Leuba and Garey [26] do not contain such corrections. Readers interested in volume data corrected for tissue shrinkage are referred to Ref. [23].

[a] No neuronal density value was available for the exact age. Values for the nearest available ages are shown.

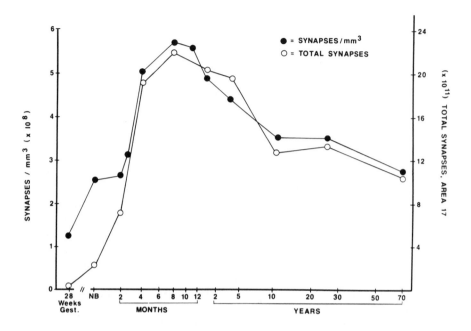

Figure 7.1 Synaptic density and total synapses in visual cortex as a function of age.

slowly. Much of the later gain in brain weight may also be related to myelination of subcortical white matter which continues throughout the childhood years [47]. The slight decrease in volume of visual cortex observed during late childhood may reflect certain regressive changes in cerebral cortex that occur late in development, and that are subsequently detailed.

Neuronal Number in Visual Cortex

Extensive data on the density of neurons in visual cortex during development have recently been reported by Leuba and Garey [26]. These data are especially useful for comparisons of synaptic and neuronal numbers during development (see below), since many of the cell counts were on semithin sections fixed in glutaraldehyde and embedded in Spurr's medium, with adjacent, identically prepared blocks of tissue used for synapse quantitation [22, 23]. Values obtained at ages when cortical volume measurements were also available are listed in table 7.1. The density of neurons decreases markedly during fetal and early postnatal development, from about 62×10^4 neurons per mm^3 at 28 weeks gestational age to about 4×10^4 in the adult. These values become meaningful only when they are related to cortical volume. Comparison with volume data for visual cortex show that total neuronal number remains constant through the life span, at least from gestational age (GA) 28 weeks to about age 70 years (table 7.1). By GA 28 weeks all cortical neurons have arrived at the cortical plate where they are densely crowded together. The decrease in packing density observed during development appears to be entirely secondary to expansion of the volume of cortex, which in turn is related to the growth of axons, dendrites, and glia. The data provide no evidence that cortical neurons are lost during normal development or during the adult years. The total numbers of neurons in visual cortex in different brains show fluctuations from about 9 to 16×10^7 which are not age related. Some of this variability may be related to inaccuracies in cell counts and volume measurements. It may also reflect normal variations in brain size. It is well known that the human brain can be organized into normal functioning units over a fairly large range in brain size, with total brain weight ranging from about 1 000 to 1 800 g in normal adults.

Dendritic Development in Visual Cortex

Human cortical neurons are characterized by great complexity and length of dendritic arborizations. The function of cerebral cortex is thought to be closely linked to dendritic morphology. Stunted growth of cortical dendrites has been found in some forms of mental retardation [20, 42]. Defective morphology of dendritic spines – the specialized regions on dendrites in which many synaptic contacts are located – has also been reported in brains from the mentally retarded [29, 30, 34, 35].

Several aspects of dendritic development have been quantitated in human cerebral cortex, including dendritic spine formation, dendritic length, and complexity of branching patterns. Michel and Garey [31] examined the density of spines on apical dendrites[b] of pyramidal neurons in layer III of visual cortex (area 17). They found that the mean number of dendritic spines[c] increases to a maximum of about 79 per 50 μm of dendritic length at about age five months. It declines thereafter, and the adult value of about 50 spines/50 μm is reached by age 21 months. These data *per se* do not provide information as to whether there is actual loss of spines – and hence presumably of synapses related to spines – after age five months, or whether the decrease in spine density is related to progressive elongation of dendrites, the number of spines per neuron remaining constant. Data published by Becker *et al.* [4] show that progressive elongation of dendrites occurs between ages 5 and 21 months. These authors obtained measurements of total dendritic length of pyramidal neurons in layers III and V of area 17. Total length of apical dendrites in layer III, the structures studied by Michel and Garey, increased from about 800 μm at age five months to 1 400 μm at age 24 months. The increase in dendritic length is very close to the figure that would have been predicted on the assumption that the decrease in dendritic spine density that occurs during the same period is due to increase in dendritic length alone. The combined data therefore do not provide evidence for actual loss of spines.

[b] Apical dendrites are the prominent leading dendrites which extend from the top of pyramidal cell bodies toward the upper layers of the cortex. (Editor's note.)

[c] Dendritic spines are small protuberances on the surface of dendrites upon which is a synapse.

The study of Becker *et al.* [4] suggests that the time course of dendritic growth varies in different cortical layers. The dendritic trees of pyramidal cells in layer V grow earlier than those in layer III. The mean total length of dendrites for pyramidal cells in layer III is only about 30 percent of the maximum at birth, while in layer V it is already about 60 percent of maximum. In addition, a higher degree of dendritic branching was observed in layer V neurons at birth than in layer III neurons. Dendritic development appears to reflect differences in the time course of neurogenesis in general. The birth of neurons and neuronal migration in the lower layers of cortex precede these events in the upper layers, in what is referred to as the inside-out pattern of cortical development [41]. A pattern of earlier dendritic development in the lower cortical layers has also been reported in human motor cortex [28].

The study of Becker *et al.* [4] provides no evidence for regressive changes in dendritic development. There appears to be no significant overall pruning of dendrites on cortical neurons as development progresses, at least up to age seven years. Elongation of dendrites on pyramidal neurons in visual cortex appears to end by about age 18 months, and dendritic length shows no significant change between that age and seven years. The study leaves unanswered whether changes in dendritic length occur after seven years, the oldest age examined by these authors.

Synaptogenesis in Visual Cortex

Dendritic geometry of neurons relates to function of the system through cellular interactions that occur along the dendritic membranes at synapses. Data on synaptogenesis in area 17 are available for all cortical layers, from GA 28 weeks to the adult [22, 23]. Synaptic profiles are detectable already in the fetal brain at GA 28 weeks, but synaptic density at that stage is low, about 1×10^8 synapses per mm^3 of tissue, or 1/3 of the adult value. Synaptic density increases during late fetal life and in early infancy. A sudden spurt occurs between ages two and four months, when synaptic density almost doubles. After age one year synaptic density begins to decline to an adult value about 60 percent of the maximum, which is reached by age 11 years (figure 7.1). Analysis of synaptic density by cortical layers does not show an inside-out pattern of development, i.e. synaptogenesis in the lower cortical layers does not precede that in the upper ones. This has also been noted by Rakic *et al.* in the monkey [36]. In humans, there is some difference between layers, with a trend toward later synaptogenesis in the lower layers: in layer V maximum synaptic density is reached by age 11 months, and in layer VI by 19 months, while density in layer III is maximum already at four months. In visual cortex, synaptogenesis in regions concerned with processing of afferent inputs appears to lead that in efferent systems.

Availability of synaptic density and volume data on the same brains has made it possible to calculate the approximate total number of synapses in area 17 at various ages (figure 7.1). Only about 1 percent of the maximum are present at GA 28 weeks, and about 10 percent at birth. The maximum is reached at postnatal age eight months. Subsequently, there is a decrease to 50–60 percent of maximum, which is reached by age 11 years. The data indicate a very significant loss of synapses during postnatal development of cerebral cortex.

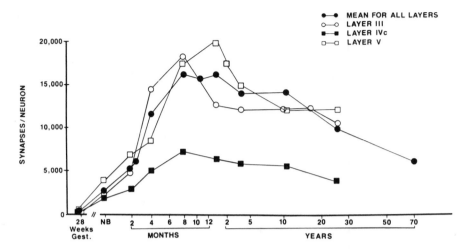

Figure 7.2 Mean number of synapses per neuron in visual cortex as a whole and in selected cortical layers as a function of age.

Several derived values can be calculated from extant data on synaptic density, neuronal density, and dendritic length. The average calculated number of synapses per neuron at various ages is given in figure 7.2. This value reaches a maximum of over 15 000 at age eight months and declines to about 10 000 in the adult, for area 17 as a whole. It is lower for layer IVc, as would be expected from the fact that small neurons predominate in this cortical layer. The average number of synapses per micron of dendritic length also declines during childhood. These values have been calculated, using data for total dendritic length in layers III and V provided by Becker *et al.* [4], and synaptic density and neuronal density values for the same layers, obtained from Huttenlocher and de Courten [23] and Leuba and Garey [26]. The results are shown in figure 7.3. The findings appear to differ between the two cortical layers, with greater crowding of synapses on dendrites during development of layer III than of layer V. Maximum density of synapses on dendrites is reached earlier in layer III, at about age eight months, *vs* about 18 months in layer V. However, the values calculated at age seven years are almost identical for the two cortical layers. These derived values are very gross approximations, since the calculations include the incorrect assumptions that all synapses are axodendritic, and that all neurons in layers III and V are pyramidal cells. However, the errors introduced by these assumptions are likely to remain constant across age, and are unlikely to affect the age-related trends indicated in figure 7.3.

Frontal Cortex

Available information on the development of cortical areas other than 17 in humans is limited. The only other area for which combined data on neuronal

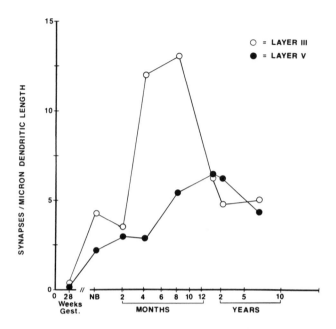

Figure 7.3 Estimate of distribution of synapses on dendrites as a function of age.

number, synaptic density and dendritic development are available is the middle
frontal gyrus. The findings in frontal cortex form an interesting contrast to those
in visual cortex, in that they indicate different developmental schedules in the
two cortical areas. In frontal cortex, neuronal density in layer III at birth is about
$100\,000/mm^3$, similar to that in area 17. The subsequent decline in density is
slower. While neuronal density in visual cortex reaches the adult value by about
postnatal age five months, in frontal cortex it is still 55 percent above adult mean
at age two years, and 10 percent above adult mean at seven years. No volume
data are available for frontal cortex, and it is therefore unknown whether the
decrease in density is related to expansion of cortex or to neuronal loss. The
adult value for neuronal density in layer III of middle frontal gyrus is about
$13\,000/mm^3$ [19, 38]. Published values for motor cortex vary from about 10 000
to 26 000 neurons/mm^3. Values for both of these frontal regions are considerably
smaller than that for visual cortex, which is about 40 000 for layer III [12, 26,
39].

Dendritic development in middle frontal gyrus also progresses considerably
more slowly than in visual cortex. In area 17, the total dendritic length of
pyramidal neurons approaches the adult value by age four months in layer V and
by 18 months in layer III [4]. In contrast, dendritic length in layer III of middle
frontal gyrus is only about 50 percent of the adult at age two years [38].

By age two years, mean total dendritic length of pyramidal neurons in layer
III of middle frontal gyrus is already more than twice that of visual cortex. This,
as well as the lower density of neurons, undoubtedly reflects the greater

complexity and size of pyramidal neurons in the frontal areas. In general, a decrease in density of cortical neurons has been observed as one progresses from simpler to more complex cortical systems, both within a species and phylogenetically [12, 18, 32, 39, 40, 44]. The limited available data also suggest that growth of some neural elements, especially dendrites, continues for a longer period of time in frontal cortex. Buell and Coleman [6, 7] have found that dendritic elongation continues even in old age, where it may provide compensation for neuronal loss.

Synaptic density data during development of middle frontal gyrus are available for layer III only [21]. They show a slower postnatal increase in synaptic density than in visual cortex. Maximum density is reached at about age one year, *vs* age four months in visual cortex. Subsequently, synaptic density declines, but again more slowly than in visual cortex. The decrease in synaptic density does not become evident until after age seven years, at which age synaptic density in visual cortex is already near the adult value, i.e. at about 60 percent of maximum. Synaptic density in frontal cortex is at adult level by age 16 years. The synaptic density data therefore show regional differences in the time course of cortical synaptogenesis in the human. In that respect, synaptogenesis in human brain appears to differ from that in the monkey, where concurrent overproduction of synapses in diverse regions of cerebral cortex has been found [36]. Available data indicate that synaptic density in adult frontal cortex exceeds that in visual cortex. Cragg [12, 13], who obtained synapse quantitations in motor and visual cortex in the same brains, found synaptic density in area 4 to be about 50 percent greater than in area 17.

Calculated values derived from neuronal density, dendritic length and synaptic density figures in frontal cortex show trends similar to those in visual cortex, but with a slower time course. The number of synapses per neuron appears to decrease between late childhood and age 16 years. The number of synapses per micron of dendritic length also decreases, the adult value being about 50 percent of the value obtained at age two years. It is not possible to be certain that actual loss of synapses occurs during development of middle frontal gyrus, since no volume data are available. However, the fact that synaptic density declines after neuronal density has stabilized, i.e. after age seven years, suggests that loss of synapses does occur, similar in extent but later in age than in visual cortex.

Discussion

The quantitative anatomy approach to cortical development has clear limitations which need to be spelled out in order to put the present data into proper perspective. Development is an ongoing, dynamic process. The anatomical method is a static one, providing a glimpse of only one point in time for any given case. In the human, the material that is available for study may be affected by such uncontrollable events as effects of the agonal illness on the tissue and postmortem changes [45]. Even at best, the quantitative method gives only mean values. Growth and regressive changes may occur at the same time and may balance each other, in which case quantitation would show no change at all, and would suggest a static rather than a dynamic system. This may well be the case in the adult brain. It is quite likely that new synapses are constantly formed and old connections disappear, a phenomenon that is not reflected in the data on total synapse number in adults, which show little evidence of change. Finally, the anatomical methods are tedious, and they require the availability of samples of brain tissue. Both of these factors make it impractical to study the large number of subjects that would be required for the statistical analyses needed for the detection of small changes.

Nevertheless, important information has resulted from morphometric analysis of cerebral cortex. Some widely held notions have been put in question. For example, programmed neuronal death, i.e. the normal loss of neurons during development [11], is often assumed to be a universal developmental event. In fact, the extant developmental data show no evidence that neuronal death is important during development of the largest and most complex aggregate of neurons, the human cerebral cortex. Interestingly, this could not have been predicted from animal studies. In the mouse, a 30 percent loss of cortical neurons has been shown during development [18, 19]. A smaller neuronal loss, about 15 percent, has been reported between birth and adulthood in area 17 in the monkey [32]. The data suggest that programmed cell death may be more important in less complex neural systems. It is generally accepted that programmed cell death relates to the failure of developing neurons to find targets for innervation. Target finding may be easier in systems of great complexity, such as human cerebral cortex, where potential targets are available on large populations of nearby neurons.

The data for synapse elimination during cortical development show phylo-genetic changes which are opposite those for programmed neuronal death. In rodents, there is little evidence for overproduction of synapses. Aghajanian and Bloom [1] found that synaptic density in the rat brain reaches a maximum at about postnatal day 35, which is less than 10 percent greater than the adult value. More definite evidence for synapse elimination has been found in the kitten, where the maximum, about 50 percent above the adult value, is reached at about age 36 days [14]. The findings in the monkey resemble those in humans, with synaptic density values during infancy (age six months) that are 75–95 percent above the adult value [32, 36].

It therefore appears that synapse elimination in cerebral cortex becomes a more important developmental event as the complexity of the system increases. This result conforms to expectations that derive from a theory concerning synaptogen-esis proposed by Changeux [8, 9]. It is argued that genetic determination of synaptogenesis in complex systems is incomplete, the genome being insufficient in size to allow for specification of all synaptic connections. "The genetic program directs the proper interaction between main categories of neurons. During development within a category several contacts form at the same site; in other words a significant . . . redundancy . . . of the connections exists" [8]. These early synaptic contacts are viewed as being labile (synaptic plasticity). Some connec-tions are stabilized by being incorporated into functioning systems either through the establishment of intrinsic neuronal circuits or through afferent activity transmitted from sense organs. The stabilized synaptic contacts persist, while labile contacts that fail to be incorporated into functioning units regress. The theory thus implies overproduction of synaptic contacts during development, followed by synapse elimination. The recent computer simulations of nerve nets provide evidence that randomly connected systems can develop considerable organization in terms of strength of internal connections and output, provided that they are subjected to non-random input [15].

The anatomical findings in humans are consistent with Changeux's theory, and they also provide data as to the ages at which synapses are most numerous, as well as the time course of their regression. The postnatal occurrence of these events is of particular interest. It suggests that the anatomical changes may be directly related to the development of cortical functions, including learning, memory and language.

Parallels between the anatomical changes and functional development are easily discernible in visual cortex, since the functions of this cortical region are well understood. Relatively few synaptic connections (about 10 percent of the maximum) are found at birth, a time when visual alertness is as yet very low and visual fixation and following are just beginning to be demonstrable. The rapid burst in synaptogenesis at age four months correlates well with a sudden increase in visual alertness at about that time. Binocular interactions, which are clearly dependent on cortical rather than primarily retinal or lateral geniculate function, first appear between ages four and five months. These include stereopsis, stereoacuity, equalization of the optokinetic nsytagmus to nasotemporal and temporonasal motion, and binocular summation of the light reflex [5, 17, 43]. Clinical observations confirm the importance of afferent input for the formation of functional connections during this period. Strabismic amblyopia, i.e. blindness in the squinting eye, and amblyopia due to absence of formed visual inputs, as occurs in congenital cataract, have been observed to occur at this age [16, 25, 27].

Synaptic density – and hence presumably the number of unspecified or labile synaptic contacts – continues to be high in visual cortex until at least age four years. Functionally, this correlates with persistence of plasticity in the visual system. Most notably, strabismic amblyopia can be reversed during this time, provided that the good eye is occluded and the child is forced to use the squinting eye [2, 3].

The persistence of large numbers of labile synapses may provide the anatomical substrate for neural plasticity in the child [24]. If so, then one would expect plasticity to persist later in middle frontal gyrus, where synapse elimination does not begin until about age seven years. Unfortunately, we have no clear information about the functions of this cortical area. However, it is known that plasticity for some functions persists into late childhood. An example is the ability to recover language functions after large dominant hemisphere lesions. This appears to persist until at least age eight years [46] and appears to depend on changes in the functional organization of the non-dominant hemisphere.

The presence of large numbers of synaptic contacts during postnatal development probably influences cortical function in ways other than through imparting plasticity to the system. Available evidence suggests that at least some of the exuberant synapses may be active rather than silent. This evidence derives from studies of cerebral metabolism. Cerebral metabolic rate is closely linked to the synaptic activity of cortical neurons. Developmental data show a remarkable parallel between synaptic density and cerebral metabolic rate as determined by positron emission tomography [10]. The metabolic rate in human cerebral cortex rises rapidly during the first postnatal years, remains above adult levels throughout childhood, and declines to adult values during adolescence. These changes show a rough parallel to the age-related variations in synaptic density observed in frontal cortex, but they correlate less well with changes in synaptic density in primary visual cortex. It may well be that area 17 has an unusual, early developmental schedule that differs from that of most other cortical regions.

The presence of excess synaptic activity may well have certain negative effects on brain function in the child. Activity in large pools of unspecified synapses may to some extent interfere with cortical processing. It may account for the well-known high susceptibility of the young child to seizures. The high metabolic demand of immature brain also may make it more susceptible to damage related to deficiency of metabolic substrates, including oxygen. Many components of the complex interactions between structure and function in developing cerebral cortex are as yet unknown. Newer methodologies, including *in vivo* imaging techniques [10] and computerized quantitation [33], are likely to bring significant future advances in this field.

REFERENCES

1 Aghajanian, G. K. and Bloom, F. E. The formation of synaptic junctions in developing rat brain: a quantitative electron microscopic study. *Brain Res.* 6, 716–727, 1967.

2 Assaf, A. A. The sensitive period: transfer of fixation after occlusion for strabismic amblyopia. *Br. J. Ophthalmol.* 66, 64–70, 1982.

3 Awaya, S., Miyake, Y., Imaizumi, Y., Shoise, Y., Kanda, T. and Komuro, K. Amblyopia in man, suggestive of stimulus deprivation amblyopia. *Jpn. J. Ophthalmol.* 17, 69–82, 1973.

4 Becker, L. E., Armstrong, D. L., Chan, F. and Wood, M. M. Dendritic development in human occipital cortical neurons. *Devl Brain Res.* 13, 117–124, 1984.

5 Birch, E. E. and Held, R. The development of binocular summation in human infants. *Invest. Ophthalmol. Vis. Sci.* 14, 1103–1107, 1983.

6 Buell, S. J. and Coleman, P. D. Dendritic growth in the aged human brain and failure of growth in senile dementia. *Science* 206, 854–856, 1979.

7 Buell, S. J. and Coleman, P. D. Quantitative evidence for selective dendritic growth in normal human aging but not in senile dementia. *Brain Res.* 214, 23–41, 1981.

8 Changeux, J.-P. and Danchin, A. Selective stabilization of developing synapses as a mechanism for the specification of neuronal networks. *Nature* 264, 705–712, 1976.

9 Changeux, J. P., Heidmann, T. and Patte, P. Learning by selection. In *The Biology of Learning*, P. Marler and H. S. Terrace (Editors), pp. 115–137. Springer-Verlag, New York, 1984.

10 Chugani, H. T. Phelps, M. E. and Mazziotta, J. C. Positron emission tomography study of human brain functional development. *Ann. Neurol.* 22, 487–497, 1987.

11 Cowan, W. M. Neuronal death as a regulative mechanism in the control of cell number in the nervous system. In *Development and Aging in the Nervous System*, M. Rockstein (ed.), pp. 19–41. Academic Press, New York, 1973.

12 Cragg, B. G. The density of synapses and neurons in the motor and visual areas of the cerebral cortex. *J. Anat.* 101, 639–654, 1967.

13 Cragg, B. G. The density of synapses and neurons in normal, mentally defective and aging human brains. *Brain* 98,. 81–90, 1975.

14 Cragg, B. G. The development of synapses in the visual system of the cat. *J. comp. Neurol.* 160, 147–166, 1975.

15 Edelman, G. M. *Neural Darwinism. The Theory of Neuronal Group Selection.* Basic Books, New York, 1987.

16 Gelbert, S. S., Hoyt, C. S., Jastrebski, G. and Marg, E. Long-term visual results in bilateral congenital cataracts. *Am. J. Ophthalmol.* 93, 615–621, 1982.

17 Held, R., Birch, E. and Gwiazda, J. Stereoacuity of human infants. *Proc. Natl Acad. Sci. U.S.A.* 77, 5572–5574, 1980.

18 Heumann, D., Leuba, G. and Rabinowicz, T. Postnatal development of the mouse cerebral neocortex. IV. Evolution of the total cortical volume, of the population of neurons and glial cells. *J. Hirnforsch.* 19, 385–393, 1978.

19 Heumann, D. and Leuba, G. Neuronal death in the development and aging of the cerebral cortex of the mouse. *Neuropath. Appl. Neurobiol.* 9, 297–311, 1983.

20 Huttenlocher, P. R. Dendritic development in neocortex of children with mental defect and infantile spasms. *Neurology* 24, 203–210, 1974.

21 Huttenlocher, P. R. Synaptic density in human frontal cortex. Developmental changes and effects of aging. *Brain Res.* 163, 195–205, 1979.

22 Huttenlocher, P. R., De Courten, C., Garey, L. G. and Van Der Loos, H. Synaptogenesis in human visual cortex – evidence for synapse elimination during normal development. *Neurosci. Lett.* 33, 247–252, 1982.

23 Huttenlocher, P. R. and De Courten, C. The development of synapses in striate cortex of man. *Hum. Neurobiol.* 6, 1–9, 1987.

24 Huttenlocher, P. R. Synapse elimination and plasticity in developing human cerebral cortex. *Am. J. Mental Deficiency* 88, 488–496, 1984.

25 Jacobsen, S. G., Mohindra, I. and Held, R. Age of onset of amblyopia in infants with esotropia. *Doc. Ophthal. Proc. Ser.*, Vol. 30. L. Maffei (ed.), pp. 210–216. Dr W. Junk, Publishers. The Hague. 1981.

26 Leuba, G. and Garey, L. J. Evolution of neuronal numerical density in the developing and aging human visual cortex. *Hum. Neurobiol.* 6, 11–18, 1987.

27 Lewis, T. L., Maurer, D. and Brent, H. P. Effect on perceptual development of visual deprivation during infancy, *Br J. Ophthalmol.* 70, 214–220, 1986.

28 Marin-Padilla, M. Prenatal and early postnatal ontogenesis of the human motor cortex: a Golgi study. I. The sequential development of the cortical layers. *Brain Res.* 23, 167–183, 1970.

29 Marin-Padilla, M. Structural abnormalities of the cerebral cortex in human chromosomal aberrations. A Golgi study. *Brain Res.* 44, 625–629, 1972.

30 Marin-Padilla, M. Pyramidal cell abnormalities in the motor cortex of a child with Down's syndrome. A Golgi study. *J. comp. Neurol.* 167, 63–82, 1976.

31 Michel, A. E. and Garey, L. J. The development of dendritic spines in the human visual cortex. *Hum. Neurobiol.* 3, 223–227, 1984.

32 O'Kusky, J. and Colonnier, M. Postnatal changes in the number of neurons and synapses in the visual cortex (A17) of the macaque monkey. *J. Comp. Neurol.* 210, 291–296, 1982.

33 Paldino, A. M. and Purpura, D. P. Quantitative analysis of the spatial distribution of axonal and dendritic terminals of hippocampal pyramidal neurons in immature human brain. *Expl Neurol.* 64, 604–619, 1979.

34 Purpura, D. P. Dendritic spine 'dysgenesis' and mental retardation. *Science* 186, 1126–1128, 1974.

35 Purpura, D. P. Normal and aberrant neuronal development in the cerebral cortex of human fetus and young infants. In *Brain Mechanisms in Mental Retardation.* N. A. Buchwald and M. A. B. Brazier (eds), pp. 141–169. Academic Press, New York, 1975.

36 Rakic, P., Bourgeois, J.-P., Eckenhoff, M. F., Zecevic, M. and Golman-Rakic, P. S. Concurrent overproduction of synapses in diverse regions of primate cerebral cortex. *Science* 232, 232–234, 1986.

37 Sauer, N., Kammaradt. G., Krauthausen, I., Kretschmann, H.-T., Lange, H. W. and

Wingert, F. Qualitative and quantitative development of the visual cortex in man. *J. Comp. Neurol.* 214, 441–450, 1983.

38   Schade, J. P. and Van Groenigen, W. B. Structural organization of the human cerebral cortex. I. Maturation of the middle frontal gyrus. *Acta Anat.* 47, 74–111, 1961.

39   Shariff, G. A. Cell counts in the primate cerebral cortex. *J. Comp. Neurol.* 98, 381–400, 1953.

40   Sholl, D. A. A comparative study of the neuronal packing density in the cerebral cortex. *J. Anat.* 93, 143–158. 1959.

41   Sidman, R. L. and Rakic, P. Neuronal migration, with special reference to developing human brain: a review. *Brain Res.* 62, 1–35, 1973

42   Takashima, S., Becker, L. E., Armstrong, D. A. and Chan, F. Abnormal neuronal development in the visual cortex of the human fetus and infant with Down's syndrome. A quantitative and qualitative Golgi study. *Brain Res.* 225, 1–21, 1981.

43   Teller, D. Y. Scotopic vision, color vision and stereopsis in infants. *Curr. Eye Res.* 2, 199–210, 1983.

44   Tower, D. B. Structural and functional organization of mammalian cerebral cortex: the correlation of neurone density with brain size. *J. Comp. Neurol.* 101, 19–51, 1954.

45   Williams, R. S., Ferrante, R. J. and Caviness, V. S. The rapid Golgi method in clinical neuropathology: the morphologic consequences of suboptimal fixation. *J. Neuropath. Exp. Neurol.* 37, 13–33, 1978.

46   Woods, B. T. and Teuber, H. L. Changing patterns of childhood aphasia, *Ann. Neurol.* 3, 273–280, 1978.

47   Yakovlev, P. I. and Lecours, A.-R. The myelogenetic cycles of regional maturation of the brain. In *Regional Development of the Brain in Early Life*, A. Minkowsky (ed.), pp. 3–70. Blackwell, Oxford, 1967.

8

Positron Emission Tomography Study of Human Brain Functional Development

HARRY T. CHUGANI, MICHAEL E. PHELPS AND
JOHN C. MAZZIOTTA

During development, the brain undergoes the sequential anatomical, functional, and organizational changes necessary to support the complex adaptive behavior of a fully mature normal individual. The delineation of developmental changes occuring in different brain regions would provide a means of relating various behavioral phenomena to maturation of specific brain structures, thereby enhancing our understanding of structure–function relationships in both normal and disease states.

One approach to the study of these relationships has been to measure regional substrate utilization at different stages of cerebral maturation. Since the principal brain substrates for energy production are glucose and oxygen, the determination of their regional alterations would provide a measure of the local energy requirement for maintenance processes and functional activity. This approach has been used in the study of brain–behavior relationships in various animal models [1, 18, 31], and has generated important concepts in our understanding of brain function. Alternatively, because of the close relationship between local cerebral blood flow (ICBF) and local cerebral metabolic rate under normal conditions [54], an indirect assessment of local functional activity can also be obtained by the measurement of ICBF during development [4, 29, 30, 43].

The development of positron emission tomography (PET) [47], which employs tracer kinetic measurements of compounds labelled with positron-emitting isotopes [48, 49], has enabled us to apply directly the regional substrate utilization approach in studying human brain development. Using 2-deoxy-2{^{18}F}fluoro-

"Positron Emission Tomography Study of Human Brain Functional Development" first appeared in *Annals of Neurology* 22 (1987), pp. 487–97, and is reprinted by kind permission.

D-glucose (FDG) and PET, we have measured local cerebral metabolic rates for glucose (lCMRGlc) in infants and children during postnatal brain development.

In an earlier communication [6], we used relative measures of lCMRGlc to determine the temporal relationship of human functional development during the first 18 months of life. These studies demonstrated that the order of functional development, from the relatively earlier maturation of phylogenetically older brain structures to the later maturation of newer structures, is in general agreement with behavioral, neurophysiological, and anatomical alterations known to accompany infant development. We now report absolute values of lCMRGlc for different brain regions from birth to adolescence and compare them with normal adult values.

Materials and Methods

Patient Population

We have retrospectively selected 29 subjects from over 100 infants and children studied with FDG-PET at UCLA School of Medicine since 1983. Clinical summaries of these 29 children are provided in Table 8.1. Of the 29 individuals, 24 were selected from our research protocol designed to evaluate the role of PET in seizures and epilepsy. Each had suffered transient neurological events not significantly altering neurological development on close follow-up. Informed consent was obtained in all cases. The remaining five subjects were asymptomatic, but because they had facial capillary nevi they were evaluated with FDG-PET for possible Sturge–Weber syndrome. The parents of each of these five subjects were anxious to accept any noninvasive procedure with potential diagnostic value. FDG-PET did not disclose any hemispheric asymmetry of lCMRGlc in any one of these five patients. We believe that these 29 children are reasonably representative of normal children and provide an opportunity to measure lCMRGlc changes during normal brain development, since entirely normal children cannot be studied with PET for ethical reasons. Indeed, the older children in this subpopulation were all attending school and performing well in classes for normal children. Of the infants studied, none had been born prematurely and all continue to develop normally. There were 16 males and 13 females, and their ages ranged from five days to 15.1 years at the time of study. Although 18 of the 29 subjects were taking daily anticonvulsants at the time of PET, none displayed sedation or other side-effects.

PET Procedure

All studies were performed in accordance with the policies of the UCLA Human Subject Protection Committee. Subjects were fasted (except for water) for 4 hours prior to PET. One hour prior to the study, golden disk electrodes were applied to the patient's scalp for later electroencephalographic (EEG) monitoring. Then a venous catheter was inserted in a hand vein for blood collection. The blood was arterialized by placing the hand into a water chamber heated to 44°C [48]. Radial arterial catheters were used in three subjects.

Table 8.1 Patient Summary

Age, Sex	Clinical information	Laboratory data	Medication on day of study	Period of follow-up after onset of neurological event
5 days, M	42 weeks gestation; mild fetal distress; Apgar scores 2 at 1 minute, 8 at 5 minutes; seizures on days 1 and 2	EEG multifocal spikes, CT scan normal	Phenobarbital	24 months
5 weeks, M	Tonic seizures at age 4 weeks	EEG normal, CT scan normal	Phenobarbital	16 months
8 weeks, F	Onset of myoclonic jerks at age 2 weeks	EEG normal, CT scan normal	None	4 months
13.5 weeks, F	Asymptomatic, left facial port-wine nevus (? Sturge-Weber syndrome)	EEG normal, CT scan normal	None	22 months
4 months, M	Normal birth; one seizure on day 1, none since	EEG normal, CT scan normal	Phenobarbital	17 months
6.25 months, F	Onset of seizures at age 5 months	EEG normal, CT and MRI scans normal	Phenobarbital	3 months
7.6 months, M	Opsoclonus and myoclonus developed at age 6.5 months, responded well to adrenocorticotropic hormone	EEG paroxysmal generalized spike and wave activity, CT scan normal	Phenobarbital, clonazepam	22 months
1 year, F	Asymptomatic, left facial port-wine nevus (? Sturge-Weber syndrome)	EEG normal, CT scan normal	None	32 months
1.5 years, F	Glaucoma OS, bilateral facial port-wine nevi (? Sturge-Weber syndrome)	EEG normal	None	36 months
1.5 years, M	Glaucoma OD, right facial port-wine nevus (? Sturge-Weber syndrome)	EEG normal, CT scan normal	None	27 months
1.6 years, M	Onset of apneic episodes at age 9 months	EEG normal, CT scan normal	None	18 months
3.5 years, F	Onset of seizures at age 1.5 years	EEG normal, CT scan normal	Carbamazepine	26 months
3.7 years, F	Complex febrile seizures	EEG normal	Phenobarbital	43 months

Table 8.1 (continued)

Age, Sex	Clinical information	Laboratory data	Medication on day of study	Period of follow-up after onset of neurological event
5.7 years, F	Onset of rolandic epilepsy at age 2.5 years	EEG right centrotemporal spike-wave discharges, CT scan normal	Carbamazepine	4 years
6.7 years, M	Episodic generalized paresthesias (? seizures)	EEG normal, CT and MRI scans normal	None	11 months
6.8 years, M	Visual hallucinations beginning at age 5.5 years	EEG normal, CT and MRI scans normal	Carbamazepine, clorazepate	18 months
7 years, F	2 grand mal seizures at age 5 years	EEG normal, CT scan normal	Carbamazepine	34 months
7.1 years, F	A single nocturnal seizure at age 7 years	EEG infrequent right centrotemporal spike-wave discharges, CT scan normal	Carbamazepine	5 months
7.2 years, M	15 episodes of tunnel vision at age 7 years	EEG normal, CT and MRI scans normal	None	18 months
7.5 years, F	Onset of complex partial seizures at age 6 years	EEG occasional generalized spike-wave discharges, CT and MRI scans normal	Phenobarbital carbamazepine	24 months
8.4 years, M	Rolandic seizures beginning at age 5 years	EEG left centrotemporal spikes, CT scan normal	Phenobarbital	4 years
8.5 years, M	Hypoplastic kidneys, on chronic ambulatory peritoneal dialysis; febrile seizures in infancy (? myo-clonic seizures at age 6 years)	EEG generalized irregular spike-wave activity only during sleep, CT scan normal	Clonazepam	32 months
8.6 years, M	Hemolytic–uremic syndrome at age 8 years with convulsion in acute phase	EEG normal, CT scan normal	None	9 months
9.3 years, M	Onset of complex partial seizures at age 9 months, infrequent episodes	EEG normal, CT scan normal	Carbamazepine	7 months
9.5 years, F	Asymptomatic, left facial port-wine nevus (? Sturge–Weber syndrome)	EEG normal, CT scan normal	None	10 years

9.8 years, M	Onset of left simple partial motor seizures at age 3 years	EEG right paracentral spikes, CT and MRI scans normal	Carbamazepine, phenytoin	6 years
12 years, F	Onset of complex partial seizures at age 2 years, infrequent episodes	EEG normal, CT scan normal	Carbamazepine	10 years
13.5 years, M	Onset of complex partial seizures at age 10 years, infrequent episodes	EEG normal, CT scan normal	Carbamazepine	3 years
15.1 years, M	Onset of seizures with migraine at age 11 years	EEG normal, CT scan normal	None	4 years

M = male; F = female; EEG = electroencephalogram; CT = computed tomography; MRI = magnetic resonance imaging; OS = left eye; OD = right eye.

FDG (0.143 mCi/kg) was administered intravenously as a pulse at a different site from the catheter, and serial blood samples were collected to determine plasma FDG and glucose concentrations as described elsewhere [48]. In infants younger than two years, microtechniques were employed to minimize total blood collected (5 ml). The dose of FDG was approximately 25 percent lower than that used in adults, and in children results in a whole body radiation exposure of approximately 300 mrads. The dose to the brain is about 500 mrads (as compared to 1–3 rads in X-ray computed tomography).

EEG activity was monitored, and the children were closely observed for seizure activity. The EEG recordings were also useful in the early detection of drowsiness in some children. When a child became drowsy, as evidenced by diminishing amplitude and slowing of EEG activity, he or she was gently tapped on the shoulder to be kept awake and alert. Other than this occasional stimulus, all visual, auditory, and other sensory stimuli were minimized by dimming the lights and discouraging talking and other forms of interaction. Patients eyes and ears were open during the study.

Forty minutes after FDG injection scanning of the brain was initiated using the NeuroECAT positron tomograph (CTI, Knoxville, TN) with a spatial resolution of 8.4 mm in the plane of section and a 12.4 mm slice thickness [19]. A head holder minimized head movement during scanning [38]. To confirm true axial positioning two rectilinear images (anteroposterior and lateral views) were obtained prior to generating a standard set of 12 tomographic images parallel to the canthomeatal line.

Data Analysis

Patterns of lCMRGlc on the PET images were initially assessed by inspection. Then the images were displayed on a display monitor, and regions of interest were drawn for different brain structures using anatomical atlases, patients' CT scans, and standard lCMRGlc functional maps as references [39]. Using the operational equation of Sokoloff and associates [55] as modified by Phelps and associates [48] and Huang and associates [21], lCMRGlc for the different brain regions was then calculated and expressed in μmol/min/100 gm. Whenever a brain region appeared on more than one tomographic level, the lCMRGlc value used for that region was a bilateral average (weighted by area) of the values for each tomographic plane where that region appeared. The lumped constant and rate constants employed were those measured previously for normal young adults [21, 48].

The anatomical distribution and absolute values of lCMRGlc in the children were compared to those of adults studied under similar conditions. The latter group consisted of seven young healthy volunteers (aged 19–30 years; mean age 24.4 years; five males, two females) whose detailed neurological and psychological examinations disclosed no abnormalities.

Results

The PET images revealed several distinct patterns of lCMRGlc in the first year of life (figure 8.1) as described below. Although the anatomical distribution of

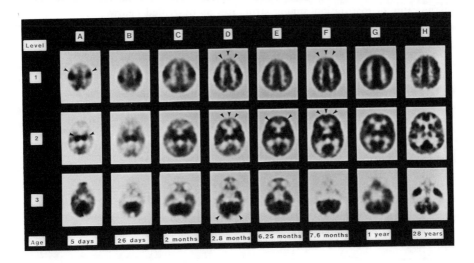

Figure 8.1 2-Deoxy-2{^{18}F} fluoro-D-glucose (FDG)-positron emission tomography (PET) images illustrating developmental changes in local cerebral metabolic rates for glucose (lCMRGlc) in the normal human infant with increasing age, as compared to lCMRGlc of the adult (image sizes not on same scale). Level 1 is a superior section, at the level of the cingulate gyrus. Level 2 is more inferior, at the level of caudate, putamen, and thalamus. Level 3 is an inferior section of the brain, at the level of cerebellum and inferior portion of the temporal lobes. Gray scale is proportional to lCMRGlc with black being highest. Images from all subjects are not shown on the same absolute gray scale of lCMRGlc: instead, images of each subject are shown with the full grey scale to maximize grey scale display of lCMRGlc at each age. Changes in absolute lCMRGlc with age appear in figure 8.2 and table 8.2. In each image, the anterior portion of the brain is at the top of the image and the left side of the brain is at the left of the image. (A) In the five-day-old, lCMRGlc is highest in sensorimotor cortex, thalamus, cerebellar vermis (arrows), and brainstem (not shown). (B,C,D) lCMRGlc gradually increases in parietal, temporal, and calcarine cortices: basal ganglia: and cerebellar cortex (arrows), particularly during the second and third months. (E) In the frontal cortex, lCMRGlc increases first in the lateral prefrontal regions by approximately six months. (F) By approximately eight months, lCMRGlc also increases in the medial aspects of the frontal cortex (arrows), as well as the dorsolateral occipital cortex. (G) By one year, the lCMRGlc pattern resembles that of adults (H).

lCMRGlc by one year of age was similar to that of adults, absolute values of lCMRGlc were lower than adult rates (figure 8.2 and table 8.2). Adult rates were reached by approximately two years of age; however, lCMRGlc for all regions measured continued to increase, and by three to four years attained values that exceeded those of adults by a factor of approximately 2 (see table 8.2). These high values of lCMRGlc were maintained until approximately 9 years of age, when they began to decline, and reached adult rates again by the end of the second decade. Although this general pattern of maturational rise and decline of lCMRGlc was seen in all brain regions studied, there were individual differences in the rates of maturation among structures as described below.

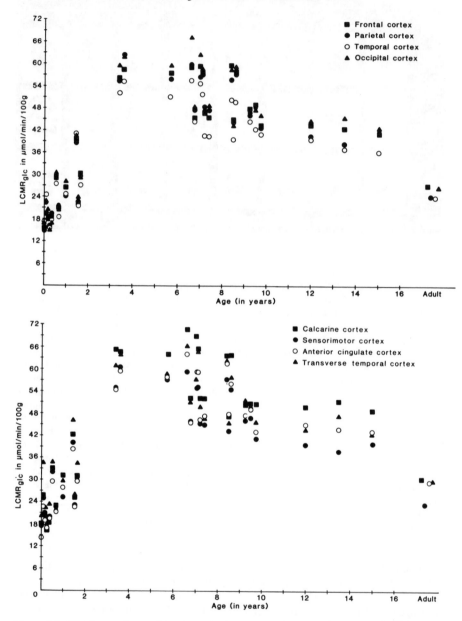

Figure 8.2 Absolute values of local cerebral metabolic rates for glucose (lCMRGlc) for selected brain regions plotted as a function of age for all 29 infants and children, and corresponding adult values. In the infants and children, points represent individual values

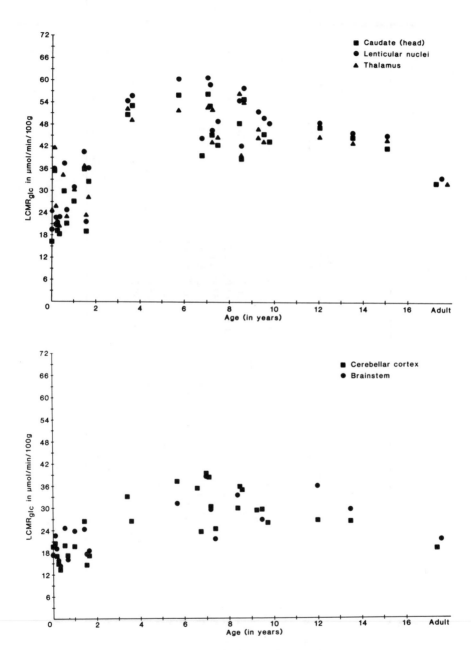

of lCMRGlc: in adults, points are mean values from seven subjects, in which the size of the symbols equals the standard error of the mean (also see table 8.2). (A, B) Selected regions of cerebral cortex: (C) basal ganglia and thalamus: (D) cerebellar cortex and brainstem.

Table 8.2 Local cerebral metabolic rates for glucose[a] (ICMRGlc) in μmol/min/100 gm and as a ratio[b] to adult rates for selected brain regions during development

Structure	Birth–1 year (n = 7)		1–2 years (n = 4)		3–8 years (n = 12)		9–15 years (n = 6)		Adult 19–30 years (n = 7)
	ICMRGlc	Ratio	ICMRGlc	Ratio	ICMRGlc	Ratio	ICMRGlc	Ratio	ICMRGlc
Cerebral hemisphere	20.35 ± 1.81	0.84	27.36 ± 3.23	1.13	48.07 ± 1.68	1.98	39.23 ± 0.79	1.62	24.27 ± 1.09
Cerebral cortex									
Frontal cortex	19.68 ± 1.83	0.73	29.65 ± 3.65	1.09	54.01 ± 1.82	1.99	44.59 ± 1.21	1.64	27.11 ± 1.26
Parietal cortex	20.23 ± 1.90	0.84	28.76 ± 3.54	1.19	53.98 ± 1.66	2.24	43.10 ± 1.50	1.78	24.15 ± 1.40
Temporal cortex	20.00 ± 1.60	0.83	28.64 ± 4.27	1.19	48.94 ± 1.69	2.04	40.05 ± 1.31	1.67	23.98 ± 1.15
Occipital cortex	20.54 ± 1.92	0.76	30.39 ± 3.50	1.16	56.35 ± 2.11	2.10	45.66 ± 0.78	1.70	26.85 ± 1.09
Calcarine cortex	22.07 ± 2.20	0.72	32.39 ± 3.55	1.06	61.01 ± 2.22	1.99	50.45 ± 0.35	1.65	30.59 ± 1.15
Sensorimotor cortex	22.17 ± 1.93	0.93	29.73 ± 3.72	1.25	52.85 ± 1.75	2.22	42.04 ± 1.52	1.76	23.83 ± 1.30
Anterior cingulate cortex	20.53 ± 1.85	0.69	29.61 ± 3.20	0.99	55.08 ± 1.88	1.85	45.36 ± 1.01	1.52	29.79 ± 1.33
Transverse temporal cortex	25.47 ± 2.44	0.86	34.00 ± 4.38	1.14	57.25 ± 2.10	1.92	47.00 ± 1.41	1.57	29.86 ± 1.33
Basal ganglia and thalamus									
Caudate (head)	22.95 ± 2.67	0.71	28.77 ± 3.67	0.89	48.86 ± 1.96	1.52	44.76 ± 0.83	1.39	32.20 ± 1.34
Lenticular nuclei	26.42 ± 2.70	0.79	32.36 ± 4.02	0.97	53.08 ± 1.98	1.58	48.15 ± 0.96	1.44	33.50 ± 1.27
Thalamus	27.15 ± 2.97	0.84	29.48 ± 2.95	0.92	49.54 ± 1.71	1.54	43.81 ± 0.28	1.36	32.19 ± 1.96
Cerebellum									
Cerebellar cortex	17.59 ± 1.02	0.93	19.50 ± 2.50	1.03	32.28 ± 1.56	1.71	27.38 ± 0.75	1.45	18.85 ± 0.86
Brainstem	18.63 ± 1.44	0.89	21.17 ± 1.80	1.01	30.74 ± 2.75	1.46	30.61 ± 2.68	1.45	21.04 ± 1.12

[a] Mean ± SEM
[b] Ratio to mean adult ICMRGlc

Statistical analysis of these data consisted of multiple *t*-tests between age groups for each structure using the Bonferroni adjustment for multiple testing. An acceptance criterion of $p < 0.05$ or better was employed for statistical significance. Although mean lCMRGlc values at one to two years were higher than those from birth to 1 year for all structures (see table 8.2), the differences were not statistically significant at the 5 percent level except for frontal cortex because of the use of multiple testing adjustment. Differences between the birth to one year and three to eight years groups were statistically significant for all structures measured ($p < 0.01$). Differences between the 3 to 8 years and 9 to 15 years groups were statistically significant ($p < 0.05$) for all structures except the caudate and lenticular nuclei, brainstem, and cerebellum. Comparisons with the adult group were significantly different for the 3 to 8 and 9 to 15 years age groups, except for brainstem and cerebellum (cerebellum showed a significant difference for the 3 to 8 years age group only). Finally, comparisons between adult and 1 to 2 years age groups were not statistically significant throughout.

Cerebral Cortex

In the neonatal period (less than 4 weeks of age), the most prominent area of metabolic activity in the cerebral cortex was the primary sensorimotor area (see figure 8.1 A). The remaining cerebral cortical regions had comparatively lower lCMRGlc. By approximately 4 weeks, lCMRGlc in parietal cortex had increased only slightly (see figure 8.1B), and by approximately the second postnatal month, lCMRGlc had slightly increased in calcarine and temporal cortices also (see figure 8.1C). Considerable maturational rises in lCMRGlc were seen in the anterior parietal, temporal, and calcarine cortices by approximately three months postnatally (see figure 8.1D). However, most of the frontal cortex, as well as dorsolateral occipital (visual association) cortical regions, was slower to display a developmental increase. Although lCMRGlc in frontal cortex, particularly the lateral prefrontal regions, had increased slightly by 6 months (see figure 8.1E), both frontal and visual-association cortical lCMRGlc continued to rise considerably during the next several months (see figure 8.1F, G). By one year, the lCMRGlc pattern resembled that in adults (see figure 8.1G, H).

As depicted in table 8.2 mean lCMRGlc for cerebral cortical regions in the first year of life ranged from 65 to 86 percent of the corresponding adult values. The lCMRGlc for the sensorimotor cortex, which was the earliest cortical region to display its maturational rise, was the closest to the adult rates during the first year compared to other cortical structures. After the first year, the maturational curves for all cerebral cortical regions displayed a similar pattern (see figure 8.2A, B). Between 3 and 8 years, mean lCMRGlc for most cerebral cortical regions were 190–226 percent of corresponding adult values. As a whole, cerebral cortical structures underwent the highest proportional increase in lCMRGlc over their mature rates when compared to other portions of the brain.

Basal Ganglia and Thalamus

The basal ganglia and thalamus displayed developmental increases in lCMRGlc earlier than most areas of the cerebral cortex (see figures 8.1A–C, 8.2C). The thalamus was one of the earliest structures to show a maturational rise in lCMRGlc and was prominently active even in the five-day-old infant (see figure 8.1A). Indeed, mean lCMRGlc for the thalamus was already 84 percent of its adult rates during the first year; for lenticular nuclei it was 75 percent and for caudate nuclei 69 percent. Although peak values of lCMRGlc attained by the basal ganglia and thalamus during childhood exceeded those of corresponding structures in the adult, the magnitude of increase (155 to 162 percent) was less than that of cerebral cortex (see table 8.2).

Cerebellum

During the first year, lCMRGlc for the cerebellum as a whole was closer to adult rates than any other portion of the brain (see table 8.2). Within the cerebellum, however, a heterogeneous pattern of maturation was observed. The centrally located, phylogenetically older portion (vermis) of the cerebellum was the first to display a maturational rise (see figure 8.1A, B), showing relatively high lCMRGlc as early as five days of age. The cerebellar hemispheres, or neocerebellum, had comparatively lower lCMRGlc in the neonatal period, and only displayed a maturational rise in lCMRGlc by the third postnatal month (see figure 8.1D). During childhood, peak values of lCMRGlc in the cerebellum were approximately 175 percent of adult rates for this structure (see table 8.2).

Brainstem

The maturational pattern of the brainstem was similar to that of the cerebellum in that rates were relatively advanced at birth. During the first year, mean lCMRGlc for brainstem was approximately 82 percent of mature rates, and subsequent peak values were approximately 170 percent of corresponding adult values (see table 8.2).

Discussion

Methodological Issues

Although approximately two-thirds of the subjects in this study were taking anticonvulsants daily, sedative effects were not seen. Nevertheless, in PET studies of adult intractable epileptics taking multiple anticonvulsants, lCMRGlc in cerebral cortex increased by a mean of 37 percent after withdrawal of phenobarbital or primidone [58], and a mean of 13 percent after withdrawal of phenytoin [57]. It seems unlikely that our findings were significantly affected by anticonvulsant use, since subjects of all ages were taking drugs at the time of PET and drug effects on lCMRGlc, if they occurred, would tend to be random.

A second methodological issue in our study involves the use of rate constants from normal young adults for calculating lCMRGlc in children. This has relatively little impact on the absolute values of lCMRGlc, because the rate constants appear with terms in the equation that contain exponentials to a negative power multiplied by time. Thus, at the late times after measurement these factors are small, and variations in the exact values of the rate constants cause only small errors over the range of calculated lCMRGlc values in this study [21, 22, 48, 55].

Earlier Studies of Cerebral Blood Flow and Substrate Utilization During Development

Prior to the development of PET, there had been no adequate noninvasive method to study changes of local substrate utilization in the developing human brain. Nevertheless, in their studies of cerebral blood flow and oxygen utilization, Kennedy and Sokoloff [32] demonstrated that the average global cerebral blood flow in nine normal children (aged three to 11 years) was approximately 1.8 times that of normal young adults. Similarly, average cerebral oxygen utilization was approximately 1.3 times higher in children than in adults.

The subsequent development of autoradiographic techniques for measuring lCBF [33, 52] and lCMRGlc [55] in laboratory animals enabled substrate utilization to be determined in individual anatomical structures during cerebral maturation. These previous investigations have suggested that during different stages of development cerebral structures with relatively high lCBF or lCMRGlc in general determine the predominant behavioral pattern at the particular stage [1, 4, 29–31, 43]. For example, using [^{14}C]2-deoxyglucose autoradiography, Kennedy and associates [31] found lCMRGlc in neonatal monkeys to be lower than adult rates in structures above the midbrain, particularly striate and the inferior temporal cortex. In contrast, lCMRGlc in neonatal auditory and soma-tosensory cortical areas were similar to mature rates, and neonatal thalamic rates were also relatively high when compared to other structures. These findings supported the concept that, in general, a rise in metabolic rate of a particular structure marks the time of its contribution to the animal's behavior. In the case of the monkey, structures with the highest lCMRGlc in the neonatal period dominated the behavior at that age [31].

Correlation Between lCMRGlc and Behavior During Human Development

Our data on the patterns of lCMRGlc in human neonates are congruous with the thesis that there is a relationship between a metabolic increase within neuroanatomical structures and the emergence of corresponding function. Neo-natal behavior is primarily dominated by subcortical brain structure activity. Intrinsic brainstem reflexes, such as the Moro, root, and grasp reflexes, are prominent. Visuomotor function is present only in rudimentary form [60], and cortical function is mostly limited to primary sensory and motor areas. The prominent metabolic activity in sensorimotor cortex (see figure8.1A) is also consistent with its relatively early morphological maturation compared to other cortical areas [51].

An interesting finding in the neonatal PET images is the relatively low lCMRGlc in the striatum compared to the more functionally mature thalamus (see figure 8.1A, B). This lCMRGlc relationship is also seen in adults with Huntington's disease [35]. Since normal newborn infants manifest nonpurposeful limb movements similar to those seen in Huntington's disease, the mechanism of chorea may be related to a functional imbalance in the interaction among striatum, thalamus, and cerebral cortex. Pathological chorea may result from striatal loss of function, whereas newborn physiological chorea occurs prior to emergence of significant lCMRGlc in the striatum and much of the cerebral cortex. It would, therefore, be of interest to determine whether a similar relationship in lCMRGlc among these structures exists in other clinical entities where chorea is a prominent feature.

By approximately three months, when striatal lCMRGlc has approached that of thalamus (see figure 8.1D), nonpurposeful limb movements have been replaced by more coordinated reaching movements. During this time, lCMRGlc has also increased in structures important for visuospatial and visuo-sensorimotor integration, such as parietal cortex, primary visual (calcarine) cortex, and cerebellar hemispheres. Indeed, infants between two and three months of age often open their hands during forward extension of the arm while visually fixing on an object as a preparatory maneuver to manipulate the object [59]. The increasingly sophisticated nature of these reaching movements is consistent with the notion that, whereas visual function in newborns may be mediated by phylogenetically older (subcortical) visual structures, the primary visual (calcarine) cortex begins to play a more important role in visual function by two to three months [3]. The lCMRGlc in the visual association areas, however, remains relatively low during this period, a finding consistent with the delayed anatomical maturation of the dorsolateral occipital cortex compared to calcarine cortex [51].

Another behavioral hallmark of two to four month-old infants is the attenuation and gradual disappearance of intrinsic brainsteam reflexes, presumably as a result of increasing cortical influence [2, 45]. Since the frontal cortex remains relatively hypometabolic compared to parietal, temporal, and calcarine cortices during this time (see figure 8.1C, D), cortical suppression of brainstem reflexes (assuming this to be the mechanism) is probably not exclusively the result of frontal cortical input. These primitive newborn reflexes are also often seen in demented individuals suffering from Alzheimer's disease [46], where PET has demonstrated the early decrease of parietal, prior to frontal lobe, metabolism [9, 15, 34]. Therefore, the concept of *frontal release signs*, a phrase often used to denote the emergence of primitive reflexes in both demented and normal elderly individuals, may be more accurately referred to as *cortical release signs*.

The EEG, another measure of cerebral cortical activity, also undergoes considerable maturation during the second and third postnatal months. During this time, newborn EEG patterns, such as trace alternant, frontal rhythmic delta, and frontal sharp transients, disappear, and the precursors of alpha rhythm appear [28]. Thus, it is not surprising that increases of lCMRGlc in cerebral cortical structures should occur during this period of cortical structures should occur during this period of cortical maturation as evidenced by dramatic EEG changes.

By eight months postnatally, lCMRGlc had increased in dorsolateral occipital cortex and much of the frontal cortex (see figure 8.1F). These increases coincide with the appearance of higher cortical and cognitive function [27]. The infant now shows a more sophisticated interaction with his or her surroundings and exhibits the phenomenon of stranger anxiety [12]. In addition, the infant improves his or her performance on the delayed response task, a commonly used neuropsychological paradigm for evaluating prefrontal lobe integrity [16, 17]. Together, these changes in the skills of the infant imply increasing function in the prefrontal cortex. Neuroanatomically, this stage is accompanied by an expansion of dendritic fields [53] and an increase in capillary density [8] of human frontal cortex.

Possible Causes of High lCMRGlc During Development

Although by eight to 12 months of age the anatomical distribution of lCMRGlc seen with PET qualitatively resembled that of young adults, and by two years absolute lCMRGlc for most structures were similar to those of adults, brain development was far from complete. In virtually all brain regions measured, lCMRGlc continued to increase, although to varying degrees depending upon the specific structures, reaching very high values compared to adults. Only during the second decade did lCMRGlc decline to approximate adult values (see figure 8.2). Evidence in support of these high metabolic rates during childhood was first reported by Kennedy and Sokoloff [32] some 30 years ago in a study alluded to earlier in this discussion.

There are a number of possible explanations for the high energy demands of the brain during development. First, there is now ample evidence in humans [51] and in other species [10, 36, 44] that during development the brain produces a vast excess of neurons, synapses, and dendritic spines. For example, the phenomenon of polyneuronal innervation, where synaptic targets receive innervation from more neurons during development than will remain in the adult, has been well documented (reviewed in [50]). The overproduction of neurons and their synaptic contacts is biologically advantageous in reducing the genetic load that would otherwise be required for specifically programming the enormous numbers of synaptic contacts in the nervous system [5, 25]. Many neurons subsequently die, and there is a regression of dendritic spines and synapses [7]. This form of cell death occurs early in development – by two years of age in humans [51] – but the loss of synaptic elements is a more protracted process. For example, the concentration of synaptic contacts in both human frontal [23] and visual [24] cortices of children up to 11 years old exceeds those of corresponding regions in adults. Specifically, at age seven years, when the child's brain is almost identical in size and weight to that of the adult, average synaptic density in frontal cortex is about 1.4 times the adult value [23].

The biological rules governing regression of neuroanatomical elements are poorly understood, but these phenomena are believed to account, at least in part, for nervous system plasticity [11]. The concept that there are mechanisms that act to retain those pathways in which patterns of external stimuli induce activity and eliminate potential connections not so activated has been termed *functional validation* by Jacobson [25], and *selective stabilization* by Changeux and Danchin [5]. This process would account for the contribution of early experience of the developing individual toward the final neuroanatomical composition and neurophysiological representation within the nervous system. This notion is supported by data from animal studies [13, 40, 41, 56, 61].

Our finding of higher lCMRGlc in children compared to adults is consistent with the excessive numbers of dendritic processes and synapses in childhood, since these elements account for most of the glucose utilized [26, 37, 42]. Therefore, the large surface area of an excess number of processes might lead to high resting glucose metabolic rates for maintenance of membrane potentials. As the density of processes diminishes, lCMRGlc also decreases to approach adult levels.

A second cause for high lCMRGlc in the developing brain may be excessive fuel expenditure by oligodendroglia during myelination, which continues, in the human brain, throughout the first decade of life [20, 62], and undergoes remodelling throughout life [14]. Conversely, incomplete myelination of brain pathways may result in suboptimal conduction efficiency, thus requiring greater energy expenditure. The relative contributions of these possible mechanisms in accounting for the high lCMRGlc in the developing brain can only be speculated. Since myelin remodelling is a slow process, it is unlikely to contribute significantly to immediate energy expenditure in the brain. Nevertheless, it is possible that all of these factors, and perhaps others, collectively account for the high lCMRGlc in the developing brain.

Conclusion

Our findings support the commonly accepted view that brain maturation in humans proceeds at least into the second decade of life. This study illustrates the potentially powerful approach PET provides in the study of human brain development. PET has opened a new window on our understanding of neuroanatomical correlation with brain function and behavior. Since both the anatomical distribution and absolute values of lCMRGlc in children are age dependent, the precise mapping of these maturational changes in the normally developing brain is a prerequisite to PET studies of abnormal brain development in children ranging from various learning disabilities to severe psychomotor retardation. Finally, by establishing changes in lCMRGlc during normal development, it will be possible to use PET in the study of central nervous system plasticity in children with early brain injury and other disease processes.

ACKNOWLEDGEMENTS

Supported by Department of Energy contract No DE–AC03–SF7600012 and by USPHS grants nos 5R01-MH37916-04 and 2P01-NS15654-06. Dr Chugani is the recipient of Teacher-Investigator Developmental Award 1-K07-NS00886-03, and Dr Mazziotta is the recipient of Teacher-Investigator Developmental Award 1-K07-NS00588-05-NSBA from the National Institute of Neurological and Communicative Diseases and Stroke.

We thank Drs C. Kennedy, P. Phelps, P. Nelson, P. Huttenlocher, F. Gilles, D. Holtzman, L. Sokoloff, and C. Smith for helpful comments, and Ms Marybeth Literarus for typing the manuscript. The support and assistance of the UCLA Pediatrics housestaff are greatly appreciated.

REFERENCES

1 Abrams R. M., Ito M., Frisinger J. E., et al. Local cerebral glucose utilization in fetal and neonatal sheep. *Am J Physiol* 246:R608–R618, 1984.

2 Andre-Thomas C. Y., Saint-Anne Dargassies S. *The neurological examination of the infant.* London, Medical Advisory Committee of the National Spastics Society, 1960.

3 Bronson G.: The postnatal growth of visual capacity. *Child Dev* 45:873–890, 1974.

4 Cavazzuti M., Duffy T. E. Regulation of local cerebral blood flow in normal and hypoxic newborn dogs. *Ann Neurol* 11:247–257, 1982.

5 Changeux J. P., Danchin A. Selective stabilization of developing synapses as a mechanism for the specification of neuronal networks. *Nature* 264:705–712, 1976.

6 Chugani H. T., Phelps M. E. Maturational changes in cerebral function in infants determined by [18]FDG positron emission tomography. *Science* 231:840–843, 1986.

7 Cowan W. M., Fawcett J. W., O'Leary D. D. M., Stanfield B. B. Regressive events in neurogenesis. *Science* 225:1258–1265, 1984

8 Diemer K. Capillarisation and oxygen supply of the brain. In Lubbers D. W., Luft U. C., Thews G., Witzleb E. (eds): *Oxygen transport in blood and tissue.* Stuttgart, Thieme Inc, 1968, pp 118–123.

9 Duara R., Grady C., Haxby J., et al. Positron emission tomography in Alzheimer's disease. *Neurology* 36:879–887, 1986.

10 Duffy C. J., Rakic P. Differentiation of granule cell dendrites in the dentate gyrus of the rhesus monkey: a quantitative Golgi study. *J Comp Neurol* 214:224–237, 1983.

11 Easter S. S. Jr, Purves D., Rakic P., Spitzer N. C. The changing view of neural specificity. *Science* 230:507–511, 1985.

12 Emde R. N., Gaensbauer T. J., Harmon R. J. *Emotional expression in infancy: a behavioral study, vol 10.* New York, Intl University Press, 1976.

13 Fiala B. A., Joyce J. N., Greenough W. T. Environmental complexity modulates growth of granule cell dendrites in developing but not adult hippocampus of rats. *Exp Neurol* 59:372–383, 1978

14 Fishman M. A., Agrawal H. C., Alexander A. et al. Biochemical maturation of human central nervous system myelin. *J Neurochem* 24:689–694, 1975.

15 Frackowiak R. S. J., Pozzilli C., Legg N. J., et al. Regional cerebral oxygen supply and utilization in dementia. A clinical and physiological study with oxygen-15 and positron emission tomography. *Brain* 104:753–778, 1981.

16 Fuster J. M. Behavioral electrophysiology of the prefrontal cortex. *Trends Neurosci* 7:408–414; 1984.

17 Goldman-Rakic P. S. The frontal lobes: uncharted provinces of the brain. *Trends Neurosci* 7:425–429, 1984.

18 Himwich H. E., Fazekas J. F. Comparative studies of the metabolism of the brain in infant and adult dogs. *Am J Physiol* 132:454–459, 1941.

19 Hottman E. J., Phelps M. E., Huang S. C. Performance evaluation of a positron tomograph designed for brain imaging. *J Nucl Med* 24:245–257, 1983.

20 Holland B. A., Haas D. K., Norman D., et al: MRI of normal brain maturation. *AJNR* 7:201–208, 1986.

21 Huang S. C., Phelps M. E., Hoffman E. J., et al. Noninvasive determination of local cerebral metabolic rate of glucose in man. *Am J Physiol* 238:E69–E82, 1980.

22 Huang S. C., Phelps M. E., Hoffman E. J., Kuhl D. E. Error sensitivity of fluorodeoxyglucose method for measurement of cerebral metabolic rate of glucose. *J Cereb Blood Flow Metab* 1:391–401, 1981.

23 Huttenlocher P. R. Synaptic density in human frontal cortex – developmental changes and effects of aging. *Brain Res* 163:195–205, 1979.

24 Huttenlocher P. R., de Courten C., Gary L. J., van der Loos H. Synaptogenesis in human visual cortex – evidence for synapse elimination during normal development. *Neurosci Lett* 33:247–252, 1982.

25 Jacobson M., Abrahams R. M. *Developmental Neurobiology*, 2nd edn. New York, Plenum, 1978, pp 302–307.

26 Kadekaro M., Crane A. M., Sokoloff L. Differential effects of electrical stimulation of sciatic nerve on metabolic activity in spinal cord and dorsal root ganglion in the rat. *Proc Natl Acad Sci USA* 82:6010–6013, 1985.

27 Kagan J. Do infants think? *Scientific American* 226:74–82, 1972.

28 Kellaway P. An orderly approach to visual analysis: parameters of the normal EEG in adults and children. In Klass D. W., Daly D. D. eds: *Current practice of clinical electroencephalography*. New York, Raven, 1979, pp 69–147.

29 Kennedy C., Grave G. D., Jehle J. W., Sokoloff L. Blood flow to white matter during maturation of the brain. *Neurology* 20:613–618, 1970.

30 Kennedy C., Grave G. D., Jehle J. W., Sokoloff L. Changes in blood flow in the component structures of the dog brain during postnatal maturation. *J Neurochem* 19:2423–2433, 1972.

31 Kennedy C., Sakurada O., Shinohara M., Miyaoka M.: Local cerebral glucose utilization in the newborn macaque monkey. *Ann Neurol* 12:333–340, 1982.

32 Kennedy C., Sokoloff L. An adaptation of the nitrous oxide method to the study of the cerebral circulation in children; normal values for cerebral blood flow and cerebral metabolic rate in childhood. *J Clin Invest* 36:1130–1137, 1957.

33 Kety S. S. Measurement of local blood flow by the exchange of an inert, diffusible substance. *Methods Med Res* 8:228–236, 1960.

34 Kuhl D. E., Metter E. J., Riege W. H. Patterns of cerebral glucose utilization in depression, multiple infarct dementia, and Alzheimer's disease. In Sokoloff L. ed: *Brain imaging and brain function*. New York, Raven, 1985, pp 211–226.

35 Kuhl D. E., Phelps M. E., Markham C. H., et al. Cerebral metabolism and atrophy in Huntington's disease determined by 18-FDG and computed tomographic scan. *Ann Neurol* 12:425–434, 1982.

36 Lund J. S., Boothe R. G., Lund R. D. Development of neurons in the visual cortex (area 17) of the monkey (Macaca nemestrina): a Golgi study from fetal day 127 to postnatal maturity. *J Comp Neurol* 176:149–188, 1977.

37 Mata M., Fink D. J., Gainer H., et al. Activity-dependent energy metabolism in rat posterior pituitary primarily reflects sodium pump activity. *J Neurochem* 34:213–215, 1980.

38 Mazziotta J. C., Phelps M. E., Meadors A. K., et al. Anatomical localization schemes for use in positron computed tomography using a specially designed head holder. *J Comput Assist Tomogr* 6:848–853, 1982.

39 Mazziotta J. C., Phelps M. E., Plummer D., et al. Optimization and standardization of anatomical data in neuro-behavioral investigations using positron computed tomography. *J Cereb Blood Flow Metab* 3(Suppl 1):S266–S267, 1983.

40 Mistretta C. M., Bradley R. M. Effects of early sensory experience on brain and behavioral development. In Gottlieb G (ed): *Studies on the development of behavior and the nervous system, vol 4. Early influences*. New York, Academic Press, 1978. pp 215–247.

41 Mollgaard K., Diamond M. C., Bennett E. L., et al. Quantitative synaptic changes with differential experience in rat brain. *Int J Neurosci* 2:113–128, 1971.

42 Nudo R. J., Masterton R. B. Stimulation-induced [14C]2-deoxy-glucose labeling of synaptic activity in the central auditory system. *J Comp Neurol* 245:553–565, 1986.

43 Ohata M., Sundaram U., Fredericks W. R., et al. Regional cerebral blood flow during development and ageing of the rat brain. *Brain* 104:319–332, 1981.

44 Oppenheim R. W. Naturally occurring cell death during neural development. *Trends Neurosci* 8:487–493, 1985.

45 Parmelee A. H. Jr, Sigman M. D. Perinatal brain development and behavior. In Haith M., Campos J. (eds): *Biology and infancy, vol II*, New York, Wiley, 1983, pp 95–155.

46 Paulson G., Gottlieb G. Development reflexes: the reappearance of fetal and neonatal reflexes in aged patients. *Brain* 91:37–52, 1968.

47 Phelps M. E., Hoffman E. J., Mullani N. A., Ter-Pogossian M. M.: Application of annihilation coincidence detection to transaxial reconstruction tomography. *J Nucl Med* 16:210–224, 1975.

48 Phelps M. E., Huang S. C., Hoffman E. J., et al. Tomographic measurement of local cerebral glucose metabolicrate in humans with (F-18)2-Fluoro-2-deoxyglucose: validation of method. *Ann Neurol* 6:371–388, 1979.

49 Phelps M. E., Mazziotta J. C. Positron emission tomography: human brain function and biochemistry. *Science* 228:799–809, 1985.

50 Purves D., Lichtman J. W. Elimination of synapses in the developing nervous system. *Science* 210:153–157, 1980.

51 Rabinowicz T. The differentiate maturation of the human cerebral cortex. In Falkner F., Tanner J. M. (eds): *Human growth, vol 3, Neurobiology and nutrition.* New York, Plenum, 1979, pp 97–123.

52 Sakurada O., Kennedy C., Jehle J., et al. Measurement of local cerebral blood flow with iodo[14C]antipyrine. *Am J Physiol* 234:H59–H66, 1978.

53 Schade J. P., van Groenigen W. B. Structural organization of the human cerebral cortex. *Acta Anat* 47:74–111, 1961.

54 Sokoloff L. Localization of functional activity in the central nervous system by measurement of glucose utilization with radioactive deoxyglucose. *J Cereb Blood Flow Metab* 1:7–36, 1981.

55 Sokoloff L., Reivich M., Kennedy C., et al. The (14-C) deoxyglucose method for the measurement of local cerebral glucose utilization: theory, procedure, and normal values in the conscious and anesthetized albino rat. *J Neurochem* 28:897–916, 1977.

56 Spinelli D. N., Jensen F. E., di Prisco G. V. Early experience effect on dendritic branching in normally reared kittens. *Exp Neurol* 68:1–11, 1980.

57 Theodore W. H., Bairamian D., Newmark M. E., et al. Effect of phenytoin on human cerebral glucose metabolism. *J Cereb Blood Flow Metab* 6:315–320, 1986.

58 Theodore W. H., DiChiro G., Margolin R., et al. Barbiturates reduce human cerebral glucose metabolism. *Neurology* 36:60–64, 1986.

59 Von Hofsten C. Developmental changes in the organization of prereaching movements. *Dev Psychobiol* 20:378–388, 1984.

60 Von Hofsten C. Eye-hand coordination in the newborn. *Dev Psychol* 18:450–461, 1982.

61 Wiesel T. N., Hubel D. H. Effects of visual deprivation on morphology and physiology of cells in the car's lateral geniculate body. *J Neurophysiol* 26:978–993, 1963.

62 Yakovlev P. I., Lecours A. R. The myelogenetic cycles of regional maturation of the brain. In Minkowski A. (ed): *Regional development of the brain in early life.* Philadelphia. Davis Co, 1967, pp 3–70.

Part III

Brain Maturation and Cognition

Introduction

Perhaps the most obvious way to relate brain development and cognition is to attribute the onset of a certain cognitive ability to the maturation of underlying neural circuitry. This part presents several variants of this general class of hypothesis. Although this type of argument has commonly been applied to the onset of an ability, it may also be applied to the termination of an ability (see the reading by Johnson and Newport). The variations on the general claim usually take one of the following forms: (a) specific neural developments at a certain age are posited to give rise to a specific computational advance at that same age (Held; Diamond), (b) considerations of sequences of brain maturation are used to predict the *sequence* of development of certain cognitive abilities (Bachevalier and Mishkin; Johnson).

In the first reading of this section, Held reviews converging evidence that binocular vision comes in toward the end of the fourth month of life in human infants (although it is worth noting that this can vary from two to five months in different infants). One of the abilities associated with binocular vision, stereoacuity, increases very rapidly from the onset of stereopsis, such that it reaches adult levels within a few weeks. This is in contrast to other measures of acuity, such as grating acuity, which increase much more gradually. Held suggests that this very rapid, sudden spurt in stereoacuity requires some radical change in the neural substrate supporting it. On the basis of evidence from animal studies, he proposes that this substrate is the development of ocular dominance columns found in layer IV of the primary visual cortex.

Neurophysiological studies have demonstrated that the geniculocortical afferents from the two eyes are initially mixed so that they synapse on common cortical neurones in layer IV (see figure 9.1, in the Held reading). These layer IV cells project to disparity selective cells (possibly in layers II and III). During ontogeny, geniculate axons originating from one eye withdraw from the region, leaving behind axons from the other eye. Held posits that it is these events at the neural level that give rise to the sudden increase in streoacuity observed by behavioral measures at around four months of age in the human infant. It is also worth noting that this age corresponds fairly well to the age at which layers II and III are showing rapid dendritic growth (see the Johnson reading in this part). Thus, another limitation may be the state of maturity of the putative disparity cells in these layers.

In an update to his original article, Held explores implications of the fact that prior to segregation of neuronal input, both eyes project to the same cells in layer 4 of the primary visual cortex. Thus, there will be a certain degree of integration between the eyes that will decline once each neuron only receives innervation from one eye. This is elegantly demonstrated in an experiment (see figure 9.2) in which Held and colleagues demonstrate that younger infants (under four months) can perform certain types of integration between the two eyes that older infants cannot.

Clearly, the fact that a behavioral change occurs rapidly cannot be taken as a strong indication that it is unaffected by environmental influence. Instead, it only suggests that we should expect the concomitant neural changes to be more obvious than those that occur gradually. A rapid transition also means that the strategy (employed by Held and others) of using a temporal correlation to infer cause is likely to be more convincing.

My own paper adopts the second of the approaches outlined earlier: I attempt to use evidence about patterns of postnatal brain growth to make predictions about the sequence of development of components of cognition, specifically visual attention and orienting. The conclusions of the paper are the result of putting together some neuroanatomical observations. These are (a) that the primary visual cortex is the main "gateway" to several pathways that underlie components of visual attention and orienting; (b) that primary visual cortex, like other areas of cortex, has a layer-specific pattern of connectivity to these other neural structures and pathways; and (c) that some measures of postnatal cortical growth show a layer-specific pattern of development from deeper layers to more superficial ones (as we saw in part II). The combination of these facts allows predictions to be made about the sequence of development of certain cortical pathways. Since these pathways underlie particular components of visual orienting and attention, we can also make predictions about the sequence of development of abilities at the cognitive level. By reviewing a large amount of evidence on the development of visual orienting in human infants, I attempt to provide some support for the predicted sequence.

The striking dissociations in memory found in amnesic patients have led to the discovery of similar dissociations following limbic lesions in the monkey. Bachevalier and Mishkin find evidence for a similar striking ontogenetic dissociation between two forms of memory, which they refer to as "habit formation" and "cognitive memory." Habit formation, the formation of simple "noncognitive" associations, is found to be almost as good between birth and three months as it is in adulthood. In contrast, the limbic-dependent memory system involved in cognitive memory shows a much more protracted and gradual improvement over the entire first year in infant monkeys.

The authors consider a number of possible explanations for this dissociation, including that the problem-solving abilities of young monkeys are less well developed than those in adults, and that infant monkeys are less able to abstract information about familiarity from objects. Their final conclusion, however, is that their evidence is most consistent with the interpretation that cognitive memory is later developing simply because the limbic circuitry on which it depends undergoes relatively slow ontogenetic development. Thus, they posit that the differential maturation of brain circuits gives rise to the differential maturation of the cognitive functions which they subserve.

Using similar tasks to those used to assess cognitive memory by Bachevalier and Mishkin, Diamond argues that the successful performance attained around ten months of age in the human infant is mediated by the maturation of the dorsolateral prefrontal cortex. Diamond's claims are based on the realization that a test commonly used to assess the psychological capacities of human infants, the *object-permanence test*, shows many similarities to tasks which have proved very sensitive to damage to the dorsolateral prefrontal cortex in the monkey, the *delayed response* task and the *object retrieval* task. In collaboration with Patricia Goldman-Rakic she proceeded to test the hypothesis that maturation of the prefrontal cortex is primarily responsible for human infants' ability to overcome the errors that they show in the object permanence test before age ten months.

Having marshalled evidence for the role of the prefrontal cortex in these tasks, Diamond goes on to consider what aspects of these tasks engage the functioning of this structure. She proposes two functions that the frontal lobe may subserve: (a) relating information separated in time or space, and (b) inhibiting a prepotent response. Only when both of these functions are required are the frontal lobes likely to be involved. While both of these functions would be required by the cognitive memory task discussed by Bachevalier and Mishkin, delayed non-match to sample, they would not both be required by a delayed match to sample. Whether this prediction is upheld remains to be seen. Clearly, Diamond would be of the view that the transition attributed to hippocampal maturation by Bachevalier and Mishkin might be better accounted for in terms of frontal lobe maturation (see also Janowsky, part VIII).

Diamond is prepared to allow that there is some limited role for experience in the behavioral transitions that she describes. Indeed, she reports that repeated testing on any of the tasks can accelerate the performance of human infants by two or three weeks. However, she argues that these accelerations are limited by the maturational state of the brain. This is because the transitions occur at around the same age in three types of task which appear to require very different forms of experience. Much like Lenneberg (part I), Diamond believes that the underlying maturation of neural circuitry allows certain types of experience to have effects at certain points only. Some of the evidence for this is that in an object retrieval task, the infants always go through the same sequence of stages before succeeding. Experience cannot push them straight to the final behavior.

The reading by Lenneberg on language acquisition in part I also introduced us to the notion of a "critical period"; that is, the view that the brain is "maturationally ready" to acquire language at certain ages, and that it subsequently loses this ability. Johnson and Newport investigate this claim with regard to second language learning. Second language learning is important to study, since it helps differentiate between two types of critical period hypotheses. The first is the *exercise hypothesis*. It states that if the superior capacity to acquire language early in life is not exercised, then it will disappear or decline with maturation. If it is exercised, then the capacity for further language learning will remain throughout life. This hypothesis is consistent with some of the existing literature on first language learning and with some animal studies on critical periods. The second view is the *maturational state hypothesis*. This "purer" form of critical period hypothesis implies that there is a particular age at which all languages are learned more readily, and that this ability then declines regardless of experience. By this second account, there ought to be the same critical period for second language learning as there is for the first.

Johnson and Newport investigate the acquisition of a second language by Korean and Chinese speakers who immigrated to the United States between the ages of 3 and 39 years. They find that level of proficiency in English is clearly related to whether arrival occurred before or after puberty. On the other hand, it is not related to the length of time that subjects had been exposed to the language. This is strong evidence for the maturationally determined termination of plasticity around the age of puberty, i.e. for the maturational state hypothesis. In contrast to some interpretations of Lenneberg's account, however, the end of the sensitive period is not sudden – it is a gradual decline from about age seven years to adulthood. Moreover, we know that many aspects of grammar remain readily learnable by adults.

FURTHER READING

Atkinson, J. (1984) Human visual development over the first six months of life: a review and a hypothesis. *Human Neurobiology*, 3, 61–74. (A comprehensive review of the development of vision and its neural basis.)

Bates, E., Thal, D. and Janowsky, J. S. (1992) Early language development and its neural correlates. In I. Rapin and S. Segalowitz (eds), *Handbook of Neuropsychology, Vol. 6: Child Neurology*. Amsterdam: Elsevier. (A recent review of neurodevelopmental correlates of language acquisition.)

Bronson, G. W. (1974) The postnatal growth of visual capacity. *Child Development*, 45, 873–90. (The now classic original statement proposing that the development of visually guided behavior in the human infant can be viewed in terms of a transition from subcortical to cortical processing.)

Carey, S. (1980) Maturational factors in human development. In D. Caplan (ed.), *Biological Studies of Mental Processes*. Cambridge, MA: MIT Press, 1–7. (An introduction to some of the issues about the relation between brain development and cognitive development.)

Carey, S. and Diamond, R. (1980) Maturational determination of the developmental course of face encoding. In D. Caplan (ed.), *Studies of Mental Processes*. Cambridge, MA: MIT Press, 60–96. (Evidence for a maturationally determined "dip" in face recognition abilities around the time of puberty.)

Dehaene, S. and Changeux, J.-P. (1989) A simple model of prefrontal cortex function in delayed-response tasks. *Journal of Cognitive Neuroscience*, 1, 244–61. (An attempt to simulate some of the tasks, and types of errors, discussed in the Diamond reading.)

Goldman-Rakic, P. S. (1987) Development of cortical circuitry and cognitive function. *Child Development*, 58, 601–22. (A review of the possible effects of prefrontal cortex maturation on cognition.)

Goldman-Rakic, P. S., Isseroff, A., Schwartz, M. L. and Bugbee, N. M. (1983) The neurobiology of cognitive development. In P. Mussen (ed.), *Handbook of Child Psychology: Biology and Infancy Development*. New York: Wiley, 281–334. (A comprehensive overview of the relation between the anatomical development of the cortex, especially the prefrontal cortex, and some aspects of behavioral development.)

Muir, D. W., Clifton, R. K. and Clarkson, M. G. (1989) The development of a human auditory localization response: a U-shaped function. *Canadian Journal of Psychology*, 43, 199–216. (A review of experiments indicating that auditory orienting in the human infant goes through a similar subcortical to cortical shift to that described in the visual system.)

Newport, E. L. (1990) Maturational constraints on language learning. *Cognitive Science*, 14, 11–28. (Argues for maturational constraints of language acquisition.)

Witelson, S. F. (1987) Neurobiological aspects of language in children. *Child Development*, 58, 653–88. (Explores some parallels between aspects of brain and language development.)

9

Binocular Vision – Behavioral and Neuronal Development

RICHARD HELD

In the course of the last decade or so, interest in the developing vision of infants has proceeded apace. Methods of testing infants for visual resolution including grating, stereo, and vernier acuities, contrast sensitivity, refraction, oculomotor control, and other functions have been evolved. At least one compendium of the new knowledge has appeared quite recently (Aslin et al., 1981). A principal source of interest in this work has been the advances in understanding of the function and structure of the visual nervous system and of their developmental courses. This research has of necessity been largely performed on animals, chiefly cats and monkeys, but its implications for the study of human vision have had profound effects, of which the burgeoning interest in infant vision is one facet.

In this chapter I review briefly some of the relevant results concerning neuronal systems and their development. I also review some of the behavioral and psychophysical findings on young animals and human infants concerning binocular vision. From these results I draw a speculative interpretation in terms of the development and modifiability of these neuronal mechanisms. My excuse for doing this exercise is an effort to draw together some of the ideas expressed by different participants in this volume.

The questions that I address deal largely with the development of binocularity. Obviously the two eyes work together insofar as the normally sighted person sees one world despite using two eyes and consequently having slightly different images on the retinas. This phenomenon, called fusion, is the most elementary form of binocularity. The condition under which fusion occurs requires that the two images be aligned on the retinas in corresponding positions. The maintenance of correspondence depends of course on maintaining proper convergence of the

"Binocular Vision – Behavioral and Neuronal Development" first appeared in *Neonate Cognition: Beyond the Blooming Buzzing Confusion*, edited by Jacques Mehler and Robin Fox (Lawrence Erlbaum Associates, 1985, pp. 37–44), and is reprinted by kind permission.

eyes so that both look at the same object. But assuming proper convergence, images may very well not correspond in retinal positions. For example, if two objects differ in distance from the eyes, their images will not fall on corresponding retinal loci for obvious geometric reasons (Foley, 1978). When the lack of correspondence involves distances across the retinal of more than a degree or two, doubling of the nonfixated object will be seen. Parenthetically, one may note that in a reasonably crowded environment most objects should in fact be seen double. The curious fact is that such doubling is rarely seen in normal circumstances. When the non-correspondences are of the order of a degree or less, fusion is maintained and a new phenomenon emerges, that of stereopsis.

Stereopsis

The small non-correspondences between the images of objects at different distances from the eyes are interpreted by the visual system as actual depth differences, and the scene gains the three-dimensional appearance that characterizes stereopsis. Because stereopsis involves a comparison of small differences between the images in the two eyes, and because the neuronal substrate for such comparison doesn't occur below the level of the visual cortex as seems to be the case, stereopsis gives us direct access to cortical visual processing. This implication is examined in great detail by Bela Julesz (1971).

In recent years, investigators working in a number of laboratories have developed techniques for testing stereopsis in very young infants. The results have shown a very satisfying agreement (Teller, 1983). Stereopsis appears to emerge on the average toward the end of the fourth postnatal month, based on full-term gestational age, with a range such that 20 percent appear to have it by two months and 80 percent before five months. More striking from a developmental point of view is the finding that the fineness of stereopsis, called stereoacuity, increases very rapidly from the onset of stereopsis, such that within a few weeks it approaches adult levels (Birch, et al., 1982; Held et al., 1980). This result contrasts strikingly with the rate of development of grating acuity, which increases rapidly over the first six months after birth and then more slowly over the first few years (Birch et al., 1983; Teller, 1981). Grating acuity barely changes during the period in which stereoacuity changes rapidly. The sharpness of the change in stereoacuity implies that some radical change in the neuronal substrate is occurring, and that substrate is very probably cortical. Before considering the possibilities for modeling this underlying process, I want to consider three other developmental findings that confirm and amplify the importance of the timing of the changes under discussion.

Binocular Function

When part or all of the visual field before an observer moves in one direction, the eyes will follow up to some limiting displacement and then saccade back to their former positions. This process then repeats itself in a periodic manner that is called optokinetic nystagmus. In normally sighted adults the following response is equally well elicited by motion in either rightward or leftward directions. If only one eye is used, the same equivalence is observed. However, in observers who suffer from anomalies of binocular vision such as strabismus (crossed eyes), the following response of an eye to both directions of motion is not equivalent. The following tends to be better for motion running from the side toward the midline, called the temporonasal direction, than it is for motion in the opposite direction, called nasotemporal. In this regard the optokinetic response of those who suffer from these binocular anomalies resembles that of many animals who have lateralized eyes (Tauber and Atkin, 1968). In the former case it appears that the neuronal substrate for symmetrical OKN has a cortical component related to binocularity, whereas in the latter the animal with predominantly lateral eyes has little binocular overlap and accordingly limited central convergence of the inputs from the two eyes. The goodness of the following response can be quantified in terms of the measure called gain. Gain is the ratio of the velocity of the eye to that of the moving field, where the ratio one to one is the optimal.

In recent experiments we have managed to measure the gain of the nasotemporal relative to that of temporonasal response in infants ranging in age from one to six months (Naegele and Held, 1982). The results show that very young infants behave like strabismics and show little or no following to nasotemporal motion but relatively normal following to temporonasal motion. However, the gain of the response to nasotemporal motion increases steadily through the first four months, until it reaches equivalence between the two directions. In summary, the equalization of the gains of the optokinetic responses to the two directions occurs on the average toward the end of the fourth month, just as does the achievement of stereopsis.

A process similar to the aforementioned occurs in the case of binocular summation of the pupillary response. When one eye of a normally sighted adult views a large illuminated field, the other eye being closed, its pupil constricts to some steady state diameter. If the other eye is now opened, the pupil of the first eye will further constrict by a small but significant increment. One of the investigators of this phenomenon, Matthew Alpern (1970), has observed no such summation in his own pupillary responses, but he has strabismus. The lack of summation has since been observed in many observers suffering from binocular imbalance, implying that binocular convergence at the cortex may be involved in this summation. Eileen Birch in our laboratory decided to test infants for this form of binocularity. She soon found that very young infants did not show the effect, but that it appeared on the average toward the end of the fourth month of life (Birch and Held, 1983). Once again, this age emerges as a transition point in the evolution of binocular function.

Thus far I have described three types of evidence that binocular function is perfected sometime during the fourth month on average. The evidence is drawn from sources that show enhanced capabilities resulting from either direct or implied interaction between inputs to the two eyes. A fourth form of evidence comes from a source in which reduced function actually occurs. This source is the evidence for what appears to be the onset of amblyopia, resulting from congenital esotropia (crossed-eyes) with strong fixation preference by one eye. This condition is well known to be frequently accompanied by low acuity in the habitually deviated eye, a condition known as amblyopia (lazy eye).

Amblyopia

We have asked the question, what is the time course of development of this abnormally low acuity? The answer to this question could help decide between the two possibilities that either amblyopia is a consequence of esotropia, or esotropia is the consequence of poor vision in one eye. Of course, both could be true, and probably are, but the developmental sequence of the two events might distinguish cause from effect.

Using measures of grating acuity derived from a two-choice preference procedure (Gwiazda et al., 1980), we have made serial measurements on four congenital esotropes and found the following result in all cases. When first measured, the two eyes were found to be equal in acuity and at a level normal for the age tested. However, in all four cases, measurement at a later age showed significant differences in acuity, with the acuity of the deviating eye found to be less than that of the straight eye (Jacobson et al., 1981). Moreover, in every case the deviating eye showed a lesser acuity; it had actually decreased from the previous test. The average age at which the transition from equal to unequal acuities occurred turned out once again to be toward the end of the fourth month of life.

Thus it appears that at some point during development when binocularity becomes perfected, not only is the visual system capable of enhanced performance in at least three ways, it also becomes subject to the deleterious effects of binocular imbalance resulting from esotropia.

Neuronal Mechanism

The abrupt onset of binocular function suggests the sudden availability of an underlying neuronal mechanism for processing information combined from the two eyes. Do we have any candidates for such a process? So far we have discussed only data drawn from the study of human infants. The search for a neuronal mechanism must draw information from the study of animals in which the development of the visual nervous system has been delineated. Several indices of binocularity have been examined in both cat and monkey. Consider the cat first.

Timney (1981) has studied the development of depth discrimination in the kitten. He finds a rapid rise in such discrimination specific to the use of both eyes during the fifth and subsequent weeks of life. He argues that this ability depends on stereopsis. Recording from single cells in the visual cortex of kittens, Pettigrew (1974) claims that sensitivity to disparity matures at this time. Thus the times of onset are the same for both physiological and behavioral evidence for stereopsis in the cat.

Other evidence indicates that the sensitive period for loss of stereopsis resulting from monocular occlusion begins in the fifth week after birth, peaks during the next few weeks, and falls off over the next several weeks (Timney, 1983). Moreover, results coming from surgically induced squint imply that the deviating eye becomes amblyopic if surgery is performed before 12 weeks of age and not

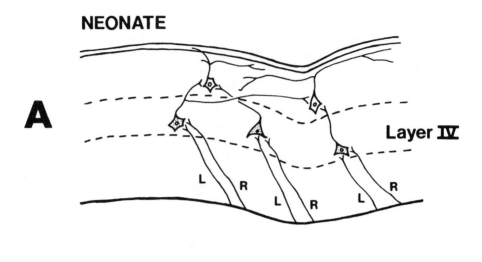

NEONATE

A

Layer IV

L R L R L R

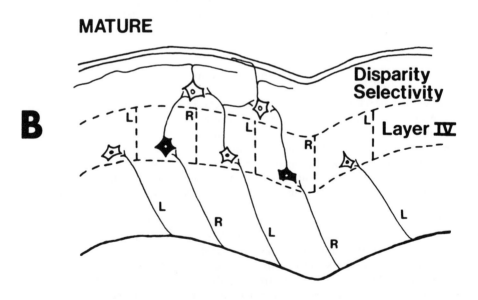

MATURE

B

Disparity
Selectivity

Layer IV

L R L R L

L R L R L

Figure 9.1 A. Geniculostriate afferents from both eyes (R and L) synapse on the same cells in layer IV, thereby losing information about the eye of origin. B. Geniculostriate afferents are segregated on the basis of eye origin (R and L) and consequently recipient cells in layer IV may send their axons to cells outside of that layer so as to synapse on cells that may be disparity selective. Reprinted with permission from *Vision Research* 26 (3), 501–10, of Shimojo, Shinsuke et al. (1986). Copyright Pergamon Press Plc.

after that time (Jacobson and Ikeda, 1979). This result is again consistent with a sensitive period for the development of amblyopia immediately following the development of stereopsis. Finally, van Hof-van Duin (1978) reports that optokinetic nystagmus becomes symmetrical in the kitten between five and eight weeks of age.

Only two of these indices of the onset of binocularity in the monkey are currently to be found. Kiorpes and Boothe (1980) report that the onset of amblyopia in animals made esotropic by surgery occurs between five and six weeks of age. Atkinson (1979) reports that the symmetrization of optokinetic nystagmus is achieved during the fifth week of age.

According to these indices, binocularity in both cat and monkey appears to have its onset during the fifth week of life. What neural developments in cat and monkey could account for this behavioral development? Elsewhere we have cited the evidence for completion of segregation of the ocular dominance columns in layer IV in the cat (LeVay et al., 1978) and layer IV C in the monkey (LeVay et al., 1980). Prior to such segregation, it appears that the geniculocortical afferents from the two eyes are mixed so that they synapse on common cortical neurons in those layers (see figure 9.1A). Unless one assumes that the disparity selective neurons responsible for stereopsis are to be found in these layers, which appears most doubtful, one must look to the extragranular layers (outside layer IV) for such cells. In these layers axons from the cells of layer IV carrying information from non-corresponding (disparate) retinal loci may be expected to synapse so as to yield disparity selective neurons in the mature system (Poggio and Fisher, 1977) (figure 9.1B). However, in the immature system, prior to segregation of the columns, the output from cells of layer IV may be so mixed as to eye of origin, as to preclude the formation of disparity selective cells (figure 9.1A). Whereas the process that is responsible for the segregation of the columns is not yet well understood, it appears that the geniculate axons originating from one eye withdraw (atrophy?) from the region to be occupied only by axons originating from the other eye. This process may correspond to that of selective stabilization discussed in detail by Changeux and Danchin (1976).

Although this explanation of the onset of binocular function may be plausible, it is not complete. Study of the development of vernier acuity has shown that its onset and increase occur in the human infant over a time course much like that of stereopsis (Shimojo et al., 1983). However, vernier acuity does not depend on having two eyes with binocular combination of their information. It can equally well be observed with the use of one eye only. Consequently, it appears that, whereas segregation of the ocular dominance columns is a necessary condition for binocular function, it is not sufficient. In addition, during this early period the cortex develops the capacity to compute the positions of edges with the precision necessary to account for both stereopsis and vernier acuities.

REFERENCES

Alpern, M. The pupillary light reflex and binocular interaction. In F. Young and D. Lindsley (eds). Early experience and visual information processing in perceptual and reading disorders. *National Academy of Science*, 1970.

Aslin. R. N., Alberts. J. R., & Petersen, M. R. (eds). *Development of perception* (Vol. 2). New York: Academic Press. 1981.

Atkinson, J. Development of optokinetic nystagmus in the human infant and monkey infant: An analogue to development in kittens. In R. D. Freeman (ed.), *Developmental neurobiology of vision*. New York: Plenum Press. 1979.

Birch. E., Gwiazda. J., Bauer, J. A., Jr., Naegele. J., & Held, R. Visual acuity and its meridional variations in children aged 7 to 60 months. *Vision Research*, 1983, 23(10), 1019–1024.

Birch. E. Gwiazda, J., & Held. R. Stereoacuity development for crossed and uncrossed disparities in human infants. *Vision Research*, 1982, 22, 507–513.

Birch, E., & Held. R. The development of binocular summation in human infants. *Investigative Ophthalmology and Visual Science*, 1983, 24, 1103–1107.

Changeux. J. P., & Danchin. A. Selective stablization of developing synapses as a mechanism for the specification of neuronal networks. *Nature*, 1976, 264, 705–712.

Foley. J. M. Primary distance perception. In R. Held, H. W. Leibowitz, & H.-L. Teuber (eds), *Handbook of sensory physiology* (Vol. 8). New York: Springer, 1978.

Gwiazda. J., Brill, S., Mohindra, I., & Held. R. Preferential looking acuity in infants from 2 to 58 weeks of age. *American Journal of Optometry and Physiological Optics*, 1980, 57, 428–432.

Held, R., Birch. E., & Gwiazda, J. Stereoacuity of human infants. *Proceedings of the National Academy of Sciences. USA*, 1980, 77, 5572–5574.

Jacobson. S. G., & Ikeda. H. Behavioral studies of spatial vision in cats reared with convergent squint: Is amblyopia due to arrest of development? *Experimental Brain Research*, 1979, 34, 11–26.

Jacobson. S. G., Mohindra, I., & Held. R. Age of onset of amblyopia in infants with esotropia *Documenta Ophthalmologica*, Proceedings Series, 1981, 30, 210–216.

Julesz. B. *Foundations of cyclopean perception*, University of Chicago Press. 1971.

Kiorpes. L., & Boothe. R. G. Strabismic amblyopia development in infant monkeys. *Investigative Ophthalmology and Visual Science*, 1980, 19, 841–845.

LeVay, S., Stryker, M. P., & Shatz, C. J. Ocular dominance columns and their development in layer IV of the cat's visual cortex: A quantitative study. *Journal of Comparative Neurology*, 1978, 179, 223–224.

LeVay. S., Wiesel. T. N., & Hubel, D. H. The development of ocular dominance columns in normal and visually deprived monkeys. *J. Comp. Neurol.*, 1980, 191, 1–51.

Naegele. J. R., & Held, R. The postnatal development of monocular optokinetic nystagmus in infants. *Vision Research*, 1982, 22, 341–346.

Pettigrew, J. D. The effect of visual experience on the development of stimulus specificity by kitten cortical neurons. *Journal of Physiology*, 1974, 237, 49.

Poggio. G. F., & Fischer, B. *Journal of Neurophysiology*, 1977, 40, 1392–1405.

Shimojo. S., Birch, E., & Held. R. Development of vernier acuity assessed by preferential looking. *Supplement: Investigative Ophthalmology & Visual Science*, 1983, 24, 93.

Tauber, E., & Atkin, A. Optomotor responses to monocular stimulation: Relation to visual system organization. *Science*, 1968, 160, 1365–1367.

Teller. D. Y. The development of visual acuity in human and monkey infants. *Trends in Neuroscience*, 1981, 4, 22–24.

Teller. D. Y. Scotopic vision, color vision, and stereopsis in infants. *Current Eye Research*, 1983, 2, 199–210.

Timney. B. Development of binocular depth perception in kittens. *Investigative Ophthalmology and Visual Sci.*, 1981, 21, 493–496.

Timney. B. The effects of early and late monocular deprivation on binocular depth perception in cats. *Brain Research*, 1983, 283, 235–43.

Van Hof-Van Duin. J. Direction preference of optokinetic responses in monocularly tested normal kittens and light deprived cats. *Arch. Ital. Biol.*, 1978, 116, 471–477.

Development of Binocular Vision Revisited

The original draft of this paper was presented in 1982 although it was not published until 1985. As is inevitable in an active area of research, relevant new results require revision and additions to earlier reports. Rather than rewrite the original, I add this supplement. It consists of additions to, deletions from, and amplifications of the original report. When read together with the original it may have the virtue of revealing something of the dynamics of change in one small area of science. Of particular interest is the fate of the model of development proposed in the original paper. One might claim, paraphrasing General MacArthur on the occasion of his enforced retirement, that old models never die. They may be superseded, but mostly they are altered to fit new conditions. I shall let the reader decide as to the fate our model deserves.

Further Results and Considerations From The MIT Laboratory

To my thinking the most impressive supplements to the original paper are new data that were gathered from experimental tests performed under hypotheses suggested by the original model. To some extent these data confirm the relevance of the model but they also raise new questions about it.

Interocular Rivalry

The most impressive of these model-testing experiments were performed by my postdoctoral fellow, Eileen Birch, and my graduate student, Shinsuke Shimojo, in collaboration with the staff of our laboratory. The original model purported to explain the absence of stereopsis in the early and immature stage of development. It did so by assuming the absence of eye-addressed (monocular) single cells in layer 4 of the visual cortex based upon the cited anatomical and physiological studies. In their absence there could be no further combination of the outputs of such cells to form disparity selective neurons. With segregation of the ocular dominance columns in the mature stage such cells become the rule and are, presumably, a necessary but not sufficient condition for the formation of the disparity sensitive cells that account for stereopsis. By the same reasoning we should not expect to find evidence for other interocular interactions that require combination of single eye-addressed cells. One of these interactions is the phenomenon of binocular rivalry. Stimuli that fall on corresponding loci on the two retina but that differ substantially in luminance, color, edge orientation, or size are not seen simultaneously by normal viewers. Instead they alternate in appearance, presumably because of a mutually inhibitory process at the cortical level. Clearly such a process requires that the addresses of the eyes of origin be tied to the representations of the inhibited features at the level of the rivalry process.

An experiment was performed to test the sensitivity of infants of various ages to such rivalry. In a two-alternative preferential looking experiment the infant was stereoscopically presented with binocularly rivalrous versus binocularly fusible stimuli (Birch et al., 1985). Preferential responses were not found until the infants were of an average age not significantly different from that at which stereopsis appears. Hence, one prediction of the model was confirmed. Later tests showed that the ages of onset of stereopsis and of binocular rivalry measured in a group of individuals are highly correlated, thereby arguing that the same internal changes are responsible for both (Gwiazda et al., 1989). These data also reveal the sex difference we have repeatedly seen in the development of binocular visual functions (Bauer et al., 1986) as well as the development of vernier acuity (Held et al., 1984). During the fourth to sixth months females appear to develop more rapidly than males. We do not now know the source of this difference but one expects that when found it should be revealing of one of the origins of sexual dimorphism in the brain.

Summation versus Rivalry

Based upon the results of the above experiment, an even more strongly confirming demonstration was made by Shimojo et al. (1986). The model implies what binocular vision should be like in pre-stereoptic infants. During the neonatal or primitive stage, optic tract neurons from both eyes overlap and often synapse on the same cells in layer 4. That state of affairs implies that information from the two eyes is undergoing summation at the synapse in layer 4. If so, then differing stimuli falling on corresponding loci of the two retinas will cause an averaging of their neural responses in the cells of layer 4. Rivalry between the two eyes is ruled out. As one consequence, stimuli with edges of different orientations in the two eyes will be represented to a first approximation as combined crossing edges. A grating in one eye orthogonal to that in the other will form a gridlike representation. This reasoning was embodied in the experiment illustrated in figure 9.2. Control tests (C) showed that infants during the first few months of life prefer ordinary (non-stereoscopic) grids over gratings of comparable spatial frequencies. In the experiment (E), interocularly orthogonal gratings were paired with parallel ones in a two-alternative preferential looking test. In accord with the above reasoning, the infants might be expected to prefer the orthogonal gratings during the primitive stage since they summate to some appoximation of a grid. However, upon achieving the mature stage, as the previously discussed experiment demonstrated, the infants should prefer binocularly fusible stimuli over rivalrous ones. Consequently, if the above reasoning from the model is correct, the subjects of this experiment should completely shift preference from orthogonal to parallel gratings when the mature stage occurs. The results of the experiment bore out the prediction. The infants shifted suddenly, at about the same age as they acquire stereopsis, from a preference for the orthogonal gratings to one for the parallel gratings. In fact, this shift in preference often occurred from one testing session to another only one or two weeks apart. Such an abrupt change actually raises a question as to whether the underlying neuronal transition from non-segregated to segregated columns, presupposed by our model, could occur with such rapidity. This issue is discussed below.

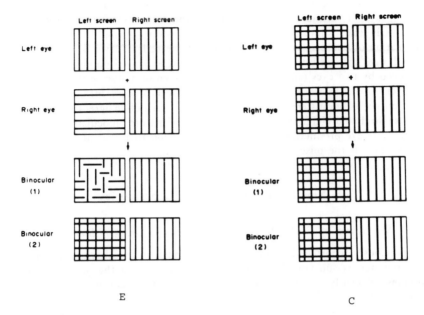

E   C

Figure 9.2 Both control (C) and experiment (E) are performed with separation of separate eye views produced by crossed polarization. Left and right eye views are superimposed by binocular fusion of the outline squares. The stereoscopic combination of the two views yields the two alternative hypothetical appearances Binocular (1) and Binocular (2) in the E condition but only the fused appearance in C. Reprinted with permission from *Vision Research* 26 (3), 501–10, of Shimojo, Shinsuke et al. (1986). Copyright Pergamon Press Plc.

Symmetry of OKN

Recent developments in our understanding of the symmetrization of the opto-kinetic response raise questions as to what relation the phenomenon has with the development of binocularity. The achievement of full symmetry of the pursuit response occurs on average at roughly the time of onset of stereopsis. But its development is gradual and extends over the early months, unlike the abrupt onset of stereopsis and of the preference for interocularly fusible over rivalrous stimuli. For this reason and others (see discussions in Braddick and Atkinson, 1988; Lewis et al., 1989), we conclude that although the development of symmetrical OKN shows a certain parallelism with that of mature binocularity, the two processes may not be produced by a common mechanism.

Binocular Summation of the Pupillary Response

Further thinking about the pupillary response in relation to our model has led to the following conception. Neuronal pathways leading from visual cortex to the oculomotor nuclei exist and may be presumed to influence pupillary activity (Benevento et al., 1977). According to our model, during the primitive stage stimulation of one eye only will suffice to produce activity at the synapses of all cells in layer 4. Stimulation of both eyes cannot then extend activation to any more cells than stimulation of one eye. However, during the mature stage, stimulation of one eye will activate only half the cells of layer 4 but stimulation of both eyes will activate all cells. Consequently, enhanced pupillary constriction produced by two eyes (summation) should be seen only during the mature stage in layer 4. If, as we have argued, this cortical process influences pupillary function via its brain stem connections, then this prediction agrees with the actual results (Birch and Held, 1983). With the onset of mature binocularity, stimulation of only one eye produces less pupillary constriction than that of both eyes. The consequence is the onset of binocular summation.

New Results from Other Laboratories

Segregation of Ocular Dominance Columns and Onset of Binocularity

We previously reported that the onset of stereopsis in the kitten occurs at about the same age as substantial completion of segregation of the ocular dominance columns. Recently, study of the development of stereopsis in the macaque monkey (O'Dell et al., 1991) has revealed an average age of onset between three and four weeks of age. Completion of segregation of the monkey's ocular dominance columns occurs at a similar age (Le Vay et al., 1980). As mentioned above, the process of columnar segregation, as reported for the cat and monkey, is relatively gradual compared to the transition from primitive to mature binocularity. It is reported to occur in the cat between birth and six weeks of age. In the monkey it appears to begin before birth but not to be completed until several weeks after birth. Consequently, we can only account for the rapid transition from primitive to mature binocularity, as measured behaviorally (psychophysically), by recognizing that while segregation may be a necessary condition for mature binocularity, it is not a sufficient condition. Connections must also be made with cells outside of layer 4 that analyze for disparity and rivalry. Furthermore, it may be that some threshold in terms of number of functioning analyzers must be exceeded before mature binocular function is evident (Held, 1988).

Binocular Beats

When stimuli flickering at slightly different frequencies are presented to left and right eyes of adult viewers with normal vision, they report seeing a beat at the frequency of the difference between the two originating frequencies. Evoked potentials recorded from the heads of such observers also reveal the beat frequencies. This result is in accord with the fact that the production of such a beat frequency requires a nonlinear interaction between the two frequencies of the sort that is produced by binocular combination. In the stereoblind individual, neuronal evidence suggests that binocular combination is rare and, in fact, in viewers lacking stereopsis the beat frequency is either reduced or eliminated. Will the beat frequency be evident in the primitive stage of binocularity? The infants are stereoblind but do they have binocular interaction? The answer is that the beat has been found in infants before the age of onset of stereopsis (Baitch and Srebro, 1990). The authors argue that the infants have some form of binocular interaction before onset of stereopsis, a result in accord with our model.

Probability Summation at Threshold

In general, visual thresholds for binocular stimulation are lower than those for monocular stimulation. The most common explanation is that the probability of detection by two independent detectors of equal sensitivity is greater than that of one. Recently Birch and Swanson (1991) reported that infants do not show such summation before four months of age but do at later ages. They argue that the pathways from the two eyes converge before detection and therefore preclude probability summation. This result is also in accord with our model.

Binocularity and Eye Alignment

Recent studies of the development of eye alignment suggest a parallel with that of binocularity. The relation between stereopsis and the control of vergent eye movements is reciprocal. Alignment of the eyes to ensure that both lines of sight intersect a target object is required for producing stereoptic depth perception by

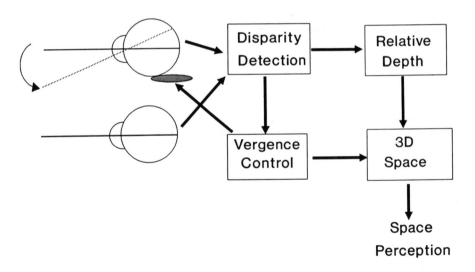

Figure 9.3 When disparity signals become available they will input to vergence control at the same time as they allow of stereopsis. Activation of vergence by disparity will yield orthotropy (solid lines of sight) in the normal infant but esotropy (dashed line of sight) in the at-risk infant. Stereopsis is presumed to include processing for relative depth and a metric for 3D space when combined with an input from vergence control.

optimizing retinal disparities. But the same binocular disparities control vergent eye movements. Figure 9.3 depicts this relation. While disparity signals are not the only source of such control, they may be expected on theoretical grounds to make vergent movements more efficient. Existing data on the development of these eye movements of infants bear out this conjecture. Aslin (1977) demonstrated that accurate convergence of the eyes in order to follow an abrupt stepwise movement of a target in depth is not found prior to the fourth month of life.

Recent accounts of the ages of onset of infantile esotropia (cross-eyes) (Nixon et al., 1985) and of orthotropia (correctly aligned eyes) (Archer, 1992) reveal an agreement with the ages of onset of stereopsis (Held, 1992). The few data from studies of the onset of esotropia in monkeys are consistent with this conclusion (Kiorpes et al., 1985). The agreement suggests a relation between the development of mature binocularity and the achievement of habitually correct alignment of the eyes. We have suggested (see figure 9.3) that when disparity information becomes available to drive vergence it will either improve eye alignment (orthotropia) in the normal infant or produce esotropia in the at-risk infant (Held, 1992).

Development of Amblyopia and Loss of Stereopsis

Amblyopia is a loss of normal vision resulting from causes not attributable to changes in the eyeball, including the retina. Well-known causes include occlusion of one eye, early reduction in image clarity in one eye, and early esotropia. The underlying cause of the loss is generally attributed to the competition for synaptic space where neurons from the two eyes converge on single central neurons. More weakly excited neurons from one eye will suffer reduction in their effective synaptic connections relative to those of the other eye. The locus of interocular competition will be determined in part by the stage of binocularity in accord with our model. During the primitive stage binocular convergence first occurs in layer 4. To the extent that layer 4 contains only concentric on- and off-center cells (as does layer 4c in monkey), differences between the eyes in terms of edge orientation alone should not cause competition whereas non-correspondences in contrast, color, and luminance begin in the entry layer and should cause competition. In the mature stage, non-correspondence of retinal images of any sort, including that produced by strabismus (non-aligned eyes), should have no effect upon the neurons of layer 4 to the extent that these neurons are monocular. Where known, the effects of early deprivation and strabismus appear to be consistent with these predictions. Very early monocular occlusion appears to produce loss of acuity in the occluded eye, whereas strabismus appears to have little effect before the mature stage of binocularity.

It might be supposed that a lack of mature binocularity in the form of fusional capability is responsible for infantile strabismus. That conclusion is contraindicated by reports from several laboratories of evidence for stereopsis before the onset of infantile esotropia (reviewed in Held, 1992). Those findings do not, of course, argue against the possibility that esotropia of later onset might be caused by a lack of mature binocularity. They do strongly suggest that loss of binocularity results from habitual misalignment of the eyes.

Conclusion

I would like to conclude that our model has been useful in suggesting new tests, some carried out and some still to be done, and in accounting for previously unanticipated results. It does leave problematic the question, among others, of the abrupt appearance of mature binocularity in light of the slower process of segregation of ocular dominance columns. I am under no illusions as to the resemblance of the model to the underlying reality of the visual nervous system. The latter is inordinately more complex than is even hinted by the model.

REFERENCES

Archer, S. M. (in press) Detection and treatment of congenital esotropia. In K. Simons (ed.), *Infant Vision*.

Aslin, R. N. (1977) Development of binocular fixation in human infants. *Journal of Experimental Child Psychology*, 23, 133–50.

Baitch, L. W. and Srebro, R. (1990) Binocular interactions in sleeping and awake human infants. *Investigative Ophthalmology and Visual Science (Supplement)*, 31, 251.

Bauer, J., Shimojo, S., Gwiazda, J. and Held, R. (1986) Sex differences in the development of binocularity in human infants. *Investigative Ophthalmology and Visual Science (Supplement)*, 27, 265.

Benevento, L. A., Rezak, M. and Santos-Anderson, R. (1977) An autoradiographic study of the projections of the pretectum in the rhesus monkey (*Macaca mulatta*): evidence for sensorimotor links to the thalamus and oculomotor nuclei. *Brain Research*, 127, 197–218.

Birch, E. E. and Held, R. (1983) The development of binocular summation in human infants. *Investigative Ophthalmolgy and Visual Science*, 24, 1103.

Birch, E. E., Shimojo, S. and Held, R. (1985) Preferential looking assessment of fusion and steropsis in infants aged 1 to 6 months. *Investigative Ophthalmolgy and Visual Science*, 26, 366–70.

Birch, E. E. and Swanson, W. H. (1991) Probability summation of grating acuity in the human infant. *Investigative Ophthalmolgy and Visual Science (Supplement)*, 32, 964.

Braddick, O. and Atkinson, J. (1988). Sensory selectivity, attentional control, and cross-channel integration in early visual development. In A. Yonas (ed.), *Perceptual Development in Infancy*, vol. 20. Hillsdale, NJ: Lawrence Erlbaum Associates, 105–43.

Gwiazda, J., Bauer, J. and Held, R. (1989) Binocular function in human infants: correlation of stereoptic and fusion-rivalry discriminations. *Journal of Pediatric Ophthalmology and Strabismus*, 26, 128–32.

Held, R. (1988) Normal visual development and its deviations. In G. Lennerstrand, G. von Noorden and E. Campos (eds), *Strabismus and Amblyopia*, vol. 49. London: Macmillan Press, 247–57.

Held, R. (in press) Two stages in the development of binocular vision and eye alignment. In K. Simons (ed.), *Infant Vision*. New York: Oxford University Press.

Held, R., Shimojo, S. and Gwiazda, J. (1984) Gender differences in the early development of human visual resolution. *Investigative Ophthalmology and Visual Science (Supplement)*, 25, 220.

Kiorpes, L., Boothe, R. G., Carlson, M. R. and Alfi, D. (1985) Frequency of naturally occurring strabismus in monkeys. *Journal of Pediatric Ophthalmology and Strabismus*, 22, 60–4.

Le Vay, S., Wiesel, T. N. and Hubel, D. H. (1980) The development of ocular dominance columns in normal and visually deprived monkeys. *Journal of Comparative Neurology*, 191, 1–51.

Lewis, T. L., Maurer, D. and Brent, H. P. (1989) Optokinetic nystagmus in normal and visually deprived children:implications for cortical development. *Canadian Journal of Psychology*, 43, 121–40.

Nixon, R. B., Helveston, E. M., Miller, K., Archer, S. M. and Ellis, F. D. (1985) Incidence of strabismus in neonates. *American Journal of Ophthalmology*, 100, 798–801.

O'Dell, C. D., Quick, M. W. and Boothe, R. G. (1991) The development of stereoacuity in infant Rhesus monkeys. *Investigative Ophthalmolgy and Visual Science (Supplement)*, 32, 1044.

Shimojo, S., Bauer, J. A., O'Connell, K. M. and Held, R. (1986) Pre-stereoptic binocular vision in infants. *Vision Research*, 26, 501–10.

10

Cortical Maturation and the Development of Visual Attention in Early Infancy

MARK H. JOHNSON

Introduction

There are a number of possible approaches to studying the neural basis of cognition, including the use of neuroimaging techniques, lesion or drug studies in animals, and the study of brain damage in humans. An alternative to these approaches is to consider how the postnatal maturation of neural pathways and structures may mediate steps in normal cognitive development. This approach to studying the neural basis of cognition is not without difficulties, however, e.g. identifying changes in behavior appropriate for a particular brain region and defining the specific criteria for the maturation of a brain structure or pathway.

There are several ways to attempt to minimize these problems. First, although notable attempts have been made to relate physical changes indicating puberty to cognitive changes (e.g. Carey and Diamond, 1980), since most gross morphological changes in brain development occur within the first year of life, a cognitive neuroscience approach to development during infancy, rather than during childhood, would seem more feasible. Second, no single marker of neural maturation should be used in isolation. Ideally, rapid change in several neuroanatomical variables should be required. Third, arguments based on the *comparative* state of development of two or more neural systems will be strongest since they circumvent the difficulty of defining full functional maturation of an individual structure or pathway. Given these considerations, the differential development of the two visual pathways over the first few months of life should provide a promising area of study.

Reprinted from *Journal of Cognitive Neuroscience*, Vol. 2:2, 1990. Johnson: 'Cortical Maturation and the Development of Visual Attention in Early Infancy' by permission of the MIT Press, Cambridge, Massachusetts.

Bronson (1974, 1982) proposed that the newborn human infant "sees" primarily by means of the subcortical retinocollicular pathway and that only by around two or three months of age does the primary visual pathway become functional. The development of visually guided behavior can thus be viewed as shift from subcortical to cortical processing. The claim that the primary visual pathway is not functionally mature until around two or three months postnatal has been supported by a variety of electrophysiological, neuroanatomical, and behavioral studies (see later section). However, two main factors have led to criticism of Bronson's original proposals. First, more recent knowledge about the visual pathways of the mamalian brain has led to a reconsideration of the original two pathways account. It is now known that there are several cortical streams of processing held to have differing information-processing functions (e.g. Kaas, 1989; Van Essen, 1985). Thus, the original cortical–subcortical dichotomy for visual processing may be oversimplistic. Second, the striking psychological abilities of the very young infant in visual tasks have led many psychologists to question the validity of the "decorticate" newborn (e.g. Bushnell et al., 1989; Slater et al., 1988). As a result of this conflict some commentators have adopted the compromise position that there are "islands of cortical functioning" or partial cortical functioning in newborns (e.g. Maurer and Lewis, 1979; Posner and Rothbart, 1980; Atkinson, 1984; Atkinson et al., 1988). However, as yet this partial functioning has been poorly defined. Thus, in the light of recent evidence about the pathways underlying vision and oculomotor control it seems appropriate to re-evaluate Bronson's original enterprise. In the present paper a more specific hypothesis about the computational consequences of the developmental cortical neuroanatomy is put forward in an attempt to specify more precisely partial cortical functioning in newborns and its expansion over the first six months of life.

I will begin by describing proposals put forward by Schiller (1985) concerning the neuroanatomical pathways subserving oculomotor control in the adult primate. In subsequent sections these proposals will be used as a framework within which to relate observations of behavioral development with postnatal developmental neuroanatomy. It will be argued that the visually guided behavior of the infant at various stages can be accounted for in terms of the functioning or otherwise of particular pathways. Furthermore, which of the pathways is functional at a given age dependent on the maturational state within layers of the primary visual cortex. That is, the maturational state of the primary visual cortex is the limiting factor determining the presence or absence of these attentional systems.

The Functional Neuroanatomy of Overt Visual Attention

In reviewing the neuroanatomical pathways related to overt visual attention[1] a modified version of the model originally proposed for the adult by Schiller (1985) will be used as a basis (see figure 10.1A). The original model is based on extensive evidence from lesion and electrophysiological studies in nonhuman primates together with clinical evidence in humans. This evidence has been extensively reviewed elsewhere (e.g. Schiller, 1985; Harter and Aine, 1984; Robinson and Peterson, 1986) and only the main conclusions will be presented here.

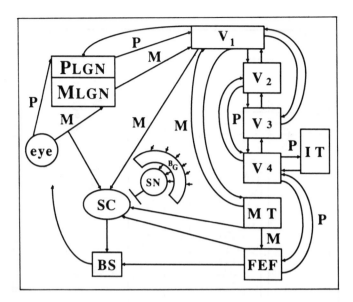

Figure 10.1A A schematic representation of the model proposed by Schiller (1985) for the neuroanatomical pathways thought to underlie oculomotor control in primates. LGN, lateral geniculate nucleus; SC, superior colliculus; SN, substantia nigra; BG, basal ganglia; BS, brainstem; FEF, frontal eye fields; MT, middle temporal area; VI, primary visual cortex; M, broad-band (magnocellular) stream; P, color opponent (parvocellular) stream. (Adapted, with permission, from Schiller, 1985.)

In line with other authors, Schiller points to a difference originating in the retina between a broad-band stream of processing and a color-opponent stream. The former responds transiently, has low spatial frequency resolution, lacks color opponency, and conducts at higher velocity. The latter has high spatial frequency resolution, is color selective, responds in a sustained fashion, and conducts at slower velocities (Gouras, 1969; Schiller and Malpali, 1977; Schiller et al., 1990). This difference corresponds to that between parvocellular and magnocellular streams (Van Essen, 1985; De Yoe and Van Essen, 1988). These two streams appear to remain segregated through several stages of visual processing and, to some extent, through the four pathways Schiller outlines for the control of eye movements. These pathways are as follows.

1 A pathway from the retina to the superior colliculus (SC). This pathway is fed mainly from the peripheral visual field, and the broad-band stream (Schiller et al., 1979). I will refer to this pathway subsequently as the *SC pathway*. Schiller proposes, as many had before him, that the SC pathway is involved in the generation of eye movements toward simple, easily discriminable stimuli. This system is thought to sacrifice accuracy for a quick, reflex-like response in the adult.

2 A broad-band cortical pathway. This system has two output pathways to influence the superior colliculus, one directly from V1 (primary visual cortex) and the other from V1 to MT (middle temporal area) and subsequently to the

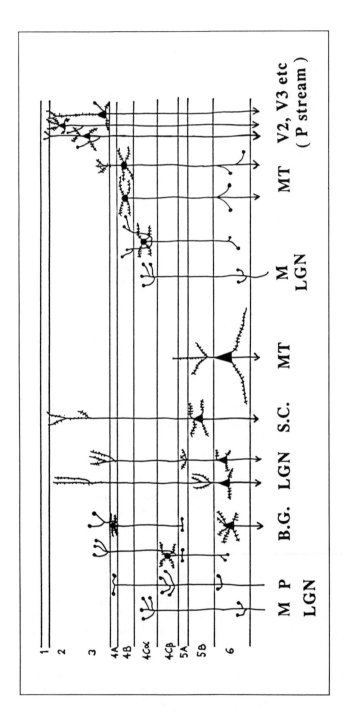

Figure 10.1B A schematic representation of primary visual cortex adapted from a diagram of the macaque visual cortex (Lund, 1981). Not all cell types or connections are shown.

SC. The latter pathway I will subsequently refer to as the *MT pathway*. The corticotectal projections are exclusively driven by the broad-band system (Hoffman and Sherman, 1974; Schiller et al., 1979). The superior colliculus then appears to be processing information primarily derived from the broad-band pathway.

3 A third pathway appears to converge broad-band and the color opponent streams in the frontal eye fields (FEF). The *FEF pathway*, as I shall subsequently refer to it, undertakes more detailed and complex analyses of visual information, · such as may be required for search strategies when viewing complex stimuli. Lesions to FEF appear to result in short-term deficits in visual search and in the temporal sequencing of eye movements within complex arrays (Butter, 1983; Newsome et al., 1985).

4 The final aspect of Schiller's model, and a fourth pathway for the control of visual attention, is that while all the cortical pathways discussed so far have an excitatory influence on the SC, there is also an inhibitory input to the colliculus from the substantia nigra (SN) (Hikosaka and Wurtz, 1983). Efferents from several cortical areas feed into the SN via the basal ganglia. Schiller suggests that this inhibitory input ensures that the activity of the SC can be regulated. I will refer to this pathway as the *inhibitory pathway*.

Now let us consider, in the light of evidence from both developmental neuroanatomy and behavior, which of these visual information processing pathways may be subserving behavior at different ages over the first six months.

The Postnatal Development of Visual Pathways

Some of the neural evidence in support of the idea that the development of visually guided behavior represents a shift from subcortical to cortical processing will now be briefly reviewed (for full reviews see Bronson, 1974; Atkinson, 1984). Since no single anatomical criterion for functional maturation has met with universal acceptance, I either discuss several such measures or adopt other authors' conclusions regarding functional maturation where they are based on several anatomical variables.

The Maturation of Subcortical Visual Structures

The retina: little anatomical information is available with regard to the structural development of the human retina due to its great delicacy and the difficulty in obtaining samples. However, a study of the retinal morphology of an eight-day-old infant (Abramov et al., 1982) confirmed the earlier suggestion that while the peripheral retina is relatively mature at birth, the macular region is still very immature. This observation led Abramov and his colleagues to suggest that neonatal visual acuity is mainly due to extrafoveal vision. Myelination of the optic nerve proceeds rapidly in the first four months of life, thereafter progressing less rapidly to reach adult levels at about two years of age.

The lateral geniculate: in the human this structure doubles in total volume between birth and six months (Huttenlocher et al., 1982). Although most cell types can be recognized at birth (de Courten and Garey, 1982), they differ from their mature forms by possessing many more spiny processes on the dendritic shafts and soma. Hairs and spines reach a maximum at about four months after birth, before reducing to adult numbers by nine months. During this time the cell body size increases although the total dendritic length decreases due to the more complex branching pattern at birth (Leuba and Garey, 1982).

The superior colliculus: by 24 weeks of gestation the adult pattern of lamination in the superior colliculus can be observed (Stampalija and Kostovic, 1981). In general, the retinocollicular visual pathway begins to myelinate about two months prenatally and the process is completed by about three months after birth. In contrast, the retinocortical pathway begins the process of myelinization only around the time of birth but is largely complete by about four months (Yakovlev and Lecours, 1967).

The Maturation of Visual Cortex

An assumption made in this paper is that the critical limiting "bottleneck" in the development of three of the four Schiller pathways is the maturational state of the primary visual cortex. There are two reasons for making this assumption. First, in humans, the vast majority of geniculate inputs to the cortex enter the primary visual cortex (Schiller, 1985). Second, although the maturational state of the primary visual cortex is generally thought to be in advance of many cortical association areas, it may not necessarily be in advance of the other visual cortical or subcortical areas to which it projects directly (see Conel, 1939–67).

As well as differential rates of maturation between major visual pathways, we should consider the possibility of differential maturation within the cortex. Anatomical studies suggest that, on the basis of several maturational criteria, the deeper layers of the cortex develop before the more superficial layers (Conel, 1939–67; Rabinowicz, 1979; Purpura, 1975). In particular, layer 5 maturing before layer 2 seems to be a very reliably observed sequence for many cortical regions in the human infant (Rabinowicz, 1979). The observation that cortical layers develop from deeper to more superficial layers is a critical one for the hypothesis put forward in this article.

Although the computational consequences of the characteristic elimination of synapses during postnatal development will not be discussed further in this paper (but see Johnson and Karmiloff-Smith, 1990), it is worth noting that this process occurs only after early infancy and shows little or no differential pattern between cortical layers (Huttenlocher and de Courten, 1987). In primary visual cortex spines become more numerous in the weeks following birth, reaching a peak at about four or five months, before declining to adult levels in the second year of life. A parallel rise and fall are found in synaptic density, which reaches a peak at eight months postnatal before declining to adult levels, 40 percent lower, by 11 years of age (Huttenlocher et al., 1982).

Electrophysiological Evidence

Many studies have been undertaken on visually evoked potentials (VEP) in young infants (see Atkinson, 1984; Vaughan and Kurtzberg, 1989, for reviews). In general, they show that components of the VEP thought to be related to the subcortex are present from birth, but only some components related to the striate cortex are present from around the time of birth. More specific components of cortical origin (fast high frequency wavelets) do not appear in infants under four weeks (Schanel-Klitsch and Siegfried, 1987). Further, responses to changes in the orientation of moving bars (thought to be cortically mediated) are not manifest until six weeks. The electrophysiological evidence thus gives general credance to the idea that cortical functioning develops over the first few months, and that some major changes occur in the second month of life. However, the evidence is also indicative of some limited cortical activity at birth.

The Development of Visual Attention and its Neural Basis: a Hypothesis

In this section I will go through the first six months of the human infant's life. At each of the ages specified the most notable characteristics of the visually guided behavior at that age will initially be described before discussion of the oculomotor pathways thought to underlie them. This will be followed by an account of how the maturational state of the primary visual cortex may enable the systems postulated to be operating and to function.

The Newborn

When in an alert and attentive state (Brazelton, 1973) the newborn responds to a wide variety of visual stimuli. Three aspects of the newborn's visually guided behavior are often noticed.

1 *Tracking of Slowly Moving Stimuli* This behavior is very easily elicited in newborns. However, the tracking is not smooth but "saccadic" in nature (McGinnis, 1930; Dayton et al., 1964; Barten et al., 1971). Where brief components of smooth tracking have been observed they are probably mediated by peripheral visual areas (see Aslin, 1981). Figure 10.2 illustrates the typical saccadic following of a moving stimulus in a five week old. The saccades tend to be of fixed size inversely related to the velocity of the moving target. The fixed size of the saccades does not appear to be a limitation of the motor system since young infants are capable of making eye movements of greater magnitude (Aslin, 1981). Furthermore, the eye movements always follow behind the movement of the stimulus. That is, they are "pursuit" rather than "anticipatory" in nature. Unlike older infants and adults, newborns' eye movements rarely appear to anticipate the future location of the stimulus.[2]

2 *Preferential Orienting toward Temporal Visual Field* Newborns will much more readily orient toward stimuli presented in the temporal visual field than in the nasal visual field. For example, Lewis et al. (1979) showed infants a line 3.3° wide located at 30° in the temporal field and at 20° in the nasal field under monocular viewing conditions. Although two month olds oriented toward the line at either location more often than they oriented in the same direction on blank control trials, newborns and one month olds oriented toward the line only in the temporal field. However, newborns are influenced by the presence of a central

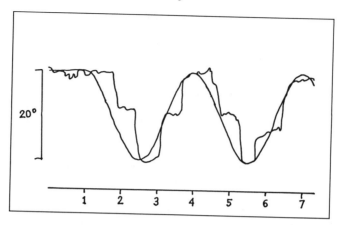

Figure 10.2 The visual following of a moving target by a typical five week old. The smooth line indicates the movement of the target while the other line indicates the movement of the eyes while attempting to track the stimulus. (Adapted from Aslin (1981) with permission.)

stimulus in detecting a peripheral one, an observation that suggests that foveal vision has some role (Haith and Campos, 1977). Even in adults temporal visual field input has more direct access to systems controlling exogenously produced eye movements than does nasal visual field input (Posner, 1980).

3 *The "Externality Effect"* Young infants do not appear to attend to small stationary pattern elements within a larger frame or pattern, a phenomenon known as the "externality effect" (Salapatek, 1975; Milewski, 1976; Maurer, 1983). Since the internal pattern elements are chosen to be above infant acuity values and may be discriminable when presented in isolation, spatial vision in isolation cannot account for the effect (Aslin and Smith, 1988). However, manipulating the internal elements by movement or increasing contour density may overcome the effect (Bushnell, 1979; Garon and Swartz, 1980). Although attempts have been made to account for the externality effect in terms of the linear systems model of infant preference (Banks and Salapatek, 1981; Banks and Ginsburg, 1985; Aslin and Smith, 1988), separate accounts of the first two characteristics of newborn visual behavior (saccadic pursuit tracking and preferential orienting) would then still be required. An alternative approach can accommodate facts from all three phenomena reviewed here.

As mentioned earlier, the peripheral retina and midbrain appear to be close to fully mature around the time of birth (Abramov et al., 1982; Atkinson, 1984; Bronson, 1974). Further, it is claimed that localization of targets in the peripheral visual field can be mediated by subcortical circuits in adult humans with cortical damage (Weiskrantz, 1986). Thus, any overall account of the control of visual attention in newborns may be based primarily on the capacities of subcortical structures such as the superior colliculus. Posner and Rothbart (1980) describe such a mechanism capable of bringing the fovea to areas of importance in the visual field as follows:

powerful links between the peripheral visual field of each eye and midbrain structures subserving eye movements of the opposite side . . . [ensure that] . . . temporal visual stimuli to the left eye operate via the right midbrain to move the conjugate eye movement system, so that both foveae become aligned with the visual stimulation (Arbib, 1972; Posner and Cohen, 1980). Powerful inhibitory connections between the two sides allow each eye to control the conjugate saccadic movements of both eyes. Thus, evolution has designed a system in which each eye can operate more or less independently on its own temporal field input to drive the whole system. (Posner and Rothbart, 1980, pp. 8–9)

In my view, the operation of such a (collicular) mechanism could account for a number of the phenomena just described in the following way. Tracking would be saccadic since while the object was in the central visual field it would not engage the eye control mechanism. Only when the object passed into the temporal field of one or the other eye would the mechanism described operate to refoveate the stimulus. If the object continues to move, then further saccades would be initiated. The saccadic tracking of a moving object by such a system would necessarily involve pursuit. No calculation of the future location of a moving object is computed. Furthermore, the operation of such a mechanism may account for the inverse relationship between saccade size and target velocity mentioned earlier since the greater the velocity of the object, the quicker it will enter the temporal field and reinitiate a saccade. The relative ease of detection of stimuli in the temporal field is obviously easily accounted for in similar terms by this mechanism.

What about the "externality effect"? Although a (collicular) mechanism similar to that outlined above could account for infants attempting to foveate the largest frame or pattern elements in a stimulus array, it does not in itself provide an account of the "rules" for foveation.[3] That is, given a stimulus array composed of particular elements sufficiently far apart, the mechanism gives an account only of why eye movements should oscillate between the most visible elements of that array. For example, an infant might foveate only regions of the high contrast frame of a stimulus and not the detailed pattern contained within. The (collicular) mechanism in isolation does not give an account of why one particular stimulus element, or pattern of stimulus elements, should be preferred over another.

The linear systems (LSM) approach[4] to predicting infant stimulus preferences proposes that the visual system "filters" the visual stimulus through a contrast sensitivity function appropriate for that particular age. Up to about three months of age versions of this model can predict certain infant pattern preferences involving paired presentations of high contrast geometric patterns with a correlation of 0.96 (Banks and Ginsburg, 1985). After this age the model may become less successful (Aslin and Smith, 1988).

There are two reasons to believe that the LSM model is a reflection of the functioning of the SC pathway. First, the model declines in its predictive effectiveness around the same age as indicators of cortical maturity (see subsequent sections). Second, the model has difficulty predicting preferences in testing situations in which only a single stimulus is presented at any one time (Slater and Morison, 1985). If two stimuli are presented simultaneously, the viewing conditions are likely to be such that part or all of both stimuli fall on the temporal visual field of the infant. Thus, although the (collicular) mechanism

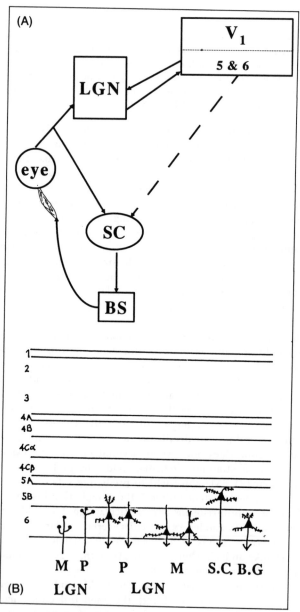

Figure 10.3 (A) The neuroanatomical pathways underlying oculomotor control hypothesized to be functional in the newborn. For abbreviations see legend to figure 10.1A. (B) A schematic representation of the maturational state of the primary visual cortex around the time of birth. The neurons shown are those thought, by a variety of maturational criteria, to be capable of supporting normal functioning. Cells in upper layers are present but may not be capable of supporting organized activity.

outlined by Posner and Rothbart can be extended to account for the scanning patterns and saccadic eye movements of the newborn, the LSM model may be required to account for the overall pattern preferences. Both may reflect the functioning of the SC pathway.

Evidence was presented in earlier sections that the primary visual pathway is developmentally immature at birth. Further evidence was advanced showing that the visually guided behavior of the newborn is mainly controlled by collicular pathways. However, there is also considerable data suggesting that information from the eye enters cortical pathways even in newborns. How are we to reconcile these observations and move beyond the much criticized cortical versus subcortical dichotomy in infancy? Examination of the development of the internal cytoarchitectonics of the primary visual cortex may shed some light on the matter.

Although thalamic afferents to layers 4a and 4c may be in place around three weeks before birth in macaques (Rakic, 1976, 1983), Conel (1939–67) found that in the human the majority of afferents entering the newborn primary visual cortex terminate in layers 5 and 6, rather than at their mature termination sites in layer 4. Whether these immature projections form synaptic contacts is, as yet, unclear. However, I will proceed with the assumption that transient synaptic contacts are made in the termination layer of thalamic afferents during postnatal development (see also Purpura, 1975). This assumption seems reasonable in view of the evidence for transient synaptic contacts from thalamic afferents being established in "inappropriate" cortical layers during development in other primates (Rakic, 1976, 1983).

Proceeding with the assumption that there is geniculate input to the deepest layers of primary visual cortex at, or shortly after birth, what computational consequences result? Taking a number of different criteria of maturation, in all cortical areas large pyramidals in layer 5 show most rapid development (Conel, 1939–67; Rabinowicz, 1979). Shortly after birth axons of these cells begin to myelinate (Conel, 1939–67). These layer 5 pyramidals project to subcortical structures such as the superior colliculus and pulvinar (see figure 10.3A) and their activation may provide some minimal cortical influence over the activity of the colliculus at birth. Pyramidal cells in the upper and lower parts of layer 6 project to the magnocellular and parvocellular layers of the lateral geniculate nucleus, respectively. These cells may provide the feedback thought to be essential for the developmental "fine-tuning" in the lateral geniculate. Normally, at least for early visual areas, feedforward cortico–cortico projections from cortical areas leave from pyramidals in layers 2 and 3 (Rockland and Pandya, 1979; Maunsell and Van Essen, 1983). These layers of the cortex are without thalamic afferent innervation and comparatively undeveloped in the newborn infant (Conel, 1939–67), suggesting that feedforward mechanisms in early visual cortical processing are not functioning at this age. In primary visual cortex there is one exception to the normal pattern of feedforward projection. At least in the macaque, large pyramidals in layer 6 project to area MT (for review see Lund, 1981). However, it is unlikely that this projection plays a significant role in information processing in the newborn since (a) the maturational state of area MT will not be in advance of that in V1, and (b) the main input to these layer 6 pyramidal cells may be from spiny neurones in layer 4b (which, in turn, may not be functionally mature until around two months of age).

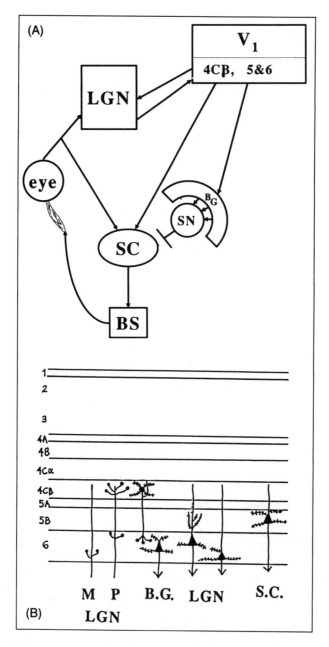

Figure 10.4 (A) The neuroanatomical pathways underlying oculomotor control hypothesized to be functional in the one month old. For abbreviations see legend to figure 10.1A. (B) A schematic representation of the maturational state of the primary visual cortex in the one month old infant. See legend to figure 10.3B for further details.

In general, therefore, the functional cortical activity of the newborn may be confined to layers 5 and 6 and mainly serves the purpose of regulatory feedback to the still maturing lateral geniculate. As mentioned in the section on the visually guided behavior of the newborn, most of the characteristics can be accounted for in terms of a fully functioning collicular system. Later I will discuss how some apparently sophisticated perceptual abilities in the newborn relating to face recognition can be accounted for without recourse to full cortical functioning.

The One Month Old

Stechlar and Latz (1966) coined the phrase "obligatory attention" for the periods of very prolonged fixation of a stimulus (sometimes more than 30 min), which can be observed in infants around the first month of life. Often the fixation is terminated by great distress. Similar phenomena have been described in infants four to eight weeks old by Tennes et al. (1972), who reported that at around this age they often seem "compelled" to look at a target, and by Slater (1988), who reports that one month old infants take much longer to habituate to a simple visual form even than newborns. These and other observations suggest that infants of around one month may be unable to disengage their gaze from a stimulus easily. This impression is supported by results suggesting that, under certain conditions, the extent of the infants' measurable visual field may actually decline between birth and one month of age (Schwartz et al., 1987), before expanding again by two months (Mohn and van Hof-van Duin, 1986; Schwartz et al., 1987).

Under monocular viewing conditions, one month olds, like newborns, will orient toward targets only if presented in the temporal visual field. In contrast, two month olds, like adults, are more sensitive to targets at 20° in the nasal visual field than at 30° in the temporal field (Lewis, 1979; Lewis et al., 1985). Tracking behavior at one month is similar to that described for newborns (Aslin, 1981) and the "externality effect" remains present.

Figure 10.4B indicates the supposed maturational state of the primary visual cortex in infants around one month. In the human infant around one month of age layer 4 follows layers 5 and 6 in maturation. A few afferent fibers reach the lower parts of layer 4 (4cβ) at this age (Conel, 1939–67) and the exogenous fibres are more developed than the others. Layers 2 and 3 and upper layer 4 still remain comparatively undeveloped by a variety of maturational criteria (Conel, 1939–67; Rabinowicz, 1979). What might be the computational consequence of the afferentation and development of lower layer 4 (4cβ)? Spiny stellate neurons in layer 4cβ are strongly innervated by parvocellular input from the LGN. Indeed, layer 4cβ is the primary target of parvocellular afferents from the LGN. These spiny stellates project mainly to layer 3 but also to upper layer 6. Which of the four pathways involved in the control of overt visual attention would be influenced by this development? The MT pathway requires the adequate functioning of spiny neurons in layer 4b, and also would require the LGN magnocellular innervation of layer 4cα. Due to the less advanced maturational state of upper layer 4, this pathway may be only weakly activated around one month of age. Similarly, the parvocellular pathway to FEF is unlikely to be functional since it requires the adequate maturation of layers 2 and 3. However, the development of layer 4cβ may allow a pathway from the parvocellular input to cells in the deeper layers that project the basal ganglia and the inhibitory pathway to the colliculus (figure 10.4B). I propose that the function of this pathway is to inhibit orienting toward peripheral stimuli and its development may account for the "obligatory attention" characteristic of infants around one month old. That is, stimuli in the peripheral visual field that trigger orienting in the newborn no longer do so at one month due to the increased inhibition of collicular activity.

The Two Month Old

Two changes in visually guided behavior relative to younger infants are notable around this age.

Onset of Smooth Pursuit Tracking   Smooth pursuit is not thought to be present prior to the sixth postnatal week, at least with small targets moving at low velocities. Segments of smooth pursuit start to become interspersed with saccadic tracking between six and eight weeks postnatal (McGinnis, 1930; Aslin and Salapatek, 1975). Initially the accuracy of these short periods of smooth tracking is poor and always lags behind the movement of the stimulus. Figure 10.5 shows a typical following trace from an eight week old. Saccadic following is interspersed with brief periods of smooth tracking, although the tracking still lags behind the stimulus movement.

Unlike in the adult, in the infant saccades tend to be of similar size. Aslin (1981) suggests that if only the direction and not the angular distance of a peripheral target is available to the saccadic programming system this will result in a particular saccadic step size being reapplied until the target is foveated.[5] This proposal raises the further possibility that smooth pursuit emerges devel-

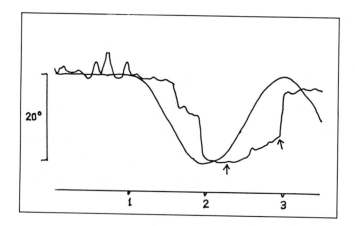

Figure 10.5   The visual following of a moving target by an eight week old. The smooth line indicates the movement of the target while the other line represents the movements of the eyes while attempting to follow it. The arrows indicate the period for which some smooth tracking occurred. See text for further details. (Adapted from Aslin (1981).)

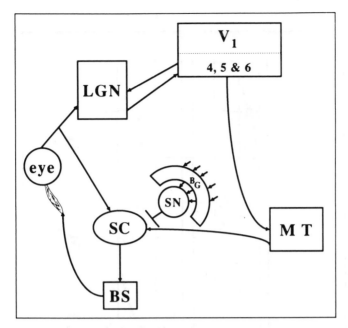

Figure 10.6A The neuroanatomical pathways underlying oculomotor control thought to be functional in the two month old. For abbreviations see legend to figure 10.1A.

opmentally from a steady reduction in the size of saccades. However, Aslin (1981) provides evidence that this is not the case. That is, the control mechanisms for smooth tracking appear to be largely independent of those for saccadic movements.

Onset of Attention toward Internal Features of Patterns and the Ability to Detect Stimuli in the Nasal Visual Field   Lewis et al. (1985) investigated the ability of one and two month old infants to detect single lines of varying width in the temporal and nasal visual fields. For one month olds to detect a line it needed to be at least eight times wider in the nasal visual field than in the temporal field. By contrast, two month olds detected thinner lines in the nasal visual field than in the temporal field. These age differences appear to be due exclusively to improvement in sensitivity in the nasal visual field.

Since Conel's analysis of the postnatal growth of the human cortex goes from one to three months, the details of the neural development between one and two months are a matter for speculation. However, on the basis of several maturational criteria, Conel considers that by three months layers 4, 5, and 6 may be capable of supporting activity, whereas layer 2 is not. It thus seems plausible to suggest that during the second and third month of life the rest of layer 4 becomes functionally mature (figure 10.6B). This would have the consequence that the layer 4cα interneurons that connect magnocellular afferents from the LGN with neurons projecting to MT from layers 4B and 6 are functionally mature. This, in turn, would provide a "cortical" pathway to MT and may allow functioning of the third of the proposed pathways for visual attention, the MT pathway.

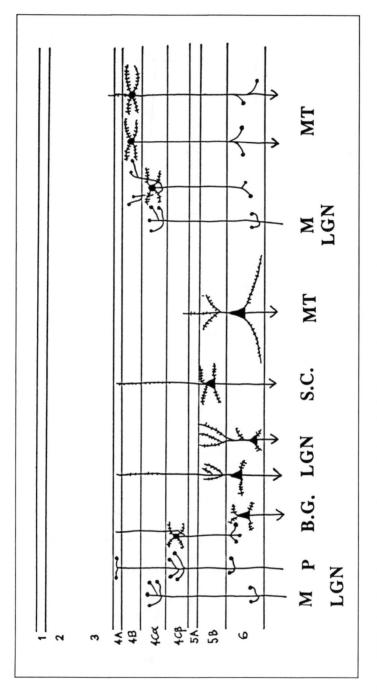

Figure 10.6B A schematic representation of the hypothesized maturational state of the primary visual cortex in the two month old infant. See figure 10.3B for further details.

With these developments in mind the two aspects of change in the visually guided behavior of 2 month olds mentioned earlier can be accounted for in the following way. As mentioned earlier, the MT pathway is thought to be crucially involved in smooth pursuit tracking, so its development at this age would give rise to the onset of nonsaccadic pursuit. The onset of attention toward internal features of patterns and the ability to detect stimuli in the nasal visual field can be accounted for because the cortex, which is mainly receiving input from the central visual field, now has greater control over eye movements. That is, information in the central visual field is now not only processed, but also influences motor output. The externality effect, a product of the earlier lack of sensitivity to the central visual field, begins to decline around this age.

Three to Six Month Olds

Figure 10.7 shows a typical tracking record from a 12 week old. From this age the smooth pursuit gain is often greater than 1.0. That is, the tracking moves faster than the stimulus, "anticipating" its future location. This suggests the functioning of a mechanism capable of computing the trajectory of a moving object. This conclusion is supported by the observation that tracking error is reduced following multiple exposures to the same oscillation of a target (Aslin, 1981). Like in adults, in three month olds saccadic eye movements are required only when the peak velocity of a target exceeds maximum smooth pursuit velocity.

Further evidence for the ability to make anticipatory eye movements at around this age comes from a study by Haith et al. (1988) with 3.5 month old infants. Infants viewed one of two series of slides that appeared on the right- or left-hand side of the infant either alternating with regular interstimulus intervals (ISI) or with an irregular alternation pattern and ISI. The regular ISI series generated more stimulus anticipations and fast reaction times than did the irregular series.

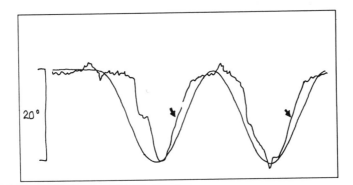

Figure 10.7 The visual following of a moving target by a three month old. The smooth line indicates the movements of the target, while the other line indicates the eye movements. The arrow indicates areas of smooth pursuit with gain greater than 1.0. At these two points the movement of the eye "anticipates" the future location of the object. (After Aslin (1981) with permission.)

The authors argue that their evidence demonstrates that infants of this age can develop expectancies for noncontrollable spatiotemporal events. Robinson et al. (1988) report that they were unable to obtain these effects as strongly in infants of six or nine weeks of age.

Several more "cognitive" factors associated with the input begin to influence looking behavior after three months. For example, using habituation techniques with three and four month olds, Spelke and her collaborators (e.g. Spelke 1988) have domonstrated infants' ability to utilize the perceptual properties of objects (e.g. cohesion, boundaries, substance, and spatiotemporal continuity). Similarly, Leslie and Keeble (1987) have provided evidence that by six months infants can perceive a specifically causal relationship between two moving objects.

Turning to the developmental neuroanatomy, between three and six months Conel reports rapid maturation of layers 2 and 3, although layer 2 may take still longer to fully mature. I propose that the maturation of these layers allows the functioning of the parvocellular pathway via V2, V3, and the frontal eye fields (figure 10.1A). As discussed earlier, the functioning of the FEF pathway may allow the onset of anticipatory eye movements in tracking and the sequencing of scanning patterns within particular objects. Note also that this pathway is interconnected with the temporal lobe pathway, a pathway associated with the identification of objects (Mishkin and Appenzeller, 1987). This latter connectivity may allow pattern and object specifications along the temporal lobe pathway to influence looking sequences and to control scanning patterns for particular classes of object. Further, it may be related to the onset of the ability to identify the properties of objects investigated by Spelke, Leslie, and others.

Held (1985) has argued that the end of the fourth month is a transition point in the development of various aspects of binocular function such as optokinetic nystagmus and steropsis. The neural basis of this development is argued, on evidence from the cat and monkey, to be due to the segregation of occular dominance columns in layer 4c. Prior to this age the geniculocortical afferents from the two eyes are mixed so that they synapse on common neurons within this layer. The output from these segregated cells converges on disparity selective cells, the latter being located probably in layer 3. Held (1985) has proposed that the limitation in the immature cortex is due to the lack of segregation of the inputs from the two eyes. Although this may be the case, the evidence discussed in the present paper suggests that the maturity of layer 3 cells may also be a limiting factor. Whatever the exact neural basis of the computational limitation, the timing of the emergence of binocularity corresponds well with the maturation of the middle cortical layers of visual cortex.

To summarize the argument so far: by around the middle of the first year of life the human infant possesses the four pathways involved in the control of overt visual attention in the adult. These four pathways mature at different ages. This differential maturation can:

1 be accounted for in terms of the maturation of layers in the primary visual cortex; and
2 account for changes in visually guided behaviors in the infant over the first six months.

Table 10.1

Age	Functional anatomy	Behaviour
Newborn	SC Pathway, + layer 5 and 6 pyramidal output to LGN and SC	Saccadic pursuit tracking Preferential orienting to temporal visual field "Externality effect"
One month	As above + inhibitory pathway to SC via BG	As above + "obligatory attention"
Two months	As above + MT (magnocellular) pathway to SC	Onset of smooth pursuit tracking and increased sensitivity to nasal visual field
Three months and over	As above + FEF (parvocellular) pathway to SC and BS	Increase in "anticipatory" tracking and sequential scanning patterns

Briefly, I have proposed that the newborn has a functioning SC pathway and that changes in behavior around one month can be accounted for in terms of the maturation of the inhibitory pathway from cortex to SC. Following further maturation of primary visual cortex layer 4 around two months of age, I have argued that the cortical pathway via MT becomes functional. Maturation of layers 2 and 3 allows functioning of the fourth pathway via the FEF, and results in the onset of anticipatory eye movements in tracking and the sequencing of scanning patterns for particular objects. See table 10.1 for an outline of these changes.

The Development of Attention Toward Face-like Stimuli

It has been argued that the visual preference behavior of newborn infants can be accounted for mainly by the functioning of the SC pathway. How then are we to account for evidence of apparently sophisticated perceptual processing in the newborn infant. For example, Goren et al. (1975) claimed that newborn infants (around 10 min after birth) will track a slowly moving face-like pattern further than they will various patterns with "scrambled" face features. Although this finding was initially regarded as controversal, it has recently been replicated twice under more rigorous conditions (Johnson et al., 1990b). How are we to reconcile this evidence for seemingly sophisticated visual cognition with the maturational state of the newborn's cortex?

A number of observations suggest that the preferential tracking of face-like patterns may be primarily mediated by the SC pathway.

1 The preferential tracking of face-like patterns appears to decline in the second month of life (Johnson et al., 1990b). Several newborn sensorimotor behaviors appear to decline around this age, possibly due to inhibition by developing cortical circuits (e.g., Muir et al., 1989; Johnson, 1990).

2 The lateralization effects found in adult face processing, and thought to be characteristic of cortical functioning, are not present in early infancy (DeSchonen and Mathivet, 1989).

3 The face preference is found in newborns with tasks where the infant is required to track a moving stimulus, but not until around two months of age when using habituation or infant-control preference procedures (Maurer and Barrera, 1981; Johnson et al., 1990a). Why should the tracking task be so sensitive to newborns' preferences whereas the standard testing to procedures with static stimuli are ineffective? As discussed earlier, tracking behavior in the newborn infant can be accounted for by functioning in the collicular pathway. It was argued that it is the movement of the stimulus out of the central visual field that initiates a saccade. This consistent movement toward the periphery would not necessarily arise with static presentations. Therefore, it may be that tracking tasks access information present in the collicular pathway better than do other preference testing techniques. This proposal implies that some information about the structure or characteristics of faces is contained within the SC pathway. This would not be surprising in view of the other complex information-processing functions that this structure is known to subserve (e.g. Stein and Gordon, 1981).

What about the emergence of face preferences around two months of age using habituation and other testing techniques? It will be argued in the next section that habituation is a product of cortical activity. Consequently, the re-emergence of face-specific preference at this time may reflect the adequate maturation of cortical circuits supporting attention within the central visual field (see also Johnson and Morton, 1990).

Habituation, and the Relation to Other Models of Visual Preference

In the discussion so far the phenomenon of habituation, the gradual decline of length of gaze at a repeatedly presented stimulus, has been mentioned only breifly. The issue of the neural and information-processing basis of habituation in early infancy is a controversial one. Until the past few years it was commonly thought that habituation could not be obtained in infants until they were several months old. Recently, it has been established that this is not the case. Habituation can be reliably demonstrated even in newborns (Slater et al., 1982; Cohen, 1988). Furthermore, even shortly after birth the locus of habituation is "central" rather than "peripheral." For example, experiments by Slater et al. (1983) in which newborns were habituated to a stimulus with one eye and subsequent novelty preference was investigated with the other eye established that adaptation at the retinal level can be ruled out. There is still considerable debate about the extent to which habituation requires information processing rather than selective sensory adaptation, and whether its locus is at the collicular or cortical level (see Dannemillar and Banks, 1983; Slater and Morrison, 1985). In an earlier section it was argued that the linear systems model is indicative of subcortical activity.[6] How might this be related to habituation over the first few months of life?

Slater et al. (1985) obtained results suggesting that natural preferences based on infants' peak contrast sensitivity cannot be changed by habituating infants either to the preferred or nonpreferred member of a stimulus pair. However, where no prior spontaneous preference exists between two discriminable stimuli, strong novelty preferences can be obtained following repeated exposures. Further evidence for a degree of independence between the predicted preference of the linear systems model and habituation was provided in a study by Aposhyan et al. (1988). These authors established that while spatial frequency models are fairly accurate in predicting initial and overall fixation time to a stimulus by two month old infants, the models do not predict the habituation component, i.e. the slope of the decline in gaze lengths.

There is, then, evidence that the mechanisms underlying habituation in the newborn are not the same as those argued to be mediated by the collicular circuit. I therefore propose that habituation in the newborn is mediated via the weakly functioning inhibitory pathway to SC. By one month this pathway is more developed and strongly inhibits collicular activity, resulting in the inhibition of the specific preferential tracking of faces and the general difficulty in disengaging from a stimulus. As an infant grows past one month of age, the looking times in a habituation paradigm decrease (Cohen, 1988). Arguably this is due to the increasing excitatory control over the superior colliculus and brainstem by the cortical attentional pathways via MT and FEF.[7]

Within the overall framework put forward in this paper, let me take the example of a two month old infant and consider what internal processes will result from exposure to a static, repeatedly presented, visual pattern.

1   Assuming that the pattern is visible, the collicular pathway will ensure head and eye movements to foveate the pattern. If more than one pattern is present, which pattern is attended to would be determined by their relative spatial frequencies.

2   Once within the nasal visual field, visual information about the pattern will enter the primary visual cortex and "activate" both the MT and inhibitory feedback pathways.

3   Diffuse cortical activation of the SN inhibitory feedback pathway ensures that the SC system is inhibited, "locking" gaze to the foveated pattern.

4   This activation decreases with time, while the inputs from stimuli in the peripheral visual field continue.

5   Eventually, stimulation from the peripheral field exceeds the waning inhibition of SC by the SN inhibitory pathway, and head/eye movements toward one of these patterns will ensue, i.e., the infant will "disengage" from the initial pattern and shift fixation to another.

6   On representation of the same static pattern (such as during a habituation experiment) step (1) will ensure refoveation and the subsequent sequence of events will take place as previously. At each exposure, however, the inhibitory feedback pathway will be activated less and consequently the stimulation from the peripheral field will exceed the waning inhibition of the SC sooner.

Comparison with the Bronson Theory

The theory put forward in this paper shares its general aims with that put forward by Bronson (1974). Both theories attempt to address the issue of how postnatal cortical maturation influences the development of visually guided behaviour. However, aside from the incorporation of more recent evidence from both neuroscience and infant psychology, my account concentrates more on the control of behavior (eye movements) than on the input pathways. This change in emphasis allows an interesting possibility, namely that the infant can be processing a level of complexity of information that it cannot act on. For example, with regard to face recognition, although information about the detailed characteristics of faces may be entering particular cortical circuits in the newborn, this may not be evident from the infant's behavior. That is, such information may influence the development of certain cortical circuits, but these cortical circuits do not have access to motor output until weeks or months later.

The present analysis also differs from that of Bronson in that it speculatively attempts to incorporate evidence relating to the maturation of cortical layers, and in that it moves beyond a simple subcortical/cortical dichotomy to discussing the role of four pathways, three of which have both cortical and subcortical components. This results in a clearer notion of what partial cortical functioning in early infancy might imply. A final area in which the current analysis departs from the earlier Bronson attempt is with regard to the nature of inborn biases in the visually guided behavior of the newborn infant. Although Bronson believed the newborn to possess no ability for discriminating the configurational attributes of a pattern, this has now been shown not to be the case, especially with regard to face-like patterns.

Relation to Covert Attention

The analysis presented in this paper has been confined to overt visual attention, i.e. involving eye movements. In adults overt visual attention has been demonstrated to be dissociable from covert (internal) attentional processes (Posner, 1980). While covert attention in infancy has not been extensively studied, Posner and Rothbart (1990) make the intriguing suggestion that the onset of the ability of the infant to make anticipatory eye movements may coincide with the development of covert attention. Prior to this stage the overt (eye movement) system is incapable of "marking" the future location of a stimulus. Once a covert attentional "spotlight" has developed this can mark a particular point as the target for overt saccades, allowing the magnitude and direction of a saccade to be programmed in advance.

Maturation or Learning?

A confusion often arises in the developmental literature between the explanatory level (psychological or neural) and the extent to which it is open to influence by experiential factors. For example, if a particular cognitive change is correlated with a particular neural development it is sometimes assumed that no experiential factors are involved. However, since at least some characteristics of cortical structure may be entirely a product of activity-dependent competition (e.g. Miller et al., 1989), this assumption is not necessarily valid. Therefore, although it is clear that a change in cognitive capacity may be attributable to the adequate development of a neural pathway or structure, this need not necessarily imply a rigid or inflexible maturational timetable. Consequently, the ages given in this paper should be treated as approximate and are likely to vary to some extent between individuals. However, the explicit (and testable) claims that are being made include the following.

1   Both the behavioral and neural events will unfold in the general sequence described for any individual infant.

2   The neural events described will precede or coincide with the associated behavioral change.

3   The main limitation on the developmental sequence described is the maturational state of the primary visual cortex. This assumption, while speculative, seems reasonable since in the human the LGN projections terminate almost exclusively in the striate cortex, which thereby forms the major gateway for visual information to the rest of the cortex (Schiller, 1985). Thus, the argument presented here is one of limitations on systems. The functioning of three information-processing systems is constrained by the maturational state of one structure.

NOTES

1   This article is largely confined to the discussion of overt attention, i.e. attentional shifts involving eye and head movements.

2   Evidence discussed in this article mainly pertains to eye movements. Even in the very young infant eye and head movements appear to be coordinated (Regal et al., 1983).

3   Note that from estimates of the extent of newborns' nasal visual field it should be possible to generate testable predictions about the retinal size of visible stimuli that will yield the externality effect (see also Bronson, 1974).

4   Fourier transform analysis of two-dimensional stimuli yields two components: the *amplitude spectrum*, comprising the amplitude and orientation of the component spatial frequencies, and the *phase spectrum*, comprised of the phases and orientation of the components. The LSM holds that newborns' pattern preferences are influenced only by the amplitude spectrum.

5   Posner and Rothbart (1990) discuss evidence from studies of the "inhibition of return" phenomenon in infants suggesting that they may be unable to program the magnitude of saccades over the first few months of life.

6   It has been argued that the preferential attention toward faces in newborns, although possibly also mediated by the SC circuit, is unrelated to preferences elicited by the LSM (Morton et al., 1990).

7   Recent evidence indicates that infants' difficulty in disengaging from a stimulus may persist until 3 months of age (Johnson et al., 1990c).

ACKNOWLEDGMENTS

I have benefited from presenting and discussing portions of this text at MRC Cognitive Development Unit internal seminars, University of Oregon cognitive seminars, and the Chateau de Rosay workshop on Sensory Motor Development in Infancy. In particular, I wish to thank Martyn Bracewell, Jeri Janowsky, Annette Karmiloff-Smith, Jean Mandler, John Morton, Mike Posner, and Mary Rothbart for their comments on earlier drafts. Financial support from the MRC (UK) and McDonnell Foundation is gratefully acknowledged.

REFERENCES

Abramov, I., Gordon, J., Hendrickson, A., Hainline, L., Dobson, V., & Laboussier, E. (1982). The retina of the newborn human infant. *Science*, 217, 265–267.

Aposhyan, H. M., Kaplan, P. S., Peterzell, D. H., Werner, J. S. (1988). Spatial frequency analysis and infant habituation. *Infant Behavior Development*, 11, 145–157.

Arbib, M. A. (1972). *The Metaphorical Brain*. New York: Wiley.

Aslin, R. N. (1981). Development of smooth pursuit in human infants. In D. F. Fisher, R. A. Monty, & J. W. Senders (eds), *Eye Movements: Cognition and Visual Perception*, Hillsdale, NJ: Lawrence Erlbaum, 31–51.

Aslin, R. N. & Salapatek, P. (1975). Saccadic localization of visual targets by the very young human infant. *Perception and Psychophysics*, 17, 293–302.

Aslin, R. N. & Smith, L. B. (1988). Perceptual development. *Annual Review of Psychology*, 39, 435–473.

Atkinson, J. (1984). Human visual development over the first six months of life: A review and a hypothesis. *Human Neurobiology* 3, 61–74.

Atkinson, J., Hood, B., Wattam-Bell, J., Anker, S., & Tricklebank, J. (1988). Development of orientation discrimination in infants. *Perception*, 17, 587–595.

Banks, M. S. & Ginsburg, A. P. (1985). Early visual preferences: a review and new theoretical treatment. In H. W. Reese (ed.), *Advances in Child Development and Behavior*. New York: Academic Press.

Banks, M. S. & Salapatek, P. (1981). Infant pattern vision; a new approach based on the contrast sensitivity function. *Journal of Experimental Child Psychology*, 31, 1–45.

Barten, S., Birns, B., & Ronch, J. (1971). Individual differences in the visual pursuit behavior of neonates. *Child Development*, 42, 313–319.

Braddick, O. J., Wattam-Bell, J. and Atkinson, J. (1986). Orientation-specific cortical responses develop in early infancy. *Nature*, 320, 617–619.

Brazelton, T. B. (1973). Neonatal Behavioral Assessment Scale. *Clinics in Development Medicine*, No. 50. London: Heinemann.

Bronson, G. W. (1974). The postnatal growth of visual capacity. *Child Development*, 45, 873–890.

Bronson, G. W. (1982). Structure, status and characteristics of the nervous system at birth. In P. Stratton (ed.), *Psychobiology of the Human Newborn*. Chichester: Wiley.

Bushnell, I. W. R. (1979). Modification of the externality effect in young infants. *Journal of Experimental Child Psychology*, 28, 211–229.

Bushnell, I. W. R., Sai, F., & Mullin, J. T. (1989). Neonatal recognition of the mother's face. *British Journal of Developmental Psychology*, 7, 3–15.

Butter, C. M. (1983). The role of polysensory neuronal structures in spatially-directed attention and orienting responses to external stimuli. In D. Shear & K. Pribram (eds), *Attention: Neural Mechanisms, Models and Clinical Applications*. New York: Academic Press.

Carey, S. & Diamond, R. (1980). Maturational determination of the developmental course of face encoding. In D. Caplan (ed.), *Biological Studies of Mental Processes*. Cambridge, MA: MIT Press.

Cohen, L. B. (1988). An information-processing approach to infant cognitive development. In L. Weiskrantz (ed.), *Thought without Language*. Oxford: Clarendon Press.

Conel, J. L. (1939–1967). *The Postnatal Development of the Human Cerebral Cortex*, Vols. I–VIII. Cambridge, MA: Harvard University Press.

Dannemiller, J. L. & Banks, M. S. (1983). Can selective adaptation account for early infant habituation? *Merrill-Palmer Quarterly*, 29, 151–158.

Dayton, G. O., Jones, M. H., Steele, B., & Rose, M. (1964). Developmental study of coordinated eye movements in the human infant. II. An electrooculographic study of the fixation reflex in the newborn. *Archives of Ophthalmology*, 71, 871–875.

de Courten, C. & Garey, L. J. (1982). Morphology of the neurones in the human lateral geniculate nucleus and their normal development. *Experimental Brain Research*, 47, 259–271.

de Schonen, S. & Mathivet, H. (1989). First come, first served: A scenario about the development of hemispheric specialisation in face recognition during infancy. *European Bulletin of Cognitive Psychology*, 9, 3–44.

de Yoe, E. A. & Van Essen, D. C. (1988). Concurrent processing streams in monkey visual cortex. *TINS*, 11, 219–226.

Garon, E. C. & Swartz, K. B. (1980). Perception of internal elements of compound figures by one-month-olds. *Journal of Experimental Child Psychology*, 30, 159–170.

Goren, C. C., Sarty, M., & Wu, P. Y. K. (1975). Visual following and pattern discrimination of face-like stimuli by newborn infants. *Pediatrics*, 56, 544–549.

Gouras, P. (1969). Antichromic responses of orthochromically identified ganglion cells in monkey retina. *Journal of Physiology*, 204, 407–419.

Haith, M. M. & Campos, J. J. (1977). Human infancy. *Annual Review of Psychology*, 28, 251–293.

Haith, M. M., Hazan, C., & Goodman, G. S. (1988). Expectation and anticipation of dynamic visual events by 3.5-month-old babies. *Child Development*, 59, 467–479.

Harter, M. R. & Aine, C. J. (1984). Brain mechanisms of visual selective attention. In R. Parasuranian & D. R. Davies (eds), *Varieties of Attention*. New York: Academic Press.

Held, R. (1985). Binocular vision: Behavioural and neuronal development. In J. Mehler & R. Fox (eds), *Neonate Cognition: Beyond the Booming, Buzzing, Confusion*. Hillsdale, NJ: Lawrence Erlbaum.

Hikosaka, O. & Wurtz, R. H. (1983). Visual and oculomotor functions of monkey substantia nigra pats reticulata I, II, III, IV. *Journal of Neurophysiology*, 37, 1230–1253, 1254–1267, 1268–1284, 1285–1301.

Hoffman, K. P. & Sherman, S. M. (1974). Effects of early monocular deprivation on visual input to cat superior colliculus. *Journal of Neurophysiology*, 49, 1276–1286.

Huttenlocher, P. R. & de Courten, C. (1987). The development of synapses in the striate cortex of man. *Human Neurobiology*, 6, 1–9.

Huttenlocher, P. R., de Courten, C., Garey, L. G., & Van der Loos, H. (1982). Synaptogenesis in human visual cortex–evidence for synapse elimination during normal development. *Neuroscience Letters*, 33, 247–252.

Johnson, M. H. (1990). Cortical maturation and perceptual development. In H. Bloch & B. Bertenthal. (eds.), *Sensory Motor Organisation and Development in Infancy and Early Childhood*. Dordrecht: Kluwer Academic Press (NATO series).

Johnson, M. H. & Karmiloff-Smith, A. (1990). Neural development and language acquisition: Parcellation and selective stabilisation. Submitted for publication.

Johnson, M. H. & Morton, J. (1990). *The Development of Face Recognition*. Oxford: Blackwells, in press.

Johnson, M. H., Posner, M. I., & Rothbart, M. (1990c). The development of visual attention in infancy: Contingency learning, anticipations and disengaging. Manuscript in preparation.

Johnson, M. H., Dziurawiec, S., Bartrip, J., & Morton, J. (1990a). Infants' preferences for face-like stimuli: Effects of the movement of internal features. Submitted for publication.

Johnson, M. H., Dziurawiec, S., Ellis, H. D., & Morton, J. (1990b). Newborns' preferential tracking of face-like stimuli and its subsequent decline. Submitted for publication.

Kaas, J. H. (1989). Why does the brain have so many visual areas? *Journal of Cognitive Neuroscience*, 1, 121–135.

Leslie, A. M. & Keeble, S. (1987). Do six-month-olds perceive causality? *Cognition*, 25, 265–288.

Leuba, G. & Garey, L. J. (1982). A morphometric developmental study of dendrites in the lateral geniculate of the monkey. *Neuroscience, 7 (Suppl.)* 131.

Lewis, T. L. (1979). The development of nasal field detection in young infants. *Dissertation Abstracts International*, 41B, 1547.

Lewis, T. L., Maurer, D., & Milewski, A. (1979). The development of nasal detection in young infants. *Investigating Ophthalmology and Visual Science Supplement*, 271.

Lewis, T. L., Maurer, D., & Blackburn, K. (1985). The development of young infants' ability to detect stimuli in the nasal visual field. *Vision Research*, 25, 943–950.

Lund, J. S. (1981). Intrinsic organization of the primate visual cortex, area 17, as seen in Golgi preparations. In F. O. Schmitt, et al. (eds.), *The Organisation of the Cerebral Cortex*. Cambridge MA: MIT Press.

Maunsell, J. H. R. & van Essen, D. C. (1983). The connections of the middle temporal visual area (MT) and their relation to a cortical hierarchy in the macaque monkey. *Journal of Neuroscience*, 3, 2563–2586.

Maurer, D. (1983). The scanning of compound figures by young infants. *Journal of Experimental Child Psychology*, 35, 437–448.

Maurer, D. & Barrera, M. (1981). Infants' perception of natural and distorted arrangements of a schematic face. *Child Development*, 47, 523–527.

Maurer, D. & Lewis, T. L. (1979). A physiological explanation of infants' early visual development. *Canadian Journal of Psychology*, 33, 232–252.

McGinnis, J. M. (1930). Eye movements and optic nystagmus in early infancy. *Genetic Psychology Monographs*, 8, 321–430.

Milewski, A. E. (1976). Infants' discrimination of internal and external pattern elements. *Journal of Experimental Child Psychology*, 22, 229–246.

Miller, K. D., Keller, J. B., & Stryker, M. P. (1989). Ocular dominance column development: Analysis and simulation. *Science*, 245, 605–615.

Mishkin, M. & Appenzeller, T. (1987). The anatomy of memory. *Scientific American*, June, 2–12.

Mohn, G. & von Hof-van Duin, J. (1986). Development of the binocular and monocular visual fields of human infants during the first year of life. *Clinical Vision Sciences*, 1, 51–64.

Morton, J., Johnson, M. H., & Maurer, D. (1990). On the reasons for newborns responses to faces. *Infant Behavior & Development*, 13, 99–103.

Muir, D. W., Clifton, R. K., & Clarkson, M. G. (1989). The development of a human auditory localization response: A U-shaped function. *Canadian Journal of Psychology*, 43, 199–216.

Newsome, W. T., Wurtz, R. H., Dursteler, M. R., & Mikami, A. (1985). Punctate chemical lesions of striate cortex in the macaque monkey: Effect on visually guided saccades. *Experimental Brain Research*, 58, 392–399.

Posner, M. I. (1980). Orienting of attention. *Quarterly Journal of Experimental Psychology*, 32, 3–25.

Posner, M. I. & Cohen, Y. (1980). Attention and the control of movements. In G. E. Stelmach & J. Roguiro (eds), *Tutorials in Motor Behavior*. Amsterdam: North Holland.

Posner, M. I. & Rothbart, M. K. (1980). The development of attentional mechanisms. In J. H. Flower (ed.), *Nebraska Symposium on Motivation*. Lincoln, NE: University of Nebraska Press.

Posner, M. I. & Rothbart, M. K. (1990). Regulatory mechanisms in infant temperament. In J. Enns (ed.), *The Development of Attention: Research and Theory*. Amsterdam: North Holland.

Purpura, D. P. (1975). Normal and abberant neuronal development in the cerebral cortex of human fetus and young infant. In N. A. Buchwald & M. A. B. Brazier (eds), *Brain Mechanisms of Mental Retardation*. New York: Academic Press.

Rabinowicz, T. (1979). The different maturation of the human cerebral cortex. In F. Falkner & J. M. Tanner (eds), *Human Growth*, Vol. 3. *Neurobiology and Nutrition*. New York: Plenum.

Rakic, P. (1976). Prenatal genesis of connections subserving ocular dominance in the rhesus monkey. *Nature (London)*, 261, 467–471.

Rakic, P. (1983). Geniculo-cortical connections in primates: normal and experimentally altered development. *Progress in Brain Research*, 58, 393–404.

Regal, D. M., Ashmead, D. H., & Salapatek, P. (1983). The coordination of eye and head movements during early infancy: A selective review. *Behavioral and Brain Research*, 10, 125–132.

Robinson, D. L., & Peterson, S. E. (1986). The neurobiology of attention. In *Mind and Brain: Dialogues in Cognitive Neuroscience*. Cambridge: Cambridge University Press.

Robinson, N. S., McCarty, M. E., & Haith, M. M. (1988). *Visual Expectations in Early Infancy*. Paper presented at the international conference on infant studies, Washington, DC.

Rockland, K. S. & Pandya, D. N. (1979). Laminar origins and terminations of cortical connections of the occipital lobe in the rhesus monkey. *Brain Research*, 179, 3–20.

Salapatek, P. (1975). Pattern perception in early infancy. In L. Cohen & P. Salapatek (eds.), *Infant Perception: From Sensation to Cognition*, Vol. 1. New York: Academic Press.

Schanel-Klitsch, E. and Siegfried, J. B. (1987). High-frequency VEP wavelets in early infancy: A preliminary study. *Infant Behavior and Development*, 10, 325–336.

Schiller, P. H. (1985). A model for the generation of visually guided sacadic eye movements. In D. Rose & V. G. Dobson, *Models of the Visual Cortex*. Chichester: Wiley.

Schiller, P. H. & Malpeli, J. G. (1977). Properties and tectal projections of the monkey retinal ganglion cells. *Journal of Neurophysiology*, 40, 428–445.

Schiller, P. H., Malpeli, J. G., & Schein, S. J. (1979). Composition of geniculo-striate input to superior colliculus of the rhesus monkey. *Journal of Neurophysiology*, 42, 1124–1133.

Schiller, P. H., Logothetis, N. K., & Charles, E. R. (1990). Functions of the colour-opponent and broad-band channels of the visual system. *Nature (London)*, 343, 68–70.

Schwartz, T. L., Dobson, V., Sandstrom, D. J., & van Hof-van Duin, J. (1987). Kinetic perimetry assessment of binocular visual field shape and size in young infants. *Vision Research*, 27, 2163–2175.

Slater, A. (1988). Habituation and visual fixation in infants: Information processing, reinforcement and what else? *European Bulletin of Cognitive Psychology*, 8, 517–523.

Slater, A., Earle, D. C., Morison, V. & Rose, D. (1985). Pattern preferences at birth and their interaction with habituation-induced novelty preferences. *Journal of Experimental Child Psychology*, 39, 37–54.

Slater, A. M. & Morison, V. (1985). Selective adaptation cannot account for early infant habituation: A response to Dannemiller and Banks. *Merrill-Palmer Quarterly*, 31, 99–103.

Slater, A. M. Morison, V., & Rose, D. (1982). Perception of shape by the newborn baby. *British Journal of Developmental Psychology*, 1, 135–142.

Slater, A. M., Morison, V., & Rose, D. (1983). Locus of habituation in the human newborn. *Perception*, 12, 289–295.

Slater, A., Morison, V., & Somers, M. (1988). Orientation discrimination and cortical function in the human newborn. *Perception*, 17, 597–602.

Spelke, E. S. (1988). The origins of physical knowledge. In L. Weiskrantz (ed.), *Thought without Language*. Oxford: Clarendon Press.

Stampalija, A. & Kostovic, I. (1981). The laminar organization of the superior colliculus (SC) in the human fetus. In A. Huber & D. Klein (eds), *Neurogenetics and Neuro-ophthalmology*. North Holland: Elsevier.

Stechler, G. & Latz, E. (1966). Some observations on attention and arousal in the human infant. *Journal of the American Academy of Child Psychiatry*, 5, 517–525.

Stein, B. E. & Gordon, B. G. (1981). Maturation of the superior colliculus. In R. D. Aslin, J. R. Alberts, & M. R. Peterson (eds), *The Development of Perception: Psychobiological Perspectives*. Vol. 2. New York: Academic Press.

Tennes, K., Emde, R., Kisley, A., & Metcalf, D. (1972). The stimulus barrier in early infancy: An exploration of some formulations of John Benjamin. In R. R. Holt & E. Peterfreund (eds), *Psychoanalysis and Contemporary Science*. New York: Macmillan.

Van Essen, D. C. (1985). Functional organisation of primate visual cortex. In A. Peters & E. G. Jones (eds), *Cerebral Cortex*, Vol. 3. New York: Plenum.

Vaughan, H. G. & Kurtzberg, D. (1989). Electrophysiologic indices of normal and aberrant cortical maturation. In P. Kellaway & J. Noebels (eds.), *Problems and Concepts of Developmental Neurophysiology*. Baltimore: The Johns Hopkins University Press.

Weiskrantz, L. (1986). Blindsight: A case study and its implications. Oxford: Oxford University Press.

Yakovlev, P. I. & Lecours, A. (1967). The myelogenetic cycles of regional maturation of the brain. In A. Minokowski (ed.), *Regional Development of the Brain in Early Life*. Philadelphia: Davis.

11

An Early and a Late Developing System for Learning and Retention in Infant Monkeys

JOCELYNE BACHEVALIER AND MORTIMER MISHKIN

One of the most intriguing aspects of the amnesic syndrome is the preserved ability of profoundly amnesic subjects to learn many tasks almost normally. A particularly dramatic example of this paradox was described in a companion article (Malamut et al., 1984). There it was shown that monkeys made amnesic by bilateral removal of the amygdalo-hippocampal complex, and as a result failed to recognize objects only a minute or so after they were presented, nevertheless learned to discriminate a long list of pairs of objects as rapidly as normal animals even though this list was presented only once every 24 hours. The dichotomy of performance on different learning tasks that has now been seen in amnesic monkeys (Malamut et al., 1984; Zola-Morgan et al., 1982) was discovered initially in amnesic patients (Corkin, 1968; Milner, 1962; Warrington and Weiskrantz, 1971) and soon after in rats with hippocampal lesions (Hirsh, 1974; O'Keefe and Dostrovsky, 1971). One proposal that has been advanced to explain these paradoxical results is that retention of the effects of experience depends on two fundamentally different neural systems (Hirsh, 1974; Mishkin et al., in press). One of these is considered to be a memory system that serves both recognition and association and appears to utilize a cortico-limbo-diencephalic circuit; this is the system that is presumed to be impaired in subjects rendered amnesic by limbic or diencephalic lesions. The other is a habit system that mediates retention of stimulus–response connections and, it has been speculated, depends in large part on a cortico-striatal circuit; this is the system that is presumed to be preserved in amnesic subjects.

"An Early and a Late Developing System for Learning and Retention in Infant Monkeys" first appeared in *Behavioral Neuroscience* 98 (1984), pp. 770–8, and is reprinted by kind permission.

On the hypothesis that memory and habit formation in the adult monkey are qualitatively different learning processes based on separate neural systems, we sought to compare the functional development of the two systems ontogenetically. Separate groups of monkeys of different ages were tested on a delayed nonmatching-to-sample task and on a 24-hour concurrent discrimination task to evaluate their developing capacity for memory formation and habit formation, respectively. The purpose of the study was to determine whether the dissociation between the two abilities that was found in amnesic monkeys might also be present in infant monkeys. In fact, the results we obtained are consistent with the view that whereas the habit system is already mature early in infancy, the memory system develops only slowly.

Experiment 1

In the first experiment, the visual recognition ability of monkeys aged three, six, and 12 months was measured by the delayed nonmatching-to-sample task with trial-unique objects. This particular task was chosen from among the various one-trial memory tasks with which normal adult animals have been tested because it has proven to be the easiest one for them to learn (Gaffan, 1974, 1979; Mishkin and Delacour, 1975).

Method

Subjects.   The subjects were 17 infant rhesus monkeys (*Macaca mulatta*). Nine were received at birth and raised in our laboratory; the remainder were born and raised in a breeding colony and received in the laboratory at least one month prior to training. Because the performance of these two subgroups did not appear to differ, this variable is not considered further. The animals were housed in a nursery in individual wire mesh cages which allowed them visual, auditory, and manual contact with each other but nogross body contact. Contact comfort for the younger infants was provided by a cotton towel hung from the top of the cage and several towels placed on the floor; these were changed daily. The infants were fed Similac with iron (Ross Laboratories, Columbus, Ohio) supplemented with banana pellets (P. J. Noyes Co., Lancaster, New Hampshire) for the three month group and with banana pellets and monkey chow for the two older groups. Throughout training, when banana pellets were used as rewards, the daily milk ration (supplemented by monkey chow for the one-year group) was manipulated to provide each animal with the highest ration consistent with prompt responding in the testing situation. The monkeys were fed twice a day, once immediately after the training session and again approximately 14 hours before the next session. Water was provided *ad lib*.

The animals were assigned to one of the three age-groups: three months (two males, two females), six months (three males, three females), and one year (two males, five females). The group designation indicates the age at which the infants began the training procedure. These three groups were compared with each other and with a group of young adults (three males and three females, approximately three years of age) that had been trained in the same way in an earlier study (Mishkin, 1978).

Apparatus. Training of the three- and six-month groups was conducted in a reduced version of the Wisconsin General Test Apparatus (WGTA) containing a stationary test tray with three recessed food wells 10 cm apart and 6 cm from the front of the cage. The animals in the one-year group, like the adults, were trained in a standard WGTA containing a test tray with three recessed food wells 14 cm apart and 12 cm from the front of the cage. For all groups, a stock of approximately 300 variegated objects were used as stimuli, although the objects presented to the three infant groups were smaller than those that had been presented to the adults. In addition, the rewards for the infants were 190-mg banana pellets, whereas for the adults the rewards had been peanuts.

Procedure. The infants were food deprived for two days before they were adapted to the WGTA. They were trained first to retrieve pellets from the open food wells by a method of successive approximation in which more and more of the well was covered by the object. For this phase, three objects were presented one at a time over one of the three wells in random order, and this preliminary training continued until the monkeys unhesitatingly displaced the baited object on ten successive trials.

After completion of the preliminary training, which required from one to six days, the infants were trained on the one-trial object recognition task, delayed nonmatching to sample. On each acquisition or familiarization trial, the central well was baited and covered by a single object which the animal displaced to obtain the reward. Ten seconds later a test trial was presented in which the sample object and a new object were placed over the lateral wells, and the animal was rewarded only for choosing the new object, the sample object now being unbaited. Thirty seconds later another set of trials was presented in the same way, but with a new pair of objects, and so on for 20 trials a day. The monkeys were trained in this manner for five to six days per week until they reached the criterion of 90 correct choices in 100 trials. A noncorrection technique was used throughout.

Fifteen days after completion of the task, retention was assessed by retraining the monkeys to criterion on the basic recognition problem. Subsequently, their recognition memory was evaluated more fully by a performance test in which, first, the delay between the presentation of the sample and the test was lengthened in stages from the initial 10 second delay to 30, 60, and finally 120 seconds; then, the number of objects to be remembered was increased progressively from the initial single object to three, five, and finally ten objects. In the list-length tests, the samples were presented successively at 20 second intervals followed by presentation of the test trials also at 20-second intervals. At every delay, the animals were trained for five consecutive blocks of 20 trials each, and for every list length, they received five consecutive blocks of 30 trials each.

Results

The learning curves for the three infant groups and the adults are shown in figure 11.1, where each point represents the mean percentage of correct responses

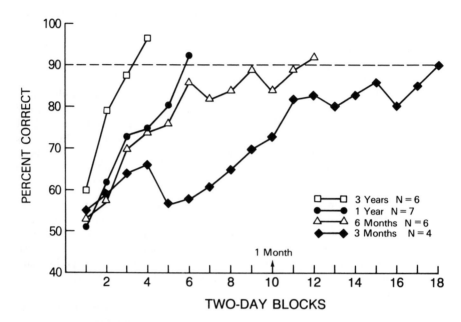

Figure 11.1 Learning curves on the delayed nonmatching-to-sample task for three groups of infants and one group of adults. For computation of these curves, criterion was set at 90 percent correct responses in a two-day block (rather than in the five-day block actually required), and scores were then averaged in two-day blocks until criterion was met. Animals that met criterion prior to the last two-day block for the group were given a score of 90 percent on all blocks following their attainment of criterion. The arrow on the abscissa indicates that approximately one month elapsed for ten blocks of testing.

during two days of training (40 trails). It is apparent that speed of learning varied systematically with age. At the start of training, the four groups did not differ significantly (Kruskal–Wallis H test), each scoring 50–60 percent correct. As training progressed, however, the adult animals showed a sharp improvement in score from the first two-day block to the second (Mann–Whitney U test, $P = 0.04$) and continued to improve rapidly thereafter, whereas both the one-year and the six-month group improved significantly only on the third block ($P = 0.001$ and 0.047, respectively). The learning curves of the latter two groups remained parallel during the first five blocks of training (ten days) but separated on the sixth block when the one-year group improved sharply, reaching the learning criterion, whereas the six-month group remained just under this criterion for five more blocks. The most striking result, however, was the absence of improvement in the curve for the three-month group through the first nine blocks (18 days) of training. It was only on the tenth block that the mean scores of these animals differed significantly from their initial scores ($P < 0.04$). Thereafter, the three-month group showed a progressive improvement, similar in slope to that shown by the six-month group seven blocks earlier.

After a rest period of 15 days, all animals except three of the seven one-year monkeys and three of the six adults were retrained on the basic recognition task (single sample with 10 second delay). The six animals excluded were ones that received cerebral lesions for the purpose of another study; their learning scores on the delayed nonmatching-to-sample task did not differ significantly from those of the remaining animals. The mean numbers·of trials and errors to learn and relearn the task for each age-group are presented in figure 11.2. As already indicated, the original learning scores decreased systematically with the age of the animals: Kruskal–Wallis $H(3) = 15.67$, $P < 0.01$ for trials; $H(3) = 16.91$, $P < 0.001$ for errors. The individual comparisons indicate further that each age-group differed significantly from all the others in both trials and errors (Mann–Whitney U test, $P < 0.05$ in each case). In relearning, although all groups showed a sharp decline in the number of trials they required to reattain the criterion, which indicates a high level of retention by each, the four groups retained the same rank order as before, $H(3) = 9.68$, $P < 0.025$ for trials. The individual comparisons again show that the youngest group, now six months old, required significantly more trials to relearn the task than any other group ($P < 0.05$ in all cases) and that the six-month group, now 7.5 months old, required significantly more trials to relearn than the two oldest groups ($P < 0.05$ in both cases). The one-year group, on the other hand, did not differ from the adult group.

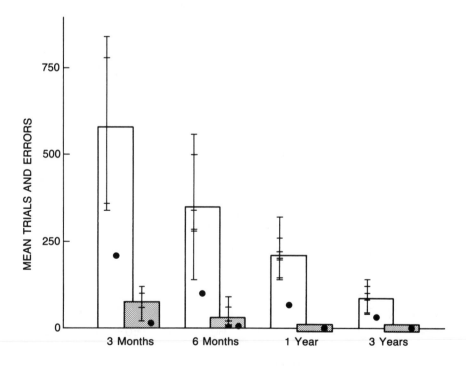

Figure 11.2 Scores for learning (white bars) and relearning (stippled bars) the delayed nonmatching-to-sample task to the criterion of 90 correct responses in 100 trials. (A rest period of 15 days separated the two measurements. The horizontal lines represent individual trial scores, and the filled circles indicate mean error scores.)

As described in Procedure, the monkeys' recognition memory was then taxed further through progressive increase of the delays and then of the list lengths of objects to be remembered. The results are shown in figure 11.3 where the mean percentage of correct responses on each condition has been plotted for the four age-groups. The main effects of both age and condition were significant, $F(3, 13) = 7.26$, $P < 0.01$ and $F(6, 13) = 21.91$, $P < 0.0005$, respectively, although the age by condition interaction was not. Multiple comparisons reveal that the memory performance of the three- and six-month infants, though not different from each other, were significantly poorer than those of the two oldest groups (Newman–Keuls, $P < 0.05$ for each case) and, further, that the performance of the one-year group had not yet reached adult levels of proficiency (Newman–Keuls, $P < 0.05$).

To determine whether results in a delayed matching-to-sample test might lead to a different conclusion from that described above, we trained a single three-month monkey in the delayed matching principle. This animal took 600 trials to learn the task and 60 trials to relearn it, compared with a mean of 565 and 70

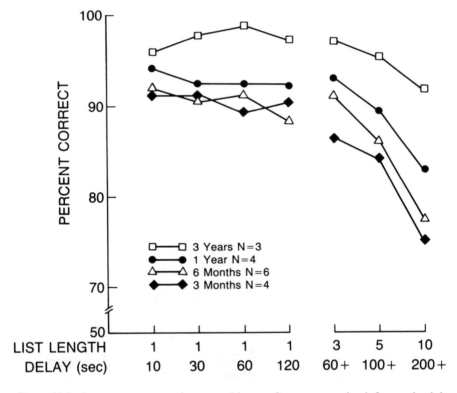

Figure 11.3 Average scores on the recognition performance test by infant and adult monkeys. (The first point of the curve indicates the average final score achieved during the relearning of the basic task, which entailed recognizing a single object after 10 s. Animals were tested on the six remaining conditions, involving gradually increasing delays and list lengths, for one week each.)

trials, respectively, for the three-month infants trained in nonmatching. Furthermore, the average score on the performance test for the animal trained in matching was 86 percent, compared with 85.9 percent for the animals trained in nonmatching. These results indicate that the performance of infant monkeys on the two versions of the recognition task are nearly identical.

Experiment 2

As described by Malamut et al. (1984), adult monkeys with severe impairment in visual recognition memory may nevertheless show normal acquisition of visual discrimination habits, even though the successive trials are separated by 24 hours. After discovering that three-month-old infant monkeys showed particularly poor learning and performance in the visual recognition task, we asked in a second experiment whether such infants, like amnesic adults, would still be able to form and retain discriminations in which the intertrial intervals lasted 24 hours. To answer this question, we compared a new group of three-month infants with normal adults on the 24-hour concurrent object discrimination task.

Method

Subjects. The subjects consisted of seven naive three-month rhesus monkeys (Macaca mulatta, four females and three males). Three were received at birth and raised in our nursery; the remaining four were born and raised in a breeding colony and received in our nursery one month prior to testing. Again, the performance of these two subgroups did not differ. The caging, handling, feeding, and pretraining procedures were identical to those used with the animals in experiment 1. The learning scores of the infants were compared with those of a group of ten naive young adult rhesus monkeys (three females and seven males, approximately three years old) that had been trained similarly as described by Malamut et al. (1984). Seven of the adults were subjects in that study, and the three others are from an unpublished study (B. Malamut and M. Mishkin, 1980).

Apparatus. As in experiment 1, the testing of the infants was conducted in a reduced version of the standard WGTA in which the adults had been tested. Comparison between the groups was based on their rate of acquisition of two different sets of discriminations, A and B, each set consisting of 20 pairs of objects. As before, the objects used with the infants were smaller in size than those used with the adults. Banana pellets rather than peanuts served as the rewards.

Procedure. A pair of objects, one baited and one unbaited, were presented simultaneously over the lateral wells of the test tray. After the animal made a choice by displacing one of the objects, there was a 20-second delay, following which the second pair of objects were presented for choice, and so on until all 20 pairs had been presented once each. The same series of objects was then repeated once every 24 hours. The baited and unbaited objects within each pair as well as the serial order of the pairs remained constant across sessions, but the left–right positions of the objects were randomized daily. Testing was continued in this way until the monkeys attained the criterion of 90 correct responses in five daily sessions (100 trials), first on set A and then on set B. Again, a noncorrection technique was used throughout. Fifteen days after completion of the learning of these two sets, all of the infants and four of the adults were retrained to criterion on the two sets.

Results

Table 11.1 shows the number of daily sessions and total errors that each monkey required to learn and relearn the two sets of object discriminations. For set A, the infant monkeys took significantly longer than the adults to reach the criterion in terms of both sessions and errors, $t(15) = 3.48$, $P < 0.005$ and $t(15) = 4.55$, $P < 0.005$ respectively. This retardation in learning is illustrated in the curves shown on the left in figure 11.4. The retardation was brief, however, lasting no more than four to six daily sessions (two to three blocks), after which the slopes of the two learning curves were nearly identical.

The efficiency with which infant monkeys can learn such discriminations became particularly evident, however, in the acquisition of set B. On this set they attained criterion even more quickly than the adults, though the difference

Table 11.1 Number of daily sessions (S) and total number of errors (E) preceding criterion on the 24-h concurrent object discrimination task by 3-month-old infants and 3-year-old adults

| Monkey | Acquisition | | | | Retention | | | |
| | Set A | | Set B | | Set A | | Set B | |
	S	E	S	E	S	E	S	E
Infant								
1	12	87	8	44	2	9	1	4
2	13	104	2	15	1	5	0	0
3	14	102	8	41	0	0	0	0
4	12	88	3	15	2	9	0	0
5	26	165	15	97	3	21	0	0
6	24	92	2	16	0	0	0	0
7	12	190	11	80	0	0	0	0
Adult								
1	11	76	11	102	0	0	0	0
2	9	56	13	78	12	45	1	6
3	9	40	3	16	0	0	0	0
4	10	59	14	66	1	4	0	0
5	9	61	7	41				
6	10	48	13	91				
7	11	62	17	111				
8	7	41	6	40				
9	9	58	8	64				
10	8	63	8	49				

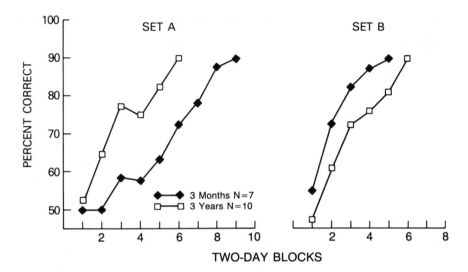

Figure 11.4 Learning curves on the two sets of 24-hr concurrent object discriminations for three month old infants and three year old adults. For each age-group, scores for two-day blocks were averaged until the criterion of 90 percent correct in a two-day block was met. As in figure 11.1, animals that met criterion prior to the last two-day block for the group were given a score of 90 percent on all blocks following their attainment of criterion.

did not reach significance (table 11.1 and figure 11.4, right). The difference in the results obtained on the two sets is attributable to a significant improvement in the infants' but not in the adults' scores on set B compared with scores on set A: age × set interaction, $F(1, 15) = 7.79, P < 0.01$; set A *vs* set B for the infants, $t(6) = 3.57, P < 0.01$; set A *vs* set B for the adults, $t(9) = 0.62, ns$.

The results on the relearning of these two sets after a 15-day interval indicate that the infants retained the two sets of concurrent object discriminations just as well as the adults, both age-groups showing nearly perfect retention (table 11.1).

Discussion

Infant rhesus monkeys failed to solve the delayed nonmatching-to-sample task until they were approximately four months of age. On further maturation, there was a gradual improvement in learning ability, yet it did not reach adult levels of proficiency even at one year. Only at about two years of age do monkeys master the recognition task as efficiently as adult animals (Bachevalier and Mishkin, unpublished data, 1982). These results substantiate a suggestion by Elliott et al. (1977) that their failure to observe the anticipated rapid learning of delayed nonmatching (Mishkin and Delacour, 1975) was due in part to the immaturity of the animals in the Elliott et al. study. In short, as has already been shown for discrimination learning sets (Harlow, 1959), oddity problems (Harlow, 1959), delayed-response (Harlow et al., 1960), patterned strings (Mason and Harlow, 1961), and object discrimination reversal (Mahut and Zola-Morgan, 1977), there is an age at which a delayed nonmatching-to-sample task can first be solved and a considerably greater age before it can be solved with full adult proficiency.

Despite their poor performance on the one-trial recognition task, infant monkeys between three and four months old were clearly able to form discrimination habits as quickly as adult animals. Rapid acquisition of visual discrimination habits was already known to occur in infant monkeys even younger than one month of age (for review, see Zimmerman and Torrey, 1965). In the earlier studies, however, the discriminations were presented one pair at a time and with massed practice and short intertrial intervals. The results of the present study extend those findings by demonstrating that infant monkeys are equally successful when they are required to discriminate long lists of object-pairs and to learn and retain their reward values on the basis of distributed practice on single trials separated by 24 hours. At this time, we have not identified the age at which 24-hour concurrent object discrimination learning can first be mastered, but it is clear that the ability must be present even earlier than three months of age. As in the case of mature monkeys rendered amnesic by limbic lesions, the success of the normal infant monkeys in 24-hour concurrent learning demonstrates that their retardation in learning a delayed nonmatching-to-sample task cannot be attributed to any inadequacy of perception, attention, motivation, or general learning ability.

One possible explanation for the striking dissociation in the acquisition of the two tasks is a slow maturation of problem-solving strategies. Although little information exists on such strategies in infant monkeys, Harlow (1959) showed that whereas animals of all ages seem to approach an object discrimination problem in a systematic manner, the younger monkeys persisted in their incorrect hypotheses longer than older monkeys did. Similar findings have been obtained in studies of complex versions of matching in children. Levin and Maurer (1969) proposed that in acquiring a matching principle, younger children reject old hypotheses and sample new ones less readily than older children in part because they have a less developed "lose–shift" mechanism. Yet, if this particular mechanism is not well developed in infants, it should affect the learning not only of matching principles but of 24-hour concurrent object discrimination as well.

Another possible explanation for the poor performance of infant monkeys in delayed nonmatching relates instead to the problem of abstraction. Perhaps infants can readily learn to associate reward value with particular object qualities as required in discrimination tasks but not with any of the object's abstract qualities. To learn a delayed matching or nonmatching principle, the animal must first be able to separate and abstract the relatively subtle mnemonic cue of that object's familiarity (or novelty) from the salient perceptual cue of that object's physical quality and then be able to associate the abstraction with the reward. It is reasonable to suppose that the congnitive step from object–reward association to familiarity–reward (or novelty–reward) association involves a considerable step in functional neuronal development.

But although an inadequately developed cognitive system undoubtedly underlies the infants' retardation in learning delayed nonmatching, there is perhaps an even more fundamental inadequacy that underlies their lack of cognitive development. The proposal is that the basic functional inadequacy in infant monkeys, just as in adult monkeys with limbic lesions, is a deficient memory. This proposal is supported by the finding that even after the animals had mastered the delayed nonmatching principle, their scores on the memory performance test with increasing delay intervals and list lengths declined systematically in inverse relation to their age. The scores of the youngest (three-month) animals, given the performance test when they were between six and eight months old, averaged approximately 10 percent below those of the adults, and even the scores of the oldest (one year) averaged about 6 percent below the adults'. To place these scores in perspective, we can say that the degree of impairment of the infants in the oldest group is about the same as that of adult animals given either bilateral amygdalectomy or bilateral hippocampectomy (Mishkin, 1978), whereas the impairment of the youngest infants is about twice as great. Neither impairment, of course, approaches in severity the 30 percent reduction in score produced by combined amygdalo-hippocampal ablations (Mishkin, 1978).

The poorer memory of the infants could have led to the retardation in their learning of the basic task for at least two reasons. First, poorer memory implies poorer recognition memory, and recognition is of course essential if the quality of familiarity (or novelty) is to be abstracted. Second, poorer memory also implies poorer associative memory between this abstraction and the reward, even though the association is repeated trial after trial within a session. As indicated by Malamut et al. (1984), this type of cognitive association, which is presumed to take place between two items of information in memory, can be distinguished from the type of noncognitive association that takes place between a particular stimulus and a particular response under appropriate conditions of reinforcement (Mishkin et al., in press; Mishkin and Petri, in press). The system for noncognitive association, which we and others (Hirsh, 1974) have referred to as habit formation and which is preserved in adult monkeys rendered amnesic by limbic lesions, seems to be present in very early infancy. By contrast, the system for cognitive associations, which we have referred to as memory formation and which is severely impaired in adult monkeys with limbic lesions, develops later in infancy, presumably because the limbic circuitry on which it depends undergoes a relatively slow ontogenetic development. This notion, which has also been discussed recently by others (Nadel and Zola-Morgan, in press; Rose, 1980; Schacter and Moscovitch, in press), opens up new avenues of investigation aimed at detailing precisely what forms of learning and retention become available to animal and human infants at different points in their behavioral development and how these correlate with different points in their neuronal development (Macko et al., 1983). Besides providing further tests of the proposal that memory and habit systems are dissociable ontogenetically, such studies should ultimately provide the explanation for one of the most intriguing amnestic phenomenon of all, namely, our global amnesia for the experiences of infancy and early childhood.

ACKNOWLEDGEMENTS

Portions of this material were presented at the meeting of the International Organization of Psychophysiology, Montreal, 1982 (Bachevalier and Mishkin, 1983) and at a conference on the Neurobiology of Learning and Memory, Irvine, California, 1982 (Mishkin, Malamut and Bachevalier, in press).

The first author was a postdoctoral fellow, supported by the Quebec Government, during the time of this study.

We thank Howard Crawford for his valuable help with testing of the animals, and Laura Parkinson for supervising their care.

REFERENCES

Corkin, S. (1968). Acquisition of motor skill after bilateral medial temporal-lobe excision. *Neuropsychologia*, 6, 255–265.

Elliott, R. C., Norris, E., Ettlinger, G., & Mishkin, M. (1977). Some factors influencing nonmatching-to-sample in the monkey. *Bulletin of the Psychonomic Society*, 9, 395–396.

Gaffan, D. (1974). Recognition impaired and association intact in the memory of monkeys after transection of the fornix. *Journal of Comparative and Physiological Psychology*, 86, 1100–1109.

Gaffan, D. (1979). Acquisition and forgetting in monkey's memory of informational object-reward associations. *Learning and Motivation*, 10, 419–444.

Harlow, H. F. (1959). The development of learning in the rhesus monkeys. *American Scientist*, 47, 458–479.

Harlow, H. F., Harlow, M. K., Rueping, R. R., & Mason, W. A. (1960). Performance of infant rhesus monkeys on discrimination learning, delayed response, and discrimination learning set. *Journal of Comparative and Physiological Psychology*, 53, 113–121.

Hirsh, R. (1974). The hippocampus and contextual retrieval of information from memory: A theory. *Behavioral Biology*, 12, 421–445.

Levin, G. R., & Maurer, D. M. (1969). The solution process in children's matching-to-sample. *Developmental Psychology*, 1, 679–690.

Macko, K. A., Bachevalier, J., Kennedy, C., Suda, S., Sokoloff, L., & Mishkin, M. (1983) Functional development of the ventral cortical visual pathway measured by the 2-deoxyglucose method. *Society for Neuroscience Abstracts*, 9, 375.

Mahut, H., & Zola-Morgan, S. (1977). Ontogenetic time-table for the development of three functions in infant macaques and the effects of early hippocampal damage upon them. *Society for Neuroscience Abstracts*, 3, 428.

Malamut, B. L., Saunders, R. C., & Mishkin, M. (1984). Monkeys with combined amygdalo-hippocampal lesions succeed in object discrimination learning despite 24-hour intertrial intervals. *Behavioral Neuroscience*, 98, 759–769.

Mason, W. A., & Harlow, H. F. (1961). The effects of age and previous training on patterned-strings performance of rhesus monkeys. *Journal of Comparative and Physiological Psychology*, 54, 704–709.

Milner, B. (1962). Les troubles de la mémoire accompagnant des lésions hippocampiques bilatérales [Memory disorders following bilateral hippocampal removal]. *Physiologie de l'Hippocampe*, 107, 257–272.

Mishkin, M. (1978). Memory in monkeys severely impaired by combined but not separate removal of the amygdala and hippocampus. *Nature*, 273, 297–298.

Mishkin, M., & Delacour, J. (1975). An analysis of short-term visual memory in the monkey. *Journal of Experimental Psychology: Animal Behavior Processes*, 1, 326–334.

Mishkin, M., Malamut, B. L., & Bachevalier, J. (in press). Memories and habits: Two neural systems. In J. L. McGaugh, G. Lynch, & N. M. Weinberger (eds), *The neurobiology of learning and memory*. New York: Guilford Press.

Mishkin, M., & Petri, H. L. (in press). Memories and habits: Some implications for the analysis of learning and retention. In N. Butters & L. Squire (eds), *Neuropsychology of memory*. New York: Guilford Press.

Nadel, L., & Zola-Morgan, S. (in press). Infantile amnesia: A neurobiological perspective. In M. Moscovitch (ed.), *Infant memory*. New York: Plenum Press.

O'Keefe, J., & Dostrovsky, J. (1971). The hippocampus as a spatial map: Preliminary evidence from unit activity in the freely moving rat. *Brain Research*, 34, 171–175.

Rose, D. (1980). Some functional correlates of the maturation of neural systems. In D. Caplan (ed.), *Biological studies of mental processes* (pp. 27–43). Cambridge, MA: MIT Press.

Schacter, D. L., & Moscovitch, M. (in press). Infants, amnesics, and dissociable memory systems. In M. Moscovitch (ed.), *Infant memory*. New York: Plenum Press.

Warrington, E. K., & Weiskrantz, L. (1971). Organizational aspects of memory in amnesic patients. *Neuropsychologia*, 9, 67–73.

Zimmermann, R. R., & Torrey, C. C. (1965). Ontogeny of learning. In A. M. Schrier, H. F. Harlow, & F. Stollnitz (eds.), *Behavior of nonhuman primates: Modern research trends* (Vol. 2, pp. 405–447). New York: Academic Press.

Zola-Morgan, S., Squire, L. R., & Mishkin, M. (1982). The neuroanatomy of amnesia: Amygdala-hippocampus versus temporal stem. *Science*, 218, 1337–1339.

12

Neuropsychological Insights into the Meaning of Object Concept Development

ADELE DIAMOND

I propose that infants know a good deal more about objects than Piaget gave them credit for knowing. For Piaget, many of the developments between 5 and 12 months of age concerned the elaboration of the concept of the object and the concept of space. The thesis of this chapter is (a) that what emerges between 5 and 12 months is, instead, the ability to *demonstrate* an understanding of these concepts, the understanding already having been present, and (b) that these behavioral developments between 5 and 12 months are intimately tied to maturation of frontal cortex.

If infants understand the object concept and spatial relationships, why can't they demonstrate this in their behavior? There appear to be two reasons. First, behavioral predispositions get in the way. Infants must be able to inhibit these action tendencies if they are to demonstrate what they know. Second, the demonstrations that Piaget required of infants often involve relating two actions together in a sequence or relating information over a separation in space or time. These inhibitory and relational abilities are not in place early in the first year. Frontal cortex and its network of neural interconnections must reach a certain level of maturity before these abilities begin to appear.

Inhibitory Control

Cognitive development can be conceived of, not only as the progressive *acquisition* of knowledge, but also as the enhanced *inhibition* of reactions that get in the way

"Neuropsychological Insights into the Meaning of Object Concept Development" first appeared in *The Epigenesis of Mind: Essays on Biology and Cognition*, edited by S. Carey and R. Gelman (Lawrence Erlbaum Associates, 1991, pp. 67–110), and is reprinted by kind permission.

of demonstrating knowledge that is already present. Reflexes of the hand, which are invaluable aids during the first months of life, must be inhibited if more mature manipulatory behavior is to emerge. Over the period of *5–8 months of age* infants become able to inhibit their *reflexive reactions to contact*, such as the grasp reflex. Inhibition of these reflexes depends on maturation of the supplementary motor area (SMA) (see figure 12.1).

Between *8 and 12 months of age* infants first become able to inhibit *predominant response tendencies*, that is, they first become able to resist the strongest response of the moment. (A response tendency can be inherently predominant, such as reaching straight for a visible goal: If you see what you want, the tendency to go toward it does not have to be learned. Indeed, it requires effort and discipline to resist this tendency when a more circuitous route is appropriate. A predominant response can also be acquired or learned, e.g. on the basis of reinforcement

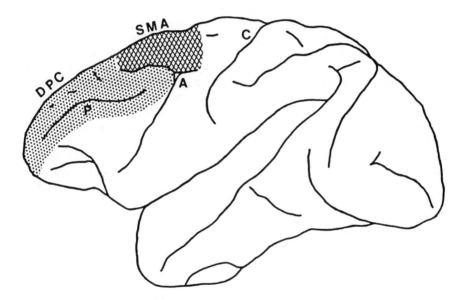

Figure 12.1 A lateral view of the rhesus monkey (*Macaca mulatta*) brain. The area covered by hatched lines just behind the arcuate sulcus represents the supplementary motor area (SMA), which extends further to the midline than can be shown in this diagram. SMA occupies the anterior medial surface of Brodmann's Area 8. In the terminology of other maps of the macaque brain, SMA corresponds to Area 6aβ of the Vogts and Areas FC and FB of von Bonin and Bailey (see Welsendanger, 1981). The dotted area just in front of the arcuate sulcus represents dorsolateral prefrontal cortex (DPC). Dorsolateral prefrontal cortex centers around the principal sulcus and extends from the anterior bank of the arcuate sulcus to the frontal pole. It includes most of Brodmann's Area 9, Area 8, and some of Area 10. In the terminology of other maps of the macaque brain, it corresponds to Area 9, much of Area 8, and some of Area 10 of the Vogts, and corresponds most closely to Area 46 of Walker, including Walker's Areas 8 and 9 as well. C = central sulcus. All cortex in front of the central sulcus is part of frontal cortex. A = arcuate sulcus. This is the principal boundary between SMA and dorsolateral prefrontal cortex. P = principal sulcus. This is the "heart" of dorsolateral prefrontal cortex.

experience.) Inhibition of the dominant or habitual response depends upon maturation of dorsolateral prefrontal cortex. Dorsolateral prefrontal cortex borders SMA and is immediately anterior to it (see figure 12.1).

Relational Abilities

Inhibition is only one of the abilities dependent on frontal cortex that appears to underlie behavioral changes between 5 and 12 months. Piaget correctly saw that many of the advances of this period are made possible by the increasing ability to "put into relation" (Piaget, 1952, pp. 237–9). Part of the task solved by infants between *5 and 8 months of age* is to *combine actions together into a behavioral sequence*, whether it be a means–end sequence or a reaching sequence consisting of two different movements. Relating two or more movements into a sequence in this way is dependent upon SMA.

Over the period of *8–12 months*, infants become able, for the first time, to relate two different movements together *simultaneously*. That is, they become able to do one action with one hand while at the same time doing something else with the other hand. This complementary use of the two hands is dependent upon maturation of the interhemispheric connections via the corpus callosum between the two SMAs on either side of the brain. Such bimanual coordination is an achievement of relational ability *and* inhibition, in as much as it requires not only coordinating the actions of the two hands but also inhibiting the tendency of both hands to do the same thing.

From *8 to 12 months* one also sees important advances in the ability to *relate information over temporal delays or spatial separations*. (Note that relating information over a temporal delay requires memory, or sustained attention, to keep something in mind in the absence of perceptual supports. This is seen here as part of a more general ability to relate information separated in space or time.) This ability is tied to dorsolateral prefrontal cortex. Whereas SMA is required for executing a sequence of actions, dorsolateral prefrontal cortex is required for remembering a sequence of actions (as in temporal order memory).

Frontal Cortex Maturation

Thus, I am proposing that some of the critical behavioral changes in the second half of the first year of life are made possible by maturational changes in frontal cortex and in its neural connections. More precisely, the hypothesis is that those maturational changes begin more posteriorly (involving the supplementary motor area, SMA) and progress toward the frontal pole (dorsolateral prefrontal cortex) over these months, and include the emergence of interhemispheric communication between the frontal cortices on the two sides of the brain.

Plan of the Chapter

First, evidence is presented that an understanding of the object concept and of the spatial relations among objects, such as contiguity, are present early in the first year. Given that, the question of why infants make the striking mistakes Piaget so astutely observed is considered. (If infants are as smart as I claim, why do they act so "dumb"?) Finally, evidence is provided linking the behavioral advances during the first year, and the abilities that underlie them, to frontal cortex. Contiguous objects, hidden objects, and detour reaching are considered. The chapter is organized, not by problem or task, but by age. First, the changes between 5 and 9 months are considered, that is, tasks on which infants of 5–7 months fail but infants of 7½–9 months succeed. Second, the changes between 8 and 12 months are considered, that is, tasks on which infants of 7½–9 months fail but infants 9½–12 months succeed.

Changes between 5 and 9 Months of Age: Relating Actions Together in a Sequence and Inhibition of the Reflexes of the Hand

Contiguous Objects

Piaget (1937/1954) concluded that infants do not understand the spatial concept of contiguity, that is, that an object continues to exist independently even when it shares a boundary with another object: "[T]here is a general difficulty in conceiving of the relations of objects among themselves (in contrast to the relations of objects with the subject himself). It is this general difficulty which prevents the child from realizing that two objects can be independent of each other when the first is placed upon the second" (p. 177).

The behavioral observation on which this was based was that although infants can retrieve a small free-standing object, they fail to retrieve that same object if it is placed on top of a slightly larger object. This was confirmed by Bower (1974), who also demonstrated that infants fail to retrieve an object if it is placed directly behind a slightly larger object. For example, infants will retrieve a small object if it is several inches behind a screen but not if it is directly behind the screen. Bower's (1977) conclusion echoed that of Piaget: "It seems that what the baby doesn't understand is that two objects can be in a spatial relationship to one another, so that they share a common boundary. Evidently it is the common boundary that is critical" (pp. 116–17).

We have confirmed Bower's observations, using a plexiglass box open at the top rather than a screen. We found that infants could retrieve a building block from the center of the plexiglass box (2 inches from the front wall of the box), but they failed to retrieve the building block when it was directly behind the front wall of the box (Diamond and Gilbert, 1989). However, we also found that infants succeeded in retrieving the building block when it was outside the box, bordering the front wall. Moreover, when a thinner building block was used, infants failed to retrieve that when it was a half-inch behind the front wall of the box (not touching the wall), although they successfully retrieved the thin block when it was in the center of the box (2 inches from the front wall). Here, infants succeeded in a condition of contiguity ("in front of") but failed in a condition where the wall and toy shared no common boundary (thin toy a half-inch from wall). These findings cannot be accounted for by a problem in understanding the concept of contiguity. Sharing a common boundary seems not to be the critical factor.

Infants did not fail because they did not try. All tried to retrieve the toy, and gave clear evidence that they were reaching for the toy and not the box. Their behavior indicated that they knew the toy was there even when it bordered the wall of the box. For example, infants showed little interest in reaching for the box alone, but when the toy was inside (even when it bordered the wall) they reached persistently. They showed great frustration at not being able to retrieve the toy. Although they typically made contact with the box rather than the toy, their reaches all appeared to be directed at the toy.

In studying the frame-by-frame record of the infants' performance, we noticed that unsuccessful reaches often ended with the infants grasping the edge

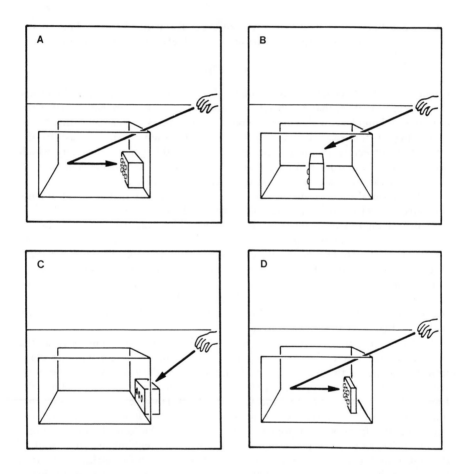

Figure 12.2 Infants could reach on a straight line for the toy when (C) the toy was outside the box, bordering the front wall, and when (B) the toy was in the center of the box. However, when (A) the toy was inside the box, bordering the front wall, or when (D) a thinner toy was one-half inch behind the front wall, infants could not get to the toy by reaching on a straight line. They had to reach over the front wall of the box and then change direction to reach back for the toy. (Adapted from Diamond and Gilbert, 1989.)

of the box (grasp reflex) or grazing the edge of the box and then jerking their hand back (avoidance reflex). Grasping the edge or withdrawing their hand would then be followed by another attempt to reach, and another, and another, each ending with the same frustrating result.

In short, it seemed to us that the infants were trying to retrieve the toy, but were having difficulty in getting their hand to the toy. The problem seemed to be that (a) the infants could not guide their reaches accurately enough to avoid touching the edge of the box en route to the toy, and (b) once they touched the edge of the box they could not inhibit reflexive grasp or avoidance reactions. (A touch too slight to trigger a reflexive grasp is often sufficient to trigger the avoidance reaction, which consists of withdrawing or springing the hand back in response to contact: Twitchell, 1965, 1970.)[1]

Seven-month-old infants can accurately reach to a free-standing object and can retrieve a toy from the center of the box. Why, then, should they have had difficulty aiming their hand to the toy when it was touching, or near, the front wall of the box? We reasoned that by 7 months infants could execute a straight reach with ease, but they had difficulty executing a reach that required changing direction (i.e. reaching away from the goal and then back toward it). When the toy was in front of the box touching the front wall, or in the center of the box, infants could reach for it on a straight line. However, when the toy was directly behind the front wall of the box, infants had to first reach over the wall and then back for the toy (see figure 12.2).

To test this, we predicted that infants would perform better if the box were closer to them (so that they could reach straight down for the toy), if the walls of the box were lower, if the toy were placed vertically so that it was as tall as the box, or if the toy were placed perpendicular to the wall (so that although a side of the toy still bordered the wall, the toy extended into the middle of the box and could be reached on a straight line). In all of these conditions, a straight line of reach would be possible, even though the toy bordered the front wall in every case. All predictions were confirmed (figure 12.3). Infants succeeded even though the toy was directly behind the front wall; these same infants failed the baseline condition with the same toy in the horizontal position, directly behind the front wall (see figure 12.3).

Frame-by-frame analysis of the videotapes indicated that infants touched the edge of the front wall much more often in conditions requiring a two-directional reach than in conditions permitting a unidirectional reach for the toy. For example, when the toy was directly behind the front wall of the box, 7-month-old infants touched the edge of the box an average of 7.31 times per trial, whereas when the toy was in the center of the box they touched the edge of the box only an average of 1.53 times per trial (matched pairs $t(15) = 4.74$, $P = 0.0005$). By 10 months of age, infants touched the edge of the box significantly less often, even when a two-directional reach was required for success. For example, when the toy was directly behind the front wall of the box, 10-month-old infants touched the edge of the box only an average of 3.13 times per trial (*vs* 7.31 for 7-month-olds: $t(7) = 4.21$, $P = 0.01$). Thus, when a direct line of reach was possible, infants of both 7 and 10 months of age reached accurately enough to avoid touching the box. When a two-directional reach was necessary, however, infants of 7 months had much more difficulty than infants of 10 months in

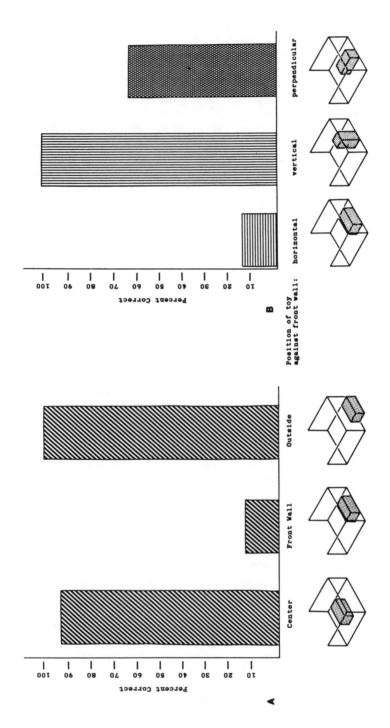

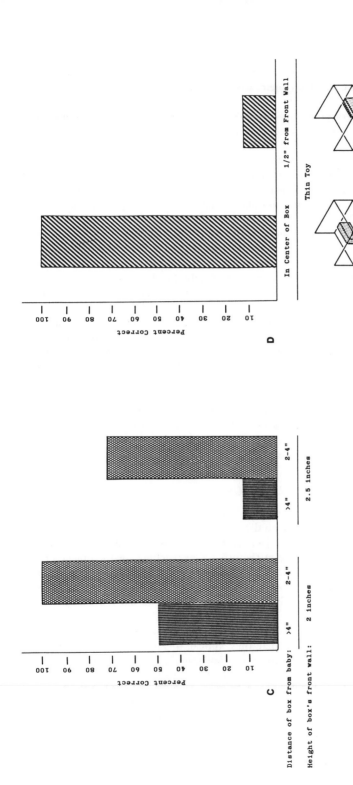

Figure 12.3 (a) Percent correct with toy in the center of the box, directly behind front wall, and outside directly in front of the front wall. (b) Percent correct with the toy horizontal, vertical, or perpendicular to the front wall. (In all instances, the toy bordered the front wall.) (c) Percent correct by distance of box from the infant and height of the front wall of the box. Note that percent correct is lowest when the taller box was farther away, and highest when the shorter box was closer. (d) Percent correct for thin toy in the center of the box and 0.5 inches from the front wall. The box is drawn with the front of the box toward the right side of the page. Top and back of box are open. (From Diamond and Gilbert, 1989.)

accurately executing that sequence of movements and so touched the edge of the box significantly more often on their way to the toy.

Moreover, infants of 7 months typically reacted to touching the edge of the box by reflexively grasping the box (68 percent of the time) or reflexively withdrawing their hand (15 percent of the time). Infants of 7 months rarely continued a reach despite grazing the edge of box and rarely continued a reach after grasping the box. Instead, they recoiled their hand and began the reach again from the starting position. Infants of 10 months, on the other hand, were much less likely to react reflexively when they touched the box (grasping the edge only 25 percent of the time and almost never reflexively pulling their hand back) and were much more likely to continue their reach despite contacting the box (10-month-olds *vs* 7-month-olds: $t(7) = 14.18$, $P < 0.0001$).

We interpret these findings to indicate that infants of 7 months do, indeed, know that an object that shares a boundary with another object is still there. They give clear evidence of reaching specifically for that object, and under diverse conditions of a shared boundary they are able to successfully retrieve the object. They fail under certain conditions of contiguity (and, indeed, under other conditions where no common boundary is shared) because of difficulty in executing a reach which changes direction and difficulty inhibiting reflexive reactions of the hand.[2] We conclude that infants of 7 months (and even infants as young as 5 months, see Diamond, 1990b) understand the concept that an object continues to exist as a separate entity when it shares a boundary with another object. Their behavior often fails to reflect this understanding, however, because of their imperfect control of the movements of their hands. By at least 10 months of age, and perhaps earlier, infants have sufficient control of their actions to enable them to demonstrate in their behavior the conceptual understanding that was present much earlier.

Hidden Objects

Piaget was the first to observe that infants of 5–7 months will not reach for an object hidden under a cover or behind a screen, even if the experimenter rattles or squeaks the object, even if the object creates a large bulge under a cloth cover, and indeed even if the infant were in the process of reaching for the object when it was covered (e.g. Gratch, 1972; Piaget, 1936/1952; 1937/1954). Piaget concluded from this that infants below 8 months do not have the concept of object permanence; they do not know that an object continues to exist when it is out of sight.

When looking rather than reaching is the dependent measure, however, infants of only 4–5 months demonstrate that they appear to know that an object they can no longer see does continue to exist (Baillargéon, 1987; Baillargéon et al., 1985). Baillargéon habituated infants to the movement of a screen back and forth through a 180° arc, like a drawbridge. A box was then placed behind the screen. In one test condition, infants were shown the screen moving along its arc until it reached the occluded box (movement of 112°; a possible event). In the other condition, the screen moved through its full 180° arc as though the box were no longer behind it (an impossible event). Infants of 4 and 5 months, and some infants of 3 months, looked significantly longer at the impossible, than at the possible, event, suggesting that they knew the box hidden behind the screen was still there. When no box was placed behind the screen, all infants looked reliably longer when the screen stopped before completing its 180° arc (movement of 112°: same movement as in the possible condition above) than when the screen repeated the boring 180° arc to which they had habituated (see table 12.1). Thus, the presence of an object which the infants could no longer see behind the screen significantly affected their looking time; the infants seemed to expect the screen to stop when it reached the object and were surprised (looked longer) when the screen continued beyond this point. The 4- and 5-month-old infants knew that an object they could no longer see was still there; they understood the concept of object permanence.

Why should there be this décalage between when infants' looking and reaching behaviors reveal their knowledge about objects? One possibility is that visual habituation requires only a simple response (looking at what one is interested in), whereas reaching measures have required a more complicated means–end response, such as removing a cover or detouring around a screen in order to then reach for the desired object. In visual habituation studies, the subject does not look at something in order to produce anything else. In reaching studies, however, subjects have had to act on one object in order to obtain another. The requirement that they execute a sequence of actions might account for why infants do not uncover a hidden object, or reach around an opaque screen to obtain a hidden object, until about 7½–8 months of age, although they know and remember that the hidden object is still there by at least 4–5 months of age. Note that infants begin to reach for hidden objects at about the same age as they first organize other actions into means–end sequences (e.g. pulling a cloth closer to retrieve a distant toy on the cloth) (Piaget, 1937/1954; Willatts, 1987). Note also that infants of 5 months appear to reach for objects in the dark (Wishart et al. 1978) – this might be because they can reach directly for the object there, without first acting on anything else.

To explore whether the crucial variable might be a simple response versus a means–end action sequence, we have tested infants on two versions of the same task. In one version the response is made by reaching; in the other version the response is made by looking; but in *both* versions the response is simple and direct (Diamond, 1990c). In both versions, infants are presented with a sample object until they habituate, a delay is imposed, and then the sample object is presented again paired with an object the infants have never been exposed to before.

Table 12.1 Looking responses of 4–5 month-old infants to the movement of a screen after they had habituated to the screen moving 180° by whether or not a solid object was placed behind the screen after habituation (based on Baillargéon, 1987; Baillargéon et al., 1985)

	Infants' responses to movement of screen 180°	*Infants' responses to movement of screen 112°*
No object behind screen	looked little (bored)	looked long (surprised)
Solid object behind screen	looked long (surprised)	looked little (bored)

Note: Once the screen was raised 90° or more, the object was no longer visible.

This task has been widely used with infants with looking as the dependent measure, where it has been called the "visual paired comparison" task (e.g. Caron et al., 1977; Fagan, 1970; Pancratz and Cohen, 1970; Rose et al., 1982; Werner and Perlmutter, 1979). By 4 months of age, infants show that they remember a sample object by looking preferentially at the novel object after delays of 10–15 sec. (Albarran, n. d.; Pancratz and Cohen, 1970; Stinson, 1971). A similar task using reaching as the dependent measure, called the "delayed non-matching to sample" task, was originally devised to study brain function in monkeys (e.g. Gaffan, 1974; Mishkin and Delacour, 1975; Zola-Morgan and Squire, 1986; Zola-Morgan et al., 1989). Here, subjects must displace the object in order to retrieve the reward underneath (a means–end sequence). Children reach randomly on this task with a 5- or 10-sec. delay until almost 2 years of age, when they begin to reach consistently to the new object (Diamond, 1990c; Overman, 1990) – compare this to their consistent looking to the new stimulus on the visual paired comparison task with delays of 10 sec. at only 4–5 months of age. A similar décalage is seen in the performance of infant monkeys: They consistently prefer to look at the novel stimulus in the visual paired comparison task with delays of 10 sec. as early as 15 *days* of age and perhaps earlier (Brickson and Bachevalier, 1984), but they fail to consistently reach to the novel stimulus in the delayed non-matching to sample task with delays of 10 sec. until at least 4 months of age (Bachevalier and Mishkin, 1984).

We hypothesized that success on delayed non-matching to sample may appear much later than success on visual paired comparison because the former requires subjects to act on one object to retrieve another, whereas the latter requires only the simple act of looking. To test this, we modified the delayed non-matching to sample task so that it no longer required a means–end sequence, but only a simple reach. Instead of rewarding infants with something underneath the object, we allowed the infants to have the object they reached for as the reward. Because babies have a natural preference for novelty we reasoned that if we gave them enough time with the sample object to begin to get bored with it, they would want to reach for something new when later given the chance, rather than that old sample object again.

We now had a version of the task that required a simple looking response (the traditional visual paired comparison task) and a version of the task that required a simple reaching response (the modified delayed non-matching to sample task). In both versions, the same 10 pairs of three-dimensional objects were used, and infants were tested for two trials each at delays of 10 sec., 15 sec., 1 min, 3 min, and 10 min. Half of the infants were shown an object to look at until they habituated to it and then, following a delay, were given the choice of looking at that same object or a new one. Half of the infants were shown an object to reach for and were allowed to keep the object until they habituated to it; then, following a delay, they were given the choice of reaching for the same object or a new one.

We replicated the finding from previous studies of visual paired comparison that infants of 4 months look preferentially at the novel stimulus after delays of 10 sec. Additionally, infants performed every bit as well on the modified delayed non-matching to sample task as they did on visual paired comparison, from roughly the earliest age infants can retrieve free-standing objects. That is, by 6 months of age, infants succeeded on the looking version of the task with delays

Table 12.2 Percent of infants choosing the non-matching (novel) object by age, task, and delay

Delays	4 months old VPC	4 months old DNMS	6 months old VPC	6 months old DNMS	9 months old VPC	9 months old DNMS	12 months old VPC	12 months old DNMS
10 sec	70**		90**	85**	80**	85**		90**
15 sec	55		60	80**	80**	85**		85**
1 min	60		75**	70**	80**	90**		85**
3 min	50		70**	65*	65*	85**		90**
10 min	50		60	70**	70**	80**		85**

VPC = visual paired comparison task. DNMS = delayed non-matching to sample task (modified). Choice of non-matching (novel) object in VPC = looked at novel object at least 67 percent of the time during 20-sec. paired presentation. Choice of non-matching (novel) object in DNMS = reached for novel object. All N = 20. Each subject was tested on only one task and at only one age. All received two trials at each delay; these two scores are averaged for each subject. Significance levels (binomial distribution); 90% = 0.0002, 85% = 0.0008, 80% = 0.004, 75% = 0.01, 70% = 0.03, 65% = 0.065, 60% = 0.10, 55% = 0.15. * significant at $P = 0.065$. ** significant at $P < 0.05$

of at least 1–3 min and succeeded on the reaching version with delays of at least 10 min. By 9 months of age, they succeeded on both versions with delays of at least 10 min (Diamond, 1990c; see table 12.2).

Although our task did not involve reaching for a hidden object, we believe that the two versions of our task address the same conundrum as that posed by (a) Baillargéon's evidence that infants demonstrate knowledge of object permanence prior to 7½–8 months when judged by where they look, and (b) the wealth of evidence that infants cannot demonstrate this knowledge until after 7½–8 months when judged by where they reach. Baillargéon (Baillargéon, 1987; Baillargéon et al., 1985) demonstrated that the conceptual understanding appears to be present by at least 4–5 months. Why, then, do infants fail to demonstrate this understanding in their actions until 7½–8 months or later? Perhaps it is because infants cannot organize a means–end action sequence at 4–5 months, but they can at 7½–8 months, and the actions which infants have been required to make to demonstrate that they understand object permanence have always involved a sequence of actions (e.g. removing a cloth as the means to retrieving the toy underneath it). In another situation where a cognitive competence has been seen earlier when assessed by looking (visual paired comparison task) than by reaching (delayed non-matching to sample task), we have demonstrated that when a simple reaching act is required (instead of a means–end sequence) infants demonstrate acquisition of the cognitive competence as early in their reaching as they do through their looking, and much earlier than they do when required to demonstrate this by putting two actions together in a means–end sequence. Note that the ability to uncover a hidden object comes in at roughly the same age as the ability to retrieve one object directly behind another, which also requires linking two sequential actions together (reaching over the barrier and then reaching back for the toy).

In short, infants of 5–7 months appear to understand that an object continues to exist when it is out of sight or when it shares a boundary with another object. They have often failed to demonstrate this conceptual understanding in their behavior because the tasks we have used have required action skills that are beyond the ability of infants this age. Infants of 5–7 months cannot accurately put two actions together in a sequence and cannot inhibit reacting reflexively to touch. These shortcomings in the control of the movements of their hands, and not a failure to understand that contiguous objects, or hidden objects, are still there, have been the critical factor. By 7½–9 months, infants have these action skills and so succeed at the tasks that developmental psychologists have been using.

Functions of the Supplementary Motor Area (SMA): Relating Actions Together in a Sequence and Inhibition of the Reflexes of the Hand

Reflexive grasping, which is present in earliest infancy and is thereafter inhibited, is released in adults by lesions in medial, anterior portions of Brodmann's Area 6 of frontal cortex (SMA). No other cortical area besides Area 6 has been implicated in the release of this reflexive behavior. The effect of Area 6 lesions on reflexive grasping was first noted in monkeys by Richter and Hines (1932) and has been confirmed by Fulton et al. (1932), Penfield and Welch (1951), Travis (1955), Denny-Brown (1966), and Goldberger (1972). Observations of this in human patients are abundant (Addie and Critchley, 1927; Davis and Currier, 1931; Freeman and Crosby, 1929; Goldberg et al., 1981; Kennard et al., 1934; Luria, 1973; Penfield and Jasper, 1954; Walshe and Robertson, 1933). Kennard et al. (1934) offered this representative description of the behavior: "Forced grasping was also observed; very gentle contact with the skin of the palm did not in itself evoke grasping with the body in any position, but contact with the palm or skin at the base of the digits, especially when the patient's attention was diverted, caused a fairly prompt, involuntary grasp, which became more exaggerated as one pulled slightly on the flexor tendons" (p. 78).

Little has been written about the release, following brain damage in adults, of the avoidance reaction, the other reflexive reaction to contact seen in 5–7 month old infants. The only mention of it that I know of is by Denny-Brown (Denny-Brown, 1966; Denny-Brown and Chambers, 1958), who has linked it to lesions of parietal cortex.

Infants of 5–7 months might still succeed in retrieving contiguous objects, despite their inability to inhibit the grasp and avoidance reactions, if they could correctly aim their reach so they did not touch the neighboring object (the front wall of the box in our situation). However, the precision of the reach appears to suffer when infants must first aim to clear the front wall of the box and then change direction to retrieve the object inside. Errors in aiming a reach are often observed after lesions to parietal cortex (e.g. *monkeys*: Lamotte and Acuna, 1977; Stein, 1976, 1978; *humans*: Allison et al., 1969; Bender and Teuber, 1947; Cole et al., 1962; Damasio and Benton, 1979). An example of such misreaching errors would be to try to reach inside a box, but instead reach to the box's side. Often the reach is too high, too low, too far to the right, or too far to the left. Infants sometimes make mistakes reminiscent of this (Diamond, 1981), but their errors in reaching for contiguous objects do not seem to be of this type. The reaching errors seen after lesions of frontal cortex, on the other hand, are errors in putting two different movements together, such as are seen in 7-month-old children. For example, instead of reaching over a barrier and then back for the goal object, a monkey with a lesion to frontal cortex may keep on reaching in the initial direction and go well past the goal object. Here, the problem seems to be inhibiting the first movement. The animal continues the first movement instead of switching to the second. Errors in switching are common after lesions in various areas of frontal cortex, but errors at this level of concreteness are most common following lesions of medial, anterior Area 6 (see e.g. Luria, 1973).

Another typical problem following lesions to Area 6, especially SMA, is in linking two or more movements together in the proper order. For example, having been taught to execute a sequence of three movements (push, turn, lift), monkeys with bilateral lesions to SMA were severely impaired in relearning the sequence, although they were unimpaired in executing the individual movements (Halsband, 1982). (In humans see: Orgogozo and Larsen, 1979; Roland et al., 1980.) This is reminiscent of the inability of 5–7-month-old infants to string together two actions into a means–end sequence, even though they are perfectly capable of executing the two actions individually.

In short, I propose that maturational changes in SMA may contribute to the ability of infants older than 7 months to successfully retrieve contiguous objects and hidden objects. By 5–7 months of age, and probably much earlier, infants understand that an object contiguous with another, or an object obscured by another, is still there. Thereafter, their developmental task is not so much to elaborate these concepts, but to gain control of their behavior so that it accurately reflects what they know.

Changes between 8 and 12 Months of Age: Relating Actions Together Simultaneously, Relating Information over a Temporal or Spatial Separation, and Inhibition of Prepotent Response Tendencies

Hidden Objects

The characteristic error with hidden objects seen in sensorimotor stage IV (7½–9 months of age) is called the $\overline{AB}$("A, not B") error. By stage IV, infants are able to find a hidden object. However, having found an object at one place (A), if the object is then hidden at another place (B), infants often search at A, even though they have watched the object being hidden at B only moments before. Piaget believed that infants make this mistake because they still do not understand that objects are permanent, enduring things, independent of the child's actions. Infants somehow believe that no matter where an object is hidden, it can be found where the infant first found it. As Piaget (1937/1954) put it, "[The child] seems to reason as if the place where the object was found the first time remains where he will find it when he wants to do so" (pp. 44–45). ". . . [T]he child looks for and conceives of the object only in a special position, the first place where it was hidden and found.... [T]he original screen seems to him to constitute the special place where the action of finding is successful" (p. 50).

Infants continue to make the A$\overline{\text{B}}$ error from about 7½ to 12 months of age, as long as the delay between hiding and retrieval is incremented as the infants get older (Diamond, 1985). The testing procedure has become quite standard by now. Typically, the hiding places consist of two wells embedded in a tabletop, identical except for their left–right position. The infant watches as a toy is hidden in one of the wells. Both wells are covered simultaneously by identical covers and a brief delay is imposed (0–10 sec.). We prevent infants from staring, or straining, toward the correct well during the delay. Then the infant is allowed to reach. The youngest infants often make the A$\overline{\text{B}}$ error with almost no delay at all. If anything interrupts their visual fixation on the correct well, or their bodily orientation in that direction, they fail, no matter how brief the interruption. Their plan or intention to reach to B seems extremely fragile. Indeed, infants of 6½–7½ months sometimes start reaching to the correct well and then stop in mid-reach, as if they have forgotten why they started reaching. Often they reach to a hiding well, but then in removing the cover get distracted by it, and lose the train of what they were doing. It is difficult to tell at this age, but it appears as if the infants are reaching for the toy, not for the cloth. Once they get the cloth in their hand, however, they attend to that instead of continuing to retrieve the toy. Unlike older infants, infants who can uncover a hidden object at 6½–7½ months of age rarely correct themselves if they reach to the wrong hiding well on the A$\overline{\text{B}}$ task (Diamond, 1983). Older infants spontaneously try to reach to the correct well straightaway if their first reach is wrong (i.e. they try to "self-correct"). The failure of the younger infants to self-correct suggests that they forget why they were reaching if their first reach does not produce the toy.

The fragility of the plan of action indicated here, with the infants easily distracted, easily diverted from their course of action, is very similar to the behavior of patients with frontal cortex damage. They are very easily distracted and have great difficulty sustaining a train of thought. It is remarkably difficult, for example, to obtain a simple personal history from a frontal patient because the patient gets distracted by associations to the history and goes off on tangents. Frontal patients will start to respond to a question or instruction but then get sidetracked so that one must continually remind them what they were doing. As Luria (1973) noted: "Usually these patients begin to perform the task set, but as soon as a stranger enters the ward, or the person in the next bed whispers to the nurse, the patient ceases to perform the task and transfers his gaze to the newcomer or joins in conversation with his neighbor" (p. 275).

At 7½–8 months of age, the average delay between hiding and retrieval required for the A$\overline{\text{B}}$ error is 2sec.. By 9 months it is 5sec., and by 12 months infants perform well on the A$\overline{\text{B}}$ task at delays as long as 10 sec. or more (Diamond, 1985).[3] At all ages, infants perform well if allowed to look at or strain toward the correct well throughout the delay (Cornell, 1979; Fox et al., 1979; Diamond, 1985). At each age, if the delay is reduced 2–3 sec. below the level at which the A$\overline{\text{B}}$ error is found, infants reach correctly whether the toy is hidden at A or at B. If the delay is increased 2–3 sec. above the level at which the A$\overline{\text{B}}$ error is found, infants err even on the trials at A and they become very distressed

(Diamond, 1985). They cry or fuss and refuse to reach at all or perseverate excessively in reaching to the wrong well.[4] All of this suggests that memory ability is crucially important for infants' success on AB̄. If delays are brief, infants succeed; if delays are longer, they fail. If allowed to circumvent the memory requirements of the task by orienting themselves toward the correct well throughout the delay, infants succeed.[5] Older infants only continue to err if increasingly long delays are imposed. Because infants can succeed with short delays or with uninterrupted attention to where the toy was hidden, it is unlikely that their problem is that they think A is the special place where they can find the toy regardless of where it is hidden, as Piaget believed. If this were true, errors should occur regardless of delay or memory load.

Inadequate memory cannot account for all of the findings with the AB̄ task, however. First, because the basic procedures, including delay, are the same on all trials, the memory requirements of all trials should be the same. Hence, errors should be no more likely on one trial than another; errors should be randomly distributed over trials – but they are not. Infants perform very well on "repeat following correct" trials (roughly equivalent to trials at A) but perform poorly on reversal trials (e.g. when the location of hiding changes to well B) and on "repeat following error" trials (roughly equivalent to the subsequent trials at B), even though the delay is the same on all trials (Diamond, 1985). (See table 12.3 for a description of these three types of trials.)

Second, infants show a similar error pattern on the AB̄ task even with transparent covers, although they err less often (Butterworth, 1977). Memory should not be taxed at all when the toy remains visible under a transparent cover. Third, infants, beyond the age of about 7½ months typically reach immediately to the correct well if their initial reach is incorrect. Indeed, often when they reach incorrectly to A, they do *not* look in to see if the toy is there, but reach immediately to B, and then look in for the toy. It is as if they know the toy is at B, even though their first reach was to A. Occasionally, an infant will look fixedly at B even as he or she reaches to A (see figure 12.4). Although this behavior is not common, it has been observed by many researchers in many laboratories; it is very striking when it does occur because at this age infants almost always look where they are reaching. Here, infants appear to be showing

Table 12.3 Types of trials

| Performance on previous trial | Side of hiding | |
	Same as on previous trial	Changed
Correct	Repeat-following-correct trials	Reversal-following-correct trials
Wrong	Repeat-following-error trials	Reversal-following-error trials

Note: Type of trial is determined by whether side of hiding is the same as on the previous trial or not and by whether the subject was correct or not on the previous trial. Reversal-following-error trials occur in delayed response, but not in AB̄, as reversals are only administered in AB̄ following a correct reach. Thus, when discussing AB̄, the term "reversal trials" always refers to Reversal-After-Correct trials.

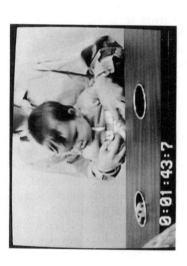

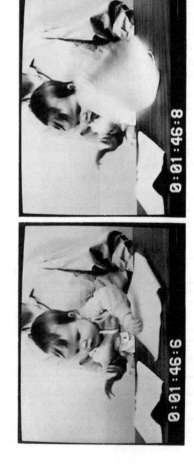

Figure 12.4 Instance of an infant looking at B while reaching to A. Infant had successfully retrieved the toy at A. Side of hiding is now reversed to B. Infant clearly sees the hiding (top row). Following a brief delay, infant was allowed to reach. Although infant was looking fixedly at B, his hand went back to A (bottom row).

with their eyes that they know where the toy is hidden, even though they reach back to A anyway. This is another instance where infants appear to know more than they can demonstrate in their reaching behavior. They seem to understand the concept of object permanence; their problem is demonstrating this under-standing through their behavior.

Adults with damage to dorsolateral prefrontal cortex also indicate, on occasion, that they know the correct answer, despite the fact that they cannot indicate this in their reaching behavior. The classic test for frontal cortex function in adult patients is the Wisconsin Card Sort. The patient is presented with a deck of cards that can be sorted by color, shape, or number. Frontal patients are able to deduce the first criterion by which to sort the cards as well as anyone else. However, after being rewarded for sorting by the first criterion, when the experimenter changes the criterion, patients with frontal cortex damage are impaired in switching to the new criterion. They continue to sort the cards by the first criterion. These patients can sometimes tell you, however, what the new criterion is. Indeed, a patient will sometimes say, as he or she is sorting the cards by the old criterion, "This is wrong, and this is wrong, . . ." (Luria and Homskaya, 1964; Milner, 1964). Here, as when infants look at B while reaching to A, patients appear to know the correct answer but cannot gain control of their behavior to reflect what they know.[6] (This might be considered, in some sense, the inverse of what is seen in amnesia. Amnesic patients often fail to consciously remember information, but they show evidence of "memory" of this information in their behavior. Patients with frontal cortex damage appear to consciously remember the information, but they are often unable to show evidence of this in their reaching behavior.)

In summary, there are two abilities required by the $A\overline{B}$ task: One is memory, and the other is the ability to inhibit the tendency to repeat the rewarded reach at A. When the initial reaches to A are reinforced, the tendency to reach to A is thereby strengthened; it is that response tendency that must be inhibited.[7] This explains the pattern of errors (poor performance at B, excellent performance at A). It also explains why some errors still occur at B (although far fewer) even when there is no memory load (as when transparent covers are used) – here, inhibitory control is taxed (hence some errors) but memory is not (hence fewer errors than when both abilities are required). The pull to reach back toward A can be seen even with multiple wells when the hiding places are arranged so that infants can reach to wells on the side of B away from A or to wells on the side of B toward A. Here, errors are not randomly distributed around B (as a memory interpretation might predict) but are found disproportionately on the side of B toward A (Diamond et al., 1989). Finally, the present interpretation can also account for why some errors (although only a few) are found at well A when a delay is used (e.g. Sophian and Wellman, 1983) – here, memory is taxed (hence some errors) but inhibitory control is not (hence, fewer errors than when both abilities are required).

There appear to be several characteristics of the type of memory ability required for $A\overline{B}$:

1 It is very brief (2–5 sec.).
2 It must be maintained on-line to link together the various components of a trial to guide behavior. That is, the delay is imposed within a trial

(between hiding and response), as opposed to between trials or between testing sessions. When a delay is imposed between trials or between sessions, one is typically studying whether subjects can remember an association they have already learned; in AB̄, subjects must bridge a temporal gap in order to establish the association.

3 Infants must pay attention to the hiding on each trial and continually update their mental record of where the reward has been hidden. Once the toy has been hidden at well A on at least one trial and at well B on at least one trial, one might consider the task to be one of temporal order memory ("Where was the toy hidden most recently?")

4 Because the hiding wells typically differ only in location, one might consider the task to be one of memory for spatial position ("Was the toy hidden on the left or the right?")

5 The information that infants must remember is presented briefly and only once in AB̄ – on any given trial, infants see the toy hidden only once and then the well is quickly covered. The subject "is not trained to the correct response by making it . . . but instead must respond on the basis of a single unrewarded and unpunished presentation" (Jacobsen & Nissen, 1937, p. 132).

The type of memory required for AB̄ can be contrasted with memory abilities seen in infants much younger than 7½–9 months. Once they have learned an association between a cue and response, they can remember it for long periods (hours, days, and even weeks e.g. Rovee-Collier, 1984). Here, they are typically given repeated presentations and long exposure times to learn the association, and once it is learned they never need to update it. As long as they remember it, that single rule leads to correct performance across all trials and all testing sessions.

Indeed, within the AB̄ situation, infants can learn to associate the hidden toy with a landmark, and to use the landmark's location to guide their reaching (Diamond, 1983). Memory is required here, for the infant must remember the association between the landmark and the reward. However, once this single association is learned, the infant can use that to guide performance on all trials; memory does not need to be updated on each trial.

Visual paired comparison and delayed non-matching to sample require that memory be updated on each trial, and they require that memory of the sample be maintained on-line during the delay period within a trial. Yet infants show evidence of memory on visual paired comparison and on our modified version of delayed non-matching to sample at delays of at least 1 minute at 6 months and delays of at least 10 minutes at 9 months – delays far longer than the 2–5 sec. at which they fail AB̄ at the ages of 7½–9 months. The differences in the memory requirements are that visual paired comparison and delayed non-matching to sample do not pose problems of temporal order memory, as unique stimuli are used on each trial, and they do not require memory of spatial information. Moreover, if an infant remembers which stimulus was the sample, the infant need only do what comes naturally (i.e. choose the new stimulus); whereas on AB̄ the infant must not only remember where the object was hidden, but must also resist a strong response tendency to reach to the previously correct location.

Detour Reaching

Over the same ages that infants' ability to find hidden objects improves, infants also improve in their ability to detour around a barrier to retrieve objects. The detour task I have studied, called "object retrieval," involves a small, clear box. The box can be placed so that the front, top, left, or right side is open. The infant's task is to retrieve a toy from inside the open box; the toy being clearly visible through the transparent walls of the box (Diamond, 1981).

Infants of 6½–7 months reach only at the side of the box through which they see the toy. If they see the toy through the opening, they reach in and retrieve it, but if they see the toy through a closed side, they reach repeatedly to that side, trying no other approach to the toy. This is typical of sensorimotor stage III behavior: alternative approaches are not generated, behavior is not varied; rather, the same way of attempting to retrieve the toy is tried over and over again.[8]

The tendency to reach straight through the side at which they are looking is remarkably strong. Even when an infant has successfully retrieved the toy from the front of the box on three trials in a row, if the box is moved so that the infant now sees the toy through the top of the box, he or she will not reach to the open front but will reach only to the top of the box. Here, the infant's failure to inhibit the strong urge to reach straight to the toy results not in perseveration, as it does on AB̄, but in a change in where the reach is directed. If the infant repeated the previous response (i.e. if the infant continued to reach to the front of the box), the infant would succeed, but infants fail by not perseverating.

When the left or right side of the box is open, they can retrieve the toy if it extends partially outside the box opening, but not if it is totally inside the box. This is because they reach only at the sides through which they see the toy, which are the top and front sides of the box.

At 7½–8 months of age, infants take active steps for the first time to change the side of the box through which they see the toy. They bend down to look in the front of the box, or raise the box so they can see in through the front. They are no longer restricted to acting on only one side of the box. On their own initiative, they reach to both the top and the front of the box on the same trial. This is the kind of change from a reactive, passive approach to a more active orientation that marks Piaget's sensorimotor stage IV. Indeed, the same infants tested on object retrieval and on object permanence first show this active orientation on object retrieval at the same age at which they can first find a hidden object (Diamond, 1988). A similar change occurs in attachment behavior at this time: infants progress from just reacting to the overtures of their caregivers (phase 2 attachment) to actively initiating overtures to their caregivers on their own (phase 3 attachment) (Bowlby, 1969).

Infants of 7½–8 months still reach only to the side of the box through which they are looking, however. When they see the toy through the top, they reach to the top; when they see the toy through the front, they reach to the front. Moreover, their efforts to raise the box are of little help to infants at 7½–8 months. They cannot raise the box *and* reach for the toy at the same time, and after the box comes back down and they see the toy again through the top of the box, they reach only there (see figure 12.5).

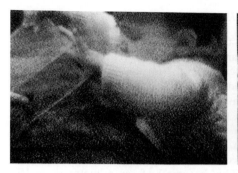

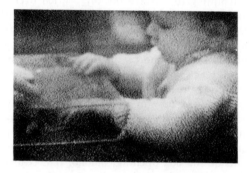

Figure 12.5 Frame 1: Front of box is open. Nina raises box, establishing a direct line of sight to the toy through the opening. (Experimenter is holding back of box, exerting downward pressure on it.) Frame 2: Nina starts to reach for the toy through the opening, but when one hand comes down to reach, the hand left holding onto the box comes down, too. Note that Nina's hand is now inside the box, perhaps a half inch from the toy, but her line of sight to the toy is now through the top. Frame 3: Nina withdraws her hand from inside the box and tries to reach for the toy through the top, i.e. she tries to reach through the side she is looking. (From Diamond, 1981.)

Often, infants of 7½–8 months raise the box with both hands, but with both hands thus occupied, there is no free hand with which to retrieve the toy. The infants lean forward, their head just inches from the toy, but the toy remains inaccessible. Often, too, an infant will raise the front of the box with both hands, remove one hand from the box and attempt to reach for the toy, but the box comes down, halting the reach. The box comes down because when one hand is lowered to reach for the toy, infants have great difficulty *not* lowering the other hand. They try repeatedly to reach while the box is raised, but the hand left to hold up the box keeps failing at its task. Bruner et al. (1968) noted similar behaviors with a slightly different task. Their apparatus was a box with a transparent lid. The lid was mounted on sliding ball bushings. To retrieve the toy, the child had to slide the lid up its track, which was tilted 30° from the horizontal and would fall back down if not held. Bruner et al. (1968) observed that infants of seven months have "great difficulty holding the panel with one hand while reaching underneath with the other. Indeed, the first compromise solutions to the problem consist of pushing the panel up with both hands, then attempting to free one hand in order to slip it under the panel. One notes how often the infant fails because the two hands operate in concert" (p. 222).

By 8½–9 months of age, infants can bend down to look in the front of the box, then sit up, look through the top, and reach into the front. For the first time, one sees a separation of line of sight from line of reach: infants can look through one side of the box while reaching through another. Similarly, they can raise the box, let the box come back down, and reach into the front while looking through the top. Although they are still not able to hold the box up with one hand and reach in with the other, they are able to do this sequentially, first raising the box and then reaching in.

Millar and Schaffer (1972, 1973) also found that the ability to look one place and reach another emerged at around 9 months of age. Using an operant conditioning paradigm, they trained infants to depress a lever in order to see a colored light display. Even infants of 6 months could learn this when the lights and lever were in the same visual field. When the lights and lever were not in the same visual field, however, 6-month-olds failed to acquire the response, although 9-month-olds succeeded. Nine-month-olds succeeded by looking one place (at the lights) while simultaneously acting at another (the lever). This strategy was not in evidence at 6 months.

Infants of 8½–9 months still need to have seen the toy through the opening on each trial to succeed, but success no longer depends on maintaining that line of sight. For the first time, the memory of having seen the toy through the opening is enough. Raising the box aids performance now, not because infants are able to reach in for the toy with one hand while raising the box with the other, but because once the box is back down on the table, they can reach in while looking through the top, having looked into the opening while the box was raised.

When the top of the box is open and the box is far from the infant, infants of 8½–9 months begin to raise one hand to reach for the toy as they extend the other to pull the box closer to themselves. As the pull begins, the other hand is raised in readiness, and the reach is timed to meet the toy as the box draws near. For the first time, the action sequence gives the clear appearance of having been planned from the start. By 9 months this is very smooth and skillful.

When the right or left side of the box is open, infants of 8½–9 months reach with the hand contralateral to the opening. That is, they reach to the right side of the box with their left hand and to the left side with their right hand (Bruner et al., 1969; Diamond, 1981; Gaiter, 1973; Schonen and Bresson, 1984). Reaching with the hand farthest from the opening makes the action maximally contorted and awkward, and is therefore called an "awkward reach." This reach may occur because infants need to look into the opening *and maintain that line of sight* in order to succeed. Infants need to lean over quite far to look into the opening. In that leaning position, the hand ipsilateral to the opening is almost trapped under the body, and there is a tendency to want to leave it available to break one's fall if the pull of gravity becomes too strong. Hence, the awkward reach may be a consequence of the need to match up the infant's line of sight and line of reach to the toy. On the other hand, from an upright position, the only way to retrieve the toy through the left or right side of the box is to reach away from the toy at the midline (toward the opening), and then reach back to the toy (midline) – a two-directional reach. When an infant is leaning over and the hand is coiled to reach, the hand can shoot in for the toy on a straight line. Hence, the awkward reach may be consequence of the need to make a direct, straight movement rather than a sequence of two movements.[9] Finally, if the box is the visual world of the infant for the moment, and the toy is all the way over in the far corner of the box, the image of the toy may fall on the visual field of only one hemisphere, in which case infants reaching with the "awkward hand" would be reaching with the hand controlled by the same hemisphere as the one receiving the visual image of the toy.

By 9½–10 months, infants can coordinate looking through the top of the box while reaching through the front, without ever having looked in the front opening. They can also coordinate raising the box with one hand and simultaneously reaching in for the toy with the other. Note, however, that there is less need to raise the box at this age because infants have less need to see in the front opening. When the left or right side of the box is open, most infants need to have leaned and looked in the opening before they reach to the opening. However, they can now lean and look, then sit up straight, and reach through the side opening while looking through the top of the box. The awkward reach no longer is seen.

Finally, by 11–12 months, infants are perfect on the object retrieval task. They can retrieve the toy from any side of the box efficiently, speedily, and without ever having looked in the opening.

One of the major problems posed by object retrieval is the need to inhibit the pull to reach directly to the visible goal. Indeed, infants perform much better when the box is opaque (Diamond, 1981, 1990b; see Bruner et al., 1969; Church, 1971; Lockman, 1984; Schonen and Bresson, 1984, for similar results with transparent and opaque barriers).

Most infants early in the second half of the first year attend to the sight of the toy, ignoring abundant tactile information about the closed and open surfaces of the box. For example, if they see the toy through the top of the box, they reach only at the box's top, even if they happen to be touching or grasping the opening of the box. A minority of infants at 9½–10 months appear to attend only to tactile information. For example, one child kept getting her thumb caught on the top edge of the opening when the left or right side of the box was open. To help her, the experimenter tipped the box to enlarge the size of the opening, but then the child reached yet higher and still got her thumb stuck on the top edge of the opening! She seemed to search for the opening the way a blind person would, by feeling for the edge. When the opening was made very large, she still went for the edge. Other infants, upon feeling the back edge of the opening, bent their hand around the back of the box as if they thought they had touched the front edge of the opening and were entering the box. No infants, however, until close to 1 year of age, give evidence of attending to both visual and tactile information.

The developmental progression in the use of visual and tactile information nicely illustrates Piaget's point that differentiation and intercoordination are part and parcel of the same development. As infants become better able to intercoordinate vision and touch, attending to both, they also become better able to dissociate them so that they can look one place and reach another.

For Piaget, many of the advances during the second half of the first year of life reflect infants' newly acquired ability to "put into relation": relating one action to another in a means–end sequence, relating two objects to one another in a spatial relation, and so forth. In this, Piaget was most certainly correct. For example, infants progress from straight line reaches to reaches that require relating a movement in one direction to another movement in a different direction; infants become able to relate the movements of their two hands so that what each hand does complements the other. In particular, infants become able to do different things simultaneously – for example, they can look one place, or along one route, while reaching at another place, or along another route; they can reach simultaneously for two different objects (Diamond, 1988); they can simultaneously concentrate on both visual and tactile information. They also become able to relate information over increasingly large temporal separations (increasingly long delays in A$\overline{\text{B}}$) and increasingly large spatial separations (increasing distances between the toy and box opening in object retrieval).

Advances of the second half-year also reflect (more than Piaget appreciated) infants' emerging ability to resist or inhibit the reflexes of the hand and later to resist or inhibit response tendencies strengthened by reinforcement (as in A$\overline{\text{B}}$) or innately strong (such as the response tendency to reach straight to one's goal seen in object retrieval). Instead of reacting automatically with the strongest response of the moment, infants begin to gain more control over their behavior and begin to demonstrate intentionality, which Piaget saw as the crowning achievement of the sensorimotor period.[10] The execution of intentional behavior requires not only planning and "putting into relationship," as Piaget so clearly saw, but also resisting more automatic action tendencies that lead the behavior astray.

Interhemispheric Communication between the Supplementary Motor Areas (SMAs) on the Left and Right Sides of the Brain: Relating Actions Together Simultaneously

Human adults, and monkeys, with lesions of SMA have difficulty with the complementary use of the two hands. Their hands tend to do the same thing, making bimanual coordination difficult. Brinkman (1984) provides an excellent example of this in the monkey following an SMA lesion. Removal of SMA in human adults results in similar lasting deficits when simultaneous, but different, movements of the two hands are required (Laplane et al., 1977; Luria, 1973). For example, these patients have great difficulty making a fist with one hand while simultaneously turning their other hand palm-up. They either do the same thing with both hands or execute the movements sequentially. This is very similar to the behavior seen in 7½–9-month-old infants. In their reaching, for example, infants of 7 months move both hands in the same direction, instead of in opposite (complementary) directions, as do infants by 11 months (Goldfield and Michel, 1986). When infants of 7½–9 months raise the object retrieval box with both hands, they have great difficulty not lowering the second hand when one hand goes down to reach in the box. By 8½–9 months, infants can solve this sequentially by first raising the box and then reaching in, but it is still beyond

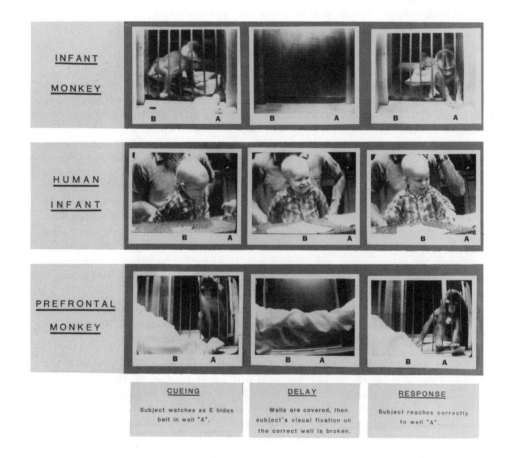

Figure 12.6 Example of the A̅B̅ error in an infant monkey, human infant, and an adult monkey with bilateral lesions of dorsolateral prefrontal cortex. (a) Illustration of performance on trials at the initial hiding place (A).

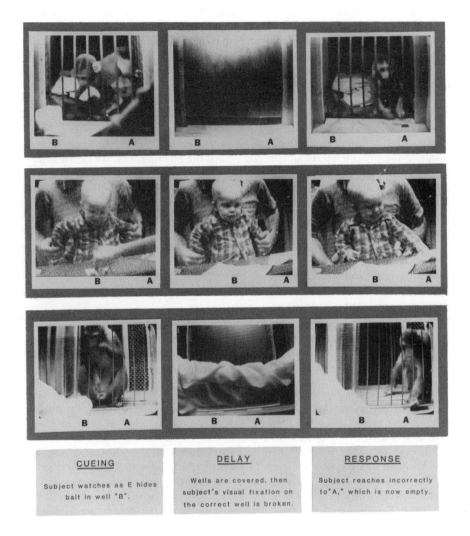

CUEING	DELAY	RESPONSE
Subject watches as E hides bait in well "B".	Wells are covered, then subject's visual fixation on the correct well is broken.	Subject reaches incorrectly to "A," which is now empty.

Figure 12.6 (b) Illustration of performance when side of hiding changes, i.e. trials at B̲. AB̄ testing procedures for monkeys and human infants were virtually identical. The AB̄ performance of 1½ – 2½ month-old infent monkeys, 7½ – 9 month-old human infants, and adult monkeys with lesions of dorsolateral prefrontal cortex is fully comparable in all respects.

their ability to simultaneously raise the box and reach inside. Simultaneous integration of the movements of the two hands requires not only involvement of SMA, but inhibitory projections via the corpus callosum so that the tendency of one hand to do the same thing as the other hand can be suppressed.

Integrating movements, whether sequentially or simultaneously, is dependent on SMA. Sequential integration is seen earlier, however, because simultaneous integration requires interhemispheric communication through the corpus callosum between the left and right SMA, whereas sequential integration does not require callosal connections. Involvement of the corpus callosum in the changes occurring around 9½–10 months can also be seen in the disappearance of the "awkward reach." One explanation for the awkward reach is that the sight of the toy may fall on the visual field of only one hemisphere, and, lacking, callosal connections to communicate this information to the other hemisphere, infants reach with the hand controlled by the same hemisphere as that receiving the image of the toy (i.e. the hand contralateral to the opening, the "awkward hand"). This explanation has gained support from the finding of Lamantia, Simmons, and Goldman-Rakic (personal communication) that monkeys in whom the corpus callosum has been prenatally removed continue to show the awkward reach long after the age when monkeys normally cease showing this behavior and, indeed, may continue to show this behavior indefinitely.

Adults who were born without a corpus callosum (congenital acallosals) have difficulty suppressing "associated movements"; that is, they have difficulty inhibiting one hand from doing what the other is doing (Dennis, 1976). Indeed, inhibitory control of callosal fibers on movement has been well documented (e.g. Asanuma and Okamoto, 1959).

Functions of Dorsolateral Prefrontal Cortex: Relating Information over a Temporal or Spatial Separation and Inhibition of Prepotent Response Tendencies

Adult monkeys are able to succeed easily on the $\overline{AB}$ and object retrieval tasks. Lesions of dorsolateral prefrontal cortex in the monkey disrupt performance, producing exactly the same sorts of errors, on both tasks, as seen in human infants at the age of 7½–9 months (Diamond and Goldman-Rakic, 1985, 1989).

For example, adult monkeys with lesions of dorsolateral prefrontal cortex show the $\overline{AB}$ error at delays of 2–5 secs. (Diamond and Goldman-Rakic, 1989) just as do human infants of 7½–9 months. Prefrontal monkeys, like human infants, perform well when the hiding is at A, but they err when the reward is then hidden at B. They perform well if there is no delay, or if they are allowed to stare at, or orient their body, toward the correct well throughout the delay. They immediately try to self-correct after an error. They can learn to associate a landmark with the correct well and can use the landmark to help them reach correctly on every trial (Diamond, 1990a). In all respects, their performance is comparable to that of 7½–9-month-old human infants. Lesions to no other area of the brain produce this pattern of results. Monkeys with lesions to parietal cortex (Diamond and Goldman-Rakic, 1989) or the hippocampal formation (Diamond et al., 1989) perform perfectly on the $\overline{AB}$ task at delays of 2–5 secs., and even at longer delays never show the $\overline{AB}$ error pattern.

Indeed, $A\overline{B}$ is almost identical to the task that has been most strongly linked to dorsolateral prefrontal cortex (the delayed response task) (Fuster, 1989; Jacobsen, 1936; Nauta, 1971; Rosenkilde, 1979). In delayed response, as in $A\overline{B}$, the subject watches as the experimenter hides a reward in one of two identical wells, a delay of 0–10 secs. is imposed, and then the subject is allowed to uncover one of the wells. Over decades of research, using a wide array of physiological, pharmacological and anatomical procedures, performance on delayed response has been consistently shown to depend specifically on the functioning of dorsolateral prefrontal cortex (see e.g. Diamond, in press, for review). Further evidence of the close association between these two tasks is that infants show the same developmental progression on delayed response between 7½–12 months as they show on $A\overline{B}$ (Diamond, 1990a; Diamond and Doar, 1989).

Adult monkeys with lesions of dorsolateral prefrontal cortex also fail the object retrieval task, showing the same behaviors as do human infants of 7½–9 months (Diamond, 1990b; Diamond and Goldman-Rakic, 1985). They have great difficulty inhibiting the urge to reach straight to their goal, and so persist in trying to reach directly through the side of the box through which they are looking. When the opening of the box is on the left or right side, they lean and look, and then reach with the "awkward hand," just as do human infants. Lesions of the hippocampus have no effect on performance of the task (Diamond et al., 1989). Parietal cortex lesions produce misreaching errors (reminiscent of the few 9½–10-month-old infants who appeared to ignore available visual information) but produce no other deficit on the task (Diamond and Goldman-Rakic, 1985).

Importantly, lesions of dorsolateral prefrontal cortex produce the same effects on performance of these tasks in infant monkeys as they do in adult monkeys. Infant monkeys show the same developmental progression on the $A\overline{B}$ and object retrieval tasks between 1½ and 4 months of age as do human infants between 7½ and 12 months (Diamond, 1990a, 1990b, 1990c, in press; Diamond and Goldman-Rakic, 1986). On $A\overline{B}$, they show the same pattern of performance over trials as do human infants and as do monkeys with lesions of dorsolateral prefrontal cortex: Their errors are confined to only certain types of trials, rather than being randomly distributed; they reach correctly if they orient themselves toward the correct well throughout the delay; and they try to correct themselves immediately if they reach to the wrong well. At 1½–2½ months, they make the $A\overline{B}$ error at delays of 2–5 secs. (just as do human infants of 7½–9 months and prefrontally operated adult monkeys), and by 4 months they are perfect at delays of at least 10 sec. (like human infants of 12 months) (see figures 12.6 and 12.7). If infant monkeys then receive lesions of dorsolateral prefrontal cortex at 4 months, their performance on $A\overline{B}$ at 5 months is once again as it was at 1½–2½ months of age (i.e. they make the $A\overline{B}$ error at delays of 2–5 secs., although prior to surgery they were performing perfectly at delays of 15 sec. or longer) (Diamond, 1990a; Diamond and Goldman-Rakic, 1986).

On the object retrieval task, infant monkeys of 1½ months perform much like human infants of 7½–8 months (i.e. they reach only at the side of the box through which they are looking), and at 2 months of age infant monkeys show the "awkward reach" (seen in human infants at 8½–9 months). That is, on object retrieval, as on $A\overline{B}$, infant monkeys of 1½–2½ months perform as do human infants aged 7½–9 months and as do monkeys with lesions of dorsolateral prefrontal cortex (see figures 12.8 and 12.9). By 4 months, infant monkeys are

AB̄ PERFORMANCE WITH DELAY OF 2-5 SEC

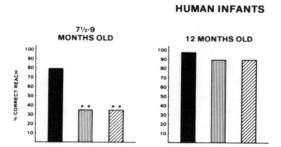

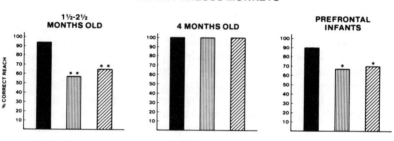

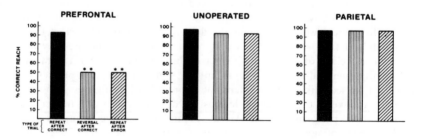

Figure 12.7 The AB̄ error is characterized by a particular pattern of performance by type of trial. The subject performs very well on repeat-following-correct-trials, but errs on reversal trials and repeat-following-error trials. With delays of 2–5 secs., the AB̄ error pattern is seen in 7½–9-month-old human infants, adult monkeys with dorsolateral prefrontal cortex lesions, infant monkeys of 1½–2½ months, and 5 month old infant monkeys who received lesions of dorsolateral prefrontal cortex at 4 months. On the other hand, infants of 12 months, infant monkeys of 4 months, unoperated adult monkeys, and adult monkeys with lesions of parietal cortex or the hippocampus all perform perfectly on AB̄ at delays of 2–5 secs.

ADULT CYNOMOLGUS MONKEYS

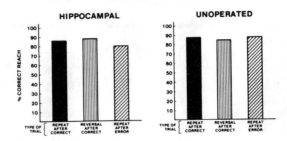

Figure 12.7 (contd.)

perfect on the object retrieval task, as are human infants of 12 months (Diamond, 1990a, in press; Diamond and Goldman-Rakic, 1986; see table 12.4).

This body of evidence suggests that the improved performance of human infants on these tasks from 7½–12 months of age may reflect maturational changes in dorsolateral prefrontal cortex. Infants of 7½–9 months may fail these tests because dorsolateral prefrontal cortex is too immature to support the abilities that the tasks require. Dorsolateral prefrontal cortex is not fully mature at 12 months; indeed, it will not be fully mature until many years later; but by 12 months it appears to have reached the level where it can support certain critical cognitive functions.

Dorsolateral prefrontal cortex is required for those tasks, such as $A\overline{B}$, delayed response, and object retrieval, where subjects must integrate information that is

Table 12.4 Performance of human infants, infant monkeys, and monkeys with selective lesions of the brain on the $A\overline{B}$, delayed response, and object retrieval tasks

	$A\overline{B}$	*delayed response*	*object retrieval*
Human infants show a clear developmental progression from 7½–12 months.	Diamond, 1985	Diamond and Doar, 1989	Diamond, 1981
Adult monkeys with lesions of frontal cortex fail.	Diamond and Goldman-Rakic, 1989	Diamond and Goldman-Rakic, 1989	Diamond and Goldman-Rakic, 1985
Adult monkeys with lesions of parietal cortex succeed.	Diamond and Goldman-Rakic, 1989	Diamond and Goldman-Rakic, 1989	Diamond and Goldman-Rakic, 1985
Adult monkeys with lesions of hippocampus succeed.	Diamond et al., 1989	Squire and Zola-Morgan, 1983	Diamond et al., 1989
Infant monkeys show a clear developmental progression from 1½–4 months.	Diamond and Goldman-Rakic, 1986	Diamond and Goldman-Rakic, 1986	Diamond and Goldman-Rakic, 1986
5-month-old infant monkeys, who received lesions of frontal cortex at 4 mo, fail.	Diamond and Goldman-Rakic, 1986	Diamond and Goldman-Rakic, 1986	

Figure 12.8 The awkward reach in a 2-month-old infant monkey, a 9-month-old human infant, and an adult monkey with a bilateral lesion of dorsolateral prefrontal cortex. Frame 1: Subject leans and looks at bait through opening of box. Frame 2: Subject reaches in awkwardly with the far hand. Frame 3: Opening is on the other side of the box. Performance is the same. Subject leans and looks into the opening. Frame 4: Subject reaches in awkwardly with the far hand. (From Diamond 1981, 1990b; Diamond and Goldman-Rakic, 1985, 1986.)

HUMAN INFANTS

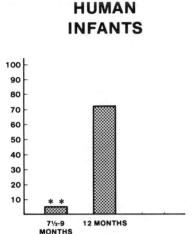

INFANT RHESUS MONKEYS

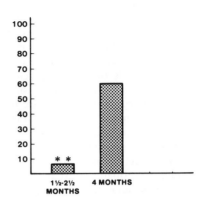

ADULT RHESUS MONKEYS

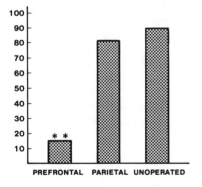

ADULT CYNOMOLGUS MONKEYS

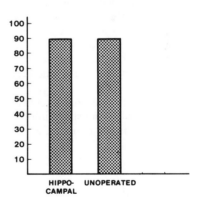

Figure 12.9 Percent of trials during object retrieval testing where subjects reached to the box opening without ever having looked into the opening on that trial. Human infants of 7½–9 months, adult monkeys with lesions of dorsolateral prefrontal cortex, and infant monkeys of 1½–2½ months, almost never reach to the opening unless they have looked into the opening on that trial. On the other hand, 12-month-old human infants, 4-month-old infant monkeys, unoperated adult monkeys, and adult monkeys with lesions of parietal cortex or the hippocampus often reach to the opening without ever having looked into the opening on that trial. This figure summarizes work from Diamond 1981; Diamond and Goldman-Rakic, 1985; 1986; Diamond et al., 1989.

separated in space or time *and* must inhibit a predominant response. If only one of these abilities is required, involvement of dorsolateral prefrontal cortex is not necessary. Tasks that require only inhibitory control or only memory do not depend on dorsolateral prefrontal cortex.

The object retrieval task requires the subject to relate the opening of the box to the bait over a spatial separation. When bait and opening are superimposed (as when the bait is in the opening, partially out of the box), even the youngest infants, and even monkeys without prefrontal cortex, succeed. However, as the spatial separation between bait and opening widens (i.e. as the bait is placed deeper inside the box), the age at which infants succeed progressively increases.

The AB̄ task requires the subject to relate two temporally separated events – cue and response. When there is no delay between hiding and retrieval, even the youngest infants, and even monkeys without prefrontal cortex, succeed. However, as the time interval between hiding and retrieval increases, the age at which infants succeed progressively increases.

In object retrieval, the tendency to reach straight to a visible target must be inhibited. Infants must instead reach around to the opening. Results when the box is opaque provide particularly strong evidence here: infants perform better with the opaque box, where the toy cannot be seen through a closed side (Diamond, 1981). The counterintuitive finding that the task is easier when the goal is not visible supports the hypothesis that *seeing* the goal through a closed side makes the task harder, because the tendency to reach straight to the goal must then be inhibited.

The predominant response is often the response a subject has been making, in which case lack of inhibitory control will be manifest as perseveration. However, when the prepotent response is different from the response just made, lack of inhibitory control is manifest by a failure to persevere. This is seen in object retrieval as when, after three successful reaches into the front opening, the box is moved an inch closer to the infant and the toy a half-inch deeper in the box, so that the infant now sees the toy through the top of the box – instead of perseverating the infant deserts the front opening and reaches to the top of the box.

In AB̄, a conditioned tendency or "habit" to reach to "A" (where the infant was rewarded) must be inhibited when the toy is hidden at "B." When such inhibition is not required, as on the initial trials at A, infants perform quite well.

Summary

Evidence that by at least 5–7 months of age infants understand that a hidden object remains where it was last seen and that an object contiguous with another continues to exist as an independent entity has been reviewed. An explanation has been offered for why infants at this age often fail to demonstrate these understandings in their behavior. Infants of 5–7 months have great difficulty inhibiting reflexive reactions to objects they touch and they have great difficulty combining two actions together in a behavior sequence, whether it be a means–end sequence or a reaching sequence consisting of two different movements. I have suggested that it is for these reasons that infants at this age cannot retrieve a contiguous object, uncover a hidden object, or detour around a barrier. The problem for the infants is not to acquire an understanding that objects continue to exist when they share a boundary or are no longer visible; by at least 5–7 months infants understand this. The problem for the infants is to gain control of their actions so they can demonstrate this understanding. By 7½–9 months, infants begin to be able to retrieve contiguous objects, uncover hidden objects, and detour around barriers. It is suggested that these advances may be due in part to maturation in the SMA neural system.

Infants of 7½ –9 months can find a hidden object, but they fail the A̅B̅ hiding task if a delay is introduced. Indeed, even with no delay or with transparent covers, they still have some difficulty *not* repeating the previously reinforced response of reaching to A. They also have difficulty inhibiting the pull to reach straight to their goal in the object retrieval task and inhibiting the tendency to do the same action with both hands. They can link two actions together in a sequence, but they still have great difficulty doing, or attending to, two things simultaneously, whether it be bimanual coordination or the coordination of vision and reaching or vision and touch. They know where to reach for a hidden toy if allowed to reach immediately and can retrieve a toy from the object retrieval box if the toy is sitting in the box opening; however, they run into difficulty if a temporal gap is imposed between when the toy is hidden and when they are allowed to reach (as in A̅B̅) or if a spatial gap is imposed between the toy and the box opening by placing the toy deep inside the box (in object retrieval). By 12 months, infants begin to be able to do all of these things skillfully. It is suggested that these advances are made possible partly through maturational changes in the dorsolateral prefrontal cortex neural system and in callosal connections between the supplementary motor areas (SMAs) of the left and right hemispheres.

It may be that inhibitory control makes possible infants' emerging ability to construct relations. To relate two stimuli to one another, one must fight the tendency to attend only to the more salient stimulus. To relate two movements in a two-directional reach, one must stop the first movement so that the second one can begin. Reasoning and planning require that one inhibit focusing exclusively on one stimulus or idea so that more than one thing can be taken into account and interrelated.

The ability to inhibit making the predominant response frees us to exercise choice and control over what we do. That is, it makes possible the emergence of intentionality. All organisms have prepotent response tendencies, innate and conditioned. It is not clear, however, that all organisms have the capacity to *resist* the strongest response of the moment or an engrained habit. That seems to depend upon the highest levels of cortical control, and may not be possible for organisms without frontal cortex.

ACKNOWLEDGEMENTS

The work summarized here was carried out at: (a) Harvard University, in the laboratory of Jerome Kagan, with funding from the National Science Foundation (NSF) (Doctoral Dissertation Grant BNS-8013–447) and the National Institute of Child Health and Development (NICHD) (HD-10094) and support to the author from NSF and Danforth Graduate Fellowships; (b) Yale University School of Medicine, in the laboratory of Patricia Goldman-Rakic, with funding from the National Institute of Mental Health (NIMH) (MH-00298 & MH-38456) and support to the author from a Sloan Foundation award and

NIMH Postdoctoral Fellowship (MH-09007); (c) University of California, San Diego, in the laboratory of Stuart Zola-Morgan, with funding from the Medical Research Service of the Veterans Administration, National Institutes of Health (NIH) and the Office of Naval Research and support to the author from a grant from Washington University; and (d) Washington University, St Louis, and the University of Pennysylvania, in the laboratories of the author, with funding from the McDonnell Center for Studies of Higher Brain Function at Washington University School of Medicine, NIMH (MH-41842), and Basic Research Science Grants (BRSG) (RR07054 & RR07083).

NOTES

1 According to Twitchell, the grasp reaction is not fully formed until after 4 months and then becomes less easily and reliably elicited by the last months of the first year. The avoidance reaction is fully formed by 24–40 weeks. Note that the experimental situation described here should be particularly well suited to elicit the grasp reaction because the infant is reaching out for the toy, primed to grasp, so that when the infant touches the box that which was primed gets released.

2 Note that if 7-month-old infants were able to execute two-directional reaches with precision *or* were able to inhibit reflexive reactions to touch, they would succeed in all conditions. It is only because they have problems both with executing the reach precisely and with reflex inhibition that they fail under certain conditions. If they could put the two parts of the reach together smoothly, they would never touch the edge of the box. Similarly, if they did not react to touching the box by grasping it or pulling their hand back, it would not matter if they touched the edge of the box. The slightest reorientation of the hand would suffice to give them access to the toy; but instead they halt the reach, back up, and try again.

3 Once delays are introduced, I wonder if $A\overline{B}$ does not properly become a stage V task. Piaget used no delay when he administered it to his children.

4 The progression from accurate performance at short delays, to the $A\overline{B}$ error, to deteriorated performance at long delays, marks a linear decrement in performance, not a curvilinear trend, as Wellman, Cross, and Bartsch (1987, p. 36) seemed to think. At short delays, infants are correct at both A and B. At slightly longer delays, infants are still correct at A, but they err at B (hence, performance is significantly worse at B than at A). At long delays, infants err at both A and B (so that there is again no significant difference between performance at A and B, not because performance at B has improved, but because performance at A has worsened).

5 The role of memory in $A\overline{B}$ performance has recently been questioned because infants have performed better when multiple hiding wells are used (where one would think the memory requirements are more severe) than they do when only two hiding wells are used. However, this performance difference may be an artifact of a difference in hiding procedures. When two wells are used, the experimenter typically covers both wells simultaneously. When multiple wells are used, the experimenters have changed the procedure to accomodate to the fact that we only have two hands: They have uncovered only the correct well, hidden the toy, and then re-covered that well alone (the other wells remaining covered the entire time). Harris (1973, experiment III) demonstrated that infants perform better with two wells if A is covered and then B, as the last action by the experimenter draws the Infant's attention to B. Diamond, Cruttenden, and Neiderman (1989) demonstrated that when multiple wells are used and all wells are covered simultaneously, performance is significantly worse than when only the correct well is uncovered and covered, and it is much worse than performance typically found in experiments with only two wells (see Diamond, 1990a).

6 Patients with acute damage to SMA also show a dissociation between consciousness

and action. The phenomenon is called the "alien hand" (Goldberg, 1985; Goldberg et al., 1981) where "the limb performs normally organized acts directed toward goals linked to objects in extrapersonal space in which the patient does not perceive himself as a causal agent. . . . The alien hand sign can be interpreted as a disorder of intention because the patient reports that the behavior of the limb is dissociated from the patients' own volition" (Goldberg, 1985, p. 605). This behavior usually disappears within a few months after the injury to SMA.

7 One successful reach to A is sufficient to produce a pull to reach to A, and within the range of 1–5, the number of successful reaches to A does not seem to matter (Butterworth, 1977; Diamond, 1983; Evan, 1973). However, infants repeat the error of reaching back to A over significantly more trials after 8–10 successful reaches to A than after only 2 successful reaches to A (Landers, 1971).

8 Frontal patients are also poor at generating alternative solutions, such as generating abstract drawings using only four lines or generating all the words they can think of beginning with the letters "F", "A", or "S" (FAS test) (e.g. Benton, 1968).

9 Performance with the opening of the box at the side always lagged behind performance with the opening at the top or front of the box. For a discussion of possible reasons for this, see Diamond (1981).

10 Here, the presence of intentionality is distinguished from the ability to provide evidence of it in behavior. The intention may be there early, but the ability to demonstrate it may depend on frontal cortex maturation.

REFERENCES

Addie, W. J., & Critchley, M. (1927). Forced grasping and groping. *Brain*, 50, 142–170.

Albarran, L. (n. d.). *The maturation of delayed recognition memory in infants between ages of 11 and 24 weeks*. Unpublished manuscript, Harvard University, Cambridge, MA.

Atlison, R. S., Hurwitz, L. J. Graham White, J., & Wilmot, T. J. (1969), A follow-up study of a patient with Balint's syndrome. *Neuropsychologia*, 7, 319–333.

Asanuma, H., & Oksmoto, K. (1959). Unitary study on evoked activity of callosal neurons and its effect on pyramidal tract cell activity in cat. *Japanese Journal of Neurophysiology*, 9, 437–483.

Bachevalier, J., & Mishkin, M. (1984). An early and a late developing system for learning and retention in infant monkeys. *Behavioral Neuroscience*, 98, 770–778.

Baillargoon, R. (1987). Object permanence in very young infants. *Developmental Psychology*, 23, 655–664.

Baillargoon, R., Spelke, E. S., & Wasserman, S. (1985). Object permanence in five-month-old infants. *Cognition*, 20, 191–208.

Beader, M.B., & Teuber, H. L. (1947). Spatial organization of visual perception following injury to the brain. *Archives of Neurology and Psychiatry*, 58, 721–739.

Benton, A. L. (1968). Differential behavioral effects of frontal lobe disease. *Neuropsychologia*, 6, 53–60.

Bower, T. G. R. (1974). *Development in infancy*. San Francisco: Freeman & Co.

Bower, T. G. R. (1977). *The perceptual world of the child*. Cambridge, MA: Harvard University Press.

Bowlby, J. (1969). *Attachment and loss, Vol. I: Attachment*. New York: Basic Books.

Brickson, M., & Bachevalier, J. (1984). Visual recognition in infant rhesus monkeys: Evidence for a primitive memory system. *Society for Neuroscience Abstracts*, 10, 137.

Brinkman, C. (1984). Supplementary motor area of the monkey's cerebral cortex: Short- and long-term deficits after unilateral ablation and the effects of subsequent callosal section. *Journal of Neuroscience*, 4, 918–929.

Bruner, J. S., Kaye, K., & Lyons, K. (1969). *The growth of human manual intelligence:*

III. The development of detour reaching. Unpublished manuscript, Center for Cognitive Studies, Harvard University, Cambridge, MA.

Bruner, J. S., Lyons, K., & Watkins, D. (1968). *The growth of human manual intelligence: II. Acquisition of complementary two-handedness.* Unpublished manuscript, Center for Cognitive Studies, Harvard University, Cambridge, MA.

Butterworth, G. (1977). Object disappearance and error in Piaget's Stage IV task. *Journal of Experimental Child Psychology*, 23, 391–401.

Caron, A. J., Caron, R. F., Minichiello, M. D., Weiss, S. J., & Friedman, S. L. (1977). Constraints on the use of the familiarization novelty method in the assessment of infant discrimination. *Child Development*, 48, 747–762.

Church, J. (1971). Techniques for the differential study of cognition in early childhood. In J. Hellmuth (ed.), *Cognitive studies* (pp. 1–23). New York: Bruner/Mazel.

Cole, M., Soutle, H. S., & Warrington, E. K. (1962). Visual disorientation in homonymous half-fields, *Neurology*, 12, 257–263.

Cornell, B. H. (1979). The effects of cue reliability on infants' manual search. *Journal of Experimental Child Psychology*, 28, 81–91.

Damasio, A. R., & Benton, A. L. (1979). Impairment of hand movements under visual guidance. *Neurology*, 29, 170–174.

Davis, D. B., & Currier, F. P. (1931). Forced grasping and groping. *Archives of Neurology and Psychiatry*, 26, 600–607.

Dennis, M. (1976). Impaired sensory and motor differentiation with corpus callosum agenesis: A lack of callosal inhibition during ontogeny? *Neuropsychologia*, 14, 455–469.

Denny-Brown, D. (1966). *The cerebral control of movements.* Liverpool: Liverpool University Press.

Denny-Brown, D., & Chambers, R. A. (1958). The parietal lobe and behavior. *Research Publications of the Association for Research of Nervous and Mental Diseases*, 36, 35–117.

Diamond, A. (1981). Retrieval of an object from an open box: The development of visual-tactile control of reaching in the first year of life. *Society for Research in Child Development Abstracts*, 3, 78.

Diamond, A. (1983). *Behavior changes between 6 to 12 months of age: What can they tell us about how the mind of the infant is changing?* Unpublished doctoral dissertation, Harvard University, Cambridge, MA.

Diamond, A. (1985). The development of the ability to use recall to guide action, as indicated by infants' performance on A$\overline{B}$. *Child Development*, 56, 868–883.

Diamond, A. (1988). Difference between adult and infant cognition: Is the crucial variation presence or absence of language? In L. Weiskrantz (ed.), *Thought without language* (p. 337–370). Oxford: Oxford University Press.

Diamond, A. (1990a). The development and neural bases of memory functions, as indexed by the A$\overline{B}$ and delayed response tasks, in human infants and infant monkeys. *Annals of the New York Academy of Sciences*, 608, 267–317.

Diamond, A. (1990b). Developmental time course in human infants and infant monkeys, and the neural bases, of inhibitory control in reaching. *Annals of the New York Academy of Sciences*, 608, 637–676.

Diamond, A. (1990c). Rate of maturation of the hippocampus and the developmental progression of children's performance on the delayed non-matching to sample and visual paired comparison tasks. *Annals of the New York Academy of Sciences*, 608, 394–426.

Diamond, A. (in press). Frontal lobe involvement in cognitive changes during the first year of life. In K. Gibson, M. Konner, & A. Patterson (eds), *Brain and behavioral development.* New York: Aldine Press.

Diamond, A., Cruttenden, L., & Neiderman, D. (1989). Why have studies found better performance with multiple wells than with only two wells on A$\overline{B}$? *Society for Research in Child Development Abstracts*, 6, 227.

Diamond, A., & Doar, B. (1989). The performance of human infants on a measures of frontal cortex function, the delayed response task. *Developmental Psychobiology*, 22, 271–294.

Diamond, A., & Gilbert, J. (1989). Development as progressive inhibitory control of action: retrieval of a contiguous object. *Cognitive Development*, 12, 223–249.

Diamond, A., & Goldman-Rakic, P. S. (1985). Evidence for involvement of prefrontal cortex in cognitive changes during the first year of life: Comparison of performance of human infant and rhesus monkeys on a detour task with transparent barrier. *Neuroscience Abstracts (Part II)*, 11, 832.

Diamond, A., & Goldman-Rakic, P. S. (1986). Comparative development in human infants and infant rhesus monkeys of cognitive functions that depend on prefrontal cortex. *Neuroscience Abstracts*, 12, 742.

Diamond, A., & Goldman-Rakic, P. S. (1989). Comparison of human infants and rhesus monkeys on Piaget's AB task: Evidence for dependence on dorsolateral prefrontal cortex. *Experimental Brain Research*, 74, 24–40.

Diamond, A., Zola-Morgan, S., & Squire, L. R. (1989). Successful performance by monkeys with lesions of the hippocampal formation on AB and object retrieval, two tasks that mark developmental changes in human infants. *Behavioral Neuroscience*, 103, 526–537.

Evans, W. F. (1973). *The stage IV error in Piaget's theory of concept development: An investigation of the rise of activity*. Unpublished doctoral dissertation, University of Houston.

Fagan, J. F. (1970). Memory in the infant. *Journal of Experimental Child Psychology*, 9, 217–226.

Freeman, W., & Crosby, P. T. (1929). Reflex grasping and groping: Its significance in cerebral localisation. *Journal of the American Medical Association*, 93, 712.

Fox, N., Kagan, J., & Weiskopf, S. (1979). The growth of memory during infancy. *Genetic Psychology Monographs*, 99, 91–130.

Fulton, J. F., Jacobsen, C. F., & Kennard, M. A. (1932). A note concerning the relation of the frontal lobes to posture and forced grasping in monkeys. *Brain*, 55, 524–536.

Fuster, J. M. (1989). *The prefrontal cortex* (2nd ed.). New York: Raven Press.

Gaffan, D. (1974). Recognition impaired and association intact in the memory of monkeys after transaction of the fornix. *Journal of Comparative and Physiological Psychology*, 86, 1100–1109.

Gaiter, J. L. (1973). *The development of detour reaching in infants*. Unpublished doctoral dissertation, Brown University, Providence, RI.

Goldberg, G. (1985). Supplementary motor area structure and function: Review and hypotheses. *The Behavioral and Brain Sciences*, 8, 567–616.

Goldberg, G., Mayer, N. H., & Toglia, J. U. (1981). Medial frontal cortex and the alien hand sign. *Acta Neurologica*, 38, 683–686.

Goldberger, M. E. (1972). Restitution of function in the CNS: The pathologic grasp in *Massaca mulatta*, *Experimental Brain Research*, 15, 79–96.

Goldfield, E. C., & Michel, G. F. (1986). Spatiotemporal link age in infant interlimb coordination. *Developmental Psychobiology*, 19, 259–264.

Gratch, G. A. (1972). A study of the relative dominance of vision and touch in six month old infants, *Child Development*, 43, 615–623.

Halsband, U. (1982). *Higher movement disorders in monkeys*. Unpublished doctorial dissertation, University of Oxford, Oxford, UK.

Harris, P. L., (1973). Perseverative errors in search by young infants. *Child Development*, 44, 29–33.

Jacobsen, C. F. (1936). Studies of cerebral functions in primates. I. The function of the frontal association areas in monkeys. *Comparative Psychology Monographs*, 13, 1–60.

Jacobsen, C. F., & Nissen, H. W. (1937). Studies of cerebral function in primates. IV. The effects of frontal lobe lesions on the delayed alternation habit in monkeys. *Journal of Comparative and Physiological Psychology*, 23, 101–142.

Kennard, M. A., Viets, H. R., & Fulton, J. F. (1934). The syndrome of the premotor cortex in man: Impairment of skilled movements, forced grasping, spasticity, and vasomotor disturbance. *Brain*, 57, 69–84.

Lamotte, R. H., & Acuna, C. (1977). Defects in accuracy of reaching after removal of posterior parietal cortex in monkeys. *Brain Research*, 139, 309–326.

Landers, W. F. (1971). The effect of differential experience in infants' performance in a Piagetian stage IV object-concept task. *Developmental Psychology*, 5, 48–54.

Laplanc, D., Talairach, J., Meininger, V., Bancaud, J., & Orgogozo, J. M. (1977). Clinical consequences of conticeclomics involving the supplementary motor area in man. *Journal of Neurological Science*, 34, 310–314.

Lockman, J. J. (1984). The development of detour ability during infancy. *Child Development*, 55, 482–491.

Luria, A. R. (1973). *Higher cortical functions in man*. New York: Basic Books.

Luria, A. R., & Homskaya, E. D. (1964). Disturbance in the regulative role of speech with frontal lobe lesions. In J. M. Warren & K. Akert (eds), *The frontal granular cortex and behavior* (pp. 353–371). New York: McGraw-Hill.

Millar, W. S., & Schaffer, H. R. (1972). The influence of spatially displaced feedback on infant operant conditioning. *Journal of Experimental Child Psychology*, 14, 442–453.

Millar, W. S., & Schaffer, H. R. (1973). Visual-manipulative response strategies in infant operant conditioning with spatially displaced feedback. *British Journal of Psychology*, 64, 545–552.

Milner, B. (1964). Some effects of frontal lobectomy in man. In J. M. Warren & K. Akert (eds), *The frontal granular cortex and behavior* (pp. 313–334). New York: McGraw-Hill.

Mishkin, M., & Delacour, J. (1975). An analysis of short-term visual memory in the monkey. *Journal of Experimental Psychology: Animal Behavior*, 1, 326–334.

Nauta, W. J. H. (1971). The problem of the frontal lobe: A reinterpretation. *Journal of Psychiatric Research*, 8, 167–187.

Orgogozo, J. M., & Larsen, B. (1979). Activation of the supplementary motor area during voluntary movements in man suggests it works as a supramotor area. *Science*, 206, 847–850.

Overman, W. H. (1990). Performance on traditional matching-to-sample, nonmatching-to-sample, and object discrimination tasks by 12 to 32 month-old children: A developmental progression. In A. Diamond (ed.), *The development and neural bases of higher cognitive functions*. New York: New York Academy of Sciences Press.

Pancratz, C. N., & Cohen, L. B. (1970). Recovery of habituation in infants. *Journal of Experimental Child Psychology*, 9, 208–216.

Penfield, W., & Jasper, H. (1954). *Epilepsy and the functional anatomy of the human brain*. Boston: Little, Brown.

Penfield, W., & Wetch, K. (1951). The supplementary motor area of the cerebral cortex. *Archives of Neurology and Psychiatry*, 66, 289–317.

Piaget, J. (1952). *The origins of intelligence in children* (M. Cook, Trans.). New York: Basic Books. (Original work published 1936.)

Piaget, J. (1954). *The construction of reality in the child* (M. Cook, Trans.). New York: Basic Books. (Original work published 1937.)

Richter, C. P., & Hines, M. (1932). Experimental production of the grasp reflex in the adult monkey by lesions of the frontal lobe. *American Journal of Physiology*, 101, 87–88.

Roland, P. E., Larsen, B., Larsen, N. A., & Skinhoj, B. (1980). Supplementary motor area and other cortical areas in organization of voluntary movements in man. *Journal of Neurophysiology*, 43, 118–136.

Rose, S. A., Gottfried, A. W., Melloy-Carminar, P., & Bridger, W. H. (1982). Familiarity and novelty preferences in infant recognition memory: Implications for information processing. *Developmental Psychology*, 18, 704–713.

Rosenkilde, C. E. (1979). Functional heterogeneity of the prefrontal cortex in the monkey: A review. *Behavioral and Neural Biology*, 25, 301–345.

Rovee-Collier, C. (1984). The ontogeny of learning and memory in human infancy. In R. Kail & N. E. Spear (eds), *Comparative perspectives on the development of memory* (pp. 103–134). Hillsdale, NJ: Lawrence Erlbaum.

Schonen, S. de, & Bresson, F. (1984). Development de l'atleinte manuelle d'un objet chez l'enfant, *Omportements*, 1, 99–114.

Sophian, C., & Wellman, H. M. (1983). Selective information use and perservation in the search behavior of infants and young children. *Journal of Experimental Child Psychology*, 35, 369–390.

Squire, L. R., & Zola-Morgan, S. (1983). The neurology of memory: The case for correspondence between the findings for human and nonhuman primate. In J. A. Deutsch (ed.), *The physiological basis of memory* (pp. 199–268). New York: Academic Press.

Stein, J. F. (1976). The effect of cooling parietal lobe areas 5 and 7 upon voluntary movement in awake rhesus monkeys. *Journal of Physiology*, 258, 62–63.

Stein, J. F. (1978). Effects of parietal lobe cooling on manipulative behavior in the conscious monkey. In G. Gordon (ed.), *Active touch. The mechanisms of recognition of objects by manipulation: A multidisciplinary approach* (pp. 79–90). Oxford: Pergamon Press.

Stinson, F. S. (1971). *Visual short-term memory in four-month-old infants*. Unpublished doctoral dissertation, Brown University.

Travis, A. M. (1955). Neurological deficiencies following supplementary motor area lesions in *Macaca midatta*, *Brain*, 78, 174–201.

Twitchell, T. E. (1965). The automatic grasping responses of infants. *Neuropsychologia*, 3, 247–259.

Twitchell, T. E. (1970). Reflex mechanisms and the development of prehension. In K. Connolly (ed.), *Mechanisms of motor skill development* (pp. 25–45). New York: Academic Press.

Walshe, F., & Robertson, E. G. (1933). Observations upon the form and nature of the "grasping" movements and "tonic innervation" seen in certain cases of lesion of the frontal lobe. *Brain*, 56, 40–70.

Weisendanger, M. (1981). Organization of the secondary motor areas of cerebral cortex. In V. B. Brooks (ed.), *Handbook of physiology: The nervous system: Vol. 2. Motor control* (pp. 112–147). Bethesda, MD: American Physiological Society.

Wellman, H. M., Cross, D., & Bartsch, K. (1987). Infant search and object permanence: A meta-analysis of the A-not-B error. *Monographs of the Society for Research in Child Development*, 51(3, Serial No. 214).

Werner, J. S., & Perimutter, M. (1979). Development of visual memory in infants. *Advances in Child Development and Behavior*, 14, 2–56.

Willatts, P. (1987). Development of problem-solving. In A. Slater & J. G. Bremner (eds), *Infant development* (pp. 143–147). Hillsdale, NJ: Lawrence Erlbaum Associates.

Wishart, J. G., Bower, T. G. R., & Dunkeld, J. (1978). Reaching in the dark. *Perception*, 7, 507–512.

Zola-Morgan, S., & Squire, L. R. (1986). Memory impairment in monkeys following lesions limited to the hippocampus. *Behavioral Neuroscience*, 100, 155–160.

Zola-Morgan, S., Squire, L. R., & Amaral, D. G. (1989). Lesions of the hippocampal formation but not lesions of the fornix or mammilary nuclei produce long-lasting memory impairment in monkeys. *Journal of Neuroscience*, 9, 897–912.

13

Critical Period Effects in Second Language Learning: the Influence of Maturational State on the Acquisition of English as a Second Language

JACQUELINE S. JOHNSON AND ELISSA L. NEWPORT

In most behavioral domains, competence is expected to increase over development, whether gradually or in stages. However, in some domains, it has been suggested that competence does not monotonically increase with development, but rather reaches its peak during a "critical period,"[1] which may be relatively early in life, and then declines when this period is over. For example, in the development of early visual abilities, the development of attachment, or – in the case considered here – the acquisition of language, it has been suggested that learners are best able to achieve the skill in question during a maturationally limited period, early in life. Elsewhere we have presented evidence that first language learning is indeed limited in this way (Newport and Supalla, 1987). The present paper focuses on the acquisition of a *second* language, asking whether this type of learning, undertaken only after a native language is already acquired, is neverthless still maturationally constrained.

We will begin by reviewing prior evidence on this hypothesis, for both first and second language learning, and will then present a new empirical study which we believe shows evidence for a maturational function in second language learning. Such evidence leaves open, however, whether the underlying maturational change occurs in a specific language faculty, or rather in more general

"Critical Period Effects in Second Language Learning: the Influence of Maturational State on the Acquisition of English as a Second Language" by Jacqueline S. Johnson and Elissa L. Newport in *Cognitive Psychology* 21, 60–99 (1989) (Copyright © 1989 by Academic Press, Inc.)

cognitive abilities involved in language learning. We will conclude by considering the types of mechanisms which are consistent with our findings.

Evidence for a Critical Period Effect in First Language Acquisition

The critical period hypothesis, as advanced by Lenneberg (1967), holds that language acquisition must occur before the onset of puberty in order for language to develop fully. As will be detailed in the subsequent section, Lenneberg's hypothesis concerned only first language acquisition; he left open the question of whether this critical period extended to second language acquisition, which would occur after a first language was already in place.

Lenneberg's argument contained two parts. First, he reviewed available behavioral evidence suggesting that normal language learning occurred primarily or exclusively within childhood. At the time his book was written, no direct evidence for the hypothesis (from normal individuals who had been deprived of exposure to a first language for varying lengths of time in early life) was available. His review therefore included various types of indirect evidence; for example, differences in recovery from aphasia for children *vs* adults, and differences in progress in language acquisition, before *vs* after puberty, in the mentally retarded.

Second, he proposed a mechanism which might be responsible for a maturational change in learning abilities. The proposed mechanism was fundamentally neurological in nature. He suggested that the brain, having reached its adult values by puberty, has lost the plasticity and reorganizational capacities necessary for acquiring language. Subsequent research has questioned whether all of the neurological events he cited occur at an appropriate time for them to serve as the basis for a critical period (Krashen, 1975). Nevertheless, the hypothesis that there *is* such a critical period for language learning has remained viable.

Since Lenneberg's writing, behavioral studies approximating a direct test of the critical period hypothesis for first language acquisition have become available. One such study is a well-known case of Genie, a girl who was deprived of language and social interaction until her discovery at the age of 13 (Curtiss, 1977). Her lack of linguistic competence, particularly in syntax, after seven years of rehabilitation supports the critical period hypothesis. However, the abnormal conditions under which Genie was reared, including nutritional, cognitive, and social deprivation, have led some investigators to question whether her language difficulties have resulted only from lack of linguistic exposure during early life.

More recently, Newport and Supalla (Newport, 1984; Newport and Supalla, 1987) have studied language acquisition in the congenitally deaf, a population in which exposure to a first language may occur at varying ages while other aspects of social and cognitive development remain normal. Their data come from congenitally deaf subjects for whom American Sign Language (ASL) is the first language. However, since 90 percent of the congenitally deaf have hearing (speaking) parents, only a few deaf individuals are exposed to this language from birth. The majority of deaf people are exposed to ASL only when they enter residential school for the deaf and first associate with other deaf individuals; this can be as early as age four or as late as early adulthood.

Newport and Supalla separated subjects by their age of exposure into three groups: *native learners*, who were exposed to ASL from birth by their deaf parents; *early learners*, who were first exposed to ASL between the ages of four and six; and *late learners*, who were first exposed to ASL at age 12 or later. Wishing to test asymptotic performance (i.e. ultimate command of the language), they chose subjects who had at least 40 years of experience with the language as their primary, everyday communication system. The subjects were tested on their production and comprehension of ASL verb morphology. The results show a linear decline in performance with increasing age of exposure, on virtually every morpheme tested. That is, native learners scored better than early learners, who scored better than late learners, on both production and comprehension.

This study thus provides direct evidence that there is a decline over age in the ability to acquire a first language. It also tells us, however, that Lenneberg's portrayal is at least partially incorrect in two regards. First, the results show a continuous linear decline in ability, instead of a sudden drop-off at puberty as his hypothesis implies. (This study does not tell us whether the linear function asymptotes or continues to decline after puberty, since separate groups of later learners, before *vs* after puberty, were not tested.) Second, it should be noted that, while the postpubescent learners did not reach as high a level of proficiency as the native or early learners, language had not become totally unlearnable for them. This rules out any extreme interpretation of the critical period hypothesis.

In sum, current evidence supports the notion of a maturationally delimited critical period for first language acquisition, with some modifications from Lenneberg's original formulation. However, this evidence is compatible with a number of quite different accounts of the nature of the underlying maturational change. Evidence concerning age effects on *second* language learning can contribute to a further delineation of critical period accounts.

Second Language Acquisition

What It Can and Cannot Tell Us about the Critical Period

Given the early difficulties of performing a direct test of the critical period hypothesis on first language acquisition, many researchers undertook studies of second language acquisition over age as a test of the hypothesis. Some investigators have suggested that a critical period theory must predict that children are better than adults at learning second languages, as well as first languages. Consequently, they have viewed any evidence to the contrary as evidence against the critical period hypothesis (see Snow, 1983, for discussion).

In our opinion, data on this issue do have an important consequence for a critical period theory of language acquisition. However, it is not that the critical period hypothesis could be rejected on such evidence but rather that it can be refined or clarified by such evidence. A critical period theory for language acquisition would have quite a different character depending upon whether second language acquisition were included in its effects.

To capture this distinction there are two different ways we can state the critical period hypothesis, one that does not include second language acquisition in its effects and one that does:

Version one: the exercise hypothesis. Early in life, humans have a superior capacity for acquiring languages. If the capacity is not exercised during this time, it will disappear or decline with maturation. If the capacity is exercised, however, further language learning abilities will remain intact throughout life.

Version two: the maturational state hypothesis. Early in life, humans have a superior capacity for acquiring languages. This capacity disappears or declines with maturation.

Notice that, although very different in character, the two versions make the same predictions with regard to first language acquisition. They differ, however, in their predictions for second language acquisition.

The exercise hypothesis predicts that children will be superior to adults in acquiring a first language. By this account, if learners are not exposed to a first language during childhood, they will be unable to acquire any language fully at a later date. However, as long as they have acquired a first language during childhood, the ability to acquire language will remain intact and can be utilized at any age. On such a hypothesis, second language learning should be equivalent in children and adults, or perhaps even superior in adults owing to their greater skills in their first language as well as in many related domains.

This hypothesis is not unlike the conception of the visual critical period described for cats (Hubel and Wiesel, 1963), where early visual experience is required to maintain and refine the structure of the visual cortex, or the conception of the critical period described for attachment in dogs (Scott, 1980), where early attachment to one dog is required for subsequently normal socialization and permits unlimited later attachments to other members of the same species. Indeed, as will be discussed below, some of the current evidence on second language learning could be interpreted to support an exercise hypothesis.

In contrast, the maturational state hypothesis claims that there is something special about the maturational state of the child's brain which makes children particularly adept at acquiring *any* language, first as well as second. This hypothesis predicts that language learning abilities decline with maturation, regardless of early linguistic experience: acquiring a first language early in life will not guarantee the ability to acquire a second language later in life. In this version, then, children will be better in second language learning as well as first.

With certain qualifications, the critical period hypothesis that Lenneberg put forth can be subsumed under either version. In fact, it is not absolutely clear which version he would have favored. Some comments he made suggest that he thinks the young learner has a superior capacity for acquiring second languages, and therefore that he would favor the maturational state hypothesis:

> the incidence of "language learning blocks" rapidly increases after puberty. Also automatic acquisition from mere exposure to a given language seems to disappear after this age and foreign languages have to be taught and learned through a conscious and labored effort. Foreign accents cannot be overcome easily after puberty. (Lenneberg, 1967, p. 176)

However, other comments within the same paragraph sound as if he would have favored the exercise hypothesis:

> our ability to learn foreign languages tends to confuse the picture. Most individuals of average intelligence are able to learn a second language after the beginning of their second decade . . . a person can learn to communicate in a foreign language

at the age of forty. This does not trouble our basic hypothesis on age limitation because we may assume that the cerebral organization for language learning as such has taken place during childhood, and since natural languages tend to resemble one another in many fundamental aspects the matrix for language skills is present. (Lenneberg, 1967, p. 176)

Since Lenneberg's was one of the first proposals in this area, it is not surprising that he did not take a definitive stand on this issue, particularly since there were at that time few data to support either view. Nevertheless, it is a crucial distinction that should be made in any subsequent account of a critical period.

Research on Age Effects on Second Language Acquisition

Is there an age-related limitation on the learning of a second language? A number of studies have investigated this question since the time of Lenneberg's book, focusing particularly on the acquisition of phonology and grammar. Superficially, these studies appear to contradict one another; some have been said to demonstrate an adult advantage, some a child advantage.

This apparent contradiction is resolved when one separates performance in the early stages of learning from eventual attainment in the language (for a review of these studies, with a conclusion similar to the one presented here, see Krashen et al., 1982). Most of the studies of second language learning have examined just the early stages of learning; these studies tend to show an adult advantage in both phonology (Asher and Price, 1967; Olson and Samuels, 1973; Snow and Hoefnagel-Hohle, 1977) and syntax (Snow and Hoefnagel-Hohle, 1978). Adults thus seem to begin moving toward second language proficiency more quickly. However, this advantage appears to be short-lived.

In contrast, studies of eventual attainment in the language show a superiority for subjects who began learning in childhood, both in phonology (Asher and Garcia, 1969; Seliger et al., 1975; Oyama, 1976) and in syntax (Oyama, 1978; Patkowski, 1980). However, most of the studies of child–adult differences in ultimate attainment have focused on pronunciation. With anecdotal evidence that late learners do carry an accent and experimental findings that support it, most investigators will concede a child advantage for acquiring phonology (though not necessarily a maturational one; see, for example, Snow and Hoefnagel-Hohle, 1977; Olson and Samuels, 1973).

There is much less available evidence on child–adult differences in the ultimate attainment of grammar. To our knowledge, only two studies have been done. In both, the subjects were US immigrants who were exposed to English upon moving to the United States and who had lived in the United States for at least five years at time of the test.

In one study, subjects' syntactic ability was assessed by trained judges who assigned syntactic ratings to written transcripts of the subjects' speech from tape recorded interviews (Patkowski, 1980). For purposes of analysis, subjects' scores were divided along two variables: age of arrival in the United States (before *vs* after age 15), and years in the United States (under *vs* over 18 years). Additionally, measures of the subjects' exposure to English in both natural and classroom settings were taken. Using either the results from the analysis of variance test or correlations, age of arrival was the only significant predictor of syntactic proficiency, with the prepubescent learners outperforming the postpubescent learners. The correlation of age of arrival with score was -0.74, which indicates a linear trend; however, the exact shape of the relationship cannot be determined from the reported results.

In the second study mentioned, subjects were measured on their ability to repeat spoken English sentences which had been masked with white noise (Oyama, 1978). This task was meant to tap the ability to integrate different sources of linguistic knowledge including phonology, syntax, intonation, and redundancy patterns. Admittedly this is not a pure measure of syntactic ability; however, it presumably involves syntactic knowledge (along with other factors). This study found the same pattern of results just reported: age of arrival was the only significant predictor of test performance.

In addition, the Oyama study addressed important claims regarding whether children's superiority over adults in final attainment is due to factors other than maturation, which happen to be correlated with age. For example, it has been argued that the adult is less *motivated* than the child to learn the language fully, is more *self-conscious* about speaking (i.e. practicing and making errors), does not have the cultural *identification* with the host country necessary to become fluent, and in general is less able to achieve the open attitudinal and affective state required for language acquisition to take place (for reviews of this view, see Schumann, 1975; Krashen, 1982). To test these claims, Oyama measured each of these variables, plus other candidate predictors, using interview and question-naire material. Simple correlations showed a good association between these variables and test score; however, partial correlations removing the effects of age of arrival became essentially zero. In contrast, when the reverse procedure was performed, removing each of these variables from the relationship between age of arrival and test score, the partial correlation remained large and significant. In short, age of arrival, rather than the attitudinal variables, predicted language performance.

These are important findings, for they support the view that age effects are not simply an artifact of child–adult differences in affective conditions of learning. However, a more rigorous test of this question could be performed. Nonmaturational hypothesis do not typically propose that one attitudinal variable, for example, self-consciousness, will alone predict performance; rather, they propose that the combination of all of these variables favors children over adults. Thus a more stringent test would involve partialling out all of the attitudinal variables together from age of arrival, and then determining whether there is any predictive power left.

The study we present in the present paper is an attempt to supplement the findings of these earlier studies. It is similar to the two studies discussed above, in that the focus is on ultimate command of the grammar of the second language as a function of age of exposure to that language. It differs from previous studies, however, in the way subjects' proficiency in the language is assessed and in the types of analyses performed. First, a detailed evaluation of subjects' knowledge of numerous aspects of English morphology and syntax is performed. This allows us to examine the relationship between age of exposure and an overall measure of English proficiency, as well as the possible differential effects of age of exposure on various aspects of grammatical structure. Second, a wide range of ages of exposure is examined, so that the precise shape of the function relating age to proficiency can be determined. Third, multivariate analyses are used to evaluate the relative contributions to proficiency of age as well as a number of affective, sociological, and environmental conditions of learning.

In detail, the primary questions that we address are as follows:

1   Is there an age-related effect on learning the grammer of a second language?
2   If so, what is the nature of this relationship? What is the shape of the function relating age to learning and ultimate performance, and where (if anywhere) does the relationship plateau or decline?
3   Can experimental or attitudinal variables, separately or together, explain the effects obtained for age of learning?
4   What areas of the grammar are the most and least problematic for learners of different age groups?

In answering these questions we hope to gain a better understanding of the nature of the critical period and, most particularly, to be able to decide between the two versions of the critical period outlined above.

Method

Subjects

Subjects were 46 native Chinese or Korean speakers who learned English as a second language. Chinese and Korean were chosen as the native languages because of their typological dissimilarity to English. (For consideration of the effects of the first language on the second, see Discussion.) No differences were found in the results for the two language groups, so they will be presented together throughout the paper.

The primary criterion for selecting subjects was that they varied in the age at which they moved to the United States and thereby first became immersed in English. All subjects were exposed to English by native speakers in the United States. In addition, to be sure that subjects had sufficient experience with English to be considered at their ultimate attainment in the language, every attempt was made to obtain subjects who had lived in the United States for many years. Minimum criteria were as follows: all subjects had to have at least five years of exposure to English and had to have lived in the United States for an inbroken stay of at least three years prior to the time of test. Finally, to ensure ample exposure to english and to ensure some homogeneity of social background, all subjects were selected from the student and faculty population at an American university (University of Illinois). Subjects were recruited through posted sign-up sheets, letters, and by word of mouth.

The resulting 46 subjects varied in age of arrival in the United States from ages 3 to 39; throughout that range there was a fairly even distribution of ages of arrival. Age of arrival was considered the age of first exposure to English.

Three additional subjects were tested but eliminated from data analysis when our posttest interview revealed that they did not meet the above criteria: one did not have an unbroken stay in the United States for three years prior to test; the second did not arrive in the United States until adulthood but was immersed in English through attending an all-English-speaking school in a foreign country. For both of these subjects, then, age of immersion could not be determined unambiguously. The third subject was eliminated because her early exposure to English was from her Chinese parents, who had no prior experience with English but neverthless decided to speak only English in the home upon their arrival in the United States. Most of her early exposure to English was therefore not to standard English.

Additional experiential characteristics of the subjects varied for subjects arriving in the United States early *vs* late in life, and will be discussed separately for these two groups. In all cases, these experiential characteristics, as well as age of arrival, will be evaluated for their relationship to performance in English.

Early arrivals. There were 23 subjects, 12 males and 11 females, who had arrived in the United States before age 15. These early arrivals were, at the time of test, for the most part freshman or sophomore undergraduates who received money or class credit for their participation. All of these subjects, from the time of arrival until college, lived in an environment where their native language was spoken in the home and English spoken outside of the home. Once they entered college, all lived predominantly in an English-speaking environment.

Late arrivals. The remaining 23 subjects were 17 males and six females who had arrived in the United States after age 17. Prior to coming to the United States, all of these subjects had had between 2 and 12 years of mandatory formal English instruction in their native country. This raised two possible concerns. One, the classroom experience might reduce the effect of age of arrival on learning, since age of first exposure to English for these subjects is earlier than age of arrival. Two, "age of learning" may turn out to be better defined by age of starting classes rather than age of arrival, which would result in a narrower range of ages than desired. Whether point two is true is an interesting question itself and will be examined empirically in the results section.

At the time of test, these subjects were primarily professors, research associates, and graduate students. All subjects, in both the early and late arrivals groups, had at least some years of schooling while in the United States. Within the late arrivals, the smallest number of years of school in the United States was three years, the largest ten, with an average of six years for the group.

For some of the subjects, the language environment was analogous to that of the early arrivals, in which the native language was spoken in the home and English spoken at school and work; for others, particularly those that were unmarried, the language environment was almost all English. Thus in terms of exposure on a day to day basis, it does not appear that the early arrivals have any advantage over the late arrivals.

In terms of years of exposure in the United States the late and early arrivals also are fairly even see table 13.1. The average number of years in the United States for early and late arrivals is 9.8 and 9.9, respectively. The main difference between the two groups is that the late arrivals have a larger range of years in the United States.

Table 13.1 The distribution of early and late arrival in terms of the number of years they lived in the USA

Years in the USA	Age of arrival	
	3–15	*17–39*
3–6	4	7
7–10	10	11
11–15	9	3
23–26	0	2

To provide a baseline performance on tests of English, 23 native speakers of English were run. Two additional native subjects participated but were not included in the analysis, one because the posttest interview revealed that he acquired English outside of the United States, and one because she spoke a nonstandard dialect of English.

Procedure

The subjects were tested on their knowledge of English syntax and morphology by being asked to judge the grammaticality of spoken English sentences of varying types (see Materials). While such a task, of course, in principle requires metalinguistic skills in addition to knowledge of the language, virtually perfect performance is shown on the same task by six and seven year old native speakers in subsequent studies (Johnson, Newport, & Strauss, in press). This suggests that the metalinguistic skills necessary for our task can only be minimally demanding for an adult and that any variation obtained in performance on the task among adults must be due to variation in knowledge of the language.

The test sentences were recorded on tape by a native American female voice (E.N.). Each sentence was read twice, with a 1–2 second pause separating the repetitions. They were said clearly, with normal intonation at a slow to moderate speed. The ungrammatical sentences were spoken with the intonation pattern of the grammatical counterpart. There was a 3–4 second delay between the different sentences.

Subjects were tested individually in the laboratory. They were instructed to make a grammaticality judgement for each sentence, guessing if they were not sure. It was made clear to the subject that if the sentence was incomplete or otherwise wrong for any reason, they should regard it as ungrammatical. The subject recorded yes/no responses on an answer sheet by circling Y or N. To avoid giving cues to the subject, the experimenter did not face the subject during the testing session while the tape was going. Subjects were given a break halfway through the test, but were told prior to starting that they should tell the experimenter to stop the tape at any time if they need to break sooner, either if the tape was too fast for them or if they were simply getting tired.

Following the grammaticality judgement test, subjects were interviewed for approximately half an hour about their language background. Information was gathered about the type and amount of exposure to English they had, from when they were first learning the language until the time of test. Motivational and additudinal measures were also taken, by having the subjects rate themselves on a scale of 1 to 5 with regard to those measures.

None of the subjects were blind as to the nature of the experiment. They were told prior to participating that we were interested in determining whether children or adults are better at learning second languages; they were not told, however, what type of results were expected.

Materials

The judgements of grammaticality test was modeled loosely after one used by Linebarger et al. (1983) in a study unrelated to the present one. Our test, however, has a different set of English constructions and corresponding test sentences than those of Linebarger et al., with the exception of two rule types which are noted.[2]

Our test was composed of 276 sentences.[3] Of these, 140 were ungrammatical. The other 136 formed the grammatical counterparts of these sentences.[4] The pairs that were formed, between the ungrammatical and grammatical counterparts, were sentences that were exactly the same except for one rule violation contained in the ungrammatical sentence. The pairs of sentences were constructed to test 12 types of rules of English, listed in table 13.2. The test contained between six and 16 pairs of sentences testing each rule type. The members of a pair were, however, not adjacent to each other, but rather were placed in opposite halves of the test. Within each half, sentences were presented in random order (see Design for further details).

To ensure as much as possible that the sentences tested the rules under study and not extraneous factors, sentences were constructed to contain only relatively high frequency words, most of which were only one or two syllables in length. The location of the grammatical error (at the beginning, middle, or end of the sentence), the basic phrase structure of the sentence, and the sentence length (ranging from five to eleven words per sentence) were balanced across pairs of sentences testing each rule type, so that each rule type was tested by a set of sentences comparable in all of these regards.

The 12 rule types we tested were chosen to represent a wide variety of the most basic aspects of English sentence structure. (Indeed, according to our expectations, native speakers of English found the test very easy, with ungrammatical sentences producing strong feelings of ungrammaticality.) Within the 12 rules types, there were four rule types which dealt specifically with English morphology: past tense, plural, third person singular, and present progressive. They will be discussed together since many of the violations were constructed

Table 13.2 Twelve rule types tested in gramaticality judgement task

1	Past tense	7	Particle movement
2	Plural	8	Subcategorization
3	Third person singular	9	Auxiliaries
4	Present progressive	10	Yes/no questions
5	Determiners	11	Wh-questions
6	Pronominalization	12	Word order

along similar lines. The other eight types involved various rules of English syntax. Within each rule type, the violations were formed on the basis of a few basic formats, with several pairs of sentences (typically four) using each format. These are discussed in more detail, with examples of the structure of the pairs, below.

Morphology: Past tense, plural, third person singular, and present progressive. For morphology, the grammatical sentence always contained the target morpheme in a required context, while the grammatical violation was created using one of four formats:

1 by omitting the required morpheme;
2 by replacing the required morpheme with an inappropriate morpheme from a different class;
3 by making an irregular item regular;
4 by attaching a regular marking to an already irregularly marked item.

The first format was used to make ungrammatical sentences for all four types of morphology. The sentence pairs were constructed so that the grammatical context required the target morpheme, making it a grammatical violation when the morpheme was omitted in one of the sentences of the pair. For example, in sentences (1a) and (1b), a plural marker is required on the noun "pig," and is present in (1a) but is omitted in (1b). In sentences (2a) and (2b), the present progressive ending is required on the verb "speak"; it is present in (2a) but omitted in (2b).

(1a)   The farmer bought two pigs at the market.
*(1b)   The farmer bought two pig at the market.
(2a)   The little boy is speaking to a policeman.
*(2b)   The little boy is speak to a policeman.

Sentences were structured similarly for the other classes of morphemes.

The second format applied only to the verb morphology. One sentence of the pair was correct; the other had an inappropriate tense marking for the context. Consider, for example, sentences (3a) and (3b).

(3a)   Yesterday the hunter shot a deer.
*(3b)   Yesterday the hunter shoots a deer.

In (3a), the verb is in the past tense form as required, while in (3b) the verb "shoot" occurs in present tense form in a past tense context.

The last two formats for creating the ill-formed sentences could be used only for past tense and plural forms. An ill-formed sentence created by making an irregular item regular is exemplified in sentence (4b), with its gramatical counterpart in (4a). Similarly, the ungrammatical sentence (5b) has a regular marking added on an already marked irregular.

(4a)   A shoe salesman sees many feet throughout the day.
*(4b)   A shoe salesman sees many foots throughout the day.

(5a)   A bat flew into our attic last night.

*(5b)   A bat flewed into our attic last night.

The test was constructed so that there was an equal number of sentence pairs (4) in each format used for each type of morphology. However, due to the nature of the morphemes, it was impossible for all of the formats to be applied to all of the four rule types. Therefore the past tense and plural are tested by more sentence pairs than are the third person or the present progressive.

Determiners. To test subjects' knowledge of determiners, the grammatical member of the sentence pairs was constructed so that a determiner in a particular position was either necessary or not allowed. The ungrammatical counterparts were then formed by one of three methods: (a) by omitting them in required contexts, as in sentence (6b); (b) by substituting the indefinite for the definite, as in (7b); and (c) by inserting them where neither article is allowed, see (8b). These examples can be contrasted with their grammatical counterparts (6a), (7a), and (8a), respectively:

(6a)   Tom is reading a book in the bathtub.

*(6b)   Tom is reading book in the bathtub.

(7a)   The boys are going to the zoo this Saturday.

*(7b)   A boys are going to the zoo this Saturday.

(8a)   Larry went home after the party.

*(8b)   Larry went the home after the party.

In many cases, there are other ways of construing the errors; for example, (6b) may be construed as a plural error, instead of a determiner error, for not having the plural marking on the noun "book." In cases like these, where the error classification was ambiguous, the semantic contexts were created to try to bias the listener into the preferred reading. For example, in (6) the reason Tom is in the bathtub is to sway the subject into expecting that he is reading only one book rather than many.

Pronominalization. The sentence pairs for this rule type contain some type of pronominal. The ungrammatical sentences were formed to include one of the following violations: (a) the wrong case marking on the pronoun; (b) an error in gender or number agreement for the pronoun; or (c) an erroneous form of the possessive adjective.

The violations of case involved using nominative pronouns in objective positions (see (9a) and (9b), and objective pronouns in nominative positions:

(9a)   Susan is making some cookies for us.

*(9b)   Susan is making some cookies for we.

Gender and number were tested by capitalizing on the fact that reflexive pronouns have to agree with the noun they are coindexed with. Sentence (10a) is an example of correct gender agreement, while (10b) shows a gender agreement violation:

(10a) The girl cut herself on a piece of glass.

*(10b) The girl cut himself on a piece of glass.

For possessive adjectives, the error is in the form the word takes. So, for example, some ungrammatical items have a possessive adjective with the possessive marker added, as in (11b). Compare this to the correct form in (11a):

(11a)   Carol is cooking dinner for her family.
*(11b) Carol is cooking dinner for hers family.

Particle movement. With some minor changes, all of the items in this rule type are from Linebarger et al. (1983). Here the sentences take advantage of the differences between particles and prepositions. The ill-formed sentences were created by treating prepositions as particles, that is, by moving the preposition to the right of the object NP as in (12b), as compared to the correct from in (12a). These were contrasted with grammatical sentences with particles in their moved and unmoved positions, as in (13a) and (13b). Additionally, other sentences were ill-formed by moving the particle outside its own clause, as in (13c). Notice that, for this rule type, the sets of counterpart sentences are not pairs but triples:

(12a)   The man climbed up the ladder carefully.
*(12b) The man climbed the ladder up carefully.
(13a)   Kevin called up Nancy for a date.
(13b)   Kevin called Nancy up for a date.
*(13c) Kevin called Nancy for a date up.

Subcategorization. The items in this rule type are also from Linebarger et al. (1983). These items test subjects' knowledge of the subcategorization frames of various verbs. In English, individual verbs determine the type of syntactic frames that may follow them. For example, some verbs require a direct object, while others require propositional phrases. Because the details of these frames are lexically determined, ill-formed sentences could be created by changing the structure of the required frame for a particular verb while keeping the meaning intact. Thus, the change in these sentences involved using the subcategorization frame of a semantically similar verb. See, for example, the contrasts below.

(14a)   The man allows his son to watch TV.
*(14b) The man allows his son watch TV.
(15a)   The man lets his son watch TV.
*(15b) The man lets his son to watch TV.

The ungrammatical sentences were formed by exchanging the different subcategorization frames of the two semantically similar verbs "allow" and "let."

Auxilliaries. In this rule type, the affix requirements for different auxiliary verbs were tested. In particular, the ungrammatical sentences were formed by violating three rules of auxiliaries. Each rule, with an example of the correct and incorrect forms, is given below:

"Have" requires a past participle.
(16a)   The baby bird has fallen from the oak tree.
*(16b) The baby bird has fall from the oak tree.

Following any form of "be," the main verb must take the progressive.

(17a) Fred will be getting a raise next month.

*(17b) Fred will be get a raise next month.

Only the first element of Aux is tensed.

(18a) Leonard should have written a letter to his mother.

*(18b) Leonard should has written a letter to his mother.

Yes/no questions. For this rule type, the ungrammatical sentences contain primarily errors in subject–aux inversion. The errors are of three types. In one, two auxiliaries are moved in front of the subject, as in (19b). In another, both the auxiliary and the verb are fronted (20b); and in the third, the verb is fronted in a sentence where do-insertion would normally occur, as in (21b). The grammatical counterparts are (19a), (20a), and (21a), respectively.

(19a) Has the king been served his dinner?

*(19b) Has been the king served his dinner?

(20a) Can the little girl ride a bicycle?

*(20b) Can ride the little girl a bicycle?

(21a) Did Bill dance at the party last night?

*(21b) Danced Bill at the party last night?

Additionally, there were some ungrammatical sentences formed by copying, instead of moving, the auxiliary verb, the difference being shown in (22a) and (22b):

(22a) Can the boy drive a tractor?

*(22b) Can the boy can drive a tractor?

Wh-questions. The ungrammatical wh-questions have three forms, two of them also dealing with aux. In one form, no subject–aux inversion occurs, as in (23b) as compared with (23a); in the other, do-insertion is omitted, as in (24b) compared to (24a):

(23a) When will Sam fix his car?

*(23b) When Sam will fix his car?

(24a) What do they sell at the corner store?

*(24b) What they sell at the corner store?

The third form of the ungrammatical wh-questions was lexical. A question was ill-formed by substituting an incorrect wh-word for a correct one. In sentence (25b), for example, "why" cannot be used unless the subcategorization frame of the verb "put" is satisfied by supplying a locative. Sentence (25a) satisfies this restriction by replacing the locative with a locative wh-word.

(25a) Where did she put the book?

*(25b) Why did she put the book?

Word Order. In this last rule type, basic word order rules are tested. Sentences of three types were used: intransitive (NP–V), transitive (NP–V–NP), and dative (NP–V–NP–NP). Within each type, the ungrammatical sentences were formed by systematically rearranging the verbs and noun phrases so that all of the possible orders of constituents occurred. Thus the simplest ill-formed sentence involves the reversal of an NP and intransitive verb, as in (26a) versus (26b); the most complex involves the rearrangement of NPs and V in double-object structures, as in (27a) versus (27b).

(26a)   The woman paints.
*(26b)   Paints the woman.
(27a)   Martha asked the policeman a question.
*(27b)   Martha a question asked the policeman.

Design

The test was divided into two halves. An equal number of exemplars of each rule type and subrule type were represented in each half. The grammatical and ungrammatical members of a pair were in opposite halves of the test. Within each half, sentences were randomized in such a way that no rule type was concentrated in one section of the test, and no run of grammatical or ungrammatical sentences was longer than four.

Results

Age of Acquisition

Age of acquisition and ultimate performance. The primary questions of this study involved examining the relationship between age of learning English as a second language and performance on the test of English grammar. The results show a clear and strong relationship between age of arrival in the United States and performance. Subjects who began acquiring English in the United States at an earlier age obtained higher scores on the test than those that began later, $r = -0.77$, $P < 0.01$.

A more detailed understanding of this relationship can be gained from table 13.3 and figure 13.1. Subjects were grouped by age of arrival into categories similar to those used in past research (e.g. Snow and Hoefnagel-Hohle, 1978). Table 13.3 presents the mean score, standard deviation, and the ranges of the number of correct responses and the number of errors for each group and for the native English comparison group. The means are also presented graphically in figure 13.1. The adjacent age groups were compared, two at a time, by a set of two-sample *t* tests using separate variance estimates.[5]

The first comparison involved determining whether there was any difference between the age 3–7 group and the native group in their performance in English. The two groups were not significantly different from each other, $t(10.4) = 1.28$, $P > 0.05$; indeed, the two groups were entirely overlapping in performance. In contrast, all of the other age groups performed significantly below the natives

Table 13.3 Mean scores of nonnative and native speakers of english

| | | Age of arrival | | | |
	Natives (n = 23)	*3–7* (n = 7)	*8–10* (n = 8)	*11–15* (n = 8)	*17–39* (n = 23)
Means	268.8	269.3	256.0	235.9	210.3
SD	2.9	2.8	6.0	13.6	22.8
Range	275–265	272–264	263–247	251–212	254–163
(Errors)	(1–11)	(4–12)	(13–29)	(25–64)	(22–113)

Note: Maximum score = 276

(for natives *vs* the next closest group (8–10), $t(8.1) = 6.67$, $P < 0.01$). This suggests that, if one is immersed in a second language before the age of seven, one is able to achieve native fluency in the language;[6] however, immersion even soon after that age results in a decrement in ultimate performance.

Given that the 3–7 group is the only group that reached native performance, it is perhaps not surprising that the difference between the means of the 3–7 and 8–10 age groups is significant, $t(10) = 5.59$, $P > 0.01$. As can be seen in table 13.3, while the absolute difference between the means of these two groups is small, both groups have very small SDs, and the range of scores for the 3–7 group is entirely nonoverlapping with the 8–10 group. All of the later adjacent age groups are also significantly different from each other. The age 8–10 group obtained higher scores than the 11–15 group, $t(9.7) = 3.83$, $P < 0.01$, with almost nonoverlapping distributions between the two groups, and the age 11–15 group obtained higher scores than the 17–39 (adult) group, $t(21) = 3.78$, $P < 0.01$.

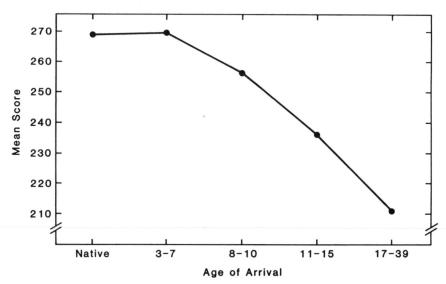

Figure 13.1 The relationship between age of arrival in the United States and total score correct on a test of English grammar.

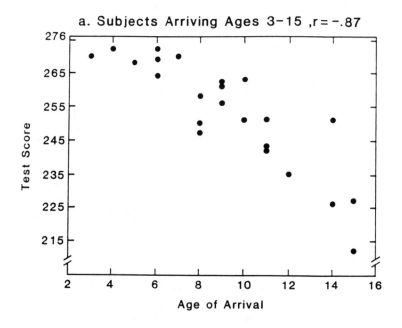

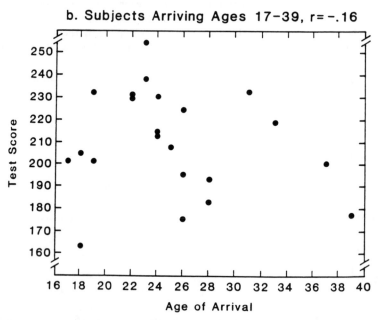

*Note: The Y-axes are on different scales.

Figure 13.2 Scatterplots of test score in relation to age of arrival for subjects arriving in the USA before versus after puberty.

In sum, there appears to be a strong linear relationship between age of exposure to the language and ultimate performance in that language, up to adulthood. In the next section we examine the shape of this function in more detail.

The effects of age of acquisition before versus after puberty.   An important question to answer is whether, throughout adulthood, performance continues to decline as a function of age of exposure or whether it plateaus at some point (H. Gleitman, personal communication). If the explanation for late learners' poorer performance relates to maturation, performance should not continue to decline over age, for presumably there are not many important maturational differences between, for example, the brain of a 17 year old and the brain of a 27 year old. Instead, there should be a consistent decline in performance over age for those exposed to the language before puberty, but no systematic relationship to age of exposure, and a leveling off of ultimate performance, among those exposed to the language after puberty. This is precisely what was found.

Subjects were divided into two groups in terms of age of exposure, from age 3–15, versus 17–39, with an equal number of subjects ($N = 23$) in each group. The correlations between age of exposure and performance for these two groups were strikingly different. For the group first exposed to English between the ages of 3 and 15, the correlation was $- 0.87$, $P < 0.01$. Note that this correlation is even more substantial than that for the subjects as a whole. In contrast, for the group first exposed to English between the ages of 17 and 39, there is no significant correlation, $r = - 0.16$, $P > 0.05$. Scatterplots demonstrating this effect are presented in figure 13.2a and b.

Age of acquisition and variance in ultimate performance.   Another age-related result, which is obvious from inspecting the scatterplots of figure 13.2 and the SDs in table 13.3, is the heterogeneous variance. For groups who acquired English at early ages, the variance is very small; with increasing age of exposure, variance gets larger, creating a megaphone shape, so that for subjects exposed to English after 15 the variance is very large. Note that it would have been quite possible to find that the means of these groups increased but the variance stayed constant over the age groups. The heterogeneity of variance obtained, and the relation between age of acquisition and variance, is an independent result.

This heterogeneity of variance underscores two simple but important points:

1   Before age 15, and most particularly before age 10, there are very few individual differences in ultimate ability to learn language within any particular age group; success in learning is almost entirely predicted by the age at which it begins.
2   For adults, later age of acquisition determines that one will not become native or near-native in a language; however, there are large individual variations in ultimate ability in the language, within the lowered range of performance.

Age of exposure to formal instruction.   It has been assumed thus far that age of arrival in the United States is the best measure of age of exposure to the language. For early arrivals it is the only measure available, since these subjects had no prior experience with English at all. However, for the late arrivals there are two measures possible: age of arrival in the United States, or age of beginning English instruction in school within the native country. There is already a high correlation between age of arrival and test score for the subjects as a whole, $r = -0.77$; if age of classes is a better measure of first exposure for the late arrivals, then the correlation should be even higher when using that as a measure of time of exposure. This is not what was found. The correlation for the subjects as a whole between age of exposure, defined as classes or immersion (whichever came first), and test score is -0.67. These correlations, however, are not statistically different from each other, $t(43) = 1.26$, $P > 0.05$. This is not surprising since, due to the early arrivals, half of the measurements are exactly the same; moreover, most of the late arrivals are defined as later learners (pubescent or postpubescent) either way they are measured. Because of this overlap in measurement, the best way to evaluate the effect of age of classes is to do so using only the subjects who had classroom instruction. For these subjects alone ($N = 23$), the correlation between age of classes and test score is -0.33, which is not significant, $P > 0.05$.

This result has two implications. First, it means that we are using the right measure for "age of exposure"; age of arrival in the United States, with its resulting immersion in English, is more strongly related to ultimate performance in English than is age of beginning formal English instruction. More profoundly, it means that the learning which occurs in the formal language classroom may be unlike the learning which occurs during immersion, such that early instruction does not necessarily have the advantage for ultimate performance that is held by early immersion. It should be noted, however, that this last conclusion may be limited by the relatively narrow age range for formal instruction found in our subjects: our subjects all began their English classes between the ages of 7 and 16, with most subjects beginning at ages 12–15. This conclusion may also be restricted to the type of formal instruction received in Chinese and Korean schools (and, of course, any other schools in which the instruction is similarly formal), and should be less true the more formal instruction approximates immersion in the United States. In any event, age of arrival in the United States appears to be the better measure of age of acquisition for the population we studied.

Experiential and Attitudinal Variables

Experiential variables. Years of exposure in the United States was also a variable of interest in this study. First, careful attention was paid to balance the years of exposure between early and late learners. This was done in order to avoid the possibility that obtained age effects would be due to differences in years of exposure, rather than to true differences in age of exposure. That we were successful in controlling for years of exposure between the early and late learners is apparent from the lack of correlation between age of arrival and years in the US, $r = -0.09$, $P > 0.05$.

Beyond controlling for this potential confound, it is also important to ask what effect years of exposure has on learning, independent of the age effects. It is known that number of years has some effect on subjects' competence during the initial stages of learning a second language (see, for example, Snow and Hoef-nagel-Hohle, 1978). At an extreme, people who have been in a host country for one and a half years must perform better than those who have only been there half a year. The question here is, however, do people continue to improve over time through continued exposure to the language, or do they reach an asymptote after a certain number of years? To answer this question, a correlation coefficient was computed between years of exposure in the United States and test perfor-mance. The resulting correlation, $r = 0.16$, is not significant, $P > 0.05$ (see also table 13.4). This is in agreement with other studies (Oyama, 1978; Patkowski, 1980), also showing no significant effect of the number of years of exposure on language performance for learners beyond the first few years of exposure.

In addition to years of exposure, table 13.4 also presents other variables which we considered possible experiential correlates with ultimate performance, such as amount of initial exposure to English, classroom experience, and attitude. Most of these variables were computed from information provided by the subjects; amount of initial exposure (measured as the percentage of time English was used during the first year or two in the United States) and motivation to learn in English classes (rated 1 to 5) were estimates provided by the subjects. None of the correlations are significant.

Regarding amount of initial exposure, the mean percentage for the group is 51.4 percent, with a standard deviation of 20.2 percent. Unless subjects' estimates are inaccurate, it appears that ultimate performance is not sensitive to fairly large differences in amount of initial exposure to the language, at least not after the subjects have been immersed in the language for a number of years.

The classroom variables include the age at which the subjects began English classes in their native country (already discussed in the previous section), the number of years they took English classes, and their ratings of how motivated they were to learn English in the classroom. Again, none of these variables correlates significantly with performance. It may be of interest for future research, however, that age of starting English classes is the highest of the (nonsignificant) experiential correlations. This may suggest some benefit of early classroom exposure, if classroom exposure occurred earlier than in the population we studied, and particularly if the classroom were more like immersion.

Attitudinal variables. Some investigators (see Schumann, 1975, and Krashen, 1982, for reviews) have suggested that age effects are secondary by-products of changes in people's level of self-consciousness, in their cultural identification,

Table 13.4 Correlation coefficients of experiential variables with score

Interview variable	*Correlation w/score*
Length of exposure (years in the USA)	0.16
Amount of initial exposure (first year or two in USA)	0.03
Age of English classes[a]	− 0.33
Years of English classes[a]	0.25
Motivation to learn in classes[a]	0.05

[a] Correlation for late learners only; measure not applicable to other subjects.

Table 13.5 Correlation coefficients of attitudinal variables with test score and age of arrival

Attitudinal variables	Test score	Age of arrival
Identification	0.63^{**}	-0.55^{**}
Self-consciousness	-0.36^{*}	0.19
Motivation	0.39^{**}	-0.48^{**}

* $P < 0.05$.
** $P < 0.01$.

Questions:

1 How strongly would you say you identify with American culture? (subject's reply). If 5 means you identify with the American culture, that is, you feel like a complete American, and 1 means not at all, how would you rate your identification?

2 Did you feel self-concious while learning English in the United States? (most often an explanation was needed here). How would you rate that on a scale from 1 to 5, where 5 is very self-conscious and 1 is not at all?

3 Motivation is a composite of two questions. (a) Is it important to you to be able to speak English well? (subject's reply). On a scle of 1 to 5, where 5 means very important and 1 means not at all, how would you rate it? (b) Do you plan on staying in the United states? The composite was formed by adding one point to their importance rating if they planned on staying in the United States, and by subtracting one point if they did not.

and in their motivation to learn a second language well, rather than maturational changes in learning. To address this claim, correlation and regression analyses were performed. Table 13.5 presents correlations of such attitudinal variables with test score as well as with age of arrival. These variables were measured by asking subjects to rate themselves according to the questions presented at the bottom of table 13.5.

The correlations show a strong relationship between these attitudinal variables and both test score and age of arrival. Higher ratings of American identification and increased measures of motivation were associated with better performance in English and with younger age of arrival, while higher ratings of self-consciousness were associated with poorer performance and with later age of arrival. Both of these sets of results would be predicted by a theory which attempted to explain age differences in language learning as a function of attitudinal variables correlated with age, rather than a function of maturation. The other possibility is, of course, the reverse; the attitudinal variables may have obtained their correlations with test score as a result of the correlation with age of arrival. Thus it becomes a question as to which is the better measure: age of arrival or attitudinal variables?

It is clear that age of arrival is the better measure over any of the attitudinal variables considered alone. The correlation between age of arrival and test score ($r = -0.77$) surpasses the correlation between any of the attitudinal variables and test score. Furthermore, the attitudinal variables are more adversely affected when age of arrival is partialled out than is age of arrival when each of the attitudinal variables is partialled out, as shown in table 13.6. This is in complete agreement with Oyama's (1978) results.

As stated earlier, however, the most powerful evidence against this alternative hypothesis is to show that age of arrival can account for variance not accounted

Table 13.6 Partial correlation of age of arrival and attitudinal variables with test score

	Attitudinal variables w/ age of arrival removed	Age of arrival w/ attitudinal variables removed
Identification	0.39^*	-0.65^{**}
Self-consciousness	-0.34^*	-0.76^{**}
Motivation	-0.04	-0.72^{**}

*　$P < 0.05$.
**　$P < 0.01$.

for by the attitudinal variables combined. To test this, a regression analysis was performed using the three attitudinal variables together, which resulted in a regression coefficient of 0.47. This was compared to the 0.69 regression coefficient obtained with the three attitudinal variables plus age of arrival. The contribution made by age of arrival is statistically significant $F(1,41) = 28.1$, $P < 0.01$. This shows that, independent of any possible attitudinal effects, age of arrival has an effect on learning a second language.

Of independent interest is whether the attitudinal variables can account for any of the variance not accounted for by age of arrival. Even though it is clear that age of exposure to a language is an important variable for predicting ultimate performance, other variables may contribute to this as well. Unlike previous studies (e.g. Oyama, 1978), we did find added predictive value with two attitudinal variables: self-consciousness and American identification. Each of the two makes a significant contribution to a regression model including only age of arrival $(F(1,43) = 5.6$, $P < 0.05$, for self-consciousness, and $F(1,43) = 7.5$, $P < 0.05$, for indentification), as well as a significant contribution to a regression model including age of arrival and the other attitudinal variable $(F(1,42) = 5.0$, $P < 0.05$, for the addition of self-consciousness to age plus identification, and $F(1,42) = 6.9$, $P < 0.05$. for the addition of identification to age plus self-consciousness). Motivation, whether analyzed separately or in conjunction with the other two variables, failed to add significantly to the regression coefficient. Thus it appears at first glance that a model of second language learning would have to include both age effects and the effects of self-consciousness and identification, though not the effects of motivation. Such a model might argue, for example, that while age of arrival affects language learning, so does the self-consciousness and the cultural identification of the learner.

At this time one might, however, be cautious about inferring a direct causal link between self-consciousness and cultural identification to language learning, until this result is corroborated in future studies. Not only are the effects of self-consciousness and cultural identification not supported in other studies, but also possible mediating variables have not been ruled out. For example, language performance may be correlated with subjects' evaluation of their performance, which may in turn affect how self-conscious they are and how much they identify with the host country. Thus poorer learners may, as a result of their performance problems, become more self-conscious and identify less with the United States. In this account, greater self-consciousness and less identification would be the result rather than the cause of the performance problems. In any case, apart from whether attitudinal variables do or do not play a role, there is a clear independent effect of age of arrival on ultimate performance.

Age of Acquisition and Rule Type

The results show a striking effect of age of acquisition on performance in our test of English syntax and morphology. It is of interest to know what particular areas of the grammar create the most and least problems for second language learners. Are the errors random, with an even dispersal across rule type, or do late learners err more frequently on a particular type of rule? To answer this question, an analysis was performed on age of learning in relation to the differing types of rules evaluated on the test. This analysis used only the ungrammatical items, since it is only the ungrammatical items which can be said to be testing any particular rule type. That is, when a subject marks a grammatical sentence as ungrammatical, it is unclear what part of the sentence, or grammar, (s)he is having problems with. In contrast, when a subject marks an ungrammatical sentence as grammatical, (s)he must have failed to represent just that structure under test as a native speaker would. For purposes of this analysis, the age groups were the same as those used previously, except that the late learner group was further divided into two groups, (17–24) and (25–39), with an approximately equal number of subjects in each. This was done to reach a more nearly equal number of subjects in each of the age of learning groups. A two-way analysis of variance was performed, using the 12 rule types (outlined in the Methods section above) and six ages of acquisition.

The results of the anova showed a significant effect of rule type $F(11,693) = 53.2$, $P < 0.01$, a significant effect of age of acquisition, $F(5,63) = 32.3$, $P < 0.01$, and an interaction between rule type and age of acquisition, $F(55,693) = 8.3$, $P < 0.01$. The age effect here is simply a reproduction of the finding that early learners perform better than the late learners; apparently there is no reduction of this effect when scoring only the ungrammatical test items. The effect of rule type shows that subjects made more errors on certain rule types than on others. Finally, the interaction appears mainly to be the result of late learners making proportionately more errors on some rule types, and proportionately fewer on others. Thus, many of the late learners' errors do not appear to be random; rather, there are particular parts of the grammar that seem more difficult.

The pattern of errors for each age group across the 12 rule types can be seen in figure 13.3. In figure 13.3, rule types are ordered along the *x*-axis in decreasing order of difficulty for later learners.[7] As can be seen, determiners and plural morphology appear to be the most difficult for the two latest groups of learners, with scores significantly worse than chance for determiners ($t = 3.35$, $P < 0.01$), and no different from chance for plurals ($t = 0.16$, $P > 0.05$). While all of the remaining rule types receive scores significantly better than chance (t ranges from 3.46 to 26.1, $P < 0.01$), they vary widely in level of performance. Most notably, basic word order rules and the present progressive are giving very few problems, with most subjects getting virtually all of the items of these types correct.[8]

Why are subjects performing better on some rule types and worse on others? One uninteresting possibility is that the items testing some rule types are

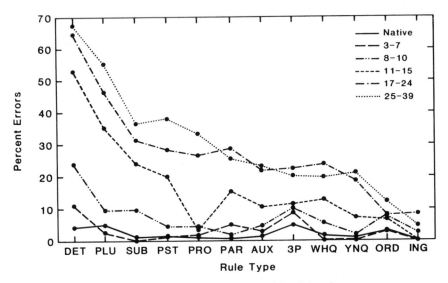

Figure 13.3 Mean percentage of errors in 12 types of English rules.

inherently easier than those testing other rule types, since in some cases different rules are tested by quite different sentential variations. On the other hand, it is clear that this is not the whole account of our effects. Rule types tested in very similar ways on our test (e.g. the various rule types involving morphology) did not show similar degrees of difficulty for late learners, suggesting that these rule type effects are not due to the difficulty of the format by which we tested the rules.

A second possibility is that the subjects suffered from phonological difficulties which made the items for that rule type difficult to process. Again, although we cannot definitely eliminate this possibility, we do not believe it is the whole account of the rule type effects. Rule types with exactly the same phonological form (e.g. plural and third person singular, both -s) did not show similar degrees of difficulty for late learners. Also, rule types testing forms which were phonologically more substantial and therefore easier to hear (e.g. rule types with whole words reversed or eliminated) were not necessarily easier for late learners than those that involved smaller phonological units.

A third possibility is that subjects suffered from interference from the nature of their first language (Chinese or Korean), and so should show special difficulty with rule types most different from the first language. Once again this did not appear to be the full account of our effects. Rule types equally absent from Chinese and Korean (e.g. past tense and present progressive) did not show similar degrees of difficulty for late learners.

Most important, our rule type ordering corresponds in certain striking ways to the order of difficulty obtained in studies of second language learners from other first language backgrounds, as well as in studies of the isolated girl Genie. In particular, the relative ease of word order and the present progressive show

Table 13.7 Correlation coefficients between age of arrival and rule type[a]

Rule type	Correlations
Determiners	0.64[**]
Plural	0.75[**]
Subcategorization	0.53[**]
Past tense	0.79[**]
Pronouns	0.73[**]
Particles	0.44[**]
Auxiliaries	0.45[**]
Third person singular	0.29[*]
Wh-questions	0.39[**]
Yes/no questions	0.50[**]
Word order	0.48[**]
Present progressive	0.32[*]

[a] These correlations, unlike others with age of arrival, are positive correlations, since they relate age of arrival to number of errors.
[*] $P < 0.05$.
[**] $P < 0.01$.

up in all of these studies. We believe, then, that the rule type effects we obtained are at least in part reflections of what is generally difficult or easy for a late learner. We will return to this issue in the Discussion section below.

One final question involved the relationship between age of arrival and each of the individual rule types. Given that late learners' competence varies over rule types, it is of interest to know whether age of arrival predicts performance on only certain selected rules of the second language. The data show, however, that this is not the case. Table 13.7 presents the correlations between age of arrival and the scores on each of the 12 rule types. Despite late learners' proficiency on some rule types, all of the rule types showed significant correlations with age of arrival. This result shows that age of exposure to the language affects all of the structures we examined, despite variations across rule types in the absolute level of performance late learners achieved.

Discussion

This study was designed to answer certain empirical questions about critical period effects in second language learning, and thereby to clarify and refine theoretical proposals regarding a critical period for language acquisition more generally. We will begin our discussion by reviewing the empirical findings, and then turn to the general theoretical issues.

The Basic Empirical Findings

Age of acquisition and ultimate performance. The first question we asked was whether there was a relation between age of acquisition and ultimate performance in the grammar of a second language. The results of this study clearly show such a relation, and therefore support the notion that children have an advantage over adults in acquiring a second language. The overall correlation between age of arrival in the United States and performance on our test of English grammar was − 0.77; and, for those subjects arriving in the United States before puberty, this correlation was − 0.87. Indeed, there was a significant correlation between age of arrival and performance on every type of syntactic and morphological rule we tested.

These findings are in accord with the results of the previous studies which have tested asymptotic performance, despite the fact that these studies used very different measures of English proficiency. (Oyama, (1978) measured number of words detected through white noise; Patkowski (1980) measured syntactic ratings of production.) The 'present study enhances the previous studies' findings by providing a much more detailed examination of English syntax and morphology. The three studies, however, complement each other well, for each emphasizes a different aspect of language use. Oyama's study, for example, taps some aspect of on-line processing in comprehension, Patkowski's measures free production, and in our study we presume to be measuring underlying grammatical competence via sentence judgements. Because these studies complement each other, the compatibility of the results is all the more impressive. Together they provide a strong case for the conclusion that children are indeed better than adults in their ultimate attainment in a second language.

The effects of age of acquisition before versus after puberty. The second question we asked concerned the shape of the relationship between age of acquisition and ultimate performance. Due to the large range of ages in the learners we tested, and our division of the early learners into small age groups, we are able to make a fairly good generalization about the shape of this relationship. Subjects who arrived in the United States before the age of seven reached native performance on the test. For arrivals after that age, there was a linear decline in performance up through puberty. Subjects who arrived in the United States after puberty performed on the average much more poorly than those who arrived earlier. After puberty, however, performance did not continue to decline with increasing age. Instead, the late arrival group, while performing on the whole more poorly than the younger arrivals, distinguished itself by having marked individual differences in performance, something which was not found in the earlier arrivals.

The pattern of this relationship supports a maturational account of the age effects found. It does this by the fact that the age effect is present during a time of ongoing biological and cognitive maturation and absent after maturation is complete (i.e. at puberty). Thus it appears as if language learning ability slowly declines as the human matures and plateaus at a low level after puberty. The precise level of this plateau differs between individuals.

Again, these findings are in line with previous studies, although no previous study has asked this question in detail. Both Oyama (1978) and Patkowski (1980) reported only overall correlations and grouped means, with groupings which were larger and slightly different from our own and with a more limited range of ages of acquisition than our own. Both studies found the general linear decline of performance with age of acquisition that we found, but the groupings of their subjects make it difficult to tell whether the precise ages at which we found changes in the function are supported by their results as well. In addition, in a study of age of acquisition in relation to first (rather than second) language acquisition, Newport and Supalla (1987) and Newport (1984) found a linear decline in ultimate performance over three age groups: subjects exposed to American Sign Language from birth *vs* at age 4–6 *vs* after age 12.[9] In short, the surrounding literature on both first and second language acquisition appears to be generally consistent with the more detailed results obtained in the present study.

Experiential and attitudinal variables. The third question we asked was whether the effects of age of acquisition could be due to experiential or attitudinal variables coincidentally related to age, rather than to maturational changes in language learning. Our results suggest that entirely nonmaturational explanations for the age effects would be difficult to support. Certainly the attitudinal variables (motivation, American identification, and self-consciousness) were unable to explain away the age effects, in accord with Oyama's (1978) study. This held true in the present data even when all three variables together were pitted against age.

It is also doubtful that the age effects are the result of differences in the amount of English exposure between the younger and older arrivals. This is true for several reasons. First, the younger arrivals did not differ significantly, if at all, from the adult arrivals in the amount of English they were exposed to during learning (see the Method section for description of the subjects' experiential characteristics). Second, the nonsignificant correlation between amount of initial exposure and performance suggests that second language learning is not particularly sensitive to differences in the amount of exposure, at least when that exposure has occurred over a number of years and is fairly high in the first place.

Some reserachers have claimed that there are differences in the quality of the exposure that adults and children receive, rather than in the mere quantity, and that this difference may account for the age differences found in language learning success. According to this view, children receive the ideal type of input for successful language learning, while adults do not. Many have said, for example, that children receive "simple," reduced input which refers to concrete objects, existing in the here and now. Adults, on the other hand, are exposed to syntactically more complex input which most often refers to abstract concepts and events that are displaced in space and time. The simple concrete input of the child is thought to be helpful for language acquisition, while the complex input of the adult is thought to interfere with language acquisition (Dulay et al., 1982).

Both the empirical and theoretical assumptions underlying this approach have been disputed. First, the assumption that language is easier to learn from limited simple input has been questioned (Wexler and Culicover, 1980; Gleitman et al., 1984). Second, the empirical evidence for this claim has also been brought into question. Freed (1980) performed a study which compared the type of input given to adult and child second language learners and found that adults and children actually receive comparable input in terms of syntactic complexity (as measured by the number of clause boundaries). Interestingly, however, the adult-directed input contained a more limited range of constructions than the child-directed input. Adults received input which tended to maintain the canonical shape of a sentence, while children received sentences with more deformations. Thus in terms of transformational complexity, adults received the simpler input. From this it would be just as reasonable to argue that adults learn less well because their input is not as complex and varied as the child's. In any case, the role of input in second language learning needs to be better formulated before we can decide whether children have any advantage in learning a language due to the type of input they receive.

Age of acquisition and rule type. The fourth question we asked concerned the nature of the effects of age on the attained grammar of the second language. Our results suggested that, although there was an effect of age of acquisition on every rule type we examined, some rules of English grammar were more profoundly affected by age of acquisition than others. In particular, knowledge of the basic word order of the language was acquired by all of our subjects, regardless of their age of learning. Similarly, knowledge of the present progressive (-ing) was acquired by all of our subjects. These areas of competence likewise appear in other studies of second language learning (see Krashen (1982) for a review of the order of morpheme difficulty in second language learning). Perhaps even more striking, they are the only two aspects of English which were successfully acquired by Genie, who was exposed to English as a first language only after puberty (Curtiss, 1977; Goldin-Meadow, 1978). In contrast, other aspects of English syntax and morphology gave late learners much more difficulty.

We believe that these rule type results are at least in part reflections of universal factors in learnability, and not merely the result of item difficulty or transfer from the first language. Newport et al. (1977), Gleitman et al. (1984), and Goldin-Meadow (1978) have suggested that basic word order is a highly resilient property of languages, appearing in the acquisition of a first language under widely varying conditions of both input and age of exposure. The present results on the acquisition of a second language under varying conditions of age of exposure are in accord with these claims. However, accounting for why word order and -ing are particularly easy for learners remains for future research.

Before turning to a more general discussion of critical period hypotheses in language learning, we must consider whether the set of results we have obtained will be replicable on other second language learning groups or whether they are confined in any way to the particular second language learners (Chinese and Koreans) we have studied.

Possible effects of the first language on second language learning. We have thus far presented our results as though the findings were generalizable to second language learning, regardless of the nature of the first language or the relationship between the grammar of the first language and that of the second language. Indeed we believe this is the case, although we also recognize that certain aspects of the structure of one's first language are likely to have some effects on the learning of the second language (see, for example, Zehler (1982) and Hakuta and Cancino (1977) for a review of transfer effects in second language learning). Here we wish to raise two points of relevance to the question of whether our results are limited in any way to the Chinese and Korean speakers we studied.

First, we do not believe that the relationship found here between age of exposure and ultimate performance in the second language is unique to the circumstances where Chinese or Korean is the first language and English is the second. We did purposely choose to concentrate on first and second languages where the grammars were sufficiently different that a significant second language learning problem would arise. Chinese and Korean are relatively more isolating languages than English and have syntaxes which are different in many ways from that of English. However, studies currently underway, as well as certain details of our present results, suggest that the basic findings do not depend on these particular language combinations.

Several studies in progress (Johnson and Newport, in press) examine performance on our test by subjects with a wide variety of first languages. It is too early to say from these data whether there is any effect of the nature of the first language (we expect that there might be); however, it is already clear that the strong correlation between age of arrival and test performance replicates with subjects from these other first-language backgrounds.

In addition, the detailed results of the present study suggest that the nature of the first language cannot fully explain the difficulties of the second language learner. The examination of performance on the 12 rule types reveals relationships to age of arrival on every structure we examined, regardless of how similar or different these structures were to ones in the first language. For example, determiners and plural inflection, which gave late learners their most serious difficulties on our test, are notably lacking in Chinese and Korean; but so are inflections for the present progressive, on which late learners performed exceptionally well. A more detailed understanding of which of our effects, if any, may arise from first language characteristics should emerge from our studies in progress.

Second, we do not believe that our results derive in any important way from the input or cultural circumstances which characterize Chinese and Korean speakers. The Chinese and Korean speakers we tested were perhaps unusual, compared with many second language learners of English, in that they often continued close associations with other speakers of their first language. One might wonder, therefore, whether their exposure to English or their maintenance of their first language somehow influenced their second language learning. Again, this is an empirical question which is best resolved by the results of our studies in progress, which include many speakers isolated from their first language group as well as speakers of first languages with large communities. Within the present study, all of our subjects (both early and late learners) continued speaking their first language with their families and others into adulthood, and all were exposed to English from native English speakers. In addition, all had a significant amount of exposure to English, since they were all active members of an English-speaking community (that is, American schools and universities). These factors therefore could not be responsible for the differences we found between early and late learners of English. Whether these factors have an additional effect on learning, beyond the effect of age of exposure, was not the focus of our study, although some of our results do bear on this question.

In sum, we believe that in other language groups the strong effects of age of acquisition may be accompanied by effects of input, first language typology, or other variables that do not appear in our data on Chinese and Korean learners. Most importantly, however, we have reason to expect, on the basis of our data, that these effects of age of acquisition will persist.

Theoretical Conclusions for a Critical Period Hypothesis in Language Acquisition

The present study was performed primarily for the purpose of understanding the nature of the critical period for language acquisition. In particular, we wanted first to discover whether the critical period occurs at all in second language acquisition or whether it is exclusively a first-language phenomenon. To delineate this distinction we began by presenting two possible versions of a critical period hypothesis. They are repeated here for convenience.

Version one: the exercise hypothesis. Early in life, humans have a superior capacity for acquiring languages. If the capacity is not exercised during this time, it will disappear or decline with maturation. If the capacity is exercised, however, further language learning abilities will remain intact throughout life.

Version two: the maturational state hypothesis. Early in life, humans have a superior capacity for acquiring languages. This capacity disappears or declines with maturation.

To reiterate the differences between these two versions, the exercise hypothesis only requires that a first language be acquired during childhood; as long as this occurs, the capacity for successful language learning will remain intact. Thus it predicts no differences between child and adult learners, due to maturation itself, in the ability to acquire a second language to native proficiency. In contrast, the maturational state hypothesis says that any language, be it first or second, must be acquired during childhood in order for that language to develop fully. Our results support the maturational state hypothesis, and not the exercise hypothesis. Human beings appear to have a special capacity for acquiring language in childhood, regardless of whether the language is their first or second.

The maturational state hypothesis is, however, not itself an explanation of critical period phenomena in language; rather, it merely outlines a class of explanations which would be compatible with our results (namely, those which posit maturational changes in general language learning abilities). In order to approach a more precise theoretical account of the phenomena, our study has also provided additional information which should aid in understanding the nature of the critical period: namely, information about the shape of the function relating age of acquisition and ultimate performance. Our results provide three sets of facts which any theory regarding critical periods would have to account for: the gradual decline of performance, the age at which a decline in performance is first detected, and the nature of adult performance.

The gradual decline of performance. Lenneberg's original proposal of a critical period in language acquisition seemed to predict a rectangular function in the relationship between age of acquisition and ultimate performance. That is, Lenneberg hypothesized that "normal" language learning was possible during the period from infancy to puberty, with a loss of abilities after puberty. However, the data on second language learning in the present study did not have this shape. We did not find a flat relationship between performance and age of learning throughout childhood, with a sudden drop in performance marking the end of the critical period; instead, performance gradually declined from about age seven on, until adulthood. Insofar as such data are available from other studies of first and second language acquisition, the same linear trend seems to appear (Oyama, 1978; Patkowski, 1980; Newport, 1984; Newport and Supalla, 1987).

Although this gradual decline is not in accord with Lenneberg's implied function, it is in accord with results from other behavioral domains in which critical periods have been hypothesized. As research accumulates on critical periods, whether it be in imprinting in ducks (Hess, 1973), socialization in dogs (Scott, 1978), or song learning in birds (Kroodsma, 1981), it is becoming apparent that most, if not all, critical periods conform to the more gradual function. This point has recently been noted by several investigators (Tanner, 1970; Immelman and Suomi, 1981).

> usually these periods consist of . . . beginning and end parts . . . [during] which the organism is slightly sensitive to the specic influence, with a period of maximum sensitivity in the middle. It is not as a rule an all-or none phenomenon. (Tanner, 1970, p. 131)

Whatever mechanisms underlie a critical period effect in language learning, then, must be compatible with this gradual decline of performance over age.

The age at which a decline in performance is first detected.   Lenneberg's proposal also seemed to imply that a decline in performance should first appear at puberty. Instead of puberty, we found a small but significant decline in performance in subjects who had arrived in the United States as early as age 8–10. Indeed, the only discrepancy we know of between our results and other data is that, in first language acquisition, this decline may occur even earlier (Newport, 1984; Newport and Supalla, 1987); in the Newport and Supalla data, a 4–6 age group scored consistently, although not always significantly, below native performance. It is possible that a similarly early decline may occur in second language acquisition as well on a test that included more complex aspects of syntax than our own; on our present test, the age 3–7 group scored at ceiling.

Further research is therefore necessary to determine with certainty the exact point at which a decline in learning begins for second language acquisition. It is clear from the present data, however, that this decline begins well before puberty. It also appears that this early decline is small, and that another more major change occurs around puberty. Proposed mechanisms underlying a critical period effect in language learning must therefore account for the details of timing of these changes and, particularly, for the fact that the decline in learning ability begins earlier than initially thought by most researchers.

The nature of adult performance.   There are two aspects of adult performance with which any theoretical account of the critical period must be compatible. The first is that language does not become totally unlearnable during adulthood. This has held true in all of the studies which have tested age differences in asymptotic performance, including both first and second language learning. In the present study, late learners scored significantly above chance on all of the rule types tested except for determiners and plurals. It appears to be the case, then, that quite a few aspects of language are learnable to a fair degree at any age, even though deficiencies in this learning occur.

The second aspect of adult performance with which any theory must be compatible is the great variability found among individuals. For adult learners, age does not continue to be a predictor of performance; thus any proposed mechanism accounting for adult performance likewise cannot be correlated with age. Moreover, while early learners are uniformly successful in acquiring their language to a high degree of proficiency, later learners show much greater individual variation (see also Patkowski, 1980, for related comments). A theoretical account of critical period effects in language learning must therefore consider whether the skills underlying children's uniformly superior performance are similar to those used by adult learners, or rather whether adult language learning skill is controlled by a different set of variables.

Final remarks on a critical period theory of language acquisition. In sum, we now have a number of findings which should be accounted for in any explanation of a critical period. There is the nature of the relationship between age of arrival and performance: a linear decline in performance up through puberty and a subsequent lack of linearity and great variability after puberty. There is also the pattern of errors found for the wide range of aspects of syntax and morphology of English studied: age effects were found for every rule type, with low levels of performance on every rule type except word order and present progressive. The primary and most general finding to accommodate for any critical period theory, of course, is that the critical period is not just a first language phenomenon, but extends to a second language as well.

These findings rule out certain types of accounts of critical period for language acquisition and make other types of accounts more plausible. We have suggested that our results are most naturally accommodated by some type of maturational account, in which there is a gradual decline in language learning skills over the period of on-going maturational growth and a stabilization of language learning skills at a low but variable level of performance at the final mature state. This leaves open, however, the precise explanation of such a phenomenon. The traditional view of critical period effects in language learning has been that there is maturational change in a specific language acquisition device (Lenneberg, 1967; Chomsky, 1981). Such a view, with some modifications to incorporate the detailed points of maturational change, is consistent with our results. Also consistent with our results are views which hypothesize more general cognitive changes over maturation (see, for example, Newport, 1984). From this view, an increase in certain cognitive abilities may, paradoxically, make language learning more difficult. We are hopeful that future research will provide more detailed results which may differentiate these views from one another. In any event, the present study makes clear that some type of critical period account for language acquisition is necessary and that the proper account of a critical period will include both first and second language in its effects.

ACKNOWLEDGEMENTS

This research was supported in part by NIH Grant NS16878 to E. Newport and T. Supalla, and by NIH Training Grant HD07205 to the University of Illinois. We are grateful to Geoff Coulter, Henry Gleitman, and all of the members of our research group for discussion of the issues raised here, to Lloyd Humphreys for advice on statistical matters, to Marcia Linebarger for the loan of test materials, and to Carol Dweck, John Flavell, Dedre Gentner, Doug Medin, and two anonymous reviewers for helpful comments on earlier drafts of this paper.

NOTES

1 In this paper we use the term *critical period* broadly, for the general phenomenon of changes over maturation in the ability to learn (in the case under consideration in this paper, to learn language). We therefore include within this term maturational phenomena which other investigators have called sensitive, rather than critical, periods. By using the term in this broad fashion, we mean to avoid prejudging what the degree or quality of such maturational change may be (e.g. is it a sharp qualitative change *vs* a gradual quantitative one?) and what the nature of the underlying maturational mechanism may be (e.g. is it a change in a special language faculty *vs* a more general change in cognitive abilities?). These further questions will be addressed in part by the nature of our findings, and in part by future research.

2 We thank Marcia Linebarger for making these and other tests available to us.

3 An additional six sentences, three ungrammatical and three the grammatical counterparts of these, were included in the test but were eliminated from scoring because native speakers of English made large numbers of errors in judging their grammaticality, due to either auditory problems or dialect variations.

4 The numbers of ungrammatical and grammatical sentences are unequal because some rule types have more than one grammatical sentence, or more than one ungrammatical sentence, within each set of counterparts (see, for example, the section on particle movement). For the most part, however, the grammatical and ungrammatical sentences form pairs, and for ease of presentation they will be referred to as "pairs" throughout the paper.

5 Using a two-sample *t* statistic where the variance of each group is estimated separately is appropriate whenever the population variances are not assumed to be equal, as is the case here.

6 It is always possible, however, that the equivalence in performance between natives and the 3–7 group is due to a ceiling effect on our test, and that tests of more complex aspects of English syntax would show differences even between these groups.

7 This ranking of rule type difficulty remains the same when using other criteria; for example, ordering rule type according to the number of subjects who score almost perfectly on that rule (that is, 0 or 1 item wrong, out of 6 to 16 possible, depending on the rule type).

8 Some other rule type scores also benefited from subjects' apparent ease with basic word order rules. For example, those items testing yes/no question formation by presenting questions in a V-N-N order (e.g. "Learns Jane math from Mr Thompson?") were particularly easy for subjects. This pattern fit in with a general tendency for V-first items to be easily judged ungrammatical.

9 One discrepancy between the Newport and Supalla results for first language acquisition and the present results for second language acquisition is in the level of performance

attained by subjects who began learning the language between the ages of 3 and 7. In the Newport and Supalla data, the 4–6 age group performed consistently, although not always significantly, below natives. In the present study, the 3–7 age group was entirely within native performance. This difference will be discussed below, in the section entitled "The age at which a decline in performance is first detected."

REFERENCES

Asher, J., & Garcia, R. (1969). The optimal age to learn a foreign language. *Modern Language Journal*, 53, 334–341.

Asher, J., & Price, B. (1967). The learning strategy of total physical response: Some age differences. *Child Development*, 38, 1219–1227.

Chomsky, N. (1981). *Lectures on government and binding*. Dordrecht, Netherlands: Foris.

Curtiss, S. (1977) *Genie: A psycholinguistic study of a modern day "wild child."* New York: Academic Press.

Dulay, H., Burt, M., & Krashen, S. (1982) *Language two*. New York: Oxford University Press.

Freed, B. (1980). Talking to foreigners versus talking to children: Similarities and differences. In R. Scarcella and S. Krashen (eds), *Research in second language acquisition*. Rowley, MA: Newbury House.

Goldin-Meadow, S. (1978). A study in human capacities. *Science*, 200, 649–651.

Gleitman, L. R., Newport, E. L., & Gleitman, H. (1984). The current status of the motherese hypothesis. *Journal of Child Language*, 11, 43–79.

Hakuta, K., & Cancino, H. (1977). Trends in second language acquisition research. *Harvard Educational Review*, 47, 294–316.

Hess, E. H. (1973). *Imprinting*. New York: Van Nostrand.

Hubel, D., & Weisel, T. (1963). Receptive fields of cells in striate cortex of very young, visually inexperienced kittens. *Journal of Neurophysiology*, 26, 994–1002.

Immelmann, K., & Suomi, S. J. (1981). Sensitive phases in development. In K. Immelmann, G. W. Barlow, L. Petrinovich, & M. Main (eds), *Behavioral development: The Bielefeld Interdisciplinary Project*. Cambridge: Cambridge University Press.

Krashen, S. (1975). The development of cerebral dominance and language learning: More new evidence. In D. Dato (ed.), *Developmental psycholinguistics: Theory and applications: Georgetown Round Table on Language and Linguistics*. Washington, DC: Georgetown University.

Krashen, S. (1982). Accounting for child-adult differences in second language rate and attainment. In S. Krashen, R. Scarcella, & M. Long (eds), *Child–adult differences in second language acquisition*. Rowley, MA: Newbury House.

Krashen, S., Long, M., & Scarcella, R. (1982). Age, rate, and eventual attainment in second language acquisition. In S. Krashen, R. Scarcella, & M. Long (eds), *Child–adult differences in second language acquisition*. Rowley, MA: Newbury House.

Kroodsma, D. E. (1981). Ontogeny of bird song. In K. Immelmann, G. W. Barlow, L. Petrinovich, & M. Main (eds), *Behavioral development: The Bielefeld Interdisciplinary Project*. Cambridge: Cambridge University Press.

Lenneberg, E. (1967). *Biological foundations of language*. New York: Wiley.

Linebarger, M. C., Schwartz, M. F., & Saffran, E. M. (1983). Sensitivity to grammatical structure in so-called a grammatic aphasics. *Cognition*, 13, 361–392.

Newport, E. L. (1984). Constraints on learning: Studies in the acquisition of American Sign Language. *Papers and Reports on Child Language Development*, 23, 1–22.

Newport, E. L., Gleitman, H., & Gleitman, L. R. (1977). Mother, I'd rather do it myself: Some effects and non-effects of maternal speech style. In C. E. Snow & C. A. Ferguson (eds.), *Talking to children: Language input and acquisition*. Cambridge: Cambridge University Press.

Newport, E. L., & Supalla, T. (1987) *A critical period effect in the acquisition of a primary language*. University of Illinois, manuscript under review.

Olson, L., & Samuels, S. (1973). The relationship between age and accuracy of foreign language pronunciation. *Journal of Educational Research*, 66, 263–267.

Oyama, S. (1976). A sensitive period for the acquisition of a nonnative phonological system. *Journal of Psycholinguistic Research*, 5, 261–285.

Oyama, S. (1978). The sensitive period and comprehension of speech. *Working Papers on Bilingualism*, 16, 1–17.

Patkowski, M. (1980). The sensitive period for the acquisition of syntax in a second language. *Language Learning*, 30, 449–472.

Schumann, J. (1975). Affective factors and the problem of age in second language acquisition. *Language Learning*, 2, 209–235.

Scott, J. P. (1978). Critical periods for the development of social behavior in dogs. In J. P. Scott (ed.), *Critical periods*. Stroudsburg, PA: Dowden, Hutchinson, & Ross.

Scott, J. P. (1980). The domestic dog: A case of multiple identities. In M. A. Roy (ed.), *Species identity and attachment: A phylogentic evaluation*. New York: Garland STPM Press.

Seliger, H., Krashen, S., & Ladefoged, P. (1975). Maturational constraints in the acquisition of a native-like accent in second language learning. *Language Sciences*, 36, 20–22.

Snow, C. (1983). Age differences in second language acquisition: Research findings and folk psychology. In K. Bailey, M. Long, and S. Peck (eds), *Second language acquisition studies*. Rowley MA: Newbury House.

Snow, C., & Hoefnagel-Hohle, M. (1977). Age differences in pronunciation of foreign sounds. *Language and Speech*, 20, 357–365.

Snow, C., & Hoefnagel-Hohle, M. (1978). The critical period for language acquisition: Evidence from second language learning. *Child Development*, 49, 1114–1128.

Tanner, J. M. (1970). Physical growth. In P. H. Mussen (Ed.), *Carmichael's manual of child psychology*. New York: Wiley.

Wexler, K., & Culicover, P. (1980). *Formal principles of language acquisition*. Cambridge, MA: The MIT Press.

Zehler, A. M. (1982). *The reflection of first language-derived experience in second language acquisition*. Unpublished doctoral dissertation, University of Illinois.

Part IV

Brain Plasticity

Introduction

A confusion is often made between the level of explanation for a developmental change, cognitive or neural, and the extent to which that change is attributable to experience rather than maturation. Thus, evidence that a change at the behavioral level is due to developments at the neural level is often taken as evidence for that change being due to maturation. The readings in this section should dispel this myth, and reveal how open to the effects of experience some aspects of brain development are. It is also important to realize that this plasticity in the brain goes down to the expression of genes themselves. To the biologist this is no surprise. Ever since the time of Ramon y Cajal (1911) it has been believed that information is encoded in the brain by changes in the contacts between neurons. As any biologist knows, constructive changes in the structure of neuronal elements requires the production of their building blocks, proteins, and the instruction to the cell to produce proteins comes from the genes. Thus, to the biologist, the notion that information storage in the brain requires gene expression is obvious. To the developmental psychologist, used to thinking in terms of learning as being distinct from maturation, by contrast, the fact that learning involves the expression of genes may be somewhat surprising. While it had been known for some time that gene expression is influenced by temporal, locational, and biochemical factors such as those alluded to by Rakic in part II, recent experiments have indicated that specific postnatal sensory experience, such as exposure to patterned light, can also play a role in regulating gene expression (see, for example, writings by Black and colleagues in suggestions for further reading).

In part I, Oyama described why we need to move beyond the nature–nurture dichotomy. But there is a problem in doing this. Discarding this dichotomy results in the loss of one of the most powerful analytic tools in development. How are we then to unpack developmental processes?

One possible way out of this impasse is to analyse development in terms of components of environmental influence. This is the approach taken by Greenough and colleagues. The reading is concerned with the effects of experience on neuroanatomical measures of neuronal structure in the cortex. After reviewing a series of studies on the effects of rearing rats in impoverished as opposed to comparatively enriched environments, these authors propose a distinction between two types of information storage in the brain induced by the environment.

The first, *experience-expectant* information storage, refers to changes induced by aspects of the environment that are common to all species members. For example, the developing visual system will almost always be exposed to patterned light. There is no need for the genes to code for every detail of a complex nervous system when certain aspects of the environment can be sure to help in sculpting connectivity. Greenough et al. propose that this class of information storage is commonly associated with a particular form of neuronal change: the selective loss of synapses (such as that reviewed by Huttenlocher in part II). The second type of information incorporated by the brain from the environment is referred to as *experience-dependent*. This refers to information absorbed from the environment that is, or can be, unique to the individual. Examples of such information include learning about characteristics of particular conspecifics, or acquiring a particular vocabulary. The authors present some evidence in support of their claim that this type of information storage involves the generation of new synaptic connections, possibly even in the adult.

The dissociation discussed by Greenough and colleagues is similar to one which I have developed independently with John Morton (see Johnson and Morton, 1991). Our proposal was that a way out of the interactionist impasse outlined earlier is to clearly separate out classes of environmental influence on phenotypes. Instead of the dichotomy being reduced to necessity or otherwise of environmental input, we put forward a framework which, like Greenough and colleagues, distinguishes between the various levels of environmental input. There are at least three levels at which "environment" interacts with genotype. First, there is the environment within the genetic material. The location of a gene in the genetic material will determine when it is expressed, and with which other genes. Second, there is the local biochemical environment, which can either act with gene products, or act upon the gene itself. Third, there is the interaction between the product of the first two levels and the world outside the organism. It is only this latter level of environmental influence that is directly relevant to those interested in cognitive development. We (Johnson and Morton) invoked the phrase *internal* environment for the first two levels of environmental influence, and *external* environment for the third. At the level of the external environmental input we proposed another distinction, that between the *species-typical environment* (STE) (roughly equivalent to experience-expectant information storage) and the *individual-specific environment* (ISE) (roughly equivalent to experience-dependent storage). For example, while being exposed to spoken language would be an aspect of the human STE, being exposed to English, rather than French, in early childhood would be an aspect of the ISE.

One difference between the Johnson and Morton analysis and that discussed by Greenough and colleagues is that the latter see their categories of experience-expectant and experience-dependent as being forms of information storage in the brain, with the one form of experience giving rise to different synaptic mechanisms from the other. This means that any single aspect of experience would give rise to one or the other class of neuronal change. In contrast, in the Johnson and Morton account, it is quite possible for some aspects of the environment to act as both STE and ISE for the same species. For example, the language input to a human child provides both STE and ISE. Language input itself is species-typical, and any language input will serve to develop the language-specific structures of the brain. In this sense, all languages are equivalent. At the same time, the particular language we hear as an infant is part of the ISE. Such an analysis can be carried further by identifying particular aspects of the grammar that are part of the STE. Note that even if certain aspects of grammar turn out to be universal to all cultures, this does not mean that they are "genetic." It does imply, however, that it is part of the environment that the developing human brain can expect to encounter.

The next reading (O'Leary) addresses the issue of plasticity with regard to one particular mammalian brain structure, the cerebral cortex. This structure appears to be considerably more open to influence by sensory experience than any other region of the mammalian brain. In order further to understand the extent to which this structure is organized by sensory input, we may divide cortical differentiation into three types (see also Sur et al., 1990): first, *radial specification* (the laminar pattern discussed by Rakic in part II); second, the development of *external connections* with both subcortical and other cortical structures; and third, the development of the *internal microcircuitry* within the cortex.

The first of these, the laminar structure of the cortex, deviates very little with varying sensory experience. Both from one area of cortex to another, and across species, the characteristic six-layered structure of the cortex seems to be maintained, with each layer possessing particular cell types and the same general patterns of connectivity. In experiments where the thalamic (sensory) input to an area of cortex is drastically reduced, the six-layered structure of the cortex is still maintained, despite corresponding reductions in the area of cortex innervated by those inputs. For example, a reduction of 50 percent in the thalamic input to the primary visual cortex results in a 50 percent reduction in the size of this structure – area 18 (V2) now occupies much of the area of cortex which was previously V1 (see figure 15.3 from O'Leary). Despite this reduction in its size, the depth of the remaining V1 is identical to that found normally, and all six layers with their corresponding neuron types are present. Thus, as discussed in the reading by Rakic in part II, it appears that the radial structure of the cortex is extremely robust, and not open to influence by sensory factors.

The story with regard to the external connections of the cortex is a little different. O'Leary describes some experimental manipulations in which visual input is rerouted to the primary auditory or somatosensory cortices. Not only does the visual input find its way to these primary cortices and innervate them, but these cortices then develop at least some of the information processing properties normally found in the primary visual cortex. For example, in the ferret, visual input can be induced to innervate the auditory cortex. Such rewiring results not only in cells in the auditory cortex being sensitive to visual input, but also in some of them becoming orientation selective, direction selective, and even binocular (see also Sur et al., 1990). Furthermore, the auditory cortex sometimes develops a two-dimensional map of visual space, very different from the normal one-dimensional tonotopic map found in the auditory cortex. Thus, the nature of the thalamic afferents to a region of cortex appears to determine to some extent the nature of the representations that it deals with, and presumably therefore some aspects of its internal microcircuitry.

With regard to the outputs, or efferents, from the cortex to subcortical regions, O'Leary describes experiments involving the transplantation of cortex from one region to another. These experiments lead to the conclusion that the regional location of a developing piece of cortex is the most important determiner of its subsequent subcortical projections. For example, visual cortical neurones which are transplanted into the motor region of a newborn rat develop, and permanently retain, projections to subcortical regions characteristic of motor, and not visual, cortex (see figure 15.4 from O'Leary). Outputs to subcortical regions, therefore, also appear to depend on location within the cortex as a whole, rather than the origins of the developing piece of cortex. In conclusion, the findings described by O'Leary strongly suggest that the cortex is composed of basic building blocks (those described in the reading by Rakic in part II), which are equipotential. If the location of any unit within the whole is changed early in development, this unit will develop inputs, outputs and cortico–cortico connections quite appropriate for the region within which it finds itself. Furthermore, it may also perform, at least to some extent, information processing functions appropriate for that location.

The plasticity of cortex can also be studied by investigating the extent to which it can recover or compensate following damage. In the 1930s Kennard proposed, on the basis of her experiments with monkeys, that the younger cortical damage occurs, the less severe the subsequent behavioral deficits (see also Stiles and Thal, part VIII). This principle dominated thinking in developmental neuropsychology for many years, and is the starting point for some of the experimental investigations reported in the reading by Kolb. Kolb describes results obtained from experimental studies in which rats receive lesions of one hemisphere, or bilaterally to the prefrontal cortex, at various postnatal ages.

In accordance with the Kennard effect, it is the case that brain damage at different ages often has different consequences. However, the effects are not always that the earlier the damage occurs, the less the behavioral consequence (but see Stiles and Thal, part VIII, for some examples where this is the case). Sometimes the reverse effect is found, with early damage having more profound consequences than does later damage. The research of Kolb and others has been concerned to identify the variables that predict the extent of recovery in various behavioral domains following early and late brain damage.

The variables identified by Kolb include: (a) the site and extent of the lesion, e.g. removal of a cerebral hemisphere has widespread effects on many behavioral tasks, while early prefrontal damage has more selective effects; (b) the types of tasks studied, e.g. frontal damage in rats appears to have a far greater effect on species-typical behaviors than on learning tasks; (c) rearing in enriched environments, such as those described by Greenough and colleagues (this section), result in greater recovery of function than does rearing in social isolation. Finally, Kolb discusses the very complex and still poorly understood neural correlates of functional recovery. All that can be said at present is that when the Kennard effect is observed, there is a corresponding increase in dendritic arbors. In contrast, when behavior suffers to a greater extent following early damage, there is a decreased dendritic arbor observed in cortical neurones.

FURTHER READING

Black, I. B. et al. (1984) Neurotransmitter plasticity at the molecular level. *Science*, 225, 1266–70.

Black, I. B. (1991) *Information in the Brain: a Molecular Perspective.* Cambridge, MA: Bradford Books/MIT Press.

Jenkins, W. M., Merzenich, M. M. and Recanzone, G. (1990) Neocortical representational dynamics in adult primates: Implications for neuropsychology. *Neuropsychologia*, 28, 573–84. (Reviews studies concerned with representational plasticity in the adult primate brain.)

Johnson, M. H. and Morton, J. (1991) *Biology and Cognitive Development: the Case of Face Recognition.* Oxford: Blackwell. (Chapter 1 is relevant to the issues addressed in this section.)

Killackey, H. P. (1990). Neocortical expansion: an attempt toward relating phylogeny and ontogeny. *Journal of Cognitive Neuroscience*, 2, 1–17. (Argues that both phylogenetic and ontogenetic development can be understood in terms of the addition of cortical "units.")

Rauschecker, J. P. and Marler, P. (eds) (1987) *Imprinting and Cortical Plasticity: Comparative Aspects of Sensitive Periods.* New York: John Wiley & Sons. (A useful and well-edited collection of chapters about cortical plasticity and sensitive periods in a variety of species and contexts.)

Schoups, A. and Black, I. B. (1991) Visual experience specifically regulates synaptic molecules in rat visual cortex. *Journal of Cognitive Neuroscience*, 3, 252–7. (Further evidence that visual experience can affect gene expression.)

Sur, M., Pallas, S. L. and Roe, A. W. (1990) Cross-modal plasticity in cortical development: differentiation and specification of sensory neocortex. *Trends in the Neurosciences*, 13, 227–33. (A review of the authors' work on "rewiring" the inputs to regions of cortex.)

14

Experience and Brain Development

WILLIAM T. GREENOUGH, JAMES E. BLACK AND
CHRISTOPHER S. WALLACE

> What is the Meaning of Infancy? What is the meaning of the fact that man is born
> into the world more helpless than any other creature, and needs for a much longer
> season than any other living thing the tender care and wise counsel of his elders?
> (John Fiske, 1883/1909, p. 1)

The extended period of infancy reflects the importance of incorporating enormous amounts of information into the brain. It has been estimated that, even within the much smaller brain of the rat, perhaps a quarter of a million connections between nerve cells are formed each second during the first month of postnatal development (Schüz, 1978). These connections, at least those that persist, comprise the combination of intrinsic and experiential information, recorded in neural circuitry, upon which behavior is based. Although research has demonstrated substantial effects of experience on brain connections, we do not yet understand just how the infant's brain is specialized to organize and incorporate experience, or the ways in which the infant may program its own experience. However, biological research using animals has helped outline basic mechanisms whereby experience affects the brain, and has provided a new view of how the brain may adapt to different types of experience.

Such studies of animal development have suggested a fundamentally different view of what have been called "sensitive- period" or "critical-period" phenomena. The traditional concept has been likened by Bateson (1979) to the brief opening of a window, with experience influencing development only while the window is open. A window for visual development in kittens, for example, might open at the time the eyes first open, and close a few weeks later. Although the term "sensitive period" is a useful label for such a process, it does little to explain the underlying mechanisms. We propose a new classification based on the type of information that is stored and the brain mechanisms used to store it. This

"Experience and Brain Development" first appeared in *Child Development* 58 (1987), pp.
539–59, and is reprinted by kind permission.

approach allows consideration of the evolutionary origins of a process, its adaptive value for the individual, the required timing and character of experience, and the organism's potentially active role in obtaining appropriate experience for itself.

We propose that mammalian brain development relies upon two different categories of plasticity for the storage of environmentally originating information. The first of these probably underlies many sensitive- or critical-period phenomena. This process, which we term *experience-expectant*, is designed to utilize the sort of environmental information that is ubiquitous and has been so throughout much of the evolutionary history of the species. Since the normal environment reliably provides all species members with certain experiences, such as seeing contrast borders, many mammalian species have evolved neural mechanisms that take advantage of such experiences to shape developing sensory and motor systems. An important component of the neural processes underlying experience-expectant information storage appears to be the intrinsically governed generation of an excess of synaptic connections among neurons, with experiential input subsequently determining which of them survive. The second type of plasticity, which we call *experience-dependent*, is involved in the storage of information that is unique to the individual. Mammals in particular have evolved nervous systems that can take advantage of such information, as of sources of food and haven, and individual survival depends upon it to a very great extent. Since such experience will differ in both timing and character among individuals, the nervous system must be ready to incorporate the information when it becomes available. An important aspect of the mechanism underlying experience-dependent information storage appears to be the generation of new synaptic connections in response to the occurrence of a to-be-remembered event.

Sensitive Periods in Sensory-System Development: Experience-expectant Information Storage

That there are sensitive periods during which experience manipulations profoundly affect sensory-system development in mammals is well known, and this will be reviewed only briefly here. For more extensive reviews, the reader is referred to Mitchell and Timney (1984) or Movshon and Van Sluyters (1981). The vast majority of data regarding experience effects on sensory development have come from studies of the visual system. However, to the extent that other modalities have been examined, relatively similar results have been obtained (Clopton and Winfield, 1976; Feng and Rogowski, 1980; Meisami, 1975). The visual manipulations range from total pattern deprivation (bilateral eyelid suture or dark rearing) to selective deprivation (e.g. of certain contours or of movement). Monocular deprivation in species with binocularly overlapping visual fields and binocular depth perception is a special case that will be discussed separately. Each of these manipulations interferes with an experience that otherwise would be common to the young of the species.

Behavior

Total pattern deprivation may occasionally involve interpretational problems, since dark rearing can disturb endocrine rhythms, parental behavior, and feeding

(Eayrs and Ireland, 1950; Mos, 1976) and can damage the retinae of some species (Rasch et al., 1961), and eyelid suture can lengthen the optical axis of the eye, causing nearsightedness (Wiesel and Raviola, 1977). Nonetheless, an extensive literature demonstrates that behavioral deficits resulting from total pattern deprivation arise primarily from impairment of visual information processing by the brain. In rats, for example, Tees (1979) has noted that particular aspects of visual discrimination tasks, such as the relation among elements within the stimulus, rather than task difficulty *per se* (measured as number of trials required for learning), are sensitive indicators of visual deprivation induced impairment. Moreover, visually deprived rats are not impaired on similarly complex tasks involving nonvisual modalities (Tees and Cartwright, 1972). A human parallel to this process is the impaired vision of the surgically corrected congenital cataract patients of Senden (1960). For at least two weeks, such patients could discriminate forms such as squares and triangles only by counting their corners. In general, total deprivation effects become less reversible by later visual experience with longer periods of deprivation (Crabtree and Riesen, 1979; Timney et al., 1980). This may result in part because deprived animals tend increasingly to rely on nonvisual cues (Fox, 1966), but it certainly reflects impairment of visual processing ability as well.

Physiology

Deficits at the neurophysiological level parallel, and presumably underlie, the behavioral impairments. The neurophysiological deficits described to date probably relate more closely to differences in acuity than to ones in complex aspects of form and pattern perception – the latter processes having not yet been understood at the neurophysiological level. What have been studied are the stimuli that best activate single neurons in the visual system, recognizing generally that such neurons are merely components of a quite complicated circuit. In kittens at the time the eyes open, somewhat less than half of primary visual cortex neurons respond selectively to the orientation or direction of movement of a stimulus (Blakemore and Van Sluyters, 1975; Buisseret and Imbert, 1976). Over several weeks in normal light, virtually all cells gain orientation sensitivity, and there is a general tendency for cells to become much more selective to specific orientations as well. In the absence of patterned visual stimulation, visual cortex neurons gradually lose responsiveness to stimulus orientation. As with behavior, the degree to which recovery toward normal physiological responsiveness can be achieved with exposure to patterned stimulation declines as deprivation is prolonged (Cynader et al., 1976). Moreover, the recovered animal, if it has binocularly overlapping vision, is quite different from the normal: about half of its neurons never recover, and the ability to orient to stimuli across the midline is lost from both eyes (Sherman, 1973, 1977).

More selective effects have been obtained with selective forms of deprivation. In the most extensively studied paradigm, animals have been reared such that their visual experience is limited to a pattern of lines at a particular (usually horizontal or vertical) orientation. Initial neurophysiological studies indicated that visual cortex neurons fired strongly when the animal saw lines at angles close to those of the rearing stimuli (Hirsch and Spinelli, 1970). Later work has qualified these findings to some extent (e.g. Gordon et al., 1979; Leventhal and Hirsch, 1975), but the essential details remain intact. As expected, these animals were also better at resolving lines at those same angles in behavioral tasks (e.g. Blasdel et al., 1977; Corrigan and Carpenter, 1979). Similar results have been obtained for cortical neurons sensitive to direction of stimulus movement. Cynader and Chernenko (1976), for example, deprived cats of visual movement perception by rearing them in a stroboscopic environment. Because the flashes of light were very brief, these cats saw the world as a series of "still pictures" rather than one of continuous movement. In these animals, cells sensitive to movement were much less frequently found. Thus cells in visual cortex were impaired in responding to specific stimulus characteristics that were missing from the rearing environment. A behavioral parallel to this in humans has been suggested by a persistent reduction in acuity, even while wearing glasses, if astigmatism went uncorrected in childhood (Mitchell et al., 1973).

Morphology

Total pattern deprivation has pronounced effects on central visual structures, and particularly upon the visual cortex. Most nerve cell connections in the visual cortex occur on spines (see figure 14.1). There are fewer of these spines on dendrites of neurons in visually deprived animals (Fifkova, 1968, 1970; Rothblat and Schwartz, 1979; Valverde, 1971). This indicates that the nerve cells of visually deprived animals make fewer interconnections. While later exposure to light can reverse differences to some extent, at least in dark-reared mice (Valverde, 1971), significant differences persist (Ruiz-Marcos and Valverde, 1969). Reduction in the overall amount of dendrite has also been reported for visual cortex neurons following dark rearing in some species, again indicating fewer connections among neurons (Coleman and Riesen, 1968; Valverde, 1970). Finally, an overall measure of synaptic connectivity, the number of synapses per visual cortex nerve cell, was lower in visually deprived than in normal cats (Cragg, 1975a; Winfield, 1981). A straightforward interpretation is that the complexity of the visual cortex "wiring diagram" is reduced in animals deprived of visual experience during early postnatal sensitive periods.

While the results will not be detailed here, differences in the morphology of subcortical visual structures (see figure 14.1) have also been reported following visual deprivation (e.g. Fifkova, 1979; for review, see Globus, 1975). Overstimulation (constant lighting), a procedure that eventually damages the rat retina, has been reported to increase spine frequency on neurons above that seen with normal diurnal lighting in the lateral geniculate nucleus (Parnavelas et al., 1973) and also in the visual cortex (Parnavelas and Globus, 1976). These findings indicate that many brain structures may be affected simultaneously by experience.

Particularly interesting morphological results have been reported in a selective visual experience paradigm. Coleman et al. (1981) studied the orientation of dendrites of visual cortex neurons in cats raised with their visual experience limited to either horizontal or vertical lines, as described above. They found that the outer dendrites were oriented at about 90° from each other in the two groups, a result that could correspond to the visual cortex neurons selectively modifying their dendrites such that they responded to the exposure orientation. Tieman

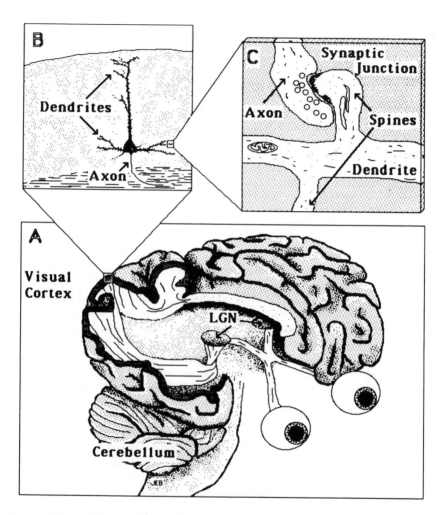

Figure 14.1 A, A human brain, with much of the right hemisphere removed and many subcortical structures omitted to reveal a simplified view of the visual system. Visual information travels from the retina to visual cortex via the lateral geniculate nucleus (LGN). As fibers from the retina pass back toward the LGN, some of them cross to the other side, reflecting the general principle that a sensory input originating on one side of the body is processed by brain structures in the hemisphere on the opposite side. Fibers from each retina which receive light from the *right* half of the visual field project to visual cortex on the *left* hemisphere. Hence, the visual cortex in the left hemisphere "sees" only the right half of the world, through both eyes. Within visual cortex, inputs from each eye are organized into adjacent bands called "ocular dominance columns." B, A section of visual cortex showing a neuron, as would be seen through a light microscope. Visual cortex, which is approximately 2 mm thick in a two year old infant, is actually much more densely packed with neurons and their interconnecting fibers than is depicted by this figure. A neuron in visual cortex might receive, depending on cell type, 10 000–30 000 synaptic

and Hirsch (1982) similarly reported approximately perpendicularly oriented visual cortex dendrites in vertical and horizontal stripe reared cats. These studies indicate that the pattern of connections among visual cortex neurons, not merely the number of connections, is influenced by visual experience during early development.

Expected Experience

An important question is *why* there are experience–expectant or sensitive periods in sensory development. On the surface, it may not seem to make much evolutionary sense to have designed an organism that will be forever impaired in its sensory performance if the proper sorts of experiences do not occur at relatively specific developmental time points. The offsetting advantage appears to be that sensory system can develop much greater performance capabilities by taking advantage of experiences that can be expected to be available in the environment of all young animals. Thus many species seem to have evolved such that the genes need only roughly outline the pattern of neural connectivity in a sensory system, leaving the more specific details to be determined through the organism's interactions with its environment.

The way in which this finer tuning of both sensory and motor systems is often accomplished has provided us with some real insight into the circumstances that may give rise to sensitive-period phenomena. Studies of a number of developing sensory systems as well as of peripheral connections in the autonomic and skeletal musculature systems have indicated that synapses are overproduced in early development (Boothe et al., 1979; Brown et al., 1976; Brunjes et al., 1982; Cragg, 1975b; Purves and Lichtman, 1980). Similar findings have been described in the human visual and frontal cortex (Huttenlocher, 1979; Huttenlocher et al., 1982). As development proceeds, the extra synapses are lost, such that the final wiring diagram consists of those synapses that remain. Two examples serve to illustrate how a refined pattern can emerge from relatively more chaotic beginnings through selective retention of synapses: synapse elimination at the neuromuscular junction and ocular dominance column (see figure 14.1 caption) formation in the visual cortex.

Motor neurons in the spinal cord connect with fibers of skeletal muscle. While a specific spinal location projects to each muscle, the pattern is quite different in the newborn rat from that in the adult. Brown et al. (1976) reported an overlapping pattern in the newborn rat, such that individual motor neurons connect to several muscle fibers, and each muscle fiber receives connections from several motor neurons. During the first two weeks after birth, these overlapping multiple connections disappear, as all but one of the synapses on each muscle

inputs to its dendrites, most of which will occur on spines. At this level of magnification, spines appear as tiny dots along the dendrites. C, Detail of a portion of dendrite containing a synapse between an axon terminal (distinguished by the presence of spheres called vesicles) and a dendritic spine, a small projection from the dendrite tunk. For perspective, note that spines are somewhat less than 1/1 000 of a millimeter wide. Thus, to see a synapse requires the resolving power of an electron microscope.

fiber drop out. Brown et al. (1976) suggest that a selection process occurs that involves competition between the various neurons innervating a muscle fiber, leaving behind a one-to-one pattern. Precisely what leads to competitive success is not known, but at least some experiments have suggested that neuronal activity is a necessary part of the process (Gouze et al., 1983; O'Brien et al., 1978; Thompson et al., 1979). The important point is that, if the proper connections are selectively retained (or if improper ones are selectively eliminated), a highly ordered pattern can emerge from a much less organized one by the loss of synaptic connections (Changeux and Danchin, 1977).

The development of ocular dominance columns in mammals with binocularly overlapping visual systems provides an example of a similar selection process in the central nervous system. In species such as cats or monkeys, closure of one eye during a relatively brief postnatal sensitive period causes a severe visual impairment when the eye is later reopened (Wiesel and Hubel, 1963). The effect is far more pronounced and lasting than that seen with binocular deprivation (Wiesel and Hubel, 1965). At the neurophysiological level, the deprived eye loses most of its ability to control the activity of visual cortex neurons, while the open eye correspondingly gains in control. Thus it appears that the deprived eye becomes functionally disconnected from visual cortex neurons. LeVay et al. (1980) have shown that the monocular deprivation effect involves a competitive process in which connections actually are lost in the visual cortex. In the binocular regions of normal adult monkey visual cortex, inputs from the two eyes terminate in alternating bands termed "columns" which are about 400 micrometers wide. In monkeys in which one eye has been closed during development, the bands are still present, but those arising from the deprived eye are much narrower than normal, and those arising from the open eye are correspondingly wider. LeVay et al. (1980), studying the development of these bands, found that axons from the two eyes initially have overlapping terminal fields (figure 14.2), such that distinct columns are not present. In normal development, the terminal fields of axons from both eyes gradually and simultaneously regress, such that the sharply defined ocular dominance bands of the adult emerge. When one eye is deprived, its terminals regress more than normally, whereas those of the open eye retain a larger part of initial dually innervated territory, thus generating the alternating pattern of narrow and wide bands. This work, along with supportive evidence (e.g. Guillery, 1972), points to the view that a competition process occurs in the visual cortex, in which inputs from experienced eyes are advantaged. Hypotheses regarding the neural bases of the advantage have proposed that actively firing synapses are more likely to be preserved, or that synchronous firing of the presynaptic terminal and the postsynaptic neuron may stabilize the synapse (see e.g. Singer, 1986), a process similar to that proposed by Hebb (1949).

These two examples illustrate a major point. In both cases, during a relatively restricted period, an *expected experience* (motor activity or visual stimulation) participates in the organization of a detailed neural pattern. The neural manifestation of expectation or sensitivity appears to be the production of an excess number of synapses, a subset of which will be selectively preserved by experience-generated neural activity. If the normal pattern of experience occurs, a normal pattern of neural organization results. If an abnormal pattern of experience occurs, an abnormal neural organization pattern will occur. We do not, of course, know that similar processes underlie all phenomena proposed to involve sensitive periods, and we shall see below that other factors may be involved in the determination of sensitive periods. Nonetheless, it seems clear that the production of more synapses than can eventually survive, combined with an experience-based selection process, is a central aspect of the sensitive-period phenomena that have been most extensively studied. Because the developing mammal's experience has been predictable throughout the evolutionary history of the species, the species has come to count on or expect its occurrence in the developmental process. We refer to this as *experience-expectant* information storage.

Schüz (1978), comparing altricial (born underdeveloped) with precocial species, has similarly noted that the overproduction of synapses might be an indication of readiness for expected experience. With its eyes open and able to move about, the precocial guinea pig's cerebral cortex shows many more dendritic spines at birth than that of the newborn mouse, which is born in a relatively altricial state. However, at the time the mouse's eyes open, about two weeks after birth, its cortical neurons have developed a density of spines comparable to that of the newborn guinea pig. Thus spines matured at the time the animal became able to actively explore the environment.

Control of Experience-expectant Processes

The character or quality of expected experiences may also play a role in determining the length of time that the developing nervous system remains

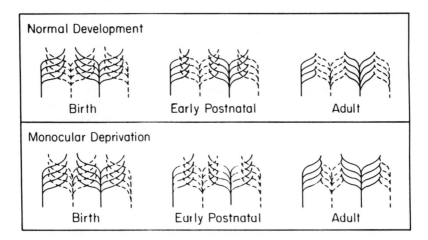

Figure 14.2 Schematic depiction of ocular dominance column development in monkeys reared normally or monocularly deprived. The left panels represent the substantial overlap of the axonal branches from the two eyes at birth. In normal development (top), the competitive interactions result in equal pruning back of axons from each eye in the adult (right panels). After monocular deprivation, however, axons from the nondeprived eye (solid lines) retain more branches, while the axons from the deprived eye (dashed lines) retain fewer branches (from Greenough and Schwark, 1984; copyright 1984 by Plenum Publishing; reprinted by permission).

sensitive to their effects. For example, since success in competition and consequent elimination of alternative neural patterns is promoted by experience-based
neural activity, a relative reduction in that activity may prolong the competition
process. Cynader and Mitchell (1980) found that kittens dark reared until six,
eight, or ten months remained highly sensitive to monocular deprivation effects.
This is in contrast to light-reared kittens, in which peak sensitivity to monocular
deprivation normally occurs within the first two months of life, and negligible
effects of monocular deprivation are seen in kittens reared normally if deprivation
begins after three or four months (Hubel and Wiesel, 1970; Olson and Freeman,
1978). Relatively small amounts of normal visual experience appear to set in
motion processes that can protect the organism against later deprivation (Mower
et al., 1983).

The character of experience may not be the only factor regulating the temporal
aspects of sensitive periods. Kasamatsu and Pettigrew (1976) initially proposed
that the chemical neurotransmitter norepinephrine regulated sensitivity to monocular deprivation. They found that treatment with 6-hydroxydopamine, which
reduces brain norepinephrine, prevented the shift in control of visual cortex
neurons from the deprived eye in cats that were monocularly deprived during
the sensitive period. If norepinephrine was replaced by local administration into
visual cortex, however, the ocular dominance shift did occur in 6-hydroxy-
dopamine-treated cats (Pettigrew and Kasamatsu, 1978). More recent work (Bear
and Singer, 1986) has suggested that two neurotransmitters, norepinephrine and
acetylcholine, may be involved in regulating developmental sensitivity of the
visual cortex. There have also been some reports that drugs that interfere with
norepinephrine action reduce or prevent the brain and behavioral effects of
environmental complexity that are discussed in a later section of this article
(Mirmiran and Uylings, 1983; O'Shea et al., 1983; Pearlman, 1983). These results
suggest that neurotransmitters such as norepinephrine and acetylcholine may be
involved in initiating or maintaining neuronal sensitivity to experience, a role
consistent with the term "neuromodulator," often applied to norepinephrine.
Parallel reports of noradrenergic regulation of adult memory storage processes
(e.g. Gold, 1984) suggest the possibility of a quite general role for norepinephrine
systems in the governance of plastic neural processes.

On the "Chalkboard" Metaphor

An important question involves the extent to which developing sensory systems
merely follow the pattern imposed upon them by sensory experience, in the
manner of a "blank slate," as opposed to selectively utilizing or actively creating
information in experience. At the level of the neuron, an equivalent question is
whether all input promotes similar structural change. It is clear that sensory
systems have strong predispositions at the time of birth; for example, the initial
stages of the binocular segregation process precede eye opening in the monkey
visual cortex (LeVay et al., 1980), and oriented receptive fields are present to
some extent at birth (Blakemore and Van Sluyters, 1975) and certain orientations
appear to be more predisposed to arise in the absence of appropriate input in

the cat (Leventhal and Hirsch, 1975). The rudimentary neural organization imposes order on its input. A phenomenon that may illustrate this is the apparent compensatory change that has been reported in intact modalities' central representations with damage to or deprivation of other modalities. For example, the auditory cortex increases in size in visually deprived or blinded animals (Gyllensten et al., 1966; Ryugo et al., 1975). Since auditory stimulation is equivalent in deprived and sighted animals, the size increase must depend upon some aspect of the increased reliance upon audition that becomes necessary in the absence of visual input. That is, the brain's differential use of the same auditory information determines the information's effect on brain structure. It is but a small extension of this idea to note that individual differences could be preserved even in the face of identical environmental experience.

Possible human behavioral reflections of neural predispositions to select and organize experience are also evident. For example, infants may have "hard-wired" capacities for categorical perception of phonemes (Eimas, 1975) and syntactic structure (Chomsky, 1980). The infant's behavioral and affective responses to caretaker speech can make the social interaction highly rewarding for both participants, perhaps even encouraging a phonetic adjustment to match the perceptual limitations of the infant (Fernald, 1984). An innate predisposition of the infant to smile and make noises, if it exists, could serve the infant by shaping the caretaker's speech toward an optimal form of linguistic input. Thelen (1980) has suggested that kicking and other behaviors, while serving as neural foundations of mature motor systems, can also help the infant control experience (e.g. as in communicating distress or pleasure). From this perspective, the infant may often pick and choose from an experiential smorgasbord available during development. In fact, we suspect that some types of "expected" experience may rely largely on the infant to produce them.

Early Sensory-System Development: Summary

The primary quality of experience effects in early sensory-system development that sets them apart from many later developmental processes, as well as from adult learning and memory, is the degree to which they are age dependent and subsequently irreversible. At the behavioral level, a relevant human example may be the loss of perceived phonemic boundaries present in infants if the language to which they are exposed does not utilize them (Werker and Tees, 1984). At the neural level, the irreversibility appears to arise in at least some cases because a set of synapses has become committed to a particular pattern of organization, while synapses that could have subserved alternative patterns have been lost. A process seen in the brain that may underlie this is a rapid peaking of synapse numbers, followed by the loss of a significant proportion of them, as shown in figure 14.3. The rate and extent of commitment of synapses may be regulated by both the quality of experience and intrinsic factors such as broadly acting neurochemical systems. In at least some cases, it seems clear that central system organization is not merely "painted" on the brain by experience, since both the quality of information and the way in which it is used can affect the rate of pattern formation as well as the character of the pattern.

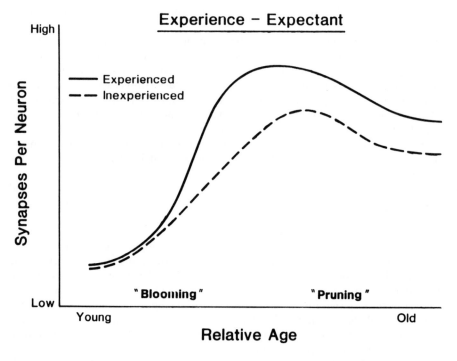

Figure 14.3 Schematic diagram of synapse overproduction ("blooming") and deletion ("pruning"; Schneider, 1981) during an experience-expectant process (from Black and Greenough, 1986, Vol. 4, p. 28; copyright 1986 by Lawrence Erlbaum Associates; reprinted by permission).

Experience-dependent Information Storage in Later Development and Adulthood

Many of the effects of experience upon behavioral development do not appear to exhibit the relatively strict age-dependent character associated with early sensory system development. One reason for this may be that a species cannot count on certain important experiences to occur at particular points in the lifespan. Another is that much of the information that an animal or human must acquire during development or adulthood is unique to its own particular environment: information about the physical characteristics of the surroundings, the social system and the roles of specific individuals, and, in humans, the details of one's language(s) and other formally specified cognitive capacities. It is not clear *a priori* whether the brain mechanisms involved in storing these kinds of information are the same as those used for experience-expectant processes, although evolution tends to produce new adaptations (such as the unique plasticity of the mammalian brain) by modifying existing systems, as opposed to creating entirely new ones. We will review some of what is known about these more mature categories of information storage and will then return to our consideration of neural mechanisms.

The Environmental Complexity Paradigm

The research that has perhaps taught us the most about mechanisms of cognitive development in animals utilizes variations in the physical and social complexity of the rearing environment. This line of research began with Hebb's (1949) rearing of rats as pets in his home for comparison with laboratory-reared animals, but most researchers have adopted less life-disrupting laboratory versions of Hebb's home. Most commonly, two or all of the following three conditions have been employed. (1) *Environmental complexity* (EC) animals are housed in groups of about a dozen in large cages filled with various objects with which the animals are free to play and explore. Often the animals are given additional daily exposure to a maze or a toy-filled field. In our work and most others', the play objects are changed and rearranged daily. (2) *Social cage* (SC) animals are housed in pairs or small groups in standard laboratory cages, without objects beyond food and water containers. (3) *Individual cage* (IC) animals are housed alone in similar or identical laboratory cages. The term "enriched condition" has been used to describe what we call environmental complexity, but we prefer the latter to emphasize that these conditions represent an incomplete attempt to mimic some aspects of the wild environment and should be considered "enriched" only in comparison to the humdrum life of the typical laboratory animal.

Behavior. Since Hebb's (1949) initial demonstration that home-reared rats were superior to laboratory-reared rats at learning a series of complex maze patterns, a large number of experiments have confirmed that rats and mice reared in complex environments are generally superior on complex, appetitive tasks. A significant number of experiments have been directed at particular behavioral characteristics that differentiate EC from SC and IC animals, and it seems safe to conclude that no single explanation, such as differential emotional reactivity, better use of extra-maze cues, or differential visual ability, can account for the pattern of behavioral differences that have been reported (Greenough et al., 1972; Krech et al., 1962; Ravizza and Herschberger, 1966; see Greenough, 1976, for review). All of these may play a role under certain circumstances, of course (Brown, 1968; Hymovitch, 1952; Myers and Fox, 1963), but the differences appear to be quite general, extending even to models of Piagetian volume-conservation tasks (Thinus-Blanc, 1981), such that the most likely explanation (if not the most satisfying in specificity) may well be that the groups differ in the amount of stored knowledge upon which they can draw in novel situations.

It appears that active interaction with the environment is necessary for the animal to extract very much appropriate information. Not only do the EC and SC conditions differ little with regard to the average intensity of energy impinging upon most sensory modalities, but merely making visual experience of a complex environment available to animals otherwise unable to interact with it has little behavioral effect. Forgays and Forgays (1952), for example, found little benefit to maze performance of having been housed in small cages within the EC environment. Similar results have been reported with regard to some of the brain effects of EC rearing that are described below (Ferchmin et al., 1975).

Morphology. Following initial reports that several regions of the cerebral cortex were heavier and thicker in EC than in IC rats (Bennett et al., 1964) and had larger neuronal cell bodies and more glial (i.e. supportive) cells (Diamond, 1967; Diamond et al., 1972), detailed studies began to indicate probable differences in the number of synaptic connections. Differences in the amount of dendrite per neuron, that is, the amount of surface available for synaptic connections, of up to 20 percent were reported in the upper visual cortex of rats reared in EC versus IC environments from weaning to late adolescence (Greenough and Volkmar, 1973; Holloway, 1966). Values for SC rats were intermediate, although generally closer to those of IC rats, in the Greenough and Volkmar study, and this has tended to be the case in other experiments in which such a group has been included. Small differences in the frequency of postsynaptic spines (see figure 14.1) favoring EC rats were also reported (Globus et al., 1973), suggesting that synapses were not merely spaced farther apart on the longer dendrites of the EC rats. A direct demonstration that EC rats exceeded IC rats in synapses per neuron in upper visual cortex by 20–25 percent (Turner and Greenough, 1985) led us to consider what similar extremes might result if all neurons in the human brain were equally plastic. The difference of about 2 000 synapses per neuron in the rat would translate into many trillions of synapses on the 100–200 billion neurons of the human brain!

While EC–IC differences (in male rats) are greatest in the occipital, or visual, region of the cerebral cortex, they occur in other neocortical regions as well, including those associated with audition and somesthesis and also regions somewhat functionally comparable to the human frontal cortex (Greenough et al., 1973; Rosenzweig et al., 1972; Uylings et al., 1978). Differences in dendritic field size following similar differential rearing have also been reported in subcortical regions such as the rat hippocampal formation and monkey and rat cerebellum (Floeter and Greenough, 1979; Juraska et al., 1985; Pysh and Weiss, 1979), suggesting that this later plasticity is not a phenomenon unique to regions like cerebral cortex that are most prominent in mammals. A surprising finding is that different patterns of EC–IC differences in visual cortex and hippocampus are found in males and females (Juraska, 1984; Juraska et al., 1985). Males show greater differences across environmental extremes in the visual cortex, whereas females show greater differences in some regions of the hippocampus. Although the behavioral significance of this is still under investigation, it suggests that very similar experiences may have different effects on individually different brains.

Adult Brain Morphology

Until relatively recently, it was widely assumed that, except for certain cases of response to brain damage, the brain acquired all of the synapses it was going to have during development, and that further plastic change was probably accomplished through modification of the strength of preexisting connections. While some morphological and electrophysiological data suggest that changes in the strength of existing connections may occur in response to experience manipulations (see Greenough and Chang, 1985, for review), it has now become quite clear that new connections may arise as a result of differential housing conditions and other manipulations throughout much, if not all, of the life of the rat, and presumably of other higher mammals as well. Bennett et al. (1964) had actually reported quite early that cortical weight differences induced by EC versus IC housing occurred in adult rats, but over a decade passed before reports appeared that dendritic field size was affected by these conditions in both young adult (Juraska et al., 1980; Uylings et al., 1978) and middle-aged (Green et al., 1983) rats. While direct measurements of synapses per neuron have yet to be reported in adults under these conditions, the correspondence between dendritic field and synapse-per-neuron measures in younger animals (Greenough and Volkmar, 1973; Juraska, 1984; Turner and Greenough, 1985) gives us considerable confidence that the increase in adult postsynaptic surface is paralleled by an increase in synapse numbers. While not all neuron types affected by postweaning exposure to differential environmental complexity may be affected by these environments in adult animals, there is little question at this point that the cerebral cortex, and also the cerebellar cortex (Greenough et al., 1986), retain the capacity to form new synaptic connections in response to new experiences.

Effects of Training on Adult Brain Morphology

There has not yet been a specific demonstration of what might be represented by the changes in synaptic connections brought about by differential environmental complexity, nor are the details of the relationships between brain structure and behavioral performance very clear. If we follow the rather hazy terminology of "accumulated knowledge" used above, then one might suggest that these changes have something to do with storing (and/or accessing) that knowledge. A simple view of nearly a century ago (Ramon y Cajal, 1893; Tanzi, 1893), which has been embellished by the more detailed theorizing of Hebb (1949) and many others, is that memory, in both the very broad and the psychologically more specific sense, might be encoded in the functional pattern of connections between neurons. While demonstrating unequivocally the involvement of brain phenomena in learning or memory has been a difficult process for a variety of reasons, it is possible to perform experiments the outcomes of which would be either compatible or incompatible with such an interpretation. For example, if the changes in synaptic organization that occur in complex environments are involved in storage of information from the experience, then we might be able to detect similar morphological changes in animals trained on specific learning tasks.

Since the experience of training probably provides a more limited range of information than that available in the complex environment, we might expect the morphological effects of training to be more limited (and harder to detect). In the first experiment of this sort, young adult rats were trained on a changing series of patterns in the Hebb–Williams maze (the maze Hebb used in the initial test of home-reared rats) over a period of about 25 days (Greenough et al., 1979). In the visual cortex of the trained animals, two types of neurons had more dendrite than in nontrained animals, while a third type was unaffected. The unaffected type was one that had been altered in previous EC studies. Thus training affected a measure related to synaptic connectivity, and the effects were more localized and specific than were those of the complex environment experience.

In a similar experiment, Bennett et al. (1979) exposed weanling rats to a changing series of mazes in their rearing cages for 30 days. The visual cortices of these animals were heavier than those of rats kept in IC cages for the same period. Rats housed with an unchanging simple maze pattern were intermediate between these groups, suggesting that the information available in the changing-maze patterns was an important aspect of their results.

A problem in the interpretation of these results and, in fact, in the interpretation of the environmental complexity findings as well, is the possibility that brain effects might arise from stress, sensory stimulation, motor activity, or other nonspecific consequences of the training procedure, rather than from the information acquired through training. This problem is, of course, not trivial, and it has been one of the major difficulties in a long history of previous experiments designed to elucidate the molecular biological underpinnings of the memory process (see Dunn, 1980; Greenough and Maier, 1972; Rose, 1981, for perspectives on this work). No single experiment (and maybe no set of experiments) can rule out all alternatives, but the involvement of generally acting factors such as hormonal or metabolic consequences of a training procedure can be examined using a within-animal control. One advantage of the rat for such work is that the bulk of fibers from each eye cross to the opposite side of the brain, such that the use of a split-brain procedure, combined with occlusion of one eye, can restrict visual input from training largely to one hemisphere. Chang and Greenough (1982) performed such an experiment, again using the changing maze patterns. A control group indicated that there were no interhemispheric differences as a result of insertion of the eye occluder (an opaque ratsized contact lens) for a few hours each day. The group trained with the same eye covered each day, in contrast, had more apical dendritic branches on visual cortex neurons in the hemisphere opposite the trained eye, a result incompatible with effects of generally acting hormonal or metabolic effects. Thus the changes brought about by maze training were specifically a consequence of visual input from the training experience.

One further experiment increases our confidence in both the generality of the morphological effects of training in adult rats and in the unlikelihood that these effects result from general hormonal or metabolic causes (Greenough et al., 1985b). In it, rats were trained to reach, bilaterally or unilaterally, either with the forepaw they preferred to use or the nonpreferred forepaw, into a tube for food. A strong preference for reaching with one paw was accomplished by placing a partition next to the tube that made reaching with the opposite forepaw difficult. Extensive training on the nonpreferred paw permanently reversed reaching preference, as had been demonstrated previously (Peterson, 1951). It is not clear that something like "handedness" in humans is being reversed in these rats, as opposed to the animals' merely using the paw with which they had developed more skill or even thinking that the contingency required them to continue reaching with the trained paw. We examined the neurons in the forelimb region of the cortex whose axons project to the spinal region that governs reaching. Animals trained with both paws had dendrites that were more highly branched than those of nontrained animals, and hemispheres opposite trained forelimbs in unilaterally trained animals had more branches than the other hemisphere. Analysis of the hindlimb region of motor cortex in unilaterally trained rats indicated no similar pattern of assymetry, so the structural change was specific to both the hemisphere and the cortical area most directly involved in the learned task. We must realize, however, that this reaching task involves many other areas of the brain, as became evident when we examined metabolism of various brain areas in rats performing the task (see Greenough, 1984). The complex tasks used in developmental psychology research are similarly likely to involve multiple brain areas, and explanations of the role of the brain in such tasks that focus on a single region (e.g. Diamond, 1985), while interesting, are likely to be incomplete.

Experience-dependent Information Storage: Possible Mechanisms

Given that complex environment experience and experience in learning tasks alter these estimates of synapse number, the process whereby the new synapses arise is of significant interest. There appear to be two obvious possibilities. (1) The process of synapse overproduction that we described with regard to early sensory-system development might continue. That is, excess synapses, the existence of which would be transient unless they were confirmed by some aspect of neural activity, might be continually produced on a nonsystematic basis. Since the nature and timing of these sorts of experiences could not be anticipated, synapse formation would have to occur chronically throughout the brain (or in regions that remain plastic). The effects of environmental complexity or training would arise because a proportion of these synapses became permanent as a result of experience-associated neural activity (Changeux and Danchin, 1977; Cotman and Nieto-Sampedro, 1984; Greenough, 1978). (2) The production of new synapses in later development and adulthood might be dependent upon experience-associated neural activity. That is, synapses would be formed as a result of the activity of neurons in information-processing and/or neuromodulatory systems. The synapses might be generated nonsystematically at the outset, with some aspect of patterned neuronal activity determining the survival of a subset of them (Greenough, 1984). The synapses formed in this case would be localized to regions involved in the information-processing activity that caused their formation.

The first hypothesis is attractive, given the tendency of evolution to conserve mechanisms. It also provides a very simple way for a proper set of connections to come to encode a memory. The second hypothesis has its own attractions, such as the relatively lower amount of metabolic resources required for local, experience-dependent synapse formation and the reduction in potential "noise" in the nervous system that might be associated with chronic generation and degeneration of synapses. Most of the same genes would probably be involved in the construction or stabilization of synapses, regardless of the initiating event. Moreover, the initiating event for intrinsic and extrinsic triggering of synapse formation could involve a final common pathway or common mechanism, such as the activation of neuromodulatory systems. Finally, the second hypothesis has been made far more attractive by the recent appearance of data that are more consonant with it than with the first.

Rapid, Active Synapse Formation in the Adult Brain

Two lines of evidence have emerged that can be interpreted as suggesting a dynamic synapse-formation process in response to experience-associated neural activity in the adult brain. The first arises from a phenomenon induced by electrical stimulation of neurons that has been proposed as a model for adult long-term memory, long-term potentiation (LTP). In the hippocampus and a number of other brain regions, stimulation of axons at high frequencies can give rise to an increased postsynaptic response to test stimuli (Bliss and Lømo, 1973; see Teyler and Fountain, 1987, in this issue). With proper stimulus sequences, this elevated responsiveness can persist for up to several weeks. There are several hypotheses as to its neural basis. One, that additional synapses are formed, is based on the work of Lee et al. (1980, 1981), who reported that synapses form in the hippocampus *in vivo* and in an *in vitro* tissue slice preparation following LTP-inducing stimulation. The synapses form surprisingly rapidly. Chang and Greenough (1984) noted that synapses formed within 10–15 minutes *in vitro*. This rate of formation is simply too rapid to arise from the chronic synapse turnover proposed in the first hypothesis. Regardless of whether LTP is related to memory, or synapse formation to LTP, the fact remains that the adult brain, or at least the hippocampus, is capable of generating new synapses rapidly in response to neural activity.

The second finding involves what we believe to be a marker of newly forming synapses, polyribosomal aggregates (PRA), the protein-synthesizing "factories" of cells. Steward (1983) reported that PRA were found frequently within postsynaptic spines (otherwise rare) during the process of re-formation of synapses that occurs following damage to a part of the hippocampus. Hwang and Greenough (1984) similarly found, in a developmental study, a large increase in the number of PRA in spines in rat visual cortex during periods of peak synapse formation, compared to adult values. Thus, in both situations, PRA in spines appear to indicate the formation of new synapses. We do not know, of course, that synapse formation in late development or adulthood resembles early development or the response to damage. However, if it does, a recent finding suggests that behavioral experience can promote synapse formation, as the second hypothesis above suggests. If animals in environments of different complexity formed equivalent numbers of synapses, but more synapses were confirmed or stabilized in ECs, we might expect the frequency of PRA in spines to be equivalent across the groups. Greenough et al. (1985b) studied synapses in upper visual cortex of rats reared for 30 days after weaning in EC, SC, or IC environments. PRA were considerably more frequent in spines in the EC animals, suggesting that more new synapses were forming.

Given our knowledge that there are more synapses per neuron in EC rats, and other data indicating that PRA in spines marks newly formed synapses, this result suggests that experience-dependent synapse formation occurs in the developmental environmental complexity paradigm. Of course we must keep in mind that PRA may aggregate in spines to perform functions associated with increased activity of synapses or modification of their strength. We now need to find other ways to identify newly forming synapses and must determine whether similar increases in spine-located PRA occur in adult animals during learning. The data to this point, however, suggest that synapses form *in response to experience from which information is to be stored* in the postweaning environmental complexity paradigm.

Summary of Later Development and Adult Learning

The data reviewed here suggest that there is a fundamental difference between the processes governing the formation of synapses in early, age-locked sensory system development and those governing synapses formation during later development and adulthood. Experience-expectant processes found in early development appear to produce a surplus of synapses, which are then pruned back by experience to a functional subset. In later development and adulthood, synapses appear to be generated in response to events that provide information to be encoded in the nervous system. This later experience-dependent synapse formation may differ from that of early development in that it is localized to regions involved in processing information arising from the event, but may be similar in that synapses are initially formed on a relatively unpatterned basis, with aspects of neural activity resulting from the event determining the selective preservation of a subset of them. The cumulative effect of many such individual experiences may appear to be a smoothly increasing supply of synapses, as shown in figure 14.4.

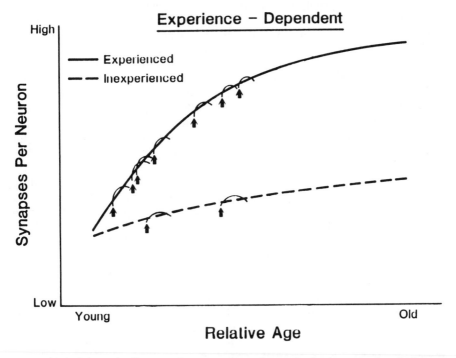

Figure 14.4 Schematic diagram of synapse formation and selective retention during an experience-dependent process. The arrowheads mark salient experiences that generate local synaptic overproduction and deletion (small curves). The cumulative effect of such synaptic blooms and prunes is a smooth increase in synapses per neuron, which is greater for the animals with more experience (from Black and Greenough, 1986, Vol. 4, p. 38; copyright 1986 by Lawrence Erlbaum Associates; reprinted by permission).

Some Cautionary Notes

Presumably we need not point out to most readers that neuroscience involves significant amounts of disagreement and controversy, as do other disciplines, and some of what is said here would be considered controversial by certain of our colleagues. For simplicity, we have painted a much more straightforward picture here than probably exists. For example, there is significant evidence for an active synapse-formation component in early sensory development. Winfield (1981), for example, noted that the peak number of synapses per neuron was lower in visually deprived than in normal kittens, suggesting that visual stimulation promotes extra synapse formation (although it remains possible that this reflects reduced preservation of synapses in a population that is intrinsically generated over time). There is also evidence for a burst of synapse formation and axonal and/or dendritic growth at eye opening or first exposure to light in rodents. Several studies have indicated a burst of synapse formation at about the time of eye opening (Blue and Parnavelas, 1983; Hwang and Greenough, 1984; Miller, 1981; Miller and Peters, 1981), although there is some evidence that the burst may begin prior to eye opening (e.g. Valverde, 1971), leaving open the possibility of an intrinsic trigger. Exposure of rats to light for the first time at later than the normal age of eye opening may also trigger some synapse formation (Cragg, 1967), as well as the synthesis of protein (Rose, 1967), including tubulin, a major molecular component of axons and dendrites (Cronly-Dillon and Perry, 1979). In an artificial imprinting situation, in which chicks were exposed to light for the first time in the form of a flashing amber stimulus, RNA and protein synthesis in the forebrain increased dramatically (Bateson et al., 1973; Horn et al., 1973). And, during the recovery that can be made to occur in monocularly deprived monkeys by reversing which eye is sutured shut, there is evidence for active extension of the axons associated with the previously deprived eye (LeVay et al., 1980). Thus, while synapse overproduction appears to be a dominant aspect of the early organization of the visual system, it is likely to be accompanied by some experience-dependent growth. Nonetheless, on the basis of the evidence to date, the relative emphasis on intrinsic generation and experiential selection on a sensory system-wide basis seems quite clear in early development, and the generation of synapses in later development and adulthood appears to be much more dependent upon extrinsically originating events. It thus seems reasonable to view sensitive period versus continuing developmental information-storage phenomena from this perspective.

Finally, our dichotomy of information-storage mechanisms is based upon studies of a limited number of brain regions. Although many developing systems within the brain other than the visual system go through phases of synapse overproduction, and experience effects on various aspects of the development of these systems have been reported, it remains quite possible that other systems may operate in different ways. Similarly, experience-dependent synapse formation is quite probably not characteristic of all regions of the later-developing and adult nervous system, and there may be other mechanisms with quite different properties whereby nervous systems store information. Recently, for example, we found that an electrophysiologically detectable phenomenon in the hippocampal dentate gyrus (perhaps similar to LTP), which was apparent immediately after postwean-ing rearing in a complex environment, had entirely disappeared within 30 days (Green and Greenough, 1986). In contrast, dendritic branching differences induced in visual cortex in this paradigm are relatively stable for at least that long (Camel et al., 1986).

Thus, while the separation of experience effects upon brain development into categories based upon the existence of neural anticipation of the experience is compatible with current data, these categories may well not be comprehensive. Nonetheless, recognition (1) that a common aspect of early development of sensory systems may be overproduction of synapses in expectation of experiences that will determine their selective survival, and (2) that later developmental and adult information storage may involve synapse formation triggered by experience, may offer a new level of understanding of phenomena previously described as merely related or unrelated to sensitive periods in development.

Some Guidelines for Studying Effects of Experience on Development

Monolithic approaches, in which the development of the brain (or the organism) is treated as a unitary phenomenon, are unlikely to be very useful and, in fact, may be misleading. For example, Epstein (1974a, b) has proposed that "phreno-blysis," or spurts of growth of the whole brain during selected periods of development (purportedly corresponding to stages of cognitive development), characterizes species as diverse as humans and mice. While findings of others have failed to replicate Epstein's observations in either species (e.g. Hahn et al., 1983; McCall et al., 1983) and Epstein's analytical procedures have been dis-credited (Marsh, 1985), the general concept, that the brain as a whole develops in bursts or stages, continues to attract attention to phenomena that probably do not exist (e.g. Spreen et al., 1984). Certainly any recommendations that educa-tional practices be modified to accomodate such bursts (e.g. Epstein and Toepfer, 1978) are not appropriate at this stage. Several lines of evidence indicate that, while discrete brain regions definitely progress through something like "spurts," in terms of such processes as the generation of nerve cells and of connections between them, different brain regions do so out of synchrony and in a reliable developmental sequence. First, some older but generally ignored data on human cerebral cortex development (Conel, 1939–1967), which we have plotted in figure 14.5, show rather striking differences in the pattern of growth across brain regions. While many regions of the cortex show some synchrony in the pattern of thickness fluctuations with age, other regions are not in synchrony with them. Rather than showing clear peaks, for example, the prefrontal cortex appears to continue to grow thicker throughout the first six years of life. A similar relative delay in the development of frontal brain regions is evident in the protracted (10–14 years) process of achieving stable synaptic density values in human frontal cortex (Huttenlocher, 1979), compared with the rapid stabilization (1–2 years) seen in human visual cortex (Huttenlocher et al., 1982). A metabolic parallel, perhaps, to these reports is the Chugani and Phelps (1986) report that glucose utilization in human infants was initially highest in sensorimotor cortex and only later rose in the frontal cortex.

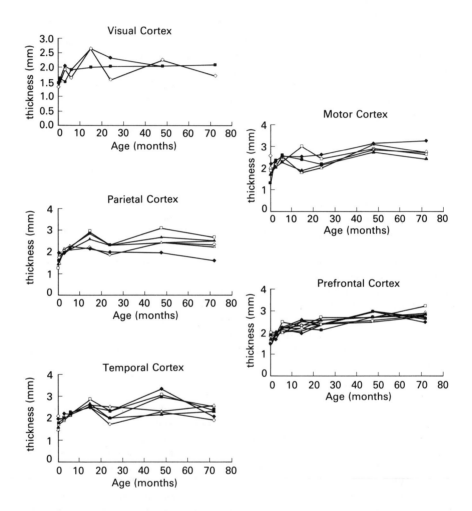

Figure 14.5 Cortical thickness in humans is plotted as a function of age and region of the cerebral cortex. Symbols within regions identify particular sites that were measured (data from Conel, 1939–1967). Postnatal changes in cortical thickness indirectly reflect the addition or deletion of brain components, for example, synapses, neurons and supporting cells, blood vessels. A tendency for a peak in cortical thickness between 10 and 20 months of age is evident at many sites in visual, parietal, temporal, and motor cortex, and a second peak may also occur near 50 months of age at some sites. A clear pattern of peaks and troughs is much less evident in prefrontal cortex, which seems to increase gradually in thickness over the first four years of life.

In the light of these findings, the report by Rakic et al. (1986) that there is a striking temporal synchrony across cortical areas in developmental changes in density of synapses is rather surprising. Interpreting synaptic density measures can be difficult, since they do not clearly reflect either the number of synapses within a functional area or the number of synapses per nerve cell. Turner and Greenough (1985) found that while the number of synapses per neuron was about 20 percent higher in rats reared in complex environments, the density of synapses (in neuropil, as in Rakic et al., 1986) did not differ in these groups, apparently because the tissue volume of the dendrites, axons, glial cells, blood vessels, etc. necessary for additional synapses pushed the new synapses as far apart as they were in IC rats. As Bennett et al. (1964) had shown years earlier, the volume of the cortex as a whole simply increases to accommodate these needs.

Thus, while counterexamples exist, it seems clear that asynchrony in brain development merits theoretical attention. Theorists have argued that by staggering the developmental schedule for maturation of different brain regions, the human species (and other mammals, for which such patterns are also evident) may have gained substantial advantages, most importantly by allowing one developmental system to provide a suitable framework for a subsequent, experience-sensitive system (Black and Greenough, 1986; Turkewitz and Kenny, 1982). This "stage setting" possibility is most interesting for human development, for example, where early social and communicative skills can establish the foundations for adult language, and where early visual and motor skills can help the infant master spatial and causal relations. The active participation of the infant in acquiring and organizing experience becomes paramount if one process is setting the stage for a subsequent experience-dependent process. In summary, sensitive periods must be characterized in terms of their time course, the brain regions and mechanisms employed, and the organism's involvement in shaping experience.

This perspective may be helpful to both developmental psychologists and neuroscientists in explaining the meaning of infancy. For example, a conjecture that a particular developmental process has a sensitive period(s) (e.g. language acquisition) can now generate testable hypotheses about neural changes that must accompany it. For example, a fixed time course for language acquisition would suggest a peak in cortical thickness or synaptic numbers shortly before the start of a hypothetical experience-expectant period. Such predictions could be quite specific about what brain regions are involved and when the changes occur. After examination of appropriate brain tissue, findings of different time courses or the involvement of other brain regions can reflect back on the original theory, suggesting different influences and constraints. Given the complex and long period of language acquisition, a theory invoking a single, protracted "sensitive period" may eventually be expanded to reflect the multiple involvement of many brain regions, each with its own time course and experiential sensitivities, as has recently been proposed for visual development (Harwerth et al., 1986).

ACKNOWLEDGEMENTS

Preparation of this paper and ressearch not otherwise reported was supported by NIMH 40631, NIMH 35321, NIH RR 07030, PHS 5 T-32EY07005, PHS 5 T-32GM7143, ONR

N00014-85-K-0587, the Retirement Research Foundation, the System Development Foundation, and the University of Illinois Research Board.

REFERENCES

Bateson, P. P. G. (1979). How do sensitive periods arise and what are they for? *Animal Behavior*, 27, 470–486.

Bateson, P. P. G., Rose, S. P. R., & Horn, G. (1973). Imprinting: Lasting effects on uracil incorporation into chick brain. *Science*, 181, 576–578.

Bear, M. F., & Singer, W. (1986). Modulation of visual cortical plasticity by acetylcholine and noradrenaline. *Nature*, 320, 172–176.

Bennett, E. L., Diamond, M. C., Krech, D., & Rosenzweig, M. R. (1964). Chemical and anatomical plasticity of brain. *Science*, 146, 610–619.

Bennett, E. L., Rosenzweig, M. R. Morimoto, H., & Hebert, M. (1979). Maze training alters brain weights and cortical RNA/DNA ratios. *Behavioral and Neural Biology*, 26, 1–22.

Black, J. E., & Greenough, W. T. (1986). Induction of pattern in neural structure by experience: Implications for cognitive development. In M. E. Lamb, A. L. Brown, & B. Rogoff (eds), *Advances in developmental psychology* (Vol. 4, pp. 1–50). Hillsdale, NJ: Erlbaum.

Blakemore, C., & Van Sluyters, R. C. (1975). Innate and environmental factors in the development of the kitten's visual cortex. *Journal of Physiology*, 248, 663–716.

Blasdel, G. G., Mitchell, D. E., Muir, D. W., & Pettigrew, J. D. (1977). A physiological and behavioural study in cats of the effect of early visual experience with contours of a single orientation. *Journal of Physiology*, 265, 615–636.

Bliss, T. V. P., & Lømo, T. (1973). Long-lasting potentiation of synaptic transmission in the dentate area of the anaesthetized rabbit following stimulation of the perforant path. *Journal of Physiology*, 232, 331–356.

Blue, M. E., & Parnavelas, J. G. (1983). The formation and maturation of synapses in the visual cortex of the rat: I. Quantitative analysis. *Journal of Neurocytology*, 12, 697–712.

Boothe, R. G., Greenough, W. T., Lund, J. S., & Wrege, K. (1979). A quantitative investigation of spine and dendritic development of neurons in visual cortex (area 17) of *Macaca nemestrina* monkeys. *Journal of Comparative Neurology*, 186, 473–490.

Brown, M. C., Jansen, J. K. S., & Van Essen, D. (1976). Polyneuronal innervation of skeletal muscle in new-born rats and its elimination during maturation. *Journal of Physiology*, 261, 387–422.

Brown, R. T. (1968). Early experience and problem solving ability. *Journal of Comparative and Physiological Psychology*, 65, 433–440.

Brunjes, P. C., Schwark, H. D., & Greenough, W. T. (1982). Olfactory granule cell development in normal and hyperthyroid rats. *Developmental Brain Research*, 5, 149–159.

Buisseret, P., & Imbert, M. (1976). Visual cortical cells: Their developmental properties in normal and dark-reared kittens. *Journal of Physiology*, 255, 511–525.

Camel, J. E., Withers, G. S., & Greenough, W. T. (1986). Persistence of visual cortex dendritic alterations induced by postweaning exposure to a "superenriched" environment in rats. *Behavioral Neuroscience*, 100, 810–813.

Chang, F.-L. F., & Greenough, W. T. (1982). Lateralized effects of monocular training on dendritic branching in adult split-brain rats. *Brain Research*, 232, 283–292.

Chang, F.-L. F., & Greenough, W. T. (1984). Transient and enduring morphological correlates of synaptic activity and efficacy change in the rat hippocampal slice. *Brain Research*, 309, 35–46.

Changeux, J.-P., & Danchin, A. (1977). Biochemical models for the selective stabilization of developing synapses. In G. A. Cottrell & P. M. Usherwood (eds.), *Synapses* (pp. 705–712). New York: Academic Press.

Chomsky, N. (1980). On cognitive structures and their development: A reply to Piaget. In M. Piatelli-Palmarini (ed.), *Language and learning* (pp. 35–52). Cambridge, MA: Harvard University Press.

Chugani, H. T., & Phelps, M. E. (1986). Maturational changes in cerebral function in infants determined by [18]FDG positron emission to mography. *Science*, 231, 840–843.

Clopton, B. M., & Winfield, J. A. (1976). Effect of early exposure to patterned sound on unit activity in rat inferior colliculus. *Journal of Neurophysiology*, 39, 1081–1089.

Coleman, P. D., Flood, D. G., Whitehead, M. C., & Emerson, R. C. (1981). Spatial sampling by dendritic trees in visual cortex. *Brain Research*, 214, 1–21.

Coleman, P. D., & Riesen, A. H. (1968). Environmental effects on cortical dendritic fields: I. Rearing in the dark. *Journal of Anatomy*, 102, 363–374.

Conel, J. L. (1939–1967). *The postnatal development of the human cerebral cortex* (Vols. 1–8). Cambridge, MA: Harvard University Press.

Corrigan, J. G., & Carpenter, D. L. (1979). Early selective visual experience and pattern discrimination in hooded rats. *Developmental Psychobiology*, 12, 67–72.

Cotman, C. W., & Nieto-Sampedro, M. (1984). Cell biology of synaptic plasticity. *Science*, 225, 1287–1294.

Crabtree, J. W., & Riesen, A. H. (1979). Effects of the duration of dark rearing on visually guided behavior in the kitten. *Developmental Psychobiology*, 12, 291–303.

Cragg, B. G. (1967). Changes in visual cortex on first exposure of rats to light: Effect on synaptic dimensions. *Nature*, 215, 251–253.

Cragg, B. G. (1975a). The development of synapses in kitten visual cortex during visual deprivation. *Experimental Neurology*, 46, 445–451.

Cragg, B. G. (1975b). The development of synapses in the visual system of the cat. *Journal of Comparative Neurology*, 160, 147–166.

Cronly-Dillon, J., & Perry, G. W. (1979). The effect of visual experience on tubulin synthesis during a critical period of visual cortex development in the hooded rat. *Journal of Physiology*, 293, 469–484.

Cynader, M., Berman, N., & Hein, A. (1976). Recovery of function in cat visual cortex following prolonged deprivation. *Experimental Brain Research*, 25, 139–156.

Cynader, M., & Chernenko, G. (1976). Abolition of direction selectivity in the visual cortex of the cat. *Science*, 193, 504–505.

Cynader, M., & Mitchell, D. E. (1980). Prolonged sensitivity to monocular deprivation in dark-reared cats. *Journal of Neurophysiology*, 43, 1026–1040.

Diamond, A. (1985). Development of the ability to use recall to guide action, as indicated by infants' performance on AB̄. *Child Development*, 56, 868–883.

Diamond, M. C. (1967). Extensive cortical depth measurements and neuron size increases in the cortex of environmentally enriched rats. *Journal of Comparative Neurology*, 131, 357–364.

Diamond, M. C., Rosenzweig, M. R., Bennett, E. L., Lindner, B., & Lyon, L. (1972). Effects of environmental enrichment and impoverishment on rat cerebral cortex. *Journal of Neurobiology*, 3, 47–64.

Dunn, A. J. (1980). Neurochemistry of learning and memory: An evaluation of recent data. *Annual Review of Psychology*, 31, 343–390.

Eayrs, J. T., & Ireland, K. F. (1950). The effect of total darkness on the growth of the newborn albino rat. *Journal of Endocrinology*, 6, 386–397.

Eimas, P. D. (1975). Speech perception in early infancy. In L. B. Cohen & P. Salapatek (eds), *Infant perception* (pp. 193–231). New York: Academic Press.

Epstein, H. T. (1974a). Phrenoblysis: Special brain and mind growth periods: I. Human brain and skull development. *Developmental Psychobiology*, 7, 207–216.

Epstein, H. T. (1974b). Phrenoblysis: Special brain and mind growth periods: II. Human mental development. *Developmental Psychobiology*, 7, 217–224.

Epstein, H. T., & Toepfer, C. F., Jr. (1978). A neuroscience basis for reorganizing middle grades education. *Educational Leadership*, 35, 656–660.

Feng, A. S., & Rogowski, B. A. (1980). Effects of monaural and binaural occlusion on the morphology of neurons in the medial superior olivary nucleus of the rat. *Brain Research*, 189, 530–534.

Ferchmin, P. A., Bennett, E. L., & Rosenzweig, M. R. (1975). Direct contact with enriched environments is required to alter cerebral weights in rats. *Journal of Comparative and Physiological Psychology*, 88, 360–367.

Fernald, A. (1984). The perceptual and affective salience of mother's speech to infants. In L. Feagans, C. Garvey, & R. Golinkoff (eds.), *The origins and growth of communication* (pp. 5–29). Norwood, NJ: Ablex.

Fifkova, E. (1968). Changes in the visual cortex of rats after unilateral deprivation. *Nature*, 220, 379–381.

Fifkova, E. (1970). The effect of unilateral deprivation on visual centers in rats. *Journal of Comparative Neurology*, 140, 431–438.

Fiske, J. (1909). *The meaning of infancy*. Boston: Houghton Mifflin. (Original work published 1883)

Floeter, M. K. & Greenough, W. T. (1979). Cerebellar plasticity: Modification of purkinje cell structure by differential rearing in monkeys. *Science*, 206, 227–229.

Forgays, D. G., & Forgays, J. W. (1952). The nature of the effect of free-environmental experience in the rat. *Journal of Comparative and Physiological Psychology*, 45, 322–328.

Fox, M. W. (1966). Neuro-behavioral ontogeny: A synthesis of ethological and neurophysiological concepts. *Brain Research*, 2, 3–20.

Globus, A. (1975). Brain morphology as a function of presynaptic morphology and activity. In A. H. Riesen (ed.), *The developmental neuropsychology of sensory deprivation* (pp. 9–91). New York: Academic Press.

Globus, A., Rosenzweig, M. R., Bennett, E. L., & Diamond, M. C. (1973). Effects of differential experience on dendritic spine counts in rat cerebral cortex. *Journal of Comparative and Physiological Psychology*, 82, 175–181.

Gold, P. E. (1984). Memory modulation: Neurobiological contexts. In G. Lynch, J. L. McGaugh, & N. M. Weinberger (eds.), *Neurobiology of learning and memory* (pp. 374–382). New York: Guilford.

Goldman-Rakic, P. S. (1987). Development of cortical circuitry and cognitive function. *Child Development*, 58, 601–622.

Gordon, B., Presson, J., Packwood, J., & Scheer, R. (1979). Alteration of cortical orientation selectivity: Importance of asymmetric input. *Science*, 204, 1109–1111.

Gouze, J.-L., Lasry, J.-M., & Changeux, J.-P. (1983). Selective stabilization of muscle innervation during development: A mathematical model. *Biological Cybernetics*, 46, 207–215.

Green, E. J., & Greenough, W. T. (1986). Altered synaptic transmission in dentate gyrus of rats reared in complex environments: Evidence from hippocampal slices maintained in vivo. *Journal of Neurophysiology*, 55, 739–750.

Green, E. J., Greenough, W. T., & Schlumpf, B. E. (1983). Effects of complex or isolated environments on cortical dendrites of middle-aged rats. *Brain Research*, 264, 233–240.

Greenough, W. T. (1976). Enduring brain effects of differential experience and training. In M. R. Rosenzweig & E. L. Bennett (eds), *Neural mechanisms of learning and memory* (pp. 255–278). Cambridge, MA: MIT Press.

Greenough, W. T. (1978). Development and memory: The synaptic connection. In T. Teyler (ed.), *Brain and learning* (pp. 127–145). Stamford, CT: Greylock.

Greenough, W. T. (1984). Structural correlates of information storage in the mammalian brain: A review and hypothesis. *Trends in Neurosciences*, 7, 229–233.

Greenough, W. T., & Chang, F.-L. C. (1985). Synaptic structural correlates of information storage in mammalian nervous systems. In C. W. Cotman (ed.), *Synaptic plasticity and remodeling* (pp. 335–372). New York: Guilford.

Greenough, W. T., Hwang, H. M., & Gorman, C. (1985a). Evidence for active synapse formation, or altered postsynaptic metabolism, in visual cortex of rats reared in complex environments. *Proceedings of the National Academy of Sciences* (USA), 82, 4549–4552.

Greenough, W. T., Juraska, J. M., & Volkmar, F. R. (1979). Maze training effects on dendritic branching in occipital cortex of adult rats. *Behavioral and Neural Biology*, 26, 287–297.

Greenough, W. T., Larson, J. R., & Withers, G. S. (1985b). Effects of unilateral and bilateral training in a reaching task on dendritic branching of neurons in the rat motor-sensory forelimb cortex. *Behavioral and Neural Biology*, 44, 301–314.

Greenough, W. T., Madden, T. C., & Fleishmann, T. B. (1972). Effects of isolation, daily handling, and enriched rearing on maze learning. *Psychonomic Science*, 27, 279–280.

Greenough, W. T., & Maier, S. F. (1972). Molecular changes during learning: Behavioral strategy: A comment on Gaito and Bonnet. *Psychological Bulletin*, 78, 480–482.

Greenough, W. T., McDonald, J., Parnisari, R., & Camel, J. E. (1986). Environmental conditions modulate degeneration and new dendrite growth in cerebellum of senescent rats. *Brain Research*, 380, 136–143.

Greenough, W. T., & Schwark, H. D. (1984). Age-related aspects of experience effects upon brain structure. In R. N. Emde & R. J. Harmon (eds.), *Continuities and discontinuities in development* (pp. 69–91). Hillsdale, NJ: Plenum.

Greenough, W. T., & Volkmar, F. R. (1973). Pattern of dendritic branching in occipital cortex of rats reared in complex environments. *Experimental Neurology*, 40, 491–504.

Greenough, W. T., Volkmar, F. R., & Juraska, J. M. (1973). Effects of rearing complexity on dendritic branching in frontolateral and temporal cortex of the rat. *Experimental Neurology*, 41, 371–378.

Guillery, R. W. (1972). Binocular competition in the control of geniculate cell growth. *Journal of Comparative Neurology*, 144, 117–130.

Gyllensten, L., Malmfors, T., & Norrlin, M. L. (1966). Growth alteration in the auditory cortex of visually deprived mice. *Journal of Comparative Neurology*, 126, 463–470.

Hahn, M. E., Walters, J. K., Lavooy, J., & DeLuca, J. (1983). Brain growth in young mice: Evidence on the theory of phrenoblysis. *Developmental Psychobiology*, 16, 377–383.

Harwerth, R. S., Smith III, E. L., Duncan, G. C., Crawford, M. L. J., & von Noorden, G. K. (1986). Multiple sensitive periods in the development of the primate visual system. *Science*, 232, 235–238.

Hebb, D. O. (1949). *The organization of behavior*. New York: Wiley.

Hirsch, H. V. B., & Spinelli, D. N. (1970). Visual experience modifies distribution of horizontally and vertically oriented receptive fields in cats. *Science*, 168, 869–871.

Holloway, R. L. (1966). Dendritic branching: Some preliminary results of training and complexity in rat visual cortex. *Brain Research*, 2, 393–396.

Horn, G., Rose, S. P. R., & Bateson, P. P. G. (1973). Monocular imprinting and regional incorporation of tritiated uracil into the brains of intact and "split-brain" chicks. *Brain Research*, 56, 227–237.

Hubel, D. H., & Wiesel, T. N. (1970). The period of susceptibility to the physiological effects of unilateral eye closure in kittens. *Journal of Physiology*, 206, 419–436.

Huttenlocher, P. R. (1979). Synaptic density in human frontal cortex–developmental changes and effects of aging. *Brain Research*, 163, 195–205.

Huttenlocher, P. R., de Courten, C., Garey, L. J., & Van Der Loos, H. (1982). Synaptogenesis in human visual cortex–evidence for synapse elimination during normal development. *Neuroscience Letters*, 33, 247–252.

Hwang, H. M., & Greenough, W. T. (1984). Spine formation and synaptogenesis in rat visual cortex: A serial section developmental study. *Society for Neuroscience Abstracts*, 14, 579.

Hymovitch, B. (1952). The effects of experimental variations on problem solving in the rat. *Journal of Comparative and Physiological Psychology*, 45, 313–321.

Juraska, J. M. (1984). Sex differences in dendritic response to differential experience in the rat visual cortex. *Brain Research*, 295, 27–34.

Juraska, J. M., Fitch, J., Henderson, C., & Rivers, N. (1985). Sex differences in the dendritic branching of dentate granule cells following differential experience. *Brain Research*, 333, 73–80.

Juraska, J. M., Greenough, W. T., Elliott, C., Mack, K. J., & Berkowitz, R. (1980). Plasticity in adult rat visual cortex: An examination of several cell populations after differential rearing. *Behavioral and Neural Biology*, 29, 157–167.

Kasamatsu, T., & Pettigrew, J. D. (1976). Depletion of brain catecholamines: Failure of ocular dominance shift after monocular occlusion in kittens. *Science*, 194, 206–209.

Krech, D., Rosenzweig, M. R., & Bennett, E. L. (1962). Relations between brain chemistry and problem-solving among rats raised in enriched and impoverished environments. *Journal of Comparative and Physiological Psychology*, 55, 801–807.

Lee, K. S., Oliver, M., Schottler, F., & Lynch, G. (1981). Electron microscopic studies of brain slices: The effects of high-frequency stimulation on dendritic ultrastructure. In G. A. Kerkut and H. V. Wheal (eds), *Electrophysiology of isolated mammalian CNS preparations* (pp. 189–212). New York: Academic Press.

Lee, K. S., Schottler, F., Oliver, M., & Lynch, G. (1980). Brief bursts of high-frequency stimulation produce two types of structural change in rat hippocampus. *Journal of Neurophysiology*, 44, 247–258.

LeVay, S., Wiesel, T. N., & Hubel, D. H. (1980). The development of ocular dominance columns in normal and visually deprived monkeys. *Journal of Comparative Neurology*, 191, 1–51.

Leventhal, A. G., & Hirsch, H. V. B. (1975). Cortical effect of early selective exposure to diagonal lines. *Science*, 190, 902–904.

Marsh, R. W. (1985). Phrenoblysis: Real or chimera? *Child Development*, 56, 1059–1061.

McCall, R. B., Meyers, E. C., Jr., Hartman, J., & Roche, A. F. (1983). Developmental changes in head-circumference and mental-performance growth rates: A test of Epstein's phrenoblysis hypothesis. *Developmental Psychobiology*, 16, 457–468.

Meisami, E. (1975). Early sensory influences on regional activity of brain ATPases in developing rats. In M. A. B. Brazier (ed.), *Growth and development of the brain* (pp. 51–74). New York: Raven.

Miller, M. (1981). Maturation of rat visual cortex: I. A quantitative study of Golgi-impregnated pyramidal neurons. *Journal of Neurocytology*, 10, 859–878.

Miller, M., & Peters, A. (1981). Maturation of rat visual cortex: II. A combined Golgi-electron microscope study of pyramidal neurons. *Journal of Comparative Neurology*, 203, 555–573.

Mirmiran, M., & Uylings, H. (1983). The environmental enrichment effect upon cortical growth is neutralized by concomitant pharmacological suppression of active sleep in female rats. *Brain Research*, 261, 331–334.

Mitchell, D. E., Freeman, R. D., Millodot, M., & Haegerstrom, G. (1973). Meridional amblyopia: Evidence for modification of the human visual system by early visual experience. *Vision Research*, 13, 535–558.

Mitchell, D. E., & Timney, B. (1984). Postnatal development of function in the mammalian nervous system. In J. M. Brookhart & V. R. Mountcastle (eds), *Handbook of physiology, Section 1: The nervous system* (Vol. 3, pp. 507–555). Bethesda, MD: American Physiological Society.

Mos, L. P. (1976). Light rearing effects on factors of mouse emotionality and endocrine organ weight. *Physiological Psychology*, 4, 503–510.

Movshon, J. A., & Van Sluyters, R. C. (1981). Visual neuronal development. *Annual Review of Psychology*, 32, 477–522.

Mower, G. D., Christen, W. G., & Caplan, C. J. (1983). Very brief visual experience eliminates plasticity in the cat visual cortex. *Science*, 221, 178–180.

Myers, R. D., & Fox, J. (1963). Differences in maze performance of group- vs. isolation-reared rats. *Psychological Reports*, 12, 199–202.

O'Brien, R. A. D., Ostberg, A. J., & Vrbova, G. (1978). Observations on the elimination of polyneural innervation in developing mammalian skeletal muscle. *Journal of Physiology*, 282, 571–582.

Olson, C. R., & Freeman, R. D. (1978). Monocular deprivation and recovery during sensitive period in kittens. *Journal of Neurophysiology*, 41, 65–74.

O'Shea, L., Saari, M., Pappas, B., Ings, R., & Stange, K. (1983). Neonatal 6-hydroxydopamine attenuates the neural and behavioral effects of enriched rearing in the rat. *European Journal of Pharmacology*, 92, 43–47.

Parnavelas, J. G., & Globus, A. (1976). The effect of continuous illumination on the development of cortical neurons in the rat: A Golgi study. *Experimental Neurology*, 51, 637–647.

Parnavelas, J. G., Globus, A., & Kaups, P. (1973). Continuous illumination from birth affects spine density of neurons in the visual cortex of the rat. *Experimental Neurology*, 40, 742–747.

Pearlman, C. (1983). Impairment of environmental effects on brain weight by adrenergic drugs in rats. *Physiology and Behavior*, 30, 161–163.

Peterson, G. M. (1951). Transfers of handedness in the rat from forced practice. *Journal of Comparative and Physiological Psychology*, 44, 184–190.

Pettigrew, J. D., & Kasamatsu, T. (1978). Local perfusion of noradrenaline maintains visual cortical plasticity. *Nature*, 271, 761–763.

Purves, D., & Lichtman, J. W. (1980). Elimination of synapses in the developing nervous system. *Science*, 210, 153–157.

Pysh, J. J., & Weiss, M. (1979). Exercise during development induces an increase in Purkinje cell dendritic tree size. *Science*, 206, 230–232.

Rakic, P., Bourgeois, J.-P., Eckenhoff, M. F., Zecevic, N., & Goldman-Rakic, P. S. (1986). Concurrent overproduction of synapses in diverse regions of the primate cerebral cortex. *Science*, 232, 232–235.

Ramon y Cajal, S. (1893). New findings about the histological structure of the central nervous system. *Archiv fur Anatomie und Physiologie (Anatomie)*, pp. 319–428.

Rasch, E., Swift, H., Riesen, A. H., & Chow, K. L. (1961). Altered structure and composition of retinal cells in dark-reared mammals. *Experimental Cell Research*, 25, 348–363.

Ravizza, R. J., & Herschberger, A. C. (1966). The effect of prolonged motor restriction upon later behavior of the rat. *Psychological Record*, 16, 73–80.

Rose, S. P. R. (1967). Changes in visual cortex on first exposure to light. *Nature*, 215, 253–255.

Rose, S. P. R. (1981). What should a biochemistry of learning and memory be about? *Neuroscience*, 6, 811–821.

Rosenzweig, M. R., Bennett, E. L., & Diamond, M. C. (1972). Chemical and anatomical plasticity of brain: Replications and extensions. In J. Gaito (ed.), *Macromolecules and behavior* (2d ed., pp. 205–277). New York: Appleton-Century-Crofts.

Rothblat, L. A., & Schwartz, M. (1979). The effect of monocular deprivation on dendritic spines in visual cortex of young and adult albino rats: Evidence for a sensitive period. *Brain Research*, 161, 156–161.

Ruiz-Marcos, A., & Valverde, F. (1969). The temporal evolution of the distribution of dendritic spines in the visual cortex of normal and dark raised mice. *Experimental Brain Research*, 8, 284–294.

Ryugo, D. K., Ryugo, R., Globus, A., & Killackey, H. P. (1975). Increased spine density in auditory cortex following visual or somatic deafferentation. *Brain Research*, 90, 143–146.

Schneider, G. E. (1981). Early lesions and abnormal neural connections. *Trends in Neurosciences*, 4, 187–192.

Schüz, A. (1978). Some facts and hypotheses concerning dendritic spines and learning. In M. A. B. Brazier & H. Petsche (eds), *Architectonics of the cerebral cortex* (pp. 129–135). New York: Raven.

Senden, M. von (1960). *Space and sight: The perception of space and shape in the congenitally blind before and after operation.* Glencoe, IL: Free Press.

Sherman, S. M. (1973). Visual field defects in monocularly and binocularly deprived cats. *Brain Research*, 49, 25–45.

Sherman, S. M. (1977). The effect of cortical and tectal lesions on the visual fields of binocularly deprived cats. *Journal of Comparative Neurology*, 172, 231–246.

Singer, W. (1986). Neuronal activity as a shaping factor in postnatal development of visual cortex. In W. T. Greenough & J. M. Juraska (eds), *Developmental neuropsychobiology.* New York: Academic Press.

Spreen, O., Tupper, D., Risser, A., Tuokko, H., & Edgell, D. (1984). *Human developmental neuropsychology.* New York: Oxford University Press.

Steward, O. (1983). Polyribosomes at the base of dendritic spines of CNS neurons: Their possible role in synapse construction and modification. *Cold Spring Harbor Symposia on Quantitative Biology*, 48, 745–759.

Tanzi, E. (1893). Facts and inductions in current histology of the nervous system. *Rivista sperimentale di freniatria e medicina legale delle mentali alienazioni*, 19, 419–472.

Tees, R. C. (1979). The effect of visual deprivation on pattern recognition in the rat. *Developmental Psychobiology*, 12, 485–497.

Tees, R. C., & Cartwright, J. (1972). Sensory preconditioning in rats following early visual deprivation. *Journal of Comparative and Physiological Psychology*, 81, 12–20.

Teyler, T. J., & Fountain, S. B. (1987). Neuronal plasticity in the mammalian brain: Relevance to behavioral learning and memory. *Child Development*, 58, 698–712.

Thelen, E. (1980). Rhythmical behavior in infancy: An ethological perspective. *Developmental Psychology*, 17, 237–257.

Thinus-Blanc, C. (1981). Volume discrimination learning in golden hamsters: Effects of the structure of complex rearing cages. *Developmental Psychobiology*, 14, 397–403.

Thompson, W., Kuffler, D. P., & Jansen, J. K. S. (1979). The effect of prolonged reversible block of nerve impulses on the elimination of polyneural innervation of newborn rat skeletal muscle fibres. *Neuroscience*, 4, 271–281.

Tieman, S. B., & Hirsch, H. (1982). Exposure to lines of only one orientation modifies dendritic morphology of cells in the visual cortex of the cat. *Journal of Comparative Neurology*, 211, 353–362.

Timney, B., Mitchell, D. E., & Cynader, M. (1980). Behavioral evidence for prolonged sensitivity to effects of monocular deprivation in dark-reared cats. *Journal of Neurophysiology*, 43, 1041–1054.

Turkewitz, G., & Kenny, P. A. (1982). Limitations on input as a basis for neural organization and perceptual development: A preliminary theoretical statement. *Developmental Psychobiology*, 15, 357–368.

Turner, A. M., & Greenough, W. T. (1985). Differential rearing effects on rat visual cortex synapses. I. Synaptic and neuronal density and synapses per neuron. *Brain Research*, 329, 195–203.

Uylings, H. B. M., Kuypers, K., Diamond, M. C., & Veltman, W. A. M. (1978). Effects of differential environments on plasticity of dendrites of cortical pyramidal neurons in adult rats. *Experimental Neurology*, 62, 658–677.

Uylings, H. B. M., Kuypers, K., & Veltman, W. A. M. (1978). Environmental influences on neocortex in later life. *Progress in Brain Research*, 48, 261–274.

Valverde, F. (1970). The Golgi method: A tool for comparative structural analyses. In W. J. H. Nauta & S. O. E. Ebbesson (eds), *Contemporary research methods in neuroanatomy* (pp. 12–31). New York: Springer-Verlag.

Valverde, F. (1971). Rate and extent of recovery from dark-rearing in the mouse. *Brain Research*, 33, 1–11.

Werker, J. F., & Tees, R. C. (1984). Cross-language speech perception: Evidence for perceptual reorganization during the first year of life. *Infant Behavior and Development*, 7, 49–63.

Wiesel, T. N., & Hubel, D. H. (1963). Single-cell responses in striate cortex of kittens deprived of vision in one eye. *Journal of Neurophysiology*, 26, 1003–1017.

Wiesel, T. N., & Hubel, D. H. (1965). Comparison of the effects of unilateral and bilateral eye closure on cortical unit responses in kittens. *Journal of Neurophysiology*, 28, 1029–1040.

Wiesel, T., & Raviola, E. (1977). Myopia and eye enlargement after neonatal lid fusion in monkeys. *Nature*, 266, 66–68.

Winfield, D. A. (1981). The postnatal development of synapses in the visual cortex of the cat and the effects of eyelid closure. *Brain Research*, 206, 166–171.

Brain Adaptation to Experience: an Update

WILLIAM T. GREENOUGH

Since the Greenough, Black and Wallace paper was published in 1987, a number of findings have increased our understanding of the function of brain differences arising from experience. In particular, we have found that the synaptic changes are accompanied by an orchestrated set of changes in other elements of the brain tissue. In addition, a recent experiment makes us more confident that the synaptic and dendritic changes, which alter the "wiring diagram" of the brain, are specifically associated with learning. The results of this experiment have also provided a new perspective on mechanisms of brain adaptation to behavioral demands.

Changes in Nonsynaptic Brain Components

A major advance in our understanding of the brain's response to experience, still unfolding to some degree, was the finding that the experience-dependent formation of synapses is accompanied by changes in the brain's *blood supply* and in *astrocytes*, cells that metabolically support the activities of nerve cells and their synapses. When we wrote "apparently because the tissue volume of the dendrites, axons, glial cells, blood vessels, etc. necessary for additional synapses pushed the new synapses as far apart as they were in IC rats," in late 1986, we had very little to back it up. In fact, the only study published on EC (environmental complexity), SC (social condition) and IC (individual cage) rat blood vessels had reported that the density of vessels was *lower* in EC rats (Diamond et al., 1964). Our more recent work has indicated that work to be in error; in fact, blood vessel density is dramatically higher in young EC rats, while the capacity to generate new vessels declines with age. In young animals placed in the EC housing condition, the number of *capillaries*, the blood vessels that mediate transfer of nutrients from blood to brain, increases dramatically (Black et al., 1987). Similarly, the amount of astrocyte tissue is increased in young EC rats relative to SC and IC rats (Sirevaag and Greenough, 1991). Astrocytes are glial cells that maintain the metabolic environment of neurons and their synapses in a manner that optimizes synaptic and neuronal function. Synapses use a very large amount of metabolic energy and the developing brain apparently adapts itself to their numbers, and perhaps also to their level of activity, which is likely to be considerably higher in the exciting and stimulating world of the EC rat.

For capillaries, at least, the dramatic adaptation of the young rat, in which the amount of capillary per nerve cell is nearly double that of the IC rat, is not an ability that the animal retains if its exposure to EC is delayed to young adulthood. Adult EC rats can increase capillary numbers somewhat, but only enough to keep the same density within the expanding cortical tissue volume, in contrast to the greatly increased capillary density in the young EC rat (Black et al., 1991). Middle-age rats first exposed to EC show an even smaller capillary response to EC exposure in the visual cortex, although other areas or conditions may exhibit greater responsiveness (Black et al., 1989). We have not studied age effects on astrocytes.

In short, the brain retains in this case the ability to generate new synapses but it loses to a significant degree the ability to support them metabolically with advancing age. Whether this may lead to what Smith (1984) called a "power failure" for synapses – a situation in which they cannot keep up with the demands of behavior – remains an open question.

Do the Brain Differences Arise from Learning or from Neural Activity?

While it makes sense that changing the wiring diagram of the brain would alter its functional organization such that new information could be incorporated, there is no direct evidence that this is the case. One could conceive that neurons, like muscles, simply grow larger with increased levels of use and that brain blood vessels, like muscle vessels, proliferate to support the neurons. An experiment that addressed this issue compared animals learning a long series of complicated motor skills with animals that exercised by running on a treadmill or in an activity wheel such that little new learning was possible. A control group had neither exercise nor learning but were handled by the experimenters each day in a manner comparable to that of the other groups. (The rats were ten months old, about half the way to the "middle-age" groups described earlier.) The experiment used the cerebellum, a sensorimotor part of the brain (we had previously found that the complexity of housing conditions affects the cerebellum in a manner similar to its effects on the visual cortex: Floeter and Greenough, 1979; Greenough et al., 1986). The results of this experiment (Black et al., 1990) showed that both learning and exercise had effects, but that they were quite different. In the animals that learned, the number of synapses per cerebellar output cell increased, as we would have expected based upon our visual cortical results with the complex environment animals. The blood vessels in the learning animals just "kept up" with the changes in the tissue volume necessary to accommodate the new synapses. In contrast, both exercise groups exhibited no change in the number of synapses, but substantially increased the density of capillaries. Clearly, in cases where sufficient demand exists, the mature adult brain becomes capable of a response that we previously thought was limited to the juvenile.

The results of this experiment really revised the way we think about *learning*, or experience-expectant information storage in general, as an independent process as opposed to brain adaptation to the demands placed upon it by the animal's behavior. As psychologists oriented towards higher mental processes, we had tended to think of learning as something special and different from the sort of thing that the blood supply does in a muscle when it is repeatedly exercised. There are still ways in which this is true – other evidence from our laboratory also indicates that mere activation of neurons is insufficient to bring about synaptic change (Chang and Greenough, 1984). But the fundamental change that has occurred in our thinking has come from looking at how the cerebellum "views" the problems in this experiment. The appropriate role for any part of the body is to adapt in an optimal way to the conditions that the organism's needs are placing upon it. In the cases of the conditions used in this experiment, one adaptation apparently required establishing more capillaries such that the cerebellum could comfortably support sustained involvement in mediating routine but taxing motor output over long periods. The other adaptation involved changing the wiring diagram to incorporate the ability to perform novel skills. One might easily argue that from the point of view of the role of the cerebellum in optimizing its owner's chances of surviving in the natural environment, the two adaptations are equivalent. Both capillary increases and synapse increases are appropriate to the rats' behavioral needs. In short, from a survival viewpoint, what we call learning is not unique. It is just one of a range of adaptations that nervous systems may adopt to optimize behavioral performance.

REFERENCES

Black, J. E., Isaacs, K. R., Anderson, B. J., Alcantara, A. A. and Greenough, W. T. (1990) Learning causes synaptogenesis, whereas motor activity causes angiogenesis, in cerebellar cortex of adult rats. *Proceedings of the National Academy of Sciences (USA)*, 87, 5568–72.

Black, J. E., Polinsky, M. and Greenough, W. T. (1989) Progressive failure of cerebral angiogenesis supporting neural plasticity in aging rats. *Neurobiology of Aging*, 10, 353–8.

Black, J. E., Sirevaag, A. M. and Greenough, W. T. (1987) Complex experience promotes capillary formation in young rat visual cortex. *Neuroscience Letters*, 83, 351–5.

Black, J. E., Zelazny, A. M. and Greenough, W. T. (1991) Capillary and mitochondrial support of neural plasticity in adult rat visual cortex. *Experimental Neurology*, 111, 204–9.

Chang, F.-L. F. and Greenough, W. T. (1984) Transient and enduring morphological correlates of synaptic activity and efficacy change in the rat hippocampal slice. *Brain Research*, 309, 35–46.

Diamond, M. C., Krech, D. and Rosenzweig, M. R. (1964) The effects of an enriched environment on the histology of the rat cerebral cortex. *Journal of Comparative Neurology*, 123, 111–20.

Floeter, M. K. and Greenough, W. T. (1979). Cerebellar plasticity: modification of Purkinje cell structure by differential rearing in monkeys. *Science*, 206, 227–9.

Greenough, W. T., McDonald, J. W., Parnisari, R. M. and Camel, J. E. (1986) Environmental conditions modulate degeneration and new dendrite growth in cerebellum of senescent rats. *Brain Research*, 380, 136–43.

Sirevaag, A. M. and Greenough, W. T. (1991) Plasticity of GFAP-immunoreactive astrocyte size and number in visual cortex of rats reared in complex environments. *Brain Research*, 540, 273–8.

Smith, C. B. (1984) Aging and changes in cerebral energy metabolism. *Trends in Neuroscience*, 7, 203–8.

15

Do Cortical Areas Emerge from a Protocortex?

DENNIS D. M. O'LEARY

The neocortex is unique to mammals. Although it differs greatly in complexity between mammalian species, in all mammals it can be divided on both morphological and functional grounds into a sizable number of "areas."[1, 2] There are phylogenetic differences in neocortical parcellation which reflect the addition of higher order "associational" areas and an increase in the specialization of regions of neocortex to perform specific functions.[3] Much attention has been directed toward understanding the organization and operation of the neocortex. Recently, though, an increased amount of effort has been focused on determining how areas of the neocortex acquire their unique characteristics.[4] Although this question relates to an understanding of the mechanisms underlying the phylogenetic expansion of the neocortex in terms of the size and the number of definable areas, studies of neocortical development provide the best opportunity for answers. One can imagine two extreme positions of how distinct areas are developed: the neuroepithelium which gives rise to the neocortex may be regionally specified to generate area-unique lineages of neurons that reflect the area-specific features of the adult neocortex, or alternatively, the neocortical neuroepithelium may generate uniform lineages across its extent and rely on subsequent interactions to bring about the differentiation of areas. I will consider here an increasing body of evidence which suggests that many prominent features distinctive of the differentiation of areas of the neocortex are not determined at the time of neurogenesis, but rather are established through subsequent epigenetic interactions involving a variety of mechanisms.

"Do Cortical Areas Emerge from a Protocortex?" first appeared in *Trends in the Neurosciences* 12 (Elsevier Trends Journals 1989), pp. 400–6, and is reprinted by kind permission.

Some Distinctions and Similarities between Cortical Areas
in the Adult

Areas of the adult neocortex are clearly dissimilar. Neocortical areas can be distinguished from one another by differences in connections, both outputs and inputs, as well as by distinctions in architecture, from different distributions of receptors for neurotransmitters to variations in cell sizes and densities. These area-specific characteristics contribute to the unique functional properties of the various neocortical areas. But, in spite of the many striking differences between areas, certain features are shared. The most obvious common feature is that by convention all neocortical areas have six primary layers. Although the appearance of individual layers changes at the borders between areas, the chief characteristics of each layer are retained. For example, the same basic scheme of laminar organization of sources of cortical outputs applies to all: neurons in layer 6 project to the thalamus and claustrum, neurons in layer 5 send their axons to all other subcortical targets, and layers 2 and 3 are the principal source of projections to other neocortical areas, ipsilaterally and contralaterally.[5, 6]

Even the basic cellular constituents seem to be consistent from one area to another. Although cortical thickness varies considerably, the number of neurons found in a "radial traverse" through the six layers is surprisingly constant between diverse cortical areas within a species, as well as across species.[7, 8] A notable exception is that the number of neurons found in a radial traverse in primary visual cortex (area 17) is higher than in other areas.[7-9] The proportion of cells classified by shape as pyramidal or non-pyramidal is also constant between two very different areas, the primary motor and visual areas.[10] Similarly, the predominant cortical inhibitory cell, the GABAergic neuron, is present in roughly equivalent proportions in all areas examined.[8] Cortical neurons that might use other neurotransmitters or modulators, for example those immunoreactive for choline acetyltransferase (the synthesizing enzyme for the neurotransmitter acetylcholine),[11] as well as interneurons of various peptide phenotypes,[12-15] are also found in all neocortical areas. In short, all of the basic morphological and chemically defined types of cortical neurons identified to date are widely distributed within the adult neocortex.

Based on these and other structural and functional consistencies between areas of the adult neocortex, it has been proposed by both neuroanatomists and neurophysiologists, especially Lorente de No,[16] Creutzfeld,[17] Mountcastle,[18] Powell[19] and Eccles,[20] that different primary cortical areas share a common organizational scheme. This suggestion has been addressed experimentally in two independent sets of experiments in which somatosensory or auditory cortex was induced to process visual information by misrouting, during development, retinal axons to somatosensory thalamus[21] or to auditory thalamus[22] (figure 15.1). In these animals, the receptive field and response properties of cells in somatosensory or auditory cortex to visual stimuli resemble those normally seen in visual cortex. The most straightforward explanation for these findings is that the primary sensory areas of the neocortex normally process sensory information relayed through the thalamus in a fundamentally similar way, implying that the basic organization of cells and connections that underlie functional properties is also similar. This interpretation is supported by the finding that some cells in the somatosensory cortex to which visual input is directed can respond both to visual and somatosensory stimuli in modality-appropriate ways.[21] An alternative explanation is that the intrinsic organizations of neocortical sensory areas are not normally similar at mature stages, but that their development can be altered by visual input. However, even this suggests that primary sensory areas arise from regions of developing neocortex that are initially similar or to some extent pluripotent.

In summary, it appears that areas of the adult neocortex are constructed with the same basic set of cells organized in a fundamentally similar way, yet, by definition, each area has distinctive features.

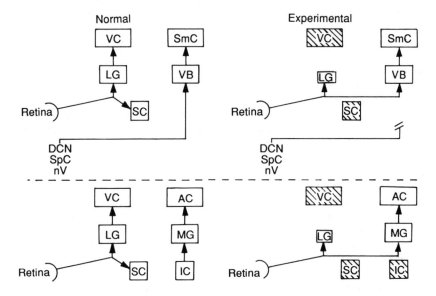

Figure 15.1 Aberrant routing of visual input into somatosensory and auditory cortex. Top left: in normal hamsters, the retina projects to the primary visual thalamic nucleus, the lateral geniculate nucleus (LG), and the superior colliculus (SC). The LG relays visual information to the visual cortex (VC). Somatosensory information is sent from the dorsal column nuclei (DCN), spinal cord (SpC) and the trigeminal nuclei (nV) to the primary somatosensory thalamic nuclei, termed the ventrobasal complex (VB), which in turn relays it to the somatosensory cortex (SmC). Top right: the retina can be induced to project to VB, by reducing its normal targets (by removing at birth the SC and the VC, which results in atrophy of the LG) and making terminal space available in the VB (by removing at birth its normal input). Under these conditions, SmC receives visual input from VB (see ref. 21). Bottom left: in normal ferrets, the retina projects to the LG and the SC. The LG projects to several visual cortical areas. The primary auditory thalamic nucleus, the medial geniculate (MG), receives auditory information from the inferior colliculus (IC), and relays it to the auditory cortex (AC). Bottom right: the retina can be induced to project to MG by a similar strategy to that described above; retinal targets are reduced (by removing the SC and visual cortical areas 17 and 18, which results in atrophy of the LG) and terminal space is made available in MG (by removing IC). Under these conditions, AC receives visual input from MG (see ref. 22). (Figure modified from figures appearing in refs 22 and 23.)

Early Events in Cortical Development

A discussion of differentiation of the areas of the neocortex should include the early stages of cortical development. Cortical neurons are generated in the neuroepithelium of the lateral ventricle. They migrate away from this site along the processes of radial glial cells and form the cortical layers in a deep-to-superficial sequence.[4, 24] Previous studies have suggested that the young neurons are deposited in a radial fashion within the developing cortical plate. The first direct demonstration of this has come recently from studies in which a progenitor cell is infected with a recombinant retrovirus carrying a marker gene which allows for later identification of its progeny. Using this approach, it has been shown that clonally related cortical neurons are usually distributed in roughly radial arrays.[25, 26] Occasionally, though, clonally related cells can be tangentially displaced within the cortex over distances that are substantial relative to the size of individual cortical areas.[26] These findings bear on the issue of area differentiation, since in its simplest form the concept of a specification of the neuroepithelium to give rise to specific cortical areas requires that neurons generated by a specific proliferative region remain segregated within the overlying cortical plate from neurons produced by neighboring proliferative regions.[4] A re-examination of this issue using two distinguishable viral markers that are now available[27] should allow for a firm determination of the frequency and magnitude of tangential displacements of clonally related neurons.

The findings from mouse chimera studies suggest that if the neocortical neuroepithelium does become regionally specified, specification must be a relatively late event. Neurons derived from blastula fusions of two strains of mice seem to be randomly dispersed within the mature neocortex,[28] implying that proliferative cells mix within the neocortical neuroepithelium close to the time that the first neurons become postmitotic. At these and later stages, morphological distinctions that could suggest the subdivision of the neocortical neuroepithelium into regions are not apparent,[29] while discontinuities indicative of the mosaic organization of certain other proliferative zones, for example the thalamic neuroepithelium, can be clearly discerned.[30] But any regional specification of the neocortical neuroepithelium should be revealed by a parallel expression of unique molecules in distinct patterns. Interestingly, antibodies to the peptides encoded by four proto-oncogenes (*sis-*, *src-*, *ras-*, and *myc-*), and against the intermediate filament protein vimentin, co-stain patches of radial glial cells spanning the neocortical neuroepithelium of rats,[31] whereas other antibodies to components of the neuroepithelium, D1.1[31, 32] and Rat-401,[33] stain it homogeneously. Presently, this is the best evidence for a structural or molecular regionalization within the neocortical neuroepithelium. However, since the patchy pattern of peptide staining emerges from a uniformly stained neuroepithelium only at very *late* stages of neurogenesis,[31] it is not clear how such regionalization would play a role in an early specialization of the neuroepithelium.

Generation of a "Protocortex"

The developing neocortex is distinct from the adult form in notable ways. First, it contains transient structures. The earliest recognized cortical structure is a cellular layer,[34] termed the preplate, that does not persist into adulthood. The neurons that populate this layer are the first to be generated by the neocortical neuroepithelium, but die over the course of development.[35] Later generated neurons that form the cortical plate aggregate within the preplate and split it into two layers. The upper layer develops into layer 1, while the lower layer, termed the subplate, becomes part of the axon tracts underlying layer 6. Presently, it is not clear if the preplate is simply a phylogenetic remnant, or if it plays a critical role in cortical development before its demise.[36]

Additionally, the neocortex is more uniform across its extent during development than at maturity, as it lacks many of the area-specific features characteristic of the adult. For instance, the primary somatosensory cortex of adult rodents contains a one-to-one representation of the mystacial vibrissae found on the muzzle, and sinus hairs present on the head and limbs, in the form of aggregations of layer 4 neurons and thalamic afferents referred to as barrels[37] (see figure 15.2). However, barrels are not apparent as the cortex is assembled, but emerge later from an initially uniform cortical plate.[38] Another example of uniformity in the developing neocortex can be taken from the development of area-specific outputs. In the adult neocortex, the unique outputs of specific areas are reflected in part by the limited distributions of types of cortical projection neurons, including those that send axons to subcortical targets such as the superior colliculus (corticotectal neurons), certain medullary nuclei and the spinal cord (pyramidal tract neurons), or through the corpus callosum to the contralateral cortex (callosal neurons). However, during development all of these classes of projection neurons are widely distributed across the neocortex (table 15.1). The restricted distributions of projection neurons in the adult, then, do not reflect regional differences in the ability of the neocortical neuroepithelium to generate general classes of cortical projection neurons.

Taken together, these comparisons of the organization of developing and adult neocortex lead to a reasonable conclusion that the entire extent of the neocortical neuroepithelium is competent to generate most, if not all, of the basic classes of cortical neurons, both permanent and transient. Further, early in its development, the neocortex not only contains large, transient populations of neurons, but also lacks the architectonic divisions characteristic of area diversity in the adult neocortex. The relative uniformity of the early neocortex compared with its adult

Table 15.1 Selected reports of developmentally widespread distributions of cortical projection neurons

Type of projection neuron	Mammalian order	References
Pyramidal tract/Corticospinal	Rodents	39, 40, 41
	Marsupials	42
	Lagomorphs	43
Corticotectal	Rodents	44
Callosal (commissural)	Rodents	45, 46
	Marsupials	47
	Lagomorphs	48
	Carnivores	49, 50, 51
	Primates	52, 53

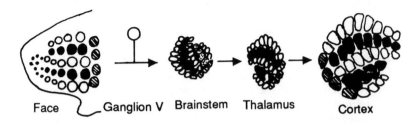

Figure 15.2 Patterning of cytoarchitectural units in somatosensory cortex. The pattern of 'barrels' in the posteromedial barrel subfield of somatosensory cortex of rodents is an isomorphic representation of the geometric arrangement of mystacial vibrissae found on the animal's face. Similar patterns are present in the brainstem and thalamic nuclei that relay inputs from the face to the barrel cortex. Alterations of the pattern of mystacial vibrissae, either genetically or by removal of vibrissae follicles during a critical period of development, result in a corresponding alteration of the cortical barrel pattern. Cutting the axons of trigeminal ganglion (ganglion V) neurons (thus blocking the flow of sensory information from the periphery to the brainstem) early on prevents barrel formation (see refs 38, 69–71).

form suggests that many of the area-specific features characteristic of the adult are not predetermined within the neuroepithelium. The neocortical neuroepithelium may generate a "protocortex" from which well-defined areas gradually emerge in a manner dependent upon influences that operate after neurogenesis. If different regions of the protocortex are indeed similar and their differentiation is not rigidly predetermined, one would expect that they would be capable of considerable plasticity in their expression of area-specific features. In the following sections, this issue will be examined.

Development of Area-Specific Outputs

The set of output projections of a given neocortical area in the adult is a subset of the projections that it originally elaborates. Although just a subset is retained by a given area, these early, widespread projections are made only to specific sets of targets appropriate for the general class of projection neuron from which they arise;[54, 55, 57] the subset retained in the adult varies between areas. The output of a neocortical area is remodeled chiefly through the selective elimination of particular axon collaterals or long distal segments of the primary axons without a concomitant death of the projection neurons. For example, in adult rats, pyramidal tract neurons (which extend a long axon through the pyramidal tract and innervate medullary nuclei and the spinal cord) are restricted to cortical layer 5, but of sensorimotor areas only. In neonates, though, while already limited to layer 5, these neurons are distributed throughout the entire neocortex.[39, 40] Pyramidal tract neurons located in regions of developing neocortex completely devoid of them in adults, such as the primary visual and auditory areas, subsequently lose their pyramidal tract axons,[39, 56] but retain collateral branches to other subcortical targets appropriate for their cortical location.[57] The fate of this axon is not a fixed property of pyramidal tract neurons, but is dependent on the area location of the neuron in the developing cortex.[58, 59] Thus, although the appropriate laminar position of cortical projection neurons is probably specified at or near the time they become postmitotic,[60] their adult areal distribution is achieved through a process of selective axon elimination that occurs well after the cortex is assembled.

Selective axon elimination also brings about the developmental restriction of initially widely distributed populations of callosally projecting neurons.[61-64] The stabilization or elimination of callosal axons seems to be influenced by sensory input. This is suggested by the presence of an abnormally widespread distribution of callosal neurons in visual cortical areas of adult rodents, cats and primates in which visual input to the developing cortex was altered naturally by genetics (Siamese cats)[65] or experimentally by removing or changing, in a number of ways, retinal inputs to visual thalamus.[66, 67] Such findings imply that thalamocortical input, or inputs relayed through thalamus, may regulate the process of selective axon elimination, and thus the output of a given region of neocortex.

Differentiation of Area-Specific Architecture

The cytoarchitectural differentiation of a region of neocortex is not a fixed property, and is capable of considerable plasticity. To illustrate this point, we return to the barrel-field of rodents. Cortical barrels develop through an interaction with thalamic afferents that relay sensory information from the periphery. The existence of cortical barrels is the manifestation of a series of afferent-induced barrel-like parcellations beginning in the brainstem and passing through the thalamus to the cortex[38] (figure 15.2). A number of markers, including certain lectins, can reveal early stages of this process.[68] Manipulations of the sensory periphery, all of which modify or block sensory input through the trigeminal system, alter or even prevent barrel formation.[38, 69] Somatosensory cortex is able also to reorganize and form a normal pattern of barrels following small lesions made in the barrel-field during an early postnatal critical period.[70] Perhaps the best evidence that the barrel pattern is not predetermined comes from observations made on strains of mice inbred for abnormal sets of mystacial vibrissae. In these mice, supernumerary vibrissae are represented in the cortex through the induced formation of additional barrels, but only if the anomalous vibrissa follicle is innervated by a suprathreshold number of sensory axons.[71] These observations indicate that the differentiation of barrel morphology and the unique patterning of groups of barrels are not fixed properties of somatosensory cortex, but are induced by inputs relayed to the cortex from the sensory periphery, suggesting that at least this feature of cortical cytoarchitecture is not predetermined within the neuroepithelium.

Are the Borders between Cortical Areas Fixed?

How is an extra barrel accommodated in somatosensory cortex? Does the area undergo some local or overall reorganization to allow for the space occupied by

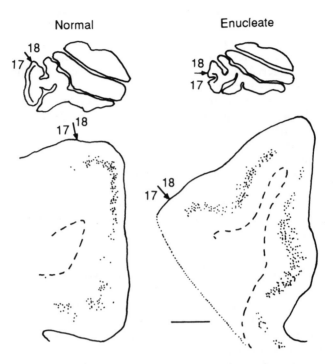

Figure 15.3 Borders between cortical areas are not fixed. A border shift between visual cortical areas 17 and 18 seems to occur in macaques bilaterally enucleated during the third month of gestation. The drawings are of sagittal sections of brains from normal (left) and bilaterally enucleated (right) newborn macaques. The top illustrations are low-power drawings to show the extent of area 17 (bold line) and the location of its border with area 18. The bottom drawings are higher power plots of callosally projecting neurons (which are normally present in area 18 but not area 17) taken from the same sections displayed above. (Figure modified from ref. 67.) In similarly enucleated macaques analysed as adults, the total number of neurons is reduced by about 50 percent within the region defined by cytoarchitecture as area 17, but the thickness and appearance of the layers, the number of neurons in a traverse across the six layers, and cell density in this region are comparable to that in area 17 of normal adults.[4,70] The reduced number of neurons cannot be attributed to fewer cells generated since the enucleations are done after neurogenesis. Further, it is unlikely that the result is a consequence of increased cell death since a selective loss of entire columns of cortical neurons has never been observed (and is highly improbable), and neuronal death distributed across all of area 17 would result in a substantial reduction of the number of neurons per column and a thinning of the cortex rather than the observed reduction in surface area. Thus, a reasonable conclusion is that a part of cortex that normally would mature into area 17 has instead developed properties characteristic of the adjacent area 18. (See ref. 4 for detailed arguments in support of a border shift.)

the barrel, or does the area expand its size at the expense of neighboring neocortical areas? Unfortunately, the size of an individual barrel is too small to make any firm statements. But recent findings in primates suggest that the border between primary visual cortex (area 17) and a secondary visual area (area 18) appears to be capable of a large shift with dramatic consequences on the subsequent differentiation of the affected piece of cortex.[4,67] Such a border shift seems to occur in macaque monkeys bilaterally enucleated at mid-fetal stages (see figure 15.3 legend, and reference 4 for arguments). This manipulation results in a 50 percent loss in the number of lateral geniculate neurons, the primary source of thalamic input to area 17. The total number of neurons in area 17, and its overall size, are correspondingly reduced, but the thickness and appearance of the layers are normal.[72] Features characteristic of area 17, including the unique laminar distributions of receptors for neurotransmitters and the presence of functional subunits specific to area 17, are retained within the reduced area identified as area 17 based on cytoarchitectural appearance.[4] But more importantly, a region of cortex normally contained within area 17 takes on the architectural appearance of area 18, and appaently lacks other characteristics which define area 17. Even the output of this region is altered and resembles that of area 18. A large numbr of callosally projecting neurons are present within area 18 up to its new border with area 17, with few or none found in the region cytoarchitecturally identified as area 17;[67] callosal neurons are rarely, if at all, encountered in area 17 of normal macaque monkeys.[53] These findings indicate that the biochemical, cytoarchitectural, and connectional differentiation of a part of neocortex can be developmentally controlled by epigenetic factors. Again, a critical, regulatory role for thalamic input in this phenomenon has been suggested.[4]

Are Cortical Areas Interchangeable?

Similar conclusions can be drawn from a set of studies that indicate that the regional location of a piece of developing neocortex has a decisive influence on the subsequent acquisition of many area-specific properties. This has been demonstrated by transplanting pieces of late fetal neocortex to be heterotopic positions within the neocortex of newbron rodents. The layer 5 projections to subcortical targets permanently established by such transplants are dependent upon the transplant's position within the neocortex (figure 15.4). Visual cortical neurons transplanted to the sensorimotor region extend and permanently retain axons to the spinal cord, a subcortical target of sensorimotor cortex.[58, 59] Conversely, sensorimotor cortical neurons transplanted to the visual region extend and then lose spinal axons, but retain a projection to a subcortical target of visual cortex, the superior colliculus.[59] The heterotopic transplants also establish callosal and thalamic connections, both input and output, appropriate for their *new* location.[59, 73, 74] In sum, the inputs and outputs of heterotopically transplanted neurons resemble those of the neurons normally present in that cortical location. Heterotopic transplants of neocortex can also take on the cytoarchitectural appearance of the host cortical region. For example, pieces of occipital (visual) cortex placed in the presumptive barrel-field of primary somatosensory cortex develop morphological features that resemble barrels when innervated by thalamic afferents.[75] From this observation it can be inferred that thalamic afferents are able to organize in a foreign piece of cortex, and that the transplanted cells can respond to the afferents in ways necessary to express the cytoarchitectural features appropriate to their new cortical locale. It can be concluded from this class of experiments that different regions of the protocortex are sufficiently alike that, if heterotopically placed in the developing neocortex, they will come

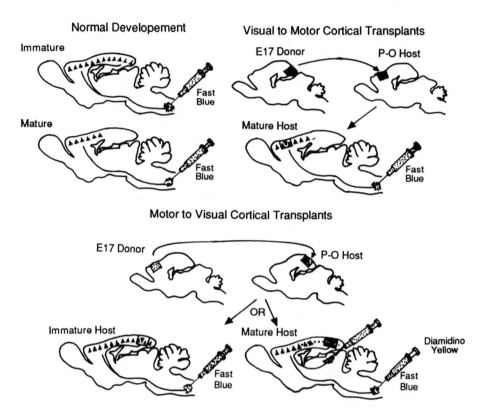

Figure 15.4 Development of area-specific outputs is not a fixed property of cortical areas. Top left: during normal development in rats, layer 5 neurons in all regions of the immature neocortex develop a pyramidal tract axon and can be labeled retrogradely with the dye Fast Blue injected into the pyramidal decussation. A similar injection made in mature rats labels layer 5 neurons confined to sensorimotor areas of cortex. The restriction from the widespread, immature distribution to the limited, mature one is achieved through a selective elimination of pyramidal tract axons without neuron loss (see ref. 39). Heterotopic transplantation of fetal cortex shows that this elimination of pyramidal tract axons is dependent upon the cortical location of developing neurons (see refs 58, 59). Top right: embryonic day 17 (E17) visual cortical neurons transplanted to the motor region of a newborn (P-O) host develop and permanently retain pyramidal tract axons as demonstrated by Fast Blue labeling from the pyramidal decussation after maturation. Bottom: motor cortical neurons transplanted to the visual region can be labeled with Fast Blue injected into the pyramidal decussation (PD) at immature stages, but not at maturity. However, in the same mature hosts, the transplanted neurons can be labeled with a second dye, Diamidino Yellow, injected into the superior colliculus, a permanent target of visual cortex but only a transient target of motor cortex. Thus, the transplants form permanent projections characteristic of their new cortical location. (Figure modified from ref. 59.)

to acquire many of the area-specific properties normally associated with their new location.

Mechanisms Involved in the Differentiation of the Protocortex

All, or most, of the epigenetically influenced developmental processes that operate throughout the developing nervous system[76] are likely to play a role in the differentiation of the protocortex. Some of these processes elaborate upon existing components. For instance, the shapes and sizes of the dendritic arbors of specific classes of neurons, which contribute to differences in cytoarchitecture, can be greatly influenced by afferent input[38] and target-derived factors.[77] Other processes, such as selective axon elimination, synapse elimination and neuronal death, which can be thought of as regressive in nature, serve to remove, in a regionally specific manner, excess of functionally inappropriate components. We have already seen that selective axon elimination contributes to the development of area-specific outputs. Synapse elimination has been reported to occur in several diverse cortical areas,[70] and is probably involved in the shaping of many cortical features. It is best documented as underlying the developmental remodeling of geniculocortical inputs to visual cortex,[79] a process driven by a relative asynchrony in activity patterns among competing sets of inputs.[80] Neuronal death is a likely contributor to the sculpting of inter-area differences in the number of neurons found in specific layers. In rodents, about 30 percent of cortical neurons die.[81] Most of this loss occurs in the superficial layers, primarily in layers 2 and 3, and to a lesser extent in layer 4.[9, 81] There is evidence that the number of cells in layer 4 is governed by the density of thalamic input, and that the number of cells present in the superficial layers is determined by a combination of differential cell loss and changes in neuronal differentiation,[9, 82] factors which are believed to contribute to the greater number of neurons found in a radial traverse in area 17 compared with other areas.[9] Although I have only briefly considered a few, clearly a wide range of developmental processes can act on the protocortex to establish area-specific features characteristic of the adult neocortex.

Regional Differences in the Protocortex

The processes just described contribute to the differentiation of the protocortex, but can they account for all of the differences seen between neocortical areas in the adult? Let us consider two features reported for area 17 of monkeys of the genus *Macaca*. First, in adult macaques area 17 has more than twice as many neurons in a radial traverse compared with other primary sensory areas, with the extra neurons contained in layers 4 and above.[7, 8] The increased number of neurons in area 17 might reflect not only a reduced amount of cell loss, but also a regionally specific increase in neuronal production. Here it is worth recalling the patchy distribution of radial glial cells that stain in rats with antibodies to proto-oncogene peptides.[31] Within a patch, an increased proportion of neuroepithelial cells can be labeled with [³H]thymidine (a marker of DNA synthesis), and the patches appear over the period that neurons which will populate the most superficial corrical layers are being generated. Although this observation can be interpreted in several ways, one intriguing possibility is that it reflects localized increases in the generation of superficial neurons.[31] Second, area 17 of macaques reportedly does not have a callosal projection even during development,[53] and in this sense is unlike area 17 in all non-primate mammals examined to date, where, as mentioned earlier, neurons throughout area 17 transiently extend callosal axons. Macaques may have evolved a higher degree of specification of the output of area 17. If true, this feature may prove to be unique for area 17, since other cortical areas in macaques, namely the secondary visual area 18[53] and primary somatosensory cortex,[52] do develop transiently widespread callosal connections. However, an argument against this possibility is the finding in macaques that parts of cortex that normally are contained within area 17 do have callosal connections following eye removal at mid-fetal stages.[67]

Nevertheless, there are likely to be differences across the protocortex, whether present as subtle gradients or as sharp discontinuities. One likely possibility would be molecular distinctions between regions, and even within regions, of the protocortex, which promote the formation of appropriate connectional relationships, for example between thalamic nuclei and cortical areas, as well as underlie the topographic ordering of the input and output connections of the neocortex. These molecules would probably be present on the surface of select subsets of cells. To date, though, cells immunoreactive for antibodies that recognize distinct neuronal surface antigens are present in all neocortical areas, whether the number stained is substantial, as for Cat-301-positive neurons,[83] or exceedingly small, as for Tor-23-positive neurons.[84] However, specific areas of limbic cortex (often termed allocortex and distinct from neocortex), do stain selectively for an antibody that recognizes a surface molecule (named limbic-associated membrane protein), both in the mature[85] and developing brain.[86] The same molecule is associated with subcortical components of the limbic system.[85] Similar markers will probably be found for neocortex.

Concluding Remarks

The neocortical neuroepithelium generates a fairly uniform structure, here termed the protocortex, that does not have the architectonic divisions present in the adult neocortex. Many of the area-specific features characteristic of well-defined cortical areas emerge from the protocortex long after the conclusion of neurogenesis through a process that can be regulated by influences, for example afferent inputs, that vary across the developing neocortex. However, differences are likely to exist from one region of the protocortex to another – differences laid down at the time of neurogenesis that contribute to the development of area-specific properties. The extent to which area-specific properties are determined at the time of neurogenesis, that is, the degree to which the neocortical neuroepithelium is regionally specified to generate the definable characteristics of specific neocortical areas,[4] is presently not resolved and may well vary from species to species. However, most studies relevant to this issue provide evidence for epigenetic regulation of area differentiation; the mere existence of cytoarchitectonically defined areas in the adult neocortex is presently the most compelling evidence for their predetermination within the neocortical neuroepithelium. The neocortex shows considerable plasticity in the development of area-specific features, but many of these findings are based on perturbation studies, and therefore such plasticity does not unequivocally demonstrate that area-specific features are not predetermined, but rather that they are not irreversibly predetermined. Nonetheless, different regions of the developing neocortex have the capability to acquire many of the area-specific characteristics normally associated with other cortical areas, indicating that there are significant similarities among these regions. These similarities may reflect a phylogenetic conservation of the ability of all parts of the neocortical neuroepithelium to generate the ensemble of basic structural components of the neocortex, thereby establishing a protocortex from which defined areas emerge.

ACKNOWLEDGEMENTS

I thank B. Stanfield for valuable discussions, A. Burkhalter, J. Lichtman, B. Schlaggar, C. Shatz and T. Woolsey for their thoughtful comments on the manuscript, T. Woolsey for help with making figures 15.1 and 15.2 and the NEI, NINCDS, the McKnight Endowment Fund for Neuroscience and the Sloan Foundation for support.

REFERENCES

1 Brodmann, K. (1909) *Lokalisationslehre der Groshirnrinde in ihren Pricipen dargestellt aus Grund des Zellenbaue*, Barth.
2 Krieg, W. J. S. (1946) *J. Comp. Neurol.* 84, 221–275.
3 Van Essen, D. C. (1985) in *Cerebral Cortex, Vol. 3: Visual Cortex* (Peters, A. and Jones, E. G., eds), pp. 259–330, Plenum.
4 Rakic, P. (1988) *Science* 241, 170–176.
5 Gilbert, C. D. (1983) *Annu. Rev. Neurosci.* 6, 217–248.
6 Jones, E. G. (1984) in *Cerebral Cortex, Vol. 1: Cellular Components of the Cerebral Cortex* (Peters, A. and Jones, E. G. eds), pp. 521–553, Plenum.
7 Rockel, A. J., Hiorns, R. W. and Powell, T. P. S. (1980) *Brain* 103, 221–244.
8 Hendry, S. H. C., Schwark, H. D., Jones, E. G. and Yan, J. (1987) *J. Neurosci.* 4, 2497–2517.
9 Finlay, B. L. and Slattery, M. (1983) *Science* 219, 1349–1351.
10 Winfield, D. A., Gatter, K. C. and Powell, T. P. S. (1980) *Brain* 103, 245–258.
11 Sofroniew, M. V., Campbell, P. E., Cuello, A. C. and Eckenstein, F. (1985) in *The Rat Nervous System, Vol. 1: Forebrain and Midbrain* (Paxinos, G., ed.), pp. 471–486, Academic Press.
12 Fuxe, K., Hokfelt, T., Said, S. I. and Mutt, V. (1979) *Neurosci. Lett.* 5, 241–246.
13 Hendry, S. H. C., Jones, E. G. and Emson, P. C. (1984) *J. Neurosci.* 4, 2497–2517.
14 Peters, A., Miller, M. and Kimerer, L. M. (1983) *Neuroscience* 8, 431–448.
15 Morrison, J. H., Benoit, P. J., Magistretti, P. J. and Bloom, F. E. (1983) *Brain Res.* 262, 344–351.
16 Lorente de No, R. (1949) in *Physiology of the Nervous System* (Fulton, J. F., ed.), pp. 288–315, Oxford University Press.
17 Creutzfeld, O. D. (1977) *Naturwissenschaft* 64, 507–517.
18 Mountcastle, V. B. (1978) in *The Mindful Brain* (Mountcastle, V. B. and Edelman, G. M., eds), pp. 7–50, MIT.

19 Powell, T. P. S. (1981) in *Brain Mechanisms and Perceptual Awareness* (Pompeiano, O. and Ajmone Marsan, C., eds), pp. 1–19, Raven.
20 Eccles, J. C. (1984) in *Cerebral Cortex, Vol. 2: Functional Properties of Cortical Cells* (Jones, E. G. and Peters, A., eds), pp. 1–36, Plenum.
21 Metin, C. and Frost, D. O. (1989) *Proc. Natl Acad. Sci. USA* 86, 357–361.
22 Sur, M., Garraghty, P. E. and Roe, A. W. (1988) *Science* 242, 1437–1441.
23 Frost, D. O. (1981) *J. Comp. Neurol.* 203, 227–256.
24 Rakic, P. (1974) *Science* 183, 425–427.
25 Luskin, M. B., Pearlman, A. L. and Sanes, J. R. (1988) *Neuron* 1, 635–647.
26 Walsh, C. and Cepko, C. L. (1988) *Science* 241, 1342–1345.
27 Galileo, D. S., Gray, G. E., Owens, G. C., Majors, J. and Sanes, J. R. *Soc. Neurosci. Abstr.* (in press).
28 Goldwitz, D. (1987) *Dev. Brain Res.* 35, 1–9.
29 Smart, I. H. M. and Sturrock, R. R. (1979) in *The Neostriatum* (Divac, I. and Oberg, R. G. E., eds), pp. 127–146, Pergamon.
30 Altman, J. and Bayer, S. A. (1988) *J. Comp. Neurol.* 275, 346–377.
31 Johnson, J. G. and Van Der Kooy, D. (1989) *Proc. Natl Acad. Sci. USA* 86, 1066–1070.
32 Levine, J. M., Beasley, L. and Stallcup, W. B. (1984) *J. Neurosci.* 4, 820–831.
33 Frederikson, K. and McKay, R. D. G. (1988) *J. Neurosci.* 8, 1144–1151.
34 Marin-Padilla, M. (1978) *Anat. Embryol.* 152, 109–126.
35 Luskin, M. B. and Shatz, C. J. (1985) *J. Neurosci.* 5, 1062–1075.
36 Shatz, C. J., Chun, J. J. M. and Luskin, M. B. in *Cerebral Cortex, Vol. 7* (Jones, E. G. and Peters, A., eds), Plenum (in press).
37 Woolsey, T. A. and Van Der Loos, H. (1970) *Brain Res.* 17, 205–242.
38 Woolsey, T. A. in *Development of Sensory Systems in Mammals* (Coleman, J. R., ed.), Wiley (in press).
39 Stanfield, B. B., O'Leary, D. D. M., and Fricks, C. (1982) *Nature* 298, 371–373.
40 Bates, C. A. and Killackey, H. P. (1984) *Dev. Brain Res.* 13, 265–273.
41 O'Leary, D. D. M. and Stanfield, B. B. (1986) *Dev. Brain Res.* 27, 87–99.
42 Cabana, T. and Martin, G. F. (1984) *Dev. Brain Res.* 15, 247–263.
43 Distel, H. and Hollander, H. (1980) *J. Comp. Neurol.* 192, 505–518.
44 Thong, I. G. and Dreher, B. (1986) *Dev. Brain Res.* 25, 227–238.
45 Ivy, G. O. and Killackey, H. P. (1981) *J. Comp. Neurol.* 195, 367–389.
46 Olavarria, J. and Van Sluyters, R. C. (1985) *J. Comp. Neurol.* 239, 1–26.
47 Cabana, T. and Martin, G. F. (1985) *Anat. Embryol.* 17, 121–128.
48 Chow, K. K., Baumbach, H. D. and Lawson, R. (1981) *Exp. Brain Res.* 42, 122–126.
49 Innocenti, G. M., Fiore, L. and Caminiti, R. (1977) *Neurosci. Lett.* 4, 237–242.
50 Innocenti, G. M. and Caminiti, R. (1980) *Exp. Brain Res.* 38, 824–827.
51 Feng, J. Z. and Brugge, J. F. (1983) *J. Comp. Neurol.* 214, 416–426.
52 Killackey, H. P. and Chalupa, L. M. (1986) *J. Comp. Neurol.* 244, 331–348.
53 Dehay, C., Kennedy, H., Bullier, J. and Berland, M. (1988) *Nature* 331, 348–359.
54 O'Leary, D. D. M. and Terashima, T. *Soc. Neurosci. Abstr.* (in press).
55 Koester, S. E. and O'Leary, D. D. M. *Soc. Neurosci. Abstr.* (in press).
56 O'Leary, D. D. M. and Terashima, T. (1988) *Neuron* 1, 901–910.
57 O'Leary, D. D. M. and Stanfield, B. B. (1985) *Brain Res.* 336, 326–333.
58 Stanfield, B. B. and O'Leary, D. D. M. (1985) *Nature* 313, 135–137.
59 O'Leary, D. D. M. and Stanfield, B. B. (1989) *J. Neurosci.* 9, 2230–2246.
60 McConnell, S. K. (1988) *J. Neurosci.* 8, 945–974.
61 Innocenti, G. M. (1981) *Science* 212, 824–827.
62 O'Leary, D. D. M., Stanfield, B. B. and Cowan, M. W. (1981) *Dev. Brain Res.* 1, 607–617.

63 Ivy, G. O. and Killackey, H. P. (1982) *J. Neurosci.* 6, 735–743.
64 Chalupa, L. M. and Killackey, H. P. (1989) *Proc. Natl Acad. Sci. USA* 86, 1076–1079.
65 Shatz, C. J. (1977) *J. Comp. Neurol.* 173, 497–518.
66 Innocenti, G. M. (1985) in *Cerebral Cortex, Vol. 5: Sensory-motor Areas and Aspects of Cortical Connectivity* (Jones, E. G. and Peters, A., eds), pp. 291–353, Plenum.
67 Dehay, C., Horsburgh, G., Berland, M., Killackey, H. and Kennedy, H. (1989) *Nature* 337, 265–267.
68 Cooper, N. G. F. and Steindler, D. A. (1986) *J. Comp. Neurol.* 249, 157–186.
69 Van der Loos, H. and Welker, E. (1985) in *Development, Organization, and Processing in Somatosensory Pathways*, pp. 53–67, Alan R. Liss.
70 Seo, M. L. and Ito, M. (1987) *Exp. Brain Res.* 65, 251–260.
71 Welker, E. and van der Loos, H. (1986) *J. Neurosci.* 6, 3355–3373.
72 Rakic, P. and Williams, R. W. (1986) *Soc. Neurosci. Abstr.* 12, 1499.
73 Chang, F. L. F., Steedman, J. G. and Lund, R. D. (1986) *J. Comp. Neurol.* 244, 401–411.
74 O'Leary, D. D. M. (1988) *Soc. Neurosci. Abstr.* 14, 1113.
75 Schlaggar, B. L. and O'Leary, D. D. M. (1988) *Soc. Neurosci. Abstr.* 14, 475.
76 Purves, D. and Lichtman, J. W. (1985) *Principles of Neural Development Sinauer.*
77 Voyvodic, J. T. (1989) *J. Neurosci* 9, 1997–2010.
78 Rakic, P., Bourgeois, J. P., Eckenhoff, M. F., Zecevic, N. and Goldman-Rakic, P. S. (1986) *Science* 232, 232–235.
79 LeVay, S., Wiesel, T. N. and Hubel, D. H. (1981) in *The Organization of the Cerebral Cortex* pp. 29–45, MIT.
80 Stryker, M. P. and Harris, W. A. (1986) *J. Neurosci.* 6, 2 17–2133.
81 Huemann, D., Lueba, G. and Rabinowicz, G. (1978) *J. Hirnforsch.* 19, 385–393.
82 Windrem, M. S., Jan de Beur, S. M. and Finlay, B. L. (1986) *Soc. Neurosci. Abstr.* 12, 867.
83 Hendry, S. H. C., Jones, E. G., Hockfield, S. and McKay, R. D. G. (1988) *J. Neurosci.* 8, 518–542.
84 Stephenson, D. T. and Kushner, P. D. (1988) *J. Neurosci.* 8, 3035–3056.
85 Levitt, P. (1984) *Science* 223, 299–301.
86 Horton, H. L. and Levitt, P. (1988) *J. Neurosci.* 8, 4653–4661.

16

Brain Development, Plasticity, and Behavior

BRYAN KOLB

Nearly one half million people will suffer traumatic brain injury in the United States alone this year [1989]. When one adds the people who will suffer a stroke, develop dementing disorders, or suffer from other types of brain dysfunctions such as mental retardation, cerebral palsy, or epilepsy, it becomes clear that there are a large number of people who have permanent behavioral abnormalities that may include disorders of movement, perception, or memory; loss of language; and the alteration of social behavior and personality. Thus, whereas the study of brain–behavior relationships was once restricted largely to physiological psychologists, the development of neuropsychology has moved the study of brain and behavior into the mainstream of psychology to involve significant numbers of human experimental and clinical psychologists. One problem, however, is that most of the basic work in neuroscience is largely divorced from psychology and is inaccessible to the bulk of psychologists who quite rightly have difficulty in seeing the direct relevance of this work to psychological issues. My goal in this article is to review recent work on the nature of brain development and plasticity and its relation to the understanding of behavior.

There are numerous approaches to the study of brain–behavior relationships. The first is to study how normal mature brains work. This can be done either by examining the morphological and physiological correlates of behavior or by studying the structure of cognitive processes and making predictions about how the brain must be processing information. Studies of morphological changes during learning provide an example of the former type, and psychophysical experiments provide examples of the latter. A second approach is to study the behavioral correlates of brain dysfunction, with the goal of making predictions about normal function. This has been the principle method of neuropsychology for over 100 years. A third approach is to study the manner in which the brain and behavior normally develop, with the hope of gaining insight into both how the brain comes to produce behavior and how one might gain control of the processes of development. In the latter case it is proposed that it might be possible to re-initiate developmental processes to repair injury. Indeed, because both fish and amphibian brains can do this after injury and some birds annually regrow structures necessary for song each spring, it is possible that under certain conditions, hormonal events may re-initiate neural growth in mammals. A final approach is to alter the brain during development in order to see how the anatomical and behavioral organization changes. This allows an opportunity not only to look at the processes involved in brain development but also to try to determine what rules can predict when restitution of function is likely to occur and what anatomical changes might correlate with behavioral recovery. Furthermore, this approach allows one to look at the nature of localization of functions in the brain, which is an issue that has fascinated psychologists since the time of Gall. It is this final approach that I wish to examine in detail, and I will begin with an illustrative example.

Consider the following case histories of two young women. The first, P.B., is a 22-year-old business school graduate who was struck by a car and suffered a serious head injury, requiring emergency surgery to repair her skull and to relieve the pressure from subdural bleeding. It was necessary to remove a large portion of her right posterior temporo-parietal cortex. After the accident she had a left visual field defect but was able to return to her job as a typist/clerk. Upon neuropsychological examination six years after the injury, she obtained an average IQ score, although she was relatively better at verbal tests than those requiring manipulation of pictorial information. She had particular difficulty drawing and remembering pictorial information, including faces. Her motor skills were good, and although she initially had difficulty reading because of the visual loss, she overcame this handicap and could read as well as IQ-matched controls. The second case, S.S., is an 18-year-old woman who had a difficult birth and forceps delivery and began having epileptic seizures at 14 years of age. Neurological examination revealed a right parietal cyst; this was removed surgically, and the seizures were arrested. She was an average student in school but had difficulty in 12th grade, especially with English and mathematics. Her neuropsychological assessment at age 18 revealed an average IQ, but she was relatively better at pictorial tests than verbal ones, which is in direct contrast to P.B. Furthermore, she had a poor vocabulary score considering her education, IQ, and socioeconomic group, and she had a difficult time with arithmetic. She also had difficulty in repeating sequences of movements shown to her by the examiner, especially those of the face, and had difficulty on tests that are typically sensitive to frontal-lobe injury. In contrast, she had no difficulty on tests of drawing or visual memory. In short, P.B. and S.S. had similar brain damage, but at different ages, and the consequences could not have been much more different. I note, parenthetically, that because P.B. had a closed head injury, one might expect some nonspecific damage, such as tearing of connections or bruising elsewhere in the brain, in addition to her focal lesions. Her symptoms were typical of patients with vascular lesions in adulthood, however, and there was some evidence of nonspecific damage on tests of interhemispheric transfer (see Kolb and Whishaw, 1985, chapter 16, for more examples).

Several questions arise from these two cases. If functions are localized in the cortex, why are the symptoms different when the damage included the same tissue? Why did S.S. have symptoms typical of frontal-lobe injury when there is no evidence of any damage to her frontal lobe? Was the age at which brain damage was sustained responsible for her behavioral differences? Why was there a permanent loss of functions in both cases, even with years of recovery? How did the function of the remaining tissue in the two brains change after the injuries? Were the changes the same? I return to these questions later.

Brain Development

One of the wonders of human development is the manner in which the human brain, which consists of over 100 billion neurons, can develop so quickly from just a few initial neural cells. According to Cowan (1979), during the time the brain is growing *in utero* it must be generating neurons at a rate of more than 250 000 per minute. Furthermore, once the neurons are "born," they must move to their correct locations and form connections, which have been estimated at up to 15 000 per neuron.

The gross development of the human brain is summarized in figure 16.1, but these general morphological changes provide little insight into the details, most of which have been discovered in the last two decades by studies on laboratory animals, especially rats and monkeys. It is now known that the development of the cortex in any species occurs in several stages (e.g. Cowan, 1979; Rakic, 1988). These include cell proliferation, cell migration, cell differentiation, dendritic and axonal growth, cell and axonal death, and gliogenesis. I consider these stages briefly.

Like all mammalian brains, the human brain begins as a hollow tube and gradually develops the features of the adult brain. The hollow area in the tube forms the ventricular system, and the cells of the brain are generated along the ventricular wall and then migrate out to their proper locations. As the brain develops, the newly formed cells must travel farther and farther to reach their final locations. As might be predicted, the precise timing of the development and migration of cells to different cortical regions varies with the particular area in question. Once cells find their correct location in the cortex, they develop the characteristics of the cell type that they are to be (e.g. stellate or pyramidal cell) and begin to grow their dendrites and axons and to form synapses. One particularly interesting aspect of neural development is that the brain overproduces neurons, possibly by a factor of two, and the extra cells are lost by a process of cell death. Similarly, a large proportion of the cortical synapses are lost during development, perhaps as many as 50 percent. This cell and synaptic loss is probably not random, although the controlling factors are still unknown. Curiously, it has been suggested that a failure of cell death or synaptic loss may lead to retardation or contribute to the emergence of developmental disorders, possibly even schizophrenia (e.g. Feinberg, 1982).

It has been possible to determine the timetable for many of these stages by labeling cells with various tracers. For example, thymidine is a compound that is incorporated into cells only during cell division. If a radioactive isotope is attached to the thymidine, the radioactivity will be detectable later only in those

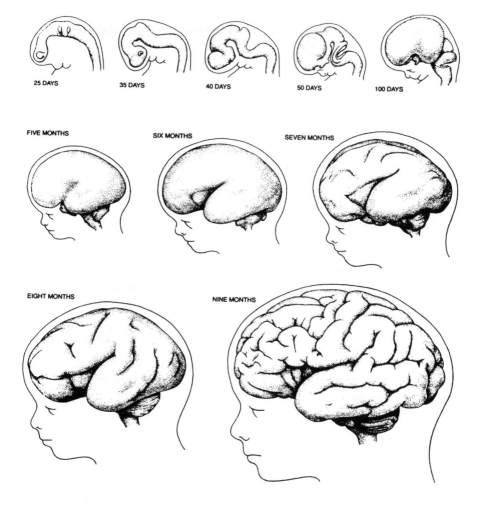

Figure 16.1 The development of the human brain.
Note: Adapted from "The Development of the Brain" by W. M. Cowan. In *The Brain*, (p. 59), 1979, San Francisco: Freeman. Copyright 1979 by W. H. Freeman. Adapted by permission.

cells that were exposed to the thymidine during their mitosis. Cells born before or after this time will not be labeled. By labeling cells at different points in development, it is possible not only to chart the time of birth of cells but also to track their route during migration (see figure 16.2). Thus, the thymidine technique has shown that cells that form the innermost layers of the cortex are born first, followed by those in the external layers. One consequence of this arrangement is that newly produced cells must migrate through the existing layers to reach their correct locations. It is also known that all cells forming a particular layer in a particular region of the cortex proliferate and migrate at the same time.

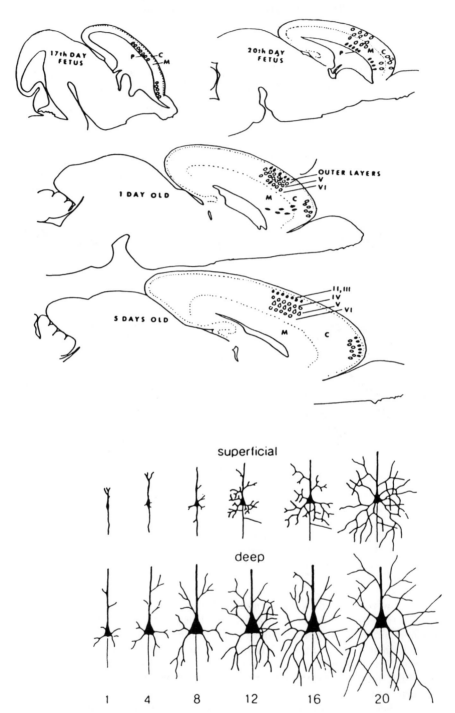

Figure 16.2 Migration of cells.

Thus, brief prenatal events (e.g. drugs, toxins, or stress) that jeopardize developing cells could lead to the development of a brain without a particular cell group, the anomoly depending upon the precise timing of the prenatal event.

Detailed studies of brain development have shown that in most altricial mammals such as rats, cats, monkeys, or humans the stages of cell proliferation and migration are largely prenatal and much of the development of neuropil (axons and dendrites) and cell death are postnatal. Thus, most mammals are born with practically a full complement of neurons, and few, if any, neurons are born postnatally. One exception is the hippocampus, which continues to develop neurons throughout the life of some species. In general, however, if the brain is damaged after cell proliferation has ceased, it is obvious that any compensation will have to be accomplished by changes in the remaining cells. The fact that the growth of neuropil and the loss of cells is postnatal is important for it is obvious that the extrauterine environment could have a direct influence on these processes.

Consider the following analogy. If one were to make a statue, it would be possible to do it either by starting with grains of sand and glueing them together to form the desired shape or by starting with a block of stone and chiseling the unwanted pieces away. The brain uses the latter procedure. The "chisel" in the brain could be of several forms including genetic signal, environmental stimulation, gonadal hormones, stress, and so on. Similarly, the same processes are likely to affect the development of dendrites, axons, and synapses. Cell death and neuropil development do not end in infancy but rather may continue well into adolescence. For example, it appears that cell death continues in the human frontal lobe until about 16 years of age (Huttenlocher, 1979). I should note here that cell death continues at a greatly slowed pace throughout adult life, but it is unclear what role environmental events may play in this process.

One example of the effect of environmental stimulation on brain development comes from the work of Janet Werker and Richard Tees (1984). They studied the ability of infants to discriminate phonemes taken from widely disparate languages, such as English, Hindi, and Salish. Their results showed that infants can discriminate speech sounds of different languages without previous experience, but there is a decline in this ability, over the first year of life, as a function of specific language experience. One might speculate that neurons in the auditory system that are not stimulated early in life may be selected against and die, although there are other explanations.

Note: The top panel (left) is adapted from "Cell Migrations to the Isocortex of the Rat" by S. P. Hicks and C. J. D'Amato, 1968, *Anatomical Record*, 160, p. 621. Copyright 1968 by Allen R. Liss, Inc. Adapted by permission.

The top panel is a diagram of labeled cells that originated in the 17th (ovals) or 20th (black) intrauterine day in the rat brain. Notice that migration continues after birth.

The bottom panel is adapted from "Cellular differentiation: development of dendritic arborizations under normal and experimentally altered conditions" by M. Berry, 1980, *Neurosciences Research Program Bulletin*, 20, p. 456. Copyright 1980 by MIT Press. Adapted by permission.

The bottom panel is a schematic illustration of the rate of acquisition of basal and apical dendrites of the pyramidal cells of the superficial and deep layers of the cerebral cortex of the rat.

The postnatal stages of brain development provide not only an explanation for how early experience could affect later behavior but also why brain damage at different ages might have very different effects and lead to different cerebral organizations.

Behavioral Effects of Early Brain Damage

In the 1930s Margaret Kennard was studying the effects of cortical lesions on motor performance in monkeys and reported the provocative finding that lesions in infant monkeys had less severe effects on behavior than similar lesions occurring in adulthood. This claim led to the development of the Kennard doctrine (1936), which stated that the earlier one suffers brain damage, the less severe the behavioral loss. This view was reinforced by Lenneberg (1967), who reviewed the effects of cortical lesions on language in children and concluded that left hemisphere damage in the first few years of life allowed substantial recovery of language processes, presumably because of some sort of cortical reorganization. By the mid-1970s, the Kennard doctrine was being challenged on the basis of studies using a variety of laboratory animals including monkeys, cats, and rats. For example, Patricia Goldman and her colleagues began to find that early cortical injury in monkeys was not always advantageous; the outcome depended on when behavior was assessed, the type of behavioral test employed, and the sex of the animal (e.g. Goldman, 1974). Indeed, even Kennard's experiments recently failed replication when redone using more modern behavioral methods (Passingham et al., 1983). Similarly, although the initial studies done by me and my colleagues on the effects of cortical lesions on infant rats supported the Kennard doctrine, we fell victim to the general principle of science that the more one studies something, the smaller the effects become (e.g. Kolb, 1987)!

Studies using children have also failed to support either Kennard's or Lenneberg's findings. Although there clearly is recovery of language after early left hemisphere lesions to the language areas and there is evidence that the language zones can shift either to the other hemisphere, if the damage is in the first two years of life (or within the left hemisphere, if the damage occurs between two and five years), children with early brain injuries suffer significant cognitive loss. For example, Woods (1980) found that the IQs of children with brain damage in the first year of life were well below average (WISC-R = ~85) as well as below those of children who suffered brain damage later in life. Similar results have been found by others, and it now appears that the period of severe IQ loss may extend as late as four to five years of age. In sum, there is little support for Kennard's original conclusions. Nonetheless, we have now identified a variety of factors that influence the outcome of early brain injury, and there is some evidence that a limited version of Kennard's principle may have some validity.

Behavioral Recovery in Rats

Over the past 15 years my colleagues and I have removed virtually every region of the rat's neocortex and have devised a neuropsychological test battery for the

Table 16.1 Behavioral assessment of the rat: a partial summary of features of behavior for examination

Measure	Specific feature
1 Appearance	Body weight, core temperature, eyes, feces, fur, genitals, muscle tone, pupils, responsiveness, saliva, teeth, toenails, vocalizations
2 Sensory and sensorimotor behavior	Response to stimuli of each sensory modality presented both in home cage and in novel place such as open field
3 Posture and immobility	Behavior when spontaneously immobile, immobile without posture or tone; tonic immobility or animal hypnosis; environmental influences on immobility
4 Movement	General activity, movement initiation, turning, climbing, walking, swimming, righting responses, limb movements in different activities such as reaching or bar-pressing, oral movements such as in licking or chewing, environmental influences on movement
5 Species-typical behaviors	All species-typical behaviors such as grooming, food hoarding, foraging, sleep, maternal or sexual behavior, play, and burying
6 Learning	Operant and respondent conditioning, and learning sets, especially including measures of spatial learning, avoidance learning, and memory (for details, see Whishaw et al., 1983)

rat that is conceptually similar to that used for people. In contrast to the "rat studies" of the 1930s to 1960s, which assumed that a rat should be used for just a single experiment, our test battery assumes that the best way in which to study behavior in any species is to administer multiple measures of many aspects of behavior including both learned and species-typical behaviors (e.g. Kolb, 1984; Whishaw et al., 1983), as summarized in table 16.1.

Contrasting models. To simplify the following discussion, I will focus on two of the preparations that we have used: (a) the hemidecorticate preparation and (b) the bilateral frontal preparation. In the hemidecorticate preparation, the entire neocortical mantle of one hemisphere is removed at different ages. This procedure is especially interesting in that it parallels the surgical procedure used in the treatment of children with major injuries restricted to one hemisphere, for which there is virtually no empirical basis in the primate literature (but see Villablanca et al., 1984, for parallel studies in kittens). In the bilateral frontal preparation, the frontal cortex that is analogous to the prefrontal and anterior cingulate region of primates is removed at different ages. We chose this preparation because the bulk of the work on infant lesions in primates has been done in animals with frontal lesions and because more is known about the frontal cortex of the rat than any other region of the rodent cortex.

We have varied the age at lesion and found the behavioral and anatomical effects to vary with age at insult (Kolb et al., 1987; Kolb, 1987; Kolb and Tomie, 1988). Such a finding would be expected given the different stages of development that would be interrupted (e.g. see figure 16.2). Thus, lesions on the first day of life, which we call postnatal day 1 (P1), perturb a brain in which cell migration is not yet complete and in which neuropil development has barely begun. In contrast, lesions on postnatal day 5 or 10 (P5, P10) affect a brain in which there is active development of neuropil. In human terms, the P10 lesions would be well into the first year, or even later.

Following adult rat hemidecortication there is a loss, or impairment, in a wide variety of behaviors. For example, there is a significant impairment in control of the limbs contralateral to the removal, a reduced ability to respond to stimuli contralateral to the lesion, and a deficit in most learning tasks requiring visuospatial guidance. Neonatal hemidecortication produces parallel deficits although the earliest operates (P1) were less impaired than adult operates. This advantage was not present in rats operated at P10. An example will illustrate.

Richard Morris (1981) devised an ingeneous test of spatial navigation in the rat in which an animal is placed in a large tank of water. The water is made opaque by a small amount of skimmed milk powder, and there is a hidden

Figure 16.3 Illustration of the Morris water task.
Note: Adapted from "Plasticity in the neocortex: mechanisms underlying recovery from early brain damage by B. Kolb and I. Q. Whishaw, 1989, *Progress in Neurobiology*, 32, p. 242. Copyright 1989 by Pergamon Press. Adapted by permission.

The rat's task is to locate a submerged, hidden platform by using visuospation cues available in the room.

platform that the rat must locate to escape from the water (see figure 16.3). Because rats are excellent swimmers, they need little training to learn the location of the platform on the basis of visual cues in the environment. Rats hemidecor-

A. Hemidecortication

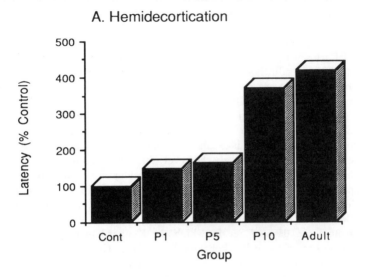

B. Bilateral Frontal

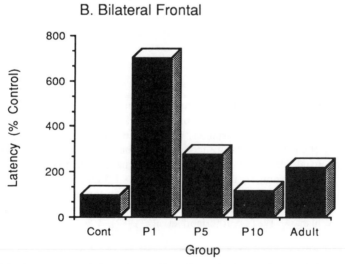

Figure 16.4 Comparison of the effects of hemidecortication or frontal lesions on performance on the Morris water task
Note: The data are graphed as a percentage of control performance. All animals were tested as adults. Con = control. Ad = adult. P1 = surgery on postnatal day 1. P5 = surgery on postnatal day 5. P10 = surgery on postnatal day 10.

ticated as adults are impaired at this task, however, even if preoperatively trained. Although P1 hemidecorticates are also impaired when tested as adults, they are significantly superior to rats with P10 or adult lesions (see figure 16.4). Parallel results are obtained from other measures, such as of motor abilities. Thus, for the hemidecorticate there is evidence that something like the Kennard principle is operating.

The effect of frontal lesions is different, however. Rats with bilateral frontal lesions at P1 are not only worse at most behavioral tasks than animals with lesions at P5, P10, P25, or adulthood, but they are also impaired on tasks at which the P10 and older animals are not. In short, they are much like those children with early lesions who have low IQs and poor recovery. The Morris water task again provides a good example. In contrast to rats with restricted lesions in other neocortical regions, rats with frontal lesions are slow to master this task. Rats with lesions at P1 are truly incapable of completing this task and never learn where the platform is. Surprisingly, however, rats with lesions at P10 are virtually indistinguishable from control animals. If the lesions are made later in life, the deficit appears, although we do not know the exact age at which it occurs. Nonetheless, in contrast to rats with hemidecortications, in which the earliest lesions allowed the best recovery, in the frontal preparation there is a window of time around ten days of age in which the Kennard principle holds. Similar results can be shown for other behavioral tests (e.g. Kolb, 1987).

The contrasting effects of hemidecortication and frontal lesions are important because they have provided a behavioral marker that we can use to look for an anatomical correlate. Thus, the task is to find an anatomical change that occurs in P1 hemidecorticates and P10 frontals and that correlates with the Kennard effect, and an absence of this change (or possibly the onset of other changes) that correlates with the poor behavioral performance of the P1 frontal animals. Before describing such a correlate, I will consider some factors that influence recovery.

Factors Influencing Recovery

It has long been known that in different people the severity of symptoms resulting from the same brain damage varies considerably. This is presumably because of differences in a number of variables, such as handedness, IQ, and personality. We have searched for modulating factors other than age that might influence the effect of neonatal (or adult) lesions in rats and have identified a large number, including sex, environmental experiences, size of brain lesion, nature of the behavioral test used, age at behavioral testing, and the level of endogenous cortical norepinephrine (e.g. Kolb and Elliott, 1987; Kolb and Sutherland, 1986; Kolb and Whishaw, 1981; Sutherland et al., 1982). I will briefly describe two examples.

Behavioral test. It is typical in neuropsychology to use tests of learned habits to assess behavior. When we began our studies, we also emphasized these measures, but as we expanded our tests, we were surprised to find little correspondence between the performance on tests of learned behaviors and measures of species-typical behavior such as hoarding or nest building. An example will serve to illustrate. John Pinel and his colleagues (e.g. Pinel and Treit, 1983) devised a test of natural avoidance behavior in rats in which a noxious stimulus, such as an electrified prod, was introduced into a rat's living

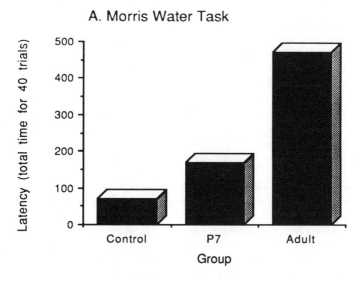

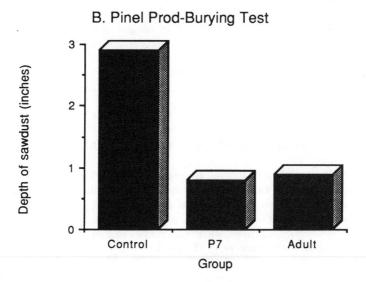

Figure 16.5 Comparison of the effects of frontal lesions at postoperative day 7 on the performance of the Morris water task and the Pinel burying task
Note: The same animals who showed sparing of function on the learned task showed no sparing on the species typical test.

quarters. Pinel found that rats, being curious, approached this stimulus but once they were "stung" by it, and recovered from the immediate startle of the experience, they began to bury the stimulus. This highly reliable behavior proved simple to quantify with measures such as the depth of sawdust piled upon the electric prod. When we used Pinel's test with adult rats with frontal lesions, we found that they failed to bury the prod at all, although they clearly learned that the prod was noxious because no animal was shocked a second time; they simply avoided it. When rats with P7 lesions were tested on this task, they too failed to bury the prod. In contrast to the adult operates, however, the P7 animals showed nearly normal performance on several tests of learned behaviors, including delayed response, active avoidance, and spatial reversal learning. Further study showed that the animals that were nearly normal on a variety of tests of learned habits were as impaired at a variety of species-typical tests as were animals with adult lesions (e.g. figure 16.5). Thus, it is evident that there is limited generality to the Kennard effect, even when it is present on some tests.

Environmental effects.   Because it is now well accepted that environmental stimulation has major effects upon the neocortex (e.g. Greenough, 1986), it is reasonable to predict that some environmental conditions may influence the extent to which lesions influence behavior. In particular, we predicted that if animals with early lesions were housed in complex environments in which they were given considerable opportunity to move about and to explore a frequently changing world, they would show better recovery than those who were raised in standard laboratory cages. This proved to be the case: in contrast to the large impairments in isolated rats, enriched animals with P1 or P5 frontal lesions were significantly better at nearly all behaviors that we assessed, and in some cases the P5 animals were nearly as proficient as control animals (Kolb and Elliott, 1987). For example, when tested in the Morris water task the animals with P5 lesions performed as well as our P10 animals. Furthermore, those with P1 lesions, although still seriously impaired, performed as well as adult operates. In sum, we again showed that the Kennard effect is flexible and is not simply a function of the time of surgery, but may also interact with other factors.

Anatomical Effects of Early Brain Injury

As we began to search for anatomical correlates of our behavioral findings, we were immediately struck by one observation: animals with early lesions had visibly smaller brains, even when lesion size was held constant (e.g. Kolb et al., 1983). This led us to measure the brain and its parts in order to find the cause of this small brain syndrome. Although we found many changes in the brain, we were most impressed with the changes in the thickness of the remaining cortex. This was intriguing because these changes correlated with behavior. For example, hemidecortication at P1 led to a thicker cortex than similar lesions at P10. The problem was to find the cause of the variability in cortical thickness. There seemed to be several obvious places to look.

First, others have shown that unilateral cortical lesions, including hemidecortication, lead to the development of abnormal connections. Perhaps lesions at different ages produce major changes in cortico-cortical or cortico-subcortical connections. An increase or decrease in the number of connections would not only affect the number of fibers in the cortex but also the number of synapses. This could be reflected in changes in cortical thickness. Second, perhaps the early lesions differentially affect cell death such that the cortex is thicker or thinner depending on the number of neurons present. Third, there could be a difference in the development of myelin in the cortex. Because myelin takes considerable space, this too could affect cortical thickness. Fourth, it is reasonable to suppose that the lesions affect neuropil development, independent of gross changes in connections. Thus, there could be significant changes in the extent of dendritic or axonal arborization, and these changes could contribute to cortical thickness. Finally, because it is known that strokes in humans lead to changes in vascular flow and in metabolic activity, it is reasonable to suppose that these too are changed by lesions in rats and may be changed differently at different ages.

We began by looking at the connections of the cortex. There has been a revolution in techniques of neural tracing in the past decade. When injected in very small quantities (e.g. 0.05 μl) into the brain, various compounds (amino acids, proteins, or dyes) are transported either to the cell body from the terminal field of an axon (retrograde transport) or to the terminal field from the cell body (anterograde transport). Using such techniques, it has proven possible to demonstrate numerous, previously unknown, connections in the brain. Thus, there is a new understanding of the principles of cortical connectivity, and function (e.g. Pandya and Yeterian, 1985). In addition, this new technology has provided an opportunity to look for changes in normal connectivity, changes that might underlie behavioral recovery. Although we were able to replicate many of the peculiarities in rewiring that others already had observed (e.g. Kolb and Whishaw, 1989), as well as finding many others, these changes could not account for the large changes in cortical thickness, especially in the frontal operates. The biggest changes in cortical connectivity were seen in new connections in the animals with the earliest lesions, but these animals also had the thinnest cortices. Furthermore, it seemed unlikely that factors that affected behavior, such as environment or sex, had any effect on the development of anomolous connections.

Our examination of cell numbers was equally unrevealing for there were simply no differences in the number of cells in a given column of cortical tissue. In retrospect, this finding might have been anticipated because there are no differences across mammalian species either, even though there are up to twofold differences in cortical thickness in different species (Rockel et al., 1980). Thus, if mice and humans have the same number of cells in cortices that are wildly different in thickness, we ought not be surprised when treatments fail to affect the numbers within a species. Furthermore, within a species the number of cells in different cortical areas is constant even though cortical thickness varies considerably. It appears as though there is a genetic signal for the number of cells in a column of cortical tissue. It is the neuropil that varies from area to area and species to species.

When we examined myelin, we did find abnormalities, but they were idiosyncratic from animal to animal and seemed unlikely to allow us to make reliable correlations with behavior. Finally, we began to study the neuropil, and it was here that we began to find correlations with our behavioral data.

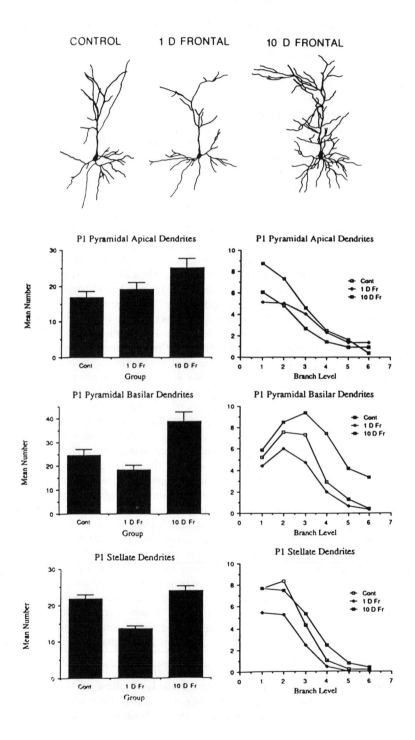

Dendritic arborization. The neuropil of cortical neurons is composed of the dendritic and axonal branches of neurons. The dendritic arbor can be visualized by using a Golgi stain in which a small percentage of cortical neurons and their dendrites and unmyelinated axons are stained. Although the reason for the incomplete staining of cortical neurons is still unknown, this property makes it possible to draw neurons and all their processes, and then to quantify them in a number of ways. This procedure is not adequate for axons, however, in part because only the unmyelinated portions are well stained and in part because axons are fine and difficult to identify. Axonal staining must be done using a different procedure. To date, we have studied only dendritic arbor, and so my discussion will be restricted to this.

Our major finding was that changes in the dendritic arbor correlate with changes in behavior. Thus, hemidecortication at P1 and frontal lesions at P10 both increase dendritic arbor in the intact cortex relative to littermate control animals (Kolb and Whishaw, 1989). In contrast, frontal lesions at P1 decrease dendritic arbor in the intact cortex (figure 16.6). In other words, in those instances in which we have evidence of at least a limited Kennard effect we have evidence of increased dendritic arbor. Similarly, in the case of worsened behavior, we have decreased dendritic arbor. Furthermore, we know from the work of others, as well as from our own preliminary observations, that dendritic arbor is affected by environmental conditions and by norepinephrine levels, and both factors influence the Kennard effect. As might be expected, however, there are some difficulties that must be considered.

First, the changes in dendritic arborization are not found everywhere in the cortex. Why not? Second, although the increase in dendritic arbor in the P10 frontals is equivalent to that in the P1 hemidecorticates, the cortical thickness is by no means comparable. The P10 frontals still have a significant thinning of the cortex relative to control animals. Why? Third, are the same factors influencing the changes in dendritic arbor in the hemidecorticate and frontal animals? Fourth, how do changes in dendritic arbor translate into changes in behavior? It is reasonable to argue that if there is an increase in dendritic space, there will be a corresponding increase in the number of synapses. Indeed, this appears to be true in other experimental conditions that affect dendritic arbor, such as environmental enrichment. If there are increased synapses, then we must wonder *what* is synapsing? In sum, we believe that we have made meaningful anatomical correlations of behavioral recovery, but we do not yet understand the mechanism. Future work will have to determine both the mechanism and the variables that affect it.

Figure 16.6 Effects of frontal lesions at P1 and P10
Note: The top panel shows examples of layer 11/111 pyramidal cells from the parietal cortex of a normal rat and a rat with a P1 frontal lesion in one hemisphere and a P10 frontal lesion in the other hemisphere.

The bottom panel shows the quantification of the differences in dendritic arbor of layer 11/111 pyramidal cells and stellate cells in parietal cortex. The apical dendrites are those that extend directly upward on the main dendritic shaft, whereas the basilar dendrites are those that originate from the cell body. The total number of branches is summarized on the left, and the distribution of the differences in different branches is summarized on the right.

Generalizations and Conclusions

It is now possible to reach several conclusions regarding the nature of brain plasticity and recovery from early brain injury. First, it is clear that early brain injury has different anatomical and behavioral effects depending on the nature of the injury, the age of the brain at injury, and the presence of various modulating factors such as the environment or the levels of endogenous trans-mitters or hormones. Second, it is difficult to make simple generalizations about whether functions are spared after early lesions. Different measures of behavior yield different results. Third, although the relationship between the anatomical and behavioral changes is complex, there appears to be a strong correlation between dendritic arborization and behavioral recovery.

The rat has proved to be a convenient and useful model for use in studying the effects of early cortical lesions. It is reasonable to wonder, however, if this work has any generalizability to humans. I believe it does. First, we have already seen in our comparison of two cases with right parietal injury that early lesions in humans can produce paradoxical behavioral effects. Of particular interest in this regard is the brain of Case S.S., the woman with the birth injury. Figure 16.7 illustrates her computerized tomography (CT) scan, and it is immediately evident that the entire right hemisphere is smaller than the left, even though the lesion is clearly restricted to the parietal cortex. This result is strikingly similar to what we have seen in our rats. Furthermore, because the right frontal lobe is normally somewhat larger than the left (Le May, 1982), the magnitude of the effect on the right hemisphere may even be larger than it appears. Second, we have had an opportunity to study a small sample of patients who had perinatal injuries to their frontal lobes and to compare these patients, as adults, to other adults who had frontal lobe injuries acquired in adulthood. The results are

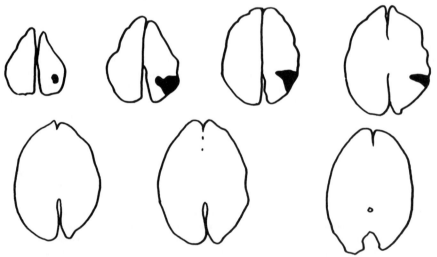

Figure 16.7 Drawing from a CT-scan of the brain of case S.S. who had a birth-related injury to the right posterior cortex

unequivocal: frontal-lobe injury in the first year leads to a lowered IQ and poor performance on all tests sensitive to frontal lobe injury in adulthood. Frontal-lobe injury in later childhood has a somewhat better outcome, but these people all have significant social difficulties. These results are reminiscent of two findings in our rats: (a) the earliest lesions produce the worst behavioral outcome; and (b) recovery is much better on tests of learned behaviors than on tests of species-typical behavior (Kolb and Whishaw, 1981).

To conclude, it is evident that cortical lesions produce different behavioral and anatomical effects depending on the age at which the brain is damaged. These observations have now provided us with a model to make predictions concerning the processes underlying restitution of function and to search for ways to control the effects of brain damage not only in our laboratory animals but also, someday, in humans. One of the major challenges in the future will be to learn how to control the anatomical changes so that we can gain control over the behavioral outcomes of early brain injury.

REFERENCES

Berry, M. J. (1980). Cellular differentiation: Development of dendritic arborizations under normal and experimentally altered conditions. *Neurosciences Research Program Bulletin*, 20, 451–461.

Cowan, W. M. (1979). The development of the brain. In *The brain* (pp. 56–69). San Francisco: Freeman.

Goldman, P. S. (1974). An alternative to developmental plasticity: Heterology of CNS structures in infants and adults. In D. G. Stein, J. J. Rosen, & N. Butters (eds), *Plasticity and recovery from brain damage* (pp. 149–174). New York: Academic Press.

Greenough, W. T. (1986). What's special about development? Thoughts on the bases of experience-sensitive synaptic plasticity. In W. T. Greenough & J. M. Juraska (eds), *Developmental neuropsychology* (pp. 387–408). New York: Academic Press.

Hicks, S. P., & D'Amato, C. J. (1968). Cell migrations to the isocortex of the rat. *Anatomical Record*, 160, 619–634.

Huttenlocher, P. R. (1979). Synaptic density in human frontal cortex–developmental changes and effects of ageing. *Brain Research*, 163, 195–205.

Kennard, M. A. (1936). Age and other factors in motor recovery from precentral lesions in monkeys. *Journal of Neurophysiology*, 1, 477–496.

Kolb, B. (1984). Functions of the frontal cortex of the rat: a comparative review. *Brain Research Reviews*, 8, 65–98.

Kolb, B. (1987). Recovery from early cortical damage in rats: I. Differential behavioral and anatomical effects of frontal lesions at different ages of neural maturation. *Behavioural Brain Research*, 25, 205–220.

Kolb, B., & Elliott, W. (1987). Recovery from early cortical lesions in rats: II. Effects of experience on anatomy and behavior following frontal lesions at 1 or 5 days of age. *Behavioural Brain Research*, 26, 47–56.

Kolb, B., Holmes, C., & Whishaw, I. Q. (1987). Recovery from early cortical lesions in rats: III. Neonatal removal of posterior parietal cortex has greater behavioral and anatomical effects than similar removals in adulthood. *Behavioural Brain Research*, 26, 119–137.

Kolb, B., & Sutherland, R. J. (1986). A critical period for noradrenergic modulation of sparing from neocortical parietal cortex damage in the rat. *Neuroscience Abstracts*, 12, 322.

Kolb, B., Sutherland, R. J., & Whishaw, I. Q. (1983). Abnormalities in cortical and subcortical morphology after neonatal neocortical lesions in rats. *Experimental Neurology*, 79, 223–244.

Kolb, B., & Tomie, J. (1988). Recovery from early cortical damage in rats: IV. Effects of hemidecortication at 1, 5, or 10 days of age on cerebral anatomy and behavior. *Behavioural Brain Research*, 28, 259–274.

Kolb, B., & Whishaw, I. Q. (1981). Neonatal frontal lesions in the rat: Sparing of learned but not species typical behavior in the presence of reduced brain weight and cortical thickness. *Journal of Comparative and Physiological Psychology*, 95, 863–879.

Kolb, B., & Whishaw, I. Q. (1985). *Fundamentals of human neuropsychology* (2nd ed.). New York: Freeman.

Kolb, B., & Whishaw, I. Q. (1989). Plasticity in the neocortex: Mechanisms underlying recovery from early brain damage. *Progress in Neurobiology*, 32, 235–276.

Le May, M. (1982). Morphological aspects of human brain asymmetry. *Trends in Neurosciences*, 5, 273–275.

Lenneberg, E. (1967). *Biological foundations of language*. New York: John Wiley.

Morris, R. G. M. (1981). Spatial localization does not require the presence of local cues. *Learning and Motivation*, 12, 239–260.

Pandya, D. N., & Yeterian, E. H. (1985). Architecture and connections of cortical association areas. In A. Peters & E. G. Jones (eds), *Cerebral cortex: Vol. 4. Association and auditory cortices* (pp. 3–61). New York: Plenum.

Passingham, R. E., Perry, V. H., & Wilkinson, F. (1983). The long-term effects of removal of sensorimotor cortex in infant and adult rhesus monkeys. *Brain*, 106, 675–705.

Pinel, J. P. J., & Treit, D. (1983). The conditioned burying paradigm and behavioral neuroscience. In T. E. Robinson (ed.), *Behavioral approaches to brain research* (pp. 212–234). New York: Oxford University Press.

Rakic, P. (1988). Specification of cerebral cortical areas. *Science*, 241, 170–176.

Rockel, A. J., Hiorns, R. W., & Powell, T. D. S. (1980). The basic uniformity in structure of the neocortex. *Brain*, 103, 221–244.

Sutherland, R. J., Kolb, B., Whishaw, I. Q., & Becker, J. (1982). Cortical noradrenaline depletion eliminates sparing of spatial learning after neonatal frontal cortex damage in the rat. *Neuroscience Letters*, 32, 125–130.

Villablanca, J. R., Burgess, J. W., & Sonnier, B. J. (1984). Neonatal cerebral hemispherectomy: A model for postlesion reorganization of the brain. In S. Finger & C. R. Almli (eds), *Recovery from brain damage* (Vol. 2, pp. 179–210). New York: Academic Press.

Werker, J. F., & Tees, R. C. (1984). Cross language speech perception: Evidence for perceptual reorganization during the first year of life. *Infant Behavior and Development*, 7, 49–63.

Whishaw, I. Q., Kolb, B., & Sutherland, R. J. (1983). Analysis of the behavior of the laboratory rat. In T. E. Robinson (ed.), *Behavioral approaches to brain research* (pp. 141–211). New York: Oxford University Press.

Woods, B. T. (1980). The restricted effects of right-hemisphere lesions after age one: Wechsler test data. *Neuropsychologia*, 18, 65–70.

Part V

Brain Plasticity and Cognition

Introduction

In the previous parts evidence regarding regressive events in brain development was reviewed (Chugani et al., Huttenlocher, Greenough et al.). In the first reading in this part, Changeux and Dehaene posit that these regressive events are the basis of plasticity in the brain. In support of this contention they present an elegant and wide ranging "selectionist" framework, which they attempt to apply to both neural and cognitive development. They begin with the premise that there are definable biological levels in the brain (e.g. the molecular level, the circuit level, and the metacircuit or cognitive level), and that the challenge is to understand how to relate these levels. It is also necessary to understand how the levels relate since the lower ones provide powerful constraints upon the higher ones. The gist of Changeux and Dehaene's argument is that, at an abstract level, the mechanisms of change at the neural and the cognitive level both involve "Darwinian" selection.

A "Darwinian" change has two components, the first being some mechanism for generating a range of possible options, and the second being a mechanism for selecting among the options. At the neural level the authors discuss evidence in support of the notion that the commonly found exuberance of connections during ontogeny occurs within a particular genetic envelope. That is, genes code for a particular exuberant patterns of connections, and this provides the range of options from which subsequent selection can take place. The selection of particular synapses, or groups of synapses, then takes place either as a result of spontaneous activity within neural circuitry, or as a direct result of sensory input. This viewpoint accounts for a number of previously puzzling phenomena, such as the fact that animals with identical genetical material may show some variations in their neural circuitry prior to any experience of the external world.

While there is less direct evidence in support of a similar mechanism of change at the cognitive level, the authors outline how such a mechanism might operate. The first step, the generation of variability, is achieved by the presence of "pre-representations" which are transient, dynamic, "privileged" spontaneous activity states in neural circuits. The second step, that of selection, is achieved by particular pre-representations "resonating" with particular sensory inputs. Clearly the temporal dimension of this process is of the order of tenths or hundredths of a second, rather than the weeks and months that might be involved in the analogous process at the neural level. However, both processes, like evolution itself, involve "Darwinian" selection.

The viewpoint put forward by Changeux and Dehaene stands in clear contrast to the classical view of cognitive processing as championed by Fodor, Pylyshyn and others. Rather than the challenge of understanding the mind being seen as to provide an adequate single level information processing account of what occurs between a sensory input and a motor output, the view put forward by Changeux and Dehaene insists on the crucial importance of considering information from neural circuitry, ontogeny, and phylogeny in order to understand the adult mind at a cognitive level. The study of developmental processes should not be seen merely as a subset of cognitive science. Rather, the authors argue, an understanding of the human mind at the cognitive level is one of the benefits that we will reap from an improved understanding of the mechanisms of change.

O'Leary (part IV) presented evidence that the cortex could, at least to some extent, be regarded as equipotential. If this is the case, we have to account for how particular areas, or hemispheres, of the cortex become specialized for processing particular functions in a fairly invariant way. While this is clearly an unresolved issue (and one taken up in the next part), the other two readings in this part begin to address it by focusing on the left hemisphere specialization for language processing. It is apparent from neuropsychological studies that the left cerebral hemisphere in man is specialized for language processing. How does this specialization normally come about, and how can we account for data implying that if damage to the left hemisphere occurs early enough, then the right can take over at least some of its language processing functions?

The paper by Bellugi, Poizner and Klima involves the detailed analysis of the acquisition of sign language, and its breakdown following brain injury. First, they present evidence that human capacity for language is not due to some privileged cognitive-auditory connection. Sign language appears to have many of the same formal properties that spoken language possesses, while clearly having a different surface form. Bellugi et al. use the difference in surface form between signed and spoken language to investigate the extent to which the left hemisphere might be predetermined for modality-free language processing. They do this by giving a battery of tests (associated with sign language, spatial cognition, and motor function) to deaf signers with focal brain injury.

Signers with left hemisphere lesions proved to be aphasic for sign language, but were relatively preserved in visuospatial tasks. In contrast, signers with right hemisphere lesions were not aphasic for sign language, but showed very clear visuospatial impairments. In this latter group, signing was fluent even in areas of space which they severely neglected outside language. This striking dissociation extends to signers with right hemisphere damage being able to converse about the contents of their room fluently, while showing gross spatial distortion in their description of its contents. This, and other evidence, leads the authors to propose that primary specialization of the left hemisphere rests not on the *form* of the signal, but rather on the linguistic *function* that it serves (see also McManus and Bryden, part VIII).

Given that the left hemisphere has a predisposition to support language, how are we to account for the ability of the right hemisphere to take over after damage early in life to the left? Neville begins by reviewing evidence concerning intersensory competition during development, and suggests that this form of plasticity may be mediated by the mechanisms proposed by Changeux (in this part): the elimination of exuberance following sensory input. Neville addresses these issues by the use of event-related potentials (ERPs). In these experiments, she looks at two aspects of intersensory competition. First, she provides evidence from visual and spatial tasks in deaf subjects that cortically mediated visual processing is different among subjects reared in the absence of auditory input. Specifically, the congenitally deaf seem more sensitive to events in the peripheral visual field than are hearing subjects. ERPs recorded over classical auditory regions, such as the temporal lobe, are two or three times larger for deaf than for hearing subjects following peripheral visual field stimulation.

The second line of evidence discussed by Neville concerns language and hemispheric specialization. ERP studies reveal greater activation of areas of the left hemisphere in normal hearing subjects during a word reading task. In contrast to this, deaf subjects did not show this lateralization. A group of subjects who had learned sign language as their first language, but who were not themselves deaf, showed the lateralization found in the normal hearing subjects, suggesting that it is not the acquisition of sign language *per se* that gives rise to this difference. Rather, the difference may index the activity of processes involved in either phonological or grammatical decoding. However, the lateralization effect was found in deaf signers when they were presented with signed gestures, indicating that the left hemisphere becomes specialized for language regardless of the modality involved, and may develop in association with the acquisition of competence in the grammar.

Neville concludes by suggesting that her data support the idea that, in the absence of auditory input to auditory and polysensory areas of cortex, visual afferents that are normally lost either stabilize or increase. This is clearly consistent with the general position put forward by Changeux and others. Changeux and Dehaene proposed that the stablization of afferents required neural activity. Consistent with this, Neville argues that the acquisition of competence in grammar is essential for the left hemisphere specialization in language. This specialization may not otherwise emerge.

FURTHER READING

Poizner, H., Klima, E. S. and Bellugi, U. (1987) *What the Hands Reveal about the Brain.* Cambridge, MA: MIT Press/Bradford books. (A detailed account of the Salk group studies in the neural basis of sign language.)

Selectionism
Changeux, J.-P. (1983) *L'homme neuronal.* Paris: Fayard. Translated (1985) as *Neuronal Man: the Biology of Mind.* New York: Pantheon Books. (An expanded account of Changeux's selectionist ideas.)
Ebbesson, S. O. E. (1984) Evolution and ontogeny of neural circuits. *Behavioral and Brain Sciences*, 7, 321–6. (A target article putting forward an alternative selectionist theory to Changeux's – see also the commentaries.)
Johnson, M. H. (1988) Parcellation and plasticity: implications for ontogeny. *Behavioral and Brain Sciences*, 11, 547–9. (A continuing commentary on the Ebbesson article that

brings out the contrasts between that theory and the ideas of Changeux – see also reply by Ebbesson.)

Edelman, G. M. (1987) *Neural Darwinism: the Theory of Neuronal Group Selection.* New York: Basic Books. (A wide ranging theory including some neural selectionist components.)

Crick, F. (1989) Neural Edelmanism. *Trends in Neurosciences,* 12, 240–8. (A critique of the Edelman theory.)

Piattelli-Palmarini, M. (1989) Evolution, selection and cognition: from "learning" to parameter setting in biology and the study of language. *Cognition,* 31, 1–44. (An attempt to contrast "selection" to theories that involve new learning, and to show that the former can be more usefully applied to many developmental issues.)

Johnson, M. H. and Karmiloff-Smith, A. (1992) Can neural selectionism be applied to cognitive development and its disorders? *New Ideas in Psychology,* 10, 35–46. (Compares and contrasts the various types of selectionist theory, and illustrates some direct and indirect ways that they can inform thinking about cognitive development.)

17

Neuronal Models of Cognitive Functions

JEAN-PIERRE CHANGEUX AND STANISLAS DEHAENE

Introduction

To think is to make selections
W. James (1909)

In the course of the past decade, the development of the cognitive sciences has resulted in many significant contributions, and, for many, the science of mental life constitutes a "special science" (Fodor, 1975). But still one must ask how the physical world supports mental processes. The radical proposal was made (Johnson-Laird, 1983) that "the physical nature [of the brain] places no constraints on the pattern of thought . . . any future themes of the mind [being] completely expressible within computational terms." The computer thus became the last metaphor, which "needs never be supplanted" (Johnson-Laird, 1983).

In parallel, the sciences of the nervous system have made considerable progress. Studies of single nerve cells and of their molecular components unambiguously rooted the elementary processes of neurons in physical chemistry, thereby introducing a wide spectrum of constraints, in particular upon their dynamics. Moreover, comparative anatomical investigations of higher vertebrate (see Goldman-Rakic, 1987; Rakic, 1988) and human (Geschwind and Galaburda, 1987; Luria, 1973) brain connectivity, biochemistry (e.g. Hökfelt et al., 1986) and physiology (e.g. Edelman et al., 1984) have yielded novel views about the complexity of adult brain organization and about its morphogenesis (Changeux, 1983a, b; Edelman, 1987; Geschwind and Galaburda, 1987). On such bases, the alternative radical program was proffered that, ultimately, the science of mental life will be reduced to neural sciences and the tenets of psychology will be eliminated (Churchland, 1986).

"Neuronal Models of Cognitive Functions" first appeared in *Cognition* 33 (1989), pp. 63–109, and is reprinted by permission of Elsevier Science Publishers B.V.

The aim of this paper is *not* to deal, once more, with this philosophical debate (Churchland, 1986; Fodor, 1975; see also Mehler et al., 1984; Stent, 1987), but rather to report recent theoretical and experimental work that actually lies at the frontier between cognitive science and neuroscience and that might ultimately bridge these two disciplines. It is hoped that such neurocognitive approaches will serve to create positive contacts between the two disciplines rather than to stress their differences. The real issue becomes the specification of the relationships between a given cognitive function and a given physical organization of the human brain. From an experimental point of view, our working hypothesis (rather than philosophical commitment) is that levels of organization exist within the brain at which a type-to-type physical identity (Fodor, 1975) might be demonstrated with cognitive processes. Yet, it should be stressed that we address this problem from the neurobiological point of view in an attempt to *reconstruct* (rather than reduce) a function from (rather than to) its neural components. This is, of course, not to deny the bridges that some psychologists have already thrown to the neural sciences in areas like language, neonate cognition, memory or neuropsychology. Our aim is to review recent contributions from the neurosciences to psychological concepts like innateness, learning, internal representations, and intentionality, and to offer relevant models that, in many cases, still remain speculative.

It is beyond the scope of this article to present an exhaustive review of data and models that fall within this approach. The discussion is limited to a few selected issues. First, the notion of level of organization and the relationship between structure and function in biological systems is introduced, together with evidence for the existence of multiple levels of functional organization within the human brain. A generalized Darwinian-like theory is proposed to describe the relationships between levels of organization and, in particular, the transition from one level to the next higher one. This empirically testable theory assumes that selection at a given level takes place in real time as a result of pressure from the immediately higher level, yielding a two-way dependency. Such Darwinian views are applied to the epigenesis of developing neuronal networks. The last two parts deal with the more conjectural neural bases of mental representations and "mental Darwinism," where the above-mentioned two-way dependency is assumed to take place at a higher level, between representations and the goals they subserve. In both instances, Darwinian views are extended to evolutive systems that are *not* based on variations of their genetic material itself, but of their phenotypic expression in developmental and psychological time-scales.

We have deliberately omitted from the discussion complex cognitive functions such as problem solving or language processing, especially those aspects of language interpretation that require access to very large stores of knowledge. Our feeling is that, at this stage, the neurobiological basis is too complex and the relevant data still too scarce for pertinent modelling in neuronal terms.

1   The Notion of Level of Organization in Biological Systems

The debate over the relative contributions of cognitive psychology, connectionist modelling and neurobiology to the understanding of the higher functions of the human brain hinges primarily upon a basic confusion about the levels of organization at which models of cognitive function and their neural implementations have been designed. The specification of such levels should precede any theoretical approach, and might even constitute the substance of a full theory. The cleavage of the world into pertinent units – from atoms, molecules and cells, up to, for example, syntactic structures and social classes – is neither trivial nor unequivocal. In highly evolved organisms, the relevant levels are expected to be multiple and intricate. Before dealing with the cognitive level(s), three basic questions must be answered:

1   What characterizes a given level of organization within a living organism?
2   To what extent are the levels dependent on each other?
3   Does a general mechanism account for the transition from one level to the next?

The definition of a given level relies upon the anatomical organization of its elementary components and upon characteristic properties or functions that are unique to this level. The programme of the life sciences is, of course, to specify functions but, most of all, to relate a given function to an appropriate anatomical organization of its components in a causal and reciprocal manner. A quick look at the history of biology shows that unravelling the actual "physical" implementation of a given function has always been at the origin of considerable progress in the understanding of biological functions (see Clarke and O'Malley, 1968, in the case of neurobiology). As a metaphor to illustrate this point, let us consider the well-known example of the catalytic activity of enzymes. Enzymes are proteins made up of linear chains of amino acids that spontaneously fold into three-dimensional edifices of rather large size – macromolecules. At the turn of the century, such a macromolecular organization of enzymes was not known, but their function as catalysts was already well recognized (see Debru, 1983, for a review). The laws of their action on substrates were described in great detail, and in still valid computational terms, by the Henri and Michaelis–Menten *algorithms*, which, to a first approximation, adequately fit the measured kinetics. The rapid progress of molecular biology, in particular the unravelling of the three-dimensional topology of folded polypeptide chains by X-ray diffraction methods at the atomic level, led to an explanation of the way their active sites function. If showed, for instance, that the fixed orientation in space of a few of the protein amino acid side chains suffices for matching to the shape of the substrate and, through chemical bonding, for activating the transformation of the enzyme – substrate complex, a feature that disappears upon unfolding of the protein. The function of the enzyme (which Jacques Monod (1970) already referred to as "cognitive") is thus directly bound to the macromolecular level of organization and may even be viewed as characteristic of this level. The implementation of the function in terms of chemical bonds, including their nature, strength and topology, would never have been predicted from the algorithmic description of the active site function. Yet, this new understanding did not lead to an abandonment of the Michaelis–Menten algorithm, but rather raised many novel functional questions at a more microscopic level.

Another example is that of the material bases of inheritance. Mendel's observations on the heredity of flower colour in peas, and its description in simple algorithmic terms which constitute the Mendelian laws, may, at a glance, appear sufficient from a functional point of view. Yet, the identification of chromosomes and (subsequently) DNA as the physical basis of heredity opened many new avenues of research without, at any moment, contradicting the Mendelian algorithm.

2   The Multiple Levels of Functional Organization within the Nervous System

The notion of organization and the relationship between physical structure (architecture) and function can legitimately be extended to the nervous system (Changeux, 1983b; Chomsky, 1979; Jackson, 1932). However, to what extent can the entire nervous system be viewed as one such level, above which would stand both a functional algorithmic level and a formal level of abstract grammatical rules (Marr 1982)? Should we follow the classical view (Fodor and Pylyshyn, 1988), which distinguishes among physical, syntactic and knowledge (semantic) "levels," and further assumes that the "functional organization of the nervous system crosscuts its neurological organization" (Fodor, 1975)? Or even, to be more schematic, may we say that the nervous system is the mechanism, the hardware of the machine, above which would stand autonomously the program with its semantic and syntactic levels? We deliberately reject such a view, for within the nervous system, several distinct levels of organization can be defined. Distinct levels of cognitive function relate to these different levels of physical organization, thus shattering the simple-minded (and actually reductionistic) behaviour/algorithm/hardware metaphor for the relationship between psychology and neural science.

The first level, the architecture of which can be related to functional characteristics of the nervous system, is the "*cellular level*," because of the unique ability of nerve cells to make topologically defined networks through their axonal and dendritic branches and their synaptic contacts. This physical architecture is described by the topology of the cell arborization and its synaptic connections. Its function includes both the patterns of electrical and chemical signals produced by the cell (Prince and Huguenard, 1988) and the actions of these signals on effector cells, which lead to either overt behaviour or a covert process that might contribute to further operations within the system. At the single-cell level, the ability of the neuron to generate electrical impulses (or modulate its spontaneous firing) as a function of the inputs it receives (and several other functions it displays) can be expressed in a global algorithmic form, and implemented in terms of the molecular properties of its synaptic and cell membrane components. Yet, in this instance already, the algorithmic level cannot be viewed simply as autonomous or distinct from the physical one. It would, of course, be absurd to infer from such cellular and molecular data the nature of the architecture of cognitive functions. Yet, nerve cells are the building blocks of cognitive architectures, and as such they exert severe constraints on the coding of mental representations, on the computations accessible to these representations, and on the modalities of storage and retrieval. After all, the rates of propagation of impulses in nerves and across synapses impose inescapable limits on the speed of higher computations; storage of memory traces has to be considered in terms of changes of molecular properties of nerve cells and synapses; and the production of internal thought processes independently of outside world stimulation relies upon the existence of a spontaneous self-sustained and organized firing of nerve cells (see section 6).

Another level of organization, referred to as the *"circuit level,"* is reached with the nervous system of invertebrates (sea-slugs like *Aplysia* or *Hermissenda*, insects like *Drosophila* and worms like *Hirudo*). Circuits are made up of thousands (or even millions) of nerve cells organized in well-defined ganglia, with each (or nearly each) cell possessing a well-defined individual connectivity and function within the organism. Satisfactory attempts have been made to account for simple behaviours strictly on the basis of the anatomy of small circuits and the electrical and chemical activity displayed by the circuit (Alkon et al., 1987; Grillner, 1975; Grillner et al., 1987; Kandel et al., 1983; Kleinfeld and Sompolinsky, 1987; Stent et al., 1978). The architecture of the most advanced connectionist models, which aim at imitating human-like brains, are no more complex than these rather primitive nervous systems, and often remain inferior in complexity even in the most elaborate attempts.

The mutual relations of individual neural circuits define another level of organization. Thus, for example, classical physiology has emphasized the roles of the spinal cord and brainstem in the mediation of reflexes and various other sensorimotor operations. A vast amount of anatomical, physiological and neuro-psychological data, moreover, has led to a closer understanding of the participation of various cortical and other brain domains in sensory perception, motor control, language comprehension and production, memory, etc. (Geschwind and Galaburda, 1987; Kolb and Wishaw, 1980; Luria, 1973). The number of these specialized domains appears much larger than initially suspected (Rakic and Singer, 1988): in the primate brain, for instance, there are about a dozen representations of the visual world and half a dozen each of auditory and somatic representations. Many of these are interdigitated, and yet, each fragment displays a distinct characteristic, thus "constructing categories in an unlabeled world" (Zeki, 1988).

The cognitive level lies within reach of this "meta-circuit" level, since the parsing of psychological tasks into elementary operations correlates well with a decomposition of the brain into separate areas (Posner et al., 1988). However, even these ultimate cognitive functions might themselves be cleaved into distinct faculties. Seventeenth-and eighteenth-century philosophers, Kant in particular, distinguished *"reason"* as the "faculty which contains the principles by which we know things absolutely *a priori"* from *"intendment"* which, from the perceived elements, produces concepts and evaluates them. In a simplified manner, the intendment would make the synthesis of sensible elements into concepts, while pure reason would make computations upon the concepts produced by the intendment. Such distinction of different levels of abstraction bears a relation to recent concepts from experimental psychology (see Kihlstrom, 1987). According-ly, intendment processes would be mostly modular, automatic and unconscious, although attention may regulate their inputs and their access to memory stores, while in pure reason the processing would essentially (though not exclusively) be conscious, non-modular and require attention. What then are the brain structures, if any, for intendment and reasoning?

In attempting to build bridges across disciplines, it may be useful to relate the intendment/reason distinction with a distinction reached through a different approach in the field of artificial intelligence. Newell (1982) raised questions of levels in computers, of their autonomy and reducibility to lower levels, questions that are indeed familiar to neuroscientists. Thus, he proposed that immediately above the symbol (program) level of standard computers stands a knowledge level, where the agent processes its own knowledge to determine the actions to take. The law governing behaviour is the principle of rationality: actions are selected to attain the agent's goal. "If an agent has the knowledge that one of its actions will lead to one of its goals it will select that action" (4.2, p. 17). According to Newell, the "knowledge level is exactly the level that abstracts away from symbolic processes" (4.3, p. 23), a conclusion not far from Kant's definition of reason. Moreover, and this is a crucial point, the actions may add knowledge to the already existing body of knowledge. As mentioned by Simon (1969) in the case of economic agents, "the adjustment to its outer environment (its substantive rationality) is conditioned by its ability to *discover* an appropriate adaptive behaviour (its procedural rationality)." In other words, in selecting actions to achieve a goal, the agent not only relies upon judgements but, in situations of uncertainty, it computes expectations and possible scenarios of complex interactions.

A crucial issue then becomes the specification of the neural architectures that characterize the knowledge level thus defined. Yet, the feasibility of this attempt is under debate. For instance, Pylyshyn (1985) has argued, on the basis of Newell's (1982) views, that one should distinguish knowledge-based from mechanism-based explanations. We quote him: "the mechanism is part of the process that itself is not knowledge dependent (it is cognitively impenetrable) hence it does not change according to rational principles based upon decisions, inferences, and the like, but on other sorts of principles, ones that depend on intrinsic properties, which are presumably governed by biological laws" (p. 408). "Ignoring the physics and biology may even be necessary because the categories over which the system's behaviour is regular may include such things as the meaning of certain signals and because the entire equivalence class of signals having the same meaning need not have a description that is finitely statable in a physical vocabulary" (p. 405). Our view is that even if the distinction between cognitively penetrable and the impenetrable processes may, to some extent and within a limited time-scale, be justified, the separation between the cognitively penetrable and the "biological or biochemical properties" of organisms is not valid. In fact, as will become clear in the following paragraphs, there is hardly any structure in the brain which does not incorporate exterior knowledge during its epigenesis and functioning. We realize that there is more to Pylyshyn's cognitive penetrability than the simple notion of knowledge dependence. For instance, Pylyshyn's mechanistic level, as far as we understand it, comprises the processes that do not vary following a change in conscious beliefs and intentions of an agent. However, the usefulness of this notion is questionable on the grounds that: (1) this particular mechanistic level is not identical to the level of biological laws, since there may be encapsulated psychological processes that cannot be accessed and modified intentionally; (2) its definition depends on the time-scale chosen, since conscious, attention-demanding processes may become automatic and impenetrable in the course of learning (see Baddeley, 1976, 1986); and (3) its definition puts exceptional emphasis on the notions of consciousness and belief, the scientific status of which is now questioned on philosophical as well as neuropsychological grounds.

It is thus part of a concrete scientific programme to describe which (and to what extent) biological structures are penetrable by knowledge at a given level. This programme is necessary if we are to have a biology of goal, knowledge and rational decisions, as well as to know the neural architectures underlying the faculty of reason.

If such a research programme looks plausible, it is far from being achieved (or even undertaken) in neuroscience for many reasons. First of all, in humans, processes as elementary as visual perception, which take place at the intendment level, are deeply impregnated by knowledge from the earliest stages of development (see sections 4 and 5). Similarly, since storage seems to rely more on semantic than on perceptual cues (Baddeley, 1976, 1986, 1988), it seems almost impossible to analyse the function of long-term memory stores without considering what information they encode. Moreover, from both the phylogenetic and embryological points of view, the faculties for reasoning and for concept formation, among others, cannot be assigned to unique brain domains or areas and, of course, the operations taking place at any level are expected to mobilize important populations of nerve cells with a distributed topology which will *a priori* be difficult to map.

Nevertheless, one may theorize, for example, that the frontal areas of the cortex contribute to the neural architectures of reason (for reviews see Struss and Benson, 1986; Goldman-Rakic, 1987). Among the many observations supporting this view is the fact that the differential expansion of prefrontal cortical areas from the lowest mammals up to man parallels the development of cognition. Neuropsychological observations of Lhermitte (1983) and Shallice (1982), among others, also relate frontal cortex to high-level cognitive processes. Patients with frontal lobe lesions, for example, display an interesting "utilization" behaviour. They grasp and utilize any object presented to them as if they had become dependent upon sensory stimulation. They also fail in tests such as the "Tower of London," which require planning strategies and control of the execution. Patients no longer employ a general mode of regulation that lets them plan their interactions with the environment, makes them aware of novel situations or errors in the executions of their own strategies, and allows them to generate new hypotheses. Although few studies have investigated the neuronal architecture underlying these functions, brain lesions indicate a dissociation of two levels *within* cognition, which closely approximate the levels of reason and intendment discussed previously.

3 The Transition between Levels of Organization: Generalized Variation–Selection (Darwinian) Scheme

A given function (including a cognitive one) may be assigned to a given level of organization and, in our view, can in no way be considered to be *autonomous*. Functions obviously obey the laws of the underlying level but also display, importantly, clear-cut dependence on higher levels. Coming back to our favourite metaphor, the function of the enzyme active site is determined by the amino acid sequence of the protein; yet the amino acid sequence is itself the product of a long genetic evolution, which ultimately rested upon survival (stabilization) rules that constrained the structure of the macromolecule. The macromolecular state, which determines the enzyme catalytic function, is rooted, by its structure, in the underlying levels of physics and chemistry, but also contributes, by its function at a higher level, to the metabolism of the cell and thus to its own existence.

The same interdependence holds for the various levels of neurofunctional organization. If, for instance, the function of the reflex arc can be viewed as strictly determined by a well-defined spinal cord neuronal circuit, its detailed organization is such that higher brain centres may control its actualization within a coordinated motor act. At any level of the nervous system, multiple feedback loops are known to create re-entrant (Edelman and Mountcastle, 1978) mechanisms and to make possible higher-order regulations between the levels.

Our view is that the dual dependence between any two levels must be framed in an evolutionary perspective (see Changeux, 1983b; Delbrück, 1986; Edelman, 1987) and is governed by a generalized variation–selection (Darwinian) scheme. Accordingly, a minimum of two distinct components is required: a generator and a test. "The task of the generator is to produce variety, new forms that have not existed previously, whereas the the task of the test is to cut out the newly generated forms so that only those that are well fitted to the environment will survive" (Simon, 1969; p. 52). The initial diversity may arise from combinatorial mechanisms that produce organizations that are novel (or rare) for the considered level and become transitional forms, bridging it to the next higher level. The rules of stabilization (survival) are governed by the function associated with the novel form, thus creating feedback stabilization loops of function upon structure.

Such a scheme is classical in the case of the evolution of species and is evidenced in the development of the immune response, where diversity arises from genomic reorganization and gene expression, and the test arises from the survival of the fittest (including matching to the antigen). The scheme may also account for the transition from cellular to multicellular organisms and for the general morphogenesis of the brain. Our view, in addition, (Changeux & Danchin, 1974, 1976; Changeux et all., 1973, 1984; Edelman, 1978, 1985, 1987; Jerne, 1967; Young, 1973; see also Ramon y Cajal, 1909; Taine, 1870; references in Heidmann et al., 1984), is that the interaction between the nervous system and the outside world during the course of postnatal development through adulthood, during which the acquisition of some of its highest abilities, including language and reasoning, occur (see section 5), also follows an analogous Darwinian scheme. Yet, such evolution is expected to take place *within* the brain without any necessary change in the genetic material (at variance with the view of Piaget, 1979, or Wilson, 1975), and inside of short time-scales: days or months in the case of embryonic and early postnatal development and tens of seconds in the case of the processing and reorganization of mental representations. At each level, the generator of variety and the test must be specified, and the time-scale of the evolution must be defined. Moreover, such time-scales are short enough (compared to those spanning the evolution of species) to render the theory experimentally testable.

The justification of such views will constitute the matter of the subsequent sections. In essence the brain will be considered constantly and internally to generate varieties of hypotheses and to test them upon the outside world, instead of having the environment impose (instruct) solutions directly upon the internal structure of the brain (see Changeux, 1983b). The view of the brain as a hardware construct, knowledge-independent, that would be programmed by a computationally autonomous, cognitively penetrable mind has, thus, to be reconsidered for the following reasons:

1 There exists, within the brain, multiple levels of functional organization associated with distinct neural architectures (see section 2).
2 Several of these neurofunctional levels are cognitively penetrable at some stage of development, and these multiple levels are heavily interconnected via feedback loops, or re-entrant mechanisms, that make possible high-order regulations *between levels* (further examples of such interactions appear below).
3 The information-processing/input–output scheme has to be abandoned in favour of an internal "generator of variations" continuously anticipating and testing the outside world with reference to its own invariant representation of the world.

4 The Ontogenesis of Neural Form

A basic principle of cognition is the recognition, storage and internal production of forms in space (patterns) or time (melodies). The Gestalt psychologists have emphasized that this faculty relies on the existence of physiological forms within the organism that display some physical relationship with the psychological ones. Without entering into a debate on the exact nature of this relationship – whether it is insomorphic or not – it is evident that the brain must be viewed as a highly organized system of intertwined architectures whose forms result from pre- and postanal development. Moreover, as discussed in the preceding section, several distinct levels of functional organization exist within the brain and develop according to defined biological constraints during both phylo-and ontogenesis. Understanding the formation of neural forms and their hierarchical organizations, for example those involved in the architectures of reason, concept formation or pattern recognition, becomes a fundamental step in the understanding of cognition.

Preformation and epigenesis. The problem of the origin of animal form has been at the centre of a long controversy from classical times to the present. According to the extreme *performationist* view, ontogenesis proceeded strictly as the enlargement of forms that were thought to be already present in the egg (Swammerdam) or in the spermatozoon (Van Leeuwenhoek). Related views are still found in the theory of morphological archetypes advocated by D'Arcy-Thompson (1917), and they have recently been revived by Thom (1980). Accordingly, such archetypes, mathematically formalized in a set of abstract rules, would impose global morphological constraints on, or even direct the ontogenesis of, the adult form. Also, contemporary molecular biologists frequently refer to a DNA-encoded genetic program according to which development would proceed in a strictly autonomous manner (see Stent, 1981, for a criticism of the concept of genetic program). Finally, some contemporary linguists and psychologists posit the innateness of knowledge (or at least of a certain body of information) (Chomsky, 1965) or of mental faculties or structures (Fodor, 1983), although without referring to the actual neural bases of their development. According to such extreme Cartesian views, the internal innate structures are rich and diverse, and their interaction with the environment, although capable of "setting parameters," does not create new order.

The alternative attitude, illustrated by epigenesis, contrasts with radical pre-formationism by postulating a progressive increase of embryonic complexity (rather than simple enlargement by post-generation and after-production). Such epigenetic conceptualization of the development of animal forms shows analogies in psychology to the associationist attitude (Helmholtz), or mental atomism, which assumes, for instance, that perception relies upon the analysis of external objects into elements and upon their synthesis through association by continuity in time and repetition. According to such views, in their most extreme formulation, mental forms would build up strictly from experience, starting from an initial empty state or *tabula rasa*.

The developmental genetics of brain forms. Both the extreme preformationist attitude and the strict epigenetic views are incompatible with current knowledge about development. The contribution of strictly innate, DNA-encoded mechanisms to the development of animal forms is supported by a large body of experimental evidence. Yet, the genes involved are not expressed all at once, whether in the egg or in the early embryo, as postulated by the extreme preformationist view. Rather, they are activated (or blocked) throughout embryogenesis and postnatal development in a sequential and intricate manner and according to well-defined patterns.

The straightforward comparison of the genetic endowment of the organism with the complexity of the adult brain produces, however, two *apparent* paradoxes (Changeux, 1983a, b). The total amount of DNA present in the fertilized egg is limited to a maximum of 2 million average-sized genes which, because a large number of them consist of non coding sequences, might in fact be in the range of 100 000 genes. There is thus striking parsimony of genetic information available to code for brain complexity. The second paradox is raised by the evolution of the global amount of DNA in mammals, which appears rather stable from primitive species such as rodents up to humans, whereas the functional organization of the brain becomes increasingly complex. There thus exists remarkable non linearity between the evolution of total DNA content and that of brain anatomy.

The analysis of the early steps of embryonic development by the methods of molecular genetics primarily in *Drosophila* (see Akam, 1987; Doe et al., 1988; Gehring, 1985; Nüsslein-Volhard et al., 1987) and in the mouse (see Johnson et al., 1984) begins to resolve these paradoxes. For instance, in *Drosophila*, a variety of gene mutations have been identified that affect early embryonic development. The genes involved have been grouped into three main categories. The first controls the Cartesian coordinates of the embryo; the second controls the segmentation of the body; and the third, called homeotic, specifies the identity of the body segments in well-defined territories of the egg and embryo during oogenesis and embryonic development, respectively, both in a hierarchical and parallel manner, and with cross-regulatory interactions. In the course of expression, the symmetry properties of the developing oocyte or embryo change: symmetry breakings (Turing, 1952) take place. In *Drosophila* the expression of the genes that specify the Cartesian coordinates of the embryo occurs in the mother's ovary through the asymmetric diffusion of morphogens from specialized ovary cells into the egg during the latter's maturation. In the mouse (and most likely in humans), the fertilized egg and early embryo (until the eight-cell stage) appear entirely isotropic. All symmetry breakings take place within the embryo after fertilization. Turing (1952) and followers (Meinhardt and Gierer, 1974) have demonstrated mathematically that such symmetry breakings may be created by random fluctuations that generate defined and reproducible patterns within an initially homogeneous system of morphogens reacting together and diffusing throughout the organism. A spatio-temporal network of gene interactions, with convergence, divergence and re-utilization of regulatory signals, thus governs development of the body plan and, as we shall see, governs the plan of the brain.

Several segmentation and homeotic genes are expressed in the nervous system (Awgulewitsch et al., 1986) and are most likely members of a larger but still unidentified population of genes directly concerned with brain morphogenesis, the parsing of the brain into definite centres and areas and even into asymmetric hemispheres. Their combinatorial expression during development thus offers a first answer to the above-mentioned paradox of gene parsimony. Moreover, a quantitative variation in the expression of a few genes at early stages of development may suffice to account for the increase (or decrease) of surface (or volume) of some brain regions such as the cerebral cortex (or the olfactory bulb) in higher mammals (see Changeux, 1983b), thereby providing an explanation for the paradox of nonlinear evolution between the complexity of the genome and that of the organization of the nervous system. For instance, since the total number of neurons in the thickness of cerebral cortex appears uniform throughout vertebrate species (Rockwell et al., 1980), its surface area has been the primary target of evolutive changes (Rakic, 1988). One may then speculate that the extremely fast expansion of the frontal lobe surface that, in part, led to the human brain resulted from the prolonged action of some of these genes in the anterior part of the brain (see Changeux, 1983b). The genomic evolution that underlies this process has been extensively discussed in terms of (classical and non-classical) Darwinian mechanisms (Mayr, 1963).

Later in the course of the cellular organization of the nervous system by the mechanism just mentioned, synaptic connections begin to form. In the higher vertebrates, large ensembles of cells are found to project into other large ensembles of cells, and maps develop. The best-known maps correspond to the projections of sensory organs, but maps also exist that represent projections from one brain region to another. In the course of such transformations symmetry breaking does not, in general, take place, but regular, geometrical deformations frequently occur. They can be mathematically analysed in terms of the theory of transformations (D'Arcy-Thompson, 1917). The actual mechanisms involved in the establishment of ordered connections of neural maps are still largely unknown. In addition to long-range tropism by chemical substances, the conservation of topological relationships between growing axons and a temporal coding by differential outgrowth of nerve fibres have been invoked. Processes of cell surface recognition might also be seminal in these transformations (Edelman, 1985, 1987).

In conclusion, the main forms of brain architecture develop by principles that can be summarized as follows:

1   The basic operations of symmetry breaking and transformation that occur during the genesis of the geometric outlines and patterns of central nervous system organization are determined by an ensemble of rules. These rules are genetically coded as defined physicochemical organizations of the brain. The notion of *tabula rasa* does not hold for the developing brain.

2   The expression of the genes involved in the determination of brain forms follows well-determined spatio-temporal patterns that lead to the progressive establishment of the adult organization. As a consequence, relationships become established between the progressively laid-down forms, with built-in hierarchies, parallelisms and re-entries.

5   Epigenesis of Neuronal Networks by Active Selection of Synapses

5.1   Biological Premises

If our view of the development of neural forms accounts for species-specific traits of brain organization and function, it does not suffice for a more detailed description of neural anatomy. Indeed, a significant variability of the phenotype of the nervous system is apparent at several levels of its organization. Examination by electron microscopy of identified neurons from genetically identical (isogenic) individuals reveals minor but significant variability. In the small invertebrate *Daphnia magna*, the number of cells is fixed and the main categories of contacts (between optic sensory cells and optic ganglion neurons) are preserved from one isogenic individual to another. Yet, the exact number of synapses and the precise form of the axonal branches varies between pairs of identical twins (Macagno et al., 1973). Similar findings have been reported in the case of the Müller cells of a parthenogenetic fish (Levinthal et al., 1976) and thus they are not restricted to invertebrates. A fluctuation in the details of the connectivity exists. In mammals, the variation also affects the number of neurons. For instance, in the case of the cerebellum of the mouse, the division and migration of Purkinje cells in consanguineous strains are not subject to as rigorous and precise a determinism as the laying down of neurons in invertebrates (Oster-Granite and Gearhart, 1981; Goldowitz and Mullen, 1982). The variability becomes microscopic and may even affect the chemistry (such as the pattern of transmitters and coexisting messengers synthesized (Hökfelt et al., 1986) of entire populations of neurons. In humans, most of the information available on anatomy derives from individuals taken from genetically heterogeneous populations. Nevertheless, the substantial variability noticed in the topology of sites specialized for such language functions as naming, syntax or short-term memory, as identified by electrical stimulation mapping (Ojemann, 1983), cannot be accounted for solely by this heterogeneity.

In the extreme case where the left hemisphere has been ablated in infants, the right hemisphere systematically takes over the language functions (Geschwind and Galaburda, 1984; Nass et al., 1985, 1989). More subtle is the topological distinction of sites, the stimulation of which causes different errors in the two languages spoken by bilingual subjects (Ojemann, 1983), a situation which, of course, relies upon reorganization by learning. Finally, in monkeys, transection of peripheral sensory nerves or their functional alternation causes striking reorganization of the topology of the relevant sensory cortical maps (Merzenich, 1987; Edelman, 1987). Thus, an important degree of variation of neural phenotype is manifest at several levels of organization of the nervous system, and this variability seems to increase with the complexity of the brain.

It may be useful to introduce the notion of a *genetic envelope* to delimit invariant characteristics from those that show some phenotypic variance (Changeux, 1983a). Thus, as animals evolve from primitive mammals to humans, the genetic envelope opens to more and more variability. This variability in the organization of the adult brain reflects characteristic features of its developmental history, in particular the way neural networks become interconnected. The growth cones of the dendrite and axon tip navigate by trial and error through the developing neural tissue toward their targets and thus contribute to the variability of the adult neuronal network. Another source of variability resides in recognition of, and adhesion to, the target cells. Little evidence exists for a point-to-point pre-addressing between individual neurons by specific chemical cues (the chemo-affinity hypothesis), except perhaps in small invertebrates (Goodman et al., 1985). On the contrary, the emerging view is that growing nerve endings identify ensembles of target cells further grouped into wider categories by a few inter-cellular adhesion molecules (N-CAM, for instance; Edelman, 1985, 1987). Discrimination between cell categories would emerge from the temporal sequence of the expression of such adhesion molecules on the surface of the cells, from their differential topological distribution in regular patterns within populations of cells, and from their graded combination of the surface of cells. In any case, within a given cell category, a limited randomness and even some overlap between growing nerve fibres and individual target neurons from a given category are expected to occur.

At a critical stage (or sensitive period) of development, the axonal and dendritic trees branch and spread exuberantly. There is redundancy but also maximal diversity in the connections of the network. Yet, as mentioned, this transient fluctuation of the growing connections remains bounded within stringent limits of the genetic envelope. These include, in addition to the overall plan of the nervous system, the rules that command the behaviour of growing tips of nerves (the growth cones) regarding recognition among cell categories and the formation and evolution of synapses. Such limited fuzziness of the network makes a final tuning of the connectivity necessary, but also offers the opportunity for an adaptive shaping.

The classical information-processing scheme of the nervous system is based on the notion that its internal states of activity directly result from interactions with the outside world. In fact, from very early on, there is intense spontaneous electrical and chemical activity within the nervous system of the embryo and of the fetus (Hamburger, 1970). Chick embryos move within the egg as early as two and a half days of incubation. These spontaneous movements are blocked by curare and coincide with electrical activity of the same frequency arising in spinal cord neurons. In the human, these movements start during the eighth week of embryonic development and continue and diversify during the following months. Such spontaneous activity develops in a strictly endogenous manner and results from molecular oscillators consisting of slow and fast ionic channels (Berridge and Rapp, 1979). The cost of this activity in terms of structural genes is very small and bears no relation to its enormous potential for interaction and combination, which results from the activity's eventual contribution to the epigenesis of neuronal synaptic networks.

5.2 A Model for Active Selection of Synapses

The proposed theory (Changeux and Danchin, 1976; Changeux et al., 1973, 1984; also see Edelman, 1987) deals with the stability of the connections. It postulates that the selection of connections by the activity of the developing network (endogenous, or evoked, or both) contributes to the final establishment of the adult organization. Accordingly, the generator of internal diversity would not be based upon genetically determined recombinations, as in the case for the evolution of species or antibody synthesis, but rather stems from multiple neural configurations with connectivities drawn up during the epigenetic formation of a network at the stage(s) of transient redundancy (figure 17.1).

According to our theory, during the sensitive period of maximal connectivity, any given excitatory or inhibitory synapse exists in three states: labile, stable and degenerate. Nerve impulses can be transmitted only in the labile and stable states. A given synapse may undergo transitions from labile to stable states (stabilization), from labile to degenerate states (regression), and from stable to labile states (labilization). The ontogenetic evolution of each synaptic contact is governed by the combined signals received by the cell on which it terminates. The activity of the postsynaptic cell within a given time-window regulates the stability of the synapse in a retrograde manner (Changeux et al., 1973). As a consequence, a given afferent message will cause the long-term stabilization of a matching set of synapses from the maximally connected neuronal network, while the others will regress.

Detailed models of molecular mechanisms possibly involved in this activity-dependent synapse selection have been proposed. Some deal with the topology of the postsynaptic clusters of receptors (Changeux et al., 1981), whereas others deal with the selection of multiple afferent nerve endings (Edelman, 1987; Fraser, 1985; Gouzé et al., 1983). In both instances, the competition takes place for a limited component: in the first case, the receptor for a neurotransmitter; and, in the second, a diffusible growth (or stability) factor produced by the postsynaptic cell and taken up by the nerve ending in a differential manner by active and inactive nerve endings. In both cases, the firing of the postsynaptic cell is assumed to limit the component by repressing its biosynthesis. In addition, rules of release (by the postsynaptic cell) and/or uptake (by the presynaptic nerve endings) based upon the timing relationships between pre- and postsynaptic activity have to be specified in order to yield stable morphogenesis (Kerszberg et al., in preparation).

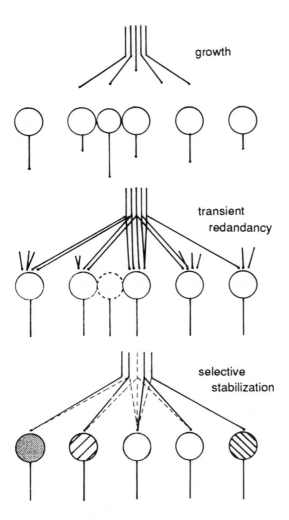

Figure 17.1 A diagrammatic representation of the model of epigenesis by selective stabilization. An initial stage of growth precedes the pruning of circuits through elimination and stabilization of synapses. From Changeux (1983b); reproduced by permission of the publishers, Artheme Fayard, Paris.

A straightforward consequence of this theory is that the postulated epigenesis contributes to the specification of the network at a low cost in terms of genetic information, which, in addition, can be shared by different systems of neurons. Such a mechanism offers a plausible way for coding organizational complexity from a small set of genes. By the same token, it also accounts for the paradoxical non-linear increase in complexity of the functional organization of the nervous system compared with that of the genome during the course of mammalian evolution.

5.3 The Theorem of Variability

In the course of the proposed epigenesis, diversification of neurons belonging to the same category occurs. Each one acquires its individuality or singularity by the precise pattern of connections it establishes (and neurotransmitters it synthesizes) (see Changeux, 1983a, b, 1986). A major consequence of the theory is that the distribution of these singular qualities may also vary significantly from one individual to the next. Moreover, it can be mathematically demonstrated that the same afferent message may stabilize different connective organizations, which nevertheless results in the same input–output relationship (Changeux et al., 1973). The variability referred to in the theory, therefore may account for the phenotypic variance observed between different isogenic individuals. At the same time, however, if offers a neural implementation for the often-mentioned paradox that there exists a non-unique mapping of a given function to the underlying neural organization.

5.4 Test of the Model

Still, only fragmentary experimental data are available as tests of the theory. Elimination of synapses (and sometimes neurons) during development is well documented at the neuromuscular junction (Redfern, 1970; Van Essen, 1982), at the synapses between climbing fibres and Purkinje cells in the cerebellum (Mariani and Changeux, 1981a, b), and at the autonomic ganglia (Purves and Lichtman, 1980), whereby in each case individual synapses can be easily counted. The phenomenon had already been noticed by Ramon y Cajal (1909) and interpreted as "a kind of competitive struggle" in Darwinian terms. It looks, in fact, to be rather widespread in the central nervous system (Clarke and Innocenti, 1986; Cowan et al., 1984; Huttenlocher et al., 1982; Innocenti and Caminiti, 1980; Price and Blakemore, 1985).

Particularly pertinent to the theory is the effect of nerve activity on these regressive phenomena. As noted, the developing nervous system is already spontaneously active at early stages of embryogenesis. This activity persists into maturity, being eventually modulated by the activity evoked by interaction with the outside world. Chronic blocking of the spontaneous undergoing activity prevents or delays the elimination of connections (Benoit and Changeux, 1975; Callaway et al., 1987; Fraser, 1985; Reiter and Stryker, 1988; Ribchester 1988; Schmidt, 1985; Sretavan et al., 1988). In contrast with the classical empiricist views, activity does not create novel connections but, rather, contributes to the elimination of pre-existing ones. Long-term learning results from disconnection but in a growing network. "To learn is to eliminate" (Changeux, 1983b: p. 246, English translation).

At the larger scale comprising neural maps, activity has also been shown to contribute to the shaping of the adult network. Blocking activity by tetrodotoxin in regenerating fish retinotectal connections interferes with the development of a normal map, both by leading to the maintenance of a diffuse topology of connections and by restricting the receptive fields (Edelman, 1987; Fraser, 1985; Schmidt, 1985). The effect of activity on the segregation of ocular dominance columns in the newborn (but also possibly in the fetus) is well documented (Hubel and Wiesel, 1977; also see references in Reiter and Stryker, 1988; Stryker and Harris, 1986). Lastly, the long-term coordination among maps required, for example, for stereoscopic vision or for the unitary perception of visual and auditory spaces, has also been shown to depend on experience, and models for the synaptic mechanisms involved have been proposed (see Bear et al., 1987).

Finally, the theory also accounts for the sensitive phases of learning and imprinting, which may correspond to the transient stage of maximal innervation (or diversity) in which the synaptic contacts are still in a labile state. This stage is well defined in the case of a single category of synapses. In the case of complex systems, such as the cerebral cortex, multiple categories of circuits become successively established, and, accordingly, many outgrowth and regression steps may take place in a succession of sensitive periods. In this sense the whole period of postnatal development becomes critical, but for different sensory inputs and performances! It is worth recalling that in humans this period is exceptionally long. A prolonged epigenesis of the cerebral cortex would not cost many genes, but for the reasons given above would have a considerable impact on the increased complexity and performance of the adult brain. Possible implications of epigenesis by selective stabilization of synapses in left-right hemispheric differentiation (Nass et al., 1985, 1989) for all aspects of language learning have already been extensively discussed (see Changeux, 1983b; Gazzaniga, 1987). The developmental loss of the perceptual ability to distinguish certain phonemes in different languages, such as the initial sounds of *ra* and *la* in Japanese, in contrast to Western languages (Eimas, 1975; Miyawaki et al., 1975), the variability in topological distribution of brain areas in different individuals (Ojemann, 1983), and the remarkable segregation of the cerebral territories utilized in the processing of Japanese Kanji and Kana writings (Sasanuma, 1975) may all be interpreted in such terms. But, convincing demonstrations remain to be established on the basis of neurofunctional data.

In summary:

1 The brain-computer metaphor does not apply to the development of the brain. The brain does not develop via the part-by-part assembly of prewired circuits.

2 On the contrary, its morphogenesis is progressive, with forms becoming intricated within forms, including possibly, at each step, sensitive phases of limited transient variability and exuberance followed by drastic elimination of connections.

3 The proposal is made that a selection of synapses takes place at these sensitive steps and is governed by the state of activity of the developing nervous system.

4 According to this view, the effect of experience is intertwined with innate processes from development through the adult stage. The formation of brain architectures is not independent of cognitive processes but, rather, is deeply impregnated by them, starting from the early stages of postnatal development.

6 Mental Objects and Mental Darwinism

6.1 *"Representations" and Hebbian Assemblies*

J. Z. Young (1964) introduced his insightful book, *Models of the Brain*, by defining the brain as the "computer of a homeostat" (p. 14). Being a homeostat the organism can exist in several states, and its adaptation is achieved by selection among possible actions provided by some antecedent process. Young further speculated that such selection is appropriate in that the homeostat continues its self-maintenance. For it to do so, the organism must adequately represent the situation as a set of physical events (signals) that transmit information. Thus, "The organism is (or contains) a representation of its environment" (p. 20).

The word "representation" has several different meanings. In the cognitive and computer sciences, it refers equally to the structure of internalized information as to its content. Thus, theorists who postulate a "language of thought" (Fodor, 1975) take mental representations to have a combinatorial syntax and semantic content. These representations are often contrasted with the operations performed with them, which are described in algorithmic terms. On the other hand, in neuroscience, the word representation mainly refers to the projections of sensory organs onto defined areas of the brain, or to the mappings of given domains of the brain upon others (Mountcastle, 1978). In his book, *The Organization of Behavior*, Hebb (1949) introduced the first bridge between the neural and the mental by postulating that "an assembly of association-area cells which can act briefly as a closed system after stimulation has ceased . . . constitutes the simplest instance of representative process (image or idea)" (p. 60). For Hebb, the assembly is described by the firing of an anatomically defined population of cells, and "an individual cell or transmission unit may enter in more than one assembly, at different times" (p. 196). Hebb thus posits the assembly as a "three-dimensional lattice", or as a net of neurons, with *coordinated* activity.

Alternative views to Hebb's concept of assembly have been advocated by various authors. For instance, Barlow (1972) has assumed that the coding units of concepts or representations can be identified with the activity of single neurons named "grandmother" or "pontifical" cells. Consistent with such a notion, single cells have been recorded that respond to particular objects, faces or even words (references in Heit et al., 1988; Perrett et al., 1987). In between, there are neuronal groups (Edelman and Mountcastle, 1978) or clusters of cells (Dehaene et al., 1987; Feldman, 1986). Depending on the level at which the coding takes place, pontifical cells or clusters of such cells may be viewed either as autonomous (individual) units or as building blocks for higher order assemblies (Hopfield, 1982).

From both an experimental and theoretical point of view, the actual size of the population of neurons involved in the coding of mental representations remains a debated issue. A wide range of plausible sizes has been suggested, from a single nerve cell to the whole brain. Nevertheless, extensive single-unit recording of populations of cells in awake animals (references in Georgopoulos et al., 1986; Llinás, 1987; Motter et al., 1987; Steinmetz et al., 1987) as well as large-scale high-resolution imaging (Posner et al., 1988; Roland and Friberg, 1985) give credence to the notion that these mental objects correspond to privileged activity states of widely distributed domains of the brain and have an identifiable, if not yet specified, physical basis.

Nevertheless, Von der Malsburg (1981, 1987) and Von der Malsburg and Bienenstock (1986) have criticized the cell-assembly concept as formalized by Little (1974) and Hopfield (1982), for two main reasons: (1) in a given brain area, a coding assembly is expected to correspond to only a fraction of a larger ensemble of active units; and (2) states which have the same global distribution of features might be confused with each other. Von der Malsburg and Bienenstock thus propose that the discrimination between coding and non-coding units relies on the temporal correlation between active units rather than on the fact that they are active or not. Such correlations become established between action potentials within a time-scale of a few milliseconds, during the overall time-scale of a representation (tenths of second), and are mediated by fast changes of synaptic strength. On this basis, Von der Malsburg and Bienenstock have developed a formalism whereby topologically organized synaptic patterns can be stored and retrieved, and whereby invariant pattern recognition finds a natural solution. The critical aspect of this formalism is to specify the notion of a firing correlation. Two final remarks have to be made about this view. First, the formalism is fully consistent with Hebb's original proposal of synchronization of activity between active cells, and thus only conflicts with the recent reformulations of the cell assembly concept in terms of statistical physics. Second, under physiological conditions, *both* the actual firing of individual nerve cells and the correlation of firing between cells are likely to contribute to the coding of mental representations.

6.2   Mental Darwinism

According to Hebb (1949), the growth of the cell assembly is determined by the repeated simultaneous excitation of cells consecutive to sensory stimulation in such a manner that each cell assists each other in firing. The time coincidence of firing between two cells increases the efficiency of the synapse linking the cells. In other words, the genesis of mental representations would occur through an instructive or "Lamarckian" mechanism (see Rolls, 1987). As noted, the thesis we wish to defend in the following is the opposite; namely, that the production and storage of mental representations, including their chaining into meaningful propositions and the development of reasoning, can also be interpreted, by analogy, in variation – selection (Darwinian) terms within psychological time-scales (Changeux, 1983b; Changeux et al., 1973, 1984; Dehaene et al., 1987; Edelman and Mountcastle, 1978; Edelman and Finkel, 1984; Finkel and Edelman, 1987; Heidmann et al., 1984).

A basic requirement for such "mental Darwinism" is the existence of a generator of variety (diversity), which would internally produce the so-called Darwinian variations. At psychological time-scales, and at the two levels of intendment and reason, such variations may be viewed as resulting from spontaneous activity of nerve cells. Hebb and many of his followers did not make explicit a possible differential contribution of spontaneous and evoked activity in coding mental representations. But the occurrence of spontaneous firing by cellular oscillators (see Berridge and Rapp, 1979) and/or oscillatory circuits (see Grillner et al., 1987; Stent et al., 1978) makes possible a strictly internal production of representations.

In a selectionist framework (Changeux, 1983b; Heidmann et al., 1984; Toulouse et al., 1986), one may thus schematically distinguish: (1) percepts in which the correlation of firing among the component neurons is directly determined by the interaction with the outside world and ceases when the stimulation has stopped; (2) images, concepts and intentions that are actualized objects of memory resulting from the activation of a stabilized trace; and (3) *pre-representations* (analogous to the Darwinian variations), which may be spontaneously developed, multiple, labile, and transient, and which may be selected or eliminated.

Pre-representations would be produced by the neural forms described in the preceding section with both their genetically encoded components (resulting from the evolution of the genome in geological time-scales) and their epigenetic ones (resulting from the consequences of embryonic and postnatal development). Pre-representations would correspond to privileged spontaneous activity states of these wired-in forms, occurring in shorter time-scales (0.1 seconds) and in a transient, dynamic and fleeting manner. At any given time, these pre-representations would be composed of sets of neurons from much larger populations of cells. As a consequence, the correlated firing of diverse combinations of neurons or groups of neurons (or even already stored assemblies) and a wide variety of active neural graphs would be produced successively and transiently. Such pre-representations may arise at the level of intendment and take part in the elaboration and storage of percepts at concepts. They may also arise at the level of reason and contribute to the genesis of higher-order programs and intentions representing the synthesis of concepts (see section 7). The genesis of pre-representations by such a mechanism would thus offer one neural component for the so-called productivity of cognitive processes (Fodor and Pylyshyn, 1988).

At a given stage of the evolution of the organism, some of these spontaneously generated pre-representations may not match any defined feature of the environment (or any item from long-term memory stores) and may thus be transiently meaningless. But, some of them will ultimately be selected in novel situations, thus becoming "meaning full." The achievement of such adequacy (fitness) with the environment (or with a given cognitive state) would then become the basic criterion for selection. The matching between a percept and a pre-representation has been referred to as resonance (Changeux, 1983b; Toulouse et al., 1986) and its unmatching as dissonance. Matching is likely to take place with global, invariant representations of the outside world resulting from the transformation of a set of sensory vectorial components into an invariant functional state (Llinás, 1987; Teuber, 1972).

Finally, mental representations are *not* static states of the brain, but are produced and chained within a system in constant dynamic interaction with the outside world and within itself. They are part of a system in constant evolution within psychological time-scales.

6.3   The Hebb Synapse and Elementary Mechanism of Resonance

To account for the growth of the assembly at the first stage of perception, Hebb (1949) postulates that "when an axon of cell A is near enough to excite cell B and repeatedly, or persistently, takes part in firing it, some growth process or metabolic change takes place in one or both cells such that A's efficiency as one of the cells firing B is increased" (p. 62). This proposal has been much debated from both theoretical and experimental points of view, and many cellular implementations of the Hebb synapse have been suggested since Hebb's original proposal (for instance, see Stent, 1973; Kelso et al., 1986; and for a recent review, see Bear et al., 1987).

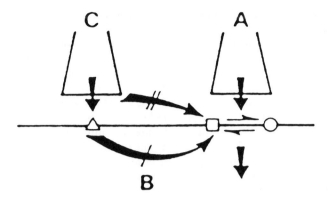

Figure 17.2 A model of the regulation of synapse efficacy at the postsynaptic level based on the allosteric properties of the acetylcholine receptor (from Dehaene et al., 1987). The conformation of receptor molecules can be affected by intra- or extracellular chemical potential of the postsynaptic cell.

Heidmann and Changeux (1982) (see also Changeux and Heidmann, 1987; Finkel and Edelman, 1987) have proposed a molecular mechanism whereby synaptic efficacy is governed by the conformational states of the postsynaptic receptor for a given neurotransmitter. The percentage of receptor molecules in activable and inactivable conformations would be a measure of efficacy, and could be modulated by converging electrical and/or chemical postsynaptic signals within a given time-window (figure 17.2). This model can account for a variety of modes of regulation of synapse efficacy, as found for instance in *Aplysia* (Abrams and Kandel, 1988; Changeux et al., 1987a; Hawkins and Kandel, 1984) where presynaptic changes appear postsynaptic to a true Hebbian process, or in the cerebellum (Ito et al., 1982), and may include so-called non-Hebbian cases.

Most important to our present purpose, such allosteric mechanisms for the Hebb rule and for other rules for synaptic enhancement may serve as basic devices to implement the resonance process defined above. It must be stressed that these mechanisms and rules do not imply any revival of "associationist" ideas (Fodor and Pylyshyn, 1988). Spontaneous firing may also regulate the efficacy of afferent synapses by the same rules. Conditions may be defined to occur for synaptic modifications only during a state of resonance between the activity of afferent synapses and the spontaneous firing of the target neuron (Dehaene et al., 1987). Thus, there is no intrinsic empiricist feature in the way these molecular regulatory devices operate.

6.4 Modelling Mental Objects by Statistical Physics

The test of a biological theory may sometimes be carried out succesfully on qualitative grounds without the help of a mathematical formalism. In most instances, however, the predictions appear difficult to derive intuitively, and the elaboration of a formal model in a coherent and simplified form becomes necessary. This is particularly true for assemblies of neurons, and an abundant literature has recently been published on this matter.

McCulloch and Pitts (1943) first described neurons as simple, all-or-none threshold devices. The further introduction of an analogue of temperature (Little, 1974; see Burnod and Korn, 1989) and of variable but symmetrical synapses (Hopfield, 1982) made possible the application of the ready-made formalism of statistical physics to neuronal networks. Hopfield (1982) showed how a content-addressable memory could be constructed, whereby information is stored as stable attractors of the dynamics via synaptic modifications. Several unrealistic features of the model were later revised, such as symmetrical interactions between neurons (Sompolinsky and Kanter, 1986; Derrida et al., 1987) or catastrophic deterioration of the memory with overloading (Mézard et al., 1986; Nadal et al., 1986a).

An important aspect of the attempt to formalize neural networks concerns the actual origin of the firing activity and of the interactions between neurons. In the instructive framework, which is the most commonly adopted (Amit et al., 1985a, b; Hopfield, 1982), the interaction with the outside world imposes the internal state of activity of the network. In the initial state, the interactions are vanishingly small, and the energy landscape flat. Among several drawbacks, this hypothesis does not take into account the existence of an already heavily connected network and the occurrence of spontaneous activity within the network (see above). In terms of the spin glass formalism (Toulouse et al., 1986), a selectionist model, in contrast, posits an initially rich energy landscape with pre-existing interactions between neurons and an abundance of hierarchically organized attractors. The interaction with the outside world would not enrich the landscape, but rather would select pre-existing energy minima or pre-representations and enlarge them at the expense of other valleys. As a consequence, the whole energy landscape would evolve, the already stored information influencing the pre-representations available for the next learning event. The system possesses internal rigidity so that not every external stimulus would be equally stored. The crucial issue remains to find a learning rule coherent with such a Darwinian picture. A relatively simple initial model was proposed in Toulouse et al. (1986). It begins with a random distribution of synaptic efficacies, and stores patterns using the same rule as the original Hopfield model. Although this does not allow one to make use of the hierarchical structure of pre-existing attractors, such networks do possess an internal rigidity. Moreover, additional biological constraints, such as excitatory synapses not becoming inhibitory and vice versa, are easily implemented, taking this model a step further toward the selective model. Still, one of the major limitations of this model is that it deals with "spin glass" under static conditions, while selection of mental states in the brain always takes place under constant dynamic conditions (see section 7).

In summary:

1 Experimental and theoretical evidence from cellular neurophysiology and statistical physics make plausible the hypothesis that mental representations can be defined as states of activity of brain cells.

2 Models for the Darwinian selection of mental states can be proposed on the basis of:

(a) the spontaneous productions of transient, dynamic and coherent but fleeting activity states referred to as pre-representations, which would be analogues of the Darwinian variations;

(b) the selection and stabilization of some of these pre-representations by matching percepts arising from external and somatic internal stimuli with already selected internal states.

7 Neural Architecture and the Application of Theoretical Models to Cognitive Science

Models inspired from statistical physics deal mostly with networks of fully interconnected neurons, whereby neither the singularity of each individual neuron nor higher-order architectural principles of the networks are specified. To better approach a more realistic neurobiology, some modellists have studied simple systems such as *Limax* (Hopfield and Tank, 1986) or *Tritonia* (Kanter and Sompolinsky, 1987) despite the fact that the cognitive abilities of these creatures are rather rudimentary. Our approach is the opposite. While anatomists, physiologists and neuropsychologists decipher the real functional organization of brain connectivity in mammals (see Goldman-Rakic, 1987; Rakic, 1988) and in humans (Geschwind and Galaburda, 1987), it may be possible starting from simple networks to reconstruct cognitive functions by introducing architectural and functional constraints within, and between, neuronal networks and, in a second step, to look for their presence in real brains. In the following section, we try to establish a parallel between the behaviour of networks and well-known cognitive functions, knowing, *a priori*, that such attempts are a simplistic but necessary preliminary to more complex and plausible reconstruction.

7.1 Short-term memory of a neuronal network

The simplest feature displayed by formal neuronal networks is the storage of memories within a limited-capacity network. As described above, the Hopfield model can be specified and completed in order to retain only the most recent information it received. A direct relation exists between the steady-state, memory capacity of this network and its connectivity. For instance, a network in which each neuron is connected to 500 other neurons has a memory capacity of seven items (Nadal et al., 1986a, b). Both numbers are within a plausible range. Extension of such evaluations to short-term memory in humans is attractive but still highly hypothetical. Yet, at least for the most perceptually driven memory stores, the application of the Hopfield instructive scheme seems legitimate. A long-standing debate in the field has been the origin of forgetting (see Baddeley, 1976, for discussion). Erasure of the short-term memory traces might result from a spontaneous decay or, alternatively, from an interference of recent memories over older ones. Spontaneous decay may simply result from the relaxation kinetics of the molecular transitions of proteins engaged in synaptic transmission. The modelling of formal neuronal networks according to the Hopfield scheme, as exemplified by the palimpsest model (Nadal et al., 1986a, b), illustrates, however, the physical plausibility of an interference mechanism. It further accounts for characteristic features of short-term memory stores such as the "primacy effect," according to which the first item stored is more easily recalled than the subsequent ones (Nadal et al., 1986a, b).

An important feature of this model is that it points to the dependence of global functional features (a fixed memory span) upon elementary synaptic parameters such as the average number of synapses per neuron (see figure 17.3). As emphasized by Simon (1969), "the most striking limits to subjects' capacities to employ efficient strategies arise from the very small capacity of the short-term memory structure" (p. 76). These models, at variance with the classical functionalist point of view, thus illustrate how elementary parameters of the brain may place fundamental constraints on the pattern of thought.

7.2   Organization of Long-term Memory

The long-term memory stores in humans possess an apparent unlimited capacity, are strongly hierarchical, and are organized along a semantic, rather than perceptual, space (Baddeley, 1976, 1986, 1988; Massaro, 1975). Storage into long-term memory appears as a rare and slow event compared to the short-term storage of information, and may be viewed as a semantically driven, Darwinist selection from representations present in the short-term store.

Several models for storing a hierarchical tree of memories in a neural network have been proposed (Feigelman and Toffe, 1987; Gutfreund, 1988; Parga and

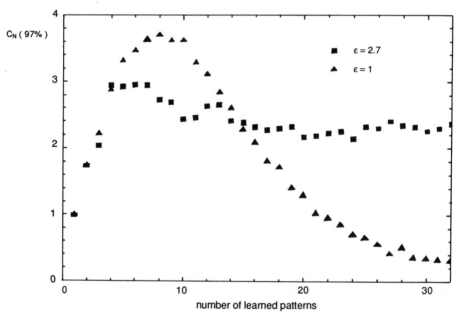

Figure 17.3 Model of memory palimpsest. The percentage of memorized patterns drops catastrophically as more and more patterns are added into the Hopfield (1982) model (triangles). A minor modification yields a stationary regime (squares) where only recently learned patterns can be retrieved (palimpsest model: from Nadal et al., 1986a; reproduced by permission of the publishers, Editions de Physique, Les Ulis, France).

Virasoro, 1985). One of them (Gutfreund, 1988) relies on an architecture based upon multiple distinct networks, one for each level of the tree. The retrieval of a particular memory is achieved at the lowest network, and is assisted by the retrieval of its ancestors, and mimics access to long-term stores in humans (see Baddeley, 1986b, 1988). The models inspired from statistical physics thus offer an elementary physical implementation of semantic relationships in long-term memory, which partially covers the notion of "meaning" (Amit, 1988). In this respect it is worth noting that blood-flow studies involving retrieval of specific memories, such as numbers, nine-word jingles or sequence of visual fields reveal something in the activation of topographically distinct though interconnected cortical areas (Roland and Friberg, 1985). Neuropsychological investigations show that even words belonging to different semantic categories may be represented at different loci in the brain (e.g. McCarthy and Warrington, 1988).

Finally, the so-called unlimited capacity of the long-term store is more apparent than real. First of all, reasonable evaluations of its capacity converge at a value of 10^9 bits (see Mitchinson, 1987), which is a small number compared to the 10^{11} neurons of the human brain and its 10^{15} synapses. Second, the transfer from short- to long-term memory looks rather limited considering the large number of representations transiently circulating in the short-term store. Third, only truly new items, distinct from those already present in long-term memory, are stored at any given time. The transfer from short- to long-term stores may thus be viewed as a selection for novelty occurring via the validation of pre-existing hierarchies and the stabilization of small branches, thereby saving considerable space.

7.3 Plausible Molecular Mechanism for Long-term Storage

Mental objects have been defined as transient physical states of neuronal networks with durations in the time-scale of fractions of seconds. Such activity-dependent changes of neuronal and synaptic properties may be extended to longer time-scales by covalent modifications of neuronal and synaptic proteins and, ultimately, by the regulation of protein synthesis.

Yet, at variance with currently accepted views (Goelet et al., 1986; Montarolo et al., 1986), Changeux and Heidmann (1987) have argued that long-term regulations cannot be equated to regulation of protein synthesis, but rather to the perpetuation of an activity-dependent trace beyond protein turnover. The simplest and most plausible general mechanism is that of a self-sustained metabolic steady-state that includes a *positive* feedback loop (or negative ones in *even* numbers (Delbrück, 1949; Thomas, 1981). Such self-reinforcing circuits may be built at the level of neuronal receptors (Changeux and Heidmann, 1987; Crick, 1984; Lisman, 1985), gene receptors (Britten and Davidson, 1969; Monod and Jacob, 1961), and even at the level of the synapse on the basis of a sequence of chemical reactions. In this last instance (Changeux et al., 1987a) a positive feedback loop may be created by the activity-dependent regulation of the production (by the postsynaptic cell) of a growth factor required for the stability of the afferent nerve ending. There is no theoretical time limit to the maintenance of a trace in a system of that sort up to the life span of the organism.

Plausible molecular mechanisms for the extension to long-term changes of synapse efficacies may thus be envisioned at the level of the synapse in which the short-term modification took place. On the other hand, the occurrence of neuropsychological disconnections in the transfer from short- to long-term stores in human patients supports the notion that in the human brain these two compartments might be topographically distinct though highly interconnected.

7.4 Recognition, Production and Storage of Time Sequences

The attempts to model neuronal networks that have been mentioned concern either stable states or relaxation to stable states. However, as emphasized, the nervous system does not process information under static conditions. At the cellular or simple circuits level, it produces coherent patterns of linear or cyclic sequences of activity (Getting, 1981; Grillner, 1975; Grillner et al., 1987; Stent et al., 1978). At higher levels, including the knowledge level, the nervous system possesses the striking faculty to recognize, produce and store time sequences (Lashley, 1951). One basic function of the frontal cortex mentioned in section 2 is the control of the temporal evolution of overt behaviour and internal chains of mental representations. An important issue is thus: what are the minimal requirements of neural architecture and function for a network to process temporal sequences?

Complex networks that recognize and produce sequences of higher order have recently been proposed that rely on two sets of synaptic connections: one set which stabilizes the network in its current memory state, while a second set, the action of which is delayed in time, causes the network to make transitions between memories (Kleinfeld, 1986; Sompolinsky and Kanter, 1986; Peretto and Niez, 1986; Amit, 1988). Others (Tank and Hopfield, 1987) are based on delay filters, one for each known sequence. In all these instances, the time delay is built-in as an intrinsic physical parameter of individual neurons, such as postsynaptic potential or axon length.

The network model we have proposed (Dehaene et al., 1987) displays capacities for recognition and production of temporal sequences and for their acquisition by selection. It was inspired by the learning of songs in birds such as *Melospiza* by selective attrition of syllables (Konishi, 1985; Marler and Peters, 1982), whereby identified neurons, called song-specific neurons, detect sequences of syllables. It also makes use of the known properties of allosteric receptors (Changeux, 1981; Changeux and Heidmann, 1987; Heidmann and Changeux, 1982), which may potentially serve as regulators of synapse efficacy at the postsynaptic level (including Hebbian mechanisms: see section V).

The model is based on four assumptions about neural architecture (figure 17.4): (1) synaptic triads are composed of three neurons A, B, and C. These are connected so that the efficacy of a synapse of A on B is influenced by the activity of a third modulator neuron C, under conditions that make the postsynaptic neuron B behave as a sequence detector for neurons A and C; (2) a Hebbian learning rule increases the maximal efficacy of the A–B synapse toward an absolute maximum if, after its activation, postsynaptic neuron B fires; (3) the network is formed of juxtaposed clusters of synergic neurons densely interconnected by excitatory synapses, thus able to maintain self-sustained stable activity; and (4) the network is subdivided into three superimposed layers: a sensory layer on which percepts are merely imposed, and an internal production network subdivided into two layers for input clusters and internal clusters, respectively. The network displays several original properties:

(a) *Passive recognition and production of temporal patterns.* The few architectural designs of the network, the presence of synaptic triads and the existence of clusters with a linear or hierarchical organization, suffice for the recognition of time sequences. As a consequence of the self-excitatory connections within clusters, the activity of previous states remains within the cluster. Individual triads acting as elementary sequence detectors, and the linear and hierarchical arrays of clusters thus behave as detectors of complex sequences that may include repetitions.

Furthermore, the same network produces time sequences. A set of triads between clusters transmits activity with a delay. A memory of previous activity is kept through the persistence, or *remanence*, of former activity within the clusters. Remanent activity may thus influence the pathways that the system takes. The temporal span of this remanence will thus determine the complexity of the sequence produced. It is an elementary neural implementation of context dependence which is basic to cognitive psychology and linguistics. Amit (1988)

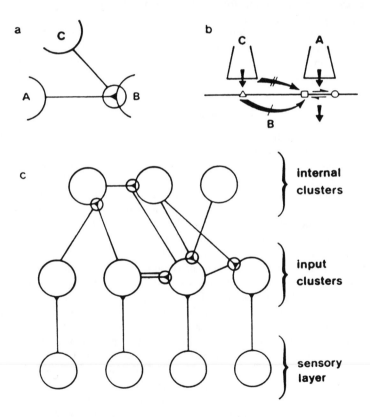

Figure 17.4 Model of formal neuron networks capable of recognition, production and storage of temporal sequences (from Dehaene et al., 1987) (for explanation see text).

provides a similar demonstration, although in a different framework, that the same stimulus can elicit different network responses depending on the remanent internal state.

(b) *Genesis of internal organization by learning.* Introduction of the Hebbian learning rule and the subdivision of the network in two distinct layers, one for the input and the other strictly for internal representations, makes possible the differentiation of hierarchically organized sequence detectors from randomly connected clusters. Conditions can be found in which the imposition of a melody to the input clusters leads progressively to elimination of the initial redundancy and to stabilization of hierarchies of sequence detectors. Conversely, sequences of arbitrary complexity may be produced in the network by stabilization of ongoing spontaneous activity during interaction (resonance) with an externally applied melody.

The model thus illustrates how neurons coding for a temporal relationship between activity clusters may differentiate through experience according to a Darwinian mechanism. It also suggests that abstract relations (rules) may be extracted and stored in hierarchically organized neurons or, conversely, imposed to lower-level neurons coding for a variety of more concrete features.

From an experimental point of view the model points to the role of synaptic triads and to the differentiation through experience of neuronal hierarchies. It has global predictions about variability and its reduction in the course of learning, which are strikingly consonant with observations made on children in the course of phonology acquisition (see Ferguson, 1985).

7.5   Intentions and Inventions

Intentionality and meaning appear so basic to cognition that those who do not address these issues are often viewed as missing the whole field! An elementary step toward the physical implementation of meaning has already been made. On the other hand, the problem of intentionality, even in a very limited sense, has not been considered. Any attempt to unravel its neural bases appears unrealistic *a priori* (Searle, 1983). Our aim is not to propose a neural theory of intentionality. Rather, we limit ourselves to a few remarks and arguments illustrating how such a theory might be constructed, with respect to goals and plans.

(a) *Intentions and the frontal cortex.* The brief discussion on the contribution of the frontal lobe to the architecture of reason (section 2) led to the suggestion that this region of the brain contributes to the elaboration of plans, and controls the temporal unfolding of patterned mental operations or behavioural actions according to a goal. Frontal lesions do interfere with planning behaviour and result in a typical unintentional utilization behaviour (Lhermitte, 1983) that one may associate with the lower intendment level. The prefrontal cortex must thus have a *prospective* function in anticipating and planning and a *retrospective* one in maintaining it in a provisional memory until the goal is reached (Fuster, 1980).

Single-unit recordings in the prefrontal cortex during the delay period of a delayed alternation task disclose cells that remain active for seconds before the response and code for the anticipated direction of the motor response (Bruce, 1988; Niki, 1974). Neural activity therefore can be related to the achievement of a goal. From this it is reasonable to conclude that there exists a neural basis for intentions in humans, as there exists a neural basis for goals in monkeys. Intentions may concern both motor acts and thought processes (Searle, 1983). Accordingly, an intention will be viewed as a particular category of mental object characterized by (1) its occurrence at a high level of organization, such as the level of reason in the frontal cortex, and (2) a long-lasting, *predictive*, activity. Self-excitatory clusters of neurons would offer one implementation for the maintenance of intentions, but the involvement of cellular oscillators or, more likely, of reverbatory closed circuits involving positive feedback loops appears equally plausible (see Changeux, 1983b). The intervention of attentional processes (see Posner and Presti, 1987) would contribute to the fixation of such self-sustained states of activity, which would be determined either externally through percepts or internally through the evocation of memory objects.

(b) *Intentionality and context dependence.* Intentions are viewed as occurring on top of the hierarchy of brain networks and may create a context for underlying motor actions on the environment and the chaining of mental objects by imposing a frame of semantic constraints on these processes. The model proposed for the recognition, storage and retrieval of time sequences (Dehaene et al., 1987) bases context dependence on the joint contribution of the remanence of activity in self-excitatory clusters and of the recognition (or production) of time sequences by synaptic triads. It might serve as a general framework for the elaboration of more complex models for the context created by intentions, for the development of reasonings and in a more general manner for what Fodor and Pylyshyn (1988) refer to as structure-sensitive operations.

(c) *The selectionist (Darwinian) test for intentions and inventions.* A basic function of the frontal cortex is to capture errors in the unfolding of a motor program. Similarly, intentions might be subjected to internal tests. The validation of a proposition, for example, would then result from a context-dependent compatibility of a chain of mental objects within a given semantic frame with already-stored mental objects. Such tests for compatibility or adequateness might be viewed, from a neural point of view, as analogues of the matching by resonance (or un-matching by dissonance) of percepts with pre-representations.

The contribution of attention to the processing of sensory information is currently being investigated in great detail by joint psychological and neurological approaches (Posner and Presti, 1987; Posner et al., 1988). It appears plausible that similar, if not identical, attentional systems are involved in maintaining coherent patterns designed to reach a goal (Posner, 1980; Posner and Presti, 1987). "Attention for action" (Posner et al., 1988) is a generic name for the attentional processes involved in the selection of actions, intentions or goals. As in the case of the selection of meaning, but at a different level and on a different time-scale, the selection of actions and intentions may take place via a Darwinian mechanism among internally evoked and context-dependent pre-representations. Of course, such selection will concern higher-order representations including complex chains of objects from the long-term memory stores. Combinatorial processes may produce novel intentions or inventions at this level. The selection will then be carried out by testing their realism from the cognitive as well as affective point of view. The connections existing between the limbic system and the prefrontal cortex offer a material basis for relationships between the emotional and cognitive spheres (Goldman-Rakic, 1987; Nauta, 1971, 1973).

In summary, on the basis of rather simple architectural designs, physical models of neural networks can be proposed that account for some characteristic features of short-term and long-term memory and for the recognition, production and storage of time sequences. Such models make plausible a neural theory of intentions.

8 Conclusions

Despite the rather speculative character of some sections of this presentation, we conclude that it is timely to approach cognition in a synthetic manner with the aim to relate a given cognitive function to its corresponding neural organization and activity state. Such a neurocognitive trend (see also Arbib, 1985; Luria, 1973; Struss and Benson, 1986) contrasts with the classical functionalist approach to cognition (Fodor, 1975; Johnson-Laird, 1983), although it is more compatible with a revised, more recent version (Fodor and Pylyshyn, 1988). This approach has several important consequences.

It contends that data from cognitive psychology often overlook many highly intricate levels of functional organization that have to be distinguished within the human brain. Reconstructing architecture on the basis of external observations alone is a complex matter, if not an ill-defined task, with no unique solution. Neuropsychology and neuro-imagery (Posner et al., 1988) usefully complement the psychological approach by offering ways to dissect such global functions into elementary operations that are localized in the brain, and help to show that the cleavage of brain functions into the classical neurological, algorithmic and semantic levels is no longer appropriate and may even be misleading. Ultimately, both theoretical models and experiments must be devised in such a manner that they specify the particular level of neural organization to which a given function is casually related.

It further argues that the classical artificial intelligence approach, which tries to identify the programs run by the hardware of the human brain, loses much of its attractive power. This may be overcome if one conceives brain-style computers based on the actual architectural principles of the human brain and possessing some of its authentic competences rather than simply mimicking some of its surface performances (for references, see Sejnowski et al., 1988). Models of highly evolved functions, for example the acquisition of past tense in English (Rumelhart and McClelland, 1987) or the ability to read a text aloud (Sejnowsky and Rosenberg, 1986) among others (Lehkey and Sejnowski, 1988; Zipser and Andersen, 1988) have been implemented in simplistic connectionist machines. But, despite an "appearance of neural plausibility" (Fodor and Pylyshyn, 1988), the architectures involved are far too simple and even naive compared to those that the human brain actually uses for such multimodal performances with deep cultural impregnation (Pinker and Prince, 1988). As stated by Fodor and Pylyshyn (1988), these systems cannot "exhibit intelligent behavior without storing, retrieving or otherwise operating on structured symbolic expressions" (p. 5). A basic requirement of a plausible neurocognitive approach is thus to unravel the physics of meaning or, in other words, the neural bases of mental representations. The attempt to find the implementation of the semantic content of symbolic expressions in neural terms cannot be viewed as secondary to a psychological theory of meaning (Fodor and Pylyshyn, 1988). Theories of the neural implementation of mental representations may raise useful issues such as the capacity of short-term memory, the hierarchical organization of long-term memory, the recognition and storage of time sequences, and context dependence, as illustrated in a still rather primitive form in this paper. An important issue will be the search for the neural representation of rules (in particular, syntax) and their application to restricted classes of mental representations. In this respect, the model of learning temporal sequences by selection (Dehaene et al., 1987) illustrates how neurons coding for relations between mental objects may differentiate as a consequence of experience. The model recently served as a starting point for an investigation of the role of prefrontal cortex in delayed-response tasks (Dehaene and Changeux, 1989), which are elementary rule-governed behaviours. Such implementations will one day be described in terms of real neural connections and will thus point to critical experimental predictions. Such abstract neurological theories based upon the most advanced progress of brain anatomy and physiology may ultimately unravel novel algorithms and architectures out of the still largely unexplored universe of human brain connectivity. Our view is that there is much more to expect from such an approach than from strict psychological and/or mathematical theorizing.

Another conclusion that we wish to draw from this discussion is that the brain should be viewed as an evolutive system rather than as a static input–output processing machine. The brain is part of an organism belonging to a species that has evolved (and is still evolving) in geological time-scales according to Darwinian mechanisms at the level of the genome. But the complexity of the brain is such that it may itself be considered as a system evolving *within* the organism with, at least, two distinct time-scales; that of embryonic and postnatal development for the process of organizing neuronal somas and connectivity networks, and that of psychological times for the storage, retrieval and chaining of mental objects and for their assembly into higher-order motor programs, behavioural strategies and schemas. The extension of *selectionist* mechanisms to all these levels breaks down the rigidity (sphexishness; Dennett, 1984) of the strictly nativist or Cartesian schemes (Fodor, 1983) by introducing, at each level, a degree of freedom linked with the production of variations. But as long as these variations are constrained by the genetic envelope, it escapes the pitfalls of Lamarckian associationism. The generator of internal diversity produces, at each of these levels, intrinsic richness, and thereby offers possibilities for creating structures within a given level but also between levels, yielding again one plausible component for the productivity requirements of Fodor and Pylyshyn (1988). Moreover, the number of such choices need not be large to cause an important diversity as long as variability exists at all hierarchically organized levels. The criteria for selection of the pre-representations must be defined at each level. At the lower levels, an obvious criterion is the adequateness or fitness to the environment. At a higher one, the internal thought (Gedanken) experiments might refer to the outcome of former experiences stored in the long-term memory and in the genetic endowment of the species which, *in fine*, ensure its survival (see Dennett, 1984, 1987).

Brain would thus be an evolutive system constantly anticipating the evolution of its physical, social and cultural environment by producing expectations and even intentions that create a lasting frame of reference for a selected set of long-term memories. Brain would not only be a semantic engine (Dennett, 1984) but an intentional engine. At no level would such a machine be neutral about the nature of cognitive processes. Rather, it would be "knowledge-impregnated" from the organization of its genome up to the production of its more labile intentions.

REFERENCES

Abrams, T., & Kandel, E. (1988). Is contiguity detection in classical conditioning a system or a cellular property? Learning in *Aplysia* suggests a possible molecular site. *Trends in Neuroscience*, 11, 128–135.

Akam, M. (1987). The molecular basis for metameric pattern genes of *Drosophila*. *Development*, 101, 1–22.

Alkon, D., Disterhoft, J., & Coulter, D. (1987). Conditioning-specific modifications of postsynaptic membrane currents in mollusc and mammal: In J. P. Changeux & M. Konishi (eds), *The neural and molecular bases of learning*. New York: Wiley.

Amit, D. J. (1988). Neural networks counting chimes. *Proceedings of the National Academy of Science USA*, 85, 2141–2145.

Amit, D. J., Gutfreund, H., & Sompolinsky, H. (1985a). Spin glass models of neural networks. *Physical Review*, A32, 1007–1018.

Amit, D. J., Gutfreund, H., & Sompolinsky, H. (1985b). Storing infinite numbers of patterns in a spin-glass model of neural networks. *Physical Review Letters*, 55, 1530–1533.

Arbib, M. (1985). *In search of the person*. Amherst, MA: University of Massachusetts Press.

Awgulewitsch, A., Utset, M. F., Hart, C. P., McGinnis, W., & Ruddle, F. (1986). Spatial restriction in expression of a mouse homeobox locus within the central nervous system. *Nature*, 320, 328–335.

Baddeley, A. D. (1976). *The psychology of memory*. New York: Harper & Row.

Baddeley, A. D. (1986). *Working memory*. Oxford: Clarendon Press.

Baddeley, A. D. (1988). Cognitive psychology and human memory. *Trends in Neuroscience*, 11, 176–181.

Barlow, H. B. (1972). Single units and sensations: a neuron doctrine for perceptual physiology? *Perception*, 1, 371–394.

Bear, M. F., Cooper, L. N., & Ebner, F. F. (1987). A physiological basis for a theory of synapse modification. *Science*, 237, 42–48.

Benoit, P., & Changeux, J. P. (1975). Consequences of tenotomy on the evolution of multi-innervation in developing rat soleus muscle. *Brain Research*, 99, 354–358.

Berridge, M., & Rapp, P. (1979). A comparative survey of the function, mechanism and control of cellular oscillations. *Journal of Experimental Biology*, 81, 217–280.

Britten, R. J., & Davidson, E. H. (1969). Gene regulation for higher cells: a theory. *Science*, 165, 349–357.

Bruce, C. (1988). What does single unit analysis in the prefrontal areas tell us about cortical processing? In P. Rakic & W. Singer (eds), *Neurobiology of neocortex*, Dahlem Konferenzen. Chichester: Wiley.

Burnod, Y., & Korn, H. (1989). Consequence of stochastic release of neurotransmitters for network computation in the central nervous system. *Proceedings of the National Academy of Science USA*, 86, 352–356.

Callaway, E., Soha, J., & Von Essen, D. (1987). Competition favoring inactive over active motor neurons during synapse elimination. *Nature*, 328, 422–426.

Cavalli-Sforza, L., & Fedelman, M. (1981). *Cultural transmission and evolution: A quantitative approach*. Princeton, NJ: Princeton University Press.

Changeux, J. P. (1981). The acetylcholine receptor: An "allosteric" membrane protein. *Harvey Lectures*, 75, 85–254.

Changeux, J. P. (1983a). Concluding remarks on the "singularity" of nerve cells and its ontogenesis. *Progress in Brain Research*, 58, 465–478.

Changeux, J. P. (1983b). *L'homme neuronal*, Paris: Fayard. English translation by L. Garey (1985). *Neuronal Man*. New York: Pantheon Books.

Changeux, J. P. (1984). Le regard du collectionneur. *Catalogue de la donation Othon Kaufmann et François Schlageter au Departement des peintures, Musée du Louvre*. Paris: Edition de la Réunion des Musées Nationaux.

Changeux, J. P. (1986). Coexistence of neuronal messengers and molecular selection. *Progress in Brain Research*, 68, 373–403.

Changeux, J. P., Courrège, P., & Danchin, A. (1973). A theory of the epigenesis of neural networks by selective stabilization of synapses. *Proceedings of the National Academy of Science USA*, 70, 2974–2978.

Changeux, J. P., Courrège, P., Danchin, A., & Lasry, J. M. (1981). Un mécanisme biochimique pour l'épigénèse de la jonction neuromusculaire. *C. R. Acad. Sci. Paris*, 292, 449–453.

Changeux, J. P., & Danchin, A. (1974). Apprendre par stabilisation sélective de synapses en cours de développement. In E. Morin & M. Piattelli (eds), *L'unité de l'homme*. Paris: Le Seuil.

Changeux, J. P., & Danchin, A. (1976). Selective stabilization of developing synapses as a mechanism for the specification of neuronal networks. *Nature*, 264, 705–712.

Changeux, J. P., Devillers-Thiéry, A., Giraudat, J., Dennis, M., Heidmann, T., Revah, F., Mulle, C., Heidmann, O., Klarsfeld, A., Fontaine, B., Laufer, R., Nghiêm, H. O., Kordeli, E., & Cartaud, J. (1987b). The acetylcholine receptor: Functional organization and evolution during synapse formation. In O. Hayaishi (ed.), *Strategy and prospects in neuroscience*. Utrecht: VNU Science Press.

Changeux, J. P., & Heidmann, T. (1987). Allosteric receptors and molecular models of learning. In G. Edelman, W. E. Gall, & W. M. Cowan (eds), *Synaptic function*. New York: Wiley.

Changeux, J. P., Heidmann, T., & Patte, P. (1984). Learning by selection. In P. Marler & H. Terrace (eds), *The biology of learning*. Berlin: Springer-Verlag.

Changeux, J. P., Klarsfeld, A., & Heidmann, T. (1987a). The acetylcholine receptor and molecular models for short and long term learning. In J. P. Changeux & M. Konishi (eds), *The cellular and molecular bases of learning*. Chichester: Wiley.

Chomsky, N. (1965). *Aspects of the theory of syntax*. Cambridge, MA: MIT Press.

Chomsky, N. (1979). Le débat entre Jean Piaget et Noam Chomsky. In M. Piattelli-Palmarini (ed.), *Théories du langage – théories de l'apprentissage*. Paris: Le Seuil.

Churchland, P. (1986). *Neurophilosophy*. Cambridge, MA: MIT Press.

Clarke, E., & O'Malley, C. (1968). *The human brain and spinal cord. A historical study illustrated by writings from antiquity to the twentieth century*. Berkeley, CA: University of California Press.

Clarke, S., & Innocenti, G. (1986). Organization of immature intrahemispheric connection. *Journal of Comparative Neurology*, 251, 1–22.

Cowan, M. W., Fawcett, J. W., O'Leary, D., & Stanfield, B. B. (1984). Regressive phenomena in the development of the vertebrate nervous system. *Science*, 225, 1258–1265.

Crick, F. (1984). Memory and molecular turnover. *Nature*, 312, 101.

D'Arcy-Thompson, W. (1917). *On growth and form*. Cambridge: Cambridge University Press.

Debru, C. (1983). *L'esprit des protéines*. Paris: Hermann.

Dehaene, S., & Changeux, J. P. (1989). A single model of prefrontal cortex function in delayed-response tasks. *Journal of Cognitive Neuroscience*.

Dehaene, S., Changeux, J. P., & Nadal, J. P. (1987). Neural networks that learn temporal sequences by selection. *Proceedings of the National Academy of Sciences USA*, 84, 2727–2731.

Delbrück, M. (1949). *In Unités biologiques douées de continuité génétique (Publication CNRS)*, 33–35.

Delbrück, M. (1986). *Mind from matter*. Palo Alto, CA: Blackwell.

Dennett, D. (1984). *Elbow room*. Cambridge, MA: MIT Press.

Dennett, D. (1987). *The intentional stance*. New York: Basic Books.

Derrida, B., Gardner, E., & Zippelius, A. (1987). An exactly solvable asymmetric neural network model.

Derrida, B., & Nadal, J. P. (1987). Learning and forgetting on a symmetric diluted neural network. *Journal of Statistical Physics*, 49, 993–1009.

Doe, C. Q. Hiromi, Y., Gehring, W. J., & Goodman, C. S. (1988). Expression and function of the representation gene *fushi tarazu* during *Drosophila* neurogenesis. *Science*, 239, 170–175.

Edelman, G. M. (1978). Group selection and phasic reentrant signaling: a theory of higher brain function. In G. M. Edelman and V. B. Mountcastle (eds), *The mindful brain: Cortical organization and the group-selective theory of higher brain function* (pp. 51–100). Cambridge, MA: MIT Press.

Edelman, G. M., (1985). Molecular regulation of neural morphogenesis. In G. M. Edelman, W. E. Gall, & W. M. Cowan (eds), *Molecular bases of neural development*. New York: Wiley.

Edelman, G. M. (1987). *Neural Darwinism*. New York: Basic Books.

Edelman, G. M., & Finkel, L. (1984). Neuronal group selection in the cerebral cortex. In G. Edelman, W. E. Gall, & W. M. Cowan (eds), *Dynamic aspects of neocortical function*. New York: Wiley.

Edelman, G. M., Gall, W. E., & Cowan, W. M. (eds) (1984). *Dynamic aspects of neocortical function*. New York: Wiley.

Edelman, G. M., & Mountcastle, V. (eds) (1978). *The mindful brain; Cortical organization and the group-selective theory of higher brain function*. Cambridge, MA: MIT Press.

Eimas, P. D. (1975). In L. B. Cohen & P. Salapatek (eds), *Infant perception: From sensation to cognition* (Vol. 2). New York: Academic Press.

Feigelman, M. V., & Toffe, L. B. (1987). The augmented model of associative memory asymmetric interaction and hierarchy of pattern. *International Journal of Modern Physics, B*, 1, 51–68.

Feldman, J. A. (1986). Neural representation of conceptual knowledge. *Technical report, Department of Computer Science, University of Rochester*, TR189, June 1986.

Ferguson, C. A. (1985). Discovering sound units and constructing sound systems: It's child's play. In J. S. Perkell & D. H. Klatt (eds), *Invariance and variability in speech processes*. Hillsdale, NJ: Erlbaum.

Finkel, L. H., & Edelman, G. M. (1987). Population rules for synapses in networks. In G. M. Edelman, W. E. Gall, & M. W. Cowan (eds), *Synaptic function*. New York: Wiley.

Fodor, J. (1975). *The language of thought*. Cambridge, MA: Harvard University Press.

Fodor, J. (1983). *The modularity of mind*. Cambridge, MA: MIT Press.

Fodor, J., & Pylyshyn, Z. (1988). Connectionism and cognitive architecture: A critical analysis. *Cognition*, 28, 3–71.

Fraser, S. E. (1985). Cell interactions involved in neuronal patterning: An experimental and theoretical approach. In G. M. Edelman, W. E. Gall, & W. M. Cowan (eds), *Molecular bases of neural development*. New York: Wiley.

Fuster, J. M. (1980). *The prefrontal cortex*. New York: Raven.

Fuster, J. M. (1984). Electrophysiology of the prefrontal cortex. *Trends in Neuroscience*, 1, 408–414.

Gazzaniga, M. S. (1987). The dynamics of cerebral specilization and modular interactions. In L. Weiskrantz (ed.), *Thought without language*. Oxford: Clarendon Press.

Georgopoulos, A. P., Schwartz, A. B., & Kettner, R. E. (1986). Neuronal population coding of movement direction. *Science*, 233, 1357–1460.

Geschwind, N., & Galaburda, A. (eds) (1984). *Cerebral dominance: The biological foundations*. Cambridge, MA: Harvard University Press.

Geschwind, N., & Galaburda, A. M. (1987). *Cerebral lateralization*. Cambridge MA: MIT Press.

Getting, P. A. (1981). Mechanism of pattern generation underlying swimming in *Tritonia*. I. Neuronal network formed by monosynaptic connections. *Journal of Neurophysiology*, 46, 65–79.

Ghering, W. (1985). Homeotic genes, the homeobox and the genetic control of development. *Cold Spring Harbor Symposium for Quantitative Biology*, 50, 243–251.

Goelet, P., Castellucci, V., Schacher, S., & Kandel, E. (1986). The long and the short of long-term memory: A molecular framework. *Nature*, 322, 419–422. representational knowledge. In V. Mountcastle & K. F. Plum (eds), *The nervous system: Higher functions of the brain, Vol. 5, Handbook of Physiology*. Washington, DC: American Physiological Society.

Goldowitz, D., & Mullen, R. (1982). Granule cell as a site of gene action in the weaver mouse cerebellum. Evidence from heterozygous mutant chimerae. *Journal of Neuroscience*, 2, 1474–1485.

Gombrich, E. H. (1960). *Art and illusion*. Oxford: Phaidon Press.

Gombrich, E. H. (1983). *L'écologie des images*. Paris: Flammarion.

Goodman, C. S., Bastiani, M. J., Raper, J. A., & Thomas, J. B. (1985). Cell recognition during neuronal development in grasshopper and *Drosophila*. In G. M. Edelman, W. E. Gall, & W. M. Cowan (eds), *Molecular bases of neural development*. New York: Wiley.

Gouzé, J. L., Lasry, J. M., & Changeux, J. P. (1983). Selective stabilization of muscle innervation during development: A mathematical model. *Biological Cybernetics*, 46, 207–215.

Grillner, S. (1975). Locomotion in vertebrates. Central mechanisms and reflex interaction. *Physiological Review*, 55, 247–304.

Grillner, S., Wallén, P., Dale, N., Brodin, L., Buchanan, J., & Hill, R. (1987). Transmitters, membrane properties and network circuitry in the control of locomotion in lamprey. *Trend in Neuroscience*, 10, 34–41.

Gutfreund, H. (1988). Neural networks with hierarchically correlated patterns. *Physical Review*, 91, 375–391.

Hamburger, V. (1970). Embryonic mobility in vertebrates. In F. O. Schmitt (ed.), *The Neurosciences: Second study program*. New York: Rockefeller University Press.

Hawkins, R. D., & Kandel, E. (1984). Is there a cell-biological alphabet for simple forms of learning? *Psychological Review*, 91, 375–391.

Hebb, D. O. (1949). *The organization of behavior: A neuropsychological theory*. New York: Wiley.

Heidmann, A., Heidmann, T., & Changeux, J. P. (1984). Stabilisation selective de représentations neuronales par résonance entre "pré-représentations" spontanées du réseau cérébral et "percepts" évoqués par interaction avec le monde extérieur. *C. R. Acad. Sci. Paris* (série 3), 299, 839–844.

Heidmann, T., & Changeux, J. P. (1982). Un modèle moléculaire de régulation d'efficacité d'un synapes chimique au niveau postsynaptique. *C. R. Acad. Sci. Paris* (série 3), 295, 665–670.

Heit, G., Smith, M. E., & Halgren, E. (1988). Neural encoding of individual words and faces by the human hippocampus and amygdala. *Nature*, 333, 773–775.

Hökfelt, T., Holets, V. R., Staines, W., Meister, B., Melander, T., Schalling, M., Schultzberg, M., Freedman, J., Björklund, H., Olson, L., Lindk, B., Elfvin, L. G.,

Lundberg, J., Lindgren, J. A., Samuelsson, B., Terenius, L., Post, C., Everitt, B., & Goldstein, M. (1986). Coexistence of neuronal messengers: As overview. *Progress in Brain Research*, 68, 33–70.

Hopfield, J. (1982). Neural networks and physical systems with emergent collective computational abilities. *Proceedings of the National Academy of Sciences USA*, 79, 2554–2558.

Hopfield, J., & Tank, D. W. (1986). Computing with neural circuits: A model. *Science*, 233, 625–635.

Hubel, P., & Wiesel, T. (1977). Functional architecture of macaque monkey visual cortex. Ferrier Lecture. *Proceedings of the Royal Society (London) B*, 198, 1–59.

Huttenlocher, P. R., De Courten, C., Garey, L. J., & Vander Loos, H. (1982). Synaptogenesis in human visual cortex. Evidence for synapse elimination during normal development. *Neuroscience Letters*, 33, 247–252.

Innocenti, G. M., & Caminiti, R. (1980). Postnatal shaping of callosal connections from sensory areas. *Experimental Brain Research*, 38, 381–394.

Ito, M., Sakurai, M., & Tongroach, P. (1982). Climbing fibre induced depression of both mossy fibre responsiveness and glutamate sensitivity of cerebellar Purkinje cells. *Journal of Physiology (London)*, 324, 112–121.

F. O. Schmitt (eds.), *The Neurosciences*. New York: Rockefeller University Press.

Johnson, M. H., McConnell, J., & Van Blerkom, J. (1984). Programmed development in the mouse embryo. *Journal of Embryology and Experimental Morphology*, 83 (Suppl.), 197–231.

Johnson-Laird, P. N. (1983). *Mental models*. Cambridge: Cambridge University Press.

Kandel, E. R., Abrams, T., Bernier, L., Carew, T. J., Hawkins, R. D., & Schwartz, J. H. (1983). Classical conditioning and sensitization share aspects of the same molecular cascade in *Aplysia*. *Cold Spring Harbor Symposium on Quantitative Biology*, 48, 821–830.

Kanter, I., & Sompolinsky, H. (1987). Associative recall of memory without errors. *Physical Review A*, 35, 380–392.

Kelos, S. R., Ganong, A. H., & Brown, T. H. (1986). Hebbian synapses in hippocampus. *Proceedings of the National Academy of Science USA*, 83, 5326–5330.

Kihlstrom, J. (1987). The cognitive unconscious. *Science*, 237, 1445–1452.

Kleinfeld, D. (1986). Sequential state generation by model neural networks. *Proceedings of the National Academy of Sciences USA*, 83, 9469–9473.

Kleinfeld, D., & Sompolinsky, H. (1987). Associative neural network model for the generation of temporal patterns: Theory and application to central pattern generators. Unpublished paper.

Kolb, B., & Whishaw, I. (1980). *Fundamentals of human neuropsychology*. San Francisco: Freeman.

Konishi, M. (1985). Bird songs: From behavior to neuron. *Annual Review of Neurophysiology*, 8, 125–170.

Lashley, K. S. (1951). *Central mechanisms in behavior*. New York: Wiley.

Lehkey, S. R., & Sejnowski, T. J. (1988). Network model of shape-from-shading: Neural function arises from both receptive and projective fields. *Nature*, 333, 452–454.

Levinthal, F., Macagno, E., & Levinthal, C. (1976). Anatomy and development of identified cells in isogenic organisms. *Cold Spring Harbor Symposium on Quantitative Biology*, 40, 321–332.

Lhermitte, F. (1983). "Utilization behavior" and its relation to lesions of the frontal lobe. *Brain*, 106, 237–235.

Lisman, J. E. (1985). A mechanism for memory storage insensitive to molecular turnover: A bistable autophosphorylating kinase. *Proceedings of the National Academy of Science USA*, 82, 3055–3057.

Little, W. A. (1974). Existence of persistent states in the brain. *Mathematical Bioscience*, 9, 101–120.

Llinás, R. R. (1987). "Mindness" as a functional state of the brain. In C. Blakemore & S. Greenfield (eds), *Mindwaves*. London: Basil Blackwell.

Lumsden, C., & Wilson, E. O. (1981). *Genes, mind and culture: The coevolutionary process.* Cambridge, MA: Harvard University Press.

Luria, A. R. (1973). *The working brain: An introduction to neuropsychology.* New York: Basic Books.

Macagno, F., Lopresti, U., & Levinthal, C. (1973). Structural development of neuronal connections in isogenic organisms: Variations and similarities in the optic tectum of *Daphnia magna*. *Proceedings of the National Academy of Science USA*, 70, 57–61.

McCarthy, R. A., & Warrington, E. K. (1988). Evidence for modality-specific meaning systems in the brain. *Nature*, 334, 428–430.

McCulloch, W. S., & Pitts, W. A. (1943). Logical calculus of the ideas immanent in nervous activity. *Bulletin of Mathematical Biophysics*, 5, 115.

Marr, D. (1982). *Vision*. San Francisco: Freeman.

Mariani, J., & Changeux, J. P. (1981a). Ontogenesis of olivocerebellar relationships: I – Studies by intracellular recordings of the multiple innervation of Purkinje cells by climbing fibers in the developing rat cerebellum. *Journal of Neuroscience*, 1, 696–702.

Mariani, J., & Changeux, J. P. (1981b). Ontogenesis of olivocerebellar relationships: II – Spontaneous activity of inferior olivary neurons and climbing fiber-mediated activity of cerebellar Purkinje cells in developing rats and in adult cerebellar mutant mice. *Journal of Neuroscience*, 1, 703–709.

Massaro, D. (1975). *Experimental psychology and information processing*. Chicago: Rand McNally.

Mayr, E. (1963). *Animal species and evolution*. Cambridge, MA: Harvard University Press.

Mehler, J., Morton, J., & Jusczyk, P. W. (1984). On reducing language to biology. *Cognitive Neuropsychology*, 1, 83–116.

Meinhardt, H., & Gierer, A. (1974). Application of a theory of biological pattern formation based on lateral inhibition. *Journal of Cell Science*, 15, 321–346.

Merzenich, M. M. (1987). Dynamic neocortical processes and the origins of higher brain functions. In J. P. Changeux & M. Konishi (eds), *The neural and molecular bases of learning*, New York: Wiley.

Mézard, M., Nadal, J. P., & Toulouse, G. (1986). Solvable models of working memories. *Journal de Physique (Paris)*, 47, 1457–1462.

Mitchinson, G. (1987). The organization of sequential memory: Sparse representations and the targeting problem. *Proceedings of the Bad Homburg meeting on Brain Theory*, 16–19 September, 1986.

Miyawaki, K., Strange, W., Verbrugge, R., Liberman, A., Jenkins, J., & Fujimura, O. (1975). An effect of linguistic experience: the discrimination of |r| and |l| by native speakers of Japanese and English. *Perception and Psychophysics*, 18, 331–340.

Monod, J., & Jacob, F. (1961). General conclusions: Teleonomic mechanisms in cellular metabolism, growth and differentiation. *Cold Spring Harbor Symposium for Quantitative Biology*, 26, 389–401.

Monod, J. (1970). *Le hasard et la nécessité*. Paris: Le Seuil.

Montarolo, P. G., Goelet, P., Castellucci, V. F., Morgan, T., Kandel, E., & Schacher, S. (1986). A critical period for macromolecular synthesis in long-term heterosynaptic facilitation in *Aplysia*. *Science*, 234, 1249–1254.

Motter, B. C. Steinmetz, M. A., Duffy, C. J., & Mountcastle, V. B. (1987). Functional properties of parietal visual neurons: Mechanisms of directionality along a single axis. *Journal of Neuroscience*, 7, 154–175.

Mountcastle, V. (1978). An organizing principle for cerebral function: The unit module and the distributed system. In G. M. Edelman & V. Mountcastle (eds), *The mindful brain: Cortical organization and the group-selective theory of higher brain function*. Cambridge, MA: MIT Press.

Nadal, J. P., Toulouse, G., Changeux, J. P., & Dehaene, S. (1986a). Networks of formal neurons and memory palimpsests. *Europhysics Letters*, 1, 535–542.

Nadal, J. P., Toulouse, G., Mézard, M., Changeux, J. P., & Dehaene, S. (1986b). Neural networks: Learning and forgetting. In R. J. Cotteril (ed.), *Computer simulations and brain science*. Cambridge: Cambridge University Press.

Nass, R. D., Koch, D. A., Janowsky, J., & Stile-Davis, J. (1985). Differential effects on intelligence of early left versus right brain injury. *Annals of Neurology*, 18, 393.

Nass, R. D., Koch, D. A., Janowsky, J., & Stile-Davis, J. (1989). Differential effects of congenital left and right brain injury on intelligence.

Nauta, W. J. H. (1971). The problem of the frontal lobe: A reinterpretation. *Journal of Psychiatric Research*, 8, 167–187.

Nauta, W. J. H. (1973). Connections of the frontal lobe with the limbic system. In L. V. Laitiven & K. E. Livingston (eds), *Surgical approaches in psychiatry*. Baltimore, MD: University Pack Press.

Newell, A. (1982). The knowledge level. *Artificial Intelligence*, 18, 87–127.

Niki, H. (1974). Prefrontal unit activity during delayed alternation in the monkey. I. Relation to direction of response. II. Relation to absolute versus relative direction of response. *Brain Research*, 68, 185–196.

Nüsslein-Volhard, C., Frohnhöffer, H. G., & Lehmann, R. (1987). Determination of anteroposterior polarity in Drosophila. *Science*, 238, 1675–1681.

Ojemann, G. (1983). Brain organization for language from the perspective of electrical stimulation mapping. *Behavioral and Brain Science*, 6, 189–230.

Oster-Granite, M., & Gearhart, J. (1981). Cell lineage analysis of cerebellar Purkinje cells in mouse chimaeras. *Development Biology*, 85, 199–208.

Peretto, P., & Niez, J. J. (1986). Collective properties of neural networks. In E. Bienenstock, F. Fogelmann & G. Weisbuch (eds), *Disordered systems and biological organization*. Berlin: Springer-Verlag.

Perrett, D. I., Mistlin, A. J., & Chitty, A. J. (1987). Visual neurons responsive to faces. *Trends in Neurosciences*, 10, 358–364.

Personnaz, L., Guyon, I., & Dreyfus, G. (1985). Information storage and retrieval in spin-glass like neural networks. *Journal de Physique Lettres*, 46, L359.

Petersen, S. E., Fox, P. T., Posner, M. I., Mintun, M., & Raichle, M. E. (1988). Positron emission tomographic studies of the cortical anatomy of single-word processing. *Nature*, 331, 585–589.

Piaget, J. (1979). *Behavior and evolution*. London: Routledge & Kegan Paul.

Pinker, S., & Prince, A. (1988). On language and connectionism: Analysis of a parallel model of language acquisition. *Cognition*, 28, 73–913.

Posner, M. I. (1980). Orienting of attention. *Quarterly Journal of Experimental Psychology*, 32, 3–25.

Posner, M. I., Petersen, S. E., Fox, P. T., & Raichle, M. E. (1988). Localization of cognitive operations in human brain. *Science*, 240, 1627–1631.

Posner, M., & Presti, D. F. (1987). Selective attention and cognitive control. *Trends in Neuroscience*, 10, 13.

Price, D. J., & Blakemore, C. (1985). Regressive events in the postnatal development of association projections in the visual cortex. *Nature*, 316, 721–723.

Prince, A., & Pinker, S. (1988). Rules and connections in human language. *Trends in Neuroscience*, 11, 195–202.

Prince, D. A., & Huguenard, J. R. (1988). Functional properties of neocortical neurons. In P. Rakic & V. Singer (eds), *Neurobiology of the neocortex*. Chichester: Wiley.

Purves, D., & Lichtman, J. W. (1980). Elimination of synapses in the developing nervous system. *Science*, 210, 153–157.

Pylyshyn, Z. (1985). Plasticity and invariance in cognitive development. In J. Mehler & R. Fox (eds), *Neonate cognition*. Hillsdale, NJ: Erlbaum.

Rakic, P. (1988). Intrinsic and extrinsic determinants of neocortical parcellation: a radial unit model. In P. Rakic & W. Singer (eds), *Neurobiology of neocortex*. Chichester: Wiley.

Rakic, P., & Singer, W. (eds) (1988). *Neurobiology of the neocortex*. Chichester: Wiley.

Ramon y Cajal, S. (1909). *Histologie du système nerveux de l'homme et des vertébrés* (2 vols.). Paris: Maloine.

Redfern, P. A. (1970). Neuromuscular transmission in newborn rats. *Journal of Physiology (London)*, 20, 701–709.

Reiter, H. O., & Stryker, M. P. (1988). Neural plasticity without postsynaptic action potentials: Less-active inputs become dominant when kitten visual cortical cells are pharmacologically inhibited. *Proceedings of the National Academy of Science USA*, 85, 3623–3627.

Ribchester, R. R. (1988). Activity-dependent and -independent synaptic interactions during reinnervation of partially denervated rat muscle. *Journal of Physiology*, 401, 53–75.

Rockwell, A., Hiorns, R., & Powell, T. (1980). The basic uniformity in structure of the neocortex. *Brain*, 103, 221–224.

Roland, P. E., & Friberg (1985). Localization of cortical areas activated by thinking. *Journal of Neurophysiology*, 53, 1219–1243.

Rolls, E. (1987). Information representation, processing and storage in the brain: Analysis at the single neuron level. In J. P. Changeux & M. Konishi (eds). *The neural and molecular bases of learning*. Chichester: Wiley.

Rugg, M. (1988). Stimulus selectivity of single neurons in the temporal lobe. *Nature*, 333, 700.

Rumelhart, D. E., & McClelland, J. L. (1987). Learning the past tenses of English verbs: Implicit rules or parallel distributed processing? In B. MacWhinney (ed.), *Mechanisms of language acquisition*. Hillsdale, NJ: Erlbaum.

Searle, J. R. (1983). *Intentionality: An essay in the philosophy of mind*. New York: Cambridge University Press.

Sejnowsky, T. J., Koch, C., & Churchland, P. S. (1988). Computational neuroscience. *Science*, 241, 1299–1306.

Sejnowsky, T. J., & Rosenberg, C. R. (1986) *NET-talk: A parallel network that learns to read aloud*. Technical report JHU/EECS-86/01. Department of Electrical Engineering and Computer Science, John Hopkins University.

Shallice, T. (1982). Specific impairments of planning. *Philosophical Transactions of the Royal Society of London B*, 298, 199–209.

Simon, H. A. (1969). *The sciences of the artificial*. Cambridge, MA: MIT Press.

Sompolinsky, H., & Kanter, I. (1986). Temporal association in asymmetric neural networks. *Physical Review Letters*, 57, 2861–2864.

Sperber, D. (1984). Anthropology and psychology: Towards an epidemiology of representations. *Man* (N.S.), 20, 73–89.

Sretavan, D. W., Shatz, C. J., & Stryker, M. P. (1988). Modification of retinal ganglion cell axon morphology by frontal infusion of tetrodotoxin. *Nature*, 336.

Steinmetz, M. A., Motter, B. C., Duffy, C. J., & Mountcastle, V. (1987). Functional properties of parietal visual neurons: Radial organization of directionalities within the visual field. *Journal of Neuroscience*, 7, 177–191.

Stent, G. (1973). A physiological mechanism for Hebb's postulate of learning. *Proceedings of the National Academy of Science USA*, 70, 997–1001.

Stent, G. (1981). Strength and weakness of the genetic approach to the development of the nervous system. *Annual Review of Neuroscience*, 4, 163–194.

Stent, G. (1987). The mind-body problem. *Science*, 236, 990–992.

Stent, G. S., Kristan, W. B., Friesen, W. O., Ort, C. A., Poon, M., & Calabrese, R. L. (1978). Neurosal generation of the leech swimming movement. *Science*, 200, 1348–1356.

Stryker, M. P., & Harris, W. A. (1986). Binocular impulse blockage prevents the formation of ocular dominance columns in cat visual cortex. *Journal of Neuroscience*, 6, 2117–2133.

Stuss, D., & Benson, F. (1986). *The frontal lobes*. New York: Raven.

Taine, H. (1870). *De l'intelligence*. Paris: Hachette.

Tank, D. W., & Hopfield, J. J. (1987). Neural computation by concentrating information in time. *Proceedings of the National Academy of Science USA*, 84, 1896–1900.

Teuber, H. L. (1972). Unity and diversity of frontal lobe functions. *Acta Neurobiology Experiments (Warst.)*, 32, 615–656.

Thom, R. (1980). *Modéles mathèmatiques de la morphogènése*. Paris: Bourgeois.

Thomas, R. (1981). On the relation between the logical structure of systems and their ability to generate multiple steady-states or sustained oscillations. *Springer Series in Synergetics*, 9, 180–193.

Toulouse, G., Dehaene, S., & Changeux, J. P. (1986). Spin glass model of learning by selection. *Proceedings of the National Academy of Science USA*, 83, 1695–1698.

Turing, A. M. (1952). The chemical basis of morphogenesis. *Philosophical Transactions of the Royal Society (London)*, 237, 37–72.

Van Essen, D. G. (1982). Neuromuscular synapse elimination: Structural, functional and mechanistic aspects. In N. C. Spitzer (ed.), *Neuronal development*. New York: Plenum.

Von der Malsburg, C. (1981). *The correlation theory of brain function*. Internal report 8–12 July 1981, Department of Neurobiology, Max Plank Institute for Biophysical Chemistry, Göttingen.

Von der Malsburg, C., & Bienenstock, E. (1986). Statistical coding and short-term plasticity: A scheme for knowledge representation. In E. Bienenstock, F. Fogelman, & G. Weisbuch (eds), *Disordered systems and biological organization*. Berlin: Springer-Verlag.

Wilson, E. O. (1975). *Sociobiology*. Cambridge, MA: Harvard University Press.

Young, J. Z. (1964). *A model of the brain*. Oxford: Clarendon Press.

Young, J. Z. (1973). Memory as a selective process. *Australian Academy of Science Reports: Symposium on the Biology of Memory*, 25–45.

Zeki, S. (1988). Anatomical guides to the functional organization of the visual cortex. In P. Rakic & W. Singer (eds), *Neurobiology of neocortex*. Chichester: Wiley.

Zipser, D., & Andersen, R. A. (1988). A back-propagation programmed network that stimulates response properties of a subset of posterior parietal neurons. *Nature*, 331, 679–684.

18

Language, Modality and the Brain

URSULA BELLUGI, HOWARD POIZNER AND EDWARD S. KLIMA

Biological Foundations of Language

Until recently, nearly everything learned about the human capacity for language has come from the study of spoken languages. It has been assumed that the organizational properties of language are inseparably connected with the sounds of speech, and that the fact that language is normally spoken and heard determines the basic principles of grammar.[1] There is good evidence that structures involved in breathing, chewing and the ingestion of food have evolved into a versatile and more efficient system for producing sound. Studies of brain organization indicate that the left cerebral hemisphere is specialized for processing linguistic information in the auditory–vocal mode and that the major language-mediating areas of the brain are intimately connected with the auditory–vocal channel. It has even been argued that hearing and the development of speech are necessary precursors to this cerebral specialization for language.[2] Thus, the link between biology and linguistic behavior has been identified with the particular sensory modality in which language has developed.

The existence of signed languages allows us to inquire about the determinants of language organization from a different perspective. What would language be like if its transmission were not based on the vocal tract and the ear? How is language organized when it is based instead on the hands and eyes? Do these transmission channel differences result in any deeper differences? Over the past decade, we have been specifying the ways in which the formal properties of languages are shaped by their modalities of expression, sifting properties peculiar to a particular language mode from more general properties common to all languages.[3,4] American Sign Language (ASL) exhibits formal structuring at the same levels as spoken languages (the internal structure of lexical units and the grammatical scaffolding underlying sentences) as well as the same kinds of organizational principles as spoken languages. Yet the form this grammatical

"Language, Modality and the Brain" first appeared in *Trends in the Neurosciences* 12 (1989), pp. 380–8, and is reprinted by kind permission.

structuring assumes in a visual–manual language is apparently deeply influenced by the modality in which the language is cast.

Language in a Visuospatial Modality

American Sign Language, a primary linguistic system passed down from one generation of deaf people to the next, has been forged into an autonomous language with its own internal mechanisms for relating visual form with meaning. The grammatical processes of ASL are totally unrelated to those of English and thus add to the evidence that ASL is a separate language, though it uses hands in space.[3-6] It can serve not only everyday conversation, but intellectual argumentation, scientific discussion, wit and poetry. ASL shares underlying principles of organization with spoken languages, but the physical realization of those principles occurs in formal devices arising out of the very different possibilities of the visual–gestural mode.[7] We consider briefly the structure of ASL at three different linguistic levels: "phonology" without sound, vertically arrayed morphology, and spatially organized syntax.

"Phonology" without sound. Research on the structure of lexical signs in ASL has shown that signs are fractionated into sublexical elements just like the words of spoken languages. The contrasts that distinguish signs from one another (analogous to consonants and vowels of spoken languages) are a small set of "Handshapes," "Movements," and "Locations" that co-occur throughout the sign. Recent analyses focus on the segmental structure of signed languages, suggesting a sequential structure analogous to phonemes and syllables of spoken language.[8, 9] Signed languages differ from one another, much as do spoken languages, and there are many different signed languages. We note that ASL and British Sign Language are mutually incomprehensible, having independent histories. Furthermore, analyses of unrelated signed languages reveal not only differences in lexicon and grammar, but even systematic phonetic differences that may cause native signers from one sign language to have an "accent" in a newly learned sign language.[4, 10]

Vertically arrayed morphology. The grammatical mechanisms of ASL take full advantage of the spatial medium and of the possibility of simultaneous and multidimensional articulation. Like spoken languages, ASL has developed grammatical devices that serve as inflectional and derivational markers. These are regular changes in form across syntactic classes of lexical items associated with systematic changes in meaning. In ASL, families of sign forms are related via an underlying stem: the forms share Handshape, Location, and Movement shape. Grammatical processes represent the interaction of the stem with other features of movement in space (dynamics of movement, directions of movement, spatial array and the like all *layered* with the sign stem (see figure 18.1A).

In ASL, such grammatical processes can apply in combinations to signs, creating different levels of form and meaning. In these combinations, the output of one morphological process can serve as the input for another, and there are alternative orderings producing different levels of semantic structure as well, as figure 18.1A shows. The creation of complex expressions through the recursive application of hierarchically organized rules is also characteristic of the structure of spoken languages.[11] However, the form such expression takes in a visual–gestural language is unique: the sign stem embedded in the pattern created by a morphological process, and nested spatially in a pattern created by the same or a different morphological process.

Spatially organized syntax. All spoken languages have grammatical elements and structure relating items to one another in sentences, providing the underlying scaffolding on which to build sentential meaning. Languages have different ways of marking grammatical relations among their lexical items. In English, it is primarily the order of the lexical items that marks the basic relations among verbs and their related nouns. ASL, by contrast, specifies relations among signs primarily through the manipulation of sign forms in space. In sign language, space itself bears linguistic meaning. The most striking and distinctive use of space in ASL is in syntax and discourse. Noun phrases introduced into ASL sentences may be associated with specific points in a plane of signing space: pointing again to a specific locus clearly 'refers back' to a previously mentioned noun, even with many other signs intervening.

The ASL system of verb agreement, like its system of pronouns, is also spatialized. Verb signs move between abstract loci in signing space, bearing obligatory markers for person and number via spatial indices, thereby specifying subject and object of the verb, as shown in figure 18.1B. This spatialized system thus allows explicit reference through pronouns and agreement markers to distinct, third-person referents. The same signs in the same order, but with different spatial endpoints of the verb, may specify a reversal of grammatical relations. Furthermore, sentences with signs in different temporal orders can still have the same meaning, since grammatical relations are signified spatially. Different spaces may be used to contrast events, to indicate reference to time preceding the utterance, or to express hypotheticals and counterfactuals. This use of spatial loci for referential indexing, verb agreement, and grammatical relations is clearly a unique property of visual–gestural systems.[4]

ASL has developed as a fully autonomous language, with complex organizational properties not derived from spoken languages, thus illuminating the biological determinants of language. ASL exhibits formal structuring at the same levels as spoken language, and principles similar to those of spoken language (constrained systems of features, rules based on underlying forms, and recursive grammatical processes). Yet the surface form of grammatical processes in a visuospatial language is rooted in the modality in which the language developed. This difference in surface form between signed and spoken languages makes possible new investigations into the perception and production of language.

Perception, Language and Experience

Dynamic point-light displays. Linguistic analyses and experimental studies of sign language have been linked together, allowing the study of the interplay between the perception of language and the perception of motion. Specifically, one can now investigate the nature of perception of movement organized into a linguistic system.[12] To investigate linguistic movement in ASL experimentally, a method was developed to isolate movement of the hands and arms, adapting a technique

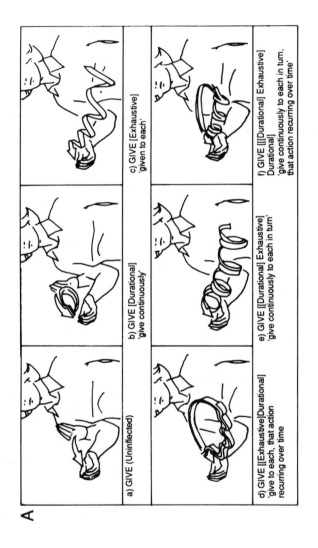

A

a) GIVE (Uninflected)

b) GIVE [Durational]
'give continuously'

c) GIVE [Exhaustive]
'given to each'

d) GIVE [[Exhaustive]Durational]
'give to each, that action
recurring over time

e) GIVE [[Durational] Exhaustive]
'give continuously to each in turn'

f) GIVE [[[Durational] Exhaustive]
Durational]
'give continuously to each in turn,
that action recurring over time'

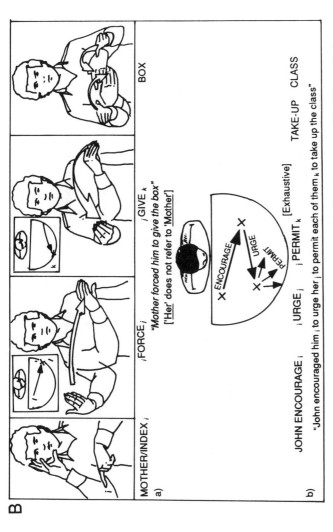

Figure 18.1 Layered morphology and spatially organized syntax in American Sign Language. (A) Hierarchical processes governing ASL grammatical inflections. The uninflected sign GIVE is shown in (a), together with the sign GIVE under single inflections (b and c). The figure shows an ordered combination of inflections (Exhaustive in Durational, d) as well as a different ordering of inflections (Durational in Exhaustive with a distinct meaning, e). Finally, (f) illustrates the recursive applications of rules (Durational in Exhaustive in Durational). We note that ASL packages its grammatical information systematically in simultaneously occurring layers of structure. (B) Syntactic spatial mechanisms in ASL. The figure shows a spatially organized sentence in ASL, illustrating association of nouns with loci in space, and movement of verbs between spatial endpoints (verb agreement). Also shown is a spatial reference diagram for sentences with complex embedded structures in which co-referential nominals are indexed to the same locus point.

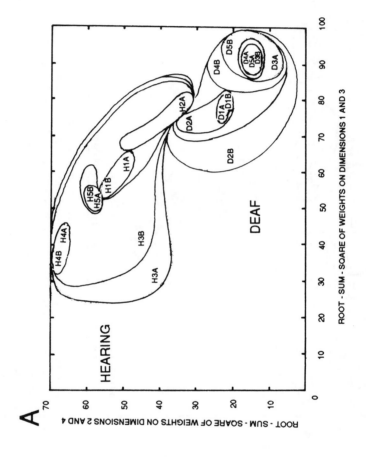

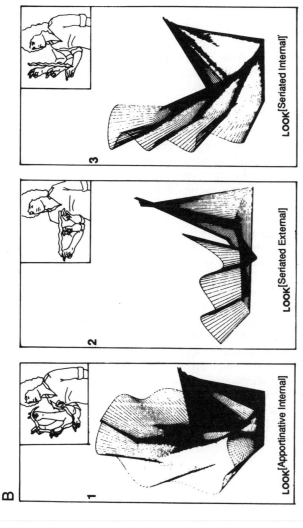

Figure 18.2 Multidimensional analysis of movement organized into a linguistic system. (A) Hierarchical clustering of correlations among subjects (closed contours) superimposed on the multidimensional scaling of judgements of movement similarity by deaf and hearing subjects. The position of each replication (A or B) of each deaf subject (D1 through D5) and each hearing subject (H1 through H5) was determined from each subject's combined weights on dimensions 2 (plane) and 4 (direction) versus his combined weights on dimensions 1 (repetition) and 3 (direction) of the scaling solution. Note the virtually complete separation between deaf and hearing subjects, reflecting the different perceptual salience of dimensions of movement for the two groups. (B) Three-dimensional reconstructions of the positions of the arm and hand for grammatical inflections in ASL contrasting in both planar locus and geometric array. The first and third reconstructions contrast minimally in geometric array (circular versus linear path movement), whereas the second and third reconstructions contrast minimally in planar locus (horizontal versus vertical).

introduced by Johansson[13] to study the perception of biological motion.[14] Small incandescent bulbs were placed at the major joints of the arms and hands, and signing recorded in a darkened room so that only the patterns of moving lights appeared against a black background. Even with such greatly reduced information, deaf signers identified morphological processes of ASL presented in these point-light displays with a high degree of accuracy, demonstrating that these patterns of dynamic contours of movement form a distinct, isolable layer of structure in ASL.

The interplay between perceptual and linguistic processes. To investigate the relation between basic perceptual processes and higher order linguistic ones, the psychological representation of ASL movement by native deaf signers was contrasted with that of hearing non-signers. Triads of ASL signs were presented as point-light displays for judgements of movement similarity. Multidimensional scaling and hierarchical clustering of judgements for both groups of subjects revealed that the inflectional movements were perceived in terms of a limited number of underlying dimensions. Furthermore, the psychological representation of movement differs for deaf and hearing subjects, with perception of movement form tied to linguistically relevant dimensions for deaf, but not for hearing subjects (figure 18.2A). Thus, the data suggest that acquisition of a visual–gestural language can modify the natural perceptual categories into which linguistically relevant forms fall.[15, 16]

The study of sign languages provides a powerful vehicle for analysing language production since in sign language, but not in spoken language, movements of the hands are directly observable. In order to analyse the structure of movements that have been forged into a linguistic system, methods have been developed to track movements in three-dimensional space and reconstruct them computer-graphically.[17, 18] Figure 18.2B presents three-dimensional reconstructions of the sequential positions of the arm and hand throughout the course of three grammatical inflections expressed in ASL through modulations of movement. These illustrate the essential nature of grammatical contrasts that have developed in ASL, conveyed through dimensions unique to visual–spatial language, such as planar locus and geometric array. Thus, processing grammatical relations in sign language also requires the processing of spatial relations, since in sign language the two are intimately intertwined. These powerful techniques for the three-dimensional computergraphic analysis of movement are now being coupled with linguistic analysis to explore how the brain controls movement at different levels – *linguistic*, *symbolic* and *motoric*.[19, 20]

Brain Organization: Clues from a Visuospatial Language

American Sign Language (ASL) displays the complex linguistic structure found in spoken languages but conveys much of its structure by manipulating spatial relations, thus exhibiting properties for which each of the hemispheres of hearing people shows a different predominant functioning. The study of brain-damaged deaf signers offers special insight into the organization of higher cognitive functions in the brain, and how modifiable that organization may be. How is language represented in the brain when linguistic relations are expressed spatially?

Systematic studies of the grammatical structure of sign language have only recently become available,[4, 5, 21-26] allowing analyses of the nature of ASL breakdown following localized lesions to the brain.

The relative contributions of each cerebral hemisphere with special reference to the interplay between linguistic functions and the spatial mechanisms that convey them has recently been systematically investigated, focusing on the nature of the linguistic breakdown following localized lesions to the brains of deaf signers. We carried out three series of experimental studies, each bringing to bear a special property of the visual–gestural modality on the investigation of brain–language relationships. Right- and left-lesioned deaf signers (and matched controls) were given a battery of tests designed to assess their capacities for sign language, spatial cognition and motor function.[27-30] Figure 18.3 shows the background characteristics and lateral reconstructions of brain lesions of six deaf signers reviewed below.

Language capacities of left- and right-lesioned signers. Signers with left hemisphere damage showed clear sign language aphasias, as indicated by results on tests for processing the structural levels of ASL, on a sign aphasia examination, and on linguistic analyses of their signing. To illustrate the nature of the aphasias that occur for a visual–gestural language, the deficits of several left-lesioned deaf signers with aphasia are briefly described. One left hemisphere damaged signer (GD) was agrammatic for ASL. After her stroke, her signing was severely impaired; it was halting and effortful, and reduced to single sign utterances, shorn of the syntactic and morphological markings of ASL (figure 18.4A). Her lesion was typical of those that produce agrammatic aphasia for spoken language. Another left hemisphere damaged signer (KL) had motorically facile signing, but made selection errors in the formational elements of signs, producing the ASL equivalent of phonemic paraphasias (figure 18.4B). She had a severe and lasting sign comprehension loss, although both major language-mediating areas for spoken language (Broca's and Wernicke's areas) were intact. Her lesion was in the parietal area known to function in higher spatial analysis. A third left hemisphere damaged signer (PD) showed primary impairment at the grammatical level. His signing before his stroke was articulate, even eloquent. After his stroke, he produced grammatically inappropriate signs (paragrammatisms) in the context of fluent sign output. Furthermore, he displayed errors of spatially organized syntax of ASL (figure 18.4C). Thus, differential damage within the left hemisphere produced sign language impairments that were not uniform, but rather broke down along lines of linguistically relevant components.[31]

Quite remarkably, considering the spatial nature of sign language, the signers with right hemisphere damage were not aphasic. They exhibited fluent, grammatical, virtually error-free signing, with a good range of grammatical forms, no agrammatism, and no signing deficits. Their performance on our Sign Diagnostic Aphasia Battery (adapted from Goodglass and Kaplan[32]) revealed intact sign language capacities for right-lesioned signers. Furthermore, only the right hemisphere damaged signers were unimpaired on our tests of ASL grammatical structure (phonology, morphology, syntax). Figure 18.5A shows the results of an ASL test equivalent of 'rhyming'. Importantly, right-lesioned signers had no impairment in the grammatical aspects of their signing, including their spatially

LEFT HEMISPHERE DAMAGED SIGNERS

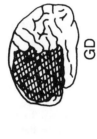

PD

81yr. old ♂

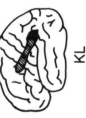

KL

67yr. ♀
Rt. Hemiplegia

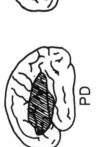

GD

38yr. ♀
Rt. Hemiplegia

Patient	Age at testing	Sex	Age at onset of deafness	Handed-ness	Language environment				Primary commu-nication	Hemiplegia	Lesion
					Parents and siblings	School	Spouse	Cultural group			
Paul D.	81	M	5 yrs.	Right	Hearing	Residential deaf	Deaf	Deaf	Sign	—	Left subcortical; deep to Broca's area extending posteriorly beneath parietal lobe.
Karen L.	67	F	6 mos.	Right	Hearing	Residential deaf	Hard of hearing	Deaf	Sign	Right hemiplegic	Left pariental: supramarginal and angular gyri; extending subcortically into middle frontal gyrus.
Gail D.	38	F	Birth	Right	Older deaf siblings	Residential deaf	Deaf	Deaf	Sign	Right hemiplegic	Most of convexity of left frontal lobe; Broca's area damaged.

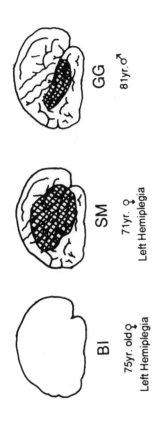

RIGHT HEMISPHERE DAMAGED SIGNERS

Brenda I.	75	F	Birth	Right	Hearing	Residential deaf	Deaf	Sign	Right hemisphere
Sarah M.	71	F	Birth	Right	Hearing	Residential deaf	Deaf	Sign	Right temporoparietal area; most of territory of right middle cerebral artery damaged
Gilbert G.	81	M	5 yrs.	Right	Hearing	Residential deaf	Deaf	Sign	Right superior temporal and middle temporal gyri extending into the angular gyrus.

BI — 75yr. old ♀ — Left Hemiplegia

SM — 71yr. ♀ — Left Hemiplegia

GG — 81yr. ♂ — Left hemiplegic / Right hemiplegic — —

Figure 18.3 Summary characteristics and lateral reconstructions of lesions of three left and three right hemisphere damaged deaf signers. All six were right-handed, had gone to residential schools for deaf children, married deaf spouses, and had used sign language as the primary form of communication throughout their lives. Note that no CT scan was available for BI.

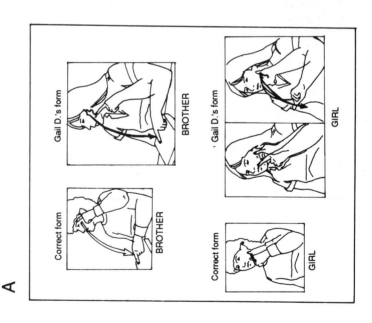

A

Correct form — BROTHER

Gail D.'s form — BROTHER

Correct form — GIRL

Gail D.'s form — GIRL

B

Correct form — CAREFUL

Karen L.'s Sublexical errors

Correct form — ENJOY

Karen L.'s Handshape errors
(/ W / for / K /)

Karen L.'s Movement errors
(/ N / for / @ /)

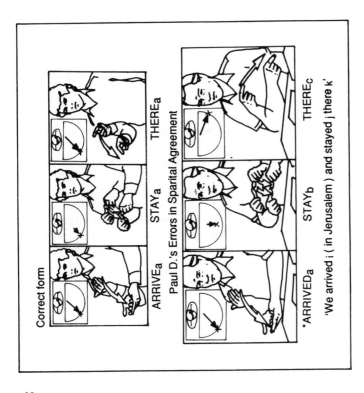

Figure 18.4 Characteristic errors of left-lesioned signers showing breakdown of American Sign Language at different structural levels. (A) Articulatory difficulty characteristic of GD's signing. In the example, she searches for the handshape, movement, and location of two signs, although on other occasions she can produce the signs smoothly. (B) Sublexical (or 'phonological') errors typical of KL's signing. Note selection errors within major formational parameters of ASL of handshape and movement. These are the equivalent of phonemic paraphasias in spoken language. (C) Failure of spatially organized syntax in PD's signing. Note the lack of spatial agreement in PD's sentence, rendering it ungrammatical in ASL.

organized syntax; they even used the left side of signing space to represent syntactic relations, despite their neglect of left hemispace in non-language tasks.[28]

Spatial cognition in signers with left and right hemisphere lesions. The preserved signing of the right-lesioned signers was in the face of their marked deficits in processing non-language spatial relationships. Across a range of tasks, including drawing, spatial construction, spatial attention, judgement of line orientation, facial discrimination, right-lesioned signers showed the classical visuospatial impairments seen in hearing patients with right hemisphere damage. In contrast, left-lesioned signers showed relatively preserved non-language spatial functioning. The severe disorganization of the spatial constructions of right-lesioned signers in contrast to relatively good constructions of the left-lesioned signers is shown in figure 18.5B. Even the right-lesioned signer who was an artist before her stroke showed disorganization, failure to indicate perspective, and neglect of left hemispace in her drawings afterwards. These data show that the right hemisphere in deaf signers can develop cerebral specialization for non-language visuospatial functions. In light of their major non-language spatial deficits, the impeccable use of the spatial mechanisms for syntax in right-lesioned signers shows how little effect right hemisphere damage can have on language, even when spatial contrasts are crucial at all linguistic levels.[30, 31]

The contrast between spatial syntax and spatial mapping. Spatial contrasts and spatial manipulations figure structurally at all linguistic levels in ASL. For syntactic functions, spatial loci and relations among these loci are actively manipulated to represent grammatical relations. As opposed to its syntactic use, space in ASL also functions in a topographic way: the space within which signs are articulated can be used to describe the layout of objects in space. In such mapping, spatial relations among signs correspond topographically to actual spatial relations among the objects described. We investigated the breakdown of two uses of space within sign language, one for syntax and the other for mapping. Subjects were asked to describe the spatial layout of their living quarters from memory; in this task, signing space is to describe space and actual spatial relations are thus significant. The descriptions given by the right-lesioned signers were grossly distorted spatially. In contrast, room descriptions of the left hemisphere damaged signers were linguistically impaired (matching their linguistic breakdown in other domains) but without spatial distortions.

When space was used in ASL to represent syntactic relations, however, the pattern was reversed. The left hemisphere damaged signer, who showed consistent failure in his spatially organized syntax, was able to describe the layout of his room with some omissions but no spatial distortions. A dissociation was also dramatically displayed in a right-lesioned signer. The description she gave of her room showed severe spatial disorganization: furniture piled in helter-skelter fashion on the right, and the entire left side of signing space left bare. However, in her use of the spatial framework for syntax in ASL, she established loci freely throughout the signing space (including on the left) and maintained consistent reference to spatial loci. Thus even within signing, the use of space to represent *syntactic* relations and the use of space to represent *spatial* relations may be differentially affected by brain damage, with the syntactic relations disrupted by left hemisphere damage and the spatial relations disrupted by right hemisphere damage.[28, 30]

The separation between apraxia and sign aphasia. In a long-standing controversy over the nature of aphasic disorders, certain investigators have proposed a common underlying basis for disorders of gesture and disorders of language. One position is that disorders of language occur as a result of more primary disorders of movement control. A second position is that both apraxia and aphasia result from an underlying deficit in the capacity to express and comprehend symbols.

Since gesture and linguistic symbols are transmitted in the same modality in sign language, the breakdown of the two can be directly compared. In addition to an array of language tests, a series of apraxia tests was administered to brain-damaged deaf subjects, including tests of production and imitation of representational and non-representational movements. The right hemisphere damaged signers were neither aphasic nor apraxic. However, for the left hemisphere damaged signers, all of whom were aphasic for sign language, some strong dissociations emerged between their language and non-language gesture and motor capacities.[30] The language deficits of these signers were on the whole related to specific linguistic components of sign language rather than to an underlying motor disorder, or to an underlying disorder in the capacity to express and comprehend symbols of any kind. This separation between linguistic and non- linguistic functioning is all the more striking since sign language and gesture are transmitted in the same modality.

Converging evidence regarding brain organization for signing. A recent study (Damasio *et al.*) analyzed the sign language of a hearing signer proficient in ASL during a left intracarotid injection of sodium amytal (Wada Test), and before and after a right temporal lobectomy for her epilepsy.[33] Neuropsychological and anatomical asymmetries suggested left cerebral dominance for auditory-based language. Single photon emission tomography (SPET) revealed lateralized activity of left Broca's and Wernicke's areas for spoken language (figure 18.6A). The Wada Test, during which all left language areas were rendered inoperative, caused a marked aphasia in both English and ASL. The patient's signing was markedly impaired, with many incorrect sign responses and sign neologisms. Interestingly, since she was hearing and could sign and speak at the same time, it was possible to compare her responses in two languages simultaneously – a unique possibility for languages in different modalities. This revealed a frequent mismatch between word and sign, the sign being frequently incorrect both in meaning and in form (figure 18.6B). Subsequently, the patient had the anterior portion of her right temporal lobe removed surgically (figure 18.6C). Analysis of her language after the surgery revealed no impairment of either English or sign language. These findings add further support to the notion that the left cerebral hemisphere subserves language in a visuospatial as well as an auditory mode.[33]

Converging evidence also comes from a combination of behavioral and neurophysiological studies in deaf signers without lesions (Neville[34-36]). In Neville's studies, digitized sequences of ASL signs were presented to the left and right visual fields of deaf native signers and hearing non-signers. The deaf native signers, but not the hearing non-signers, showed a left hemisphere specialization for processing signs of ASL, providing further evidence for left hemisphere specialization for sign language. From these converging perspectives, it is becoming clear that the primary specialization of the left hemisphere rests not on the form of the signal, but rather on the linguistic function it subserves.

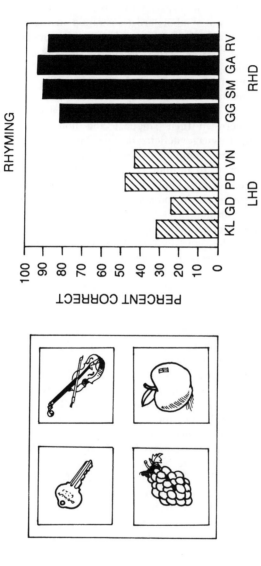

a) Test For Processing Sublexical Structure in ASL: Rhyming

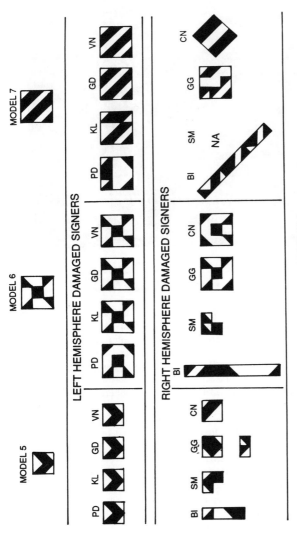

WAIS-R BLOCK DESIGN

Figure 18.5 Impaired linguistic performance of left-lesioned signers contrasted with impaired spatial capacity of right-lesioned signers. (A) Results from a test of ASL phonology, the sign equivalent of 'rhyming' in ASL. Subjects were asked to indicate the two pictures that represented the sign equivalent of 'rhyme' in ASL. In the figure, the correct answer is 'apple' and 'key', since their associated signs are the same in all but one of the three major parameters of ASL (e.g. they have the same handshape and movement, and differ only in location). Right-lesioned signers (RHD) show far superior performance to left-lesioned signers (LHD) on this test. (B) Sample performance on a block arrangement task in which subjects must assemble either four or nine three-dimensional blocks to match a two-dimensional model of the top surface. On this non-language visuospatial task, left-lesioned signers were markedly superior to right-lesioned signers. The left-lesioned signers (upper row) produced correct constructions on the simple block designs and made only featural errors on the more complex designs; in contrast, the right-lesioned signers (lower row) produced erratic and incorrect constructions and tended to break the overall configurations of the arrangements.

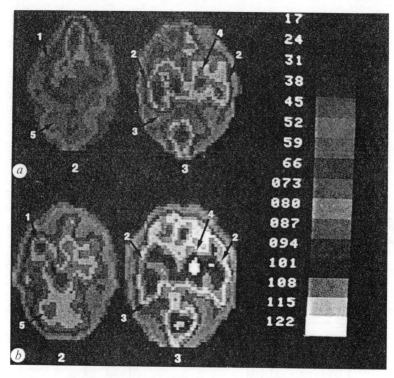

SPET Study At Rest (a) and During a
Verbal Rhyme Detection Task(b).

Figure 18.6 Left hemisphere specialization for both spoken and signed language in a hearing signer. (A) Cuts 2 and 3 of a six-slice SPET study at rest and during an auditory rhyme detection task. During activation, there is an increase of radiosignal in Broca's region (the left frontal fields 44 and 45, indicated by arrow 1), and a bilateral increase of signal in auditory cortices (indicated by arrow 2). In the left hemisphere, the signal increase extends into Wernicke's area (the posterior sector of area 22, arrow 3), suggesting that the processing of spoken language is lateralized to the left hemisphere. During activation, there is also an increase in the right basal ganglia (arrow 4) and left cerebellar hemisphere (arrow 5), two motor structures that are engaged by the movement of the left foot required to signal appropriate rhyme detection. (B) Three errors produced by the patient during left Wada injection. Asked to name an object, the patient often produced simultaneously a correct English word and an incorrect ASL sign. Some sign errors were blends of formational components from different ASL signs, producing nonsense forms that were well-formed in ASL, but meaningless. During recovery from the left Wada injection, the patient frequently responded in speech and sign simultaneously (a possibility confined to languages using different transmission channels). The two languages were frequently mismatched and the sign was more often in error. Inserts in the upper left-hand corner of the illustrations indicate the correct ASL signs. (C) Magnetic resonance images obtained after surgical removal of portions of the right hemisphere. The top left-hand image is a mid-sagittal cut, showing the mesial aspect of one hemisphere. The vertical lines represent the level and incidence of the coronal cuts. Cuts 2, 4 and 5 are reproduced depicting the area of right ten poral lobe ablation. Hippocampus, parahippocampal gyrus, fourth, third and second temporal gyri are missing. (Taken, with permission, from Ref. 33. Copyright © 1986 Macmillan Magazines.)

B

speech: ['cigarette']
sign: [SCISSORS]

speech: ['orange']
sign: [Neologism]
ORANGE / SCISSORS blend

speech: ['cat']
sign: [Neologism]
different ORANGE / SCISSORS blend

The Conflict Between Sign and Speech
Errors During left Wada Test

C

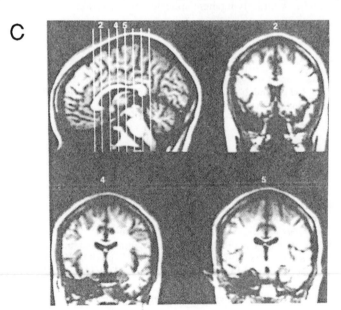

MRI Brain Scan Following Right
Temporal Lobectomy

U. Bellugi et al.

Concluding Remarks

We have reviewed studies that investigate language, its formal architecture, and its representation in the brain, by analysing visuospatial languages passed down from one generation of deaf people to the next. Analysis of patterns of breakdown in deaf signers provides new perspectives on the determinants of hemispheric specialization for language. First, the data show that hearing and speech are not necessary for the development of hemispheric specialization: sound is *not* crucial. Second, it is the left hemisphere that is dominant for sign language. Deaf signers with damage to the left hemisphere show marked sign language deficits but a relatively intact capacity for processing non-language visuospatial relations. Signers with damage to the right hemisphere show the reverse pattern. Thus, not only is there left hemisphere specialization for language functioning, but there is also complementary specialization for non-language spatial functioning. The fact that grammatical information in sign language is conveyed via spatial manipulation does not alter this complementary specialization. Furthermore, components of sign language (lexicon and grammar) can be selectively impaired, reflecting differential breakdown of sign language along linguistically relevant lines. These data suggest that the left hemisphere in man may have an innate predisposition for language, regardless of the modality. Since sign language involves an interplay between visuospatial and linguistic relations, studies of sign language breakdown in deaf signers may, in the long run, bring us closer to the fundamental principles underlying hemispheric specialization.

ACKNOWLEDGEMENTS

We acknowledge the support of National Institutes of Health grants NS 15175, NS 19096, NS 25149 and HD 13249, and National Science Foundation grant BNS86–09085 to the Salk Institute for Biological Studies.

REFERENCES

1 Liberman, A. (1982) *Am. Psychol.* 37, 148–167.
2 McKeever, W. F., Hoemann, H. W., Florian, V. A. and VanDeventer, A. D. (1976) *Neuropsychologia* 14, 413–423.
3 Bellugi, U. and Studdert-Kennedy, M., eds (1980) *Signed and Spoken Language: Biological Constraints on Linguistic Form.* Verlag Chemie.
4 Klima, E. S. and Bellugi, U. (1988) *The Signs of Language.* Harvard University Press.
5 Bellugi, U. and Klima, E. S. (1979) In *Brain and Mind*, pp. 99–117. Excerpta Medica.
6 Stokoe, W., Croneberg, C. and Casterline, D. (1965) *A Dictionary of ASL on Linguistic Principles.* Gallaudet College Press.
7 Bellugi, U. (1983) In *Psychobiology of Language* (Studdert-Kennedy, M., ed.), pp. 152–176. MIT Press.
8 Liddell, S. K. and Johnson, R. E. (1986) *Nat. Lang. Ling. Theory* 4, 445–513.
9 Perlmutter, D. (1990) In *Sign Language Research: Theoretical Issues* (Lucas, C., ed.), Gallaudet University Press.

10 Fok, Y. Y. A., Bellugi, U. and Lillo-Martin, D. (1986) In *Linguistics, Psychology and the Chinese Language* (Kao, H. and Hoosain, R., eds), pp. 336–362. University of Hong Kong Press.
11 Chomsky, N. (1982) *Lectures on Government and Binding.* Dordrecht-Holland.
12 Poizner, H., Wooten, E. and Salot, D. (1986) *Behav. Res. Meth. Inst. Comp.* 18, 427–433 [special issue].
13 Johansson, G. (1975) *Sci. Am.* 232, 76–89.
14 Poizner, H. (1981) *Science* 212, 691–693.
15 Poizner, H. (1983) *Percept. Psychophys.* 33, 215–231.
16 Poizner, H., Bellugi, U. and Lutes-Driscoll, V. (1981) *J. Exp. Psychol.* 7, 430–440.
17 Jennings, P. and Poizner, H. (1988) *J. Neurosci. Meth.* 24, 45–55.
18 Poizner, H., Klima, E. S., Bellugi, U. and Livingston, R. (1986) in *Event Cognition* (McCabe, V. and Balzano, G., eds), pp. 155–174. Erlbaum Press.
19 Poizner, H., Bellugi, U. and Klima, E. S. (1990) In *Modularity and the Motor Theory of Speech Perception* (Mattingly, I. and Studdert-Kennedy, M., eds), Erlbaum Press.
20 Poizner, H., Mack, L., Verfaillie, M., Rothi, L. and Heilman, K. (1990) *Brain.*
21 Bellugi, U. (1980) in *Signed and Spoken Language: Biological Constraints on Linguistic Form* (Bellugi, U. and Studdert-Kennedy, M., eds), pp. 115–140. Verlag Chemie.
22 Lane, H. and Grosjean, F., eds (1980) *Recent Perspectives on American Sign Language.* Erlbaum Press.
23 Liddell, S. K. (1984) *Language*, 60, 372–399.
24 Padden, C. and Perlmutter, D. M. (1987) *Nat. Lang. Ling. Theory* 5, 335–375.
25 Lillo-Martin, D. and Klima, E. S. (1990) In *Theoretical Issues in Sign Language Research* (Siple, P. and Fischer, S., eds). Springer-Verlag.
26 Wilbur, R. (1987) *American Sign Language.* Little, Brown and Company.
27 Bellugi, U., Poizner, H. and Klima, E. S. (1983) *Hum. Neurobiol.* 2, 155–170.
28 Bellugi, U., Poizner, H. and Klima, E. S. (1990) In *Signal and Sense: Local and Global Order in Perceptual Maps* (Edelman, G., Gall, W. E. and Cowan, M., eds), John Wiley & Sons.
29 Klima, E. S., Bellugi, U. and Poizner, H. (1988) *Aphasiology* 2, 319–328.
30 Poizner, H., Klima, E. S. and Bellugi, U. (1987) *What the Hands Reveal About the Brain* MIT Press/Bradford Books.
31 Bellugi, U., Klima, E. S. and Poizner, H. (1988) In *Language, Communication, and the Brain* (Plum, F., ed.), pp. 39–56, Raven Press.
32 Goodglass, H. and Kaplan, E. (1983) *The Assessment of Aphasia and Related Disorders.* Lea and Febiger.
33 Damasio, A., Bellugi, U., Damasio, H., Poizner, H. and Van Gilder, J. (1986) *Nature* 322, 363–365.
34 Neville, H. J. (1991) In *Brain Maturation and Behavioral Development: Biosocial Dimensions* (Gibson, K. and Petersen, A. C., eds), Aldine Grutyer Press.
35 Neville, H. J. (1988) In *Spatial Cognition: Brain Bases and Development* (Stiles-Davis, J., Kritchevsky, M. and Bellugi, U., eds), pp. 327–342, Erlbaum Press.
36 Neville, H. J. and Lawson, D. (1987) *Brain Res.* 405, 253–294.

19

Neurobiology of Cognitive and Language Processing: Effects of Early Experience

HELEN J. NEVILLE

Introduction

Philosophers have discussed the contribution of experience to normal neural and behavioral development over the past several hundred years, at least since the time of Descartes. This is currently a key issue in the neurosciences, both because this information is critical to an understanding of how functional neural systems are formed in normal development, and also because knowledge about the extent of neural plasticity in response to environmental stimulation will have important clinical implications in cases of abnormal neural development. In spite of the long-standing interest in this issue, systematic research on the effects of experience on neural development began only about 20 years ago. Most of this work has been performed on the visual system of cats and monkeys, and includes the work of Wiesel and Hubel, which showed that following deprivation of visual input to one eye, most cells in primary visual cortex respond only to stimulation of the experienced eye (Wiesel and Hubel, 1963). These results by themselves were not necessarily strong evidence for the role of experience in the development of visual cortex. It could be, for example, that a genetically determined program that specifies visual development requires a trigger in the form of visual input to run its maturational course. By this view, however, total (i.e. binocular) visual deprivation should lead to even more abnormalities in visual cortex than monocular deprivation. However, it has been shown that neurons in primary visual

"Neurobiology of Cognitive and Language Processing: Effects of Early Experience" first appeared in *Brain Maturation and Cognitive Development: Comparative and Cross-cultural Perspectives*, edited by K. R. Gibson and A. C. Petersen (Aladine de Gruyter Press, 1991, pp. 355–80), and is reprinted by kind permission. Copyright © 1991 by Social Science Research Council.

cortex are in fact more normal following total visual deprivation than after monocular deprivation (e.g. after total visual deprivation there are more binocularly driven neurons, with more normal receptive fields and they can even display ocular dominance columns, i.e. whereby each eye innervates different neurons; Wiesel and Hubel, 1965). These results documented an important role for visual experience in the development of striate cortex, and further they led to the proposal that one important mechanism underlying neural organization in striate cortex is competition between the different inputs from the two eyes for cortical synaptic sites.

Competition in Development

More generally these results imply that active neural systems compete for and take over cortical synaptic sites that do not receive input from other sources. Additionally, and more relevant to the data presented in this chapter, there is evidence that this type of competition between inputs within both the visual system and the somatosensory system (Merzenich and Kaas, 1982) may also occur between different sensory modalities. For example, there is evidence that in polymodal brain regions (including superior colliculus and parietal cortex), when input from one modality is missing, the number of neurons responsive to remaining modalities is increased. In early blinded animals in the superior colliculus, in extrastriate cortex, and in parietal cortex there is both a marked reduction in the number of visually responsive neurons to somatosensory stimulation (Cynader, 1979; Hyvarinen, 1982). It is conceivable that these specific neurophysiological changes could account for the behavioral consequences of visual deprivation that have been well described in humans. The reduction of visually responsive neurons in these areas could account for the marked deficits in visual functioning that occur following even limited periods of early visual deprivation, and the increase in neurons responsive to somatosensory input could account for the reports of superior somatosensory skills in blind individuals. However, typically in research on animals, the physiological consequences of altered sensory experience have not been linked to behavior, and, conversely, in humans while the behavioral consequences of sensory deprivation have been extensively studied, little is known about the changes in neural organization that underlie these behavioural consequences.

Neural Development in Humans

It seems likely that early experience could significantly impact neural development in humans. The postnatal development of the human brain is very protracted and, according to most parameters studied, including the size of neurons, the extent of dendritic branching, myelinization, and number of synapses, these parameters do not reach mature values until at least 15 years after birth (Conel, 1939–1963; Schade, 1961; Huttenlocher, 1979). For example, the number of synapses in human frontal and occipital cortex displays a prolonged developmental course that does not stabilize until 20 years of age (Huttenlocher, 1979; Huttenlocher et al., 1982). Moreover, the developmental course is similar to that observed in other animals. During an early period (in humans from birth to two years of age), there is a rapid rise or transient exuberance in the number of synapses followed, from 2 to 15 years of age, by substantial elimination of synapses. In at least some animal neural systems, one important factor in determining which synapses are stabilized and which are eliminated is the pattern of activity of cortical inputs (e.g. as occurs in the formation of ocular dominance columns; Wiesel and Hubel, 1965). It is our working hypothesis that a similar situation exists in humans. Clinical studies of humans have shown that during the time from birth to puberty, structural damage to the brain can produce very marked changes in cerebral organization. Moreover, these changes are often associated with relatively preserved behavior (Smith, 1981; Dennis and Whitaker, 1977). For example, even if one entire cerebral hemisphere is removed during this time period, an individual can develop relatively normal cognitive and language skills. Thus, during this time there must be a substantial degree of redundancy and/or plasticity of cerebral connections. Further, it is conceivable that as in other animals, experience (i.e. functional activity) acts to reduce the redundancy and increase the specificity of neural connections during this period.

Epigenesis

One conception of how this might work, based on research on animals, has been presented by Changeux (1985) in his theory of epigenesis by selective stabilization of synapses. The idea is that there is an initial period of growth of neurons, axons, and dendrites, much of which occurs prenatally, and that this growth is determined genetically – or as Changeux puts it, occurs within a genetic envelop of possibilities. This would include, for example, the formation of ocular dominance columns that can occur, as mentioned above, in the absence of visual input. We also know that these initial baises are not immutable, as they can be substantially altered by visual experience (e.g. monocular deprivation). Following the period of initial growth there is a transient period of redundancy or exuberance of connections that has been documented in several species, in several brain regions both in humans (Huttenlocher, 1979; Huttenlocher, 1982) and animals (Cowan et al., 1984). This transient redundancy may underlie the ability of inputs from an experienced eye to take over neurons that would normally receive input from an unexperienced eye as occurs following monocular deprivation. It has also been shown that there are early, transient connections between different sensory modalities, for example, from the retina to the ventrobasal (somatosensory) nucleus of the thalamus (Frost, 1984); and there are cortical connections between auditory and visual cortex that are present in the neonatal kitten but that are eliminated around three months of age (Innocenti and Clark, 1984). Additionally, there is an early period when the callosal fibers that join the two hemispheres are considerably more numerous than in the mature animal (Innocenti, 1981). So, during this time, which is probably different for different brain regions, there is maximal diversity of connections. The subsequent pruning of these diverse connections occurs in a few well-documented cases as a direct consequence of activity that selectively stabilizes certain connections, while others that do not receive input are eliminated or suppressed. It is further hypothesized that in addition to competition between inputs the temporal patterning between inputs is an important variable in setting up neuronal systems or groups; that is, neurons that are active together tend to aggregate. A major question in our research program has been to determine in humans both what is innately biased (i.e. which aspects of cerebral organization are similar following different types of early experience), and what aspects of cerebral organization can be altered by specific experiences.

Electrophysiological Method

Our approach to the study of cerebral organization in humans is to obtain behavioral data employing standard measures of signal detection and reaction time and to simultaneously record, from electrodes placed over different regions of the scalp, the electrical signals that are time locked to discrete sensory or cognitive events such as the presentation of a flash of light, or the correct recognition of a work. Averages of epochs of electrophysiological activity associated with similar stimuli or responses are termed event-related brain potentials or ERPs. Over the past two decades this approach has proven to be valuable in assessing the integrity of neural systems and in elucidating the time course and subprocesses of several cognitive functions (see Hillyard and Kutas, 1983; Kutas and Hillyard, 1984, for review).

Subjects

We have employed the combined behavioral–electrophysiological approach in the study of individuals who have had a very extreme and highly specific form of altered experience. These are deaf individuals who have sustained total auditory deprivation since birth. All of our deaf subjects were born bilaterally and profoundly deaf, and they were born to deaf parents. Thus, their deafness is genetic, in which case the cochlea does not differentiate normally. The central nervous system (CNS) is not directly affected by the disease, and our subjects are otherwise neurologically normal and tend to be college students as are our normally hearing control subjects.

In humans, and probably in other animals as well, the impact of unimodal deprivation extends well beyond the development of sensory functions. Thus, our deaf subjects, as a consequence of their auditory deprivation, have also had markedly abnormal language experience. None of them has acquired speech, nor any auditory language comprehension. Instead they learned, from their deaf parents, at the normal age for language acquisition, American Sign Language (ASL). The perception of ASL relies heavily on peripheral vision since in sign discourse the eyes are typically focused on the eyes and face of the signer, so that much of the signed information falls outside the foveal region. The vocabulary and grammar of ASL make extensive use of visual space and of modulations of hand movements. For example, the same handshape presented at different locations, or with different motions, can convey different semantic or grammatical information (Klima and Bellugi, 1979).

In several studies we compared cerebral organization in deaf and hearing subjects during different sensory, cognitive, and language tasks. To dissociate the influences of auditory deprivation and the acquisition of a visual language on the differences between deaf and hearing subjects we compare these results with a third group of subjects: these are normal hearing subjects, who were born to deaf parents and so have acquired ASL as a first language like the deaf subjects, but have not experienced any auditory deprivation (hearing subjects born to deaf parents or HD subjects).

Visual Sensory Processing

In one study we tested the hypothesis that the visual system might be organized differently following auditory deprivation, in view of the evidence for competition between inputs from different modalities (Neville et al., 1983). Briefly, we recorded the evoked response to a small square of light presented in the periphery of the left or right visual fields, or in the foveal region. A major result was that over classical auditory brain regions, i.e. over temporal cortex, hearing and deaf subjects displayed similar evoked responses to the foveal stimuli, but the peripheral stimuli elicited responses that were two to three times larger in the deaf than in the hearing subjects. To assess the possibility that the acquisition of sign language contributed to this group difference we tested the HD subjects on this paradigm as well (see Neville and Lawson, 1987c). As seen in figure 19.1, the HD subjects, like the hearing subjects, displayed considerably smaller ERPs over these brain regions than did the deaf subjects, suggesting the effect was due to auditory deprivation, not to acquisition of ASL. This pattern of group differences was similar over both hemispheres and was obtained only for the peripheral stimuli.

These results suggest that the visual system may be organized differently after auditory deprivation, and moreover that the systems involved in processing peripheral visual information may undergo more compensatory changes than do the systems that mediate the processing of foveal visual information. This could arise because, whereas normal hearing subjects rely on audition to detect important events in the periphery, deaf subjects must rely on peripheral vision. A related possibility is that the structures of the peripheral visual system may be more modifiable than are the structures of the primary visual system. In agreement with this hypothesis, it has been reported that the Y cells in the retina, which are more abundant in the peripheral retina, develop later and are more altered by visual experience than are the X cells, which are clustered in the foveal region (Sherman, 1985). The increased response amplitude in the deaf may be the result of early, normally transient, visual afferents to auditory and/or superior temporal polysensory cortex that become stabilized when auditory input to these areas is absent.

Visual Attention

To explore further the hypothesis that the systems that subserve the processing of foveal and peripheral visual information are differentially affected by auditory deprivation since birth, we compared processes associated with attention to peripheral and central visual space. We first had to determine whether attention to peripheral and central space would be associated with different ERPs in normal

VEP RECOVERY CYCLE
Peripheral Stimuli

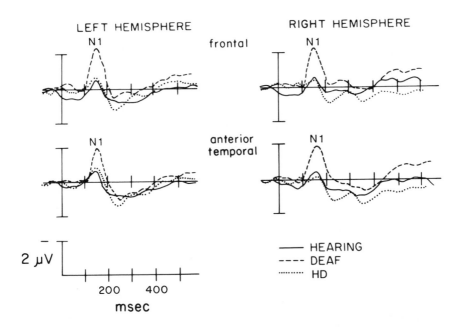

Figure 19.1 ERPs to peripheral visual stimuli in the paradigm described in Neville and Lawson (1987c). ERPs from hearing, deaf, and HD Ss recorded over frontal and anterior temporal regions of the left and right hemispheres. Copyright © 1987. Reprinted with permission of Elsevier Science Publishers.

hearing adults, and then determine whether ERPs associated with attention to the peripheral and foveal regions would be differentially altered in the deaf subjects (Ss). To tax the secondary visual system we designed a difficult task that required the perception of direction of motion.

Methods

The stimuli were presented on a darkened video screen. In the center of the screen was a small black dot that subjects fixated during recording blocks. The standard stimuli were small, 1/2° white squares presented 18° in the left and right visual field and in the center of the field. Stimuli were presented for 33 mseconds in these three positions randomly with variable interstimulus interval of 280–480 mseconds. On different blocks of trials Ss were asked to attend without moving their eyes to the stimuli in the left or right visual field, or to the center, in order to detect occasional (20 percent probable) apparent movements of these stimuli in the attended field only. The movement actually consisted of the illumination for another 33 msec of the adjacent 1/2° square.

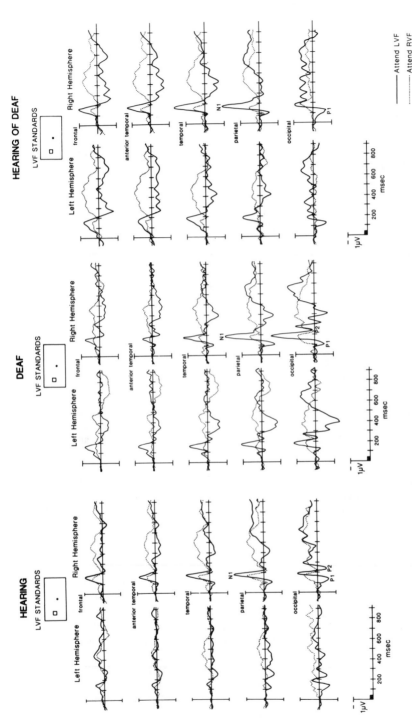

Figure 19.2 ERPs averaged across 12 hearing Ss (left panel), 12 deaf Ss (center panel), and 12 HD Ss (right panel) to standard stimuli presented to the left visual field (lvf) when attended (attend lvf) and when inattended (attend rvf). Recordings from left and right frontal, anterior temporal, temporal, parietal, and occipital cortex. From H. L. Neville, Cerebral organization for spatial attention: Effects of early sensory and language experience. In J. Stiles-Davis, U. Bellugi and M. Kritchevsky (eds), *Spatial Cognition: ainBases and Development.* Copyright © 1988. Reprinted by permission of Elsevier Science Publishers.

This resulted in an impression of smooth motion of about $1/2°$, which occurred randomly along the vertical, horizontal or diagonal axes. Ss pressed one of eight different keys as accurately and quickly as possible to indicate the direction of motion in the attended visual field.

ERPs were recorded from electrodes placed over frontal, anterior temporal, temporal, parietal, and occipital brain regions of each hemisphere. All electrodes were referenced to the linked mastoids (bandpass 0.01–100 percent Hz). Blinks and vertical eye movements were monitored from an electrode beneath the left eye, and horizontal eye movements were monitored via bipolar recordings from the external canthi. As seen in figure 19.2, the ERPs to these stimuli displayed two early positivities around 130 and 230 mseconds (P1 and P2) separated by a prominent negative peak around 160 mseconds (N1). Following these peaks there occurred broad shifts in amplitude whose polarity depended on the direction of attention. The peak and area voltages of each of the components were measured by computer and the values were subjected to analyses of variance with repeated measures (see Neville and Lawson, 1987a, b, c, for complete details).

Hearing Subjects

Hearing subjects were more accurate at detecting the direction of motion when it occurred in the left (lvf) rather than the right (rvf) visual field. In figure 19.2 (left panel) are superimposed ERPs to stimuli in the lvf when Ss were attending the lvf and to the same stimuli when they were attending the rvf. Since the stimulus and task are identical in the two conditions, differences in the ERPs reflect the effects of focused attention.

A prominent effect of attention was to increase the amplitude of N1. For peripheral stimuli this effect was most prominent over the parietal and temporal regions of the hemisphere contralateral to the attended visual field (see figures 19.2 and 19.3 left, bottom). By contrast, with attention to the central field the major increase occurred over the occipital regions where it was bilaterally symmetric (figure 19.3 left, top). Later attention-related changes, where the ERP was negative to inattended stimuli but slightly positive to attended stimuli, were largest over temporoparietal regions. These effects were symmetrical with attention to the center, but were larger from the right than the left hemisphere with attention to both the lvf and rvf.

These results suggest that in normal hearing Ss attention to peripheral and central regions of visual space are mediated by different neural systems. Moreover, the distributions of these effects are in agreement with considerable data from nonhuman animals showing that information presented to the fovea is processed by the retinogeniculostriate pathway, while processing of and attention to peripheral visual information is associated with increased activity in parietal cortex. They further suggest, in agreement with clinical studies, a greater role for the right hemisphere in visuospatial attention, especially to the periphery.

Deaf Subjects

With attention to the center, deaf Ss' behavior and the attention-related changes in the ERPs were similar to those of the hearing Ss (see figure 19.3 right, top).

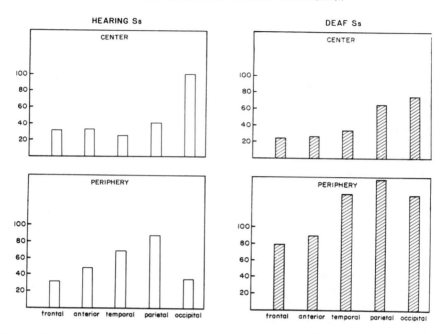

Figure 19.3 Percentage by which N1 amplitude was increased from inattend to attend conditions for hearing and deaf subjects. Top: center standards, mean of left and right frontal, anterior temporal, temporal, parietal, and occipital sites. Bottom: peripheral standards, mean of contralateral frontal, anterior temporal, temporal, parietal, and occipital sites. From Neville and Lawson (1987b). Copyright © 1987. Reprinted with permission of Elsevier Science Publishers.

However, deaf Ss responded more quickly than hearing Ss to motion in the periphery and, in contrast to the hearing Ss, they detected the direction of motion more accurately when it occurred in the rvf than the lvf. In addition, the attention-related changes in the ERPs were considerably larger in deaf than hearing Ss under conditions of attending the periphery (see figure 19.3 bottom). As seen in figure 19.2, whereas both deaf and hearing Ss displayed attention increases in N1 amplitude over the parietal and temporal regions of the hemisphere contralateral to the attended periphery, the deaf Ss, unlike the hearing Ss, also displayed attention-related increases in N1 and in the 300–600 mseconds positivity over the occipital regions of both hemispheres. In addition, deaf Ss displayed considerably larger attention-related increases over the left temporal and parietal regions than did the hearing Ss. Both of the group differences, the increased occipital ERPs and the increased amplitudes over the left hemisphere in deaf Ss, occurred independently of whether attention was focused on the lvf or rvf.

The specific pattern of group differences can be considered with respect to anatomical and physiological evidence from experimental animals that shows that two major types of changes can occur following unimodal sensory deprivation since birth. First there is evidence for increased growth and activity of remaining sensory systems or "compensatory hypertrophy" (Burnstine et al., 1984). The bilateral increase of attention-related changes in occipital regions in the deaf Ss may represent this type of change and may be due to increased visual activity in posterior polymodal brain regions and/or to the stabilizations of visual afferents on what would normally be auditorily responsive cells in these regions. Second, there is evidence that brain systems that would normally subserve functions that are lost – in the case of the deaf Ss these are audition, speech, and auditory language skills – may maintain rather than eliminate early, exuberant input from the remaining modality (Burnstine et al., 1984). These results suggest that areas within the left hemisphere that would normally subserve speech and auditory language comprehension are active in attention to and perception of movement in the peripheral visual fields in deaf Ss.

It may be that since these regions of the left hemisphere are not used for the production and comprehension of speech, they instead come to process this type of visual material through the stabilization of visual afferents in these areas. Alternatively, it could be that the observed increase in left hemisphere activity in the deaf Ss in this task was not a consequence of auditory deprivation but rather arose in conjunction with the acquisition of a visual, sign language. If the acquisition of sign language is mediated by the left hemisphere, as is the case in the acquisition of speech, perhaps nonlanguage information that is temporally coincident with and critical to the production and perception of sign language – such as attention to space and perception of motion – is also mediated by the left hemisphere, by virtue of their temporal correlation. This would be analogous to the situation in hearing Ss where the perception of temporal order of rapidly presented nonlanguage material is mediated by the left hemisphere, perhaps because the perception of temporal order is critical in the production and perception of speech (Albert, 1972; Efron, 1963).

Hearing Subjects Born to Deaf Parents

We dissociated the possibly separate effects of the deaf Ss' auditory deprivation from the effects of acquiring a visual language whose grammar relies on the perception of motion on this pattern of group differences by testing the hearing Ss who were born to deaf parents (HD Ss). If the enhanced attention effects over the bilateral occipital regions seen in the deaf Ss were a consequence of auditory deprivation, the HD Ss should not display these results. On the other hand, if the increased attention effects over the left temporoparietal regions are attributable to acquisition of ASL, the HD Ss should display results similar to those of the deaf subjects.

As seen in figure 19.4, the HD Ss, like the hearing Ss, were significantly slower than those of the deaf Ss in responding to peripheral motion. Likewise, over the occipital regions bilaterally, the attention effects in the ERPs were considerably smaller in the hearing and HD Ss than in the deaf Ss (see figure 19.2, right panel). These results are in agreement with the hypothesis that the faster reaction times and increased occipital attention effects are a consequence of auditory deprivation since birth, and are not due to the acquisition of a visual language.

REACTION TIME

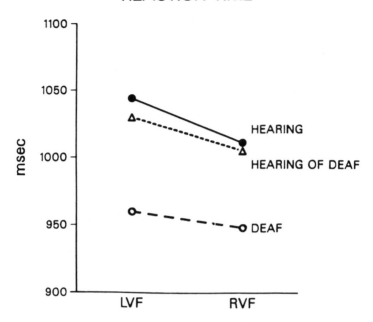

Figure 19.4 Reaction times (in mseconds) to detect the direction of motion of target stimuli in the left (LVF) and right (RVF) visual fields. Data from hearing Ss, deaf Ss, and hearing Ss born to deaf parents.

In contrast to these results, over temporal and parietal regions of the left hemisphere, hearing Ss display small attention effects on N1, but both deaf and HD Ss displayed large, and equivalent attention effects. Additionally, whereas hearing Ss detected the direction of motion more accurately when it occurred in the lvf, both deaf and HD Ss displayed the opposite pattern (figure 19.5).

Thus, these results suggest that the increased attention effects over the left temporoparietal regions in the deaf and HD Ss in this task may be attributable to the acquisition of a language that relies critically on the perception of motion. If the left hemisphere plays the greater role in acquisition of ASL, as in the acquisition of speech, then perhaps it also mediates the perception of motion even in a nonlanguage task like this one.

Taken together, these results suggest that aspects of the anterior–posterior organization of the visual system within both hemispheres are significantly affected by early auditory deprivation. This reorganization of the visual system may include both an anterior expansion, into areas normally used for auditory processing (as seen in the first experiment described), as well as increased activity of the posterior visual cortical areas. Both of these effects could be accounted for by early exuberant visual afferents that are stabilized when competing input from the auditory modality is absent. Additionally, the results suggest that aspects of the different cerebral specializations of the two hemispheres may be deter-

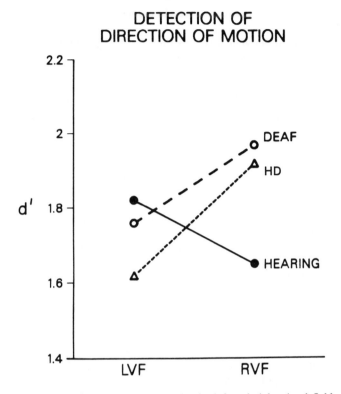

Figure 19.5 Detection (d′) of moving targets in the left and right visual fields (LVF and RVF) for hearing, deaf, and HD Ss. From Neville and Lawson (1987c). Copyright © 1987b. Reprinted with permission of Elsevier Science Publishers.

mined by the nature and modality of language acquisition. Since part of our interpretation of these results rests on the assumption that the left hemisphere is specialized for both signed and spoken languages, we conducted research, described below, in which we tested this hypothesis and further explored the effects of language experience on the different functional specializations of the hemispheres in these subjects.

Language Processing

Considerable controversy still surrounds the nature of the special role of the left hemisphere in language processing, the degree to which it may be determined at birth, and the role that experience might play in its development. As mentioned above, clinical studies of hemispherectomized patients show that early in development each hemisphere has similar, if not identical, capabilities to sustain language and other cognitive skills. However, little is known about the role of language experience in reducing the redundancy and increasing the specificity of hemispheric function in adults. If language experience does impact cerebral development, then aspects of cerebral specialization ought to be different in deaf and hearing Ss when they read English. Hearing people learn English first through the auditory modality and they utilize this information in learning to read. According to several studies, when hearing Ss read they translate the visual word to an auditory sound (so-called phonological decoding). On the other hand, deaf Ss apparently do not perform this visual–auditory phonological conversion (Conrad, 1977). Would these different experiences result in different patterns of cerebral activity during reading?

Hemifield Studies

English. To study this issue we developed a paradigm that produced reliable evidence of cerebral specialization during reading in normal adults, and then compared results from deaf Ss. Briefly (see Neville et al., 1982a), words were projected to the left or right visual fields or bilaterally for 100 mseconds, and, 2 seconds following word onset, Ss wrote the word. Every hearing S reported the words more accurately after they were presented to the rvf, i.e. to the left hemisphere, thus providing behavioral evidence that the left hemisphere was more active than the right in this task. The simultaneously recorded ERPs to each word presentation displayed a different pattern of activity depending on where, within and between the hemispheres, they were recorded. ERPs from over left and right occipital regions reflected the anatomy of the visual system, i.e. the N1 component was larger from the hemisphere contralateral to the visual field in which the word was presented. By contrast, ERPs recorded over anterior temporal regions were asymmetrical in the same way regardless of where in the visual field a word appeared. In each case the left hemisphere response displayed a negative (410 mseconds)–positive (560 mseconds) shift that was absent or smaller than in ERPs from over the right hemisphere (see figure 19.6). This asymmetry, like the behavioral asymmetry, was evident in each of the hearing Ss, and appeared to index some aspect of the left hemisphere's greater role in this reading task.

The results from the congenitally deaf adults (all were bilaterally and profoundly deaf, had acquired ASL as a first language, and had not acquired speech) were markedly different from those of the hearing Ss (see Neville et al., 1982b). Neither the behavioral data nor the ERPs displayed evidence of left hemisphere specialization in this task. The deaf subjects reported the words as accurately as the hearing Ss, but they were equally accurate when words were presented to the lvf and rvf. In addition, whereas over the left anterior temporal region hearing Ss displayed a prominent negative–positive shift, deaf Ss did not (see figure 19.6). However, deaf Ss displayed a negative potential in right temporal region that was much less prominent in hearing Ss ERPs.

There are several possible reasons why deaf Ss did not display the pattern of left hemisphere specialization observed in the hearing Ss. It could be, as has been proposed, that the left hemisphere is specifically specialized for the phonological decoding that characterizes reading by hearing but not deaf Ss. On the other hand, it has also been proposed that the special role of the left hemisphere for language arises in conjunction with the acquisition of the grammatical or

HEMIFIELD WORDS

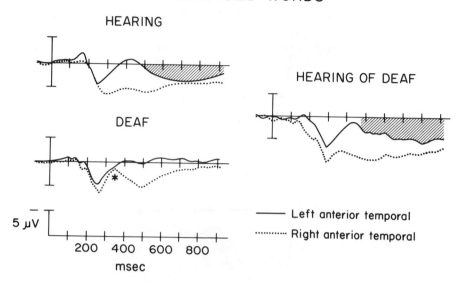

Figure 19.6 ERPs recorded to English words presented to the right visual field. Recordings from over left and right anterior temporal regions. Grand mean ERPs from ten hearing, eight congenitally deaf, and ten hearing Ss born to deaf parents.

propositional coding strategies that characterize hearing subjects' language use (Liberman, 1974). Since deaf Ss typically do not acquire full grammatical competence in English, this may be the reason they do not display left hemisphere specialization during reading. Alternatively, a third possibility is that the acquisition of two languages by the deaf Ss (i.e. ASL and English) would account for these results. One way we investigated this third possibility was to test the hearing Ss born to deaf parents (HD) on this task. If the acquisition of two languages was an important variable in determining this pattern of results their data should parallel those of the deaf Ss. On the other hand, if the left greater than right asymmetry is a manifestation of phonological decoding or grammatical encoding of English then the HD Ss should display results similar to those of the hearing Ss, even though in the perception of motion task they displayed lateral asymmetries opposite in direction to those of the hearing Ss.

The HD Ss, like the hearing Ss, reported the words more accurately after presentation to the rvf than to the lvf, suggesting left hemisphere specialization. The ERPs from this group (see figure 19.6) over the anterior temporal region displayed an asymmetry similar to that observed in the hearing Ss. This pattern occurred independently of the visual field to which words were presented. These results suggest that the absence of this negative component in the deaf subjects was not attributable to the acquisition of ASL as a first language, but may instead index the activity of processes involved in either phonological or grammatical decoding.

DEAF SUBJECTS
Hemi-field Signs

RIGHT VISUAL FIELD

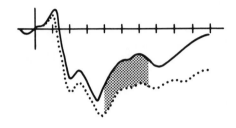

BILATERAL

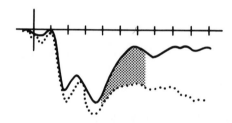

LEFT VISUAL FIELD

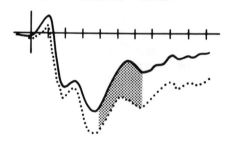

4μV

200 400 600 800
msec

—— LEFT BROCA'S
········· RIGHT BROCA'S

Figure 19.7 ERPs from nine congenitally deaf Ss recorded over left and right frontal regions (over Broca's area) to signs presented in the right or left visual field or to two different signs in each visual field.

American Sign Language. To assess the roles of phonological processing versus acquisition of grammatical competence in producing left hemisphere specialization for English (observed in the hearing but not the deaf subjects), we performed a version of this experiment with ASL. Since ASL is not phonological (i.e. not sound based), but is highly grammatical (Klima and Bellugi, 1979), if grammatical recoding is an important variable and if phonological decoding is not essential in the development of left hemisphere specialization for a language, deaf Ss should display left hemisphere specialization in processing ASL. We digitized filmed sequences of a person signing (six frames per sign, 180 mseconds) and presented each sign once to the left and once to the right visual field as we had presented the English words. Two seconds after sign onset, Ss made the sign just presented. Every deaf subject reported the signs more accurately after they were presented to the rvf, suggesting a greater role for the left hemisphere. This is what was observed when hearing Ss read English, and contrasts with the results for deaf subjects reading English. Moreover, these signs – which are physically very dissimilar from printed words – elicited ERPs from over anterior temporal regions that displayed a similar pattern of results to that seen in hearing Ss reading English. That is, they were characterized by a negative–positive shift that was larger from the left than the right hemisphere (see figure 19.7). Moreover, this asymmetry occurred independently of where in the visual field a sign appeared, as we had observed in ERPs from hearing Ss reading English words. We also recorded ERPs from normally hearing subjects to the ASL stimuli. These Ss did not know ASL, but were asked to mimic the signs as best they could. ERPs from these subjects did not display the asymmetrical negativity characteristic of the deaf Ss but instead displayed a prolonged positive shift that was symmetrical from the two hemispheres (see figure 19.8).

These data suggest that (1) similar neural systems within the left hemisphere mediate the processing of formal (i.e. grammatical) languages that have evolved through different modalities, (2) phonological processing is not necessary for the development of left hemisphere specialization for language, and (3) the special role of the left hemisphere in language processing may develop along with the acquisition of competence in the grammar of language.

Sentence Processing. We have further tested this hypothesis in studies of the processing of English sentences where we have compared and contrasted cerebral organization during aspects of grammatical and semantic processing. Briefly (more fully reported in Neville et al., 1990), we presented sentences, one word (duration 200 mseconds) at a time, to the central 2° of vision. ERPs to the words in the middle of the sentences were coded according to whether they were content or "open class" words (nouns, verbs, and adjectives, i.e. words that make reference to specific objects and events) or whether they were function or "closed class" words (e.g. pronouns, prepositions, articles, conjunctions, i.e. the small, "closed" set of words that specifies the relations between content words). The closed class words are viewed as providing much of the syntactic structure to sentences, while the open class words carry semantic information. Clinical data documenting the effects of lesions suggest that nonidentical neural systems mediate these two aspects of language processing. For example, lesions to the anterior regions of the left hemisphere disrupt the use and comprehension of the

HEARING SUBJECTS
Hemi-field Signs

RIGHT VISUAL FIELD

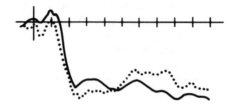

BILATERAL

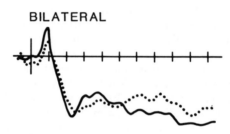

LEFT VISUAL FIELD

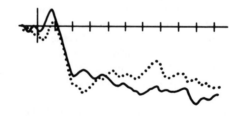

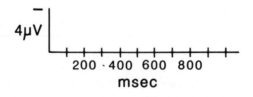

4μV

200 · 400 600 800
msec

—— LEFT BROCA'S
········· RIGHT BROCA'S

Figure 19.8 ERPs from ten normally hearing Ss recorded over left and right frontal regions (over Broca's area) to signs presented in the right or left visual field or to two different signs in each visual field.

closed class vocabulary, while lesions to posterior regions of the left hemisphere disrupt the use of open class words. Additionally, lesions to posterior areas of the right hemisphere diminish some aspects of semantic functioning (Wapner et al., 1981). ERPs from hearing Ss ($N = 17$) also provide evidence that different systems are active in processing these different types of words. As seen in figure 19.9, ERPs to closed class words display a negative peak around 280 mseconds (N280) that was most evident over the left hemisphere. This peak was evident from anterior brain regions but not over parietal cortex. By contrast, ERPs to open class words did not display a prominent N280 in ERPs from the anterior areas, but (from over parietal) regions they displayed a negative component around 350 mseconds (N350) that was evident in ERPs from both hemispheres. We determined that the different morphologies and distributions of ERPs to these different classes of words were not attributable to the frequencies of the words in the language, their lengths, or their imagability scores. Thus, the ERP differences likely index different functions in language processing.

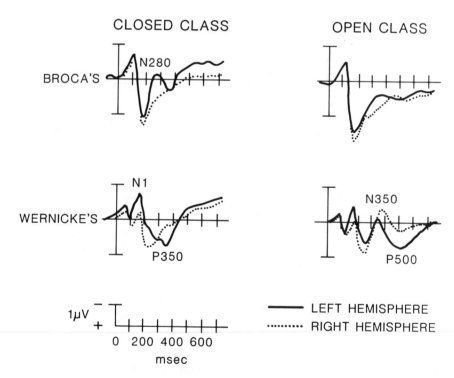

ENGLISH SENTENCES
17 HEARING SUBJECTS

Figure 19.9 ERPs to open and closed class words within English sentences, from normal hearing Ss, recorded anterior temporal (near Broca's area) and parietal (over Wernicke's area) sites of the left hemisphere and homologous positions over the right hemisphere.

To further explore the hypothesis that incomplete acquisition of the grammar of English by deaf Ss may have been an important variable in their lack of left hemisphere specialization for English (as was observed in the studies reported above) we recorded ERPs to these same sentences from ten congenitally deaf adults. As seen in figure 19.10, ERPs to the closed class words, in contrast to those of the hearing Ss, did not display the N280 component, nor any asymmetries in amplitude, from anterior or posterior brain regions. Each of these deaf Ss scored significantly lower (mean 75 percent correct) on tests of English grammar than did our hearing Ss (range 95–100 percent correct). We also studied four congenitally deaf Ss who scored perfectly on the tests of English grammar (figure 19.11). These Ss, like the other deaf Ss, were congenitally, bilaterally, and profoundly deaf, had not acquired speech, and used ASL as their major form of communication. Nonetheless, they did display a pattern of hemispheric specialization similar to that observed in the hearing Ss. Thus these data are

ENGLISH SENTENCES
10 DEAF SUBJECTS

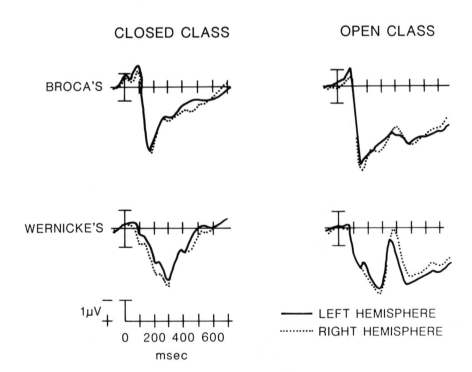

Figure 19.10 ERPs to open and closed class words within English sentences, from congenitally deaf Ss, recorded over anterior temporal (near Broca's area) and parietal (over Wernicke's area) sites of the left hemisphere and homologous positions over the right hemisphere.

compatible with the idea that grammatical competence in a language is an important factor in the development or stabilization of left hemisphere specialization for that language.

In contrast to these results for the closed class words, deaf and hearing Ss displayed ERPs more similar to the open class words. In each group ERPs to these words displayed a prominent negative peak between 350 and 400 mseconds over left and right parietal regions. To the extent that this component reflects aspects of semantic processing, these results suggest that there are strong similarities in this aspect of processing, the different early language experience of the deaf Ss notwithstanding. Further studies of semantic priming in deaf and hearing Ss are consistent with this view (Neville, 1985; Kutas et al., 1987).

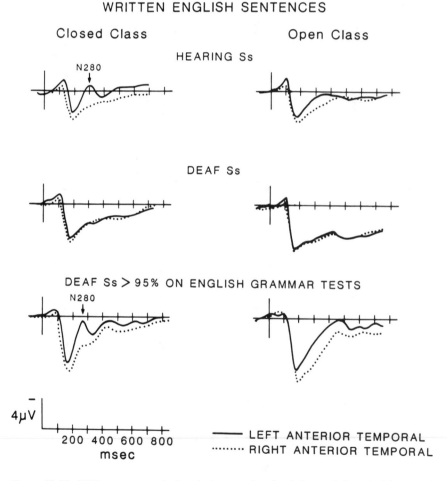

Figure 19.11 ERPs to open and closed class words recorded over left and right anterior temporal regions. Recordings from normal hearing Ss and from congenitally deaf Ss who scored poorly (middle) and well (bottom) on tests of English grammar.

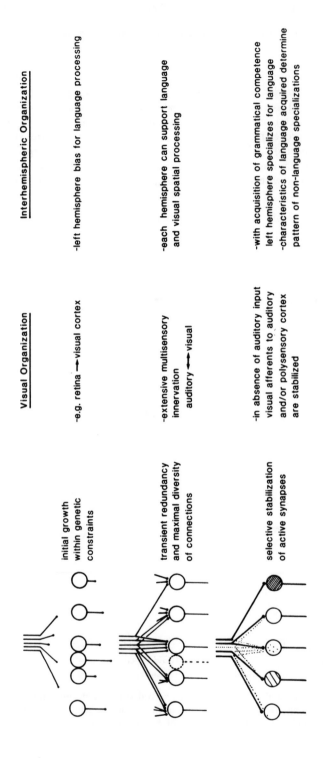

Visual Organization

initial growth within genetic constraints

- e.g. retina → visual cortex

transient redundancy and maximal diversity of connections

- extensive multisensory innervation
  auditory ⟷ visual

selective stabilization of active synapses

- in absence of auditory input visual afferents to auditory and/or polysensory cortex are stabilized

Interhemispheric Organization

- left hemisphere bias for language processing

- each hemisphere can support language and visual spatial processing

- with acquisition of grammatical competence left hemisphere specializes for language
- characteristics of language acquired determine pattern of non-language specializations

Figure 19.12 Summary of results presented within the framework of Changeux's (1985) conception of the epigenesis of functional neural systems. Translation Copyright © 1985 by Random House, Inc. Reprinted by permission of Pantheon Books, a division of Random House, Inc.

In summary, these data suggest that the systems that mediate the acquisition of aspects of syntactic processing appear to be more vulnerable to and dependent on specific aspects of early language experience, but that aspects of semantic processing develop in a very similar fashion under widely varying conditions of early language experience. This may be because there are strong biological constraints on the development of the systems that are used to process semantic information, or it may be that they are more dependent on more general cognitive experience that is more similar in deaf and hearing Ss than is language experience *per se*.

These results are of interest in view of studies of language development that show earlier acquisition of the open than the closed class elements of language. Of additional interest are reports that variations in maternal speech have virtually no effect on the time of acquisition of open class elements of the language, but that they do affect the rate of acquisition of closed class items (Newport et al., 1977). Moreover, it is of interest that deaf children who have not been formally exposed to a sign language and have not acquired speech invent signs for objects and events in the world (open class items) and that the age of acquisition of these language milestones occurs as in normal children. In contrast, these children display little evidence of acquiring any grammer, i.e. they do not invent closed class items (Goldin-Meadow, 1979). Thus it appears that whereas the acquisition of lexical semantics is not dependent on language input, some grammatical input is necessary for the systems that mediate the acquisition of grammar to unfold. It will be important for future research to determine whether there are critical or sensitive periods when particular types of language input are necessary for language acquisition to proceed normally.

Summary and Conclusions

The results presented in this chapter concerning effects of sensory and language experience on neural development can be summarized within the framework discussed initially, which is outlined in figure 19.12. The left-hand column of figure 19.12 is taken (and modified) from *Neuronal Man*, by Changeux (1985). According to this view, there is an initial period of growth that is genetically influenced. In the visual system this includes, for example, the growth of retinal afferents to primary visual cortex, where they form ocular dominance columns. Following this time there is transient, exuberant growth of connections that includes extensive multisensory innervation (e.g. visual afferents into auditory and polysensory cortex). Our data on visual processing in congenitally deaf Ss are compatible with the idea that in the absence of auditory input to these regions, visual afferents are stabilized and in some cases their activity is increased. This would account for our observations of increased visual ERP amplitudes over temporal cortex and over posterior brain regions of both hemispheres.

The studies of the functional specializations of the two hemispheres, which show a greater role for the left hemisphere in the processing of both spoken and signed languages (by competent users of the language), indicate a strong initial bias for the left hemisphere to mediate language. This bias may also underlie the anatomical asymmetry in the planum temporal, observed by Geschwind and colleagues, where the left side is larger than the right, by 28 weeks gestation (Geschwind and Levitsky, 1968). Later on, in postnatal development at least until ten years of age, as shown by clinical data on hemispherectomy cases, there is considerable redundancy such that each hemisphere can support many aspects of both language and visuospatial processing. This redundancy may be supported by extensive callosal fibers, which, at least in other species, are more abundant in the immature than the mature animal (Innocenti, 1981).

Our work suggests that one factor that is important in establishing or maintaining the specialization of the left hemisphere for language is the acquisition of competence in the grammar of language. This would account for the data showing that hearing but not deaf subjects display left hemisphere specialization for English, and for the data showing that deaf but not hearing subjects show left hemisphere specialization for ASL.

Finally, the data from the visual attention study showing opposite patterns of cerebral asymmetries in the perception of motion suggest that characteristics of the language first acquired determine aspects of hemispheric specialization for certain nonlanguage material. For example, the temporal coincidence of motion perception and of the grammer of ASL may result in these functions being organized together within the province of the language-specialized left hemisphere.

Future research will focus on the possibility that there are specific times or critical periods in human development when auditory deprivation and language experience can lead to changes in cerebral organization. This will include the study of postnatally deafened individuals and also individuals who, although deaf since birth, were not exposed to a formal language until late in development. In summary, the results presented here clearly show that sensory experience and language experience have marked and different effects on human neurobehavioral development. The combined behavioral–electrophysiological approach can be useful in further studies of the nature and timing of these effects.

ACKNOWLEDGMENTS

Supported by Grants NS 14365 and NS 22343 from National Institute of Health and National Institute of Neurological and Communicative Disorders and Stroke.

REFERENCES

Albert, M. L. (1972). Auditory sequencing and left cerebral dominance for language, *Neuropsychologia*, 10, 245–248.

Burnstine, T. H., Greenough, W. T., and Tees, R. C. (1984). Intermodal compensation following damage or deprivation: A review of behavioral and neural evidence. In C. R. Almli and S. Finger (eds), *Early brain damage, I, Research orientation and clinical observations* (pp. 3–34). New York: Academic Press.

Conel, J. L. (1939–1963). *The postnatal development of the human cerebral cortex*, Vols I-VI Cambridge, MA: Harvard University Press.

Changeux, J. P. (1985). *Neuronal man*. New York: Pantheon Books.

Conrad, R. (1977). The reading ability of deaf school-leavers. *British Journal of Educational Psychology*, 47, 138–148.

Cowan, W. M., Fawcett, J. W., O'Leary, D. D. M., and Stanfield, B. B. (1984). Regressive events in neurogenesis, *Science*, 225, 1258–1265.

Cynader, M. (1979). Competitive interactions in the development of the kitten's visual system. In R. D. Freeman (ed.), *Developmental neurobiology of vision*. New York: Plenum Press.

Dennis, M. D., and Whitaker, H. A. (1977). Hemispheric equipotentiality and language acquisition. In S. J. Segalowitz and F. A. Gruber (eds), *Language development and neurological theory* (pp. 93–106). New York: Academic Press.

Efron, E. (1963). Temporal perception, aphasia, and deja vu. *Brain*, 86, 403–424.

Frost, D. O. (1984). Axonal growth and target selection during development: Retinal projections to the ventrobasal complex and other 'nonvisual' structures in neonatal Syrian Hamsters. *Journal of Comparative Neurology*, 230, 576–592.

Geschwind, N., and Levitsky, W. (1968). Left-right asymmetry in temporal speech region. *Science*, 161, 186–187.

Goldin-Meadow, S. (1979). Structure in a manual communication system developed without a conventional language model: Language without a helping hand. In H. Whitaker and H. A. Whitaker (eds), *Studies in neurolinguistics*, Vol. 4, (pp. 125–209). New York: Academic Press.

Hillyard, S. A., and Kutas, M. (1983). Electrophysiology of cognitive processing. *Annual Review of Psychology*, 34, 33–61.

Huttenlocher, P. R. (1979). Synaptic density in human frontal cortex-developmental changes and effects of aging. *Brain Research*, 163, 195–205.

Huttenlobher, P. R., Courten, C., Garey, L., and Van Der Loos, D. (1982). Synaptogenesis in human visual cortex-evidence for synapse elimination during normal development, *Neuroscience Letters*, 33, 247–252.

Hyvarinen, J. (1982). *The parietal cortex of monkey and man*. New York: Springer-Verlag.

Innocenti, G. M. (1981). Growth and reshaping of axons in the establishment of visual callosal connections. *Science*, 212, 824–827.

Innocenti, G. M., and Clark, S. (1984). Bilateral transitory projection to visual areas from auditory cortex in kittens. *Developmental Brain Research*, 14, 143–148.

Klima, E. S., and Bellugi, U. (1979). *The signs of language*. Cambridge, MA: Harvard University Press.

Kutas, M., and Hillyard, S. A. (184). Event-related potentials in cognitive science. In M. S. Gazzaniga (ed.), *Handbook of cognitive neuroscience* (pp. 387–409). New York: Plenum Press.

Kutas, M., Neville, H., and Holcomb, P. (1987). A preliminary comparison of the N400 response to semantic anomalies during reading, listening and signing. *EEG Supplement*, 39, 325–330.

Liberman, A. M. (1974). The specialization of the language hemisphere, In F. O. Schmitt and F. G. Worden (eds), *The neurosciences third study program* (pp. 43–56). Cambridge, MA: MIT Press.

Merzenich, M. M., and Kaas, J. H. (1982). Reorganization of mammalian somatosensory cortex following peripheral nerve injury. *Trends in Neurosciences*, 5, 434–436.

Neville, H. (1985). Biological constraints on semantic processing: A comparison of spoken and signed languages. *Psychophysiology*, 22(5), 576.

Neville, H. J. (1988). Cerebral organization for spatial attention: Effects of early sensory and language experience. In J. Stiles-Davis, U. Bellugi and M. Kritchevsky (eds), *Spatial cognition: Brain bases and development* (pp. 327–341). Hillsdale, NJ: Erlbaum Associates.

Neville, H. J., Kutas, M., and Schmidt, A. (1982a). Event-related potential studies of cerebral specialization during reading: I. Studies of normal adults. *Brain and Language*, 16, 300–315.

Neville, H. J., Kutas, M., and Schmidt, A. (1982b). Event-related potential studies of cerebral specialization during reading: II. Studies of congenitally deaf adults. *Brain and Language*, 16, 300–315.

Neville, H. J., and Lawson, D. (1987a). Attention to central and peripheral visual space in a movement detection task: An event-related potential and behavioral study. I. Normal hearing adults. *Brain Research*, 405, 253–267.

Neville, H. J., and Lawson, D. (1987b). Attention to central and peripheral visual space in a movement detection task: An event-related potential and behavioral study. II. Congenitally deaf adults. *Brain Research*, 405, 268–283.

Neville, H. J., and Lawson, D. (1987c). Attention to central and peripheral visual space in a movement detection task: III. Separate effects of auditory deprivation and acquisition of a visual language. *Brain Research*, 405, 284–294.

Neville, H. J., Schmidt, A., and Kutas, M. (1983). Altered visual-evoked potentials in congenitally deaf adults. *Brain research*, 266, 127–132.

Newport, E. L., Gleitman, H., and Gleitman, L. R. (1977). Mother I'd rather do it myself: Some effects and noneffects of maternal speech style. In C. E. Snow and C. A. Ferguson (eds), *Talking to children: Language imput and acquisition* (pp. 109–149). Cambridge, MA: Cambridge University Press.

Schade, J. P., and Van Groenigen, W. B. (1961). Structural organization of the human cerebral cortex. *Acta Anatomica*, 47, 74–111.

Sherman, S. M. (1985). Development of retinal projections to the cat's lateral geniculate nucleus. *Trends in Neuroscience*, 86, 350–355.

Smith, A. (1981). Principles underlying human brain functions in neuropsychological sequelae of different neuropathological processes. In S. Filskov and T. Ball (eds) *Handbook of clinical neuropsychology*, Vol. 6. New York: Wiley Press.

Wapner, W., Hamby, S., and Gardner, H. (1981). The role of the right hemisphere in the apprehension of complex linguistic materials. *Brain and Language*, 14, 15–33.

Wiesel, T. N., and Hubel, D. H. (1963). Effects of visual deprivation on morphology and physiology of cells in the cat's lateral geniculate body. *Journal of Neurophysiology*, 26, 978–993.

Wiesel, T. N., and Hubel, D. H. (1965). Comparison of the effects of unilateral and bilateral eye closure on cortical unit responses in kittens. *Journal of Neurophysiology*, 28, 1029–1040.

Part VI

Constraints on Plasticity

Introduction

The realization that many aspects of brain development are open to influence by sensory experience raises the issue of how this latent plasticity is constrained. On the one hand, we have the observations reported in the earlier parts about the seeming equipotentiality of cortex: within certain broad constraints, any part of cortex can replace any other, and different parts of cortex may subserve the same function at different points in development. On the other hand, we have the commonly observed correspondence between particular regions of cortex and particular functions. Indeed, most of classical neuropsychology and behavioral neuroscience is based upon this assumption.

One way to begin to resolve this apparent paradox is to consider the various constraints that might operate on the plasticity latent in the brain (see also the reading by Johnson in Part VIII). All of the readings in this part illustrate factors which may provide such constraints.

Marler discusses some examples of how specific species of birds acquire the characteristic song of their species. In several of these cases, Marler argues, rather than instinct and learning being opposing, they may be viewed as complementary. Marler develops some of the concepts first put forward by the founders of ethology, Tinbergen and Lorenz (see Part I), such as the notions of *sensitive period*, *releasers* (or sign stimuli) and *innate releasing mechanisms*, to argue that such forms of innate responsiveness may also facilitate and guide learning. Studies have revealed that certain species of young sparrows are able to learn about their species-specific song even if they are exposed to several songs during development. For example, young swamp sparrows "tune in" to the song syllables of their own species, even when the experimenter attempts to fool the young birds by exposing them to synthetic songs structured like that of a closely related species. Thus, the young of many songbird species start with some form of "innate" song template which helps them to select their species song from the many other sounds to which they are exposed.

Another point made by Marler concerns the differences in mechanisms that result in the acquisition of the species-specific song in the wild, even between quite closely related species, such as song sparrows and swamp sparrows. For example, while the swamp sparrow responds to its species syllables within a song, song sparrows base their learning preferences more on a number of "syntactic" features, such as number of segments, phrase structure, and tempo. This, and several other examples, help to make the point that selection pressures operate on behavioral phenotypes, not directly on genotypes. When studying the mechanisms underlying the ontogeny of a behavior, we should expect to find a variety of degrees of genotypic contribution as long as they produce the same result. To a certain extent then, evolution doesn't care about the exact mechanisms that give rise to an outcome, it only cares about the outcome itself.

Another source of constraint on brain plasticity is the developmental state of the sensory organs and pathways. The role of these constraints is elegantly pointed out in the reading by Turkewitz and Kenny. Traditionally, it has been thought that the limited vision of the human infant is a restrictive limitation. By this view, if a human infant happened to be born with perfect adult vision it should be better off than normal infants with their comparatively poor vision. In contrast, Turkewitz and Kenny argue that sensory limitations (and motor limitations) provide both current and subsequent adaptive advantages, and prevent the infant from living in William James's "blooming, buzzing confusion."

Since competition between neural elements is crucial for both intra- and intersensory development (see reading by Neville, Part V), it is important that sources of competition are sequentially arranged over time. That is, for many sensory regions of the brain, it is often important that intrasensory competition occurs in advance of intersensory competition. This results in a sequential development of sensory channels with, for example, auditory development often preceding visual development. Another reason for the sequential development of sensory channels is that the more developed channel can often "tutor" the less developed. For example, turning toward mother's voice means that the infant is exposed to mother's face, and that it will learn more about this socially relevant stimulus.

According to these authors, the limitations on sensory modalities after birth may also promote subsequent perceptual and cognitive integration. For example, the poor visual capacities of the human infant mean that it can only focus clearly on stimuli that are within its grasp. Thus, the authors argue, temporal contiguity between visual and tactile stimulation from an object would be developed more readily than if the infant could resolve the details of distant objects which it could not reach. This view leads to the prediction that, for example, abnormally precocial visual input should impair normal development, rather than enhancing it. Evidence obtained since the article was written has confirmed this prediction (see Turkewitz and Kenny, 1985).

A particularly well studied example of how learning can be constrained by instincts or predispositions is described by Horn in the final reading of this section. The example discussed by this author concerns the form of learning commonly referred to as imprinting. In a long research program spanning several decades, Horn and his collaborators have studied the neural basis of this form of learning, identifying particular regions of the domestic chick brain that are crucially involved. While the bird forebrain differs in many respects from the mammalian cortex, many believe that the same neural and biochemical principles underlie plasticity in the two structures (see, for example, Rauschecker and Marler, further reading, Part IV). It is also likely that the constraints which operate on this plasticity are similar.

In the absence of a mother hen, newly hatched chicks will imprint on a wide variety of brightly colored moving objects (see Bolhuis, 1991 for review). In the natural rearing context, however, chicks learn about the visual characteristics of their mother hen. What constrains this learning? Horn presents evidence for an independent neural system which ensures that the young chick attends more toward objects resembling conspecifics, regardless of earlier experience. This predisposition serves to bias the input to the learning mechanisms underlying imprinting.

FURTHER READING

Bolhuis, J. J. (1991) Mechanisms of avain imprinting: a review. *Biological Reviews*, 66, 303–45. (A recent review of most of what is known from experimental studies of imprinting in precocial birds.)

Bolhuis, J. J. and Johnson, M. H. (1991) Sensory templates: mechanism or metaphor? *Behavioral and Brain Sciences*, 14, 349–50. (Argues that imprinting in the chick should not be viewed as a form of "template" learning.)

de Schonen, S. and Mathivet, E. (1989) First come, first served: a scenario about the development of hemispheric specialization in face recognition during infancy. *European Bulletin of Cognitive Psychology*, 9, 3–44. (An example of how intrinsic and extrinsic factors can combine to ensure that a particular cerebral hemisphere develops specialization for particular class of representations – also see the commentaries.)

Gleitman, L. (1984) Biological predispositions to learn language. In P. Marler and H. S. Terrace (eds), *The biology of learning*. Berlin: Springer-Verlag. (Argues for predispositions that facilitate language learning in the human infant.)

Horn, G. (1985) *Memory, Imprinting and the Brain*. Oxford: Oxford University Press. (The complete and detailed account of the neural basis of imprinting in the chick up to 1985 – see also chapter 3 of Johnson and Morton, 1991.)

Johnson, M. H. and Bolhuis, J. J. (1991) Imprinting, predispositions, and filial preference in the chick. In R. Andrew (ed.) *Neural and Behavioral Plasticity*. Cambridge: Cambridge University Press. (Reviews recent evidence on the interaction between predispositions and learning in the chick.)

Johnson, M. H. and Morton, J. (1991) *Biology and Cognitive Development: the Case of Face Recognition*. Oxford: Blackwell. (Argues that a two process theory, similar to that put forward for the chick, can be applied to the development of face recognition in the human infant.)

Turkewitz, G. and Kenny, P. A. (1985) The role of development limitations of sensory input on sensory/perceptual organization. *Developmental and Behavioral Pediatrics*, 6, 302–6. (Contains experimental evidence in support of the idea that sensory limitations facilitate development.)

von der Marlsburg, C. and Singer, W. (1988) Principles of cortical network organization. In P. Rakic and W. Singer (eds), *Neurobiology of the Neocortex*. Chichester: John Wiley & Sons.

20

The Instinct to Learn

PETER MARLER

I sense from the classical debate between Piaget and Chomsky (Piattelli-Palmarini, 1980) that at least some of us are all too prone to think of learning and instinct as being virtually antithetical. According to this common view, behavior is one or the other, but it is rarely, if ever, both. Lower animals display instincts, but our own species, apart from a few very basic drives, displays instincts rarely. Instead, we are supposed to be the manifestation of what can be achieved by the emancipation from instinctive control (Gould and Marler, 1987).

It is self-evident that this antithesis is false. Just as instincts are products of interactions between genome and environment, even the most extreme case of purely arbitrary, culturally transmitted behavior must, in some sense, be the result of an instinct at work. Functions of instincts may be generalized or highly specialized, but without them learning could not occur. Thus, the question I pose is not "Do instincts to learn exist?" but rather "What is their nature, and by what behavioral and physiological mechanism do they operate?" How do they impinge on the pervasive plasticity that behavior displays at so many points in the course of its development? I suggest that concepts from the classical ethology of Konrad Lorenz (1950) and Niko Tinbergen (1951) are instructive in a search for answers to these questions.

Of the several concepts with which Lorenz and Tinbergen sought to capture the essence of instinctive behavior in animals (listed in table 20.1), I concentrate especially on three. First is the notion of *sensitive periods as phases* of development with unusual potential for lability. Second and third are the complementary ideas of *releasers (or sign stimuli) and innate release mechanisms*, invoked by ethologists to explain the remarkable fact that many organisms, especially in infancy, are responsive to certain key stimuli during interactions with their social companions and with their physical environments, when they first encounter them. This responsiveness implies the possession of brain mechanisms that attune them innately to certain kinds of stimulation.

"The Instinct to Learn" first appeared in *The Epigenesis of Mind: Essays on Biology and Cognition*, edited by S. Carey and R. Gelman (Lawrence Erlbaum Associates, 1991, pp. 37–66), and is reprinted by kind permission.

Table 20.1 Concepts from classical ethology relevant to the instinct to learn

Sensitive periods
Imprinting
Fixed action patterns
Releasers
Innate release mechanisms
(Instincts to learn)

In recent years, I have come to believe that many such mechanisms have richer and more interesting functions than simply to serve as design features for animal as automata. They also provide the physiological machinery to facilitate and guide learning processes, as one set of components in what I think can be appropriately viewed as instincts to learn.

I use birdsong to make the case for instincts to learn as an approach that is productive and logical, even with behavior that is clearly and obviously learned. As a research strategy, it prepares us directly for posing the right kinds of questions in neurophysiological investigations of the underlying mechanisms. It is a position that follows naturally, once the crucial point is appreciated that instincts are not immutable and completely lacking in ontogenetic plasticity, as has so often been assumed in the past, but are themselves, by definition, susceptible to the influence of experience. I present evidence that even the most creative aspects of song development are imbued with instinctive influences, by which I refer to the aspects of the phenotype of the learning organism that are attributable to its genetic constitution (Johnston, 1988). These influences pervade all aspects of ontogeny. We cannot begin to understand how a young bird learning to sing interacts with its social and physical environments, and assimilates information from these interactions, without taking full account of innate contributions to the assimilation process. Each species accommodates most readily to those aspects of experience that are compatible with its nature.

One of the best illustrations of local dialects in birdsong is the white-crowned sparrow (figure 20.1). This is a very simple case. With rare exceptions, each male has a single song type, which has about a 2-second duration. Some song features conform very closely to the local dialect, and others are unique to each individual male. The dialects are so marked that someone with a cultivated ear would be able to tell where he or she was in California, blindfolded, simply by listening to their songs (Baker and Cunningham, 1985; Baptista, 1975, 1977). The fact that the dialects are learned becomes obvious when a male bird is reared without hearing the song of its own kind. A much simpler song develops, lacking all traces of the local accent (Marler, 1970; Petrinovich, 1985). What is the nature of this learning process, and what, if any, are the contributions of instinctive processes? We can detect such contributions in many aspects of the process of learning to sing.

Innate Learning Preferences

If we present a young bird with an array of different songs or tutors to learn from, are they equipotential as stimuli, or are some preferred over others? If

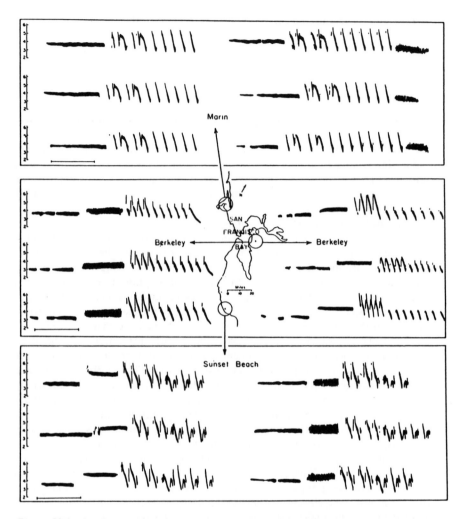

Figure 20.1 An illustration of song dialects in the white-crowned sparrow in the San Francisco Bay area. Songs of 18 males are illustrated, 6 from Marin County, 6 in the Berkeley area, and 6 from Sunset Beach, to the south. Each male has a single song type, for the most part. Local dialects are most evident in the second, trilled portion of the song (from Marler, 1970). These dialects have been studied in much greater detail by Baptista (1975).

there are preferences, do species differ in the songs they favor, or is a song that is a strong learning stimulus for one species, strong for others as well?

As a key feature of the research on which this report is based, a comparative approach has been taken. The underlying principle is simple. Young males of two species, the swamp and the song sparrow, were brought into the laboratory and reared under identical conditions. This gave us the opportunity to observe whether they interacted similarly or differently with the experimental situations in which they were reared. Despite their close genetic relatedness, their songs are very different (figure 20.2). One is simple; the other is complex. They differ in the overall "syntax" of their songs and in the "phonology" of the individual notes. They differ in repertoire size, a male song sparrow having about three times as many song types as a male swamp sparrow (three in one case, 10 to 12 in the other).

How do males of these two species react if we bring them into the laboratory as nestlings, raise them by hand so that their opportunity to hear song in nature is limited, and expose them to tape recordings with equal numbers of swamp sparrow songs and song sparrow songs? When we analyze the songs that they produce, it becomes clear that each displays a preference for songs of its own species (figure 20.3).

Normal, Crystallized
Song Sparrow Song

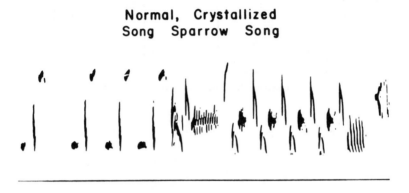

Normal, Crystallized
Swamp Sparrow Song

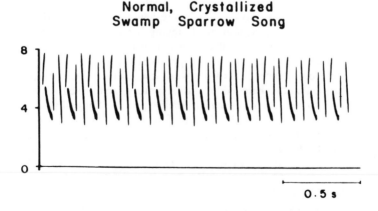

0.5 s

Figure 20.2 Sound spectrograms of normal song and swamp sparrow songs. They differ in both syntax and phonology, and also in the size of individual song repertoires, which average about three song types in swamp sparrows and 10–12 in song sparrows.

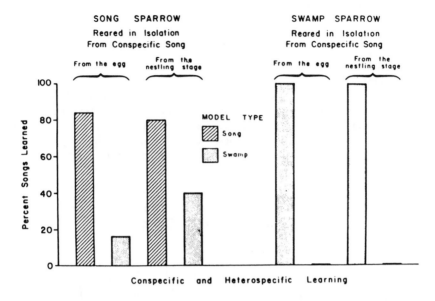

Figure 20.3 Learning preferences of male song and swamp sparrows either raised in the laboratory from the egg or exposed to song in nature during the nestling phase and only then brought into the laboratory. Birds were given a choice of tape recordings to learn, some of their own species' song and some of the other species. The results show that both have an innate preference for learning songs of their own species, but the preference is stronger in swamp sparrows than in song sparrows. Song experience during the nestling phase evidently has no effect on learning preferences.

In most of the experiments I report on, birds were raised by hand, after being taken as nestlings from the field at an age of 3–5 days. We do this because it is more difficult to raise them from the egg. Might they have learned something in the egg, or the first few days of life before being brought into the laboratory that has an influence on development of singing behavior, perhaps leading them to favor songs of the species heard during that period?

To check on the possibility of pre- or perinatal experience of species-specific song on learning preferences, eggs from wild nests of the same two species were taken early in incubation, hatched in the laboratory, and raised with absolutely no opportunity to hear adult song of their species. They displayed similar learning preferences (figure 20.3). The preference for conspecific song is thus innate (Marler and Peters, 1989). Interestingly, the song sparrow preference is less extreme in birds raised under both conditions. Dooling and Searcy (1980) uncovered a similar trend by looking at heart-rate changes in three-week-old song and swamp sparrows in response to song (figure 20.4). It may be that, as found in some other birds (Baptista and Petrinovich, 1984, 1986; Clayton, 1988; Pepperberg, 1988), social interaction with live tutors is more important in song sparrows than in swamp sparrows, because song sparrows are not known to imitate swamp sparrows in nature, even though they live in close proximity. In swamp sparrows, learning from tape recordings and live tutors has been shown to take place in a very similar fashion (Marler and Peters, 1988b). Social influences notwithstanding, in both species the preference *can* be sustained solely on the basis of acoustic features of song. What are the acoustic features on which these preferences are based? The answer is different in the two species.

By using computer-synthesized songs in which different acoustic features were independently varied, we found that the learning preference of male swamp sparrows is based not on syntactical features of the song but on the phonology

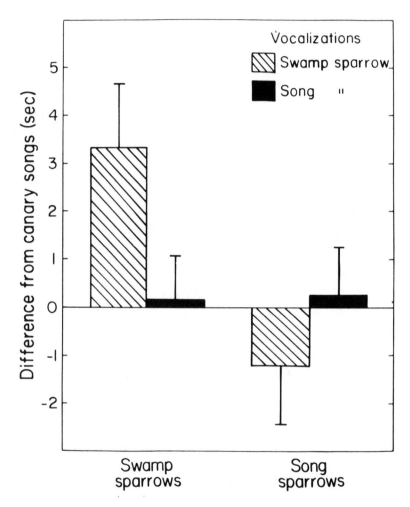

Figure 20.4 Cardiac responses of young swamp and song sparrows to recorded songs of their own and of the other species. The responses are calibrated in relation to the neutral stimulus of a canary song. Each responds most strongly to songs of its own species. The swamp sparrows discriminated more strongly than the song sparrows, in which the preference was not statistically significant. The trend matches that in song learning preferences (figure 20.3). These data were gathered at an age of 3–4 weeks, prior to any song production. (After Doding and Searcy, 1980.)

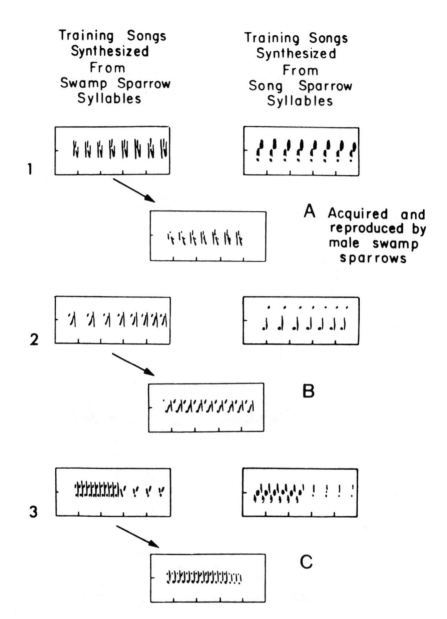

Figure 20.5 A diagram of song learning preference in male swamp sparrows. Three pairs of computer-synthesized songs are illustrated with the same syntax but composed of syllables either from song sparrow or from swamp sparrow songs. In each case, male swamp sparrows preferred syllables of their own species, irrespective of the syntactical arrangement in which they were presented. In each case, the syllable chosen was produced with typical swamp sparrow syntax, regardless of the syntactical structure of the learned model.

of the syllables. As illustrated in figure 20.5, male swamp sparrows presented with simplified songs consisting either of swamp sparrow syllables or song sparrow syllables unerringly favor those with conspecific syllables, irrespective of the temporal pattern in which they are presented. They then recast them in the normal syntactical pattern, whether or not this pattern has been available to them in the songs they have heard. In choosing models for learning, the song syllable is clearly the primary focus of interest for a swamp sparrow.

In contrast, song sparrows, with their more complex songs, base their learning preference not only on syllabic structure but also on a number of syntactical features, including the number of segments, their internal phrase structure – whether syllables are trilled or unrepeated, and such attributes as the tempo in which they are delivered. There is no evidence that young male swamp sparrows refer to any of these syntactical features when they choose models for song learning (Marler and Peters, 1980, 1988a, 1989).

The evidence of differences in innate responsiveness to song features from species to species is thus clear and unequivocal, implying the existence of something like Lorenzian "innate-release mechanisms." This innate responsiveness is employed not to develop fixed behaviors, as we might once have thought, but as the basis for a learning process. Having focused attention on the particular set of exemplars that satisfy the innate criteria, sparrows then learn them, in specific detail, including the local dialect (if this is a species that possesses dialects). In the swamp sparrow, the dialects are defined by the patterning of notes within a syllable (Marler and Pickert, 1984) as displayed in figure 20.6. Balaban (1988) has shown that both males and females acquire responsiveness to these dialect variations. Thus, the birds go far beyond the dictates of the initial ethological lock-and-key mechanism.

A further point, the importance of which cannot be overstressed, is that birds are not completely bound by these innate preferences. If conspecific songs are withheld, sparrows can be persuaded to learn nonpreferred songs (Figure 20.7), especially if these are accompanied by further, strong stimulation, as with a live interactive tutor of another species (Baptista and Petrinovich, 1984, 1986). Thus, the process of choosing models for song learning is probabilistically controlled, not absolutely determined. Given the normal ecology of the species, however, conspecific song tutoring will usually be available for innate preferences to be exercised, thus establishing a certain predictable trajectory to the learning process.

How might one model the mechanisms underlying such learning preferences? There is ample experimental evidence that birds can hear the songs of other species perfectly well and can discriminate between them with precision, even at the level of individual differences (Dooling, 1989). Yet they either fail to learn them in retrievable form in the normal course of song acquisition, or, if they do learn them, they forget them again. One caveat here is that we still lack a direct test of what has been memorized, and we have to rely instead on what is produced as a memorization index. Even in the earliest productions of imitations, in plastic song, copies of songs of other species are not usually in evidence. By this criterion, these sparrows behave as though any song presented as a stimulus is subjected to normal sensory processing but is then quickly lost from memory in the usual course of events, unless the exposure is massive, continuing day after

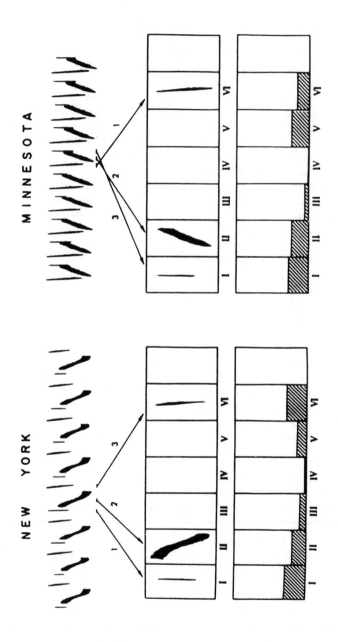

Figure 20.6 Swamp sparrow songs are constructed from six basic note types (I–VI), present in similar proportions in different populations (histograms at the bottom). Two typical songs from New York and Minnesota are illustrated, with different rules for ordering note types within syllables. In New York three-note syllables, type I notes are typically in first position and type VI notes in final position, with one of the other note types between. In Minnesota three-note songs an opposite rule tends to prevail, as illustrated (Marler and Pickert, 1984). Wild males and females are both responsive to these differences in syllable construction (Balaban, 1988).

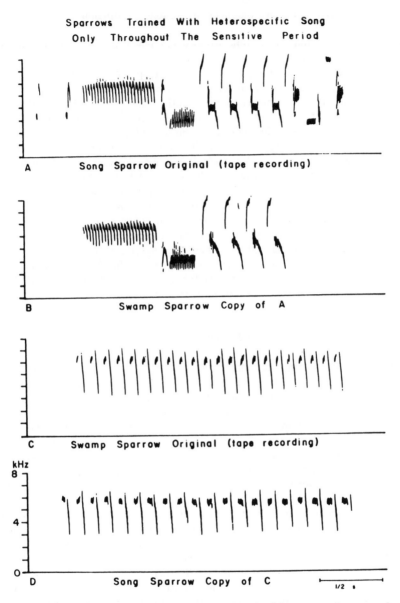

A   Song Sparrow Original (tape recording)

B   Swamp Sparrow Copy of A

C   Swamp Sparrow Original (tape recording)

kHz
8

4

0
D   Song Sparrow Copy of C   1/2 s

Figure 20.7 If song and swamp sparrows are raised in the laboratory and presented only
with tape-recorded songs of the other species, on rare occasions they will imitate them.
Examples are illustrated of a swamp sparrow copy (B) of part of a song sparrow model
(A) and a song sparrow copy (D) of a swamp sparrow model (C). Male swamp sparrows
rarely imitate song sparrow song. Song sparrows imitate swamp sparrow song more often
(cf. figure 20.3), but when they do so they usually recast the swamp sparrow syllables
into song sparrow-like syntax (cf. figure 20.20).

day, and associated with strong arousal. There is an urgent need to develop memorization assays that are independent of song production.

When conspecific stimuli are presented, it is as though the bird suddenly becomes attentive, and a brief time window is opened during which the stimulus cluster in view becomes more salient, more likely to be memorized, and probably destined to be used later for guiding song development. One tends to think in terms of parallel processing, with certain circuits responsible for general auditory processing and others committed to the identification of stimuli as worthy of the special attention of the general processing machinery, if and when they are encountered. This interaction might be thought of as a teaching process, with special mechanisms serving – especially in infancy – to instruct general mechanisms about what to pay special attention to during learning and about how the learning process can most efficiently be structured. In adulthood, once their function of establishing certain developmental trajectories has been accomplished, special mechanisms may cease to function or even cease to exist.

One may think of the sign stimuli present in conspecific songs operating not only as behavioral triggers but also as cues for learning, serving as what might be thought of as "enabling signals," their presence increasing the probability of learning other associated stimuli that might otherwise be neglected (Rauschecker and Marler, 1987). I believe that this function is served by many ethological "releasers," and it may even be the *primary* function for many of them.

Vocal Learning Templates

Sparrows are able to generate some aspects of normal, species-specific song syntax irrespective of the syntax of the models to which they have been exposed in the past. This potential is most clearly displayed in the songs of birds raised in isolation, completely deprived of access to adult song of their own or any other species. Figure 20.8 shows examples of natural song and examples of the simpler form of song that develops in males reared in isolation. There are many abnormalities in the songs of males raised in isolation, and quantitative study reveals that the variation is great. Nevertheless, by using a comparative approach, it can be clearly shown that each species is capable of generating some basic features of normal song syntax irrespective of whether these have been experienced in the form of song stimulation by others. The syntax of a swamp sparrow is rather resistant to change by experience, in comparison with the song sparrow, although stimulation by multipartite songs does result in the production of a certain proportion of bipartite song patterns (Marler and Peters, 1980). Male swamp sparrows copy syllables more readily than whole songs. This is less true of song sparrows. When they are allowed to hear conspecific song, they will sometimes imitate the entire syntax of the particular model experienced (figure 20.8), even though they are innately responsive to conspecific syntax. Once more, the invocation of innate influences in no way implies a commitment to immutability.

Again, we may pose the question, "What kind of physiological mechanism underlies this ability?" Some insight is gained by studying the singing behavior of birds that are deaf. We know that the sense of hearing is important not only to permit a bird to hear the songs of others but also to enable it to hear its own voice (Konishi, 1965; Nottebohm, 1968). Male sparrows deafened early in life, prior to any singing, develop songs that are highly abnormal, exceedingly variable, almost amorphous in structure (figure 20.8), although certain basic species differences are sometimes still detectable (Marler and Sherman, 1983).

This highly degraded form of song results both if a male is deafened before song stimulation and also after song stimulation but before the development of singing (Konishi, 1965). Thus, there seems to be no internal brain circuitry that makes memorized songs directly available to guide motor development. To transform a memorized song into a produced song, the bird must be able to hear its own voice.

This contrast between the songs of hearing and deaf birds inspired the concept of vocal learning templates, existing in two forms: one innate and the other

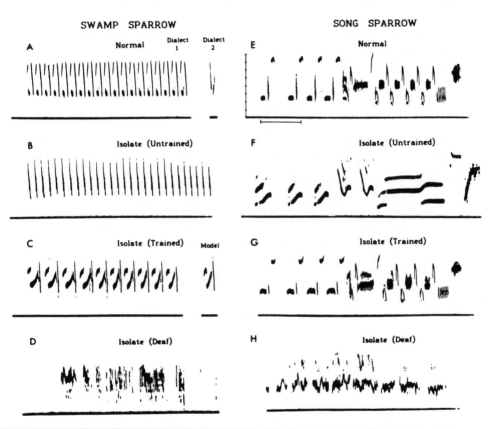

Figure 20.8 Sound spectrograms illustrating typical songs of swamp and song sparrows produced under four conditions. First row: normal learning in the wild (A and E, with one syllable of a second dialect also shown in A). Row 2: acoustic isolation, but with intact hearing (B and F). Row 3: isolated, but trained with tape recordings of normal songs of their species (C and G). Row 4: isolated and deafened (D and H). Frequency markers indicate 1 kHz intervals and the time marker 0.5 secs.

acquired. Acquired templates, resulting from enrichment, modification, substitution, or interaction with other mechanisms as a consequence of experience, were originally conceived of as transforms of the same basic mechanisms as innate templates (Konishi, 1965; Marler, 1976; Marler and Sherman, 1983). It now seems possible that they are functionally and neuroanatomically separate, although interconnected and interreactive, as indicated earlier. Innate auditory song templates have a potential direct influence on early learning preferences, in some circumstances, and on the later production of songs. They also serve as a vehicle for bringing innate influences to bear on the effects of intervening experience. Auditory templates for vocal learning provide one model of the kind of brain mechanisms underlying this particular instinct to learn. Many of the attributes of this model are applicable to other systems of behavioral development. Ontogeny is guided by sensory feedback from motor activity, with referral of this feedback to templates with specifications that can be supplemented, modified, or overridden by experience. The specifications incorporate innate contributions that may be unique to one species, as is the case with those stressed in this paper, or they may be more generally distributed across species, such as specifications for the tonality that characterizes many birdsongs (Nowicki and Marler, 1988).

Plans for Motor Development

Songs of many birds, such as sub-oscine flycatchers, develop completely normally in isolation. When such a song begins to be performed, the first efforts are clearly identifiable as immature versions of what will ultimately be the normal crystallized song. These early attempts may be noisy and fragmented, but the maturational progression is clear and predictable (Kroodsma, 1984). In birds that learn their songs, the developmental progression is quite different. There is a more complex ontogenetic sequence, from subsong, through plastic song, to crystallized song (figure 20.9). The general pattern of song development in 16 male swamp sparrows in the laboratory is diagrammed in figure 20.10. There is considerable individual variation, but a modal pattern can nevertheless be discerned that

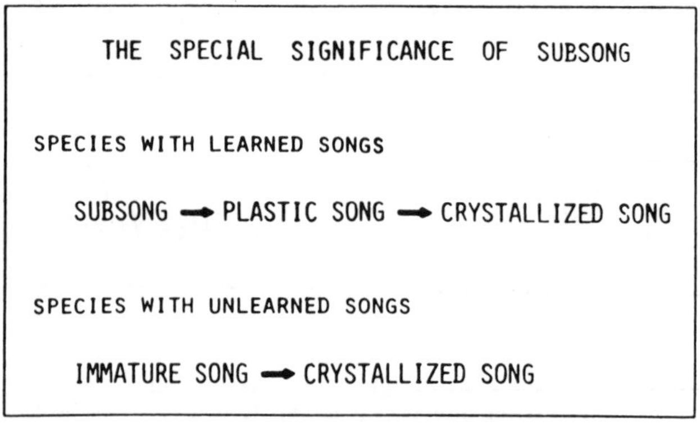

```
THE  SPECIAL  SIGNIFICANCE  OF  SUBSONG


SPECIES WITH LEARNED SONGS

    SUBSONG ➡ PLASTIC SONG ➡ CRYSTALLIZED SONG


SPECIES WITH UNLEARNED SONGS

    IMMATURE SONG ➡ CRYSTALLIZED SONG
```

Figure 20.9 The developmental sequence is different in bird species with learned and unlearned songs. Subsong is radically different from mature song in structure, and undergoes a metamorphosis in the progression through plastic song.

comprises three stages: subsong, plastic song, and crystallized song. This program unfolds similarly in males raised in isolation, suggesting that it is hormonally controlled (but see Marler et al., 1988).

We still know less about subsong than any other aspect of birdsong development. Figure 20.11 shows examples of early subsong from male swamp and song sparrows. It illustrates the fact that the structure of subsong is quite different from that of mature song. It is typical of bird species with learned songs that a kind of metamorphosis intervenes between subsong and later stages of song development. The amorphous structure and noisy spectral organization of sparrow subsong is typical.

Despite its lack of structure, careful analysis reveals subtle species differences. Auditory templates appear to be operating even at this early stage. A difference in note duration present in normal song and in those of isolates (Marler and Sherman, 1985) also occurs in the subsong of hearing song and swamp sparrows (figure 20.11) but is lacking in the early subsong of deaf birds (figure 20.12). Subsong is believed to be critical for several aspects of the development of the general motor skills of singing and also for honing the ability to guide the voice by the ear, which is a prerequisite for vocal imitation (Nottebohm, 1972; Marler and Peters, 1982b); however, direct evidence has been hard to obtain.

Only in the second stage, plastic song, do the more obvious signs of mature song structure appear. Figure 20.13 presents samples of developing song in a

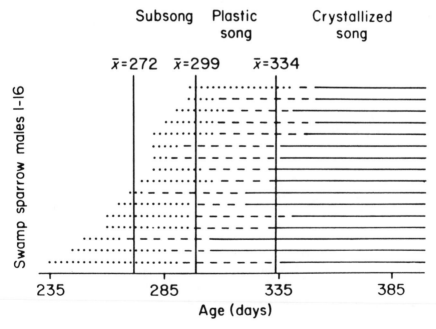

Figure 20.10 Patterns of song development in 16 male swamp sparrows, each raised in individual isolation. They are displayed with the latest developers at the top and the earliest developers at the bottom. Despite considerable individual variation, a species-typical pattern can be discerned.

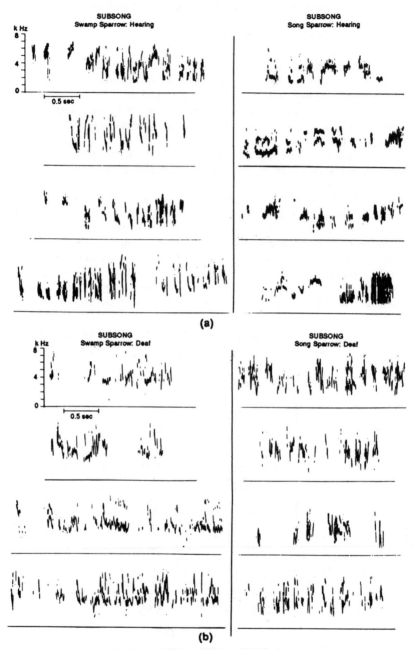

Figure 20.11 Sound spectrograms of early subsong from swamp and song sparrows with hearing intact, as compared with subsong produced after early deafening. In the birds with hearing intact, note duration averages longer in the song sparrows. This difference is absent in subsong of deaf birds produced at the same age.

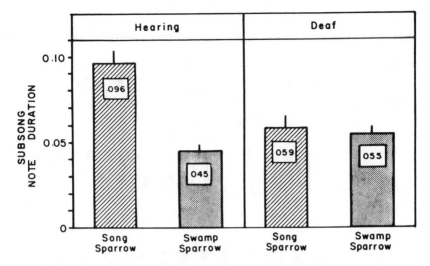

Figure 20.12 Histograms of mean note durations in subsong of song and swamp sparrows with hearing intact and after deafening. It is evident that auditory song templates are already operating even at this early age, to generate species differences in subsong structure.

single male swamp sparrow, starting with subsong and proceeding through plastic song to the stable form of crystallized song. As plastic song progresses, rehearsal of previously memorized song patterns begins. These continue to stabilize gradually until crystallization occurs. Note that normal species-specific syntax – a single trill – emerges late in swamp sparrows, irrespective of whether such patterns have been heard from others or not, suggesting that an innately specified central motor program is accessed at this stage.

Larger repertoires of songs occur during plastic song than in crystallized song (Marler and Peters, 1982a). Male swamp sparrows greatly overproduce song material at intermediate stages of development, as can be seen more clearly by summing data on numbers of songs present in an individual repertoire during the transition from plastic to crystallized song (figure 20.14). A typical crystallized repertoire consists of two or three song types, but in early plastic song the repertoire may be four or five times greater. Thus, more is memorized than is manifest in the final products of motor development.

The process of discarding songs during crystallization is not a random one. For one thing, birds that have been persuaded to learn songs of other species by "hybridizing" them with conspecific song elements are more likely to reject these "hybrid" songs during the attrition process (Marler and Peters, 1982a). In addition, there are also opportunities for experience to interact with development to influence the final outcome. There is often a premium in songbirds on countersinging against rivals with similar themes if they are available. The transition from plastic song to full song takes place at a stage of life when a young male is striving to establish his first territory, and, by a "pseudolearning" process, stimulation by the songs of rivals at this time may favor the retention of song themes that most closely match those of rivals in the attrition process.

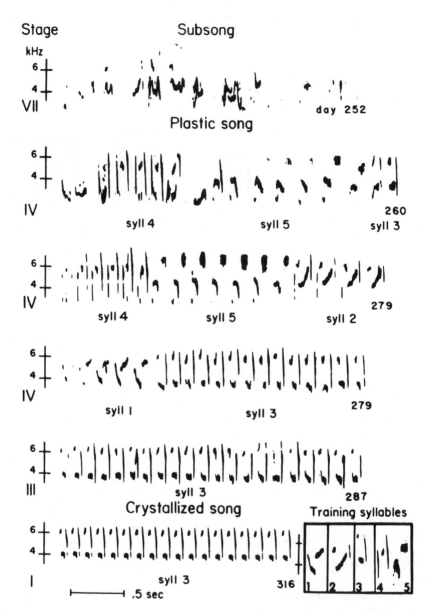

Figure 20.13 Samples from the process of song development in a single male swamp sparrow, ranging from subsong to crystallized song. The age of the bird is indicated on the right ranging from 252 to 316 days of age. This bird was trained with tape-recorded songs, syllables of some of which are indicated in the boxed insert (1–5). As indicated by the labels, early efforts to reproduce imitations of these months later are imperfect in early plastic song, but they improve as progress towards crystallized song is made. The overproduction of song types during plastic song can also be seen. The two song types in the crystallized repertoire of this male consisted of syllable types 2 and 3.

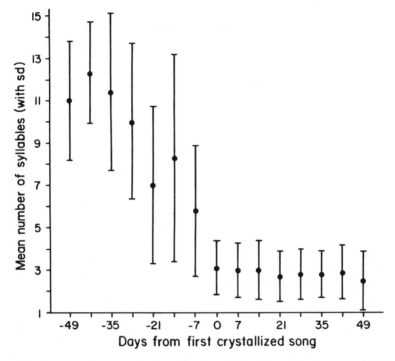

Figure 20.14 A plot of mean syllable repertoires of 16 male swamp sparrows at different stages of song development, arranged around day 0 as the time of crystallization. There is extensive overproduction of song types during plastic song, and the repertoire is drastically reduced as development proceeds towards crystallization of the mature repertoire, averaging three song types per bird (from Marler and Peters, 1982).

There is also a fascinating suggestion from the work of King and West (1988) on the brown-headed cowbird that females can influence the choice of crystallized song by giving courtship responses to song types that they favor during the plastic song phase.

Steps in Learning to Sing

The diverse strategies that different birds use in learning to sing are accompanied by certain underlying consistencies. For example, there are always several phases in the process of learning to sing. Sensory and perceptual processing tends to precede production (figure 20.15). Songs pass into storage during the acquisition phase, when a bird subjects songs to auditory processing, and commits some of them to memory. It seems logical that the knowledge necessary to develop patterns of action should be acquired before development of these actions commences. After acquisition, internalized representations of songs, or parts of them, may be stored for an appreciable time before the male embarks on the process of retrieving them and generating imitations. In figure 20.16, time

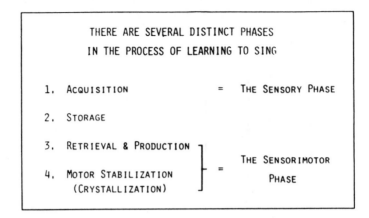

THERE ARE SEVERAL DISTINCT PHASES
IN THE PROCESS OF LEARNING TO SING

1. ACQUISITION   = THE SENSORY PHASE

2. STORAGE

3. RETRIEVAL & PRODUCTION ⌉
                                        THE SENSORIMOTOR
                              ⎬ =
4. MOTOR STABILIZATION ⌋   PHASE
   (CRYSTALLIZATION)

Figure 20.15 Steps in the process of learning and reproducing a song.

intervals are plotted between the last exposure to tape-recorded songs of 16 male
swamp sparrows, each separately housed, ending at about 60 days of age, and
production of the very first hints of identifiable imitations. This storage interval
was surprisingly long, on the order of 8 months, an impressive achievement.

The period of storage before retrieval of stored representations from memory
begins varies greatly from species to species. It is not known whether this is a
phase of passive storage or whether consolidation or active reorganization of
memorized material is taking place. Subsong may occur during storage, and even
during acquisition, but the onset of rehearsal is the sign that plastic song has begun.
Themes are rehearsed and stabilized, and eventually song crystallization occurs.

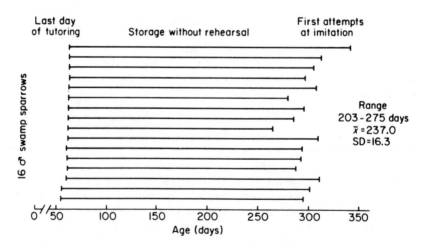

Figure 20.16 The period of storage of learned songs without rehearsal in 16 male swamp
sparrows trained with tape-recorded song prior to 60 days of age. Songs were recorded
and analyzed every two weeks, and the age was noted at which the first identifiable
imitations were reproduced, some eight months after last exposure to the models.

Sensitive Periods for Acquisition

Another aspect of instincts to learn is the timing of the acquisition phase. Is it brief, or extended? Does it occur only once, or repeatedly during life? There are striking differences between species in the timing of song acquisition (figure 20.17). In some birds, acquisition is age-dependent and is restricted to a short period early in life. In other species, song remains changeable from year to year, apparently with a continuing ability to acquire new songs throughout life. Even close relatives, such as sparrows and canaries, may differ strikingly in the timing of sensitive periods, providing ideal opportunities for comparative investigation of variations in the neural and hormonal physiology that correlate with song acquisition. Such species differences can have a direct and profound impact on the potential for behavioral plasticity.

Much of the behavioral information on sensitive periods is inadequate to serve well as a springboard for comparative physiological investigation. In an effort to develop a more systematic, experimental approach to this problem, we played tape-recorded songs to male sparrows in the laboratory throughout their first year of life, changing song types every week or two (Marler and Peters, 1987, 1988b; Marler, 1987). By recording and analyzing the songs produced, we were able to extrapolate back to the time when acquisition occurred. Figure 20.18 shows the results for a group of male swamp sparrows, with a clear sensitive period for song acquisition beginning at about 20 days of age and then closing out about 3–4 months later, before the onset of plastic song. A similar picture of song acquisition was obtained with a changing roster of live tutors, brought into song by testosterone therapy (figure 20.18). Differences between species in the timing of sensitive periods are sometimes gross but may also be subtle, as

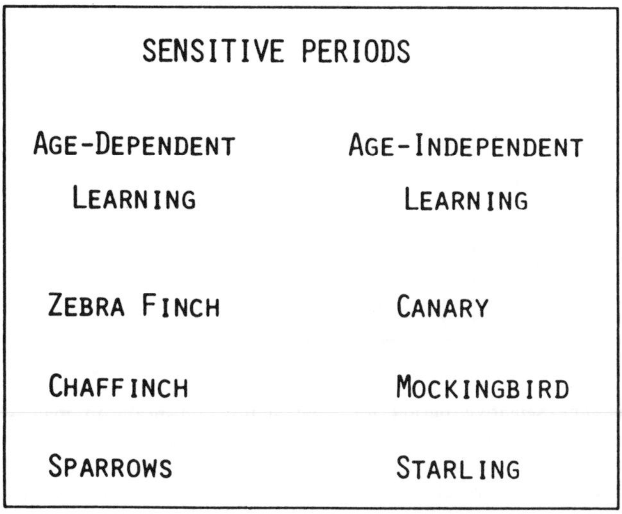

SENSITIVE PERIODS	
AGE-DEPENDENT LEARNING	AGE-INDEPENDENT LEARNING
ZEBRA FINCH	CANARY
CHAFFINCH	MOCKINGBIRD
SPARROWS	STARLING

Figure 20.17 Examples of bird species with age-dependent and age-independent song learning.

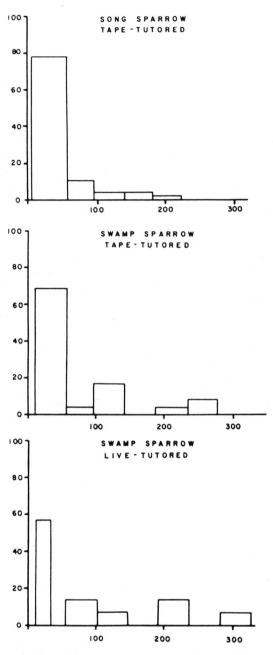

Figure 20.18 The sensitive period for song acquisition peaks in male song sparrows between 20 and 50 days of age (top). The peak is attenuated somewhat in male swamp sparrows and extends to a later age, both when they are tutored with tape recordings (middle) and when they are given live tutors (bottom). These results were obtained by training birds with a constantly changing program of either tape recordings or live tutors and then inferring the age at which acquisition occurred from analyses of songs produced later (from Marler and Peters, 1987, 1988b).

can be seen by comparing the timing of song acquisition from tape recordings in male song sparrows (figure 20.18). Here, the sensitive period is even more compressed into early adolescence. These birds provide ideal opportunities for pursuing questions about the neural and hormonal changes that are correlated with these sensitive periods and perhaps bear a causal relationship with them (Marler et al., 1987, 1988; Nordeen et al., 1988).

Although sensitive periods for song acquisition are clearly significant components of instincts to learn, it is important to be aware once again that these are not fixed traits (Marler, 1987). There are degrees of lability, depending on such factors as the strength of stimulation – whether a tape recording or a live tutor is used (Baptista and Petrinovich, 1984, 1986). Physiological factors that correlate with the season are also relevant. In some species, young may be hatched so late that singing, which is a seasonal activity in most species, has ceased for the year. In such cases, it has been shown that closure of the sensitive period may be delayed until the following spring, apparently in response to the changing photoperiod (Kroodsma and Pickert, 1984). Deprivation of access to conspecific models can also delay closure of the sensitive period (Clayton, 1988). Once more, the invocation of innate influences does not mean sacrifice of the potential for behavioral flexibility; rather, instincts to learn set a species-specific context within which experience operates.

Innate Inventiveness

Thus far in this account of song learning, the emphasis has been placed on the production of more-or-less precise imitations of songs heard from other birds. In fact, an element of inventiveness often intrudes. This may take several forms. One revelation from the sensitive period experiments described in the previous section is that sparrows are able to recombine components both of the same song and of songs acquired at different times. Recasting or re-editing of components of learned models into new sequences is commonly exploited as one means for generating novelty and also for producing the very large individual repertoires that some birds possess (Krebs and Kroodsma, 1980). Often, models are broken down into phrases or syllables and then reordered into several different sequences that become stable themes (Marler, 1984). Song sparrows are especially prone to indulge in such recombinations with songs acquired in later phases of the sensitive period (Marler and Peters, 1988b). This correlates with a decline in the completeness with which entire learned songs are accurately reproduced (figure 20.19). This tendency to recombine segments of learned models has the effect of creating new songs from old, by reuse of the same basic raw materials.

Species differ greatly in the faithfulness with which they adhere to learned models, although imitations are rarely identical with their models, even in the best mimics. Some species imitate learned models closely, and local dialects are common in birds, but a degree of personal individuality is also virtually universal. In every case examined, this individuality has proved to provide a basis in nature for personal identification of companions and for distinguishing neighbors from strangers (reviewed in Falls, 1982).

Some degree of inventiveness is, in fact, universal, but species differ greatly in the extent to which they indulge in creative activity in song development.

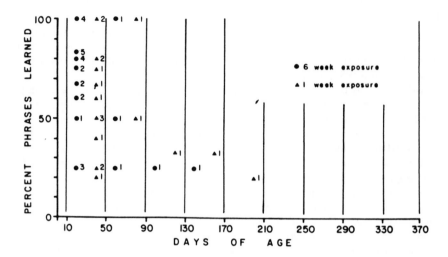

Figure 20.19 When song sparrows reproduce songs acquired early in the sensitive period, they are more likely to reproduce them with the original syntax of the model than with songs acquired later in the sensitive period. For each age block, two sets of data are illustrated, from tape recorded songs heard for a six-week period (left) and for a one-week period (right). Songs acquired later are more likely to be broken up into separate phrases that are then recombined in different ways to produce new songs (from Marler and Peters, 1987).

Figure 20.20 illustrates just one example of a song sparrow exposed in the laboratory to a variety of simple synthetic songs. This bird generated an approximation of typical song sparrow syntax in highly creative fashion by drawing two components from one model and one from another model. Some species provide abundant illustrations of this kind of innovative process, both in the laboratory and in the field.

The rules for parsing acquired songs down into components and recombining them are species-specific, however. There is also species variation in the faithfulness with which a bird adheres to the structure of a given imitation. Some, like sparrows, are conservative. They recast syllables often, but they adhere to the basic syllabic structure, which makes them good subjects for studies of learning. Other species, such as the red-winged blackbird, are compulsive improvisers (Marler et al., 1972), subjecting themes to continuous experimentation and embroidery during development, until the originals are barely recognizable.

Even more intriguing is the suggestion that improvisation and invention may be most consistently applied to certain segments of songs, with other segments left as pure, unadulterated imitations. A species like the white-crowned sparrow, in which birds in a given locality adhere closely to a given dialect, nevertheless has song segments or features that are more free for individual improvisation. Thus cues for personal identification may be encoded in one segment or feature, cues for the local dialect in another, and cues for species recognition in yet another set, the arrangement varying from species to species (Marler, 1960).

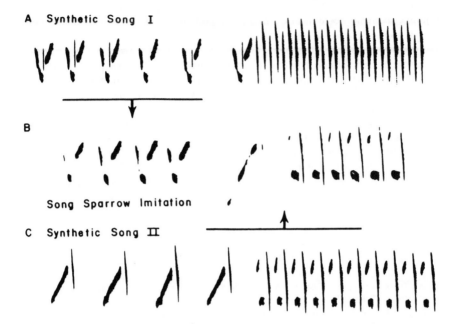

Figure 20.20 Song sparrows often create new themes by breaking learned songs down into their component syllables and recombining them in various ways. Illustrated here is the song of a laboratory-reared song sparrow exposed to an array of synthetic songs. It learned two of these (A and C) and recombined parts of them, as illustrated, to create a crude approximation of normal song sparrow song syntax.

Conclusions

It is less illogical than it first appears to speak of instincts for inventiveness. Song development is a creative process, but the inventiveness that birds often display is governed by sets of rules. Each species has its own distinctive set of physiological mechanisms for constraining or facilitating improvisation, guiding learning preferences, directing motor development, and establishing the timing of sensitive periods. Songs are learned, and yet instinctive influences on the learning process intrude at every turn.

Instincts to learn offer priceless opportunities to pinpoint the ways in which physiological or neuroanatomical changes can affect the process of learning a new behavior. Given the striking contrasts in song development in birds that are very close genetic relatives and are otherwise very similar in structure and physiology, presumably quite limited changes in neural organization or the timing of a hormonal event can have profound effects on the course of learning. Already the proverbial bird brain has yielded many secrets about the neural biology of vocal plasticity (Konishi, 1985; Nottebohm, 1987). Yet there is a sense in which we have hardly begun to exploit the potential of comparative studies as a source of new insights into the role of innate species differences in structure and physiology in the operation of instincts to learn.

There is a need in studies of behavioral development to overcome behavioristic prejudice against the invocation of innate contributions. It is as a consequence of such prejudice against the term "innate" that most students of animal behavior have eschewed its use altogether. The result is that ethological investigations of processes of behavioral epigenetics have, for the most part, been rendered impotent. The initiative has been left to geneticists and developmental biologists, who take it for granted that the genome plays a major role in all aspects of behavioral development (Marler and Sherman, 1985).

There is nothing illogical in applying the term "innate" to *differences* between organisms. As Hinde (1970) asserted, "Evidence that a difference in behavior is to be ascribed to genetic differences must come ultimately from the rearing of animals, known to differ genetically, in similar environments" (p. 431). It is both valid and productive for students of development to address Dobzhansky's (1962) question, "To what extent are the *differences* observed between persons due to genotypic or to environmental causes?" (p. 44).

ACKNOWLEDGMENTS

Research was conducted in collaboration with Susan Peters and supported in part by grant No. BRSG SO7 RR07065, awarded by the Biomedical Research Support Grant Program, Division of Research Resources, National Institutes of Health, and by grant number MH 14651. Esther Arruza prepared the figures and typed the manuscript. I thank Judith and Cathy Marler and Eileen McCue for rearing the birds. I am indebted to Susan Peters, Stephen Nowicki, Susan Carey, and Rochel Gelman for discussion and valuable criticism of the manuscript and to the New York Botanical Garden Institute of Ecosystem Studies at the Mary Flagler Cary Arboretum for access to study areas.

REFERENCES

Baker, M. C., & Cunningham, M. A. (1985). The biology of birdsong dialects. *Behavioral and Brain Sciences*, 8, 85–133.

Balaban, E. (1988). Cultural and genetic variation in swamp sparrows (*Melospiza georgiana*). II. Behavioral salience of geographic song variants. *Behaviour*, 105, 292–322.

Baptista, L. F. (1975). Song dialects and demes in sedentary populations of the white-crowned sparrow (*Zonotrichia leucophrys nuttalli*). *University of California Publications in Zoology*, 105, 1–52.

Baptista, L. F. (1977). Geographic variation in song and dialects of the Puget Sound white-crowned sparrow. *Condor*, 79, 356–370.

Baptista, L. F., & Petrinovich, L. (1984). Social interaction, sensitive phases and the song template hypothesis in the white-crowned sparrow. *Animal Behaviour*, 32, 172–181.

Baptista, L. F., & Petrinovich, L. (1986). Song development in the white-crowned sparrow: social factors and sex differences. *Animal Behaviour*, 34, 1359–1371.

Clayton, N. S. (1988). Song tutor choice in zebra finches and Bengalese finches: the relative importance of visual and vocal cues. *Behaviour*, 104, 281–299.

Dobzhanksy, T. (1962). *Mankind evolving*. New Haven, CT: Yale University Press.

Dooling, R. J. (1989). Perception of complex, species-specific vocalizations by birds and humans. In R. J. Dooling & S. Hulse (eds), *The comparative psychology of audition* (pp. 423–444). Hillsdale, NJ: Lawrence Erlbaum Associates.

Dooling, R. J., & Searcy, M. H. (1980). Early perceptual selectivity in the swamp sparrow. *Developmental Psychobiology*, 13, 499–506.

Falls, J. B. (1982). Individual recognition by sounds in birds. In D. E. Kroodsma & E. H. Miller (eds), *Acoustic communication in birds*, *Vol. 2* (pp. 237–278). New York: Academic Press.

Gould, J. L., & Marler, P. (1987). Learning by instinct. *Scientific American*, 256, 74–85.

Hinde, R. A. (1970). *Animal behaviour: A synthesis of ethology and comparative psychology*, 2nd edn. New York: McGraw-Hill.

Johnston, T. D. (1988). Developmental explanation and the ontogeny of birdsong: Nature/nurture redux. *Behavioural and Brain Sciences*, 11, 631–675.

King, A. P., & West, J. J. (1988). Searching for the functional origins of song in eastern brown-headed cowbirds, *Molothrus ater ater*. *Animal Behaviour*, 36, 1575–1588.

Konishi, M. (1965). The role of auditory feedback in the control of vocalization in the white-crowned sparrow. *Zeitschrift für Tierpsychologie*, 22, 770–783.

Konishi, M. (1985). Birdsong: From behavior to neuron. *Annual Review of Neuroscience*, 8, 125–170.

Krebs, J. R., & Kroodsma, D. E. (1980). Repertoires and geographical variation in bird song. In J. S. Rosenblatt, R. A. Hinde, C. Beer & M. C. Busnel (eds), *Advances in the study of behavior* (pp. 143–177). New York: Academic Press.

Kroodsma, D. E. (1984). Songs of the alder flycatcher (*Empidonax alnorum*) and willow flycatcher (*Empidonax traillii*) are innate. *Auk*, 101, 13–24.

Kroodsma, D. E., & Pickert, R. (1984). Sensitive phases for song learning: Effects of social interaction and individual variation. *Animal Behaviour*, 32, 389–394.

Lorenz, K. Z. (1950). The comparative method in studying innate behavior patterns. *Symposium Society Experimental Biology*, 4, 221–268.

Marler, P. (1960). Bird songs and mate selection. In W. N. Tavolga (ed.), *Animal sounds and communication* (pp. 348–367). American Institute of Biological Sciences Symposium Proceedings.

Marler, P. (1970). A comparative approach to vocal learning: song development in white-crowned sparrows. *Journal of Comparative and Physiological Psychology*, 71, 1–25.

Marler, P. (1976). Sensory templates in species-specific behavior. In J. Fentress (ed.), *Simpler networks and behavior* (pp. 314–329). Sunderland, MA: Sinauer Associates.

Marler, P. (1984). Song learning: Innate species differences in the learning process. In P. Marler & H. S. Terrace (eds), *The biology of learning* (pp. 289–309). Berlin: Springe-Verlag.

Marler, P. (1987). Sensitive periods and the role of specific and general sensory stimulation in birdsong learning. In J. P. Rauschecker & P. Marler (eds), *Imprinting and cortical plasticity* (pp. 99–135). New York: John Wiley & Sons.

Marler, P., Mundinger, P., Waser, M. S., & Lutjen, A. (1972). Effects of acoustical stimulation and deprivation on song development in red-winged black birds (*Agelaius phoeniceus*). *Animal Behaviour*, 20, 586–606.

Marler, P., & Peters, S. (1980). Birdsong and speech: evidence for special processing: In P. Eimas & J. Miller (eds), *Perspectives on the study of speech* (pp. 75–112). Hillsdale, NJ: Lawrence Erlbaum Associates.

Marler, P., & Peters, S. (1982a). Developmental overproduction and selective attrition: new processes in the epigenesis of birdsong. *Developmental Psychobiology*, 15, 369–378.

Marler, P., & Peters, S. (1982b). Subsong and plastic song: their role in the vocal learning process. In D. E. Kroodsma & E. H. Miller (eds), *Acoustic communication in birds: Vol. 2* (pp. 25–50). New York: Academic Press.

Marler, P., & Peters, S. (1987). A sensitive period for song acquisition in the song sparrow, *Melospiza melodia*: a case of age-limited learning. *Ethology*, 76, 89–100.

Marler, P., & Peters, S. (1988a). The role of song phonology and syntax in vocal learning preferences in the song sparrow, *Melospiza melodia*. *Ethology*, 77, 125–149.

Marler, P., & Peters, S. (1988b). Sensitive periods for song acquisition from tape recordings and live tutors in the swamp sparrow, *Melospiza georgiana*. *Ethology*, 77, 76–84.

Marler, P., & Peters, S. (1989). Species differences in auditory responsiveness in early vocal learning. In S. Hulse & R. Dooling (eds), *The comparative psychology of audition* (pp. 243–273). Hillsdale, NJ: Lawrence Erlbaum Associates.

Marler, P., & Peters, S., Ball, G. F., Dufty, A. M., Jr, & Wingfield, J. C. (1988). The role of sex steriods in the acquisition of birdsong. *Nature*, 336, 770–772.

Marler, P., Peters, S., & Wingfield, J. (1987). Correlations between song acquisition, song production, and plasma levels of testosterone and estradiol in sparrows. *Journal of Neurobiology*, 18, 531–548.

Marler, P., & Pickert, R. (1984). Species-universal microstructure in the learned song of the swamp sparrow (*Melospiza georgiana*). *Animal Behaviour*, 32, 673–689.

Marler, P., & Sherman, V. (1983). Song structure without auditory feedback: Emendations of the auditory template hypothesis. *Journal of Neuroscience*, 3, 517–531.

Marler, P., & Sherman, V. (1985). Innate differences in singing behaviour of sparrows reared in isolation from adult conspecific song. *Animal Behaviour*, 33, 57–71.

Nordeen, K. W., Marler, P., & Nordeen, E. J. (1988). Changes in neuron number during sensory learning in swamp sparrows. *Society of Neuroscience Abstracts*, 14, 89.

Nottebohm, F. (1968). Auditory experience and song development in the chaffinch (*Fringilla coelebs*). *Ibis*, 110, 549–568.

Nottebohm, F. (1972). Neural lateralization of vocal control in a passerine bird. II. Subsong, calls and a theory of vocal learning. *Journal of Experimental Zoology*, 1979, 35–49.

Nottebohm, F. (1987). Plasticity in adult avian central nervous system: possible relation between hormones, learning, and brain repair. In F. Plum (ed.), *Higher functions of the nervous system* (pp. 85–108). Washington: American Physiological Society.

Nowicki, S., & Marler, P. (1988). How do birds sing? *Music Perception*, 5, 391–426.

Pepperberg, I. M. (1988). The importance of social interaction and observation in the acquisition of communicative competence: Possible parallels between avian and human learning. In T. R. Zentall & B. G. Galef, Jr (eds), *Social learning: A comparative approach* (pp. 279–299). Hillsdale, NJ: Lawrence Erlbaum Associates.

Petrinovich, L. (1985). Factors influencing song development in the white-crowned sparrow (*Zonotrichia leucophrys*). *Journal of Comparative Psychology*, 99, 15–29.

Piattelli-Palmarini, M. (ed.). (1980). *Language and learning*. Cambridge, MA: Harvard University Press.

Rauschecker, J. P., & Marler, P. (1987). Cortical plasticity and imprinting: Behavioral and physiological contrasts and parallels. In J. P. Rauschecker & P. Marler (eds), *Imprinting and cortical plasticity* (pp. 349–366). New York: John Wiley & Sons.

Tinbergen, N. (1951). *The study of instinct*. Oxford: Clarendon Press.

21

Brain Mechanisms of Memory and Predispositions: Interactive Studies of Cerebral Function and Behavior

GABRIEL HORN

During the 1960s substantial advances were made in the neural analyses of a simple form of learning, habituation. At that time, however, the prospect of similar success in analyzing other forms of learning and memory was not encouraging. There are probably many reasons for this state of affairs, but one reason may be that many neurobiologists interested in this field were still in the slough of despond which followed the publication in 1950 of Karl Lashley's article "In search of the engram." In summarizing his own contributions, and those of others, he wrote:

> The series of experiments has yielded a good bit of information about what and where the memory trace is not. It has discovered nothing directly of the real nature of the engram. I sometimes feel, in reviewing the evidence on the localization of the memory trace, that the necessary conclusion is that learning just is not possible. (Lashley, 1950, pp. 477–8).

The series of experiments to which Lashley referred had been conducted on adult mammals, especially on rats and monkeys, and the techniques involved either purely behavioral observations or behavioral observations made before and after the destruction of parts of the brain (Lashley, 1950, p. 455). This neurosurgical technique has an invaluable part to play in analyzing neural function, but as the sole method of analysis the technique is necessarily a limited one. By

This chapter is a substantially modified version of a chapter originally entitled "Cerebral function and behaviour investigated though a study of filial imprinting" that appeared in *The Development and Integration of Behaviour. Essays in Honour of Robert Hinde* Edited by Patrick Bateson (Cambridge University Press 1991). Reprinted with the permission of Cambridge University Press.

the 1950s, however, many new methods for studying the nervous system were becoming available. In addition, behavioral scientists were drawing attention to a variety of forms of learning, including habituation, imprinting, and vocal learning in songbirds (see Thorpe, 1950), which had been relatively neglected during the time of, and in the years that immediately followed, the powerful behavioral analysis of conditioned reflexes by Pavlov and Konorski (see Konorski, 1950). The three relatively neglected forms of learning to which Thorpe drew attention, in the same volume as that in which Lashley's review had appeared, were to be the subjects of intensive study, at the neural level, in the following decades.

The analysis of birdsong was pursued through a beautiful series of experiments by Nottebohm and by Konishi and their collaborators (see Konishi, 1985; Nottebohm et al., 1991). My own experimental work on the neuronal mechanisms of habituation was carried out in the 1960s (see Horn, 1970, 1971). At that time several laboratories were analyzing this form of learning, and at the end of the decade the evidence suggested that: (a) the habituation of at least some behavioral responses could be accounted for in terms of a progressive reduction of impulse discharges in the neural circuit mediating the response; (b) this depression was brought about by activity in the circuit, and in this sense was "self-generated"; (c) the depression was a consequence of a reduction in the release of neurotransmitter at certain synapses in the circuit; (d) the change in transmitter release was probably brought about through a change in the movement of calcium ions at the depressed synapses; (e) dishabituation could be brought about by changing the membrane potential of the depressed presynaptic terminals; and (f) many of the more subtle aspects of behavioral habituation could be accounted for by relatively simple arrangements of neural circuits possessing synapses with the above properties (see various contributions in Horn and Hinde, 1970). In the years that followed many of these hypotheses and experimental observations were confirmed, and the analysis of habituation was extended further, especially to the cellular level (for review see Castelucci et al., 1978; Carew, 1989).

Work described below on the analysis of imprinting was to start at the behavioral level and work "downward" toward the neural level. But some surprises were to come and the direction of analysis was to be a two-way affair. I have attempted to give a flavor of this interaction in what follows.

From Behavior to Brain

Soon after hatching, young domestic chicks (*Gallus gallus domesticus*) follow their mothers. This following response is not only elicited by the natural mother: a chick will approach a wide range of visually conspicuous objects, especially if they are moving. After a period of exposure to such an object the chick develops a social attachment to it. When this "training" or "imprinting" object is near, the chick emits contentment calls, and approaches it; if the object is moving away, the chick follows it. In addition, instead of approaching other conspicuous objects as it would have done in the naive state, the chick now avoids them (see Spalding, 1873). As a result, when given a choice between a novel and a familiar object the chick approaches the familiar one. In this sense the chick recognizes the object it had seen previously; so we may infer that the chick learned the characteristics of the object during the period of exposure. The learning process is known as filial imprinting (Lorenz, 1935, 1937; Hinde, 1955; Bateson, 1966; Sluckin, 1972; Bolhuis, 1991).

Because filial imprinting is usually measured by a locomotor approach response, this form of learning has been studied most extensively in precocial species – those whose young show well-coordinated locomotor activity within a few hours of birth or hatching. However, there is no *requirement* that the underlying learning process must be tied to a locomotor response. Klopfer and Hailman (1964), for example, exposed domestic Vantress-Cross chicks to models of life-sized mallard duck decoys. Those chicks that did not follow the decoy during training, but sat watching it, showed the same subsequent preference as the initial "followers," although not as strongly (see also Baer and Gray, 1960).

Imprinting is a particularly attractive form of learning for analysing mechanisms at the neural level. One important attraction is that some of the consequences of exposing a chick to a training object are often dramatic and may easily be measured: a chick may run the equivalent of 1 kilometer in an hour in attempting to reach the training object (Horn et al., 1973a). An additional attraction is that, by incubating eggs in darkness and by maintaining the chicks in darkness until they see the training object, a few hours after hatching, the experimenter may be confident that no other information derived from visual experience has been stored in the brain; and the chances of successfully detecting neural changes which are associated with the first visual experience are accordingly increased.

In the studies of imprinting described below, chicks were trained by exposing them to a visually conspicuous object. Most experiments employed the following procedures (see McCabe et al., 1982). After hatching, chicks were reared in individual compartments in a dark incubator until they were between 15 and 30 hours old. The chicks were then placed individually in running wheels (figure 21.1d), the centre of which stands some 50 cm from an imprinting stimulus (see figure 21.1). The chicks were exposed to the stimulus for between 1 and 4 hours, depending on the experiment, and the number of revolutions made by the wheel as the chick attempted to approach the training object was recorded ("approach activity"). A chick's preference was subsequently determined by exposing the chick to the familiar object and to a novel object in succession. A measure of preference is given by the relative strength of the chick's approach to these objects.

If the storage process underlying imprinting involves changes in the connections between neurones then changes in protein and RNA metabolism may be expected to occur in those brain regions in which storage takes place. To examine this possibility one group of chicks was exposed to a conspicuous object, one group was exposed to diffuse light from an overhead lamp and one group was maintained in darkness. Training was found to be associated with an increase in the incorporation of radioactive lysine into protein and of radioactive uracil into RNA in the dorsal part (forebrain roof) of the cerebral hemispheres (Bateson et al., 1972). Although these results were clear-cut their interpretation is not since there are many ways in which the trained chicks differed from their controls and the biochemical changes may have been related to some or all of these differences. A number of control procedures was therefore devised to determine whether the

biochemical changes were specifically related to the learning process, or whether
they reflected some side-effects of training. The evidence provided by these
procedures suggested that the biochemical changes were closely related to the
learning process because: (a) when visual input was restricted to one cerebral
hemisphere by dividing the supra-optic commissure and occluding one eye with

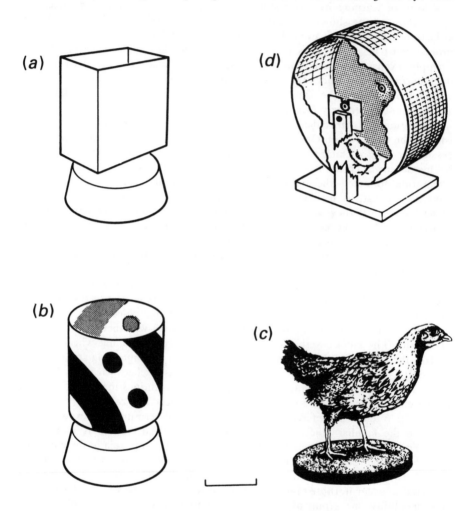

Figure 21.1 Training procedures and some training objects. In many of the experiments
described in this chapter chicks were placed individually in a running wheel (d) facing
the training object which was placed some 50 cm away (a). For the purposes of illustration
one of the opaque sides of the running wheel is shown partly removed. The chick ran on
the wire mesh. The training object illustrated in (a) is a box which, when activated, rotated
about the base and was illuminated from within. The two larger surfaces were often colored
red, the narrower sides being black. The cylinder in object (b) was also illuminated from
within and rotated about the base. (c) is the stuffed skin of a jungle fowl. Scale bar· 10 cm.

a black patch, incorporation was higher in the forebrain roof of the "trained" hemisphere than the "untrained" hemisphere (Horn et al., 1973b); (b) the magnitude of incorporation was positively correlated with a measure of how much the chicks had learned, but was not correlated with a variety of other measures of the chicks' performance (Bateson et al., 1975); and (c) the increase associated with training is not a result of some short-lasting effect of sensory stimulation (Bateson et al., 1973).

Since the biochemical changes were closely tied to the learning process of imprinting it was necessary, for a more detailed analysis of these changes, to enquire whether they were localized to restricted regions within the forebrain roof. Using an autoradiographic technique (Horn and McCabe, 1978), an increased incorporation of radioactive uracil into RNA was found in the intermediate and medial part of the hyperstriatum ventrale (Horn et al., 1979), a region referred to as IMHV (see figure 21.2). Subsequently, the same region, and an adjacent part of the medial hyperstriatum ventrale, have been reported by other research groups to be involved in visual (Kohsaka et al., 1979) and auditory imprinting (Maier and Scheich, 1983), as well as in passive avoidance learning (Rose and Csillag, 1985; Davies et al., 1988).

If IMHV plays a crucial role in the storage of information, then destruction of the region should prevent the acquisition of a preference through imprinting, and impair the retention of an acquired preference. Both of these predictions were confirmed in a number of lesion studies which involved the bilateral destruction of IMHV (McCabe et al., 1981, 1982; Takamatsu and Tsukada, 1985). Similar lesions to other brain regions – a visual projection area known as the Wulst, and the lateral cerebral area – had no such effects (Johnson and Horn, 1987; McCabe et al., 1982; Takamatsu and Tsukada, 1985).

The poor performance of the IMHV-lesioned chicks in the preference test could be accounted for if, for example, some sensory or motor functions were impaired by the lesion, or if the chicks lacked the motivation to approach the

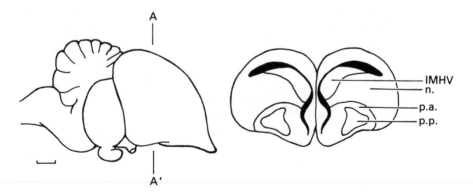

Figure 21.2 Outline drawing of the chick brain. The vertical lines AA' above and below the drawing of the lateral aspect (left diagram) indicate the plane of the coronal section outline (right diagram) of the brain. Abbreviations: IMHV, the intermediate and medial part of the hyperstriatum ventrale; n., neostriatum; p.a., paleostriatum augmentatum; p.p., paleostriatum primativum. Scale bar: 2 mm.

training object. However, the fact that chicks with these lesions peck at objects as accurately as sham-operated controls and that lesioned and control chicks, allowed to move about freely, could not be distinguished from each other even by experienced observers (McCabe et al., 1981, 1982) implies that there were no gross motor or motivational deficits in the lesioned birds. This implication is supported by the finding that these birds are successfully able to perform certain other learning tasks (see below). It is also worth emphasizing that the biochemical studies, which first implicated IMHV in imprinting, were correlative and did not involve any intervention that might impair the chicks' behavior; the lesion studies served to test predictions based on the correlative studies, and the predictions were met. When all the experimental results are taken together, the most likely explanation of the behavior of the IMHV-lesioned chicks is that they are unable to recognize the training object.

Many theories of the neural basis of memory suppose that a particular experience or event leads to the formation or strengthening of pathways in the brain (James, 1890) through changes in the size or number of synaptic junctions (Tanzi, 1893; Cajal, 1911; Hebb, 1949). Such changes occur widely in the central and peripheral nervous systems during normal growth and development, and frequently occur after injury. Thus the occurrence of these changes is not by itself evidence that they play a role in memory. To be confident that a neural change plays such a role, it is necessary to demonstrate that the change is exclusive to learning and occurs in a brain region in which information is known to be stored (see Horn et al., 1973a). The evidence presented above suggests that IMHV is such a region. A series of experiments was therefore conducted to enquire whether imprinting leads to changes in the structure of synapses in the left and right IMHV (Bradley et al., 1979, 1981; Horn et al., 1985).

In the first experiments two groups of chicks were used. Both groups were dark-reared until they were approximately 21 hours old. One group was then exposed to an artificial imprinting stimulus for 20 minutes (undertrained), the other group exposed to the stimulus for 140 minutes (overtrained). After training, the right and left IMHV regions were removed and studied using the electron microscope. Quantitative sampling techniques were used to measure various aspects of synapse morphology, including the number of synapses per unit volume of brain tissue, and the mean size of axonal terminal swellings, the synaptic boutons. At chemical synapses, in which transmission is mediated by a neurotransmitter, pre- and postsynaptic elements are separated by a narrow cleft. At vertebrate synapses part of the postsynaptic membrane is thickened and is known as the postsynaptic density (PSD); the mean lengths of the PSD in right and left IMHV respectively were determined. Overtrained chicks differed from the undertrained chicks in only one measure of synapse structure: the mean length of the PSD was increased. This change occurred only in left IMHV synapses (figure 21.3). Synapses on dendrites occur in two forms, axodendritic and axospinous. Axodendritic synapses are found on the shafts of dendrites; axospinous synapses are found on small, balloon-shaped structures, the dendritic spines. The data shown in figure 21.3 are based on measurements from the two types of synapses without distinction. The study of Bradley et al. (1981) was subsequently extended by increasing the number of chicks and adding a group of dark-reared chicks (Horn et al., 1985). With this larger sample enough data were

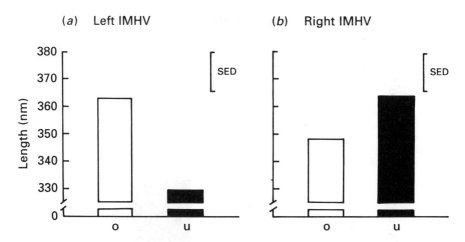

Figure 21.3 Effects of training on the length of the postsynaptic densities of synapses in IMHV. Mean values are shown according to hemisphere and treatment. Data for axospinous and axodendritic synapses are combined. Chicks were either exposed to the imprinting stimulus for 20 minutes (u, undertrained chicks, black bars) or for 140 minutes (o, overtrained chicks, open bars). Data for the left IMHV are shown in (a) and for the right IMHV in (b). For each side the standard error of the difference (SED) between mean values from undertrained and overtrained chicks is shown. Further training led to a significant increase in the lengths of the postsynaptic densities in the left IMHV only. (After Bradley et al., 1981.)

available to analyze separately the measurements from each type of synapse. When this was done the effects of training were found to be restricted to axospinous synapses: the mean length of the PSDs in the left IMHV of overtrained chicks was approximately 17 percent greater than the corresponding mean values for the two other groups of birds.

When neurotransmitter molecules are liberated from the presynaptic bouton they diffuse into the synaptic cleft and bind to receptors that are present in the postsynaptic density (Fagg and Matus, 1984). A consequence of this interaction between neurotransmitter and receptor protein is that ion channels may open. If the synapse is excitatory, the net ion flux will depolarize the postsynaptic cell membrane and may lead to the discharge of an impulse along the axon. At least some axospinous synapses in the mammalian central nervous system are excitatory and possess receptors for the excitatory amino acid L-glutamate (Errington et al., 1987; Nadler et al., 1978; Nafstad, 1967; Storm-Mathisen, 1977). Membranes with these receptors bind the radioactive isotope L-[³H]glutamate. If imprinting leads to an increased number of receptors for this amino acid, then membranes prepared from the left IMHV of trained chicks should bind more L-[³H]glutamate than corresponding membranes from dark-reared chicks. McCabe and Horn (1988) found that this was indeed the case. However, there are several subtypes of receptor for L-glutamate. One of these subtypes is defined by the action of the selective agonist N-methyl-D-aspartate (NMDA). McCabe and Horn (1988) found a significant increase in NMDA-sensitive binding in the left IMHV of

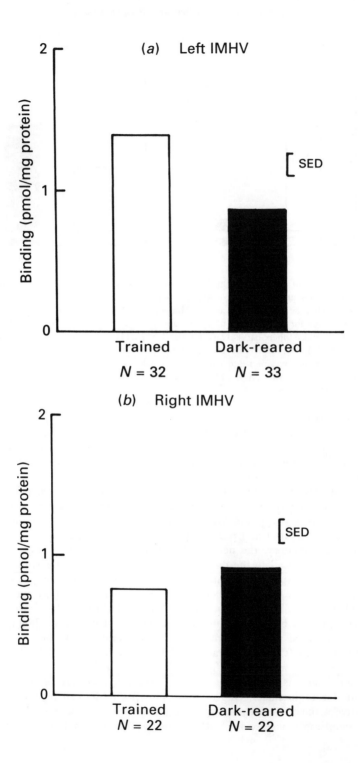

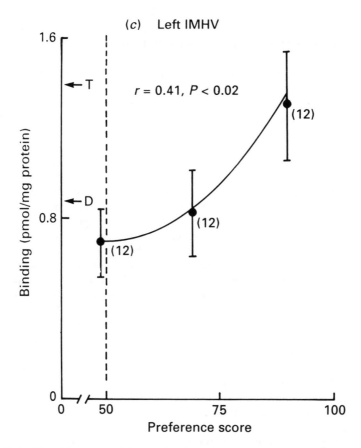

(c)   Left IMHV

$r = 0.41, P < 0.02$

Figure 21.4 The effects of training on NMDA-sensitive binding of L-[^{3}H]glutamate to membranes from the IMHV. Data for the left and right IMHV are shown in (a) and (b) respectively. In these figures mean values are shown together with the standard error of the differences (SED) between the means from trained and dark-reared chicks. N = number of samples, each sample comprising material from three chicks. (a) Left IMHV. Binding in the trained group was significantly higher than in the dark-reared group (matched-pairs $t = 3.46$; df = 30; $P < 0.005$). (b) Right IMHV. These samples were taken from the chicks which also contributed to the samples summarized in (a). There were no significant effects of training on binding in the right IMHV samples ($t = 0.91$). (c) Relationship between NMDA-sensitive binding in the left IMHV and preference score, both corrected by linear regression to constant approach during training as a result of a partial correlation analysis. The higher the preference score, the greater the chick's preference for the training stimulus and the greater the strength of imprinting. Preference scores of 100 and 0 indicate that in the preference test all activity was directed to the imprinting and novel objects respectively. The "no preference" score of 50 is indicated by the vertical broken line. Arrow D indicates the mean binding in the left IMHV of dark-reared chicks and arrow T the mean binding in trained chicks in the experiments on which (a) is based. Each point represents a mean of 12 values. The standard error bars for binding (vertical) and for preference score (horizontal) are given. The curve is a polynomial fitted to all 36 points by least-squares regression. Note that T is close to the mean of the group with the highest mean preference score. (After McCabe and Horn, 1988.)

trained chicks compared with that in dark-reared controls; there were no such differences in right IMHV binding (figure 21.4a,b).

While these results were consistent with the results of the electron microscope studies of IMHV described above (compare the pattern of mean values in figures 21.3a, b and 21.4a, b), many ambiguities remained in the interpretation of the data. The trained birds were visually experienced, the dark-reared birds were not, so that the differences in NMDA-sensitive binding could be a result of these and other, consequential differences. To clarify these ambiguities, a group of chicks was exposed to the training stimulus and given a preference test immediately before being killed. The strength of the chick's preference for the familiar object relative to a novel object was measured and expressed as a preference score (McCabe et al., 1982). The preference score was positively correlated with NMDA-sensitive binding in the left IMHV. The corresponding correlation coefficient for sensitive binding in the right IMHV was not significant. Bateson and Jaeckel (1976) found that approach activity during training is correlated with preference score. It is therefore possible that the observed correlation between NMDA-sensitive binding and preference score reflects a relation between binding and locomotor activity during training. Binding and preference scores were therefore corrected for training approach activity, using the method of partial correlation. There was a significant positive partial correlation between NMDA-sensitive binding in the left IMHV and preference score (see figure 21.4c). The chicks with the lowest mean corrected preference score performed at chance; the corresponding mean binding for this group is not significantly different from that in the left IMHV of the dark-reared chicks of the previous experiments (see figure 21.4a). The partial correlation between NMDA-sensitive binding in the right IMHV and preference score was not significant.

The increase in binding in the left IMHV is very likely due to an increase in the number of receptors (McCabe and Horn, 1988). This increase cannot simply be attributed to side-effects of the training procedure for several reasons. (a) The studies that led to the localization of IMHV and to the demonstration of the crucial role of this region, especially of the left IMHV (Cipolla-Neto et al., 1982), in information storage had controlled for these and other side-effects of training. (b) An effect of arousal would be expected to be expressed in behavior, e.g. the more aroused the chicks, the more vigorously would they be expected to approach the red box during training. However, the partial correlation coefficient between NMDA-sensitive binding and preference score was significant when the effect of approach activity during training was held constant. This latter finding also demonstrates that differences in locomotor activity during training cannot account for the correlation between binding and corrected preference score. (c) Light exposure *per se* does not account for the findings, since the corrected mean left IMHV binding in chicks that had been exposed to the red box for 140 minutes, but had not developed a preference for it, was closely similar to the mean left IMHV binding of dark-reared chicks. These considerations suggest that the change in receptor binding is not a side-effect of training, but that learning leads to an increase in the number of NMDA-type receptors in the left IMHV.

The selective preference of the imprinted chicks for the familiar object is evidence that these chicks recognize this object. It is therefore possible (Horn, 1962) that the increased number of excitatory receptors leads to an increased efficacy of synaptic transmission in the left IMHV and hence forms a basis for this recognition memory (see also McCabe and Horn, 1991). Although the molecular mechanisms which bring about the changes in the postsynaptic density are not known, the consequences of the changes, and of the increased number of NMDA receptors, are likely to be subtle in several ways. (a) The ion channels associated with the NMDA receptors will pass current only under certain conditions: the receptors must be activated by their neurotransmitter and the postsynaptic cell must be excited through ion channels associated with other receptors (Nowak et al., 1984). At the behavioral level, such conditions could have interesting consequences. For example, the presentation of a familiar object may activate the afferent fibres to the synapses which, through training, have an increased number of NMDA receptors. The activated afferent fibres may release L-glutamate, which binds to these receptors. The postsynaptic cell may not respond to the presynaptic signal unless the cell is depolarized by some other input. This input may be generated by, for example, neurons whose activity is controlled by the attentional state of the animal; that is, attentional mechanisms may exercise some control of the flow of signals through the memory systems of the brain (Horn, 1970). Other controlling inputs may be from neural systems underlying affective states of the animal or from neuronal assemblies representing other memories. (b) Calcium ions flow inwards through NMDA-channels (Mac-Dermot et al., 1986). This influx may lead to and maintain changes in the structure of the postsynaptic density and influence its interactions with proteins in the cytoskeleton of the dendritic spine. If this view proves to be correct it may be that prolonged inactivity of a previously modified synapse may lead to a regression of the modification and so to a corresponding loss of the specific memory with which these synapses are involved.

It is clear that many questions remain to be answered in addition to those which are implicit in the considerations outlined in the above paragraph. For example, do the structural changes in axospinous synapses, and the changes in NMDA receptors occur at the same synapses; are all axospinous synapses in the left IMHV affected by training or are the changes restricted to a sub-population of them; and are the changed synapses interconnected as in a Hebbian cell-assembly (Hebb, 1949)? While a change in number of NMDA receptors might, as suggested, increase synaptic efficiency, other possibilities exist and need to be explored. For example, the increase in NMDA receptors may play only a "permissive" role in the cellular mechanisms of memory: the increase might permit a relatively large influx of calcium into the cell to initiate other changes, for example in synapse structure, after which NMDA receptor numbers may return to lower levels.

NMDA receptors have been implicated in the processes that control certain forms of plasticity in the developing nervous system (Cline et al., 1987; Kleinschmidt et al., 1987; Rauschecker and Hahn, 1987). The implied link between developmental and growth processes on the one hand and learning on the other is not wholly unexpected. Changes occur in the morphological and functional properties of neurons during the course of ontogeny. In some systems the direction of these changes is such that neurons largely lose their capacity for plastic change as their synaptic connections become stabilized in the course of development and maturation (Hubel and Wiesel, 1970; Knudsen and Knudsen,

1986; Olson and Freeman, 1980). A similar direction of change may occur, as a result of learning, in neural circuits specialized for storage. Thus Horn et al. (1973a) suggested that neurons within the memory systems of the brain may remain plastic until they become engaged in the storage process associated with a specific learning experience. Thereafter the synaptic connections may become stabilized although, as suggested above, this stabilization may require active maintenance.

That the neural mechanisms underlying memory formation engage growth processes was hinted at by a study of changes in protein synthesis after imprinting (Brown and Horn, 1990). It was found that the more chicks ran toward the imprinting object during training, the higher was the synthesis of one or more proteins with a molecular mass of approximately 80 kDa. This result was found for the left IMHV, but not for two other samples from the left cerebral hemisphere. However, since preference score was not measured in this study it was not possible to say how closely the change in protein synthesis was related to learning. In a further set of experiments a slightly different molecular approach was followed. Protein kinase C is a family of proteins with enzymological properties. When an external signal, mediated by a neurotransmitter (or, more generally, a ligand), impinges on a cell, the ligand binds to certain receptors on the cell surface. Substances may then be produced that act as "second messengers." These transmit the external signal to the interior of the cell and may do so by activating protein kinase C. The properties of protein kinase C strongly suggest that it plays a key role in many aspects of the growth and metabolism of cells (see Nishizuka, 1988). In brain tissue, protein kinase C phosphorylates several substrate proteins. The effects of imprinting on the phosphorylation of these proteins in various parts of the chick brain were studied (McCabe et al., 1991; Sheu et al., 1992). Three protein kinase C substrate proteins were identified. The phosphorylation of one of them in the left IMHV, but not in the right IMHV, was correlated with the strength of imprinting. The protein is known as myristoylated alanine-rich C kinase substrate (MARCKS) (Stumpo et al., 1989). In mammals the protein has a molecular mass of approximately 80 kDa although the molecular mass of chicken MARCKS protein is rather less than this. In the young chick MARCKS protein has two acidic components. Only the phosphorylation of the less acidic component was significantly greater in trained than in dark-reared chicks ($t = 4.0$, 22 d.f., $P < 0.001$); in trained chicks phosphorylation was significantly correlated with preference score ($r = 0.62$, 10 d.f., $P < 0.05$). The partial correlation between preference score and phosphorylation, holding constant the effects of training approach, was also significant ($r = 0.75$, 9 d.f., $P < 0.01$). The phosphorylation of the more acidic component of MARCKS was not significantly affected by training and was not significantly correlated with preference score, even after correcting for the effects of training approach. These results suggest that the learning-related increase in the phosphorylation of the less acidic component of MARCKS protein may be implicated in the mechanism of recognition memory for imprinting. In studies of MARCKS protein in white blood cells (neutrofils) it was found that protein kinase C-dependent phosphorylation displaces the protein from the membrane (Thelen et al., 1991). These workers suggested that there may be a cycle of membrane attachment and detachment of MARCKS, providing a reversible cross-link between the plasma membrane and the cytoskeleton of the cell. Such interactions, if they occur at synapses, may be involved in the changes of synaptic structure that accompany imprinting and which are described above. The phosphorylation of the MARCKS protein may, through an interaction with calmodulin (Graff et al., 1989), also modify synaptic function in ways which are still unknown.

Given the sensitive way in which the molecular and morphological organization of the left IMHV changes with learning, it might be expected that the activity of neurons in this region would also be modified when chicks are exposed to an imprinting object. There is indeed evidence that the spontaneous discharge of neurons in the left IMHV is influenced by training (Payne and Horn, 1984; Davey and Horn, 1991; Bradford and McCabe, 1992). The IMHV region receives connections from several sensory projection areas of the forebrain (Bradley et al., 1985), but in anesthetized chicks the neuronal responses recorded through a microelectrode to such visual imprinting objects as a rotating red box or a rotating blue box are very weak. However, specific effects of imprinting were found when measures of neuronal activity at several recording sites in the left IMHV were combined (McLennan and Horn, 1991, 1992). These learning-specific effects were also regionally specific since they were not found in a visual projection area, the left hyperstriatum accessorium. In these experiments chicks were exposed to, and developed a strong preference for, either a rotating blue box or a rotating red box. After the preference test the chicks were anesthetized and the responses of neurons in the left IMHV to the red or blue box were recorded. The combined neuronal response of the left IMHV to a given stimulus was then calculated. Recordings were also made from the left IMHV of dark-reared anesthetized chicks. In this group of chicks the combined left IMHV response to a rotating red box differed from that to a rotating blue box. After training with the red box the responses to both boxes were similar to the response to the red box in dark-reared birds. After training with the blue box the responses to both boxes were similar to the response to the blue box in dark-reared birds. The two training boxes were virtually identical (see figure 21.1a) apart from differences in color and brightness. Training thus appeared to stabilize the response of the visually naive left IMHV to the training stimulus, but changed its response to the alternative, but similar, stimulus. So one consequence of training is that the two stimuli are placed in the same "category" of neuronal responses. If one of the functions of the left IMHV is to classify together similar stimuli, it became a matter of some importance to know whether there was any evidence that such categorization occurs at the behavioral level. That is, if after training chicks selectively approach the imprinting object, is this selectivity extended to other objects which are similar to the imprinting object?

Whether or not such behavioral generalization occurs, chicks are able to distinguish between the red and blue boxes if they have been trained by exposing them to one or the other. In anesthetized chicks, perhaps because the responses of neurons at specific recording sites are very weak, no specific effects of training on these responses were observed. Brown and Horn (1992) therefore recorded from the left IMHV of unanesthetized chicks. A striking feature of this study was that many neurons responded strongly to visual imprinting stimuli and/or to auditory stimuli. The vigor of these responses suggests that the responsiveness of neurons in the left IMHV is profoundly depressed by anesthesia. The work of Brown and Horn (1992) is still in progress, but it is already clear that in imprinted chicks some neurons in the left IMHV respond preferentially to the imprinting object. Taking these results together with those of McLennan and Horn (1991, 1992) the evidence suggests that, in imprinted chicks, some left IMHV neurones classify together similar objects, and so "generalize" from one object to the other, while other neurons respond in a highly specific way to the training object. The latter property may provide a basis for the specificity of the chick's preferences, while the property of stimulus generalization may also have its counterpart in the chick's behavior (see below). These findings not only allow us to explore the neural basis of recognition in the chick during the course of imprinting, but more generally allow us to study the basis of pattern recognition in a physiological system that learns.

From Brain to Behavior

1 Stimulus Recognition and Stimulus Generalization

In the experiments of McLennan and Horn (1991, 1992) chicks had been exposed to either a rotating red box or a rotating blue box. Those birds which had been trained to the blue box preferred it to the red one; conversely those birds which had been trained to the red box preferred it to the blue box. If the familiar object is regarded as a "mother" surrogate, an object that shares major features with it might be construed as an "aunt" surrogate. Clearly the chicks can distinguish between them after appropriate training. But the results of the neuronal study of the left IMHV raise the question of whether, after training on one box, there is also some generalization to the other. In experiments designed to examine this possibility, Bolhuis and Horn (1992) trained chicks by exposing them to the red box which rotated at 28 r.p.m. The chicks were then given a preference test during which they were exposed to two novel objects. One of these, a blue box, was similar in shape to the imprinting object (see figure 21.1a), while the other was a blue cylinder (see figure 21.1b). Both stimuli rotated at 28 r.p.m. The red-box-trained chicks significantly preferred the blue box to the blue cylinder. As expected, when the chicks were given a choice between the familiar red box and the blue box, they preferred the red box. These findings demonstrate that when chicks are trained by exposing them to an object, they selectively approach that object; they discriminate it from other, novel objects even though the familiar and novel objects may be similar in a number of ways. However, the preference for the familiar object is not absolute: given a choice between an object which is similar to the imprinting object and one which is very different, they prefer the similar one. The similar stimuli may thus be considered to have been placed in the same category (e.g. rotating, illuminated boxes). Thus at the behavioral and the neural levels, recognition involves both specificity and generalization.

2 Predispositions and Preferences

In the study in which autoradiography was used to determine whether or not training led to localized biochemical changes in the forebrain, the training object was an artificial one (Horn et al., 1979). Indeed, artificial visual objects had been used as training stimuli in all our earlier experiments as well. However, in a series of four experiments in which the effects of brain lesions on imprinting were studied, one of the training objects was artificial (figure 21.1a) and the other was the stuffed skin of a jungle fowl (figure 21.1c). Both of these stimuli were illuminated and moved. After a given period of training (see p. 5) the chicks were given a sequential preference test and a preference score was calculated (see legend to figure 21.4). In a preliminary experiment the "attractiveness" of the box and fowl were adjusted by varying the intensity of illumination and the speed of movement, so that for a given period of training, the mean preference score of box-trained chicks did not differ significantly from that of the fowl-trained chicks.

The type of training stimulus (box or fowl) used in the four lesion experiments referred to above did not seem to influence the outcome of the results. Therefore, the preference scores of the box-trained chicks had been combined with those of the fowl-trained chicks in each experiment. However, when the data for all four experiments were analyzed together, a different picture emerged (Horn and McCabe, 1984). IMHV-lesioned chicks which had been trained on the box performed at chance, achieving an overall mean preference score which was not significantly different from 50 percent (figure 21.5a); IMHV-lesioned chicks which had been trained on the fowl had a clear preference for that object (figure 21.5b), a preference which was slightly, though significantly, smaller than that of their sham-operated controls. The mean preference scores of the two sham-operated control groups were not significantly different from each other. In contrast, the mean preference scores of the two lesioned groups differed significantly from each other. Thus lesions to IMHV had a profound effect on the mean preference score of box-trained birds, but only a small effect on the mean preference score of the fowl-trained birds.

Two other procedures also teased apart an effect of the training object. In the first experiment one group of chicks received a drug (DSP4) that reduces the concentration of catecholamines in the brain. Chicks that had received an injection of this drug and had been exposed to a rotating red box performed at chance in the sequential preference test. In contrast, drug-treated chicks that had been exposed to the fowl had a strong preference for the fowl in the test, although the strength of the preference was significantly less than that of the fowl-trained controls which had received an injection of distilled water instead of the drug (Davies et al., 1985). This pattern of results – a strong preference for the training object by the controls, performance at chance by the box-trained experimental birds, and a clear, though slightly impaired, preference for the training object by the fowl-trained experimentals – is very similar to that found in the lesion studies (figure 21.5). The second procedure which provided further evidence of stimulus-dependent effects involved an analysis of plasma testosterone concentrations. The mean preference score of fowl-trained chicks which had received an injection of testosterone was higher than for those chicks which had not received the hormone. Furthermore, there was a significant positive correlation between plasma testosterone concentration and preference score in the fowl-trained birds. This correlation was significant even among fowl-trained birds which had not received testosterone; that is, the correlation between preference score and testosterone concentration held over the physiological range of concentrations of the hormone. In contrast to these findings in fowl-trained birds, exogenous testosterone was without effect on the preference scores of box-trained chicks; nor was there a significant correlation between preference score and plasma testosterone concentration in these birds (Bolhuis et al., 1986).

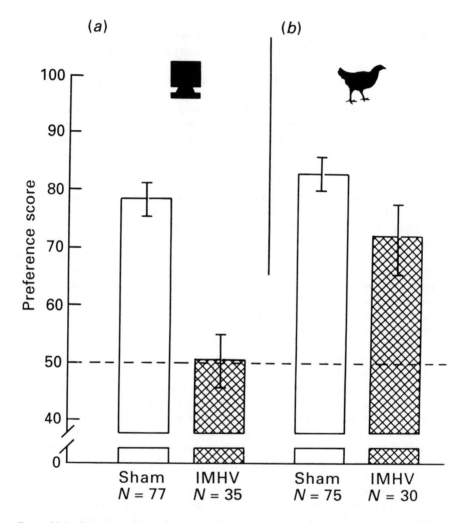

Figure 21.5 Summary of data from experiments in which preference scores were impaired by lesions of IMHV. The scores (see legend to figure 21.4) for chicks with lesions of IMHV and sham-operated controls are set out according to the stimulus to which the chicks were exposed during the training period. Means ± SEM for chicks trained with the box (a) and with the jungle fowl (b). The standard errors may be used to compare the means against the chance, no preference scores of 50. Sham = sham operated control chicks; IMHV refers to chicks with lesions of this brain region. N = number of chicks. (Based on data from Horn and McCabe, 1984.)

Although we had no clear evidence that the behavioral responses elicited by the naturalistic stuffed fowl differed from those elicited by the artificial red box, the results of the neural and endocrine studies compelled us to be alert to the possibility that such differences might exist. We had been forced, so to speak, to move "upwards" from studying brain function to studying behavior.

Evidence for such differences came from a different experimental approach (Bolhuis et al., 1985; Johnson et al., 1985). In these studies chicks were subjected to various procedures and the chicks' preferences for the box and fowl were then tested. These experiments differed from earlier ones in that the chicks had not seen either the box or the stuffed fowl before the test. Furthermore, unlike most of the previous studies in which a chick's preference was measured in a test which involved presenting novel and familiar stimuli separately (the sequential test), in this study the two objects were presented together using the simultaneous choice test of Bateson and Wainwright (1972). Apart from the obvious differences between the two tests, the simultaneous test provides a more sensitive measure of the chick's preference by providing a more sensitive measure of the chick's approach activity (see Horn, 1985, pp. 156–7).

The central finding of the experiments of Bolhuis et al. (1985) and Johnson et al. (1985) can be summarized quite briefly. Chicks were raised in individual compartments of an incubator and when they were approximately 24 hours old were placed in a running wheel for a total of 2 hours. They were then returned to the incubator. The chicks were given a simultaneous choice test either 2 hours (test 1) or 24 hours (test 2) after having been removed from the wheel. *Until the chicks were given the preference test they had been kept in darkness.* At test 1, the chicks performed at chance, expressing no preference. At test 2, the chicks preferred the jungle fowl. Control chicks which had remained in the incubator all the time, until the test, performed at chance in the test.

These experiments suggest that some aspects of the chicks' experiences of the wheel (e.g. handling, opportunity to move about in the wheel) were necessary for the expression of the preference for the fowl. The experiments also suggest that, over the period studied, this preference does not appear simply with the passage of time. Because the preference appeared in the absence of prior visual experience, it was referred to as an emerging predisposition.

The emerging predisposition can be detected in previously trained as well as in visually naive chicks. Thus in the experiments of Johnson et al. (1985) the preferences of young chicks were measured either approximately 2 hours (test 1) or 24 hours (test 2) after exposure to a red box or a stuffed fowl. Preferences were measured using the simultaneous choice test. At test 1 the chicks preferred the object to which they had been exposed previously, whether it had been the stuffed fowl or the red box (figure 21.6a, b). However, at test 2 the pattern of results was different. The mean preference of the fowl-trained chicks in this test was significantly stronger than that of the fowl-trained chicks in test 1; in contrast the mean preference score of the box-trained chicks in test 2 was significantly less than that of the box-trained chicks in test 1 (figure 21.6a, b). In other words it appeared as if the preferences of the fowl-trained chicks had strengthened with the passage of time, whereas those of the box-trained chicks had weakened. Johnson et al. (1985) found that chicks (light-exposed) which had been placed in a running wheel and exposed to diffuse white light, but not to the box or to

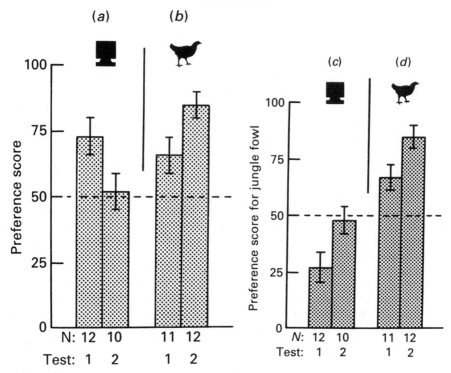

Figure 21.6 Mean preference scores (+ SEM) in test 1 and test 2 for box-exposed (a),
(c) and fowl-exposed (b), (d) chicks. In (a) and (b), preference scores were calculated from
the expression:

$$\frac{100 \times \text{distance traveled by trolley as chick attempted to approach the familiar conspicuous object}}{\text{total distance traveled by the trolley}}$$

Thus the score of 100 indicates that the chicks directed all their approach activity toward
the training object, 0 that all the approach activity was directed toward the novel object;
a score of 50 indicates that activity was directed equally to the two objects. In (c) and
(d) the preference scores in (a) and (b) were expressed as preferences for the stuffed
jungle-fowl (thus 100 signifies that all approach was directed toward the fowl, 0 that
approach was directed towards the box). N = number of chicks in each group. (Results
based on data from Johnson et al., 1985.)

the fowl, showed a similarly increasing preference for the fowl over time when
tested in the same way.

Since the box and fowl were both present in the simultaneous choice test, the
preferences may be expressed in terms of approach to the stuffed fowl irrespective
of a chick's prior experience. The mean preference scores shown in figure 21.6a,
b are used in figure 21.6c, d, but expressed now as mean preferences for the
stuffed fowl. Chicks which had been exposed to the box and which preferred
this object in test 1 necessarily had a low preference for the stuffed fowl. All

chicks tested approximately 24 hours after training (test 2), however, showed a significantly greater preference for the stuffed fowl than those tested at approximately 2 hours (test 1), regardless of the training stimulus. The mean values shown figure 21.6c, d are plotted in figure 21.7. This figure also includes the mean preference scores of the light-exposed chicks referred to above. These scores may be used as a baseline for measuring the effects of training on mean preference scores at the appropriate testing times. The mean preference scores of the light-exposed chicks changed over time. Accordingly the baseline level from which the acquired preferences were measured also changes with time (figure 21.7, ΔY), and so is different at test 2 from that at test 1. The difference between the mean preference score of an experimental group and that of the light-exposed group is k_i. This difference provides a measure of the preferences acquired by the chick for one of the conspicuous objects as a result of being exposed to it during training. In test 1 the mean preference score of the chicks exposed to the box was less than that of the light-exposed controls by 19.2 percent (figure 21.7, k_1). The corresponding difference for the chicks exposed to the fowl is almost identical at 20.7 percent (figure 21.7, k_2), but in the opposite direction of the scale used in this figure. The preferences of all three groups of chicks shift towards the jungle fowl from test 1 to test 2. Is this shift associated with the loss of the preference acquired through training? If the acquired preference is lost we should expect k_3 to be less than k_1 and k_4 to be less than k_2. In order to test this hypothesis the mean preference score of the light-exposed birds in each test was subtracted from the preference score of each trained bird at the same test. The resulting adjusted scores were subjected to an analysis of variance. The adjusted scores of the experimental birds were not significantly affected by the time of testing (test 1 or test 2), implying that the acquired preferences are not lost; they are stable over the period studied notwithstanding the emergence of the predisposition for the fowl.

This result, together with the finding that the relative preference for the jungle fowl increases from test 1 to test 2 suggest that the preferences of the experimental chicks are affected by two underlying processes: (a) a developing predisposition which becomes apparent as an increase in preference for the jungle fowl by the light-exposed chicks; and (b) a learning process through which chicks come to recognize particular objects to which they have been exposed. Whether or not these two processes may be related in some way to the activity of the different neural systems revealed by the physiological studies (pp. 499–500) is an issue which is taken up below (pp. 505–6).

In all the experiments in which the emerging preference haa been studied, the chicks were placed in the running wheels when they were approximately a day old. The results of further experiments suggested that there is a sensitive period for the emergence of the preference: if chicks are placed in the wheel before or after this period the preference for the fowl is not present in the 24 hour test (Johnson et al., 1989).

Once developed, the predisposition might serve as a filter for incoming signals, allowing only information about stimuli that resemble conspecifics to be processed for learning. If this were so, not only might the bird preferentially approach such stimuli, but it might be unable to learn about other objects through being exposed to them. However, Bolhuis et al. (1989a) have shown that chicks

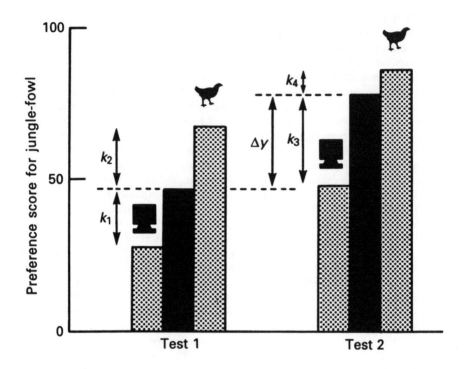

Figure 21.7 A model for the interaction between acquired preferences and a developing predisposition. All mean preference scores are expressed as preferences for the stuffed fowl. Broken lines represent the base lines in test 1 and test 2 set by the respective groups of light-exposed chicks (black bars). ΔY represents the difference in mean preference score between the light-exposed chicks in test 1 and test 2. k_i represents the effects of prior exposure to the red box (k_1 and k_3) or to the jungle fowl (k_2 and k_4). See text for further discussion. (After Johnson et al., 1985.)

are able to learn the characteristics of, and come to prefer, an artificial object even though there is strong presumptive evidence that the chicks' predisposition to approach the fowl has appeared. Nevertheless, if chicks are exposed to an imprinting object during the sensitive period for the predisposition, they form a stronger attachment to an object resembling a conspecific than to an artificial object (Boakes and Panter, 1985; Bolhuis and Trooster, 1988). This effect is not revealed by a preference test (see figure 21.7: $|k_1| = |k_2|$) but has been revealed by experiments designed to change an acquired preference (Bolhuis and Trooster, 1988). These authors showed that it is more difficult to modify the preference of a fowl-trained chick than that of a box-trained chicks. These findings are consistent with the interaction model of preference formation described above (see Horn and McCabe, 1984; Johnson et al., 1985). If exposed to a conspecific at the appropriate time chicks have a predisposition to approach it and so to learn the characteristics of that individual. At the neural level at least two systems are engaged, IMHV in the learning process and the system outside IMHV in the process controlling the predisposition. If an artificial stimulus, such as the box, is first presented the chick learns about it and is subsequently able to recognize it (Bolhuis et al., 1989a). But if given a choice between the box and the fowl, the predisposition and the learning process seem, at both the behavioral and neural levels of analysis, to "pull" in opposite directions. In the case, then, of attachment to the natural mother the interactions between predisposition and learning appear to be synergistic; whereas for the box, an artificial mother surrogate, the interaction does not appear to be synergistic and may even be antagonistic. It should follow from these considerations that when the sensitive period for the predisposition has passed the strength of attachment to the fowl should no longer be greater than to an artificial object. Work by Johnson et al. (1992) suggests that this is indeed the case.

What aspects of the stuffed fowl are critical, and serve as "targets" for the emerging preference? This question was addressed in a series of experiments that involved giving chicks a simultaneous choice test. In this test one object was always the intact stuffed fowl (see figure 21.1), but the second test object was varied (Johnson and Horn, 1988). These experiments suggested that the target of the emerging preference was the head and neck region of the fowl. However, experiments using as test objects a stuffed gadwall duck or a stuffed polecat demonstrated that *the configuration of features essential for the predisposition is neither species-specific nor even class-specific*. It remains unclear whether or not certain features of the region are more important than others. That the eyes may play a role (see for example Coss 1972; Scaife 1976a, b) is consistent with a lack of species specificity in this change of behaviour.

In considering the possible implications of their findings, Horn and McCabe (1984) suggested *inter alia* that two neural systems may be involved in controlling the response of a chick to the fowl. One of these systems, they suggested, is within IMHV and the other outside this brain region. The two systems were considered to play different roles in the recognition of conspecifics: the system outside IMHV is concerned with the recognition of the general features of conspecifics whereas IMHV is involved in recognizing the features of particular individuals. These features must be learned; and IMHV, it was proposed, is involved in the learning process whether the chick learns the markings of its own mother or the characteristics of an artificial object, such as the red box.

Three predictions arise from these proposals concerning conspecifics. First, intact young chicks are capable of learning the characteristics of individual adult fowl; second, ablation of IMHV precludes such learning. These two predictions have been confirmed (Johnson and Horn, 1987). Moreover, the impaired ability of IMHV-lesioned birds to recognize individual conspecifics extends into adult life (Bolhuis et al., 1989b). A third prediction is that ablation of IMHV will not impair the emerging predisposition. This prediction has also been confirmed (Johnson and Horn, 1986).

The evidence that the emerging predisposition is to the face and neck region, or to features contained within it, raises the possibility that the putative recognition system involved, lying outside IMHV, is responsive to the features of the face and neck, and may have some of the properties of "face neurones" which have been described in the temporal cortex of monkeys (Bruce et al., 1981; Perret et al., 1982) and sheep (Kendrick and Baldwin, 1987). Whether or not this is so will only be known if it proves possible to localize a region of the brain which is crucially involved in the predisposition.

We do not yet know what it is about the period in the running wheel that gives rise to the emergence of the predisposition. Handling the chick is an obvious possibility, but other nonspecific experiences have not been excluded. The finding of an emerging predisposition for some features possessed by conspecifics is reminiscent of the findings of Klopfer (1967) in his studies of the preferences of young Peking ducklings. From these studies he concluded: "It looked as if some kind of innate preference existed that had to be activated by the experience of following". Whether movement was the important factor in Klopfer's studies, or some other nonspecific factor associated with following, is not known. One way of thinking about the action of nonspecific factors, such as arousal (see Davey and Horn, 1991), is to suppose that they have physiological consequences which lead to a modification of chicks' preferences. What these physiological consequences may be is not known, although the possibility that they involve hormones may be worth exploring. Thus arousal, and even minor degrees of stress, may lead to a change in the hormonal state of an animal (see Kruhlich et al., 1974). Furthermore, Bolhuis et al. (1986) have shown that the strength of preference of fowl-trained chicks for the fowl is correlated with the concentration of testosterone in the plasma. In addition, the relatively long time taken by some hormones to exert certain of their effects is consistent with the relatively long time taken for the predisposition to be expressed. While these views are speculative they at least have the merit of being testable experimentally. Testable speculation may be pushed still further by supposing (see above) that neurons in the putative system outside IMHV, which support the emerging preference for the jungle-fowl, have properties similar to face-detecting neurones. In the chick such a system would not be expected to be functional prior to the emergence of the predisposition, perhaps because transmission between neurones in the system is ineffective. Transmission across these synapses may become effective, and the system "functionally validated," soon after the chick has been in the running wheel – or, in more natural circumstances, soon after it begins to move about. Such functional validation could be achieved through hormonal action, the hormone initiating intraneuronal events that lead to efficient synaptic transmission. Once operational, neurones in the face-detecting system may be excited by impulses evoked by the sight of the natural mother, who may possess a combination of features which optimally trigger these neurones. If such neurones control orientation and approach behavior, the chick is likely to direct its activity selectively to the parent and, as suggested above, gradually learn its characteristics in a process which engages neurones in IMHV.

The term "imprinting" was originally used by Lorenz (1935, 1937) in the context of the following response of birds. Hence it is easy enough to suppose that the rules governing the following response also apply to the learning process. While there is good evidence of a sensitive period for the following response, as there is for the predisposition, it does not follow that there is a sensitive period for the learning process, or that there is anything "peculiar" about this process (see Lorenz 1935, 1937). Sluckin and Salzen (1961) have emphasized the perceptual side of the learning process, as have Hinde (1962), Bateson (1966, 1971), and Kovach et al. (1966). Sluckin used the term "exposure learning," since it "refers unambiguously to the perceptual registration by the organism of the environment to which it is exposed" (Sluckin, 1972, p. 109; see also Thorpe, 1944). Such learning is not restricted to birds, but occurs widely even among mammals (see, for example, Hinde, 1962; Sluckin, 1972).

The general situation or context in which learning takes place influences the outcome of a training procedure (see Mackintosh, 1983). So also, of course, does the motivational state, previous experience and age of the animal. Furthermore, it has become apparent that animals have predispositions to learn some things and not others even though the tasks seem of similar difficulty. In other words, learning is constrained and predisposed in many ways (see, for example, Hinde and Stevenson-Hinde, 1973). The influence of such predispositions is, perhaps, nowhere more powerful than in very young animals. The central nervous system of the newborn or newly hatched animal cannot be thought of as a *tabula rasa* on which are inscribed the characteristics of viewed objects. Thus Goren et al. (1975) found that human newborns, whose median age was 9 minutes post-partum, turned their eyes and heads further to follow a schematic face than to follow a variety of "scrambled" faces. Goren et al. wrote that all the persons with whom the infant could have had visual contact were capped, gowned and masked so that the infant had not been exposed to a face before testing. Nevertheless, the infants may have "seen" their attendants' eyes, become familiar with them and later followed the eye stimuli of the schematic face. This is not a plausible explanation of the infants' responses since two of the scrambled faces also contained eye stimuli, but were not followed as far as the schematic face. In the light of their findings Goren et al. considered that an infant "enters the world predisposed to respond to any face" (see also Johnson and Morton, 1991). Chicks also have predispositions, responding differently to objects of certain colours, size and contrast (see Schaefer and Hess, 1959; Kovach, 1971; Fabricius and Boyd, 1953). Hinde (1961) suggested that for some species objects resembling the natural mother may be optimal for eliciting following behavior, a prescient suggestion given the evidence set out above concerning the emerging predisposition. This predisposition interacts with information acquired through learning. In the natural situation, where the chick is exposed to patterned light and is able to move around freely, the predisposition may emerge very rapidly (Bolhuis et al., 1985). The young chick may then attend to the face and neck of its own mother, rather than to inanimate objects, learn specifically about the features of this region and so come to recognize her on the basis of these features.

Conclusions

The experiments on imprinting which have been described in this chapter were initiated because of an interest in the neural mechanisms of learning and memory. The studies have thrown some light on these mechanisms, but the analysis has not been one-way. Some questions posed at the behavioral level were answered at the neural level; in turn these answers generated further questions, the answers to which were to be found at the behavioral level. Only some of this two-way "traffic" has been discussed – no reference has been made, for example, to the neural and behavioral significance of the asymmetry of cerebral function (see Horn, 1981, 1985). But perhaps sufficient has been said to illustrate the need for a dynamic intercourse between levels of analysis as we seek to understand brain mechanisms of behavior.

REFERENCES

Baer, D. M. and Gray, P. H. (1960) Imprinting to different species without overt following. *Perceptual Motor Skills*, 10, 171–4.

Bateson, P. P. G. (1966) The characteristics and context of imprinting. *Biological Reviews*, 41, 177–220.

Bateson, P. P. G. (1971) Imprinting. In H. Moltz (ed.), *Ontogeny of Vertebrate Behavior*. New York: Academic Press, pp. 369–87.

Bateson, P. P. G., Horn, G. and Rose, S. P. R. (1972) Effects of early experience on regional incorporation of precursors into RNA and protein in the chick brain. *Brain Research*, 39, 449–65.

Bateson, P. P. G., Horn, G. and Rose, S. P. R. (1975) Imprinting: Correlations between behaviour and incorporation of (14C) Uracil into chick brain. *Brain Research*, 84, 207–20.

Bateson, P. P. G. and Jaeckel, J. B. (1976) Chick's preferences for familiar and novel conspicuous objects after different periods of exposure. *Animal Behaviour*, 24, 386–90.

Bateson, P. P. G., Rose, S. P. R. and Horn, G. (1973) Imprinting: lasting effects on uracil incorporation into chick brain. *Science*, 181, 576–8.

Bateson, P. P. G. and Wainwright, A. A. P. (1972) The effects of prior exposure to light on the imprinting process in domestic chicks. *Behaviour*, 42, 279–90.

Boakes, R. and Panter, D. (1985) Secondary imprinting in the domestic chick blocked by previous exposure to a live hen. *Animal Behaviour*, 33, 353–65.

Bolhuis, J. J. (1991) Mechanisms of avian imprinting: a review. *Biological Reviews*, 66, 303–45.

Bolhuis, J. J. and Horn, G. (1992) Generalization of learned preferences in filial imprinting. *Animal Behaviour*, 44, 185–7.

Bolhuis, J. J., Johnson, M. H. and Horn, G. (1985) Effects of early experience on the development of filial preferences in the domestic chick. *Developmental Psychobiology*, 18, 299–308.

Bolhuis, J. J., McCabe, B. J. and Horn, G. (1986) Androgens and imprinting. Differential effects of testosterone on filial preferences in the domestic chick. *Behavioral Neuroscience*, 100, 51–6.

Bolhuis, J. J., Johnson, M. H. and Horn, G. (1989a). Interacting mechanisms during the formation of filial preferences: the development of a predisposition does not prevent learning. *Journal of Experimental Psychology: Animal Behavior Processes*, 15, 376–82.

Bolhuis, J. J., Johnson, M., Horn, G. and Bateson, P. (1989b). Long-lasting effects of IMHV lesions on social preferences in domestic fowl. *Behavioral Neuroscience*, 103, 438–41.

Bolhuis, J. J. and Trooster, W. J. (1988) Reversibility revisited: stimulus-dependent stability of filial preference in the chick. *Animal Behaviour*, 36, 668–74.

Bradford, C. M. and McCabe, B. J. (1992) An association between imprinting and spontaneous neuronal activity in the hyperstriatum ventrale of the domestic chick. *Journal of Physiology*, 452, 238 p.

Bradley, P., Davies, D. C. and Horn, G. (1985) Connections of hyperstriatum ventrale in the domestic chick (*Gallus domesticus*). *Journal of Anatomy*, 140, 577–89.

Bradley, P., Horn, G. and Bateson, P. P. G. (1979) Morphological correlates of imprinting in the chick brain. *Neurosciences Letters Supplement*, 3, S84.

Bradley, P., Horn, G. and Bateson, P. (1981) Imprinting: an electron microscopic study of chick hyperstriatum· ventrale. *Experimental Brain Research*, 41, 115–20.

Brown, M. W. and Horn, G. (1990) Are specific proteins implicated in the learning process of imprinting? *Developmental Brain Research*, 52, 294–7.

Brown, M. W. and Horn, G. (1992): The influence of learning (imprinting) on the visual responsiveness of neurones of the intermediate and medial part of the hyperstriatum ventrale (IMHV) of freely moving chicks respond to visual and/or auditory stimuli. *Journal of Physiology* (in the press).

Bruce, C., Desimone, R. and Gross, C. G. (1981) Visual properties of neurons in a polysensory area in superior temporal sulcus of the macaque. *Journal of Neurophysiology*, 46, 369–84.

Cajal, S. R. (1911) *Histologiè du Système Nerveux de l'Homme et des Vertébrés*, Vol. 2. Paris: Maloine.

Carew, T. J. (1989) Developmental assembly of learning in *Aplysia*. *Trends in Neuroscience*, 12, 389–94.

Castelluci, V. F., Carew, T. J. and Kandel, E. R. (1978) Cellular analysis of long-term habitation of the gill-withdrawal reflex of Aplysia californica. *Science*, 202, 1306–8.

Cipolla-Neto, J., Horn, G. and McCabe, B. J. (1982) Hemispheric asymmetry and imprinting: the effect of sequential lesions to the hyperstriatum ventrale. *Experimental Brain Research*, 48, 22–7.

Cline, H. T., Debski, E. A. and Constantine-Paton, M. (1987) N-methyl-D-aspartate receptor antagonist desegregates eye-specific stripes. *Proceedings of the National Academy of Sciences, USA*, 84, 4342–5.

Coss, R. G. (1972) Eye-like schemata: their effect on behaviour. PhD dissertation, University of Reading.

Davey, J. E. and Horn, G. (1991) The development of hemispheric asymmetries in neuronal activity in the domestic chick after visual experience. *Behavioural Brain Research*, 45, 81–6.

Davies, D. C., Horn, G. and McCabe, B. J. (1985) Noradrenaline and learning: the effects of the noradrenergic neurotoxin DSP4 on imprinting in the domestic chick. *Behavioral Neuroscience*, 100, 51–6.

Davies, D. C., Taylor, D. A. and Johnson, M. H. (1988) The effects of hyperstriatal lesions on one-trial passive-avoidance learning in the chick. *Journal of Neuroscience*, 8, 4662–6.

Errington, M. L., Lynch, M. A. and Bliss, T. V. P. (1987) Long-term potentiation in the dentate gyrus: induction and increased glutamate release are blocked by D(−) aminophonovalerate. *Neuroscience*, 20, 279–94.

Fabricius, E. and Boyd, H. (1952/53) Experiments on the following reactions of ducklings. *Wildfowl Trust Annual Report*, 6, 84–9.

Fagg, G. E. and Matus, A. (1984) Selective association of N-methyl aspartate and quisqualate types of L-glutamate receptor with postsynaptic densities. *Proceedings of the National Academy of Sciences, USA*, 81, 6876–80.

Goren, C. C., Sarty, M. and Wu., P. Y. K. (1975) Visual following and pattern discrimination of face-like stimuli by newborn infants. *Pediatrics*, 56, 544–9.

Graff, J. M., Young, T. N., Johnson, J. D. and Blackshear, P. J. (1989) Phosphorylation-regulated calmodulin binding to a prominent cellular substrate for protein kinase C. *Journal of Biological Chemistry*, 264, 21818–23.

Hebb, D. O. (1949) *The Organization of Behavior*. New York: Wiley.

Hinde, R. A. (1955) The modifiability of instinctive behaviour. *Advances in Science*, 12, 19–24.

Hinde, R. A. (1961) The establishment of the parent- offspring relation in birds, with some mammalian analogies. In W. H. Thorpe and O. L. Zangwill (eds) *Current Problems in Animal Behaviour*. Cambridge: Cambridge University Press, pp. 175–93.

Hinde, R. A. (1962) Some aspects of the imprinting problem. In *Evolutionary Aspects of Animal Communications: Imprinting and Early Learning*. Symposium of the Zoological Society of London, vol. 8, pp. 129–38.

Hinde, R. A. and Stevenson-Hinde, J. (eds) (1973) *Constraints on Learning*. London: Academic Press.

Horn, G. (1962) Some neural correlates of perception. In J. D. Carthy and C. L. Duddington (eds), *Viewpoints in Biology*. London, Butterworth, pp. 242–85.

Horn, G. (1970) Changes in neuronal activity and their relationship to behaviour. In G. Horn and R. A. Hinde (eds), *Short-term Changes in Neural Activity and Behaviour*. Cambridge: Cambridge University Press, pp. 567–606.

Horn, G. (1971) Habituation and memory. In B. Adam (ed.), *Biology of Memory*. Budapest: Hungarian Academy of Sciences, pp. 267–84.

Horn, G. (1981) Neural mechanisms of learning: an analysis of imprinting in the domestic chick. *Proceedings of the Royal Society of London, Series B*, 213, 101–37.

Horn, G. (1985) *Memory, Imprinting, and the Brain*. Oxford: Clarendon Press.

Horn, G., Bradley, P. and McCabe, B. J. (1985) Changes in the structure of synapses associated with learning. *Journal of Neuroscience*, 5, 3161–8.

Horn, G. and Hinde, R. A. (eds) (1970) *Short-term Changes in Neural Activity and Behaviour*. Cambridge: Cambridge University Press.

Horn, G. and McCabe, B. J. (1978) An autoradiographic method for studying the incorporation of uracil into acid-insoluble compounds in the brain. *Journal of Physiology*, 275, 2–3P.

Horn, G. and McCabe, B. J. (1984) Predispositions and preferences. Effects on imprinting of lesions to the chick brain. *Animal Behaviour*, 32, 288–92.

Horn, G., McCabe, B. J. and Bateson, P. P. G. (1979) An autoradiographic study of the chick brain after imprinting. *Brain Research*, 168, 361–73.

Horn, G., Rose, S. P. R. and Bateson, P. P. G. (1973a) Experience and plasticity in the central nervous system. *Science*, 181, 506–14.

Horn, G., Rose, S. P. R. and Bateson, P. P. G. (1973b) Monocular imprinting and regional incorporation of tritiated uracil into the brains of intact and 'split-brain' chicks. *Brain Research*, 56, 227–37.

Hubel, D. H. and Wiesel, T. N. (1970) The period of susceptibility to the physiological effects of unilateral eye closure in kittens. *Journal of Physiology*, 206, 419–36.

James, W. J. (1890) *The Principles of Psychology*. New York: Henry Holt.

Johnson, M. H., Bolhuis, J. J. and Horn, G. (1985) Interaction between acquired preferences and developing predispositions during imprinting. *Animal Behaviour*, 33, 1000–6.

Johnson, M. H., Bolhuis, J. J. and Horn, G. (1992) Predispositions and learning: Behavioural dissociations in the chick. *Animal Behaviour* (in the press).

Johnson, M. H., Davies, D. C. and Horn, G. (1989) A sensitive period for the development of a predisposition in dark-reared chicks. *Animal Behaviour*, 37, 1044–5.

Johnson, M. H. and Horn, G. (1986) Dissociation of recognition memory and associative learning by a restricted lesion of the chick forebrain. *Neuropsychologia*, 24, 329–40.

Johnson, M. H. and Horn, G. (1987) The role of a restricted region of the chick forebrain in the recognition of individual conspecifics. *Behavioral Brain Research*, 23, 269–75.

Johnson, M. H. and Horn, G. (1988) Development of filial preferences in dark-reared chicks. *Animal Behaviour*, 36, 675–83.

Johnson, M. H. and Morton, J. (1991) *Biology and Cognitive Development: the Case of Face Recognition*. Oxford: Blackwell.

Kendrick, K. M. and Baldwin, B. A. (1987) Cells in temporal cortex of conscious sheep can respond preferentially to the sight of faces. *Science*, 236, 448–50.

Kleinschmidt, A., Bear, M. F. and Singer, W. (1987) Blockade of "NMDA" receptors disrupts experience-dependent plasticity of kitten striate cortex. *Science*, 238, 355–8.

Klopfer, P. H. (1967) Is imprinting a Cheshire cat? *Behavioral Science*, 12, 122–9.

Klopfer, P. and Hailman, J. P. (1964) Perceptual preferences and imprinting in chicks. *Science*, 145, 1333–4.

Knudsen, E. I. and Knudsen, P. F. (1986) The sensitive period for auditory localisation in barn owls is limited by age, not by experience. *Journal of Neuroscience*, 6, 1918–24.

Kohsaka, S.-I., Takamatsu, K., Aoki, E. and Tsukada, Y. (1979) Metabolic mapping of chick brain after imprinting using [^{14}C]2-deoxyglucose. *Brain Research*, 172, 539–44.

Konishi, M. (1985) Birdsong: from behavior to neuron. *Annual Review of Neuroscience*, 8, 125–70.

Konorski, J. (1950) Mechanisms of learning. *Symposia of the Society for Experimental Biology*, 4, 409–31.

Kovach, J. K. (1971) Effectiveness of different colors in the elicitation and development of approach behaviour in chicks. *Behaviour*, 38, 154–68.

Kovach, J. K., Fabricius, E. and Fält, L. (1966) Relationship between imprinting and perceptual learning. *Journal of Comparative and Physiological Psychology*, 61, 449–54.

Kruhlich, L., Hefco, E. and Read, C. B. (1974) The effects of acute stress on the secretion of LH, FSH, Prolactin and GH in the normal rat, with comments on their statistical evaluation. *Neuroendocrinology*, 16, 293–331.

Lashley, K. S. (1950) In search of the engram. *Symposia of the Society for Experimental Biology*, 4, 454–82.

Lorenz, K. (1935) Der Kumpan in der Umwelt des Vogels. *Journal für Ornithologie*, 83, 137–213; 289–413.

Lorenz, K. (1937) The companion in the bird's world. *Auk*, 245–73.

MacDermot, A. B., Mayer, M. L., Westbrook, G. L., Smith, F. J. and Barker, J. L. (1986) NMDA-receptor adrenalin increased cytoplasmic calcium concentration in cultured spine neurones. *Nature*, 321, 519–22.

Mackintosh, N. J. (1983) *Conditioning and Associative Learning*. Oxford: Clarendon Press.

Maier, V. and Scheich, H. (1983) Acoustic imprinting leads to differential 2-deoxy-D-glucose uptake in the chick forebrain. *Proceedings of the National Academy of Sciences, USA*, 80, 3860–4.

McCabe, B. J., Cipolla-Neto, J., Horn, G. and Bateson, P. (1982) Amnesic effects of bilateral lesions in the hyperstriatum ventrale of the chick after imprinting. *Experimental Brain Research*, 48, 13–21.

McCabe, B. J. and Horn, G. (1988) Learning and memory: regional changes in N-methyl-D-aspartate receptors in the chick brain after imprinting. *Proceedings of the National Academy of Sciences, USA*, 85, 2849–53.

McCabe, B. J. and Horn, G. (1991) Synaptic transmission and learning: N-methyl-D-aspartate receptors are involved in recognition memory. *Behavioural Neuroscience*, 105, 289–94.

McCabe, B. J., Horn, G. and Bateson, P. P. G. (1981) Effects of restricted lesions of the chick forebrain on the acquisition of filial preferences during imprinting. *Brain Research*, 205, 29–37.

McCabe, B. J., Sheu, F.-S., Horn, G. and Routtenberg, A. (1991) Memory alters protein kinase C substrate (MARCKS) phosphorylation. *Society for Neuroscience*, Abstracts, 17, 140.

McLennan, J. G. and Horn, G. (1991) Learning-dependent responses to visual stimuli of units in a recognition memory system. *European Journal of Neuroscience*, Supplement 4, 61.

McLennan, J. G. and Horn, G. (1992) Learning-dependent changes in the responses to visual stimuli of neurones in a recognition memory system. *European Journal of Neuroscience* (in press).

Nadler, J. V., White, W. F., Vaca, K. W., Perry, B. W. and Cotman, C. W. (1978) Biochemical correlates of transmission mediated by glutamate and aspartate. *Journal of Neurochemistry*, 31, 147–55.

Nafstad, P. H. J. (1967) An electron microscope study of the termination of the perforant path fibers in the hippocampus and the fascia dentata. *Zeitschrift für Zellforschung Mikroskopische Anatomie*, 76, 532–42.

Nishizuka, Y. (1988) The molecular heterogeneity of protein kinase C and its implications for cellular regulation. *Nature*, 334, 661–5.

Nottebohm, F., Alvarez-Buylla, A., Cynx, J., Kirn, J., Ling, C.-Y., Nottebohm, M., Sutter, R., Tolles, A. and Williams, H. (1991) Song-learning in birds: the relation between perception and production. In J. R. Krebs and G. Horn (eds.) *Behavioural and Neural Aspects of Learning and Memory*. Oxford: Clarendon Press, pp. 17–26.

Nowak, L., Bregestovski, P., Ascher, P., Herbert, A. and Prochiantz, A. (1984) Magnesium gates glutamate-activated channels in mouse central neurones. *Nature*, 307, 462–5.

Olson, C. R. and Freeman, R. D. (1980) Profile of the sensitive period for monocular deprivation in kittens. *Experimental Brain Research*, 39, 17–21.

Payne, J. K. and Horn, G. (1984) Long-term consequences of exposure to an imprinting stimulus on "spontaneous" impulse activity in the chick brain. *Behavioral Brain Research*, 13, 155–62.

Perret, D. I., Rolls, E. T. and Caan, W. (1982) Visual neurones responsive to faces in the monkey temporal cortex. *Experimental Brain Research*, 47, 329–42.

Rauschecker, J. P. and Hahn, S. (1987) Ketamine-xylazine anaesthesia blocks consolidation of ocular dominance. *Nature*, 326, 183–5.

Rose, S. P. R. and Csillag, A. (1985) Passive avoidance training results in lasting changes in deoxyglucose metabolism in left hemisphere regions of chick brain. *Behavioral and Neural Biology*, 44, 315–24.

Salzen, E. A. (1966) The interaction of experience, stimulus characteristics and exogenous androgen in the behaviour of domestic chicks. *Behaviour*, 26, 286–322.

Scaife, M. (1976a) The response to eye-like shapes by birds. I. The effect of context: a predator and a strange bird. *Animal Behaviour*, 24, 195–9.

Scaife, M. (1976b) The response to eye-like shapes by birds. II. The importance of staring, pairedness and shape. effect of context: a predator and a strange bird. *Animal Behaviour*, 24, 200–6.

Schaefer, H. H. and Hess, E. H. (1959) Color preferences in imprinting objects. *Zeitschrift für Tierpsychologie*, 16, 161–72.

Sheu, F.-S., McCabe, B. J., Horn, G. and Routtenberg, A. (1992) Learning selectively increases protein kinase C substrate (MARCKS) phosphorylation in specific regions of the chick brain. Submitted.

Sluckin, W. (1972) *Imprinting and Early Learning*. London: Methuen.

Sluckin, W. and Salzen, E. A. (1961) Imprinting and perceptual learning. *Quarterly Journal of Experimental Psychology*, 13, 65–77.

Spalding, D. A. (1873) Instinct, with original observations on young animals. *Macmillan's Magazine*, 27, 282–93. Reprinted in 1954 in *British Journal of Animal Behaviour*, 2, 2–11.

Storm-Mathisen, J. (1977) Glutamic acid and excitatory nerve endings: reduction of glutamic acid uptake after axotomy. *Brain Research*, 120, 379–86.

Stumpo, D. J., Graff, J. M., Albert, K. A., Greengard, P. and Blackshear, P. J. (1989) Molecular cloning, characterization, and expression of cDNA encoding the "80- to 87-kDa" myristoylated alanine-rich C kinase substrate: a major cellular substrate for protein kinase C. *Proceedings of the National Academy of Sciences, USA*, 86, 4012–16.

Takamatsu, K. and Tsukada, Y. (1985) Neurobiological basis of imprinting in chick and duckling. In Y. Tsukada (ed.), *Perspectives on Neuroscience from Molecule to Mind.* Berlin: Springer, pp. 187–206.

Tanzi, E. (1893) I fatti e le induzioni nell' odierna istologia del sistema nervoso. *Riv. sper. Freniat. Med. leg Alien. ment*, 19, 419–72.

Thelen, M., Rosen, A., Nairn, A. C. and Aderem, A. (1991) Regulation by phosphorylation of reversible association of a myristoylated protein kinase C substrate with the plasma membrane. *Nature*, 351, 320–2.

Thorpe, W. H. (1944) Some problems of animal learning. *Proceedings of the Linnaen Society, London*, 156, 70–83. ·

Thorpe, W. H. (1950) The concepts of learning and their relation to those of instinct. *Symposia of the Society for Experimental Biology*, 4, 387–408.

22

Limitations on Input as a Basis for Neural Organization and Perceptual Development: a Preliminary Theoretical Statement

GERALD TURKEWITZ AND PATRICIA A. KENNY

It has been tacitly assumed by most students of normal and aberrant development that differences between adults and infants reflect deficiencies in the infant, and therefore represent handicaps which must be overcome if development is to proceed normally. Barnett (1960) raised serious questions concerning the value of this assumption with regard to kidney function and more recently Fantz and Yeh (1979) have questioned it with regard to the development of visual functioning.

The widespread use of the term "immature" to describe the infant and child attests to the dominance of the view that structure and function are best understood in terms of what they will become, rather than in terms of what they are. It is possible, however, and probably meaningful to view the somatic and behavioral capacities of the developing organism as uniquely adapted to that organism's current stage of development. For example, the limited motor capacity of many newly born mammals serves to prevent their wandering from a nest site and from their mother and thereby facilitates feeding, temperature maintenance, etc. This notion of the developing organism's capacities and attributes as adaptive for current functioning has been clearly stated by Oppenheim (1981), who has made a very appealing comparison between the metamorphic transformations undergone by insects and amphibians (where the different stages, e.g. caterpillars and butterflies, are each considered integrated, functioning organisms) and the

"Limitations on Input as a Basis for Neural Organization and Perceptual Development: a Preliminary Theoretical Statement" first appeared in *Developmental Psychobiology* 15 (1982), pp. 357–68, © 1982 by John Wiley & Sons Inc., and is reprinted by kind permission.

ontogenetic changes of birds and mammals. Rather than viewing the former processes as qualitatively different from the latter, Oppenheim suggests that metamorphosis may "merely represent an exaggeration . . . of developmental processes common in most animals" (p. 76). Accordingly, infancy in mammalian and avian organisms, with its accompanying modes of functioning, might be viewed as representing as harmoniously integrated and uniquely adapted a state as is the larval stage of invertebrates.

Although it is important to keep in mind the contribution of a given aspect of structure or function to meeting the current needs of the organism, it is also necessary to recognize that some adaptations go beyond meeting current needs and also contribute to the development of new structures or new modes of function which will be advantageous at later stages of development. Therefore, in a developmental analysis of any structure of function, it is important to consider both current and subsequent advantages for the organism. Although concerned with both types of advantage, the present paper is principally concerned with the subsequent adaptive advantages that accrue to the sensory limitations which are characteristic of most young organisms. It should be noted that the possibility that adaptive advantages result from motor limitations has long been part of the psychological literature, a prime example being the view that man owes his cognitive preeminence, in part, to the long period of infancy which includes motoric limitations. According to this view, the motoric limitations increase the period of dependency with a concomitant increase in socialization and opportunity for learning.

The position which we will advance maintains that sensory limitations, as well as motor limitations, produce both current and subsequent adaptive advantages. Despite the fact that some organisms are born or hatched with relatively well-developed sensory capacities, all have limited sensory functioning at some stage in their development. In this paper, we will try to indicate why we believe that these limitations in sensory functioning may, in fact, facilitate the organization of the sensory systems and the processing of sensory information, thereby promoting current adaptive functioning and providing a basis for subsequent perceptual development.

Role of Competition

We propose that limitations in function affect the presence or absence of competition both within and between sense systems. These limitations, in turn, play a major role in shaping both development within a system and relationships between systems. The role which we are proposing for competition is a complex modulating one with reduction or enhancement of competition at various stages responsible for the ultimate organization of perception. Because sensory systems develop at different rates, competition within and between them undergoes marked changes during ontogenesis. In our view, early stages in development are characterized by competition within a system, but little or no competition between sensory systems. This is followed by a period during which the emergence of new functions results in increasing competition, which is responsible for restructuring earlier systems and organizing later developing ones. The extent and timing of competition determines the nature of the developmental competitive relationships. Thus, reduced intersensory and limited intrasensory competition at early stages in development allows for organization to occur in the absence of interference from competing input. Once a system has become organized, the introduction of input from a competing system can result in something analogous to what Piaget has referred to as disequilibration. Although Piaget has emphasized the concept principally with regard to cognitive development, we feel that it is equally useful in understanding perceptual development. Thus, according to our view, the emergence of competition at certain stages results in the disruption of a stabilized organization and provides the basis for a subsequently more advanced reorganization of function.

In view of the earlier development of intrasensory competition, it is apt to be more important early in life, with intersensory competition becoming important only later on. We would therefore propose that interference with or elimination of intrasensory competition early in development or interference with intersensory competition later would both hinder development. Such interference could come either from the premature introduction of competition or from delaying the time when competition occurs.

Prenatal Influences

One major determinant of competitive relationships is limitation on sensory functioning at varying times during development. One period during which there are likely to be significant influences on functions is the one before birth or hatching (Kuo, 1924; Lehrman, 1953; Schneirla, 1956, 1965). It is our contention that limitations on functioning during this period play a substantial role in subsequent sensory and perceptual organization. Limitations and their consequences during the prenatal period are likely to stem from both the buffered nature of the prenatal environment and the incomplete development of the end organ and the nervous system. What we are suggesting here is that the uneven rate of development and sequential onset of functioning of the sensory systems have consequences for the development of relationships between them. In reviewing possible types of intersensory relationships, Mendelson and Haith (1976) suggest independence between systems as one possibility, although they point out that there is no evidence for such independence in infants. Intersensory independence might, however, characterize various phases of embryogenesis owing to the uneven rate of development of sense systems (Turkewitz and McGuire, 1978). Because of its consequences for reducing and regulating competition between emerging systems, such independence of sense systems may play an important role in the development of sensory function. Schneirla (1965) and Birch (1962) have proposed that the developing organism's behavior is first under the control of proximal sense systems, i.e. vestibular, cutaneous, etc., and that only gradually does a shift to distal (visual and auditory) control of behavior occur. Although he deals with the onset of sensory function rather than the control of behavior Gottlieb (1971) offers convincing evidence that some such sequence, i.e. cutaneous, vestibular, olfactory, auditory, visual, is invariant in at least those birds and mammals which have thus far been studied. It should be noted that the sequential onset of sensory function should not be taken for granted, as there is no *a priori* reason to exclude the possibility of parallel and simultaneous development of the senses leading to the simultaneous onset of functioning in the various modalities. Although the existence of a regular sequence of functional onset may be the result of constraints having to do with the development of other aspects of structure or function, its apparent uniformity throughout a large segment of the animal kingdom raises the question of its potential selective advantage. One such advantage might be the elimination or reduction of competition between input in various modalities. For example, during the period when only the cutaneous system is functional, embryonic behavior might more easily be organized around such input than would be the case if the organism also had to contend with vestibular input at the same time. Once behavior has begun to be organized around cutaneous input, the addition of vestibular input is less likely to disrupt behavioral organization, but rather would be assimilated into the existing framework.

Although we can think of no examples of enhanced behavioral organization in the absence of competition during the prental period, there is considerable information available concerning what has been termed compensatory functioning in individuals who have been deprived of the use of one or another modality at or around birth. Instances of the highly organized use of auditory information in congenitally blind individuals have been noted. Such extreme examples of integrated behavior as a congenitally blind boy being able to ride his bike through the streets of Boston by using auditory cues have been reported (Gibson, 1969). It should be noted that in no reports of compensatory functioning with which we are familiar have there been any indications of enhanced sensory capacity; rather the effects of deprivation in one modality appear to be on the attention paid to the remaining systems rather than to changes in sensitivity as such.

The Relationship Between Sensory Limitations and Neurogenesis

Not only are limitations involved in the determination of sensory functions, there is also considerable evidence suggesting that limitations of a number of different types can function to influence biochemical, neuroanatomical, and neurophysiological development. In these cases, competition, albeit of a very different nature from that involved in the competition between sensory systems, appears to be a major shaping force for structural organization. Studies indicate that modification of the patterns of competition encountered during normal development can markedly influence structural relationships. In a series of experiments, Krech et al., (1963) examined the brains of visually deprived rats for anatomical and biochemical changes resulting from such deprivation. He found that dark-raised rats developed heavier somesthetic cortical areas than did control (lightraised) littermates, and that the biochemical activity of nonvisual areas of the cortex was greater than in the control animals. These effects are likely to reflect the influence of absence of competition from the visual system on the organization of other sensory systems. In a somewhat similar vein, Gyllensten, et al. (1966) compared changes of the auditory cortex in visually deprived mice with changes in the visual cortex. They reported two primary findings: after two months in the dark, they found hypotrophy of both cortical areas, i.e. a decrease in amount of internuclear material and in the diameter of the nuclei of visual and auditory cortical cells, the decrease being much greater in the visual than in the auditory cortex. After four months, however, this hypotrophy persisted in the visual cortex and was succeeded by hypertrophy, or increased internuclear material and nuclear diameter of cells in the auditory cortex. Of particular interest here is Gyllensten et al.'s (1966) discussion of the eventual hypertrophy in the auditory cortex. They suggest it might be attributable to the increased use of the auditory mode by the visually deprived animal. Thus, if the relationship between audition and vision is a competitive one during development, visual deprivation allows audition a competitive edge. A marked effect of intramodal (visual) competition on the responsivity of individual cells within the visual system was demonstrated by Wiesel and Hubel (1963a, b), who showed that the effects of visual deprivation were much more severe when only a single eye was sutured closed than was the case when both eyes have been deprived; stimuli presented through the deprived eye failed to stimulate the majority of cortical cells, while the nondeprived eye became the sole effective route for visual stimuli. When intraocular competition was eliminated by suturing both eyes closed, there was less of an effect than was the case when one eye was placed at a competitive disadvantage. This suggests that during normal development, the presence of intramodal competition helps to establish binocularity.

Cynader (1979) provides further evidence for the existence of a competitive relationship within the visual system. Investigating the locus of visual competitive interaction, he reared kittens with one eye viewing through a lens that allowed clear vision of horizontal contours but defocused the image progressively more as the stimulus orientation approached vertical, thus simulating the clinical condition of astigmatism. He found that while the overall distribution of orientation-selective cells in the visual cortex remained the same, "the normal eye [seemed] to have made compensatory orientation selective inroads into the cortical territory normally occupied by the astigmatic eye" (p. 6). This "expansion of territory" provided evidence suggestive of a normally occuring intramodel competitive relationship.

It is worth noting that there is some evidence regarding the role of intramodal competition for the development of systems other than the visual. Thus, when Spinelli and Jensen (1978) used a conditioning procedure involving shock to the forelimb of otherwise normally reared kittens, they found a marked increase in the size of the area of somatosensory cortex which could be stimulated by contact with or movement of the conditioned limb.

Of even greater significance for our present concern is Cynader's investigation of intermodal effects on neural organization. He recorded the effects of dark rearing on responses of cells in the superior colliculus of cats and found intriguing effects. In the normal cat, cells in the superficial layers of the superior colliculus are driven exclusively by visual stimuli, while cells in the intermediate and deep layers are responsive to somatic and auditory, as well as visual, stimuli. As expected, following a period of dark rearing, Cynader found a loss of directional selectivity in the superficial layers and a shift of ocular dominance in favor of the contralateral eye; visual responses could be elicited, however, from nearly all cells encountered in these layers. However, in the deeper collicular layers, where multimodal receptivity is normally found, responses to visual stimuli were depressed while responses to auditory and tactile stimuli were not. Cynader interpreted this loss of visual responsivity in the intermediate and deep collicular layers as the result of a competitive interaction similar to the intramodal effect observed in the visual cortex following monocular deprivation, where competition is between the two eyes. In the superficial layers of the colliculus, visual responsivity is maintained in the dark-teared animal due to the absence of competitive input. In the intermediate and deeper layers, however, visual afferents are at a "competitive disadvantage" relative to somatic and auditory inputs, and hence lose their ability to influence cells in these layers.

The evidence therefore suggests that competition has a marked influence on neural organization and that a variety of conditions effecting differential input to the senses can influence the competitive relationships between them. In our view, the normal course of ontogeny, entailing as it does unequal rates of development of sensory systems, serves to modulate and orchestrate the competitive relationships among sensory systems and so makes possible an optimal or at least highly functional sharing of neural space. We suggest that differences in the rate of development of various sensory systems result in limited functioning in one or another modality at various times and that those limitations are responsible for at least certain features of neural organization.

Effects of Postnatal Limitations on Perceptual Development

Thus far, we have been considering the effect of limitations in sensory functioning on neurogenesis. In addition to these effects, which stem largely from the unequal rate of development of the sense systems, there are also important organizational consequences of the sensory limitations which are frequently present at birth. In this section of the paper, we will try to indicate why we believe that limitations shortly after birth promote organized responding by the infant, which may underlie subsequent perceptual and cognitive integration.

In recent years, it has become abundantly clear that William James' (1890, vol. 1, p. 499) characterization of the world of the infant as a "blooming buzzing confusion" is simply wrong. There is evidence that the infant's world is structured and that far from being overwhelmed by a barrage of stimulation which only slowly comes to be sorted out, the infant from his earliest days is quite properly characterized as competent and organized. It is our contention that one of the major sources for this organization is the infant's limited sensory capacity. This limitation includes a fixed accommodative system in which objects that are approximately 10 in. away are most clearly in focus (Haynes et al., 1965), and an acuity level such that only relatively large objects or large features (Salapatek and Banks, 1978) are resolvable. Although there is some controversy over just how limited the accommodative functioning of the infant is (Banks, 1980), there is general agreement that accommodation is restricted. Furthermore, the infant's responsiveness to visual stimuli with only low spatial frequencies ensures that large segments of the external world will not be resolved by the infant's visual system, further reducing the amount of visual information available for processing (Salapatek and Banks, 1978). By reducing the number of effective sources of stimulation in the infant's surroundings, such limitations reduce the amount of information which the infant must contend with and assimilate. Further, because those stimuli which are close to the infant, i.e. which are within reach, are most clearly focused, temporal contiguity between visual and tactile stimulation from an object would be promoted. Such contiguity might provide a basis for associations between multimodal attributes of an object (Humphrey et al., 1979; Lawson, 1980), and thereby promote the early appearance of intersensory equivalence (Bryant et al., 1972; Gottfried et al., 1977; Ruff and Kohler, 1978). It is probably not accidental that mothers tend to hold their infants approximately 20 cm away from them, irrespective of the mother's visual acuity (Papousek and Papousek, 1979). This behavior of the mothers, when coupled with the infant's visual restrictions, could account for the observed salience achieved by faces during early development (Fantz, 1963).

Sensory limitation during infancy may not only promote subsequent perceptual organization, but it may also substitute for perceptual organization during early infancy by providing an orderly world for the infant. An illustration of this type of substitution is provided by a consideration of the phenomenon of size constancy. Size constancy probably owes its importance as a subject for investigation to the general view that, if order is to be maintained in a world in which objects change their position relative to a viewer, and therefore change their projected size on the retina, it is necessary for some perceptual process like size constancy to exist. However, if vision is effectively restricted to objects within a narrowly circumscribed distance from the viewer, the requirement for size constancy is obviated and an orderly world is attained even in the absence of a level of perceptual organization necessary for the achievement of size constancy. Thus, the infant's limited depth of field may make it possible to respond to and learn the relative size of objects even in the absence of size constancy. In that known size is a strong cue for size constancy (Ittelson, 1951), the early opportunity to learn relative sizes provided by the infant's limited depth of field may facilitate the development of size constancy. That such is the case is suggested by the recent finding that size constancy, when it appears (at between four and six months), is initially restricted to very near distances (probably not greater than 70 cm) (McKenzie et al., 1980). Based on the logic which we have previously offered, we would expect size constancy for faces to be present at an earlier age than would be the case for other familiar objects which were not so consistently presented at an optimal viewing distance. Such a prediction is readily testable.

The view we are advancing suggests adaptive advantages for certain sensory limitations at particular times during development. That this advantage applies to an organism only at a stage when perceptual organization is limited or nonexistent is suggested by the fact that when intraocular lenses are inserted in the eye of cataract removal patients, the lens is set for distances from 10 feet to infinity rather than for near distances. We contend that such a prosthesis is useful for the adult only because he has already developed the perceptual mechanisms necessary for organizing the volumes of information simultaneously available with such a system. However, the use of such a prosthesis with an infant suffering from congenital cataracts would be detrimental rather than beneficial to his perceptual development. In support of this view, it should be noted that Von Senden's report (1932) of visual functioning in postoperative children and adults who had suffered from early cataracts noted a failure to cope with visual information on the part of those patients who had been blind from the earliest ages and who, therefore, did not have the opportunity to gradually develop an appropriate perceptual framework. A particularly dramatic instance was cited in which a patient began going around with her eyes closed because of the disturbance which vision produced to her functioning. In the absence of the necessary perceptual framework, the sudden availability of relatively unrestricted visual information led to disruption rather than enhancement of functioning. Because we are dealing here with adult organisms, the implications for infant development are unclear. Although not enough is known about visual functioning in nonhuman primate infants, it is likely that they have similar limitations to those of human infants. It might, therefore, be possible to test some of the inferences we are drawing by equipping primate infants with intraocular lenses fixed for varying distances, and subsequently testing for the presence of such perceptual characteristics as size constancy.

Although our focus thus far has been on the role of sensory limitations on human perceptual development, the view that we are propounding is a broadly based comparative one which has support from and implications for the perceptual development of many organisms. Organisms other than humans also exhibit early restrictions of input. For example, kittens, which at birth have a neurophysiologically functional visual system (Hubel and Wiesel, 1963), are born with their eyes sealed. It is not until six or seven days after birth that the eyes begin to open. In that there is sufficient variation in the age of eye opening to provide an easy path to the evolution of earlier eye opening if this conferred any selective advantage, it seems reasonable to believe that the opposite is the case, i.e. that it is reduction of visual input which provides the selective advantage. Whatever the evolutionary basis for the early limitation on visual functioning, it may facilitate the kitten's organizing its behavior around tactile, thermal, and olfactory inputs, thereby providing an organized framework into which vision can be incorporated. In fact, there is some evidence suggesting that such is the case. Examination of the homing behavior of kittens indicates that such behavior is initially under the control of thermal or olfactory cues (Freeman and Rosenblatt, 1978); several days after the eyes open there is a gradual transition to joint visual and olfactory control, succeeded by visual dominance and the modification of the entire pattern of homing (Rosenblatt et al., 1969).

It should be noted that the transition to visual control of behavior is gradual, and follows a sequence in which more and more detailed information becomes available to the visual system. Thus, at birth, and for approximately six days thereafter (the period when the eyes are sealed), the kitten has no pattern information available, but does have information about light and dark transmitted through the lids. Although there is no evidence that kittens are responsive to such information, there is evidence suggesting that rat pups respond to light even when their lids are sealed (Crozier and Pincus, 1937; Fleischer and Tukewitz, 1981). Even when pattern vision becomes available, it does not do so abruptly; when the eyes open, they do so gradually (eye opening typically takes place over a period of days), so that the kitten is spared the sudden confrontation with a potentially overwhelming stimulus load. The view that sensory limitation facilitates organization would suggest that if kittens were born with their eyes open at birth, or had them surgically opened, homing behavior would be less efficient both during the phase when it would ordinarily be accomplished under olfactory control and during the phase when it was ordinarily under visual control. That is, because of competition between visual and olfactory input, olfactorily based homing would not develop, and because of this, visually based homing would also fail to develop. There is some slight evidence which suggests that precocial availability of visual input does indeed interfere with organized functioning in other modalities. Thus, prematurely born human infants exhibit markedly reduced orientation to auditory stimuli at an age when full-term infants reliably orient (Kurtzberg et al., 1979). Although there are a number of explanations available for this effect (Lawson et al., 1977), the data are certainly in line with our expectations.

On the other side of the coin, if homing ordinarily disappears because the introduction of visual functioning leads to the reorganization of behavior, preventing the use of vision at the age at which it ordinarily appears should result in the maintenance of homing behavior beyond the age of its normal disappearance. Unfortunately, studies involving examination of the effects of reduced input in one modality on functioning in other modalities are very rare. In one such study, in which olfactory functioning in neonatal hamsters was interfered with via transection of the lateral olfactory tract or olfactory bulbectomy, the pups continued to show a thermal preference at an age when such preference has normally declined and been replaced by responsiveness to olfactory stimuli (Small, 1978). This finding suggests that the basis for the normal transition is not the independent maturation of the thermal system but rather the consequence of increasing competition from the olfactory system. This sequence emphasized the possibility that had both the thermal and olfactory systems been operating at fully mature levels at birth, neither system might have been able to successfully mediate organized patterns of behavior such as those exhibited in responding to a thermal gradient.

Thus far, we have provided some evidence indicating that when input is made available earlier than normal, it may disrupt functioning. We have also provided some support for the view that delaying or preventing the onset of a particular input results in the failure to reorganize behavior. A third possibility regarding consequences of alterations in the typical timing of relationships between systems, for which there is also limited support, is that when input from an earlier developing system is reduced, it leads to the precocial utilization of a later developing system. Thus, when the vibrissae of kittens are clipped, thereby reducing tactile input, kittens respond appropriately on a visual cliff at an earlier age than is the case in the absence of such reduced input (Turkewitz et al., 1974).

Finally there is some evidence suggesting that during normal development in infants and young children, the availability of multimodal input may disrupt rather than enhance functioning. Thus, Rose, et al. (1978) report that when six month-old infants are allowed to simultaneously see and manipulate objects, there is no evidence that they subsequently recognize the object visually, although such recognition is clearly evidenced when they are given only visual preexposure. Lawson, Ruff, McCarter-Daum, Kurtzberg and Vaughan (unpublished) found that three-month-old infants who give clear evidence of recognizing a stationary object which they have previously seen moving fail to give any such indication of recognition when exposure of the object is accompanied by a sound emanating from it. In a similar vein, Renshaw et al. (1930) report that the ability of young children to localize a touched spot on their body surface is interfered with if they are allowed to use vision during localization. The same procedure results in improved localization in older children and adults.

The evidence thus far presented suggests that the effect which either the onset of functioning in a particular modality or of changes in the nature of functioning in a particular modality will have on perceptual development is a function of the stage of organization of other modalities at the time of onset or change. Thus, according to our view, any radical increase in input during a period of rapid acquisition in other modalities would be disruptive of function. Increases in input during a period of slower development could lead to a reorganization to a higher level of functioning while similar increases in input following stabilization of functioning might have relatively little effect on existing organization.

The argument that we have been advancing raises the question of differences in the level of perceptual functioning achieved by precocial and altricial organisms. These organisms differ in the extent of sensory system development that occurs prenatally; the precocial organism is born with its full complement of sensory systems operating to at least some extent, whereas the altricial organism has more limited functioning in some or all of its sensory systems. This difference may limit the degree of sensory integration achieved by precocially born organisms and enhance sensory integration in altricially born organisms. Inasmuch as all sensory systems other than the visual have the opportunity to be stimulated prenatally, it is particularly with regard to the integration of vision with other modalities that we would expect precocial and altricial organisms to differ as mature adults. That is, since at birth precocial infants must suddenly contend with visual input as well as input from other modalities, the opportunities for integrating large amounts of new information with previously developed patterns of functioning may be more limited in such organisms than is the case for altricial organisms, or for those organisms born with some means of limiting visual input. Although there is virtually no information available concerning the relative capacity for sensory integration of newborn precocial and altricial animals, it should be noted that there are differences in the manner of functioning of such organisms which are at least suggestive of differences in intersensory integration. It is quite obvious that precocial animals have a number of potential selective advantages in both reduced predation and reduced the requirements for parental care and feeding. Despite these advantages, many animal species are altricially born. Obviously, when we speak of the advantages of precocity, we mean all else being equal. However, all else is never equal, and one of the inequalities is with regard to the influence of precocity on subsequent intersensory functioning. To the extent that successful predators require a greater ability to modify their behavior than do equally successful grazers and browsers, the distribution of altricial births among such organisms provides support for our position. Thus, predatory species of birds and mammals are for the most part altricial. In that increased modifiability has been attributed, at least in part, to increased intersensory integration (Birch, 1962; Gottlieb, 1971; Maier and Schneirla, 1935; Sherrington, 1941), this would suggest that altricial predators owe their superior modifiability to their superior intersensory capabilities, and further suggests the possibility that such intersensory superiority is in part based on their altricial condition at birth. Although such differences in intersensory functioning would clearly follow from our position, there have been no comparative studies of the intersensory functioning of predators and grazers and browsers nor of altricial and precocial animals. Such investigations, particularly if made among closely related species, would provide a clear test of some aspects of the position we are advancing.

We are currently examining the relative capacity for auditory–visual sensory integration of the precocial chinchilla and the altricial rat, both members of order Rodentia, and therefore closely related species, differing in the extent of sensory system functioning at birth. While there are other important distinctions between the two species, differences in the degree of intersensory integration capability may stem from their differing birth conditions. It may also be possible to reverse the direction of this difference by altering the normal sensory environment of these organisms at birth. Thus, early opening of rat pups' eyelids and dark-rearing of chinchilla newborns may result in adult rats that exhibit a level of intersensory functioning more like that of the normal chinchilla and, similarly, adult chinchillas that function more like the normal rat.

There is not yet as much empirical evidence as we would like with which to directly substantiate the position which we have been advocating. Furthermore, much of the evidence we cite in support of our position is open to alternative interpretations. Despite the limited empirical support thus far available for our position, we believe it provides a useful alternative to the generally uncritically accepted position that "earlier is better" and that "better is better." That is, it has generally been felt that we improve infant functioning whenever we can advance the age at which a particular behavior or function occurs or that if we would improve visual acuity or auditory responsivity, we would of necessity promote the development of higher levels of perceptual or cognitive functioning. In our view, such thinking fails to be properly respectful of the integrity of the organism and fails to take into account the possibility that different types of organization are advantageous at different stages of development. We believe our view to be particularly valuable because it provides ample opportunities for its own rejection within a framework which suggests numerous unique questions for comparative and developmental analysis.

NOTE

We thank the following colleagues for their thoughtful comments on an earlier draft of this manuscript: Judith Gardner, Gilbert Gottlieb, Sam Korn, Katherine Lawson, Mary O'Connell, Ronald Oppenheim, Susan Rose, Holly Ruff, and Howard Topoff.

REFERENCES

Barnett, H. L. (1960). Attitudes in pediatric research. *Arch. Dis. Children*, 100, 459–464.
Birch, H. G. (1962). Dyslexia and the maturation of visual function. In J. Money (ed.), *Reading Disability*. Baltimore: Johns Hopkins University Press.

Bryant, P. E., Jones, P., Claxton, V., and Perkins, G. M. (1972). Recognition of shapes across modalities by infants. *Nature*, 240, 303.

Crozier, W. J., and Pincus, G. (1937). Photic stimulation of young rats. *J. Gen. Psychol.*, 17, 105.

Cynader, M. (1979). Competitive interactions in postnatal development of the kitten's visual system. In R. Freeman (ed.), *Developmental Neurobiology of Vision*. New York: Plenum.

Fantz, R. L. (1963). Pattern vision in newborn infants. *Science*, 140, 296–297.

Fantz, R. L., and Yeh, J. (1979). Configurational variations as critical in development of visual perception and attention. *Can. J. Psychol.*, 33, 277–287.

Fleischer, S., and Turkewitz, G. (1981). Sensory influence on homing of stunted rat pups. *Dev. Psychobiol.*, 14, 29–39.

Freeman, N. C. G., and Rosenblatt, J. S. (1978). The interrelationship between thermal and olfactory stimulation in the development of home orientation in newborn kittens. *Dev. Psychobiol.*, 11, 437–457.

Gibson, E. J. (1969). *Principles of Perceptual Learning and Development*. Engelwood Cliffs, NJ: Prentice Hall.

Gottfried, A., Rose, S. A., and Bridger, W. H. (1977). Cross-modal transfer in human infants. *Child Dev.*, 48, 118–123.

Gottlieb, G. (1971). Ontogenesis of sensory function in birds and mammals. In E. Tobach, L. R. Aronson, and E. F. Shaw (eds), *The Biopsychology of Development*. New York: Academic Press.

Gottlieb, G. (1976). Conceptions of prenatal development: Behavioral embryology. *Psychol. Rev.*, 83, 215–234.

Gould, S. J., and Lewontin, R. C. (1979). The spandrels of San Marco and the Panglossian paradigm: A critique of the adaptationist programme. *Proc. R. Soc. Lond.*, 205, 581–598.

Gyllensten, L., Malmfors, T., and Noylin, M. (1966). Growth alteration in the auditory cortex of visually deprived mice. *J. Comp. Neurol.*, 126, 463–470.

Haynes, II., White, B. L., and Held, R. (1965). Visual accommodation in human infants. *Science*, 148, 528–530.

Hubel, D. H., and Wiesel, T. N. (1963). Receptive fields of cells in striate cortex of very young, visually inexperienced kittens. *J. Neurophysiol.*, 26, 994–1002.

Humphrey, K., Tees. R. C., and Werker, J. (1979). Auditory-visual integration of temporal relations in infants, *Can. J. Psychol.*, 33, 347–352.

Ittelson, W. H. (1951). Size as a cue to distance: Static localization. *Am. J. Psychol.*, 64, 54–67.

James, W. (1890). *The Principles of Psychology, Volume 1*. New York: Holt.

Krech, D., Rosenzweig, M. R., and Bennett, E. L. (1963). Effects of complex environment and blindness on rat brain. *Arch, Neurol.*, 8, 403–412.

Kuo, Z. Y. (1924). A psychology without heredity. *Psychol. Rev.*, 31, 427–448.

Kurtzberg, D., Vaughan, H. G. Jr. Daum, C., Grellong, B., Albin, S., and Rotkin, L. (1979). Neurobehavioral performance of low-birthweight infants at 40 weeks conceptional age: Comparison with normal fullterm infants. *Dev. Med. Child Neurol.*, 21, 590–607.

Lawson, K. R., (1980). Spatial and temporal congruity and audiotry-visual integration in infants. *Dev, Psychol.*, 16, 195.

Lawson, K. R., Daum, C., and Turkewitz, G. (1977). Environmental characteristics of a neonatal intensive care unit. *Child Dev.* 48, 1633–1639.

Lehrman, D. S. (1953). A critique of Konrad Lorenz's theory of instinctive behavior. *Q. Rev. Biol.*, 28, 337–363.

Maier, N. R., and Schneirla, T. C. (1935) *Principles of Animal Psychology*. New York: Dover.

McKenzie, B. E., Tootell, II. E., and Day, R. H. (1980). Development of visual size constancy during the first year of human infancy. *Dev. Psychol.*, 16, 163–174.

Mendelson, M. J., and Haith, M. M. (1976). The relation between audition and vision in the human newborn. *Lon. Soc. Res. Child Dev.*, 41 (Serial No. 167).

Papousek, and Papousek, (1979) *Human Ethology: Claims and Limits of a New Discipline.* Cambridge: Maison des Science de Homme and Cambridge University Press.

Renshaw, S., Wherry, R. J., and Newlin, J. C. (1930). Cutaneous localization in congenitally blind versus seeing children and adults. *J. Gen. Psychol.*, 38, 223–238.

Rose, S. A., Gottfried, A. W., and Bridger, W. H. (1978). Cross-modal transfer in infants: Relationship to prematurity and socioeconomic background. *Dev. Psychol.* 14, 643–652.

Rosenblatt, J. S., Turkewitz, G., and Schneirla, T. C. (1969). Development of home orientation in newly born kittens. *Trans. N. Y. Acad. Sci.*, 231.

Ruff, H. A., and Kohler, C. J. (1978). Tactual-visual transfer in six-months-old infants. *Infant Behav. Dev.*, 1, 259–264.

Salapatck, P., and Banks, M. S. (1978). Infant sensory assessment: Vision. In F. Minifie and L. Lloyd (eds), *Early Behavioral Assessment of the Communicative and Cognitive Abilities of the Developmentally Disabled.*

Schneirla, T. C. (1956). Inter-relationships of the 'innate' and the 'acquired' in instinctive behaviour. In P. P. Grassé (ed.), *L'instinct dans les Comportement des Animaux et de l'Homme.* Paris: Masson, pp. 387–439.

Schneirla, T. C. (1965). Aspects of stimulation and organization in approach/withdrawal processes underlying vertebrate behavioral development. In D. S. Lehrman, R. A. Hinde, and E. Shaw (eds), *Advances in the Study of Behavior, Volume 1.* New York: Academic Press.

Senden, M. von (1932). *Raum-und Gestaltauffassung bei Operierten Blind-Geborenen vor und nach der Operation.* Leipzig: Barth.

Sherrington, C. S. (1941). *Man on His Nature*, Cambridge: University Press.

Small, R. (1978). Functional and anatomical reorganization in developing hamsters after early postnatal lesions of the olfactory system. Unpublished doctoral dissertation. City University of New York.

Spinelli, D. A. N., and Jensen, F. E. (1978). Plasticity: The mirror of experience. *Science*, 203, 75–78.

Turkewitz, G., and McGuire, I. (1978). Intersensory functioning during early development. *Int. J. Men. Health*, 7, 165–182.

Turkewitz, G., Gilbert, M., and Birch, H. G. (1974). Early restriction of tactile stimulation and visual functioning in the kitten. *Dev. Psychol.*, 7, 243–248.

Wiesel, T. N., and Hubel, D. H. (1963a). Single cell response in the striate cortex of kittens deprived of vision in one eye. *J. Neurophysiol.*, 26, 1003.

Wiesel, T. N., and Hubel, D. H. (1963b). Effects of visual deprivation on morphology and physiology of cells in the cat's lateral geniculate body. *J. Neurophysiol.*, 26, 978.

Part VII

Self-organization and Development

Introduction

In part I we saw that an alternative to analyzing development into nature and nurture components was to view development as a constructive process in which structure emerges from the interaction of lower level components (Oyama, Piaget). Specific examples of attempts to provide constructive accounts of developmental change at the neural, cognitive, and behavioral levels are contained in this part.

Commonly studied aspects of neuronal structure in the visual cortex are the ocular dominance columns alluded to earlier by Held (part III). The clustering of cells with similar functional properties into patches or columns within the cortex appears to be widespread, and may be of computational significance. For example, cells in the superior temporal sulcus that are sensitive to faces appear to be clustered in patches about 3–4 mm across (Harries and Perrett (1991) *Journal of Cognitive Neuroscience*, 3, 9–24). One question has been to what extent these distinctive segregation patterns in the cortex are predetermined. In the first reading of this section, Miller and colleagues analyze the starting conditions and rules of organization that give rise to clustering patterns similar to those found in the primary visual cortex, and argue that the emergence of such a pattern is a robust property of certain types of self-organizing system.

By modeling the projection from the lateral geniculate to layer 4 of the primary visual cortex, including some intrinsic connections within layer 4, Miller and colleagues find that ocular dominance columns emerge under a variety of conditions and learning rules. There are, however, a number of core computational requirements for this form of periodicity to emerge. One of these is the "arbor function" – this relates to the fact that the projection pattern from the lateral geniculate cell to cortical cells is such that cortical cells at the center of the projection fan receive stronger input from the lateral geniculate neuron than do those at the periphery of the projection. Another computational requirement is that cortico–cortico interactions should be excitatory locally, but not at greater distances (as yet, there is no strong empirical evidence to support this). A third important aspect of the model for the emergence of regular ocular dominance patterns is the assumption that the input to the two eyes comes from spontaneous activity. Further, this spontaneous activity is assumed to yield greater positive correlations in activity within local areas of each retina than between the right and left retina. Whether this requirement is met in reality remains to be established.

Many other features of biological development also emerge from the Miller et al. model (although these are less robust), such as a critical period for monocular deprivation effects, and an increase in monocularity following artificially simulated strabismus, or other manipulations that reduce correlations in activity between the two eyes. These observations lead Miller and colleagues to propose that "simple mechanisms of activity-dependent competition may underlie many of the phenomena seen in the developing visual nervous system." Thus, the correlational structure of the input from the external world, taken together with the local rules governing intracortical interactions, may be sufficient to give rise to complex structures and developmental phenomena associated with the cerebral cortex.

The second reading in this section, that by Thelen, discusses the description of behavioral development in terms of a framework called "dynamical systems theory." This framework provides formalisms for accounting for characteristics of changes of states, and has been especially successfully applied to the developmental of rhythmical activities such as walking and sleep/wake cycles. Within dynamical systems theory, as in Piagetian theory (part I), apparent stable states are, in fact, the result of the interaction between several dynamic processes. When one or more of the factors contributing to the dynamic stability change to a sufficient extent, this can push the state out of one local energy minima and into another.

Addressing issues at the cognitive level, Karmiloff-Smith discusses how the Piagetian constructivist view of development (see the reading by Piaget, part I) fails to take into account the fact that the newborn human infant has many predispositions to attend to specific stimuli, such as speech, faces and so on. On the other hand, nativists (see the reading by Lenneberg, part I) often fail to appreciate the extent to which psychological development is a self-organizing process subject to certain intrinsic constraints. Karmiloff-Smith argues for an intermediate viewpoint in which hierarchical levels of representations are developed partly as a result of the inborn biases of the newborn, and partly as a result of processes of "re-representation." One example of the self-organization argued for by Karmiloff-Smith is the progressive modularization of some representational systems. While Fodor and others have argued that self-contained and encapsulated modular information processing systems are switched on by maturational factors (for example, in the same way as binocularity could be said to be enabled by underlying neural developments – see Held, part III), Karmiloff-Smith proposes that in many cases they may also be a *product* of development. That is, development gives rise to the increasing encapsulation of certain information processing systems. This has the consequence that such systems would be less accessible to other information processing systems within the mind. Such developmental processes at the cognitive level may have their counterparts at the neural level. For example, Ebbesson (see further reading, part VI) has proposed that neural development involves a process of encapsulation in which certain neural circuits become increasingly isolated from others (see Johnson and Karmiloff-Smith, further reading, part VI, for a more detailed account of these parallels).

While the framework provided by dynamical systems theory is at the same level as the representational redescription described by Karmiloff-Smith, it is worth noting that they yield quite different predictions about the variation of responses prior to a change in state. Dynamical systems theory predicts that, prior to a change of state, the system should become unstable. In terms of behavior this means that one should expect both the inter- and intra-subject variability to increase markedly just before a change of state. In contrast, Karmiloff-Smith proposes that the process of representational redescription takes place only following the achievement of stable output ("behavioral mastery") by the child. Interestingly, this suggests that there may be at least some classes of developmental change in higher cognition that do not obey the general principles underlying dynamical systems theory.

With regard to the interrelation between brain development and cognitive change, Thelen uses the dynamical systems framework to make several points. The first is that we should not assume that a sudden change of state at the cognitive level is a result of either a particular neural development or a particular environmental transition. A graded change in some combination of environmental and neural development is as likely to be the cause. Second, dynamical systems theory can be equally well applied to the neural level as it is to the cognitive level, and the same process of change may occur at both levels (see discussion of this class of attempt to relate brain to behavior by Johnson and Morton (1991), further reading, part VI).

All three papers in this section put forward what we might refer to as *process* accounts of developmental change, as opposed to discussing detailed *mechanisms* of development. In this context, process refers to the dynamics of change, while mechanism refers to the particular instantiation of that process. For example, selectionism may occur at both the neural and the cognitive level (see part V). Selectionism implemented by a mechanism of selective loss has been established at the neural level, but may or may not be the case at the cognitive level. That process and mechanism are, to some extent, independent is most evident in the reading by Miller and colleagues. They explicitly demonstrate that a variety of different learning rules and starting conditions yield a patchy "ocular dominance" pattern. The robustness with which this pattern develops (also in a variety of other biological and nonbiological systems) implies that it is the product of a developmental process, and may be subserved by a wide variety of detailed mechanisms. As demonstrated by Miller et al., however, the particular mechanisms employed do influence many more detailed developmental phenomena, such as the width of the "ocular dominance" stripes and the presence and strengh of a sensitive period.

23

Ocular Dominance Column Development: Analysis and Simulation

KENNETH D. MILLER, JOSEPH B. KELLER
AND MICHAEL P. STRYKER

In the visual systems of many mammals, including cats, monkeys, and humans, the optic nerves from the two eyes project to separate layers of a relay nucleus, the lateral geniculate nucleus (LGN) of the thalamus. Fibers from the LGN in turn project to cortical layer 4, the input layer of the primary visual cortex. There they terminate in alternate patches called "ocular dominance columns" serving the left eye and right eye, respectively (figure 23.1). The nonoverlapping pattern of connections evolves during development. Initially the connections representing the two eyes are distributed throughout layer 4, overlapping completely. Subsequently, they become segregated into two sets of patches, one for each eye.

Ocular dominance patch formation appears to depend on competition between the activity patterns originating within the two eyes (*1*). The patches do not develop when neural activity is blocked in the eyes or in the cortex or when a pattern of neural activity is given synchronously to the nerves from both eyes. They do develop when the activity patterns in the nerves from the two eyes are asynchronous. Closing one eye during a critical period early in development (monocular deprivation) results in larger patches for the open eye and smaller patches for the closed eye. Closing of both eyes during the same period causes no abnormal effect. Thus, both development of ocular dominance patches and the effects of monocular deprivation involve competition between activity patterns; they do not result simply from the presence or absence of activity.

This competition provides a model system for understanding activity-dependent synaptic plasticity. We presume that the strengthening of some

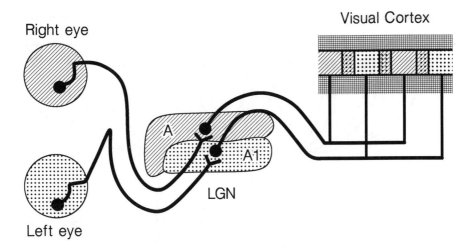

Figure 23.1 Schematic of the visual system after development of ocular dominance patches. The left lateral geniculate nucleus (LGN) and visual cortex are pictured. Retinal ganglion cells from the two eyes project to separate laminae of the LGN. The right (contralateral) eye projects to lamina A, and the left (ipsilateral) eye projects to lamina A1. Neurons from these two layers in turn project to separate patches or stripes within layer 4 of the primary visual cortex. The cortex is depicted in cross section, so that layers 1 through 3 are above and layers 5 and 6 are below the layer 4 projection region. Binocular regions are pictured at the borders between patches in layer 4.

synapses and the weakening of others are governed by cellular-level rules involving the patterns of neural activity onto and by each cortical cell. These small-scale changes, occuring on many individual cells during development, result in the large-scale structure of ocular dominance.

Various cellular-level mechanisms for plasticity have been proposed (2). Simulations by von der Malsburg and others (3) have demonstrated that some of these mechanisms can produce ocular dominance patches. We have developed a mathematical model that describes several such mechanisms. From it, we can determine the ocular dominance structure that would result from each mechanism, given experimental values for biological parameters (4).

Our analysis focuses on four biological features that are thought to play a role in organizing ocular dominance patches (figure 23.2):

1 The patterns of initial connectivity of the geniculocortical afferents (inputs from geniculate to visual cortex) onto the cortical cells. These patterns involve the spread of afferent arbors and of cortical dendrites and are described by an "arbor function," A.

2 The patterns of activity in the afferents. These patterns are described by a set of four "correlation functions," C^{LL}, C^{RR}, C^{LR}, and C^{RL}. They describe correlations in activity between afferents serving the same eye, left or right (C^{LL} and C^{RR}) or serving different eyes (C^{LR} and C^{RL}).

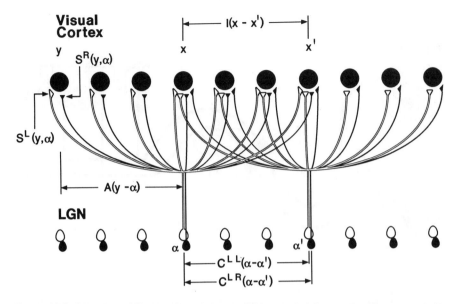

Figure 23.2 Notation. Afferents from left-eye (white) and right-eye (black) layers of the LGN innervate layer 4 of the visual cortex. α and α' label positions in the LGN, and x and x' label the retinotopically corresponding points in the cortex; y labels an additional position in the cortex. The afferent correlation functions C^{LL} (correlation in activity between two left-eye afferents) and C^{LR} (correlation in activity between a left-eye and a right-eye afferent) are functions of separation across the LGN. The arbor function A measures anatomical connectivity (number of synapses) from a geniculate point to a cortical point, as a function of the retinotopic distance between them. The cortical interaction function I depends on a distance across cortex. The left-eye and right-eye synaptic strengths, S^L and S^R from a geniculate location to a cortical location, depend upon both locations.

3   Influences acting laterally within the cortex, whereby synapses on one cell can influence the competition occurring on nearby cells. These influences, described by a "cortical interaction function," I, may occur through corticocortical synaptic connections or diffusion of modulatory substances.

4   Constraints limiting the total synaptic strength supported by an afferent or cortical cell.

The sizes of some of these features have been measured in the visual cortex of adult cats. The final patches have periodicity of about 850 μm (5, 6). Initial arbors may fill a region with diameter 1 to 1.5 mm (X cells) or larger than 2 mm (Y cells) (7). Afferents from a single eye appear positively correlated in darkness over distances of from 1/2 (for X cells) to 3/2 (for Y cells) of a geniculocortical arbor radius (8). Corticocortical synaptic interactions may be excitatory at short range and are inhibitory at further distances to about 400 μm; longer range, periodic cortical connections also exist (9). Most of these features have not yet been measured in kittens, when columns are developing.

The purpose of this analysis is to demonstrate the role of each of these four features in ocular dominance segregation. The model shows that ocular dominance patches emerge from an initially uniform state when the state is unstable to small perturbations. The model also describes the development of structure within individual cortical receptive fields and geniculate axon terminal arborizations ("arbors"). We shall characterize the general conditions on the four features under which a pattern-forming instability exists and determine the width of the ocular dominance patches that emerge. The results predict the patterns of ocular dominance organization that should result under various experimental conditions and thereby permit discrimination among proposed mechanisms of plasticity.

Formulation of the Equations

We model layer 4 of the cortex and two geniculate laminae, each serving one eye, as three two-dimensional sheets. Consider afferents serving the left eye with cell body at position α in the LGN (figure 23.2) (10). Suppose the terminal arborizations of these cells make synaptic contact with cortical cells at the position x. We denote the number of such synapses by the arbor function $A(x - \alpha)$ and their total synaptic strength at time t by $S^L(x,\alpha,t)$. Similarly, $S^R(x,\alpha,t)$ denotes the corresponding strength for the right eye. $A(x - \alpha)$ is taken to be a decreasing function of the retinotopic distance between geniculate and cortical cells and is the same for both eyes.

We begin by formulating an equation for Hebbian synapses, which are strengthened when presynaptic activity is sufficiently correlated with activation of the postsynaptic cell and weakened otherwise (11). This equation can be written for individual synapses as $\Delta s = [(post)(pre) - (decay)]\Delta t$, where Δs is the change in the synaptic strength in a small time interval Δt, and *post* and *pre* are functions of postsynaptic and presynaptic activities, respectively.

We assume that cortical activity is determined by the combined activity of all the afferents from the LGN to the cortex. Then *post* can be replaced by a function of presynaptic activities and of synaptic strengths. We then obtain the following equation governing $S^L(x,\alpha,t)$ (12–15):

$$\frac{dS^L(x,\alpha,t)}{dt} = \lambda A(x - \alpha) \sum_{y\beta} I(x - y) \, [C^{LL}(\alpha - \beta)S^L(y,\beta,t)$$

$$+ C^{LR}(\alpha - \beta)S^R(y,\beta,t)] - \gamma S^L(x,\alpha,t) - \varepsilon A(x - \alpha) \tag{1}$$

Interchanging L and R yields the equation for S^R. Similar equations have been derived by a number of investigators (16–21).

In eqn 1, $C^{LL}(\alpha - \beta)$ is a measure of the correlation between the activities of the left-eye afferents from points α and β in the LGN. $C^{LR}(\alpha - \beta)$ is the corresponding correlation measure for left-eye afferents from α and right-eye afferents from β. The cortical interaction function $I(x - y)$ describes the total influence on the cortical cell at x of geniculate excitation of the cortical cell at y. This includes direct excitation, if $y = x$, and indirect effects via excitation of intermediate cortical cells that may excite or inhibit the cell at x.

Equation 1 for S^L and the corresponding equation for S^R constitute our basic mathematical model of synaptic strength development. The data used in the model are the arbor function $A(x - \alpha)$, the cortical interaction function $I(x - y)$, and the correlation functions such as $C^{LL}(\alpha - \beta)$. When the initial values of S^L and S^R are given at time $t = 0$, the equations determine S^L and S^R at any later time t.

This basic model must be modified to prevent synaptic strength from becoming negative or from becoming too large. Nonlinearities must be included in the equation to enforce these conditions. In addition, the model may be modified to limit the total synaptic strength supported by a cortical or afferent cell (22). Terms must be added to the equations to enforce such limits.

We have investigated eqn 1, subject to these conditions, by using computer simulations and analytical methods to determine the conditions on the functions A, I, and C under which column development and other features of visual cortical development occur. We choose a particular model for the conditions limiting synaptic strengths in the simulations and explore the role of these conditions more generally in the analysis.

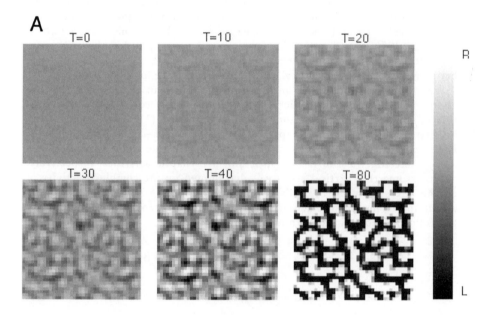

Figure 23.3 Typical development of ocular dominance patches (A), cortical cell receptive fields (B), and geniculocortical afferent arbors (C). (A) Ocular dominance of cortex at timesteps T = 0, 10, 20, 30, 40, 80. Each pixel represents a single cortical cell. The shades represent ocular dominance of each cell, that is, the difference between the total (summed) strength of right eye and of left-eye geniculate inputs to the cell. White indicates complete dominance by the right-eye, black indicates complete dominance by the left eye, and gray represents equality of the two eyes. The ocular dominance varies linearly along the gray scale at right. Final (timestep 200) cortex can be seen in the upper left of figure 23.6. (B) Receptive fields (ignoring the contribution of corticocortical connections) of eight cortical cells at timesteps 0, 30, 60, and 200. Each vertical pair of shaded squares shows strengths of the 49 left-eye and 49 right-eye synapses onto a cortical cell. The gray scale

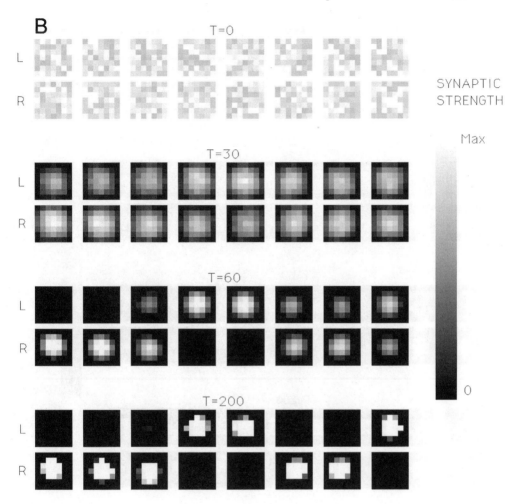

varies linearly in synaptic strength from 0 (black) to the maximum strength present at the given timestep (white). These maximum strengths are: timestep 0, 1.2; timestep 30, 3.5; and timesteps 60 and 200, 8.0. Cortical cells shown are the eight leftmost cells in the bottom row of the cortices of (A). Receptive fields first refine in size, then become monocular with synaptic strength confined to left-or right-eye inputs. (C) Afferent arbors at timesteps 0, 30, 60 and 200. Conventions as in (B), except that strengths of synapses made by eight left-eye and eight right-eye LGN afferents are shown. The afferents shown are the eight leftmost cells in the bottom row of the geniculate grids. Note that arbors first refine, then break up into patches confined to complementary ocular dominance stripes. This development used the following functions: The correlation functions have same-eye correlations only, with Gaussian parameter 2.8 (figure 23.5A). The intracortical interactions are mixed excitatory-inhibitory (figure 23.5B). The arbor function is taken to be 1 over a 7×7 arbor, 0 elsewhere. Conventions for all simulations: Illustrations of cortex show 40×40 grids, although the model cortex is 25×25. Periodic boundary conditions

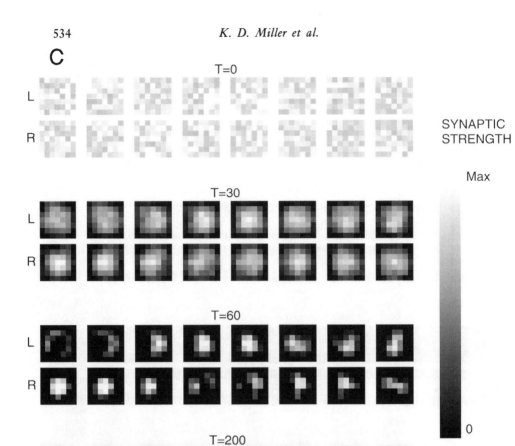

were used, so this display shows continuity of the pattern across what would otherwise appear to be a boundary. Simulations in most cases were run through timestep (iteration) 200; the cortex was mature by timestep 60 to 100, and very few or no changes were visible in the cortical maps after timestep 150. For the range of functions considered in this article, all but 2 500 to 4 000 of the 61 250 synapses had limiting values of 8.0 or 0.0 at timestep 200.

Simulations

We represent layer 4 of the cortex and two LGN laminae, one representing each eye, as three 25×25 grids of cells. Periodic boundary conditions are used, so that the topmost and bottommost rows within each grid are regarded as neighbors, as are the leftmost and rightmost columns within each grid. Each LGN cell arborizes to contact a 7×7 square of cortical cells centered on its retinotopic position in the cortex. Thus there are $2 \times (25 \times 25) \times (7 \times 7) = 61\ 250$ synapses. Initially the strength of each synapse is assigned a value chosen randomly from a distribution uniform between 0.8 and 1.2. We limit synaptic strengths to a range between 0 and 8.0 and impose constraints fixing the total synaptic strength supported by a cortical cell and limiting or fixing the total synaptic strength over an afferent arbor. We solve eqn 1 beginning from the random initial conditions and subject to these limits and constraints (23).

Figure 23.3 shows typical development under the model. Initially the cortex is binocular everywhere with approximately equal input from the two eyes, indicated by the gray in figure 23.3A. Gradually, synapses driven by the right and left eyes segregate, indicated by white and black, respectively, dividing the cortical territory into ocular dominance patches. Biologically, the development of ocular dominance patches is accompanied by (i) development of monocular receptive fields of cortical neurons, (ii) topographic refinement of receptive fields, and (iii) the progressive confinement of individual LGN axon arbors to patches. We examine the set of LGN inputs to a cortical cell as representative of the cell's receptive field. Figure 23.3B shows the development of eight such sets. Initially, each cortical cell has synapses of uniform strength from both eyes throughout the field. The inputs from each eye become concentrated in the centers of each receptive field, producing topographic refinement. Subsequently, the cells become monocular, that is, one eye gives strong input (black) and the other eye's input is lost (gray). Geniculate afferent arbors (figure 23.3C) also are initially uniform and then concentrate their strength centrally. Subsequently, the two axonal arbors from the two eyes stemming from a single retinotopic position

Figure 23.4 Cortex, timestep 100, for four different random initial conditions. Cortical interaction, arbor, and correlation functions and conventions as in figure 23.3A. Results are qualitatively and quantitatively similar for all initial conditions we have tried; that is, the two-dimensional Fourier transforms yield similar power spectra.

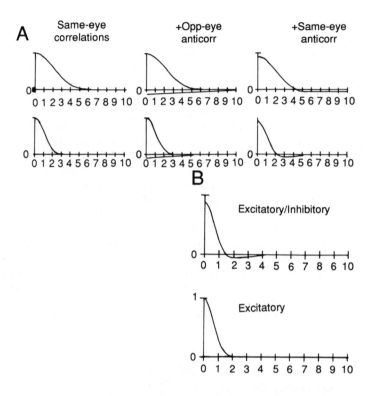

Figure 23.5 Correlation functions (A) and cortical interaction functions (B) used in simulations and computations. Horizontal axes are in units of grid intervals. All functions are circularly symmetric in two dimensions. (A) Correlation functions. Functions labeled "same-eye correlations" represent positive correlations, as illustrated, between afferents within each eye, with zero correlation between the eyes. The functions illustrated are Gaussians e^{-x^2/ξ^2}, with parameters $\xi = 2.8$ and 1.4, respectively. Results do not depend on the Gaussian tails. Results with $\xi = 2.8$ are virtually identical if the function is set to zero outside a square of ± 3 grid intervals; that is, outside an arbor radius. Results with $\xi = 1.4$ change only slightly if the function is set to zero outside a square of ± 1 grid interval. Functions labeled "+opp-eye anticorr" include anticorrelations between afferents from the two different eyes, illustrated by the curve below the axis, in addition to the positive correlations within each eye as in the same-eye correlations case. Functions labeled "+same-eye anticorr" have anticorrelations added within each eye, in addition to the positive correlations within each eye, while correlations between the two eyes remain zero. Both opposite-eye and same-eye anticorrelations are given by the Gaussian $-(1/9)$ $e^{-x^2/(3\xi)^2}$ with ξ the same as for the same-eye correlations. (B) Cortical interaction functions. The mixed "excitatory/inhibitory" function is given by $e^{-x^2/\xi^2} - (1/9)e^{-x^2/(3\xi)^2}$ with $\xi = 0.933$. It was explicitly set to zero outside a square of ± 7 grid intervals. Results are identical if the cutoff is ± 5 grid intervals, and only small changes are seen if the cutoff is ± 3 grid intervals. The "excitatory" function consists of the excitatory Gaussian alone, explicitly set to zero outside a square of ± 2 grid intervals. Results are indistinguishable with a cutoff of ± 1 grid interval.

in the LGN segregate into complementary regions. These regions correspond to the cortical patches.

These results are completely robust, because qualitatively identical results were obtained for every set of random initial conditions tried. Figure 23.4 shows the final cortical layer 4 patterns of ocular dominance resulting from four different random initial conditions. Although the precise locations of the patches vary from

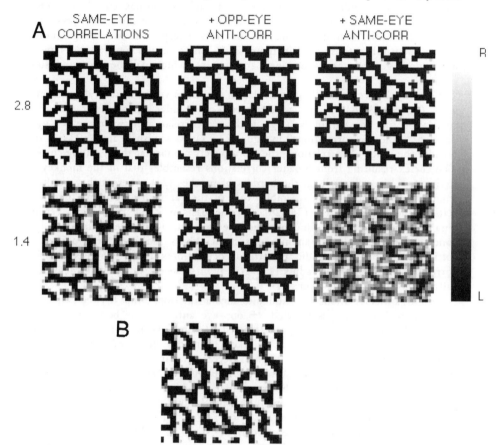

Figure 23.6 Development of ocular dominance using different correlation (A) and cortical interaction (B) functions. Initial conditions, conventions, and all functions (correlation, cortical interaction, arbor) except the one being studied are as in figure 23.3A. (A) Cortex, timestep 200, resulting from development from timestep 0 with each of the six afferent correlation functions illustrated in figure 23.5A. (B) Cortex, timestep 200, resulting from development from timestep 0 with the purely excitatory cortical interaction function (figure 23.5B). For these simulations, constraints were used fixing the total synaptic strength over each afferent arbor. In (A), these constraints make little difference in the final results (for example, compare the lower right panel of figure 23.7, which used only partial constraints, with the upper right panel of figure 23.6A). In (B), results depend crucially on these constraints. The theoretical basis for this difference is discussed in the text and in figure 23.9B.

trial to trial, the qualitative and essential quantitative nature of the patches remains invariant.

The precise afferent correlations, cortical interactions, and spread of afferent connections in kittens are not yet known. Furthermore, these functions will vary among species and under experimental perturbations. Therefore, it is important to determine how the developmental outcome depends on these functions. To do so, we simulated development with each of various correlation functions, cortical interaction functions, and arbor functions. In the results presented below, the initial conditions and all functions except the one being studied remain identical to those used in figure 23.3. These results confirm and supplement more general results obtained analytically, which will be discussed subsequently.

We studied development with correlation functions varied in several systematic ways (figure 23.5A). First, we considered a broader or narrower Gaussian correlation function within each eye, with zero correlation between the two eyes (labeled "same-eye correlations" in figure 23.5A). As shown in figure 23.6A, the broader the range of correlations, the more purely monocular the resulting cortex. The cortex resulting from broader correlations resembles that of the monkey in having few binocular cells at the borders of patches (24), whereas that resulting from narrower correlations resembles that of the cat in having many binocular cells at the patch borders (25, 26). On the basis of these results and results obtained with correlation functions that are constant over some finite range, we conclude that correlation among nearest neighbors (adjacent grid points) is sufficient to give a periodic pattern of ocular dominance, whereas positive correlation over an arbor radius (± 3 grid points) seems sufficient to achieve a fully monocular cortical layer 4.

Second, anticorrelations were added to such a function, either between afferents of the two different eyes (labeled "+ opp-eye anticorr") or between distantly spaced afferents within a single eye (labeled "+ same-eye anticorr"). Addition of opposite-eye anticorrelations can be taken to model strabismus or alternating monocular deprivation, treatments that increase the monocularity of cortex, or to reflect a possible feature of normal LGN circuitry (27). Addition of opposite-eye anticorrelations increases the monocularity of the simulated layer 4, as in experiments. In contrast, addition of anticorrelations within each eye decreases monocularity. If present within an arbor radius, such anticorrelation largely destroys monocularity (same-eye anticorr 1.4, figure 23.6A).

An alternative type of cortical interaction function that is purely excitatory is shown in figure 23.5B. With this interaction, one eye tends to dominate most or all of cortex. However, if the total synaptic strength supported by each arbor is fixed, the two eyes must remain equal in their total synaptic strength. The result is that a pattern of ocular dominance patches forms, with the width of left-eye plus right-eye patches slightly larger than before and approximately equal to an arbor diameter (figure 23.6B). Thus, periodic segregation of ocular dominance can occur in the absence of lateral inhibition.

The arbor function was modified to decrease with distance over the 7 × 7 range of connection. This represents decreasing connectivity. The result (not shown) is to decrease the period of the ocular dominance patches and to reduce the sizes of the final receptive fields and arbors.

The model thus reproduces many features of normal development for a wide range of correlations, cortical interactions, and arbors. The degree of monocularity of the final cortex depends on afferent correlations, whereas the widths of the patches can be altered by varying the intracortical interactions or the arbor function.

We studied monocular deprivation, modeling it as a reduction in the amount of activity in the deprived eye without alteration of the correlational structure of that activity. This corresponds to a reduction in the amplitude of the correlation function within that eye. Disruption of the correlations would only increase the effects of deprivation. The result of deprivation, both in the model and experimentally, is that the normal eye takes over more than its normal share of the cortex (figure 23.7). There is a critical period for this effect in the model, as is seen biologically; that is, the effect of deprivation is progressively weaker for later onset.

The critical period in the model has two causes. One cause is strictly dynamical, requiring neither changes in plasticity rules nor stabilization of synapses. Once the cortex has a sufficient degree of ocular dominance organiz-

Figure 23.7 Results of monocular deprivation. Results at timestep 200 are shown for initiation of monocular deprivation at five different times (timestep 0, 10, 20, 30, and 40). The sixth panel shows, for comparison, timestep 200 in an identical run but without deprivation. Arbor, correlation, and cortical interaction functions, initial conditions, and conventions as in figure 23.3A except as follows. Monocular deprivation is modeled as 30 percent decrease of amplitude of correlation function within deprived eye. Constraints on total synaptic strength over afferent arbors allow each arbor to decrease or increase its total synaptic strength by up to 50 percent. Without some constraint limiting changes in total synaptic strength over an arbor, one eye would completely take over cortex with early onset of deprivation. Although the choices of activity and constraint levels are arbitrary, the qualitative results are robust: with early onset of deprivation, the open eye takes over cortex to the limits imposed by constraints; with later onset, deprivation has progressively less effect.

ation, the deprived eye's greater synaptic strength, within its dominance domains, more than compensates for its weaker activity. In these domains the deprived eye therefore remains stable against competition from the normal eye. However, cells that remain binocular remain susceptible to domination by the more active eye. Binocular cells will become resistant to such domination if individual synapses are stabilized (rendered no longer modifiable) when they reach a saturating strength. Hence, stabilization of saturated synapses is the second cause of the critical period in the model. The dynamical mechanism is sufficient to completely account for the critical period when, as in figure 23.7, cells in layer 4 become fully monocular in the absence of deprivation. If, as in the cat, many cells in layer 4 normally remain binocular, the dynamical mechanism can nonetheless contribute to the critical period by ensuring that regions that become sufficiently dominated by one eye are no longer subject to an ocular dominance shift.

When cortical cells, but not afferents, are pharmacologically inhibited during monocular deprivation, the experimental result is a shift in responsiveness in favor of the closed eye (28). To model this, we note that *post* in the Hebbian equation $\Delta S = [(post)\,(pre) - (decay)]\Delta t$ becomes equal to a negative constant, because all cortical cells are inhibited (see eqn 3 in (15)). Then there is no coupling between synapses; each synapse decays in proportion to *pre*, which is a measure of its presynaptic activity. This "punishes" the more active synapses and, given constraints to preserve total synaptic strength over a cell, favors the afferents from the less active eye as in experiment.

Analysis

The simulations demonstrate that both normal and experimentally perturbed development of ocular dominance columns are reproduced by the model. These results can largely be explained by the following intuitive analysis. First, consider geniculate synapses onto a single cortical cell in the absence of interactions with synapses on other cortical cells. Each synapse then grows in proportion to the sum of its correlations with all other synapses on the cell, weighted by the strengths of those synapses. Receptive fields refine topographically, because synapses representing the center of the receptive field are strongly correlated with larger numbers of synapses than are synapses representing the periphery. This causes the central synapses to grow more rapidly than the peripheral ones. Similarly, receptive fields become monocular, because synapses serving each eye are better correlated with other synapses serving the same eye. This causes synapses of the eye with an initial advantage in overall synaptic strength to grow faster. Because this initial advantage is very slight compared to the advantage of central over peripheral synapses, monocularity develops more slowly than receptive field refinement.

Broader correlations within each eye enhance the growth of a monocular pattern of inputs compared to that of a binocular pattern and thus enhance monocularity. Broader correlations also reduce the advantage of central synapses over peripheral ones. Anticorrelations between the two eyes enhance the difference in growth rate between synapses of the two eyes and hence also enhance development of monocularity. Same-eye anticorrelations within an arbor radius cause a synapse's growth to be reduced by the presence of synapses of the same eye in an adjacent part of the receptive field. This causes binocular cells to develop, because a binocular pattern of inputs then grows more quickly than a monocular one. Thus, the development of monocularity and of receptive field refinement can be understood from the correlation functions.

Now consider the effects of intracortical interactions on the growth of a monocular set of inputs to one cortical cell. The set's growth is most enhanced if inputs to surrounding cortical cells fire in correlation over distances at which intracortical interactions are excitatory, and fire without correlation over distances at which intracortical interactions are inhibitory. Hence, the monocular inputs grow fastest if surrounded by a "bull's eye" of inputs from the same eye at excitatory distances and of inputs from the opposite eye at inhibitory distances. Although each monocularly driven cortical cell cannot be at the center of its own bull's eye, a compromise can be reached through a periodic organization such as patches or stripes. The period of this organization is like that of the bull's eye and is determined by the intracortical interactions.

To gain a more precise understanding of the roles played by afferent correlations, arbors, and cortical interactions in causing ocular dominance segregation and in determining patch widths, we analyze the equations mathematically. To do so, we assume that the two eyes are equivalent in their activities and their initial projections. Thus we ignore the effects of slight (5–10 percent) overall bias toward the contralateral eye in the cat (26) and we restrict our analysis to exclude monocular deprivation. Equivalence of the eyes implies $C^{LL} = C^{RR}$, $C^{LR} = C^{RL}$. Subtracting eqn 3 for S^L from eqn 3 for S^R yields an equation for the time evolution of the difference, $S^D \equiv S^R - S^L$, between the synaptic strengths of the two eyes at a given location in the cortex:

$$\frac{dS^D(x,\alpha,t)}{dt} = \lambda A(x - \alpha) \sum_{\beta y} I(x - y) C^D(\alpha - \beta) \, S^D(y,\beta,t) - \gamma S^D(x,\alpha,t) \quad (2)$$

Here $C^D \equiv C^{LL} - C^{LR}$. The function $C^D(\alpha - \beta)$ measures the extent to which afferents at geniculate locations α and β are more correlated if they are from the same eye than if they are from opposite eyes.

Initially the difference in synaptic strengths S^D, is very close to zero. We examine the stability of the state $S^D \equiv 0$ by examining whether a small initial perturbation of this state will grow or decay. Growth will result in a pattern of ocular dominance, whereas decay will yield a state of complete equality of the two eyes. If $S^D \equiv 0$ is unstable, many geniculocortical patterns of S^D may grow from the initial perturbation. The fastest growing such pattern will quickly dominate. Its characteristic periodicity will determine the width of the patches or stripes. The initial pattern-forming instability occurs when S^D is small, so only linear terms in an equation for S^D are relevant to this analysis. Thus the results will be robust to nonlinearities such as those inherent in biological development (29).

The Characteristic Patterns of Ocular Dominance

We refer to the patterns that grow exponentially, from a perturbation of $S^D \equiv 0$, as characteristic patterns of ocular dominance. Technically, these are the eigenfunctions of the operator in eqn 2. Each characteristic pattern of ocular dominance is of a form similar to $S^D(x,\alpha) = \cos k \cdot x \, R(x - \alpha)$ (30). Figure 23.8 shows the fastest growing such pattern for the functions used in the simulation of figure 23.3. The factor $R(x - \alpha)$ represents a characteristic receptive field. This is the pattern of differences between left- and right-eye synaptic strengths in the input to a cortical cell. Where it is positive one eye is dominant, and where it is negative the opposite eye is dominant. A monocular characteristic receptive field, like that of figure 23.8, is one dominated by a single eye throughout, so that R can be taken positive everywhere. Characteristic receptive fields need not be monocular: they may show division of the receptive field into domains dominated by opposite eyes.

CHARACTERISTIC RECEPTIVE FIELDS

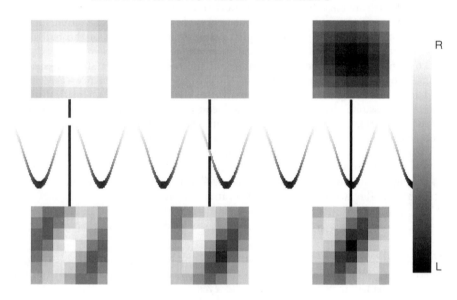

CHARACTERISTIC ARBORS

Figure 23.8 Illustration of typical monocular characteristic pattern of ocular dominance. The characteristic receptive field, and associated characteristic arbor, at three cortical points are illustrated. The sinusoid indicates the oscillation of ocular dominance across cortex associated with a characteristic pattern. Gray level codes S^D, the difference between the synaptic strengths of the two eyes, varying from dominance by one eye to dominance by the other. At the cortical point corresponding to the leftmost receptive field, cortical cell inputs are dominated by the right eye. Afferents with the corresponding retinotopic position therefore project arbors such that the right eye afferents preferentially project to the central patch of the arbor (cortical right-eye stripe) and the left-eye afferents preferentially project to the peripheral patches (left-eye cortical stripe). Similarly, the central receptive field is at the border between left-eye and right-eye stripes, where the two eyes have equal innervation, and the rightmost receptive field is in the center of a left-eye stripe. The pattern shown here is one of the set (identical except for rotations of the direction of the oscillation) of fastest growing characteristic patterns for the functions used in figure 23.3. The oscillation is shown correctly scaled to the arbor and receptive field sizes. The oscillation projects in a direction perpendicular to the stripes across the arbors rather than horizontally as depicted.

The factor $\cos k \cdot x$ represents an oscillation in the degree of dominance of receptive fields across the cortex. In figure 23.8, the leftmost receptive field occurs at a cortical point x where $\cos k \cdot x = 1$, so the right eye is dominant. The central receptive field occurs at a point x' where $\cos k \cdot x' = 0$, so the two eyes are equal. The rightmost receptive field occurs at a point x'' where $\cos k \cdot x'' = -1$, so the left eye is dominant. In the case of monocular characteristic fields, it is this oscillation, between ocular dominance by one eye and by the other, that causes organization of monocular cortical cells into ocular dominance patches. We refer to the spatial period or wavelength of this oscillation as the wavelength of the characteristic pattern. This wavelength corresponds to the width of left-eye patch plus right-eye patch, which we refer to simply as the patch width.

As figure 23.8 indicates, the characteristic receptive fields have associated with them characteristic afferent arbors, given by multiplying the receptive field by the oscillation in ocular dominance. In other words, when characteristic receptive fields are monocular, so that ocular dominance patches arise, the afferent arbors will only innervate the patches from the relevant eye. Thus, characteristic arbors show patches with a periodicity equal to that of the cortical oscillation, as is seen both in the simulations and in actual biological development.

Determining the Monocularity and Periodicity of Cortex

If the fastest growing characteristic receptive field is monocular, then a pattern of ocular dominance patches will form. The patch width is given by the wavelength of the fastest growing pattern. Thus, our problem can be reduced to two questions. (i) Under what circumstances will the fastest growing field be monocular? (ii) If it is monocular, what determines its wavelength?

Solution of the equation in simple limiting cases suggests that the correlation function C^D determines the wavelength of oscillations of ocular dominance across a receptive field, whereas the cortical interaction function I determines the wavelength of oscillations across an arbor. In these limits, each wavelength is given by the dominant wavelength in the corresponding function. This is the wavelength corresponding to the peak of that function's Fourier transform. The oscillation of ocular dominance across the cortex is the superposition of these two oscillations. Thus, if C^D does not oscillate within an arbor radius, the fastest growing receptive field does not oscillate and hence is monocular. The wavelength of the fastest growing pattern is then given by the dominant wavelength in I. Each limiting case leads to an analytic expression for the growth rate of each cortical wavelength of ocular dominance in terms of arbors, correlations, and cortical interactions (12, 13).

Direct computation of the characteristic patterns of ocular dominance for a variety of parameters confirms these basic results (31). Figure 23.9A shows the growth rates of characteristic patterns as a function of their wavelength, for the functions used in figure 23.6A. Gray level indicates the monocularity of the corresponding receptive fields, where lightest is fully monocular and darkest is fully binocular. The fastest growing field is monocular whenever $C^D(\alpha - \beta)$ is locally positive, that is, positive at least between nearest neighbors on a grid, and nonnegative within an arbor radius. Broader correlations or opposite-eye

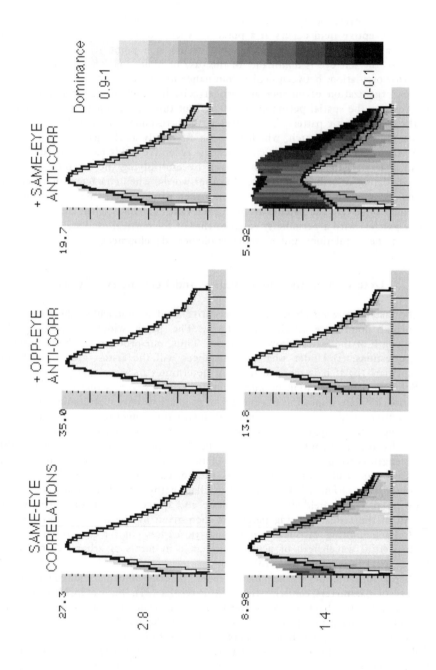

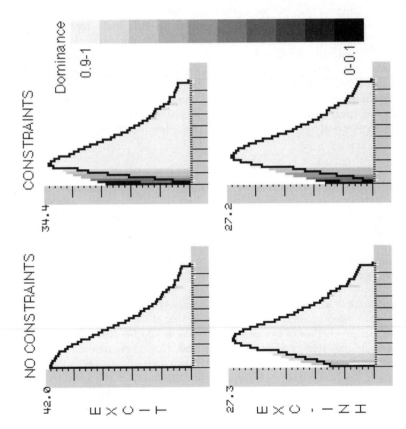

Figure 23.9 Computed growth rate (vertical axes) of characteristic patterns of ocular dominance, as a function of inverse wavelength of the pattern (horizontal axes), for varying choice of (A) correlation and (B) cortical interaction functions. Grayscale indicates maximum dominance of any characteristic pattern with the given wave number and growth rate. Dominance is a measure of the degree of monocularity of the pattern's characteristic receptive field, on a scale from 0 for complete binocularity to 1 for perfect monocularity. Number beside the vertical axis indicates the maximum growth rate of any pattern. The horizontal axis represents wave number; the wavelength in units of grid intervals is 25 divided by the wave number. The first bin on the horizontal axis represents wave numbers 0 to 0.23; subsequent bins represent increments of 0.4 in wave number, so that the second bin represents wave numbers 0.23 to 0.63, and so forth. Bins representing wave numbers for which there can be no characteristic pattern, because of the nature of our grid, are indicated with a white mark on the horizontal axis; for each dominance, these bins are assigned a growth rate that is the average of that of the two adjoining bins. (A) The six correlation functions of figure 23.5A. Arbor and cortical interaction functions are as in figure 23.3; there are no constraints on total synaptic strength over an arbor. The heavy lines show an analytic prediction for growth rate of each cortical wavelength of ocular dominance in terms of the cortical interaction and arbor functions and the correlation functions in each case. This prediction is normalized to the maximum growth rate of characteristic patterns with dominance ≥ 0.5. The light lines show the Fourier transform of the cortical interaction function, identically normalized. We derived the analytic expression by assuming that correlations change slowly over an arbor diameter. However, it accurately predicts the growth of monocular patterns over a wide range of correlation functions. At its peak, which is the dominant wavelength in the cortical interaction, the degree of monocularity and the growth rate of monocular patterns are enhanced. (B) The two cortical interaction functions of figure 23.5B. Arbor and correlation functions are as in figure 23.3. Two cases are shown: with constraints that fix the total synaptic strength over each afferent arbor and without any constraints on that total synaptic strength.

Black lines indicate predictions of the analytic expression obtained as described in (A). The constraints suppress the growth of monocular patterns with wavelength longer than an arbor diameter. Constraints have a profound effect on the outcome when the excitatory cortical interaction function is used. They select a wavelength of an arbor diameter: the maximum growth rate in the figure for this case occurs at wavelengths of 7.3 to 8.3 grid intervals. Constraints have little effect on the outcome when the mixed excitatory-inhibitory interaction function is used. This function normally selects a wavelength shorter than an arbor diameter. In this case, the maximum growth rate occurs at wavelengths of 5.4 to 5.9 grid intervals.

anticorrelations increase the monocularity of fields and the advantage in growth rate of monocular over binocular fields. Same-eye anticorrelations have the opposite effects. Their presence within an arbor radius (same-eye anticorr 1.4) leads binocular fields to grow fastest. In all cases, the wavelength of the fastest growing monocular pattern is determined by the peak of the Fourier transform of the cortical interaction function $I(x - y)$ (light lines in figure 23.9A) in close accordance with predictions from limiting cases (heavy lines in figure 23.9A).

There is an exception if the wavelength of a monocular pattern is much larger than an arbor diameter. Then in order for the pattern to grow, entire arbors centered within a dominance patch must either increase in strength or decrease in strength. If there is a constraint limiting the total synaptic strength supported by a single arbor, arbors will be constrained to break up, so that a gain in synaptic strength in one part of the arbor is offset by a loss in another part. Such a constraint can limit the patch width to approximately one arbor diameter (32). Figure 23.9B shows the growth rates of patterns, in the presence and absence of these constraints, for the two intracortical interactions of figure 23.5B. The excitatory cortical interaction normally selects a long wavelength but selects a wavelength of about an arbor diameter in the presence of constraints. The excitatory–inhibitory cortical interaction normally selects a smaller wavelength, and development under this interaction is not affected by these constraints.

To summarize, suppose that the correlation functions are such that C^D is locally positive and nonnegative within an arbor radius, so that cells tend toward monocularity. Then the patch width is determined by the dominant wavelength in the cortical interaction function $I(x - y)$. If the dominant wavelength is no larger than an arbor diameter, the patch width is equal to this wavelength. If it is larger than an arbor diameter and the total afferent arbor synaptic strength is sufficiently constrained, then the patch width is equal to the arbor diameter. The wavelengths of cortical ocular dominance in simulations, as determined by the two-dimensional Fourier transform of the patterns, develop in accordance with these rules (13).

Many Biological Mechanisms Can Be Modeled in This Framework

The results we have presented are not unique to a Hebbian synapse mechanism. A variety of other correlation-based mechanisms can be expressed in terms of an effective arbor function, an afferent correlation function, and a cortical interaction function. Therefore, they can be studied within our mathematical framework, as we shall now show for simplified versions of three alternative mechanisms.

First, suppose that cortical cells release diffusible or actively transported substances in proportion to their activity. Suppose that these substances are taken up by synapses in proportion to synaptic activity, as would be expected if uptake occurs in conjunction with vesicle reuptake, and that they modify synaptic strength. Let $E(x - z)$ describe an effective concentration of the substance at cortical site x resulting from release of a unit amount of the substance at cortical site z. Then, if we assume a plasticity rule for individual synapses of the form $\Delta s = [(conc)(pre) - decay]\Delta t$, where *conc* is a linear function of the substance's concentration, and *pre* is again a function of presynaptic activity, we obtain eqn 1. In this case the intracortical interaction $I(x - y) = \sum_z E(x - z) H(z - y)$ where $H(z - y)$ is the intracortical interaction of the Hebbian case arising from intracortical synaptic interactions (33).

Second, we suppose a plasticity rule as just described, except that afferents rather than cortical cells release the modification factor in proportion to the strength of their activity. This leads to eqn 1, with the intracortical interaction $I(x - y) = E(x - y)$. In this case the activity of cortical cells has no influence on plasticity (34).

Third, suppose that in addition to modifiable synapses, we consider chemospecific adhesion between afferent and cortical cells. Such "retinotopic" adhesion has been considered important in many models of retinotectal connections (19, 35). Suppose the degree of chemospecific adhesion between the afferent from α and the cortical cell at x depends only on $x - \alpha$. In this case, the retinotopic adhesion can be represented by a factor $f(x - \alpha)$ multiplying some of the terms on the right side of eqn 1. This is formally the role played by the arbor function. Hence, by letting $A(x - \alpha)$ represent the product of the chemospecific adhesion times the arbor strength, we can take account of retinotopic adhesion.

Discussion

We have formulated and analyzed a class of models of cortical ocular dominance development. They predict the development of a periodic pattern of ocular dominance like that seen experimentally. The organization of periodicity requires three conditions:

1   The correlation function $C^D = C^{LL} - C^{LR}$ must favor formation of monocular cells, by being positive locally and not significantly negative within an arbor radius.
2   There must be intracortical interactions, which should be locally excitatory (36).
3   If the intracortical interactions are purely excitatory, there must be constraints on the total synaptic strength over an arbor.

Given these conditions, a patch width of left-eye plus right-eye ocular dominance patches is determined. It corresponds to the wavelength at which the Fourier transform of $I(x)$ is maximized, provided that wavelength is less than an arbor diameter. Otherwise, if arbor constraints exist, the patch width will be approximately an arbor diameter. These results are very robust, being independent of initial conditions, nonlinearities, and the detailed form of the three functions.

These results are consistent with the measured sizes of ocular dominance patches, correlations, cortical interactions, and arbors in the adult cat (5–9). The observed patch width of about 850 μm can be produced by a variety of intracortical interactions ranging from excitation over a radius of 50 μm or less surrounded by weak inhibition to excitation over 200 μm or more surrounded by strong inhibition. Periodic longer range corticocortical connections, if present in the young animal, could enhance the growth of patterns with a similar period. Alternatively, a variety of arbor sizes, ranging from flat arbors of diameter about 850 μm to larger tapering arbors, would yield 850-μm patch widths by an arbor-driven mechanism. Such a mechanism is consistent with X-cell, though not with Y-cell, initial arbor sizes.

Many other observed features of biological development emerge from the mechanisms studied. These include refinement of receptive fields and development of monocularity, refinement of arbors and their confinement to patches, monocular deprivation plasticity with a critical period, and an increase in monocularity resulting from treatments such as artificial strabismus or alternating monocular deprivation that reduce correlations or produce anticorrelations between activity in the two eyes.

Many of these developmental details are less robust than the development and organization of periodicity. The robust elements of these results involve relative rates of growth and depend on interactions between synapses. Periodicity develops because one eye's synapses grow faster than the other's within each ocular dominance patch. Similarly, central synapses in a receptive field grow faster than peripheral ones. The less robust elements of the results involve absolute rates of growth and depend on the range of total synaptic strength allowed for each synapse and for the summed synaptic strength over each cell. For example, when a periodic difference in the strengths of the two eyes develops, the synapses of the weaker eye in a patch may decrease in strength or they may simply grow more slowly than the dominant eye's synapses. Only in the former case will individual cells become monocular. This can occur if there is a constraint limiting the total synaptic strength over a cortical cell and if individual synapses can grow sufficiently so that a single eye's synapses can saturate a cortical cell. In the absence of such constraints, one may see periodicity in each eye's innervation without seeing organization of monocular patches. Such a result may be seen in some New World monkeys (37).

Limitations on the range of synaptic strengths can be achieved by many means (16, 17, 19–22, 38). Because little is known about the actual mechanisms involved biologically, we prefer to use simple mechanisms, which can be analyzed more easily, for modeling purposes (39).

Other Models

Some earlier models of ocular dominance (3) showed that patches could form from simple mechanisms like those studied here. Others (20, 40) focused on the development of monocularity in isolated cells, as well as on dynamical means of limiting synaptic strengths. Legendy (18) studied a Hebb-like model and concluded that intracortical synaptic interactions will determine the distances over which cortical cells are similar in their response properties.

Swindale (41) formulated a model in terms of an effective interaction across cortex between right-eye and left-eye synapses, which produced stripes like those obtained here. The precise nature of this interaction was not specified. In the limit in which the correlation function C^D is constant or slowly varying, the influence of one synapse on another depends only on their cortical locations and their eyes of origin, and not on their retinotopic locations. Then the present model can be reduced mathematically to Swindale's (12, 13). We can then express his effective interaction in terms of arbors, cortical interactions, and afferent correlations.

Linsker (21) developed a model of plasticity very much like ours, which he used to study the development of orientation selectivity in visual cortex. It differs from ours in allowing modifiable input synapses to be excitatory or inhibitory, in using Gaussian arbors, in using constraints that ultimately fix the summed excitatory and the summed inhibitory input to a cortical cell, and in studying input from only a single eye. Our eigenfunction analysis can provide insight into his results. Thus, our equation for S^D can alternatively be regarded as an equation for the strength of synapses, of one eye, that can be positive or negative. "Center-surround" cells develop in his model, because the fastest growing eigenfunctions have receptive fields that concentrate their strength centrally. When combined with constraints that force 35 percent of final synapses to be negative (42), this can lead to a center of positive synapses with a surround of negative synapses. Therefore, the development of "center-surround" cells and the corresponding development of anticorrelations in the afferent correlation function depend on the negative synapses and the constraints. Given an afferent correlation function with strong anticorrelations within an arbor radius, oriented cells can develop. This is related to the fact that the fastest growing eigenfunctions for such a case (same-eye anticorr 1.4) have receptive fields that are striped.

Pearson et al. (43) developed a similar, but more complex, model to study somatosensory development and plasticity. By examining this model in terms of arbors, correlations, and cortical interactions, we conclude that the periodicity that develops in it should scale with the cortical interactions. If these interactions extend over several hundred micrometers, the "groups" found in that model also extend over several hundred micrometers. Physiologically, no such structures exist on such a large scale (44). Hence, our analysis would rule out their model without significant modification.

These points will be discussed elsewhere at greater length (13, 14, 45).

Experimental Implications

Our model can serve as a guide for experiment. We have found that local correlations over an arbor radius determine the development of monocularity, whereas cortical interactions determine the width of ocular dominance patches up to a possible limit set by arbor diameters. Measurement of initial correlation, cortical interaction, and arbor functions in various brain regions or species can test whether a proposed developmental mechanism is consistent with the patch width that emerges in each case. For example, area 18 of the cat has patches 1.5 to 2 times wider than those in area 17; arbors, and perhaps correlations, are also more widespread (5, 6, 46). If a Hebbian mechanism is responsible, we predict that kittens will show either a difference between the two regions in intracortical connectivities sufficient to account for the difference in patch width or predominantly excitatory intracortical connections in both regions resulting in arbor-limited patch widths.

Perturbation of the three functions in an experimental preparation before the onset of segregation, and comparison of the resulting patch width to the unperturbed case, can also test mechanisms. Under the hypothesis that a Hebbian mechanism underlies ocular dominance plasticity, periodic segregation is driven by intracortical synaptic connections. Local infusion of muscimol, a γ-aminobutyric acid (GABA) agonist, which inhibits postsynaptic cells, will eliminate activation of such connections. Therefore, we would predict that no pattern of ocular dominance organization would be seen in the muscimol-infused region, although individual cells might become monocular. Alternatively, intracortical inhibitory connections may be blocked by local infusion of bicuculline, a GABA antagonist. An increase in patch width would be consistent with a Hebbian mechanism, with width determined by the intracortical interactions. If patch width were unchanged by bicuculline, one would conclude either that the period was normally arbor-limited (which could be tested by measuring whether intracortical interactions were predominantly excitatory during initial column development) or that a non-Hebbian mechanism was involved.

The model predicts that broader correlations within each eye would increase monocularity of layer 4 for mechanisms of the type we study. This could be tested by inducing broader correlations through pharmacological interventions in the retinas. One could also measure whether retinal correlations are broadened in animals deprived of pattern vision. Such animals have increased numbers of monocular cortical neurons (47). It would also be of interest to determine whether geniculate correlations are broader, relative to a geniculocortical arbor radius, in the developing monkey than in the kitten, because the monkey develops a more fully monocular layer 4 (24, 26).

Conclusion

A variety of biological mechanisms will robustly cause development of a periodic structure of ocular dominance. The patch width can be predicted from a few biological functions that are, in principle, measurable. Given biologically plausible conditions to limit the synaptic strengths, these mechanisms also result in refinement and development of monocularity in individual receptive fields, the confinement of arbors to patches, and monocular deprivation plasticity including a critical period. These results lend plausibility to the notion that simple mechanisms of activity-dependent competition may underlie many of the phenomena seen in the developing visual nervous system.

REFERENCES AND NOTES

1. T. N. Wiesel and D. H. Hubel, *J. Neurophysiol.* 28, 1029 (1965); R. W. Guillery, *J. Comp. Neurol.* 144, 117 (1972). For a review of the material summarized in this paragraph, see M. P. Stryker, in *The Biology of Change in Otolaryngology*, R. J. Ruben, T. R. Van De Water, E. W. Rubel, eds (Elsevier Science, Amsterdam, 1986), pp. 211–224.

2. G. S. Stent, *Proc. Natl Acad. Sci. USA* 70, 997 (1973); J.-P. Changeux and A. Danchin, *Nature* 264, 705 (1976); H. Wigstrom and B. Gustafsson, *Acta Physiol. Scand.* 123, 519 (1985).

3. C. von der Malsburg and D. J. Willshaw, *Exp. Brain Res. Suppl.* 1, 463 (1976); C. von der Malsburg, *Biol. Cybern.* 32, 49 (1979).

4. Some of these results have appeared previously in abstracts: K. D. Miller, J. B. Keller, M. P. Stryker, *Soc. Neurosci. Abstr.* 12, 1373 (1986); K. D. Miller and M. P. Stryker, *ibid.* 14, 1122 (1988); K. D. Miller, J. B. Keller, M. P. Stryker, *Neural Networks* 1, S266 (1988); K. D. Miller, M. P. Stryker, J. B. Keller, *ibid.*, p. S267.

5. C. J. Shatz, S. Lindstrom, T. N. Wiesel, *Brain Res.* 131, 103 (1977); S. Lowel and W. Singer, *Exp. Brain Res.* 68, 661 (1987); N. V. Swindale, *J. Comp. Neurol.* 267, 472 (1988).

6. P. A. Anderson, J. Olavarria, R. C. Van Shryters, *J. Neurosci.* 8, 2183 (1988).

7. Putative Y-cell geniculocortical axon: S. LeVay and M. P. Stryker, *Soc. Neurosci. Symp.* 4, 83 (1979). X-cell arbors have not been filled in the kitten; based on fills in adults, X cells may have initial arborizations 1 to 1.5 mm in diameter (A. L. Humphrey, M. Sur, D. J. Uhlrich, S. M. Sherman, *J. Comp. Neurol.* 233, 159 (1985)).

8. Correlations in spontaneous firing, enduring over times of 1 to 10 ms in uniform light and about 50 ms in the dark, have been measured between retinal ganglion cells of adult cats (D. N. Mastronarde, *J. Neurophysiol.* 49, 303 (1983); *ibid.*, p. 325). The degree of correlation of two cells depends on the separation of their receptive field centers, which we may express as a distance across cortex (R. J. Tusa, L. A. Palmer, A. C. Rosenquist, *J. Comp. Neurol.* 177, 213 (1978)). Among cells of the same center type (on-cells or off-cells), X cells are correlated over distances representing about 350 μm across cortex, Y cells over about 1.6 mm; X cells are correlated with Y cells over about 1 mm. Cells of opposite center type are anticorrelated over similar distances. Fluctuations in spontaneous discharge of retinal and geniculate cells in adult cats in darkness over longer time scales (30 s to 30 min) appear to be synchronized throughout each eye but unsynchronized between eyes (R. W. Rodieck and P. S. Smith, *J. Neurophysiol.* 29, 942 (1966); W. R. Levick and W. O. Williams, *J. Physiol. (London)* 170, 582 (1964)).

9. R. Hess, K. Negishi, O. Creutzfeldt, *Exp. Brain Res.* 22, 415 (1975); K. Toyama, M. Kimura, K. Tanaka, *J. Neurophysiol.* 46, 191 (1981); C. D. Gilbert and T. N. Wiesel, *J. Neurosci.* 3, 1116 (1983); H. J. Luhmann, L. Martinez Milan, W. Singer, *Exp. Brain Res.* 63, 443 (1986); Y. Hata, T. Tsumoto, H. Sato, K. Hagihara, H. Tamura, *Nature* 335, 815 (1988).

10. The quantities α and x are two-dimensional indices, for example, $\alpha = (\alpha_1, \alpha_2)$. They represent retinotopic positions in the LGN and cortex, respectively. To each α in the LGN there is a retinotopically corresponding $x(\alpha)$ in the cortex. We use $x - \alpha$ to mean $x - x(\alpha)$. Cells in the visual cortex are generated early (unlike retinotectal development) so that cortical growth need not alter retinotopy.

11. D. O. Hebb, *The Organization of Behavior* (Wiley, New York, 1949). N-methyl-D-aspartate (NMDA) receptors may provide a biological mechanism for Hebbian plasticity. See G. L. Collingridge and T. V. P. Bliss, *Trends Neurosci.* 10, 288 (1987).

12. K. D. Miller and J. B. Keller, in preparation.

13. K. D. Miller and M. P. Stryker, in *Connectionist Modeling and Brain Function: The Developing Interface*, S. J. Hanson and C. R. Olson, eds (MIT Press/Bradford, Cambridge, MA, 1990), pp. 267–353.

14. K. D. Miller, in *Neuroscience and Connectionist Theory*, M. A. Gluck and D. E. Rumelhart, eds (Erlbaum, Hillsboro, NJ, 1990), pp. 267–353.

15. Let $c(x,t)$ represent activity (firing rate or membrane potential) of the cortical cell at location x at time t. Similarly, let $a^L(\alpha,t), a^R(\alpha,t)$ represent firing rates of afferents serving the left or right eye, respectively, from locations α at time t. The equation used to describe Hebbian synapses is

$$\frac{dS^L(x,\alpha,t)}{dt} = \lambda A(x - \alpha)\,[c(x,t) - c_1]\,f_1[a^L(\alpha,t)] - \gamma S^L(x,\alpha,t) - \varepsilon'A(x - \alpha) \tag{3}$$

Let the geniculate input to y at time t be $G(y,t) = \sum_\alpha \{S^L(y,\alpha,t)\,f_2[a^L(\alpha,t)] + S^R(y,\alpha,t)\,f_2[a^R(\alpha,t)]\}$. The equation used to describe cortical activation is $c(x,t) = \sum_y I(x - y)G(y,t) + c_2$. In these equations, λ, γ, ε', c_1 and c_2 are constants; f_1 and f_2 are functions incorporating threshold and saturation effects. If $c(x,t) = G(x,t) + \sum_y B(x - y)c(y,t) + c'$, where **B** summarizes corticocortical interconnections, then the-matrix $I = (1 - B)^{-1}$.

We substitute the expression for $c(x,t)$ into eqn 3, average the resulting equation over afferent activity patterns, and ignore higher order terms. Then we obtain eqn 1, with $C^{LL}(\alpha - \beta) \equiv \langle f_1[a^L(\alpha,t)]f_2[a^L(\beta,t)]\rangle$, $C^{LR}(\alpha - \beta) \equiv \langle f_1[a^L(\alpha,t)]f_2[a^R(\beta,t)]\rangle$, and $\varepsilon \equiv \varepsilon' - \lambda(c_2 - c_1)\langle f_1[a^L(\alpha,t)]\rangle$, where pointed brackets indicate average value. We have kept the notation S for $\langle S\rangle$.

This model includes only a single type of afferent. Corticocortical connectivity is considered to be uniform and unchanging. Changes in geniculocortical synaptic strengths are assumed to produce the initial pattern of ocular dominance, so that sprouting or retraction of terminal branches is not considered. These changes are governed by activity correlations over a time scale determined by the plasticity mechanism (G. G. Blasdel and J. D. Pettigrew, *J. Neurophysiol.* 42, 1692 (1979); L. Altmann, H. J. Luhmann, J. M. Greuel, W. Singer, *ibid.* 58, 965 (1987); B. Gustaffsson, H. Wigstrom, A. C. Abraham, Y. Y. Huang, *J. Neurosci.* 7, 774 (1987)). Interactions on this or finer time scales are considered instantaneous. Rationales for simplifications are discussed in (13, 14).

16. D. J. Willshaw and C. von der Malsburg, *Proc. R. Soc. London Ser. B* 194, 431 (1976).
17. S. Grossberg, *Biol. Cybern.* 21, 145 (1976).
18. C. R. Legendy, *Brain Res.* 158, 89 (1978).
19. V. A. Whitelaw and J. D. Cowan, *J. Neurosci.* 1, 1369 (1981).
20. E. L. Bienenstock, L. N. Cooper, P. W. Munro, *ibid.* 2, 32 (1982).
21. R. Linsker, *Proc. Natl Acad. Sci. USA* 83, 7508 (1986); *ibid.*, p. 8390; *ibid.*, p. 8779.
22. C. von der Malsburg, *Kybernetik* 14, 85 (1973). We implement conservation of total synaptic strength over a cortical cell by subtraction of the same time-dependent quantity from each synapse on a cell, whereas von der Malsburg subtracted a time-dependent quantity times the synapse's strength. The latter method suppresses the development of ocular dominance unless opposite-eye anticorrelations are present. This is discussed in (14) and in K. D. Miller and D. J. C. MacKay, in preparation.
23. At each timestep, synapses are updated as follows: (i) Compute derivative (change per timestep) of each synapse from eqn 1. $\gamma = \varepsilon = 0$. λ is set, for each choice of functions A, I, and C, so that the average change in S^D per timestep should initially be about 0.003. This yields $0.003 < \lambda < 0.015$. (ii) Modify derivatives with constraints. Constraints subtract a constant, weighted by $A(x - \alpha)$, from the derivative of each synapse $S^L(x - \alpha)$ or $S^R(x - \alpha)$ associated with a cell. The constant is determined for each cell so that the sum of derivatives over that cell becomes zero. First all cortical cells, and then all afferents, are constrained. (iii) Use these derivatives plus derivatives from previous timesteps to compute total change in each synapse by a three-step method (G. Birkhoff and G. Rota, *Ordinary Differential Equations* (Wiley, New York, 1978), p. 221), and update synaptic strengths. (iv) If $S^L(x,\alpha,t) < 0$ or $> 8A(x - \alpha)$, cut off value at 0 or $8A(x - \alpha)$, respectively; similarly for S^R. (v) If any synapses have been cut off, correct the normalization of cortical cells. Each synaptic strength on the cortical cell at x is multiplied by a constant that sets total synaptic strength on the cell to $2\Sigma_\beta A(x - \beta)$.

In simulations of figure 23.7, only partial constraints on afferent arbors were used. The term subtracted from the derivative of $S^L(x,\alpha)$ was multiplied by

$$\text{minimum}\left[1.0,\left(1-\frac{\sum_z S^L(z,\alpha)}{\sum_z A(z-\alpha)}\right)^2\middle/(0.5)^2\right]$$

and similarly for $S^R(x,\alpha)$. This allows total synaptic strength over each arbor to vary between 0.5 and 1.5 times its original value.

Runs illustrated used stabilization: when synapses reached $8A(x-\alpha)$ or 0, they were frozen so that no further changes in their strengths were allowed. Stabilization has no effect on final results, with one exception involving some cases of late onset of monocular deprivation, discussed in the text. To implement stabilization, frozen synapses were assigned a derivative of 0, and steps (ii) and (v) were applied only to unfrozen synapses. The multiplicative constants of step (v) were restricted to remain between 0.8 and 1.2.

24. D. H. Hubel, T. N. Wiesel, S. LeVay, *Phil. Trans. R. Soc. London Ser. B* 278, 377 (1977).
25. C. D. Gilbert, *J. Physiol. (London)* 268, 391 (1977).
26. C. J. Shatz and M. P. Stryker, *ibid.* 281, 267 (1978).
27. D. H. Hubel and T. N. Wiesel, *J. Neurophysiol.* 28, 1041 (1965); P. O. Bishop, G. H. Henry, C. J. Smith, *J. Physiol. (London)* 216, 39 (1971).
28. H. O. Reiter and M. P. Stryker, *Proc. Natl Acad. Sci. USA* 85, 3623 (1988).
29. The linear analysis determines the initial development of a periodic pattern. The fastest growing patterns dominate exponentially, so their period determines the width of the patches. The form of the pattern of patches (for example, stripes versus patches versus hexagons, or long parallel stripes versus shorter branching stripes) is determined by nonlinear interactions between these fastest growing patterns and so is not addressed by our analysis. It is possible for such an initial pattern to be only metastable, so that eventually it may reorganize into a pattern with a different period determined by nonlinearities. This is unlikely in the ocular dominance system, as studies of development of ocular dominance columns (S. LeVay, M. P. Stryker, C. J. Shatz, *J. Comp. Neurol.* 179, 223 (1978)) show no obvious change in periodicity between its earliest detection and the final adult pattern. With the use of voltage-sensitive dyes (G. G. Blasdel and G. Salama, *Nature* 321, 579 (1986)), it may be possible to test this by following development of the columns within a single animal. Derivation of eqn 2 using nonlinear functions for *post* in eqn 3 and for cortical activation is discussed in (*13*) and in K. D. Miller, *Neural Comp.* 2, 319 (1990).
30. Let $r \equiv x - \alpha$ and transform variables from (x,α) to (x,r). Then the right side of eqn 2 becomes a simple convolution in the variable x. By Fourier transform in x the eigenfunctions must be of the form $e^{ik \cdot x}R_k\xi(r)$, where k is a pair of rational numbers and serves as one index for the eigenfunctions, and ξ is an additional index enumerating the receptive field modes for a given k. $e^{ik \cdot x}$ represents a cortical oscillation with wavelength $2\pi/|k|$. $R_k\xi(r)$ is a (complex) characteristic receptive field, because it represents the variation of the eigenfunction as r varies while cortical location x is fixed. The eigenfunctions can also be written $e^{ik \cdot \alpha}B_k\xi(r)$, where $B_k\xi(r) = e^{ik \cdot r}R_k\xi(r)$. B is a characteristic arbor, as it represents the variation of the eigenfunction as r varies while afferent location α is fixed.
   If $I(x) = I(-x)$ and $C^D(\alpha) = C^D(-\alpha)$, the real part and imaginary part of a complex eigenfunction are both real eigenfunctions, with the same eigenvalue. These real eigenfunctions can be chosen of the form $\cos k \cdot x\, R^+(r) + \sin k \cdot x\, R^0(r)$, where R^0 has zero net ocular dominance ($\sum R^0(r) = 0$) and R^+ may have net ocular dominance

(12, 13). If, as for the eigenfunction of figure 23.8, $R^0 \equiv 0$, then the eigenfunction is precisely of the simpler form discussed in the text.

31. Eigenfunctions were computed by applying eqn 2 to 25×25 grids with 7×7 uniform arbors as in the simulations. An eigenvalue equation was obtained for $R_k(r)$ for each of the 625 cortical wave numbers k. By symmetry, only 91 of these equations are distinct. We diagonalize the resulting 49×49 complex matrix for each distinct k, using routines from the International Mathematical and Statistical Libraries.

32. More specifically, the constraint on arbors suppresses the growth of monocular modes with long enough wavelength to contribute significantly to the Fourier transform of the arbor function. One can also consider the effect of a constraint on the total synaptic strength supported by a cortical cell. Such a constraint can be imposed directly on the equation determining $S^S \equiv S^L + S^R$ and need not affect the equation determining S^D; hence, such a constraint can be imposed without influence on the development of periodicity.

33. Equation 3 is altered by substitution of $\sum_y E(x-y)c(y,t)$ for $c(x,t)$.

34. Equation 3 is altered by substitution of $\sum_y E(x-y)G(y,t)$ for $c(x,t)$, where $G(y,t)$ is defined in (15). This mechanism could not account for the results of pharmacological inhibition of visual cortical cells during monocular deprivation (28) and hence can be ruled out in visual cortex. However, formation of periodic patches is also seen in many other locations in the nervous system.

35. S. E. Fraser, *Dev. Biol.* 79, 453 (1980).

36. This condition allows a positive peak in the Fourier transform of $I(x)$. This may also be achieved by other forms of $I(x)$, for example, a purely inhibitory $I(x)$ with fairly sharp edges. We have not explored whether such an $I(x)$ could produce patches robustly.

37. Reviewed by S. LeVay and S. B. Nelson, in *The Electrophysiology of Vision*, A. Leventhal, ed. (Macmillan, London, in press).

38. T. J. Sejnowski, *J. Theor. Biol.* 69, 385 (1977); E. Oja, *J. Math. Biol.* 15, 267 (1982).

39. See discussion of realistic versus simplifying brain models in T. J. Sejnowski, C. Koch, P. S. Churchland, *Science* 241, 1299 (1988).

40. M. F. Bear, L. N. Cooper, F. F. Ebner, *ibid.* 237, 42 (1987).

41. N. V. Swindale, *Proc. R. Soc. London Ser. B* 208, 243 (1980).

42. This is the case when Linsker's parameter $g = 0.15$ (21).

43. J. C. Pearson, L. H. Finkel, G. M. Edelman, *J. Neurosci.* 7, 4209 (1987).

44. M. M. Merzenich et al., *J. Comp. Neurol.* 258, 281 (1987).

45. D. J. C. MacKay and K. D. Miller, *Neural Comp.* 2, 169 (1990); D. J. C. Mackay and K. D. Miller, *Network* 1, 257 (1990).

46. A. L. Humphrey, M. Sur, D. J. Uhlrich, S. M. Sherman, *ibid.* 233, 190 (1985).

47. Reviewed in S. M. Sherman and P. D. Spear, *Physiol. Rev.* 62, 738 (1982).

48. We thank R. Durbin and C. J. Shatz for helpful comments on the manuscript. Supported by a National Science Foundation (NSF) predoctoral fellowship to K. D. M. and by grants from the McKnight and System Development Foundations to M. P. S. Simulations were done at the San Diego Supercomputer Center supported by the NSF.

24

Self-organization in Developmental Processes: Can Systems Approaches Work?

ESTHER THELEN

The induction of novel behavioral forms may be the single most important unresolved problem for all the developmental and cognitive sciences.

Wolff, 1987, p. 240

What does behavior come from? As modest observers of humans and other animals in their early times of life, we must ask this question every day. It is the most profound of questions. Nearly every field of human inquiry – philosophy, theology, cosmology, physics, geology, history, biology, anthropology – asks in some way about the origins of new forms. How can we start with a state that is somehow less and get more? What is the ultimate source of the "more"?

Traditionally, developmentalists have sought the source of the "more" either in the organism or in the environment. In one case, new structures and functions arise as a result of instructions stored beforehand, encoded in the genes or in the nervous system (and ultimately in the genes) and read out during ontogeny like the program on a computer tape. Alternatively, the organism gains in form by absorbing the structure and patterning of its physical or social environment through its interactions with that environment.

Of course, no contemporary developmentalist would advocate either pole in the nature–nurture dichotomy. Everyone now is an interactionist or a transactionalist or a systems theorist. We have example after example in both human and other animal research of the reciprocal effects of organism and environment in effecting developmental change. We would likely find no cases that would

"Self-organization in Developmental Processes: Can Systems Approaches Work?" first appeared in *Systems and Development. The Minnesota Symposium in Child Psychology, volume 22*, edited by M. Gunnar and E. Thelen (Lawrence Erlbaum Associates, 1989, pp. 77–117), and is reprinted by kind permission.

show anything else. Why then, can Wolff claim that the induction of new forms remains a great unsolved problem?

At one level, it seems clear that no current developmental models – whether they invoke interactional, transactional, or systems concepts, have been especially successful in accounting for a wide range of empirical data. That is, we lack general principles of development that apply across species or across domains in one species, and that can account for both the exquisite regularities and the often frustrating nonlinearities, regressions, and variabilities that characterize the emergence of new forms.

Recently, several authors have criticized current developmental theorizing on perhaps an even deeper level. Oyama (1985), for example, cogently argued that by assigning the sources of ontogenetic change to either instructions from within the organism or information in the environment we have never come to grips with the ultimate origins of new forms. We seek to find the plans pre-existing somewhere that impose structure on the organism. Nativism and empiricism thus both share the assumption that "information can pre-exist the processes that give rise to it" (p. 13). This assumption of prior design located inside or "out there," leads to an inevitable logical trap – who or what "turns on" the genes, who or what decides what information out there is "good." However elaborate our story of regulator genes, feedback loops, comparators, and schema, Oyama claimed that we finally require a cause – and the old homunculus rears its head, although in more sophisticated guise. *Postulating an interaction of genes and environment in no way removes this logical impasse.* It merely assigns the pre-existing plans to two sources instead of one.

In a similar vein, Haroutunian (1983) criticized Piaget – surely our most thorough going interactionist – for failing to acknowledge the logical consequences of equilibration through accommodation and assimilation. Piaget's logical nemesis is also infinite regress. How can equilibration produce new forms through accommodation and assimilation that are not properties of these functions themselves? How does the organism know to differentiate schema in the right direction? If the organism is testing hypotheses about the world, against what standards are those hypotheses tested? Piaget's solution, Haroutunian claimed, was an implicit genetic nativism.

Are there, then, any candidates for general developmental principles that will avoid the logical pitfalls of dualistic theories and yet provide more than just rhetoric, principles that will provide structure to guide empirical research, formulate testable hypotheses, and integrate data within and across species and domains?

For many years, developmentalists have recognized that systems principles of biological organization offer a conceptually elegant solution to the problem of new forms. Systems principles are well-known: wholeness and order, adaptive self-stabilization, adaptive self-organization, hierarchical structuring (Laszlo, 1972). In addition to the classic statements of Von Bertalanffy (1968), Laszlo (1972), Waddington (1972), and Weiss (1969), a number of recent excellent essays and reviews detail the application of systems theory to development (e.g. Brent, 1978, 1984; Kitchener, 1982; Lerner, 1978; Overton, 1975; Sameroff, 1983; Wolff, 1987).

It is specifically the principle of *self-organization* that rescues developmentalists from the logical hole of infinite regress. That is, in biological systems, *pattern and order can emerge from the process of the interactions of the components of a complex system* without the need for explicit instructions. In Oyama's (1985) terminology:

> Form emerges in successive interactions. Far from being imposed on matter by some agent, it is a function of the reactivity of matter at many hierarchical levels, and of the responsiveness of those interactions to each other.... Organismic form ... is constructed in developmental processes.

Systems formulations are intuitively attractive for many developmental issues, in addition to the question of the origins of novel forms. Despite this, systems remain more of an abstraction for most working developmentalists than a coherent guide to investigation or synthesis. I believe there are a number of reasons why systems have not "worked."

Oyama suggested that the resistance to concepts like emergent order stems both from the prevailing reductionist and mechanistic approaches in biology and from a long tradition of belief in causation by design. Invoking emergent order seems like a retreat into vitalism. Equally important, I believe, is that we have had no accessible translation of systems principles to empirical design, methodology, and interpretation. By their very nature, systems are complex, multicausal, nonlinear, nonstationary, and contingent. The inherent nonlinearity and nonstationarity poses a real challenge to our needs for prescription and predictability. As a result, workers will often resort to a systems explanation only after their more direct main-effect or interactional models fail to explain a body of data. Systems views are often relegated to the discussion sections of papers: If everything affects everything else in a complicated way, then it must be a system (Woodson, 1988). Such *post hoc* incantation can dilute systems concepts to the point of vacuousness. Thus, although we need complexity and multicausality in our models because we have complexity and multicausality in our organisms, systems views seemingly lead to insurmountable obstacles for empirical analysis.

Certain contemporary work in physics, chemistry, biology, and psychology may now weaken the traditional resistance to the idea that organisms can produce pattern without prescription. The active fields of synergetics and nonlinear dynamics in physics, chemistry, and mathematics, for example, show in mathematically precise ways, how complex systems may produce emergent order, that is, without a prescription for the pattern existing beforehand (see, for example, Haken, 1983, 1985; Madore and Freedman, 1987; Prigogine, 1980; Prigogine and Stengers, 1984). Where is the "design" that allows aggregations of molecules to form laser lights, flow patterns in fluids, crystals, cloud formations, and other nonrandom collectives of simple subunits? In biology, field theories of morphogenesis in plants and animals allow for the highly complex differentiation of structural and functional elements from more simple, nongenetic factors such as gradients, nearest neighbor calculations, cell-packing patterns, and so on (e.g. French et al., 1976; Gierer, 1981; Meakin, 1986; Mittenthal, 1981). Developmental neurophysiologists are using terms such as *self-assembly* to describe the establishment and refinement of neural networks as a dynamic and contingent process (e.g. Barnes, 1986; Dammasch et al., 1986; Singer, 1986).

There is a growing trend toward viewing adult nervous system function also as a dynamic and self-organizing process; that is, modeling function as the emergent property of the assembly of elemental units, none of which contains the prescription or command center (Skarda and Freeman, 1987; Szentagothai, 1984). This work ranges from mathematical formulations of simple behaviors in relatively primitive organisms – locomotion in the lamprey eel, for example (Cohen et al., 1982), to computational models of the highest human brain functions such as memory and language (e.g. Hopfield and Tank, 1986; Rumelhart and McClelland, 1986; Shrager et al., 1987). I rely especially on the theoretical and empirical studies of human motor behavior of Kelso and his colleagues (Kelso et al., 1980; Kelso and Tuller, 1984; Kugler et al., 1980) based on dynamic principles, and in which the details of coordinated movement are seen to arise from the synergetic assembly of muscle collectives.

What these diverse formulations share – and what offers the empirical challenge to students of behavioral development – is the assumption that a higher order complexity can result from the cooperativity of simpler components. Vitalistic forces need not be invoked; it is the unique utilization of energy that can create "order out of chaos." Thus, the order and regularity observed in living organisms is a fundamental consequence of their thermodynamics; that they are open systems that use energy flow to organize and maintain stability. This means that unlike machines, biological systems can actively evolve toward a state of higher organization (Von Bertalanffy, 1968).

But will systems work for developmentalists? In the remainder of this chapter, I outline a number of principles derived from the field of synergetics (the physics of complex systems) that have special relevance for the study of developing systems. I then suggest that these principles may be useful in two ways. First, on a metaphoric or heuristic level, I offer a characterization of developing systems that may serve as a guide for examining and understanding multicausal and nonlinear phenomena in ontogeny. I apply the systems metaphor to several domains of early sensorimotor development in humans and other animals, and I suggest how synergetic principles may lead to testable systems hypotheses about the origins of new forms. Finally, I present examples from an ongoing study of infant motor coordination designed to use synergetic principles. Please note that I invoke these concepts with great caution and in the spirit of exploration. When the principles of complex systems have been applied to biological systems (e.g. Kelso and Schöner, in press), the phenomena modeled have been relatively simple and many variables could be rigorously controlled. We normally do not have that level of control over naturally developing organisms, nor can we be confident of the stationarity of our behaviour over the measurement interval.

My introduction to synergetic principles came through my interest in early motor development. A fundamental question for understanding motor behavior is how a system composed of many, many "degrees of freedom" – muscle groups, joints, neuronal elements, and so on – "compressed" these degrees of freedom into coordinated movement with precise spatial and temporal patterning. The traditional theories invoking either "motor programs" or feedback-based machine models were beset with the same logical problem that faces developmental theories: the origins of new forms. Kelso and his colleagues have used synergetic principles to show how the neuromuscular system can be "self-organizing"; that is, how trajectories and coordinative modes can emerge without the need for prescriptive solutions (see Kelso and Tuller, 1984). A basic assumption is that synergetic principles of organization are so general that they may be applied across systems and time spans; that new forms arise in development by the same processes by which they arise in "real-time" action (see Fogel and Thelen, 1987; Kugler et al., 1982; Thelen, 1986b; Thelen and Fogel, in press; Thelen et al., 1987).

Pattern Formation in Complex and Developing Systems

Compression of the Degrees of Freedom and Self-organization

Complex systems are systems with many elements or subsystems. These elements can combine with each other in a potentially very large number of ways; the

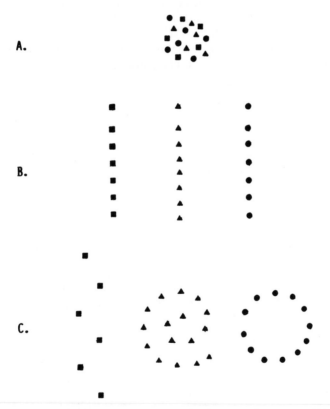

Figure 24.1 Schematic depiction of self-organization in a complex system. (A) A complex system consists of a very large number of noisy elements or subsystems with very many degrees of freedom. (B) Under certain thermodynamic conditions, such systems can self-organize to produce lower dimensional dynamics; the degrees of freedom are reduced. (C) The dynamical system, in turn, exhibits behavioral complexity; It can have multiple patterns, multiple stable states, and adaptable configurations.

system has an enormous number of "degrees of freedom" (figure 24.1). Under certain thermodynamic conditions – thermodynamic non-equilibrium (a directed flow of energy) – these elements can self-organize to generate patterned behavior that has much fewer dimensions than the original elements. That is, when the participating elements or subsystems interact, the original degrees of freedom are compressed to produce spatial and temporal order. The multiple variables can then be expressed as one or a few *collective variables*.

At any point in time, the behavior of the complex system is dynamically assembled as a product of the interactions of the elements in a particular context. At the same time that information is compressed, the resulting lower dimensional behavior can be highly complex and patterned. Behavioral complexity may be manifest in patterns evolving in space and time, in multiple patterns and stable states, and in remarkable adaptability to perturbations. Note that there is no prescription for this order existing prior to the dynamic assembly, either in the individual elements or in the context; the order grows out of the relations.

These phenomena are best illustrated by a dramatic, nonbiological example: the now-famous Belousov–Zhabotinskii autocatalytic chemical reaction. When simple chemicals – bromate ions in highly acidic medium – are placed in a shallow glass dish, a remarkable series of events begins (see figure 24.2):

> A dish, thinly spread with a lightly colored liquid, sits quietly for a moment after its preparation. The liquid is then suddenly swept by a spontaneous burst of colored centers of chemical activity. Each newly formed region creates expanding patterns of concentric, circular rings. These collide with neighboring waves but never penetrate. In some rare cases, rotating one-, two- or three-armed spirals may emerge. Each pattern grows, impinging on its neighboring patterns, winning on some fronts and losing on others, organizing the entire surface into a unique pattern. Finally, the patterns decay and the system dies, as secondary reactions drain the flow of the primary reaction. (Madore and Freedman, 1987, p. 253)

It would, of course, be impossible to describe the Belousov–Zhabotinskii reaction in terms of the behavior of the individual ions. There are too many of them and a nearly infinite number of degrees of freedom. The dramatic patterns, however, represent a much more compressed description. Whereas the behavior of the individual atoms is random and chaotic, the patterns show order in both space and time. Although they compress the original degrees of freedom, these patterns are themselves complex.

Where do these beautiful patterns and elaborate designs come from? No pattern generator or schema can be found. The order is truly emergent from the initial conditions: the mix of the chemicals and the constraints of the container, the room temperature, and so on. Scientists can simulate these self-organizing properties by a computer program that sets up very simple initial conditions. When the program runs, the sequence of pattern emerges, but a program for the pattern itself was never written.

The parallel between the Belousov–Zhabotinskii reaction and the events of early biological morphogenesis is striking. From the fertilized egg, a seeming homogeneous bag of chemicals, the embryo divides, cleaves, invaginates, becomes polarized and lateralized, develops layers, and so on. Models of early morphogenesis have much in common with those used to simulate the Belousov–Zhabotinskii reaction as they call on gradient fields, states of excitation, nearest neighbor effects, and simple rules of interaction.

But unlike the chemical reaction, which decays as the elements reach thermodynamic equilibrium, the embryo is supplied with a continual supply of energy through metabolic processes. It remains in this thermodynamic nonequilibrium, and as it utilizes energy, its emergent forms not only remain, but become more elaborated, each pattern generating its own subpatterns and so on until a great number of functional structures have been generated. Of course the process is not random as species quite precisely reproduce themselves. In this case however, the genome may be thought to greatly underspecify the resultant product. Much

Figure 24.2 Evolving forms in the Belousov-Zhabotinkll reaction. The spontaneous development of structure can be seen in a sequence of photographs (left panels in each pair) that shows waves of chemical activity propagating through a receptive liquid medium. These complex forms can be remarkably well modeled by a simple computer simulation (right panels). (From Madore and Freedman, 1987, reprinted with permission.)

evidence exists that genetic information sets the initial conditions, so to speak, but does not encode the topology that enfolds.

On a different level, behavior in developing organisms is likewise a result of the unique cooperativity of the subsystems in a context. Because of the thermodynamic status of living organisms, complexity in behavior may be an emergent property. No iconic representations of the behavior, either in the form of genetic codes, maturational timetables, reflexes, or cognitive schemes need exist *a priori*. As such, behavior is never hard-wired, but flexibly assembled within certain organismic constraints and the demands of the context or task. Order, therefore, is a product of *process*, not instruction. It is noteworthy that contemporary parallel models of neuronal and higher brain function are predicated on the processing of many individual subunits, none of which contains the icon or command of the resultant memory unit, perceptual trace, or word representation.

This formulation allows us to make another important claim. Because biological systems are openly exchanging energy with their surrounds, the state of the organism and the context for action (the task demands) are formally equivalent in the assembly of the cooperative interaction. Therefore, there is no dichotomy between organism and environment. Neither has privileged status in effecting change. It is as meaningless to talk of a decontextualized organism as of an environment without biological meaning to the animal. However, we may identify parameters either within or without the organism which act as agents of change, without being prescriptives for change.

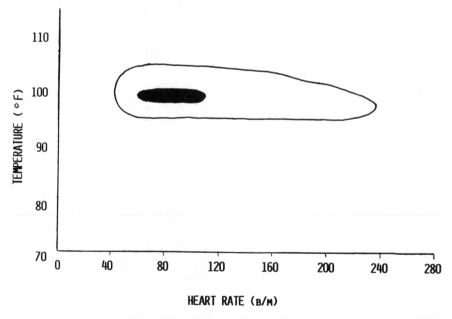

Figure 24.3 Hypothetical "fitness space" of a normal human individual showing dynamic range of heart rate and temperature. Individual "prefers" to spend time in the dark center portion, but is not limited to it. When perturbed, the system normally returns to the center oval.

Dynamic Stability

Self-assembled behavior of complex systems is dynamically stable in any given context. Given a particular biological organization, and a particular context, we can say that the system prefers a certain range of behavioral outputs (characterized in dynamic terminology as an abstract *attractor* state; Abraham and Shaw, 1982). The system will "settle into" this dynamic stability from a number of initial states and will tend to return to its attractor regimes when perturbed. In figure 24.3, I have illustrated a hypothetical state space, the "fitness space" of an individual. The two axes of this state space are defined as the possible states of two measured variables of fitness, body temperature, and heart rate. Normal adult humans occupy a certain preferred part of this space. Illness or exercise may shift you temporarily to one portion of the space, but your system "wants" to return to the dark central spot and will do so after the perturbation of illness or exercise. This is a dynamic stability because the system is not rigidly fixed to a confined region of the state space, but tends to stay in and return to a constrained region.

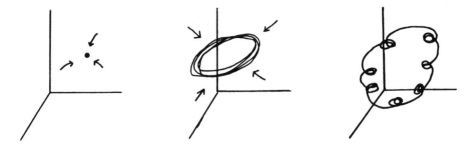

Figure 24.4 Three hypothetical attractors plotted in three-dimensional state space. (A) Point attractor. (B) Limit cycle attractor. (C) Chaotic attractor. Arrows indicate that dynamic trajectories tend to converge on these behavior patterns of the collective variable.

Dynamic systems theory identifies a number of such attractor regimes (figure 24.4). Behavior that tends to converge around a single or several output states are called *point attractor* systems, whereas repetitive or cyclical behavior is characterized as a *limit cycle attractor*. A special attractor regime currently of great biological interest is the *chaotic* or strange attractor. Chaotic systems are globally deterministic, but locally nondeterministic. They look noisy by conventional statistical tests, but they are not. Their behavior can be captured by certain sets of equations, thus, they have fewer degrees of freedom than truly random noise (Skarda and Freeman, 1987).

The attractor concept helps to understand how behavior can be both stable and variable. Developing organisms are neither stereotyped and "hard-wired" nor are they random. Behavior fluctuates, but within limits. That is, organisms tend to show a delimited number of behavioral patterns, which within certain boundary conditions, will act like dynamic attractors. These states will be the preferred configuration from a number of initial conditions, and they will be relatively resistant to perturbation. As a consequence of this dynamic assembly, developing organisms remain flexible in the face of tasks, but only within the constraints of their energetically stable possible states.

Attractors Stabilize and Destabilize during Ontogeny

Because the components of developing systems are always in flux, the attractor states themselves have dynamic trajectories. Some behavior becomes more stable, more tightly constrained, more skilled, and less subject to perturbations. New walkers, like new drivers, must focus all their attention to the task and are easily distracted and dislodged. With experience, the skill becomes so stable that conversation, even chewing gum, is possible, and the walker can compensate for all manner of obstacles. Increasing skill can be conceptualized as an increasingly stable attractor.

Likewise, many ontogenetic phenemona require attractors to destabilize; behavior becomes less reliable, more disruptable, and more variable. For example, in infant mammals, sucking is a highly stable attractor state. All intact infant mammals must suckle in a skilled and reliable manner at birth. However, with weaning, suckling becomes more context dependent, less obligatory, more variable, and more likely to be interrupted. Eventually, the motor pattern itself disappears, as adults cannot reproduce the behavior.

I have characterized the continual and gradual changes during development as the stabilization and destablization of preferred attractor states. What about the notorious discontinuities in development? As I discuss in the following sections, discontinuous changes also require the disruption of stable states.

Discontinuous Phase Shifts

Complex systems may exhibit multiple behavioral patterns. An important characteristic of such complex systems is that they switch between patterns *in a discontinuous manner*, by exhibiting discrete phase transitions. That is, the shift from one stable behavioral mode (attractor regime) to another behavioral regime occurs without stable intermediate states (Haken, 1983). *Bifurcations* are phase shifts where the collective variable jumps into two or more discrete, stable modes. Complex systems may undergo multiple bifurcations (figure 24.5), resulting in increasing behavioral complexity. Phase shifts and bifurcations give rise, therefore, to new forms and multiple states.

Developing organisms are well known to display qualitatively discrete phases during ontogeny. Sometimes, the animal seems even to lose behavioral forms or regress to less mature performance. The premier developmental question is, of course, the nature of the transition from one developmental stage to another – the emergence of new forms. How does a system retain continuity and yet produce discontinuous mainfestations?

Control Parameters

Developmental theorists may well look to synergetic principles for help with the perennial puzzle of continuity-within-discontinuity. In complex systems, behavior

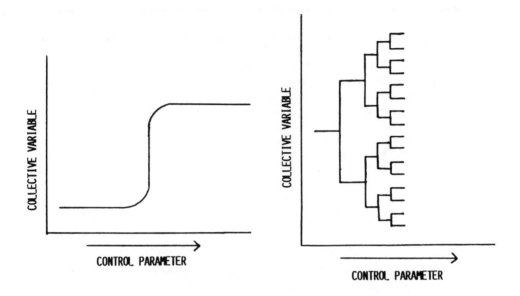

Figure 24.5   The appearance of new forms through discontinuous phase shift. (A) Scaling on a control parameter shifts the system into a new state without a stable intermediate. (B) Scaling on a control parameter induces multiple stable behavioral states.

that is ordered results from the cooperativity of the subsystems. But at points of change – phase shifts – not all of the elements drive the system into a new phase. An important synergetic principle is that at a phase transition, scaling on only one or a few *control parameters* shifts the entire system. Because of the holistic nature of cooperative systems, this change in a crucial variable beyond a critical point reverberates to a system-wide reorganization (Kelso and Schöner, in press). Again, because organismic and contextual variables are equally important in the dynamic assembly of behavior, there is no formal difference between exogenous and endogenous sources of change. The control parameter must in no way be envisioned as a prescription for change. Control parameters do not themselves encode or represent change. They may be rather unspecific, like physical parameters of pressure, temperature, or energy to the system, but they act to reorganize the system in specific ways. Continuity is maintained because most of the components of the system have not materially changed; discontinuity is manifest because the components relate to one another in a different fashion, and their low-dimensional, collective behavior has undergone a qualitative shift.

Here I would like to illustrate such a nonequilibrium phase shift and the role of the control parameter with a compelling real-time example from the human motor system, which has been elegantly modeled by Kelso and his colleagues using synergetic principles (Haken et al., 1985; Kelso et al., 1986; Schöner et al., 1986). Kelso asked human subjects to flex and extend their index fingers in time to a metronome, beginning at a slow pace and with the fingers moving out-of-phase, that is, with one finger flexing while the other was extending. As the experimenter increased the metronome pacing, subjects spontaneously and instantaneously shifted their coordination pattern from out-of-phase to in-phase at repeatable critical points in the speed scalar. (No such shift occurs if subjects begin with in-phase movements.) The degrees of freedom contributing to finger-flexing movements were compressed by the motor system such that the behavior could be described by much fewer variables – in this case the relative phasing between fingers. Although out-of-phase movements were stable at lower speeds, at a critical point the system assumed a new, and presumably more stable regime. No prescription for this phase shift is assumed; the new coordinative pattern arose from the task demands and the thermodynamics of the combined elements that produced it. In this case, a single control parameter – the energy delivered to the system to increase the speed, appeared to drive the phase shift. The anatomical and physiological elements participating in the ensemble were reorganized to produce a different output while themselves remaining stable.

Control Parameters in Developing Systems

We have proposed that at developmental transitions, one or several components of the complex system may act as control parameters, including variables in the context or in the environment (Fogel and Thelen, 1987; Thelen, 1988). Although all of the elements or subsystems are essential for the systems output, only one or a few of the subsystems will trigger transitions, which, in turn, will lead to system-wide reorganization.

This principle helps explain the heterochronic, asynchronous, and often non-linear character of behavioral ontogeny. We commonly observe "pieces" of a functional behavior long before the performance of the mature behavior. These pieces seem to be used out of sequence, in inappropriate or different functional contexts, only under certain experimental conditions, or otherwise not properly "connected" with the other elements needed for goal-directed activity.

Theories that assume that developmental change is driven by a unified timetable in the form of maturational plans, neurological reorganizations, or cognitive structures have had difficulty accounting for both the anticipations of function and regressions. In this systems approach, we strongly emphasize that contributing components may mature at different rates. The component processes are thus developing in parallel, but not synchronously or symmetric-ally. Figure 24.6 depicts a developing system composed of many component profiles in a heterarchical, rather than a hierarchical assembly. At any point in time, behavior is a compression of these components within a specific task context. This means that some elements of functional actions may be in place long before the performance but may not be manifest until the slowest component allows the system to dynamically assemble in a new form (the *rate-limiting* component).

Because it is the task, not instructions that exist prior to the task, which assembles the components, these subsystems may be opportunistically appropri-ated for different actions for different ontogenetic goals. The component is continuously available, but as it is only manifest in a task, its expression is task

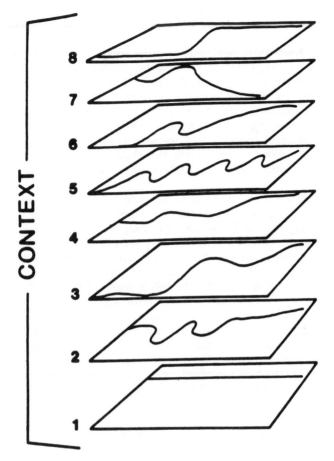

Figure 24.6 Developing systems pictured as a layered ensemble of subsystems, each with its own developmental trajectory. The low-dimensional behavior (collective variable) is assembled only within a contextual frame. No subsystem has hierarchical priority.

specific. For example, leg kicks may be used by young infants as expressive or exploratory behaviors, although these coordinated activities may be later recruited for locomotor systems. Fogel and Thelen (1987) and Thelen (1981) give other examples of coordinative patterns transiently recruited for tasks quite unrelated to their mature forms.

How Control Parameters Drive Developmental Change

Scalar Changes in a Single Control Parameter. In particular, we have proposed that control parameters can act to trigger developmental transitions in two ways. First, there may be scalar changes in one or more existing components that reach the critical values that initiate a phase shift. These may be identified at many levels of analysis: incremental growth in anatomical systems, increase (or decrease) of neural elements or concentrations of neurotransmitters, changing perceptual, cognitive or motor abilities or memory capacity, or change of attentional mechanisms.

Contextual factors may, however, be equally potent in effecting the appearance of new forms. We have especially stressed the role of the social partners of young animals in promoting developmental change (Fogel and Thelen, 1987). Social conspecifics often create contexts that support or facilitate the organization of systems by substituting for organismic elements that are later developing. Human parents, for example, continually provide access to objects, appropriate "frames" for social dialogue, correctly scaled language opportunities, and so on, which provide a task context within which the child's organismic capabilities may coalesce. Without these supportive contexts, the infant performs at a less mature level.

I offer the phenomenon of the newborn stepping response as an illustration of how, in a systems approach, a scalar change in a crucial control parameter can lead to the emergence (or in this case, the disappearance!) of ontogenetic forms. The regression of the coordinated stepping seen in normal newborns has conventionally been interpreted as the result of maturing cortical inhibitory centers. Donna Fisher and I (Thelen and Fisher, 1982) found, however, that a simple contextual manipulation – placing the infant supine – "restored" the patterned behavior even in infants who performed no steps when held upright. We proposed that the developmental transition from stepping to no-stepping was triggered by a simple, nonneural scaling of a body composition parameter, the increase of nonmuscular or fat tissue, which made the legs comparatively heavy and weak and prevented the infant from lifting the leg upright, but only when the infant was in the biomechanically demanding upright posture (Thelen and Fisher, 1982). My colleagues and I have shown that stepping in young infants can be elicited or supressed by a number of contextual manipulations that systematically change the biomechanical demands on the legs, including postural changes, submerging in water, adding weights, and placing infants on motorized treadmills (Thelen, 1986a; Thelen et al., 1984; Thelen et al., 1982).

In dynamic systems terminology, then, the low-dimensional behavior of stepping, characterized by a definable relation between the excursions of the joints of each limb and between the two legs, is not a product of some abstract "program" for stepping that exists before the performance. Rather, it is the interaction of the contributing components, including the biomechanical elements in relation to a specific task context, which determines whether the infant steps or does not step. The body composition control parameter effects a developmental shift in one context, but perhaps not in other contexts. In other words, under certain conditions, the stepping topography represents a preferred and stable output of the system. Changing the internal or external conditions causes the system to reassemble in another attractor state. We therefore cannot define the system removed from the context.

The Control Parameters Themselves Change During Ontogeny. Conventional single-causal models of developmental change assume that the control parameter in any one domain remains stationary over long periods of developmental time (i.e. that cognitive reorganizations or cortical growth organize diverse aspects of

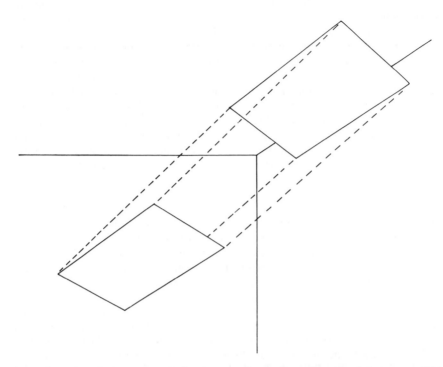

Figure 24.7 Developing system depicted as a surface in three-dimensional state space. With time, the surface itself migrates in the space, resulting in changing control parameters.

behavior over a long time span). Our systems view, however, proposes that the control parameters themselves shift as the contributing components grow and differentiate and as the physical and social contexts of the organism change as a result of its development. This is the second source of transitions. The process of development itself is nonlinear, and as the systems regroup and coalesce, these nonlinearities serve as a continuing wellspring for new forms. In figure 24.7, I represent these changing control parameters as the migration of a surface in three-dimensional state space.

Control parameters for developmental shifts at different ages and in different domains cannot be identified *a priori*. Identifying the sources of change remains an empirical exercise at every level of analysis. This is important because sometimes it is the nonobvious contributions to the system that drive the shift, as I illustrated with the newborn stepping system. Although, for example, the onset of verbal language appears to reflect a major cognitive reorganization, it is at least an open possibility that what in fact delimits the appearance of words is articulatory control over the vocal apparatus. Thus, although brain development may be a necessary condition for the appearance of new behavioral modes, it may not be sufficient, because we can never assume a one-to-one mapping of the structural basis of behavior and its performance in any individual or at any time. We can find many other instances of developing systems where only careful experimental analysis can dissect the interacting systems to reveal the driving subsystems.

For example, coordinated stepping behavior while upright reappears in the repertoire of normal infants at about ten months. I have proposed elsewhere that the control parameter driving this developmental shift (from no-stepping to stepping) is different from the one responsible for the earlier transition (Thelen, 1984). In particular, voluntary walking emerges when elements of both balance and extensor muscle strength reach values critical for allowing infants to support their weight on one leg in a stable manner while the other is lifted for the step. When we support newly stepping infants by holding their hands, or by providing then with walkers, we augment these control parameters and allow the system to display its more mature patterns (i.e. infants can successfully step).

Adaptive Behavior Emerges from Successive Bifurcations

Ontogenetic systems thus increase in complexity by a cascade of successive bifurcations or phase shifts. As the system reorganizes through the scalar change in a component, the newly emergent forms themselves act as control parameters. Changes in any one domain therefore may become amplified and have system-wide reverberations. What may appear to be a small change or acquisition may trigger a succession of major developmental landmarks – I provide examples here. I emphasize, however, that the track of successive bifurcations is a stochastic rather than a deterministic process. Ontogenetic outcomes are similar in the members of a species because certain attractor regimes are dynamically stable and certain configurations are more likely than others. Individual differences are possible because the fluctuations of the internal and external millieu provide elements of uncertainty and because the collective variable is exquisitely sensitive to the task. That is, the system may find alternative configurations to meet task constraints. For example, the task of moving toward a goal may be accomplished by young infants by a variety of locomotor modes – rolling, crawling, creeping, scooting, propelling in a wheeled device, and so on. The precise configuration is a function of the maturational and motivational state of the infant and the constraints of the support surface, provision of the wheeled device and so on.

Phase Transitions Result from the Amplification of Fluctuations

By what processes do control parameters induce changes of form? In complex systems, change results from the amplification of naturally occurring fluctuations or instabilities as the control parameter is scaled passed a critical value (Kelso et al., 1986).

As a result of their complexity and multiple degrees of freedom, biological systems are *dynamically* stable. This means that they exist within a range of possible states and fluctuate among those states. As one component is gradually changed, there exists a point where the coalition of elements is no longer stable. Normal fluctuations become amplified until this noise disrupts the dynamic stability and the system autonomously reorganizes into a new stable state. Note again that fluctuations may become amplified from such control parameters acting outside as well as within the organism (figure 24.8).

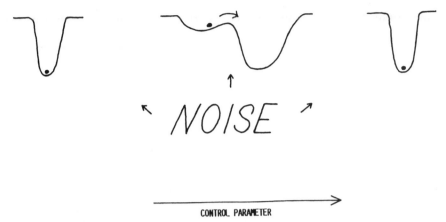

CONTROL PARAMETER

Figure 24.8 Phase shifts result from the amplification of normally occuring fluctuations or noise. The stability of a complex system is depicted in the steepness of a potential well; stable systems have steep wells. It is difficult to dislodge the ball from the steep well. At certain values of a control parameter, the internal fluctuations overwhelm the system stability and the system seeks new stable modes.

Stability can be measured in complex systems in two ways. First, if the system is driven by a small perturbation away from its stationary state, it will tend to return to that stationary state. The time it takes to return to stationarity is a function of the stability of the system, and surprisingly, independent of the size of the perturbation, if it is small. Second, the inherent noise in any system acts as perturbations on the behavior. If the system is stable, the noise produces few variations from the stable state. At points of instability, however, the noise drives the collective behavior into more variable manifestations (figure 24.8).

From these considerations, we can make two powerful predictions about nonequilibrium systems at the point of phase transitions. First, that we should be able to detect the essential enhanced fluctuations at phase transitions in the form of increased variability in our behavioral measure. (This assumes we have chosen the correct collective variable to describe the behavior of interest, a nontrivial problem and one I discuss further later.) Second, because the system is inherently less stable at these transitions, it should be more sensitive to perturbations and thus restore itself to its stable attractor more slowly when perturbed.

These predictions were rigorously confirmed in the bilateral rhythmical finger movement experiments by Kelso and colleagues previously mentioned. These investigators found clear evidence of enhanced fluctuations in the relative phase measure just before and during the spontaneous phase shift from out-of-phase to in-phase coordination (Kelso et al., 1986). In addition, when they mechanically perturbed the movements, they observed a slower return to an equilibrium state at or near the phase transition (Scholz et al., 1987).

What does this mean for developing organisms? That ontogenic change results from a dialetic process of equilibrium arising from disequilibrium has long been a feature of developmental theories, including those of Piaget, Vygotsky, Lerner,

Langer, Riegel, Overton, and Werner. However, the empirical instantiation of equilibration has been of little concern. Certainly, contemporary Piagetian research has centered more on the validity of a structural approach and the validation of invariant sequences than on Piaget's actual process of change.

If phase shifts through amplification of fluctuations are characteristic of systems in general, we should, by using the appropriate empirical strategy, be able to detect these phenomona. Indeed, such a demonstration would offer strong support to the autonomous or self-organizing abilities of developing systems.

Using Dynamical Systems Principles to Understand Development: Some Examples

Thelen et al. (1987) and Fogel and Thelen (1987) show how dynamic principles can help explain persistent puzzling aspects of early motor and expressive-communicative development. Here I present some additional examples.

Behavioral States in the Newborn Period: Self-organization and Phase Shifts

Thelen et al. (1987) suggested that the clustering of discrete variables seen in newborn state behavior was an important illustration of phase shifts or discontinuities in behavioral organization. Wolff (1987) has recently written an eloquent analysis of state behavior from a dynamic systems perspective.

In this treatment, Wolff emphasized the nonlinearity of state as a behavioral organizer in the newborn period. This nonlinearity means that there is no one-to-one correspondence between the input to the system and its response. Newborns are indeed very nonlinear: Their motor patterns form discrete clusters, and a stimulus presented in one cluster (such as sleep) may lead to a very different response than when the identical stimulus is presented during another cluster (such as alert wakefulness). Transitions from one behavioral state to another usually occur relatively abruptly, with unstable intermediate conditions.

Wolff explicitly rejected the traditional conceptualization of infant state as points along a continuum of behavioral arousal or activation. The traditional view assumes that one central agency such as the brainstem drives the discrete motor patterns, but is extrinsic to them. Rather, the cluster of behaviors we identify as state, Wolff argued, represent self-organizing aggregates of movement patterns, which are stable and resist perturbation. No outside executive assembles these clusters; states "fall out" because the system can exist only in one of several stable attractor regimes. These attractor regimes may themselves be different as development progresses; that is, the ensemble of interactive motor patterns may change with age.

Presumably, a number of control parameters can disrupt the dynamic stability of one state and lead to a qualitative shift to a new state. If a sleeping infant is tickled very gently, he or she may remain asleep, however, if we increase the tactile stimulation, there will likely be a point where the stability of the sleep state is disrupted, and the infant awakens. If he or she immediately falls asleep again, we would judge the infants sleep state to be very deep; that is, the attractor regime is very stable. If the infant stays awake, we could assume that she was close to the transition point to wakefulness and the tickling acted as a control parameter driving the phase shift. Likewise, nonnutritive sucking may be the control parameter to shift the fussy infant into a more quiet state (see also Fogel and Thelen, 1987).

Evidence from the early development of sleep states supports this self-assembly view. In premature infants, differentiation of active and quiet sleep states occurs progressively with age from a more indeterminate sleep type. Curzi-Dascalova et al. (1988) showed that this differentiation could be characterized by the association of increasing numbers of state criteria behaviors from 31 to 41 weeks of gestational age. 'They recorded EEG, eye movements, tonic chin EMG, gross limb movements, and respiration. In the youngest premature infants, only the EEG and eye movement patterns "hung together" to distinguish active and quiet states from indeterminate sleep. By 41 weeks, states were reliably characterized by larger constellations of variables. As sleep states entrap more components, they also become more stable, in terms of well-defined and regular cycles. State development looks not so much like the maturation of a single controlling structure as the progressive strengthening of stable attractor states that serve, in turn, as major organizers of behavior.

Variability and Instability at Phase Shifts: Three Examples

The three examples I offer – two recent human studies and the well-studied weaning period in rat pups – fulfill dynamic predictions: that increased variability and more sensitivity to perturbation will accompany ontogenetic transitions.

Postural Stability. Shumway-Cook and Woollacott (1985) studied the development of postural stability in three groups of children aged 15–31 months, 4–6 years, and 7–10 years. The children stood on a moveable platform that provided a rapid forward or backward displacement of a few centimeters to which subjects respond by an appropriate postural compensation. The experimenters measured the onset latency of the contraction of the stabilizing muscle groups in the lower leg and the delay between the onset of the activation of the lower leg and thigh muscles over a number of trials. The oldest group of children and adults showed consistent responses that rapidly adapted over succeeding trials; that is, the subjects damped their responses to minimize overcompensation to the perturbation. The youngest children also showed consistent, rather longer latency responses, but they did not habituate to the destablizing trials – a less mature strategy. In the transition group of four to six-year-olds, the response latencies were not only significantly longer than in the younger and older groups, but also the variability was greatly increased, both within and between subjects (figure 24.9). Postural compensation, like stepping, is a dynamic product of the neurological mechanisms detecting the perturbation and producing the corrective response and biomechanical considerations, in this case, the natural sway frequency of the body. (Children have a faster sway rate than adults, Forssberg and Nashner, 1982.) These authors speculated that the rapid change of body proportion seen in the 4–6 age range may have disrupted the stable, but less adaptable, earlier stage. In dynamic terminology, the body proportion may have acted as one (although likely not the only) control parameter. In addition, the

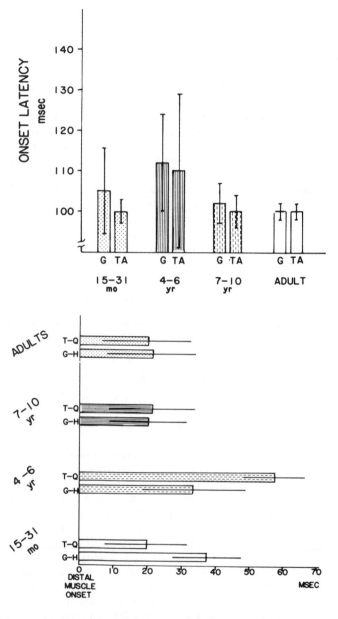

Figure 24.9 (A) Average onset latency (+ SD) In the appropriate distal muscle in response to a forward sway translation (G) or backward sway translation (TA) as a function of age. Response latencies are slower and more variable in children 4–6. (B) Temporal delay between distal and proximal muscle activation as a function of age. Children ages 4–6 demonstrate greatest temporal delay in activation of proximal muscles suggesting diminished synergic coupling between distal and proximal muscles. (From Shumway-Cook and Woollacott, 1985, reprinted with permission.)

four to six year-old group performed more poorly when they were given discrepant information about their postural stability from two sensory modalities, vision and ankle and foot proprioception. Younger infants apparently rely largely on visual input, whereas older subjects are able to rapidly integrate the two sources. In the transition group, however, the perturbation proved to be much more disruptive.

Piagetian Conservation. Church and Goldin-Meadow (1986) presented a compelling measure of instability in transitions in a classic Piagetian conservation task. When these authors asked five to eight year-old children to explain their conservation judgments nearly all children gestured spontaneously as they spoke. Some children, however, conveyed information in their gestures about the task that did not match the information of their spoken explanation. These "discordant" children were far less consistent in the nature of their explanations of the various conservation tasks and in matching the actual judgment of conservation with their explanation. These authors suggested that the discordant children "appeared to have pieces of information that they had not yet consolidated into a coherent explanatory system" (p. 59). In dynamic terms, the tasks did not elicit a stable attractor state – either conservation or nonconservation. If we consider verbal production as one compression of the degrees of freedom and gestural production as yet another way that the system can reduce the dimensionality for a lower dimensional output, we have a dramatic example of the fluid assembly of the components, especially at a time when system has not settled in to a more stable regime.

Indeed, the children in the discordant group proved to be much more sensitive to environmental perturbations. When the experimenters explicitly trained these children on conservation principles or even just allowed them practice with the materials, the children improved both on their judgments and on their explanations. Concordant children did not benefit from training. This intervention, therefore, acted as the crucial control parameter that pushed the unstable system into new forms. The stable systems of the concordant children could not be disrupted. It is consistent with a Piagetian interpretation to conclude that naturally occurring experience with conservation-like tasks would eventually shift the system into the conserving mode.

Weaning in Rat Pups. In the rat pup, the shift from suckling to independent ingestion of food is a well-defined behavioral transition. In the first two weeks of life, rats meet their nutritional needs exclusively by suckling and after 28 days they only eat and drink independently. The shift in feeding modes is most pronounced between days 21 and 24 (Hall and Williams, 1983).

Although under natural conditions the transition is relatively discrete, experimental manipulations have revealed that the process is a complex one, reflecting the synergetic and symbiotic relationship between the behavior and physiology of both the mother and the pup. Noteworthy from the present systems view is the mobility of the component subsystems and their ability to coalesce in particular task-specific configurations that can be relatively independent of age.

For example, although the rat pups do not normally eat and drink independently for several weeks after birth, Hall and Bryan (1980) have shown that even newborn rat pups will ingest liquid or semisolid food from the floor of a test chamber. In young pups, this oral activity was activated only when the ambient temperature was high. The presence of food and external warmth served as control parameters to shift the rat pups into an ontogenetically more mature performance, independent ingestion.

Equally intriguing is the demonstration by Pfister et al. (1986) of a context-determined prolongation of suckling. These experimenters provided weaning-aged rat pups with a succession of nursing dams and their 16- to 21-day-old litters. Under these conditions, rats continued to nurse until as much as 70 days of age, long beyond the time they were eating independently, but they attached to the nipple and withdrew milk only when the younger littermates had attached. A combination of the social facilitation of nursing littermates, a dam who allowed continued nursing, and the continuation of the suckling experience here coalesced to maintain the animal in a stable state characteristic of an earlier ontogenetic stage.

It is noteworthy that during the natural weaning transition, ingestive behavior in a choice situation was highly variable and subject to disruption. The youngest rat pups in Stoloff and Blass's (1983) forced choice experiment consistently chose to suckle and the over 28-day group never chose suckling over eating. However, the 21–24 day transition group exhibited highly unstable and variable responses, and their choice behavior was described as "markedly affected by each manipulation undertaken in this experiment" (p. 451).

These results make it unlikely that there is a "weaning clock" somewhere in the rat pup, ticking off time or metering out some "weaning substance." Rather, weaning may be a phenomena emergent from this confluence of ongoing systems, each with constraints and demands. In recently completed work, Thiels (1987) has shown that at the weaning transition, rat pups show increases not only in independent eating and drinking, *but also in many other actions as well* (see figure 24.10). The increased locomotor ability of the pup, its increased size and energy demands, its abilities to move away from the mother to seek food, and so on, are all contributions to the weaning transition and potential control parameters. No specific weaning instructions need be invoked. Weaning falls out, so to speak, from an ensemble of dynamic processes.

The Development of Early Lateral Preferences: Phase Shifts and Attractors

By the age of two, human children show lateral preferences for hand use almost as consistently as adults. Developmentalists have long been intrigued with the developmental origins of laterality, especially because hemispheric specialization for manual behavior may be related to specialization for speech. Nonetheless, it is not easy to determine when and how this preference is manifested in infancy. Lateral preferences often appear to wax and wane, making prediction from infant hand use to adult handedness very difficult.

The strong, predominantly rightward, asymmetrical head posture seen in the newborn period makes it likely that the central nervous system is laterally biased from birth. Indeed, neonatal head preference is a good predictor of hand-use preference in the second year (Michel and Harkins, 1986). There is considerable

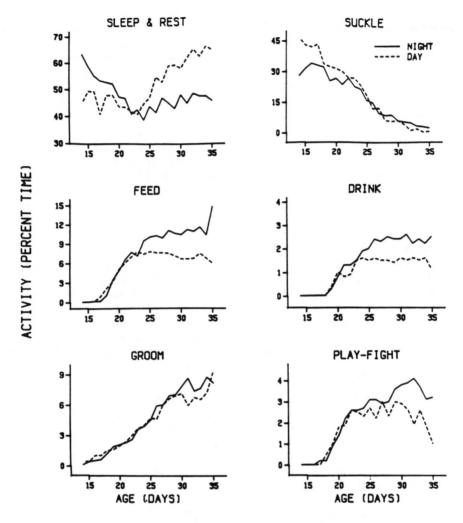

Figure 24.10 Percent time rat pups spend in various activities as a function of age. Note increase of many independent functions between ages 20–25 days. (From Thiels, 1987, reprinted with permission.)

debate over whether the asymmetries of head posture are manifestations of the same lateralities that are later expressed in handedness, or whether these head postures induce handedness through biasing hand–eye contact and arm movements (see Young et al. (1983) for further elaboration of this debate and several models of laterality development).

In a recent review, Michel (in press) offered a plausible scenario by which the initial head biasing has cascading effects leading to eventual laterality in handedness. Head orientation leads to an asymmetry of visual regard of the hand and arm movement, which in turn, may induce asymmetrical reaching, and later manipulation. Thus, the infant's own experiences generate laterality in progress- ively developing skills.

If, however, the system is inherently biased, why is infant handedness so shifting and unstable? Michel suggested that the actual manifestation of the preferred hand is a function of both the infant's level of manual skill and the particular task. For example, Michel et al. (1986) tested 6- to 13-month-old infants for lateral preference in three manual skills: reaching for objects, manipulating objects, and coordinating complementary bimanual actions. Infants generally showed consistent hand-use preferences among the tasks (and about 75 percent were right handed). However, there were some surprising shifts. Although all of the 12-month-old infants preferred the same hand for reaching and bimanual manipulation, 56 percent of the 13-month-olds chose the opposite hand for bimanual manipulations from the hand they used for reaching. It is important to note that bimanual manipulation becomes a common skill for infants only in about the twelfth month. Michel speculated that many of the reaches of the 13-month-old infants were with the nonpreferred hand so that the preferred hand could be left free to begin bimanual manipulation. When bimanual manipulation becomes practiced, presum- ably infants could both reach and manipulate with the preferred hand. Lateral preference is a useful metric only when combined with a task analysis.

This account of lateral preference is consistent with a dynamic systems view. Let us depict strong, adult-like lateral preferences for hand use as two point attractors whose stability is represented by the steepness of the well seen at the bottom left of figure 24.11. The attractor for the right hand is very strong; the ball "prefers" to roll to the bottom of the well and will return there very quickly when perturbed. Right-handed people may be able to use the left hand for some tasks, but they prefer not to under ordinary circumstances. However, if their right arms were in a cast and sling, they would recruit the left hand to do tasks not ordinarily undertaken. That is, given a strong perturbation (broken arm), the ball can be shaken out of the deep well into another attractor state (left hand use), as a qualitative phase shift.

We can characterize newborn head posture as a relatively strong attractor, which entrains the arm and hand system to become progressively more laterally differentiated. However, in the transitional period, the attractor basins are shallow. Even rather small perturbations will drive the ball out of the well, up over the wall, and into the opposite hand attractor. The system is especially sensitive to the task and skill-level interaction because each new demand acts as a perturbation. Thus, the onset of bimanual manipulation acts as a control parameter and disrupts the stability of the reaching laterality, leading to a phase shift.

How does this account differ from a model of development as simply increasing hemispheric laterality? Here I emphasize the systems nature of lateral preference, which is always assembled "softly" in relation to the task and action patterns available to the infant. The system prefers certain places in the state space, but it is not restricted to them. Accomplishing the task is always a higher priority than the particular means by which the infant executes the action, so that the attractors are shallow enough to allow for flexibility in the face of obstacles. Likewise, the system becomes lateralized only as it supports adaptive actions. At the same time, the hand use attractors are becoming lateralized and stable, the

LATERALITY STATUS

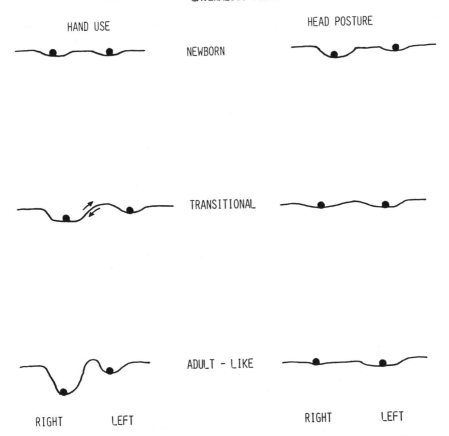

Figure 24.11 Lateral preference depicted as a series of point attractor states. Hand use attractors are the left-hand panel, head posture attractors on the right hand panel. Transitional states are bistable and are especially sensitive to task context.

head posture attractors are becoming progressively weaker. It is not adaptive for action to have an obligatory, or even strongly preferred head posture. Similarly, spontaneous leg movements develop from an initial strong asymmetry to symmetrical activity, reflecting the demands of locomotion and postural support for bilateral symmetry (Thelen et al., 1983).

Although hand use preference may indeed reflect an increasing hemispheric specialization, this explanation alone misses the richness and complexity of the process of change over time. We sometimes view the nonlinearity and nonstationary of behavior over time as noise in the smooth trajectory toward maturity. The lesson from nonlinear dynamical systems is that these aberrations are the very stuff of ontogenetic change. It is at these transitions that the system reveals what holds it together and what drives it to new forms. A synergetic strategy of development will exploit these nonlinearities for a deeper understanding of process.

An Empirical Strategy Based on Systems Principles

We know that self-organizing phenomena in physics, chemistry, and some biological systems may be modeled with precision and elegance. This goal may not be attainable with behaving and developing organisms. Can principles of complex systems help developmentalists in our everyday unraveling of real life behavior? Do we have just another set of agreeable postulates which are neither objectionable nor useful?

I believe the lessons from complex systems analysis can serve developmentalists well, not only as a conceptual framework, but as an empirical strategy that is independent of level and content domain. Nothing I propose here for operationalizing systems is, in itself, new. Developmentalists have been using these methods – observational, longitudinal, experimental – since the adoption of scientific methods for studying ontogeny. What may be new, however, is the systematic linking of these strategies to synergetic principles:

1 The focus is on process not just outcome measures.
2 No component or subsystem has ontological priority.
3 Task and context, not instructions, assemble behavior.
4 Control parameters are not stationary. (The state space itself evolves through time.)

The first requirement for a systems approach is to identify the essential collective variables and their behavior. What is the best way to describe, for any particular organism and set of developmental questions, how the system compresses the degrees of freedom? Note that this description of the collective states can be done in many domains and at many levels of analysis. For infant animals, this may be a measure of perceptual performance or motor output, a psycho-physiological measure, or variables indexing social interaction. The dynamical description is level-independent. However, the choice of an appropriate collective variable is neither a trivial nor a simple matter because ontogeny is so often nonlinear. Because we are interested in the processes of developmental change, it is likely that our first approach would be longitudinal. For animals like humans, where significant individual variability often renders group means meaningless, the analysis may require a case-study design.

Because we assume in this perspective that the task or context, not pre-existing instructions, assembles the system into a measurable collective variable, it is essential that our developmental descriptions also contain a task analysis. This also may be difficult, especially in long-term longitudinal studies, because the meaning of the task or context itself changes with the development of the infant. For example, grasping a 1-inch cube is not the same task for a three-month-old as for a 12-month-old simply because of the body scale changes in the dimensions of the hand relative to the object (Newell, 1986). Nonetheless, it is a mistake to assume that sources of developmental shifts are organismic when they may indeed be in the match between the organism and the task.

The second step in this analysis is to identify the developmental transitions or where the organism shifts from one stable mode of performance to a new mode. Again, if there is variability in the age-dependent onset of new behaviors, or if complex contextual eliciting factors are involved, such shifts may be best discovered in the course of individual developmental profiles. Synergetic theory predicts that at such transitions, the system will show enhanced fluctuations and loss of stability. In developmental data we would expect an increase in the variability of our collective variable – that is, an increase in the deviations from the mean performance when compared to either the earlier stable performance or the new behavioral mode.

Experimentally induced perturbations or facilitations at the point of transitions can test the stability of the system. Developmentalists may probe a transition by experimentally perturbing the infant with an appropriate contextual manipulation (or, in nonhuman species, a surgical or pharmacological intervention). Systems near phase transitions are predicted to recover more slowly than those in more stable states.

The third, and crucial, step is to try to identify the control parameters: the one or few variables in the complex system that drives the shift. How can this be done? First, we would expect that a component or subsystem acting as a control parameter would itself show scalar changes in the time period of the phase transition. One clue to identifying control parameters is to look for variables that themselves change rapidly prior to or during the phase shift. This is not foolproof, however! In dynamic systems even small changes in crucial scalars can amplify fluctuations and lead to new equilibrium states.

If we understand our developing organism fairly well, we can make reasonable guesses about which components may drive developmental systems. Nonetheless, it may be a mistake to assume a control parameter *a priori*. A more fruitful strategy would be to map several likely control parameters so that they may be tested individually.

Once candidates for control parameters are identified, we can perform experimental manipulations or exploit the natural variability among individuals to confirm whether changes in the single parameter drive the system reorganization. The former tactic is more easily employed if we can discover a contextual manipulation that will serve as a substitute for a natural control parameter. In humans, neural or organismic variables may need correlational methods or observation of nonnormal populations.

The final step in a synergetic strategy would be the integration of the different levels of description. In the abstract, the dynamics at the neural level should be coupled to the dynamics at the behavioral level, and so on, regardless of the level used. For example, Kelso and Scholz (1985) have related amplifications in fluctuations at phase transitions seen in the kinematics of finger movements to similar phenomena measured at the level of muscle contractions. Such elegant mappings may be quite difficult over developmental time.

A Synergetic Approach to Locomotor Development

The onset of independent, upright locomotion – learning to walk – can be viewed as a dramatic phase shift in motor development. One day, the infant cannot walk alone, and the next day he or she toddles by herself. Traditional explanations attribute this milestone to maturational changes in an executive function as increasing cortical or cognitive control of movement. My colleagues and I have suggested that walking

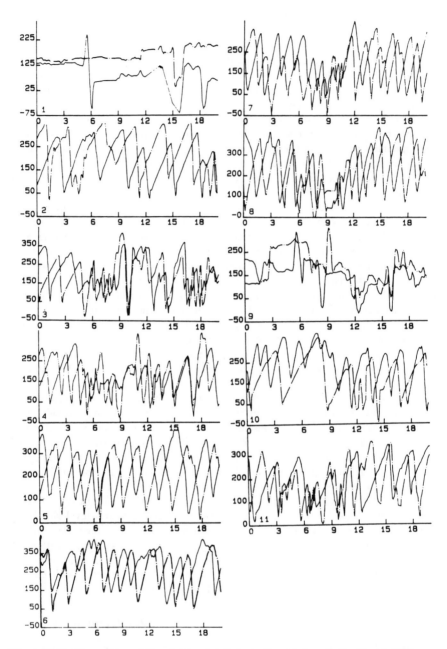

Figure 24.12 Excursions of the right and left foot of an eight-month-old girl (CH) as a function of treadmill speed condition. Trials 1 and 9 are with the belt turned off. In trials 2–8 the speed is gradually increased; the increase occurs after 5 seconds of the trial. Note CH's adjustment. Trials 10 and 11 are "split-belt" trials, where one belt is moving at twice the speed of the opposite belt. Note the continuation of alternation.

alone is not so much commanded as emergent. No "walking" schema *per se* need exist; the behavior is rather the stable compression of many variables in an organism with a particular neural, anatomical, and biomechanical configuration, with certain motivations and goals, and supported on a permissive substrate. The benefit of viewing walking as a multicomponent emergent phenomena is to open a window on how the skill is actually constructed during development.

For a synergetic strategy we must first ask: By what collective variable can we capture the compression of the degrees of freedom involved when people walk? A number of kinematic and kinetic variables might suffice. We focus on one essential characteristic of human bipedal walking: the regular, 180 degrees out-of-phase alternation of the legs needed to maintain both upright stability and forward progress. (Humans could use other symmetrical gait patterns such as hopping or galloping, but presumably they are less efficient.) When infants begin to locomote in the upright position, they use an alternating gait, although they are more variable in their phasing than in older toddlers and children (Clark et al., 1988). How do they acquire this ability? Is this a pattern that emerges with independent locomotion? What component skills do infants need to step? How does the environment support this skill?

Infants are capable of regularly alternating movements of their legs long before the onset of upright locomotion. Even in the newborn period, supine leg kicks may alternate, but the limbs appear loosely coupled. Throughout the first year, leg kicks seem to be like a weak, cyclic attractor. Alternation is a preferred, but not very stable state (Thelen, 1985).

This stability greatly increased, however, with a simple contextual manipulation. When I supported seven-month-old infants, who normally do not step, over a motorized treadmill, I saw dramatic increases not only in their step rate, but in the strictly alternating excursions of their limbs (Thelen, 1986). These treadmill steps were not simple reflexes, but dynamic and adaptive motor coordinations. Infants not only adjusted their step rate in accord with the speed of the treadmill in a manner identical to independent walkers, but also were able to compensate for extreme perturbations – one leg driven at twice the speed of the opposite leg – to maintain the right–left alternation (Thelen et al., 1987). It is unlikely that, at seven months, either the onset of stepping or the continual compensations were mediated by conscious or voluntary processes.

Figure 24.12 illustrates such leg alternation in a single eight-month-old infant girl (CH). CH's leg excursions were tracked by means of an optico-electronic motion detection system through a series of trials beginning with the treadmill belts turned off and continuing through seven more trials where the speed of the belts was gradually scaled up. The speed adjustment was made after 5 seconds in each trial except the first moving belt trial. It is easy to see where the 5-second perturbation occurred and CH's subsequent adjustment to maintain alternation. After the eighth trial, the belt was again turned off. In this second no-movement trial, CH performed some leg movements, but they were poorly coordinated. Finally, we perturbed coordination by moving one belt twice as fast as the other, but the infant still kept on walking!

Thus, the collective variable of interest is a measure of interlimb phasing – the relative coordination of one limb to another. These patterned movements represent the low-dimensional output of a system composed of many components

– neurological networks, bones, joints, muscles with characteristic strength and tone, and motivational and attentional elements, including the infant's state, physiological parameters, and so on.

We may ask about the developmental course of this coordinative ability, and especially about two transitions. First, at what point in ontogeny does this neuromotor ability develop? Second, what allows coordinated upright stepping to become manifest during the last few months of the first year? Our ultimate question is, which of the essential elements in the system will serve as control parameters in effecting the development shifts?

Beverly Ulrich, my collaborator in this work, and I began our synergetic strategy with an effort to understand the dynamics of our collective variable over developmental time. We used a multiple case-study, longitudinal design by observing nine infants each month from age one month until they walked independently or refused the treadmill (usually between seven and nine months). Each infant participated in two identical experimental sessions each month to assess within-age variability and to elicit optimal performance. The treadmill task is identical to the series of trials just described for infant CH, one of the subjects in the study. In addition, we obtained Bayley scales of motor development, behavioral state assessments, and anthropometric measurements because previous research suggested that these variables affected stepping performance.

I present here some preliminary results in the single infant, CH, to illustrate the paradigm. In figure 24.13, we plot the cycle durations of alternating steps taken by infant CH as a function of age and treadmill speed trial. (Remember that trials 1 and 9 are on stationary belts and that the belt speed was gradually increased in trials 2–8). In general, cycle duration was inversely related to belt speed, but in months 1–3, CH's performance was erratic. By month 4, however, she adjusted her steps to the belt speed, and she continued to do so, although the very fastest belt speeds sometimes appeared to inhibit performance. (We do not know whether this reflected an inability of the legs to cycle at such a high frequency or a fatigue effect, but other infants also showed this decrement at the highest speeds.)

We can also look at a more precise index of bilateral coordination, the relative phasing between the movements of each leg. In mature stepping, the step of cycle of one leg is initiated at 50 percent of the cycle duration of the opposite leg (the limbs are precisely 180 degrees out-of-phase). In figure 24.14, we can see that in the early months, CH's interlimb phasing is very variable, but that it approaches the adult-like 50 percent value more consistently in the second half of the year. The coupling between the limbs becomes tighter. The other infants in our sample showed remarkably similar developmental trends.

These descriptive data give us a picture of the dynamics of change of the ability to coordinate the two legs. Some ability, albeit rather primitive, is manifest at the first month. In CH, we saw no abrupt transitions from no stepping to fully articulated stepping on the treadmill, but rather a gradual increase in steps with age. This suggested that the basic mechanism whereby limbs respond to a backward stretch by alternating swings is in place at a very early age, but that the system is not very stable. The attractor becomes progressively stronger with age.

These results are only the first step in a synergetic strategy; an understanding of the dynamics of our collective variable over developmental time. It is an

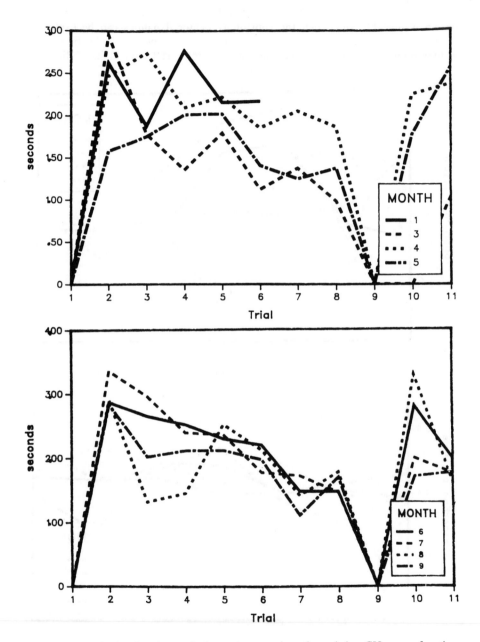

Figure 24.13 Cycle durations of alternating steps performed by CH. as a function of treadmill speed. Each trace represents the "better" day of each month's testing. Trials as in figure 24.12. Note decrease in cycle durations as belt speed increases and increased sensitivity to treadmill speed in especially in months 5–8. CH did not step at all in month 2.

essential (but often laborious) step to identify the points of transition when the system is unstable and when the control parameter dynamics can be explored. In the case of treadmill-elicited stepping, this analysis points to the first three to four months as the period of most rapid change, reflected in instability and

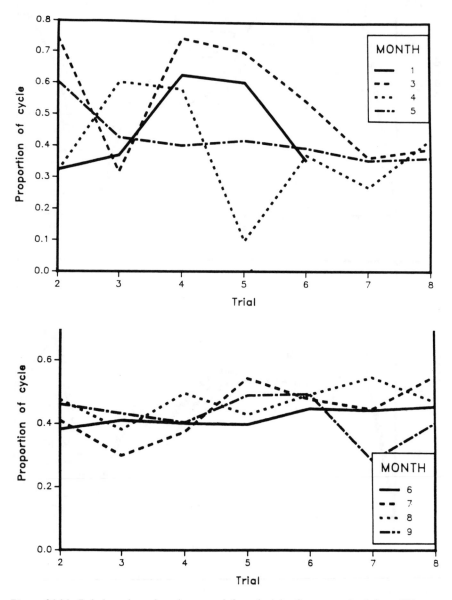

Figure 24.14 Relative phase lags between left and right foot steps in infant CH as a function of age and treadmill speed. Lags are expressed as the proportion of the step cycle of one leg when step in the opposite leg was initiated.

variability. We have some indication of a relative decrement in treadmill performance at months 1 and 2 and then a more rapid improvement. What, then, are the control parameters shifting the system at these transition times?

One source of clues is to look at the other elements of the system indexed by the anthropometric, state, and motor maturity measures. In figure 24.15, for example, we show CH's stepping performance plotted with several other anthropometric indices. The first few months are a time of especially rapid changes in the rate of weight gain, and in measures of chubbiness and leg volume. Do these other system variables act as control parameters for treadmill stepping? Clearly, we cannot answer this question on the basis of correlational and case-study data. Many other things change very rapidly in the first few months of life that may affect this behavior. Nonetheless, this method does allow us to dissect our system to see what components are in place and what components are rapidly changing and may be candidates for control parameters. This then suggests possible experimental manipulations to test causal hypotheses.

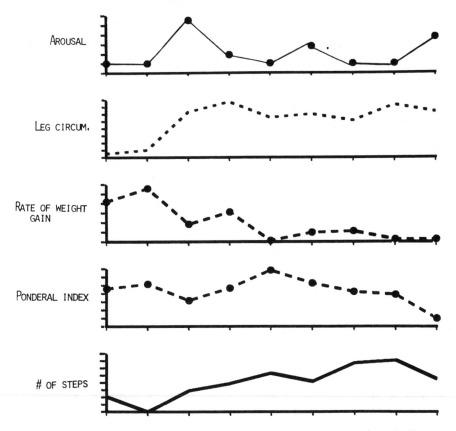

Figure 24.15 Anthropometric measures, "arousal" scale, and number of treadmill steps of infant CH from months 1 through 10. Anthropometric indices include rate of weight gain, summed circumferences of the thigh and calf, and Ponderal Index, weight/length^3. Note that there are rapid changes in the first four months on all variables.

Conclusion

In this view, ontogenetic change is the reorganization of components to meet adaptive tasks. It assigns the sources of new forms to the self-organizing properties of systems that use energy in a particular configuration. Pattern and complexity can emerge from the cooperativity of more simple elements. It says that developing systems are stable and predictable where their adaptive demands have constrained, through phylogenetic mechanisms, their range of solutions. (All mammals must suckle; at birth, the architecture of the suckling system leads to a very stable periodic attractor.) But this view also accounts for the variability and flexibility of these same systems when the task demands are not strict, or when experimental manipulations challenge the developing organisms with unique circumstances. (Suckling can also be curtailed, or prolonged, or the action patterns used for other goals, such as exploration.) Because prescriptions for action do not exist outside of the context that elicits action, components are free to assemble and reassemble within the constraints of the organism and the task. The physical and social context of the developing animal is more than just a supportive frame; it is an essential component of the assembled system. In such systems, new forms arise when the stability of the system is disrupted when random fluctuations are amplified by the scaling of a critical component. The process of developmental change is thus normally accompanied by a period of instability, where the system is exploring, so to speak, another level of stability.

A dynamic systems perspective may require new empirical strategies in which variability is the substance rather than the noise. By identifying developmental transitions, where the system may be "fooled" into progressions and regressions, we can then test the limits of the organism and the context in eliciting new forms. In reality, many developmentalists have implicitly adopted such an empirical strategy; this perspective provides a rationale consistent with pattern-formation processes in other physical and biological systems.

ACKNOWLEDGEMENTS

I thank Scott Kelso and Alan Fogel for their important contributions to the ideas presented here and Beverly Ulrich and David Niles for their invaluable collaboration on the research. This chapter was supported by National Science Foundation Grant BNS 85 09793, National Institutes of Health Grant ROI HD 22830, and a Research Career Development Award from the National Institutes of Health.

REFERENCES

Abraham, R. H., & Shaw, C. D. (1982). *Dynamics – The geomentry of behavior*. Santa Cruz, CA: Aerial Press.

Barnes, D. M. (1986). Brain architecture: Beyond genes. *Science*, 233, 155–156.

Brent, S. B. (1978). Prigogine's model for self-organization in nonequilibrium systems: Its relevance for developmental psychology. *Human Development*, 21, 374–387.

Brent, S. B. (1984). *Psychological and social structures*. Hillsdale, NJ: Lawrence Erlbaum Associates.

Church, R. B., & Goldin-Meadow, S. (1986). The mismatch between gesture and speech as an index of transitional knowledge. *Cognition*, 23, 43–71.

Clark, J. E., Whitall, J., & Phillips, S. J. (1988). Human interlimb coordination: The first 6 months of independent walking. *Developmental Psychobiology*, 21, 445–456.

Cohen, A. H., Holmes, P. J., & Rand, R. H. (1982). The nature of coupling between segmental oscillators of the lamprey spinal generator for locomotion: A mathematical model. *Journal of Mathematical Biology*, 13, 345–369.

Curzi-Dascalova, L., Peirano, P., & Morel-Kahn, F. (1988). Development of sleep states in normal premature and full-term newborns. *Developmental Psychobiology*, 21, 431–444.

Dammasch, I. E., Wagner, G. P., & Wolff, J. R. (1986). Self-stabilization of neural networks, 1: The compensation algorithm for synaptogenesis. *Biological Cybernetics*, 54, 211–222.

Fogel, A., & Thelen, E. (1987). The development of expressive and communicative action in the first year: Reinterpreting the evidence from a dynamic systems perspective. *Developmental Psychology*, 23, 747–761.

Forssberg, H., & Nashner, L. M. (1982). Ontogenetic development of postural control in man: Adaptation to altered support and visual conditions during stance. *Journal of Neuroscience*, 2, 545–552.

French, V., Bryant, P. J., & Bryant, S. V. (1976). Pattern regulation in epimorphic fields. *Science*, 193, 969–981.

Gierer, A. (1981). Generation of biological patterns and form: Some physical, mathematical, and logical aspects. *Progress in Biophysics and Molecular Biology*, 37, 1–47.

Haken, H. (1983). *Synergetics: An introduction*, 3rd edn. Heidelberg, Berlin: Springer-Verlag.

Haken, H. (ed.). (1985). *Complex systems: Operational approaches in neurobiology, physics, and computers*. Heidelberg, Berlin: Springer.

Haken, H., Kelso, J. A. S., & Bunz, H. (1985). A theoretical model of phase transitions in human hand movements. *Biological Cybernetics*, 51, 347–356.

Hall, W. G., & Bryan, T. E. (1980). The ontogeny of feeding in rats. II. Independent ingestive behavior. *Journal of Comparative and Physiological Psychology*, 93, 746–756.

Hall, W. G., & Williams, C. L. (1983). Suckling isn't feeding, or is it? A search for developmental continuities. *Advances in the Study of Behavior*, 13, 219–254.

Haroutunian, S. (1983). *Equilibrium in the balance: A study of psychological explanation*. New York: Springer-Verlag.

Hopfield, J. J., & Tank, D. W. (1986). Computing with neural circuits: A model. *Science*, 233, 625–633.

Kelso, J. A. S., Holt, K. G., Kugler, P. N., & Turvey, M. T. (1980). On the concept of coordinative structures as dissipative structures: II. Empirical lines of convergence. In G. E. Stelmach & J. Requin (eds), *Tutorials in motor behavior* (pp. 49–70). New York: North-Holland.

Kelso, J. A. S., & Scholz, J. P. (1985). Cooperative phenomena in biological motion. In H. Haken (ed.), *Complex systems: Operational approaches in neurobiology, physical systems, and computers* (pp. 124–149). Berlin: Springer.

Kelso, J. A. S., Scholz, J. P., & Schöner, G. (1986). Non-equilibrium phase transitions in coordinated biological motion: Critical fluctuations. *Physics Letters A*, 118, 279–284.

Kelso, J. A. S., & Schöner, G. (in press). Toward a physical (synergetic) theory of biological coordination. In R. Graham (ed.), *Lasers and synergetics*. Heidelberg, Berlin: Springer.

Kelso, J. A. S., & Tuller, B. (1984). A dynamical basis for action systems. In M. S. Gazzaniga (ed.), *Handbook of cognitive neuroscience* (pp. 321–356). New York: Plenum Press.

Kitchener, R. F. (1982). Holism and the organismic model in developmental psychology. *Human Development*, 25, 233–249.

Kugler, P. N., Kelso, J. A. S., & Turvey, M. T. (1980). On the concept of coordinative structures as dissipative structures. I. Theoretical lines of convergence. In G. E. Stelmach & J. Requin (eds), *Tutorials in motor behavior* (pp. 3–47). New York: North Holland.

Kugler, P. N., Kelso, J. A. S., & Turvey, M. T. (1982). On the control and co-ordination of naturally developing systems. In J. A. S. Kelso & J. E. Clark (eds), *The development of movement control and co-ordination* (pp. 5–78). New York: Wiley.

Laszlo, E. (1972). *Introduction to systems philosophy*. New York: Harper & Row.

Lerner, R. M. (1978). Nature, nurture, and dynamic interaction. *Human Development*, 21, 1–20.

Madore, B. F., & Freedman, W. L. (1987). Self-organizing structures. *American Scientist*, 75, 252–259.

Meakin, P. (1986). A new model for biological pattern formation. *Journal of Theoretical Biology*, 118, 101–113.

Michel, G. F. (in press). Self-generated experience and the development of lateralized neurobehavioral organization in infants. In J. S. Rosenblatt (ed.), *Advances in the study of behavior* (Vol. 17). New York: Academic Press.

Michel, G. F., & Harkins, D. A. (1986). Postural and lateral asymmetries in the ontogeny of handedness during infancy. *Developmental Psychobiology*, 19, 247–258.

Michel, G. F., Ovrut, M. R., & Harkins, D. A. (1986). Hand-use preference for reaching and object manipulation in 6- through 13-month-old infants. *Genetic, Social, and General Psychology Monographs*, 111, 409–427.

Mittenthal, J. E. (1981). The rule of normal neighbors: a hypothesis for morphogenetic pattern regulation. *Developmental Biology*, 88, 15–26.

Newell, K. M. (1986). Constraints on the development of coordination. In M. G. Wade & H. T. A. Whiting (eds), *Motor development in children: Aspects of coordination and control* (pp. 341–360). Dordrecht, Netherlands: Martinus Nijhoff Publishers.

Overton, W. F. (1975). General systems, structure, and development. In K. F. Riegel & G. C. Rosenwald (eds), *Structure and transformation: Developmental and historical aspects* (pp. 61–81). New York: Wiley.

Oyama, S. (1985). *The ontogeny of information: Developmental systems and evolution*. Cambridge: Cambridge University Press.

Pfister, J. F., Cramer, C. P., & Blass, E. M. (1986). Suckling in rats extended by continuous living with dams and their preweanling litters. *Animal Behaviour*, 34, 415–420.

Prigogine, I. (1980). *From being to becoming*. San Francisco: W. H. Freeman.

Prigogine, I., & Stengers, I. (1984). *Order out of chaos: Man's new dialogue with nature*. New York: Bantam.

Rumelhart, D. E., & McClelland, J. L. (eds), (1986). *Parallel distributed processing: Explorations in the microstructure of cognition. Vol. I: Foundations*. Cambridge, MA: Bradford Books/MIT Press.

Sameroff, A. J. (1983). Developmental systems: Contexts and evolution. In P. H. Mussen (ed.), *Handbook of child psychology. Vol. I. History, theory, and methods*, 4th edn. (pp. 237–294). New York: Wiley.

Scholz, J. P., Kelso, J. A. S., & Schöner, G. (1987). *Nonequilibrium phase transitions in coordinated biological motion: Critical slowing down and switching time*. Manuscript.

Schöner, G., Haken, H., & Kelso, J. A. S. (1986). A stochastic theory of phase transitions in human hand movement. *Biological Cybernetics*, 53, 1–11.

Shrager, J., Hogg, T., & Huberman, B. A. (1987). Observation of phase transitions in spreading activation networks. *Science*, 236, 1092–1094.

Shumway-Cook, A., & Woollacott, M. H. (1985). The growth of stability: Postural control from a developmental perspective. *Journal of Motor Behavior*, 17, 131–147.

Singer, W. (1986). The brain as a self-organizing system. *European Archives of Psychiatry and Neurological Sciences*, 236, 4–9.

Skarda, C. A., & Freeman, W. J. (1987). How brains make chaos in order to make sense of the world. *Behavioral and Brain Sciences*, 10, 161–195.

Stoloff, M. L., & Blass, E. M. (1983). Changes in appetitive behavior in weanling-age rats: Transitions from suckling to feeding behavior. *Developmental Psychobiology*, 16, 439–453.

Szentagothai, J. (1984). Downward causation? *Annual Review of Neuroscience*, 7, 1–11.

Thelen, E. (1981). Kicking, rocking, and waving: Contextual analysis of rhythmical stereotypes in normal human infants. *Animal Behavior*, 29, 3–11.

Thelen, E. (1984). Learning to walk: Ecological demands and phylogenetic constraints. In L. P. Lipsitt (ed.), *Advances in infancy research, Vol. 3*, (pp. 213–250). Norwood, NJ: Ablex.

Thelen, E. (1985). Developmental origins of motor coordination: Leg movements in human infants. *Developmental Psychobiology*, 18, 1–22.

Thelen, E. (1986a). Treadmill-elicited stepping in seven-month- old infants. *Child Development*, 57, 1498–1506.

Thelen, E. (1986b). Development of coordinated movement: Implications for early development. In H. T. A. Whiting & M. G. Wade (eds), *Motor skill acquisition in children (pp. 107–124). Dordrecht, Netherlands: Martinus Nijhoff.*

Thelen, E. (1988). Dynamical approaches to the development of behavior. In J. A. S. Kelso, A. J. Mandell, & M. R. Shlesinger (eds), *Dynamic patterns in complex systems* (pp. 348–369). Singapore: World Scientific Publishers.

Thelen, E., & Fisher, D. M. (1982). Newborn stepping: An explanation for a "disappearing reflex." *Developmental Psychology*, 18, 760–775.

Thelen, E., Fisher, D. M., & Ridley-Johnson, R. (1983). Shifting patterns of bilateral coordination and lateral dominance in the leg movements of young infants. *Developmental Psychobiology*, 16, 29–46.

Thelen, E., Fisher, D. M., & Ridley-Johnson, R. (1984). The relationship between physical growth and a newborn reflex. *Infant Behavior and Development*, 7, 479–493.

Thelen, E., Fisher, D. M., Ridley-Johnson, R., & Griffin, N. (1982). The effects of body build and arousal on newborn infant stepping. *Developmental Psychobiology*, 15, 447–453.

Thelen, E., & Fogel, A. (in press). Toward an action-based theory of infant development. In J. Lockman & N. Hazen (eds), *Action in social context*. New York: Plenum.

Thelen, E., Kelso, J. A. S., & Fogel, A. (1987). Self-organizing systems and infant motor development. *Developmental Review*, 7, 39–65.

Thelen, E., Ulrich, B., & Niles, D. (1987). Bilateral coordination in human infants: Stepping on a split-belt treadmill. *Journal of Experimental Psychology: Human Perception and Performance*, 13, 405–410.

Thiels, E. (1987). *Behavioral and energetic factors in weaning in Norway rats*. Unpublished doctoral dissertation, Indiana University.

Von Bertalanffy, L. (1968). *General system theory*. New York: George Braziller.

Waddington, C. H. (1972). Form and information. In C. H. Waddington (ed.), *Towards a theoretical biology, Vol. 4* (pp. 109–145). Edinburgh: Edinburgh University Press.

Weiss, P. A. (1969). The living system: determinism stratified. In A. Koestler & J. R. Smithies (eds), *Beyond reductionism: New perspectives in the life sciences* (pp. 3–55). Boston: Beacon Press.

Wolff, P. H. (1987). *The development of behavioral states and the expression of emotions in early infancy: New proposals for investigation*. Chicago: University of Chicago Press.

Woodson, R. H. (1988). Individual, development, and ontogeny. Manuscript. Dept of Psychology. University of Texas at Austin.

Young, G., Segalowitz, S. J., Corter, C. M., & Trehub, S. E. (eds), (1983). *Manual specialization and the developing brain*. New York: Academic Press.

25

Self-organization and Cognitive Change

ANNETTE KARMILOFF-SMITH

1 Introduction

Some years ago Gleitman et al. (1972) made a simple yet thought-provoking statement, which I used as a colophon to an article published in the same journal some 14 years later (Karmiloff-Smith, 1986). What they wrote was: "Young children know something about language that the spider does not know about web weaving." My chapter will not, of course, be about spiders. Rather, my intention is to explore a number of speculations about what it is for a mind to "know" (about language, the physical environment, etc.) and what makes the human mind special in contrast to the innately specified procedures by which the spider produces its seemingly complex web. How can we account for human flexibility and creativity? I shall argue that the only way to understand human cognitive change is to espouse an epistemology that integrates both innate predispositions and constructivism.[1]

Some developmentalists reject any form of innate predispositions as far as the human infant is concerned. Yet they would not hesitate to attribute some innate knowledge to the ant, the spider, the bee or the chimpanzee. Why would Nature have endowed every species except the human with some innate, domain-specific predispositions? Yet, if it turns out that all species have innately specified predispositions, if many can maintain a goal in the face of changing environmental conditions, and if many have the capacity for learning on the basis of interaction with conspecifics and the physical environment, what is special about human

This chapter is an abridged, reorganized and substantially modified version of a chapter entitled "Beyond modularity: innate constraints and developmental change," which appeared in S. Carey and R. Gelmen (eds) (1991) Epigenesis of the Mind: Essays in Biology and Knowledge. Hillsdale, NJ: Erlbaum, 171–97. Retained sections are reprinted here with permission. A few extracts are also taken from Karmiloff-Smith (1992) Beyond Modularity: a Developmental Perspective on Cognitive Science. Cambridge, MA: MIT Press/Bradford Books.

cognition? Is it simply that the *content* of knowledge between species is different? Is it language which makes humans special? Or are there qualitatively different processes at work in the human mind? If we accept innate predispositions for the human infant, does that rule out a constructivist explanation of development?

For many psychologists, accepting a nativist viewpoint precludes constructivism completely. Yet innate predispositions and constructivism are not necessarily incompatible. A now growing number of developmentalists have become dissatisfied with Piaget's account of the human infant as a purely sensorimotor organism with nothing more to start life than a few sensory reflexes and three ill-defined processes like assimilation, accommodation, and equilibration. In the light of the spate of recent infancy research, we have to invoke *some* domain-specific predispositions for the initial architecture of the human mind. Yet, both the early plasticity of the brain and the flexibility of the human mind with subsequent development suggest that a radical nativist/maturational position must be wrong, and that Piaget's constructivism is still a viable way of thinking about development. However, rather than the specifics of Piaget's *psychological* stage theory, it is the more general aspects of Piaget's *epistemology* – his epigenetic view of biology, his constructivist view of knowledge acquistion, his vision of the cognizer as a very active participant in her own cognitive development, and his focus on emergent forms (Piaget, 1967) – that should retain our interest. An attempt at reconciliation between domain-specific innate predispositions and constructivism will thus be an an important thread throughout this essay.

2 Changes in Our View of the Infant Mind

The now growing data on neonates and young infants suggest the existence of some innately constrained, domain-specific attention biases or predispositions. The infant is not assailed by buzzing blooming confusion *à la* James (1892), nor by undifferentiated and chaotically assimilated input *à la* Piaget (1955). Rather, from early infancy, special attention biases channel the way in which the child processes constrained classes of inputs that are numerically relevant, linguistically relevant, relevant to physical properties of objects, to cause – effect relations, and so forth (Anderson, 1992; Baillargéon, 1987a, b; Butterworth, 1981; Cohen, 1988; Diamond and Gilbert, 1989; Gelman, 1990; Jusczyk, 1986; Kellman, 1988; Leslie, 1984; Mehler and Fox, 1985; Rutkowska, 1987; Slater et al., 1983; Spelke, 1988, 1990, 1991; Starkey et al., 1983; and many others too numerous to mention). However, accepting that there are *some* innate underpinnings to human development does not amount to an extreme nativist position. While we need to invoke some built-in constraints, development clearly involves a more dynamic process of interaction between mind and environment than the strict nativist stance presupposes. For indeed, whatever innate component we invoke, it only becomes part of our biological potential in interaction with the environment; it is only latent until it receives input (Johnson, 1988, 1990; Marler, 1991; Oyama, 1985; Thelen, 1989). And that input affects development in return. So we can endorse Piaget's constructivism but give the infant a head start by means of domain-specific predispositions.

The infancy literature abounds with examples of the domain-specific[2] knowledge available to very young infants. The details of the many different experiments need not concern us here (see Karmiloff-Smith, 1992, and Spelke, 1985, for description and discussion). My aim is simply to point to a few examples of what we have recently discovered about infant capacities. For example, Alan Slater and his colleagues (Slater, 1990; Slater and Morison, 1992; Slater et al., 1983, 1990) have demonstrated that newborns already have capacities for shape and size discriminations and constancies. Elizabeth Spelke and her collaborators (Spelke, 1988, 1990, 1991; Kellman and Spelke, 1983; Baillargéon et al., 1986) have shown that three to four month old infants are surprised when viewing an impossible event in which one solid object passes through another. However, it is not until somewhat later that infants show surprise if objects behave as if they were not subject to gravity and in need of stable support. A ball which stops in mid-air before reaching a supporting surface does not surprise three month olds; but it does seven month olds. Renée Baillargéon and her collaborators (Baillargéon, 1987a, 1992, Baillargéon and Hanko-Summers, 1990) also provide examples suggesting that young infants understand certain characteristics of gravity and support relations between objects. Seven to nine month old infants show surprise at certain impossible support relations, but not others that require further learning. Thus, when a symmetrical block is placed on top of another block but the center of gravity of the top object does not lie on the surface of the supporting object, infants show surprise when it does not fall. But when the top object is assymmetrical, it is not until they are older that they show surprise when it does not fall. Baillargéon has also shown that three to four month old infants understand that if one places an object behind a screen that was rotating 180°, the screen can subsequently only rotate some 45°; they show surprise if the screen continues to rotate 180° indicating that they expect objects to persist after they go out of view. Furthermore, four to six month olds show sensitivity to object properties, such as precise height and location. Other experiments have demonstrated young infants' capacity for cross-modal matching between number of objects displayed visually and number of drum beats (Starkey et al., 1983). All of this is a far cry from the picture Piaget depicted of early infancy.

A particularly interesting theoretical discussion of innately specified knowledge and subsequent learning is to be found in the work of Johnson, Morton and their colleagues on infant face recognition (Johnson, 1988, 1990; Johnson and Morton, 1991; Johnson et al., 1991). Extending Johnson's theory of species recognition and imprinting in the domestic chick, the existence of two mechanisms was also postulated for human species recognition. The first mechanism operates from birth and is predominantly mediated by subcortical structures. Newborn infants (within the first hour of life) will track certain types of face- like patterns further than other patterns. The exact stimulus characteristics that give rise to this preferential orientating (which may be as minimal as three high contrast blobs in the appropriate locations for eyes and mouth, or as detailed as the actual features of a human face in their correct locations) are still under investigation. The second mechanism is controlled by cortical structures, but is constrained by the functioning of the first and gains control over behavior at around two months of age. Two months is the age which many authors have identified as the time of onset of cortical control over visually guided behavior (Johnson, 1990). Thus the first system serves to constrain the range of inputs processed by the second system and in some sense "tutors" it before it gains subsequent control over behaviour.

The neonate and infancy data that are now accumulating serve to suggest that the nativists have won the battle in accounting for the *initial structure* of the human mind. So, does that put the constructivists completely out of business? Not necessarily, and for two reasons. First, the infancy research suggests that development involves both some innately specified information *and* subsequent learning, and in both cases the infant is highly dependent on information from the environment, which affects development in return. Second, we know that human cognition manifests flexibility with development. Now, it is true that the greater the amount of primitively fixed formal properties of the infant mind, the more constrained its computational system will be (Chomsky, 1988). In other words, there is a trade-off between the efficiency and automaticity of the infant's innately specified systems, on the one hand, and the rigidity of such systems, on the other. But if systems were to remain rigid, there would be little if any room for cognitive flexibility and creativity. This is where a constructivist stance is essential to understanding development in infancy and beyond. As we draw up a much more complex picture of the rich innate structure of the infant mind and its complex interaction with environmental constraints, cognitive flexibility and creativity require specific theoretical focus within a constructivist epistemology. Thus, for a comprehensive account of human development one must invoke *both* innately specified predispositions and a constructivist view of development.

This leads me to three assumptions about the initial architecture of the human mind that corporate innately specified predispositions and processes which allow for a more constructivist view of development. They are as follows:

1 The human mind has some innately specified information that allows it to attend to persons, objects, space, cause–effect relations, number, language, and so forth, and that channels the way in which it computes these particular inputs. This leads to the establishment of domain-specific representations. Such innately specified predispositions do not, of course, preclude the need for subsequent learning, but they constrain what is subsequently learnt.

2 The human mind has a number of innately specified processes which enable self-description and self-organization. Further, the mind possesses mechanisms for inferential processes, for deductive reasoning and for hypothesis testing.

3 The human mind not only tries to appropriate the external environment that it is set to begin exploring and representing from birth, but it also tries to appropriate its own *internal* representations. I shall argue for a repeated process of representational redescription, i.e. that the human mind re-represents recursively its own internal representations.

3 Different Types of Knowledge Acquisition

How does information get stored in the child's mind? I posit that there are several different ways. First, it is innately specified as a result of evolutionary processes. Innately specified predispositions can either be specific or nonspecific (Johnson and Bolhuis, 1991). When the innate component is specified in detail, environmental input is necessary, but it is likely that in such cases the environment acts simply as a trigger for the organism to select one parameter or circuit over others (Changeux, 1985; Chomsky, 1981; Piattelli-Palmerini, 1989; see also Johnson and Karmiloff-Smith, 1992, for discussion). By contrast, when the innate predisposition is specified merely as a bias or skeletal outline, then it is likely that the environment acts as much more than a trigger, i.e. that it actually influences the subsequent structure of the brain via a rich epigenetic interaction between mind and physical/sociocultural environments. The skeletal outline specifies attention biases towards particular inputs and a certain number of principles constraining the computation of those inputs. Note that I am hypothesizing that the human mind has *both* a certain amount of detailed specification as well as some very skeletal domain-specific predispositions, depending on the domain.

There are several other ways in which new information gets stored in the child's mind. One is when the child fails to reach a goal and has to take into account information from the physical environment. The child uses this feedback information about error to modify its subsequent behavior. Another way in which new information gets stored in the child's mind provided by linguistic statements from others which the child must learn to represent. These are both external sources of change.[3]

Internal sources of change are those which occur without external mediation. One such source might involve a process of modularization, such that input and output processing becomes progressively less influenced by other processes in the brain. This causes knowledge to become more encapsulated and less accessible to other systems. I speculate that a process of modularization, as opposed to the existence of prespecified modules (Fodor, 1983), can occur as the *product* of development (Karmiloff-Smith, 1986; see also Jusczyk and Cohen, 1985). In other words, to the extent that the mind becomes modularized, this occurs *as development proceeds*. It is plausible that a number of innately specified predispositions would suffice to constrain the class of inputs that the infant mind computes. With time, brain circuits would be progressively selected for different domain-specific computations and the formation of domain-specific representations, leading, in certain cases, to relatively encapsulated modules. Note that when I use the term "innately specified" I do not mean to imply anything like a genetic blueprint for prespecified modules. Rather, I argue for a form of development that is more dynamic and epigenetic than Fodor's nativism.

While one direction of development involves a process of modularization in which information becomes *less* accessible, another essential facet of cognitive change goes in the opposite direction. It is one in which knowledge becomes progressively *more* accessible. This leads me to another way in which new knowledge can be acquired.

My claim is that a specifically human way to gain knowledge is for the mind to exploit internally the information that it has already stored by redescribing its representations or, more precisely, by iteratively *re*-representing in different representational formats what its internal representations represent. This process may be triggered by external constraints but it is often self-generating, i.e. it can occur outside input/output relations. I shall return to this in more detail below.

Finally, there is a form of knowledge change which is more obviously solely the prerogative of the human species, i.e. explicit theory change. This involves conscious construction and exploration of analogies, thought experiments, real experiments, limiting case analyses, etc., typical of older children and adults (Carey, 1985; Inhelder and Piaget, 1958; Karmiloff-Smith, 1988; Klahr and Dunbar, 1988; Kuhn et al., 1988; Piaget et al., 1978). But I will argue that this more obvious characteristic of human cognition is only possible on the basis of prior representational redescription, which turns *implicit* information into *explicit* knowledge.

Gaining knowledge via the representational redescription and restructuring of knowledge already stored has been the focus of almost all my work in linguistic and cognitive development. My research strategy has thus been to focus on age groups where efficient output is already present and then to trace subsequent representational change. The process of representational redescription is posited to take place repeatedly throughout development. In other words, each level of redescription is not linked to a *stage* of development, but is part of reiterated *phases* of development within each cognitive domain.

4   The Process of Representational Redescription

Full details of the model of representational redescription and empirical examples from many different cognitive domains can be found elsewhere (Karmiloff-Smith, 1992). Here I shall merely mention some of the main aspects of the process relevant to self-organization and cognitive change. The model of representational redescription (the RR model, for short) postulates that the mind stores multiple redescriptions of knowledge at different levels and in different types of representational format which are increasingly explicit and accessible. At the initial level, I argue that representations are in the form of procedures for responding to and analyzing stimuli in the external environment. A number of constraints are operative on the type of representations that are formed at this level:

1   Information is encoded in procedural form.
2   Within procedures components are sequentially specified.
3   New representations are independently stored.
4   Representations are bracketed such that no intra- or inter-domain representational links can yet be formed.

Information embedded in procedurally encoded representations is therefore not available to other operators in the cognitive system. Thus if two procedures contain some identical component parts, this potential inter-representational commonality is not yet represented in the child's mind. A procedure *as a whole* is available to other operators; it is its component parts that are not accessible. My contention is that it takes developmental time and a process of representational redescription for component parts to become accessible to potential intra-domain links. This ultimately leads to inter-representational flexibility and creative problem-solving capacities. But at this first level, the potential representational links and the information embedded in procedures remain implicit. This allows for the computation of specific inputs in preferential ways and for effective and rapid responses to the environment. But the behavior generated from these initial representations is relatively inflexible.

The RR model posits a subsequent reiterative process of representational redescription.[4] The redescriptions are abstractions in a higher level language and are open to potential intra- and inter-domain representational links, a process which enriches the system from within.

The process of representational redescription gives rise to a loss of some of the details of the procedurally encoded information. A nice example of what I have in mind is mentioned in a recent article by Mandler (1992). Consider, for example, the details of the grated image delivered to the perceptual system when you see a zebra. A redescription of this into "striped animal" (either linguistic or image-like) has lost many of the perceptual details. To Mandler's example, I would add that the redescription allows the *cognitive* system to understand the analogy between the animal zebra and, for instance, the road sign for a zebra crossing, even though these stimuli deliver very different details to the *perceptual* system. A species without such representational redescriptions would not find the zebra and the zebra crossing sign in any way analogous. The redescribed representation is, on the one hand, less special-purpose and less detailed but, on the other, more cognitively flexible because it is transportable to other goals and makes possible inter-representational links. Unlike perceptual representations, conceptual redescriptions are productive; they make possible the invention of new terms (e.g. "zebrin," the antibody which stains certain classes of cells in striped patterns).

The passage from procedurally encoded representations to explicit redescriptions occurs whenever a component of the child's cognitive system has reached what I call "behavioral mastery." In other words, it is representations that have reached a *stable state* that are redescribed. This success-based view of cognitive change contrasts with Piaget's view. For Piaget, a system in a state of stability would not spontaneously improve itself. Rather, the Piagetian process of equilibration takes place when the system is in a state of disequilibrium. This, I agree, may explain *some* aspects of development. The RR model also runs counter to the behaviorist view that change only occurs as the result of failure or external reinforcement. Rather, for the RR model certain types of change take place *after* the child is successful, i.e. already producing the correct linguistic output or already having consistenly reached a problem-solving goal. Representational redescription is a process of "appropriating" stable states, to extract the information that they contain, which can then be used more flexibly for other purposes.

I do not of course deny the role of cognitive conflict in generating other types of change through, for instance, the mismatch between input and output in language (e.g. Clark, 1987) or between theory-driven expectations and actual outcomes (e.g. Carey, 1985), or through competition between different internal systems (e.g. Bates and MacWhinney, 1987). What I am stressing here is the additional and, I hypothesize, crucial role of *internal system stability* as the basis for generating a special type of cognitive change pervasive in human development, i.e. representational redescription. And from the repeated process of internal representational redescription, rather than simply interaction with the external environment, cognitive flexibility and consciousness ultimately emerge. I posit that the process of representational redescription can occur without ongoing analysis of incoming data or production of output. Thus, change may take place outside normal input/output relations, i.e. simply as the product of system-internal dynamics, when there are no external pressures of any kind.

Note that the process of representational redescription does not involve the destruction or overwriting of the original representations. The human mind is not, I posit, striving for economy. Thus the original, procedurally encoded representations remain intact in the child's mind and can continue to be called for particular cognitive goals which require speed and automaticity. The redescribed representations are used for other goals where more explicit knowledge is required.

Once knowledge previously embedded in procedures is explicity defined, the potential relationships between procedures can then be marked and represented internally. Moreover, once redescription has taken place and explicit representations become manipulable, the child can then introduce violations to her data-driven, veridical descriptions of the world, violations which allow for pretend play, false belief and the use of counterfactuals (see Karmiloff-Smith, 1992, for full discussion).

It is important to stress that although the initial redescriptions are available as data to the system, they are not necessarily available to conscious access and verbal report. There are numerous examples in the developmental literature of the formation of explicit representations which are not yet accessible to conscious reflection and verbal report, but which are clearly beyond the procedural level. In general, developmentalists have not distinguished between implicity stored knowledge and a representational format in which knowledge *is* explicitly represented but not yet consciously accessible. Rather, a dichotomy has been used between, on the one hand, an undefined notion of "implicit" (as if information were not represented in any form) and, on the other hand, consciously accessible knowledge stateable in verbal form. The RR model postulates that the human representational system is far more complex than a mere dichotomy would suggest. I argue that there are more than two kinds of representation. Levels exist between implicity stored procedural information and verbally stateable declarative knowledge. The end result of these various redescriptions is the existence in the mind of multiple representations of similar knowledge at different levels of detail and explicitness.

At the highest level, knowledge is recoded into a cross-system format. It is here that my disagreement with Fodor's (1983) proposals is highlighted, for in my view the system does not transform *all* input immediately into a common, propositional language of thought. Rather, the translation process is constrained by the multiplicity of representational formats (spatial, linguistic, kinesthetic, etc.) available to the human mind. Only at the highest level is there a common format. The latter is hypothesized to be close enough to natural language for easy translation into stateable, communicable form. It is possible that some knowledge learned directly in linguistic form is immediately stored at the highest level of redescription. Children learn a lot in verbal interaction with others. However, knowledge may be stored in linguistic format but not yet be linked to knowledge stored in other formats.

There are thus multiple levels at which the same knowledge is re-represented. This notion of multiple encoding is important: as noted earlier, development does *not* seem to be a drive for economy. The mind may indeed turn out to be very redundant.

5 The Status of Early Representations

I argue that none of the components of the initial, special-purpose information available to young infants is accessible to the system as data. The procedurally encoded knowledge has a similar status to knowledge in nonhuman species. Subsequently, in humans, the process of representational redescription outlined above enables certain aspects of knowledge to become accessible to other parts of the mind. Thus human development crucially involves the passage from representations which constitute information *in* the mind, to representations which acquire the status of knowledge *to* other parts of the mind.

I therefore challenge the view of some developmentalists (e.g. Baillargéon and Hanko-Summers, 1990; Leslie, 1988; Spelke, 1988) that there are innately specified "theories" in the infant mind. Despite the fact that the principles infants use form a coherent, interrelated set which support rich inductions (Spelke, 1988), they do not in my view have the status of a "theory." They are simply embedded in procedures for responding to the environment. For knowledge to have "theoretical" status for the cognizer, it must be explicitly represented (although not necessarily available to consciousness), i.e. it must undergo representational redescription.

As mentioned above, the flourishing of infancy research has shown that the neonate is biologically set to compute – and, according to some, actively to select – constrained classes of inputs that are numerically relevant, linguistically relevant, relevant to species recognition, to the identification of features of objects, of cause – effect relations, and so forth. But that being so, we are still left with the question of the *form* of the neonate's and young infant's knowledge representations.

Piaget granted no initial innately specified predispositions and no initial capacity for symbolic representations. For Piaget only sensorimotor encodings of a domain-general type existed during infancy. Not until the culmination of the sensorimotor period at around 18 months, according to Piaget, does the child represent knowledge symbolically or declaratively. By contrast, Mandler (1983, 1988, 1992) has made a very convincing case for the existence of symbolic representations in young infants (but perhaps not neonates) who show the capacity for both procedural and declarative (symbolic) representations of new knowledge. How, Mandler asks, could a young infant recall an action to be imitated after as long as 24 hours (Meltzoff, 1988, 1990), without the benefit of accessible knowledge represented in long-term memory? Likewise, how could the four to six month old infant recall the exact size of an object and precisely where it was located behind a screen (Ashmead and Perlmutter, 1980; Baillargéon, 1992) if it could not represent them in an accessible form?

Mandler speculates that young infants engage in a process of perceptual analysis which goes beyond their rapid and automatic computation of perceptual input. Perceptual analysis results in the formation of perceptual primitives, such as *Self-motion/Caused motion/Path/Support/Agent*, etc. These primitives guide the way in which infants parse events into separate entities that are supported or contained, that move from sources to goals along specific kinds of paths according to whether movement is animate or inanimate. Mandler argues that these perceptual primitives are redescribed into accessible image-schemas, thereby providing a level of representation intermediate between perception and language. And it is these accessible image-schemas that facilitate semantic development, i.e. the mapping between language and conceptual categories. Image-schemas are nonpropositional, analog representations of spatial relations and movements, i.e. they are conceptual structures mapped from spatial structure.

Hitherto, I had only applied the concept of representational redescription to post-infancy development. However, Mandler has shown how the process of redescription can also be used to account for representational change in early infancy. In previous work, Mandler argued that procedural and declarative representations developed in parallel (Mandler, 1983, 1988). Her recent intro-duction of the process of redescription (Mandler, 1992) means that the infant's procedural representations actually constrain the content, form and timing of what is ultimately in declarative form. So, already in infancy we witness the formation of a rich system of representations ripe for further representational redescription into linguistic format.

Let us now look at some empirical examples from language acquisition with respect to infant capacities and the subsequent process of representational redescription. This will be followed by work exploring the process of redescrip-tion in older children's drawing.

6 Empirical Examples: Language Acquisition

Many developmental psycholinguists accept a nativist view of language acquisi-tion (e.g. Gleitman, 1990; Hyams, 1986; Pinker, 1984; Valian, 1990), although there exist some rather compelling counterarguments (Bates et al., 1979; Bates and MacWhinney, 1987). The most thoroughly worked out nativist account of language acquisition has been offered by Chomsky (1981, 1986, 1988). Chomsky argues that what is built into the human mind is a form of universal grammar, i.e. linguistic principles that are innately specified and constrain the child's acquisition of her native tongue. Also built in are a series of parameters, either with a default setting (Hyams, 1986) or with both settings available (Valian, 1990), to be fixed one way or the other in the light of the characteristics of the particular linguistic environment in which the child finds herself. Note that, in this case, the principles and parameters are not mere skeletal outlines, but hypothesized to be specified very precisely and then selected via interaction with the constraints of the linguistic environment.

As Gleitman (1990) has stressed, however, the Chomskyan model fails to address a prior problem. Between birth and the onset of language maturationally, how does the infant build up linguistically relevant representations from the native tongue model on which to base subsequent acquisition? Gleitman and her colleagues argue that the child is preset biologically to represent the linguistically relevant aspects of sound waves and differentiate these from other, non-linguistic acoustic input. Recent research suggests that infants compute a constrained class of specifically linguistic inputs such that, in their interpretation of sound waves, they make a distinction between linguistically relevant and other, non-linguistic sounds (Mehler and Bertoncini, 1988). The normal infant attends preferentially to human language.

The development of speech perception of the particularities of the infant's mother tongue has been shown to be an innately guided learning process (Jusczyk and Bertoncini, 1988). Results of studies have suggested that well before they can talk, young infants are already sensitive to word boundaries (Gleitman et al., 1988) as well as to clause boundaries within which grammatical rules apply (Hirsh-Pasek et al., 1987). Babies show distinct preference for a recording into which pauses are inserted at natural clause boundaries, as opposed to a recording in which the pauses violate such language-specific boundaries. Experiments also indicate that infants are sensitive to relative pitch, which is linguistically relevant, versus absolute pitch (e.g. male versus female voice), which is socially relevant, that they are sensitive to rhythmic aspects of linguistic input, to vowel duration, to linguistic stress, to the contour of rising and falling intonation, and to subtle phonemic distinctions (De Many et al., 1977; Eilers et al., 1984; Eimas et al., 1971; Fernald, 1989; Fernald and Kuhl, 1981; Fowler et al., 1986; Kuhl, 1983; Spring and Dale, 1977; Sullivan and Horowitz, 1983). Moreover, according to Mehler and his colleagues in Paris, four day old infants are already sensitive to certain characteristics of their own native tongue (Mehler et al., 1986). Mehler found that 12 hours after birth, babies distinguish between linguistically relevant input and other nonlinguistic acoustic input. However, they do not yet react to differences between particular languages. Thus the nine months *in utero* do not provide the necessary input for the child to attend preferentially to its native tongue at birth. However, already by four days of age, i.e. after exceedingly little experience, the infants studied by the Parisian team discriminated between the intonation patterns of Russian and French.

What this and other infancy work on language indicates is that by the time language production begins, there is already a large bulk of linguistically relevant representations in the infant's mind, representations that support subsequent syntactic development. These are a result of multiple internal *and* external constraints that give rise to a discrete number of possible emergent functions (see discussion in Johnson and Karmiloff-Smith, 1992).

So, is that all there is to language acquisition: a set of constraining biases for attending to linguistically relevant input and subsequently, with maturation, a number of parameters to be set via some inductive mechanism? Does language acquisition involve nothing more? In my view, little more is needed to provide an adequate account of language acquisition as far as the *initial* mapping operations are concerned to generate efficient language usage. Moreover, this may be all there is to the language acquisition of certain fluent-speaking retarded children. The now attested fact that semantically and syntactically fluent language can coexist with severe cognitive retardation in children with Williams syndrome (Bellugi, 1989; Bellugi et al., 1988; Karmiloff-Smith, 1990b; Karmiloff-Smith et al., 1992; Thal et al., 1989) and in hydrocephalic children with spina bifida (Cromer, 1991; Tew, 1979) suggests that an explanation of language acquisition as merely part of general cognitive development with no linguistically relevant predispositions (e.g. Sinclair, 1971, 1987) is highly challengeable. Whereas fluent language in a very retarded child is difficult to accommodate theoretically within a traditional Piagetian perspective, it is unsurprising within a perspective that allows for domain-specific predispositions. Indeed, the progressive modularization of language, on the basis of innately specified constraints channelling the infant's attention to a class of linguistically relevant acoustic inputs, together with innately specified linguistic principles and parameters, and some form of induction and mapping mechanism, is all that the retarded child would need to carry out automatically, *without general cognitive effort*, the mapping operations between the input model and the prespecified internal constraints. With the linguistic predispositions intact, this would allow the fluent-speaking retarded child to display similar *behavior* to that of the normal child. In terms of the .RR model, only procedurally encoded representations are needed to support initial fluent language usage.

This is *not* all there is to the language acquisition of the normally developing child, however. Although the fluent-speaking retarded child probably has intact language *usage*, the normal child also has the potential to go *beyond* successful usage and become a little grammarian. By contrast, not only do other species not have a language capacity, but the constraints on spiders, ants, beavers, and the like are such that they could never become potential describers of the knowledge embedded in their procedures for interacting with the environment. In other words, they only change their representations in interaction with the external environment; they cannot exploit relations implicit in their own knowledge. One might object that chimpanzees are much closer to humans. That is certainly true to some extent. After all, we share more than 90 percent of our genes with the chimpanzee. It used to be thought that what made us specifically human was the fact that we had language and no other species did. But in recent years, researchers have taught chimpanzees to use language-like systems (lists of lexical items from American Sign Language (Gardner and Gardner, 1969), or plastic chips standing for English words (Premack, 1986, 1990). And we know that, like children, chimpanzees can solve problems and successfully learn from environmental constraints. So is there no qualitative difference between the human child and the chimpanzee? Of course there is. First, what the chimpanzee learns is not a linguistic system but a list of lexical items (Premack, 1986, 1990). Second, an equally crucial difference shows up when we look at what happens *beyond successful learning*, i.e. beyond behavioral mastery.

Here is an anecdotal example from human development that eloquently illustrates my point:

Yara (aged four years): "What's that?"
Mother: "A typewriter."
Yara: "No, you're the typewriter, that's a typewrite."

A "typewrite"! Why doesn't the child simply accept the label provided by the adult and use the correct word "typewriter"? Why has she bothered to work out that the formal function of the suffix "-er" is agentive (i.e. you can often take verb stems and add "-er" to form a word for a human agent: bak*er*, danc*er*, teach*er*, so why not typewrit*er*?). Now, whatever the chimpanzee's linguistic capacities, I speculate that it would never go as far as the human child. It would never wonder why "typewriter" isn't used to refer to human agents. It would simply repeat successfully the linguistic labels that is given.

I suggested above that the linguistic representations of normal children, although analogous *at first* to those of fluent-speaking retarded children, may subsequently be very different because of the process of representational rede-scription typical of normal development. How does development proceed in the case of learning, say, the agentive function of -er? Initially, to get linguistic representations into the mind, the child focuses on the external input model. She learns "dancer," "baker," "butcher," "teacher," and so forth, and both produces and understands each of these words in its appropriate context. But, according to the RR model, each of these representations is isolated one from the other. Only after behavioral mastery is any representation redescribed such that its component parts become available to other processes. It is at that point that the child can focus on the phonological form "-er" outside its use in particular words, and thereby challenge the information given by the adult. To do so, the child must to some extent ignore the external stimuli and focus on her internal representations and her mini-theory of how the linguistic system functions. In other words, the normal child goes beyond successful language usage to exploit the knowledge that he or she has already stored. Thus *external* reality serves as input to form initial representations, but it is the *internal* representations which serve to form mini-theories about the linguistic system. This necessitates the redescription of procedurally embedded knowledge to extract the morphological components. It is pervasive in normal children's language acquisition.

Let us now take empirical evidence to illustrate the passage from procedurally encoded linguistic representations to the normal child's subsequent spontaneous formation of theories about how language functions as a system.

The first example is from the acquisition of simple words like the articles and post-articles "the" and "my" (Karmiloff-Smith, 1979). A series of experiments demonstrated that, between the ages of two and five, children learn to use and interpret articles and post-articles correctly in a number of their different appropriate contexts. But at five they cannot give verbal explanations of the conditions of use. Yet the knowledge of conditions of use *must* be represented (as knowledge still embedded in a procedure) to make it possible for young children to produce and understand the subtle linguistic distinctions con-veyed by these words. However, the knowledge represented at that level is not available to them as consciously reportable data. A distinction must therefore be drawn between information represented explicitly in the mind and informa-tion accessible to consciousness. It is by around nine or ten years, for this particular aspect of language, that children have quite elaborate linguistic the-ories about the conditions of use of articles and post-articles and how they are related to other members of the nominal determiner system (Karmiloff-Smith, 1979, 1986). Here is one such example from a ten year old. The context was two pens, one eraser, one earring and the child's own watch. The experimenter hid the child's watch and then asked: "What did I do?" The exchange was as follows:

Child: "You hid the watch."
Experimenter: "Why did you say '*the* watch'?"
Child: "Well . . . '*my* watch' because it belongs to me, but I said 'you hid *the* watch' because there are no other watches there. If you'd put yours out, I would have had to say 'you hid *my* watch,' because it could have been confusing, but

this way it's better for me to say 'you hid the watch' so someone doesn't think yours was there too."

This is an eloquent example of how elaborate spontaneous verbal statements from children can be, once they have access to their linguistic knowledge. Note that correct usage of "the," "my," etc., occurs much earlier, around four to five years of age.

Now, if one were only to consider the difference between young children's correct usage and older children's metalinguistic statements, then one would merely postulate two levels of representation: the implicit procedurally encoded representations sustaining correct usage, on the one hand, and the verbally stateable representations sustaining the verbal explanations, on the other. To posit the existence of a level of representational redescription between the two, one needs to find other kinds of data. Spontaneous self-repairs turned out to be one source of such data (Karmiloff-Smith, 1979, 1986). Take the same hiding game as above. During testing children often make self-repairs. They sometimes make lexical repairs, e.g. "you hid the pe . . . no, the watch." At other times they make referential repairs, e.g. "you hid the blue pe . . . the red pen." But they also make what I call "systemic repairs", e.g. "you hid my wat . . . the watch." (Note that this is precisely the equivalent at the repair level to the metalinguistic statement above.) Such repairs are not corrections of errors: "my watch" identifies the referent unambiguously. Rather, they denote children's sensitivity to the force of different determiners, which are no longer independently stored but are part of a linguistic subsystem. Such subsystems, I argue, are built up from the extraction of common components, explicitly represented after representational redescription has taken place. Important is the fact that younger children do not make systemic self-repairs. But this is precisely what children of around six years of age display in such circumstances, whereas they are unable to provide verbal explanations of their linguistic knowledge about the relationship between "the" and "my" in referential communication. However, their self-repairs bear witness to the fact that something has changed in their internal representations since the period of correct usage, and that they have linked explicitly some of the component knowledge which was previously embedded in independently stored procedures for producing/interpreting each article or post-article.

The phenomenon of late-occurring repairs and errors, after behavioural mastery, which are not in the child's language earlier, has been explored in detail by several researchers (Bowerman, 1982; Karmiloff-Smith, 1979; Newport, 1981). An eloquent example comes from Elissa Newport's work on the acquisition of American Sign Language (ASL). In ASL, signs have morphological structure. Deaf parents who are non-native signers, i.e. who acquired sign language late in life, cannot analyze the signs into their morphological component parts. They produce them as unanalyzed wholes. By contrast, children acquiring ASL as a native language do analyze the morphological structure. Initially children also use signs as frozen wholes (procedurally encoded representations). But after they have been using the sign correctly for some time, i.e. after having reached behavioral mastery, children start to produce "errors" in their output. The errors involve separate staccato movements, isolating separate morphological components, instead of producing the normally flowing sign. It is something like the equivalent of first pronouncing "typewriter" correctly and then subsequently spelling out its morphological structure and pronouncing it as "type–write–er," which would make it potentially linkable to other words with similar structure. The extraction of component parts in ASL from the initially frozen signs is again suggestive of representational redescription. Important, too, is the fact that nothing in Newport's data suggests that children are consciously aware of the segmented form of their new productions. In other words, the representations are not yet in a format that allows for conscious access and verbal report. Their representations are intermediate between the procedural format and the final level which allows for conscious access and verbal report. Subsequently, the overt marking of morphological structure disappears. Older children again use signs that look like the naturally flowing ones that they used when much younger. However, the RR model posits that the later, identical output stems from more explicit representations than the procedural ones that underlie the initial productions. (For numerous other such examples of overt marking of morphological structure in the acquisition of French, see Karmiloff-Smith, 1979).

Does a similar pattern of increasing access hold for the entire linguistic system? A recent series of experiments focused on metalinguistic awareness of discourse constraints[5] in contrast to the propositional content of utterances (Karmiloff-Smith et al., 1991b). Here we looked at both adults and children. Discourse structure and propositional content are simultaneously encoded by speakers and decoded by addresses. Take the pronoun "he" as a brief example of how a linguistic marker functions both at the level of propositional content and at the discourse organizational level. From the point of view of the semantics of propositional content, the pronoun "he" provides the listener with information at the sentential level about a referent being human, male, singular, etc. But in the on-line flow of discourse, the use of the pronoun *also* conveys information about the speaker's mental model of the overall discourse structure, about whether the referent can be taken by default to be the main protagonist, and so forth. Thus, in setting up a discourse model of a span of speech, speakers usually make use of pronouns such as "he" to refer to the main protagonist of a story, whereas full noun phrases such as "the girl" are used to refer to subsidiary characters (see Karmiloff-Smith, 1985, for full discussion of the structure of cohesive devices).

Subjects were asked to explain why a narrator had used a pronoun in some cases and a full noun phrase in others. The results of the experiment show that child and adult subjects can give elaborate explanations about, say, the pronoun "he" and how it relates to "she," "they," and "it," i.e. about its propositional content, and its relation to other pronouns stored in a subsystem in long-term memory. But neither children nor adults can say almost anything about the function of pronouns at the discourse level. In the allocation of shared computational resources, the discourse organization aspect of language turns out to be unavailable to conscious access, whereas the semantics of the propositional content can be reflected on metalinguistically (Karmiloff-Smith et al., 1991b).

Discourse organizational structure is acquired rather late in development and is most unlikely to be part of the innately specified predispositions in the same way that some aspects of sentential syntax might be. Moreover, unlike the deterministic rules of sentential syntax, discourse rules are probabilistic. The feedback from each decision regarding the choice of a discourse marker (he, the old man, Jim, etc.) becomes the input for the generation of the next choice, i.e. a closed loop control. When discourse cohesion markers first appear consistently in children's output, the propositional content of their output decreases compared to younger subjects (Karmiloff-Smith, 1985; Karmiloff-Smith et al., 1991b). There seems to be competition in the allocation of processing resources between propositional content and discourse structure when encoding a fast-fading message in real time. Only one of these aspects is subsequently available to metalinguistic reflection. The discourse organizational structure seems to become modularized for rapid on-line computation, and is not accessible to metalinguistic reflection, even in adults.

Development thus seems to involve two opposite processes: on the one hand, the progressive access to knowledge previously embedded in procedures and, on the other hand, the progressive modularization of parts of the system.

7 Empirical Examples: Drawing

Earlier work within both language and other areas of cognitive development (Karmiloff-Smith, 1992) has rendered plausible the process of representational redescription. But what has *not* been addressed thus far is the nature of the constraints on the first level of representational redescription. What constraints obtain when the child moves from knowledge embedded in a procedure to redescribing that knowledge such that component parts become accessible as data? Recent research on children's drawing focused directly on this issue (Karmiloff-Smith, 1990a).

The same general research strategy was used as in my previous work, i.e. the selection of an age group of children who already have efficiently functioning procedures in the particular domain of interest. Children between four and a half and ten years of age were asked to make drawings of a house, and then to draw a house that doesn't exist. The same procedure was used for man and animal. The rationale for this design was as follows: by roughly four and a half years of age, children have efficiently functioning procedures for rapidly drawing houses, for example. Asking them to draw a house that doesn't exist should force them into operating on the component parts of the knowledge embedded in their procedures.

My hypothesis was that there would be an initial period during which the child could merely run a procedure in its entirety, i.e. be unable to access separately its component parts and operate on them. This procedurally encoded knowledge, I hypothesized, would be followed by a period during which the child would be able to access, via representational redescription, some of the knowledge embedded previously in the procedure, but that there would be some initial constraints on flexibility. Later development would show increasing flexibility and interrepresentational relations.

I shall very briefly run through some of the data. First, the hypothesis that initially children may only be able to run through a successful procedure but be unable to access the knowledge embedded in it was borne out by the results of a few of the youngest subjects. Thus, although announcing that they were going to draw a silly or a pretend house, they proceeded to run through their normal

H̄ - Jessie 4;11 years   M̄ - Leo 8;6 years

Figure 25.1 Shape and/or size of elements changed.

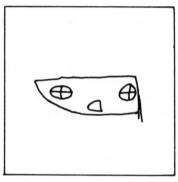
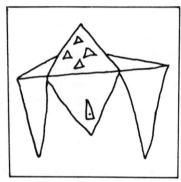

H̄ - Natasha 4;11 years   H̄ - Leo 8;6 years

Figure 25.2 Shape of whole changed.

H̄ - Peter 5;3 years   M̄ - Valerie 9;0 years

Figure 25.3 Deletion of elements.

house-drawing procedure and seemed unable to change it. Here, I shall focus on those children who did achieve some flexibility. What is of particular interest in this study is the analysis of the constraints which obtained on the types of change children made, i.e. how much flexibility they could spontaneously display.

Figures 25.1, 25.2, and 25.3 illustrate the types of change which children of all age groups introduced. They involved the following:

- shape and size of elements changed;
- shape of whole changed;
- elements deleted.

Note that in most cases, the changes do *not* involve interruption or reordering of the sequential constraints on the procedure. Although the three types of change were found in children of all ages, important differences emerged with respect to younger and older subjects who used deletion as a solution. We shall look at this once we have illustrated the other changes introduced.

Figures 25.4, 25.5, and 25.6 illustrate far more flexible and creative solutions to the task. Changes here involved:

- insertion of new elements from the same conceptual category;
- position and orientation changed;
- insertion of elements from other conceptual categories.

These changes were found almost totally in older children only. They involve reordering of sequence, interruption and insertion of subroutine, and the use of representations from other conceptual categories.

If we now reconsider figure 25.3, illustrating deletions, it can be noted that although children of both age groups used deletions, this category showed particularly interesting differences between younger and older subjects. The children from the older age group frequently made their deletions in the middle of their drawing procedure. By contrast, the younger age group made deletions of elements which are drawn towards the end of a procedure, and they did not continue drawing after making such deletions.

The very few four to six year olds who made changes classifiable in the last three categories (insertions of elements, position/orientation changes, cross-category insertions) all added elements after finishing a normal X, e.g. by adding a chimney emerging horizontally from the side wall of a house, by adding a smile on a house, etc. They did not make insertions into the middle of their drawing procedure as did older children, who, for instance, drew a man with two heads, which involves an insertion towards the beginning of the procedure.

The histogram in figure 25.7 shows the differences between the two age groups with respect to flexibility of changes. This very striking developmental difference suggests that initially, when children are able to work on a redescription of the knowledge embedded in a procedure, their flexibility is relatively constrained.

What would the overall process of learning to draw, say, a house and then a house that does not exist look like? Initially, when children build up a new procedure, like learning to draw a house, they do so laboriously, working out the different elements, watching the way others perform, and so forth. The

$\overline{\text{M}}$ - Viki 8;7 years $\overline{\text{M}}$ - Guy 9;6 years

Figure 25.4 Insertion of new elements.

M - Jessie 9;8 years   H - Justin 10;11 years

Figure 25.5 *Position/orientation changed.*

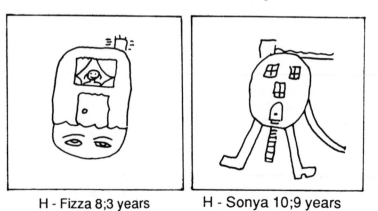

H - Fizza 8;3 years   H - Sonya 10;9 years

Figure 25.6 Insertion of cross–category elements.

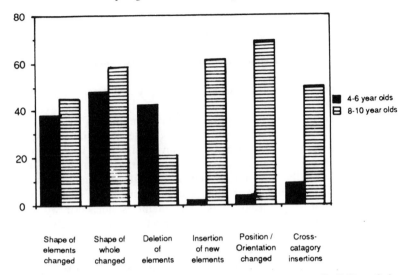

Figure 25.7 Differences between two age groups with respect to flexibility of change.

process can be long. By the time they are four to five years of age, children start to consolidate the procedure, so that it runs off more or less automatically, much in the manner of skill acquisition. Ask the child to draw a house, and now she can draw it easily and quickly. She has reached behavioral mastery and is ripe for the process of representational redescription. The results of this study suggest that although at the first level of redescription the knowledge becomes accessible, flexibility is relatively constrained. By contrast, subsequent representational redescriptions allow for greater flexibility; they are not constrained by any sequential specification. By then, the child has moved from a sequence of instructions in which order is still relatively inflexible, to a more flexibly ordered list of features in which the sequential constraint is relaxed. In computer science terms, the movement would be something like the change from a stack to an array. This makes it possible for children to be creative about insertion of new elements, change of position, orientation and so forth.

Interestingly, the interpretation in terms of sequential constraints on initial redescriptions helps to make sense of what turn out to be very similar phenomena with respect to phonological awareness in children as well as illiterate versus newly literate adults (Morais et al., 1987). Phonological awareness tasks show that it is easier for subjects to delete final phonemes than to delete initial phonemes. Initially a sequential constraint obtains for children and for the newly literate, which is surmounted by the fully literate adult.

It is important to note that the sequential specification that is often part of initial redescriptions does not only act as a curtailing constraint on flexibility. The fact that initial levels of representation are sequentially specified can in fact potentiate development in just those areas where *sequence* is an essential component – language, counting, playing an instrument, and so forth. Whereas in each case the child ultimately needs to surpass all sequential constraints, initially such constraints actually potentiate learning.

8 Conclusions

I shall conclude by summarizing the main speculations explored in this chapter:

1   Innately specified predispositions and constructivism are not necessarily incompatible.
2   Piaget's view of the initial state of the neonate mind was wrong. It is clear that at the outset some aspects of human knowledge are innately specified. Knowledge seems to be initially domain-specific and to constrain subsequent learning in complex interaction with the environment. It is not based solely on the outcome of domain-neutral sensorimotor action. But Piaget's stress on epigenesis and constructivism must incorporate some innately specified predispositions. The infant is not born with a large number of prespecified modules. Where modules do ultimately exist, they are the result of a process of modularization as development proceeds.
3   Both innately specified knowledge and newly acquired knowledge are initially procedurally encoded, activated as a response to external stimuli. The procedure as a whole is available to other operators, but its component parts are not. An exception to this is when knowledge is directly encoded in linguistic form.
4   The child is a spontaneous theory-builder (about language, physics, etc.) and exploits the knowledge that she has already stored via a process of representational redescription, in other words by representing recursively her own representations. Once redescribed, component parts of knowledge become explicitly represented and thus available as data structures to the system for theory-building and ultimately, in some cases, to conscious access.
5   The coherent sets of principles which underlie the infant's procedures for interacting with the external environment and which support rich inductions cannot be considered as innately specified "theories." To have the status of a "theory," these principles must be explicitly defined in the internal representations. I maintain that this only takes place subsequent upon a process of representational redescription.
6   Dichotomies, such as implicit/explicit, unconscious/conscious, automatic/controlled, etc., are insufficient to capture the complexities of representational change. One needs to invoke several different levels, namely a level of implicit knowledge represented but embedded in procedures, a level of explicitly defined knowledge not available to verbal report, and a level available to verbal report. A developmental perspective is crucial to identifying these different levels of representation in the human mind.
7   Although change can occur as a result of conflict and competition, change also occurs subsequent to success, i.e. after a period of behavioral mastery.
8   Development involves two opposing processes: on the one hand, progressive access to stored information and, on the other, progressive modularization.

A question that permeates the developmental literature is whether the mind is a general-purpose, domain-neutral learning mechanism *or* whether knowledge is acquired and computed in a domain-specific fashion (see the excellent discussion in Keil, 1990). I have italicized the exclusive "or" purposely, because I feel it is misplaced. It is doubtful that development will turn out to be entirely domain-specific or entirely domain-general. The more interesting developmental question for the future will hinge on the relative weights of constraints imposed by innate specifications, constraints that are domain-specific and those that are domain-general, as well as constraints emanating from the structure of the environment.

NOTES

1 Fodor uses the term "constructivism" differently from Piaget, to refer to a form of empiricism: "Specifically, if mental structures can be viewed as assembled from primitive elements, then perhaps mechanisms of learning can be shown to be responsible for effecting their construction . . . real convergence between the motivations of classical associationism and those which actuate its computational reincarnation: Both doctrines find in constructivist analyses of mental structures the promise of an empiricist (i.e. non-nativist) theory of cognitive development" (Fodor, 1983, p. 33). Piaget argued that his constructivist genetic epistemology – the notion that new cognitive structures are emergent properties of a self-organizing system – was an *alternative* to both nativism and empiricism.
2 It is important not to confuse "domain" with "module." From the point of view of the child's mind, a "domain" is the set of representations sustaining a specific area of knowledge, e.g. language, number, physics, and so forth. A "module" is an information processing unit that encapsulates that knowledge and computations on it. Considering development as domain specific does not necessarily imply modularity. In other words, storing and processing of information may be domain specific, without being encapsulated, hardwired, mandatory, and so forth.
3 Thelen (1989) argues persuasively that, in fact, in an epigenetic system there is no formal difference between exogenous (external) and endogenous (internal) sources of change in which the action of the organism plays a crucial role.
4 See also J. Campbell (1990) for a discussion of the importance of introducing the notion of re-representation to current AI modeling.
5 By discourse constraints, I have in mind discourse organizational markers: terms like pronouns and full noun phrases in their discourse functions of denoting the thematic structure of a discourse, and aspectual marking on verbs in its function of marking foregrounding and backgrounding in a span of discourse.

REFERENCES

Anderson, M. (1992) *Intelligence and Development: a Cognitive Theory.* Oxford: Blackwell.

Ashmead, D. H. and Perlmutter, M. (1980) Infant memory in everyday life. In M. Perlmutter (ed.), *New Directions for Child Development: Children's Memory, Vol. 10.* San Francisco: Jossey-Bass.

Baillargéon, R. (1987a) Object permanence in 3.5- and 4.5-month-old infants. *Developmental Psychology*, 23, 655–64.

Baillargéon, R. (1987b) Young infants' reasoning about the physical and spatial properties of a hidden object. *Cognitive Development*, 2, 170–200.

Baillargéon, R. (1992) Reasoning about the height and location of a hidden object in 4.5- and 6.5-month-old infants. *Cognition* (in the press).

Baillargéon, R. and Hanko-Summers, S. (1990) Is the top object adequately supported by the bottom object? Young infants' understanding of support relations. *Cognitive Development*, 5, 29–53.

Baillargéon, R., Spelke, E. and Wasserman, S. (1986) Object permanence in five month old infants. *Cognition*, 20, 191–208.

Bates, E., Benigni, L., Bretherton, I., Camaioni, L. and Volterra, V. (1979). *The Emergence of Symbols: Cognition and Communication in Infancy*. New York: Academic Press.

Bates, E. and MacWhinney, B. (1987) Competition, variation and language learning. In B. MacWhinney (ed.), *Mechanisms of Language Acquisition*. Hillsdale, NJ: Erlbaum, pp. 157–93.

Bellugi, U. (1989) Specific dissociations between language and cognitive functioning in a neurodevelopmental disorder. Paper given at the symposium on Neural Correlates underlying Dissociations of Higher Cortical Functioning. International Neuropsychology Society Meeting, Vancouver, February.

Bellugi, U., Marks, S., Bihrle, A. M. and Sabo, H. (1988). Dissociation between language and cognitive functions in Williams Syndrome. In D. Bishop and K. Mogford (eds), *Language Development in Exceptional Circumstances*. London: Churchill Livingstone.

Bowerman, M. (1982) Reorganizational processes in lexical and syntactic development. In E. Wanner and R. L. Gleitman (eds) *Language Acquisition: the State of the Art*. Cambridge: Cambridge University Press.

Butterworth, G. (ed.) (1981) *Infancy and Epistemology: an Evaluation of Piaget's Theory*. Brighton: Harvester Press.

Campbell, J. A. (1990) Challenges for knowledge representation. Paper presented at the International Symposium on Computational Intelligence 90, Heterogeneous Knowledge Representation Systems, Milan, Italy, September 24–28, 1990.

Carey, S. (1985) *Conceptual Change in Childhood*. Cambridge, MA: MIT Press/Bradford Books.

Carey, S. and Gelman, R. (eds) (1991) *The Epigenesis of Mind: Essays in Biology and Knowledge*. Hillsdale, NJ: Erlbaum.

Changeux, J. P. (1985) *Neuronal Man: the Biology of Mind*. New York: Pantheon Books.

Chomsky, N. (1981) *Lectures on Government and Binding*. Dordrecht: Foris Publications.

Chomsky, N. (1986) *Knowledge of Language: Its Nature, Origin and Use*. New York: Praeger.

Chomsky, N. (1988) *Language and Problems of Knowledge*. Cambridge, MA: MIT Press.

Clark, E. V. (1987) The principle of contrast: a constraint on language acquisition. In B. MacWhinney (ed.), *The 20th Annual Carnegie Symposium on Cognition*. Hillsdale, NJ: Erlbaum.

Cohen, S. R. (1988). The development of constraints on symbolmeaning structure in notation: evidence from production, interpretation and forced–choice judgements. *Child Development*, 56, 177–95.

Cromer, R. (1991) *Language and Cognition in Normal and Handicapped Children*. Oxford: Blackwell.

DeMany, L., McKenzie, B. and Vurpillot, E. (1977) Rhythm perception in early infancy. *Nature*, 266, 718–19.

Diamond, A. and Gilbert, J. (1989) Development as progressive inhibitory control of action: Retrieval of a contiguous object. *Cognitive Development*, 4, 223–49.

Eilers, R. E., Bull, D. H., Oller, K. and Lewis, D. C. (1984) The discrimination of vowel duration by infants. *Journal of the Acoustical Society of America*, 75, 1213–18.

Eimas, P. H., Siqueland, E. R., Jusczyk, P. and Vigorito, J. (1971) Speech perception in infants. *Science*, 171, 303–6.

Fernald, A. (1989) Four-month-old infants prefer to listen to Motherese. *Infant Behaviour and Development*.

Fernald, A. and Kuhl, P. (1981) Fundamental frequency as an acoustic determinant of infant preference for motherese. Paper presented at the meeting of the Society for Research in Child Development, Boston.

Fodor, J. A. (1983) *The Modularity of Mind*. Cambridge, MA: MIT Press.

Fowler, C. A., Smith, M. R. and Tassinary, L. G. (1986) Perception of syllable timing by prebabbling infants. *Journal of the Acoustical Society of America*, 79, 814–25.

Gardner, R. A. and Gardner, B. T. (1969) Teaching sign language to a chimpanzee. *Science*, 165, 664–72.

Gelman, R. (1990) First principles organize attention to and learning about relevant data: number and animate-inanimate distinction as examples. *Cognitive Science*, 14, 79–106.

Gleitman, L. (1990) The structural sources of verb meanings. *Language Acquisition*, 1, 3–55.

Gleitman, L. R., Gleitman, H., Landau, B. and Wanner, E. (1988). Where learning begins: initial representations for language learning. In F. Newmeyer (ed.), *The Cambridge Linguistic Survey, Volume III: Language: Psychological and Biological Aspects*. New York: Cambridge University Press.

Gleitman, L. R., Gleitman, H. and Shipley, E. F. (1972) The emergence of the child as grammarian. *Cognition*, 1, 137–64.

Hirsh-Pasek, K., Kemler-Nelson, D. G., Jusczyk, P. W., Wright Cassidy, K., Druss, B. and Kennedy, L. (1987) Clauses are perceptual units for young infants. *Cognition*, 26, 269–86.

Hyams, N. (1986) *Language Acquisition and the Theory of Parameters*. Dordrecht: Reidel.

Inhelder, B. and Piaget, J. (1958) *The Growth of Logical Thinking from Childhood to Adolescence*. New York: Basic Books.

James, W. (1892) *Psychology*. London: Macmillan & Co.

Johnson, M. H. (1988) Memories of mother. *New Scientist*, 18 February, 60–2.

Johnson, M. H. (1990) Cortical maturation and the development of visual attention in early infancy. *Journal of Cognitive Neuroscience*, 2, 81–95.

Johnson, M. H. and Bolhuis, J. J. (1991) Imprinting, predispositions and filial preference in the chick. In R. J. Andrew (ed.), *Neural and Behavioural Plasticity*. Oxford: Oxford University Press, 133–56.

Johnson, M. H., Dziurawiec, S., Ellis, H. and Morton, J. (1991) Newborns preferential tracking of facelike stimuli and its subsequent decline. *Cognition*, 40, 1–19.

Johnson, M. H. and Karmiloff-Smith, A. (1992) Can neural selectionism be applied to cognitive development and its disorders? *New Ideas in Psychology*, 10, 35–46.

Johnson, M. H. and Morton, J. (1991) *Biology and Cognitive Development: the Case of Face Recognition*. Oxford: Blackwell.

Jusczyk, P. W. (1986) Speech perception. In K. R. Boff, L. Kaufman and J. P. Thomas (eds), *Handbook of perception and human performance: Vol. 2. Cognitive Processes and Performance*. New York: Wiley.

Jusczyk, P. W. and Bertoncini, J. (1988) Viewing the development of speech perception as an innately guided learning process. *Language and Speech*, 31, 217–38.

Jusczyk, P. W. and Cohen, A. (1985) What constitutes a module? *Behavioural and Brain Sciences*, 8, 20–1.

Karmiloff-Smith, A. (1979) *A Functional Approach to Child Language*. Cambridge: Cambridge University Press.

Karmiloff-Smith, A. (1985) Language and cognitive processes from a developmental perspective. *Language and Cognitive Processes*, 1, 60–85.

Karmiloff-Smith, A. (1986) From metaprocesses to conscious access: evidence from children's metalinguistic and repair data. *Cognition*, 23, 95–147.

Karmiloff-Smith, A. (1988) The child is a scientist, not an inductivist. *Mind and Language*, 3(3), 183–95.

Karmiloff-Smith, A. (1990a) Constraints on representational change: evidence from children's drawing. *Cognition*, 34, 57–83.

Karmiloff-Smith, A. (1990b) Piaget and Chomsky on language acquisition: divorce or marriage? *First Language*, 10, 255–70.

Karmiloff-Smith, A. (1992) *Beyond Modularity: a Developmental Perspective on Cognitive Science*. Cambridge, MA: MIT Press/Bradford Books.

Karmiloff-Smith, A., Bellugi, U., Klima, E. and Grant, J. (1991) Talk prepared for the British Psychological Society's Developmental Section Annual Conference, Cambridge, September, 1991.

Karmiloff-Smith, A., Johnson, H., Grant, J. Jones, Karmiloff Y.-N., Bartrip, J. and Cuckle C. (1992) From sentential to discourse functions: Detection and explanation of speech repairs in children and adults. *Discourse Processes* (in the press).

Keil, F. C. (1990) Constraints on constraints: surveying the epigenetic landscape. *Cognitive Science*, 14, 135–68.

Kellman, P. J. (1988) Theories of perception and research in perceptual development. In A. Yonas (ed.), *Perceptual Development in Infancy: the Minnesota Symposium on Child Psychology, Vol. 20*. Hillsdale, NJ: Erlbaum.

Kellman, P. J. and Spelke, E. S. (1983) Perception of partly occluded objects in infancy. *Cognitive Psychology*, 15, 483–524.

Klahr, D. and Dunbar, K. (1988) Dual search space during scientific reasoning. *Cognitive Science*, 12, 1–48.

Kuhl, P. K. (1983) The perception of auditory equivalence classes for speech in early infancy. *Infant Behaviour and Development*, 6, 263–85.

Kuhn, D., Amsel, E. and O'Loughlin, M. (1988) *The Development of Scientific Thinking Skills*. San Diego: Academic Press.

Leslie, A. M. (1984) Infant perception of a manual pickup event. *British Journal of Developmental Psychology*, 2, 19–32.

Leslie, A. M. (1988) The necessity of illusion: perception and thought in infancy. In L. Weiskrantz (ed.), *Thought Without Language*. Oxford: Oxford University Press.

Mandler, J. M. (1983) Representation. In J. Flavell and E. Markman (eds), *Handbook of Child Psychology, Vol. 3*. New York: Wiley.

Mandler, J. M. (1988) How to build a baby: on the development of an accessible representational system. *Cognitive Development*, 3, 113–36.

Mandler, J. M. (1992) How to build a baby II: conceptual primitives. *Psychological Review* (in the press).

Marler, P. (1991) The instinct to learn. In S. Carey and R. Gelman (eds), *Epigenesis of the Mind: Essays in Biology and Knowledge*. Hillsdale, NJ: Erlbaum.

Mehler, J. and Bertoncini, J. (1988) Development: a question of properties, not change? *Cognition*, 115, 121–133.

Mehler, J. and Fox, R. (eds) (1985) *Neonate Cognition: Beyond the Blooming Buzzing Confusion*. Hillsdale, NJ: Erlbaum.

Mehler, J., Lambertz, G., Jusczyk, P. and Amiel-Tison, C. (1986) Discrimination de la langue maternelle par le nouveau-né. *Comptes Rendez de l'Academie des Sciences*, 303, Serie III, 637–40.

Meltzoff, A. N. (1988) Infant imitation and memory: nine-month-olds in immediate and deferred tests. *Child Development*, 59, 217–25.

Meltzoff, A. N. (1990) Towards a developmental cognitive science: the implications of cross-modal matching and imitation for the development of memory in infancy. *Annals of the New York Academy of Sciences*, 608, 1–37.

Morais, J., Alegria, J. and Content, A. (1987) The relationships between segmental analysis and alphabetic literacy: an interactive view. *Cahiers de Psychologie Cognitive*, 7, 415–38.

Newport, E. L. (1981) Constraints on structure: evidence from American Sign Language and language learning. In W. A. Collins (ed.), *Aspects of the Development of Competence: Minnesota Symposia on Child Psychology, Vol. 14*. Hillsdale, NJ: Erlbaum.

Oyama, S. (1985) *The Ontogeny of Information: Developmental Systems and Evolution*. Cambridge: Cambridge University Press.

Piaget, J. (1955) *The Child's Construction of Reality*. London: Routledge and Kegan Paul.

Piaget, J. (1967) *Biologie et Connaissance*. Paris: Gallimard.

Piaget, J., Karmiloff-Smith, A. and Bronckart, J. P. (1978) Généralisations relatives à la pression et à la réaction. In J. Piaget (ed.), *Recherches sur la Généralisation*. Paris: Presses Universitaires de France, pp. 169–91.

Piatelli-Palmarini, M. (1989) Evolution, selection, and cognition: from "learning" to parameter setting in biology and the study of language. *Cognition*, 31, 1–44.

Pinker, S. (1984) *Language Learnability and Language Development*. Cambridge, MA: Harvard University Press.

Premack, D. (1986) *Gavagai! Or the Future History of the Animal Language Controversy*. Cambridge, MA: MIT Press.

Premack, D. (1990) Words: what are they, and do animals have them? *Cognition*, 37, 197–212.

Rutkowska, J. C. (1987) Computational models and developmental psychology. In J. C. Rutkowska and C. Cook (eds), *Computation and Development*. Chichester: Wiley.

Sinclair, H. (1971) Sensorimotor action patterns as the condition for the acquisition of syntax. In R. Huxley and E. Ingrams (eds), *Language Acquisition: Models and Methods*. New York: Academic Press.

Sinclair, H. (1987) Language: a gift of nature or a homemade tool? In S. Modgil and C. Modgil (eds), *Noam Chomsky: Consensus and Controversy*. London: Falmer Press.

Slater, A. (1990) Size constancy and complex visual processing at birth. Poster presented at the IVth European Conference on Developmental Psychology, University of Stirling, August.

Slater, A. and Morison, V. (1992) Visual attention and memory at birth. In M. J. Weiss and P. Zelazo (eds), *Newborn Attention*. Norwood, NJ: Ablex.

Slater, A., Morison, V. and Rose, D. (1983) Perception of shape by the newborn baby. *British Journal of Developmental Psychology*, 1, 135–42.

Slater, A., Morison, V., Somers, M., Mattock, A., Brown, E. and Taylor, D. (1990) Newborn and older infants' perception of partly occluded objects. *Infant Behaviour and Development*, 13, 33–49.

Spelke, E. S. (1985) Preferential-looking methods as tools for the study of cognition in infancy. In G. Gottlieb and N. A. Krasnegor (eds), *Measurement of Audition and Vision in the First Year of Postnatal Life: a Methodological Overview*. Norwood, NJ: Ablex.

Spelke, E. S. (1988) Where perceiving ends and thinking begins: the apprehension of objects in infancy. In A. Yonas (ed.), *Perceptual Development in Infancy*. Hillsdale, NJ: Erlbaum.

Spelke, E. S. (1990) Principles of object perception. *Cognitive Science*, 14, 29–56.

Spelke, E. S. (1991) Physical knowledge in infancy: reflections on Piaget's theory. In S. Carey and R. Gelman (eds), *Epigenesis of the Mind: Essays in Biology and Knowledge*. Hillsdale, NJ: Erlbaum.

Spring, D. R. and Dale, P. S. (1977) Discrimination of linguistic stress in early infancy. *Journal of Speech and Hearing Research*, 20, 224–32.

Starkey, P., Spelke, E. S. and Gelman, R. (1983) Numerical abstraction by human infants. *Cognition*, 39, 167–70.

Sullivan, J. W. and Horowitz, F. D. (1983) The effects of intonation on infant attention: the role of the rising intonation contour. *Journal of Child Language*, 10, 521–34.

Tew, B. (1979) The "cocktail party syndrome" in children with hydrocephalus and spina bifida. *British Journal of Disorders of Communication*, 14, 89–101.

Thal, D., Bates, E. and Bellugi, U. (1989) Language and cognition in two children with Williams syndrome. *Journal of Speech and Hearing Research*, 32, 489–500.

Thelen, E. (1989) Self-organization in developmental processes: can systems approaches work? In M. Gunnar and E. Thelen (eds), *Systems and Development. The Minnesota Symposium in Child Psychology, vol. 22*. London: Erlbaum.

Valian, V. (1990) Null subjects: a problem for parametersetting models of language acquisition. *Cognition*, 35, 105–22.

Part VIII

New Directions

Introduction

The next decade promises an exponential increase in our knowledge about the relation between brain development and cognition. Recent technological developments in molecular biology, and in our ability to image the functioning brain, will open new vistas in our ability to test hypotheses about the relation between brain growth and cognitive development. Some of the novel theoretical directions and tools which will generate these hypotheses are illustrated in the readings in this final part. While some of these approaches may, in the long run, prove to be more useful than others, they give an indication of currently active growth points in the field.

Bates and Elman argue strongly for the utility of a new computational framework, parallel distributed processing (PDP), as a tool for understanding the mechanisms of change that may underlie both brain and cognitive development. The PDP approach may also be useful for studying how the incorporation of various types and degrees of inbuilt structure can influence the acquisition of knowledge. Stiles and Thal report on similarities and differences in the effects of early brain damage on two aspects of cognition: language and spatial cognition. Janowsky reviews evidence for independent memory systems in the brain, and proposes that a similar framework can be applied to the differential development of components of memory during infancy. McManus and Bryden present a bold argument for a gene, or small group of genes, that gives rise to the laterality of functions such as language within the cortex. Finally, I speculatively attempt to identify some of the factors responsible for constraining the plasticity of the cerebral cortex, and explore the implications of these constraints for our view of neurocognitive development in general.

FURTHER READING

Bornstein, M. H. (ed.) (1987) *Sensitive Periods in Development: Interdisciplinary Perspectives.* Hillsdale, NJ: Erlbaum. (A useful reference collection on sensitive periods in a variety of species.)

Carey, S. and Gelman, R. (eds) (1991) *Epigenesis of the Mind: Essays in Biology and Knowledge.* Hillsdale, NJ: Erlbaum. (A uniformly excellent collection of chapters at the interface between biology and cognitive development.)

Diamond, A. (ed.) (1990) *The Development and Neural Basis of Higher Cognitive Functions.* New York: New York Academy of Sciences. (A comprehensive collection of chapters related to the topic.)

Gibson, K. R. and Peterson, A. C. (eds) (1991) *Brain Maturation and Cognitive Development: Comparative and Cross-cultural Perspectives.* Hawthorne, NY: Aldine de Gruyter Press. (Contains several useful reference chapters.)

Greenough, W. T. and Juraska, J. M. (eds) (1986) *Developmental Neuropsychobiology.* London: Academic Press. (Set of chapters, mainly on animal studies, investigating the relation between aspects of brain growth and behavior.)

Gunnar, M. R. and Nelson, C. A. (1992) *Developmental Behavioral Neuroscience. The Minnesota Symposium on Child Psychology, Volume 24.* Hillsdale, NJ: Erlbaum. (Contains several useful and stimulating papers.)

Hahn, M. E., Hewitt, J. K., Henderson, N. D. and Benno, R. (eds) (1990) *Developmental Behavior Genetics: Neural, Biometrical, and Evolutionary Approaches.* Oxford: Oxford University Press. (A useful reference source for developmental behavior genetics.)

Marler, P. and Terrace, H. S. (1984) *The Biology of Learning.* Berlin: Springer-Verlag. (A useful collection of articles on the biology of learning from a developmental perspective.)

Child Development, volume 58 no. 3, 1987. (Contains special section on developmental psychology and the neurosciences, with several interesting papers and commentaries.)

26

Connectionism and the Study of Change

ELIZABETH A. BATES AND JEFFREY L. ELMAN

Developmental psychology and developmental neuropsychology have traditionally focused on the study of children. But these two fields are also supposed to be about the study of changes 5, i.e. changes in behavior, changes in the neural structures that underlie behavior, and changes in the relationship between mind and brain across the course of development. Ironically, there has been relatively little interest in the mechanisms responsible for change in the past 15–20 years of developmental research. The reasons for this de-emphasis on change have a great deal to do with a metaphor for mind and brain that has influenced most of experimental psychology, cognitive science and neuropsychology for the past few decades, i.e. the metaphor of the serial digital computer. We will refer to this particular framework for the study of mind as the *First Computer Metaphor*, to be contrasted with a new computer metaphor, variously known as connectionism, parallel distributing processing, and/or neural networks. In this brief chapter, we will argue that the First Computer Metaphor has had some particularly unhappy consequences for the study of mental and neural development. By contrast, the *Second Computer Metaphor* (despite its current and no doubt future limitations) offers some compelling advantages for the study of change, at both the mental and the neural level.

The chapter is organized as follows: (1) a brief discussion of the way that change has (or has not) been treated in the past decade of research in developmental psychology; (2) a discussion of the First Computer Metaphor, and its implications for developmental research; (3) an introduction to the Second Computer Metaphor, and the promise it offers for research on the development of mind and brain; ending with (4) a response to some common misconceptions about connectionism.

1 What Happened to the Study of Change?

Traditionally, there are three terms that have been used to describe changes in child behavior over time: maturation, learning, and development. For our purposes here, these terms can be defined as follows.

(a) *Maturation.* As the term is typically used in the psychological literature (although this use may not be entirely accurate from a biological perspective), "maturation" refers to the timely appearance or unfolding of behaviors that are predetermined, in their structure and their sequence, by a well-defined genetic program. The role of experience in a strong maturational theory is limited to a "triggering" function (providing the general or specific conditions that allow some predetermined structures to emerge) or a "blocking" function (providing conditions that inhibit the expression of some predetermined event). The environment does not, in and of itself, provide or cause behavioral structure.

(b) *Learning.* "Learning" is typically defined as a systematic change in behavior as a result of experience. Under some interpretation, learning refers to a copying or transfer of structure from the environment to the organism (as in "acquisition" or "internalization"). Under a somewhat weaker interpretation, learning may refer to a shaping or alteration of behavior that is caused by experience, although the resulting behavior does not resemble structures in the environment in any direct or interesting way.

(c) *Development.* As defined by Werner (1948) in his elaboration of the "orthogenetic principle," "development" refers to any positive change in the internal structure of a system, where "positive" is further defined as an increase in the number of internal parts (i.e. differentiation), accompanied by an increase in the amount of organization that holds among those parts. Under this definition, the term "development" is neutral to the genetic or experiential sources of change, and may include emergent forms that are not directly predictable from genes or experience considered separately (i.e. the sum is greater than and qualitatively different from the parts).

Although all three terms have been used to describe behavioral change in the psychological literature, the most difficult and (in our view) most interesting proposals are the ones that have involved emergent form, i.e. changes that are only indirectly related to structure in the genes or the environment. We are referring here not to the banal interactionism in which black and white yield gray, but to a much more challenging interactionism in which black and white converge and interact to yield an unexpected red. Because this interactionist view appears to be the only way to explain how new structures arise, it may be our only way out of a fruitless nature–nurture debate that has hampered progress in developmental psychology for most of its history.

Within our field, the most complete interactionist theory of behavioral change to date is the theory offered by Jean Piaget, across a career that spanned more than fifty years (Piaget, 1952, 1970a, b, 1971). Piaget's genetic epistemology concentrated on the way that new mental structures emerge at the interface between an active child and a structured world. The key mechanism for change in Piaget's theory is the consummate biological notion of adaptation. Starting with a restricted set of sensorimotor schemes (i.e. structured "packages" of perception and action that permit activities like sucking, reaching, tracking, and/or grasping), the child begins to act upon the world (assimilation). Actions are modified in response to feedback from that world (accommodation), and in response to the degree of internal coherence or stability that action schemes bear to one another (reciprocal assimilation). The proximal cause that brings about adaptation is a rather poorly defined notion of equilibration, i.e. the re-establishment of a stable and coherent state after a perturbation that created instability or disequilibrium. In the infant years, adaptation of simple sensorimotor schemes to a structured world leads to an increasingly complex and integrated set of schemes or "plans," structures that eventually permit the child to "re-present" the world (i.e. to call potential perceptuo-motor schemes associated with a given object or event into an organized state-of-readiness, in the absence of direct perceptual input from the represented object or event). This developmental notion of representation comprised Piaget's explanation for the appearance of mental imagery, language, and other symbolic or representational forms somewhere in the second year of life. After this point, the process of adaptation continues at both the physical and representation levels (i.e. operations on the real world, and operations on the new "mental world"), passing through a series of semi-stable "stages" or moments of system-wide equilibrium, ultimately leading to our human capacity for higher forms of logic and reasoning.

This "bootstrapping" approach to cognitive development does involve a weak form of learning (as defined above), but the mental structures that characterize each stage of development are not predictable in any direct way from either the structure of the world or the set of innate sensorimotor schemes with which the child began. Furthermore, Piaget insisted that these progressive increases in complexity were a result of activity ("construction"), and not a gradual unfolding of predetermined forms (maturation). In this fashion, Piaget strove to save us from the nature–nurture dilemma. Behavioral outcomes were determined not only by genes, or by environment, but by the mathematical, physical, and biological laws that determine the kinds of solutions that are possible for any given problem. As Piaget once stated in a criticism of his American colleague Noam Chomsky, "That which is inevitable does not have to be innate" (Piaget, 1970a).

There was a period in the history of developmental psychology in which Piagetian theory assumed a degree of orthodoxy that many found stifling. Decades later, it now appears that much of Piaget's theory was wrong in detail. For one thing, it is now clear that the infant's initial stock of innate sensorimotor schemes is far richer than Piaget believed. It is also clear that Piaget overestimated the degree of cross-domain stability that children are likely to display at any given point in development (i.e. the notion of a coherent "stage"). Once the details of his stage theory were proven inadequate, all that really remained were the principles of change that formed the bedrock of Piaget's genetic epistemology – notions of adaptation and equilibration that struck many of his critics as hopelessly vague, and a notion of emergent form that many found downright mystical. Piaget was aware of these problems, and spent the latter part of his career seeking a set of formalisms to concretize his deep insights about change. Most critics agree that these efforts failed. This failure, coupled with new empirical information showing that many other aspects of the theory were incorrect, has led to a widespread repudiation of Piaget. Indeed, we are in a period of "anti-Piagetianism" of patricidal dimensions.

What have we put in Piaget's place? We have never replaced his theory with a better account of the epistemology of change. In fact, the most influential

developmental movements of the past two decades have essentially disavowed
change. Alas, we fear that we are back on the horns of the nature–nurture
dilemma from which Piaget tried in vain to save us.

On the one hand, we have seen a series of strong nativist proposals in the past
few years, including proposals by some neo-Gibsonian theorists within the
so-called "competent infant movement" (Baillargéon and deVos, 1991; Spelke,
1990, 1991), and proposals within language acquisition inspired by Chomsky's
approach to the nature and origins of grammar (Hyams, 1986; Lightfoot, 1991;
Roeper and Williams, 1987). In both these movements, it is assumed that the
essence of what it means to be human is genetically predetermined. Change –
insofar as we see change at all – is attributed to the maturation of predetermined
mental content, to the release of preformed material by an environmental
"trigger," and/or to the gradual removal of banal sensory and motor limitations
that hid all this complex innate knowledge from view. Indeed, the term "learning" has taken on such negative connotations in some quarters that efforts are
underway to eliminate it altogether. The following quotes from Piatelli-Palmarini
(1989) illustrate how far things have gone:

> I, for one, see no advantage in the preservation of the term learning. We agree
> with those who maintain that we would gain in clarity if the scientific use of the
> term were simply discontinued. (p. 2)
>
> Problem-solving . . . adaptation, simplicity, compensation, equilibration, minimal
> disturbance and all those universal, parsimony-driven forces of which the natural
> sciences are so fond, recede into the background. They are either scaled down, at
> the physico-chemical level, where they still make a lot of sense, or dismissed
> altogether. (pp. 13–14)

On the other hand, the neo-Vygotskian movement and associated approaches
to the social bases of cognition have provided us with another form of prefor-
mationalism, insisting that the essence of what it means to be human is laid out
for the child in the structure of social interactions (Bruner and Sherwood, 1976;
Rogoff, 1990). In these theories, change is viewed primarily as a process of
internalization, as the child takes in preformed solutions to problems that lie in
the "zone of proximal development," i.e. in joint activities that are just outside
his current ability to act alone. Related ideas are often found in research on
"motherese," i.e. on the special, simplified and caricatured form of language that
adults direct to small children (for a review, see Ferguson and Snow, 1978). In
citing these examples, we do not want to deny that society has an influence on
development, because we are quite sure that it does. Our point is, simply, that
the pendulum has swung too far from the study of child-initiated change. The
most influential movements in developmental psychology for the past two decades
are those that have de-emphasized change in favor of an emphasis on some kind
of preformation: either a preformation by nature and the hand of God, or a
preformation by the competent adult.

Why have we accepted these limits? Why haven't we moved on to study the
process by which new structures really do emerge? We believe that developmental
psychology has been influenced for many years by a metaphor for mind in which
it is difficult to think about change in any interesting form – which brings us
to the First Computer Metaphor.

2   The First Computer Metaphor and Its Implications for Development

At its core, the serial digital computer is a machine that manipulates symbols. It takes individual symbols (or strings of symbols) as its input, applies a set of stored algorithms (a program) to that input, and produces more symbols (or strings of symbols) as its output. These steps are performed one at a time (albeit very quickly) by a central processor. Because of this serial constraint, problems to be solved by the First Computer must be broken down into a hierarchical structure that permits the machine to reach solutions with maximum efficiency (e.g. moving down a decision tree until a particular subproblem is solved, and then back up again to the next step in the program).

Without question, exploitation of this machine has led to huge advances in virtually every area of science, industry, and education. After all, computers can do things that human beings simply cannot do, permitting quantitative advances in information processing and numerical analysis that were unthinkable a century ago. The problem with this device for our purposes here lies not in its utility as a scientific tool, but in its utility as a scientific metaphor, in particular as a metaphor for the human mind/brain. Four properties of the serial digital computer have had particularly unfortunate consequences for the way that we have come to think about mental and neural development.

(1) *Discrete representations.* The symbols that are manipulated by a serial digital computer are discrete entities. That is, they either are or are not present in the input. There is no such thing as 50 percent of the letter **A** or 99 percent of the number **7**. For example, if a would-be user types in a password that is off by only one keystroke, the computer does not respond with "What the heck, that's close enough." Instead, the user is damned just as thoroughly as he would be if he did not know the password at all.

People (particularly children) rarely behave like this. We can respond to partial information (degraded input) in a systematic way; and we often transform our inputs (systematic or not) into partial decisions and imperfect acts (degraded output). We are error-prone, but we are also forgiving, flexible, willing and able to make the best of what we have. This mismatch between human behavior and the representations manipulated by serial digital computers has of course been known for some time. To resolve this well-known discrepancy, the usual device adopted by proponents of the First Computer Metaphor for mind is the competence/performance distinction. That is, it is argued that our knowledge (competence) takes a discrete and idealized form that is compatible with the computer metaphor, but our behavior (performance) is degraded by processing factors and other sources of noise that are irrelevant to a characterization of knowledge and (by extension) acquisition of knowledge. This is a perfectly reasonable intellectual move, but as we will see in more detail below, it has led to certain difficulties in characterizing the nature of learning that often result in the statement that learning is impossible.

(2) *Absolute rules.* Like the symbolic representations described above, the algorithms contained in a computer program also take a discrete form. If the discrete

symbols that trigger a given rule are present in the input, then that rule must apply, and give an equally discrete symbol or string of symbols as its output. Conversely, if the relevant symbols are not present in the input, then the rule in question will not apply. There is no room for anything in between, no coherent way of talking about 50 percent of a rule, or (for that matter) weak versus strong rules. Indeed, this is exactly the reason why computers are so much more reliable than human beings for many computational purposes.

Presented with the well-known mismatch between human behavior and the absolute status of rules in a serial digital computer, proponents of the First Computer Metaphor for mind usually resort to the same competence/performance described above. Alternatively, there have been attempts to model the probabilistic nature of human behavior by adding weights to rules, a device that permits the model to decide which rule to apply (or in what order of preference) when a choice has to be made. The problem is that these weights are in no way a natural product or property of the architecture in which they are embedded, nor are they produced automatically by the learning process. Instead, these weights are arbitrary, *ad hoc* devices that must be placed in the system by hand – which brings us to the next point.

(3) *Learning as programming.* The serial digital computer is not a self-organizing system. It does not learn easily. Indeed, the easiest metaphor for learning in a system of this kind is programming; that is, the rules that must be applied to inputs of some kind are placed directly into the system – by man, by nature, or by the hand of God. To be sure, there is a literature on computer learning in the field of artificial intelligence. However, most of these efforts are based on a process of hypothesis testing. In such learning models, two essential factors are provided *a priori*: a set of hypotheses that will be tested against the data, and an algorithm for deciding which hypothesis provides the best fit to those data. This is by its very nature a strong nativist approach to learning. It is not surprising that learning theories of this kind are regularly invoked by linguists and psycholinguists with a strong nativist orientation. There is no graceful way for the system to derive new hypotheses (as opposed to modifications of a pre-existing option). Everything that really counts is already there at the beginning.

Once again, however, we have an unfortunate mismatch between theory and data in cognitive science. Because the hypotheses tested by a traditional computer learning model are discrete in nature (based on the rule and representations described above), learning (a.k.a. "selection") necessarily involves a series of discrete decisions about the truth or falsity of each hypothesis. Hence we would expect change to take place in a crisp, stepwise fashion, as decisions are made, hypotheses are discarded, and new ones are put in their place. But human learning rarely proceeds in this fashion, characterized more often by error, vacillation and backsliding. In fact, the limited value of the serial digital computer as a metaphor for learning is well known. Perhaps for this reason, learning and development have receded into the background in modern cognitive psychology, while the field has concentrated instead on issues like the nature of representation, processes of recognition and retrieval, and the various stages through which discrete bits of information are processed (e.g. various buffers and checkpoints in a serial process of symbol manipulation). Developmental psychologists working within this framework (or indirectly influenced by it) have moved away from the study of change and self-organization toward a catalogue of those representations that are there at the beginning (e.g. the "competent infant" movement in cognition and perception, the parameter-setting movement in developmental psycholinguistics), and/or a characterization of how the processes that elaborate information mature or expand across the childhood years (i.e. changes in performance that "release" the expression of pre-existing knowledge).

(4) *The hardware/software distinction.* One of the most unfortunate consequences of the First Computer Metaphor for cognitive science in general and developmental psychology in particular has been the acceptance of a strong separation between software (the knowledge – symbols, rules, hypotheses, etc. – that is contained in a program) and hardware (the machine that is used to implement that program). From this perspective, the machine itself places very few constraints on our theory of knowledge and (by extension) behavior, except perhaps for some relatively banal concerns about capacity (e.g. there are some programs that one simply cannot run on a small personal computer with limited memory).

The distinction between hardware and software has provided much of the ammunition for an approach to philosophy of mind and cognitive science called Functionalism (Fodor, 1981).[1] Within the functionalist school, the essential properties of mind are derived entirely from the domains on which the mind must operate: language, logic, mathematics, three-dimensional space, etc. To be sure, these properties have to be implemented in a machine of some kind, but the machine itself does not place interesting constraints on mental representations (i.e. the objects manipulated by the mind) or functional architecture (i.e. the abstract system that manipulates those objects). This belief has justified an approach to cognition that is entirely independent of neuroscience, thereby reducing the number and range of constraints to which our cognitive theories must respond. As a by-product (since divorces usually affect both parties), this approach has also reduced the impact of cognitive theories and cognitive phenomena on the field of neuroscience.

The separation between biology and cognition has had particularly serious consequences for developmental psychology, a field in which biology has traditionally played a major role (i.e a tradition that includes Freud, Gesell, Baldwin, and Piaget, to name a few). Not only have we turned away from our traditional emphasis on change, but we have also turned away from the healthy and regular use of biological constraints on the study of developing minds. Ironically, some of the strongest claims about innateness in the current literature have been put forth in complete disregard of biological facts. Very rich forms of object perception and deep inferences about three-dimensional space are ascribed to infants before three to four months of age, conclusions which are difficult to square with (for example) well-known limitations on visual acuity and/or the immaturity of higher cortical regions in that age range. The underlying assumption appears to be that our cognitive findings have priority, and if there is a mismatch between cognitive and biological conclusions, we probably got the biology wrong (which may be the case some of the time – but surely not all the time!).

It seems to us that we need all the constraints that can be found to make sense of a growing mass of information about cognitive development, language development, perceptual development, social development. Furthermore, we suspect that developmental neuroscience would also profit from a healthy dose of knowledge about the behavioral functions of the neural systems under study. Finally, we would all be better off if we could find a computational model (or class of models) in which it would be easier to organize and study the mutual constraints that hold between mental and neural development – which brings us to the next computer metaphor.

3   The Second Computer Metaphor and Its Implications for Development

During the 1950s and 1960s, when the First Computer Metaphor for mind began to influence psychological research, some information scientists were exploring the properties of a different and competing computational device called the Perceptron (Rosenblatt, 1958, 1962). The roots of this approach can be traced to earlier work in cybernetics (Minsky, 1956; von Neumann, 1951, 1958) and in neurophysiology (Eccles, 1953; Hebb, 1949; McCulloch and Pitts, 1943). In a perceptron network, unlike the serial digital computer, there was not a clear distinction between processor and memory, nor did it operate on symbols in the usual sense of the term. Instead, the perceptron network was composed of a large number of relatively simple "local" units that worked in parallel to perceive, recognize and/or categorize an input. These local units or "nodes" were organized into two layers, an "input set" and an "output set." In the typical perceptron architecture, every unit on the input layer was connected by a single link to each and every unit on the output layer (see figure 26.1). These connections varied in degree or strength, from 0 to 1 (in a purely excitatory system) or from -1 to $+1$ (in a system with both activation and inhibition). A given output unit would "fire" as a function of the amount of input that it received from the various input units, with activation collected until a critical firing threshold was reached (see also McCulloch and Pitts, 1943). Individual acts of recognition or categorization in a Perceptron reflect the collective activity of all these units. Knowledge is a property of the connection strengths that hold between the respective input and output layers; the machine can be said to "know" a pattern when it gives the correct output for a given class of inputs (including novel members of the input class that it has never seen before, i.e. generalization).

There are some obvious analogies between this system and the form of computation carried out in real neural systems, e.g. excitatory and inhibitory links, summation of activation, firing thresholds, and above all the distribution of patterns across a large number of interconnected units. But this was not the only advantage that perceptrons offered, compared with their competitors. The most important property of perceptrons was (and is) their ability to learn by example.

During the teaching and learning phase, a stimulus is registered on the input layer in a distributed fashion, by turning units on or off to varying degrees. The

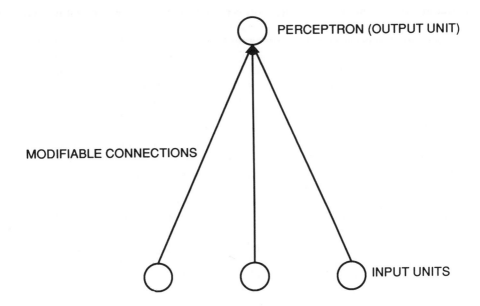

Figure 26.1   A simple perceptron network.

system produces the output that it currently prefers (based, in the most extreme *tabula rasa* case, on a random set of connections). Each unit in this distributed but "ignorant" output is then compared with the corresponding unit in the "correct" output. If a given output unit within a distributed pattern has "the right answer," its connection strengths are left unchanged. If a given output has "the wrong answer," the size of the error is calculated by a simple difference score (i.e. "delta"). All of the connections to that erroneous output are then increased or decreased in proportion to the amount of error that they were responsible for on that trial. This procedure then continues in a similar fashion for other trials. Because the network is required to find a single set of connection weights which allow it to respond correctly to all of the patterns it has seen, it typically succeeds only by discovering the underlying generalizations which relate inputs to outputs. The important and interesting result is that the network is then able to respond appropriately not only to stimuli it has seen before, but to novel stimuli as well. The learning procedure is thus an example of learning inductively.

Compared with the cumbersome hypothesis-testing procedures that constitute learning in serial digital computers, learning really appears to be a natural property of the perceptron. Indeed, perceptrons are able to master a broad range of patterns, with realistic generalization to new inputs as a function of their similarity to the initial learning set. The initial success of these artificial systems had some impact on theories of pattern recognition in humans. The most noteworthy example is Selfridge's "Pandemonium Model" (Selfridge, 1958), in which simple local feature detectors or "demons" work in parallel to recognize a complex pattern. Each demon scans the input for evidence of its preferred feature; depending on its degree of certainty that the relevant feature has appeared, each demon "shouts" or "whispers" its results. In the Pandemonium Model (as in the Perceptron), there is no final arbiter, no *homunculus* or central executive who puts all these daemonical inputs together. Rather, the "solution" is an emergent property of the system as a whole, a global pattern produced by independent, local computations. This also means that results or solutions can vary in their degree of resemblance to the "right" answer, capturing the rather fuzzy properties of human categorization that are so elusive in psychological models inspired by the serial digital computer.

So far so good. And yet this promising line of research came to a virtual end in 1969, when Minsky and Papert published their famous book *Perceptrons*. Minsky and Papert (who were initial enthusiasts and pioneers in perceptron research) were able to prove that perceptrons are only capable of learning a limited class of first-order, linearly separable patterns. These systems are incapable of learning second-order relations like "A or B but not both" (i.e. logical exclusive OR, also known as XOR), and by extension, any pattern of equivalent or greater complexity and interdependence. This fatal flaw is a direct product of the fact that perceptrons are two-layered systems, with a single direct link between each input and output unit. If A and B are both "on" in the input layer, then they each automatically "turn on" their collaborators on the output layer. There is simply no place in the system to record the fact that A and B are both on simultaneously, and hence no way to "warn" their various collaborators that they should shut up on this particular trial. It was clear even in 1969 that this problem could be addressed by adding another layer somewhere in the middle, a set of units capable of recording the fact that A and B are both on simultaneously, and therefore capable of inhibiting output nodes that would normally turn on in the presence of either A or B. So why not add a set of "in-between" units, creating three or four or N layered perceptrons? Unfortunately, the learning rules available at that time (e.g. the simple delta rule) did not work with multilayered systems. Furthermore, Minsky and Papert offered the conjecture that such a learning rule would prove impossible in principle, owing to the combinatorial complexity of delta calculations and "distribution of blame" in an N-layered system. As it turns out, this conjecture was wrong (after all, a conjecture is not a proof). Nevertheless, it was very influential. Interest in the perceptron as a model of complex mental processes dwindled in many quarters. From 1970 on, most of artificial intelligence research abandoned this architecture in favor of the fast, flexible and highly programmable serial digital computer. And most of cognitive psychology followed suit. (For a somewhat different account of this history, see Papert, 1988; a good collection of historically important documents can be found in Anderson and Rosenfeld, 1989.).

Parallel distributed processing was revived in the late 1970s and early 1980s, for a variety of reasons. In fact, the computational advantages of such systems were never entirely forgotten (Anderson, 1972; Feldman and Ballard, 1980; Hinton and Anderson, 1981; Kohonen, 1977; Willshaw et al., 1969), and their resemblance to real neural systems continued to exert some appeal (Grossberg, 1968, 1972, 1987). But the current "boom" in parallel distributed processing or "connectionism" was inspired in large measure by the discovery of a learning rule that worked for multilayered systems (Le Cun, 1985; Rumelhart et al., 1986a). The Minsky–Papert conjecture was overturned, and there are now many impressive demonstrations of learning in multilayered neural nets, including learning of *N*-order dependencies like "A or B but not both" (Rumelhart et al., 1986b).[2] Multilayer networks have been shown to be universal function approximators, which means they can approximate any function to any arbitrary degree of precision (Hornik et al., 1989). Such a network is shown in figure 26.2.

Another reason for the current popularity of connectionism derives from technical advances in the design of parallel computing systems. It has become increasingly clear to computer scientists that we are close to the absolute physical limits on speed and efficiency in serial systems – and yet the largest and fastest serial computers still cannot come close to the speed with which our small, slow, energy-efficient brains recognize patterns and decide where and how to move. As Carver Mead has pointed out (Mead, 1989), it is time to "reverse-engineer Nature," to figure out the principles by which real brains compute information. It is still the case that most connectionist simulations are actually carried out on serial digital computers (which mimic parallelism by carrying out a set of would-be parallel computations in a series, and waiting for the result until the next wave of would-be parallel computations is ready to go). But new, truly parallel architectures are coming on line (e.g. the now-famous Connection Machine) to implement those discoveries that have been made with pseudo-parallel simulations. Parallel distributed processing appears to be the solution elected by evolution, and (if Mead is right) computer science will have to move in this direction to capture the kinds of processing that human beings do so well.

For developmental psychologists, the Second Computer Metaphor holds some clear advantages for the study of change in human beings. The first set involves the same four areas in which the First Computer Metaphor has let us down: the nature of representations, rules or "mappings", learning, and the hardware/software issue. The last two are advantages peculiar to connectionist networks: nonlinear dynamics and emergent form.

(1) *Distributed representations.* The representations employed in connectionist nets differ radically from the symbols manipulated by serial digital computers. First, these representations are "coarse-coded," distributed across many different units. Because of this property, it is reasonable to talk about the degree to which a representation is active or the amount of a representation that is currently available in this system (i.e. 50 percent of an "A" or 99 percent of the number "7"). This also means that patterns can be built up or torn down in bits and pieces, accounting for the graded nature of learning in most instances, and for the gradual or graded patterns of breakdown that are typically displayed by brain-damaged individuals (Hinton and Shallice, 1991; Marchman, 1992; Schwartz et al., 1990; Seidenberg and McClelland, 1989). Second, the same units can participate in many different patterns, and many different patterns coexist in a superimposed fashion across the same set of units. This fact can be used to account for degrees of similarity between patterns, and for the ways in which patterns penetrate, facilitate and/or interfere with one another at various points

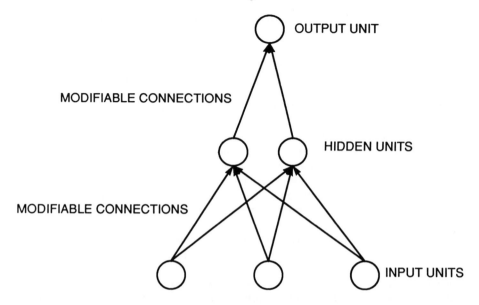

Figure 26.2 A multilayered network. The "hidden units" allow such networks to form internal representations. Multilayer networks of this sort have been shown to be able to approximate any function to any arbitrary degree of accuracy.

in learning and development (for an expanded discussion of this point, see Bates et al., 1991).

(2) *Graded rules.* Contrary to rumor, it is not the case that connectionist systems have no rules. However, the rules or "mappings" employed by connectionist nets take a very different form from the crisp algorithms contained within the programs employed by a serial digital computer. These include the learning rule itself (i.e. the principle by which the system reduces error and "decides" when it has reached a good fit between input and output), and the functions that determine when and how a unit will fire. But above all, the "rules" in a connectionist net include the connections that hold among units, i.e. the links or "weights" that embody all the potential mappings from input to output across the system as a whole. This means that rules (like representations) can exist by degree, and vary in strength.

It should also be clear from this description that it is difficult to distinguish between rules and representations in a connectionist net. The knowledge or "mapping potential" of a network comprises the units that participate in distributed patterns, and the connections among those units. Because all these potential mappings coexist across the same "territory," they must compete with one another to resolve a given input. In the course of this competition, the system does not "decide" between alternatives in the usual sense; rather, it "relaxes" or "resolves" into a (temporary) state of equilibrium. In a stochastic system of this kind, it is possible for several different networks to reach the same solution to a problem, each with a totally different set of weights. This fact runs directly counter to the tendency in traditional cognitive and linguistic research to seek "the rule" or "the grammar" that underlies a set of behavioral regularities. In other words, rules are not absolute in any sense – they can vary by degree within a given individual, and they can also vary in their internal structure from one individual to another. We believe that these properties are far more compatible with the combination of universal tendencies and individual variation that we see in the course of human development, and they are compatible with the remarkable neural and behavioral plasticity that is evident in children who have suffered early brain injury (Marchman, 1992; Thal et al., 1991).

(3) *Learning as structural change.* As we pointed out earlier, much of the current excitement about connectionist systems revolves around their capacity for learning and self-organization. Indeed, the current boom in connectionism has brought learning and development back onto center stage in cognitive science. These systems really do change as a function of learning, displaying forms of organization that were not placed there by the programmer (or by nature, or by the hand of God). To be sure, the final product is codetermined by the initial structure of the system and the data to which it is exposed. These systems are not anarchists, nor solipsists. But in no sense is the final product "copied" or programmed in. Furthermore, once the system has learned, it is difficult for it to "unlearn," if by "unlearning" we mean a return to its pristine prelearning state. This is true for the reasons described in (1) and (2): the knowledge contained in connectionist nets is contained in and defined by its very architecture, in the connection weights that currently hold among all units as a function of prior learning. Knowledge is not "retrieved" from some passive store, nor is it "placed in" or "passed between" spatially localized buffers. Learning is structural change, and experience involves the activation of potential states in that system as it is currently structured.

From this point of view, the term "acquisition" is an infelicitous way of talking about learning or change. Certain states become possible in the system, but they are not acquired in the usual sense, i.e. found or purchased or stored away like nuts in preparation for the winter. This property of connectionist systems permits us to do away with problems that have been rampant in certain areas of developmental psychology, e.g. the problem of determining "when" a given piece of knowledge is acquired, or "when" a rule finally becomes productive. Instead, development (like the representations and mappings on which it is based) can be viewed as a gradual process; there is no single moment at which learning can be said to occur (but see nonlinearity, below).

(4) *Software as hardware.* We have stated that knowledge in connectionist nets is defined by the very structure of the system. For this reason, the hardware/software distinction is impossible to maintain under the Second Computer Metaphor. This is true whether or not the structure of connectionist nets as currently conceived is "neurally real," i.e. like the structure that holds in real neural systems. We may still have the details wrong (indeed, we probably do), but the important point for present purposes is that there is no further excuse for ignoring potential neural constraints on proposed cognitive architectures. The distinction that has separated cognitive science and neuroscience for so long has

fallen, like the Berlin Wall. Some cognitive psychologists and philosophers of science believe that is not a good thing (and indeed, the same might be said someday for the Berlin Wall). But we are convinced that this historic event is a good one, especially for those of us who are interested in the codevelopment of mind and brain. We are going the right direction, even though we have a long way to go.

(5) *Nonlinear dynamics.* Connectionist networks are nonlinear dynamical systems, a fact that follows from several properties of connectionist architecture, including the existence of intervening layers between inputs and outputs (permitting the system to go beyond linear mappings), the nonlinear threshold functions that determine how and when a single unit will fire, and the learning rules that bring about a change in the weighted connections between units. Because these networks are nonlinear systems, they can behave in unexpected ways, mimicking the U-shaped learning functions and sudden moments of "insight" that challenged old stimulus–response theories of learning, and helped to bring about the cognitive revolution in the 1960s (Plunkett and Marchman, 1991a, b; MacWhinney and Leinbach, 1991).

(6) *Emergent form.* Because connectionist networks are nonlinear systems, capable of unexpected forms of change, they are also capable of producing truly novel outputs. In trying to achieve stability across a large number of superimposed, distributed patterns, the network may hit on a solution that was "hidden" in bits and pieces of the data; that solution may be transformed and generalized across the system as a whole, resulting in what must be viewed as a qualitative shift. This is the first precise, formal embodiment of the notion of emergent form – an idea that stood at the heart of Piaget's theory of change in cognitive systems. As such, connectionist systems may have the very property that we need to free ourselves from the nature–nurture controversy. New structures can emerge at the interface between "nature" (the initial architecture of the system) and "nurture" (the input to which that system is exposed). These new structures are not the result of black magic, or vital forces. They are the result of laws that govern the integration of information in nonlinear systems – which brings us to our final section.

4   Some Common Misconceptions about Connectionism

It is no doubt quite clear to the reader that we are enthusiastic about the Second Computer Metaphor, because we believe that it will help us to pick up a cold trail that Piaget first pioneered, moving toward a truly interactive theory of change. But we are aware of how much there is to do, and how many pitfalls lie before us. We are also aware of some of the doubts and worries about this movement that are currently in circulation. Perhaps it would be useful to end this essay with some answers to some common misconceptions about connectionism, with special reference to the application of connectionist principles within developmental psychology.

   Worry 1. "Connectionism is nothing but associationism, and we already know the limits of associationism" (e.g. Fodor and Pylyshyn, 1988). As we pointed out above, multilayer connectionist nets are nonlinear dynamical systems, whereas the familiar associationist models of the past rested on assumptions of linearity. This is both the good news, and the bad news. The good news is that nonlinear systems can learn relationships of considerable complexity, and they can produce surprising and (of course) nonlinear forms of change. The bad news is that no one really understands the limits and capabilities of nonlinear dynamical systems. Maybe this is also good news: we have finally met our goal, after years of physics envy, because we have finally reached the same frontiers of ignorance as the physicists! Presumably, the limits of these systems will someday be known (although probably not within our lifetimes). But right now, it would be grossly premature to claim that connectionist networks can "never" perform certain functions. Anyone who claims that we already know the limits of this kind of associationism has been misinformed.

Worry 2. "There are no interesting internal representations in connectionist nets" (e.g. Pinker and Prince, 1988). There are indeed complex and rich representations in connectionist networks, and transformations that do the same work as rules in classical systems. However, these rules and representations take a radically different form from the familiar symbols and algorithms of serial digital computers and/or generative linguistics. The representations and rules embodied in connectionist nets are implicit and highly distributed. Part of the challenge of modern research on neural networks is to understand exactly what a net has learned after is has reached some criterion of performance. So far, the answer appears to be that they do not look like anything we have ever seen before (for examples, see Elman, 1989, 1990, 1991).

Worry 3. "Connectionist nets only yield interesting performance on cognitive problems when the experiment 'sneaks in' the solution by (a) fixing the internal weights until they work, or (b) laying out the solution in the input" (e.g. Lachter and Bever, 1988). Part of the fascination of connectionist modeling lies in the fact that it offers the experimenter so many surprises. These are self-organizing systems that learn how to solve a problem. As the art is currently practiced, *no one* fiddles with the internal weights but the system itself, in the course of learning. Indeed, in a simulation of any interesting level of complexity, it would be virtually impossible to reach a solution by "hand-tweaking" of the weights. As for the issue of "sneaking the solution into the input," we have seen several simulations in which the experimenter did indeed try to make the input as explicit as possible – and yet the system stubbornly found a different way to solve the problem. Good connectionist modelers approach their simulations with the same spirit of discovery and breathless anticipation that is very familiar to those who carry out real experiments with real children. Aside from being close to impossible, cheating would not be any fun at all – and the hand-crafting of solutions is usually considered a form of cheating.

Worry 4. "The supposed commitment to neural plausibility is a scam; no one really takes it seriously." Connectionists work at many different levels between brain and behavior. In current simulations of higher cognitive processes, it is true that the architecture is "brain-like" only in a very indirect sense. In fact, the typical 100-neuron connectionist toy is "brain-like" only in comparison with the serial digital computer (which is wildly unlike nervous systems of any known kind). The many qualities that separate real brains from connectionist simulations have been described in detail elsewhere (Churchland and Sejnowski, 1992; Crick, 1989; Hertz et al., 1991). The real questions are: (a) is there anything of interest that can be learned from simulations in simplified systems; and (b) can connectionists "add in" constraints from real neural systems in a series of systematic steps, approaching something like a realistic theory of mind and brain? Of course we still do not know the answer to either of these questions, but there are many researchers in the connectionist movement who are trying to bring these systems closer to neural reality. For example, efforts are underway to study the computational properties of different neuronal types. Some researchers are exploring analogues to synaptogenesis and synaptic pruning in neural nets. Others are looking into the computational analogues of neural transmitters within a fixed network structure. The current hope is that work at all these different levels will prove to be compatible, and that a unified theory of the mind and brain will someday emerge. Of course we are a long way off, but the commitment by most of the researchers that we know in this field is a very serious one. It has launched a new spirit of interdisciplinary research in cognitive neuroscience, one with important implications for developmental psychology.

Worry 5. "Connectionism is anti-nativist, and efforts are underway to reinstate a *tabula rasa* approach to mind and development" (e.g. Kirsh, 1992). It is true that many current simulations assume something like a *tabula rasa* in the first stages of learning (e.g. a random "seeding" of weights among fully connected units before learning begins). This has proven to be a useful simplifying assumption, in order to learn something about the amount and type of structure that has to be assumed for a given type of learning to go through. But there is no logical incompatibility between connectionism and nativism. Indeed, just as many historians have argued that Franklin Delano Roosevelt saved capitalism, connectionism may prove to be the salvation of nativist approaches to mind. The problem with current nativist theories is that they offer no serious account of what it might mean in biological terms for a given structure or idea to be innate. In neural networks, it is possible to explore various avenues for building in innate structure, including minor biases that have major structural consequences across a range of environmental conditions (Jacobs et al., 1991). In fact, within connectionist models there are coherent ways to talk about 90 or 10 percent of any innate idea! This is an approach that has not been explored in any detail to date, but the possibilities are intriguing, and might (ironically enough) end up being connectionism's greatest contribution to developmental cognitive neuroscience.

To conclude, we are willing to speculate that we will soon see a revival of Piagetian theory within a connectionist framework – not a mindless reinterpretation of the old theory in modern jargon, but a return to Piaget's program of genetic epistemology, instantiating his principles of equilibration and adaptation in concrete systems that really work – and really change. As we said before, Piaget spent the later decades of his life seeking a way of formalizing the theory, to answer critics (including Piaget himself) who charged that his principles of change were much too vague. We think that Piaget would have loved these new possibilities if he had lived to see them. We now have an opportunity to pick up the threads of his old program and move it forward into an exciting new decade, incorporating all the new insights and new empirical information that has been gained in the interim, without abandoning the fundamental commitment of developmental psychology to the study of change.

ACKNOWLEDGEMENTS

We wish to thank the CNR Institute of Psychology, Via Nomentana 56 for their hospitality to the first author during her sabbatical in fall 1991; partial support to the first author during preparation of this manuscript came from NIDCD grants "Cross-linguistic studies of aphasia" and "Program Project: Origins of Communication Disorders" and from the NINDS grant "Center for the Neural Bases of Language and Learning". Support to the second author comes from Army Avionics, Fort Monmouth.

We wish to thank the John D. and Catherine T. MacArthur Foundation Research Network in Early Childhood Transitions, who furnished funds for a training program in Neural Network Modelling for Developmental Psychologists, including a conference in August 1991 where many of these ideas were discussed. We are particularly grateful to Annette Karmiloff-Smith for a number of stimulating and very helpful discussions on these topics.

NOTES

1 This particular school of Functionalism has little to do with, and is indeed diametrically opposed to, an approach within linguistics and psycholinguistics alternatively called Functional Grammar or Cognitive Linguistics. For discussions, see Bates and Mac-Whinney (1989), Givón (1984), Lakoff (1987), Langacker (1987).

2 A number of readable introductions to connectionism are now available. See Bechtel and Abrahamsen (1991), Churchland and Sejnowski (1992), Dayhoff (1990). An excellent but more technical introduction can be found in Hertz et al., (1991).

REFERENCES

Anderson, J. A. (1972) A simple neural network generating an interactive memory. *Mathematical Bio-Sciences*, 8, 137–60.

Anderson, J. A. and Rosenfeld, E. (1989) *Neurocomputing: foundations of research*. MIT Press/Bradford Books.

Baillargéon, R. and de Vos, J. (1991) Object permanence in young infants: Further evidence. *Child Development*, 62, 1227–46.

Bates, E. and MacWhinney, B. (1989) Functionalism and the competition model. In B. MacWhinney and E. Bates (eds), *The cross-linguistic study of sentence processing*. New York: Academic Press.

Bates, E., Thal, D. and Marchman, V. (1991) Symbols and syntax: a Darwinian approach to language development. In N. Krasnegor, D. Rumbaugh, E. Schiefelbusch and M. Studdert-Kennedy (eds), *The biological and behavioral determinants of language development*. Hillsdale, NJ: Erlbaum.

Bruner, J. and Sherwood, V. (1976) Peekaboo and the learning of rule structures. In J. S. Bruner, A. Jolly and K. Sylva (eds), *Play: its role in development and evolution*. New York: Basic Books, Inc.

Bechtel, W. and Abrahamsen, A. (1991) *Connectionism and the mind*. Oxford: Basil Blackwell.

Churchland, P. and Sejnowsky, T. (1992) neural computation. Cambridge, MA: MIT Press/Bradford Books.

Crick, F. (1989) The recent excitement about neural networks. *Nature*, 337, 129–132.

Dayhoff, J. (1990) *Neural network architectures*. New York: Van Nostrand Reinhold.

Eccles, J. L. (1953) *The neurophysiological basis of mind*. Oxford: Clarendon.

Elman, J. (1989) Structured representations and connectionist models. In *The Eleventh Annual Conference of the Cognitive Science Society*. Hillsdale, NJ: Erlbaum.

Elman, J. (1990) Finding structure in time. *Cognitive Science*, 14, 179–211.

Elman, J. (1991) Distributed representations, simple recurrent networks, and grammatical structure. *Machine Learning*, 7, 195–225.

Feldman, J. A. and Ballard, D. H. (1980) *Computing with connections. TR 72*. University of Rochester Computer Science Department.

Ferguson, C. and Snow, C. (1978) *Talking to children*. Cambridge: Cambridge University Press.

Fodor, J. A. (1981) *Representations*. Brighton (Sussex): Harvester Press.

Fodor, J. A. and Pylyshyn, Z. W. (1988) Connectionism and cognitive architecture: a critical analysis. In S. Pinker and J. Mehler (eds), *Connections and symbols*. Cambridge, MA: MIT Press/Bradford Books, pp. 3–71.

Givón, T. (1984) *Syntax: a functional-typological introduction. Volume I*. Amsterdam: John Benjamins.

Grossberg, S. (1968) Some physiological and biochemical consequences of psychological postulates. *Proceedings of the National Academy of Science, USA*, 60, 758–65.

Grossberg, S. (1972) Neural expectation: cerebellar and retinal analogs of cells fired by leranable or unlearned pattern classes. *Kybernetik*, 10, 49–57.

Grossberg, S. (1987) *The adaptive brain*, 2 vols. Amsterdam: Elsevier.

Hebb, D. (1949) *The organization of behavior*. New York: Wiley.

Hertz, J., Krogh, A. and Palmer, R. (1991) *Introduction to the theory of neural computation*. Redwood City, CA: Addison Wesley.

Hinton, G. E. and Anderson, J. A. (1981) *Parallel models of associative memory*. Hillsdale, NJ: Erlbaum.

Hinton, G. E. and Shallice, T. (1991) Lesioning a connectionist network: Investigations of acquired dyslexia. *Psychological Review*, 98, 74–95.

Hornik, K., Stinchcombe, M. and White, H. (1989) Multilayer feedforward networks are universal approximators. *Neural Networks*, 2, 359–66.

Hyams, N. (1986) *Language acquisition and the theory of parameters*. Dordrecht & Boston: Reidel.

Jacobs, R., Jordan, M. and Barto, A. (1991) Task decomposition through competition in a modular connectionist architecture: the what and where visual tasks. *Cognitive Science*, 15, 219–50.

Kellman, P. J., Spelke, E. S. and Short, K. R. (1986) Infant perception of object unity from translatory motion 'in depth and vertical translation. *Child Development*, 57, 72–86.

Kirsh, D. (1992) PDP Learnability and innate knowledge of language. *Center for Research in Language Newsletter Vol. 6, no. 3*. University of California, San Diego.

Kohonen, T. (1977) *Associative memory: a system-theoretical approach*. Berlin: Springer.

Lachter, J. and Bever, T. G. (1988) The relation between linguistic structure and associative theories of language learning: a constructive critique of some connectionist learning models. In S. Pinker and J. Mehler (eds), *Connections and symbols*. Cambridge, MA: MIT Press/Bradford Books, pp. 3–71.

Lakoff, G. (1987) *Fire, women, and dangerous things: what categories reveal about the mind*. Chicago: University of Chicago Press.

Langacker, R. (1987) *Foundations of cognitive grammar: theoretical perspectives. Vol. I*. Stanford: Stanford University Press.

Le Cun, Y. (1985) Une procédure d'apprentissage pour réseau à seuil assymétrique. In *Cognitiva 85: à la Frontière de l'Intelligence Artificielle des Sciences de la Connaissance des Neurosciences*, Paris, pp. 599–604.

Lightfoot, D. (1991) The child's trigger experience – degree-0 learnability. *Behavioral Brain Sciences*, 14, 2.

McClelland, J. and Rumelhart, D. (1986) *Parallel distributed processing: explorations in the microstructure of cognition, Vol. 2*. Cambridge, MA: MIT Press/Bradford Books.

McCulloch, W. and Pitts, W. (1943) A logical calculus of ideas immanent in nervous activity. *Bulletin of Mathematical Biophysics*, 5, 115–33. Reprinted in J. Anderson and E. Rosenfeld (eds), *Neurocomputing: foundations of research*. Cambridge, MA: MIT Press.

MacWhinney, B. and Leinbach, J. (1991) Implementations are not conceptualizations: revising the verb-learning model. *Cognition*, 40, 121–57.

Marchman, V. (1992) Language learning in children and neural networks: plasticity, capacity, and the critical period. (Technical Report 9201). Center for Research in Language, University of California, San Diego.

Mead, C. (1989) Analog VLSI and neural systems. Inaugural address presented to the Institute for Neural Computation, October, 1989. University of California, San Diego.

Minsky, M. (1956) Some universal elements for finite automata. In C. E. Shannon and J. McCarthy (eds), *Automata studies*. Princeton: Princeton University Press, pp. 117–28.

Minsky, M. and Papert, S. (1969) *Perceptrons*. Cambridge, MA: MIT Press.

Papert, S. (1988) One AI or Many? *Daedalus: Artificial Intelligence*, Winter.

Piaget, J. (1952) *The origins of intelligence in children*. New York: International Universities Press.

Piaget, J. (1970a) *Structuralism*. New York: Basic Books.

Piaget, J. (1970b) *Genetic epistemology*. New York: Columbia University Press.

Piaget, J. (1971) *Biology and knowledge: an essay on the relations between organic regulations and cognitive processes*. Chicago: University of Chicago Press.

Piatelli-Palmarini, M. (1989) Evolution, selection, and cognition: from "learning" to parameter setting in biology and the study of language. *Cognition*, 31, 1–44.

Pinker, S. and Prince, A. (1988) On language and connectionism: analysis of a parallel distributed processing model of language acquisition. In S. Pinker and J. Mehler (eds), *Connections and symbols*. Cambridge, MA: MIT Press/Bradford Books, pp. 3–71.

Plunkett, K. and Marchman, V. (1991a) U-shaped learning and frequency effects in a multi-layered perceptron: implications for child language acquisition. *Cognition*, 38, 43–102.

Plunkett, K. and Marchman, V. (1991b) From rote learing to system building. (Technical Report 9020). Center for Research in Language, University of California, San Diego.

Roeper, T. and Williams, E. (eds) (1987) *Parameter setting*. Dordrecht and Boston: Reidel.

Rogoff, B. (1990) *Apprenticeship in thinking: cognitive development in social context*. New York: Oxford University Press.

Rosenblatt, F. (1958) The perceptron: a probabilistic model for information storage and organization in the brain. *Psychological Review*, 65, 386–408.

Rosenblatt, F. (1962) *Principles of neurodynamics*. New York: Spartan.

Rumelhart, D., Hinton, G. and Williams, R. (1986a) Learning representations by back-propagating errors. *Nature*, 323, 533–6.

Rumelhart, D., McClelland, J. and the PDP Research Group (1986b) *Parallel distributed processing: explorations in the microstructure of cognition, Vol. 1*. Cambridge, MA: MIT/Bradford Books.

Schwartz, M. F., Saffran, E. M. and Dell, G. S. (1990) Comparing speech error patterns in normals and jargon aphasics: methodological issues and theoretical implications. Presented to the Academy of Aphasia, Baltimore, MD.

Seidenberg, M. and McClelland, J. L. (1989) A distributed developmental model of visual word recognition and naming. *Psychological Review*, 96, 523–68.

Selfridge, O. G. (1958) Pandemonium: a paradigm for learning. In *Mechanisation of Thought Processes: Proceedings of a Symposium Held at the National Physical Laboratory, November 1958*. London: HMSO, pp. 513–26.

Spelke, E. (1990) Principles of object perception. *Cognitive Science*, 14, 29–56.

Spelke, E. (1991) Physical knowledge in infancy: Reflections on Piaget's theory. In S. Carey and R. Gelman (eds), *The epigenesis of mind: essays on biology and cognition*. Hillsdale, NJ: Erlbaum, pp. 133–69.

Thal, D., Marchman, V., Stiles, J., Aram, D., Trauner, D., Nass, R. and Bates, E. (1991) Early lexical development in children with focal brain injury. *Brain and Language*, 40, 491–527.

von Neumann, J. (1951) The general and logical theory of automata. In L. A. Jeffress (ed.), *Cerebral mechanisms in behavior*. New York: Wiley.

von Neumann, J. (1958) *The computer and the brain*. New Haven: Yale University Press.

Werner, H. (1948) *Comparative psychology of mental development*. New York: International Universities Press.

Willshaw, D. J. Buneman, O. P. and Longuet-Higgins, H. C. (1969) Nonholographic associative memory. *Nature*, 222, 960–2.

27

Linguistic and Spatial Cognitive Development Following Early Focal Brain Injury: Patterns of Deficit and Recovery

JOAN STILES AND DONNA THAL

The outlook for recovery from aphasia varies with age. The chance for recovery has a natural history. This natural history is the same as the natural history of cerebral lateralization of function. Aphasia is the result of direct, structural, and local interference with neuropsychological processes of language. In childhood such interference cannot be permanent because the two sides are not yet sufficiently specialized for function, even though the left hemisphere may already show signs of speech dominance. Damage to it will interfere with language; but the right hemisphere is still involved to some extent with language, and so there is potential for language function that may be strengthened again. In the absence of pathology, a polarization of function between right and left takes place during childhood, displacing language entirely to the left and certain other functions predominantly to the right. . . . If, however, a lesion is placed in either hemisphere, this polarization cannot take place, and language function together with other functions persists in the unharmed hemisphere. . . . Notice that the earlier the lesion is incurred, the brighter is the outlook for language (Lenneberg, 1967, p. 153).

As this passage from Lenneberg's *Biological Foundations of Language* suggests, traditional views of brain development held that early occurring localized brain injury has little effect on linguistic and cognitive development (e.g. Alajouanine and Lhermitte, 1965; Carlson et al., 1968; Krashen, 1973; Lenneberg, 1967). They suggested that there is sufficient plasticity in the immature neural systems to allow for compensation and, by consequence, relatively normal development. In recent years, data have begun to accure from both human and animal studies which suggest that this view may be in need of revision. It is becoming increasingly apparent that early focal brain injury often results in persistent, but subtle, deficits. The documentation of specific deficits associated with early localized injury has important implications for our understanding of both brain plasticity and early cognitive functioning.

Data identifying specific linguistic and cognitive deficits in young children with localized brain injury suggest that even very early in life the maturing brain is not equipotential for all functions, and they argue against a strong form of the early brain plasticity hypothesis. On the other hand, deficits documented thus far tend to be less severe and they do not always follow the right/left and anterior/posterior profiles that are so familiar in the literature on focal brain injury in adults. These data, coupled with the growing body of evidence showing that early experience can affect the development of neurological systems, suggest that plasticity should not be ruled out as an important factor in development. Our task, then, is to define the extent to which both the neurological and cognitive systems can respond flexibly to insult, and to what extent flexibility is constrained by specialization. Detailed accounts of the development of linguistic and cognitive functioning in children with localized brain injury provide data that are crucial to our understanding of this issue.

The Population of Children with Early Occurring Focal Brain Injury

The studies reported in this chapter focus on children with early occurring focal brain injury. All of the children discussed here suffered localized cortical brain injury either prenatally or within the first six months of life. While more diffuse brain insult is fairly common, focal brain injury is a comparatively rare disorder in young children. The most common cause of localized injury in young children is stroke. Children with focal brain injury are typically identified in one of three ways: (1) they experience neonatal seizures; (2) they manifest signs of partial paralysis on one side of the body; or (3) the lesions are observed during routine ultrasound tests for other medical reason, such as meconium staining, premature birth, etc. The identification of lesion site is based on results of neuroimaging using either CT scan or MRI.

The unifying factor among the children in our population is the documented presence of injury to circumscribed regions of the brain. Children are excluded from our studies if there is evidence of multiple lesions, disorders with potential of more global damage such as congenital viral infection, maternal drug or alcohol, bacterial meningitis, encephalitis, severe anoxia, chronic lesions such as tumor or arteriovenus malformation. Within the population children are classified by site of lesion; that is, whether lesion is on the left or right side of the brain, and which cortical lobe or lobes are involved. Finally, on gross assessment, the children in the population do well behaviorally, both individually and as a group. They do not manifest gross cognitive deficits. In fact, they often do well, scoring within the normal range on standardized IQ measures and attending public schools.

Language Acquisition Following Early Focal Brain Injury

Studies of the relationship between brain development and language acquisition provide good examples of a literature in which contradictory views are often strongly held. The traditional view (Lenneberg, 1967) proposes that the brain is sufficiently plastic that early brain injury is not likely to have a significant effect on language development. Others (Dennis and Whitaker, 1976; Kinsbourne and Hiscock, 1977, 1983) argue for the early specialization of the brain for language processing. Studies of language acquisition in the focal lesion population provide the opportunity to clarify the issues which grow out of these disparate claims by defining the conditions which permit the emergence of compensatory forms of brain organization for language. Until recently most information about language in brain-injured children was based on retrospective studies of children with acquired aphasia (Alajounine and Lhermitte, 1965; Guttmann, 1942; Hecaen, 1976, 1983; Oelschlager and Scarborough, 1976; Woods and Teuber, 1978). This created problems of interpretation because the measures of language ability were obtained well after the period in which the basic structures of language were acquired. As a result, differences between the brain-injured children and normal controls may just as well have been caused by unmeasured maturational and/or experiential factors which intervened at any point after the lesion was acquired as from the earlier cerebral insults. In addition, results are contradictory with regard to sequellae of different lesion type and age of onset, creating more questions than answers. Nonetheless, these studies produced useful information regarding the sequelae of focal brain injury, which provided direction for more recent research.

In a recent and detailed review of the literature, Aram (1988) described patterns of linguistic and cognitive impairment which are characteristic of left-versus right-hemisphere damage, regardless of age of insult (see also Dennis, 1980; Dennis et al., 1981; Riva and Cazzaniga, 1986; Riva et al., 1987; Vargha-Khadem et al., 1985). When those data are viewed as a whole, there does appear to be some form of early left-hemisphere specialization for language. However, linguistic and cognitive deficits seen in children who have suffered early brain injury are generally relatively mild. This is a striking contrast to the frank clinical syndromes seen in adults with comparable lesions. It is also clear that correlations between patterns of impairment and site or size of lesion are less consistent in children with early focal brain injury than in adults with comparable forms of brain injury (Basso et al., 1985, 1987). Thus, there do seem to be limits on early specialization, and those limits provide evidence for functional and/or neural plasticity in early language development (also see Satz et al., 1990).

The series of studies reported here constitute one of the first detailed prospective examinations of the effects of early focal brain injury on the development of language. Children in the first two studies were identified prior to the onset of measurable language skills and were tested longitudinally from prespeech to an age when normal children make the transition from single word speech to use of grammatical sentences. In the third study, a group of school-aged children were tested on higher level language skills and compared to normal children of the same age. Data from these studies provide the first opportunity to document the *process* of language acquistion following early insult to different brain regions as it occurred. They offer insight into the issues of specification of deficit (brain specialization for language) and functional recovery (plasticity).

In the first study (Marchman et al., 1991), five infants with focal brain injury were observed longitudinally (three times) from the onset of canonical babble

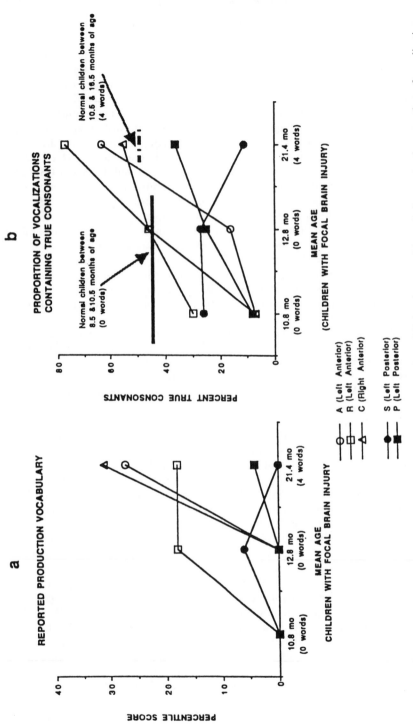

Figure 27.1 Reported production vocabulary for children with and without LP involvement (a), and the reported proportion of vocalizations containing true consonants (b) for the same children (from Thal et al., 1991).

until they were between 21 and 22 months of age. They were compared to ten normally developing children at the same level of expressive language development. Sessions included free play in which spontaneous communication was video recorded and then analyzed for number of words produced and a number of phonological measures. Parents also completed the MacArthur Communicative Development Inventory (CDI), a parental report instrument normed on children between eight and 16 months of age which assesses aspects of gestural and vocal communication including word comprehension and production (Fenson et al., 1991). Marchman et al. (1991) described the babbling, preverbal gestural communication, and vocabulary development in these five children and the ten normally developing control subjects. The CDI provided information on each child's use of gestures (e.g. giving, pointing, showing), interactive routines (e.g. pattycake), and vocabulary comprehension and production. Results from this instrument showed that the children were delayed in the production of communicative gestures and words at all test times. However, word production began to move into the normal range for a subset of the children by the third test session (see figure 27.1a). Specifically, the three children with anterior lesions had production vocabularies between the 18th and 37th percentiles for children their age, while those with left posterior damage remained below the 5th percentile. Analysis of the free play provided information about the quantity of vocalizations produced in a 30-minute sample, length of vocalizations, sophistication of syllable structure, and measures of the kinds of consonants produced. These analyses revealed that the children with focal brain injury did not vocalize less than their normally developing peers, nor did they differ in the length of vocalizations or the sophistication of syllable structure by the second and third test times. However, the phonological shape of their babble and first words was comparatively primitive: they produced fewer "true" consonants[1] than normal children. There were also signs of phonological deviance. Whereas the normally developing children produced an equal proportion of labial ($|b|$ and $|p|$) and dental ($|t|$ and $|d|$) consonants, production of labials was rare in the children with focal brain injury. Interestingly, lexical and phonological development went hand-in-hand across this short-term longitudinal study. The children who produced true consonants at or above the levels reported for children at the same language development level at the third visit (figure 27.1b) were the same ones who had improved in vocabulary production (figure 27.1a). For both measures improvement occurred in those children whose lesion did *not* involve the left posterior (LP) cortex.

Thal et al. (1991) extended these findings through analyses of parental report data from a larger sample of children (including the five children described by Marchman et al., 1991). The sample included 27 children (14 male and 13 female) from three different research sites. The children were between 12 and 35 months old during the period of the study and a subset were studied longitudinally. Two data points were available for all of the longitudinal subjects (ten children); three data points were available for five of them. Data consisted of reported vocabulary on the CDI:Infants and on a second version for children with more developed language, the CDI:Toddlers (Fenson et al., 1991). Results underscore the conclusion that infants with focal brain injury are at risk for some form of early language delay, regardless of lesion site. Thal et al. reported delays in the early

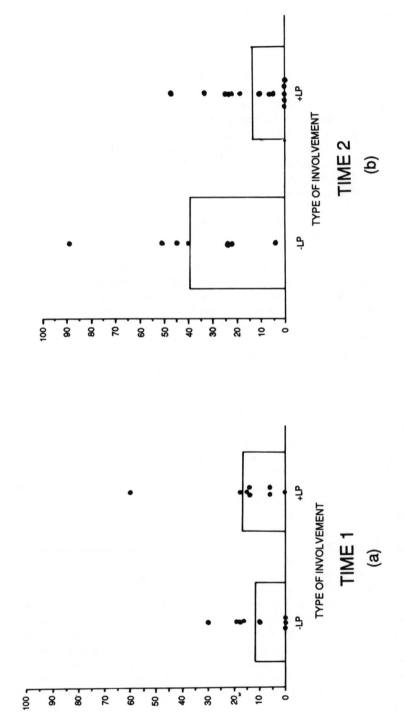

Figure 27.2 Comparison of +LP and – LP involvement on production measures (from Thal et al., 1991).

stages of lexical production for the group as a whole, throughout the 12 to 35 month age range. However, delays in comprehension occurred only in the younger age range (12 to 16 months). Although the sample size is still too small for strong conclusions, Thal et al. (1991) found some surprising associations between the behavioral profiles and site of lesion. First, although delays in expressive language were found in all children regardless of lesion site, significant delays in comprehension occured only in RH children. These analyses were only carried out on the younger children (12 to 16 months), but they suggest that, within this age range, comprehension may be more affected by RH than by LH damage. Second, children with LP injury continued to show particularly severe expressive vocabulary delays at later stages (17 to 35 months), while children with no LP involvement moved into normal percentile ranges (see figure 27.2). Recall that Marchman et al. found little or no evidence for phonological development in their LP injured subjects across the second year. In the Thal et al. study, children with LP injury were also markedly delayed in the first stages in lexical production. Putting these findings together, LP damage appears to be associated with significant delays in expressive language, including phonology and vocabulary. This pattern contrasts with typical findings in the adult aphasia literature, where deficits in expressive language are more often ascribed to left anterior damage (i.e. Broca's area and surrounding tissue) while difficulties in comprehension appear to be more severe with damage to left posterior cortex (i.e. Wernicke's area and adjacent regions). These findings lead us to seriously consider the possibility that there are developmental changes in cortical specialization for language, including changes in lateralization and changes along the anterior/posterior axis (Bates et al., 1992).

The findings reported above await replication and extension with larger populations. It is already clear, however, that prospective studies of language development in children with focal brain injury will allow us to obtain an understanding of how language abilities are built up in the first place, an understanding that is critical to adequate explanations of these brain/behavior relationships.

A third study focused on linguistic development in a small sample of children with focal brain injury, but who were not tested until the late preschool and school years (Marchman and Bates, in progress). The measures were designed to assess the relations between grammar and context, with a focus on complex morphosyntactic structures that are known to improve across the childhood years. They included the production of passives and other complex syntactic structures, the use of pronouns to signal given versus new information, the comprehension of idiomatic expressions, and the ability to construct coherent narratives. These skills were examined across a range of discourse conditions, to determine not only the presence or absence of target grammatical forms but also the frequency with which a child can access and deploy those forms to serve discourse functions.

Thus far only a small sample of children with focal brain injury have been given this comprehensive assessment of grammar and discourse, and comparisons to the longitudinal findings reported above must be taken with caution. However, preliminary analyses of data from nine school-age children provide some striking contrasts to the infant and toddler results described above, and to the patterns of deficit observed in adults with focal brain injury. For example, all of the focal lesion children performed well in their descriptions of an animated film: they were sensitive to the discourse problems posed by the experimenter (e.g. they responded appropriately when asked to describe an event from an unusual point of view), and they produced enough of the complex syntactic structures targeted by the film (e.g. passives) to place them in the normal or low-normal range for their age level. They were also within the normal range on tests of sentence comprehension, including a test designed to distinguish between idioms and novel sentences.

To summarize, we find relatively little evidence for delay in our measures of grammatical comprehension and performance after four to five years of age, in contrast with the much more serious delays that are evident in our studies of language development in infancy. Of course we must keep in mind that this contrast is based on a cross-sectional comparison. However, our preliminary findings with a small sample of school age children concur with evidence by Aram, Riva and others showing that language deficits are relatively subtle in this population when tests are administered after five years of age. At this point, however, we tentatively suggest that the most intense period of recovery-from-delay in children with·focal brain injury takes place in the transition from infancy to childhood – at least in the linguistic domain.

Spatial Analytic Functioning

Studies with adults have shown that focal brain injury results in specific disorders of spatial analytic functioning. These studies suggest that different patterns of spatial deficit are associated with left and right hemisphere lesions (e.g. Arena and Gainotti, 1978; Delis et al., 1986, 1992; Gainotti and Tiacci, 1970; Lamb et al., 1990; McFie and Zangwill, 1960; Piercy et al., 1960; Robertson and Delis, 1986; Robertson and Lamb, 1991; Swindell et al., 1988). Injury to left posterior brain regions results in disorders involving difficulty defining the parts of a spatial array. Patients with left posterior injury tend to oversimplify spatial patterns and omit pattern detail, relying upon overall configural cues and ignoring specific elements of spatial patterns. On the other hand, patients with right posterior lesions have difficulty with the configural aspects of spatial pattern analysis. They tend to focus on the parts of the pattern without attending to the overall form. Very recent studies with adults (Lamb et al., 1990; Robertson and Lamb, 1991) have begun to confirm suggestions deriving from the animal literature, suggesting that these deficits of form perception may be specifically associated with temporal brain regions, while deficits involving spatial location and movement may be associated with specific parietal systems.

Recent work in our laboratory has focused on the early development of spatial cognitive functioning in young children with congenital focal brain injury. In contrast to earlier views, this work has documented deficits of spatial cognitive functioning in young children with right- and left-hemisphere injury that provide profiles of deficit similar to those reported for adults (Stiles-Davis, 1988b; Stiles-Davis et al., 1985; 1988). Thus, even very early in development, focal brain injury does result in identifiable and persistent spatial deficits. However, those deficits are far less severe than those observed in adults, and in our longitudinal studies we have consistently observed development in children's mastery of specific spatial tasks.

The results of three studies of spatial cognitive functioning will be reviewed. These three tasks have been selected to illustrate the specificity of deficit within subject group and the range of deficit across both age and task condition. Across the tasks, clear demonstrations of the deficits associated with both right and left hemisphere injury are evident. In addition, the three very different types of tasks span the ages from three years through about nine years, thus demonstrating both the persistence of the disorders and their extent over a range of behaviors.

The first study examined spatial cognitive functioning in a large sample of young children. The study focused specifically on the ways in which three- and four-year-old children with focal brain injury spontaneously organize blocks into spatial groupings (Stiles and Nass, 1991; also see Stiles-Davis, 1988a, for data on normal children). It included two experiments. The first was a cross-sectional examination of 20 children tested at ages three and four; five children with right-hemisphere (RH) injury and five with left-hemisphere (LH) injury were included at each age. The second experiment was a longitudinal case study report of six children, three with RH and three with LH injury, tested at both ages three and four. The longitudinal data were intended to provide converging evidence for developmental patterns observed in the cross-sectional experiment. Data from both experiments were evaluated using eight measures of spatial grouping activity. The results showed that focal brain injury affected grouping activity for children with both RH and LH injury. Overall, performance of both groups was below that of normal children at three and four years of age. The profiles of deficit differed, however, for the two lesion groups. Children with RH injury were impaired on all measures of spatial construction at age three. By age four, development was observed on low-level measures assessing children's ability to combine pairs of objects, but impairment was still observed on measures designed to assess higher levels of organization. The behavior typical of this pattern of results was one in which children systematically placed blocks one by one into disordered heaps. In contrast, while children with LH injury at age four continued to produce fewer local level relations, they showed a more normal pattern of development in the kinds of global structures they produced. Like normal four-year-old children they generated arches, enclosures, and symmetries. The findings for both the RH and LH groups were consistent for the cross-sectional and the longitudinal experiments. Follow-up studies showed that by about six years of age children in both groups had achieved ceiling levels of performance on the spatial grouping task.

Data from another type of spatial construction task provide additional evidence for a spatial integrative deficit in children with RH injury. In a recent paper (Stiles-Davis et al., 1988), we reported drawing disorders in two children with RH injury that were similar to those reported for RH injured adults. Figure 27.3 shows examples of the drawings produced by children in this study. In drawing houses, RH injured children included appropriate parts, but failed to arrange them in spatially organized ways. This is consistent with reports of adults with similar injury. In their depiction of people, they portray figures with hair coming from all sides of the head and with body parts not clearly distinguished. This is consistent with Swindell and colleagues' (1988) characterization of the human figure drawings of adult patients with RH injury as, "scattered, fragmented, and

Figure 27.3 Examples of free drawings of houses and people by children with right hemisphere injury.

disorganized . . . subjects often overscored lines and added extraneous scrib-blings" (p. 19). These deficits were not observed in age and IQ matched children with LH injury (see figure 27.4).

More recent work with the focal lesion population has also suggested that with time the children's drawings improve. This improvement suggests functional recovery, but the nature of that recovery is unclear. One possibility is that the children have developed graphic formulas for depicting specific forms. That is, their improvement may reflect a process of developing a formula for drawing particular forms, rather than significant improvement in spatial analytic ability. Karmiloff-Smith (see this volume) has devised a means for testing the persistence of graphic formulas in free drawing, in which children are first asked to draw a house or a person, and then to draw an "impossible" house and person. By age six, normal children readily draw elaborate and fanciful impossible drawings, which differ significantly from their free drawings. This protocol has been used

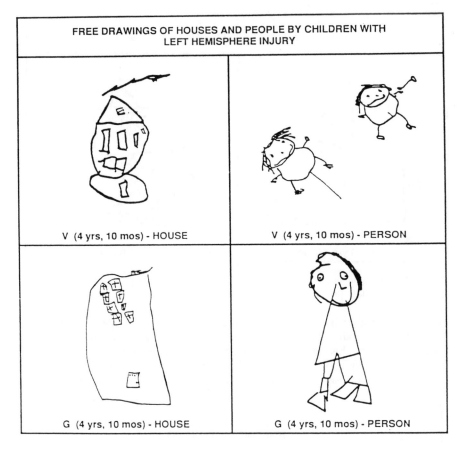

Figure 27.4 Examples of free drawings of houses and people by children with left hemisphere injury.

with six 6- to 10-year-old children, four with RH and two with LH injury (Stiles and Nass, 1991). Data from the two children with LH injury are indistinguishable from those of normal children (see figure 27.5). However, data from children with RH injury show that they have great difficulty diverging from their graphic formula. In some cases children simply produced minor variants of their free drawings, as shown in figure 27.6. Another common strategy observed in the children with RH injury, is to combine elements of two graphic formulas. This strategy simplifies the task of generating a new spatial form, in that the child can simply substitute a form from his or her existing graphic repertoire in response to the request to produce a novel figure. Figure 27.7 shows examples from two children who used this strategy. In figure 27.7a the child drew a "jet plane house" when asked to draw an impossible house. This, at first glance, appears to be a significant departure from the original house form. However, as can be seen in the final panel of figure 27.7a, the jet plane house was minimally adapted from

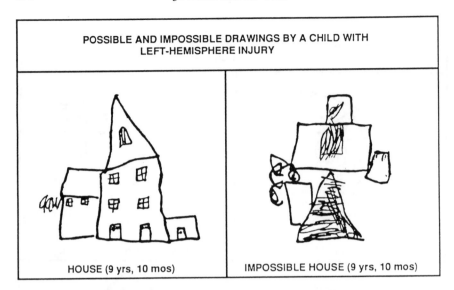

Figure 27.5 Possible and impossible houses by a child with LH injury. Note the marked change in the child's production of the impossible figure.

his formula for a jet plane. He simply substituted doors. A similar pattern is seen in the drawing produced by the child in figure 27.7b. Here the child produced a "flower house" for his impossible house, borrowing directly from his formula for a flower. This strategy of formula substitution is not observed among normal children (Karmiloff-Smith, personal communication) or children with LH injury.

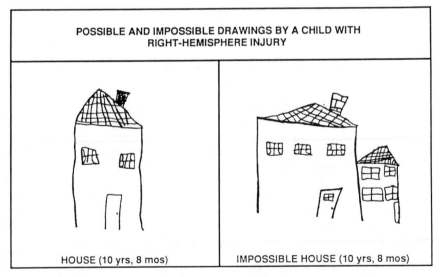

Figure 27.6 Possible and impossible houses by a child with RH injury. Note that there is only minor variation between the two figures.

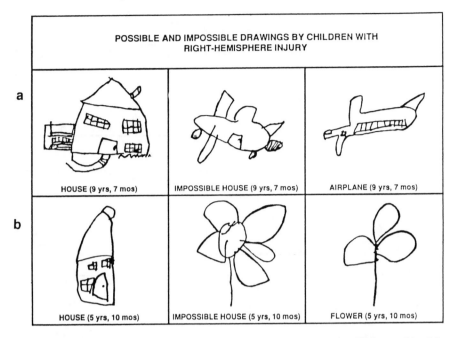

POSSIBLE AND IMPOSSIBLE DRAWINGS BY CHILDREN WITH
RIGHT-HEMISPHERE INJURY

a

HOUSE (9 yrs, 7 mos) IMPOSSIBLE HOUSE (9 yrs, 7 mos) AIRPLANE (9 yrs, 7 mos)

b

HOUSE (5 yrs, 10 mos) IMPOSSIBLE HOUSE (5 yrs, 10 mos) FLOWER (5 yrs, 10 mos)

Figure 27.7 Examples of possible and impossible houses by two children with right hemisphere injury using a formula substitution strategy. a shows the series produced by a nine-year-old child; b shows the series produced by a five-year-old.

One final task provides a particularly good demonstration of the spatial encoding deficit associated with LH injury, and provides an additional marker of integrative deficit in children with RH injury. In this task children are presented with a series of hierarchical letter stimuli (see figures 27.8 and 27.9), and asked, first, to reproduce the forms from memory, and then to copy the forms in the presence of the model. This task has been used with adult focal lesion patients to test for selective deficits of pattern integration and lower level encoding (Delis et al., 1986). Patients with LH injury produce the global pattern and omit the local level items, while patients with RH injury produce the local level items in a scattered array. In our adaptation of the task, the stimuli were presented individually and children were given as much time as they needed to reproduce the forms. Normal children as young as five years of age were proficient at this task (Dukette and Stiles, 1991).

Data from eight children, four with RH and four with LH injury, are shown in figures 27.8 and 27.9 (Stiles and Dukette, in preparation). Even a cursory examination of the data show that there are marked differences between the two groups of children. All three of the children with LH injury easily reproduced the global level of the pattern, but failed to produce local level elements. These data suggest a marked deficit of local level encoding, a pattern consistent with LH injured adult patients on this task. The children with RH injury do not appear, at least at first glance, to have had great difficulty with this task. They

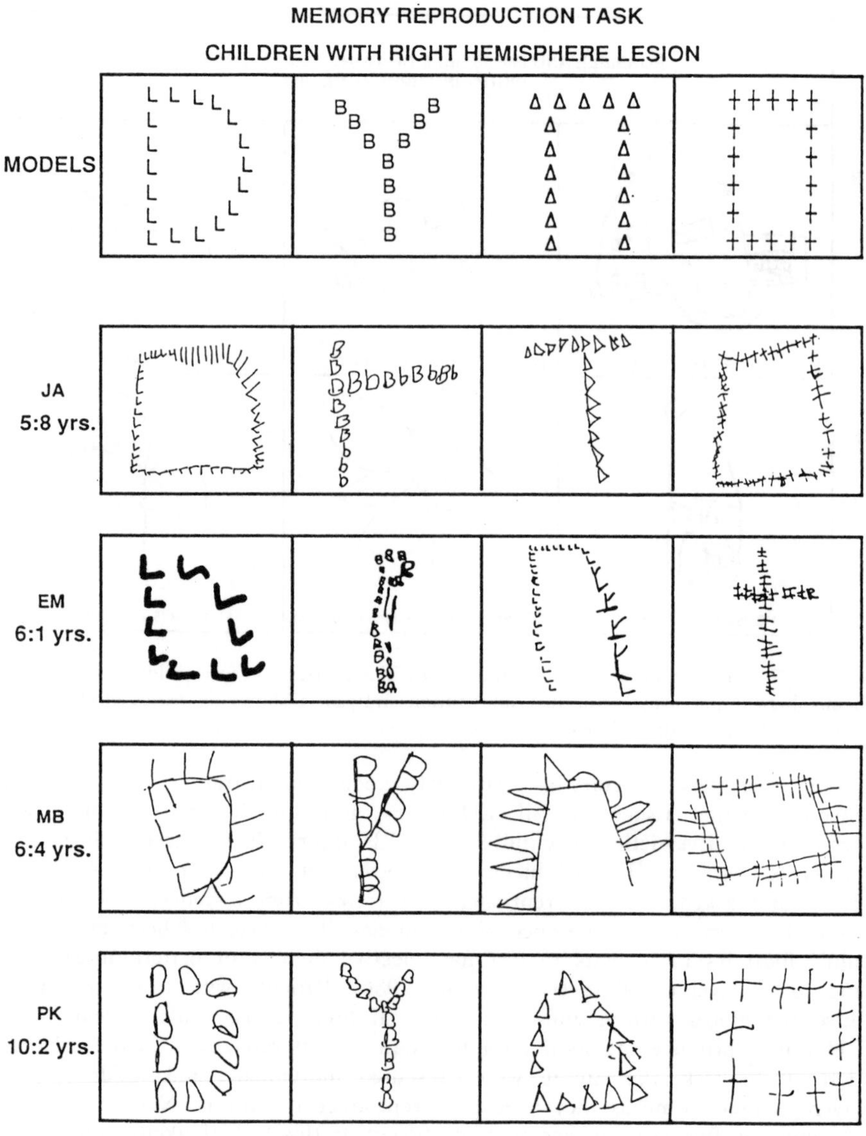

MEMORY REPRODUCTION TASK
CHILDREN WITH RIGHT HEMISPHERE LESION

Figure 27.8 Memory reproductions of hierarchical letter and form stimuli by children with RH injury.

produced both the global and the local levels of the pattern. However, a closer look at the data from these children reveals evidence of impairment on this task. Note the first, second, and fourth copies produced by child JA. In each case, she uses both upper and lower case letters in reproducing the form from memory (as indicated by the arrow, she apparently interpreted the plus in stimulus four as a letter "t"). It is apparent that the child's strategy for remembering the visual

MEMORY REPRODUCTION TASK

CHILDREN WITH LEFT HEMISPHERE LESION

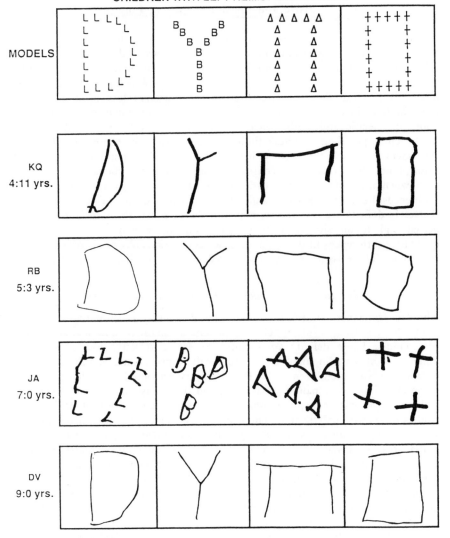

Figure 27.9 Memory reproductions of hierarchical letter and form stimuli by children with LH injury.

information was to label verbally the form and then to rely on that information at test. Child MB used another strategy, that of outlining the global form before adding the smaller letters. In this way, he generated a kind of framework or scaffold for reproducing the form. Neither strategy has been observed in our sample of more than 100 normal children tested between the ages of five and eight years.

Assessing the Effects of Early Focal Brain Injury on the Development of Linguistic and Spatial Cognitive Functions

The data from the focal lesion population suggests that a number of reformulations of our ideas concerning the effects of early localized brain injury on the subsequent development of cognitive and linguistic functioning may be in order. Consistent with traditional views of development following early focal brain injury, it is clear that the effects of early injury are less pronounced than those of later insult. Nonetheless, while the degree of impairment is less pronounced, specific and well-defined patterns of deficit have been documented in the child population. These findings suggest that there are clear limits on the extent to which the brain–behavioral system can respond flexibly to early insult, and thus there are constraints on neural and behavioral plasticity even when injury is sustained early in life. There are also a number of other differences between the child and adult populations. In addition to findings that early deficits are less severe, it is also the case that the association between deficit and lesion site is more variable, and there may also be important qualitative differences in the brain–behavior correlations observed from infancy to adulthood. These issues will be considered in more detail in the next sections.

Specific Deficits Following Early Focal Brain Injury

The data from these studies of the focal lesion population show that early brain injury does, indeed, result in selective deficits of linguistic and spatial cognitive functioning. These deficits are specific, reflecting selective loss of important dimensions of both linguistic and spatial analytic processing. Within the domain of language, young children with LP brain injury presented a profile of preserved comprehension and impaired production, and there was suggestive evidence that children with right hemisphere injury may present the reverse profile. Data from studies of spatial analytic functioning provide evidence that within the first few years of life, separate systems for encoding and integrating information in the spatial array are instantiated at the level of the brain substrate. Children as young as age two showed selective impairment of these complementary processes, depending on side of brain lesion.

The data also demonstrate, however, that documentation of selective deficit does not necessarily imply a simple structure-to-function mapping, or the loss of such mapping. The patterns of association between site of lesion and specific behavioral deficit diverge from those observed in adults. This divergence is most marked for linguistic functioning where the mapping of deficit to areas of injured brain substrate shows little conformity to adult mappings. Adults with LP brain injury typically manifest a receptive form of aphasia, in which production is preserved relative to comprehension. The opposite pattern is observed in the early phases of language acquisition for children with LP injury. One possible explanation for these differences is that what is required to comprehend and produce language early in development is quite different from what is required once language becomes a mature, integrated, and automatized system. Thus, the patterns of deficit may be quite different early in development because what is required of the language user is quite different. Alternatively, or in addition, the brain systems subserving language may undergo substantial reorganization and change with development. The evidence that injury to several distinct brain regions results in impaired language acquisition suggests that in the initial phases of acquisition diverse brain regions may participate in language processing. Thus, the distribution and organization of language areas may be quite different in the young child than in the older child or adult. The idea that diverse brain regions may participate in language processing early in development is not a new idea. It is certainly consistent with Lenneberg's claims. What is new here are the data demonstrating that *deficits* in language acquisition are associated with early brain injury, and that the patterns of structure to function mappings diverge from deficit patterns observed in the mature patient.

The most dramatic finding is that children with LP lesions showed their greatest impairment in expressive vocabulary rather than comprehension. Language comprehension was surprisingly relatively spared in children with left-hemisphere damage. In addition, we found no support for the hypothesis that LA lesions result in delays in grammatical development. Thus, the existence of a syndrome of developmental agrammatism which parallels a similar syndrome in adult aphasics has been disconfirmed. Last, size of lesion had no measurable effect on the magnitude of the language impairment in any of our studies. All of these patterns are very different from those seen in adult populations.

The data mapping structure to function for spatial analytic processing present an important contrast to the language data. Here the mapping patterns for the children with early focal brain injury are much more consistent with mappings reported for adult patients. In both groups, injury to LP brain regions resulted in encoding deficits, while injury to RP brain regions resulted in spatial integrative deficits. Visuo-spatial processing is a phylogenetically older function than linguistic processing. The brain system subserving visuo-spatial processing may be much more highly specified even in the early phases of development than the brain system mediating language. These domain specific differences in the consistency with which child and adult functional deficits map to specific brain regions have important implications for the study of brain–behavior relations in development. There may well be systematic differences in the extent to which different brain–behaviorial systems are capable of responding flexibly to early insult. The potential brain substrate for visuo-spatial processing may be more limited than the potential substrate for language. One index of these differences in the potential for reorganization may be this observed variability across domains in the early mapping of function to brain area, relative to adult patterns. The domain-specific differences in brain substrate specification for any given function may set differential ceilings on the extent to which the child may be able to compensate for the effects of early injury.

A dimension along which the data from the child and adult populations differ in both domains is the severity of deficit. The patterns of deficit observed in the child population are consistently less pronounced than those observed in adults. Even for the case of visuo-spatial processing, where the *pattern* of deficit is consistent, impairment among children is less severe. Through the course of development, the children with early focal brain injury acquire considerable spatial and linguistic skill. Indeed, it is against this backdrop of ongoing behavioral acquisition that the contrasting profiles of domain-specific deficit are observed. The profiles of deficit which emerge from this population are derived from detailed longitudinal studies of behavior on tasks that have been designed to provide detailed assessments of performance within specific linguistic and cognitive domains. These children do not lack spatial or linguistic ability. Rather, careful assessment of their performance on tasks designed to place demands on specific aspects of spatial or linguistic functioning reveal well-defined and systematic profiles of subtle behavioral impairment.

Functional Acquisition and Recovery

As indicated in the previous section, one important set of results stemming from the longitudinal approach to the study of development in children with early occurring focal brain injury has been the documentation of subtle, behavioral deficits. However, the prospective approach has a second, equally important aspect, which is the detailed study of *development* in this population. By following children over time, as they acquire new cognitive and linguistic skills, it is possible to track the course of development and from that obtain data on patterns of functional recovery or persistent deficit. This aspect of the work with this population has just begun. Only a handful of children have actually been followed from infancy through the school years, and even for them the data are incomplete. Even so, data reveal patterns of acquisition, recovery, and/or compensation for deficits which have important implications for our understanding of development in this population.

In contrast to the marked patterns of linguistic delay evident in infants and preschoolers, there is little evidence for language delay in the school age population. Children score within the normal range on measures of grammatical comprehension and production, and, in general, show good facility with language. These findings suggest that there is considerable functional recovery during the period marking the transition from preschool to the school years. Since we have not yet followed our toddler cohort into the school years, data on the critical transition from infancy to childhood are not yet available. Thus, little can be said at this point about how children achieve this crucial recovery for linguistic functioning. Early data suggest that reliance on a holistic learning style may be an important factor, but future studies are needed to test that and related hypotheses.

More persistent patterns of deficit are observed for spatial cognitive functioning. Although there is regular improvement with development on individual measures of spatial cognition, at any given point in development, children show evidence of specific deficits on tasks appropriate to the age range being tested. Thus, for example, three- to four-year-old children with LH or RH injury show clear evidence of specific deficit on tasks involving spontaneous block organization. By age six children in both groups achieve near ceiling levels of performance on the task (a level of performance reached by normal children by 42 months of age). While these data may be interpreted as indicating delay with recovery from initial impairment, evidence on tasks which are more difficult but require similar spatial analytic processing skills raises questions as to how the observed recovery, or more likely compensation, is achieved.

As suggested earlier, children with early focal brain injury manifest comparatively subtle patterns of deficit. Fairly detailed measures of performance are required to document impairment in this population. In addition, task difficulty relative to individual performance dimensions affects whether or not a particular aspect of deficit will be evident in the observed behavior of the child. Thus, free drawing provides a good medium for examining the spatial integrative deficits evident among children with RH injury, but is not an effective means of studying the encoding deficits associated with LH injury. This is because the inclusion or exclusion of pattern detail, which is necessary for detecting the encoding deficit associated with LH injury, cannot be regulated within the task. Thus, specific task demands will determine the extent to which a particular deficit is manifested in performance.

In addition, both task difficulty and task demand vary with developmental level. Tasks that may be taxing at one age are easily executed at another. This is true on many tasks for both normal children and children with focal brain injury, although the timing of task mastery may be quite different for the two groups. For any given task, there are a range of possible developmental achievements which could account for the improved performance. There is a large literature showing that in the normal course of development children employ different strategies to solve specific problems at different developmental levels (e.g. Karmiloff-Smith and Inhelder, 1974; Siegler, 1988; Stiles-Davis, 1988a; Sugarman, 1982). For the children with focal brain injury, the specific strategies employed to solve any given problem at a particular point in time could determine the extent to which a task reveals a subtle, persistent, underlying deficit. Thus, detailed assessments which document not only *whether*, but also *how* success is achieved on a given task are necessary to our understanding of development in the focal lesion population. The report of graphic formula use in free drawing discussed earlier provides an example of this approach. Even with such data, we do not yet fully understand the mechanisms of these observed improvements in performance. It is possible that plasticity of the neural substrate accounts for at least some of the observed changes. However, given the patterns of development we have observed across tasks, it is unlikely that neurological reorganization accounts for all of the changes. Rather, the children appear to develop alternative strategies for solving specific spatial problems. We have some evidence that while the strategies may be less efficient than those observed in the normal course of development, they do offer at least minimally adequate solutions to spatial problems.

Conclusions

The data from these studies of children with early occurring focal brain injury depart somewhat from traditional views of the effects of early brain injury on linguistic and cognitive development. They show that there are specific effects of early brain injury which are manifested within the first years of life in differential profiles of deficit and ability. But these deficits are subtle when compared with the effects of later occurring injury, and the patterns of association between behavior and affected brain substrate are more variable. There is also evidence of considerable change with development. The particular patterns of change vary with the age of the child and the domain of knowledge under examination. The mechanisms of change are not well understood, and they very likely involve change in both the neurological substrate and in the strategies employed by the children to achieve a given level of behavior.

In these data, we have observed selective loss within well- defined but dynamic and developing systems for linguistic and spatial cognitive functioning. The structure of the systems appears to be quite different for the two domains. The data indicating that injury to a wide range of brain areas appears to impair language acquisition suggest that diverse brain regions play a role in language acquisition. By extension, the preliminary data suggesting considerable sparing of linguistic ability by the school-age period suggest that the eventual outcome for language functioning may be enhanced by this early distribution of function. By contrast, the building blocks for the spatial analytic system appear to be in place from an early age and are susceptible to the effects of early brain injury. Specific, identifiable deficits of spatial analytic ability which are consistent with patterns of adult deficit are evident from at least the early preschool period. Yet, these deficits are mild compared to those observed among adult patterns. Thus, while the spatial cognitive system may be less flexible than the language system, the data suggest that there is still a considerable degree of plasticity, which allows for the kinds of compensation and sparing of function observed in the development of spatial functions.

NOTE

1 "True" consonants include all consonants other than glottals and glides. Thus, $|t|$, $|b|$, and $|k|$ are "true" consonants whereas $|h|$ and $|j|$ are not. Vihman et al. (1986) and Vihman and Miller (1988) have suggested that the frequency of use of "true" consonants in spontaneous speech reflects the degree to which a child's vocalizations are a part of a developing language system.

REFERENCES

Alajouanine, T. and Lhermitte, F. (1965) Acquired aphasia in children. *Brain*, 88, 553–62.

Aram, D. M. (1988) Language sequelae of unilateral brain lesions in children. In F. Plum (ed.), *Language, Communication and the Brain*. New York: Raven Press, pp. 171–97.

Arena, R. and Gainotti, G. (1978) Constructional apraxia and visuoperceptive disabilities in relation to laterality of cerebral lesions. *Cortex*, 14, 463–73.

Basso, A., Bracchini, A., Capitani, E., Laiacona, M. and Zanobio, M. (1987) Age and evolution of language area functions: A study on adult stroke patients. *Cortex*, 23, 475–83.

Basso, A., Lecours, A., Moraschini, S. and Vanier, M. (1985) Anatomoclinical correlations of the aphasias as defined through computerized tomography: Exceptions. *Brain and Language*, 26, 201–29.

Bates, E., Thal, D. and Janowsky, J. (1992) Early language development and its neural correlates. In I. Rapin and S. Segalowitz (eds), *Handbook of Neuropsychology, vol. 6, Child Neurology*. Amsterdam: Elsevier.

Carlson, J., Netley, C., Hendrick, E. and Pritchard, J. (1968) A reexamination of intellectual disabilities in hemispherctomized patients. *Transactions of the American Neurological Association*, 93, 198–201.

Delis, D. C., Kiefner, M. G. and Fridlund, A. J. (1992) Visuospatial dysfunction following unilateral brain damage: dissociations in hierarchical and hemispatial analysis. *Journal of Clinical and Experimental Neuropsychology* (in the press).

Delis, D. C., Robertson, L. C. and Efron, R. (1986) Hemispheric specialization of memory for visual hierarchical stimuli. *Neuropsychologia*, 24(2), 205–14.

Dennis, M. (1980) Capacity and strategy for syntactic comprehension after left or right hemidecortication. *Brain and Language*, 10, 287–317.

Dennis, M., Lovett, M. and Wiegel-Crump, C. (1981) Written language acquisition after left or right hemidecortication in infancy. *Brain and Language*, 12, 54–91.

Dennis, M. and Whitaker, H. A. (1976) Language acquisition following hemidecortication: linguistic superiority of the left over the right hemisphere. *Brain and Language*, 3, 404–33.

Dukette, D. and Stiles, J. (1991) Spatial pattern analysis in preschool children: Evidence from a matching task using hierarchical letter stimuli. Paper presented at the biannual meeting of the Society for Research in Child Development, Seattle, April, 1991.

Fenson, L., Dale, P., Reznick, J. S., Thal, D., Bates, E., Hartung, J., Pethnick, S. and Reilly, J. (1991). Technical Manual for the MacArthur Communicative Inventories. San Diego State University, November 1991.

Gainotti, G. and Tiacci, C. (1970) Patterns of drawing disability in right and left hemispheric patients. *Neuropsychologia*, 8, 379–84.

Guttmann, E. (1942) Aphasia in children. *Brain*, 65, 205–19.

Hecaen, H. (1976) Acquired aphasia in children and the ontogenesis of hemispheric functional specialization. *Brain and Language*, 3, 114–34.

Hecaen, H. (1983) Acquired aphasia in children: revisited. *Neuropsychologia*, 21(6), 581–7.

Karmiloff-Smith, A. and Inhelder, B. (1974) If you want to get ahead, get a theory. *Cognition*, 3(3), 195–212.

Kinsbourne, M. and Hiscock, M. (1977) Does cerebral dominance develop? In S. Segalowitz and F. Gruber (eds), *Language development and neurological theory*. NY: Academic Press.

Kinsbourne, M. & Hiscock, M. (1983) The normal and deviant development of functional lateralization of the brain. In M. Haith and J. Campos (eds), *Handbook of child psychology*, 4th edn. New York: Wiley.

Krashen, S. (1973) Lateralization, language learning, and the critical period: some new evidence. *Language Learning*, 23(1), 63–74.

Lamb, M. R., Robertson, L. C. and Knight, R. T. (1990) Component mechanisms underlying the processing of hierarchically organized patterns: Inferences from patients with unilateral cortical lesions. *Journal of Experimental Psychology: Learning, Memory, and Cognition*, 16, 471–83.

Lenneberg, E. (1967) *The biological foundations of language*. New York: Wiley.

Marchman V. A., Miller, R. and Bates, E. (1991) Babble and first words in children with focal brain injury. *Applied Psycholinguistics*, 12, 1–22.

McFie, J. and Zangwill, O. L. (1960) Visual-constructive disabilities associated with lesions of the left cerebral hemisphere. *Brain*, 83, 243–60.

Oelschlaeger, M. and Scarborough, J. (1976) Traumatic aphasia in children: a case study. *Journal of Communicative Disorders*, 9, 281–8.

Piercy, M., Hecaen, H. and Ajuriaguerra, J. (1960) Constructional apraxia associated with unilateral cerebral lesions – left and right sided cases compared. *Brain*, 83, 225–42.

Riva, D. and Cazzaniga, L. (1986) Late effects of unilateral brain lesions before and after the first year of life. *Neuropsychologia*, 24, 423–8.

Riva, D., Cazzaniga, L., Pantaleoni, C., Milani, N. and Fedrizzi, E. (1987) *Journal of Pediatric Neurosciences*, 2, 239–50.

Robertson, L. C. and Delis, D. C. (1986) "Part–whole" processing in unilateral brain damaged patients: dysfunction of hierarchical organization. *Neuropsychologia*, 24(3), 363–70.

Robertson, L. C. and Lamb, M. R. (1991) Neuropsychological contributions to theories of part whole organization. *Cognitive Psychology*, 23, 299–330.

Satz, P., Strauss, E. and Whitaker, H. (1990) The ontogeny of hemispheric specialization: some old hypotheses revisited. *Brain and Language*, 38(4), 596–614.

Siegler, R. S. (1988) Strategy choice procedures and the development of multiplication skill. *Journal of Experimental Psychology: General*, 117, 258–75.

Stiles, J. and Nass, R. (1991) Spatial grouping ability in young children with congenital right or left hemisphere brain injury. *Brain and Cognition*, 15, 201–22.

Stiles-Davis, J. (1988a) Developmental change in young children's spatial grouping activity. *Developmental Psychology*, 24(4), 522–31.

Stiles-Davis, J. (1988b) Spatial dysfunction in young children with right cerebral hemisphere injury. In J. Stiles-Davis, M. Kritchevsky and U. Bellugi (eds), *Spatial cognition: brain bases and development*. Hillsdale, NJ: Lawrence Erlbaum, pp. 251–72.

Stiles-Davis, J., Janowsky, J., Engel, M. and Nass, R. (1988) Drawing ability in four young children with congenital unilateral brain lesions. *Neuropsychologia*, 26(3), 359–71.

Stiles-Davis, J., Sugarman, S. and Nass, R. (1985) The development of spatial class relations in four young children with right-cerebral-hemisphere damage: evidence for an early spatial constructive deficit. *Brain and Cognition*, 4, 388–412.

Sugarman, S. (1982) Developmental change in early representational intelligence: evidence from spatial classification strategies and related verbal expressions. *Cognitive Psychology*, 14, 410–49.

Swindell, C. S., Holland, A. L., Fromm, D. and Greenhouse, J. B. (1988) Characteristics of recovery of drawing ability in left and right brain-damaged patients. *Brain and Cognition*, 7, 16–30.

Thal, D., Marchman, V. A., Stiles, J., Aram, D, Trauner, D., Nass, R. and Bates, E. (1991) Early lexical development in children with focal brain injury. *Brain and Language*, 40, 491–527.

Vargha-Khadem, F., O'Gorman, A. and Watters, G. (1985) Aphasia and handedness in relation to hemispheric side, age at injury and severity of cerebral lesion during childhood. *Brain*, 108, 667–96.

Woods, B. T. and Teuber, H. L. (1978) Changing patterns of childhood aphasia. *Annals of Neurology*, 3, 273–80.

28

The Development and Neural Basis of Memory Systems

JERI S. JANOWSKY

Reviews of a scientific field are often written just after a great deal of new data has been accumulated and the field is finally understood or a consensus has been reached. The former, but not the latter, describes the conditions under which I am undertaking this chapter. While the past ten years have yielded a considerable amount of information about the brain basis of different forms of learning and memory, and about the capacity of infants to learn and remember under a variety of conditions, there is little consensus on the brain basis of memory, or the primary cognitive processes underlying learning and memory during infancy. This review will briefly summarize the neural and cognitive data concerning infant memory available at this time, and present a framework for coalescing existing information on the brain basis of memory. The framework is intended to provide both guidance and constraints on future studies of infant memory.

The Problem

Infants and toddlers exasperate their parents (and developmental psychologists) by seeming to remember some things while not remembering other things. This leads one to think that memory capacity is fragile, or highly specific, early in life. In addition, people do not report memories of events that occurred in their lives before the age of two years (Sheingold and Tenney, 1982; Waldfogel, 1948). There are several possible explanations for this. One possibility is that these memories are very remote and that memory decays during the long retention interval. However, decay cannot explain the abrupt inability to recall events of early childhood. Early memories appear to be equally inaccessible regardless of whether the retention interval is three years (e.g., a child tested at the age of five regarding memories from the age of two), seven years or 50 years. It may be that early memories cannot be accessed due to a change during development in the neural mechanisms of memory storage or retrieval (Nadel and Zola-Morgan,

1984) or due to the cognitive processes involved in memory (White and Pillemer, 1979; Mandler, 1988). Alternatively the retrieval cues for early memories may not be available in later childhood or adulthood, making early memories relatively inaccessible (Schachtel, 1947).

The Neurobiology of Learning and Memory in Adults

The puzzle to be solved during development is how to achieve adult-like learning and memory at both the cognitive and neural levels. Because the trajectory of development is toward the cognitive and neural system that operates in the adult, a neural and cognitive model of adult forms of learning and memory will be reviewed here. Multiple models have been proposed for adult learning. I will use the model here for which a biological basis can be assigned to at least some of the forms of learning. Studies using animal models, memory disordered patients, and data from normal subjects suggest that the mind has multiple forms of memory, with multiple biological bases in order to accomplish all mnemonic tasks (see figure 28.1). The temporal lobe memory system, which includes the hippo-campus, overlying cortex, and medial thalamic structures, mediates the learning and remembering of declarative information (Squire and Zola-Morgan, 1991). This includes facts and events that can be brought to conscious recollection. Adult humans and animals with bilateral damage to this system are impaired at a variety of mnemonic tasks. They are impaired at learning lists of words or objects (Milner, 1966; Smith and Milner, 1981; Squire et al., 1988), and remembering stories or news events (Squire and Cohen, 1982).

The temporal lobe memory system plays a transient role in the permanent storage of information. Patients with damage to the temporal lobe have relatively preserved memory for information and events learned long before the time of

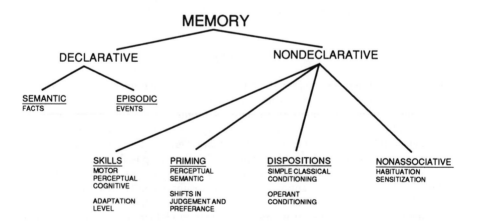

Figure 28.1 The model of memory used in this chapter. From Zola–Morgan and Squire (1990a). The neuropsychology of memory: parallel findings in humans and nonhuman primates. *Annals of the New York Academy of Sciences*, 608, 437. Reprinted with permission.

the brain injury, suggesting that the temporal lobe is not the site of memory storage (Albert et al., 1980; Cohen and Squire, 1981; Squire, 1989; Squire et al., 1989; Warrington and Weiskrantz, 1968). Recent studies using animal models show that the hippocampus and overlying cortex have a time-limited role in memory storage and retrieval. As time since learning increases, the temporal lobes' role in memory decreases, becoming negligible by several weeks (in monkey) and possibly a year or more (in human) after initial learning (Squire and Spanis, 1984; Zola-Morgan and Squire, 1990a, b). What biological and cognitive processes occur during the period of temporal lobe mediated memory "consolidation" is not yet clear.

Several features distinguish declarative from nondeclarative learning and memory. In declarative memory, representations are not built over repeated experiences but can be encoded and retrieved after only one exposure. While repeated exposures may strengthen a representation, each exposure can maintain its own distinct temporal and spatial "tag." For example, one might learn one list of words one day and a new list the second. Upon recall, one can distinguish each list by the day it was learned and even say whether any particular word occurred on both lists or only on one list (Squire, 1982; Squire et al., 1981). Likewise, our knowledge of a colleague may be built over a lifetime of conversations with the person. However, each conversation maintains its own representation. The representation includes the content of the conversation and may well contain information about each conversation's context, such as when and where the conversation occurred (Shimamura and Squire, 1987). The context of the learned information is recalled along with the information itself. Therefore, each fact or event is temporally distinguished from any other time it was experienced. Finally, the knowledge in declarative memory is flexible and can be used in domains outside the original learning situation (e.g., facts learned in school can be flexibly applied outside the original learning domain).

In contrast to declarative memory, nondeclarative memory includes learning that cannot be brought to conscious recollection in the sense that its contents cannot be "brought to mind and thought about" (Mandler, 1990, p. 487; Squire, 1987). It includes skill learning (Corkin, 1968; Cohen and Squire, 1980), priming (Graf et al., 1984; Jacoby and Witherspoon, 1982), simple conditioning, and habituation (Squire, 1987). These forms of learning may be very short-lasting, such as some forms of priming, or relatively permanent, such as the intact performance of motor skills (riding a bicycle) despite very long retention intervals. In some forms of nondeclarative memory, information may be learned through multiple exposures to the stimulus (e.g., habituation or classical conditioning). In addition, the representations are relatively inflexible. For instance, expertise on one motor skill may not result in faster learning of other motor skills. In summary, nondeclarative memory is distinguished from declarative forms of learning and memory as it cannot be brought to conscious recollection. In addition, in some forms of nondeclarative learning and memory the representation is formed over multiple exposures, not in a single unique instance as it is in declarative memory. In this way, declarative memory provides a moment-to-moment record of events as well as the association of arbitrary bits of information. In declarative learning and memory, unlike nondeclarative learning, information appears to be coded along with its unique temporal and spatial context.

The critical brain regions for nondeclarative learning and memory lie outside the temporal lobe memory system. For instance, eye blink classical conditioning requires an intact cerebellum (Thompson, 1986) and some forms of motor skill learning are dependent on the corticostriatal system (Heindel et al., 1988; Mishkin et al., 1984). The right parietal region was recently identified as a critical region for word stem completion priming (Squire et al., 1992).

Given this framework, we can now examine the mnemonic tasks that infants master very early in development versus those that appear to require months or years to attain. Do the cognitive features of these tasks follow any of the defining features of declarative versus nondeclarative learning? In addition, since the brain bases of some of the memory tasks are well delineated, we can relate the findings from infant behavior to what is known about the degree of development of the temporal lobe memory system, versus areas of the brain that are critical to nondeclarative learning.

Habituation

Infants at birth show habituation. That is, they show a decrement in responding to a previously effective stimulus (Brazelton, 1977). They will, within a few months of birth, habituate to a variety of stimuli, in a variety of modalities (sound, light, pictures of faces, etc.; Jeffrey and Cohen, 1971; Fantz, 1964). In habituation, the representation is formed over multiple exposures to the stimulus. It does not appear that each exposure is encoded with its unique spatial and temporal context. However, recent studies have shown that changes in context (e.g., the color of the crib or crying during the test session) will affect retention of a habituated stimulus (Ohr et al., 1990).

The role and character of habituation learning changes during the first year of life. For instance, between three and six months, infants require less exposure time to the stimulus in order to habituate (Bornstein et al., 1988; Columbo et al., 1987; Mayes and Kessen, 1989). While some investigators have suggested that this change in habituation is due to a change in the neural mediators of habituation, it is not clear what the neural change might be. In fact, the neural mechanism of habituation has yet to be delineated.

The biological mediator of habituation in humans is probably neurally ubiquitous in the following sense. The neural system primarily responsible for habituation may be within the neurons of the sensory modality or reflex arc of the to-be-habituated response. For instance, the acoustic startle reflex in the rat is mediated through synaptic change in one or more structures in the auditory pathway (Davis et al., 1982). In the invertebrate *Aplysia*, habituation is due to a reduction in synaptic efficacy (Kandel, 1976). One proposal is that habituation in humans is due to "neuronal fatigue" from repeated stimulation (Dannemiller and Banks, 1983). While there is evidence that individual neurons in the visual cortex will reduce responding if repeatedly stimulated at the same location in their receptive field, they will "revive" if the stimulation is moved to another location in the receptive field. This suggests that the "fatigue" is occurring somewhere else than in each feature-selective neuron (Hubel and Wiesel, 1965). Ackles and Karrer (1991) recently argued that fatigue cannot explain some of the physiological and behavioral findings in human infants. However, an alternative neural explanation has yet to be proposed.

Habituation is classed as a nondeclarative form of learning. As with other forms of nondeclarative learning, it cannot be controlled or brought to conscious recollection, each learning event or trial is not encoded with its unique temporal and spatial context, and, so far as is known, it does not require the temporal lobe diencephalic memory system.

Classical Conditioning

While it is likely that classical conditioning of a variety of responses in infants is possible, eye blink classical conditioning has been best studied. It will be used here as a specific example of a simple associative form of learning because its brain basis (Thompson, 1986) and developmental time course (Little et al., 1984; for review see Lipsett, 1990) are known. In eye blink classical conditioning, an auditory cue, such as a tone, is repeatedly paired with an air puff to the eye, causing the eye to blink. Eventually the tone alone will produce the blink response. While this form of learning is available as early as ten days of age (Little et al., 1984), as infants mature several aspects of the learning continue to develop. The rate of conditioning (percentage of conditioned responses) goes from 20–25 percent of 30 trials in the first month of life (Little et al., 1984) to the adult rate of 80 percent by four to seven years of age (Werden and Ross, 1972; Ohlrich and Ross, 1968). In addition, infants are increasingly capable of being conditioned with shorter and shorter interstimulus intervals. That is, at ten days of age they show conditioning over five blocks of trials when the time between the tone and the air puff is 1.5 seconds but little conditioning when it is 0.5 seconds (Little et al., 1984). In addition, the retention interval over which the conditioned learning is maintained also increases with age. Infants at ten days of age do not retain the learning over a ten-day retention interval, whereas infants at 20 and 30 days of age do. While very young infants show delay conditioning (tone stays on until the air puff causes the eye to blink), they do not show trace conditioning, in which the tone does not temporally overlap with the air puff (Rovee-Collier and Lipsett, 1982). Trace conditioning continues to develop through the preschool years (Werden and Ross, 1972).

The neural mediators of delay eye blink conditioning are known. The cerebellum and brainstem nuclei are critical for eye blink classical conditioning and destruction of the cerebellum may prevent conditioning (Yeo et al., 1984; Woodruff-Pak et al., 1985; for review see Woodruff-Pak et al., 1990). Specifically, the Purkinje cell decreases its influence on the interpositus nucleus (Foy and Thompson, 1986), which in turn increases its output, which eventually reaches relevant motor nuclei for the eye blink response (McCormick et al., 1982).

Can this neurobiological scenario mediate the *quality* of classically conditioned eye blink responses in human infants? The neurons for the Purkinje layer of the cerebellum form very early in development and are probably available and functional before birth (Sidman and Rakic, 1973). The same is true for the critical brainstem nuclei. The granule cell layer of the cerebellar cortex, however, forms much later in development (Sidman and Rakic, 1973). The later development of the cerebellar cortex and its late myelination (Brody et al., 1987; Jernigan and Tallal, 1990) may mediate the increased efficiency of neural transmission and the later developing changes in the conditioned response.

While the cerebellum is critical for classical conditioning of the eye blink response, the hippocampus may play a modulatory role. For instance, interference with the hippocampus, such as by stimulation (Berger, 1984) or by decreasing neural transmission (Moore et al., 1976), will enhance or inhibit classical conditioning respectively. Therefore the state of hippocampal development may modulate the efficiency of conditioning as does the development of cerebellar cortex.

Where does classical conditioning fall in the scheme of different forms of learning and memory proposed for the adult? In classical conditioning, a simple association is being formed between arbitrary or unrelated stimuli (a tone, an eye blink, an air puff). However, the formation of the association occurs over many pairings of the tone and the response. The unique aspects of each pairing are not encoded. In fact, if each trial was made unique, such as if the pitch of the tone changed from trial to trial, the learning of the association would be greatly attenuated. The association learned would then be between tones *in general* and the eye blink, not between any specific or unique tone and the blink. It may be that it is this aspect of classical conditioning that relegates this form of learning to being nondeclarative. The temporal lobe declarative memory system is specialized to make and store *unique* associations on a moment-by-moment basis. In classical conditioning, the contextual aspects of each "moment" are not encoded.

Visual Recognition Memory

The developmental time course and neural basis of visual recognition memory has been assessed in infants using three experimental techniques: eye-gaze novelty preference learning using a paired-comparison technique (Fagan, 1970; Fantz, 1964; for review see Fagan, 1990); novelty preference using a delayed nonmatching to sample technique (Bachevalier and Mishkin, 1984; Overman 1990); and memory for a familiar versus a novel mobile using an operant conditioning technique (Rovee and Fagen, 1976). The developmental time course, qualitative features and neural basis of these will be discussed and compared.

Visual Novelty Preference

Infants show a preference for looking at a novel object very early in life (Fagan, 1971; Fagan et al., 1971). This is tested using a paired-comparison paradigm in which infants are exposed to a sample stimulus (an object, a picture of a face, an abstract form, etc.) and allowed to study it. After a brief retention interval the infant is presented with a new stimulus and the sample stimulus. Infants prefer to look at the new stimulus; that is, they will show longer looking times or more frequent looks to the new than the old stimulus (Fagan, 1971). This differential visual attention between the two stimuli suggests that the infant must have at least some form of a representation still in mind for the sample stimulus. If given sufficient time to study the sample stimulus, or if the sample stimulus is a simple form, even five week old infants will show novelty preference over short retention intervals (Friedman et al., 1974; Milewski and Siqueland, 1975). As with classical conditioning, infants develop faster computation times with age. That is, infants require shorter exposures to the sample stimulus and can distinguish and recognize more complex stimuli with age (Fagan et al., 1971; Friedman, 1972; Milewski and Siqueland, 1975; for review see Fagan, 1990). The differential attention to the novel stimulus is not absolute. Infants show a *preference* on the order of approximately 60 percent of visual attention toward a novel object and 40 percent toward the old object.

Delayed Nonmatch to Sample (DNMTS)

On this task, the subject displaces a centrally located sample object to receive a reward. After a brief retention interval (ten seconds to a few minutes), the subject is presented simultaneously with the sample object and a new object. Instead of simply looking at the novel object, the subject must displace the new object to receive a reward. As in paired-comparison, the subject must maintain a representation of the sample object, but must additionally make a reward–object association and learn the rule that the reward is hidden under the novel (nonmatching) object (Zola-Morgan, 1984; for review see Overman, 1990). The criterion for competent performance is usually defined as 90 correct out of 100 trials. Unlike in the early developing paired-comparison visual novelty preference learning, human infants and infant monkeys do not show adult levels of learning and performance on this task until quite late in development. Human infants attain adult-like performance between 22 and 32 months of age (Overman, 1990), and infant monkeys around one year of age (Bachevalier and Mishkin, 1984 – this volume, chapter 11). This is in stark contrast to paired-comparison visual novelty preference learning, which is available in the first few months of life.

Mobile Conditioning

On this task, infants view objects on a mobile above their crib. The infant's ankle is tied with a cord to the mobile so that when the infant kicks the mobile moves. Infants learn an operant response that a foot kick will be reinforced by movement of the mobile. The measure of retention in this paradigm is the ratio of kicking rate at the long-term retention test divided by the kicking rate immediately after training (Rovee-Collier and Hayne, 1987). Infants at two to three months of age can learn the contingency and show specificity of memory as they kick to the training mobile but not the novel mobile. At two to three months of age infants can remember the training mobile for six to eight days; older infants can remember it for even longer (Sullivan et al., 1979). Increasing the training phase prolongs retention (Ohr et al., 1989) and changing the context of the retention test session, such as by changing the color of the crib bumper (Borovsky and Rovee-Collier, 1990) or because of the infant crying (Fagen et al., 1989; Ohr et al., 1990), disrupts retrieval.

Qualitative Differences between Visual Recognition Measures

The differences in the developmental time course of visual recognition memory using visual novelty preference learning, DNMTS or the mobile conditioning technique may be due to criteria for "competence" or the cognitive and motor demands of the task. Visual preference learning requires only that the infant gaze at the novel stimulus longer than the sample stimulus. DNMTS requires that the infant manually displace the novel object to retrieve the reward on 90 percent of the trials in a session. The mobile conditioning task requires the infant to maintain a kicking rate at the retention test that is comparable to the rate immediately after training.

The degree to which the infant must plan and execute a motor act may partially account for differences in the developmental time course between these tasks, particularly the prolonged time course of development of DNMTS. However, human infants accurately plan and reach for a desired object or to obtain a reward by eight to twelve months, as shown by the $\overline{AB}$ error task (Piaget, 1954), the delayed response task (Diamond and Doar, 1989), and object discrimination learning (Overman, 1990). Therefore, neither the planning of a reaching movement nor the associative aspects of the tasks can account entirely for the developmental differences between tasks.

The criteria for "accurate" visual recognition memory also differ between tasks but cannot account for the differences in time course of development between these three tasks. Even when the criterion for visual recognition in DNMTS is equated with that of paired-comparison novelty preference, that is when infants perform at better then chance levels, DNMTS still requires 50 days of training and by then the infants are 15–18 months old (Overman, 1990).

The qualitative characteristics of the learning and retention in the three tasks differ. The recognition memory as assessed in infants by DNMTS is extremely fragile. Information is learned very quickly, after one exposure to the object/reward pair, but is also easily forgotten with longer retention intervals or with interference from other items on a "list" of intervening object pairs (Bachevalier and Mishkin, 1984). In this way each trial is "unique" not only because different object pairs are used but also because each trial has its own unique temporal and spatial context. The infant must remember the object *on this particular trial* and distinguish this trial from all others. In contrast, the visual recognition memory as assessed by the paired-comparison and mobile conditioning tasks is remarkably robust. The information regarding the sample object is gained over multiple glances, or several exposures to the sample. Infants show retention of the sample objects over very long delays, as much as two weeks, and show few effects of interference. In addition, in paired-comparison novelty preference, the forgetting that results from interference is completely reversed and memory is restored with a one minute rest period or with a brief exposure to the previously studied sample stimulus (Fagan, 1977). "Reminder" trials in which the infant is briefly re-exposed to the sample mobile result in nearly complete restitution of the learned response (Rovee-Collier et al., 1980). This "robust" quality of infant novelty preference learning and the memory demonstrated using the mobile conditioning technique suggests that at least some aspects of the memory are different from the declarative memory form in adult learning. For example, in adult declarative forms of learning, when one forgets items on a grocery list a brief reminder may recover some of the items on the list but it is unlikely to recover all of the items.

The Brain Basis of the Development of Visual Recognition Memory

In adult monkeys (Mishkin, 1978) and humans (Squire et al., 1988) damage to the temporal lobe or diencephalic midline memory system impairs DNMTS performance. This same system is critical for paired-comparison novelty preference learning in adults as well (L. R. Squire, personal communication). Recent studies suggest that this system is critical for visual recognition memory throughout development. Early damage to the temporal lobe memory system (hippocampus, amygdala and overlying cortex) in the monkey, within a few weeks of birth, impairs novelty preference learning and DNMTS learning (for review see Bachevalier, 1990a, b) while visual discrimination is entirely intact (Bachevalier et al., 1990). The amygdala and/or entorhinal cortex are more critical than hippocampus for the development of DNMTS performance (Bachevalier and Mishkin, 1991). While early reports suggested that the loss of novelty preference learning was permanent, more recent work suggests that neonatally lesioned animals are not as impaired at maturity as animals with comparable lesions made in adulthood (Saunders et al., 1991).

This very early contribution of the temporal lobe declarative memory system to novelty preference *and* DNMTS (the neural basis of mobile conditioning is unknown) is surprising for two reasons. First, the time courses of development of these two forms of visual recognition memory are very different. Second, the task demands are also quite different. Both tasks share the necessity of the infant to maintain a representation of the sample object but DNMTS also requires a motor response and the learning of an associative "rule" (that the reward is under the novel object). One possibility is that the later developing neocortical structures are critical for DNMTS but not paired-comparison novelty preference. For instance, inferior prefrontal cortex may be needed to mediate "rule" learning in DNMTS (Overman, 1990; Weinstein et al., 1988). In addition, there may be a shift during development in the quality of object recognition and its neural basis. The earlier developing visual area TEO has early transient projections to the temporal lobe memory system and these later retract (Webster et al., 1991), possibly to be functionally replaced by later developing area TE (Hagger et al., 1987).

That neocortical areas may influence the quality of early memory is an enticing idea. Frontal cortical areas are critical for the moment-by-moment updating of representations in memory (Fuster and Bauer, 1974; Goldman-Rakic, 1987), and for associating each representation with its unique temporal and spatial context (Janowsky et al., 1989; Milner et al., 1985). In addition, there is now ample evidence that the cortical input to the hippocampal memory system is critical for the encoding and storage of information across modalities (Zola-Morgan et al., 1989). Finally, neocortical temporal and frontal areas become functionally mature later in development than primary sensory or limbic structures (Chugani et al., 1987; Goldman-Rakic, 1987; Hagger et al., 1988).

Both the "rule" learning and the degree to which representations are each contextually unique (in time and space) distinguish DNMTS from paired-comparison learning (and to some degree learning in the mobile conditioning task). It may be these aspects of DNMTS and the late development of their cortical mediators that cause the late development of DNMTS learning and late development of event memory in general in children (Bauer and Mandler, 1989) but allow the early development of paired-comparison novelty preference. The cortical influence that is necessary for these functions may also mediate the hallmark for declarative memory; that is, the ability to bring to conscious awareness information in memory (Mandler, 1988).

The comparison of mnemonic abilities across tasks, across development, and through the window of their neural mediators suggests that infants build their representations of the world using a different neural architecture from that which is used to create or maintain representations as adults. Along with the addition of cortical input to the process of learning and memory in the first years of life, come qualitative cognitive changes in the form or architecture of the representations themselves.

ACKNOWLEDGEMENTS

This work was supported in part by the Medical Research Foundation of Oregon, and the March of Dimes Birth Defects Foundation. Thanks are due to Lisa Thomas-Thrapp for assistance in the preparation of this chapter.

REFERENCES

Ackles, P. K. and Karrer, R. (1991) A critique of the Dannemiller and Banks (1983) neuronal fatigue (selective adaptation) hypothesis of young infant habituation. *Merrill-Palmer Quarterly*, 37(2), 325–34.

Albert, M. S., Butters, N. and Levin, J. (1980) Memory for remote events in chronic alcoholics and alcoholic Korsakoff patients. In Begleiter (ed.), *Biological Effects of Alcohol*. New York: Plenum, pp. 719–30.

Bachevalier, J. (1990a) Memory loss and the socio-emotional disturbances following neonatal damage of the limbic system in monkeys: An animal model for childhood autism. In C. A. Tamminga and S. C. Schultz (eds), *Advances in Psychiatry: Schizophrenia Vol. 1*. New York: Raven Press, pp. 129–40.

Bachevalier, J. (1990b) Ontogenetic development of habit and memory formation in primates. *Annals of the New York Academy of Sciences*, 608, 457–84.

Bachevalier, J. and Mishkin, M. (1984) An early and a late developing system for learning and retention in infant monkeys. *Behavioral Neuroscience*, 98(5), 770–8.

Bachevalier, J. and Mishkin, M. (1991) Effects of neonatal lesions of the amygdaloid complex or hippocampal formation on the development of visual recognition memory. *Society for Neuroscience Abstracts*, 17, 338.

Bachevalier, J., Brickson, M., Hagger, C. and Mishkin, M. (1990) Age and sex differences in the effects of selective temporal lobe lesion on the formation of visual discrimination habits in Rhesus monkeys (*Macaca mulatta*) *Behavioral Neuroscience*, 101, 885–99.

Bauer, P. J. and Mandler, J. M. (1989) One thing follows another: effects of temporal structure on 1- to 2-year-old's recall of events. *Developmental Psychology*, 25, 197–206.

Berger, T. W. (1984) Long-term potentiation of hippocampal synaptic transmission affects rate of behavioral learning. *Science*, 224, 627–30.

Bornstein, M. H., Pecheux, M.-G. and Lecuyer, R. (1988) Visual habituation in human infants: development and rearing circumstances *Psychological Research*, 50, 130–3.

Borovsky, D. B. and Rovee-Collier, C. K. (1990) Contextual constraints on memory retrieval at 6 months. *Child Development*, 61, 1569–83.

Brazelton, T. B. (1977) Neonatal behavioral assessment scale. In *Clinics in Developmental Medicine*, Vol. 50. Philadelphia: Lippincott.

Brody, B. A, Kinney H. C., Kloman, A. S., Gilles, F. H. (1987) Sequence of central nervous system myelination in human infancy. I. An autopsy study of myelination. *Journal of Neuropathology and Experimental Neurology*, 46(3), 283–301.

Chugani, H. T., Phelps, M. E. and Mazziotta, J. C. (1987) Positron emission tomography study of human brain functional development. *Annals of Neurology*, 22, 487–97.

Cohen, N. J. and Squire, L. R. (1980) Preserved learning and retention of pattern analyzing skill in amnesia: dissociation of knowing how and knowing that. *Science*, 210, 207–9.

Cohen, N. J. and Squire, L. R. (1981) Retrograde amnesia and remote memory impairment. *Neuropsychologia*, 19, 337–56.

Columbo, J., Mitchell, D. W., O'Brien, M. and Horowitz, F. D. (1987) The stability of visual habituation during the first year of life. *Child Development*, 58, 474–87.

Corkin, S. (1968) Acquisition of motor skill after bilateral medial temporal excision. *Neuropsychologia*, 6, 255–65.

Dannemiller, J. L. and Banks, M. S. (1983) Can selective adaptation account for early infant habituation? *Merrill-Palmer Quarterly*, 32, 87–91.

Davis, M., Gendelman, D. S., Tischler, M. and Gendelman, P. M. (1982) A primary acoustic startle circuit: lesion and stimulation studies. *Journal of Neuroscience*, 2, 791–805.

Diamond, A. and Doar, B. (1989) The performance of human infants on a measure of frontal cortex function, the delayed response task. *Developmental Psychobiology*, 22(3), 271–94.

Fagan, J. F. (1970) Memory in the infant. *Journal of Experimental Child Psychology*, 9, 217–26.

Fagan, J. F. (1971) Infants' recognition memory for a series of visual stimuli. *Journal of Experimental Child Psychology*, 11, 244–50.

Fagan, J. F. (1977) Infant recognition memory: studies in forgetting. *Child Development*, 48, 68–78.

Fagan, J. F. (1990) The paired-comparison paradigm and infant intelligence. *Annals of the New York Academy of Sciences*, 608, 337–64.

Fagan, J. F., Fantz R. L. and Miranda, S. B. (1971) Infants' attention to novel stimuli as a function of postnatal conceptional age. Paper presented at the Society for Research in Child Development Meeting. April, Minneapolis.

Fagen, J. W., Ohr, P. S., Singer, J. M. and Klein, S. J. (1989) Crying and retrograde amnesia in young infants. *Infant Behavior and Development*, 12, 13–24.

Fantz, R. L. (1964) Visual experience in infants: decreased attention to familiar patterns relative to novel ones. *Science*, 146, 668–70.

Foy, M. R. and Thompson R. F. (1986) Single unit analysis of Purkinje cell discharge in classically conditioned untrained rabbits. *Society for Neuroscience Abstracts*, 12, 518.

Friedman, S. B. (1972) Habituation and recovery of visual response in the alert human newborn. *Journal of Experimental Child Psychology*, 13, 339–49.

Friedman, S. B., Burno L. A. and Vietze, P. (1974) Newborn habituation to visual stimuli: a sex difference in novelty detection. *Journal of Experimental Child Psychology*, 18, 242–51.

Fuster, J. M. and Bauer, R. H. (1974) Visual short-term memory deficit from hypothermia of frontal cortex. *Brain Research*, 81, 393–400.

Goldman-Rakic, P. S. (1987) Circuitry of primate prefrontal cortex and regulation of behavior by representational memory. *Handbook of Physiology*, 5, 373–417.

Graf, P., Squire, L. R. and Mandler, G. (1984) The information that amnesic patients do not forget. *Journal of Experimental Psychology: Learning, Memory and Cognition*, 10, 164–78.

Hagger, C., Bachevalier, J. and Bercu, B. B. (1987) Sexual dimorphism in the development of habit formation: effects of perinatal gonadal hormones. *Neuroscience*, 22 (suppl.), S520.

Hagger, C., Bachevalier, J., Macko, K. A., Kennedy C., Sokoloff, L. and Mishkin, M. (1988) Functional maturation of inferior temporal cortex in infant rhesus monkeys. *Society for Neuroscience Abstracts*, 14, 2.

Heindel, W. C., Butter, N. and Salmon, D. P. (1988) Impaired learning of a motor skill in patients with Huntington's disease. *Behavioral Neuroscience*, 102, 141–7.

Hubel, D. H. and Wiesel, T. N. (1965) Receptive fields and functional architecture in two nonstriate visual areas (18 and 19) of the cat. *Journal of Neurophysiology*, 28, 229–89.

Jacoby, L. L. and Witherspoon, D. (1982) Remembering without awareness. *Canadian Journal of Psychology*, 32, 300–24.

Janowsky, J. S., Shimamura, A. P. and Squire, L. R. (1989) Source memory impairment in patients with frontal lobe lesions *Neuropsychologia*, 27, 1043–56.

Jeffrey, W. E. and Cohen, L. B. (1971) Habituation in the human infant. In H. W. Reese (ed.), *Advances in Child Development and Behavior Vol. 6*. New York: Academic Press.

Jernigan, T. L. and Tallal P. (1990) Late childhood changes in brain morphology observable with MRI. *Developmental Medicine and Child Neurology*, 32, 379–85.

Kandel, E. R. (1976) *Cellular Basis of Behavior*. San Francisco: Freeman.

Little, A. H., Lipsett, L. P. and Rovee-Collier, C. K. (1984) Classical conditioning and retention of the infant's eyelid response: effects of age and interstimulus interval. *Journal of Experimental Child Psychology*, 37, 512–24.

Lipsett, L. P. (1990) Learning processes in the human newborn: sensitization, habituation and classical conditioning *Annals of the New York Academy of Sciences*, 608, 113–127.

Mandler, J. M. (1988) How to build a baby: On the development of an accessible representational system. *Cognitive Development*, 3, 113–36.

Mandler, J. M. (1990) Recall of events by preverbal children. *Annals of the New York Academy of Sciences*, 608, 365–93.

Mayes, L. C. and Kessen, W. (1989) Maturational changes in measures of habituation. *Infant Behavior and Development*, 12(4), 437–50.

McCormick, D. A., Clark, G. A., Lavond, D. G. and Thompson, R. F. (1982) Initial localization of the memory trace for a basic form of learning. *Proceedings of the National Academy of Sciences*, 79(8), 2731–42.

Milewski, A. E. and Siqueland, E. R. (1975) Discrimination of color and pattern novelty in one-month infants. *Journal of Experimental Child Psychology*, 19, 122–36.

Milner, B. (1966) Amnesia following operation on the temporal lobes. In C. W. M. Whitty and O. L. Zangwill (eds), *Amnesia*. London: Butterworth.

Milner, B., Petrides, M. and Smith, M. L. (1985) Frontal lobes and the temporal organization of memory. *Human Neurobiology*, 4, 137–42.

Mishkin, M. (1978) Memory in monkeys severely impaired by combined but not separate removal of amygdala and hippocampus. *Nature*, 273. 297–8.

Mishkin, M., Malamut, B. and Bachevalier, J. (1984) Memories and habits: two neural systems. In G. Lynch, J. L. McGaugh and N. M. Weinberger (eds), *Neurobiology of Learning and Memory*. New York: Guildford Press.

Moore, J. W., Goodell, N. A. and Solomon P. R. (1976) Central cholinergic blockage by scopolamine and habituation, classical conditioning and latent inhibition of the rabbit's nictitating membrane response. *Physiological Psychology*, 4. 395–9.

Nadel, L. and Zola-Morgan, S. (1984) Infantile amnesia: A neurobiological perspective. In M. Moskovitch (ed.), *Infant Memory*. New York: Plenum Press, pp. 145–72.

Ohlrich, E. S. and Ross, L. E. (1968) Acquisition and differential conditioning of the eyelid response in normal and retarded children. *Journal of Experimental Child Psychology*, 6, 181–93.

Ohr, P., Fagen, J. W., Rovee-Collier, C. K., Hayne, H. and Vander Linde, E. (1989) Amount of training and retention by infants. *Developmental Psychobiology*, 22 69–80.

Ohr, P. S., Fleckenstein, L. K., Fagen, J. W., Klein, S. J. and Pioli, L. M. (1990) Crying produced forgetting in infants: a contextual analysis. *Infant Behavior and Development*, 13(3) 305–20.

Overman, W. H. (1990) Performance on traditional matching to sample, non-matching to sample, and object discrimination tasks by 12- to 32-month-old children: a developmental progression. *Annals of the New York Academy of Sciences*, 608, 365–93.

Piaget, J. (1954) *The Construction of Reality in the Child*. New York: Basic Books.

Rovee, C. K. and Fagen, J. W. (1976) Extended conditioning and 24-hour retention in infants. *Journal of Experimental Child Psychology*, 21. 1–11.

Rovee-Collier, C. K. (1990) The "memory system" of prelinguistic infants. *Annals of the New York Academy of Sciences*, 608, 517–42.

Rovee-Collier, C. K. and Hayne, H. (1987) Reactivation of infant memory: implications for cognitive development. In H. W. Reece (ed.), *Advances in Child Development and Behavior, Vol. 20*, New York: Academic Press, pp. 185–238.

Rovee-Collier, C. and Lipsett, L. P. (1982) Learning, adaptation, and memory in the newborn. In P. Stratton (ed.), *Psychobiology of the Human Newborn*. New York: Wiley.

Rovee-Collier, C. K., Sullivan, M. W., Enright, M., Lucas, D. and Fagen, J. W. (1980) Reactivation of infant memory. *Science* 208, 1159–61.

Saunders, R. C., Richards, R. S. and Bachevalier, J. (1991) The effects of neonatal limbic lesions on long-term recognition memory in the adult rhesus monkey. *Society for Neuroscience Abstracts*, 17, 133.

Schachtel, E. G. (1947) On memory and childhood amnesia. *Psychiatry*, 10, 1–26.

Sheingold, K. and Tenney, Y. J. (1982) Memory for a salient childhood event. In U. Neisser (ed.), *Memory Observed*. San Francisco, Freeman, pp. 201–12.

Shimamura, A. P. and Squire, L. R. (1987) A neuropsychological study of fact memory and source amnesia. *Journal of Experimental Psychology: Learning, Memory and Cognition*, 13, 464–73.

Sidman, R. L. and Rakic, P. (1973) Neuronal migration, with special reference to developing human brain: a review. *Brain Research*, 62, 1–35.

Smith, M. L. and Milner, B. (1981) The role of the right hippocampus in the recall of spatial location. *Neuropsychologia*, 19, 781–93.

Squire, L. R. (1982) Comparisons between forms of amnesia: some deficits are unique to Korsakoff's syndrome. *Journal of Experimental Psychology: Learning, Memory and Cognition*, 8(6), 560–71.

Squire, L. R. (1987) *Memory and Brain*. Oxford: Oxford University Press.

Squire, L. R. (1989) On the course of forgetting in very long-term memory. *Journal of Experimental Psychology: Learning, Memory and Cognition*, 15, 241–5.

Squire, L. R. and Cohen, N. J. (1982) Remote memory, retrograde amnesia, and the neuropsychology of memory. In L. Cermak (ed.), *Human Memory and Amnesia*. Hillsdale, NJ: Lawrence Erlbaum Associates.

Squire, L. R., Haist, F. and Shimamura, A. P. (1989) The neurology of memory: quantitative assessment of retrograde amnesia in two groups of amnesic patients. *Journal of Neuroscience*, 9, 828–39.

Squire, L. R., Nadel, L. and Slater, P. C. (1981) Anterograde amnesia and memory for temporal order *Neuropsychologia*, 19, 141–5.

Squire, L. R., Ojemann, J., Miezin, F., Petersen, S., Videen, T. and Raichle, M. (1992) A functional anatomical study of memory. Activation of the hippocampus in normal humans: *Proceedings of the National Academy of Sciences* 89(5), 1837–41.

Squire L. R. and Spanis, C. W. (1984) Long gradient of retrograde amnesia in mice: continuity with findings in humans. *Behavioral Neuroscience*, 98, 345–8.

Squire, L. R., and Zola-Morgan, S. (1991) The Medial temporal lobe memory system. *Science* 253, 1380–1386.

Squire, L. R., Zola-Morgan, S. and Chen, K. (1988) Human amnesia and animal models of amnesia: Performance of amnesic patients on tests designed for the monkey. *Behavioral Neuroscience*, 11, 210–21.

Sullivan, M. W., Rovee-Collier, C. K. and Tynes D. M. (1979) A conditioning analysis of infant long-term memory. *Child Development*, 50, 152–62.

Thompson, R. F. (1986) The neurobiology of learning and memory. *Science*, 233, 941–7

Waldfogel, S. (1948) The frequency and affective character of childhood memories. *Psychological Monographs*, 62 (whole no. 291).

Warrington, E. K. and Weiskrantz, L. (1968) A new method of testing long-term retention with special reference to amnesic patients. *Nature*, 217, 972–4.

Webster, M. J., Ungerleiter, L. G. and Bachevalier, J. (1991) Connections of inferior temporal areas TE and TEO with medial temporal-lobe structures in infant and adult monkeys. *Journal of Neuroscience* 11(4). 1095–1116.

Weinstein, J. A., Saunders, R. C. and Mishkin, M. (1988) Temporoprefrontal interaction in rule learning in macaques. *Society for Neuroscience Abstracts*, 14, 1230.

Werden, D. and Ross, L. E. (1972) A comparison of the trace and delay classical conditioning performance of normal children. *Journal of Experimental Child Psychology*, 59, 19–26.

White, S. H. and Pillemer, D. B. (1979) Childhood amnesia and the development of a functionally accessible memory system. In J. F. Kihlstrom and F. J. Evans (eds), *Functional Disorders of Memory*. Hillsdale, NJ: Erlbaum.

Woodruff-Pak, D. S., Logan, C. G. and Thompson, R. F. (1990) Neurobiological substrates of classical conditioning across the life span. *Annals of the New York Academy of Sciences*, 608, 150–78.

Woodruff-Pak, D. S., Lavond, D. G. and Thompson, R. F. (1985) Trace conditioning: Abolished by cerebellar nuclear lesions but not lateral cerebellar cortex aspirations. *Brain Research*, 348, 249–60.

Yeo, C. H., Hardiman, M. J. and Glickstein, M. (1984) Discrete lesions of the cerebellar cortex abolish classically conditioned nictitating membrane response of the rabbit. *Behavioral Brain Research*, 13, 261–6.

Zola-Morgan, S. (1984) Toward and animal model of human amnesia: Some critical issues. In L. R. Squire and N. Butters (eds), *Neuropsychology of Memory*. New York: Guilford Press.

Zola-Morgan, S. and Squire L. R. (1990a) The neuropsychology of memory: parallel findings in humans and nonhuman primates. *Annals of the New York Academy of Sciences*, 608, 434–56.

Zola-Morgan, S. and Squire L. R. (1990b) The primate hippocampal formation: evidence for a time-limited role in memory storage. *Science*, 250, 288–90.

Zola-Morgan, S., Squire, L. R., Amaral, D. G. and Suzuki, W. A. (1989) Lesions of perirhinal and parahippocampal cortex that spare the amygdala and hippocampal formation produce severe memory impairment. *Journal for Neuroscience*, 9, 4355–70.

29

The Neurobiology of Handedness, Language, and Cerebral Dominance: a Model for the Molecular Genetics of Behavior

I. C. McMANUS AND M. P. BRYDEN

One of the great surprises that awaited neurology and psychology in the nineteenth century was the discovery that the two halves of what seemed to be the symmetric human brain did not have the same functional properties. In this sense the hemispheres differed from the two kidneys, the two lungs, the two adrenals, the two gonads, or indeed any of the other seemingly symmetric organs. Those with a knowledge of embryology will, of course, realize that strictly speaking the right and left chambers of the heart, which *do* have very different functions, are not symmetric in any deep sense, having evolved from the complex folding of a single tube.

The important insight concerning functional asymmetry was first clearly enunciated by Paul Broca, who, in 1863, described over 25 patients, all of whom suffered from what we would now call *aphasia*, or lack of speech, and *all* of whom had suffered from lesions to the *left* side of the brain (Berker et al., 1986) (although he had undoubtedly been anticipated by Wigan and Dax – for more detailed historical accounts see Harrington, 1987; Hécaen and Dubois, 1969; Hécaen and Lanteri-Laura, 1977). The implication seemed obvious (and indeed its broad principle is as correct today as it was when Broca first enunciated it): "Nous parlons avec l'hémisphère gauche" ("we speak with the left hemisphere"; Broca, 1865). Such violation of a symmetry that had been implicitly assumed since the time of Aristotle was at first shocking; and for a while attempts were made to explain it away using the only other known functional asymmetry, that of handedness, since the majority of the population is also right-handed. Such explanations would have restored a higher order symmetry to the brain, in which left-handers simply showed the reverse pattern of language dominance to right-handers; in fact, however, they do not and, as will be seen, the relationship is much more complex.

Nineteenth-century neurologists at first talked of the "dominant" or "major" hemisphere (which does the talking), and the "non-dominant" or "minor" hemisphere (which apparently did little of real importance, for of course it was the richness of language, that dubious gift of Babel, that determined man's uniqueness in the animal kingdom). Only as cases of right-hemisphere injury were studied more closely did it become apparent that the right hemisphere also had its own typical mode of functioning, usually involving the processing of complex visuo-spatial images in a holistic or parallel fashion, and characteristically resulting in the group of syndromes broadly known as the *agnosias* (which can, however, be associated with left-hemisphere or bilateral damage). The· two hemispheres therefore seemed to show *complementary specialization*, although Bryden (1986a, b, 1990) has pointed out that a more accurate description is *statistical complementarity*, localization of the two types of function being independent, but appearing associated because each is highly biased in its distribution, one principally to the left hemisphere and the other to the right hemisphere. Modern neuropsychology (see e.g. Ellis and Young, 1988; Shallice, 1991) has now recognized a range of syndromes, many of which are lateralized, and some of which, such as prosopagnosia (deficits of face recognition), seem to require lesions in specific but different areas in both right and left hemispheres.

The Biological Problem of Asymmetry

Psychology is inevitably based in biology, in the sense that psychological functioning necessitates the existence of a neural substrate, of brain tissue, or "wetware" (just as the running of the "software" of a computer program cannot actually function in any real sense without appropriate "hardware"). If functional processes are asymmetric – and Broca's observation alone makes that conclusion indubitable – then it would seem probable that the underlying neural machinery is itself asymmetric. The problem might be biologically trivial in one sense if it were the case that exactly half of human beings spoke with their left hemisphere and the other half spoke with their right hemisphere. Chance alone might then determine in any individual person whether (s)he were right or left-brained for language, just as chance determines whether a molecule produced in a chemical (but not a biochemical) reaction takes the D- or the L-form. Chance does seem to underlie the asymmetry of many biological processes, so that, for example, almost precisely 50 percent of mice prefer to use their right paw and 50 percent prefer to use their left paw for reaching for food (Collins, 1985); and if one measures the width of the upper incisors (front teeth) in humans, then in half of individuals the right tooth is slightly larger, and in the other half the left tooth is slightly larger (Bailit et al., 1970). In each case there is the situation biologists call *fluctuating asymmetry* (Palmer and Strobeck, 1986), which results from small chance fluctuations during early development, so-called "biological noise," which eventually become magnified and fixed so that individuals are asymmetric but the population still shows symmetry.

With language dominance and with handedness in humans, however, the vast majority of the population (of the order of 90 percent) is lateralized in one particular direction, speaking with the left hemisphere and using the right hand for skilled activities (although these are not always the same 90 percent of the population for each type of dominance). Such *directional asymmetries* present a severe theoretical problem both in biology, as in explaining why the heart is almost always on the left side (Brown et al., 1991; Brown and Wolpert, 1990), and in neurobiology. The essence of the problem is that directional asymmetries cannot just happen, they have to be *maintained* by something; just as when a ball is bouncing on the top of a fountain of water, it is the force of the water that maintains what is otherwise an inherently unstable situation. The biological baseline against which all asymmetries are assessed is fluctuating asymmetry, 50 percent right and 50 percent left, and it is the situation to which directional asymmetries will inevitably revert unless they are maintained. Since human handedness and human language dominance show clear, strong, directional asymmetry, three crucial questions are immediately raised: what is it in the development of the individual human organism, in its *ontogeny*, that creates this asymmetry? When in our evolutionary past, in human *phylogeny*, did this asymmetry arise? And what were the adaptive advantages that allowed and encouraged the evolutionary shift that has apparently made humans unique in the animal kingdom in having an asymmetric brain?

It is rare in psychology for high-level, complex behaviors to have clear biological underpinnings, and such situations create unusual opportunities for studying and understanding both neurobiology and cognition. If, as we will argue is probably the case, the biological underpinning arises from the action of a single major gene, then the scope for understanding language, one of the central characteristics that seems to distinguish humans from other animals, is immense, particularly given the advent of modern techniques of molecular biology, which allow the dissection of developmental and genetic processes in immense detail. Other authors have argued that the best hope for studying the molecular basis of behavior genetics is by studying such complex, multifactorial conditions as alcoholism (McClearn et al., 1991). Here we will argue that perhaps a better strategy for molecular behavior genetics, and for cognitive neurobiology, is in understanding the biological basis of human cerebral lateralization – of language dominance and of handedness. And indeed it is the understanding of handedness that is of central importance, since language dominance is intrinsically much more difficult to study in large numbers of active, sentient, living human beings, accurate assessment and classification being neither easy nor reliable (Bryden, 1988a). In contrast, handedness is readily assessed and easily studied in large numbers of people, and therefore provides an excellent surrogate for the study of language dominance. Once the biology of handedness is understood then an understanding of the biology of language will not be far behind, since handedness and language show functional linkage, and in all probability are controlled by the same gene.

The Study of Right- and Left-handedness: the Dangers of Symbolism

Interest in right and left, particularly in why most people are right-handed but a few are left-handed, can be traced back at least to Plato and Aristotle (McManus et al., 1986), and reflects a deeper interest in the symbolic functions of right and left that can be found in Homer, in the Bible, and in other mythologies. "Right" is seen as good, correct, skilful, etc., in contrast with the sinister, evil, gauche, cack-handed nature of "left" – so that in the Bible, for instance, the (good) sheep are sorted on to the right hand whereas the (bad) goats are sorted on to the left. One consequence of this dual symbolic classification (Hertz, 1909, 1960; Needham, 1973) is that what are supposedly serious scientific studies of handedness sometimes either confuse symbolism with evidence, or are treated more seriously by other scientists or by the general public than their data strictly justify. An early example is the work of Lombroso, who tried to demonstrate that criminals were more likely to be left-handed (Lombroso, 1903) (although see Ellis, 1990, for a recent review). Recent examples are also common, and reflect ideas that refuse to die, and indeed are frequently cited in the scientific and popular literature, despite adequate evidence to refute them. Perhaps the best studied is the hypothesis, originally proposed by Bakan (1971, 1990), that left-handedness is the result of minor degress of brain damage due to birth trauma or birth stress. Large-scale prospective studies (McManus, 1981; Schwartz, 1990) have found no serious evidence to support the hypothesis, and a recent meta-analysis (Searleman et al., 1989) found almost no support for the theory. Nevertheless, claims still continue to be made on behalf of such a theory, as for instance in the variant that it is older mothers who have left-handed children (Coren, 1990), despite pre-existing evidence to the contrary (McManus, 1990) and a subsequent failure to replicate (Peters and Perry, 1992). A similar controversy is currently raging in the literature concerning the highly contentious suggestion that left-handers live less long than right-handers: despite the methodological inadequacies of the original studies (Coren and Halpern, 1991; Halpern and Coren, 1990, 1991) and the failure of other data sets to replicate the finding (Marks and Williamson, 1991; Wolf et al., 1991), serious and critical journals such as *Nature* (Pool, 1991) have devoted large amounts of space to the question, and thereby encouraged popular newspapers and magazines to report it extensively. Similar criticisms apply to the suggestion, based on a relatively small set of subjects, that homosexuals are more likely to be left-handed (McCormick et al., 1990); two large studies have failed to replicate the effect (Marchant-Haycox et al., 1991; Satz et al., 1991) yet, in an otherwise serious article (Barinaga, 1991), *Science* repeated a claim that cannot be empirically replicated.

A variant of the symbolism of "right–left" confounds it with the other potent dual symbolic classification of "male–female" (and is seen in part in the suggestion, dating back at least to the beginning of this century in the correspondence between Fliess and Freud, that homosexuals are more likely to be left-handed). That males and females differ in their lateralization seems likely from studies of deficits after unilateral brain damage (McGlone, 1980), and from the higher incidence of left-handedness in males than females, the male rate being 27 percent higher than that in females in a recent meta-analysis (McManus, 1991; Seddon and McManus, 1991). However, in recent years a very influential theory has dominated the neuropsychological literature, which combines not only laterality and sex differences, but also a vast range of diseases and other malformations in a "grand theory" of potentially awesome implication. What we will call the "Geschwind–Behan–Galaburda" (GBG) theory originated in a paper published in 1982 by Geschwind and Behan, and the theory was subsequently developed in a series of three very long papers by Geschwind and Galaburda

(1985a, b, c), and then in a book containing essentially identical material (Geschwind and Galaburda, 1987).

The Geschwind–Behan–Galaburda Theory of Lateralization

The GBG theory is complicated, as can be seen from our attempt (McManus and Bryden, 1991a) to reduce it to a causal, structural model (see figure 29.1), based on the published work of Geschwind, Behan and Galaburda (Geschwind and Behan, 1982; Geschwind and Galaburda, 1987). That the model in figure 29.1 is an oversimplification is undoubted, but it does at least make the theory tractable, and its testability can then be discussed (and we are at present preparing a critical review of the published evidence for and against the model). The absence of any independent substantial published evidence for the GBG theory has not prevented it already becoming a "citation classic," having been cited 370 times in scientific papers during the period January 1986 to June 1991.

The core of the GBG theory is that levels of testosterone in the fetus affect the relative growth of the right and left hemispheres, so that high testosterone levels, which of course will more typically be found in males than females, will result in the phenomenon of "anomalous dominance," which is defined as left-handedness, or right-hemisphere language, or left-hemisphere visuo-spatial ability, or a reduced degree of dominance for any of those characteristics, whichever hemisphere they may be in. Raised testosterone levels are also said to result in delayed growth of the posterior part of the left hemisphere, and thereby cause developmental learning disorders, such as autism, dyslexia, stuttering, hyperactivity, and poor artistic, musical, or mathematical ability. Finally, and most importantly for testing the theory, raised testosterone levels are postulated to result in modifications of immune functioning, so that there is an increased incidence of a wide range of pathological conditions, particularly those of an auto-immune nature, such as myasthenia gravis, ulcerative colitis, systemic lupus erythematosus (SLE), asthma, hayfever, and atopy, or of conditions that have a putative auto-immune status, such as migraine.

Although principally an exercise in theoretical biology, the GBG model keeps its feet on the ground by its apparent reliance on empirical data. The theory makes strong predictions that there should be associations between any of the measurable characteristics shown down the right-hand side of figure 29.1, and in their very influential 1982 paper, Geschwind and Behan reported the highly counterintuitive result that individuals with conditions such as myasthenia gravis, ulcerative colitis, and asthma are more likely to be left-handed. If correct, then those results would provide very strong evidence indeed for the GBG model – and would be totally inexplicable under any other current model of cerebral lateralization. Regrettably, however, those findings have not received the unambiguous support that a grand theory such as that of GBG really requires. Thus for instance, in two studies of allergic disorders one investigation (Smith, 1987) did find an increased incidence of left-handedness, whereas the other, a much larger and better controlled study (Bishop, 1986), found no association. Similarly, one study of ulcerative colitis and Crohn's disease (Searleman and Fugagli, 1987) did find an association as predicted, and another (Meyers and Janowitz, 1985)

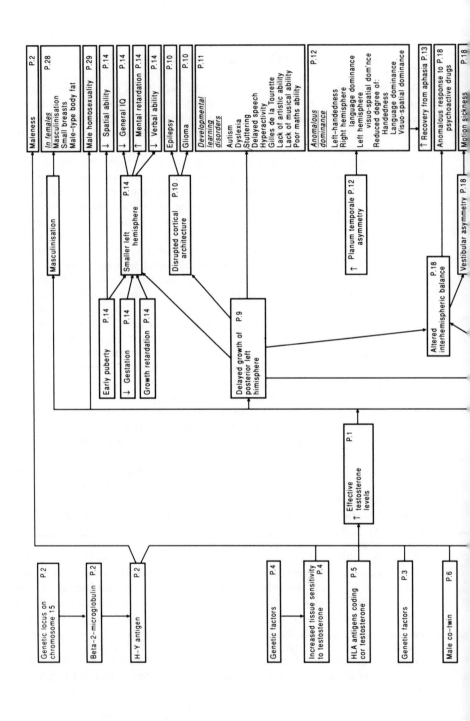

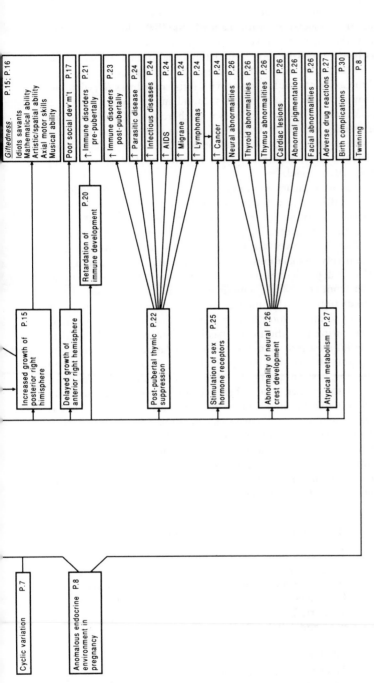

Figure 29.1 A summary diagram of the model proposed by Geschwind, Behan and Galaburda, (based on Geschwind and Galaburda, 1985a, b, c, 1987). Arrows between boxes indicate direct causal links. Reprinted with permission from I. C. McManus and M. P. Bryden (1991) Geschwind's theory of cerebral lateralization: developing a formal, causal model, *Psychological Bulletin*, 110, 237–53.

found no association. In contrast, neither of two studies of systemic lupus erythematosus found any association with handedness (Salcedo et al., 1985; Schur, 1986). In yet further distinction, two studies (Cosi et al., 1988; McManus et al., 1990) of myasthenia gravis in three populations each found evidence that left-handedness was *less* common than in the general population. A recent, more systematic review of the association of diseases with left-handedness (Bryden and McManus, 1992), using meta-analytic techniques, found suggestive evidence that there are positive associations of left-handedness with thyroiditis, Crohn's disease and colitis, negative associations with myasthenia gravis, eczema and urticaria, and no association with a wide range of conditions, including systemic lupus erythematosus and diabetes among others. Taken together such data are hardly strong support for the GBG model.

Summarizing the status of a theory as complex as that of the GBG model, as shown in figure 29.1, is difficult in a few words. Probably it is best to say that it is clearly a brave attempt at grand theorizing in neurobiology; that if it is true it is of immense importance in integrating a wide range of otherwise seemingly disparate conditions; that it receives its strength in its prediction of highly counterintuitive and unlikely associations between handedness and a range of disease conditions; that independent attempts at replicating those associations have, however, been far from consistent, sometimes contradictory and sometimes flatly refuting the predictions of the model; and accordingly it is probably premature at the moment to attach too much credence to the theory as a whole, while simultaneously accepting that the theory has been immensely influential in recent years in stimulating research into the biology of lateralization, and into the neurobiological factors underlying such conditions as mathematical and artistic ability. Perhaps the best summary in a few words is that of Galaburda, one of the proponents of the model, who, when asked whether, "The story that we left-handers are more liable to autoimmune disease, more intelligent, etc., is all nonsense?", replied, "There is no evidence to support the claim in the original observations that left-handers are more vulnerable to autoimmune diseases in general, although they may be more susceptible to some types of allergies" (Galaburda, 1991). Nevertheless, Galaburda (1990) has pointed out that there is somewhat stronger evidence for an association between learning disorders and auto-immune disorders, as the GBG theory would also predict.

What Are Right- and Left-handedness?

It was the great nineteenth-century neurologist Hughlings Jackson who said that "the study of the thing caused must precede the study of the cause of the thing" (Wilson, 1908). One of the major problems of the GBG theory is its rather uncritical acceptance of the concept of "anomalous dominance" (McManus and Bryden, 1991a). Here we will briefly look at some of the problems of classifying, measuring, and defining right and left-handedness; more extensive accounts will be found elsewhere (McManus, 1984, 1991; McManus and Bryden, 1991b).

At an everyday level handedness refers to two separate phenomena: if a person is right-handed then he is usually right-handed in the sense that he is more *skilled* at using his right hand for complex motor tasks (of which writing is the most lateralized), and he *prefers* to use his right hand for even relatively unskilled tasks which either hand could in principle carry out (for instance, picking a sweet out of a bag). In general the two phenomena are highly correlated, those with a preference for one hand also being more skilful with it. Which then comes first? It may be that we prefer to use our right hand, and as a result it gets more practice and hence becomes more skilful; or it may be that the right hand is intrinsically more skilful and hence we prefer to use it (Morgan and McManus, 1988). These hypotheses are difficult to disentangle, but recent evidence (McManus et al., 1992a) that a majority of children with autism are right-handed, and yet those right-handed children are as equally likely to be more skilful with the left hand as with the right, suggests that preference asymmetry comes before skill asymmetry during development, and thus it is preference that is probably primary, with skill differences being a secondary phenomenon.

The extent of preference can be measured more quantitatively, typically by questionnaires asking about 10, 20, or 30 tasks, or by performance, in which individuals carry out a range of tasks. The distributions of scores on such tests are typically bimodal, and it is helpful to differentiate the *direction* of handedness (right versus left) from the *degree* of handedness (if you are right-handed, are you strongly or weakly right-handed?). Very little is known about degree of handedness, although there is evidence that it strengthens during early childhood, and may show some evidence for running in families (Bryden, 1982, 1988b; Porac and Coren, 1981), although not all studies find that result (McManus, 1985a). In general, studies of handedness refer to the direction of handedness, and simply classify subjects as right- or left-handed. A meta-analysis of 88 such studies, combining data from 284,665 subjects, found an overall incidence of left-handedness of 7.78 percent, with little evidence that methods of measurement had any significant influence upon the incidence; however, there was a higher incidence of left-handedness in younger subjects and in those born in more recent cohorts, although these two effects could not be disentangled statistically.

Skill asymmetry is typically measured with tests such as the Annett pegboard (Annett, 1970), which produces a unimodal, approximately normal distribution of difference scores between the hands, or by tapping tasks, such as that of Tapley and Bryden (1985), which typically produce bimodal distributions of scores (McManus et al., 1992b; Tapley and Bryden, 1985), and which can also be broken down into components of direction and degree.

To summarize, handedness is a complex activity, with components of skill and preference, which varies in direction and degree, and can be assessed by performance measures or questionnaires. Our view is that the principal measure relevant to the genetics of handedness is the direction of preference, which can most readily be assessed by questionnaire methods.

Environmental Factors and Pathological Left-handedness

Many studies have looked at possible environmental influences upon handedness (Harris, 1990; Porac et al., 1990), and in general there is relatively poor evidence that they are of importance. An important subgroup of possible environmental causes of left-handedness concerns pathological factors, typically arising *in utero*, during delivery or in early infancy. That such factors can be of some influence is suggested by the increased incidence of left-handedness in children with mental retardation (particularly in those with very low intelligence) (Pipe, 1990). Although the concept of "pathological left-handedness" is not entirely uncontroversial (Harris and Carlson, 1988; McManus, 1983), it now seems probable that about one in twenty cases of left-handedness can be regarded as "pathological" in origin (Bishop, 1990). The precise nature of the pathology responsible for these cases is not clear, but probably it can be attributed either to early asymmetric brain damage, impairing functioning of what would otherwise have been the dominant hemisphere, or to an increased level of "developmental noise," perhaps owing to chromosomal or other defects during early ontogenesis and tissue formation, which disrupts the normal directional asymmetry and replaces it with fluctuating asymmetry, and hence results in an increased incidence of left-handedness (Batheja and McManus, 1985).

With the exception of the minority of left-handers that can be ascribed to pathological causes, there is very little solid evidence that other environmental factors modify handedness; and in particular the lack of a correlation between handedness and social class (McManus, 1981), and the extremely small correlation with intelligence (Hardyck et al., 1976; McManus and Mascie-Taylor, 1983; McManus et al., 1992b) strongly militate against the environmental influence of a range of factors, such as environmental deprivation or social disadvantage, which are strongly associated with low social class and low intelligence. In recent years researchers have therefore looked for evidence that handedness is under genetic control, and although there are still some workers who are willing to propose strong environmental models for handedness, with almost no genetic influence (Collins, 1991; Provins, 1990) most workers now seem to accept that handedness is partly or principally under genetic control. That conclusion would seem to be supported by cross-cultural evidence which suggests that the incidence of left-handedness does not differ significantly between cultures (Connolly and Bishop, 1992; McManus and Bryden, 1991c; Seddon and McManus, 1991), although there is currently still controversy on this issue and opinions do differ (Ardila et al., 1989).

Genetic Models of Handedness

Although a genetic model of handedness was suggested as long ago as 1912 (Ramaley, 1913), and many models have been proposed since then (see McManus and Bryden, 1991b), at present there are only two models that seem to be accepted as having any real success in accounting for the family and twin data. Although probably the more popular in terms of its citations, one of these models, the "right shift theory" of Annett (1985), seems to us to be unsatisfactory for a number of reasons. The model suggests that there are two alleles, RS + and RS −, which are responsible for individuals differing in their extent of "right shift." Individuals differ principally in the extent of skill differences between the hands, those who are strongly right shifted (RS +/+) showing much greater proficiency with the right hand than with the left. Individuals homozygous for a lack of right shift (RS −/−) show a distribution of differences in skill between right and left hands which is centered on zero, so that half are more proficient with the right hand and half are more proficient with the left hand. The relationship of preference to skill is essentially arbitrary, and reflects the position of a criterion, which can be altered by social and other factors, such as methods of measurement. For reasons of space the model will not be discussed in greater detail here, although elsewhere we have considered it extensively (McManus and Bryden, 1991b). We do, however, note briefly as criticisms of it that: it argues that genes determine skill rather than preference, whereas evidence suggests it is actually preference that is primary (McManus et al., 1992a); it does not provide an adequate description of observed distributions of differences between the hands in skill, which are frequently bimodal rather than unimodal (McManus, 1985b); on formal testing it provides a less adequate fit to family and twin data than does the other contending model (McManus, 1985a); it does not adequately explain the "maternal effect" (McManus and Bryden, 1991b; McManus, 1991), whereby left-handed mothers are more likely to have left-handed children than are left-handed fathers; and in its recent extension and development (Annett, 1991a, b, c; Annett and Manning, 1989, 1990a, b), it makes unrealistic assumptions about the differences in intellectual ability between heterozygotes and homozygotes (McManus et al., 1992). The model we will discuss further here, that originally proposed by McManus (1979, 1984, 1985a), and developed by us in McManus and Bryden (1991b), although indubitably far from perfect, does account for a reasonable number of phenomena, is relatively straightforward in its genetics, and has immediate implications for neurobiology and neuropsychology.

Any adequate genetic model of handedness must explain two crucial empirical results: that handedness runs in families, albeit not very strongly (summarizing data from 72,600 offspring in families, left-handedness was present in 9.5 percent of the children of two right-handers, 19.5 percent of the children of one right- and one left-hander, and 26.1 percent of the children of two left-handers); and that despite discordant twin pairs (one right- and one left-handed) being more common in dizygotic than monozygotic twins, there is still a very high proportion of monozygotic twin pairs that are discordant (21.7 percent of 2,900 pairs in our review; McManus and Bryden, 1991b). If a model also wishes to explain sex differences, which it probably should do given the statistical reliability of the sex differences, then it must also explain why the incidence of left-handedness is about 27 percent higher in males than females, and why if one parent is left-handed, then a left-handed mother produces a higher proportion of left-handed offspring (21.9 percent) than a left-handed father (16.8 percent) – the "maternal effect."

The McManus (1985a) model of the genetics of handedness proposed that there is an autosomal locus, at which there are two alleles D (for dextral) and C (for chance). (For those who are not used to the terminology of genetics, *autosomal* means that the genes are not located on the X and Y chromosomes, the sex chromosomes, but on the other chromosomes which are paired. *Alleles* are the individual units of inheritance, essentially being long strings of DNA bases. The *gene-pool* of the population may contain many types of allele for a particular *locus*, or site on a chromosome, but each individual will have only two alleles at any locus, one originating from each parent, and each located on one of the two chromosomes in the pair. Together the two alleles comprise the individual's *genotype*, and are contrasted with the individual's *phenotype*, which represents the functional, structural or behavioral characteristics displayed by the individual – handedness in this case. For an introduction to basic genetics see Cavalli-Sforza and Bodmer, 1971, and Weaver and Hedrick, 1989.) In the model, individuals with the DD genotype are all right-handed (and left-brained for language and right-brained for visuo-spatial processing). Genotype CC individuals show no systematic genetic control over the direction of their handedness, and hence fluctuating asymmetry alone determines whether they are right or left handed, and hence precisely 50 percent are right-handed and 50 percent are left-handed (see table 29.1); the model can also be extended to describe language dominance, and in the CC genotype 50 percent are right-brained for language and 50 percent are left-brained for visuo-spatial processing, the chance processes all being independent (see table 29.2). The manifestation of the heterozygotes, the DC genotype, is not specified *a priori* in the model, but model fitting finds that an acceptable fit is only obtained if the manifestation is midway between the two homozygotes, so-called "additivity" or "semi-dominance": there is therefore a 25 percent chance of a DC individual being left-handed and a 75 percent chance of being right-handed. Among other implications of this model are that little can be said with certainty about an individual's genotype based on his or her phenotype (handedness); right-handers can be DD, DC, or CC, and left-handers can be DC or CC. This is an inevitable consequence of the model containing a chance element in the form of fluctuating asymmetry, and fluctuating asymmetry seems to be necessary for any adequate genetic model of biological asymmetry (McManus and Bryden, 1991b; McManus, 1991). Formal fitting of such a model shows that it predicts well the proportions of left-handers found in the different types of family (McManus, 1985a). It also explains the high degree of discordance in monozygotic twins by making the biologically plausible assumption that the chance processes of fluctuating asymmetry in DC and CC genotypes occur independently in each member of a twin pair, and hence discordance occurs at predictably high rates (McManus, 1985a).

Table 29.1 The model of McManus (1985a) for the genetics of handedness, showing the proportion of right- and left-handers produced by each of the three genotypes

Genotype	Frequency in population	% Left-handers	% Right-handers
DD	0.7140	0	100
DC	0.2620	25	75
CC	0.0240	50	50

$p(C) = 0.155; p(D) = 0.845$

As it stands, the model of McManus (1985) cannot explain sex differences in the incidence of left-handedness. McManus and Bryden (1991b) (see also McManus, 1991) proposed that a sex-linked modifier gene, located on the X chromosome, would account for men having a higher incidence of left-handedness (just as genes on the X chromosome account for the higher incidence of color blindness and hemophilia in males). However, in the McManus–Bryden model, unlike the case of hemophilia or color blindness, it is not being suggested that the D and C alleles themselves are on the X chromosome (as stated earlier, they are autosomal). Instead there is a second gene which is located on the X chromosome, which is a *modifier gene*, acting to prevent the normal action of the D allele, and thereby making it act as if it is a C allele (see table 29.3). Modifier genes (Hartl and Clark, 1989; Moody, 1975; Roughgarden, 1979) are common in biological systems, and probably act by methylation (Bird, 1983; Weaver and Hedrick, 1989). Since the modifier gene acts as a recessive gene, it is more likely to have its effect in males (who only have one X chromosome), than in females (who have two X chromosomes). Left-handedness will therefore be more common in males. More interestingly, when the model is worked through mathematically, the hypothesis of a modifier gene also predicts that left-handed mothers will be more likely to have left-handed offspring than will left-handed fathers (intuitively this can be seen because female left-handers are more likely to be left-handed because they are truly DC or CC genotypes, whereas males are more likely to be left-handed because they are "phenocopy left-handers," probably of genotype DD, and are only left-handed as a result of the action of the modifier gene).

Table 29.2 The model of McManus (1985a) for the genetics of handedness and language dominance, showing the proportion of individuals with each combination of handedness (right or left) and language dominance (right or left) in each of the three genotypes.

Genotype	Frequency in population	R hand, L lang (%)	R hand, R lang (%)	L hand, L lang (%)	L hand, R lang (%)
DD	0.7140	100	0	0	0
DC	0.2620	56.25	18.75	18.75	6.25
CC	0.0240	25	25	25	25

$p(C) = 0.155; p(D) = 0.845$

Table 29.3 The genetic model of McManus and Bryden (1991b), showing the proportions of left-handers expected in each combination of the autosomal genotypes (DD, DC, CC) and the sex-linked modifier genotypes (M, m in males; mm, mM and mm in females). Note that the effects of the DD, DC and CC genotypes are identical to those shown in table 29.1, except in the m genotype in males and the mm genotype in females, where in each case the genotype acts as if it were the CC genotype, producing fluctuating asymmetry.

	Males		Females		
	M	m	MM	mM	mm
Frequency of modifier genotypes in population	0.955	0.045	0.9120	0.0860	0.0020
Autosomal genotype (%)					
DD	0	50	0	0	50
DC	25	50	25	25	50
CC	50	50	50	50	50

$p(m) = 0.045; p(M) = 0.955$
$p(C) = 0.135; p(D) = 0.865$

The Genetics of Cerebral Dominance for Language and Visuo-spatial Processing

Although neuropsychologists are principally interested in the neural expression of functional specializations, such as language and other high level cognitive processing, almost no studies that can properly be called genetic have been carried out on them, principally due to the practical difficulties involved. Language dominance is difficult to assess reliably in single individuals, and there are logistic problems in testing whole families, so that only one study has ever looked at dichotic listening within families (Bryden, 1975). Similarly, although it has been known for over two decades that the planum temporale is structurally asymmetric, being larger in the left hemisphere than the right (Geschwind and Levitsky, 1968), it is only recently that the asymmetry has been shown to be different in right- and left-handers (Steinmetz et al., 1991; Witelson and Kigar, 1991), and as yet there are still no studies examining whether the pattern of asymmetry runs in families.

Nevertheless, most genetic models of handedness have been partly conditioned by known data on cerebral dominance for language, and the models of Annett (1985), McManus (1985a) and McManus and Bryden (1991b) make explicit predictions about the relationship between handedness and language dominance. The key result that these models attempt to explain is that right-hemisphere language dominance is relatively rare in right-handers (about 5 percent of individuals) as compared with left-handers (about 35 percent of individuals); and it will be noted here that left-handers are *not* simply mirror-images of right-handers. The McManus–Bryden model copes with this situation by the simple method of assuming that in the CC genotype (and in the DC genotype also) there are separate and independent random processes that determine whether an individual is right- or left-handed and right- or left-hemisphere language dominant.

The McManus–Bryden model also has further implications for linguistic and other cognitive processes because of the presence of the modifier gene, which sometimes acts to prevent the normal action of the D allele. Calculations suggest that the modifier gene is fairly common, and it forms about 5 percent of genes in the gene-pool, and therefore will be expressed in about 5 percent of men (but in a far lower proportion of women, in fact $0.05^2 = 0.25$ percent). If this postulated gene indeed exists, and it operates by turning off a gene that normally acts to govern the way in which another particular gene affects the lateralization of the developing brain, then it is easy to see that the same modifier gene might also modify the action of other genes affecting high level cortical functions – such as those perhaps concerned with visual processing, speech output, or social interaction. The failure of such genes to act in a normal fashion might then result in conditions such as dyslexia, stuttering, or autism; and it should now be apparent that these conditions should not only run in families, and be more frequent in males (as has been pointed out for modifier genes in general by Comings and Comings, 1986), but should also be associated with left-handedness, as indeed has also been postulated for each of them (Bishop, 1990).

Where Did the Gene for Handedness and Language Dominance Come from, and How Do We Find It?

Genes do not just happen; they can only evolve by mutation from other genes. The gene for handedness must have arisen in some such way, and it is of great interest for understanding the evolution of humans, and their differences from the apes, particularly in characteristics such as handedness, language and social interaction, to ask when and how the gene arose. Genes that determine biological asymmetry are surprisingly rare, and the only clear, well-understood case in vertebrates is the gene for ensuring that the heart is normally on the left side of the body (as opposed to the rare situation, *situs inversus*, in which it and all of the other visceral organs are on the opposite side to normal). The most likely origin of the handedness gene is therefore that it represents a mutation in a copy of the *situs* gene, slightly modified so that it acts upon the brain rather than the heart. (It should be noted here that handedness cannot result from the action of the gene for *situs* itself, since left-handedness is no more common in individuals with *situs inversus* than in normal individuals (Torgersen, 1950)). Since population level handedness (i.e. most individuals are right-handed) is not present in the apes, as neither is language, then a parsimonious hypothesis for the evolution of the handedness gene is that it has evolved sometime since the point, probably between two and three million years ago, when *Homo* diverged from the other apes (Hill et al., 1992). That handedness has existed throughout the past five millennia, during recorded history (Coren and Porac, 1977), and there is suggestive evidence of it existing far earlier than that (de Castro et al., 1988), implies that the development of the handedness/language gene might itself have been partly responsible for the divergence of man from the apes. That hand skill was indeed a key process during the divergence of *Homo* and the apes is shown by the near simultaneity in the fossil record of the earliest evidence of stone tools, presumably requiring a high level of manual dexterity for their manufacture (Hill et al., 1992), and the occurrence of the characteristic changes in the morphology in the temporal bone of the skull (Wood, 1992), and hence by implication in the underlying temporal lobe of the brain, where important areas for language perception are now located.

Such a broad evolutionary hypothesis allows the possibility of a quick way of finding the handedness gene, which otherwise would be very difficult to find in the human genome owing to its gene having a product which is probably expressed only for a few days during early ontogeny (and it is known that at least several thousand genes are expressed during early development of the fetal brain; Adams et al., 1992). The method does require that the *situs* gene is identified, and that is indeed almost the case, molecular geneticists having reached within a million base-pairs or so of the murine version of the gene (Brueckner et al., 1989, 1991). Once that mouse gene is identified then the human *situs* gene should be almost identical, and the human gene for handedness should be very similar although not identical to the *situs* gene. The genome can therefore be searched for genes that show homology to the *situs* gene, and one of these is likely to be the handedness gene. Other homologues might be the putative genes for hand-clasping, arm-folding (McManus and Mascie-Taylor, 1979), and eye-dominance, all of which also appear to be under genetic control, and in all probability have mutated from the handedness gene (McManus, 1991). It might also be a fair prediction that since the *situs* gene is concerned with the fundamental layout of the region of the embryo around the branchial arches, then both the *situs* gene and the handedness gene may well contain homeobox sequences (Holland, 1988; Hunt et al., 1991; Leckman et al., 1991; Weaver and Hedrick 1989), a very ancient set of DNA sequences which seem to be central to early morphological development in both the animal and plant kingdoms (Gehring, 1987; Vollbrecht et al., 1991), and which are particularly concerned with development of the head and neck (Chisaka et al., 1992). An alternative approach to finding the handedness gene may capitalize on the fact that Wilm's tumor of the kidney often results in hemihypertrophy, in which one side of the body grows more quickly than the other (Björklund, 1955; Smithells, 1965); since Wilm's tumors are known to produce growth-promoting factors (Beierle et al., 1971), and the genes for such factors are expressed in human fetal brain tissue (Adams et al., 1992), it is possible that the Wilm's tumor gene represents a mutation of a gene or genes normally responsible for asymmetric brain development, so that known genetic markers for Wilm's tumor (Pelletier et al., 1991), or for other conditions resulting in asymmetric growth (Chemke et al., 1983), may also be markers for the cerebral dominance gene.

It should be noted that in using the shorthand term "a gene for handedness, language and cerebral dominance" we are not implying that the existence of language is dependent upon one and only one gene. That would be developmental nonsense. Clearly in order to have language one also requires many other genes that determine the basic structure of cerebral cortex, that organize motor control, and produce a functional larynx. However, we do mean that the majority of the variance between species with and without language may be ascribed to the presence or absence of a specific gene, which we can then regard in somewhat simplistic fashion as a "gene for language." No doubt when we have studied it in much more detail it will be apparent that it is several or even many genes.

What Will Happen When the Handedness/Language Gene Is Isolated?

Finding the DNA sequence of genes is the beginning not the end of the interesting part of developmental and evolutionary biology. From an evolutionary perspective, finding the genes will allow one to look for close and distant homologues in primates and other species, thereby providing an understanding of the origin of the gene, and an assessment of the effects of its precursors upon nonhuman cognition – and perhaps resolving the continuing controversy as to whether nonhuman primates show functional laterality.

More interesting will be the study of the process of ontogeny within the developing organism. Any gene that determines lateralization, and that presumably must be acting early during fetal development, must manifest because the gene's product is being expressed during embryogenesis. Techniques such as *in vitro* hybridization for mRNA, which allow one to visualize directly where and when a DNA-derived specific sequence is being actively transcribed, will tell us *when* the handedness/language gene is active, and in particular, *where* in the brain it is active. It will be of immense interest to know which parts of the cortex or subcortical areas are intrinsically asymmetric because of the action of the gene (and we note that although the evidence on apraxia and other high-level motor defects (Heilman, 1979) might suggest that handedness *must* be the result of cortical action of a gene, it is at least plausible that the gene instead acts on the basal ganglia, perhaps on the globus pallidus (Kooistra and Heilman, 1988), or on brainstem neurotransmitters, in the substantia nigra (Glick et al., 1977; Glick and Shapiro, 1985), or perhaps, in view of its influence on timing and force control, on the cerebellum (Ivry et al., 1988; Rosenbaum, 1991). The study of brain activity during the learning of a simple motor task involving the fingers (Seitz et al., 1990) finds evidence of altered activity in the premotor areas, supplementary motor areas, and primary motor areas of the cortex, in the basal ganglia (putamen and globus pallidus), ventrolateral thalamus, red nucleus, substantia nigra, pontine nuclei, and cerebellum. If the gene does indeed act upon cortex, how do the areas which it influences relate to our knowledge of functional activity in adults derived from conventional neuropsychology?

Identification of the gene for handedness/language will also allow the identification of allelic subtypes, of which presumably one will be the allele responsible for left-handedness; and that will immediately allow resolution of the conflicting claims of the McManus–Bryden and Annett models of handedness. Of greater scope will be the potential for assessing whether the miscellaneous range of conditions that have putatively been linked to handedness – such as dyslexia, stuttering, autism, schizophrenia, etc. – are really related: if they are, then individuals with the conditions should show a different pattern of genotypes to those without the condition. The hypothesis of an association with handedness immediately becomes rigorously testable, particularly when it is explicit, as in Crow's hypothesis that the gene for schizophrenia is specifically a mutation of the normal cerebral dominance gene (Crow, 1990a,b).

The final possibility which will arise from knowing the sequence of the handedness/language gene will perhaps at first sound like science fiction; in reality though it will have enormous potential for really understanding how this gene actually functions. Even if, at present, we are talking about a development that may be a decade or more away, the *Gedanken* (thought) experiment that it stimulates should wonderfully concentrate the minds of neuropsychologists as to the origins, purpose and function of this gene. Transgenic experimentation allows the transfer of genetic material from one species to another. If humans are unique in having handedness/language, and that is due to the presence of a particular gene, then the immediate and deceptively simple question arises as to what would happen if that gene were put into a species, such as a mouse, which does not have it. If the gene really produces directional asymmetry for handedness, then transgenic mice in which the human gene has been introduced should become right-pawed as a population, rather than, as at present, showing fluctuating asymmetry. More interestingly the transgenic mice may also show some of the cognitive capabilities that are assumed to be the ground for language processing; perhaps, say, in terms of symbolic manipulation (Corballis, 1991; Donald, 1991). It must of course be emphasized that these transgenic mice are extremely unlikely to show language as such, or to be able to talk (and this will be a relief for those who contemplate the nightmarish spectre of domestic cats, particularly whinging

Siamese, that talk to us directly, and thereby control our lives even more successfully than they do at present!). Mickey Mouse will therefore remain a creation of fantasy rather than biology. Language, it must be remembered, is, despite its biological roots, in very large part a cultural process, and therefore transgenic mice would be very unlikely to speak English or any other specific human language. More critically, speech also requires a highly evolved vocal apparatus with a very specialized laryngeal structure (which is not even shown by the apes (Lieberman, 1991), hence the failure of nineteenth-century attempts to teach monkeys to speak). The perception of speech may also require specialization of the auditory cortex in a form that is not generally available in the animal kingdom – in particular, in some form of categorical perception. Nevertheless, if the handedness gene is in any way responsible for language then mice with that gene should show different functional cognitive capacities from those without the gene. Whether it is in the existence of categorical perception, the presence of syntactic processing, the ability to comprehend other minds, or any of the other putative cognitive processes that distinguish humans from other species, the possibility of having the question answered will force us to consider the precise nature of that question far more seriously. Finally, the practical application of such a technique may mean that deliberately created mutations of the gene in transgenic mice might also allow the development of successful animal models for a wide range of human conditions, such as dyslexia, stuttering, autism, and schizophrenia. Even before the mice exist they will provide a fascinating intellectual challenge to psychologists, who will need to consider what they really believe is going on in the biology of handedness, cerebral dominance and language.

REFERENCES

Adams, M. D., Dubnick, M., Kerlavage, A. R., Moreno, R., Kelley, J. M., Utterback, T. R., Nagle, J. W., Fields, C. and Venter, J. C. (1992) Sequence identification of 2,375 human brain genes. *Nature*, 355, 632–634.

Annett, M. (1970) The growth of manual preference and speed. *British Journal of Psychology*, 61, 545–558.

Annett, M. (1985) *Left, right, hand and brain: the right shift theory*. Hillsdale, NJ: Lawrence Erlbaum.

Annett, M. (1991a) Reading upside down and mirror text in groups differing for right minus left hand skill. *European Journal of Cognitive Psychology*, 3, 363–77.

Annett, M. (1991b) Right hemisphere costs of right handedness. In J. F. Stein (ed.), *Vision and visual dyslexia*. London: Macmillan Press, pp. 84–93.

Annett, M. (1991c) Annotation: laterality and cerebral dominance. *Journal of Child Psychology and Psychiatry*, 32, 219–232.

Annett, M. and Manning, M. (1989) The disadvantages of dextrality for intelligence. *British Journal of Psychology*, 80, 213–226.

Annett, M. and Manning, M. (1990a) Reading and a balanced polymorphism for laterality and ability. *Journal of Child Psychology and Psychiatry*, 31, 511–529.

Annett, M. and Manning, M. (1990b) Arithmetic and laterality. *Neuropsychologia*, 28, 61–69.

Ardila, A., Ardila, O., Bryden, M. P., Ostrosky, F., Rosselli, M. and Steenhuis, R. E. (1989) Effects of cultural background and education on handedness. *Neuropsychologia*, 27, 893–897.

Bailit, H. L., Workman, P. L., Niswander, J. D. and Maclean, C. J. (1970) Dental asymmetry as an indicator of genetic and environmental conditions in human populations. *Human Biology*, 42, 626–638.

Bakan, P. (1971) Handedness and birth order. *Nature*, 229, 195.

Bakan, P. (1990) Nonright-handedness and the continuum of reproductive casualty. In S. Coren (ed.), *Left-handedness: behavioral implications and anomalies*. Amsterdam: North- Holland, pp. 33–74.

Barinaga, M. (1991) Is homosexuality biological? *Science*, 253, 956–957.

Batheja, M. and McManus, I. C. (1985) Handedness in the mentally handicapped. *Developmental Medicine and Child Neurology*, 27, 63–68.

Beierle, J. W. et al. (1971) Growth promotion by extracts from Wilm's tumour in vitro. *Experientia*, 27, 435–436.

Berker, E. A., Berker, A. H. and Smith, A. (1986) Translation of Broca's 1865 report: localisation of speech in the third left frontal convolution. *Archives of Neurology*, 43, 1065–1072.

Bird, A. P. (1983) DNA modification. In N. Maclean, S. P. Gregory and R. A. Flavell (eds), *Eukaryotic genes: their structure, activity and regulation*. London: Butterworth, pp. 53–67.

Bishop, D. V. M. (1986) Is there a link between handedness and hypersensitivity? *Cortex*, 22, 289–296.

Bishop, D. V. M. (1990) *Handedness and developmental disorder*. Oxford: Blackwell.

Björklund, S.-I. (1955) Hemihypertrophy and Wilm's tumour. *Acta Paediatrica*, 44, 287–292.

Broca, P. (1865) Sur le siège de la faculté du langage articulé. *Bulletin de la Société d'Anthropologie*, 6, 337–393.

Brown, N. A., McCarthy, A. and Wolpert, L. (1991) Development of handed body asymmetry in mammals. In *Biological asymmetry and handedness (Ciba foundation symposium 162)*. Chichester: John Wiley, pp. 182–201.

Brown, N. A. and Wolpert, L. (1990) The development of handedness in left/right asymmetry. *Development*, 109, 1–9.

Brueckner, M., D'Eustachio, P. and Horwich, A. L. (1989) Linkage mapping of a mouse gene, *iv*, that controls left-right asymmetry of the heart and viscera. *Proceedings of the National Academy of Sciences of the USA*, 86, 5035–5038.

Brueckner, M., McGrath, J., D'Eustachio, P. and Horwich, A. L. (1991) Establishment of left-right asymmetry in vertebrates: genetically distinct steps are involved. In *Biological asymmetry and handedness (Ciba Foundation symposium 162)*. Chichester: John Wiley, pp. 202–218.

Bryden, M. P. (1975) Speech lateralization in families: a preliminary study using dichotic listening. *Brain and Language*, 2, 201–211.

Bryden, M. P. (1982) *Laterality: functional asymmetry in the intact brain*. New York: Academic Press.

Bryden, M. P. (1986a) The nature of complementary specialization. In *Two hemispheres – one brain: functions of the corpus callosum*. New York: Alan R. Liss, pp. 463–469.

Bryden, M. P. (1986b) Dichotic listening performance, cognitive ability, and cerebral organisation. *Canadian Journal of Psychology*, 40, 445–456.

Bryden, M. P. (1988a) An overview of the dichotic listening procedure and its relation to cerebral organization. In K. Hugdahl (ed.), *Handbook of dichotic listening: theory, methods and research*. Chichester: John Wiley, pp. 1–43.

Bryden, M. P. (1988b) Cerebral specialization: clinical and experimental assessment. In F. Boller and J. Grafman (eds), *Handbook of neuropsychology, volume 1*. Amsterdam: Elsevier, pp. 143–159.

Bryden, M. P. (1990) Choosing sides: the left and right of the normal brain. *Canadian Psychology*, 31, 297–309.

Bryden, M. P. and McManus, I. C. (1992) *Relations between handedness and immune disorders. Poster presented at International Neuropsychological Society meeting, San Diego, California*, February 7, 1992.

Cavalli-Sforza, L. L. and Bodmer, W. F. (1971) *The genetics of human populations*. San Francisco: Freeman.

Chemke, J., Rappaport, S. and Etrog, R. (1983) Aberrant melanoblast migration associated with trisomy 18 mosaicism. *Journal of Medical Genetics*, 20, 135–137.

Chisaka, O., Musci, T. S. and Capecchi, M. R. (1992) Developmental defects of the ear, cranial nerves and hindbrain resulting from targeted disruption of the mouse homeobox gene *Hox-1.6. Nature*, 355, 516–520.

Collins, R. L. (1985) On the inheritance of direction and degree of asymmetry. In S. D. Glick (ed.), *Cerebral lateralization in non-human species*. New York: Academic Press, pp. 41–71.

Collins, R. L. (1991) Discussion. In *Biological asymmetry and handedness (Ciba Foundation Symposium 162)*. Chichester: John Wiley, pp. 277–280.

Comings, D. E. and Comings, B. G. (1986) Evidence for an X-linked modifier gene affecting the expression of Tourette syndrome and its relevance to the increased frequency of speech, cognitive, and behavioral disorders in males. *Proceedings of the National Academy of Sciences of the USA*, 83, 2551–2555.

Connolly, K. and Bishop, D. V. M. (1992) The measurement of handedness: a cross-cultural perspective. *Neuropsychologia* (in the press).

Corballis, M. C. (1991) *The lop-sided ape: evolution of the generative mind*. New York: Oxford University Press.

Coren, S. (1990) Left-handedness in offspring as a function of maternal age at parturition. *New England Journal of Medicine*, 322, 1673.

Coren, S. and Halpern, D. F. (1991) Left-handedness: a marker for decreased survival fitness. *Psychological Bulletin*, 109, 90–106.

Coren, S. and Porac, C. (1977) Fifty centuries of right-handedness: the historical record. *Science*, 198, 631–632.

Cosi, V., Citterio, A. and Pasquino, C. (1988) A study of hand preference in myasthenia gravis. *Cortex*, 24, 573–577.

Crow, T. J. (1990a) Strategies for biological research: psychosis as an anomaly of the cerebral dominance gene. In H. Häfner and W. F. Gattaz (eds), *Search for the causes of schizophrenia, vol. II*. Heidelberg: Springer-Verlag, pp. 383–396.

Crow, T. J. (1990b) Temporal lobe asymmetries as the key to the etiology of schizophrenia. *Schizophrenia Bulletin*, 16, 433–443.

de Castro, J. M. B., Bromage, T. G. and Jalvo, Y. F. (1988) Buccal striations on fossil human anterior teeth: evidence of handedness in the middle and early Upper Pleis-tocene. *Journal of Human Evolution*, 17, 403–412.

Donald, M. (1991) *Origins of the modern mind: three stages in the evolution of culture and cognition*. Cambridge, MA: Harvard University Press.

Ellis, A. W. and Young, A. W. (1988) *Human cognitive neuropsychology*. London: Lawrence Erlbaum.

Ellis, L. (1990) Left- and mixed-handedness and criminality: explanations for a probable relationship. In S. Coren (ed.), *Left-handedness: behavioral implications and anomalies*. Amsterdam: North-Holland, pp. 485–508.

Galaburda, A. M. (1990) The testosterone hypothesis: assessment since Geschwind and Behan, 1982. *Annals of Dyslexia*, 40, 18–37.

Galaburda, A. M. (1991) Discussion. In *Biological asymmetry and handedness (Ciba Foundation Symposium 162)*. Chichester: John Wiley, pp. 276–277.

Gehring, W. J. (1987) Homeo boxes in the study of development. *Science*, 236, 1245–1252.

Geschwind, N. and Behan, P. (1982) Left-handedness: association with immune disease, migraine and developmental learning disorder. *Proceedings of the National Academy of Sciences of the USA*, 79, 5097–5100.

Geschwind, N. and Galaburda, A. M. (1985a) Cerebral lateralization. Biological mechanisms, associations and pathology. I. A hypothesis and a program for research. *Archives of Neurology*, 42, 428–459.

Geschwind, N. and Galaburda, A. M. (1985b) Cerebral lateralization. Biological mechanisms, associations and pathology. II. A hypothesis and a program of research. *Archives of Neurology*, 42, 521–552.

Geschwind, N. and Galaburda, A. M. (1985c) Cerebral lateralization. Biological mechanisms, associations and pathology. III: A hypothesis and a program of research. *Archives of Neurology*, 42, 634–654.

Geschwind, N. and Galaburda, A. M. (1987) *Cerebral lateralization: biological mechanisms, associations, and pathology*. Cambridge, MA: MIT Press.

Geschwind, N. and Levitsky, W. (1968) Human brain: left-right asymmetries in temporal speech region. *Science*, 161, 186–187.

Glick, S. D., Jerussi, T. P. and Zimmerberg, B. (1977) Behavioral and neuropharmacological correlates of nigro-striatal asymmetry in rats. In S. Harnad, R. W. Doty, L. Goldstein, J. Jaynes and G. Krauthamer (eds), *Lateralization in the nervous system*. New York: Academic Press.

Glick, S. D. and Shapiro, R. M. (1985) Functional and neurochemical mechanisms of cerebral lateralization in rats. In S. D. Glick (ed.), *Cerebral lateralization in non-human species*. Orlando: Academic Press, pp. 157–183.

Halpern, D. F. and Coren, S. (1990) Laterality and longevity: is left-handedness associated with a younger age at death? In S. Coren (ed.), *Left-handedness: behavioral implications and anomalies*. Amsterdam: North-Holland, pp. 509–545.

Halpern, D. F. and Coren, S. (1991) Handedness and life span. *New England Journal of Medicine*, 324, 998.

Hardyck, C., Petrinovich, L. F. and Goldman, R. D. (1976) Left-handedness and cognitive deficit. *Cortex*, 12, 266–279.

Harrington, A. (1987) *Medicine, mind, and the double brain; a study in nineteenth-century thought*. Princeton, NJ: Princeton University Press.

Harris, L. J. (1990) Cultural influences on handedness: historical and contemporary theory and evidence. In S. Coren (ed.), *Left-handedness: behavioral implications and anomalies*. Amsterdam: North-Holland, pp. 195–258.

Harris, L. J. and Carlson, D. F. (1988) Pathological left-handedness: an analysis of theories and evidence. In D. L. Molfese and S. J. Segalowitz (eds), *Brain lateralization in children*. New York: Guilford Press, pp. 289–372.

Hartl, D. L. and Clark, A. G. (1989) *Principles of population genetics*. Sunderland, MA: Sinaeur Associates.

Heilman, K. M. (1979) Apraxia. In K. M. Heilman and E. Valenstein (eds), *Clinical neuropsychology*. New York: Oxford University Press, pp. 159–185.

Hertz, R. (1909) La prééminence de la main droite: étude sur la polarité religieuse. *Revue Philosophique*, 68, 553–580.

Hertz, R. (1960) *Death and the right hand*. Aberdeen: Cohen and West.

Hécaen, H. and Dubois, J. (1969) *La naissance de la neuropsychologie du langage (1825–1865)*. Paris: Flammarion.

Hécaen, H. and Lanteri-Laura, G. (1977) *Evolution des connaissances et des doctrines sur les localisations cérébrales*. Paris: Desclée de Brouwer.

Hill, A., Ward, S., Deino, A., Curtis, G. and Drake, R. (1992) Earliest *Homo*. *Nature*, 355, 719–722.

Holland, P. W. H. (1988) Homeobox genes and the vertebrate head. *Development*, 103, 17–24.

Hunt, P., Gulisano, M., Cook, M. et al. (1991) A distinct *Hox* code for the branchial region of the vertebrate head. *Nature*, 353, 861–864.

Ivry, R. I., Keele, S. W. and Diener, H. C. (1988) Dissociation of the lateral and medial cerebellum in movement timing and movement execution. *Experimental Brain Research*, 73, 167–180.

Kooistra, C. A. and Heilman, K. M. (1988) Motor dominance and the lateral asymmetry of the globus pallidus. *Neurology*, 38, 388–390.

Leckman, J. F., Lin, X., Swaroop, A., Murtha, M. T. and Ruddle, F. H. (1991) Novel antennapaedia-class homeobox genes isolated from human 11 wk fetal brain library. *Society for Neuroscience Abstracts*, 17, 1132.

Lieberman, P. (1991) *Uniquely human: the evolution of speech, thought and selfless behavior.* Cambridge, MA: Harvard University Press.

Lombroso, C. (1903) Left-sidedness. *North American Review*, 170, 440–444.

Marchant-Haycox, S. E., McManus, I. C. and Wilson, G. D. (1991) Left-handedness, homosexuality, HIV infection and AIDS. *Cortex*, 27, 49–56.

Marks, J. S. and Williamson, D. F. (1991) Left-handedness and life expectancy. *New England Journal of Medicine*, 325, 1042.

McClearn, G. E., Plomin, R., Gora-Maslak, G. and Crabbe, J. C. (1991) The gene chase in behavioural science. *Psychological Science*, 2, 222–229.

McCormick, C. M., Witelson, S. F. and Kingstone, E. (1990) Left- handedness in homosexual men and women: neuroendocrine implications. *Psychoneuroendocrinology*, 15, 69–76.

McGlone, J. (1980) Sex differences in the human brain: a critical survey. *Behavioral and Brain Sciences*, 3, 215–263.

McManus, I. C. (1979) *Determinants of laterality in man.* Unpublished PhD thesis, University of Cambridge.

McManus, I. C. (1981) Handedness and birth stress. *Psychological Medicine*, 11, 485–496.

McManus, I. C. (1983) Pathological left-handedness: does it exist? *Journal of Communication Disorders*, 16, 315–344.

McManus, I. C. (1984) The genetics of handedness in relation to language disorder. In F. C. Rose (ed.), *Advances in neurology, vol. 42: Progress in aphasiology.* New York: Raven Press, pp. 125–138.

McManus, I. C. (1985a) Handedness, language dominance and aphasia: a genetic model. *Psychological Medicine*, Monograph supplement no. 8.

McManus, I. C. (1985b) Right- and left-hand skill: failure of the right shift model. *British Journal of Psychology*, 76, 1–16.

McManus, I. C. (1990) Left-handedness and maternal age (letter). *New England Journal of Medicine*, 323, 1426–1427.

McManus, I. C. (1991) The inheritance of left-handedness. In J. Marsh (ed.), *Biological asymmetry and handedness (Ciba foundation symposium 162).* Chichester: John Wiley, pp. 251–281.

McManus, I. C. and Bryden, M. P. (1991a) Geschwind's theory of cerebral lateralization: developing a formal causal model. *Psychological Bulletin*, 110, 237–253.

McManus, I. C. and Bryden, M. P. (1991b) The genetics of handedness, cerebral dominance and lateralization. In I. Rapin and S. J. Segalowitz (eds), *Handbook of neuropsychology, section 10: Developmental neuropsychology.* Amsterdam: Elsevier.

McManus, I. C. and Bryden, M. P. (1991c) *Handedness on Tristan da Cunha: the genetic consequences of social isolation.* Unpublished manuscript.

McManus, I. C., Kemp, R. I. and Grant, J. (1986) Differences between fingers and hands in tapping ability: dissociation between speed and regularity. *Cortex*, 22, 461–474.

McManus, I. C. and Mascie-Taylor, C. G. N. (1979) Hand-clasping and arm-folding: a review and a genetic model. *Annals of Human Biology*, 6, 527–558.

McManus, I. C. and Mascie-Taylor, C. G. N. (1983) Biosocial correlates of cognitive abilities. *Journal of Biosocial Science*, 15, 289–306.

McManus, I. C., Murray, B., Doyle, K. and Baron-Cohen, S. (1992a) Handedness in childhood autism shows a dissociation of skill and preference. *Cortex* (in the press).

McManus, I. C., Naylor, J. and Booker, B. L. (1990) Left-handedness and myasthenia gravis. *Neuropsychologia*, 28, 947–955.

McManus, I. C., Shergill, S. and Bryden, M. P. (1992b) *Annett's theory that individuals heterozygous for the right shift gene are intellectually advantaged: theoretical and empirical problems.* Unpublished manuscript.

Meyers, S. and Janowitz, H. D. (1985) Left-handedness and inflammatory bowel disease. *Journal of Clinical Gastroenterology*, 71, 33–35.

Moody, P. A. (1975) *Genetics of man.* New York: W. W. Norton.

Morgan, M. J. and McManus, I. C. (1988) The relationship between brainedness and handedness. In F. C. Rose, R. Whurr and M. Wyke (eds), *Aphasia.* London: Whurr Publishers, pp. 85–130.

Needham, R. (1973) *Right and left: essays on dual symbolic classification.* Chicago: University of Chicago Press.

Palmer, A. R. and Strobeck, C. (1986) Fluctuating asymmetry: measurement, analysis, patterns. *Annual Review of Ecology and Systematics*, 17, 391–421.

Pelletier, J., Bruening, W., Li, F. P., Haber, D. A., Glaser, T. and Housman, D. E. (1991) *WT1* mutations contribute to abnormal genital system development and hereditary Wilm's tumour. *Nature*, 353, 431–434.

Peters, M. and Perry, R. (1992) No link between left-handedness and maternal age and no elevated accident rate in left-handers. *Neuropsychologia* 29, 1257–90.

Pipe, M.-E. (1990) Mental retardation and left-handedness: evidence and theories. In S. Coren (ed.), *Left-handedness: behavioral implications and anomalies.* Amsterdam: North-Holland, pp. 293–318.

Pool, R. (1991) Can lefties study be right? *Nature*, 350, 545.

Porac, C. and Coren, S. (1981) *Lateral preferences and human behaviour.* New York: Springer Verlag.

Porac, C., Rees, L. and Buller, T. (1990) Switching hands: a place for left hand use in a right hand world. In S. Coren (ed.), *Left-handedness: behavioral implications and anomalies.* Amsterdam: North-Holland, pp. 259–290.

Provins, K. A. (1990) Handedness and conformity in a small isolated community. *International Journal of Psychology*, 25, 343–350.

Ramaley, F. (1913) Inheritance of left-handedness. *American Naturalist*, 47, 730–739.

Rosenbaum, D. A. (1991) *Human motor control.* San Diego: Academic Press.

Roughgarden, J. (1979) *Theory of population genetics and evolutionary ecology: an introduction.* New York: Macmillan.

Salcedo, J. R., Spiegler, B. J., Gibson, E. and Magilavy, D. B. (1985) The auto-immune disease systemic lupus erythematosus is not associated with left-handedness. *Cortex*, 21, 645–647.

Satz, P., Miller, E. N., Selnes, O., VanGorp, W., D'Elia, L. F. and Visscher, B. (1991) Hand preference in homosexual men. *Cortex*, 27, 295–306.

Schur, P. H. (1986) Handedness in systemic lupus erythematosus. *Arthritis and Rheumatism*, 29, 419–420.

Schwartz, M. (1990) Left-handedness and prenatal complications. In S. Coren (ed.), *Left-handedness: behavioral implications and anomalies.* Amsterdam: North-Holland, pp. 75–98.

Searleman, A. and Fugagli, A. K. (1987) Suspected autoimmune disorders and left-handedness: evidence from individuals with diabetes, Crohn's disease and ulcerative colitis. *Neuropsychologia*, 25, 367–374.

Searleman, A., Porac, C. and Coren, S. (1989) Relationship between birth order, birth stress, and lateral preferences: a critical review. *Psychological Bulletin*, 105, 397–408.

Seddon, B. and McManus, I. C. (1991) *The incidence of left-handedness: a meta-analysis.* Unpublished manuscript.

Seitz, R. J., Roland, P. E., Bohm, C., Greitz, T. and Stone-Elander, S. (1990) Motor learning in man: a positron emission tomographic study. *NeuroReport*, 1, 57–66.

Shallice, T. (1991) Précis of From neuropsychology to mental structure. *Behavioral and Brain Sciences*, 14, 429–469.

Smith, J. (1987). Left-handedness: its association with allergic disease. *Neuropsychologia*, 25, 665–674.

Smithells, R. W. (1965) Congenital asymmetry. *Developmental Medicine and Child Neurology*, 7, 698–700.

Steinmetz, H., Volkmann, J., Jaencke, L. and Freund, H.-J. (1991) Anatomical left-right asymmetry of language-related temporal cortex is different in left- and right-handers. *Annals of Neurology*, 29, 315–319.

Tapley, S. M. and Bryden, M. P. (1985) A group test for the assessment of performance between the hands. *Neuropsychologia*, 23, 215–221.

Torgersen, J. (1950) Situs inversus, asymmetry and twinning. *American Journal of Human Genetics*, 2, 361–370.

Vollbrecht, E., Veit, B., Sinha, N. and Hake, S. (1991) The developmental gene *Knotted-1* is a member of a maize homeobox gene family. *Nature*, 350, 241.

Weaver, R. F. and Hedrick, P. W. (1989) *Genetics*. Dubuque, IA: William C. Brown.

Wilson, S. A. K. (1908) A contribution to the study of apraxia with a review of the literature. *Brain*, 31, 164–216.

Witelson, S. F. and Kigar, D. L. (1991) Anatomy of the planum temporale in relation to side, handedness and sex. *Society for Neuroscience Abstracts*, 17, 1044.

Wolf, P. A., D'Agostino, R. B. and Cobb, J. (1991) Left-handedness and life expectancy. *New England Journal of Medicine*, 325, 1042.

Wood, B. (1992) Old bones match old stones. *Nature*, 355, 678–679.

30

Constraints on Cortical Plasticity

MARK H. JOHNSON

1 Introduction

The postnatal development of the human brain poses a major paradox. On the one hand, there appear to be fairly consistent mappings between cortical structures or pathways and psychological functions in the adult. Indeed, the study of neuropsychology is often based on this assumption (see, for example, Posner et al., 1988). On the other hand, the ability of the brain to recover or compensate after injury early in life is often regarded as nothing short of miraculous. Despite great potential plasticity, therefore, the brain normally develops in a very consistent manner. There are two alternative ways of viewing this paradox. The first is to focus on the specialized mechanisms that may underlie plasticity in the brain early in life (e.g. Kolb, 1989 – this volume, chapter 16). The second approach, and that presented in the present paper, is to take the plasticity of the young brain for granted and enquire into what types of constraints give rise to the consistent cortical structure-to-function relations observed by adulthood. That is, to enquire into the factors which constrain plasticity during development. Reformulating the issue in this way leads one to adopt a particular viewpoint on neurocognitive development and its abnormalities.

In order to support the assumption that cortical plasticity is extensive during early life, I begin by briefly reviewing a couple of recent examples of the great plasticity of the developing cortex in mammals. The first concerns changes in cortical organization as a result of altered sensory input. Cross-modal plasticity has now been demonstrated at the neurophysiological level in several mammalian species (for review see Sur et al., 1990). For example, in the ferret projections from the retina can be induced to project to auditory thalamic areas, and thence to auditory cortex. Not only does the auditory cortex then become visually responsive, but cells also become orientation- and direction-selective and form themselves into a two-dimensional visual field map (Sur et al., 1988; Roe et al., 1988). Similar phenomena have been reported as a result of event- related potential studies in our own species. Neville (1991 – this volume, chapter 19) argues that her data on visual processing in congenitally deaf subjects are compatible with the idea that, in the absence of auditory input to certain occipital regions, visual afferents become stabilized in areas from which they normally regress. Thus, during visual tasks, increased ERP amplitudes are observed over bilateral areas of cortex which would normally contain auditorily responsive cells (Neville and Lawson 1987). In other words, parts of the cortex that normally contain auditory or polysensory cells become visual in congenitally deaf subjects.

A second example comes from the recent positron emission tomography (PET) work of Peterson and colleagues (Peterson et al., 1989, 1990). PET was used to observe brain processes during passive presentation of words. By use of a subtractive method and control stimuli such as letter strings and pronounceable nonwords, Peterson and colleagues identified particular regions of the left ventral occipital cortex which are responsive to the visual presentation of English words and pronounceable (in English) nonwords, but not to other stimuli, such as consonant strings or letter-like forms. They conclude that this area of the brain responds to visual word forms acquired through experience of English words. Since areas of cortex are unlikely to be pre-specialized to subserve such particular functions as English word recognition, some form of cortical plasticity around the age of learning to read is likely to subserve this function.

A final reason for supposing some degree of functional equipotentiality in the cortex is its remarkably general structure. Virtually all areas of cortex are composed of six distinct layers of cells, each of which contains characteristic cell types (see Rakic, chapter 6). In addition, there are gross similarities in both interlaminar and extrinsic projections. In terms of gross structure, therefore, the cortical areas thought to subserve aspects of language, for example, look very similar to those that subserve primary visual representations. With all this in mind it is hardly surprising that neurophysiologists have recently concluded that

> [sensory] neocortex appears to consist of a basic structure held in common by all cortical areas, on which is superimposed a number of area-specific differences. A reasonable hypothesis is that similar aspects are intrinsically determined, perhaps before interaction with extrinsic influences (via afferent input) has occurred. (Sur et al., 1990, p. 228)

In other words, the more detailed differences between cortical areas may only develop following exposure to environmental input. The assumption that cortical plasticity requires to be constrained during development will now be taken as established, and I will turn to consideration of the factors by which this may be achieved.

But first of all, we should note that there are two senses in which the cortex may be said to be plastic. The first of these concerns the fact that, any piece of cortex may have the potential to subserve the function of any other piece (as is suggested by, for example, the experiments by Sur and colleagues). The second sense in which the cortex could be said to be plastic concerns the fact that it could presumably encode information about a very wide range of stimuli which it encounters in the external world. However, it normally encodes information about certain classes of stimuli of relevance to survival, to the relative exclusion of others. For example, there is much evidence that parts of the cortex of the human adult are specialized for the processing of faces and language (see, for example, Johnson and Morton, 1991). It may, however, take more than a decade of consistent practice to reach the same level of specialization for other stimuli (e.g. Diamond and Carey, 1986). While this paper will be primarily concerned with the second of these senses of plasticity, we will allude to the first type in the later sections.

One objection to the second sense of cortical plasticity might be that the stimuli that the cortex encodes most information about, such as language, have evolved such that they are easier for the cortex to process. For instance, with regard to the example cited earlier from the PET studies of Peterson and colleagues, it is possible to argue that word forms have been developed such that they take advantage of the functional properties of cortical circuits. While such a position is logically possible, it is difficult to see how it could be extended to Chinese characters, for example.

The constraints on cortical plasticity to be discussed can be divided into two classes: *extrinsic* and *intrinsic*. *Extrinsic* constraints are taken to include all factors outside the cortex itself, not only aspects of the external environment but also other (subcortical) neural systems and pathways. *Intrinsic* constraints are taken to be those imposed by the cytoarchitectonics and sequences of development within the cortex itself. Let us begin with the extrinsic constraints.

2   Extrinsic Constraints on Cortical Plasticity

2.1   Environmental Constraints

Elsewhere, I have argued for a distinction between the *species-typical environment* (STE) and the *individual specific environment* (ISE) of a developing organism (Johnson 1988a; Johnson and Morton, 1991). The former represents those characteristics of the environment which are common to most or all members of a species. Such factors vary from exposure to patterned light and gravity, to exposure to spoken language in the human. The individual specific environment, however, includes aspects of environmental input that may vary from individual to individual. Thus, while being exposed to a language during early childhood would be part of the human STE, being exposed to French rather than any other language would be part of the ISE. Moving to cortical development, it is clear that alteration of the STE has major consequences for cortical structure and organization. For example, dark-rearing or monocularly depriving kittens, or raising rats in extremely impoverished or enriched environments, both influence subsequent primary sensory cortex structure (Greenough et al., 1987 – this volume, chapter 14). It is important to realize that this plasticity extends down to the molecular level. That is, altering sensory input to a neural pathway (as in dark-rearing) results in regulation of gene expression on this pathway[1] (Black et al., 1984). This, in turn, regulates the type and quantity of proteins produced that build up synapses and other neural elements.

To date most of the environmental manipulations that have given rise to observable changes in cortical structure have involved gross perturbations of the STE, such as dark-rearing. Since this constitutes a disruption of the normal developmental pathway (Oyama, 1985 – this volume, chapter 2; Johnson and

Morton, 1991) of the species, they will not be considered in more detail at this stage. Suffice it to say that the STE offers general constraints on the structure of primary sensory cortices. By this view, there is little variation on the structure and function of primary sensory and motor cortices precisely because they are configured as a result of interaction with general aspects of the STE, such as exposure to patterned light, gravity, and so forth. Indeed, several aspects of the columnar organization of the mammalian primary visual cortex, such as ocular dominance segregation and orientation columns, may be accounted for in terms of the self-organizing properties of groups of neurons receiving only spontaneous intrinsic stimulation (Miller et al., 1989 – this volume, chapter 23). In the next section the constraints arising from the developing structure and function of sensory systems are briefly considered.

2.2 Sensory Channel Constraints

This class of constraints has previously been discussed by Turkewitz and Kenny (1982, 1985 – this volume, chapter 22). These authors proposed that, in contrast to the conventional view, limitations imposed by the development of sensory systems may actually facilitate subsequent perceptual development. For example, they argue that the visual limitations on focal distance and spatial frequency in the young human infant mean that the range of stimuli that the infant has to deal with are very much reduced. By this view infancy is no longer the "blooming, buzzing confusion" of William James. For instance, objects that are in focus for the infant will also be within touching distance, thus allowing for extensive experience of the multi-modal properties of objects.

One prediction of this account is that providing better than normal sensory input at an early age should interfere with subsequent development rather than facilitate it. This turns out to be the case in several studies in which rat pups have had their eyes opened prior to the age of normal eye opening. These studies found that the experimental rats were subsequently abnormal or impaired in homing behavior and olfactory discriminations (see Turkewitz and Kenny, 1985). Notice that this argument can also be applied to the inputs to other cortical areas from primary sensory cortices. That is, the nature of the information fed forward through cortico–cortico projections will change as a result of the particular developmental state of primary sensory cortices.

2.3 Specific Orienting Biases

In this section I discuss particular examples of how orienting biases present from shortly after birth, and not primarily mediated by cortical structures, can select the appropriate classes of input to developing cortical circuitry.

Although the avian forebrain lacks the layered structure of mammalian cerebral cortex (but see Karten and Shimizu, 1989), the relation of the forebrain to subcortical structures is similar following a basic higher vertebrate brain design (Nauta and Karten, 1970; Ebbesson, 1980). With this in mind, it is appropriate to cite a well-studied example of neuronal plasticity, filial imprinting. Imprinting is the process by which young precocial birds such as chicks recognize and develop an attachment for the first conspicuous object that they see after

Figure 30.1 Examples of objects which have been used as imprinting stimuli in various experiments. Stimulus (A) a rotating colored red box illuminated from within, (B) a rotating colored cylinder illuminated from within, and (C) a rotating stuffed jungle fowl (an ancestor of the domestic chicken) illuminated from above. See Horn (1985) for further details.

hatching. In the laboratory, chicks will imprint onto a variety of objects, such as moving colored balls and cylinders (see figure 30.1). In the wild, however, imprinting may be involved in the recognition of particular individual conspecifics, including the mother hen. What mechanisms ensure that this plasticity in the chick forebrain is utilized to encode information about conspecifics, and not about the characteristics of other objects present in their early visual environment?

A series of experiments concerned with the development of filial recognition and attachment in the domestic chick have led to the proposal that there are two independent neural systems that underlie this process (Horn, 1985; Johnson et al., 1985 – see Horn, this volume, chapter 21). The first is a specific predisposition for the young chick to orient toward objects resembling conspecifics. In contrast to nonspecific color and size preferences in the chick (see Johnson and Bolhuis, 1991), the predisposition system appears to be specifically tuned to the correct spatial arrangement of elements of the head and neck region (Johnson and Horn, 1988). While the stimulus configuration triggering the predisposition is not species or genus specific, it is sufficient to pick out the mother hen from other objects the chick is likely to be exposed to in the first few days after hatching. The second system acquires information about the objects to which the young chick attends. In the natural (species-typical) environment, the first system ensures that the second system acquires information about the particular individual mother hen close by. The neural substrate of the second system has been identified to include the forebrain area known as IMHV (Intermediate and Medial part of the Hyperstriatum Ventrale). Biochemical, electrophysiological, and lesion evidence all support the conclusion that the two systems have largely independent neural substrates (for review see Horn, 1985). For example, selective lesions to IMHV impair preferences acquired through exposure to an object, but do not impair the predisposition (Johnson and Horn, 1986).

There are, of course, a number of different ways that the predisposition could constrain the information acquired by the IMHV system. For example, the information in the predisposition could act as a sensory "filter" or template through which information had to pass before reaching the IMHV system. This possibility, and a variety of other alternatives, has been rejected on the basis of recent experiments (Bolhuis et al., 1989; Bolhuis and Johnson, 1991; Johnson and Bolhuis, 1991). All the evidence available at present is consistent with the view that the two systems influence the preference behavior of the chick independently, i.e. there is no internal informational exchange between them. Instead, it appears that the input to the IMHV system is selected simply as a result of the predisposition biasing the chick to orient toward any hen-like objects in the environment. Given that the species-typical environment of the chick includes a mother hen in close proximity, and that the predisposition includes adequate information to pick the hen out from other objects in the early environment, the input to the learning system will be highly selected.

A recent analysis of the development of face recognition in the human infant has resulted in the proposal that two systems are operating, similar to those involved in the chick (Johnson 1988b; Johnson and Morton 1991; Morton and Johnson, 1991). Newborn infants will track certain kinds of face-like patterns further than they will a variety of similar patterns (Goren et al., 1975; Johnson et al., 1991a). This preference may be based on a system analogous to the predisposition in the chick mentioned earlier. It is not based purely on the filtered amplitude spectrum of the stimulus, as some theories of infant visual preferences would predict (see Morton et al., 1990; Morton and Johnson, 1991), but rather seems to require the correct spatial arrangement of high contrast "blobs" corresponding to the relative locations of the eyes and mouth. Evidence that the system is primarily mediated by subcortical circuits includes its time course[2] and the lack of any the laterality effects found in adult face recognition (De Schonen and Mathivet, 1989)

The second independent system proposed to be involved in infant face recognition first becomes manifest around the second or third month of life (Maurer and Barrera, 1981; Johnson et al., 1992), the age when several authors have argued, on the basis of a wide variety of evidence, that cortical circuits begin to control the visually guided behavior of the infant (Bronson, 1974; Atkinson, 1984; Johnson, 1990a, b). Thus, the emergence of increasingly detailed face-specific preferences between two and four months of age may reflect the development of processing in cortical circuits (Johnson, 1990b).

The available evidence is therefore consistent with the notion that a subcortical preferential orienting system biases the input set to developing cortical circuitry. This circuitry is configured in response to a certain range of input, before it itself gains control over behavior around the second month of life. Once this occurs, the system has enough experience of faces to ensure that it continues to acquire further information about them. Like in the chick, the proposal is that a specific early brain circuit acts in concert with the species-typical environment to bias the input to developing cortical circuitry. Whichever parts of the cortex are receiving the correct sensory inputs, and are in the appropriate plastic state, will configure themselves in response to this input set. According to a broadly similar analysis of the development of face recognition by De Shonen and Mathivet (1989), particular regions of the right hemisphere are timed to be in a plastic and "receptive" state just as polysensory information about faces is being attended to most avidly by the young infant. This, they propose, is why there is subsequently preferential processing of the characteristics of individual faces by the right hemisphere in normal adults, and why damage to particular parts of the right hemisphere may give rise to prosopagnosia, an inability to recognize *individual* faces, but not faces as such.

Another example of inborn attentional biases selecting the appropriate class of input for subsequent development comes from the auditory domain. Jusczyk and Bertoncini (1988) have interpreted the literature on infants' discrimination of components of speech sounds in terms of how these "innate" preferences might guide subsequent learning about speech. For example, infants are sensitive to the acoustic correlates of clausal units by at least six months of age (Hirsh-Pasek et al., 1987). This ability is proposed to be critical for language acquisition, because determining the grammatical relations that hold among words requires grouping them according to what clause they appear in. Thus, early attentional preferences may select the appropriate components of acoustical input essential for language acquisition.

Thus far we have seen how both species-typical and individual specific aspects of the external environment may interact with primitive orienting and attention mechanisms to select the input to developing cortical circuitry. Together these different sources of influence provide a major source of constraint on cortical plasticity; namely, highly selected sensory input. In the next section I focus on constraints intrinsic to the cortex itself, and enquire how processes of self-organization lead to the specificity and localization of function found within the adult cortex.

3   Instrinsic Constraints on Cortical Plasticity

Earlier, it was pointed out how uniform the general structure of the cortex is from area to area. Uniformity, however, should not be confused with simplicity.

The complex cytoarchitectonics common to all cortical regions suggest a computational mechanism with a good deal of internal structure. How, then, does the internal structure of the cortex and its sequences of postnatal growth constrain the functions which it can subserve at a given point in development? In this section two classes of intrinsic constraint on cortical plasticity are discussed: constraints in classes of input provided by attention systems involving some cortical mediation; and the role of specific cortico–cortico feedback pathways in providing information for the configuration of cortical microcircuits. These computational constraints are initially derived from consideration of two kinds of differential postnatal developmental events in the cortex: first, the differential development of the cortex from deeper layers to more superficial ones; second, the differential rates of overall postnatal development in different cortical regions.

3.1   Constraints on Input Imposed by Cortical Attention Systems

In the previous section we outlined how subcortical orienting circuits may select the appropriate input for subsequently developing cortical circuitry. In this section this general notion is extended, and it is argued that cortically mediated attention systems also select input for other cortical circuits.

The primate cerebral cortex is a six-layered structure, with each layer possessing particular cell types and patterns of interconnectivity. Inputs (afferents) and outputs (efferents) arrive and depart from particular layers. Figure 30.2 is an illustration of the postnatal growth in the primary visual cortex of man. Detailed anatomical studies of this and other cortical structures have revealed that some measures of postnatal development proceed from the deeper layers (bottom of

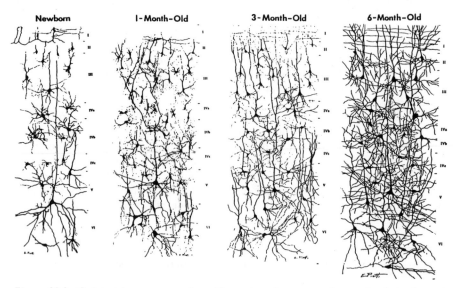

Figure 30.2 Golgi stain reconstructions illustrating the postnatal growth of the human primary visual cortex. From Conel (1939–67).

drawing) toward the more superficial (top of drawing) (e.g. Conel, 1939–67; Rabinowicz, 1979; Huttenlocher, 1990 – this volume, chapter 7).

The observation that, within a cortical area, maturation proceeds from deeper layers to more superficial ones, is a key one for the proposals reviewed in this section. This is because of the fact that particular afferent and efferents to any cortical area tend to terminate and depart from particular layers. Thus, if only some layers are functional, there is a restriction on the afferent and efferent connectivity of the area concerned. In figure 30.3 a highly schematized diagram of the inputs and outputs of primary visual cortex is shown. Several things are worth noting about this section through the visual cortex. As development proceeds upwards through the layers, more output pathways will come "on line." In fact, in primary visual cortex this effect may be exacerbated since the afferents from the lateral geniculate nucleus (LGN) slowly grow up through the deeper layers (possibly forming temporary synapses on the way) until they reach their adult termination sites in layer 4 at about two months of age in the human infant. Therefore, as the innervation passes up through the layers, different output pathways may start to feed forward information to other cortical areas. Since the primary visual cortex is the "gateway" to most cortical visual processing (Schiller, 1985), this differential maturation has some profound consequences on the control of visually guided behavior. Since this matter has been discussed in detail elsewhere (Johnson, 1990a – this volume, chapter 10), only the general conclusions will be outlined here.

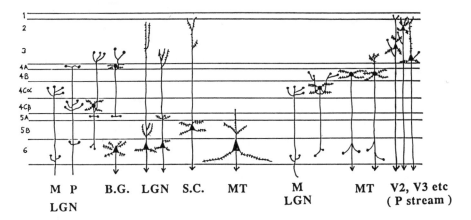

Figure 30.3 Schematic diagram of the inputs and outputs of the primary visual cortex.

The core of this account is that since particular outputs leave from particular layers of the primary visual cortex, the inside-out pattern of growth place restrictions on the functional outputs from the primary visual cortex at any point in development. This theory accounts for changes in the development of visual orienting over the ·first few months in terms of the "enabling" of outputs to three cortical pathways (see figure 30.4). These three pathways and a fourth, subcortical pathway, are initially derived from proposals ·put forward to account for adult primate electrophysiological and lesion data by Schiller (1985).

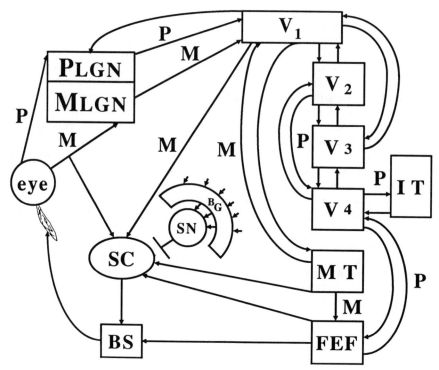

Figure 30.4 The four pathways proposed to underlie oculomotor control by Schiller (1985). These four pathways are:

(a) a pathway from the retina to the superior colliculus, the SC pathway, thought to be involved in the generation of eye movements toward simple, easily discriminable stimuli, and fed mainly by the peripheral visual field.

(b) a cortical pathway that goes both directly to the superior colliculus from the primary visual cortex and also via the middle temporal area (MT), the MT pathway. This pathway is exclusively driven by the broad-band or magnocellular system.

(c) a cortical pathway which converges both broad-band and color-opponent streams of processing in the frontal eye fields, the FEF pathway, and which is involved in the detailed and complex analysis of visual stimuli such as the temporal sequencing of eye movements within complex arrays.

(d) the final pathway for the control of eye movements is an inhibitory input to the colliculus from several cortical areas via the substantia nigra and basal ganglia, the inhibitory pathway. Schiller proposes that this final pathway ensures that the activity of the colliculus can be regulated.

LGN = lateral geniculate nucleus; SC = superior colliculus; SN = substantia nigra; BG = basal ganglia; BS = brain stem; FEF = frontal eye fields; MT = middle temporal area; V1 = primary visual cortex; M = broad band (magnocelullar) stream; P = color opponent (parvocellular) stream. Adapted, with permission, from Schiller (1985).

The proposal put forward is that, first, the characteristics of visually guided behavior in the infant at particular ages are determined by which of the pathways is functional, and second, which of the pathways is functional is determined, in turn, by the maturational state of the visual cortex. For example, by around two months infants begin to be able to track moving objects smoothly and are more sensitive to stimuli placed in the nasal visual field (Aslin, 1981). The onset of these behaviors coincides with maturation of upper layer 4 of the primary visual cortex and the consequent "enabling" of the MT pathway (see the legend to figure 30.4). This pathway provides the cortical magnocellular stream with control over the superior colliculus.

Elsewhere, I have argued that these transitions in orienting behavior in the infant may be characterized in terms of the emergence of successively more predictive stages of hierarchical control (Johnson, 1992). First, there is a transition from a purely input-driven orienting system to a system capable of making some anticipatory eye movements. Then there is a further transition to a system one step further removed from the input, which is capable of making higher order predictions about stimuli, and which can be dissociated from eye movements. Finally, there may be a further transition of control to an attention system solely concerned with focusing on internal processes.

Earlier, it was argued that subcortical orienting mechanisms play an important role in biasing the input to developing cortical circuitry. In this section, evidence in support of a developmental sequence of levels of cortically mediated attentional system was alluded to. Thus, while the early (subcortical) components of orienting may select general classes of stimuli from the external environment of the animal, later developing attention systems in the primate brain may help to select higher order temporal or spatial invariances from such stimuli. This point is argued at length in Johnson (1992).

3.2 Constraints Imposed by Cortico–Cortico Feedback Pathways

As mentioned earlier, two types of differential postnatal developments take place within the cortex. First, primary sensory and motor cortices, and a few localized regions of cortex, mature earlier than the rest of cortex. Second, by some measures the human cortex matures from deeper layers to more superficial ones. Commonly, at least for early visual processing areas, feedforward cortico–cortico projections leave pyramidal cells in layers 2 and 3 and terminate within layer 4 of the recipient area. In contrast, cortico–cortico feedback projections normally arise from the upper and lower cortical layers and terminate in the same layers in the recipient structure (Rockland and Pandya, 1979; Maunsell and Van Essen, 1983; Pandya and Yeterian, 1990).[3] Figure 30.5 is a simple schematic illustration of this characteristic cortico–cortico interconnection pattern.

If the observations about the characteristic interconnection patterns are combined with those concerning the layer-wise development of the cortex, the conclusion follows that some feedback pathways could be functional before the majority of cortico–cortico feedforward pathways. Initially this conclusion appears a little surprising because when information enters the cortex through the sensory organs it would be "trapped" in the primary sensory areas until the feedforward circuits had developed. That is, there is no apparent source of information for the feedback pathways. If there were some exceptions to the general pattern, however, such that a few "downstream" cortical areas received specific early feedforward connections from the deeper layers of a primary sensory area, then

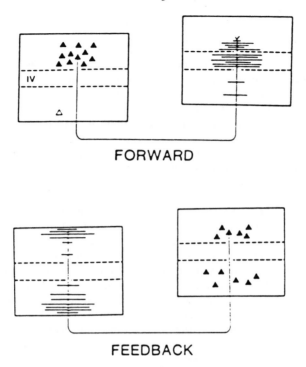

FORWARD

FEEDBACK

Figure 30.5 A schematic illustration of cortico–cortico interconnections. Feedforward pathways often project from layers 2 and 3 and terminate in layer 4. Feedback pathways often project from layers 1 and 2 and 5 and 6, and terminate in the same layers in the recipient region.

some interesting computational consequences may result. Is there any evidence for such specific exceptions?

In macaque primary visual cortex one exception to the normal pattern of cortico–cortico feedforward connection mentioned earlier is that very large pyramidals in layer 6 of the primary visual cortex[4] project to the superior temporal sulcus (STS) (Spatz, 1977; Weller and Kaas, 1978). While different parts of STS may serve different functions and be differentially interconnected with prestriate cortex (Rockland and Pandya, 1979), it is interesting to note that this is a region within which cells responsive to faces have been found in the macaque (e.g. Perrett et al., 1982).

At a certain stage of development, therefore, there may be input to primary sensory areas and a few other specific "downstream" areas such as that just described. The input to the primary sensory areas will initially be "trapped" until the feedforward circuits become capable of transmitting information. However, the input to a few "downstream" cortical areas may provide activation through feedback circuits sooner in development. When development proceeds sufficiently to allow feedforward circuits to function, I propose that local cortical microcircuits are configured in response to feedback as well as to feedforward information. At present, however, there is insufficient neurophysiological evidence to speculate on the exact temporal characteristics of the feedback and feedforward information, or on the exact way in which information becomes encoded in cortical microcircuits.

4 Constraining Representations

4.1 Constraining the Configuration of Cortical Microcircuits

What mechanisms underlie the configuration of cortical microcircuits? The postnatal events that I have discussed so far provided evidence for differential development of cortical layers. However, some neuroanatomical measures of cortical development do not reveal such a layer-wise differential pattern. For example, most cortical areas show a characteristic increase followed by a subsequent decrease in density of synaptic contacts. By such measures cortical areas show little or no layer-wise differential development. At least for any given area, all layers show loss at around the same ages (Huttenlocher, 1990 – this volume, chapter 7). Such loss can be very protracted. A number of "selectionist" theories have been put forward to account for this "pruning" of synaptic contacts, but the details of these theories need not concern us here (but see Johnson and Karmiloff-Smith, 1992).

As outlined earlier, evidence from a variety of sources suggests that a large degree of plasticity is to be found in the developing primate cortex. Some recent attempts to model this plasticity have involved variations on multilayered connectionist networks (e.g. Anderson and Zipser, 1988). While such networks appear to be able to simulate certain characteristics of the response properties of areas of cortex and individual cells, they have a number of problems associated with them which, some authors have suggested, make them biologically implausible. One of these problems is that they are essentially too powerful. In simulations the power of the network is normally constrained in two ways. First, the input is often limited by the provision of a defined input set. For example, in the model of Rumelhart and McClelland (1986) concerned with the acquisition of past tenses of regular and irregular verbs, a limited input set of verbs was initially given to the network. The model was not exposed to any inputs outside of this limited range during the first learning epochs.

A second way in which multi layered networks may be constrained is through the provision of a second source of information, other than the set of input stimuli. This second source may be a tutor signal such as is provided by the back propagation algorithm, or it may be a more information rich source of orthogonal information. Rolls (1989) has argued for a particular information processing role for the cortico–cortico back projections mentioned earlier, pointing out that while there are almost as many cortico–cortico back projections as there are forward projections, there have been very few theories put forward as to their function. Rolls's proposal is that the information passing through back projections from other cortical areas (and also the amygdala and hippocampus) is relatively rich and that it helps "neurones to learn to respond differently to (and thus to separate) input stimuli (on the forward projection lines) even when the stimuli are very similar" (Rolls, 1989, p. 258). Thus, the role of back projections from other cortical areas may be to enable the inputs to be categorized in particular ways. This cortical stage may then project back to a preceding stage resulting in still further categorization of representations. This theory requires that there be a large number of back projections which possess pattern-specific information.

With regard to development, I have argued earlier that some cortico–cortico back-projecting pathways will be functional before, or simultaneously with, the majority of cortico–cortico forward-projecting pathways. Furthermore, I proposed that these back projections contained information as a result of very specific long range forward projections from primary sensory areas. Thus, I suggest, back-projecting cortico–cortico pathways may provide an essential source of information for the configuration of cortical microcircuits during ontogeny.

4.2 *Spatial and Temporal Constraints*

It is clear that there are some spatial constraints on projections to the cortex. By spatial constraints, I refer to the fact that thalamic input innervates some regions more heavily than others. For example, in the primate the lateral geniculate nucleus innervates the area that subsequently becomes V1 more heavily than other regions. Thus, this area becomes the site of the first cortical representation of visual input. Other areas closely connected to this area are also likely to be recruited by visual input even though they may also initially receive some input from other sensory modalities (via other regions of cortex or thalamic projections). One possibility is that spatial constraints interact with temporal ones to determine whether a cortical area becomes devoted to one sensory modality or becomes polysensory.

For any given cortical area, there are waves of selective loss of synapses that occur postnatally (e.g. Lund and Holbach, 1991). In the preceding section I speculated that this process of selective loss is involved in the configuration of cortical microcircuits. Assuming that every cortical region receives some innervation, albeit indirect, from several sensory modalities at an early stage of development, one possibility is that one of these waves of selective loss occurs as a result of activity intrinsic to the area, and that another occurs as a result of competing activity between sensory inputs to the area (both direct and indirect projections). If this is the case, then the order in which these waves of selective loss take place will determine whether the area is subsequently monosensory or polysensory. That is, if the initial wave of loss affects the afferents to an area then it is likely that the loss will selectively affect one or other of the sensory inputs to the area. Normally the weaker projection to the area concerned will be selectively lost. Thus, if the auditory projection to V1 is very weak, it will be selectively pruned and the area will become "captured" by the dominant visual input. That is, the activity of circuits within the area will become more closely related to the regularities within the visual input than to those within the auditory input. In contrast, if the initial wave of synaptic loss is related to intrinsic activity, then selective loss will configure the circuits such that regularities in the input from both sensory modalities will become represented. That is, the neuronal microcircuitry within the area will become configured in response to invariances from both visual and auditory input (including common invariances), and the area will become polysensory.

Note that in the absence of sensory input from one channel (in the congenitally deaf, for example), regardless of whether intrinsic or extrinsic loss occurs first, the lack of organized input from the neglected sensory channel would mean that the area concerned will become configured to input from the functional sensory channel, no matter how weak the initial projection was. With this in mind, we can make some sense of the findings of Neville, (1991 – this volume, chapter 19) that cortical areas which are normally driven by auditory or polysensory input, become visual in the congenitally deaf.

5 Conclusions

This paper began with a paradox: despite the fact that the cortex is very plastic in early life, by adulthood particular regions of the cortex have become specialized to process information about particular classes of stimuli. Some of the extrinsic and intrinsic constraints on plasticity that gave rise to this consistent adult outcome were then reviewed. The extrinsic factors included the following:

1   Aspects of the external environment which are invariant for most members of a given species (e.g. exposure to patterned light).
2   Limitations on input imposed by immature sensory channels.
3   Specific biases for orienting toward relevant stimuli in the external world.
4   Spatial patterns of projection from the thalamus.

The factors intrinsic to the cortex which were proposed to constrain plasticity included:

1   Orienting and attention systems which are partially mediated by cortical regions and circuits. It was proposed that these systems, which become functional in the first few months of life, select even more restrictively the input to plastic areas of developing cortex.
2   Feedback pathways in the cortex, which may provide an orthogonal source of information for configuring cortical microcircuitry.
3   Temporal waves of selective loss of synapses which determine whether cortical microcircuitry within a region is configured in response to input from several sensory channels, or only one.

Clearly, some of the factors discussed are very speculative, and there are also likely to be others of importance which have not been identified in this article. However, the real challenge for the future lies in understanding how these factors interact *together* to restrict the range of mappings between cortical areas and their functions. Once we understand this constructive process, we have a chance of unravelling the relation between brain development and cognition.

NOTES

1   More specifically, pre-synaptic excitatory neurotransmitters may regulate the expression of post-synaptic nerve growth factor receptor gene (Ira Black, presentation at the

workshop on the Cognitive Neuroscience of Development, University of Oregon, October 1990).

2   Many supposedly subcortically mediated behaviors disappear around the second month of life in the human infant, possibly due to inhibition by developing cortical circuits (see, for example, Johnson, 1990b).

3   I am aware that these statements are generalizations and that there are many exceptions. It is, however, my view that the exceptions will only be understood in the light of the generalities (see also Kaas, 1989; Crick and Asanuma, 1986).

4   During the first few months of postnatal life, the thalamic afferents to V1 may terminate in the deeper cortical layers, 5 and 6. Whether or not these immature projections form synaptic contacts is as yet unclear. However, in view of the evidence for transient synaptic contacts from thalamic afferents being established in "inappropriate" cortical layers during development in other primates (Rakic, 1976, 1983), the assumption that they do seems reasonable.

ACKNOWLEDGEMENTS

Thanks are due to Annette Karmiloff-Smith, Jay McClelland, John Morton, Mike Posner, and Mary Rothbart who all provided useful comments on earlier drafts of this chapter. The paper was begun while I was at the MRC Cognitive Development Unit, London, continued while I was a Human Frontiers Research Fellow at the Center for Cognitive Neuroscience, University of Oregon, and completed at Carnegie Mellon University.

REFERENCES

Anderson, D. A. and Zipser, D. (1988) The role of the posterior parietal cortex in coordinate transformations for visual-motor integration. *Canadian Journal of Physiology and Pharmacology*, 66, 488–501.

Aslin, R. N. (1981). Development of smooth pursuit in human infants. In D. F. Fisher, R. A. Monty and J. W. Senders (eds), *Eye Movements: Cognition and Visual Perception*, Hillsdale, NJ: Lawrence Erlbaum, pp. 31–51.

Atkinson, J. (1984) Human visual development over the first six months of life: a review and a hypothesis. *Human Neurobiology*, 3, 61–74.

Black, I. B. et al. (1984) Neurotransmitter plasticity at the molecular level. *Science*, 225, 1266–1270.

Bolhuis, J. J. and Johnson, M. H. (1991) Sensory templates: mechanism or metaphor? *The Behavioral and Brain Sciences*, 14, 349–350.

Bolhuis, J. J., Johnson, M. H., Horn, G. and Bateson, P. (1989) Long-lasting effects of IMHV lesions on the social preferences of domestic fowl. *Behavioral Neuroscience*, 103, 438–441.

Bronson, G. W. (1974) The postnatal growth of visual capacity. *Child Development*, 45, 873–890.

Conel, J. L. (1939–1967) *The Postnatal Development of the Human Cerebral Cortex, Vols I–VIII*. Cambridge, MA: Harvard University Press.

Crick, F. and Asanuma, C. (1986) Certain aspects of the anatomy and physiology of the cerebral cortex. In J. L. McClelland and D. E. Rumelhart (eds), *Parallel Distributed Processing: Explorations in the Microstructure of Cognition, 2*. Cambridge, MA: Bradford Books.

de Schonen, S. and Mathivet, H. (1989) First come, first served: a scenario about the development of hemispheric specialisation in face recognition during infancy. *European Bulletin of Cognitive Psychology*, 9, 3–44.

Diamond, R. and Carey, S. (1986) Why faces are and are not special: an effect of expertise? *Journal of Experimental Psychology: General*, 115, 107–117.

Ebbesson, S. O. (1980) The parcellation theory and its relation to interspecific variability in brain organization, evolutionary and ontogenetic development, and neuronal plasticity. *Cell and Tissue Research*, 213, 179–212.

Elman, J. (1991) The importance of starting small. Unpublished manuscript.

Goldman, P. S. (1971) Functional development of the prefrontal cortex in early life and the problem of neuronal plasticity. *Experimental Neurology*, 32, 366–387.

Goren, C. C., Sarty, M. and Wu, P. Y. K. (1975). Visual following and pattern discrimination of face-like stimuli by newborn infants. *Pediatrics*, 56, 544–549.

Greenough, W. T., Black, J. E. and Wallace, C. S. (1987) Experience and brain development. *Child Development*, 58, 539–559.

Haith, M. M., Hazan, C. and Goodman, G. S. (1988) Expectation and anticipation of dynamic visual events by 3.5-month old babies. *Child Development*, 59, 467–479.

Hirsh-Pasek, K., Kemler Nelson, D. G., Jusczyk, P. W., Wright, K., Druss, B. and Kennedy, L. J. (1987) Clauses are perceptual units for young infants. *Cognition*, 26, 269–286.

Huttenlocher, P. R. (1990) Morphometric study of human cerebral cortex development. *Neuropsychologia*, 28, 517–527.

Horn, G. (1985) *Memory, Imprinting, and the Brain: an Inquiry into Mechanisms*. Oxford: Clarendon Press.

Johnson, M. H. (1988a) Parcellation and plasticity: implications for ontogeny. *Behavioral and Brain Sciences*, 11, 547–549.

Johnson, M. H. (1988b) Memories of mother. *New Scientist*, 1600, 60–62.

Johnson, M. H. (1990a) Cortical maturation and the development of visual attention in early infancy. *Journal of Cognitive Neuroscience*, 2, 81–95.

Johnson, M. H. (1990b) Cortical maturation and perceptual development. In H. Bloch and B. Bertenthal (eds), *Sensory Motor Organisation and Development in Infancy and Early Childhood*. Dordrecht: Kluwer.

Johnson, M. H. (1992) Cognition and development: four contentions about the role of visual attention. In D. J. Stein and J. E. Young (eds), *Cognitive Science and Clinical Disorders*. New York: Academic Press.

Johnson, M. H. and Bolhuis, J. J. (1991) Imprinting, predispositions and filial preference in the chick. In R. J. Andrew (ed.), *Neural and Behavioural Plasticity*. Oxford: Oxford University Press, pp. 133–156.

Johnson, M. H., Bolhuis, J. J. and Horn, G. (1985) Interaction between acquired preferences and developing predispositions during imprinting. *Animal Behaviour*, 33, 1000–1006.

Johnson, M. H., Dziurawiec, S., Bartrip, J. and Morton, J. (1992) Infants' preferences for face-like stimuli: effects of the movement of internal features. *Infant Behavior and Development*, 15, 129–136.

Johnson, M. H., Dziurawiec, S., Ellis, H. D. and Morton, J. (1991a) Newborns preferential tracking of face-like stimuli and its subsequent decline. *Cognition*, 40, 1–21.

Johnson, M. H. and Horn, G. (1986) Dissociation of recognition memory and associative learning by a restricted lesion of the chick forebrain. *Neuropsychologia*, 24, 329–340.

Johnson, M. H. and Horn, G. (1988) The development of filial preferences in the dark-reared chick. *Animal Behaviour*, 36, 675–683.

Johnson, M. H. and Karmiloff-Smith, A. (1992) Can neural selectionism be applied to cognitive development and its disorders? *New Ideas in Psychology*, 10, 35–46.

Johnson, M. H. and Morton, J. (1991). *Biology and Cognitive Development: the Case of Face Recognition*. Oxford: Blackwell.

Johnson, M. H., Posner, M. I. and Rothbart, M. (1991b) The development of visual attention in infancy: contingency learning, anticipations and disengaging. *Journal of Cognitive Neuroscience*, 3, 335–344.

Jusczyk, P. W. and Bertoncini J., (1988) Viewing the development of speech perception as an innately guided learning process. *Language and Speech*, 31, 217–238.

Kaas, J. H. (1989) Why does the brain have so many visual areas? *Journal of Cognitive Neuroscience*, 1, 121–135.

Karten, H. J. and Shimizu, T. (1989) The origins of neocortex: connections and lamination as distinct events in evolution. *Journal of Cognitive Neuroscience*, 1, 291–301.

Kolb, B. (1989) Brain development, plasticity, and behavior. *American Psychologist*, 44, 1203–1212.

Lund, J. S. (1981) Intrinsic organization of the primate visual cortex, area 17, as seen in Golgi preparations. In F. O. Schmitt et al. (eds), *The Organization of the Cerebral Cortex*. Cambridge, MA: MIT Press.

Lund, J. S. and Holbach, S. M. (1991) Postnatal development of thalamic recipient neurons in the monkey striate cortex. *Journal of Comparative Neurology*, 309, 115–128.

Maunsell, J. H. R. and Van Essen, D. C. (1983). The connections of the middle temporal visual area (MT) and their relation to a cortical hierarchy in the macaque monkey. *Journal of Neuroscience*, 3, 2563–2586.

Maurer, D. and Barrera, M. (1981) Infants' perception of natural and distorted arrangements of a schematic face. *Child Development*, 47, 523–527.

Miller, K. D., Keller, J. B. and Stryker, M. P. (1989) Ocular dominance column development: analysis and simulation. *Science*, 245, 605–615.

Morton, J. and Johnson, M. H. (1991) Conspec and conlern: a two-process theory of infant face recognition. *Psychological Review*, 98, 164–181.

Morton, J., Johnson, M. H. and Maurer, D. (1990) On the reasons for newborns responses to faces. *Infant Behavior and Development*, 13, 99–103.

Nauta, W. J. H. and Karten, H. J. (1970) A general profile of the vertebrate brain with sidelights on the ancestry of the cerebral cortex. In F. O. Schmitt (ed.), *The Neurosciences: Second Study Program*. New York: Rockefeller Press.

Neville, H. (1991) Neurobiology of cognitive and language processing: effects of early experience. In K. R. Gibson and A. C. Peterson (eds), *Brain Maturation and Cognitive Development: Comparative and Cross-Cultural Perspectives*. Hawthorne, NY: Aldine de Gruyter Press, pp. 355–380.

Neville, H. J. and Lawson D. (1987) Attention to central and peripheral visual space in a movement detection task: an event- related potential and behavioral study. II. Congenitally deaf adults. *Brain Research*, 405, 268–283.

Oyama, S. (1985) *The Ontogeny of Information*. Cambridge: Cambridge University Press.

Pandya, D. N. and Yeterian, E. H. (1990) Architecture and connections of cerebral cortex: implications for brain evolution and function. In A. B. Scheibel and A. F. Weschsler (eds), *Neurobiology of Higher Cognitive Function*. New York: Guilford Press

Perrett, D. I., Rolls, E. T. and Caan, W. (1982) Visual neurones responsive to faces in the monkey temporal cortex. *Experimental Brain Research*, 47, 229–238.

Peterson, S. E., Fox, P. T., Posner, M. I., Mintun, M. and Raichle, M. E. (1989) Positron emission tomographic studies of the processing of single words. *Journal of Cognitive Neuroscience*, 1, 153–170.

Peterson, S. E., Fox, P. T., Snyder, A. Z. and Raichle, M. E. (1990) Activation of extrastriate and frontal cortical areas by visual words and word like stimuli. *Science*, 249, 1041–1044.

Posner, M. I. and Rothbart, M. K. (1990) Attentional Mechanisms and Conscious Experience, Institute of Cognitive & Decision Sciences University of Oregon Technical Report No. 90–17.

Posner, M. I., Peterson, S. E. Fox, P. T. and Raichle, M. E. (1988) Localization of cognitive functions in the human brain. *Science*, 240, 1627–1631.

Premack, D. G. and Woodruff, G. (1978) Does the chimpanzee have a theory of mind? *Behavioral and Brain Sciences*, 1, 515–526.

Rabinowicz, T. (1979) The differential maturation of the human cerebral cortex. In Falkner, F. and J. M. Tanner, (eds), *Human Growth Vol. 3. Neurobiology and Nutrition*. New York: Plenum.

Rakic, P. (1976) Prenatal genesis of connections subserving ocular dominance in the rhesus monkey. *Nature*, 261, 467–471.

Rakic, P. (1983) Geniculo-cortical connections in primates: normal and experimentally altered development. *Progress in Brain Research*, 58, 393–404.

Robinson, N. S., McCarty, M. E. and Haith, M. M. (1988) Visual expectations in early infancy. Paper presented at the international conference on infant studies, Washington, DC.

Rockland, K. S. and Pandya, D. N. (1979) Laminar origins and terminations of cortical connections of the occipital lobe in the rhesus monkey. *Brain Research*, 179, 3–20.

Roe, A. W., Pallas, S. L., Hahm, J., Kwon, Y. H. and Sur, M. (1988) *Society for Neuroscience Abstracts* 14, 460.

Rolls, E. (1989) Functions of neuronal networks in the hippocampus and neocortex in memory. In J. Berne and W. Berry (eds), *Neural Models of Plasticity*. New York: Academic Press.

Rothbart, M. K., Posner, M. I. and Boylan, A. (1990) Regulatory mechanisms in infant development. In J. Enns (ed.), *The Development of Attention: Research and Theory*. Amsterdam: North Holland.

Rumelhart, D. E. and McClelland, J. L. (1986) On learning the past tenses of English verbs. In J. L. McClelland, D. E. Rumelhart, and the PDP Research Group, *Parallel Distributed Processing: Explorations in the Microstructure of Cognition. Vol. 2*. Cambridge, MA: MIT Press/Bradford Books.

Schiller, P. H. (1985). A model for the generation of visually guided saccadic eye movements. In D. Rose and V. G. Dobson (eds), *Models of the Visual Cortex*. Chicester: Wiley.

Spatz, W. B. (1977) Topographically organized reciprocal connections between area 17 and MT (visual area of the superior temporal sulcus) in the marmoset, *Callithrix jacchus. Experimental Brain Research*, 27, 559–572.

Sur, M., Garraghty, P. E. and Roe, A. W. (1988) *Science*, 242, 1437–1441.

Sur, M., Pallas, S. L. and Roe, A. W. (1990) Cross-modal plasticity in cortical development: differentiation and specification of sensory neocortex. *TINS*, 13, 227–233.

Turkewitz, G. and Kenny, P. A. (1982) Limitations on input as a basis for neural organization and perceptual development: a preliminary theoretical statement. *Developmental Psychobiology*, 15, 357–368.

Turkewitz, G. and Kenny, P. A. (1985) The role of developmental limitations of sensory input on sensory/perceptual organization. *Developmental and Behavioral Pediatrics*, 6, 302–306.

Weller, R. E. and Kaas, J. H. (1978) Connections of striate cortex with the posterior bank of the superior temporal sulcus in macaque monkeys. *Society for Neuroscience Abstracts*, 4, 650.

Index of Names

Index of Subjects